1990 Media Guide

A Critical Review of the Media's Recent Coverage of the World Political Economy

LIBRARY USE ONLY

Jude Wanniski
Editor

WITHDRAWN
FROM
UNIVERSITY OF PENNSYLVANIA
LIBRARIES

Peter A. Signorelli
Executive Editor

Patricia M. Koyce
Managing Editor

Claire M. Magersky
Associate Editor

ANNENBERG

PN/4867/M434/1990/Cop.2

LIBRARY
THE ANNENBERG SCHOOL
OF COMMUNICATIONS
UNIVERSITY OF PENNSYLVANIA
3620 WALNUT STREET/C5
PHILADELPHIA, PA 19104

Published by:
Polyconomics, Inc., Morristown, N. J.
In association with
Repap Enterprises, Inc., Montreal,
Canada

PENNSYLVANIA
LIBRARIES

The 1990 MediaGuide Copyright © 1986, 1987, 1988, 1989, 1990 by Polyconomics, Inc. All rights reserved. Printed in the United States of America. No part of this book may be used or reproduced in any manner whatsoever without permission except in the case of brief quotations embodied in critical articles and reviews. For information address Polyconomics, Inc., 86 Maple Avenue, Morristown, New Jersey 07960. 1-800-MEDIA 88

ISSN: 1042-2129
LIBRARY OF CONGRESS CATALOG CARD NUMBER: 87-654448

ISBN: 0-938081-06-3
ISBN: 0-938081-07-1 (pbk.)

90 91 92 93 10 9 8 7 6 5 4 3 2 1

TABLE OF CONTENTS

INTRODUCTION

Journalism has been called "the first rough draft of history" and at times in 1989, history seemed to be occurring at a dizzying pace. Every morning newspaper, every evening news broadcast, seems to bring fresh reports of events that just a year ago would have seemed unthinkable or unimaginable. From Beijing to Berlin, from Warsaw to New York, from Beirut to Brazil, all the world seems to be a stage where the actors were working with neither script nor direction. News consumers in the audience could only watch as events occurred at an ever-increasing velocity, as if the currents of time had finally caught up with the capacity of modern technology to bring history instantaneously to the world. And if news consumers had to be satisfied at times with a press that seemed just as surprised as they were by what was occurring, at least they could see history as it was happening and judge for themselves. The purpose of the *Repap 1990 MediaGuide* is not, of course, to pass judgments on the events of 1989, the historic and the transitory, but rather to review the press coverage of those events, editing the "first rough draft," as it were.

This is the fifth edition of the *MediaGuide*. Returning readers will notice some changes, starting with the new name. The *MediaGuide* is pleased to highlight the continuing sponsorship of Repap Enterprises, Inc. of Montreal, Canada. Repap ("paper" turned around) is an international pulp and paper company founded in 1978 by George S. Petty, its chairman and chief executive officer. Repap is now the third largest manufacturer of coated paper in the world, with operations across Canada and in the United States. It is, of course, Repap paper on which this book is printed. Other changes in the *MediaGuide* include sections devoted to television news and the Canadian media, along with expanded coverage in our traditional departments. This expansion is due in part to the increased editorial capabilities of the *Repap MediaGuide*, and in part to the monumental events which the press had to cover in 1989.

This fifth annual edition of the *MediaGuide*, we think, is the best we've done. We hope the editors and reporters at all levels of the news media have come to sense, if not completely understand, that the motivation behind this endeavor is solely *the strengthening of American journalism*. Our editors have their own individual notions of the way the world works and how it should look, as does every citizen of the planet. Indeed, there are incessant internal debates among us and among our contributors on all issues. Among us are liberals and conservatives, Democrats and Republicans, pro-choicers and pro-lifers, ardent environmentalists and uninhibited growth advocates. We seek to approximate a sophisticated balance of news consumers in our mix of contributors, and we energetically strive to represent in that mix almost every social, political and economic viewpoint. The common thread is a democratic one. Even more fundamentally, the common thread that binds us together at the *MediaGuide* is a profound conviction in the importance of communication. If we can talk things out — at every level, from the family at home to the family of nations — we can approach an ideal of peace and prosperity, material and spiritual.

Before the first *MediaGuide* was published in 1986, there had been no systematic attempt to critique the media, except from ideological vantage points. The watchdog organizations and newsletters are financed, generally by conservative money, to spot error and bias and make public complaint. The concept behind the *MediaGuide* is to look for excellence, to elevate the best we can find in reporting and commentary, and point out what we feel are the strengths and shortcomings of those who aspire to excellence.

1

The problems of doing anything for the first time, with no road map to follow, were more difficult than we had ever imagined. We first had to train ourselves and then train others to critically examine the communications media in a way that had never before been achieved — as free as possible from political, social or economic objectives. Unbiased. Or, at least, as objectively as humanly possible.

For the first *MediaGuide,* there were only two of us, Peter Signorelli and I, doing almost all the reading and analysis. There are now five full-time editors and analysts; Peter Signorelli in charge, others at Polyconomics contributing as much as we can. The enterprise as you see it could not be possible without the fifty or so outside "news gourmets" around the country who contribute an average of 12 reviews per month of stories they've selected from our suggested reading list. They are all specialists in the areas they are critiquing, able to judge the material they are seeing against a broader canvas of information available to them. Most of the contributors have come to us spurred by their own interest — seeing earlier editions of the *MediaGuide,* appreciating our intent, and calling to offer participation. A nominal gratuity is paid for each thumbnail review. Our contributor list has a steady turnover, and we believe it has been steadily upgraded. Our best critics are those who have been with us the longest.

By now, the early *MediaGuide* editions seem pitifully slender in their presentations and depth. A decade from now, we expect, this edition will seem frail compared to what we can present then.

The Big Story of the year was, of course, the opening of the Iron Curtain, as trends which seemed at first evolutionary quickly became revolutionary. Mikhail Gorbachev's policies of *glasnost* and *perestroika* appeared more and more to be open abandonment of the Soviet Union's failed experiment with Marxist-Leninism. While this development could have been predicted, what caught just about everyone off guard was Mr. Gorbachev's quiet encouragement, reinforced with public pronouncements, for other communist governments to open up their systems politically and economically as well, letting loose forces which had been building for decades. As Eastern European nations one by one began to undergo revolutions from top to bottom, the United States and its NATO allies began to seriously address what awaited them in a "post Cold War world" as they faced the biggest foreign policy challenge in forty years. But if the news from Europe was encouraging overall, the news from Asia was grim.

The People's Republic of China was wracked by chaos most of the year, as the government apparently remained deeply divided over economic and political policy, with students and workers pouring into the streets by the hundreds of thousands to protest as conditions deteriorated. A peaceful occupation of Tiananmen Square in May turned into a bloodbath in June, witnessed by television viewers the world over. Although afterward the Chinese leadership pledged to continue economic reforms, it instituted domestic policies that echoed the Cultural Revolution, and Western revulsion over China's oppressive policies seemed to preclude a return anytime soon to the type of relationship that existed prior to June 1989. Meanwhile, hardline elements in Eastern Europe would speak of using "the Chinese option" as demonstrations grew in their countries. If the hardliners were overruled, at least for now, one reason might be that governments learned a lesson from Tiananmen Square: in the age of the satellite hook-up, the "whole world" is, indeed, "watching."

If Vietnam was the world's first "television war," then the upheaval in the communist world may be the world's first "television revolution." Both sides seemed to understand and use the medium. In China, for instance, the protest leaders timed their occupation of Tiananmen Square to coincide with the summit visit of Mikhail Gorbachev with attendant world press coverage, making sure many of their banners were in English. The authorities later used Western television footage to identify student leaders, and beamed pictures of the "wanted criminals" to a population who had to contend with state censorship. As in most years since the medium's inception, no doubt many news consumers will think of the events of 1989 in images shown on their TV screens: the "Spirit of Democracy" standing toe-to-toe with Mao; one lone Chinese blocking a column of tanks; young East German families in an exodus stretching as far as the eye can see; candlelit protest marches in the Eastern European night; Germans dancing joyously on top of the Berlin Wall.

But words about the events in the communist world were printed as well, of course, and perhaps none were more influential than Francis Fukuyama's speech "The End of History?" which was published in the spring issue of *The National Interest*. Fukuyama, a young State Department analyst, wrote that the collapse of communism means more than an end to the Cold War, it means "the triumph of the West," in the way Western ideas and values were supposed to have made World War I "the war to end all wars," but did not. The simple notion was spiced by his tongue-in-cheek prediction: now that civilization has completed its quest for the ideal format, humankind faces a future of relative boredom. In this sense, his essay pushed conventional journalistic analytics into history's next chapter, a more provocative vantage point for viewing the closing pages of this one. Irving Kristol, publisher of *The National Interest,* said whimsically, "I don't believe a word of it." He told James Atlas of *The New York Times Magazine* that the piece has had no influence on the government. "No one in the administration has read it." But as Atlas put it, "Everyone else has." The piece palpably shaped the climate of opinion, structured the national framework of discussion about the historical events in Central and Eastern Europe, and inevitably had profound influence on policymaking. A glance at Fukuyama's citation in the index is suggestive of the essay's influence.

There were other important contributions in the media to the national debate over where America should go from here, including a series on *The New York Times* op-ed page asserting an *end to the Cold War*. But in a year when events in the Soviet Union and Europe seemed to be taking place in a collapsing timeframe from years to months to weeks to hours, it was the reporters on the scene who were put to the test, and overall they performed admirably well. In our earlier editions, we repeatedly urged that more of the media's best talent be allocated to the communist capitals to cover this emerging story, and by luck or design, when the political breakthroughs cascaded from the Kremlin Walls to the Brandenburg Gate, we had top-of-the-line, seasoned, energetic teams flooding us with sharp, smart, detailed reports. We can't say the reporting was of uniformly high quality from one publication to the next, but with so much available, we felt President Bush was probably getting as many (and more) accurate insights from his daily press clippings as he was from his National Security Council briefings.

If the great achievement of the media this year was its superb coverage of the Big Story of upheaval in the communist world, then the great challenge of the media next year will be to stay on top of this story. The media, which seems to have learned a lesson from its coverage of China, has tempered its euphoria somewhat over the developments in the Soviet Union and Eastern Europe, so that should a subsequent crackdown occur, neither the media nor news consumers will be taken so completely by surprise. But whether the Eastern Bloc continues to reform peacefully, undergoes a mild retrenchment, or suffers the fate of China, the expertise demanded of journalists trying to keep up appears to be at an unprecedented level. Even assuming no further political avalanches occur in 1990, the press will still have to follow dual tracks of political and economic developments against shifting East/West security arrangements on a grand scale of multidimensional complexities. The story of a massacre by and large tells itself; the story of slower-paced developments does not.

Elsewhere in the world, the level of reporting was not as high and in some instances was unacceptable. Given the fact that Japan is once again in an uncomfortable position in its relations with the United States and also underwent a year of domestic political upheaval, we expected a higher degree of discernment and timeliness from the press pool in Tokyo. Mexico was the central story of the ongoing Third World debt crisis this year, and for the most part we were disappointed that the the news focus was on the New York banks instead of Mexico's economy — a classic case of the tail wagging the dog. The relative calm of the Middle East, outside of Lebanon, may have been responsible for the muted press coverage of that region. One important story, the cleavage in the American Jewish community over the policies of the Shamir government in the occupied territories, was largely brushed over. The American press is uncomfortable handling such sensitive topics, while the London-based *Economist* at least had its moments.

Television coverage of Ayatollah Khomeini's funeral in June proved once again that medium's unsurpassed ability to bring a spectacle into our living room, although subsequent press coverage of Iran fell into simplistics, with reporters largely still trying to affix labels of "radical" and "moderate" to that country's political and religious leaders. The world press began reporting from South Africa once again, as press restrictions there were gradually lifted, and we noted that even some of that regime's harshest critics in the Western media were reading positive signs in the new government of F. W. de Klerk. El Salvador returned to the front pages toward the end of the year and remained the blot on the escutcheon of *The New York Times,* which seems to prefer the FMLN opposition to the elected ARENA government, and that paper's cues are still followed by the TV networks.

Domestically, it seemed to be one of those years when nobody could be really sure if things were getting better or growing worse, and this uncertainty was reflected in the media, which never really seemed to be on top of any major story. Any contribution it made to the national debate was usually on the downside. Too often this year we saw the herd instinct in the press take over, as in the coverage of the John Tower confirmation fiasco, with the press all too often putting an unsubstantiated rumor on the front page or at the top of the newscast. The year saw its fair share of important domestic political stories — the first Cabinet nominee rejected in thirty years, the first Speaker of the House forced to resign in the nation's history, the re-emergence of the abortion issue — yet the press coverage was by-and-large undistinguishable and unmemorable.

Perhaps this was because after an exhaustive Campaign '88, the political press corps was taking it easy in 1989, with more than one reporter taking time off to write one more time about what happened in 1988. Much of the political press corps clucked disapprovingly at the negative campaigning in the few big races of the year, after having written last year how brilliant campaign consultants had won the White House for George Bush by designing a negative campaign. Coverage of the Bush-Quayle administration's first year was fairly competent, after a wobbly start of pack journalists barking up tree after tree looking for the *real* George Bush. Wherever he was, he wasn't making reporters yell over the blades of a waiting helicopter or tossing off one-liners at staged "photo-ops." Unlike his predecessor, President Bush was giving more press conferences and attempting to foster a less adversarial relationship with the White House press corps, with a welcome note of civility returning to dispatches from 1600 Pennsylvania Avenue. The President, though, may still feel he is being treated unfairly by the press, which gives him one thing in common with Mikhail Gorbachev.

Other major stories were familiar, if the details were new. Major improprieties were discovered in Housing and Urban Development. Urban centers continued to deteriorate, to the accompaniment of wailing babies, emergency vehicle sirens, and the crackling of automatic weapons fire. The press seemed to zero in on one or two stories — the brutal rape of a woman jogger in Central Park, the horrible murder of an Afro-American in Queens — while news consumers wondered if the larger story was going unreported. The War on Drugs was declared once again, with newspapers, magazines, and television newscasts devoting special sections to such topics as millionaire drug lords in Colombia and underfunded treatment programs here at home. On national television, President Bush displayed a bag of crack, which had been purchased, we were told, just across the street from the White House. When it was discovered several days later that DEA agents had lured a drug dealer to Lafayette Park so the President could make his claim about the expanding availability of drugs, the press passed the information along quietly, in contrast to the Reagan years, when each presidential address was dissected and each "misstatement of fact" was trumpeted to the world. Perhaps in a year when network news shows began running staged "recreations" of actual events, at times without alerting the viewer, the media felt that discretion in this case was the better part of valor. Race was also a major story, either in the subtext of the stories mentioned above or out in the open. Virginia voted-in the nation's first elected Afro-American governor while New Yorkers elected their first Afro-American mayor, ending Ed Koch's twelve-year reign. Except for *New York* magazine, the reporting in this area was undistinguished, stories looked at separately from foxhole level, not interconnected.

The struggle between the Bush White House and the Democratic Congress culminated in the President's defeat on his capital gains tax cut proposal. The press corps missed most of this, assuming all year the President would lose in the House, then, when he won in the House, assuming he would win in the Senate, where he lost. When the loss was cinched at noon, October 13, with the White House throwing in the towel, the Dow Jones Industrial Average lost 190 points. Supply-side economists, including the chief economist of the U.S. Chamber of Commerce, *uniformly* made the connection. The financial press *uniformly* ignored the connection, except to gently ridicule the notion.

Old Guard Keynesians continue to control most of the levers of power in the business and financial press. This is *naturally* true of professional economists in industry, banking and Wall Street. It's expected. American colleges and universities have taught only demand-management concepts since the late 1940s. But in theory, journalistic reporting and analysis should be ideologically detached. Insofar as most editors and senior correspondents were also trained in the demand-management era, their old habits and influence die hard. They feel most comfortable covering the news the way they have, still uncomfortable with novelty. As a result, the preponderance of market commentary and reporting on domestic and international macro-economic news remains considerably behind the power curve. Journalists who have been dutifully advising of recessions just around the corner for the past five years continue to rely on the same sources for this wisdom.

In the way we say that generals are always fighting the last war, the news media is generally slow to handle novelty. It's best at covering what it has been covering. When an idea or a face reaches the cover of the newsmagazines, it is safe to suggest it has usually traveled already through the better part of its experience. The best and the brightest of the profession break slowly from the areas they have mastered to unexplored terrain.

Thinking back to the "energy crisis" of the mid-1970s, how foolish the press coverage seems now, conspiracy theories filling the columns of our leading newspapers and periodicals. But, of course, the United States had never before experienced an "energy crisis," the pool of talent to cover such an event was negligible. As the last decade of the century opens, though, there is an abundance of journalistic talent able to handle the most difficult energy stories. The squeaky wheel gets the grease, and in the news world, where all the wheels squeak at once, the profession has a constant struggle trying to allocate resources.

The "environmental crisis" may prove to be the "energy crisis" of the late 80s and early 90s. We say "prove to be" because we don't know for sure how serious such talked and written about phenomena as acid rain, the Greenhouse Effect, and the deteriorating ozone layer will turn out to be. They may indeed be extremely serious, or they may be as "dangerous" as two Chilean grapes. Until we know for sure, until science knows for sure, we'd like to be getting as much information from the press as we possibly can. Unfortunately, there seems to have been an almost complete breakdown in the American press over environmental issues. Sometime during the year it was determined on high that *The Debate Is Over* on all outstanding environmental issues. The Greenhouse Effect. Acid Rain. The Ozone Layer. Pesticides. If "The Debate Is Over," obviously the American press does not have to cover it anymore. Indeed, this has been a palpable professional weakness in the media, with reporters too often becoming environmentalists, thereby denying consumers of news the credible pros and cons.

When the press corps breaks down as thoroughly as it has on this, the threat of major policy error increases exponentially as political, business and labor leaders — fearful of expressing skepticism because the debate has been declared over — decide it isn't worth resurrecting the dispute. We hasten to add that it is not the *primary* responsibility of the press corps to elevate opposing ideas on one issue or another, but to report and comment on the running debate among political, business, labor and social leaders. These are the people who do have the primary responsibility to put forth the pros and cons on critical matters of public policy.

The *MediaGuide* editors, human as we are, genuinely worry about the warnings of a greenhouse warming effect, a widening ozone hole, and the *hypothesis* of acid rain as a new element and not part of nature's eternal background. We of course worry about the environment. Our admonishment to editors is this: We feel cheated out of a debate that's been accepted as being over when we haven't seen it at all in the pages of your newspapers and periodicals. The press corps should be insisting upon debate. Its readers have practically been starved for such a debate. At least, the media should be questioning assertions that the debate is over. In the *Repap 1991 MediaGuide* we will treat this issue in greater depth.

AN OVERVIEW OF
THE PRINT MEDIA

1989 PRESS DEVELOPMENTS

Most of the items that follow are examined in detail in the "Publications" section, contained in the individual publication essays. We cite the most important here in order to reemphasize them, and to call attention to those we feel will most likely affect the publications over the 1990 newsyear and beyond.

The Christian Science Monitor: Now known as the "incredible shrinking *Monitor*," the once distinguished international newspaper has shriveled to the size of a supermarket throwaway. We can't *blame* the publishers for these decisions, but color pages and redesign do not a newspaper make, and we no longer examine it critically in this book.

FW: The old *Financial World* becomes *FW,* in a sharper format to appeal to the yuppies, a la *GQ, W,* etc.

Los Angeles Times: Shelby Coffey officially takes the reins as editor. Anthony Day leaves his editorship of the editorial pages, remaining a contributor. He is succeeded by Thomas Plate, former editpage editor at *Newsday;* also moving up, editorial writer Frank del Olmo who becomes deputy editorial page editor, succeeding the outgoing Jack Burby. The *LAT* also goes to a new format, jazzing up the paper with color.

National Journal: The steady, reliable weekly on Capitol Hill goes cosmopolitan, turning to 4-color pages to better compete with the newly souped-up *Congressional Quarterly.*

The New York Times: Joseph Lelyveld is named managing editor as Arthur Gelb retires. Bernard Gwertzman becomes foreign editor and Michael Kaufman, former Warsaw bureau chief, becomes his deputy. The Washington bureau loses E. J. Dionne, Jr., to the *Washington Post* and Susan Lee leaves as op-ed editor.

The New Republic: Michael Kinsley returns to manage the magazine from his sojourn at the *Economist,* but is soon replaced by Hendrik Hertzberg a few weeks later. Kinsley remains as "TRB" columnist. The magazine, which we had grown comfortable with, is redesigned, with a new typeface making it more difficult to read.

Time: The reporters at the weekly move close to overt advocacy journalism on all topics, with the apparent blessing of the editors.

U.S.News & World Report: More musical chairs as Roger Rosenblatt leaves as editor after only a year, replaced by Michael Ruby, wooed from *Newsweek* two years earlier as a second banana.

The Wall Street Journal: Peter R. Kann is named president, in addition to his current title of publisher, of Dow Jones & Co., and is now the heir apparent to Warren H. Phillips. He edges out William Dunn, the production visionary who built the satellite system and news retrieval operations, an executive vice president who resigned after Kann's promotion. George Melloan, veteran deputy to Robert L. Bartley, departs to edit *The Wall Street Journal*/Europe's editpage. Tim Ferguson, editorial features editor, decamps as well to a West Coast assignment for the paper. Karen Elliott House becomes vice president of Dow Jones & Co. to oversee the European and Asian editions, replaced as foreign editor by her deputy, Lee Lescaze. Kathy Christiansen quits as a top inside editor for a senior producer post at ABC-TV.

The Washington Post: Robert Kaiser advances on the corporate ladder, behind Leonard Downie, who is practically running the *Post* as Ben Bradlee coasts. Michael Getler, foreign editor, moves up behind Kaiser; David Ignatius leaves the "Outlook" editorship to be foreign editor.

The Washington Times: Walter Taylor, after barely a year at the paper, is replaced as foreign editor by Marc Lerner, former Philippine correspondent.

MAJOR STORIES OF 1989

Communism's Crackup and Crackdown

The Year of Eastern Europe

Throughout the historically awesome, tumultuous events of 1989, we heard repeatedly from commentators and pundits that "no one could have predicted" the nature of the political upheaval in the communist world. This is perhaps true in the sense that what happened to the world was the equivalent of a mountain avalanche. It had been clear for several years that as long as snowflakes continued to fall on the East Bloc, as long as ice continued to form in the dark night of the communist experiment, eventually there would be one flake, one crystal that would be the margin, the way a single straw breaks a camel's back. Avalanches do not occur to accommodate those who might be interested in viewing them, a little at a time. So it happened that two and three years ago the press corps began preparing for what it could not precisely predict, identifying its best resources and sending them to the most promising vantage points. There was a general sense among the most astute observers that something would soon happen.

As the time for the avalanche approached, Meg Greenfield, *The Washington Post*'s editorial page editor, worried in her *Newsweek* column, "Misled by the 'Facts,' " 6-26, that it seemed time for us to brace ourselves, that "it is one of the ironies of the current well-documented information explosion with all its instantaneous transmission of news and data around the globe that we get the impression that we know more than we do." It is a trap that ensnares journalists as well as news consumers, a thought to bear in mind as we take a look at the coverage of the communist world in 1989.

If 1988 was the year of the Soviet Union, Mikhail Gorbachev *Time*'s "Man of the Year," 1-4-88, this was the year of Eastern Europe. It's easy to say this now, a year later, but Edward Mortimer of the London *Financial Times,* the shrewdest observer we see in the European press, said it then: "If 1988 was the year of the Soviet Union, perhaps 1989 will be the year of Eastern Europe," he prophesied in "The Dog That Failed to Bark," *FT* 1-10, a column that earned Mortimer a 10 Best selection for commentary. This was no offhand shot in the dark. Mortimer assessed the gathering forces the way a seismologist would contemplate a prospective earthquake, clearly seeing that the quiet in Eastern Europe the previous year was the calm before the storm, as the various entities drew lots to see which would test the Brezhnev Doctrine. Mortimer does not stop at that point of prophecy, but goes on to call for Western policymakers to begin preparing for a post-Brezhnev Doctrine Europe. This set the scene for the year to come.

Another important work of analysis for understanding 1989 was Robert G. Kaiser's "The U.S.S.R. In Decline," *Foreign Affairs* Winter 1988/89, cited as a 10 Best for commentary. If Mortimer was right, that Eastern Europe would test the Kremlin's hegemony this year, the test would succeed upon the acceptance in Moscow of the failure of communism as an economic model. Kaiser, who had been *The Washington Post*'s Moscow bureau chief in the early 1970s, wrote in his *FA* essay: "It is hard now to imagine how Gorbachev or any other future Soviet leader could gracefully yield to the Poles or the Hungarians — not to mention the Armenians or the Estonians — their independence. But the entire Gorbachev phenomenon was hard to imagine before it happened. The most dramatic political experiment of the century is collapsing before our eyes — slowly, but certainly."

As 1989 opened, the only real hope for the crumbling Soviet economy seemed to be a quick fix of Western joint ventures and perhaps a payoff of the co-operative movement begun a year earlier. Gorbachev's *glasnost* was also promising democratic elections in the U.S.S.R., which promised to free political reins to tackle the economic problems. In "Truly Talking Shop at the Kremlin," 1-2, Holman Jenkins, Jr. of *The Washington Times* locates the central irony that

9

Gorbachev's piecemeal move to market socialism is causing U.S. firms *to lose interest,* preferring the guaranteed orders and prices of the old command economy. He also puts his finger on the inconvertible currency as an insurmountable barrier that is not being approached: "The rub is the ruble." Meanwhile, Quentin Peel's "Moscow's Limit On Co-Operation," *FT* 1-6, told of new restrictions on the Soviet Union's fledgling new co-operative movements, threatening to strangle them in their cribs. Peter Gumbel's "Moscow Tackles No. 1 Domestic Problem," *The Wall Street Journal* 3-10, examines Gorbachev's planned agricultural reforms, and the stiff opposition it faced from orthodox communists, led by Yegor Ligachev.

Timothy Garton Ash of London's *Spectator* provided consistently incisive coverage of the changes in the East Bloc and Soviet Union, early in spotting the hairline cracks in the Iron Curtain and Berlin Wall that would widen into fissures, toppling governments and ideologies. "Safe Exit From Yalta," 1-14, poses the question of western Europe's course as the Soviet empire in Eastern Europe continues to disintegrate, and Ash argues that western Europe should continue to integrate, to ensure that West Germany remains West and to provide a more secure harbor for any central European states that, someday, may leave the Soviet orbit.

As the lots were being drawn, further reports were feeding this sense of portentiousness. Martin Sieff, in "Hard-Line Communists Are Marching Anew In Hungary," *WAT* 1-3, writes of the growing pressures on Hungarian party chief Karoly Grosz's reform efforts, noted that much of the hardliners support was coming from mid-level bureaucrats, "who risk being marginalized if they lose their power as managers." The question of what to do with party officials, or *nomenklatura,* made obsolete by economic reforms was one that would haunt other communist countries starting down the road of *glasnost* and *perestroika* in 1989.

Perhaps fittingly it was Poland, who in 1980 first gave notice to the world that time was running out on the post-World War II order in Europe, that led the way for reform in 1989, sprinting past Hungary, which had been tapped by much of the media at the start of the year as the one Eastern European nation that might try to test the boundaries of Mikhail Gorbachev's "New Thinking." John Lloyd's "The Search For An Acceptable Balance," *FT* 3-3, alerted Western readers to the changes imminent in Poland rising out of that country's desperate financial straits and political impasse, broken only by the "round table discussions" between the communist government and Solidarity. "If all goes well by the Government's lights, it will agree on elections to the Sejm (parliament), probably in June or late July, which will see a controlled move to a sort of democracy. In this the PUWP [Communist] and its parliamentary allies [Peasants' and Democratic Parties] would command a majority of seats, but a minority — mooted at 40 per cent — would be allocated to the opposition parties."

In a marvelous retrospective published late in the year, Lawrence Weschler takes readers behind the closed doors of the "round table discussions" in "A Reporter At Large — A Grand Experiment," *The New Yorker* 11-13, as well as providing an in-depth look at the June parliamentary campaign and the awesome economic problems facing the new non-communist government. " 'You don't get it, do you,' " Piotr Bikont, the documentary-film maker, said to me one evening after I had spent half an hour voicing my forebodings — ecology, union busting, exploitation. 'Yes, of course, those are all problems,' he said. 'Real problems. But that's the point — they're the real, normal problems of real, normal countries. You have no idea of how long we've been yearning for real, normal problems instead of all the surreal, abnormal problems we've had to cope with in this crazy country for so many years.' "

Before the Polish election in June, of course, there were the elections to the Soviet Congress of People's Deputies in March. We read nervously in the *Los Angeles Times* in January about "Back-Room Maneuvers Mar Soviet Vote Drive," 1-25, by Dan Fisher. If Gorbachev was going to manipulate these elections at home, it would be a clear signal he would not be able to deal with the larger issue of East Europe's independence. A promising note came in a dispatch from Michael Parks in "New-Style Election Altering Soviet Political Landscape," *LAT* 3-6 "most of the country's senior political analysts rank the changes, in terms of potential, second only to the

1917 Revolution." The elections arrived four years (or one American presidential term) into Mikhail Gorbachev's stewardship of the Soviet government and Communist Party, when his *perestroika* policy was starting to resemble more and more Napoleon's "advance" on Paris.

It was to make an end-run around conservatives like Ligachev that Gorbachev had created the Congress of People's Deputies in the first place, and this served as the subtext for virtually all the coverage we saw. Many of the articles concentrated on personalities, in time-honored American campaign coverage fashion. Michael Dobbs of *The Washington Post* zeroed in on the contest in Yaroslavl, where a lieutenant colonel was running against the commander-in-chief of Soviet Forces in Germany. Boris Yeltsin, who's name frequently appeared with the prefix "maverick" attached, was built up in the Western press as the leading opposition candidate (Esther B. Fein's "Full of Fight, Yeltsin Feels He's The One," *The New York Times* 2-23; Dobbs' "Yeltsin Given Solid Support in His Opponent's Stronghold," *WAPO* 3-22), although in "Mr. Yeltsin's Damascus," *The Spectator* 1-21, Stephen Handelman noted that "From his exile in the nether reaches of Soviet bureaucracy, the one-time Moscow Party boss appears to be having second thoughts about his earlier thesis that reforms were being sabotaged by slow-moving administrators. He told a group of Young Communist League (Komsomol) activists in Moscow last month, 'We're going too fast.' "

Nevertheless after the votes were counted on March 27th and, in the words of Gorbachev, "The Soviet man has had his say," Yeltsin won a parliamentary seat in a landslide, and Quentin Peel in "When the People Said 'Enough,' " *FT,* 3-29, addressed Yeltsin's plans to lead the opposition in the new Congress. "Mr. Yeltsin has actually united a coalition of opposition forces including many who are regarded as totally beyond the pale by the party leadership," wrote Peel. Much of the Western press echoed Peel in deciding that on balance the election and subsequent Congress would be a net plus for Gorbachev, enabling him to stay anchored in the middle while Ligachev and Yeltsin stake out the hard left and right. In a leader on the Soviet elections, *The Economist* wrote: "Mr. Gorbachev won more on Sunday than many people, including *The Economist,* thought he would. He lost some too. One disconcertingly clear message was that the Russians want a better life. . . .On Sunday the voters were allowed, for the first time, to take a swipe at individual Communists and watch them tumble." It was a phenomenon that would be repeated a little over two months later in Poland.

In April, without waiting for a test of the Brezhnev Doctrine, we read in *The New York Times* that "Gorbachev Said to Reject Soviet Right to Intervene," 4-2, by Henry Kamm in Budapest. As the dispatch made clear, he had renounced the Brezhnev Doctrine unilaterally, an event so colossal, so *incredible,* that the *Times* ran it *on page 15!!!* The commentary that followed suggested again and again that he didn't really mean what he seemed to be saying. Four days *later,* Andrew Boroweic of *The Washington Times* seemed to think he had a newsbeat in predicting that Gorbachev might be on the verge of renouncing the Brezhnev Doctrine in "Experts See Signs That Gorbachev Is Phasing Out Brezhnev Doctrine," 4-6.

In that light, the single most important sentence we saw in the press as the avalanche was about to begin was not a report at all, but an excerpt from a speech by Gorbachev printed without comment in *The New York Times,* 5-26, "The Debate in the Soviet Congress," on its first day: "I assure you, comrades, I want to dispel the illusion that information doesn't get to me and that I don't know what goes on in the country. . . .Maybe I know more than you. *I know less than all of you put together, but more than each of you individually.*" With astonishment, we realized that Gorbachev *understands* the essence of democracy *and its advantage!* The statement, of course, is the embodiment of a republican form of democracy. The Soviet leader could not then see either *legitimacy or advantage* to the Brezhnev Doctrine. The Congress itself seemed to be functioning within this framework, Bill Keller reported, "At the Soviet Congress, Watching Big Brother Squirm," 6-4, wondering himself: "Is this the birth of something like a democratic government, or is it just a big political sauna, where the country sweats out its poisons before lapsing back into apathetic languor?"

"The iron curtain is, literally, being taken down." So wrote *The Economist* in "Noblest Cut," 5-6. "On May 2nd the Hungarians began dismantling the ugly fence along their border with Austria. . ..Not everyone is happy. Austria is bracing itself for a flood of refugees. Most upset are the conservative communists in Czechoslovakia, East Germany and Romania, who fear that Hungary will become an escape route to the West."

Most of the coverage of this event did not go even as far as *The Economist* did here, with newspapers and magazines content to run the photograph of the Hungarian border guard cutting away the barbed wire with a simple caption along the lines of "New Day In Eastern Europe." There was a general sense that change was coming in Eastern Europe, although most observers were still using a time frame of years, or else referring to an open ended "some time in the next century." In "Breaching the Wall," *Time* 9-11, James O. Jackson and Frederick Painton captured the conventional wisdom of the moment, noting that "if the flood [of refugees] continues at its present rate, more than 100,000 East Germans will have crossed the border by year-end," and later "any reunification scenario that involves even modest liberalization — and virtually all of them do — would instantly be vetoed by Honecker and his hard-line allies. The East German leader only last January predicted that the Berlin Wall, the most potent symbol of the fatherland's division, could stand for a hundred years."

Passages such as the one cited above underscore the perishable nature of hard news stories on the events in Europe this year. Often the ink was barely dry on our daily newspaper before the events reported were overrun by new events. But the better reporters were able, at least, to lay some of the groundwork for what was to come. Serge Schmemann's "Succession Watch in East Germany," *NYT* 7-24, singles out Egon Krenz as the most likely successor to Erich Honecker. Later, Timothy Garton Ash cuts a sharp profile of East Germany's Egon Krenz in "Yesterday's Man," *Spectator* 10-28, persuasive on how short the tenure of this Honecker clone will be. Ash's "After the Party," *Spectator* 11-18, unfolds as three stories, the Berlin one flowing into the German one which flows into the European one. Ash does a splendid job here making the case that Europe's map will be redrawn in the wake of the dramatic changes in Berlin.

Brian Beedham in "East Of Eden," survey, *The Economist* 8-12, wrote that "Czechoslovakia. . .has a better chance than most people realize." Beedham's assertion was based not on reform from above or revolt from below, but from pressure by Mikhail Gorbachev, who "has seen that even Czechoslovakia's relatively modern economy is sinking into incompetence, and he does not want another basket-case on his hands. . ..The most hopeful view, that this will produce dramatic results before the end of 1989, may be starry eyed; but Czechoslovakia is not to be written off." Beedham also makes a passing reference to "a few rioting young people in Leipzig" later on, while discussing East Germany. And David Hoffman got one of the scoops of the year in Washington in "Bush and Gorbachev to Meet in December," *WAPO*, 11-1, where he broke the story of the shipboard summit off the coast of Malta. The year also ended with one more slide to the avalanche when Romanian President Nicolae Ceausescu, the one hardline Stalinist leader continually singled out by the press as the sure exception to the revolutionary rule in Eastern Europe, was overthrown after brief and violent public protests. In "Wrath of East Europe," 12-23, R. W. Apple, Jr. of the *NYT* wrote on its front page: "Already gone are the hard-line regimes in Poland, Hungary, Czechoslovakia, East Germany and Bulgaria, and now Rumania appears to be in the throes of revolution. These regimes jailed dissidents, disdained truth and scorned justice. Through long, dark decades, they seemed immutable, but they all began to founder in a matter of months."

Events moved so swiftly that there was barely time for commentary that would stand up over time. The best and the loftiest of the year was a conceptual framework constructed by State Department analyst Francis Fukuyama in "The End Of History?" *The National Interest*, Summer. Fukuyama stretched the envelope, going far beyond the end of the Cold War, still being debated left and right, and pronounced an epochal event in human history, the triumph of egalitarian democracy over authoritarian communism. The essay was the most discussed journalistic enterprise of the generation, written not by a journalist at all. Journalists were mostly furious, as economists get when journalists trump their expertise. Typical was Strobe Talbott's "The Beginning of Nonsense," *Time* 9-11: "Fukuyama is not really addressing the subject of history at all. He is looking through the wrong end of the telescope at current events, at a period barely twice his age (he is 36). . . .There were plenty of predatory tyrannies before Lenin arrived at the Finland Station, and there will be plenty more even if a Romanov is restored to a Kremlin throne. Genghis Khan and Caligula didn't need a course in dialectical materialism to make their periods of history interesting, and neither do today's bad actors — or tomorrow's."

A key column for understanding 1990 may turn out to be A. M. Rosenthal's "Realities of the Revolution," *NYT* 12-8. Rosenthal notes the growing discrepancy between Western policy towards reforming the Communist world by working with the Gorbachev regime in Moscow, and the fact proven by experience in Eastern Europe that the people in communist countries see reform as starting with the removal of the Communist Party from its leading role in government. Indeed, there was a generally pessimistic tone towards Gorbachev and the chances for reform in the Soviet Union as 1989 drew to a close. Western press accounts of Andrei Sakharov's funeral seemed to be sounding a death-knell for optimism about the near future for Mikhail Gorbachev and his policies as well.

Much of the scrambling at year's end among intellectuals and journalists was about who *"gets credit"* for the end of the Cold War. *The Wall Street Journal,* observing the guy in the white trunks standing up and waving, gave credit to Ronald Reagan, democracy, entrepreneurial capitalism, and steadfastness in foreign policy. *The New York Times,* having for the last decade ridiculed and opposed every feint and punch by the guy in the white trunks, claimed victory for the guy with his back on the canvas, who knew when to give up.

R. W. Apple, Jr., one of the big guns of the *NYT,* who roamed Eastern Europe during the avalanche for months doing his best work in years, did a Christmas Eve fly-by of 1989 in "The Week in Review," a first cut at history entitled "As Two Worlds Warm, a Post-Postwar Order Awaits," 12-24: "Ronald Reagan, fated to be one of the two leading players of the 1980's, was to step into the spotlight in that first year of the decade and to stay there for nine years. In the end, though, he was upstaged by Mikhail S. Gorbachev, who began the decade as an obscure apparatchik in Stavropol but ended it as the man of the decade, the father of glasnost and perestroika." *Time* agrees, right smack-dab on the cover, replacing the traditional "Man of the Year" with "Man of the Decade," 1-1-90. Reagan, who always believed you can accomplish miracles as long as you don't mind who gets the credit, surely smiled reading Apple's account, but perhaps agreed with him. Let's call it a draw, but we will predict historians will a hundred years from now refer back to "the Reagan-Gorbachev era," if you know what we mean.

The Great Leap Backward

While one of the world's communist superpowers was going though a process of political reformation, the other communist superpower was moving in the opposite direction. As the Chinese philosopher said, a journey of a thousand miles begins with a single step, then a half-step backward. China had come rather late to the experiment in authoritarian communism, in 1949, 32 years after the vanguard of the proletariat, its comrade in Moscow. But it was also the first to take the single step on that journey, deciding in December 1978 to begin inching away from the manic egalitarianism of Mao toward some undefined political economy that *would not* involve "poverty socialism," as the Old Guard in Beijing had finally concluded.

In "China Celebrates 10 Years Along the Capitalist Road," *NYT* 1-1, Nicholas Kristof writes on the 10th anniversary of Deng Xiaoping's economic reforms: "It is not that China's leaders are pursuing liberalization as such. Rather, their aim is economic liberalization, and they will accept political liberalization to get there. But they do not see political liberalization as linked to economic liberalization." Indeed, Kristof noted, an ordinary Chinese citizen has less freedom now than he did in 1979 to hang a poster in public.

This political schizophrenia was exacerbated by deteriorating economic conditions, official corruption, and the growing struggle behind the scenes over succession once Deng was gone. These would erupt four months later in large scale demonstrations that had Western commentators going back first to 1976, then to 1949, and finally all the way to 1919 in order to find historical comparisons. In "Little Dragon Model," *Far Eastern Economic Review* 3-9, Robert Delfs wrote of a growing debate between China's reformist intellectuals over " 'neo-authoritarianism' " — the theory that "economic liberalization in the country can be realized only through centralized political power." The theory is based on the models of South Korea, Singapore, Taiwan — economically successful East Asian nations. The debate, Delfs writes, "is at least partly an overt expression of anxiety over the prospects for succession after the passing of paramount Chinese leader Deng Xiaoping and a pervasive feeling among many young intellectuals that General Secretary Zhao Ziyang will only be a transitional leader."

Fang Lizhi, the former vice president of the University of Science and Technology, in "China's Despair and China's Hope," *The New York Review of Books* 2-2, assessed the road to democracy in China, against a growing democratic consciousness, and left little room for pundits who had been asserting that "democracy" is an alien concept in China. In "Power War, Chinese Way," *NYT* 3-23, Nicholas Kristof dealt with the increasingly out-in-the-open struggle between the reformer Zhao "who, more than anybody else today, embodies China's aspirations for radical change" and Prime Minister Li Peng, who "worries that too-rapid development would accelerate inflation and cause problems that would impede reform in the long run," with Li's star the one on the rise.

Dinah Lee's article "China's Next Leap Could Be Backward," *BusinessWeek* 5-8, a 10 Best selection for foreign dispatch, was accurate in relating China's current inflation to that of 1949's inflationary chaos, which paved the way for the Communist Revolution. The Old Guard remembers. For some reason we saw little on the individual protesters themselves, the Western media making little attempt to personalize any of the student leaders. Dorinda Elliott's "We Have Enthusiasm and Daring," *Newsweek* 5-8, on Wuerkaixi, was a notable exception, with Elliott relying heavily on quotes, noting that "his own methods seem more autocratic than democratic," although in the aftermath of Tiananmen Square we can understand the protesters' reluctance to draw too much attention to themselves.

There were many accounts afterwards of the government's retaliation against the demonstrators, such as Jonathan Alter's "Unwilling Informants?" *Newsweek* 6-26, which told of how Chinese authorities were using videotapes of Western news transmissions to identify protestors, then broadcasting their faces to the nation. Nicholas Kristof's "Troops Attack and Crush Beijing Protest; Thousands Fight Back, Scores Killed," *NYT* 6-4, and Daniel Southerland's "Troops Roll Through Beijing to Crush Protesters; Scores Reported Killed As Chinese Fight Back," *WAPO* 6-4, were two of the best on-the-spot reports we read on the bloody retaking of Tiananmen Square, we could almost hear the whoosh of the artillery fire and hear the crackle of the bullets, although the most memorable account we saw was BBC producer John Simpson's brief but harrowing "Tiananmen Square," *Granta*, 10th Anniversary Special. Simpson was one reporter who dropped his mask of professional detachment, was moved to act by the slaughter taking place around him and was willing to write about it afterward. Southerland's "Chinese Army Seen Near Conflict," *WAPO* 6-6, "Rival Forces Clash in China; Bush Bans Military Sales to Regime," by Adi Ignatius and James Sterba *WSJ* 6-5, with unconfirmed reports of Chinese armies clashing, was typical of Western coverage in the immediate days after the crackdown, when China was inaccurately pictured as a country on the brink of civil war.

Fox Butterfield of *The New York Times* provided the best analysis we saw in the immediate aftermath of Tiananmen Square, with essays such as "Did the Heavens Finally Fall on Deng?" *NYT* 6-16, a 10 Best selection for foreign dispatch, and "Deng Reappears With a Chilling Lesson About Power in China," *NYT* 6-11. He writes in "Chilling Lesson" that the hardliners' victory "revealed that despite a decade of stunning economic progress, politics in China remains heavily traditional. Palace intrigue, control of the army, and a web of personal relationships count far more than law or modern political institutions or international opinion."

Colina MacDougall, an astute China watcher, wrote "Economic Inequalities Test Power of Centre," *Financial Times* 6-8, an optimistic assessment of what might flow from the bloodletting. "Economic reform requires a measure of local independence, and even the hard-liners want China to become rich and powerful. While the army may be at hand to impose Deng's will for the moment, in the longer run the economic imperatives may of necessity slacken the bonds to Peking. In that case, it seems inevitable that the demand for political reform will follow again and perhaps when China's old guard have moved on, will be more successful."

The New York Review of Books was an important source of debate, discussion, and dispatches on the China story. Early it provided a forum for Fang Lizhi, critic of the Chinese regime and considered by some to be the Chinese equivalent of Andrei Sakharov, "China's Despair and China's Hope," 2-2. Orville Schell's "China's Spring," 6-29 *TNYRB,* is a magnificent account of the student democracy movement's move into Tiananmen Square and the hunger strikes. Schell, an early Mao apologist who saw the flaws early too, details with intensity the swirling, heady excitement, while keeping a firm grasp of the reality of limits and constraints on how far the movement would be able to go. In the same issue, Perry Link's "The Chinese Intellectual and the Revolt" provides rich accounts of how the "Beijing Revolt" of 1989 matured, and the depths of its influence throughout Chinese society. Both were pre-crackdown reports, but aside from perhaps an optimism about the direction of immediate events the information and insights are abundant.

Patrick Buchanan's "Caught In the Dragon's Wrath," *WAT* 6-7, summed up America's view toward China from across the political spectrum: "Mr. Deng and his gangsters have declared war on the Chinese people; and America must take sides against Mr. Deng. Not only because that is the right thing to do, but because the right thing is also the pragmatic thing. We must shove that regime to arm's length because it is a corpse; it has no legitimacy, no future." Six months later President Bush would learn that America's attitude hadn't changed when it was disclosed that Mr. Bush's National Security Advisor, Brent Scowcroft, flew to Beijing in an effort to mend ties between the two countries, which *The New Republic* labeled a "shameful retreat from principle," in "China Cad," 1-1-90. Conservatives and liberals, *The Wall Street Journal* and *The New York Times,* were beside themselves with outrage, the *Times* citing Scowcroft's hosts, whom he toasted lavishly, as "the butchers of Beijing," picking up on a phrase we first saw in *The New York Review of Books.* Taking exception to all the criticism of Bush, which we thought immensely useful, was *The New York Times*'s Tom Wicker, who argued rather persuasively that it was the correct, diplomatic thing to do at the moment, "Bush and the New Moralism About China," 12-15: "If China is going to be the last of the authoritarian communists, trapped in a corner, the former U.S. envoy to Beijing, George Herbert Walker Bush, obviously prefers coaxing them out to sealing them in."

Apple, of *The New York Times,* in that same 12-23 P. 1 analytic, mused that "The bloody and still-incomplete revolution in Rumania, the opening of the Berlin Wall at the Brandenberg Gate and the invasion of Panama, all within the final 10 days of 1989, provided a fitting denouement to a turbulent, dramatic, fascinating year in international affairs....Around the world others are watching and listening. The main Chinese group, based in Paris, said tonight, 'The wind of history blowing in Bucharest will soon reach Beijing.' "

Drugs and Crime

We were repeatedly informed during 1989 that there was a battle being fought, as the press corps elevated the drug war to national prominence. Washington DC was declared our nation's crime capital, but there were few corners of the nation that felt free of the scourge of crack cocaine, the crimes associated with it, and the strains on the social-support and criminal-justice systems. Readers could hardly glance at a headline without seeing at least one account of the latest battle in the drug war, or the casualties: crack-addicted babies, troubled youth, broken, tattered lives. Once reserved for the "Metro" sections or back pages, we found so many regional crimes and drug-related horrors on front pages and covers that we wondered at times if the larger story weren't going unreported, the press scrambling to cover the battle. The "underclass" phenomenon, the perpetual cycle of welfare dependency, had seemingly been studied to death. But this year it began to be re-examined, as it intersected with the other problems of drugs and crime and in light of the eight years of unbroken economic expansion. We were occasionally gratified to see both the causes and possible resolutions of the war probed even as the debate over drug legalization heated up again.

Fought on several different fronts, we found that spot reports from the trenches were the order of the day. The press corps was studied in its coverage of the different angles: money laundering; bombings in Colombia; interdiction; the spread of crack and drug-related crime; treatment; the tragedy of shattered souls. *Newsweek,* having been one of the first to devote major resources to the problem, continued its "The Drug Crisis" update series. As the problem strengthened its grip on the inner cities, transcending racial and socio-economic boundaries, we found the press to be well on top of each battle as the enemy pushed its way forward. Moving away from the tendency to indulge in crack-mother-babies stories, journalists and policy analysts began to debate the question of legalization and treatments.

A serious examination of Lyndon B. Johnson's Great Society as the genesis of the underclass addict, by weakening the links between effort and reward, provided a good starting point for the origins of the drug war. Nicholas Lemann, part of the neoliberal cadre of Washington journalists, began the year with "The Unfinished War," *The Atlantic* 12-88/1-89, a two-part treatise on the history of the war on poverty, from JFK to President Bush. A more accessible "No Way Out," by Carolyn Lochhead *Insight* 4-3, provides an exceptional examination of the growth of the "underclass" as distinct from the poor, as the underclass loses "a sense of hope, possibility and shared values with America's mainstream." Lochhead examines how critical shifts in policy that occurred during the Sixties cultural revolution helped shape the current situation: "Wisdom born of the Sixties reshaped ancient values and beliefs about the family, about sex, about religion and about personal behavior. . ..For the privileged and educated who originated them, many of these ideas proved to be a passing fancy. . ..But nowhere did such notions take root with greater vengeance or extract a higher price than among the poor, for whom the margin for error in life is painfully slim."

Fred Barnes sees some hope in "The Poverty Thing," *The New Republic* 1-30, with the appointment of Jack Kemp to HUD, but not much: "Concentrating on the hard-core poor is self-defeating. You won't get anywhere with them and it will cause you to lose the others. The conservative view is that lifting the entire underclass requires a moral renaissance that the government couldn't achieve if it tried." Martin Tolchin reports that Secretary Kemp is going to stand tough, "Kemp Vows to Oust Tenants on Drugs," *The New York Times* 3-8, in an effort to clean out federal housing projects long infested by dealers and addicts. As far as we could tell this was the first effort to make drug *families* responsible for addicts in their midst if they are to continue to receive federal aid. Tolchin did not examine these implications, though, and almost nothing was written directly on the possibility of extending family accountability deeper into the underclass. In a 10 Best selection from Oakland, Jane Gross connects the surge in emergency room drug-related overload on the first and fifteenth of each month to the issuance of welfare checks, "Urban Emergency Rooms: A Cocaine Nightmare," *NYT* 8-6, but there is no further development of the connection, the taxpayers financing both the drug habit and its treatment.

Additionally, the Sixties was a certain beginning point in and of itself, as shown by Walter Shapiro's drug apologia, asking how parents who did drugs as flower children or as a counterculture experience can tell their kids to just say no in good conscience, "Feeling Low Over Old Highs," *Time* 9-18. Shapiro is hardly persuasive, but such feeble thrusts were representative of the background noise: "But we are all a product of our life experiences, and I, like so many of my peers, cannot entirely abandon this *Lucy in the Sky with Diamonds* heritage." It is this first user that the Bush drug program is aimed at. There was the usual outcry that Bush wasn't doing enough, or was doing it wrong, but it wasn't as though he didn't have plenty of advice. Fred Barnes offers his in "Bennett the Drug Czar: An Agenda," *The American Spectator* 4-89, some sensible ("a joint approach on [drug kingpins] by American and Colombian forces"), some silly ("any movie treating drugs or drug dealers lightly or favorably should have a D attached to its rating") as Bill Bennett took the job nobody wanted. Bush also promised to go to the source, the drug supply-side.

This is one vow Bush kept, sending equipment, cash and advisors to Colombia, and troops to go after Panama's Gen. Manuel Noriega at the close of the year, the "political drug-dealer" surrendering on Christmas Eve. The initiative met with some moderate success, as Colombia also bravely struggled against the cancerous drug cartel in its midst, and was dutifully covered by the press, thoroughly realistic without being combative. Michael Isikoff's "U.S. Suffering Setbacks In Latin Drug Offensive," *The Washington Post* 5-27, was an excellent, if disheartening, status report of a "near breakdown of U.S. antidrug policy throughout Latin America." The article identifies the intractable political problems on the ground that account for the failure and which are now to be taken into account: "The NSC review is examining a wide range of options that include military action, an expanded role of U.S. intelligence agencies, and new economic and military aid to the region. . ."

In "Cuba Sentences Officers to Death For Corruption," *WAPO* 7-8, Julia Preston explores the different dimensions of the trial of Cuba's top war-hero General Arnaldo Ochoa Sanchez on charges of drug trafficking. Preston backs up the assessment that Fidel Castro was complicit in drug trafficking, developing the evidence that the trial also reflects his move to dispose any potential threats to his rule. Tough, Joseph Treaster's "U.S. Sending Wrong Equipment to Fight Drugs, Colombians Say," *NYT* 9-12, reveals the inefficiencies of the U.S. government, symptomatic of the bureaucracy thesis that if enough money is spent, it doesn't matter how. We got a different perspective on the source of drug traffic from *Insight*'s Stephen Brookes, with "Drug Money Soils Cleanest Hands," 8-21. A very timely cover on the global laundering of drug money, Brookes' comprehensive, steady fact-filled pace is perceptive, as launderers salivate over EEC integration, and the removal of all currency controls: "They can all park their money in Germany, which is particularly obsessed with not touching the banks." *Time*'s Jonathan Beaty and Richard Hornik produced a similar piece on "Money Laundering," 12-18. But not everyone was pleased: a Peruvian journalist, Gustavo Gorriti argued that drug interdiction policies are ineffective and only old-fashioned foreign aid will solve the problem, his analysis much more insightful than his conclusion, "How to Fight the Drug War," *The Atlantic* 7-89.

On the home front, dispatches were grimmer, as treatment centers became overloaded and crack addiction spread. A new drug, ice, turned up in California, producing a longer high and a more treacherous comedown than crack cocaine. The nation's capital became the most murderous city in the country as Mayor Marion Barry stood by. "Fighting Crime: The City is Leaderless," by Carl Rowan, *WAPO* 3-7, is an early indictment of the DC mayor: "When last seen, 'commander-in-chief' Marion Barry was on yet another walking tour of a drug-infested neighborhood mimicking (unconvincingly) Jesse Jackson's chant of 'Down with dope! Up with hope!' Even without getting into a discussion of his own alleged drug use, the mayor has been a tower of Jell-O in his self-proclaimed war on drugs. To say that the mayor lacks credibility on this topic is, unfortunately, a monumental understatement." Things were little better elsewhere. Gina Kolata in "Twins of the Streets: Homelessness and Addiction," *NYT* 5-22, finally made an important connection, linking the problems of homelessness and addiction in New York and Washington, as even homeless advocates admit that if a homeless persons' alcohol or drug addiction isn't treated, nothing else will help. Applause to *The New York Times;* now we can go to work on the real problem, of which homelessness is one symptom.

Even the traditionally "immune" all-America pockets were affected. An eye-opening pair of dispatches from Jane Mayer of *The Wall Street Journal* reveals that no place is safe from drug infestation. "Spreading Plague: Seaford, Del. Shows How Crack Can Savage Small-Town America," 5-4, is a vivid parable on small-town Seaford, a crack haven, with Mayer recounting compelling stories from a battlefield we'd not have expected. In "Street Dealers: In the War On Drugs, Toughest Foe May Be the Alienated Youth," 9-8, Mayer draws a powerful portrait of former drug dealer Robert Penn, seventeen-years-old and turned-around; Penn is from Omaha. Eric Harrison's "Jamaicans: New Faces in U.S. Crime," *Los Angeles Times* 1-3, an enterprising and fast-paced report on how Jamaican drug gangs, "Bloods & Crips," invaded Kansas City, immediately caught our attention. Andrew Malcolm picks up on this later, filing "Crack, Bane of Inner City, Is Now Gripping Suburbs," *NYT* 10-1, with powerful stories and data on new addicts to crack.

But what to do? As a sense of despair crept into the national discussion, the press corps shifted attention to a fresh discussion about legalization. A curious coalition emerged from the left and right, liberals and libertarians advocating an end to drug prohibition. William F. Buckley renewed his libertarian advocacy of the idea. Jefferson Morley recounted his experiment with crack in "What Crack Is Like," *TNR* 10-2. It perhaps was designed to ease our minds that crack's not so bad, but had the opposite effect, seeming like an advertisement for crack that reads like a 1968 LSD apologia from a zonked-out flower child. Ellen Benoit's "The Case for Legalization," *Financial World* 10-3, isn't, puffy and misinformative. But the debate really got rolling with the Friedman-Bennett-Lewis exchange. Nobel Laureate Milton Friedman, who has taken the libertarian, free-market position on drugs for decades, appeared on *The Wall Street Journal*'s op-ed page 9-7, with "An Open Letter to Bill Bennett," arguing that "had drugs been decriminalized 17 years ago, 'crack' would never have been invented. . .and there would today be far fewer addicts." Bennett's eloquent reply, "A Response to Milton Friedman," *WSJ* 9-19, points out that Friedman's policy is to surrender and see what happens. From the left, Anthony Lewis "Insisting on Disaster," *NYT* 9-24, takes off from this springboard to press perhaps the definitive case for legalization, thoughtful on the lessons Prohibition holds for the drug war.

On the other side of the equation, A. M. Rosenthal, Lewis' companion on the op-ed page, stood firmly against legalization, reasserting his opposition in several ways throughout the year. "The Drug Train," *NYT* 2-3, is plain: "The drug problem in the United States already has become too much for a sensible, self-respecting public to put up with. It is simply not sensible to put up with a society where every single day of the year hundreds of Americans are either shot, beaten, or robbed in the streets, and millions of people are afraid to even walk in them, by day or by night. It does not make sense to put up with a society in which the brains of children all over the country are being damaged without salvation. It does not make sense to permit killer gangs to hunt in our cities." He's equally trenchant in "The Japanese Mystery," 4-7, stating that Japan has no drug problem because they simply don't tolerate drug use. First offenders are treated more harshly than repeated users in the U.S. The example is worth noting, but is at this point far from the realistic center of policy probabilities. In China, after all, where offenders are executed, there is less of a drug problem than in Japan.

As Elisabeth Rubinfein points out in "U.S. Police Seek Lessons on How to Keep City Streets Crime-Free," *WSJ* 1-11, the racially and culturally homogeneous Japanese population has little in common with the problems of the varied socio-economic groups in the U.S. A *Journal* editorial, "Cracking Down," 8-10, makes the observation that the crack epidemic has eroded opposition to a forceful national anti-drug strategy, but, although most of the residents of inner-city neighborhoods being destroyed by drugs would support drug czar William Bennett's tough line, "it will be interesting to see how long liberal support for the strategy lasts," also pointing out that "It is obviously ridiculous to talk about 'rehabilitating' an Uzi-toting drug pusher who makes $5,000 a week. His problem is not lack of self-esteem." The most strenuous effort to *advise* readers on how to cope with drugs in their family and community came from *U.S.News & World Report,* whose owner and editor-in-chief, Mortimer Zuckerman, is passionately opposed to drug legalization. Several articles in its 9-11 issue are devoted to "A Family Guide" to "How You Can Beat Drugs."

We did find some particularly impressive treatises debating the wisdom of drug-legalization. *The New Republic* editors can take credit for "Crackmire," 9-11, an equally thoughtful and startling examination of Bush's drug plan, impressively evaluating its chances of success on the margin. A few months earlier, the same magazine offered "Crackdown," by James Q. Wilson and John J. DiIulio, Jr. *TNR* 7-10, a sterling effort to advance the policy debate, discussing the grave social problems that cause addiction and providing an excellent outline of perspectives that take the war on drugs to a new level of polemic. "At this stage, we are not trying to deter drug sales or reduce drug use. All we wish to do is to reassert lawful public control over public spaces. Everything else we may wish to achieve — reducing the demand for drugs, curing the users of drugs, deterring the sale of drugs — can only be done after the public and the police, not the dealers and the gangs, are in charge of the neighborhood." Another important contribution to the legalization debate came from Marlise Simons in Italy, "Rising Heroin Use and Addict Deaths Alarm Italy, Where Drug Is Legal," *NYT* 10-8, as legalization in that country open a Pandora's Box: ". . .a national law permits narcotics for personal use. There are 100,000 or so heroin users in Milan, a city that the police now call the European heroin capital. . . .'We find bodies in parks, in cars, in cellars,' said Stefano Rea, chief of the crime squad of the national police in Milan. 'Italy was a few years behind other countries with the drug problem. But like governments everywhere we are not capable of handling it.'" Simons also takes note of an ugly side effect: "Health officials say that with people widely sharing needles, more than half the country's estimated 300,000 heroin users have been infected with AIDS."

With the country far from embracing the legalization argument, the press returned to the origin of the problem. John DiIulio tells an important "underclass" success story in *The Public Interest*'s Summer issue. "The Impact of Inner-City Crime," describes Kimi Gray's and fellow tenants' work in transforming the Kenilworth-Parkside public housing development in Washington, DC from a crime and drug-infested community into a neighborhood of property owners. An effective rebuttal to the hopeless "culture of poverty" theme as well as to the idea that the underclass has to be forced to help itself, this is the cutting edge of policy. Other success stories followed.

Solutions to some of the problems of the underclass were offered by Daniel Kagan and Ben Wildavsky. Parallel reports, Kagan's cover "Fast-Food Kids," *Insight* 8-28, was among the most notable in the magazine this year, cited in *The Wall Street Journal* for its insights. Kagan reports on the poor inner-city kids of DC who *don't* peddle drugs, why they prefer flipping hamburgers, how they've made their decisions, etc., a timely and enterprising piece. Along similar lines, Wildavsky explores the story from McDonald's point of view, looking at the fast food chain as truly the largest job-training program available to inner-city kids, "McJobs," *Policy Review* Summer: "A standard lament is that the 18 million jobs created since the 1982 recession are an illusionary measure of economic expansion; a nation of hamburger-flippers, goes the argument, is a nation in decline." Wildavsky blows that apart with excellent details and organization here. This describes real work that changes the world, a real sense of solution for the poor, but not necessarily the underclass.

But all this gives us an eerie sense of *deja vu.* Despite some occasionally heavy-handed historical parallels in "How America Lost its First Drug War," *Insight* 11-20, Daniel Kagan presents an overview of the history of the first drug war of the 19th century, how frustration can lead to exaggeration and sometimes to efforts to ban all mention of drugs, which leads to ignorance in the next generation. He shows how fear-mongering and the State Department have used drug campaigns for their own ends, how statistics have been inflated or made up, and quotes experts warning against letting frustration drive our policies in directions that have failed before. The debate will continue; the crisis remain.

Charles Krauthammer's thesis in "Crime and Responsibility," *Time* 5-8, although originally penned about the Central Park "wilding" incident, is that "Entire communities are taught to find blame everywhere but in themselves." He quotes several psychologists who apologize for the Harlem youths who hunted down, raped and beat the 28-year-old jogger. A Harvard educator and psychiatrist says: "They're letting out their anger. ...There's a lot of free-floating anger and rage among a lot of our youth." Krauthammer explodes: "Rage? Upon arrest, police said, the boys joked and rapped and sang. Asked why he beat her over the head with a lead pipe, Yusaf Salaam was quoted by investigators as saying 'It was fun.' The boys have not yet been taught to say they did it because of rage, pain and despair, because of the sins whites have visited upon them and their ancestors. But they will be taught. By trial time, they will be well versed in the language of liberal guilt and exoneration."

The New York City mayoral race afforded an opportunity for the candidates to come to grips with these issues, yet they still shied from it. But Joe Klein, political columnist of *New York* magazine did not, producing some of the most pertinent writing on the subject we saw all year. In "Race: The Issue," 5-29, and "Race: Still the Issue," 11-13, he examines the racial polarization sweeping New York in 1989, with the mayoralty race in the foreground. In the 5-29 article he spotlights the vicious cycle of racial polarization that keeps blacks locked into poverty, producing a black underclass of unwed mothers and crime-prone youths, which increases racial polarization. He traces the immediate problems back to the late 1960s.

For the first time this year, the *mixture* of drugs, crime, the homeless, individual responsibility, and the current shape of the welfare state in the United States began to be addressed squarely this year, rather than each element being dissected and discussed on its own footing. It was a fair start. But this is the area we expect policymakers and the press corps will explore further as the society struggles for answers to these grave problems confronting it as the last decade of the 20th century begins.

Planet of the Year

The end of the decade saw the ending of the Cold War and the heating up of the Greenhouse Effect. Yes, we are all environmentalists, to one degree or another, with our individual priorities shifting from time to time. But it seems only natural that if the world is on a threshold of a golden age of peace and prosperity, environmental causes would rise to the top of many priority lists. After all, mankind is invariably disinterested in tending to Mother Earth during wars, recessions or depressions, of which the 20th Century has had its share. Now seems the perfect time to attend to her in earnest, before new problems arise that distract us.

Journalists, of course, are also environmentalists. But during working hours, the press corps should be covering all sides of the environmental debate, as it does on foreign policy and economic matters. We were distressed this year to see so many journalists abandoning the illusion of objectivity they maintain for open advocacy on specific environmental matters, often on the front pages and covers of important periodicals. A year ago, in *The 1989 MediaGuide,* we warned of this, where reporters "become environmentalists, detracting from the credibility of their reports, often sounding alarms instead of laying out the debates of the scientific community. We expect scientists to cry wolf at the drop of a hypothesis and expect reporters to remain skeptical even as they report the scare, acknowledging expert opinion that disputes the wolf at the door."

Taken as a whole, the news media did its worst work this year on this big, important story. Reputable scientists were forced to complain that their views were not being heard, as the media had already decided the controversy was settled across the board, slamming shut the door on debate over the "Greenhouse Effect," pesticides, toxic wastes, acid rain and the ozone layer.

What's worse, much of the press corps seemed inordinately proud of the job it was doing. At a fall conference sponsored by the Smithsonian on "The Global Environment: Are We Overreacting?" we find the science editor of *Time,* Charles Alexander, declaring "I would freely admit that on this issue we have crossed the boundary from news reporting to advocacy." Ben Bradlee, editor of *The Washington Post,* agreed with Alexander: "I don't think there's any danger in doing what you suggest."

Time, of course, helped get this all going as the year began by giving its "Man of the Year" award to the "Planet Earth," 1-2, a save-the-planet editorial that we rather liked, even though it seemed short on evidence. Our assumption was that there would be plenty of back-and-forth reporting to get to an optimum course. *The New York Times,* which devotes major resources to its Tuesday "Science Times" section, too often *acted* as if the debate was over, examining solutions but rarely offering contrasting opinion on the reality of the problem or its magnitude. *The Wall Street Journal* editorial page was open to varied opinion, but the rest of the newspaper did not even devote space to cost/benefit analysis affecting business, industry and the taxpayer. We did get from Bob Davis and Barbara Rosewicz "Poor Track Record Marks Global Climate Predictions," *WSJ* 4-10: "No one actually knows yet whether the gloomy forecasts are right, despite years of sifting through satellite data and devising computer models to predict the future." In an important story late in the year, Peter Passell of the *NYT* at least took a stab at the economics in "Curing the Greenhouse Effect Could Run Into Trillions," 11-19. Passell, an economist, starts with the assumption that the scientific debate is over, then runs through numbers showing the staggering costs of doing only very little to reverse the assumed global warming. This helped immensely in putting the discussion into perspective.

Jumping on the environmental bandwagon, *U.S.News & World Report* weighed in with a cover on "Dirty Air," 6-12, that is of little help: "Trees and ponds are dying, and many American cities are choked by a lung-searing, eye-blearing haze." The story notes good news in that the new Senate Majority Leader George Mitchell is "from the acid-polluted state of Maine," and "industry leaders who once opposed almost any clean-air strictures have changed their tune." Not one is quoted in this generally sophomoric piece. One of the best reporters in the business, Gregg Easterbrook of *Newsweek,* delivered a superlative survey that addresses many aspects of the environmental debate with satisfying detail in "Cleaning Up," 7-24, yet he too passes up a chance to examine the global warming issue: "But whether or not a greenhouse effect has officially commenced, logic says one is coming."

Among the other newsweeklies, *The Economist* also turned green in London, with "The First Green Summit," 7-15: "What defense has been to the world's leaders for the past 40 years, the environment will be for the next 40," prescribing recipes for global recession to solve the problem: "persuade people to use less fossil fuel energy, tax fossil fuels heavily, so as to drive up their price. . .Japan has to cut its fuel consumption." We thought *Insight* might try one of its patented cover packages to get its arms around the planet, but for some reason did not attempt the story. Margaret E. Kriz's "Ozone and Evidence," *National Journal* 11-11, falls short as well, advising us for openers about "the dangerous global warming trend" without presenting the "evidence." The lengthy piece is sophomoric, quoting every available hand-wringer, with no sense of debate. Philip J. Hilts in *The Washington Post* buries the good news in "Arctic Ozone Also Imperiled," 2-18, droning on about the chlorine researchers found in the Arctic Circle, where they went to find a hole in the ozone, looked for six weeks and found nothing.

Philip Shabecoff, the environmental reporter for the *NYT,* is a clear advocate in much of the material we saw from him this year. He's clearly alarmed in "Traditional Definitions of National Security Are Shaken by Global Environmental Threats," 5-29, giving no counterweight to his assertions: "Now, with the world threatened by global warming, acid rain, climate changes and the destruction of the ozone shield, environmental matters are seen as a serious threat to the internal political stability of some nations. . .." We look to the newspaper's Tuesday "Science Times" for a little more scientific method, but on this issue we were disappointed. William J. Broad's "A 30-Year Feud Divides Experts on Meteorology," *NYT* 10-24, is engrossing on a clash of methodology re the greenhouse effect between two Wisconsin academics, but Broad beats around the bush and we never do learn the pros and cons. The *Los Angeles Times* contributed little to the frontiers of the discussion, opening the year all fuzzy, squishy in a lead editorial "Caring for the Earth," 1-2: "Environmental problems, from protection of U.S. wild lands to the global atmosphere, seem immense. Still, every citizen can have an effect. It begins with caring."

The questioning of global warming came in bits and pieces for most of the year. *The Washington Post* "Outlook" section was early in running a caveat to the thesis, "The Greenhouse Climate of Fear," 1-8, by a University of Virginia professor of environmental sciences, Patrick Michaels. "None of us 'contrarians' doubts that the greenhouse effect exists. If carbon dioxide and water didn't absorb the long-wave radiation emanating from the Earth, we wouldn't be here at all — the planet would be an ice ball. What we *are* saying is that the problem is more complicated and ambiguous than it seems, if only because we are putting more into the atmosphere than just CO2." *The Post* was also the first to report on a research paper of the National Oceanographic & Atmospheric Administration that found "No Global Warming Seen in 96 Years of U.S. Data," *WAPO* 1-27 by Philip J. Hilts. The report directly challenged the congressional testimony of James Hansen of NASA, who had testified in June 1988 that he was "99% confident" the greenhouse effect was with us. *The New York Times* finally gets around to this story ten days later, but we're pleased to see it plays it high on P. 1, "U.S. Data Since 1895 Fail to Show Warming Trend," 2-6 by Philip Shabecoff, who is quick to highlight the reaction of Hansen that the U.S. is only 1.5% of global surface, without pushing further into the debate. The *NYT*'s Nicholas Wade did so in an op-ed, 7-3, based on a *Science* piece that questions the Hansen model: "The computer models of the greenhouse effect are indeed 'evolving' — they're somewhere around the amoeba stage."

Perhaps the most pregnant paragraph we read was in *Policy Review,* an excerpt from former Democratic Gov. Dixy Lee Ray's coming book, "The Greenhouse Blues," Summer: "The quantity of air-polluting materials produced by man during his entire existence on Earth does not begin to equal the quantities of toxic gases and particulates spewed forth into the atmosphere from just three volcanic eruptions: Krakatau in Indonesia in 1883, Mount Katmai in Alaska in 1912, and Hekla in Iceland in 1947. Mt. St. Helens pumped out 910,000 metric tons of carbon dioxide during six months in 1982, not including the eruption." The burden of this argument is that the biosphere is prepared to deal with shocks much greater than man-made CO2 emissions.

In October, one of the few non-alarmist pieces we came across on the biosphere was "The Ozone Hole that Didn't Eat the World," *Forbes* 10-30, by Ron Bailey: "Unfortunately, the popular press, abetted by scientists whose grants demand a public outcry, has painted ozone depletion in such apocalyptic terms that it's hard for most people to distinguish scientific facts from hysterical fears. Could the Antarctic ozone hole grow and eventually eat the world? Of course not. For one thing, the polar winds form a vortex confining the ozone hole." The piece does not dismiss the problem, but we get a reasonable context.

By November, the environmentalists seemed to have the press corps so thoroughly in the bag that we began seeing more and more assertions that "the debate is over." *Time,* with its continuing "Endangered Earth" series that spun off its "Planet Earth" cover, had already declared war against a known enemy, and any who disagreed were part of the problem. The *Wall Street Journal* editorial, "Chill Out," 11-20, picks up on this drift in the news media and properly insists that the debate ain't over, putting forth arguments that Global Warming is not a certainty. But this editorial was only a drum roll for what followed.

Without question, the best reporting we saw exploring the weaknesses in the environmental agenda came from Warren T. Brookes of *The Detroit News,* whose work we see through syndication in *The Washington Times.* "'Greenhouse Glasnost' at Sundance," 8-24, is among several salvoes Brookes fired at the unwarranted status Global Warming had achieved as a *cause celebre.* As a result of the series he did earlier in August debunking an ABC-TV acid rain hoax, Brookes was commissioned to do a story by *Fortune,* but the piece he produced so thoroughly cut against *Time*'s advocacy posture that *Fortune* gave it back to him after paying for it. It appeared soon thereafter as a *Forbes* cover, "The Global Warming Panic," 12-25, which indeed demolishes the arguments of the greenhouse alarmists. The key is an MIT study published in *Technology Review,* Nov.& Dec., that traces ocean temperatures from 1850 and finds "little or no global warming over the past century," not only in the U.S., but anywhere on the planet.

Brookes also quotes another leading global warming theorist, Stephen Schneider, as having supported in 1976 the then-popular view that we could be in for another ice age, "perhaps akin to the Little Ice Age of 1500-1850," he wrote.

William K. Stevens of *The New York Times* had drifted into the "debate is over camp," it seemed to us. But the Brookes piece in *Forbes,* which appeared two weeks earlier than its 12-25 publication date, seemed to inspire him to produce "Skeptics Are Challenging Dire 'Greenhouse' Views," 12-13, a P. 1 report that affirmed a majority of scientists are "undecided" on this matter. Where we were feeling we were going to be cheated out of a debate by the press corps, suddenly the Stevens piece indicated *The New York Times,* the newspaper of record, was opening it for further discussion.

Related to the non-debate over the greenhouse effect were the varied dispatches on clean air and acid rain. Philip Shabecoff balances a report of Bush's Ottawa trip pledge to reduce acid rain with statements of different severity on the problem, "An Emergence of Political Will on Acid Rain," *NYT* 2-19, but he's clearly alarmed: "acid rain is now recognized as destructive to fresh water life in many lakes and streams, particularly in the Northeast and Canada. Acid rain is also believed to contribute to the deterioration of forests and buildings and to threaten human health." These generalities are not incorrect, but we get no sense of the magnitude here and are left to think the worst. Again, Warren Brookes tackles these subjects superbly, actually burning shoe leather and making calls on the reportorial trail, in *The Washington Times*' acid rain series, a 10 Best selection: "Acid Rain Fakers," 8-10, "Acid Rain Failing the Acid Test," 8-13, and "Economic-Scientific Acid Rain Nonsense," 8-17. Brookes, who single-handedly has been altering policymaking in these areas, is particularly effective in debunking an ABC-TV News segment that aired 7-25, on how acid rain is killing trees in Vermont.

The clean air dispatches were marginally better, because journalists dealt with upcoming legislation and Congressional debates, rather than the science of the subject. Philip Shabecoff's handling of an EPA statement and congressional subcommittee is even-handed, "U.S. Calls Poisoning of Air Far Worse than Expected and Threat to Public," *NYT* 3-23, matching quotes from the greens and industry spokespeople. In a follow up "Bush's Call for Leadership in a World Cleanup Puts the Focus on the Mess in America's Backyard," 5-2, he presents a slightly distorted view, but this is also a useful litany of the environmental agenda in the U.S. He summarizes Bush's proposals in a straightforward manner in "President Urges Steps to Tighten Law on Clean Air," 6-13, with little addition, but this reporter says that William Reilly (EPA) "appears to have prevailed largely."

The Exxon *Valdez* oil spill of course contributed to the national concern over the ruination of the planet. Keith M. Schneider is typical, more attuned to affixing culpability than anything else. He blames Alaska for the oil spill, as the state wasn't ever vigilant in requiring the oil companies to have disaster plans, something akin to blaming the fireman for the fire, in "Under Oil's Powerful Spell, Alaska Was Off Guard," *NYT* 4-2: "One dramatic example was an industry decision in 1981 to disband a 20-member emergency team prepared for round-the-clock response to oil spills in Valdez Harbor and the sound. The reaction from Alaskan officials was modest." One of the few solidly dispassionate reports we saw on the spill came from George Church, his "The Big Spill," *Time* 4-10, one of the more impressively assembled accounts.

Marilyn Chase and Ken Wells offer "Paradise Lost: Heartbreaking Scenes of Beauty Disfigured Follow Alaska Oil Spill," *WSJ* 3-31, a more compelling account of how the scenery and delicate ecosystems were damaged, perhaps beyond repair. It was months later we found out that some of the blackened rocks had always been black, due to their composition of volcanic rock, "Now the Big Search Is on to Find Sea Otters that Use Styling Gel," by Allanna Sullivan *WSJ* 8-23. In "For the Petroleum Industry, Pouring Oil Is in Fact the Cause of Troubled Waters," 3-31, Sullivan and co-author Caleb Solomon take an excellent look at the repercussions of the Valdez spill, which could cripple further exploration in the area, using as a case in point an off shore installation which 20 years ago spewed 3 million gallons of oil into the Santa Barbara Channel, and today, oil industry officials view doing business in California in the same way they view doing business in an unstable foreign country.

Of course, given the spate of reporting on cleanup measures and environmental problems, alternative fuels and preventative measures were the order of the day. But the press corps was primed for new fuel searches. James Cook begins solidly on the natural gas bubble, "Unrealistic Expectations," *Forbes* 6-12, but he segues into a commercial for natural gas and never quite recovers his footing: "Gas is cleaner and easier to handle than coal, cheaper and more abundant than oil, and given that it's a combustible fuel, it's virtually pollution free. Low nitrogen oxide, lower sulfur dioxide, not even much carbon dioxide. So if you're worried about acid rain, the greenhouse effect, nuclear waste or the Valdez oil spill, gas is the fuel for you."

There is no industry as concerned with all this handwringing about Mother Earth than the Detroit automakers. Jerry Flint covers this track in "With Friends Like This. . ." *Forbes* 6-26, seeing no end in sight to DC regulation of Detroit, while the rules remain oddly skewed as Detroit's compact cars made abroad are the most fuel-efficient, but may not be included in their MPG accounting to the government. And now, "amid the near panic over global warming, the Exxon spill, and pollution, Washington is talking about pushing the fuel average requirement to anywhere from 33 mpg to 45 mpg." Ouch. And from Joseph B. White at *The Wall Street Journal* we get a debate with Paul Ingrassia in "Auto Anxiety: Debate over Pollution and Global Warming Has Detroit Sweating," 5-4, over the current emission standards debate.

A peripheral greening of the press corps occurred with the Alar and Chilean grape scares. It was bad enough that we couldn't breathe the air, or drink the water, but now an apple a day not only doesn't keep the doctor away but might bring the coroner. The flap occasioned two newsweekly covers ("Warning! Your Food, Nutritious and Delicious, May Be Hazardous to Your Health," *Newsweek* 3-27, and "Do You Dare to Eat a Peach," *Time* 3-27) and so frightened Keith M. Schneider of *The New York Times* that he spent the rest of the year looking for a pesticide smoking gun. We found him hyperventilating in "U.S. Urges Curbs on Deadly Insecticide," 3-21, about an EPA panel of toxicologists recommending aldicarb be eliminated from potatoes and bananas, even though a survey "may substantially underestimate the aldicarb residues to which consumers may be exposed." This comes out in the lead paragraph as: "The EPA's pesticide division has recommended barring using an acutely toxic pesticide on potatoes and imported bananas, presenting an unreasonable risk to infants and children."

More scare tactics as a rationale for abolition of the use of pesticides in "Food Industry Is Testing for Toxics To Reassure Consumers on Crops," 3-27, Schneider tells us we can't really trust either the government or the private sector to test for residue accurately. Philip J. Hilts lists different companies that offend in "F.D.A. Considering New Rules to Curb Health Food-Label Claims," *NYT* 9-31, to limit the claims that cereals and other foods can make on their labels and advertising, including a history of regulation and litigation, but this is as dry as Wheaties without milk and sugar.

It was *The Wall Street Journal* that helped set our minds at ease about the quality of foodstuffs. Months later we find the scares might not be so much the result of chemical alteration but media hysteria. Bruce Ingersoll reviewed the available evidence in the Chilean grape incident for months, coming up with the conclusion that the grapes were probably not tainted in Chile, but in Philadelphia, "In Chilean Grape Case, New Data Raise Doubt as to What Happened," 11-16, advancing different theories as to who the culprit might be, but convincing us that it wasn't the Chileans and that the problem is not likely to reoccur. A 10-3 editorial, "How a PR Firm Executed the Alar Scare" takes its cue from an internal memo from David Fenton's Fenton Communications on its work for the National Resources Defense Council, parts of which are reprinted verbatim: "In October of 1988 NRDC hired Fenton Communications to undertake the media campaign for its report. . . .The report marked the first time anyone — inside goverment or out — had calculated children's actual exposure levels to carcinogenic and neurotoxic pesticides. The study showed one of the worst pesticides to be daminozide, or Alar, used primarily on apples and peanuts. . . .It was agreed that one week after the study's release, [actress Meryl] Streep and other prominent citizens would announce the formation of NRDC's new project, Mothers and Others for Pesticide Limits. This group would direct citizen action at changing the pesticide laws, and help consumers lobby for pesticide-free produce at their grocery stores. The separation of these two events was important in ensuring that the media would have two stories, not one, about this project. Thereby, more repetition of NRDC's message was guaranteed. . . .An arrangement was made with 60 Minutes to "break the story of the report in late February. . . .On February 26th CBS 60 Minutes broke the story to an audience of 40 million viewers. . . .The next morning, NRDC held a news conference attended by more than 70 journalists and 12 camera crews." And so began the Alar story, in which the emperor's apples have no clothes.

While coverage of these varied environmental issues so frequently left us frustrated during the year, it was heartening to see some balance return at year's end. President Bush, who began his administration as a no-holds-barred environmentalist, was also reined in by reality, with price-tags of trillions flapping in the ozone. His science adviser, Dr. Allan Bromley, told a congressional committee: "My belief is that we should not move forward on major programs until we have a reasonable understanding of the scientific and economic consequences of these programs."

This sounds fair enough. But the citizenry has no way of determining what is "reasonable understanding" and what is not, unless the national press corps provides the particulars. It is in the interests of the environmental activists, whose *raison d'etre* is to cry "wolf" when a threat appears, to have a news media that will serve the rest of us by making careful inquiry about each and every wolf, and reporting evenhandedly on its relative threat to the commonweal.

THE BEST STORIES AND COLUMNS OF 1989

For the fourth consecutive year, the *MediaGuide* highlights individual efforts by ten print journalists in each of five categories: Business/Financial, Commentary, Foreign, General and Political. Journalists within each category are listed in alphabetical order, not necessarily in the order in which we would rank them. For this year's edition of the 10 Best, we reviewed nearly 1,000 articles and essays, constantly honing the list, to make the final 50 selections, many nominated by our contributors over the course of their reading for the book. We also invited editors and publishers of all the publications we review to submit material, and almost all sent in their favorites on the chance that we had missed them. Of the final 50, for the first time, all were our choices, having seen most of the editors' submissions when originally published.

Of course, we can't certify that there were no better columns or articles that appeared during the year. We're certain to have missed many, particularly as the scope of the publication automatically disqualifies the regional press. But there are no other award citations in American print journalism that we know of where the judges have read as much as we have *at the time of original publication.* As a result, some pieces selected came through on timeliness, others because they stand the test of time, still others because they challenged our perspective or answered our questions when nobody else could. The comments that follow the citation further defines the article's distinctiveness at length, in order to do justice to the work cited.

Business/Financial Reporting

1. **Adler, Stephen J.** *The Wall Street Journal.* "Former Runaway Hit Big Time at Drexel But Now Faces Prison," 3-21. Adler captures the tragedy and humanity of the huge government-Drexel fight as a low-level assistant trader, Lisa Ann Jones, 26, gets squeezed by government prosecutors as they angle for their ultimate prey, the big-money men at Drexel. While other reporters picked up on this, Adler's account was the most comprehensive, rich in detail that took us on a three-dimensional tour of the larger case by focusing on a sympathetic view of this little fish. "Eleven years ago, she ran away from her home in New Jersey and headed west. She landed a job as a bank teller in California, found an apartment, and started a new life. . .She was not quite 14 years old. . .and eventually earned a high school degree. By 1980, she was making $8,000 a year. Then she found a benefactor: Drexel Burnham Lambert Inc. Drexel worked her hard, but paid her well. In 'Working Girl' movie style, she rose from the ranks. . .But like many runaways with rich mentors, she was headed for trouble." It's easy to see, writes Adler, "why the government was so interested in breaking her down." Her boss was "high-powered" Bruce Lee Newberg, who reported directly to Michael Milken. "It was the kind of chain on which big cases are built. If Ms. Jones 'delivered' Mr. Newberg, maybe Mr. Newberg would cooperate and 'deliver' Mr. Milken." Of all the Wall Street stories this year, this was the most enlightening.

2. **Bartlett, Sarah.** *The New York Times.* "John Reed Bumps Into Reality," 2-5. Bartlett had poked around Reed and Citicorp two years back when she had the banking beat at *Business Week,* so she knew the territory. Timely and irreverent, Bartlett's interview of Citicorp's John Reed, "the Buckminster Fuller of banking," is thoroughly devoid of hype as she musses his hair, generally roughing him up for dreaming more about the bank's globalization than focusing on the current drudge work required to execute a plan: "to fulfill Citi's potential requires not more vision, but boring old nuts-and-bolts implementation. And so far, the Citi team's record on 'execution,' to use a little more Reed-speak, is spotty." One of the best overall pieces on the bank we've seen in ages, Bartlett's discriminating eye picks out the flaws in the future plans of this giant, pulling no punches and taking no prisoners. "His resources are limited. Tough new regulatory guidelines on capital — the financial cushion against losses — make growing through acquisitions an expensive strategy. To make new acquisitions and remain in compliance, Citi may have to sell some businesses, issue new stock, or raid its balance sheet for

undervalued assets like real estate. Thus, for all of Mr. Reed's vision, especially his bold move to create a special $3 billion reserve for third world loans, his toughest challenges lie ahead." At year's end, we note Citicorp's stock is still in the doldrums.

3. **Deutsch, Claudia.** *The New York Times.* "The Giant With a Black Eye," 4-2. We appreciate reporters going against the grain, when it's good of course, because it signals a potential turn in the crowd, and here Deutsch goes against the grain as the Valdez oil spill a week earlier puts Exxon and its chairman and CEO Lawrence Rawl on the defensive, telling us why Exxon's fundamentals should have it flying high. "Indeed, Exxon is in perhaps its best shape ever." Rawl may be a schmoe when it comes to public relations, but we appreciate Deutsch putting this in perspective, doing it without apology, just the facts, ma'am. "After several years of turmoil, complete with job cuts and divisional consolidations, it has struck such a nice balance between 'upstream' production of crude oil and natural gas and 'downstream' products like gasoline and chemicals that it is effectively shielded from the vicissitudes of the volatile oil market. While many oil companies are struggling in an era of depressed oil prices. . .Exxon's earnings have been positively buoyant." When a crisis like Valdez hits at Exxon, or Bhopal at Union Carbide, we look eagerly for information on the target enterprise, wondering if it can stand the shock that seems so magnified by the media. The corporate profile presented here is all we needed, professionally handled step by step. Exxon was at 44 then, at year's end at about 50.

4. **Gilder, George.** *Forbes.* "IBM-TV?" 2-20. Gilder examines the HDTV debate from a different perspective, viewing the much-hyped technology as a step in the process rather than an end in itself, competently, calmly and without mercy displays why it really doesn't much matter, an excellent expose. With all the hysterical hype over the Japanese beating us out in high-definition television, this was a breath of fresh air. *Business Week*'s William Marbach also filed a story on this, "Super Television: The High Promise — and High Risks — Of High-Definition TV," 1-30, giving more room to the criticism than any other reporter, save Gilder, who adds trenchant analytics to the mix, elevating the debate to an entirely new plane of ideas. "The whole issue is phony. Japanese HDTV will be obsolete by the time it triumphs. In the 1990s it will simply replace the technology of 1940 with the technology of 1980. The Japanese products will enter the market at precisely the time when the U.S. computer industry will be able to supply far more powerful video products at a lower price." Better still, Gilder offers far more competent advice to the electronics industry: "a competitor should never try to catch up. The goal should instead be to leap ahead, with a new technology. That's the beauty of the U.S. lead in computer technology. By applying it to television, the U.S. industry can leap ahead of HDTV." And then he goes on to demonstrate myriad possibilities.

5. **Huey, John.** *Fortune.* "Wal-Mart: Will It Take Over the World?" 1-30. By far the best article on Sam Walton and Wal-Mart that we've seen anywhere. Huey gains access inside secretive Wal-Mart in Bentonville, AR, and gives plenty of local color without going overboard on the hillbilly stuff. We see Wal-Mart is one tough, sophisticated group of operators, and that there is a thick layer of talent standing in back of Walton himself. This was the first, and brightest, of Wal-Mart articles that followed in *Financial World, U.S. News & World Report,* and elsewhere. "Most of the things you've heard about Sam Walton, America's billionaire cotton-sock retailing baron, are true enough — as far as they go. He is rich and homespun and self-made and plain-spoken; he insists you call him Sam. He is a quail-hunting fanatic, and he drives a ten-year-old Ford pickup with cages in back for Leroy and Kate, successors to the late Ol' Roy, his favorite bird dog. He is one of the world's greatest stump speakers, putting all but the best evangelists to shame when it comes to delivering a message to his 'associates,' the term he long ago substituted for 'employees.' What hasn't come yet through loudly or clearly enough from his lair in Bentonville, Arkansas, however, is just how serious a place this 70-year-old curiosity and his company are likely to hold in the history of American commerce." Judging from this, quite a distinguished one.

6. **Light, Larry.** *Business Week.* "The Power of the Pension Funds," cover 11-6. Just when we thought it time for one of the business and financial journals to get its arms around this topic, *BW* came through with this ultrasharp reconnaissance of the "$2.6 trillion stash," and how everyone is battling over it. "This magnificent machine may be the victim of its own success. People are fighting to siphon off its riches for things that often have nothing to do with paying for the work force's old age. And that may end up killing the goose that laid the golden nest egg — or at least clipping its wings. Corporations are dismantling plans, creaming off their surpluses, and leaving retirees with bare-bones annuities. Deficit-racked Washington is looking at taxing their trading gains. Fund managers, once meekly tending to their blue chips, are muscling into boardrooms to meddle with corporate policy and sinking money into risky buyouts and low-return, do-good projects." After this great overture, Light presents variations on the themes within a smart theoretical framework, highlighting the power stakes as a bigger chunk of the population faces retirement, and managers fight for a bigger piece of the pie. There are also fine pieces as accompaniment by Susan B. Garland, Leah J. Nathans, and Laura Jereski. It's an innovative, discriminating way of looking at an old friend, just when we wanted such a visit.

7. **Nazario, Sonia L.** *The Wall Street Journal.* "Policy Predicament: Many Minorities Feel Torn by Experience of Affirmative Action," 6-27. Even a year or two earlier, we would have been amazed to see a *Journal* P. 1 leder treating this subject, the recipients of government discrimination *on the minority side* wondering, or even complaining, that it does more harm than good. But there was a crack in this sacred cow in 1989, with the very first open discussions about the nature of social engineering in a welfare state, its contribution to the underclass, and the philosophy of separating effort and reward. Nazario gets only a piece of this sweeping theme, but it was like reaching an oasis after years on the desert, listening to the voices of minorities hired or promoted under an affirmative action plan, benefitting, yet torn by the policy's outcome. "At first, Roland Lee was thrilled to be the newest lieutenant in the San Francisco Fire Department. Then he learned he had beaten out a close friend in the department for the promotion. Then he discovered that his friend had scored higher on the qualifying exam. Then his friend quit," and Lee says he felt " 'disgusted' that race denied his white friend the promotion." Story after story indicates the same situation, as minorities work twice as hard just to gain credibility under affirmative action programs. While grateful for the opportunity, many find it has more costs than benefits.

8. **Rauch, Jonathan.** *National Journal.* "Bush's Economic Headaches," 1-21. Written at the threshold of the Bush White House, this lengthy, innovative perspective on what the new President faces in his first year and how he will proceed struck us as dead on when we read it, the best single piece we saw in the public press at the time, and a year later it holds up beautifully. Rauch, who left *NJ* later in the year for a sojourn at a Washington think tank, states his theme stoutly at the opening and never wavers from it: "In a complicated world, it is refreshing to discover that President Bush's economic agenda consists of only two items: No.1. Keep out of a recession. No.2. Everything else." It may seem so-what now that we look back, but at the time this simple blueprint was far from mainstream thinking, which generally held that the new President would go hammer and tongs at the budget deficit as his first priority. Rauch keys off a Bush statement in his second debate with Governor Dukakis, "What I want to do is keep this expansion going. I don't want to kill it off by a tax increase." Has the business cycle been repealed? This is where Rauch is most enterprising, surveying a range of academic economists and providing extensive discussion on the possibility of avoiding a recession. The effort by this young reporter is the first serious, comprehensive, questioning of the reality of the business cycle assumptions we'd seen in the popular press.

9. **Srodes, James.** *FW.* "How the Fed Sees 1989," 12-27-88. If the Rauch essay noted above gave us the best perspective on the new year from the White House, this piece by the *FW*'s Washington correspondent was easily the best from the Fed. Instead of asking two dozen

"experts" what they think, or trying to divine Alan Greenspan's poker face, Srodes engages in civilized chats with Vice Chairman Manuel Johnson and Gov. Wayne Angell, the team of growth-oriented Fed governors. His long quotes from Johnson and Angell are most impressive. Says Johnson: "There is no question that the Fed can fine-tune the economy all by itself while Mr. Bush battles up on Capitol Hill. Our job will be to provide the kind of stability in key areas — prices, rates, and so on — that will give the President the time he needs to get the fiscal side of the economy back into gear." Angell's prescience is remarkable: "The slow money growth we have done does not appear to be overdone. We have a high level of commodity prices and that should ensure high output levels. I'm very comfortable then to approach 1989 with very slow growth of the monetary aggregates and I think we will see price levels begin to move back down. When we see that happening, it will be hard to keep interest rates from sliding down. . .Right now, everyone is gloomy and I'm somewhat optimistic." He was right, and Srodes told us all about it.

10. **Verity, John M.** *Business Week.* "A Bold Move in Mainframes," 5-29. What's happening to IBM? The world is moving on and Big Blue, the U.S. entry in the big yacht race, seems to be sitting dead in the water. In this cover story, with IBM at 111 1/2, its lowest price since 1983, Verity produces this terrific piece that reads just as well at year's end, with IBM at 95 and looking south. It made its way in the world producing mainframes, System/370 now 19 years old, and it has not much choice but to slog ahead on this path. A graph knits together this big effort for the average Joe who reads *BW*: "Even if it dominated the rapidly growing markets for workstations or computers used for image processing or desktop publishing, these businesses are so small that the effect on IBM's $60 billion revenues would hardly show up. So in a way, IBM has no choice but to spend untold billions to save the mainframe." And away we go! Verity details the major paradox of IBM's strategy, that by making its software proprietary and trying to save the mainframe, it may be passed by in a world that is looking for open systems (Unix). With good hard quotes from John F. Akers, "IBM's determined chairman," Verity is realistic about the various plans and their chances for success, not a puff piece at all. Akers "expects his company to grow more slowly than the overall industry for two more years, perhaps — and that may be optimistic." At 95, a buying opportunity?

Commentary

1. **Baker, Russell.** *The New York Times.* "Scrap Iron and Rockettes," 11-4. Discourse about Japanese acquisitions of American assets had been taking on a harsher tone of late, and then, with Mitsubishi's purchase of Rockefeller Center, we smelled ugliness in the air. Will samurai suddenly appear to knife down the traditional Christmas tree? We had thoughts of: Yellow Peril. Protectionism. Pearl Harbor. Hmmmm. Then came this exquisite column from Russell Baker, pointing out that the Rockefeller boys were not born yesterday. In a trice, he connects up this deal and the upheaval in Eastern Europe: "As more and more people find it hard to remain awed by Russian brilliance. . .we seem to be inflating Japan into the new center of diabolical cunning." Tongue in cheek, as always, Baker congratulates the shrewd Rockefellers for fobbing their shabby center off on the Japanese, noting that the Japanese bought themselves some New York real estate that American oil companies, with their "astoundingly shrewd money sense" did not. What's going on here? Baker offers up one of the best insights of the year. It is "the primitive American fear of being the eternal rube in a slicksters world." Just as we believed for awhile that the Invincible Red would bury us, because we are essentially rubes, we now worry about the Invincible Yellows. "It's as though Americans can't stand to believe they're just as shrewd as the next target."

2. **Crovitz, L. Gordon.** *The Wall Street Journal.* "RICO Needs No Stinkin' Badges," and sidebar "No More Princeton/Newport Cases," 10-4. The *Journal's* Crovitz, a lawyer who writes editorials for the newspaper, is having more influence in shaping our opinion on criminal law

than any journalist of the period, practically alone in underscoring the Gulag implications of the Racketeering Influenced Corrupt Organization Act (RICO), originally passed as an easy way to throw mobsters into the hoosegow, now being used by eager-beaver federal prosecutors to nail jaywalkers as racketeers. Writing for both the concerned professional and the disinterested layman, Crovitz reviews the government prosecution of the trading firm of Princeton/Newport and presents a chilling example of aggressive federal prosecutors demonstrating that "RICO means they can win convictions without bothering to prove any substantive underlying crime." Tracing the use of the RICO law by prosecutors in tax evasion cases back to Rudolph Giuliani when he was U.S. Attorney in Manhattan, Crovitz writes, "Tax experts at Justice were wary of Mr. Giuliani's RICOing of Princeton/Newport, but acquiesced," resulting in a trial where the government prosecutor "urged the jury not to consider the technical tax laws but to convict with this appeal: 'Doesn't it feel wrong? Doesn't it sound sleazy? If it sounds sleazy, it's because it is sleazy. Your common sense tells you that.' " We finish the piece thinking Crovitz a national asset.

3. **Fukuyama, Francis.** *The National Interest.* "The End Of History?" Summer, 1989. "In watching the flow of events over the past decade or so, it is hard to avoid the feeling that something very fundamental has happened in world history." Thus begins "The End Of History?" easily the most influential item of journalistic commentary published in any English-language publication this year. As with any grand theme that wins immediate acceptance, this was as close as it could be to public consciousness when it appeared, amidst the historic revolution in political economy occurring in Moscow and Eastern Europe. Simply put, the message is akin to the song in the *Oklahoma!* musical: "Everything's up to date in Kansas City. We've gone about as far as we can go." Or in the World War I slogan, "the war to end all wars." Fukuyama writes with dead seriousness about the victory of West over East, egalitarian democracy over authoritarian communism as being suggestive of the attainment of an epochal search for an ideal. His tongue-in-cheek appears in the question mark at the end of his essay's title, as well as in his thought that with the ultimate completion of the Hegelian dialectic, we are henceforth doomed to intellectual boredom. Those who haven't read it or even heard about it have been influenced by its theme and its subtle influence on policymaking and opinion-making, and we realize that at the end of history, there is always more history.

4. **Grenier, Richard.** *The Washington Times.* "Prying Has Its Precedent," 11-6. There is so much sanctimoniousness, bombast and arrogance in journalistic commentary in these serious times. Which is why we so often turn to Grenier for relief, for charm and wit, erudition, obliqueness and, ultimately, persuasion. Here we find him contemplating the uproar over the "revelations" about Martin Luther King Jr.'s sexual dalliances contained in the Rev. Ralph Abernathy's autobiography. The pros and cons rage, but in a truly inspired move, Grenier, who has among his various degrees one in comparative religion from Harvard, goes back 400 years to King's namesake, Martin Luther, to put everything in perspective. Luther, we are told, "at one time or another," was charged by his enemies with: "syphilism, drunkenness, licentiousness, adultery, premarital intercourse, fathering an illegitimate child, favoring bigamy and using disgusting language," by his enemies, and Luther himself admitted to enjoying a "good drink" and to "wrestling with Satan." Luther, we see, practically created the prototype for today's televangelists. It seems to Grenier that the stories about King "go with the territory," and that "In time all will be said. All will be known. All will be written. The ideals are greater than the man." In short, don't mistake the messenger for the message. It's the oldest lesson in the book, and Grenier was able to present it in a fresh, original way.

5. **Kaiser, Robert G.** *Foreign Affairs.* "The U.S.S.R. in Decline," Winter 1988/89. The assistant managing editor of *The Washington Post,* who was its Moscow bureau chief from 1971 to 1974, writes this important assessment of the Soviet Union, Mikhail Gorbachev, and the problems awaiting them as the year 1989 opens. Kaiser's essay in this important journalistic cornerstone of Establishment thinking seemed dark and foreboding at the time it appeared, but it clearly laid

out the realities. At the end of 1989, even after the euphoric events in Berlin and Eastern Europe, it seemed more relevant than ever. "The rhetoric of Soviet reform emphasizes renewal and progress, but the facts that made reform necessary describe failure — the failure of the Soviet system. For the foreseeable future, the fact of that failure is likely to be more important for the world than Gorbachev's efforts to overcome it. That is because the failure is a fact, while the reforms — at least the practical ones affecting the economic life of the country — remain just a hope. It is likely to remain a forlorn hope for years to come." Yet Kaiser closes upbeat: "It is hard now to imagine how Gorbachev or any future Soviet leader could gracefully yield to the Poles or the Hungarians — not to mention the Armenians or the Estonians — their independence. But the entire Gorbachev phenomenon was hard to imagine before it happened. The most dramatic political experiment of the century is collapsing before our eyes — slowly, but certainly."

6. **Kinsley, Michael.** *Time.* "In Defense Of Congress," 4-17. A year ago we cited Kinsley's column in *The New Republic,* "The Hazards Of Duke," as a 10 Best in commentary, "an eccentric, refreshing celebration of Michael Dukakis." This year Kinsley provided us with an eccentric, refreshing celebration of Congress. He wrote amidst the convulsions in the House of Representatives that were bringing down Speaker Jim Wright and Majority Whip Tony Coelho and as S&L odors already wafted from the Democratic Senate. Kinsley shies from writing favorably of the current legislators, concentrating instead on defending Congress as an institution against current conservative complaints. Attacking the argument that the Democratic majority is due only to gerrymandering, Kinsley notes: "Constituency election systems inevitably exaggerate majorities; that is part of their function." As to the assertion that Congress is "immune from effective voter control," Kinsley asks: "Why is the apparent Republican lock on the White House considered to be a profound ideological message from the voters, whereas the apparent Democratic lock on Congress is considered to be a sign that the system doesn't work?" It does work, he argues. " 'The duty of an opposition,' a hoary British political maxim has it, 'is to oppose.' When the opposition controls an equal branch of government, opposition is a duty that should be pursued gaily and without remorse."

7. **Luttwak, Edward N.** *The Washington Post.* "Ready or Not: Cut Pentagon 'Readiness' Spending," 2-19. The opening line seemed harmless enough: "If you are running a hotel and no guests are coming, it is not sensible to continue putting cut flowers in every room." But this began the lead essay in Sunday's "Outlook" section of the *Post,* a powerful and persuasive argument from Luttwak, among the most conservative strategic thinkers in the business, for a more relaxed arms posture. While Mikhail Gorbachev has not yet seriously cut Soviet arms spending, Luttwak says the psychological climate he has wrought has strategic value to the West. It enables the U.S. to sharply cut those expensive elements of the Pentagon budget that keep our defenses in a state of readiness. His key paragraph: "For the first time, the West has strategic (i.e., political) warning. Even though all the totalitarian structures are still intact in the Soviet Union (*glasnost* could be abandoned literally overnight), the regime cannot possibly start a war without prolonged psychological preparation. There is always the risk of a spontaneous crisis, of course, but that too is far less likely in today's more relaxed diplomatic atmosphere." Luttwak adapted this essay from a longer piece that appeared soon after in the spring issue of *National Interest,* but its great impact was via its placement here in "Outlook." Read by virtually the entire diplomatic corps in Washington, it could not have been missed by the Soviet Embassy, an important signal to Moscow.

8. **Martin, Jurek.** *Financial Times.* "Time to Bring Japan Into the Fold," 9-26. The *FT*'s foreign editor sits in London, but he was as recently as 1987 its Tokyo bureau chief, and an excellent one at that. He thus has a better position than most senior editors in the global press to worry about Japan falling further behind in the clubby game being played out on both sides of the Atlantic and the dangerous implications. In this commentary, he worries that the debate over how to deal with Japan is dangerously one-sided and designed to lead to the conclusion that if

Japan can't or won't change it must be forced to do so. "The great American debate over Japan is taking place in the open and at many different political, journalistic and intellectual levels. It is good that it has been extracted from the narrower confines of diplomats, Japanologists, and protectionists. But, as currently constituted, the arguments are tending to flow pretty much one way." He sees Japan-bashing as the prevailing mode everywhere, citing books and magazine articles, the same drift in London and Washington, Japan "a crisis waiting to happen," awaiting some extraneous trigger. In a world of rapid change, "It is impossible to imagine the relationship between the US and Japan not changing while all about it is. In the US, most of the would-be architects of change veer toward the neo-brutalist." With so much of our attention turned to the breathtaking dynamics of Europe, this "Good Shepherd" reminder from London was appreciated.

9. **Mortimer, Edward.** *Financial Times.* "The Dog That Failed to Bark," 1-10. Mortimer's "Foreign Affairs" column in the *FT* has become one of the most reliable sources of commentary on the political revolution sweeping Europe. He did not disappoint with this early appraisal of whether Eastern Europe will test the limits of *perestroika* in the new year. It opens: "If 1988 was the year of the Soviet Union, perhaps 1989 will be the year of Eastern Europe," the dog that did not bark in 1988. Not that it can't. "It has barked audibly and repeatedly in the recent past. We know very well that it is not asleep but wide awake, hungry, discontented, kept at its master's side only by a strong and irksome physical chain. Now there is a new master who has loosened the chain and proclaims his disapproval of cruelty to animals." Mortimer predicts that soon the citizens of one or more of the East European countries will put the Brezhnev doctrine to the test, "to find out whether the Soviet Union really has renounced the right it asserted in 1968 to intervene militarily outside its frontiers 'in defense of socialism.' " On an assumption the Soviets will pass this test, Mortimer opens up the first real discussion we saw on how the world might wish to unfold after that. "That I suggest, is the goal toward which Europe's political strategists should now be bending their thoughts." The logic is flawless. Indubitably, Dr. Watson.

10. **Safire, William.** *The New York Times.* "The German Problem," 1-2. Two national security reporters for the *Times* on New Year's Day broke one of the biggest stories of the year, which we cite in the General Reporting 10 Best category, "Germans Accused of Helping Libya Build Nerve Gas Plant." With a *NYT* one-two punch, Safire followed the next day with this column that became the talk of Germany. His emotionally charged references to a "Final Solution," and "good Germans" and "Auschwitz in the sand," set off fireworks in Bonn and prodded the Germans into confessing that something was indeed amiss. In his column a week later, "Stop The Todeskramer," 1-16, Safire passes along the West German reaction: "Foreign Minister Genscher's chief apologist in the German media denounced me for 'impertinence' and trivializing the old war crimes as 'small change and slapstick'. . ..'Come on, William,' huffed the offended media mogul, 'you must have lost some of your marbles.' " But Safire then notes: "a competing publication sent a team of reporters to work investigating the covered-up charges. The magazine *Stern,* by superb on-the-spot digging, showed the denials by officials to be a tissue of lies and shamed one prosecutor into launching a criminal investigation." Did Safire take some cheap shots here? At the time it seemed he did. But his audacity carried with it risk. If he had turned out wrong, he certainly would not be cited here for one of the best advocacy commentaries of the year.

Foreign Dispatch

1. **Butterfield, Fox.** *The New York Times.* "Did the Heavens Finally Fall on Deng? Some See His Defeat in China Events," 6-16. In the reams of analysis on what was happening in China last June, this relatively short piece by Butterfield stood out, as the *Times* former China correspondent, reporting from Hong Kong, explained both why the hardliners won out in Beijing and why so many Westerners on the scene failed to predict it, in contrast to the China

watchers perched in Hong Kong. "The Hong Kong based analysts, who have pursued their craft for 20, 30 or even 40 years, tend to be more skeptical than the diplomats, less optimistic about China's condition and more prone to see continuing factional intrigue." The experts in Hong Kong, many of them Chinese themselves, base their predictions on Chinese newspapers and radio broadcasts, "the traditional tools of China watchers," while diplomats in Beijing rely on first-hand contacts with Communist officials, contacts that have increased in recent years. But the Chinese officials who talk with foreigners tend to be liberals, while the conservatives shun them. The diplomatic community was thus misled and underestimated the growing strength of the hardliners over the last few years. Working with the Hong Kong experts, Butterfield traces the tea leaves back to 1982, when the hardliners began making their comeback.

2. **Burns, John F.** *The New York Times.* "With Soviet Weapons to Lean on Kabul Is No Pushover," 3-19, and "Afghan Rebels, Divided But Resolute, Fight on From Peak Above Jalalabad," 8-12. Throughout 1988 we were told that the Najibullah regime would be overrun as soon as the Soviets withdrew. The U.S. Embassy in Kabul was evacuated in January. A month after the Soviet withdrawal, with Najibullah still in place, Burns delivered the first definitive piece on the stalemate that had developed on the ground in Afghanistan. "The Kabul regime's tenacity — political and military — appears to have surprised even Soviet advisors, who admitted to nervousness about the Afghan Army's resolve when the last Soviet troops withdrew on Feb. 15." The Soviets then provide Najibullah with heavier weapons, and Westerners in Kabul gather on their balconies to watch the government fire them at the rebel forces trying unsuccessfully to overrun the strategic town of Jalalabad. We don't hear from the rebels in this report, but the story Burns gives us here is that Najibullah, negotiating with tribal leaders, is toning down his regime's Marxism, and even starting to attend Kabul's mosques. "If the war goes on, some Western experts believe that the uneasy alliance between the main guerrilla groups could fracture, leaving Mr. Najibullah and his followers one among many competing claimants for power in an Afghanistan divided by a warlordism that no outside influence would be likely to control." In his brilliant 8-12 report, Burns is with the rebels, who are still trying to take Jalalabad, still stalemated.

3. **Friedman, Thomas L.** *The New York Times.* "Israel: Mired in the West Bank: The Politicians," *Magazine* 5-7. The *Times* two-time Pulitzer winner finished his tour of the Middle East with a book *From Beirut To Jerusalem,* that won more accolades, this time getting a National Book Award. In this article, culled from the experiences and insights related in the book, Friedman explores the political paralysis that has gripped Israeli society from the top down, digging into the roots of the impasse, and posing a question that is at the heart of their paradox. "In the course of the Six Day War, Israel occupied the West Bank and Gaza Strip, in the process extending Jewish control over virtually all the historical Land of Israel originally sought by the Zionists. From that moment on, Israelis again faced the monumental question: 'What kind of nation do we want to be?' " It is a question, Friedman writes, that Israelis have spent the last 22 years dodging, because they don't like the choices they have. They could only have two of three of their objectives. One choice was to keep all the Land of Israel and remain a Jewish state but give up democracy. The second was to annex the West Bank and Gaza, remain a democracy, but give up the Jewish character of the state. The third was to remain Jewish and democratic, but give up most of the West Bank and Gaza and with the land, the Palestinian problem. "Asking an Israeli leader to face the question, 'What is Israel?' is like inviting him to a civil war." In a nutshell, the Middle East problem.

4. **Jenkins, Holman, Jr.** *Insight.* "Truly Talking Shop at the Kremlin," 12-26-88/1-2-89. As the new year opened, we were impressed with this timely cover story on Soviet commercial overtures to the West, wondering what they were doing in line with the new economic thinking in Moscow, and what Western businessmen were thinking too. Jenkins delivers here, with a very smart, hard-headed analytical report on Soviet commercial prospects, placed in this category of foreign correspondence although it seems clear most of the reporting was done here. He digs up some

wonderful stuff, finding that the freer markets of *perestroika* is causing U.S. firms to *lose interest!* It had been *guaranteed* prices and sales that attracted them. But Jenkins has his finger on the central problem, the inconvertible Soviet ruble. "The rub is the ruble. Stuck with inconvertible currency, the Soviets must either churn out exports or borrow from foreigners to finance their will to buy." He finds Johnson & Johnson willing to "sit on the ruble until it becomes convertible, even if we're all dead by then," to grab market share when it all opens up. But there aren't that many willing to take this leap of faith. Jenkins doesn't present economic solutions here, nor do we want him to. But at the time he produced this major effort, it was the only one around that approached the good news from Moscow from this clear-eyed tack.

5. **Kempe, Frederick.** *The Wall Street Journal.* "Panama Tragedy: How the Inexperience of American Officials Helped Doom Coup," 10-6. Panama's Gen. Manuel Noriega was perhaps the biggest burr on the Bush saddle as the new President took office, a man Bush once thought a good guy, as Panamanian political leaders go, who turned out to be a major drug trafficker. The President, early in the year, seemed to openly promise that if the people of Panama became unhappy enough with Noriega to pull him down, the U.S. would be there to help. Then the fiasco. What happened, we all wanted to know? The *WSJ's* Kempe, a diplomatic correspondent who last year practically specialized in the Panamanian problem and had been writing a book on it when the story broke, dashed to Panama City to give us the best behind-the-scenes look at the failed Panamanian coup in the immediate aftermath. With his great contacts there, he was able to show how "weak communications — some of them tragically comic — combined with U.S. warnings to Panamanian coup-makers against assassination, were root causes of the botched attempt to oust Gen. Noriega." Kempe takes us step by step through the story to the fateful moment when coup leaders pleaded with U.S. officials to deal with a contingency that they had not planned for. "Apparently, neither did officials in Washington," writes Kempe, providing the epitaph for the failed coup. "Before officials there had the time to convey a response, the coup had been put down." And we marveled at Kempe's work.

6. **Lee, Dinah.** *BusinessWeek.* "China's Next Great Leap Could Be Backward," 5-8. With students already marching to Tiananmen Square and Gorbachev's visit to Beijing two weeks off, Lee sizes up the brewing crisis from her vantage point in Hong Kong, which turns out to be better than if she'd been in the midst of the action. "At stake is whether China continues down the path toward Deng-style reform and modernization or reverts to centralized, authoritarian control," she opens, moving to a fast-paced all-encompassing overview of the situation in China this spring. But the elements she adds to this otherwise good roundup that lift it to an exceptional level are her references to the inflation that is eating away at the reforms, which we know about, and parallels with the past, which we'd forgotten. "More than 2.5 million people flooded into affluent Guangdong Province, next to Hong Kong, earlier this year, in scenes reminiscent of the food crises of imperial times," she writes, and "Inflation has reached levels not seen since before the 1949 Communist takeover and far exceeds the admitted level of 20%. Even the wage benefits of Deng's decade of double-digit annual growth are gone, eaten away by inflation and pervasive corruption." It occurs to us with these reminders that the Old Guard has not forgotten and will be a tough bunch for the students to deal with. "But even if the student protests are stamped out," Lee concludes, "the underlying crisis can only deepen."

7. **Peel, Quentin.** *Financial Times.* "The Battle Lines Are Drawn," 11-20. As noteworthy as the reporting out of Moscow has been this year by the American press, it has not touched Peel's work on attentiveness to economic policymaking, which in some ways is at the center of the story. Throughout the year, the pushing and shoving in Moscow to put together a democratic forum had this ultimate aim, an elected Supreme Soviet that could help Gorbachev put together a new *perestroika* plan. At the penultimate moment we got this exquisite report from Peel and no one else: "For three days last week, while the eyes of the world were glued on the unfolding drama in East Germany, more than 1,400 of the best brains in the Soviet Union were gathered instead in awestruck contemplation of their country's domestic plight." Peel talks to Dr. Leonid

Abalkin, Gorbachev's deputy prime minister in charge of economic reform, and gets practically everything we need from him and the program laid out at the conference. It is not possible for us to imagine the U.S. Embassy in Moscow providing the kind of detail and analysis that then followed. Abalkin's radical reform plan is laid out point by point, with a timetable, rationale, and what seem to be exclusive comments from Abalkin. He has a year to make things work, he thinks, or he's convinced the conservatives will win the day. The battle lines are drawn for December's newly elected parliament. Three weeks later, the conservatives win the day as Abalkin's plan is rejected.

8. **Preston, Julia.** *The New York Review Of Books.* "The Trial That Shook Cuba," 12-7. The collapse of Marxist-Leninism in the Eastern hemisphere is of course having not ripple, but tidal wave effects on the U.S.S.R. client states in the West. How long does Fidel Castro have? We know he himself is thinking this big thought as he regularly denounces *glasnost* and *perestroika,* his back to the wall. We want to know more about all this and we get it from Preston, the veteran Central America correspondent for *The Washington Post,* who weaves these fascinating questions into the long, long report on the trials this year in Havana of some of Fidel's oldest friends. She opens: "Arnaldo Ochoa Sanchez, one of Cuba's most distinguished generals and the former commander of the Cuban forces in Angola, was arrested last June 12 in Havana and shortly afterward accused of corruption and drug-trafficking. He appeared before an honor tribunal only thirteen days later, and in his opening statement confessed to all charges against him. He said he thought the death sentence would an appropriate punishment for the crimes he had committed." This from a man who fought as a teen-ager with Fidel in the Sierra Maestra mountains. On July 13, Ochoa and three other high ranking officers went before a firing squad. The Cuban revolution, Preston reports, is now eating its children. Her dispatch, the best single piece we've read on Cuba in a decade, leaves us very nervous about what Fidel's devils have left in them before they eat him too.

9. **Rapoport, Carla.** *Fortune.* "Ready, Set, Sell — Japan is Buying," 9-11. A four-star reporter in our first *MediaGuide* in 1986 when she covered business and finance in Tokyo for the *Financial Times,* Rapoport took maternity leave, and to our delight finally re-emerged, at *Fortune* this time, where she is relieved of spot reporting. Why is her reporting so superb, as in this jewel of a piece on the revolution in Japanese retailing? The Japanese, she has written elsewhere, are decidedly a different people, despite the McDonald's and the golf. And yet, she is completely at ease covering their activities, businesses and personalities, the way we expect reporters to cover Brooklyn or Baton Rouge. This is a global marketplace, *which makes Japan a local story!* Yes, yes, she opens her piece, Tokyo is ridiculously expensive. "But step away from the Ginza. Take a trip to Chiba, 12 miles out of Tokyo, or to Fukushima, 170 miles north. There and in hundreds of other locations around the country, you'll find something quite different: discount stores, American-style shopping malls, gigantic hypermarkets, and remarkably reasonable prices. . .Here you can find a 19-inch Korean-made color TV for $43, marked down from $70." Because her word images convey so much, Rapoport tells us more in 1500 words than we get out of books on the subject, breezing through laws, regulations, trends, tastes, trade, pricing, brand names, etc., in a rich, colorful, informative whirl.

10. **Rosett, Claudia.** *The Wall Street Journal.* "Japan's Recruit Scandal in Context," 4-10. The widespread bribery and political payoffs to a flock of Japanese politicians by this executive-recruiting firm blew up into the country's biggest scandal since WWII. A Prime Minister was toppled, cabinet members resigned left and right, former government officials and prominent businessmen arrested almost daily, it seemed. "The joke in Tokyo," writes Ms. Rosett, the editorial page editor of *The Asian Wall Street Journal,* "is that in describing the recruit scandal it's more efficient to list the few politicians not involved." So what's going on here? Unlike the spot reporters on the scene, Rosett flies up from her Hong Kong home base and wanders around asking that question for us, not only the who, the what, the where, and the when. But also the why, the deep down why, the *context* in Japanese political culture. She puts a focus on Recruit's

founder and former chairman, Hiramasa Ezoe, and follows his advance out of Tokyo University, building his fortune "by creating a business so new to Japan that the bureaucracy hadn't gotten around to guiding it." Ezoe, we realize through Rosett, was an innovative entrepreneur caught up in a country where top politicians and bureaucrats have the economy in a stranglehold. There's no excuse here for his corruption, but a large message that this will continue unless the creaky regulatory apparatus is reformed to take bribery out of normal business expense.

General Reporting

1. **Brookes, Warren.** Creators Syndicate. Acid Rain Series in *The Washington Times.* "Acid Rain Fakers," 8-10; "Acid Rain Failing the Acid Test," 8-13; "Economic-Scientific Acid Rain Nonsense," 8-17. Journalists who think they are pretty hot stuff should spend a few hours leafing through Brookes' portfolio over the last several years, or a few minutes reading these awesome reports on acid rain, a problem all of us have come to accept as one of the grave threats to Mother Earth in general and Northeast woodlands in particular. President Bush is prepared to spend megataxbucks to combat this sulphur dioxide scourge. It's a hoax, we learn from Brookes, who has actually taken the trouble to pack his pencil and notebook and go looking for the monster. His dispatches from the acid-rain war zone are stunningly thorough in debunking this latest Great Hoax from the new Malthusians, most recently aided and abetted by Ned Potter of ABC News and his hair-raising 7-25 report on 50,000 deaths from acid rain. None, says Brookes, and we're almost sure he's right, after he socks us with his notebook. Of course, most of the acidity in the North American lakes comes from natural sources, such as decaying forest leaves. In part three of the series, he makes a case, with experts behind him all the way, that what President Bush wants to spend $4 billion on can be done for $4 million, and "unlike the Bush sulphur dioxide (SO2) removal program, this would actually *ensure* deacidification of lakes."

2. **Browne, Malcolm W.** *The New York Times.* "In Protecting the Atmosphere, Choices Are Costly and Complex," 3-7. As we observe the environmental lobby in Washington and around the world insist that there is simply no longer need to debate the issues, we see political leaders *and journalists* submitting to this tidal wave of assertion. The depletion of the ozone layer in the stratosphere is one of the main worries of this group, which is why we were attentive to this comprehensive report on CFCs (chlorofluorocarbons), the best we saw on the chemistry, very good too on the economics. Browne doesn't *directly* touch the debate around the legitimacy of the ozone layer; it's not within the parameters of his subject matter. But this is an important article in making it clear that "As the world moves toward a ban on ozone-destroying chemicals to head off an epidemic of skin cancer, experts searching for substitute chemicals predict that the technical and economic cost of the change will be high." And as we learn "the likely substitutes for the three main ozone-destroying CFCs may, in many cases, be less effective." Browne maps out the problems with the substitutes, some of which may be just as harmful as the original chemicals; it's just that we don't know it yet. A year ago Browne earned a 10 Best in this category simply by reporting on those in the scientific community who question the "Greenhouse Effect" projections. This "Science Times" piece was just as appreciated.

3. **Brownstein, Ronald.** *National Journal.* "Facing West Nervously," 10-28. From his Los Angeles vantage point, Brownstein produces a superior overview of the conflicts and contradictions involved in U.S.-Japanese economic linkage. Those of us who sit atop the world in New York and Washington must be reminded that in a way we are the most parochial of all. Brownstein, on temporary West Coast assignment in recent years from homebase in Washington, gives us this important perspective, loaded with fresh data, novel insights, and solid analysis, the most comprehensive reporting we saw on U.S.-Japanese relations *from the West Coast!* The state of Washington, for goodness sakes, "sends twice as many exports to Japan as to any other nation." Brownstein is completely credible, then, when he says there is somewhat less support for tough trade measures in the West, but are "surprisingly strong nevertheless."

This kind of reporting is immensely important, yet almost accidental in this case. "In the editorial and corporate boardrooms and political salons of the West Coast, there is a widespread sense that the fears of American economic decline during the 'Pacific Century,' so prevalent in the Rustbelt and Eurocentric cities of the East, are misguided. Instead, many West Coast opinion leaders argue that the economic destinies of Japan and the United States have become so intertwined that confrontation is counterproductive for either side."

4. **Engelberg, Stephen with Gordon, Michael.** *The New York Times.* "German Accused of Helping Libya Build Nerve Gas Plant," 1-1. A blockbuster with global repercussions, Engelberg and Gordon produced one of the year's major intelligence stories with their expose of the West German-assisted construction of a poison gas plant in Libya. Despite a State Department blackout on documents relating to the case, the pair is persuasive on Imhausen-Chemie being at the center of a web of western companies that have built a poison gas plant in Rabta, Libya. "Imhausen-Chemie's president, Dr. Jurgen Hippenstiel-Imhausen, acknowledged in an interview that the company has sought to obtain a contract in Libya to manufacture plastic bags, but he denied any connection to 'the plant presumed to be making chemical weapons in Libya.' 'We produce medical substances and fine chemicals and supply them to pharmaceutical companies around the world, but not so far to Libya.' he said. 'I never was in Libya. I don't even know where it is.' " There are several follow-ups, among the best, "U.S. Sees Gains in Efforts to Stop West German Aid to Libya Chemical Plant," 1-14, Engelberg's presentation icily detached. *Times* columnist William Safire trumpeted the expose in "The German Problem, 1-2, earning a 10 Best commentary for his efforts, the accolades described elsewhere in this section.

5. **Gross, Jane.** *The New York Times.* "Urban Emergency Rooms: A Cocaine Nightmare," 8-6. The continuing story of the drug wars in America has us attentive to new developments at the front. We noted dozens this year with dismay. This report from Oakland got our attention for two reasons. First it presented a vivid, horrifying picture of a battle-fatigued, inner-city emergency room wrestling with drug overdoses and other casualties of the drug trade. The opening line: "Crack has turned emergency medicine at Highland General Hospital here into a nightmare, a scene of chaos and despair that is crushing the spirits of all who encounter it." A doctor terms his work "post-mortem," as people become throwaways from a generation of crack usage: "we're talking global systematic complaints here." The magnitude of the problem is staggering. "In a 72-hour period last winter, all 500 patients in the medical emergency room regardless of age or complaint were given urine tests; 45 percent tested positive for cocaine." The other stunning revelation in Gross's report is that taxpayers are financing both sides in the drug war: "Visits to Highland's emergency rooms often coincide with the issue dates of welfare checks. 'We get to know these folks by name,' said Donna Doss, a psychiatric nurse. 'We see the same ones each month on the first and the fifteenth.' " We clipped the article and sent it to Drug Czar William Bennett, who replied that he had already read it.

6. **Ingersoll, Bruce.** *The Wall Street Journal.* "In Chilean Grape Case, New Data Raise Doubt as to What Happened," 11-16. In a breathtaking review of the evidence of the almost forgotten Chilean grape scare, Ingersoll uncovers facts that make the State Department and FDA's arguments look mighty fishy on the finding of those two contaminated grapes, a gripping story solidly documented. He begins by describing the almost absurd odds against discovery of taintings during inspection: "It was at a long line of inspection tables in a cavernous terminal here on the Delaware river that the Food and Drug Administration last March pulled off the Great Grape Catch. Out of hundreds of thousands of crates of Chilean fruit on a ship docked here, FDA inspectors plucked two cyanide-laced grapes, bearing white crystalline rings as if injected by a syringe." Those hundreds of thousands of crates adds up to about 280 million grapes! Ingersoll discovers evidence of faulty test results, strange circumstances at the dock, more grapes with white rings in the same bunch but containing no cyanide, and odd record-keeping (who, for example, took the grapes from port to the lab downtown?). A marvelous bit of investigative reporting, he comes up with a few theories: industrial espionage by a competitor; conspiracy by the State Department and FDA to undermine the Chilean economy, perhaps to hurry along the departure of its dictatorship. Why not the FDA trying to get a bigger budget?

7. **Kagan, Daniel.** *Insight.* "Fast-Food Kids," cover 8-28. The torrent of news about the inner-city underclass, the drugs, murders, rapes and collapse of families and values reached a fever pitch during the summer, especially insofar as white America thought of black America. The drug-related problems of Washington, DC Mayor Marion Barry helped this along. At exactly this moment along came this notable cover story, devoted to the black teenagers of our nation's capital who are plugging away in the mainstream of traditional values, flipping hamburgers in the city's fast-food restaurants. The article got wider attention via its favorable citation in a *Wall Street Journal* editorial, and as it was read and digested by other journalists. "Cash is an instrument of peer pressure: Youths in the drug trade flaunt their pricey possessions to those not involved, setting fashion fads that can be followed only with like amounts of cash, which can only be raised through dealing. Cash is a virtual magnet for even good adolescents who, like all teenagers, want and want and want — the right jewelry, the right clothes, the right car — and want it now." Kagan reports on the poor inner-city kids of Washington, DC, who *don't* peddle drugs, some who have and who have chosen to stop, others wise enough to stick to the straight and narrow throughout. The quotes, the anecdotes, the stories he elicits were like a slap in the face, which we seemed to need.

8. **Kolata, Gina.** *The New York Times.* "AIDS Is Spreading in Teen-Agers, A New Trend Alarming to Experts," 10-8. Kolata reports what local doctors have been warning about for years, that the teen years, normally a time for experimentation, sexual and otherwise, have deadly pitfalls in the age of AIDS. Now AIDS is off the streets and into the schools, a frightening and important finding in combating a disease where one of the greatest factors is ignorance, relevant to young and old: "Not only are teen-agers becoming infected with the virus, but it is also being transmitted through heterosexual intercourse, and equal numbers of boys and girls are infected. By contrast, among adults the virus has been transmitted primarily through homosexual sex or intravenous drug use, and the number of infected men far exceeds the number of infected women. Conditions are ripe for the virus to spread because many teen-agers have more than one sexual partner and very few use condoms." Kolata puts faces on the numbers, offering tragic examples, like the young man who tuned out when somebody came to school to talk about AIDS and then was diagnosed with the disease eight months later. Kolata effectively debunks alternate theories debating the epidemic's proportions by simply stating the facts, and quoting medical experts. In this important dispatch in cataloguing the spread of the killer, reminding us of the urgency for research both in finding a treatment and a cure, Kolata informs without sensation.

9. **Lochhead, Carolyn.** *Insight.* "No Way Out: The Brutal Snare of Poverty," 4-3. A quarter century ago, when President Johnson embarked on his War on Poverty in pursuit of a Great Society, we were among those cheering. Now, we cheer those who try to find out what went wrong and how it can be fixed. Perhaps because so many don't wish to admit they had a hand in failure, very few try. A young *Insight* staff writer in its New York bureau, Lochhead takes the best run at it we saw this year, filing a timely, ambitious report on the welfare underclass. The costs are staggering, the statistics frightening and surprising. Where does it come from? Underpinning her piece is the clear concept that in breaking down the links between effort and reward, we reaped the whirlwind. Quoting Charles Murray, author of *Losing Ground*: "There was a mind-set in the 1960s that could best be summarized as, 'It's not your fault.' If you don't study, it's not your fault. If you don't get a job, it's not your fault. If you commit a crime, it's not your fault. If you have a baby, it's not your fault. There was a message being sent out to disadvantaged, and especially young disadvantaged, and most especially poor young disadvantaged people: 'You have been wronged, it's not your fault, and it's somebody else's job to make things right.' " Potent indictments here for the Great Society and the War on Poverty, Lochhead pulls it all together in a sterling compendium.

10. **Mayer, Jane.** *The Wall Street Journal.* "Seaford, Del., Shows How Crack Can Savage Small Town America," 5-4. For the first time in a half century, the Gallup Poll this year listed "drugs" as the number one problem Americans worry about. We can see why in this frightful saga of a small town's battle against crack, how it eats away at its social fabric, a sense of desperation clouding the population of 5,500. The P. 1 leder subhead: "Once a Peaceful Place, it Reels From Murders, Muggings, Even Addicted Newborns." It tells of the citizens crowding into the fire hall "to discuss an alien invader," that confuses us as a society, catching us between compassion for the addict and growing fear of the addict and the drug, and the capacity of these to infect and kill. Andrew Malcolm of *The New York Times* produced a similar, admirable report in "Crack, Bane of Inner Cities, Is Now Gripping Suburbs," 10-2, but Mayer is five months earlier with the news that crack is everywhere, and no one is safe as entrepreneurial dealers seek out new customers. "Crack has attacked its central nervous system, almost as if poison had been dumped into the drinking water. What began as a scourge of the town's poor blacks (who represent 15% of the population) has spread to its majority white middle class, straining not only the police force but also the town's hospitals, its schools — and its vision of itself." The best reporters have to be assigned this beat. Mayer shows the way.

Political Reporting

1. **Archibald, George & Rodriguez, Paul.** *The Washington Times.* "Sex Sold from Congressman's Apartment," "Frank's Lover Was 'Call Boy,' " "School Used As Base For Sex," 8-25. In a day and age when most "scoops" are little more than political news leaks to favored journalists, this solidly documented expose of a Washington prostitution ring, operated out of a congressman's house and a suburban Virginia elementary school, was the sort of old-fashioned "Stop the presses!" exclusive that Walter Burns and Hildy Johnson would have been proud of. Representative Barney Frank, school principal Gabriel A. Massaro, and Steve Gobie (identified here as "Greg Davis") take turns playing Raskolnikov, telling all to reporters Archibald and Rodriguez, who catch their subjects more than once in discrepancies. The Massachusetts Democrat recounts his involvement with Gobie, including putting Gobie on his personal payroll and writing letters to Gobie's probation officer on his Congressional stationery, copies of which accompany the article. Frank insists that he kicked Gobie out of his apartment when he discovered what Gobie was up to. The reporters follow the trail to the Chevy Chase Elementary School, providing firsthand accounts of how Gobie was given the run of the school's facilities by the principal. The *Times* had been running exclusives earlier in the year in a similar vein, but it was this story, which involved a politician of national stature, that captured national attention.

2. **Barsky, Neil.** *The Wall Street Journal.* "Quiet Candidate: In the New York Race, Front-Runner Dinkins Remains an Enigma," 10-27. Most of the big-name political scribes took a turn writing about Manhattan Borough President David Dinkins, who this year became the first African-American to win the New York City mayoralty. None of them came close to giving us the three-dimensional look we got here from Barsky, 30, an obscure real-estate reporter. Dinkins, a mystery to New Yorkers as this P. 1 profile appeared, does not reveal the inner man here either. But Barsky, simply by talking to a lot of people who know Dinkins, filling his notebook, and then assembling the material in readable prose, does an exceptional job sketching what he sees and we are persuaded that's what we'll get. From David Garth, Mayor Ed Koch's media adviser: "He really is the personification of the patronage system. But the guy is so personally decent, people tend to forget that." From colleagues on the city's budget and land-use panel we're told of his fabled indecisiveness, keeping the board going into the wee hours: "He taught me how to drink herbal tea instead of coffee at 3 a.m., I'll give him that," says one. Procrastination fits with the problems he had in failing to file income tax returns four years running: "I always thought of this as a thing that could always been done tomorrow." Oddly enough, we're left with the feeling that if we lived in New York, we might vote for the guy.

3. **Dewar, Helen & Balz, Dan.** *The Washington Post.* "Tracing the Steps In Tower's Downfall," 3-29. Never before had the Senate rejected an incoming president's cabinet selection, a former senator as well. In this comprehensive report Dewar and Balz step beyond the emotions of the moment to show us the backstage maneuvering, infighting, and miscalculations which earned John Tower a footnote in our nation's history books, but not the position of Secretary of Defense. "The factors that brought about Tower's downfall are clear: President Bush's long delay in selecting him, which helped envelop the nominee in controversy; the cumulative impact of numerous allegations about Tower's private life and conflicts of interest in his professional life; Tower's failure to help his case in public testimony; the power of Sam Nunn, and the discipline of the Democrats in the Senate." We're led step by step through the process, from the "long, prenomination debate among Bush's advisors" to Paul Weyrich's damaging testimony. The Bush administration "poured gasoline all over him [and] sent him [Tower] up to the Senate. Paul Weyrich struck a match and he continued to burn," a senator observed. Dewar and Balz do not delve deeply into motives here, leaving that job to the historians. In fact, the lack of finger-pointing and sympathy on their part is refreshing, and brings their message home: In a story where there were no real heroes and villains, all the principal players involved were losers.

4. **Dowd, Maureen.** *The New York Times Magazine.* "The Education of Dan Quayle," 6-25. At the time Dowd, the *NYT*'s White House correspondent, wrote this marvelous cover story about the rookie Vice President, there probably wasn't a soul on the Upper West Side who didn't think of him as a lightweight Hoosier wearing a beanie and riding a tricycle, which is how the cartoonists liked to picture him. Dowd, who has become the best portraitist in the political press corps, has a marvelous way of getting into her subjects, her stereotyped preconception giving way to an absolutely honest word image, inside and out. So the man we see at first almost seems the trike and beanie Quayle. He identifies with Napoleon, for goodness sakes. He proudly points out to her, golly, that he has five offices in all. And he announces: " 'There's still an interest and intrigue on exactly who I am,' he says, sounding pleased." But a few thousand words later, we have our first real sense of the man, his intellect, his sense of humor, and a self-confidence that is reflected in the brainy cadre of advisers he's assembled. The best anecdote has Quayle telling his press secretary he's irked by people saying Marilyn is the brains in the family, and after all, he got better grades than she did in law school. Maybe now's the time to release the transcripts, says the V.P. "She might retaliate," says his aide. " 'Yeah,' Quayle says laughing. 'She might release my college records.' " This is not a trike and beanie man.

5. **Evans, Rowland & Novak, Robert.** *Chicago Tribune,* News America Syndicate. "Bush Sustains Gorbachev," in *The Washington Post* 9-28. This column on the Wyoming summit meeting between Secretary of State James Baker III and Soviet Foreign Minister Eduard Shevardnadze showed once again that when a Republican administration wants to send an important message out, Evans & Novak is still the vehicle of choice. No story was bigger this year than the upheaval in the Soviet bloc, and through this column Baker sends out the word for the first time that "President Bush is now actively committed to sustaining the Soviet reform leader in his time of trouble." Two sources of trouble are looked at, the Baltic States and strategic arms negotiations. The team reports that Baker informed Shevardnadze in a "solicitous" conversation that "Sustaining Gorbachev is more important than Baltic independence." They bolster the signal by reporting how the State Department shunted around a highly-regarded Baltic nationalist. They also signal a Bush willingness to downgrade strategic defense, freeing Gorbachev to "go for a fast-as-possible Strategic Arms Treaty (START)," to help him at home and save rubles. There were other reports on the SDI agreement in Wyoming, but this column was the clearest signal on Bush's pro-Gorbachev posture, news in itself: "If the Soviet Union is in truth near a breakup as Gorbachev relaxes force, it will not be the Bush administration that pushes it over the precipice."

6. **Hoffman, David.** *The Washington Post.* "Bush's Relentless Pragmatism," 4-30. Articles summarizing a new president's "First One Hundred Days in Office" are as inevitable in Washington as cherry blossoms and tourists, but in this piece Hoffman avoids drawing up any meaningless "legislative scorecard" comparing Bush with FDR, showing us instead the Bush "management style" in action. We especially appreciate Hoffman detaching himself from the subject, simply laying out several pertinent anecdotes that together fit into a coherent picture, as well as fine detail on the President's routine, with no attempt at psychoanalysis or judgments on whether his style will be good for us and the world or not. "In essence, Bush has suggested by his actions so far that he views ideology as a wide boulevard — giving him plenty of room to maneuver in individual decisions while still leading him in an overall direction." And "Bush, according to many of his associates, is confident that if he makes enough of what he calls the 'right decisions,' his actions will cumulatively move the country in the right direction." Hoffman adds a point made by outsiders, that an 'ad hocracy' pragmatism may be at the President's core, "a decision-making system in which the individual choices are not connected to a larger whole, but are a set of expedient responses." The conclusion we draw in this first semester, though, is of a thoughtful and thorough manager, who understands communication's importance at every level.

7. **Klein, Joe.** *New York.* "Race: The Issue," 5-29, and "Race: Still the Issue," 11-13. Coming to grips with the racial polarization sweeping New York in 1989, the mayoral race in the foreground, Klein in the 5-29 article spotlights the vicious cycle of racial polarization that keeps blacks locked into poverty, producing a black underclass of unwed mothers and crime-prone youths, which increases racial polarization. He traces the immediate problems back to the late 1960s, when black separatist impulses — which include, among other things, radicals, black big-city politicians, affirmative action programs — replaced Martin Luther King Jr.'s dream of integration into white America. Klein reaches back to a 1937 study to buttress his argument that blacks have to be assimilated into middle class society, and proposes methods to accomplish precisely that, drawing on both liberal and conservative ideas. The mayoral candidates should be addressing the issue, but they are afraid to. Klein follows up with the 11-13 article, looking back over the mayoral race and the city's year of violent racial incidents, observing that both the press and the politicians continued to duck the central issue of race, and the culpability of both. "But: Sooner or later, the complex social pathologies of these children will have to be confronted, firmly but compassionately, if the ghosts that have haunted this campaign — and this country — from the start are ever to be exorcised."

8. **Rasky, Susan F.** *The New York Times.* "For the Chairman of a Powerful Committee, the House is No Longer a Home," 11-20. It was a very difficult year for Rep. Dan Rostenkowski, the Chicago Democrat who chairs the House Ways & Means Committee. Caught between his old friendship with President Bush and the determination of the new Democratic leadership to deny the new President his appeal for a capital gains tax cut, he seemed to lose all around, especially control of his committee, but also the sense of pride and achievement that makes the grueling life of a politician bearable. There were plenty of Rosty "down-and-out" stories, but none caught him better than this unsentimental, yet sympathetic, portrait in the autumn of his discontent. Democrats on his committee, Rasky writes, are deserting him on legislation, House Democratic leaders are "leaving him out of the loop" on the S&L bailout, and elderly constituents are "chasing him down the main thoroughfare of his Chicago district shouting, 'Impeach Rotten-kowski.'" Such setbacks might sink a lesser legislator, but as Rasky makes clear, this "6 feet 2 inches tall" descendant of Chicago ward bosses, "with the shoulders of a football lineman, a gruff, street-wise voice and an expressive face that is inevitably photographed in a scowl" is made of stronger stuff. The feature displays a gift for the political personality profile, coaxing thoughts and emotions out of Rosty and presenting them with care and vitality.

9. **Shribman, David.** *The Wall Street Journal.* "Washington Mayor's Mounting Woes Spotlight Racial Tension, Suspicions Inside The Beltway," 1-11. DC's Jimmy Walkeresque mayor Marion Barry was the object of more national press attention this year than we could shake a stick at, but of all the articles, profiles, and "exposes" we saw, none told the story as well as this crisp report on the Mayor, and the political culture which produced him and now has to live with him. "The controversy involving Mr. Barry, a chemist by training but a political activist by temperament, offers a window into the racial tensions and suspicions — always present but seldom acknowledged — that govern Washington life outside the capital's shiny monuments and federal buildings." Shribman manages to stay detached, letting the facts — the late night escapades, the numerous instances of questionable judgment, the drug episodes, along with Barry's measurable achievements — speak for themselves. Shribman also captures the political and racial currents swirling just beneath the surface. "Mr. Barry's black opponents are wary of speaking out and playing into the hands of powerful white interests," he writes, quoting from Washington's black community as it grows more restive about the mayor. Without condoning or excusing the mayor, Shribman places him in context, enabling those of us living outside the capital who have been hearing and reading horror stories about Barry to understand why he has not been tossed out or moved to resign. The Marion Barry here is not a national disgrace but an almost inevitable local phenomenon.

10. **Whalen, Bill.** *Insight.* "A Party's Time For Solving Riddles," "Questions Rife On Goal Of Bradley's Fast Break," "Encore For The Top Teaser," cover series 3-27. At a time when absolutely nobody was talking about 1992, Whalen stood back for this thoughtful look on the Democrats in general, with some educated guesswork on '92. In "Riddles," he surveys the Democrats' difficulty of winning at the national level, with a great quote on '88 from Mark Siegal, a party consultant: "We've lost another election, and we've lost an election for an open seat, and that makes it worse. We didn't run against God, and that makes it worse. We lost an election that we all felt we could win, so something obviously is wrong." We get some clever thoughts on the nuts-and-bolts of the nominating process, and Whalen also provides a philosophical overview, developing William Schneider's idea that the Democrats have split into two factions: The "fundamentalists" (a la West Germany's Greens) whose viewpoint is that of the New Deal/Great Society, and "revisionists," whose temperament was forged by Vietnam and Watergate and who see the world in more practical, less ideological terms. He also hints that Bill Bradley may be more liberal than his record and manner suggest, and that for all his liberal boilerplate, New York Governor Mario Cuomo tends to be more moderate in deed, and is essentially pragmatic. Good stuff, but what elevated it for us was its early timing, the only baseball book in the dead of winter.

43

AN OVERVIEW OF THE
CANADIAN PRESS

Canadians had reason to believe that their politics would be "kinder and gentler" in 1989. Like their counterparts south of the border, they had lived through a national election campaign in the previous year — one that was far more divisive than the U.S. Presidential contest. The central issue was the free trade agreement that Prime Minister Brian Mulroney's government signed with the United States. The pact was seen solely in economic terms, but the agreement was constantly being portrayed as being vital to Canada's future cultural and political survival. This made much of the debate irrational and shrill.

Although Mulroney's Progressive Conservatives captured only slightly more than forty percent of the popular vote, they won a comfortable Parliamentary majority, enabling them to pass the necessary legislation for the free trade agreement to come into effect at the beginning of 1989. Yet there was to be no cooling off period. The federal government continually found itself in the midst of controversy throughout the year. But Mulroney and his ministers can only be held partially responsible for these political problems, as many crises were touched off by events over which he and his ministers had little control.

As an example, within a short space of time near the beginning of the year, a number of mergers were announced involving some of the largest and most visible corporations in the country. Max Ward sold his controlling interest in Wardair, Canada's third largest commercial airline, to PWA Inc., which already controlled the second largest airline, Canadian Airlines International. The second and third largest breweries in Canada, Molson's and Carling-O'keefe, also decided to merge with each other. All of these deals needed the approval of federal regulators. The press reflected widespread concerns about the effects that these mergers would have on competition and employment.

In the country's ongoing debate on abortion, events also got ahead of the government. In 1988, the Supreme Court of Canada struck down Canada's federal abortion law by declaring it unconstitutional. A year later, ruling on separate cases, provincial courts in Ontario and Quebec upheld a father's right to stop a pregnant woman from having an abortion. The woman involved in the Quebec case, Chantal Daigle, became a nationally-known figure by appealing to the Supreme Court (the father lost). While the lower court's decision was eventually reversed, the publicity given to the Daigle case increased the pressure on the federal government to introduce a new abortion law.

But Mulroney was the author of some of his own misfortune. In marked contrast to the Bush administration, his government undertook some controversial political initiatives at the beginning of its new mandate. In the election campaign, free trade overwhelmed all other issues. Budgetary matters were hardly ever discussed. But once the Tories were safely reelected, their attention was focused on ways to reduce the federal deficit. To raise revenues, the government unveiled its plans for the introduction of a widely-based consumption tax, known as the General Services Tax. Controversial spending cuts involved: the closing of military bases; lower subsidies to the Canadian Broadcasting Corporation; and less money for passenger trains, which resulted in service being completely eliminated on some routes and being significantly reduced on others. There was vocal public opposition to all of these initiatives.

In a sparsely populated country like Canada, it is relatively common for local stories to get national attention. Perhaps the cuts to VIA Rail, the national passenger train service illustrates this best. The reductions in services effected relatively few people living in more remote parts of the country. Yet they dominated headlines in most newspapers for weeks after they were released.

There is also a tendency to give national attention to local scandals. A prime example of this in 1989 was the so-called Patti Starr affair. Starr allegedly diverted funds from a local Toronto charity into the campaign coffers of a number of prominent politicians in the Ontario provincial government. A commission of inquiry was eventually established to look into the relationship between Starr and provincial politicians. The scandal received national prominence because initially it was uncovered by investigative reporters from *The Globe and Mail,* a Toronto daily with a truly country-wide circulation. Other media outlets then picked up the story, giving it national coverage. Yet it is hard to see that the story would be of any interest to many living outside the province of Ontario.

There were other provincial inquiries that received national coverage. In Manitoba, one investigated the relationship between native people and the provincial justice system. Another, in Newfoundland, looked at the alleged sexual and physical abuse of boys by priests at a Catholic orphanage. Such inquiries may have national implications because they touch on broader social issues — such as the status of native people in society and violence against children. Yet had these investigations taken place in similarly remote locations in the United States, it is hard to imagine that the pacesetters in the press would have given them coverage that was as extensive as that afforded by Canadian papers.

All of this speaks to the parochialism of the Canadian press, perhaps best reflected in their coverage of international affairs. Most of the papers do not devote more than one or two pages per day to foreign news, and most of that comes from wire copy. Only two papers, *The Globe and Mail* and *The Toronto Star* maintain a significant number of bureaus and reporters outside Canada. More typical is the practice of the *Montreal Gazette,* which has no reporters outside of Quebec, except for the two in its Ottawa bureau. This may explain why the leading American newspapers can increasingly be found at street corners in large Canadian cities.

The Globe and Mail

The Globe and Mail bills itself as "Canada's National Newspaper," boasting a circulation of 326,200. In reality, this means that it sees itself as the Canadian counterpart of both *The New York Times* and *The Wall Street Journal.* Superficially there are similarities between *The Globe* and the two leading papers in the United States. Like *The Times,* it published separate local and national editions on a daily basis. Like both of the U.S. papers, the national edition is printed in a number of locations across the country. And its "Report of Business" (known affectionately as the ROB) runs to around thirty pages daily.

Yet in trying to be both *The Times* and *The Wall Street Journal,* it ends up being neither. While it does have more bureaus than any other Canadian publication, its network of correspondents does not come close to being as extensive as those of the pacesetting dailies in the United States. For most of its foreign news, it depends on wire services. Indeed, the paper often reprints dispatches from *The New York Times* itself. And unlike *The Times, The Globe* does not do a good job of covering its local home market. Over the years, it has cut back on its coverage of Toronto. Increasingly less space has also been devoted to sports and the arts.

About ten years ago *The Globe & Mail* was purchased by newspaper baron Kenneth Thomson, who has holdings in Canada, Great Britain, and the United States. Since then, it has often been argued that *The Globe* has abandoned its role as a general newspaper, in order to become a newspaper targeted exclusively to business executives. More credence was given to this argument early in 1989 when the publisher fired Editor-in-chief Norman Webster and Managing Editor Geoffrey Stevens. The new editor is William Throsell. The new managing editor, Timothy Pritchard, had been in charge of the ROB. Under his management there have been more reductions in the editorial staff. It was also announced that the paper would be closing bureaus in China, Central America, and Africa. The bureau in Southeast Asia is to be converted from general news to business.

Yet there are some problems with the notion that *The Globe* is trying to convert itself into a business newspaper. In the first place, in the ROB, quantity has not always produced quality. There are no investigative reporters assigned to the ROB, and there are few in-depth analytical features, as one would find, for instance, on the front page of *The Wall Street Journal.* For the most part, ROB reporters are facile, rewriting corporate press releases, doing research and covering speeches, with little depth of analysis. There is foreign business news in the ROB but it comes mainly from wire services.

The ROB does have its bright spots. One of them is columnist Terence Corcoran. His "Shareholder Democracy: a Flawed and Alien Concept," 5-2, is a highly logical argument against pension fund managers using their corporate clout to achieve ideological ends. His "No Reason to Believe Market Plunge Threatens Markets System," 10-17, is a well thought-out analysis putting the October stock market mini-crash into perspective.

While on the whole the business side remained mediocre, steps were taken to beef up the general news front section. Two new columns on foreign affairs were added, by staffer John Cruckshank and by the former Canadian ambassador to the United States, Allan Gotlieb. Also new this year were columns on: the provinces, ethics, and personal health. Excepting economic coverage, where *The Globe* adheres to a middle-of-the-road market-oriented viewpoint, the paper's opinion and news section is stuck with wheels steering toward the left, the alignment out of kilter.

It is not at all clear that the front section has seen better days. Throughout the year, several series of feature articles were run in the front section. In May, Moscow correspondent Jeff Sallot and Beijing correspondent Jan Wong worked together on a series called "The New Communists" which compared the reforms in China with those in the Soviet Union. There was also a lengthy series of articles to mark the tenth anniversary of Margaret Thatcher's rule.

In its editorials *The Globe* often takes a position that would be agreeable to much of the business community. The paper led the fight for free trade in 1988. A year later it would support cuts to VIA Rail, and oppose any attempts to impose limits on the interest rate that could be charged on credit cards. But *The Globe* can hardly be considered a bastion for the right. On many foreign policy issues the paper has sided with the left. For instance, the paper has consistently opposed U.S. policy in Central America. Moreover, most columnists, such as Michael Valpy, often attack government policies that his conservative party has supported. Thus, in successive columns on 5-2 and 5-3, Valpy argued that the fiscal policies of the Mulroney government were placing the burden of fiscal restraints on the poor.

Jeffrey Simpson remains the most notable National Affairs columnist in the country. Some perceive the Ottawa columnist as a wishy-washy Scotty Reston, but his real difficulty is that he conceives his mandate to be the use of his column, the most important piece of real estate in Canadian journalism, to advocate the interests of the civil service. Nothing sinister in this — Simpson quite genuinely has this point of view on everything, but it makes him so predictable. He's competent and it's hard to find anyone that researches his work better, a Simpson column is truly educational. But standards should be absolute, not relative. Readers are exposed to a greater variety of opinions in *The Globe & Mail* than in other dailies, most notably *The Toronto Star.* But there is still as much diversity of opinion as there is in good American papers.

The Globe & Mail is, we think, the best newspaper in Canada. But it is far from being one of the world's great newspapers.

The Financial Post

Although *The Financial Post* has been published since 1907, in a very real sense the paper is the new kid on the national press block. This year was only the second year that the paper had been published as a daily. Previously it had been a weekly. The weekly edition appears much as it always has, a broadsheet that appears on weekends. The daily, which is published Tuesday through Friday, is in tabloid form. To a greater extent than most business publications the paper sticks strictly to items that are directly related to business. Even political stories that do not impact on the economy or commerce are not covered within its pages.

In keeping with the tabloid format, stories are generally shorter than in broadsheets like *The Wall Street Journal* or *The Globe & Mail.* Yet the *FP* is quite comprehensive in getting to the major stories of the day. For instance, on a daily basis, the paper carries a brief summary of trading on all of the world's major stock markets. On the other hand, *The Globe & Mail*'s ROB, on a regular daily basis, summarizes trading activity on only the New York, Vancouver, Montreal, and Toronto stock exchanges. London's *Financial Times* has an equity interest in the paper and the *FP* picks up much of its international news from this source. There is some news that the *FP* misses by necessity, however. The paper is printed on the same presses as *The Toronto Sun.* It therefore must have early deadlines. News that breaks much after the markets close in North America cannot make it into the paper. Of course, companies based in western regions of the continent often release important news late in their business day. Its publishing requirements, however, means it goes to print before the Toronto Stock Exchange closes, curious for a business paper, to say the least. These restrictions are shortcomings that continue to plague the paper, unable to attract advertising and struggling with cash flow problems, like many other startups.

There are a number of columnists that contribute on a regular or semi-regular basis to *The Financial Post.* In her column, "The Insiders," Dian Francis mixes gossip about executives with solid investigative reporting. One of her major concerns in 1989 was the handling by banks of funds received from the trade in illegal drugs. Hyman Solomon, the *FP*'s Ottawa correspondent is an excellent columnist, not a prisoner of the front page. Often Solomon focuses on a government policy that has not received much public attention, but may be important to business readers. Fred Dabbs writes an informative column on the energy industry titled "Oil Patch."

A number of academics and businessmen write regularly for the *FP.* With an American perspective on economic affairs, supply-side economist Paul Craig Roberts provides a column from Washington. William Watson, who teaches economics at Montreal's McGill University, appears frequently on the op-ed page. Along with tax lawyer Arthur Drache, Watson champions *laissez-faire* economics. Another columnist, Duncan Cameron, consistently argues for greater government intervention. The paper also runs a regular series of articles on the professions, which allows readers to follow developments in areas such as: medicine, the law, engineering, and accounting.

Out of habit, most Canadian businessmen still, reflexively, turn to *The Globe & Mail.* But if the *FP* continues to maintain its high standards, or if the paper improves significantly, that all could change.

The Toronto Star

The Washington Times does have a left-of-center counterpart — *The Toronto Star.* The management's bent is clearly displayed in virtually all of the political coverage, and there is almost no attempt to air both sides of controversial issues. It's a relative measure, however, as Canadians, on the whole, are more left-of-center than Americans, whose views tend to be more right-of-center in the mainstream. This may account for the solid subscription base (787,800 weekday; 515,227 Sunday) of the paper.

The editors, Editor John Honderich and Managing Editor Ian Urquhart, have often managed to anger individuals and groups that do not share the paper's political points of view. For instance, the Jewish community has been fighting a running battle with *The Star* since 1982. The coverage of Israel's incursion into Lebanon was seen to be so one-sided that there was a campaign to get Jewish readers to cancel their subscriptions. Many in the Jewish community are still hostile toward *The Star* because of what they see as a blatant anti-Israel bias. Their anger was aroused most recently in 1988 when, in an editorial, *The Star* intimated that Canadian Jews were more loyal to Israel than to Canada.

The Star dealt with the free trade issue in a fashion that was just plain partisan. So frustrated was Canada's negotiator, Simon Reisman, with the papers handling of free trade, that he took what is for a diplomat the highly unusual step of publicly rebuking *The Star*. Many other supporters of free trade similarly had harsh criticism of the paper.

There is not much variance between the way different papers report hard news. They really develop their distinctive identities on the editorial and op-ed pages. *The Star* probably has more in-house columnists than any other newspaper in the country. By following them on a regular basis, one could easily begin to suspect that they are in a competition with each other for the sympathies of the radical left. Moreover, the individual columnists have their own favorite hobby-horses. This makes reading their work distressingly predictable.

Of all the columnists, it is Gerald Caplan, whose work appears weekly in the Sunday edition, who tackles the widest range of subjects. Yet, he is formally a top official in the socialist New Democratic Party, and that tells you all you have to know about what he has to say about most subjects. Rarely do more than three weeks go by without Caplan attacking the one nation that he feels is most responsible for violence and injustice — the United States. Thus, in a 1-8 article, he writes favorably about a book by Noam Chomsky and Edward Herman that argues the press in the United States is not free, and that it serves the interests of the "controlling elites" of American society. In a 7-9 article, sparked by the flag-burning controversy, Caplan wrote that Ronald Reagan had appointed members of the "lunatic fringe" to the Supreme Court and asserted that violence was as American as apple pie.

Hardly a day went by in 1989 when someone writing on the editorial or op-ed page did not directly or indirectly pick up on this anti-American theme. Although the free trade agreement became law at the beginning of the year, columnists and other contributors kept attacking the pact on a regular basis. One of the most persistent crusaders against the pact is economics editor David Crane. His 10-21 column is one of a number in which Crane argues that free trade will result in the loss of Canada's economic and political independence. In a piece that appeared a day earlier, columnist Doris Anderson runs through every piece of bad economic news — and blames it all on free trade. Not exactly sophisticated economic analysis.

Opponents of free trade have always argued that only "big business" benefits from the agreement. *The Star* columnists regularly accuse the Mulroney government of being insensitive to the underprivileged. This is the theme of almost every contribution by *The Star*'s commentator on Social Policy, Leonard Shifrin, and most other columnists have taken this up. On 10-21, the paper ran "What's Happened to Our Caring Country?" by National Affairs columnist Carol Goar. In it she encouraged her readers to contribute more to charitable causes, and to get more involved in the political process. Both worthy goals. But why now? Goar blamed the federal government for policies that increased human misery.

The world view of the editorial board of *The Star* is somewhat left of center. In editorials throughout the year, *The Star* took the position that the reforms in Eastern Europe made continuation of the Cold War pointless. International Affairs columnist Richard Gwyn has taken almost exactly the same line, his views probably best summarized in one October article, in which he called Mikhail Gorbachev "courageous," while in the same piece accusing Israel of bucking the international trend toward peace.

To get the opportunity to write a guest piece for *The Star*'s op-ed page, one usually has to buy into the paper's left-of-center world point of view. One of the most outstanding examples of how the paper provides a platform for those with the most radical views was "Cambodia: Separating Legend from Reality," 10-16. In it, freelance writer Antony Black argued that the notion that the Khmer Rouge had committed genocide was a myth perpetuated by those who wanted to keep the Cold War going. *The Star* does publish dissenting views. It does carry the columns of Patrick Buchanan and George Will, but their columns are not run more than once or twice per month.

The Star has trouble keeping the views of its editors off the news pages. Blatantly, front page headlines are often manipulated to be in line with the paper's ideology. Thus, one front-page headline in *The Star* read "Ex-envoy Lewis Urges End to Destructive Tory Reign," Lewis being Mulroney's former ambassador to the UN. However, that he should now be denouncing his former masters is really not newsworthy since Lewis is a member of the New Democratic Party. The Lewis story was at the bottom of the front page. One can only speculate whether it would have been more prominently placed if it had not been competing for space with the first reports of the California earthquake.

In a similar vein, the 10-24 front page banner headline read "Moscow Offers Deal To Kill Arms Alliance." The accompanying story dealt with a speech given by Soviet Foreign Minister Eduard Shevardnadze. Of course, *The Star* consistently portrays the Soviets as peacemakers. The fact that Shevardnadze, in the same speech, also admitted that the Soviets were wrong to invade Afghanistan, and that they had violated the ABM Treaty was buried on P. 19. Increasingly, we find more and more that the real opinion page is P. 1, although *The Star*'s reporters are much less likely to inject an opinion into an article, if the subject does not fall under the prejudices of the paper's owners. But when the Hodnerich family's interests are at stake, ideological or financial, *The Star* knows no limits. This paper, which bills itself as a tribune of the people, has a long history of touting urban redevelopment projects on P. 1 that would raise land values in areas where, coincidentally, the paper has extensive real estate holdings.

In spite of its sometimes heavy-handed approach to political coverage, *The Star* compares favorably with other Canadian newspapers. Next to *The Globe & Mail* it has more bureaus than any other paper. It also devotes more space to the coverage of local news, sports, and the arts than *The Globe,* which is also based in Toronto. *The Star* also sees itself as the newspaper of the common man. As a result it carries special features for different segments of society such as small businessmen, teenagers, and persons with disabilities. With all these features, and several advertising supplements per week, *The Star,* on average, is no doubt the heaviest paper in the country.

Maclean's

Maclean's is Canada's only national weekly news magazine. The reader picking the magazine up for the first time will be struck by how much it looks like *Time, Newsweek* and *U.S.News & World Report.* The cover always features a glossy photograph. A piece by the editor on the first page of text always mentions the staff writers who wrote the cover story and this is followed by a page of one-paragraph letters from readers. Other regular sections are: "Canada;" "World;" "People;" "Business;" "Art;" and "Movies." The work of regular columnists appear at the front and back. Sound familiar? Unfortunately, the designers of North American newsweeklies have shown little imagination.

The team approach to article writing is also used at *Maclean's.* Yet this is one of the few Canadian publications that can hold its own with the American competition. *Maclean's* coverage of the news is just as comprehensive as those of the U.S. newsweeklies. It maintains its own bureaus in Ottawa, Calgary, Vancouver, Halifax, Washington, London and Moscow. Stringers gather news in smaller Canadian cities as well as in other parts of the world to be rewritten into its final form in the Toronto editorial offices.

Unlike other Canadian publications, *Maclean's* does not shy away from international news. About five stories make it into the "World" section every week, but items from outside of Canada also make it into other sections of the magazine. It is hard to detect one particular bias in *Maclean's* coverage of news. Quite frequently international news or personalities are the subject of lengthy cover stories. One of the best of the year, "Media Wars," 7-17, documented the rise of international publishing conglomerates, as good a profile of the world communications industry as we could find anywhere.

The magazine, though, does not have a strong stable of columnists. Allan Fotheringham has a lock on the back page, but it's hard to know why. From week to week he seems to be unable to decide whether he is a humorist or a serious writer. When he tries to be funny, he usually isn't. And his attempts at serious commentary almost always lack insight. Rather than informing his readers, he merely puts common prejudices into print. For example, he breaks absolutely no new ground in his 10-23 column in which he argues that "a small compact of rich families" controls the Canadian economy. In a number of other pieces, Fotheringham engages in a favorite occupation of many Canadian journalists — vilifying the United States.

Because a number of contributors share the opening column, it tends to be more uneven. One of the semi-regular columnists is Fred Bruning, who is with New York's *Newsday*. As with Fotheringham, readers will rarely be entertained or become better informed because of his column. His 6-19 article supporting gun control is filled with overstatement or exaggeration. (The NRA is the "fourth branch" of the U.S. government). In his 8-14 column, he inveighs against Sen. Jesse Helm's attempts to control grants made by the National Endowment for the Arts. Well and good, but we find his arguments could be heard by watching almost any public affairs program on American television — which is readily available in Canada. On the other hand, business columnist Dian Francis puts a great deal of research into her pieces. Her 7-10 piece on the reasons for the escalating costs of Canadian Workmen's Compensation premiums, covers an issue that the rest of the press virtually ignored. Barbara Amiel, another contributor, also often strikes out on her own. Her 6-5 analysis on the PLO's behavior since its Geneva Declaration, in which it supposedly renounced terrorism and accepted Israel's right to exist was as complete as any in the North American press.

All in all, *Maclean's* can hold its own with American newsweeklies. There is as much solid news coverage in each issue as in *Time, Newsweek* or *U.S.News & World Report.*

Saturday Night

Saturday Night is one of the last of a dying breed of magazine — the general interest monthly. In fact, it might have gone under had it not been bought a couple of years ago by the wealthy industrialist and media baron, Conrad Black.

It goes without saying that having to face the pressures of deadlines only once a month leaves an editor with considerable flexibility. John Fraser, who was brought in to head the magazine shortly after Black acquired it, has used this freedom well. In each issue, *SN* serves up a wide mix of articles on varied items such as books, politics, travel, law, and ethics.

While the focus is on Canada, the range is worldwide. In 1989, *SN* ran articles about politics in: Indonesia, Sweden, the West Bank, the Baltic States and Cuba. This year editor Fraser was able to provide an added dimension to the magazine's coverage of international affairs, as a decade ago Fraser was a foreign correspondent in China. This year, he devoted two of his monthly "Diary" pieces to events there. His March contribution is especially moving: in retelling the story of the government's mistreatment of a Chinese dissident whom he had known in the late 1970s; he was unwittingly foreshadowing the way the regime would crush the pro-democracy movement, only a few months later.

The bread and butter of *SN*'s political coverage is its articles on domestic affairs. Generally speaking there are two types of pieces: profiles of individual politicians; and the in-depth examination of individual issues or trends. The editors consistently have been able to find important stories that don't make it to the front page of the dailies.

The new owner, Conrad Black, has right-wing views, and he has never been shy to express them. At one point, Black had a regular column himself in *The Globe and Mail*'s business magazine. When he bought *SN*, many predicted that he would turn it into a Canadian version of *National Review*, which hasn't happened. It would be hard to identify an ideological slant in most of the articles, although there are a few writers who we can guess to be liberal or conservative. But only guess. For instance, the main theme of the February article on Sweden is that democratic socialism does work in that Scandinavian country. A month earlier, *SN* ran a fair but generally complimentary cover profile on a socialist Canadian politician who became the first Member of Parliament to reveal that he was a homosexual.

The articles in *SN* are not as long as the pieces that one finds in *The Atlantic Monthly,* which is similar in some ways. Yet *SN* has high standards. Virtually every article is both interesting and informative. That probably explains why well-known writers such as Mordechai Richler and Margaret Atwood contribute to the magazine.

It's becoming apparent that as borders become more blurry, the more we will become alike. These publications will be reviewed more in-depth, in the same manner as those in the sections which follow, in future editions of the *MediaGuide.*

BROADCAST NEWS

For the last several years, one of the questions asked most about the *MediaGuide* is why we haven't covered television news. Why not? Most often we've quoted Walter Cronkite's observation that the network news is at best a "picture headline service."

The reason we present the following observations on the broadcast news media is that we sense they are becoming more efficient in the communication of news, through the expansion of cablevision and the attendant competition this means for all. If we have only half an hour per day to absorb "news," it is clearly more efficient for us to get it from radio spots and television. For serious consumers of news, who must devote at least an hour or two each day to receiving news to be able to function in the business world or political economy, a basket of high-quality print publications that can be efficiently scanned is needed. Every year henceforth, as electronic breakthroughs occur, our "news" portfolio is likely to contain more of that medium.

Television's nature as a visual medium gives it both an edge over and a disadvantage to print. Television delivers strong images; certainly the scenes of East Germans desperately trying to get into embassies or marching for freedom were more heart-wrenching than the accounts in the papers. But this reliance on visuals, combined with stiff competition for viewers' attention, can control the network agenda. Producers are subject to the whims of fickle viewers with remote controls, and often go for the lowest common denominator, rather than necessarily the most newsworthy story. To carry weight, television reporting strives to impact, becoming "infotainment."

As a result, we have the practice of dramatic reenactments, posing serious credibility problems. Early in the year, CBS was accused of faking footage from Afghanistan, which spokesmen denied, and also of staging some of its China coverage, *to which a producer admitted.* ABC's use of unmarked "dramatic recreations" to illustrate the alleged transactions of Felix Bloch brought severe criticism from professional journalists. NBC pledged not to use recreations in "news programming," after the news program "Yesterday, Today and Tomorrow" was chastised.

While pictures complement a newspaper article, television can't seem to tell a story without them, relying on visuals to *make* the story, even when there is nothing new to report. This dependency on pictures was most recently demonstrated in China, as CBS and CNN led the corps with powerful live reports from Tiananmen Square. When the Chinese regime decided to pull the plug, CNN viewers saw two hours of debate between CNN officials and the Chinese before the picture went black. The networks did their best to keep the focus on China over the next few weeks, but without new footage the time devoted to the nation's turmoil shrunk day by day. Rerunning old footage as reporters called by phone grew stale after a while, and China's troubles dropped from view.

While the anchors and correspondents cited here are not rated as we do print journalists in the *MediaGuide,* our methods are similar. The observations result from literally hundreds of hours of viewing the news programs at random, although we did occasionally go to the videotape as bigger stories broke in order to make direct comparisons. The differences between print and broadcast are myriad because of the technology involved, but both still should adhere to the same *basic* principles, as they are serving the same *basic* informational function. Those requirements are fairness, accuracy, and balance or objectivity. There are some reporters who are superior to others in meeting these basic criteria, of course, and it is with this in mind we review the best and most notable of the "picture headline service."

"World News Tonight"

The Anchors

Straddling the fence between CBS and NBC, ABC's entry usually runs ahead of the competition in the Nielsen ratings. "World News Tonight" is a natural showcase for Peter Jennings. Jennings' presentation of the news is urbane and suave, despite the fact his tie always seems to be crooked. He appears more genuine than Dan Rather and is more conversational than Tom Brokaw, and his warmth pays off in dollar signs for the network. "And now we have a story for those of you concerned about health care" is not an unfamiliar Jennings opening. We see him being for the little guy, which the mass media is all about, but obliquely, without a clear prescription, perhaps reflecting a detachment and reserve that is a result from his Canadian citizenship.

After a piece on the House vote for repeal of the catastrophic health care program on 9-18, Jennings reported "Congress, having first decided that those who could afford it should pick up some of the financial burden of catastrophic insurance, is now going to be pressured into changing its mind because those who are deemed able to pay or have other insurance are so violently opposed. Which may well mean that because 5 million elderly people are angry, as many as 18 million others may suffer."

Jennings remains basically objective on domestic affairs and he also stresses this little-guy attentiveness in his foreign reporting, with no grating sense of ideology. During Gorbachev's visit to Cuba, Jennings was going to remind us that Castro did some good things too, and we appreciate that it did not come at us with a hammer, but with his engaging style, 4-3: "Education was once available to the rich and well connected. It is now free to all. . ..Medical care was once for the privileged few. Today it is available to every Cuban and it is free." That's true, and because it is, we're not especially exercised that he didn't recount Castro's many deficiencies, which we all know well.

On the weekends, ABC showcases its other anchor talents, veteran reporter Carole Simpson, and frequent "Nightline" guest host Forrest Sawyer. ABC is the only network of the Big Three to feature sports on the weekend news, good news to sports fans, but anathema to channel-flipping news hounds. Ray Gandolf reprises his TV magazine-style sports anchor role that matched well with Charles Kuralt on CBS "Sunday Morning," but seems too slow to keep up. An occasional substitution by Diane Sawyer can prove downright editorial. When the networks covered the first flight tests of the Stealth bomber on 6-10, for example, Sawyer joked "What's long overdue, way over budget, and proved today it can travel at least six miles on the ground? The new B-2 Stealth bomber. It rolled up and down the runway in California today, the first time it's gone anywhere under its own power. The plane costs half a billion dollars, and it may actually take to the air later this week." Cartooney, Diane.

Special Features

Two features differentiate "World News Tonight" from the other nightly newscasts, "American Agenda" and "Person of the Week." The "American Agenda" series was instituted after the 1988 election on the premise it would provide an opportunity to explore issues of importance to all Americans. Most segments focus on health, education, or the environment, all decidedly issues of concern. The program seems simple-minded to us, promoting more government spending on social programs as a straight line solution. On 1-30, medical correspondent George Strait called for a national health care system like that of Canada's. "It's a system that works," Strait simply asserted, with no hint of an authority. ". . .Critics say the American system is inherently inefficient because it's paid for by many competing government and private insurance companies." In a red-handed catch, syndicated columnist Warren Brookes caught environmental correspondent Ned Potter making false claims on a 7-25 "American Agenda" report. Potter built an entire segment around the claim that a Vermont forest was being destroyed by acid rain. Not so, says Brookes, and he gets a 10 Best award for his debunking.

The "Person of the Week" feature is designed to keep viewers in front of the seat on traditionally low-rated Friday nights. The segment spotlights a mixed bag of well-known political or entertainment figures and unknowns who are playing a role in a major story of the week. At its best, "Person of the Week" serves as a rare mini-profile of a public figure, as with Georgia Sen. Sam Nunn, 3-16, French President Francois Mitterrand, 7-14, or the President's National Security Advisor, Colin Powell, 8-25, outside of the combative "60 Minutes." The glowing portrait, 5-12, of former President Jimmy Carter rightly congratulated Carter for continuing his life "with distinction, considerable grace, and with a very strong commitment to peace and justice." Carter, unlike other former U.S. Chief Executives who are raking in big bucks in speaking fees and sitting on Blue Chip boards, is devoting much of his time to housing projects in Georgia. "Person of the Week" rarely goes to an undeserving character, even when it's celebrity mush: Paul Newman was highlighted for his charitable donations to relief organizations after the California earthquake, for instance. It's a nice break from the gloom-and-doom news we get, harmless enough, but rarely of import.

The Correspondents

ABC met the less confrontational Bush style with a kinder, gentler White House correspondent. The network retired A-1 attack dog Sam Donaldson, replacing him with the more reasonable Brit Hume. Hume, who grew up in the print media, often demonstrates insight not seen on the other networks, countering the established wisdom so often relayed by competitors. Especially strong on budget matters, he captures the unique Washington spectacle of constant cries for more spending and wailing over the deficit in the same breath. Hume is also refreshing in questioning federal spending increases as an automatic solution to a problem. When the fight over Bush's proposed education budget warmed up on 4-5, Hume put the burden of proof on the education lobby: "The critics may have to explain why, if money is the solution, the U.S. has a problem. This country already spends more per student on education than any country on earth." NBC and CBS missed until Bush's education summit in late September. Hume explained Congressional opposition to the President's drug plan, noting on 9-6 that the Democrats wanted new taxes so "they can spend them on the drug war, and a lot of other things."

Congressional news was dominated by a multitude of scandals during 1989, and former *New York Times* veteran Jim Wooten brought balance to ABC's Hill coverage when the heat was on. On top of the John Tower story, Wooten sorted through the gossip that became too easy to report and provided equal time for Tower supporters and detractors. Wooten's coverage of the Jim Wright flap was straightforward and balanced, neither blasting the Speaker nor sensationalizing the story, but also empathic and soft in spots. On 4-19, he describes the situation: "Much of the house on recess took the issue with them," reporting 73 percent of his home district supported the embattled Speaker, and quietly observed the rules were changing as quickly as the ethical standards, and the transition was going to catch people, including Wright, short. Later, 5-23, he again captures the gathering storm, reporting if the charges against Wright are not dismissed, House Democrats believe he must resign. On 5-31, Wooten dramatizes the situation somewhat, describing Wright as a sacrificial lamb, but noting that after 34 years of service, it took him just 44 days to fall.

Robert Zelnick's defense coverage is exceptionally satisfying, when he's on air, and we could easily see him as a network anchorman. In all the years we've been watching him, he's never disappointed us in his professionalism. Zelnick often goes beyond the easy story with the easy interpretation to explore the news behind official DoD press statements. While he has a rap among conservatives as a practicing liberal, for goodness sakes, we see only a quality newsman. Reporting on the explosion of the U.S.S. Iowa, Zelnick was punching holes in the Navy's official report as early as 5-26.

From the State Department, John McWethy probably gets the most air time of any network diplomatic correspondent. ABC regularly turns to McWethy for interpretations of the latest foreign news or details of arms control policy. He also broke one of the biggest stories of 1989 when he revealed the FBI's investigation of diplomat Felix Bloch on July 21. Unfortunately for ABC, the decision to air an unlabeled simulation of Bloch's alleged delivery of secrets to a Soviet agent put the team, and the story, in hot water.

ABC's coverage of economics is the most straightforward of the networks, except for CNN, although not the network of choice for economic and financial news. Most economic news consists of anchor reads of the latest changes in the economic indicators. Washington-based correspondent Stephen Aug is much less likely than his colleagues to make broad economic predictions, adding little to the anchor reads. He can also color a piece. Aug's biggest story of the year was his coverage of the Eastern Airlines strike, his solidarity with Eastern's employees clear, stating on 3-8 that even ruining Eastern could be a victory since "it would show employers that they cannot ignore their workers and expect them to give in." U.S.-Asian trade relations also figured prominently. A 9-26 dispatch on the purchase of Columbia by Sony bemoans the sale: "Pop culture is an export, but Americans don't own it," never examining the economic pluses of foreign investment, nor pointing out that Americans still invest more dollars overseas than foreigners do here.

"The CBS Evening News With Dan Rather"

The Anchors

More than any other network news program, the "CBS Evening News" bears the unmistakable personal stamp of its anchor, due to his active role as managing editor of the broadcast. Dan Rather's melodramatic news delivery extends to everything from natural disasters to the Soviet arms control pronouncements to U.S. economic "crises." The all-powerful anchor, Rather even went so far as to trace the path of Hurricane Hugo on a weather map, part of his "show and tell" technique of news reportage. He frequently quizzes his reporters as they finish their reads to get their "sense" of a story, probing the Pentagon, White House, Capitol Hill, and State Department reporters for some additional perspective.

In the last year or so we sense "a new Rather" the way we once contemplated "a new Nixon." A mellow Rather seems to be striving for an internal sense of journalistic excellence deeper than his internal sense of advocacy, not only with TV presence, but even moreso with his observations on WCBS radio. The Rather image was burned into the national consciousness during his prosecutorial news role in the political demise of Richard Nixon, which of course was among the most cataclysmic events in U.S. history. This recollection among conservatives is central to the high-wire Rather walks on news objectivity. Liberals defend his position. Conservatives such as North Carolina's Sen. Jesse Helms are eager to bring him down. This year or next we would not be surprised to see a Dan Rather interview with RMN. Why not?

Weekend anchors Bob Schieffer and Connie Chung remain run-of-the-mill news readers, but each has a segment to add opinions. Saturday brings Schieffer's "Washington Notebook," consisting of a brief report and related interview. Chung's "Inside Sunday" features four or five stories on the same subject for the last third of the broadcast, sometimes including an innocuous close-up on personal health or new trends in marketing. But it can also be a one-sided focus on social issues such as the drive for more federal money for contraceptive research, 8-13.

The Correspondents

As chief White House correspondent on a news program which gives the Oval Office the most coverage of all the networks, Lesley Stahl appears almost nightly, often including Congressional and State Department developments in her stories. More than her counterparts at the other networks, Stahl thrives on "palace guard" journalism, often placing much more emphasis in a story on the political fallout than the issues. With Bush only just in the Oval Office, Stahl was already critical of the President's organization, reporting on the "ethical questions" surrounding the new appointees and advising "Mr. Bush's friends are worried. They say the White House damage control operation is off to a rocky start," 2-2. A month later, things were no better, Stahl disparaging the White House for having "no strategy for dealing with the perception of an administration foundering," 3-6. In May, Stahl claimed the White House had worried that "things could start to unravel." She'd seen it all before: "It happened in Watergate," she recalled, 5-4. At the time, Bush was enjoying unprecedented national approval ratings. Still negative, Stahl informed us that "in Poland, Hungary, and the economic summit, the trip seemed to reinforce the fact that the United States no longer has the money to solve the world's problems. . .The President goes home tomorrow to confront reality, the budget deficit that created this era of limits."

Stahl's most glaring political angle came when the White House criticized the Soviets for continued aid to Nicaragua. Stahl focused on congressional dismay at the President's "cavalier" response and saw "the verbal attack on Gorbachev" as a sign of Bush's being "under rising pressure to counter Gorbachev's recent wave of arms-control initiatives." The actual existence of continued Soviet aid to Central America was all but ignored, 5-16. Stahl is backed up on the White House beat by Wyatt Andrews, a deputy who does little better with balance, as when he claimed there was "evidence that U.S.-made assault rifles are fueling the violence in Colombia." Because the Washington bureau is focused on the White House, State Department reporter Bill Plante is a relatively rare sight. He did credibly cover, though, Jim Baker's work in the Middle East and the various Central American peace plans. Following the other networks, Plante stressed the State Department's criticism of Israel for human rights violations, while adding that the Soviet's rights record was said to be "improving," 2-7.

Eric Enberg, CBS's general assignment reporter, does not have as many dimensions as we'd like to see. He covered Iran-contra, seeing the affair as a problem of "secrecy," reporting: "Freewheeling covert operators can do as they wish because an invisible policy can't be questioned." Moreover, a deception such as Iran-contra could happen again "until the President accepts the need to compromise with Congress." He does filings on occasional social issues with a clear liberal tilt, which would be okay, but we just don't get enough out of the reporting to offset the mild and irritating bias. He looked at the complaints of the Coalition for Universities in the Public Interest, which is unhappy about corporate support for universities, 6-13, with the conclusion: "Congress is also concerned about corporate money being lost. After all, universities are kept afloat with federal dollars [to] benefit the public, not some bottom line." He also doesn't put things in a historical context, which would help to give his stories more balance and credibility. "Politics didn't just turn ugly," Enberg announced 5-29, "It evolved from a nasty presidential campaign that featured the GOP's famous Willie Horton ad." Now doesn't that sound silly when you think about it?

David Martin's Pentagon coverage was exemplary. On 2-13, Martin's coverage of the Nicaraguan peace talks focused on the doubling of Soviet aid, and Nicaragua's capabilities as the most formidable Central American military power, adding that the military is "about the only thing that's gotten better in Nicaragua," and showing graphic scenes of an economy in shambles. On 7-28, in his coverage of the White House-Capitol Hill fight over the defense budget, Martin alone unmasked the Congressional sanctimony, revealing that "for all its reshuffling, the House did not cut a dime" from the budget. CBS covered every test failure of weaponry this year, but also covered the successful SDI tests.

CBS hopped on the China story early and stayed with it, with John Sheahan continuing to report on repressions and show trials months after the Tiananmen massacre. While in China, Rather irked by ascribing China's abysmal standard of living first, to "cultural traditions," 5-16, then to its "population time bomb," 5-17. CBS's coverage provided a perfect example of an event manipulated by the media. Producer Lane Venardos later confessed to having "timed" a 5-31

Rather-Sheahan interview on the program so that it would seem to be cut off live by Chinese officials, in order to recapture the drama of the previous week. In reality, Chinese Central Television announced in advance they would be turning off the satellite, so visual contact was broken, but Sheahan's telephone connection remained intact. Rather could have continued the interview but didn't, cutting Sheahan off, and making it appear the sensors and oppressors were at it again. This is not journalism; this is stage management, unacceptable in any form.

Moscow correspondent Barry Petersen was CBS's sometime cheerleader for Mikhail Gorbachev, praising him for having the "courage" to end Soviet involvement in Afghanistan, 3-11. When he followed Gorbachev to Cuba, Peterson was direct in his assessment of the Cuban military forces, calling the "equipment the best the Soviet Union can supply," 4-3, in contrast to then-ABC reporter Richard Threlkeld, who claimed "much of the equipment is old and obsolete" the same night. (Threlkeld moved to CBS in September.) In a 4-4 exchange, we get Dan Rather touting a defrosting of Cuban-American relations with no empirical evidence, "Gorbachev indicated in his speech that he and Castro will work for improved East-West relations and that he may have gotten some softening in Castro's rock-hard anti-Americanism. In at least one sense, that may have come too late. In the middle of Castro's long introduction, which included denunciations of the United States, the representative of U.S. interests here in Cuba, Jay Taylor, left the hall in protest. . .Barry, let's first detail the glimmer of hope, and that's all it is, the glimmer of hope for Central America," and Petersen responding by reading Gorby's mind: "Dan, I think we were just a heartbeat away, just a heartbeat away from Gorbachev about to say something dramatic. You know, you could see in his face, it was almost there. He wants to make a move." Well, maybe, but we think this is kiddie journalism.

CBS consistently promotes a negative economic agenda. If the news is bad, it often leads, and gets feature treatment from business correspondent Ray Brady, who would get a minus rating in our print-media guide. When news is good, it's still bad, either buried in the newscast or given a negative spin. The year was off to a bad start before it began, with Brady claiming that retailers, working to make the Christmas season pay off, could be in trouble because they'd "find themselves short of goods to sell in the new year," 12-20-88. Then when retail sales figures were up for December, Rather called that a "warning flag" for the economy "in danger of overheating," 1-13. Days later, high trade deficit figures were another cause for concern, especially for economist and former Dukakis advisor Robert Reich, whom Brady consulted in his report, 1-18. A temporary price increase that reflected the effects of the 1988 drought was quickly viewed as hitting hard at the new Bush budget, 2-10. Substitute anchor Charles Kuralt worried that "the high unemployment rate is causing problems," 3-10. In July, Brady lead the news with word of "plant closings, worker layoffs" in the second-quarter GNP figures, 7-27, but when these figures were revised upward reflecting strength in the very sectors Brady had seen as weak, the news got buried in an anchor read, 8-27. If you want economic boom reports, try another frequency. Businessmen or investors who relied on this half-hour for their economic cues surely did not do well this year.

"NBC Nightly News"

The Anchors

Of the three major networks, NBC is the least guilty of weaving political judgments into its reports. Anchor Tom Brokaw is less apt to put issues on his own terms like Jennings or play word games like Rather. His presentation is solid and straightforward, authoritative but not overbearing, a convincing mix of personality and professionalism. Brokaw is an anchor for those who want the news unadorned. For example, in contrast to ABC's substituting Diane Sawyer (see ABC), Brokaw resisted the tabloid temptation and reported the straight facts on Stealth, 6-10: "In the California desert today, the secret B-2 Stealth bomber successfully passed a critical test. For the first time, the Stealth moved under its own power, taxiing on the runway. Later this week, high-speed tests are scheduled, to be followed by a maiden flight."

But Brokaw's appeal is weakened on the weekends by the painfully flat Maria Shriver on Saturday, and on Sunday by the somewhat quirky Garrick Utley. On 3-19, Utley led off the broadcast: "The results are coming in from the election day in El Salvador: not the vote. . .but the dead." Later in the same broadcast, Utley introduced news of Soviet voting a different way: "Now we want to show you something truly extraordinary that happened in the Soviet Union today." His economics are often dizzy. On 9-17, we get this: "The debate over cutting the capital gains tax is not just about economics, it is about fairness. And if you want to know why, look at this. This is a congressional estimate of who wins and who doesn't. Those earning under $10,000 a year would win nothing. Those in the broad, middle-income range would get about 20 percent of the overall benefit from the tax cut. And those with big incomes, $100,000 a year and up, would win 80 percent of the benefit." There are smart arguments against the idea, but this is woeful class warfare baloney.

Special Features

NBC is the only network that offers viewers regular commentary. But the network made the familiar mistake of inviting back an old anchor, John Chancellor, rather than contracting with, say, a newspaper columnist who makes his living offering concise opinions. In this role, Chancellor is no better than a windbag, lacking perspective and depth, wasting precious minutes of our time on embarrassingly poor comparisons among unrelated events. Chancellor's commentary in the aftermath of the Tiananmen Square massacre on 6-20: "Thousands have been gunned down in Beijing. But what about the millions of American kids whose lives are being ruined by an enormous failure of the country's education system?. . .We can and we should agonize about the dead students in Beijing, but we've got a much bigger problem right here at home." What?

And nipping at Bush's heels only four days after he moved into the Oval Office, we get more wind: "George Herbert Walker Bush may not look like a gambler, but he has bet the farm on one risky assumption: that the American economy will continue its unabated growth. . .Fear of a recession is what drives the argument for raising government revenue through taxes while cutting government spending. Some experts say a serious attack on the deficit now would increase confidence in the government's ability to put its house in order, and increased confidence is one way of avoiding a recession." The network could do better.

The Correspondents

NBC's post-Reagan rotation of correspondents had a salutary effect, bringing freshness without amateurishness. Moving from the State Department to the White House, John Cochran does a nice job of covering President Bush. In contrast with the teflon-cracking mentality of White House correspondents during Reagan's tenure, Cochran actually presents the White House view, instead of just lining up experts to criticize it, although he'll do so when an alternate view is appropriate. In a report on Marlin Fitzwater's characterization of Gorbachev as a "drugstore cowboy," 5-16, Cochran told Brokaw "the feeling around the White House is that Gorbachev has successfully sold some snake oil to the Western media."

Cochran did get off to a shaky start covering Bush, with an erroneous inauguration day report, then got even the correction wrong. "We pointed out yesterday [Bush] referred to Benjamin Harrison dying of pneumonia after a chilly inauguration day, and of course, it was William Tyler Harrison." It was actually William *Henry* Harrison. NBC's other White House reporter, Jim Miklaszewski, better fit the Reagan-era model, spending more time with presidential critics than with the President. In a 7-21 report on Bush's "clean air" bill, Miklaszewski interviewed Richard Ayres of the National Clean Air Coalition, and added Democrats Sen. Joseph Lieberman and Rep. Gerry Sikorski, concluding: "Critics call it a bill right out of the Reagan administration." And upon William Bennett's appointment as drug czar, we find Miklaszewski winging it about Bennett's service as Education Secretary: "An ultraconservative, Bennett served as Ronald Reagan's political lightning rod, and campaigned for massive cuts in federal spending on education, a fiscal approach that concerns many in Congress." Wha?

Moving Andrea Mitchell to Capitol Hill from her number two perch at the White House was also a positive step. Permitting Mitchell's aggressive style to run loose on the legislative branch instead of the executive, unintentionally created an internal system of checks and balances at the network. We especially liked Mitchell's "Capitol Watch" segments on Rep. Les Aspin's self-promoting Pentagon think tank, 6-2; on the enormous campaign treasuries of incumbent congressmen, 6-28; and on "king of pork" Rep. Tom Bevill, 10-2. In contrast with the White House-centered approach of CBS, NBC relies heavily on Mitchell if any part of a breaking story touches Congress. Assignment editors kept Henry Champ, supposedly the network's No. 2 at the Capitol, too long on his old Pentagon beat to bring anything substantial to his new assignment.

Fred Francis remained at the Pentagon, openly departing from the line of the other networks. TV's defense correspondents are least likely to practice pack journalism, as witnessed in the aftermath of the U.S.S. Iowa explosion. Francis reported the controversial allegations that the blast was an intentional suicide by a sailor, and stuck to the basic version of this story while other reporters openly challenged it. His No. 2, Katherine Couric, spent less time at the Pentagon than Champ and more time covering her old beat as a local reporter at NBC's DC affiliate. At the State Department, John Dancy got off to a slower start and was given less opportunity to appear, especially when compared to ABC's John McWethy. Dancy's reporting is adequate; in some cases, his sense of perception is off-kilter. In a 3-7 report on the Baker plan to allow congressional committees to decide the fate of the contras, Dancy concluded "the most divisive foreign policy issue in the last ten years looks close to a solution," not realizing how long it might take to get a consensus in committee.

The network's foreign coverage suffers most at the hand of Moscow correspondent Bob Abernethy, whose reports offer no more than the official reading of events. "Until last weekend, Soviet troops just looked on at the demonstrators. Then over the weekend they moved. They didn't shoot at the crowd," Abernethy reported on a pro-independence rally in Georgia, 4-10, though Peter Jennings reported that same night that the Army had indeed opened fire. In a 4-14 report following the murder of protesters in Soviet Georgia, Abernethy reported "Moscow's delicate task in Tbilisi is to use enough force to keep order and at the same time make enough changes to restore calm." During the Castro-Gorbachev summit, 4-4, Abernethy let fly one of his PR lines: "Castro is enormously proud of such Cuban achievements as housing projects built by volunteers." And his 5-1 report from Moscow: "In Red Square, a relaxed, joyous May Day, with slogans celebrating not only labor, but peace and protection of the environment, and the reforms Mikhail Gorbachev wants to make in the way this country works. Western observers noted a turn away from hardline ideology."

On the economics beat, Mike Jensen is straightforward and prone to the conventional wisdom, as in covering Bush's first State of the Union address: "President Bush sees more people and companies paying more money and paying more taxes without an increase in the tax rate. Most experts say that's not likely to happen." Jensen had a scenario to match: "Inflation will force Alan Greenspan of the Federal Reserve to push interest rates higher. Loan rates would go up. That would slow down housing. . .and then the economy as a whole. And with that, the government would collect less money in taxes and the budget deficit would grow. It would take new taxes to reduce it," 2-10. Irving R. Levine, who lives in a bygone era, routinely covers reports on the government's economic forecasts without forever reading recession, but he can be susceptible to the "soft-landing" school of conventional economic wisdom, as on 8-11: "The danger is that as the economy picks up, it could become too much of a good thing."

Alternative News Sources

Cable News Network

At the time of its founding, Ted Turner's 24-hour Cable News Network, CNN, was welcomed mostly with skepticism from media veterans, doubtful that the new network could maintain quality when faced with the demands of a day-long news format and a cast of unknowns. But in recent years, CNN has gained a measure of respectability, which it richly deserves. CNN anchor Bernard Shaw was invited to the White House along with the Big Three network anchors for an interview with President Reagan, and Shaw's turn as a panelist in the presidential debates was unforgettable. His lead-off question to Michael Dukakis regarding his wife's hypothetical rape and murder, however inappropriate in context, was seen by many as a pivotal point of the campaign due to the governor's unemotional, bureaucratic response.

But Shaw, the closest thing CNN has to a "star," has never been given his own solo program. Whether by default or design, CNN has no "star system" by which journalists are elevated into celebrity experts whose opinions matter more than the news itself. "Headline News" broadcasts taped CNN reports and live anchor reads in a straight-from-the-hip half-hour news format. All of CNN's one-hour newscasts are co-anchored by teams of two and even three people, which gives the viewer a fresh face every so often and gives the anchor less of a spotlight. The cast of anchors and correspondents is a competent lot. Their reporters work on a story all day, in some cases providing live reports. But they should be seen as anything but a Big Three "B" team. The balance they routinely maintain in their reporting shows they have more to teach than to learn from the other networks.

There are exceptions of course, such as Moscow correspondent Steve Hurst's report from Afghanistan on 2-9: "It's the women of this country who have the most to lose if this Marxist revolution fails. . .A woman's place in such a society would be back under the head-to-toe covering of the chaterra, cooking and cleaning and bearing children." But overall, CNN is the network of choice for viewers who like their news straight up, with no ice, no twist, no nothing. Throughout these presentations, they maintain a strong commitment to balanced, accurate, timely, informative reporting.

CNN has also gained respectability in its coverage at times of crisis where on-the-scene live reporting experience is invaluable, such as May's Chinese pro-democracy protests or October's failed coup in Panama. While the other networks dart in and out of soap operas and game shows with special reports, CNN is always on the scene. Evidence continues to mount that during such events, Washington's centers of power, from the White House to the Hill, have their eyes glued on CNN for minute-to-minute details. CNN is also the satellite station of record in Eastern Europe and beyond, watched by policymakers throughout the bloc. CNN has earned a reputation as the network of record, even when in direct competition with the other networks. And in addition to CNN's regular offering of hourly newscasts interspersed with live reports, talk shows like "Larry King Live," and business programs like "Moneyline," CNN also offers "Headline News" on selected cable systems.

The format, which gives reporters the precious commodity of time unknown to the regular half-hour network evening broadcast, does not always present longer reports, but instead brings in more reports on a particular topic from different angles. CNN coverage of the Panamanian coup included stories from the White House, the State Department, the Pentagon, and Capitol Hill. But the producers must tread carefully. CNN's uninterrupted block of air time also inclines towards visual and tabloid fare. Hurricane Hugo took up almost the entire hour on CNN's "PrimeNews" on 9-22 when it hit the coast of the Carolinas.

Another example is Jeanne Moos' history of the bra on 5-30: "Most women buy them, while most men try to get by them. . ...A professor at New York's Fashion Institute of Technology maintains that the first bra was invented in the early 1800's by the Marquis de Brassiere. And then there's the titillating question about Otto Titzling in the game Trivial Pursuit." Ugh. Only by watching CNN could viewers learn who won the latest pig calling contest somewhere in Iowa, or hear about a female artist in New York who put up signs complaining about cat calls, or be treated to the latest in decoy duck racing in London.

The CNN bomb is Linda Ellerbee's commentary. Even worse than John Chancellor, Ellerbee's attempts at wit or political insight seem flatulent, either too silly or combative for the up-close-and-personal nature of television viewing. In her first commentary, 3-20, she announced: "Well, am I a liberal, a conservative, or what?. . .I believe in sunny summer mornings when the grass is sweet and the wind is green with possibilities. I believe in chili with no beans and iced tea all year round. . .And so it goes." When she does talk about politics, a sappy liberalism shows through, as on Oliver North, 4-21: "I see, you don't want to be a hero, you just want to go home. Yeah, you and every other puppet I ever saw. Okay, Ollie, you go home; we'll even give you a map to help you find your way. It's called the Constitution of the United States of America. This time, try reading it before you shred it." The bombast of Ellerbee is offset by CNN's energetic hammer-and-tongs talk-show programming, such as "The Capital Gang" on Saturday nights, and "Crossfire" on weeknights, some of the most lively political talk shows on television, right and left going head to head.

Ironically, CNN's rising respectability is only threatened by its tendency to become a vehicle for Ted Turner's personal enthusiasm, airing one-sided blasts of advocacy journalism such as the hour-long special "Climate In Crisis," 10-1. Turner, in conjunction with his Better World Society, has used television with increasing frequency to promote his own agenda. Usually, these shows are aired on his other networks, TBS and TNT. For CNN's sake, which has earned a reputation for balance, fairness, and professionalism — not to mention a growing national and international audience — this is good news.

Public Broadcasting System

The most informative news program on the air today remains the "MacNeil/Lehrer NewsHour." Hosted by Robert MacNeil and Jim Lehrer, the program consists of policymaker or government official interviews on important topics of the day. Both hosts are veterans of print, while the support staff, Judy Woodruff and Charlayne Hunter-Gault, are long-time veterans of television journalism and ultra-professional. Although the introductions, and some of the segments are produced and written by other sources, it is the interviews for which we value the show. In tandem in the New York area, where we view these programs, "MacNeil/Lehrer" follows "Nightly Business Report," the combination most satisfying and efficient.

C-Span

Now celebrating ten years of cable television, C-Span is most notable for bringing Congress' doings into the living room and for founder Brian Lamb's hour-long interviews with different behind-the-scenes newsmakers. There's little news as such presented second-hand. C-Span presents the event, with no voice-over (we get classical music for background), and no instant interpretation. C-Span's impact is in its ability to transmit visuals of Congress in action. House Minority Whip Newt Gingrich, (R-Geo.) has been noted as the first C-Span congressional leader, his orations to a near empty chamber making his reputation. C-Span went international for the 1990s at the end of 1989, adding to its live coverage of the American Houses of Congress, live coverage from London's House of Commons, a delightfully British diversion, much more raucous and entertaining than the U.S. version.

Beyond the News

On Sunday Morning

In addition to the nightly news, each network offers its own political talk show on Sunday morning. NBC's "Meet the Press," CBS's "Face the Nation" and ABC's "This Week with David Brinkley." Network management has managed to turn these from straight interview shows aimed at providing a better understanding of policymaking to adversarial newsmaking shows, in which questioners focus on current policymakers and encourage reporters to offer opinions. Indeed, these discussions regularly trigger Monday morning newspaper stories. John Tower's pledge on "This Week" to quit drinking upon Senate confirmation as Secretary of Defense landed on the front pages of major newspapers all across the country.

Roone Arledge began the recreation of the Sunday morning talk show format with "This Week With David Brinkley." "This Week" gives one of the deeper looks into all sides of one issue. Its one-hour format gives it time to explain a story's background in an opening seven-minute piece, to interview two or three different sets of guests, giving the viewer a wide spectrum of opinion and the feeling of getting the "inside" story. To add a spice of variety and keep the hour going, Brinkley presides over a reporters' chat segment (a la the syndicated political shoutfest "The McLaughlin Group") with Sam Donaldson, George Will, and a rotating guest commentator. Will offsets Donaldson's blunderbuss style with his steady eloquence, and ABC remains the only Big Three network to regularly feature a conservative opinion leader. This point-counterpoint style keeps the format lively, but we wish the powers that be at Brinkley would bring in guest commentators who could really match wits with the formidable Donaldson-Will duo. The current rotation of commentators, Tom Wicker, Hodding Carter, Cokie Roberts, Ellen Goodman, or Robert Maynard, too often wind up nodding in agreement early in the discussion. Brinkley, who is consistently our favorite television news personality, this year received the National Press Foundation's award for excellence in broadcasting.

CBS News' "Face The Nation," hosted by Lesley Stahl, is a half-hour program with an opening background report followed by one or two interview segments. Congressional leaders and Cabinet members are the usual guests, with an occasional local or state official if the issue, such as drugs or crime, has a local angle. Stahl's questions are clearly gleaned from the Sunday morning op-ed pages and tend toward the conventional wisdom. It's infrequent we get any new information from these discussions, and it's painful to watch Stahl badger her guests, rephrasing her question until she gets the answer she wants to hear, whether it's right or wrong. Occasionally, they are revealing of Stahl's own prejudices, as when she asked Richard Darman 7-23 "Won't it become necessary to raise taxes? And isn't that just a bald truth?" At the Malta summit, 12-3, she was credited with hammering at Secretary of State Baker to reveal what he got for the concessions granted Gorbachev, but we thought the grilling tiresome.

"Meet The Press," once the preeminent Sunday morning talk show, aired since the inception of television news, has degenerated from its tough, formalized press-conference feel into another faint copy of "This Week With David Brinkley." When Chris Wallace defected to ABC, NBC replaced him with Garrick Utley in an attempt to match Brinkley, but Utley's programmed wisdom is no match for Brinkley's wry cynicism and humor. The program's dependence on reporting stars like David Broder and Elizabeth Drew instead of a rotating cast of lesser-known, battle-hardened Washington reporters is another illustration of the Brinkley influence. Ending with reporter bull sessions and Utley's personal commentary (another Brinkley touch) may work well in an hour-long format, but pushes informational content out in a half-hour. It's a far cry from the long-gone glory days of the program, once designed to bring hard news for a famously slow news day. No doubt it had been anathema to come back after the last commercial break and see Lawrence Spivak chewing the fat with the reporters appearing on the show. The political talk show syndrome is another illustration of the transformation of reporters into policy players inside the beltway.

News at Dawn and After Dark

On the other end of the scale are the morning programs. ABC's "Good Morning America," "CBS This Morning" and NBC's "Today" executives may think there are great differences among their shows, but they all offer about the same product: a brief news rundown at the top and bottom of the hour, an interview or two with a political figure, and the rest of the morning filled out by movie releases, medical reports, and celebrities promoting their latest venture. Somewhat useful, if you get up that early, and certainly pleasant and entertaining.

The late-night shows, aired mostly after prime-time viewing hours, are another matter. The worst examples of the manipulation of news are found here. None, however, has yet gone so far from traditional news and interviews as NBC's "Yesterday, Today and Tomorrow" or CBS's revamped "West 57th," now creatively retitled "Saturday Night with Connie Chung." They rely heavily on re-creations of past events, making it difficult to discern whether they are supposed to be news or entertainment. Both are consistent ratings losers, Connie Chung placing at the bottom of the barrel on a regular basis out of every prime time show aired. NBC is revamping "YTT," moving it from the news to entertainment division and reassigning anchors Mary Alice Williams, Chuck Scarborough and Maria Shriver to other projects, but it might be a case of too little, too late.

ABC's entry differs slightly, but not much. "Prime Time Live," with Sam Donaldson and Diane Sawyer, though originally anchored in a live format with an actual audience, went to the standard "60 Minutes" format a few months after its premiere, and from its inception relied heavily on recreations to help fill its hour-long Thursday night timeslot. When we're not seeing a reenactment, we're getting too much happy-talk filler from Sam and Diane. And the stories the team chooses to feature are surprisingly lightweight. The premiere of the much-heralded program coincided with the execution of Marine Col. Higgins in Lebanon, yet the powers that be chose to lead off the program with the Thomas Rule airplane incident, leaving the Higgins story until mid-broadcast, and then featuring a discussion between two experts as to the best way to invade Lebanon. Sam complained publicly about the lack of hard news on the show, saying his Rolodex wasn't full of celebs. This leaves no doubt in our minds as to the priority hard news will have on the program.

These programs are the network answer to the success of Fox's "A Current Affair," the pseudo-news half-hour program which so helped to popularize dramatic recreations. All network entries are a disappointment compared to CBS's "60 Minutes," which is obviously the program to beat. On the air now for more than 20 years, and although sometimes flawed, airing irresponsible, alarmist Alar stories in May, for example, the program also produces consistently solid investigative pieces balanced with the occasional celebrity interview. ABC's "20/20," while running a definite second to "60 Minutes," sometimes does stories that rank on a par with Don Hewitt's team, but generally steers clear of anything too heavy for its Friday night audience, preferring to focus on celebrities, such as an hour with the Rolling Stones on tour, and informative consumer oriented stories.

The real late-night gem is Ted Koppel's "Nightline," ABC's live interview program. "Nightline" features a healthy mix of hard and soft news from night to night, over the years featuring everyone from Tammy Faye Bakker (on the PTL scandal) and Frank Zappa (on the PMRC "censorship" of the music industry) to Henry Kissinger and Alan Greenspan. Koppel does his homework before a program, then allows the interview to unfold relatively naturally. Koppel also is one of the rare broadcast journalists who can deal with live television effectively as a medium. The difference between Koppel and the three network anchors was painfully evident during the California earthquake, where there was no script and very little information available. Perhaps an unfair comparison, as the network anchors are not used to unscripted live television, and Koppel is. But we don't think its unreasonable for three very highly-paid "television journalists," the anchors of the major networks, no less, *to be able to handle reporting a crisis effectively.* The repeated showings of the Marina District fire, further evidence of television's dependence on image, compelled Peter Jennings to ask if the firefighters in San Francisco were mentally and emotionally ready to handle such a crisis. Dan Rather advised no one in the quake area should use the telephone, unless of course "you need help" and then began to take a body count as it came in from AP and other "unconfirmed" sources. Ah, Vietnam. NBC didn't even go on the air with the story until nearly a full hour after the tremor had been felt. Okay, nobody's perfect, especially when working under pressure, and with little confirmed information. But Koppel alone handled himself with aplomb, used to the live camera, repeating calmly *only* the information that was available, avoiding rumor and hype.

There is no question that the electronic news media are undergoing significant evolutionary changes. So rapidly is the telecommunications industry advancing, and with it, the competitive business nature of the industry, that it is difficult to predict what face the television news media will have five years from now. In 1989 NBC launched CNBC, the Consumer News and Business Channel on cable. Throughout the morning and afternoon it is targeted to consumer oriented issues; from 6:00 to 11:00 — prime time — it emphasizes interview and call-in shows, often on topical issues of the day. Business, science and health reporters from NBC News contribute stories to CNBC so it's no secret NBC wants its cable channel to become more hard news oriented. NBC's initial plan, to make CNBC go head to head with CNN during some hours, was scratched when NBC met resistance from cable operators with a stake in Turner's success with CNN. While neither ABC nor CBS has announced plans for cable news programming, it is certainly quite possible we will see them follow NBC's lead in the future.

All things considered, it wasn't such an awful year for television news. Each network scooped the others once: ABC with its earthquake coverage, CBS with China, and NBC with the Israeli-South African connection. Public pressure has ended the use of dramatic recreations for the time being, except at CBS. But the overly simplistic interpretations and inability to convey information without pictures leaves it still behind print as a source for news, in both sophistication and reliability.

PUBLICATIONS

THE PACESETTERS

The New York Times

We sometimes wondered if the nation's newspaper of record would ever be able to splash this six-column head across the broadsheet of P. 1, but there it was on November 11, 1989:

JOYOUS EAST GERMANS POUR THROUGH WALL;
PARTY PLEDGES FREEDOMS, AND WEST EXULTS

The events had unfolded the previous evening before our eyes on the network news programs, but there was a special thrill we felt in seeing the *Times* headline. This was *recorded* history the way we had experienced it so often in our lives, seeing the bold black letters (**JAPAN WARS ON U.S.**), drinking in the power of the written word (**U.S. IMPOSES ARMS BLOCKADE ON CUBA**), riveted by their finality (**KENNEDY IS KILLED BY SNIPER**). This was an especially big year for epochal headlines and the *Times* did not disappoint.

In the third year under the guidance of Executive Editor Max Frankel, the world's leading newspaper continues to steer a course that might lead to *an optimum point of financial and critical success.* The experimentation may not be noticeable to the casual eye, but over the last two years it's especially clear that Frankel doesn't quite know where that intersection might lie, but that he must maneuver until he finds it.

We don't know for sure, but we can imagine the concern at the back of his mind is the aging of newspaper readership in the United States in general and of the upscale New York City readers in particular. Throughout its illustrious history, the *Times* could always count on population growth and advancing levels of education to expand its pool of readers. These forces are still at work, but younger, educated Americans are increasingly turning to broadcast journalism for their news. With cable TV's ability to offer extended programming in sports, business, and entertainment news, the young professional finds it easier to stitch together bits and pieces of TV news during the course of a day. This self-editing of electronic news is far more satisfying than settling for the half-hour network shows, which still offer a picture-headline service.

Frankel's problem, moreso than that of any other newspaper editor, is that he must find a way to develop a replenishing pool of readers that will satisfy the *Times* advertisers, and do so in a way that does not diminish the legacy of the *Times* as the newspaper of record, committed to the highest standards of journalism. Hence, his experiments with "soft" front-page news, trend stories, top-of-the-fold news analysis. There's much more guessing at what will interest the readers and much less take-it-or-leave-it, this-is-what-the-editors-think-you-should-know attitude. Drug abuse, the environment, AIDS victims and rumored cures, experimental medicine, abortion angles, social trends are all treated. On the 11-25 front page we read of a trend toward public urination in the city streets, which we first noted in 1946.

We do not object to Frankel's experiments, although there are plenty at the *Times* who do. Two receive 10 Best honors: Jane Gross' "Urban Emergency Rooms: A Cocaine Nightmare," 8-6; and Gina Kolata's "AIDS Is Spreading in Teen-Agers, A New Trend Alarming to Experts," 10-8. When things are done for the first time, they might seem awkward and clumsy, even embarrassing. It is a fact, though, that the *Times* has to find a solution to the commercial aspects of this news dynamic. It has to compete, putting together a combination of information about the world that pulls in the younger flow of readers. Competition, in fact, is forcing it to change in ways that make it more interesting than we've ever remembered it being. There's more audacity in news judgement, more diversity of opinion, lively writing in places where we'd never seen anything but gray chronicles and sniffy analytics, individual voices appearing in the news columns instead of correct *Times*peak. As usual we have our disappointments and complaints, but judge that overall the paper is better now and we expect it will get better yet before Frankel retires in five years.

Up the Ladder

Frankel's most important personnel decision during the year was related to his retirement. He decided not to fill the managing editor's chair with a caretaker, which John Lee would have been, upon the retirement of Arthur Gelb at the end of '89. In choosing Joseph Lelyveld, 52, whom he had named foreign editor three years earlier, Frankel more or less picked his successor. Washington bureau chief Howell Raines, 46, is still in the running, and in any case would still have six years left in him after a Lelyveld tour. Insofar as the *Times* is still very much an Upper West Side liberal, Democratic newspaper, Lelyveld can be described, as we've heard, as two small clicks to the left of Frankel, Raines a click to Frankel's right. In such matters, little clicks mean a lot.

The Lelyveld appointment was very popular at the *Times,* especially given the context of Frankel's experiments and the paper's financial concerns. It means the *Times* will not likely slip to a softness that comes at the expense of international news. It does not mean he is old school, however. We understand he is very much in tune with Frankel's intent of opening up the paper, permitting distinctive voices to appear. Lelyveld's biographic in the last section of this book reveals a man who has hit every rung of the *Times* ladder. From Harvard scholar, Fulbright scholar, to *Times* copyboy, he is clearly a man of the world, *summa cum laude.*

Lelyveld's journalistic weakness, we suspect, is a personal commitment to "human rights," as he understands the term, in a way that may engage him emotionally. His stewardship at the foreign desk was, for the most part, exemplary, having the right people at the right places getting the right stories. The paper's coverage of El Salvador's civil strife was a notable exception. The dispatches of its correspondent there were reminiscent of *Times* coverage of Saigon politics in the early 1960s, the same swirl of "human rights" issues surrounding religious figures, Buddhist monks or Jesuit priests, as a friendly government struggled with Marxist terrorists. The Vietnam War, of course, grew out of this kind of political stew.

The new foreign editor is now Bernard Gwertzman, 54, who has been Lelyveld's deputy in recent years, advancing from his Washington post as chief diplomatic correspondent. Gwertzman received a three-and-a-half star rating in *The 1987 MediaGuide,* his last as a reporter, "the best of what he does." We denied him the last half star, we said at the time, because he is a little too careful, avoiding analytical initiatives. His new deputy is Michael T. Kaufman, 52, who has had postings in Nairobi, New Delhi, Ottawa, and most recently Poland, where he consistently earned a two-star rating in our guides. Another talented foreign correspondent brought home for editing chores is Steve Lohr, leaving the London bureau to be assistant business editor to Fred Andrews. We applaud Andrews again for bringing Sarah Bartlett from *BusinessWeek* in 1988 to be his chief banking reporter. She earned our highest rating this year, and receives a 10 Best selection for "John Reed Bumps into Reality," 2-5.

The Editorial Pages

Frankel's authority does not directly extend into the editpages that he did manage from 1976-86. Jack Rosenthal and his deputy, Leslie Gelb, now do this important work, and as we have noted in recent guides, they have managed to improve on the Frankel years, inviting a broader spectrum of opinion. The "Letters" column is a nice guidepost, welcoming a rich diversity of views from knowledgeable and talented people, compared to the boilerplate of earlier years that simply applauded and refined the liberal manifestos of the editorials and essays.

The editorials themselves seemed less effective this year, drifting back to the bulletin board this-is-it mode, less attempt to seek out and engage the strongest arguments *against* their views. We could frequently agree with the thrust of the editorials, as in "The Cold War Is Over," 4-1, a kind of capstone to its important occasional op-ed series, "Is the Cold War Over?" But the thread often seemed eccentric, even bombastic, in crediting Mikhail Gorbachev, the reformer, as if somehow he had won, not U.S. steadfastness and democratic capitalism, sternly counseling the Bush administration to avoid worrying "about its right flank." The three-part editorial, "More Ice Keeps Breaking," 4-17, picks up the thread, highlighting developments "flowing from Mr. Gorbachev's policies of political openness, economic reform and decentralization." On 5-21, an editorial asks us to "Imagine that a spaceship approached Earth and sent the message: 'Take me to your leader.' Who would that be? Without doubt, Mikhail Sergeyevich Gorbachev."

The editorials are by no means all this sappy. Our readers were moved to applaud the quality of argumentation in many editorials which they indicated they disagreed with. "When to Sell Secrets to Moscow," 2-10, on loosening trade restrictions, was one such. Another, "Rethink the Japan Fighter Deal," 3-18, on the FSX jet, was also effective in the points it raised. "Why Bargain About the Bloc?" 4-13, critical of a Henry Kissinger proposal on Eastern Europe, elicited a comment from our critic: "Appreciate the sophistication of *NYT*'s editorials like this, a clear sense their writers think through policy perspectives." We especially appreciated "The Utah Fusion Circus," 4-30, where they went head to head with the *WSJ* editorial columns: "for Mr. [B. Stanley] Pons and Mr. [Martin] Fleischmann, the best bet is to disappear into their laboratory and devise a clearly defined, well understood experiment that others can understand. Until they have that, they have nothing."

The two areas where there is no debate, only pronouncements, are in El Salvador and the environment. "Don't Let Salvador Become Lebanon," 1-23, is typical of its hand-wringing over the prospect that the ARENA party can win a democratic election. In its editorials and news columns, the *Times* simply can't deal with this all year. In "The Greenhouse Effect Is for Real," 1-27, we get a similar mindset. It doesn't matter that government scientists can't find the evidence to support the theory, because the theory is correct. Whether it is happening now or not is beside the point. It will, the *Times* decrees, although it would do well to insist on evidence, as it does on nuclear fusion. At year's end its greenhouse commitment pushed the *Times* into a different corner: "Revive the Atom," it urged in its 12-8 editorial, a bit forlornly, having dumped the atom earlier. The *NYT* news columns were better on the environment, among the best "Skeptics Are Challenging Dire 'Greenhouse' Views," a comprehensive front-pager by William K. Stevens 12-13, that must have shaken the dead certainty of the editpage.

In 1988, Rosenthal had hired Susan Lee, a neo-conservative supply-sider, away from *Forbes* to run the op-ed page. This was part of Frankel's new wave, opening things up. Lee left in December of '89 to write a book, but did in fact shake things up a bit during her 18 months there. Interesting people who are not of a liberal bent felt comfortable sending her material, and she solicited others, stirring the pot.

The turmoil in Israel was a particular problem here this year, as the American Jewish community divided over the Shamir government's handling of the Palestinians on the West Bank. Of the paper's regular columnists, A. M. (Abe) Rosenthal, Frankel's predecessor, devoted himself to rationalizing for Shamir, while Anthony Lewis took him on. The op-ed page of 10-8 produced a double-barrel blast at Israel, Lewis writing "Time for Straight Talk," very tough on

Israel intransigence; Hal Wyner, a Jewish reporter in Israel for a West German newspaper writing "Jewish Brutality, Press Timidity." We were excited by the *journalistic* breakthrough, the *Times* standing back and letting the fur fly on a grave matter involving Israel, a *Times* client.

Lee handled the "Is the Cold War Dead?" series, and another "new wave" idea, "Voices of the New Generation," an occasional series aimed at engaging upscale yuppies, we suppose. There were no dramatic splashes on the page during the year, but the general level of molecular action was at a higher level. We were greatly impressed with "Chinese Hardliners Did the Right Thing," by Ch-Chen Wang 6-24, an elderly lit professor at Columbia, who provided a rationale for the Tiananmen crackdown. We disagreed with his thesis, but were thrilled to be able to read it at the *Times,* and nowhere else. "Salman Rushdie, Blame Yourself," was in this vein, S. Nomanji Haq on *The Satanic Verses* 2-23, taking Rushdie to task for knowingly causing serious pain to Islam and Moslems. Op-ed must have conflicting ideas! In "The 'Mommy Track' Isn't Anti-Woman," by Felice N. Schwartz 3-22, we were delighted to see this piece excerpted from *Harvard Business Review,* asserting: "The cost of employing women in businesses is greater than the cost of employing men."

We were appalled, though, with an op-ed Lee posted, "Embarrassment in El Salvador," by Scott Greathead of the Lawyers Committee on Human Rights 6-28, a wide string of patently libelous slanders and allegations against ARENA's Roberto D'Aubuisson, accusing the Bush administration for endorsing "death squads" because V.P. Dan Quayle met with him, wild charges and no evidence. The page did then invite Quayle to make his own op-ed statement, "Get Tough on Salvador's Killers," 7-16. But we still saw nothing from D'Aubuisson.

The Sunday *Times*

There were only minor noticeable changes in the quality of the Sunday paper this year, which is to say we remain happy with it, but not especially excited. Our general impression is that "The Week in Review" section is marginally improved, if only because the editors make a bit more use of the best reporters and writers in working this section. The *Magazine* is not inspired, but at least it no longer frustrates us to look at the table of contents on a Sunday morning and see only foo-foo. The *Book Review* produces more surprises.

"Arts & Leisure" remains dreadful, but this has been the special province of Arthur Gelb, who is now retired as managing editor. For some while we have been dispensing with this section along with the real estate and want ads before ordering brunch. It does not need marginal improvement, but dynamite. The lead of the 12-10 section, written by Peter Passell, the *economics* columnist, for goodness sakes, is "Broadway and the Bottom Line," about how tough it is to make money producing Broadway plays these days. We can easily think of a few journalists who could be hired away from other publications, and who, if given "Arts & Leisure" to play around with, would have Broadway booming again within a year or two. The *Times* used to have a Sunday, as well as weekly, theatre critic, which worked well in that one served as a check against the other.

The *Magazine* will remain under the stewardship of James L. Greenfield another year as he delays his retirement. Richard Flaste, now at *Book Review,* will climb the ladder then, we gather. The magazine has improved somewhat under Greenfield these past few years — at least we spend more time with it. Among the exceptional pieces this year were: "Children After Divorce," by Judith S. Wallerstein 1-22, a psychologist, on the negative effects; Bill Keller's "Moscow's Other Mastermind," on Aleksandr Yakolev 2-19, "Gorbachev's little known alter ego"; A two-part cover on "Israel: Mired in the West Bank," 5-7, with Joel Brinkley covering the soldiers on *intifada,* Thomas L. Friedman assessing the politics, Friedman receiving a 10 Best selection; "Shaking Up Justice," an elegant profile of Attorney General Richard Thornburgh by Michael Wines 5-21; "The Education of Dan Quayle," by Maureen Dowd 6-25, a 10 Best selection. There were several misfires: "Caution at the Fed," by Louis Uchitelle 1-15, a silly piece with a focus on the chairman's love life; "The Guns of Salvador," by James LeMoyne cover 2-5, with not a word about policies or issues dividing government and rebels; "Setting Marcos Adrift," by Stanley Karnow 3-19, a baloney history of Manila in early 1985; "Can Gorbachev Feed Russia?" by Mark Kramer 4-9, "a writer," great topic, but a waste of time, not a word of structural reforms; "British Soccer: The Deadly Game," by Lesley Hazelton 5-7, pop leftist sociology that more or less blames Margaret Thatcher for nutsy soccer fans.

The *Book Review* improved under Rebecca Sinkler and Mitchell Levitas, who is now the weekend editor. It surprises us often with unexpected features and angles. It startled us twice during the year: London bureau chief Craig Whitney presenting a marvelous feature of the Moscow literary scene, "Glasnost Writing: So Where's the Golden Age?" 3-19, the best writers playing politics, with no time to write; then a rave review of Robert H. Bork's *The Tempting of America,* in "The Judge Pleads His Case," 11-19, the reviewer emphatic in asserting that the 1987 liberal victory against Judge Bork's Supreme Court nomination was "A victory won at the expense of truth, it was not liberalism's finest hour."

Sunday "Business," edited by William Stockton, delivers fluffy features on corporate America, many of them quite good, but the section occasionally floats away; the 4-16 issue gave us movies, cholesterol, light olive oil, muni funds owned by minorities, and costume jewelry. There is rarely an effort to cover the markets and finance a la *Barron's,* except in thumbnail news digests. A front-page "Prospects" column by Joel Kurtzman is fairly crisp in rounding up outside opinion on a current topic. Its second and third pages, given over to outside opinion, is turgid as a rule and should be closed down for better purpose — market commentary or even a bigger letters page.

The Washington Bureau

We have been fans of Howell Raines, the Washington bureau chief, from the earliest *MediaGuide* in 1986. The quintessential journalist, Raines manages to submerge his political, social and cultural tastes the way few can. He also has a keen sense of what is important and what is not, which enables him to economize on his resources. A soft-spoken Alabaman, Raines had been deputy then, moved to London as bureau chief where he earned two consecutive four-star ratings. Frankel brought him back to Washington 1988 as bureau chief, with a mandate to end the dissention that had emerged in his absence.

Indeed, he had the bureau humming this year, although not without some personnel flak. E. J. Dionne, Jr., one of the best political reporters in the press corps, resigned late in the year when he could not work out differences with Raines and accepted a spot on the long political bench at *The Washington Post.* Our guess is that the bureau, which has been shrunk to 35 from 40 people in the last few years for reasons of economy, did not have room for both Dionne and R. W. Apple, Jr., as bigfoot writers able to roam the political scene at will. And Dionne, with a Ph.D. in political science, is not comfortable within the disciplines of a beat reporter. The *Times* offered Dionne the Budapest post, a plum in this year of upheaval, but he chose to remain in Washington.

Some of the best work out of the bureau came from the several women there. Robin Toner got Dionne's title of national political correspondent, which she shares with Michael Oreskes. Maureen Dowd was an inspired choice for the White House, not only for her superb feature writing, but for sharing hard news duties as well with Andrew Rosenthal. Susan F. Rasky was our reporter of choice in following the capital gains issue on Capitol Hill and produced a 10 Best selection on Rep. Dan Rostenkowski (D-Ill.).

There were more musical chairs. Richard Halloran left the Pentagon beat for a think tank after a notable career at the *Times.* Michael Gordon replaced him, and he and Stephen Engelberg, the intelligence correspondent, teamed several times during the year to score newsbeats on the competition. The most notable was their "Germans Accused of Helping Libya Build Nerve Gas Plant," 1-1, a 10 Best selection. Thomas L. Friedman returned from the Middle East and wowed us as chief diplomatic correspondent, backed by Robert Pear and Elaine Sciolino. Philip Shenon kept up with the complex HUD story and Nathaniel Nash was most often in front in the S&L story. David Rosenbaum became chief financial correspondent as Peter T. Kilborn moved to the national desk. At year's end, Raines hired Jason DeParle of *The Washington Monthly*. Three of the roughly 100 top-rated journalists in this *MediaGuide* are in the bureau: Dowd, Friedman and Engelberg.

The *Times* Abroad

This was one of the best years for the *Times* foreign corps, its performance precisely the kind of outstanding effort that reminds us why *The New York Times* is acknowledged as "the paper of record." Former foreign editor Joseph Lelyveld and his successor, former deputy foreign editor Bernard Gwertzman, efficiently deployed the paper's strengths and resources to make certain that the right correspondents were in the right place at the right time.

In Moscow, bureau chief Bill Keller again earned our highest rating. The best among the corps of U.S. correspondents here, Keller continues to get deeply underneath the multidimensional layers. Esther Fein and Francis X. Clines add to the strength of the bureau, both handling important stories very well all year. As a whole the *Times* foreign corps dominated in Central and Eastern Europe. We detail elsewhere the work and ratings of the individual correspondents here, and although individually each may not receive top ratings, their collective efforts add up to the most impressive effort on the world-historic stories that broke in the East Bloc this year.

Budapest bureau chief Henry Kamm's performance bears singling out, and Bonn bureau chief Serge Schmemann's work deserves acknowledgement as the best among the U.S. corps on Germany. The *Times* had early in the year been using stringer Ferdinand Protzman for additional reports on the two Germanys, and having him in place when the wall came down was certainly fortuitous. The *Times*' coverage excelled so because the editors were able to effectively deploy their correspondents throughout the region as events began breaking. For example, Fein moved over to Czechoslovakia from Moscow as that story broke. London bureau chief Craig Whitney was effectively used throughout the East Bloc, and his marvelous reconnaissance of the Soviet literary scene, "Glasnost Writing: So Where's the Golden Age?" 3-19, was a 10 Best nomination. David Binder, a former editor of the "Washington Talk" page and political reporter R. W. Apple, Jr., who was dispatched from Washington at a moment's notice, were both impressive with their stories filed from Eastern Europe later in the year.

Similarly, the *Times* China coverage was outstanding, and again the editors deployed resources efficiently there. We'd written in last year's *Guide* that we expected great things to come from the posting of Nicholas Kristof as new Beijing bureau chief, and we were not disappointed. Kristof produced the best report on the events in Tiananmen Square, outstanding foreign correspondence in the midst of heated developments, "Troops Attack and Crush Beijing Protest," 6-4, a 10 Best nomination. A newcomer, Sheryl WuDunn, added greatly to the bureau's work, particularly with post-Tiananmen reports. Fox Butterfield and Richard Bernstein were also sent in, and both produced outstanding reports, Butterfield's "Did the Heavens Finally Fall on Deng?" 6-16, a 10 Best selection.

The *Times* picks up yet another 10 Best selection in foreign correspondence with the reports from Afghanistan by Toronto bureau chief John F. Burns, "With Soviet Weapons to Lean on Kabul Is No Pushover," 3-19, and "Afghan Rebels, Divided But Resolute, Fight on From Peak Above Jalalabad," 8-12. Burns, shipped over from Canada for this quick tour, continues to impress us as one of the best in the foreign corps. In a year in which so much of the news was in events abroad, the *Times* led overwhelmingly among the selections nominated by our readers for the 10 Best reports.

We didn't see quite the excellence out of the Tokyo bureau we'd anticipated when David Sanger became chief there, although he's among the best filing from Japan. The *Times* is beefing this bureau up, business reporter James Sterngold moving there this year, but so far *Fortune*'s Carla Rapoport is the correspondent of choice on Japan, getting every nuance.

The work in other bureaus, which ranges from acceptable to very good, is covered in the section where the individual foreign correspondents are rated. But we need to mention the one area where the *Times* has made no headway — in its San Salvador bureau. The work of its correspondent there, Lindsey Gruson, fails to meet the minimal requirements of professional journalism. Since his predecessor also failed to meet those standards, a good part of the problem lies with the *Times* editors themselves.

Editor: Max Frankel

Address: 229 West 43rd Street
                New York, NY 10036
                (212) 229-1234

Circulation: 1,068,217 Weekday
                1,628,056 Sunday

The Wall Street Journal

The big event at Dow Jones & Company this year was the elevation of Peter R. Kann, publisher, to be publisher & president of the company that publishes the *Journal.* It had more or less been expected that Kann, who rose through the journalistic ranks, would get this rung on the ladder, which means he will surely succeed Warren H. Phillips when Phillips retires. Still, there had been the possibility that William Dunn, executive VP, would get the rung instead, and when he did not, he took early retirement, a blow to the organization. Dunn, a production visionary, had built the satellite system as well as the electronic information system that now eclipses the newspaper in earning power.

As he contemplates the 1990's, Kann does not have quite the same problem as Max Frankel of *The New York Times.* Frankel must worry about declining upscale readership in his home base, the New York metropolitan area, and the resistance this will mean to advertisers and ad revenues. The *Journal*'s home base is the continental United States, which means it can grow even if the emerging generation of young adults continues to show less interest in reading newspapers. It only has to appeal to the ever-increasing pool of young professionals across the country, by offering a package of information about the nation and the world that this class cannot easily replicate by other means.

This avenue of opportunity played a large role in the decision to expand the paper to three sections, the first edition of which was unveiled October 3, 1988. The gamble by Dow Jones & Company, the publishers, was that its primary readership in the business community would accept the greater bulk and inconvenience of a third section by adapting to it. Phillips, Kann and Norman Pearlstine, the paper's managing editor (named editor of the year by the National Press Foundation), should all be immensely pleased at the results of the gamble. A readership survey taken during the year astounded the top brass with the acceptance by the readers. Our own readers, at first flustered at having to learn where things were in the new sectioning, have by now completely adjusted, almost all reporting they find the paper *more convenient* than it was in two parts. The second "Marketplace" section and the third "Money & Investing" section permit a more rational allocation of material, and we realize we feel *roomier,* as if adding a wing on a house so we can divide the living room and dining room. The added elbow room by having an additional front page, to the third section, permits the *WSJ* to add attractive graphics and sketches, to compensate for the absence of photographs in the paper.

Indeed, the attractiveness of these second front pages invites us to read material we might otherwise skip over. It also reminds us of how expressionless the traditional front page remains. Its tombstone format seemed especially rigid this year with so many exciting stories smiling across the top of the other major dailies. We think the *WSJ* should at least contemplate redesign of its front page, at least to some degree. The column 5 format is the most obvious area for revision, especially the midweek topics, "Business Bulletin," "Tax Report," and "Labor Report." The space they use is too important, given the fact that there is a second front page to highlight them. The back page of section one is already the Washington page. It could take Friday's "Washington Wire," while Monday's "Outlook" is not so definitive that it can't run in Monday's third section. The column could then be used to run two-column heads, to provide expression when appropriate, or the best analytics available on any given day, whatever the subject.

As we observed a year ago, now that the agonizing over the third section is over and done with, the editors can concentrate on improving the quality of the product. This not only means better reporting, writing and editing, but also putting the best material available where it can quickly be found. For *WSJ* reporters, knowing they can hit page one without having to write a massive leder or a frivolous ha-ha column 4 A-hed, opening up the front page has added incentives. There are now 585 journalists on the staff, including those in the 14 domestic bureaus, and the 85 posted abroad in 3 Canadian bureaus and 11 foreign bureaus. Most are reporters competing for high-priced P. 1 space on a page last redesigned when there were not many more than one hundred.

The Front Pages

In his first full year as "Page One" editor, James B. Stewart delivered the best portfolio of leders in columns one and six that we remember in this decade. Our critics are asked to rate each individual story with stars, and three quarters of the leders rated this year carried at least two stars, "very good," with quality of both substance and presentation. Stewart himself is one of the best reporters we've seen in the press corps in recent years, a lawyer by training, with a Pulitzer Prize in 1988 for a Wall Street story we had already cited as a 10 Best business piece in our guide two years ago.

We were a bit nervous early this year about his editorial stewardship, wondering if his tastes would lead to heavy weighting in criminal law and prosecution stories. But as the year progressed the steady, high-quality mix of business, political and foreign material on the page was evident to all of us. Some of our business readers early on noticed personality profiles that unnecessarily strayed into the private lives of the subjects, and we wondered if this was an attempt to boost readership. A letter to the editor 4-13, on a profile of Northwest Airline's Steve Rothmeier, noted: "Your reporter's Steve Rothmeier bears no resemblance to the Steve Rothmeier I worked with." Thereafter, perhaps by coincidence, reporting tightened up and the tone of P. 1 improved markedly.

More than 20 *WSJ* front-page stories earned 10 Best nominations from our readers and six of the 50 stories awarded were from this group: Stephen J. Adler's "Working Girl: Former Runaway Hit Big Time at Drexel But Now Faces Prison," 3-21; Jane Mayer's "Seaford, Del., Shows How Crack Can Savage Small Town America," 5-4; Sonia Nazario's "Policy Predicament: Many Minorities Feel Torn by Experience of Affirmative Action," 6-27; Frederick Kempe's "Panama Tragedy: How the Inexperience of American Officials Helped Doom Coup," 10-6; Neil Barsky's "Quiet Candidate: In the New York Race, Front-Runner Dinkins Remains an Enigma," 10-27; and Bruce Ingersoll's "In Chilean Grape Case, New Data Raise Doubts as to What Happened," 11-27. We no longer consistently find material inside the paper that should displace leders up front (although a great many of these stories are superior to columns 4 and 5). The "Outlook" column seems to be back under control this year after our observation a year ago that "it has steadily disintegrated into a front-page editorial by the several veteran ideologues on the staff who take turns pronouncing imminent doom." There are still questions raised about what might or might not result in economic slowdown, as there should be in an outlook column. But as in Alfred L. Malabre, Jr.'s "Can Expansion Last if War Ends?" 11-13, an important question on the minds of *Journal* readers, the reader is offered serious pros and cons, not simply pre-cooked opinion.

The front page of the second section, "Marketplace," pulls up the best material from the several special sections inside: Advertising, Enterprise, Health, Law, Marketing, Media, Medicine, and Technology. Since Pearlstine began overseeing the paper's big expansions almost a decade ago, bylines at first meant little because they appeared fresh by the carload. But the cream has finally come to the top, with the best of these now familiar to us as regulars in their own right, many with star ratings in this guide, others we know we will include soon. In an overkill to make sure readers would find their way around this mysterious new section, the editors have slapped labels are all over the place, the tops of pages, inserted into columns, skimming over headlines. They can start cleaning these up a bit, permitting the headlines and bylines to speak for themselves.

In the same vein, the page got series-happy this year, with logos describing continuing series on "The New Work Force," and "The American Way of Buying," plus a "Centennial Journal" that took up a big chunk of the page every day with recollections of some great event in business. We ascribe quite a bit of this to jitters, the new baby, and the page should soon grow out of this, putting itself together with confidence and style. We're still not happy with the left-hand columns on this page, preferring deeper themes and analytics to short-takes and squibs.

The third section, "Money & Investing," is much further along in giving us what we want. Its stock-exchange transaction columns are just fine, running forward at last instead of back to front in bits and pieces, much preferred to the choppy tables in *The New York Times,* and almost as good as *Investor's Daily,* which heavily influenced the *Journal*'s decision to go to a third section. The tables themselves add the stock symbols for the first time in the paper's history, fitting in well with electronic information systems being offered by the company. The best material inside gets pulled up, columns and all, and we especially appreciate this flexibility in seeing "Heard on the Street" pulled up front when it is special, as it often is with Roger Lowenstein. The feature had been anchored for practically a century at the bottom of the penultimate page. We really like the "Markets Diary" charts, but it needs reworking, to hit us at the top with the Dow, gold, D-mark and long bond, in big letters plus and minus. Like the *NYT.*

Changes at the Editpage

Editor Robert L. Bartley has seemed at a pinnacle of his career for years. Yet now at 53, in his prime as the best journalist of our time, he leaves us wondering how much better he can make this page, how much higher the pinnacle can be. Under his guidance, for starters, the page gave birth to the supply-side economic revolution, goaded the Reagan Revolution whenever it faltered, and acted as the leading edge of opinion in the western world's defense establishment, as it worked its end game against the East. He also opened the page to the first *glasnost,* bringing in the widest variety of opinion he could find, including the best leftist columnist he could find, *The Nation*'s Alexander Cockburn. He somehow sensed the strength this counterpoint would bring to his own advocacies. In these muscular struggles, we cannot say *The New York Times, Washington Post* or others lost in competition with Bartley. They were, after all, his goads as a journalist. The competition produced the kind of electric mix of opinion and analysis that can only give credit to the First Amendment.

Bartley's deputy throughout has been George Melloan, 60, who had been there when Bartley was named editor in 1972. As 1990 opens, Melloan is gone to Europe as editpage editor of the European edition, a pinnacle in itself given the events in that corner of the world. At the same time, Tim Ferguson leaves his post as features editor, moving to an editpage desk in the Los Angeles bureau, in order to have a better perspective on the Pacific rim, taking up Melloan's weekly column space. We can see Bartley moving his chess pieces around the planet. His new deputy is Dan Henninger, a neo-conservative who has trekked up from *The New Republic* and the old *National Observer,* to the *Journal* a dozen years ago, likely to succeed Bartley here, if and when RLB climbs the corporate ladder, is summoned to public service, or retires to an academic life.

The editpage is as exciting as it is because it is so unpredictably predictable. The high point of a great year, we thought, came with its lead editorial of 9-28, "Kangaroo Committee," a defense of former HUD Secretary Samuel Pierce at exactly the moment the lynch mob is about to string him up. We confess to assuming Pierce's guilt when we began to read the piece, humbled by it into retreating to suspended judgement, thinking "Only Bartley would do this." In the same vein, the editpage continues to hammer at what it argues is the basic unfairness of the federal racketeering act, RICO, in its use against violations of Wall Street securities laws. L. Gordon Crovitz, a lawyer-journalist on the editorial board, earns a 10 Best commentary citation for his extraordinary essay, "RICO Needs No Stinkin' Badges," 10-4, a compelling argument against RICO in the Princeton-Newport case that unquestionably shifted public opinion. We also note his editorial, "The $10 Million 1/8 Point," 3-24, skewering RICO in the GAF case, although the defendants were found guilty nevertheless in mid-December.

Other noteworthy editorials: "Debt Abdication," 3-14, cutting the Brady Plan on Third World debt down to midget size; "Japan's Real Scandal," 7-6, ridiculing the idea that a sex and sociology scandal is at the heart of the LDP problems when the key is its new 3% consumption tax; "The Price of Apostasy," 8-2, one of the page's continuing series on "The Black Plantation," is sulphuric in arguing the Senate has rejected the William Lucas nomination as civil rights chief because he is a black who dared quit the Democratic Party; "Cracking Down," 8-10, develops the line that while black inner-city neighborhoods will support Drug Czar's tough anti-drug line, liberals will not; "Pitiful Helpless Presidency," 10-12, is clever, sophisticated in pinning the Panama fiasco on the White House losses to Congress of foreign-policy powers; "The Lawson Legacy," 10-30, is exceptional analysis of the Nigel Lawson-Alan Walters feud over the European monetary system.

For much of the year the *Journal*'s editorial columns were the only place one could find arguments *against* the assertions of the environmentalists that mankind is doing serious damage to the atmosphere. "Chill Out," 11-20, was so emphatic in suggesting a greenhouse hoax that it could not be ignored. Curiously, *The New York Times* news columns treated the issue with balance from time to time, with a 12-13 front-pager that was rather late but noteworthy, but the news columns were practically silent at the *WSJ,* as if the story *belonged* to the editorial pages. Bartley's handling of the startling events in Europe was guarded throughout, insisting on crediting the gains to President Reagan, NATO steadfastness, and the prosperity of democratic capitalism, reserved in its enthusiasm for Gorbachev. An op-ed essay at the height of euphoria was noteworthy in its caution, Vladimir Bukovsky's "In Russia, Is It 1905 Again?" 11-27. It was as if the *NYT,* euphoric over Gorbachev, was reflecting President Bush's feeling, the *WSJ* a backdrop for Vice President Quayle's cautionary remarks. The mix of the two seemed just about right.

A highlight of the year on the op-ed page was Milton Friedman's open letter to William Bennett arguing for drug legalization, 9-7, and Bennett's reply, 9-19. The exchange prompted Anthony Lewis of the *NYT* to jump in with "Investing in Disaster," 9-24, using libertarian logic in support of the Friedman position and earning a 10 Best nomination. George Gilder also scores a 10 Best nomination with a sturdy defense of Michael Milken, "The Victim of His Virtues," 4-18. Other op-ed pieces we thought notable this year included: "Mortgages for the Masses," 6-28, by Michael S. Knoll, full of fresh news on a strategy for making home ownership affordable; "Supreme Court and Civil Rights," by Robert Bork 6-30; "Made in Japan: Low-Tech Method for Math Success," by Chester E. Finn 7-12, on the Kumon approach to teaching kids math; "The Paramount Importance of Becoming Time-Warner," by Gregg A. Jarrell 7-13, former head of the SEC's economics unit, exquisitely lucid on the legal maneuverings of the takeover; "A Jimmy Carter for Transportation," by Thomas Gale Moore 9-22, slices up Sam Skinner. Scattered over the year were exceptional commentaries on the S&L mess from John Fund ("The S&L Looters' Water-Boy," 8-28); Martin Mayer ("Now, Woefully Fast Action on S&Ls," 4-13; "The S&L Bailout's Critical Movement," 7-25; "The Latest S&L Ripoff," 11-17), Byron Harris ("S&L Busts: It Wasn't Just the Crooks," 3-2; "A PAC of Lies: The Commodore

Savings Case," 7-18), and James Ring Adams ("The Bank Dick's Dirty Linen," 2-15; "Florida Politics and the Power of Pull," 8-1). One of the most startling came from Nobel Laureate James Tobin of Yale, an old New Dealer, "Deposit Insurance Must Go," 11-22.

The Washington Bureau

We complained vigorously last year about the quality of material coming out of the newspaper's most important bureau, subjectivity creeping deeper into the reports of the economic team of Alan Murray, Jeffrey Birnbaum and Walter S. Mossberg. As the *Journal's* editorial page became a bulletin board for the Reagan Revolution in economic thinking, the Washington bureau leaned in the other direction. This competition served the paper well enough, but in recent years the tone and spin of the news dispatch seemed to us to clearly cross into unacceptable bias. We hoped the assignment of Thomas Petzinger, Jr., who had been the Houston bureau chief, to be economics editor in Washington, would alleviate the problem, and to a degree it has.

Albert R. Hunt, the bureau chief, has continued and intensified the bureau's longstanding tension with the editorial page, which goes back to the beginning of Bartley's reign in 1972. The difficulty has its roots in Bartley's innovation of what we have come to call "the reported editorial," one that contains fresh *information* as well as perspective and insight. Editorial writers roamed Washington, intruding upon the turf of the bureau and its reporters, at the same time injecting New York perspectives on material that otherwise tended to have a Beltway spin. An added difficulty we've noted previously is that neither Hunt nor his several predecessors have had experience in New York, or in covering markets, economics or finance, while these are at the core of Bartley's interests.

The two big economic stories of the year were the struggle in Congress over the President's capital gains proposal and the S&L crisis. The bureau did not do especially well in either. As in 1986, with the struggle over Reagan's supply-side tax reform, the bureau's reports *assumed* the legislation would ultimately fail, only to have it succeed. This year, the press corps generally assumed capital gains would go nowhere, being killed in the House. There was great surprise when it came to life in August and passed the House in September. Alan Murray, the chief financial correspondent in the bureau, then wrote on the assumption it would succeed in the Senate, where it failed. The S&L story should have been the bureau's throughout, with Brooks Jackson very early digging up the Lincoln S&L campaign contributions to the Keating Five. But he did not pursue the story, the editorial page finally pushing it forward to the point where the House Banking Committee Chairman Henry Gonzalez got it going in earnest. The more routine dispatches from Paulette Thomas on the S&L mess were handled very well, however.

The *Journal,* we thought, erred in assigning Peter Truell, their chief banking and finance reporter, to the bureau, where he was immediately submerged by Hunt's protege, Alan Murray. Truell, who had earlier been brought to New York from London, to cover global banking and Third World debt, is among the best in the world at this beat, but has been functioning at half speed in the bureau. It seems to our readers he more properly belongs attached to the foreign desk, operating as an international troubleshooter on global financial matters, dispatched to Mexico City, Warsaw, Brazil or Moscow to produce definitive leders and op-eds. Even when President Bush sent a Cabinet team to Warsaw in November this year, it was Murray, a novice compared to Truell, who was sent along.

With all that, there were exceptional pieces that came out of the bureau during the year. "Pierce May Have Kept Hands Off But Projects of Pals Sailed Through," by Edward T. Pound with Jill Abramson 7-12, tied HUD's Sam Pierce to friends who were doing HUD deals, with fine background on Pierce as well. David Shribman, among the best political reporters around, gave us just the big canvas piece we were looking for with "Strike at Eastern Tests Ability of Big Labor to Re-Establish Itself," 3-6, and a profile of DC Mayor Marion Barry, 1-11. Frederick Kempe, the diplomatic correspondent, served up "Most Panamanians Stop Waiting for U.S.

Godot," 10-13, very tight, sophisticated analysis after the fiasco. Truell weighed in with an early cold-eyed analytic on the coming Brady Plan, with Mossberg 3-9, another on Mexico, 7-25. Each of the above received 10 Best nominations from our readers.

Hunt wrote more this year than we've seen since he's been bureau chief, the most memorable being "How to Put a Democrat in the White House," 8-3, an op-ed feature that argued Governor Dukakis closed fast in '88 by opposing Bush on capital gains. Huh? He also suggests "moderate" trade protectionism. It is hard to imagine a *New York Times* bureau chief publicly displaying his views in this manner. Hunt is also a regular participant in a television talk show where he displays his political tastes. It strikes us as adding a burden to the reporting staff to hew to an objective standard when the boss's own tastes are so vivid in their minds. The morale in the bureau was not improved this year when it was revealed that Hunt chaired a charity event in Washington this year, selling several tables to lobbyists at $10,000 each. It took his apology to the staff to put down the furor. Skating this close to the edge may bring a reassessment by Hunt himself. We continue to recommend *perestroika*.

The *Journal* Abroad

The disappointment we expressed last year over the *Journal*'s foreign coverage is starting to turn into alarm. We noted last year that it's "not that it isn't better than adequate in its bread-and-butter business reports, but that it remains so predictable and conventional in its public policy analytics from abroad." We thought that with a new foreign editor there might be some refocusing this year, but Karen Elliott House's replacement, Lee Lescaze, and deputy foreign editor Barry Kramer, haven't changed the course. We suspect they are not up to it.

Too many major stories from abroad eluded the *Journal* this year. It was close to *adios* for South American coverage, Brazil's economy and elections getting short shrift. Roger Cohen, who is definitely among the few foreign correspondents who can do satisfying reporting on this political economy, left for *The New York Times*. With his dispatches abruptly ending, and those of his replacement, Thomas Kamm, nowhere near the quality of Cohen's, the Brazil story ended up almost totally unreported by the *WSJ*. Jonathan Kandell helped fill holes in Central and South America, as did David Asman, "Americas" column editor, but their efforts were spread thinly. Matt Moffett was doing reasonably well with Mexico, but a seriously botched, inaccurate report, ostensibly on Mexico's capital flight, should never have gotten past the editors and onto the front page. The *Journal* did have the best report out of Panama all year, "Panama Tragedy: How the Inexperience of American Officials Helped Doom the Coup," 10-6 by Frederick Kempe, but the correspondent works the national security beat out of Washington rather than on the foreign desk.

What happened on the subcontinent this year? *Journal* readers had to turn elsewhere for consistent coverage on this region. *The Asian Wall Street Journal* has a number of correspondents who do top-notch reporting out of here, Anthony Spaeth in New Delhi, for example. But they were rarely and only sporadically used for the U.S. edition. Hong Kong bureau chief, Mary Williams Walsh, a front-ranked correspondent who had consistently earned three stars in our guide, was doing fine reporting from Afghanistan and Pakistan early in the year, and we thought perhaps she'd handle the important stories on India's economy and elections. Instead, she departed to the *Los Angeles Times* at midyear with serious complaints of how the *Journal* handled her material, from Pearlstine on down, and the hole on the subcontinent was never filled.

The East Asia coverage was better. The reporting of the Tokyo bureau correspondents, as a whole, improved over last year. Jacob Schlesinger, a Detroit bureau business reporter who received a three-and-a-half star rating in last year's *Guide,* is now reporting from Tokyo, but this promising posting needs more time yet to see where he can take it. The bureau doesn't have a superstar. Its best technology reporter Stephen Kreider Yoder is no longer with the bureau, and its best correspondent, Damon Darlin, moved to Seoul to set up house there. The move took a bit of the wind out of his sails, but only a bit and we anticipate great coverage from him on northeast Asia stories. The reporting out of the Beijing bureau also improved marginally over last year, and the *Journal* backed up Adi Ignatius with former China correspondents James Sterba and Amanda Bennett during the student demonstrations and crackdown there. The resources of the *Asian WSJ* were also wisely employed. We were happy to see Julia Leung's byline appearing on stories out of China, albeit still too infrequently to suit us. *Asian WSJ* editorial page editor Claudia Rosett's reports from China were mixed, with nothing produced there to quite compare with her excellent reporting on Japan. Rosett's "Japan's Recruit Scandal in Context," 4-10, is a 10 Best selection.

Coverage of Western Europe is respectable, the collective effort at least adding up decently, although no one here is burning up the wires with hot reporting. In a year when being adequate wasn't adequate for Eastern Europe, the *Journal* did manage to carry off better efforts in its Moscow bureau under Peter Gumbel. Coverage of the East Bloc outside the U.S.S.R. is not much beyond adequate.

Overall the *Journal*'s foreign correspondence is lumbering along. We hear excuses that it has been difficult merging the foreign editions, which have different audience needs, with the paper at home. Perhaps so, but only by a smidgeon. Although spotty, with some bureaus able to keep their heads well above water, and others simply submerged, the path the *Journal* foreign corps is on is not a yellow brick road.

Editor:	Robert L. Bartley
Managing Editor:	Norman Pearlstine
Address:	200 Liberty Street New York, NY 10028 (212) 416-2000
Circulation:	1,978,259

The Washington Post

There was more slack at *The Washington Post* this year than we've seen in a while. In part, this is relative to the pace being set at *The New York Times* by Washington bureau chief Howell Raines. The *Post* can still blanket a story more manpower than the *Times*, most often on defense reports, but with Raines pushing the bureau, we see the *Times* taking stories away from the *Post* with more aggressive follow up. The capital's other paper, *The Washington Times*, also pulled off an impressive number of newsbeats, leaving the *Post* chagrined by the daring of this competition nipping at its heels. The overall competition can only be healthy and we're assuming the *Post* will swing back aggressively.

Some of the *Post*'s performance this year couldn't help but be distorted by the eventual retirement of executive editor Benjamin Bradlee as that prospect works its way through the paper. Bradlee's acting replacement, Leonard Downie, isn't the same kind of "free spirit," and this may be having a marginal effect already. Downie may represent a pendulum swing back from the years of advocacy journalism, though we hope not to the point where "objectivity" causes the *Post* to lose an edge on analysis. The subsequent reorganization has yet to be played out, but we have mixed feelings about Robert Kaiser moving up to managing editor, an administrative task that will reduce his appearance in the pages of the paper. Michael Getler will take over Kaiser's job as assistant managing editor and "Outlook" editor David Ignatius is scheduled to become foreign editor, replacing William Drozdiak, both assignments holding healthy promise for the *Post* performance next year.

The Investigative Reporting

We are somewhat surprised that, in a year of so many scandals in and around Capitol Hill, the *Post* comes away with a smaller share of investigative scoops than expected. However, when it does score, it scores big. Its outstanding work in this regard is "Coelho Campaign Listed as Junk Bonds Buyer," by Charles R. Babcock 4-13, which reports on the House majority whip's "unusual $100,000 investment in 1986 in high-yield junk bonds issued by Drexel Burnham Lambert Inc. that generally are available only to institutional investors and regular Drexel customers." Babcock's report was a major news item itself, commented on throughout the press, and although we can't step inside Rep. Tony Coelho's (D-Calif.) head, we're reasonably certain that the prospect of a *Post* investigative team ready to follow the leads on this story was a major inducement in his speedy decision to immediately resign from Congress.

The year's first major "investigative" story on the domestic scene centered on the allegations regarding incidents in the private life of former Senator and nominee for secretary of defense John Tower. The *Post* was on this trail, with several of its reporters and editors covering various aspects of the battle over his nomination, the overall efforts of which ranged from satisfactory to very good. The *Post* editors called to account Sen. Sam Nunn (D-Geo.), the principal antagonist of John Tower, noting the "elliptical, suggestive ways" in which he was making his charges against the nominee. Nunn needs to "be declarative, unambiguous and forthright," the editors advised in "The Tower Fight," 2-28, as "Those who are disposed to take Sen. Nunn's words very seriously are still waiting for him to clarify and specify the charges."

However, the *Post* rushed to print with a report that ended up fitting precisely the kind of "character assassination" campaign Tower insisted he was up against. Bob Woodward, assistant managing editor for investigative reporting, built a damaging front page story around a single, unsubstantiated allegation regarding the conduct of then-Sen. John Tower at an air force base in the late 1970s. In the context of the testy hearings over the nominee's qualifications for the appointment, Woodward's P. 1 report, "FBI Cites 2 Incidents at Base," 3-2, was very harmful. According to "informed sources," Woodward reported that "During the two tours of the base Tower had 'liquor on his breath and he had trouble talking and was staggering out of his car and up the steps.' " On this visit and a subsequent one, Tower was alleged to have fondled two women. The story received widespread circulation, and, although it was totally discredited the next day, the damage was done, with the discrediting having an effect similar to the words of a judge instructing a jury to disregard a dramatic yet libelous statement made by one of the attorneys during a trial.

If the Woodward story was a serious low point in the *Post*'s coverage, the high point in its performance came along with "Tracing the Steps in Tower's Downfall," by Helen Dewar, Capitol Hill reporter, and Dan Balz, national editor, 3-29. Lofty, detached, and yet intimate, the report was the best summary of the battle over the senator's nomination, and is a 10 Best selection for political reporting.

The *Post* was scooped on some of the more sordid improprieties on Capitol Hill, *The Washington Times* beating them on the Craig Spence story and the Barney Frank affair. The Spence story involved homosexual "call boys" and a lobbyist whose social climbing and influence peddling perhaps involved key officials among the clients. The *Post* first covered the story as a local one, reporting on a February raid of what the D.C. police and U.S. Secret Service called a male prostitution service involving credit card fraud. When the *WAT* ran a banner headline, "Homosexual Prostitution Inquiry Ensnares VIPs with Reagan, Bush," 6-29, promising disclosure of seemingly high-ranking "key officials" involved, the *Post* ran a story in its "Metro" section 7-1, treating the scandal as a matter involving credit card fraud. But the scoop at the *Times* had an impact at the *Post,* and, according to James Perry of *The Wall Street Journal,* it was executive editor Benjamin Bradlee himself who stepped in to demand full coverage of the story. However, although managing editor Leonard Downie instructed "Style" section editor Mary Hadar to produce a major profile of Craig J. Spence, the reporter assigned took a long holiday weekend, the profile not appearing until July 18. Ombudsman Richard Harwood, in a 7-9 column, chastised his paper for letting the story get away from them. Although the "story" turned out to be far less than anticipated, the *Post*'s slow reflexes in responding to it couldn't help but be noticed. Perry's report on the "heel-nipping competition" that the *WAT* is giving the *Post,* captures a significant appreciation by Leonard Downie of how the paper fared in this, which can apply even more generally: "We're a little like a supertanker. . .Our sheer size makes it difficult sometimes to turn around."

The *Post* was also scooped by Washington's other paper on the scandal involving Rep. Barney Frank's (D-Mass.) relationship with a male prostitute, even though information regarding this was first offered to the *Post.* However, the *Post* didn't shirk at all from covering the spate of scandals involving Capitol Hill. In fact, it was accused of excess in this regard in an op-ed by Beltway flak Norman Ornstein, "The Post's Campaign to Wreck Congress," 5-29. Even Ben Bradlee's wife, Sally Quinn, urged an end to the focus in the "Outlook" section with "Congress to America — This Isn't Fun Anymore," 6-4.

The *Post*'s coverage of Speaker Jim Wright's story this year was respectable, Tom Kenworthy handling most of it. Again, though, we were surprised to see less than the expected tenacity involved in developing the various leads into other stories the issue suggested. Perhaps the most significant story during the Speaker's travails to come from the *Post* was the expose of his top aide, John Paul Mack, that appeared in the "Style" section. "Memory and Anger: A Victim's Story," by Ken Ringle 5-4, was a graphic account of the 1973 bludgeoning, stabbing and slashing of a 20-year-old coed by Mack, who after release from jail went to work for Rep. Wright and became "the most powerful staff member on Capitol Hill." Although some of this information had been released to the press two years earlier, no one had ever told the story from the point of view of the victim. The effect was explosive, Mr. Mack immediately resigning, and another cloud was added over Jim Wright's head, provoking questions about the role he played in Mack's treatment by the justice system compared with that of the victim.

The Political Bench

The political bench was more depleted than usual. Heavyweight Paul Taylor was gone for the year, and David Broder rested on his laurels most of the year, part of it running around London, following his outstanding coverage of the presidential elections the previous year, while Thomas Edsall, occupied with writing a book, was less prolific than usual. Much of the press operated from the perspective of this being an "off year" for elections, and the *Post* was no exception. The broader political analyses that rise above the politics of the Beltway and are such a hallmark of the *Post* were not so much in evidence this year. The addition to the *Post* political bench next year of former *Times*man E. J. Dionne, Jr., one of the press corps top political reporters, should result in a renewed vibrancy there. Taylor and Edsall will be back as well contemplating the congressional elections.

The *Post* coverage of Beltway politics showed overall improvement, despite holes here and there. David Hoffman was magnificent with "Bush's Relentless Pragmatism," 4-30, masterfully synthesizing Bush's management style into a short recap of his first 100 days. At a time when conventional wisdom was focused on an "agenda-less" or "brain-dead" administration, Hoffman's balanced and insightful examination is refreshingly astute political reporting, a 10 Best selection for political reporting. One of his better years, he nonetheless did indulge in some inexcusably sloppy reporting, as in the P. 1 "Presidential Disability Discussed," with Judith Havemann 4-28. The story reports on an "unprecedented session" in which the President and Vice President, their wives, White House physician Burton Lee II and White House Counsel C. Boyden Gray, met to "determine the circumstances under which Quayle would take over as acting president if Bush became disabled." The report, quoting an anonymous source, tells us that "Quayle remained silent during most of the discussion. . .while Barbara Bush, Marilyn Quayle and the president questioned White House Staff members." We discover the next day that Mrs. Quayle was not asking questions while her husband sat mute, and in fact wasn't even present at the discussion.

Still, anyone can end up with egg on their faces when a source turns out to be less reliable than anticipated, and this incident isn't indicative of the two reporters' work overall. We suspect a certain biased perception of the VP may have led Havemann and Hoffman to go with their source's version of what occurred rather than establishing the veracity of his or her information. Certainly, only a bias against the VP could account for "RNC Helped Pay for Quayle Vacation. Party Provided $25,000 Last Month for Colorado Skiing Party," by deputy national editor and political editor Ann Devroy 1-11. One has to read to the end of this provocatively titled report to discover that no Republican National Committee money was used to pay for any of the personal expenses of the Veep and neither he nor his family requested any such payment.

The "Outlook" Section

A consistent strength of the *Post* is the Sunday "Outlook" section, edited by David Ignatius, who is scheduled to move on to foreign editor. The content of selections in "Outlook" stretches across a wide political spectrum, often without a definable ideological bent to the contributions appearing here. "Outlook" works, not because we get balanced or rounded views expressed on a subject, but because the intent of "Outlook" editor David Ignatius is to engage issues early, and to do so in a provocative way. Still, the section can list to one side heavily from time to time, as for example with the selections for its 1-29 issue. The lead feature — "America the Tax Haven," is particularly weak. James Henry, a New York lawyer, complains that low U.S. tax rates contribute to a class of wealthy "citizens of the world" who pay no personal income taxes. Then, also on the front page, "Giving Japan a Handout," by Clyde V. Prestowitz, is a particularly shrill version of Japan-bashing. An "Outposts" column on psychology, "How Presidents Speak Their Minds," contains dubious material on how candidates' speeches can predict election outcomes depending on their optimism or pessimism. Equally dubious is "Outlook" deputy editor Jodie T. Allen's conclusion in "A Story That Refuses to Happen," 1-29 — "Hang in There Gloomsayers, the Economy May Yet Crash." Fortunately, we didn't often see this kind of almost total disappointment from the "Outlook" selections.

Among the important selections in "Outlook" were two adaptations from essays in *The National Interest.* Any of the other press could just as easily run with these, but the *Post* seems to have been the most alert on their critical importance, and their appearance on the "Outlook" pages helped trigger subsequent focus on the issues raised in *TNI.* "Ready or Not: Cut Pentagon 'Readiness' Spending," by Edward N. Luttwak 2-19, a 10 Best selection (an adaptation of his "Do We Need a New Grand Strategy?" Spring) is a provocative, healthy intervention into the strategic debates emerging in the wake of the Gorbachev-altered situation: "Gorbachev has made it possible to reallocate U.S. defense spending away from the costly upkeep of immediate war-fighting capability and towards renewed investments in the truly innovative technology to secure our long-range interests." The other selection was "The End of History?" by Francis Fukuyama 7-30, an adaptation of Fukuyama's essay by the same name and a 10 Best selection from *TNI* Summer-89. Its appearance in the *Post* clearly helped boost circulation of the year's most provocative thesis.

"Outlook" probably led the opinion pages of the national press in providing a forum for the new critics of Japan. "Giving Japan a Handout," by outspoken protectionist Clyde V. Prestowitz 1-29, referred to above, complains about General Dynamics' agreement with Mitsubishi to produce a jet fighter that "gives" Japan U.S. technology. "The Japanese Difference," an adaptation from James Fallows' book *More Like Us* 2-5, contains some of the more provocative theses seen this year on the cultural differences between the West and Japan, and "Japan's Money Machine," by Karel van Wolferen 11-5, author of *The Enigma of Japanese Power,* carries on with the image of a politically driven economic expansion of Japan's leverage over the global financial system. While the Prestowitz feature served as a tocsin for Japan-bashers in Congress and their allies in the capital, the *Post* in an editorial, "The FSX Decision," 3-17, sided with the Defense Department and, in opposition to Commerce Secretary Mosbacher, urged the president to approve joint U.S.-Japanese production on the FSX jet fighter, a policy earlier advocated by the *Post*'s chief foreign correspondent Jim Hoagland. We noticed that despite the tendency of the editorial page to avoid any endorsement of the new critics' perspectives, the *Post* Tokyo bureau was less rigorous in preventing that intrusion into its reporting. With Ignatius slated to move on to foreign editor, we are concerned that vigilance against this bias might further slip.

Among other "Outlook" selections we noted: Bob Woodward's "The Abortion Papers," 1-22. This is one of his best investigative reports in a while, shedding new light on the murky underpinning of *Roe v. Wade*. "Bush's Start: A Presidency 'On the Edge Of a Cliff,'" by David Gergen 3-5, which caused consternation at the White House, is an articulate exposition of the conventional assessment of the Administration early on. However, "George Bush And Congress — Brain-Dead Politics of '89," by Kevin Phillips 10-1, is too predictable and without sufficient insights to have ended up in "Outlook," much less as a P. 1 item. Another provocative but very dubious item, "Is the Church Ignoring a Sexual Crisis In Its Ranks?" by Jason Berry 9-17, on pedophilia in the Roman Catholic Church, throws out wild figures on homosexuality among priests — 50% are gay according to one source — along the way in his arguing against celibacy.

The events within the Communist bloc received somewhat less coverage than we'd hoped for, although the commentary that did appear was superior: "Double Standard on Human Rights?" by Fang Lizhi 2-26, Chinese astrophysicist and human rights activist; "Is the Soviet Union on the Road to Anarchy?" by Professor Peter Reddaway 8-20; "How We Helped Solidarity Win," on the A.F.L.-C.I.O.'s decade-long critical aid to Solidarity, by Adrian Karatnycky 8-27; "A Chinese Manifesto," by student pro-democracy leader Wang Dan 5-14, which clearly establishes that the student leaders have a sophisticated understanding of democracy.

"Outposts," the P. 3 column focusing on issues in science and technology, was Ignatius' brainchild, and is capably handled by Curt Suplee. The column was initiated in response to a growing layer among the *Post* readership whose interests in this regard were not being sufficiently met by the paper. We had looked askance at the effort in the past, but our judgment was premature. Although maybe one in four columns will appeal to the general reader, the section has developed into a feature that we find rewarding on the whole. Very early in the year, we got an authoritative examination of how little evidence actually exists to support the apocalyptic view of the "Greenhouse Effect," in "The Greenhouse Climate of Fear," by U. of Va. professor of environmental affairs and executive board member of the American Association of State Climatologists Patrick Michaels 1-8. This is the most forthright critique of the issue, by a professional, and "Outlook" editors deserve credit for running with the nonconventional view so early. We get good Sunday morning reading with Suplee's "The Fusion Confusion," 4-30, on the history of a breathless breakthrough in science that didn't pan out.

The *Magazine*

After a brief skim this still ends up in our discard pile of non-nutritive Sunday morning filler. However, there seemed to be a few more items this year that arrested our attention. The 1-29 issue, for example, offered a decent cover feature on James Baker III. Henry Allen, one of our favorite writers from the "Style" section was entertaining on "Dardo, King of the Rink Rats," a sixteen-year-old at Wheaton rink. And Richard Cohen delighted us with a lovely column "Oh, Yes, I'm the Great Pretender."

Nonetheless, the rewards were few and far between, with some stories just downright ridiculous. For example, Susan Estrich, the defeated campaign manager of Michael Dukakis, was given a second chance to defend her handling of his presidential campaign with a six-page cover feature, 4-23. Her theme: "The hidden politics of the race: When George Bush made Willie Horton part of his campaign team, the issue he was raising wasn't just crime — it was racial fear."

It's hard to imagine the Sunday *Magazine* sparking controversy, but *Post* columnist Richard Cohen managed to set off an explosive reaction with his "Critic at Large" column, "Fakin' It," 8-13. Inspired by a scene in the movie "When Harry Met Sally. . .", Cohen observes that while women may fake orgasms, men have been faking conversations with women, merely pretending to listen. "The laugh's on you, ladies," he concluded. But it wasn't, as Cohen quickly backtracked all over the place under a torrent of indignant letters to the editor, among them one from Gerry Rebach, the wife of Post managing editor Leonard Downie, 9-14. "May I oink my innocence," he pleaded in "What I Meant," 10-15.

The "Style" Section

We saw more criticisms of this section of the *Post* appearing elsewhere than ever before. Both Washington DC's top weekly, *The City Paper,* and *The Washingtonian* ran extensive critiques. Our own readers saw some loss of its usual vim and vigor. Of course, the absence of Stephanie Mansfield (ranking between three-and-a-half and four stars in the last three editions) as well as political essayist Sidney Blumenthal left some holes unfilled. Henry Allen, we find, is the "Style" reporter most likely to move into the slot vacated by Mansfield, but we don't see among editor Mary Hadar's galaxy of writers a replacement for Blumenthal on these pages yet. "Style" doesn't seem to quite cover Washington as a political town. Still in all, the *Post*'s widely emulated "Style" section continues to boast some of the best writers around in the profession, as we detail in the individual ratings.

The Foreign Service

A number of significant changes took place in the bureau assignments of the *Post*'s foreign correspondents this year, with some extensive redeployments midyear. Former London bureau chief Karen DeYoung departed at the end of last year to assume duties as national editor back in the U.S. Glenn Frankel moved on to London from Jerusalem, replaced there by the *Post*'s longtime Warsaw bureau chief, Jackson Diehl. We found Diehl's replacement, former Nairobi bureau chief Blaine Harden, not quite as swift-footed as necessary to keep ahead of the fast-breaking development in Poland this year. However, an outstanding foreign correspondent (ranked three-and-a-half stars and receiving a 10 Best selection last year), we expect to see him quickly catching up to the competition now that he's been exposed to fire there. Bonn bureau chief Robert McCartney also lagged behind the pace and depth of events on his beat, the wrong guy at the wrong time in Germany. Moscow bureau chief Michael Dobbs and correspondent David Remnick had another good year covering the U.S.S.R. Neither are as alert for critical economic details as their counterparts at the *Financial Times.* A newcomer, stringer Jennifer Parmelee, worked the Italy beat with a thoroughness that was lacking among the rest of the U.S. press.

The *Post*'s China coverage was noteworthy, providing us with wide coverage of the events there this year. Bureau chief Daniel Southerland was backed by business reporter John Burgess, Los Angeles bureau chief Jay Mathews and EPA reporter Michael Weisskopf during the student demonstrations and subsequent crackdown. Southerland does deserve a rapping on the knuckles, though, for having reported unsubstantiated news about a split in the Chinese armies during a critical period. We noticed a bit of bias on the part of Tokyo bureau chief Fred Hiatt, as some of his reports suggest that he's leaning a bit too much on the perspectives of the new critics of Japan. Hiatt isn't asleep at the switch, though, having been one of the first U.S. correspondents to pick up on the breaking of an age-old taboo by a Japanese magazine's report that newly installed PM Sosuke Uno had been involved in a "scandalous" affair with a geisha, "Sex Scandal Hits Japan's Uno," 6-7. The scandal led to his resignation, but curiously the *Post* ran this important report in its "Style" section. While the competition is beefing up their Tokyo bureaus with journalists who have strong credentials as business/financial reporters, the *Post* doesn't seem to be on that track yet. Interestingly, it did deploy business writer Steve Coll to New Delhi to replace Richard Weintraub as bureau chief.

The *Post*'s reports from Latin America were a mixed bag this year. William Branigan didn't come through with the news we needed on Mexico's economic transformations, although his reporting from Panama (where he ended up being handcuffed and detained by Noriega's police) was very good. Julia Preston left the foreign service with flying colors, her reporting from Central America and the Caribbean splendid. Preston's report on the drug-trafficking trials in Cuba which appeared in *The New York Review of Books,* 12-7, is a 10 Best selection. Douglas Farah's coverage on El Salvador was marginally improved over last year, but only a step above the unacceptable reporting by his counterpart at the *NYT.* With Preston gone from the scene, there's reason to be concerned over the quality of *Post* reporting coming out of the region next year. Mr. Ignatius will have his work cut out for him.

Business and Economics Reporting

The weakest of the three pacesetters on business/financial reporting, the *Post* perftormance this year was weaker than usual. Economics editor and columnist Hobart Rowen wobbled on issues where he used to be resolute and just didn't delve deeply this year. Paul Blustein, who has the international finance beat, still is rummaging through obsolete, stale perceptions that waste his energy and talent. International trade correspondent Stuart Auerbach disappointed us particularly with his insufficiently balanced reports on trade flaps with Japan. We further detail the performance of *Post* business/financial reporters in the ratings section.

A number of the *Post*'s editorials on various aspects of economic policy seemed particularly out of focus this year. "Capital Gains and Losses," 2-1, challenges the argument that a capital gains tax rate cut would have positive effects on raising revenues, but with an assertion that is simply incorrect: "As for the supposed benefits for economic growth, the record [of tax cuts] points the other way." "Latin Debts: The Reforms," 3-26, is an unabashed defense of austerity policies for debt-burdened countries. "Paper Cuts," 4-16, shocks us with "The key to genuine deficit reduction is a tax increase."

Executive Editor:	Benjamin Bradlee
Address:	1150 15th Street, NW Washington, DC 20071 (202) 334-6000
Circulation:	849,191 Weekday 1,216,398 Sunday

THE DAILY NEWS

The Christian Science Monitor

The victim of multiple physical and editorial changes at the close of 1988, the *Monitor* is now dismissed in the trade as the "incredible shrinking *Monitor*" and the "invisible *Monitor*." Cut in half from an already tiny size and staff, the *Monitor* no longer breaks any new ground, reportorial or otherwise, looking more like the *Weekly Reader* than the prestigious daily newspaper it used to be. Longtime staff continue to resign, following former editor Katharine Fanning's lead. Charlotte Saikowski, Washington bureau chief, after twenty-seven years with the paper, decided the first week of 1989 that she and the "new" *Monitor* just couldn't coexist, asking to retire in April: "Fundamentally, I just couldn't go along with the current direction of the paper. They have gotten farther and farther away from daily news."

In agreement, this year we dropped our systematic reading of the newspaper and reporters previously cited are no longer found in the rating sections. The publishers' decision to concentrate on television and the snazzy *World Monitor* has sounded the death knell of the newspaper. *The Christian Science Monitor* now devotes fewer than half of its 20 tabloid pages to hard news items, and often those stories are not really hard news, many devoted to social or quirky issues such as marketing in New Guinea ("On the Jungle Road With Colgate Toothpaste," by David Clark Scott 1-9), adoption ("Couples Target Texas In Search for Newborns," by Howard LaFranchi 4-11), indifference ("Student Political Apathy Is Growing, Educators Report," by John Dillin 8-11) and cartoons in Asia ("It's a Hard Place to Raise Hackles," by James L. Tyson 8-11). The remaining ten pages is divided between art reviews, books and leisure, inspirational thought and commentary. Proportioning the paper thus in half might have worked for a larger newspaper; *The New York Times* probably devotes about half of its pages to soft news. But for a newspaper as small as the *Monitor* to cut its newspages in half, makes it effectively useless as a source for news. If it were not for a faithful core of church subscribers, it would certainly not exist.

The loss of Fanning and three assistants was only a first blow. Elizabeth Pond resigned, then the aforementioned Charlotte Saikowski, and Ned Temko, a four star correspondent two years ago, ceased to appear at all, busy with *Monitor* television. These losses occurred along with *planned* staff cuts. The *Monitor* did pick up former *New York Times* stringer John Battersby in Johannesburg, but this wasn't enough to stop the hemorrhage at the paper. And though some of the reporters the *Monitor* has managed to retain, such as Paul Quinn-Judge and William Echikson, are quality, they are stretched as thin as wire reporters.

World Monitor maintains a more credible air than its tabloid counterpart, but only due to the glossy printing and pages. There are few journalists who report directly for the monthly, which instead relies on freelancers, the occasional *Monitor* newspaper correspondent, and guest commentators who sometimes have an axe to grind. *World Monitor* isn't by nature a newsmagazine, comparable more to a policy-oriented *Atlantic,* with a similar smattering of socially conscious essays. Bruce Babbitt's "Reviving Mexico," 3-89, is one of the first to point out Mexico's possibilities, but offers mostly standard advice, i.e., cut the debt. William Echikson's "Bloc Buster," 6-89, is certainly solid, culled from years of experience in Hungary and the East bloc, but this is old news and reads like a compilation of all Echikson's articles, missing much of the change throughout the region. Computer programmer Daniel Chernin's stories of China, "China: A Love Story," 9-89, turns out to be his recollections of the girl he left behind from a trip, rather than the country, and is sorely in need of editing. While *World Monitor* may look great, there just isn't much value in the magazine, rarely insightful, eminently discardable.

All the changes at the *Monitor,* combined with the increased accessibility of the big dailies and *USA Today,* spell a continued decline and possibly demise for the paper. Unless the current team of editors, Richard Cattani and Richard Nenneman, can somehow turn the *Monitor* around, despite all the setbacks, there won't be much left within a year or two. It's too far on its way to becoming a pamphlet as it is.

Editor: Richard J. Cattani

Address: 8 Norway Street
                  Boston, MA 02115
                  (617) 450-2000

Circulation: 140,000

Financial Times

We noted more flexibility in the *Financial Times'* economic analyses this year than previously. Samuel Brittan, the paper's chief commentator on global political economy, set particularly laudable standards in that regard. Especially brilliant is "Teenager's Guide to UK Trade," 4-27, which demolished the mercantilist doctrine upon which so many other financial journalists seem fixated. Also challenging orthodoxy and conventionality this year, several other *FT* journalists were, at times, in advance of their U.S. counterparts. Martin Wolf's "A Budget For Saving?" 2-9, although focused on the U.K., has specific applicability to the U.S. concern with the "savings problem," as Wolf demonstrates that conventional accounts on the issue are misleading.

John Plender's "Soaring Dollar Disturbs the Party," 5-27, displays coherent logic as he reasons "the U.S. twin deficits are small numbers when taken as a percentage of anything that matters." Instead, the dollar rose because money was scarce in the U.S., so the real threat "may now lay less on the side of inflation than deflation." Christopher Lorenz's "Dogma and Reality About Exports," 6-26, is an excellent debunking of an assertion insufficiently challenged by financial reporters — that use of currency devaluations as a device for securing competitive trade advantages works. We also learn from the *FT*'s Peter Norman that the IMF now looks at commodity prices and ignores the money supply as important indicators, "IMF Calls on G7 Countries to Step Up Economic Coordination," 9-14. The news of this shift is very important and the information was made available to all the press, yet only the *FT* was swift enough to report it.

The U.S. press has been less than vigilant in covering the threats to foreign investment that are inserted like time bombs in various proposed U.S. legislation. *FT* reporters were out in front of their U.S. counterparts on this. "US Plans To Tax Foreign Buyers," by Norma Cohen 7-26, is serious reporting, as she gets the news out about a proposal being considered by a U.S. Congressional committee that would impose news taxes on foreign buyers of U.S. companies. Nancy Dunne kept abreast of these kinds of developments with "Foreign Companies to Fight US Tax Package," 9-13, an important alert on new moves to saddle foreign investment with adverse new rules. Peter Riddell's "London Fears Over US Tax Proposals," 10-13, updates us on the threats to tax incentives out of foreign investment.

FT has kept up one of the better watches on the re-emergence of protectionist sentiment within the U.S., and has been unabashedly critical whenever the administration has lessened its commitment to free trade. Martin Wolf took the U.S. to task in a "Lombard" column, "US Versus India," 6-12, on "the childish American tantrum about the unfairness of the world." Solidly rapping the Super 301 clause in the 1988 U.S. trade bill as a threat to world trade, he observes that "Things have come to a pretty pass when those who support a liberal, multilateral trading system find they must side with a country as protectionist as India against the U.S." Jurek Martin, a former Tokyo bureau chief and current foreign editor, penned the most astute and perceptive assessment and critique of the evolution toward a "neo-brutalist" U.S. policy toward Japan, "Time to Bring Japan Into the Fold," 9-26, a 10 Best selection.

Of course, while *FT*'s journalists and columnists might display more flexibility from time to time and develop angles or challenges to orthodoxy and conventionalities that would never occur to their American counterparts, the paper itself is slow to shed obsolete points of view. We still find Barry Riley lost in a labyrinth of illogic, trying to explain from a muddled Keynesian view why the U.K. is running a budget surplus, "Lawson Buries His Budget Treasure," 3-11. *FT* columnists can correctly diagnose problems, but their prescriptions this year were deadly. Michael Prowse opened the door for revival of the old Keynesian "policy mix" — raise taxes and print money — in his policy prescription for new chancellor John Major, "Tax Challenge for Mr Major," 11-3. Barry Riley was even more frank, suggesting that the chancellor raise taxes so as to deliberately provoke "a slump in domestic demand," i.e., a recession, "Making Good Use of a Scapegoat," 10-28.

There is, though, more healthy tension in the outlook at the publication than we've seen in a long time. The editors can rethink fundamental issues and come away with an entirely new perspective, as in "The Bretton Woods Twins," 4-7, where they criticize the IMF, calling into question its role. This was a real turnaround at the *FT*. Yet, they can also revert to the old standard orthodoxies, as in "Menem's Bold Steps," 7-12, endorsing "orthodoxy" for treatment of Argentina's crisis, i.e., the same devastating policies of currency devaluations and increased tax burdens that have helped pushed the country toward the abyss.

They can slip into a moral equivalency from time to time, exhibiting a bit of resentment toward the Yanks, as in "The Gaddafi Problem," 1-5, advising that "Libya has the same right, which the U.S. has, and exercises, to produce and stock chemical weapons as a deterrent." But as befits the editors as they survey the world from London, once the loftiest vantage point of all, they're also assertive in their criticism of other allies. France takes regular drubbings for its attempts to play a role in the Middle East, as in "Syria's Role in Lebanon," 4-20, where London sees peace coming only via a *Pax Syriana.* Germany, of course, receives regular advice and criticism on everything, from economic policy to relations with the East Bloc. However, *FT*'s editorials are seriously read by those who make policy, and they possess a logic that is persuasive, as in "A Flawed US Trade Policy," 5-2, warning the U.S. that "Super-301 is still a fundamentally flawed provision and incompatible with the smooth working of a multilateral trading system on which all countries, including the US, ultimately depend. . ..It sets a precedent for other countries to impose sanctions of their own against the US in future years when Washington will be seeking to run a large trade surplus."

FT's foreign corps is very impressive, and this year we found the performance of their correspondents covering Eastern Europe, the U.S.S.R. and China to be excellent. The *FT* used to have the best correspondent covering South Africa, with Anthony Robinson in Johannesburg, but he departed this year. On the Moscow beat, Quentin Peel and John Lloyd were outstanding. Both reported details of important economic policy shifts we simply didn't see covered anywhere else. Lloyd's "Wide Change in Soviet Taxes Foreshadowed," 4-18, is an example of timely news on Soviet tax plans, reporting on new rates and thresholds, the combination of which seem certain to sap *perestroika.* How hard is it to get an interview with the Minister of Finance? Peel's "Soviet Tax, Investment Rules 'Will Be Radically Reformed,' " 7-13, was the only report we saw in the press on new Finance Minister Dr. Valentin Pavlov's perspective of what appeared to be a dramatically new set of changes in the Soviet tax system and investment rules. We consistently looked for his byline, knowing that his reporting is authoritative and likely to contain critical detail we won't find anywhere else. "The Battle Lines Are Drawn," 11-20, a 10 Best selection, reports on the dramatic new plans to reform Soviet economy. Deputy prime minister Leonid Abalkin, Peel reports, envisions the reforms as leading to a social democratic U.S.S.R., with Gorbachev giving his blessings to the reform. "Hungary's Socialists Quit the Frying Pan for the Fire," by John Lloyd and Judy Dempsey 10-11, highlights the seriousness with which *FT* covered the breaking developments in central and Eastern Europe all year. *FT* has *two* correspondents covering the political changeover in Budapest, and here they hung around the party meeting until it disbanded at 1:30 a.m. to get the story.

It was also an *FT* columnist who, at the beginning of 1989, most persuasively and most presciently located the importance eastern and central Europe would have this year in testing the limits of *glasnost* and *perestroika.* Edward Mortimer's "The Dog That Failed to Bark," 1-10, a 10 Best selection, is excellent analysis of that question. Other Moscow-watchers in the London office also tried daring projections for the year, as we saw with "Perils of Perestroika," 12-30-88, by James Blitz. Blitz's argument was provocative — Gorbachev shouldn't push political freedom as economic reform will cause discontent; the state should retain authoritarian power to suppress it — but it wasn't developed persuasively.

Although it hasn't a Beijing bureau, *FT*'s coverage of China was especially impressive. Colina MacDougall continues to register with us as one of top correspondents following this story. "Hunger Rumbles Under China's Search for Viable Reform," 12-31-88, an assessment of efforts to restore central control of the economy and improve efficiency, amidst a backdrop of escalating crises, seemed a particularly ominous look into 1989, but in retrospect it was uncannily prescient. *FT* relied on an Australian journalist, stringer Peter Ellingsen, for some of its China stories. Ellingsen demonstrated a far more acute perception of what was brewing than did any other correspondent based in Beijing at the time. His 3-30 dispatch, "False Forecast Of 'Peking Spring,' " discounted the activity and high profile of liberal intellectuals as setting the stage for a more measured and successful assault on state despotism. The effort is already doomed, he warned.

The weak section within the *FT*'s foreign bureaus continues to be the Americas. The U.S. crew had a better year than previously overall, Anatole Kaletsky in particular doing much better work this year. But reporting south of the border was weaker. We noted with astonishment a "Survey" of Cuba, written by Latin America editor Robert Graham 2-17. The survey is full of ads for Cuba and its products and "A Mellowed Revolutionary," 2-17, the lead for the "Survey," is full of apologies for Fidel Castro's authoritarian "quirks." Graham advises that "In judging Cuba, so much depends upon perceptions. . .Cuban officials have no difficulty in rationalizing low living standards and low wages because they believe the right to basic nutrition, health and education is more important. The same applies to the regimentation of thinking and the lack of opposition. . .President Castro dismisses elections as unnecessary. 'The people vote for the Revolution every day.' " In "Austerity. . .and Experiment," 2-17, another part of the "Survey," we get a vast understatement of why Cuba's economic growth rate evaporated: "a combination of adverse weather, poor management and supply bottlenecks at home and debt and low commodity prices abroad have restricted growth."

Editor:	Geoffrey Owens
Address:	Bracken House, 10 Cannon Street London EC4P 4BY United Kingdom 011-441-248-8000
Circulation:	278,577 Worldwide

Investor's Daily

This smart, snappy new financial broadsheet is still looking for shots it can take at *The Wall Street Journal,* but the role it played in getting the *WSJ* changing course has to a large degree succeeded and *Investor's Daily* has to regroup. The *WSJ*, the battleship among financial dailies, had been contemplating a *perestroika* for years, but it was *ID,* a mini-submarine that appeared out of nowhere, that forced the *Journal* to act. It offered a print source for the financial community — which reads these things on trains and buses — a great, quick read of raw data, with no interpretation to mar its various charts, graphs and tables. A quick read is essential for most money managers, brokers, and serious investors, and this was *ID*'s strength.

The *Journal*'s move to a third section in October, 1988, was a mighty depth charge to the mini-sub. The third section itself was clearly influenced by the innovations of *ID,* the better graphics, the finer detail in the stock tables. *ID*'s are still a bit better for the professional, but the *WSJ* has closed off this avenue of a broader market to *ID* by renovating its archaic investment pages. *ID* still has a tiny little niche. But it must find another weakness at the *Journal* to exploit the expanding market for news in the growing, integrating world market.

The vast amount of information in *ID* is catalogued neatly in a "How to. . ." and pages and pages of charts and graphs on different stock markets, futures options, mutual funds, interest rates, convertible bonds. Different companies are spotlighted in graphic format in "Industry in the News," as opposed to the conventional article or profile. A Tuesday chart lists the 400 top computer companies for the category of the week, such as "400 Computer Companies Ranked by Total of EPS Rank and Relative Strength Rank," 9-26, impressive, but exhausting over time. With all the information there, it's still not confusing, nor difficult to find a specific figure, as long as you know what you're looking for. If not, the speedy access characteristic of *ID* can quickly turn into quicksand; this is not a newspaper for amateurs.

Amid the myriad graphics, *ID* does offer some interesting features at either end of the paper, front and back, quick but solid and to the point. The front page serves up a *Journal*-like "News Digest," which unlike the *Journal* offers only a rare non-business-related snip. On Monday, though, "The Week Ahead," a useful calendar of events which may or may not affect a businessman's livelihood, appears, telling us who's going where to meet with whom and why, precisely encapsulated. We also get bylined daily articles on the "World Economy," "Leaders & Success," "Our Economy," "Leading the News" (replacing "Top Story" but amounting to the same thing), and "Investor's Corner." These articles run with a one-sentence synopsis at the start, and begin on the front page, all finishing on the back for the really-in-a-hurry investor, who is sometimes told "It's easy to finish on the back page" when the article jumps. The short stories can be amusing, and don't have the New York-Washington focus that the *Journal* has, due to *ID*'s publishing base in California.

ID's reporting tends to focus on the top of a news pyramid, but more and more its material is getting beneath the surface of an issue. "Dictators Out of Date In Top Management," by Alexa Bell 3-10, begins delightfully "If Attila the Hun were a CEO, he might do just fine," with Bell using good examples and solid quotes from a few credibly-employed management consultants. A case of *ID* getting out in front on an important issue pleasantly surprised us. Charles Pluckhahn looks at some weaknesses in statistics, partly due to substantial revision over time, in "What Do Economic Statistics Truly Reveal?" 9-11, a hefty 40 column inches plus sidebar getting to the nitty-gritty of the subject, relating it admirably to the markets. *The Wall Street Journal* didn't pick up on this until late in the month, and then only to castigate the naysayers in an editorial; *The New York Times* waited until the end of October. *ID* makes good use of the wire services, Reuters and AP (a necessary evil due to the small size of the staff at the daily), selecting just the right material for busy investors to supplement the charts and giving an additional insight overseas or for a specific company or merger.

One great advantage of *ID* over the *Journal* is that it does not have to spend a great deal of time serving up news of interest to the business community. This should free even a small staff to fire salvoes of interest to the hefty finance community that the *Journal* is letting slide. *ID*'s daily coverage of the capital gains maneuvering was superior to the rest of the press corps which fed investors bits and pieces now and then. More probing for weaknesses on the *financial* reporting side, less on graphics and news for the businessman, might sink some ships.

Editor: Wesley Mann

Address: 1941 Armacost Avenue
              Los Angeles, CA 90025
              (213) 207-1832

Circulation: 101,000

The Journal of Commerce

We continue to maintain an appreciation of *The Journal of Commerce* for its sure and steady reporting on international trade issues. A solid industry-specific and world-oriented daily, the *JofC* holds onto its niche by providing steadily reliable coverage of events and issues the other business and financial dailies may ignore entirely. The special reports at the paper are often definitive, as we found with the 12-15-88 dispatches on Canada as it prepared for the free trade pact with the U.S.; no one else covered this as well or as thoroughly. The *JofC* also carries regular reports on the integration of Europe, done up as sub-headlined features. "1992: The European Community" is valuable in keeping us up with trade and regulatory developments during the critical maneuverings there.

Founded in 1827, 62 years before Dow Jones began *The Wall Street Journal, The Journal of Commerce* found this niche in a world of sailing ships and would not let go. Its circulation is probably not much larger than its original subscription list, compounded by family expansion. Nor do we see any signs that as we approach a new century — with the world of commerce tightening again and again through integration and reform — there will be bold, new moves at the *JofC* to enable the paper to advance beyond its corner. Nor can we argue with longevity, as much as we appreciate audacity and risk-taking in a competitive world. To live this long, the traditions of the newspaper must necessarily involve a high degree of caution. Even Publisher Don C. Becker's protectionist bent has been nicely complemented by the free-market tastes of Editor Stanford Erickson. Erickson, though, swapped jobs with General Manager Robert L. Harris effective January 1, 1990.

The *JofC* covers the world from two angles, theirs and ours, which has been so ingrained over the two centuries that it is natural for the editors to think of all stories as being local, which is precisely why we found so much here in this era of the global marketplace. Here we found a story 3-13, "Cold Took Toll on Rail Traffic in February" and another adjacent, "Panama Canal Tolls May Increase 10%," comfortably relating information that has to do with the same subject in the micro and macro. In the world of instantaneous electronic news retrieval, the *JofC* is redolent of rolltop desks and quill pens, which is how they like to be perceived. Like the Smith Barney commercial about the "old fashioned way."

As the paper is owned by a very modern and up-to-date newspaper empire, Knight-Ridder, the *JofC* editors make constructive and creative use of the empire's reporters, enabling it to cover the globe with greater speed than a telegraph and packet ship. We note here George W. Grayson's op-ed "Andean Revolution in Taxation," 2-12, with details on Bolivia's economic revolution that we didn't see anywhere else, done professionally and thoroughly. And James Bruce's "Brazil Cuts Import Duties To Foster Competition," 7-12, important news on this move away from protectionism in Brazil that wasn't covered much in the rest of the financial press. "Japan's Growing Investment In Mexico Worries Americans," by Katherine Ellison 7-27, is ironic in that while critics are alarmed about Japanese investment in Mexico, for example, the U.S. penalizes Americans for investing in Mexico by requiring them to pay a capital gains tax of 33%. These kinds of stories of some importance to global investors could frequently be found only in the *JofC,* groundbreaking and against the grain, too small for the big guys, but essential for those who want to be ahead of the crowd.

A senior editor of *The Wall Street Journal* complained to us a few years ago that we were citing the *JofC* for its coverage of Japan, when the *JofC* has only one reporter in Tokyo and the *WSJ,* he said with pride, has nine. The same A. E. Cullison is still the Tokyo bureau chief for the *JofC* in the years since we had this conversation, still a three-star reporter, and the revolving door at the *WSJ* Tokyo bureau still cannot match Cullison day in and day out. The same is true of P. T. Bangsberg, the Hong Kong bureau chief, who, with Cullison, has earned a three-star rating every year of the *MediaGuide*'s five. It's hard for us to imagine either of them at our highest rating, because they do not swing for the fences. But they are all-stars nevertheless. We keep waiting for the big guys to cover Brazil the way we'd like, but until they do, James Bruce of the *JofC* will do. Bruce Barnard puts European integration into financial and, to some degree, political perspective. The newspaper does not have correspondents in the U.S.S.R. or China, but still is the best source of news on joint ventures between U.S. and the East Bloc companies that we see. Another nice little niche. We don't know what the switching of jobs by Harris and Erickson means, but we assume it's a tradition that this sort of thing be arranged every quarter century or so, to kick up the dust.

Editor:	Robert L. Harris
Address:	110 Wall Street
	New York, NY 10005
	(212) 425-1616
Circulation:	117,000

Los Angeles Times

This was a year of important transition at the *Los Angeles Times,* with a number of significant changes taking place. The major development is that executive vice president C. Shelby Coffey III officially took over as *LAT* editor, succeeding retiring William F. Thomas, January 1, 1989. Coffey supervises a staff of 1,206 in this flagship of the Times Mirror Company. (There are more than 11,000 people in the paper's workforce.)

Coffey is an "outsider." His selection over others who've been part of the long-time regular crew at the daily was commented upon as an indication that it's precisely because he's an outsider that there's an added edge in the efforts to freshen the look and content of the *LAT.* Described as "A personable workaholic, physical fitness believer, and voracious reader," Coffey brings with him an accumulated experience as editor for several major publications. From a start as a sportswriter at *The Washington Post,* he quickly moved up the ladder there, becoming editor of its "Style" section, deputy managing editor and editor for national news. Before joining the *LAT* as deputy associate editor in 1986, he also served as editor of *U.S.News & World Report* and of the *Dallas Times Herald.* His "stamp" on the paper was evident this year.

Unsatisfied that *LAT* readers weren't seeing a "clean layout," Coffey began working on the prototype of a new layout early in the year. In October, the paper appeared with a new design, launching a new format that "builds on the *Times*'s strengths by making more accessible the information readers need and want," as he put it. The paper has been seen as "too intimidating" to new readers, but as Coffey intends to reshape the daily, the perspective is to build from its strengths. A paper of national stature, *LAT* reports are still quoted enough elsewhere to reinforce its impression of quality. It does contain a healthy amount of elegant writing, steady and solid news coverage, and competitive national and international reporting.

With the demise this year of Los Angeles's other daily, the *Los Angeles Herald Examiner,* the *LAT* will probably pick up only a few tens of thousands of those subscribers and a bit of new advertising. Many *Herald Examiner* readers will turn instead to the various suburban dailies from Santa Barbara to San Clemente. The *LAT* is swollen with ad revenues ($1 billion a year), but its circulation expansion is less than respectable, the regional dailies hotly competitive there. Part of the new format change also is intended to better help serve regional areas. Coffey acknowledges that the paper serves a Southern California audience, which, along with providing fine local coverage, is the paper's primary concern.

The *LAT* keeps the California accent up front, as we see on P. 3 of 1-2. The entire section is devoted to "California Laws, 1989," with subheads on "AIDS," "Crime," "Health," "Schools," etc., enacted laws of California legislature, and thumbnail descriptions of each. This is a great idea for any major state or regional paper.

Of course, there are always some who disapprove of format changes and the *LAT* wasn't an exception to the rule. Some disgruntled reader ran a classified ad in the "Lost and Found" section, which read: "*LOST. LA TIMES.* Last seen in a confused state disguised as *USA Today.* If found, please return to Times Mirror Square." That criticism notwithstanding, the changes do appear to be for the better. Tight summaries of each section's contents are provided in a "Highlights" column, except for section A. Instead, P. 2 of section A summarizes the major stories of each section in a "The Top of the News" column. Some stories also have summary subheads under the main title, especially those appearing on the front page.

The other area in which Coffey is restructuring the paper is on its editorial pages. Thomas Plate, who had been editorial page editor at New York *Newsday,* replaced Anthony Day as editorial page editor at the *LAT* in November. Day will continue on as a senior correspondent with essays on ideas and ideology, but "new ideas" are expected from Plate. Also moving up is editorial writer Frank del Olmo, who became deputy editorial page editor, succeeding Jack Burby. We had remarked in last year's *Guide* that we were hoping Coffey could breathe some life into *LAT*'s editorial pages, and are therefore eager to follow the changes that Plate's assignment promises for the coming year.

These changes came late in the year, so their effects were strongly apparent. The op-ed pages varied all year. We'd have days where the composition of views was rich and diverse, informative as a whole. For example, in late December, 1988, and early January, 1989, the editors gave heavy coverage to the PLO declaration of a Palestinian state, with a very finely selected variety to the views and perspectives presented in its op-eds. Likewise, the composition of the Sunday "Opinion" section front page, 1-29, was an effective one: Walter Russell Mead on the likelihood that the Bush years will be "anything but boring;" Donella H. Meadows revisiting her 1972 "Limits to Growth;" former L.A. Police Chief Ed Davis on gun control and senseless murders; and Ronald Brownstein on the 1990 census and importance of the gubernatorial races next year.

We saw decent quality throughout the year, as for example, with a midyear "Opinion" section, 6-11. The front page holds up well with the theme of "A World of Shock and Aftershock," divided into four effective essays: "China: Brutal Suppression," by Edward A. Gargan, *NYT* Beijing bureau chief, 1986 to 1988; "Iran: Funereal Depression," by Prof. Mansour Farhang; "Russia: Emboldened Expression," by Craig S. Barnes, a vice president of the Beyond the War Foundation; and "Japan: Tainted Succession," by David Williams, editorial writer for the *Japan Times.* Also within the section, "Hungary: People's Revolt Three Decades Later," by Endre Marton, who covered the 1956 revolution as an AP correspondent, after 18 months in prison on a conviction for treason and espionage, adds to the general theme. The op-eds in this issue help round out the theme with assessments and criticisms of U.S. policy: "While the World Erupts, U.S. Policy Stands Still," by Alan Tonelson; "Noriega-Bashing Has Had Its Day," by Jorge Castaneda, professor of political science at the National Autonomous University of Mexico and frequent contributor to the op-ed page; "Grand Words Don't Make an Allied Strategy," by Christoph Bertram, diplomatic correspondent for *Die Zeit* of Hamburg, Germany; and "Leftist Cacophony for Human Rights Grows Silent on the Beijing Massacre," by Alan M. Dershowitz.

However, in the realm of "fresh, new ideas," the performance wasn't as consistent. The lead "Opinion" feature "Tower Besieged. . .as Bush Team Bungles," 3-5, for example, is by David Gergen, who produces a banal observation: "There is a gathering consensus in both parties that the country needs an effective leader." Although Gergen can write and organize the conventional view most effectively, and although this essay did cause some umbrage at the White House, the mainstream, conventional observation is one that too frequently leads the Sunday "Opinion" section. Similarly the "Opinion" section 3-12, employs Kevin Phillips for its lead, "A Team of Old Pols" on the John Tower fight: "One of the least capable administrations in recent U.S. history seems to be stumbling into a four-year dogfight with an underwhelming congress." Phillips has been saying the same thing for the last eight years. He's the lead again for the 4-9 "Opinion," with "Taxes Reformed," giving us his very stale, very misinformed and unsubstantiated assessment: "Succinctly put: Public opinion appears to favor re-establishing tax-bracket progressivity — the principle of significantly higher rates for higher income groups so much eroded in the 1980s." Editor Plate and deputy del Olmo have their work cut out for them.

The paper's editorial voices are generally predictable, rarely forceful, and just too frequently without much serious impact on policy. A look at the messages sent out at the beginning of the year illustrates that. For example, on public housing policy, we know the editors will assert, as they did in a "New Look at Housing," 12-21-88, that the issue needs "more federal attention," including "an aggressive jobs program, [and] intensive training programs." We also know that the editorial will then limply conclude that "the best thing he [new HUD Secretary Jack F. Kemp] could do would be to challenge Americans from the new President down to think deeply and to care passionately about decent housing for everyone in the nation who needs it." On Central American policy, the consequences of a democratic election are so feared that in "Nightmare in El Salvador," 12-27-88, the editors warn that because "There is a possibility that deep divisions in [President Jose Napoleon] Duarte's centrist Christian Democratic party could result in the next President being a member of the ARENA party" the Bush administration ought to help "revive the stalled peace talks between the government and the rebel's political representatives, with the aim of trying to reach first a ceasefire, and then a power-sharing arrangement." Incredible!

On the environment, we get squishy ruminations, as in "Caring For The Earth," 1-2: "Environmental problems, from protection of U.S. wild lands to the global atmosphere, seem immense. Still, every citizen can have an effect. It begins with caring." The editors produce more spongy material, as with "Air Service: What Now?" 1-3: "The government must closely monitor fares to make certain that the public is not victimized by de-facto price fixing." Some moral equivalency is dished out with "American as Vigilante," 1-5: "Libya. . .is not committing outlawry by seeking to join a score of other states in acquiring chemical weapons. . .the United States is not the world's policeman, or even the Mediterranean's." We don't object to the use of pejoratives in an editorial, except, that's all we really get out of "Bennett the Menace," 1-13, on the newly-appointed "drug czar," William Bennett, an "abrasive. . . .favorite of the far right. . . .shoot-from-the-lip" type.

The *Los Angeles Times Magazine* is usually discarded after a quick skim of its generally unappealing table of contents. Even when we think we've come across an item worth reading, we find disappointment, as with the 1-29 cover story on former Gov. Jerry Brown. All we get is a reproduction of a recent Brown speech blasting Reagan and Bush and celebrating old-fashioned liberalism. This is poor judgement by the editors. Occasionally we do get something better, as with the "Eyewitness At Tian An Men Square," cover story by Edward Gargan in the 7-16 issue, or with "Making Sense of Maureen," a cover story profiling San Diego's mayor Maureen O'Connor, 12-10.

We detail the performance of the *LAT*'s journalists in the sections where individual evaluations are contained. We do note that its foreign bureaus continue to be one of the paper's strengths, although they too have a share of weaknesses. The Beijing, London, Moscow, Nairobi and Tokyo bureaus performed quite well this year. Although we were disappointed that we didn't see enough from Tokyo bureau chief Sam Jameson, Tokyo correspondent Karl Schoenberger is a strong asset to the bureau. We're looking forward to Bob Drogin's reporting this coming year, as this solid political reporter has moved to Manila from the Washington bureau. *LAT*'s Pacific perspective is healthy, its coverage continuing to satisfy. However, it needs to demand more from its Latin American bureaus.

We find that we often get more out of the *LAT*'s business-financial sections than we do from *The Washington Post*. Its coverage of the Drexel-Mike Milken stories was especially strong. We also found in the *LAT* remarkably clear reporting on the Utah fusion experiments, as in "Of Fusion and Confusion: Does It Really Work?" by Lee Dye 3-28. The material here was easier to understand than that by *The New York Times* and *Wall Street Journal* reporters several weeks later. We still find its "Board of Economists" forum more miss than hit. For example, its 1-2 column is a useless exercise in which three economists say yes to a coming recession while three say no recession. The *LAT* at least mentions the poor forecasting records of some of those cited, but the idea itself is obsolete. It would be better to have Scot Paltrow get on the phone to several with good forecasting records. We more often than not end up with obsolete or misinformed observations from the contributors in this column, as with "Can We Avert the Next Financial Crisis?" by Prof. Paul R. Krugman 10-29, misadvising that "Had the Federal Reserve acted in 1929 as it did in 1987, there would almost surely have been no Great Depression."

Still sensitive to criticism that the paper misses important local news, Coffey surely has a perspective for better covering that hole. The special format redesign will help somewhat, as an attention on the Orange County section, for instance, is heightened. The paper has, though, a relatively successful formula for linking its Pacific Rim perspective with local news. The fine reports of Nancy Yoshihara on the cultural, financial and business links between East Asia and the greater LA area are one worthy example. But it'll take awhile before California readers forget that it was the paper's former rival, the *Herald Examiner,* that broke the story on LA Mayor Tom Bradley's tangled financial dealings — especially since the *LAT* had sufficient information seven months earlier to hit the front pages with the news. All in all, though, we look forward to Mr. Coffey's tenure at the helm as he carries *perestroika* at the *Los Angeles Times* into the 1990s.

Editor: C. Shelby Coffey III

Address: Times Mirror Square
                 Los Angeles, CA 90053
                 (213) 237-5000

Circulation: 1,118,649 Weekday
                 1,433,739 Sunday

USA Today

While newspaper publishers everywhere fret about declining readership in the new electronic generation, *USA Today* not only makes headway, but also introduces the thought at the back of our mind that it has been going in the right direction as the result of what President Bush calls that "vision thing." We do not *frequent* the newspaper, as we do the pacesetting *New York Times, Wall Street Journal,* and *Washington Post.* But we have to respectfully acknowledge that the founder of this could-be white elephant, self-confessed SOB Al Neuharth, may have seen the future.

We're still not sure that *USA Today* is the future, but it is already evident that its innovation and thrust has forever changed the face of American print journalism.

The Washington Times, struggling from its own deep financial problems, was the first to emulate Neuharth's architecture, producing at least a metropolitan newspaper that looks sensational — winning awards left and right for visual appeal. We think *The Wall Street* Journal's decision to expand to a third section, reorganizing its presentation, was spurred by *Investor's Daily,* but that the original impetus came from *USA Today* and its deep insight that newspapers are not competing against each other, or other news media, but are simply competing for the consumer's time in the broadest sense. Now we have the *Los Angeles Times* and *National Journal,* both going to *Today*-like color looks, and *The New York Times* is fussing about color. Neuharth has retired, but we expect Peter Pritchard will continue to develop the newspaper around this news philosophy.

We still see the newspaper most often in an airport or at our hotel threshold, purchased for us by a generous airline or hotelier and delivered free, without asking. But in the last year or two, this has become a more pleasant experience. We find the material we see is not only presented well graphically, but is actually competitive informationally. We note this especially in the paper's spot business news. Although it's rare that a correspondent for the national daily will break a story, we find more and more that the pieces the editors run are being treated with respect rather than derision. The information is accurate and tightly packaged, becoming more confident in tone and analysis. although not particularly analytic.

"Marvin Davis Bids $2.6B for NWA," by David Landis and Jim Freschi 3-31, covers the bases as respectably as any report we saw on the Northwest Airlines buyout bid. Similarly, "Fla. Sweep Is Newest Tactic in Drug War," by Mike McQueen and Steve Marshall 7-3/4, is short and pithy on the new sweep idea that may soon sweep the country. "Sexy Ragtop Puts Buyers in Scramble," by David Landis 8-11/13, predicts early on that the Mazda Miata could be the Mustang of the '90s. There's usually a human interest piece on the front page too, capturing the quirky and the dramatic, particularly with San Francisco pitcher Dave Dravecky's cancer comeback, "Pitcher's Duel: Cancer Strikes Out," 8-11/13. The paper gets considerable attention in the broadcast media for the business newsbeats and tips from veteran columnist Dan Dorfman, who seemed to have had a good year on this score.

This is, of course, only a sample of the paper's daily fare, but it impresses us that we are so impressed with the sample. It is still a considerable distance from being a primary source of information for serious consumers of news, but it has matured and ripened into a close substitute.

Editor:	Peter S. Pritchard
Address:	1000 Wilson Boulevard Arlington, VA 22209 (703) 276-3400
Circulation:	2,127,559

The Washington Times

It's at least been an interesting year for Washington's other paper, *The Washington Times,* which continues to struggle for readers and advertising in a *Washington Post* Beltway. The *Times* really did have the scoop of the year, uncovering Massachusetts Rep. Barney Frank's liaison with and support of Greg Davis alias Stephen Gobie, a homosexual prostitute. As *Time* put it in a press story on the *Times,* "No. 2 and Trying Harder," 11-6, "*The Washington Times* bags a politician, but can it win respect?"

In last year's *MediaGuide,* we zapped the paper for mangling a story about the Democratic presidential nominee. A year earlier, we zapped it for mangling an editorial squabble about South Korea, when the newspaper's owners are one-and-all part of the Unification Church of the Rev. Sun Myung Moon. It just isn't *nice* to be getting into brawls all the time if you are going to be a respectable newspaper! After observing the fisticuffs over Barney Frank and related Washington sex scandals trumpeted by the paper this year, we must agree: the *Times* doesn't have respect in the sense of *respectability.*

But the Barney Frank story followed the deep digging the *Times* editpage did a year ago in tieing House Speaker Jim Wright to the S&L scandal, which helped topple Wright this year, the first House Speaker in U.S. history to resign, for goodness sakes. And these revelations followed the bare-knuckled, yet *completely clean,* columns of Warren Brookes in hanging Willie Horton, the homicidal maniac and his parole, around the neck of Michael Dukakis, which helped George Bush win the Big Political Enchilada on the Planet Earth. Taking all this into account, one has to acknowledge that the newspaper has achieved *some* kind of respect. It may be the kind *demanded* by Leo Gorcey and the Bowery Boys, who are otherwise uncouth. But at this cost, Editor Arnaud de Borchgrave has put this brazen newspaper on the political map.

George Archibald and Paul Rodriguez, who broke the Frank story, were led into it by an earlier scandal, "Homosexual Prostitution Inquiry Ensnares VIPs with Reagan, Bush," 6-29, about a Capitol character, Craig J. Spence, who threw parties, lobbied, and was tied to gay prostitutes who managed to get past the Secret Service for late-night tours of the White House. The piece promised much and delivered nothing at the time. Wesley Pruden, managing editor of the *Times,* did advise readers they would only release names from the "Call Boy" list that were in sensitive government positions. But there was nary a VIP on the "Call Boy" list the paper had unearthed, except, ironically, one of its own lesser editors, who resigned.

The *Times* at this point pushed the story to especially distasteful lengths, with reporters Michael Hedges and Jerry Seper, rather good investigative reporters, running around at supermarket tabloid level. "Spence Arrested in N.Y., Released," 8-9, a 6-column spread with two articles recounting an eight-hour interview with Craig J. Spence, repeating again, word-for-word some of the information previously published, and allowing Spence, suffering from AIDS, making repeated references to suicide and carrying a razor blade, to walk out of an interview into oblivion. Seper, on his own, dishes up the dirt pretty well too. "Pedophile Was Free Despite Past," 6-7, are companion pieces ("7-year-old Regains Spirit After Rape, Mutilation" and "Officials Say He Killed Girl, Molested Others") detailing the horrific story of the May 20 rape and mutilation of a seven-year-old Tacoma boy by a known child molester, screechy reporting on a particularly disturbing crime. What are these doing on the front page of *The Washington Times*? The *Times'* veteran White House reporter, Jeremiah O'Leary, now a columnist, tactfully took his paper to task in ". . .and Rumor Mongers," 6-2, noting rumor isn't always reporting: "There may or may not be pedophiles and undiscovered homosexuals in Congress. If there are, I do not look forward to reading the sordid details."

At this point, the *Times* seemed to be taking on the coloration of a sorry rag, with nothing to show for its "Call Boy" sleaze. Nary a VIP and the *Post* which pooh-poohed the story, seemed vindicated. But out of the effort developed the second, big story, a 10 Best selection, "Sex Sold Out of Congressman's House," a two-article headline spread across 6 columns, again by George Archibald and Paul Rodriguez 8-25, this time nailing a genuine VIP, Barney Frank, who admits to the whole fiasco. The avoidance of the story by other newspapers and television further intensified the importance of the coverage in the *Times.* The next few days brought about further revelations, " 'Call Boy' Caper Gets House Panel's Ear," 8-28, until Frank requested a House investigation of his conduct, "Frank Himself Asks Probe of Sex Charges," 8-29, front-page headlines with several accompanying articles, responsibly done.

Follow-up dispatches proved to be mostly sensationalist. "The Gobie Story: Frank's 'Call Boy' Tells All," 9-1, also by Archibald and Rodriguez, does tell the whole story from Gobie's point of view. We also get a detailed sexual history of Mr. Gobie, quoting him directly as he explains his first experience with oral sex, more appropriate in context for a Guccione publication; Mr. Frank is not consulted, nor does the team produce any support for Gobie's claims. Subsequent dispatches openly beat the drum for Mr. Frank's resignation, rarely quoting anyone directly: "Dump Frank Drive Has Democrats Jittery," Paul Bedard and Michael Hedges 9-1; "Embarrassed Leaders Want Frank to Go," Chris Harvey 9-8; "Deserted by Press, Frank Stands Firm Against Resigning," Michael Hedges 9-18; "Tide Is Rolling Against Frank," Ralph Hallow and Paul Rodriguez 9-19; and "Democratic Leaders Desert Frank," Rodriguez and Hallow 9-20.

Wesley Pruden, the paper's managing editor, who had been the driving force behind the coverage of these stories, weighed in with "Sweet Times in the Low House," 9-1, in his sulfuric political column, which gave us projected pillow talk between Frank and Gobie. Pruden's reasoning was that *The Washington Times* was making the city a better place for the children by exposing the "call boy scandal," "A Little Outrage for the Children?" 8-25. When the Frank frenzy finally waned in the Fall, the paper settled down to more thoughtful reportage and commentary, one item, "Propriety of Investigating Sex Lives Has House Divided," Ralph

Hallow and George Archibald 10-4, delicately probed the question of sexual conduct as a political problem, but directly contradicted an earlier story that Rep. Frank initiated the House inquiry, noting the House Ethics Committee "decided on its own" to investigate the matter. And Paul Rodriguez's piece, "Alexander, Impatient With Gingrich Probe, Hires Outside Lawyer," 10-11, is thorough and fair on Rep. Bill Alexander (D-Ark.) hiring a firm to get the ethics committee to move faster on Rep. Newt Gingrich, helping to prove the *Times* can be as non-partisan as anybody, when it wants to be.

The "Commentary" section edited by Mary Lou Forbes holds steady as a bastion of conservative thinking. Its star performer remains columnist Warren T. Brookes, whose work originates in *The Detroit News,* but whose chief national platform is in this section. His material is always on its first page and usually leads the section. The only journalist to achieve four stars in every edition of the *MediaGuide,* Brookes' work builds a viewpoint on a mountain of careful reporting. It has an impact on policymaking in the administration and on Capitol Hill. In addition to leading the pack on the Willie Horton story last year, Brookes was relentless throughout Campaign '88 in pointing out the financial difficulties of the state of Massachusetts under Governor Dukakis. Brookes again earns a 10 Best selection in general reporting for his pathbreaking work in demonstrating the weakness of the arguments made by environmentalists on acid rain and global warming.

Three other columnists who are among our highest-rated appear in this section regularly: Pat Buchanan, Richard Grenier and Thomas Sowell. Buchanan uses a hammer to nail home his conservative views. Grenier who uses a foil, dropped to three stars from four last year when we noted sour notes creeping into his material, came back to three-and-a-half stars this year, also earning a 10 Best selection for a charming column on Martin Luther and Martin Luther King. We continue to believe Grenier is being mishandled by the editors, belonging back in the "life!" section. Sowell's Scripps-Howard column, which we see in the *Times,* would be even better if he devoted more of its energy to the problems of black America.

Other "Commentary" stalwarts who are almost always worth reading include Suzanne Fields, Georgie Anne Geyer, Paul Greenberg and Paul Craig Roberts. Less consistent, but still usually making telling points, are Ben Wattenberg, Ken Adelman, and Harry Summers. John Lofton, who we noted a year ago had "an abysmal year," was dropped by the newspaper in a dispute over his material early this year. The section's right-wingedness lightened as a result, but it still needs a solid, pro-choice, pro-Gorbachev liberal to give it more vitality.

The editorial page itself improves steadily under its young editor, Tony Snow, who had been deputy editor on *The Detroit News* page, and whose first editorial in the *Times* questioning Jim Wright's ethics dated back to August '87. Snow, who is cast in the mold of *The Wall Street Journal's* Robert L. Bartley, is more a "progressive conservative" than we might otherwise expect from the *Times.* Because a good chunk of the newspaper's circulation is in the city's black community, Snow's sensitivities on African-American issues — developed in Detroit — is an asset. Snow's editorials and columns can be credited with developing a good piece of the ethical indictment against House Speaker Jim Wright. Samuel T. Francis, his deputy editorial page editor, was selected by the American Society of Newspaper Editors as a recipient of its Distinguished Writing Award for his '88 work at the *Times.* Snow's bylined material is much crisper this year than last and impresses too. "Barney Frank and 'Privacy,' " 8-31, is thoughtful on the repercussions of the case, early on.

The other development at the newspaper this year that bears noting is the improvement of its "life!" section under a new editor, John Podhoretz, the precocious son of Norman Podhoretz, editor of *Commentary.* Young Podhoretz got his foothold in journalism as movie critic of *The American Spectator,* worked as a *Time* reporter for a year, joined the *Washington Times* in '85 as features editor, became Kirk Oberfeld's deputy editor at *Insight* for a year, skipped across town to edit at *U.S. News & World Report* for a bit, returning this year, age 28, to edit "life!" After a quirky first day, in which "life!" reveals that Budget Director Richard Darman is one-quarter Jewish and takes him to task for refusing to discuss the matter, the section actually has improved steadily and has become quite a respectable product, even winning a fairly prestigious Penney-Missouri award for this kind of material. He's made good use of Cathryn Donohoe (one of the best feature writers in town), Charlotte Hays, TV critic Rick Marin, and media writer Don Kowet. He has refrained from assigning reporters to Barbara-watch, and has engaged our attention generally. A talent that developed at the "life!" section, David Mills, was hired away by the *Post*'s "Style" section at year's end. Working without the resources of *The Washington Post*'s "Style" section, Podhoretz has been a pleasant surprise, and if he can sit still for awhile, might soon be nipping at "Style."

The Korean owners of the paper are showing more concern about the big bag of money they have to spend each year subsidizing the *Times*, however. Circulation is up nicely over last year, but still a far cry from what would be necessary to pull in big ad accounts and turn a profit. The budget squeeze has been big enough to force closing down more of the foreign operations, with Marc Lerner leaving Manila with no replacement as he becomes foreign editor. de Borchgrave's contract is up this spring, and there is speculation he may choose to step down, with perhaps a portfolio to do big globe-trotting interviews for the paper.

Editor-in-Chief:	Arnaud de Borchgrave
Address:	3600 New York Avenue, NW
	Washington, DC 20002
	(202) 636-6000
Circulation:	103,539

MAJOR PERIODICALS

The American Spectator

With the usual exception, it was a good year for the irreverent monthly. Overall, *TAS* continues to improve, although it did spin out of control on one occasion this year. Once elegantly and appropriately described as "a journal of joy, reminding us in every issue of the reasons to celebrate the zest of combat, the joy of right thinking, the pleasure of language," *TAS* exhibited signs of cognitive dissonance with the editors' infantile attack on Vice President Dan Quayle, "Why Danny Can't Read," whose unflattering caricature defaces the periodical's 6-89 cover. Is R. Emmett (Bob) Tyrrell Jr. once again "bored," but this time unable to supercede that boredom with a freshly invigorating perspective on the global scene? It was from out of "boredom" that *TAS* originally sprang, RET fed up with the stupidity around him and "thrilled with the prospect of writing about it." We hope this foaming fit is a one-time only indulgence, but the experience leaves us skittish nonetheless.

One of the best developments has been the decision to use roving correspondent Micah Morrison more frequently. Morrison is an effective reporter, as his 5-89 cover "Adios Pinochet," attests. This was fine reporting from Chile, with Morrison working many dimensions and layers of the post-plebiscite situation. Morrison was also one of the few to go after his fellow professionals for lazy journalism regarding environmental stories. He targets the National Park Service with some impressive investigative reporting in "The Yellowstone Scam," 8-89, and delivers a critique of the "Let it burn!" policy that set us to rethinking the issue all over again. In "The Road To Revolt In China," 11-89, we're willing to overlook some of the rhetorical excess in his conclusions as he recounts the events in Tiananmen Square based on an interview with student democracy leader Xin Ku, the basic story well done. RET has an asset here.

TAS has an impressive list of contributors upon whom it can rely for at least one outstanding story each issue. P.J. O'Rourke appears frequently, his special brand of gonzo journalism always delightful and entertaining. His most provocative essay was "Call for A New McCarthyism," 7-89, in which he introduces a McCarthyesque enemies list, those on it not so much leftists as individuals who express "silly opinions on matters about which he or she is largely or abysmally uninformed." Donald Trump, for example, appears on the list, and O'Rourke explains why that's appropriate. "OK. So he's not a real pinko, but I don't like him. And if McCarthyism isn't good for settling grudges, what is it good for." O'Rourke's essay provided multiple belly laughs, but the editors worked the laughs into the ground by filling the October and November issues with contributions from readers of other individuals and institutions that ought to go onto the list. Unfunny and a waste of space.

Among other stories that were particularly well done was Malcolm Gladwell's "Risk, Regulation and Biotechnology," 1-89, an insightful look into the problems and challenges for genetic engineers — not just in the lab, but with winning the public's trust and regulators' understanding. James Ring Adams' on the S&L Crisis, "The Big Fix," 3-89, provided early details on the sticky relationships between that mess and Congress: "When [Federal] examiners grew too pesky, phone calls to [U.S. Congressmen] Fernand St. Germain, Tony Coelho, and Jim Wright were enough to shoo them off." Robert Novak's profile of the House majority leader, "The Shifty Richard Gephardt," 8-89, is comprehensive, Novak going over the congressman's character and beliefs with a fine-toothed comb. The October issue carried "The Asbestos Rip-Off," by Michael Fumento, a compelling expose on the expensive and deadly attempts to correct a problem that doesn't exist.

TAS doesn't suffer for any want of high quality contributors, but some of its regulars seemed a bit more sluggish than usual. Tom Bethell's "Capitol Comment" column was hit and miss, scoring perhaps one out of every three times. Irwin M. Stelzer "Business of America" column scores better, and we appreciate seeing *TAS* running a regular column on economic policy. His "Some Like It Hot," 3-89, was a respectable attempt to look at the ambiguity of evidence on the global warming trend.

We just didn't see enough of national correspondent Vic Gold, after having our appetites for his brand of humor whetted by his "Aside From That, Sam, How Did You Like the Speech?" 1-89. A light, amusing diversion on how it'd be reported if today's White House press corps had covered the Gettysburg Address, we get: *"And analyzed by Sam Donaldson on ABC News:. . .The President delivered his remarks in the same high-pitched, grating vocal style that has characterized his past public addresses. Another criticism, voiced by one Bucks Country farmer, was that, I quote, 'My family and I drove two hours in a wagon to hear the President of the United States speak. All we got for our trouble was a puny two-minute talk.' Nor was this opinion isolated. An ABC exit poll of those leaving the cemetery following the President's speech found 86 percent rating it 'Poor,' only 5 percent rating it 'Average,' with one percent 'Undecided.' "* *TAS* has beefed up its irreverent side, bringing in others beside P.J. O'Rourke as regular contributors. Joe Queenan's acidic wit reminds us of the *TAS* of yore, and we always enjoy Benjamin J. Stein's mellow mirth.

Tyrrell's own contributions vary. Among his editorials we noted a sophistication on issues of finance and debt, as in "Junk Danger," 1-89. His "Continuing Crisis" column, though, is still not up to the levels it once reached when its appearance used to be one of the most eagerly awaited events among neocons and conservatives in the Beltway. But we can live with that, as long as the rest of *TAS* keeps its vibrancy.

TAS pulls in respectable ad revenues and its subscriber base is up. However, it really depends heavily on grants and contributions. Its June cover on Dan Quayle hurt it somewhat, the outpouring of angry letters to the editor that ran for two months an indication. RET looked upon it as "vitriol under the bridge," and stated his intentions of renewing his old friendship with the Vice President. All well and good. But, *TAS* reaction to the Veep's observations about it and other publications suggests a really serious blind spot at the publication. Vice President Quayle had been quoted in *The Wall Street Journal* 3-21, as saying: "I used to. . .read *National Review* — some. I used to read *Human Events*. Don't read it as much as I used to. *The American Spectator* — it's hard to get through *The American Spectator*. And the *New Republic*. I enjoy reading *New Republic* articles." It was the last reference that particularly irked the editors at *TAS,* four of them coming together to pen the small-minded and vindictive one-page June "cover story." Tyrrell was still begrudging him that observation in his response to the letters of complaint in the August issue: "On the other hand, perhaps he [the Vice President] believes that true wisdom resides with the *New Republic*. . ." Come on now, Bob, loosen up.

Editor:	R. Emmett Tyrrell Jr.
Address:	P.O. Box 10448
	Arlington, VA 22210
	(703) 243-3733
Circulation:	39,606

The Atlantic

The Atlantic Monthly continues to be an important journal, although its primary importance is as a consensus-builder rather than as a trend-setter. Generally, its function is to consolidate establishment opinion on topics of the day, especially among old-line Democrats.

Political coverage in *The Atlantic* took on a new color in 1989, as the editors adjusted their coverage to focus more on historical issues rather than contemporary problems. William Schneider's "JFK's Children: The Class of '74," cover 3-89, received a 10 Best nomination for political reporting. Schneider's look at how the new Democrats who came into office in 1974 changed their party is the best handling we've seen of this topic. Nicholas Lemann's series wrapping up the history of the war on poverty, "The Unfinished War," 12-88/1-89, will undoubtedly be quoted by all sides in the continuing welfare-reform arguments. Another cover story, "The Last Wise Man," 4-89, excerpting George Kennan's diaries, continued *The Atlantic Monthly*'s elegiac tendencies. Oh, well, those who forget history are condemned to repeat it.

Foreign coverage was also spotty, much of it skewed and undiscerning. James Fallows shifted from straight reporting on Japan to analyzing U.S.-Japanese relations, a task to which he is not up, as one might say. Fallows is a superb writer who provides good, solid information and fresh insights; too frequently, though, we must pick out all the digs which fall within the parameters of Japan-bashing. "The Hard Life," 3-89, takes on the conventional questions — if the Japanese are so wealthy, why do they live in cramped housing and commute on cramped trains? — and delivers a too familiar answer: the Japanese just don't want to change. Still, there are mountains of sharp detail in every paragraph of this long report. He furnishes the Japanese viewpoint on defense spending, with emphasis on the FSX controversy in "Let Them Defend Themselves," 4-89. This works well, showing how unpopular the *jieitai* (self-defense force) is, and sharply poses the question of what, exactly, an expanded Japanese defense would do. If we could excise his policy proposals and his tendentious analytics from the exhaustive 5-89 cover, it would be an outstanding report, the wealth of detail, data, and insights into Japan so impressive. But his agenda is metastasized throughout the report, beginning with the title itself, "Containing Japan," which conjures up an image previously reserved only for the Communist menace. Fallows' book *More Like Us* also helped to contribute to the press corps' declaring open season on Japan, evidence of the influence of Fallows and *The Atlantic*.

Robert Kaplan's contributions declined substantially, further weakening the magazine's foreign coverage. His best offering, "Europe's Third World," 7-89, provides a concise overview of the ethnic feuds in the troubled Balkans, examining why these feuds exist, why they matter, and who the players are, including interviews with leading Yugoslavs and Hungarians.

The magazine ran several environmental pieces this year, some providing fresh insights. Kenneth Brower's "The Destruction of Dolphins," cover 7-89, is wonderfully descriptive, but emotionally manipulative on the killing of dolphins by tuna fishermen. Evan Eisenberg's "Back to Eden," cover 11-89, on modern farming's detriment to the environment, goes well beyond the pollution exposes and clean-up recommendations that have become common. Eisenberg offers a powerful and provocative look at the history of agriculture, explaining with clear logic the economics of the current problems facing the industry.

A special issue on defense, 6-89, fell short, doing more to obscure the current debate on defense spending and defense strategy than to illuminate it. The introduction, "Indefensible," 6-89, does contain the magazine's hidden agenda, but it is not clear that the writers of this editorial read all the pieces in the series. Well written and thoughtful, "A Bankrupt Military Strategy," 6-89, by Col. Harry G. Summers, Jr., is the most lucid of this cover-story collection, pointing to real problems in U.S. strategic concepts. Less impressive was Jack Beatty's contribution "The Exorbitant Anachronism," 6-89. Difficult to read through, the piece is tedious, confusing in spots, and unbalanced.

"Reports and Comment" continued to have interesting reports and dull comments. The best reports: James Pittaway on the Muslim Brotherhood of Egypt, "A Benign Brotherhood?" 1-89; Robert Kaplan on Afghanistan, "Postmortem," 4-89; Joseph Alper on the American Psychiatric Association's diagnostic manual "Order on the Couch," 5-89; and John Garvey on American members of the Eastern Orthodox faith, "Eastern Orthodoxy," 5-89.

Editor:	William Whitworth
Address:	745 Boyleston Street Boston, MA 02116 (617) 536-9500

Circulation: 450,000

Aviation Week & Space Technology

In 1989 *Aviation Week & Space Technology* made a worthy contribution to the nation's ongoing debate on the big issues facing us as the Cold War winds down. Whether the subject matter was the future of the U.S. defense budget, *perestroika,* America's space program, or the latest in technological breakthroughs in the field of national security, *AWST* consistently provided comprehensive coverage that was rarely found in more politically inspired publications.

Once again, *AWST* remained the unequalled chronicler of record of virtually every noteworthy event in the world of aviation, space and associated technologies, making it invaluable for the business executive and the engineer, the logistics and ordnance officer, and the KGB spook, as well as the future historian of technology. In accomplishing this latter task, *AWST* met its self-defined obligation to be "edited for persons with active, professional, functional responsibility in aviation, air transportation, aerospace, advanced and related technologies." The publication's clout is measurable by the fact that its over 150,000 subscription based circulation, by stated corporate policy, is "limited to executive, management, engineering and scientific levels in industry, airlines, corporate aviation, government and military. No subscriptions accepted without complete identification."

This latter clause in the corporate policy statement is not unrelated to the recurring concern, occasionally expressed in letters to the editor, that *AWST*'s thoroughness, excellence and competence in reporting may unwittingly be providing unmerited benefits to foreign intelligence services. Such, for instance, was the case with William B. Scott's coverage of the F-117A Stealth fighter in his "USAF Expands Use of F-117A, Adds More Daytime Flights," 5-1.

The publication's principal stylistic features are two: Teamwork and the complete absence of "prima donnas;" and these almost to the point of self-effacement: to this day, no bylines appear in the Table of Contents. Also, some of the best published items were the fruits of the joint labor of ad-hoc teams, such as the 5-29 Aerospace/Defense Financial Report under the lead rubric "Wall Street Upbeat on Airlines, Gloomy About Defense Stocks," the multi-issue, exhaustive coverage of the Le Bourget, Paris Airshow, with its lead-event, "Agile Sukhoi Su-27 Leads Strong Soviet Presentation," 6-19, the stunning two-part Electronic Warfare Special Report organized under "New Concepts Emerging For Electronic Warfare," 9-11, and the sobering "Special Report: The World Airline Fleet Grows Older," 7-24.

The one special report produced by such *AWST* teamwork which definitely caught history in the making in 1989 was the Soviet Aerospace Industry Report under the lead rubric "Perestroika's Changes Grip Soviet Aerospace Industry," 6-5. The package was the fruit of a three-week visit to the U.S.S.R. of an editorial team led by editor-in-chief Donald E. Fink, and included managing editor David M. North, European editor Jeffrey M. Lenorovitz and engineering editor Michael A. Dornheim. In what was a "first" for any Western nation, the *AWST* team gained access to the top management and to the production floor of every major Soviet aerospace facility. It then supplied us with what was the year's best firsthand economic intelligence on the Soviet Union published anywhere.

Matters of industry, technology and science are not merely reported competently, but they are cast in a distinctive perspective on world affairs that is inconspicuous, quiet, but ubiquitous. Only rarely does *AWST* explicitly devote articles to articulating this philosophical perspective. It does so circumspectly, but with a persuasive force characteristic of the mindset of a science-oriented engineer. One such instance was Donald Fink's editorial endorsement of *perestroika* in "Seize the Perestroika Opportunity," 6-5. Another was the superb, acerbic editorial "The Strategy Morass," 4-24, which argued that "strategy has not been allowed to interfere with the Pentagon's grotesque budget and planning system," and set the fur flying. On rare occasions, *AWST* editorials do rise to the bold and visionary, as was the case with the exceptional editorial "The

Legacy of Apollo 11," 7-17, in which it places President Bush's Moon-Mars mission objective in its earthly political context: "As the new century approaches, the U.S. needs vibrant scientific and engineering communities to help it stay the course. The Eastern and Western Blocs are being driven toward accommodations that could prompt drastic reductions in defense spending, with obvious ramifications for the global aerospace/defense industry. What better way is there to take up the slack while continuing to stoke America's critical 'technological engine' than to pursue a vigorous space exploration program?"

The practical weight of such *A WST* perspectives is measurable by the strategic position of the magazine's formidable constituency.

The layout and distribution of the news material has remained stable, without innovations over the year. Apart from the Special Reports, each issue continues to be organized around key sections such as "Headline News," "Aeronautical Engineering," "Avionics," "Missile Engineering," "Space Technology," "Air Transport," etc. Guests are accorded valuable space in the ongoing "Aerospace Forum," and the "Letters to the Editor" invariably reflect a lively exchange within the rather spirited community serviced by *A WST.* No changes have been made in the Departments, which are designed with maximum economy to serve as comprehensive intelligence summaries for the busy executive: "Who's Where" keeps track of the moves of the major players; "Market Focus" summarizes the bottom line; and "Industry Observer," "Airline Observer," and "Washington Roundup" keep in perspective the industry's entire theater of operations. These are supplemented by "News Briefs," "Filter Center," and the inevitable "Aerospace Calendar."

The already excellent art and photography work keeps improving, where no improvement was thought possible. This year's photographic feats included masterpiece-portraits of the B-2 Stealth bomber, especially in the 7-24 issue, the "unveiling" of the F-117A Stealth fighter, 5-1, and breathtaking photography from the Voyager's Neptune/Triton flyby, 8-28 and 9-4. Two other unusual photographic feats were the capture by still camera, both light and infrared, of the maneuver sequence that resulted in the crash of a MiG-29 at the Paris air show, 6-12 and 6-19, and the photos of the spectacular "Pugachev's Cobra" maneuver executed by a Soviet Sukhoi Su-27, also at the Paris air show. *A WST* was quicker than the Air Force in identifying the importance for tactical combat advantage of this maneuver, which U.S. fighters cannot execute.

Finally, during July, *A WST* marked the opening of two new bureaus, one in Hong Kong headed by chief Paul Proctor, formerly the transport editor, and the other in Yokohama, Japan, headed by contributing editor Eiichiro Sekigawa. The new transport editor is Christopher P. Fotos; John D. Morrocco also was promoted, to senior military editor. Art director Moumtaz Joukhadar has left; his replacement is Robert P. McAuley. In August, the bureau chiefs of Dallas and London switched places. Carole A. Shifrin now heads the London bureau, and David A. Brown, Dallas. The able Theresa M. Foley, who was the space technology editor, left during September to strike out on her own as editor of the newly formed *Space News.*

Editor:	Donald E. Fink
Address:	1221 Avenue of the Americas New York, NY 10020 (212) 512-2000
Circulation:	143,632

Barron's

The Saturday morning business tabloid continues to be the weekend staple of the investment community. It's still the bulkiest on Wall Street too, with reams of data, consistently important Q&As with the movers and shakers, and a bit more serious market analysis than we get on the spot from the dailies. Our readers agree, though, this was an off-year for the weekly, its curmudgeonly tone of imminent disaster in the financial markets grating on the nerves of investors who, fortunately, did not see the warnings bear bitter fruit, except for the October 13 lemon. And while the reporting at *Barron's* continues to shine, it's becoming more of a seat-of-the-pants shine, particularly the investigative dispatches, with the sharp edge dulled, the editing not as tight, the material less rewarding than we've become used to over the years.

Editor Alan Abelson, who was curmudgeonly in knee pants, is now 65, approaching retirement, and has more curmudge in him than ever. His front-page "Up & Down Wall Street" column, which picks over corporate lemons, is still read carefully by the trade, because it usually moves markets Monday morning, depending on the depth of his pans. It isn't what it used to be when he was in his prime and when he did not have to oversee the total work of the publication. His patented opening sweep of the political and economic gab on the street, pointed, smart and witty, is not nearly as consistent in quality these days, his batting average down to one in four, our statisticians advise.

But his long-time editorial partner, Robert M. Bleiberg, now 66, has gotten back a bit of a spring in his step after turning most of the editorial controls to Abelson. He now simply manages his own editorial column. We had become increasingly critical of this in recent years, but noted a comeback this year. His full-page editorials have always been windy, yet the substance of his no-nonsense warnings about going to hell in a handbasket unless we repeal the New Deal was always well-shaped, with information and logic dealing with specific complaints rather than simple, general assertion. The recent problem with his material, common to senior citizens, is his penchant for opening his columns with "I told you so, back in my column of April 12, 1953, entitled, "Hell and Handbaskets." He still indulges this maddening approach, but now that he doesn't have to run the editorial staff, he spends more time reporting fresh info. The quintessential Bleiberg column this year was "Back to the Future?" 7-24, offering a critique of U.S. manned space programs as a waste of money, one he has made before, Bleiberg arguing that private funds should seek return on investment, not public pie in sky: "As Barron's time and again has pointed out, private enterprise should be mobilized whenever possible to do the job. Bureaucracy works no better in space than it does on Earth." In "Back to the Horse and Buggy?" 5-1, Bleiberg bangs around EPA's William Reilly for regulatory excesses, the environmentalists surely taking us to hell in a horse and buggy. Good and solid, even persuasive, but ponderous.

The other notable columns in *Barron's* fare about the same. Randall Forsyth had been a three star credit-market columnist until this year, dropping a notch as his material loses some of its snap. His "Current Yield" column is still the best available over the long weekend, but for new data, less so for imaginative analytics. Peter C. Du Bois, an aristocratic gent who's been with the weekly on and off for nearly thirty years, pens "The International Trader" column, which he's been writing for a mere ten. He is quickly becoming a must flip-though, if not yet a must-read: "Tax Flap Roils Canada," 8-28, is solid coverage of the damage the Canadians are doing to their tax system that we read with interest. He updates neatly on the probably-overheated art market in "Not So Pretty Picture," 12-4, as Vincent Van Gogh's *Irises,* sold for $53.9 million to Australian Alan Bond, is now in protective custody, since Bond couldn't make his payments. Shirley Hobbs Schiebla, who has been reporting the Washington regulatory scene since Abelson was in knickers, still serves up "Potomac Potpourri" now and then, but she's much better on one subject instead of these disjointed items.

It isn't only the statistics and the columns that we read *Barron's* for. The feature stories have traditionally been provocative, muckraking in the best sense of the term. We are beginning to think the material was better when Bleiberg was overseeing it, less flashy, but with more attention to detail. We saw less of Maggie Mahar this year, more of Ben Stein, the former the detail, the latter the flash. Mahar, whom we'd been impressed with in earlier years, filed only two major pieces that we saw. "The Great S&L Bailout," 9-11, with good material, was three times longer than it needed to be, reading more like Tolstoy than *Barron's,* still impressive and months ahead of a similar treatment in the *NYT.* We also got the end story to last year's 10 Best nomination on INSLAW, "Beneath Contempt," 3-21-88, and "Rogue Justice," 4-4-88. "Justice Is Done," 12-4, finds the Justice Department guilty as charged, a federal district court ruling in favor of INSLAW, a vindication of Mahar's work that we applaud. Another *Barron's* reporter who was developing nicely, Diana Henriques, jumped to the *NYT* "Business Day" at year's end.

Benjamin Stein, one of the most unusual journalists to work at this newspaper in memory, the son of Richard Nixon's chief economic advisor, a speechwriter for Pat and Tricia Nixon at one time, a lawyer for the Federal Trade Commission, a TV critic for *The Wall Street Journal,* a scriptwriter for Norman Lear, an author of several books making fun of Hollywood and its denizens, who now moonlights as Mr. Cantwell, the droning science teacher on ABC's "The Wonder Years," has for the last few years been taken under Abelson's wing. He can impress, as with "It's About Time: Shareholders Should Be Allowed to Vote," 7-17, his considerable contribution to the flurry of information over the Time-Warner-Paramount battle regarding shareholder rights. But Stein is a free spirit who believes too much in poetic license. His material on the Columbia S&L mess would have been 10 Best quality, but he couldn't resist dragging in Michael Milken, to liven up his material, we suspect, "On the Junk Heap: The Trashing of a Multi-Billion Dollar California S&L," 10-9. One of our readers wondered why he did not drag in the Pope. We wondered, too, about the editing here.

Kathryn Welling's Q&A interviews with the smart money on Wall Street remain the most admired work in the newsweekly. In "Return of the Bull," 1-2, with Merrill Lynch's chief market analyst Robert Farrell, we get great insights and perspectives from Farrell that we thought useful and smart at the time, and which in fact held up rather well. Throughout the year our readers applauded her features, at times the only applause they gave in particular issues. Then again, with its twin pillars about ready to go fishing, *Barron's* is probably on the cusp of something or other, as they say these days.

Editor:	Alan Abelson
Address:	200 Liberty Street New York, NY 10281 (201) 416-2762
Circulation:	241,890

Business Week

"There is no publication in American journalism that improved as much in 1986 over 1985 than *Business Week,* which doesn't particularly surprise us, because the magazine has had hot and cold streaks in the many years we've been following it." We wrote this, of course, in our *1987 MediaGuide.*

Once again our ups and downs with America's foremost business newsweekly had a most pleasant upswing this year after a so-so report card in last year's guide and a bummer the year before. Celebrating its 60th anniversary, *Business Week* impressed us most this year by stressing the basics. The editors had been frustrating us with attempts to call the market and political turns in its cover stories, "Can America Compete?" or "Wake Up America!" sniffing bears and seeing lean years just ahead and getting bulls instead, smelling bulls and projecting rosy scenarios on the threshold of decline. Who needs this?

We got much less of this from *BW* this year, more nose-to-the-grindstone reporting on plain vanilla business and financial news, with so much good material so well presented that it could not be ignored by us. It scored three 10 Best selections, even one in foreign correspondence, as we got the best early bead on events in China from its Hong Kong reporter, Dinah Lee. We reach for *BW* now almost as often as anything else now.

We're especially pleased *BW* is finally getting away from what we last year called its "*crise du jour*" economic cover stories. The magazine is at its best when its cover stories are exactly right on the timing, put under our noses just at the moment we're ready for them. This year was reminiscent of the vintage '86 we cited above.

We got two satisfying cover stories from John Byrne, "The New Headhunters," 2-6, and "Is Your Company Too Big?" 3-27, the former finding new twists and angles in his coverage of executive recruiters, the latter citing the benefits of smaller, more nimble corporations. Judith Dobrzynski files "Taking Charge: Corporate Directors Start to Flex Their Muscle," 7-3, on how outside directors in some big companies are starting to get tough on management which is not producing for shareholders, providing information on action at a lot of companies, many interviews and good quotes, focusing on ideas that have been implemented and work, and on ideas that haven't been tried yet, but may be useful.

Chris Welles' "America's Gambling Fever," 4-24, is timely, laying out the story exceptionally well. The evolution of the junk bond market is covered well in Christopher Farrell's "The Bills Are Coming Due," 9-11, and "Running the Biggest LBO," by Judith Dobrzynski 10-2, on RJR. *BW*'s offering of a steady dose of news-filled stories on business issues included Larry Light's definitive "Pension Power," 11-6, a 10 Best selection, recognizing what the growth in pension funds will mean to the markets, the brokers and the consumer. Jon Friedman's "Can Shearson Regain That Old Midas Touch?" 1-23, is a densely packed review of Shearson's past and future, including the 1988 earnings debacle. His "The Remaking of Merrill Lynch," 7-17, is another Wall Street company profile in the tradition of Anthony Bianco, one of *BW*'s heaters on the Wall Street beat, who is still off writing a book. Friedman scored a third time with a cover, "Sandy Weill Is Back," 12-4, which earned a 10 Best nomination.

There were a few notable covers on foreign stories, the best material coming from Asia where *BW* is strong. A follow-up to "China's Next Great Leap Could Be Backward," 5-8, Dinah Lee's prescient 10 Best selection in foreign correspondence, was "Communism in Turmoil," 6-5, offering lengthy special reports on *both* China and the Soviet Union, the first major effort on China since the pro-democracy demonstrations began some weeks before, the writer trying to come to grips with the political and economic phenomena in the two countries, providing us with reasoned analysis and in-depth background information. Also on China, "The Great Leap Backward," by Dori Jones Yang and Dinah Lee 6-19, intelligently summarizes the dynamics at the high point of the turmoil. Inside the magazine, the foreign desk practically has a monopoly on business reporting among the periodicals. Amy Borrus sharply summarizes the roots of corruption in the Japanese political system, in "Takeshita Talks Political Reform — But Doesn't Sound Convincing," 1-23, on the Recruit scandal. Stephen Baker and Elizabeth Weiner's "One Tough Hombre," 4-3, follows a good interview with Mexico's new president, Carlos Salinas, who is pictured as very tough and smart, but faced with terrible economic and political problems, with quotes from a cross section of supporters and critics within Mexico and the U.S. on whether he can remake Mexico.

It was not totally upside for *BW* this year. A cover profile of 3M, "Masters of Innovation," by Russell Mitchell 4-10, takes the easy way, using anecdotal material from their successes (Post-It notes, wet or dry sandpaper, etc.) and failures rather than presenting hard analytics. Christopher Farrell and Chris Welles' cover "Insurers Under Siege," 8-21, slips back into the doomsday mode on the insurance industry, with dramatic tales of woe, current weakness extended out indefinitely, and socialized insurance the story.

Washington coverage was weaker than it should have been, the bureau seemingly happy enough summarizing the week's news and keeping their sources comfortable. *BW* has not produced a top-ranked Washington reporter since Blanca Riemer went to Paris, hard to believe given the big stories this year at the intersection of business and politics. We thought "The Quiet Crusader," by Howard Gleckman cover 9-18, much too puffy on Treasury Sec. Brady's plans, personality and management style, missed a chance to do a really important piece on the Bush Treasury. Gleckman was closer earlier in the year with "The Trillion Dollar Man: Can Richard Darman Tame the Deficit," with Lee Walczak cover 3-13, but he doesn't see the capital gains issue emerging as part of the plan. Mike McNamee's "Greenspan's Moment of Truth," 7-31, has a headline that makes us flinch, "In Two Years as Chairman of the Federal Reserve, Alan Greenspan Has Done a Very Good Job," but the story itself is written within bounds, a bit heavy on the "soft landing" metaphor, but McNamee gets good quotes and is focused nicely. We got a good roundup on "The Seduction of Senator Alan Cranston," by Paula Dwyer *et al.* 12-4, but with 19 people in the bureau and no daily deadline pressure, *BW* should be leading on these kinds of stories, not rounding up.

BW was clearly the best in the business this year in covering technology news, though, not because it hit many home runs, but because it devoted so much manpower and horsepower to the high-tech beat, perhaps goaded by the *Forbes* decision a year earlier to open a special section on technology. John Carey, John Verity, Otis Port, William Marbach and Jeffrey Rothfeder gave the magazine a solid core that drew in material from other reporters and bureaus. William Marbach was early on HDTV with "Super Television — The High Promise — And High Risks — Of High Definition TV," 1-30, giving some to the critics of the technology. Despite myriad bylines, "Fusion in a Bottle," 5-8, is a great cover just when we looked for it, complete with readable and informative graphics, respectful and skeptical, and there's a nice balance and detachment we appreciate. In addition to the aforementioned articles, John Carey and Otis Port filed one of the best early articles we saw on cold fusion, turning seawater into energy, "Table Top Fusion Looks Less Like a Parlor Trick," 4-24, an excellent explanation of a technical subject, with a broad survey of evidence from many academic sources. John Verity's superb "A Bold Move in Mainframes," 5-29, another 10 Best selection, clearly laid out Big Blue's strategy and challenged it, and we watched IBM's stock going down for the rest of the year. Jeffrey Rothfeder knocks out "Is Nothing Private?" 9-4, a fast-paced and informative cover on how computers are loaded with data on most citizens these days, the info is sold repeatedly as individual credit histories or to provide people who are appropriate targets for marketers.

The various columns in *Business Week* vary in quality. Gene Marcial's "Inside Wall Street" column generally throws a fresh, important item the readers' way every week. Gene Koretz's "Economic Trends" continues to survey "serious economic research and less serious opinion," as we said last year, but we appreciate it no less for its citations of data we wouldn't see otherwise. The "Economic Viewpoint" column up front runs several economists of various flavors on a regular basis, of generally high quality, which we do not skip. The important "Business Outlook" column, however, by James Cooper and Kathleen Madigan, just spins its wheels, with no framework to hang its tidbits on. The back page "Editorials" remains the biggest waste of space in the magazine. We'd much prefer a bylined column from Editor William Wolman.

Our incessant complaints about the magazine's excessive use of multiple bylines may have had some effect, at last. They still dangle aimlessly like bunches of grapes at the end of most of the stories at the back of the book. But it's nice to see so many cover stories this year attributed to individual writers. For this we commend editor-in-chief Stephen B. Shepard and managing editor John A. Dierdorff. Once we squash out the grapes inside, though, we intend to press anew our complaints about the absence of any bylines at all in the table of contents.

Editor: Stephen B. Shepard

Address: 1221 Avenue of the Americas
                New York, NY 10020
                (212) 512-2000

Circulation: 900,989 North America
                1,002,572 Worldwide

Commentary

It was hardly an "End to History" thesis, but the thrust was along that kind of provocative line, when Jerry Z. Muller wrote in "The Wave of the Future," 12-88, that "The moral and political evaluation of this global movement toward capitalism has only begun. . ... Capitalism. . .increasingly looks like the wave of the future." The thesis remained an important, but unfortunately not central, focus at this monthly journal of opinion and thought. However, in this year of deep changes in the communist world, *Commentary*'s intervention into the debates seemed to examine these developments from the other side of the cusp of history. We didn't really see examination of the new dynamics and forces in Eastern and Central Europe. Instead, the faithful old big guns were brought out to deliver salvos against any notion of a process of reversibility in the East Bloc.

"Is Communism Reversible?" by Jean-Francois Revel 1-89, was one of the stronger affirmations of the skeptical view on East Bloc changes: "Despite what so many in the West appear to regard as an extremely easy process, we cannot name a single *completed* instance of Communist reversibility." Revel puts the actions of Soviet leader Mikhail Gorbachev into historical context, squeezing out any support for the view that he represents a fundamental break with Soviet history or communist ideology. Presenting *perestroika* and *glasnost* reforms as coherent with a policy of saving communism, Revel argues the case for withholding Western embraces for Gorbachev's leadership. We, of course, could have predicted Revel's thesis without even having read his essay in *Commentary,* although we can appreciate his sober disdain for the impressionistic euphoria and simple credulity of others on the issue. Yet, there's an intrinsic inflexibility in his views that mitigate against this effort being a useful guide to policy. By October, Revel had become tendentious, arguing in "Hastening the Death of Communism" that *perestroika* is effectively dead, unable to be resuscitated, with the West therefore having no stake in Gorbachev's "revolution."

"Can Poland Be Free?" by Alain Besancon 4-89, pursues a similar thesis in its examination of transformations in Poland. As Besancon analyzes the key players — Solidarity, the Communist Party, the Roman Catholic Church, Pope John Paul II — he concludes that the only player with a policy is the party. That policy is to strengthen Leninism without employing the methods of Stalin or rhetorical excess. The Pontiff's "policy" is dismissed as too transcendent for politics, and the Church's is discounted as being too satisfied with enjoyment of the perks of acceptance. Solidarity's policy is criticized as too focused on the incremental reform of socialism rather than the revolution of the entire system. Sectarian calls, at best, this perception of Solidarity reminds us that if you think big enough — total revolution — you never really have to act. Again, as a guide to policy, this *Commentary* essay also seems inflexible. From Besancon's perception of Solidarity, the organization should not have assumed any responsibility in the government — and waited instead for the collapse of the system?

"Gorbachev's Cultural Revolution," by former state department official during the Reagan administration Charles H. Fairbanks 8-89, develops two tracks on the U.S.S.R., looking at an enigmatic Mikhail Gorbachev and an apparent collapse of communism. He places Gorbachev in the context of former Communist leaders and the dynamics of Soviet politics, raising skepticism about his ability for survival and questioning the intentions of his foreign policy initiatives. The second track explores the breakdown of Soviet society and the Communist world in general: "We are not discussing the end of an administration like that of Ferdinand Marcos in the Philippines, but of an entire social system, a civilization." He soberly concludes that fundamental Soviet reforms are inevitable, but that the Cold War is hardly over. Even if his last point should be accurate, the conceptual framework of the "Cold War" is an especially inflexible handle for working the new options presented by collapse "of an entire social system."

Commentary's contributions on the crackup of the Communist world seemed far more ideologically driven than necessary. Its intervention into domestic social policy was more refreshing.

Chester Finn, a former assistant secretary of Education in the Reagan administration, produced two especially fine, provocative essays on education policy. "A Nation Still at Risk," 5-89, examines the continuing deficiencies of the U.S. education system. Denial of problems, lack of clear goals and an insufficiently concentrated focus all hurt the system, but even more damaging is the emphasis on process learning over product learning. "Thinking critically" has become more important than learning specific knowledge, with deleterious consequences. While certainly not conclusive, nor completely persuasive on all points, Finn's critique is precisely the kind of *Commentary* article that underscores the strengths of the magazine — professionals in the specific field being discussed end up debating and discussing the ideas it raises, hopefully with positive effects on policy.

Finn was used to especially good effect at the publication, a second contribution "The Campus: 'An Island Of Repression In A Sea Of Freedom,' " is a resplendent critique of ideology on campus. Unlike his former boss, Bill Bennett, who used the hell and damnation approach, Finn employs an "isn't this so ironical" tone. The result is an essay that delivers familiar arguments with a fresh insight. Particularly well done is his examination of campus policies regulating free speech, viewed in light of the Supreme Court decision on flag burning. He's very adept at positing the contradictory policies universities attempt to maintain. For example, and here the irony is well developed, in the name of "diversity," students are actually subjected to a regimented indoctrination of certain social beliefs and political philosophies, with a "diversity" of views really not presented. Interestingly, Finn finds that while students continue to abhor the concept *loco parentis* when it comes to alcohol, drugs and promiscuity, they now consent and even help bring about required courses designed to adjust attitudes toward subjects such as affirmative action and minority rights.

"Drugs and Youth," by Joseph Adelson 5-89, was a provocative contribution to the debate over this issue. Adelson effectively builds a case against *a priori* classification of all adolescents as oppositional and radically different from their parents, establishing that their career choices and religious values are quite similar to those of their parents. Adelson points out how modernist tolerance for relativism reinforces at least the early stages of drug experimentation and other hedonist behavior, all of which contradicts the lip service paid to anti-drug programs.

Commentary carried two very well-done essays dealing with civil rights policy. "Racial Preference in Court (Again)," by Terry Eastland 1-89, is an excellent, stimulating analysis of racial preference in the courts. Eastland establishes how the Reagan administration reinforced the policymaking powers of the courts in the area of civil rights. This serves as a solid background for assessing the Supreme Court review of the *City of Richmond v. Croson,* an attempt by Richmond to set aside a percentage of contracts for minority businesses. Eastland raises the issue of the broad brush vs. the narrow remedies, and whether the courts should redress societal discrimination or whether the issue should be defined more narrowly regarding discrimination in the particular governmental entity employing racial preference.

The other essay, " 'Affirmative Action:' A Worldwide Disaster," by Thomas Sowell 12-89, is the first really global assessment of this policy we've seen. Sowell's report is relentless on the failure of the programs and on their contribution to remedies worse than the problems. The evidence he assembles is powerful and the arguments are very persuasive.

Partisan politics was subjected to respectable examinations, among the most impressive Joshua Muravchik's "Why the Democrats Lost Again," 2-89. Muravchik confronts the Democrat leadership's attribution of their 1988 presidential loss to style, luck, or racism. The article provides a substantive delineation of the liberalism of Michael Dukakis, and cites the Democratic Leadership Council and the Coalition for a Democratic Majority as minorities in the Democratic party who are trying to bring the party back to a more centrist position.

Somewhat pessimistic, he concludes that the group pulling the party "down the suicidal path of the British Labour party seems stronger." Missing, though, is a confrontation of those GOP handlers and advisers who also believe that it was style, luck, and racism, rather than substantive ideas that produced the Democrat defeat.

Editor Norman Podhoretz rarely writes for *Commentary*. In 1989, we saw very few of his columns elsewhere, but he did pen one of the magazine's most provocative essays this year, "Israel: A Lamentation From the Future," 3-89. Podhoretz not only laments Israel's historical threat from without — by the Palestinians, the PLO, the Arab world — but he is also particularly saddened by the erosion of support and defense of Israel from within the Jewish community itself. The unravelling of Israel, he feels, began in earnest with the rise of Begin, the rupture of the Israeli intelligentsia from the Israeli leadership, and the weakening of the alliance between liberalism and American Judaism. The *intifada* has forced a new intensity of debate around Israel's policies, within and without the Jewish community. *Commentary* is published by the American Jewish Committee, and anytime it intervenes on policies affecting the Jewish community, the repercussions are widespread. Podhoretz's essay didn't move policy, but his lament helped keep the debate going on Israel's policy and on U.S. policy toward Israel. The letters in response to his lamentation were especially provocative, the 7-89 issue containing an especially livid rebuttal.

Another contribution on the issue of Israel and the Palestinians, "How The PLO Was Legitimized," by Jeane Kirkpatrick 7-89, is a devastating account of the how the United Nations was led over the years into equating Zionism with racism and colonialism and how the Palestine Liberation Organization was recognized as a legitimate body in its struggle against colonialism and racism. Kirkpatrick is stark in detailing how even terrorism has come to be accepted as a legitimate weapon of struggle by the oppressed, a peculiar suspension of morality employed on behalf of the horrid evil when practiced by the PLO.

Commentary never really focused on the perspective laid out at the end of the past year in "The Wave of the Future," but it did provide a thoughtful examination of the nature of democratic capitalism with Michael Novak's "Boredom, Virtue, and Democratic Capitalism," 9-89. Novak combats the view that democratic capitalism leads to excessive individualism and that it is devoid of a spiritual base. After pointing out that democratic capitalism is not the kingdom of God but rather designed to give people the space in which their souls may soar by giving freedom from oppression, Novak argues that the society imparts the opportunity for the individual to make creative choices. Novak discusses the virtues of civic responsibility, personal economic enterprise, creativity, and a certain communitarian dimension fostered by the system. Critics might ask what keeps the individual visions within the communal society communally oriented enough for the common good? Or does a system automatically produce the most effective, creative system when the natural liberties of individuals flourish? Well-written, this was one of those *Commentary* essays that leave you still thinking and rethinking after you've finished it.

The monthly's "Letters to the Editors" columns, of course, remain a particularly strong attraction of the magazine, the level of discourse and thought that appears in them no less high than the best of the contributions gracing *Commentary*. We also find that the "Books in Review" still continues its fine tradition of erudition and intelligent criticism. Still and all, it seemed for the year that *Commentary* edged a bit away from being a forum for today's most vital issues to a forum for a specific ideological approach to those vital issues.

Editor:	Norman Podhoretz
Address:	165 East 56th Street New York, NY 10022 (212) 751-4000
Circulation:	46,000

Defense News

We have lauded the Times Journal Companies, now owned by media bigfoot Federal Cities Communications Corporation, for seeing a gap (or creating a market) in defense coverage and launching the brisk, informative weekly *Defense News* in 1986. With increased familiarity and exposure to 30,000-plus defense insiders, *DN* retains an impressive niche with its overall reportage and interviews, even if the paper experienced a year of staff upheaval and expansion.

Last year we pointed out that editor Richard Barnard was wise not to tamper with success, "as *Defense News* avoided any major staff or production turnover." Not so this year. Especially missed was Patricia Gilmartin, now plying her considerable talents at *Aviation Week & Space Technology*, the Broadway showcase of defense media. Dan Beyers has also flown the coop, Daniel Marcus decided to test the think-tank waters at the Heritage Foundation, and several other reporters were reassigned. Additionally, a new crop of editors and reporters were brought on board, and the Times Journal honchos have rolled the dice with a new weekly, *Space News,* which will copy the *DN* format and style of short, fast-breaking news pieces of interest to industry professionals (Theresa Foley has been nabbed from *AWST* as editor, a fine recruit). Finally, a new European bureau was opened in Brussels, presumably to take advantage of the Euro-92 defense scene, headed by the ballyhooed Theresa Hitchens. The upshot of all this is that it was a significant transition year for the magazine. For the most part it went well, as the overall style gained confidence and maintained reliability.

As usual, the overriding strong suits of the weekly tabloid are the timeliness, accuracy, and scope of its reporting on news and trends. No weekly publication, in or out of security affairs, gets more column inches or story ideas from its reporters than *DN*. Take newcomer staff writer Myron Struck's contribution, for example, in the issue of 2-13 alone: "Former Geneva Military Assistant Backs Tower As Confirmation Stalls;" "DoD Awards To Small Businesses Declined In 1988;" "Pentagon Outlines Long-Delayed Plan For Internal Industry Procurement Controls." Not one of these filings rehashed a public affairs office press release. Peter Adams portfolio was a notable standout this year, as he consistently churned out revealing, economically written dispatches on Soviet military affairs and arms control, e.g. "Soviet Army Is Tougher, Versatile," 9-18, on pessimistic on-site evaluation of military *perestroika,* an angle completely missed by other scribes, as was his account of an important article in a Soviet military publication, "Soviet Forces Lack Skill, Top Military Official Says," 1-30.

We also were enlightened by Washington-based staff writer David Silverberg, whose entries on 1992 defense issues were often more illuminating than those from the European bureaus. Overall reporting was very strong on land warfare and naval issues, competitive with, if not comparable to, *AWST* on air and space matters, and comprehensive on congressional defense coverage (Senators and Representatives continue to be featured prominently in full-page ads with glowing testimonials). There appears to be editorial gridlock in NATO Europe, as the new Brussels bureau competes with the Paris bureau for output and story ideas; we wonder if both are needed for this audience. Coverage also seems more targeted to industry-types, less to the lay reader, perhaps as a result of reader preferences.

The FSX story was a particularly important one within this field, and it was *DN* that first reported congressional skepticism toward the deal with "U.S.-Japanese FSX Pact Inspires Suspicion and Doubt on Capitol Hill," 12-5-88. DoD was surprised by the reaction, but David Silverberg was accurately reporting on the congressional undercurrents, as with "FSX Plan Walks Shaky Ground As Crucial Senate Vote Nears," 5-15, in which the significance of the Byrd resolution threatening the deal is first addressed. Importantly, the FSX story is placed in the context of shifting relationships within the administration, with only *DN* really alert to the implications for national security of new Commerce Secretary Mosbacher's perspectives on U.S. defense trade, illustrated by "FSX Controversy: Harbinger of Tougher Defense Trade Agreements," 3-20 and "Mosbacher Forges National Security Role for Commerce," 4-17. *DN* continues to run far ahead of others on covering the tensions between DoD and Commerce.

Defense News also is the only publication that gave thorough attention to an amendment within the U.S. trade bill of 1988 that gives the president power to block mergers and acquisitions that threaten national security. Overlooked by many others is the new life the Exon-Florio amendment gives to the Committee on Foreign Investment in the United States (CFIUS). CFIUS operations are blanketed by a number of national security restrictions that keep most of its activities classified. *DN,* though, has been breaking CFIUS stories all year.

Silverberg, *DN*'s international trade reporter, works well with new Brussels office head Theresa Hitchens and with Tokyo correspondent Daniel Sneider (who also heads *The Christian Science Monitor*'s bureau in Japan), filing stories with a fine mix of reporting and analysis. The publication is well-positioned to continue its lead role in covering the defense trade field.

Unique features of *Defense News* include "Random Notes," a potpourri of defense McNuggets that range widely across people, companies, and weapons systems in brief; "One-on-One," a regular back-of-the-book interview with a defense newsmaker conducted by a staff writer or editor, usually one of the week's highlights (our favorites: a short goodbye to Cap Weinberger, 1-30; with brilliant, bipartisan strategist and arms negotiator James Woolsey, 3-27; 4-10's coup with Israeli Defense Minister Yitzhak Rabin; and bull session with once and future Presidential contender Al Gore, 7-24); and the inimitable "Special Reports," 14 in 1989, when the entire staff seems to be assigned as a reportorial SWAT team, covering a particular issue with unrivaled depth and detail, creating true collector's items for defense mavens (this year's most special specials: a two-parter on the Defense Budget, 1-16, 1-23; 3-27 on Armor Requirements; 4-17 on Military Computers; 5-15 on Vertical Flight, a great insight on the Osprey debate; and 9-11's coverage of Anti-Submarine Warfare technology). Less innovative is the "Week in Washington," which is not as tangy as *AWST*'s "Washington Roundup."

The editorial pages receive an A for effort, since in addition to the weekly musings and regular columnists we also get "Inside View," a visiting column presenting unorthodox gadflies. We are holding the pages to a higher standard, however, and therefore must take Barnard and Co. to task for some shortcomings. Even as *DN* gathers more readers and advertising, we detect some increasing anti-defense crankiness in some editorials, as well as a holier than thou tone: "The Defense Junkie's New Toy," 1-16, was an unreasoned blast at "competitive strategies," a set of doctrinal precepts designed to give defense planners some forward guidance, something the editors think is a farrago to get more goodies — unfair posturing. We also saw some brown-nosing in "Aspin's Strategic Plan Hits Target," 1-23, on the esteemed Chairman of the House Armed Services Committee, as well as some facile whacks at the B-2 bomber. The editors also caught the-end-of-history bug, adopting freewheeling disarmament proposals in "Bring Some NATO Troops Home," 3-6 and "Time For A Few Strategic Cuts," 8-7. On the plus side was the no-nonsense plug of the FSX agreement with Japan, "FSX Deal Is Good For All Involved," 2-20, and the call for NATO solidarity, "Disarray Does Not Mean Dissolution," 5-22.

Of the regular moonlighting columnists, Center for Security Policy Director Frank Gaffney continues to excel in his second year as designated strategy Cassandra (or Chicken Little, to arms control devotees); his contributions on chemical weapons, technology exports, and Soviet negotiating behavior are as salient, and sobering, as those of any big-time pundit (cf., "Chemical Weapons And Voodoo Arms Control," 1-16, "Easing Computer Export Controls A Disaster," 8-7, and especially "Soviet Union Creeps Closer To Killing SDI," 10-2). Another noticeable entry came from Harry Summers, with an impassioned jeremiad against those who would compare Afghanistan to Vietnam, "Soviet Pullout Chaotic Compared To 'Nam," 3-6. The "Inside View" segment appeared to us to be heavy on *glasnost* chic, with numerous Soviet contributions ("NATO Must Bend During Arms Talks," by Soviet General Nikolai Chevrov 4-3, and "NATO Avoiding Arms Cuts," by Oleg Grinevsky 5-29, both more propaganda than analysis), but otherwise well balanced on the ideological spectrum.

Defense News has retained its attractive, colorful format, even if the four-color photos occasionally create unusual facial hues, and the caricature art is nowhere near *Wall Street Journal* quality. The important thing is that *DN* is neither daunting nor flip; one can breeze through it quickly or pore and ponder over items of interest. The staff additions, for the most part, retain the high standards of the recently departed, and we applaud its self-promotion efforts (as Muhammad Ali once said, "If it's true, it ain't bragging"). Our gripes, slight as they are, are with the editorial pages and their tone. We hope they aren't victimized by their success, and become parochial and unctuous. And while Europe is important, how about sending some roving correspondents to Asia, Third World hotspots, and emerging arms industries in countries such as Brazil? Such moves would make *DN* a must for an even wider audience, and we think the decision-makers at Times Journal, of FCCC, should go for it.

Editor: Richard C. Barnard

Address: 6883 Commercial Drive
              Springfield, VA 22159-0400
              (703) 642-7300

Circulation: 33,000

The Economist

If we were allowed only one source of news to keep up with what's going on in the world, and it had to be a periodical, we would take the *Economist.* In business for almost two centuries, it has figured out what's important to serious consumers of news, and once a week it gets close to delivering the goods. At the same time we confess that we spend very little time reading this periodical. The fact is, with a world of information out there to choose from, not just one, *The Economist* has been sinking closer to the bottom of the pile. Which is to say, we spend little time with it when all is said and done. Think of it this way: If we had to choose one place to eat all year long and none other, we'd stay home and take pot luck, for the convenience and nourishment. With the world to choose from, time and expense no object, we'd rather choose from the varied menus of New York and Washington.

The issues of *The Economist* that washed up in bottles onto the shores of our desert island in 1989 seemed as comprehensive as ever in coverage of the world's political economy. Just as in years past, we got interesting and varied analyses that monitored new trends or defied the conventional view, as usual served up in *TE*'s unique style of cheeky British irreverence combined with authoritative certainty, which, as former part-time "American Survey" editor Michael Kinsley has observed, makes the magazine sound 100 percent sure of itself even when it isn't.

During 1989, a most uncertain year in the world political economy, *TE*'s certainty was at least comforting, even if at times we found ourselves disagreeing with its always precise prescriptions. Once again, we were unhappy with some of the economic analysis, and too often it seemed, its forays into foreign affairs relied a bit too much on conventional wisdom, although argued in a much more literate voice than we usually find in colonial publications. *TE* continued to insist that America's budget deficit was keeping interest rates high, unable to quite explain why the U.K. runs a surplus and its rates are higher. The publication also became concerned about leadership turnover, taking a bemused view of President Bush, praising his policies while voicing doubts about his abilities. It also grew increasingly critical of Margaret Thatcher as she dug in against monetary integration with Europe. The magazine (which refers to itself as a newspaper) also maintained a detached view of Mr. Gorbachev while sympathizing with his domestic plight. *TE* often viewed the political upheaval in Eastern Europe through a 1992 prism, which was helpful to us Yanks.

While other newsweeklies opened 1989 featuring a retiring Ronald Reagan or an endangered planet Earth, *The Economist* kept its priorities straight and featured Alan Greenspan on its 1-7 cover, choosing him as "Man of the New Year" in letters the color of money, but we got old hat in the story, *TE* sniggering at the Fed chairman's chances of holding down inflation and interest rates in the face of rising trade and budget deficits and little political will to do anything about them. As it turned out, *The Economist* was wrong on these matters, as it has been persistently in recent years, viewing the U.S. from Keynesian heights. In "Just Sniffing Around," 10-21, *TE* blasted some of the ill-conceived notions about the Wall Street slide of October 13, countering that equities aren't nearly as volatile as they seem, and that neither Japanese bankers nor greedy investors were to blame for the crash. It lays the blame instead on uncertainty over interest rates, exchange rates, and the dollar, but, like so many other analyses, *TE* never plugs into the Washington tug-of-war over capital gains, which is not mentioned in the Keynesian texts.

But while *The Economist* could wear us out at times with its discourses on what it perceives as the twin debt towers, we thought it did unusually deft work in arguing the merits of free trade. "Wrong About Japan," 2-25, makes the point that Japan's non-tariff barriers have decreased while EC and U.S. barriers increased between 1981 and 1986, and that Japan buys abroad as much as expected given its GNP level, lack of raw materials and high transport costs. "Tough Traders Come Last," 9-9, tries again to persuade that U.S. trade policy is contradictory, arguing here that trade retaliation by the U.S. is based on "two profound misconceptions" that (1) its country is more open to imports than other economies and that (2) its trade strategy helps U.S. companies compete internationally. Yes, but *TE* still buys into the theory that a low U.S. savings rate is much of the problem, an assertion seemingly learned *deus ex machina.*

The newspaper became tangled in its own feet more than usual this year on macro-economics. "Of Banks, Borrowers and Brady," 4-29, also asserts that banks can afford and should join the Brady Plan on Third World debt, but doesn't address why they would *want* to. In "Trade Turns Pinker," 4-29, the magazine argues that then-U.K. Chancellor of the Exchequer Nigel Lawson could restore focus from the trade deficit figures to money-GDP growth, but we're at a loss as to what good this will do. "The Myth of Managed Trade," 5-6, says, yes, managed trade offers no benefits according to classical economics, it's what all countries practice to some extent; what may be needed is a fresh look at the Uruguay Round at the GATT, *TE* suggests, and some valid policy ideas. Hmmmm. "Driving the Dollar," 5-13, does a schoolbook on theory, arguing the dollar is about valued right against the Deutschemark in terms of purchasing-power parity. "Trade Gaps Good And Bad," 10-7, is as close as we get to seeing the editors throw up their hands in frustration. We see: The strong dollar and large U.S. current-account deficit (fed by government borrowing) and the weak pound and the large U.K. current-account deficit (created by the private sector) show that the traditional links behind deficits, currencies, and government borrowing have broken down. Ah, the Keynesian framework is okay. The links are not.

The Economist seems to generally believe that regulation is a necessary evil, and that price regulation is the best kind. It recommends such a solution to reduce use of CFCs in "High Noon for the Ozone Layer," 3-4. It does not assume the danger of ozone depletion is certain, but we're advised that "wise people do not mess with UV light. . . ." (At one time we understood that mad dogs and Englishmen stand in the noonday sun!) Like most of the U.S. news media, *The Economist* took on a clear shade of green this year now that red is no longer *au courant*. Building a theme begun in 1988, in "The First Green Summit," 7-15, *TE* predicts that what defense was to the Western alliance for the last 40 years, the environment will be for next: The U.S. should impose heavy taxes on fossil fuel use; Japan should cut oil consumption, etc. In a follow-up, "Growth Can Be Green," 8-26, *TE* argues that environmentally sound economic growth doesn't necessarily mean slower growth. Yet earlier, "A Tax to Keep Cool," 5-13, advocates an EC-wide sales tax on fossil fuels to reduce their hazardous effect on the environment. In "Set the Networks Free," 3-25, *TE* argues that FCC regulation of the U.S. networks is needed so they can better compete with the global media giants.

The Economist is one of the few institutions to have mastered the knack of being serious while never taking itself too seriously. Evincing a dry Brit wit, *TE* labels George Bush "The World's New Quarterback," cover 1-21, picturing the incoming president in an over-sized football uniform with Ronald Reagan's name on it. The insouciance doesn't extend to the inside pages, though, as *TE* joins the crowd with the article "None Dare Call It Taxes," printed under the subject heading "Revenue Enhancements," and featuring pictures of Bush in profile along with a "menu of excuses for the new president" to use when he has to break his no-new-tax pledge, with each "excuse" the president's nose grows a little longer, until by the end, "For fear of finding something worse," the presidential probiscus is jutting right out into the text. Zzzzz. In the same issue *TE* also manages to skewer American excess and one of President Bush's favorite "visions" in one swipe. Writing of inauguration festivities in "Fish Story," *TE* notes that for one ceremony 40,000 flashlights were to be handed out to the people in the crowd, "Perhaps it was assumed that 39,000 were too stupid to switch them on when Mr. Bush gave the signal." What? *TE* fumbles with "Bush Bumbles," 3-11, *TE* dramatically stating that President Bush's relationship with Congress "is in ruins" and his "reputation is crumbling" following "the John Tower fiasco." "Sure-footed Bush," 9-2, has not completely crumbled six months later, so the newspaper divines that his popularity is at a high mainly because he's stayed out of trouble. Oh.

Having used the sports motif once already for President Bush, *The Economist* cast Mikhail Gorbachev in the role of a jockey, maintaining a steely gaze towards a distant finishing line that only he could see as he was thrown off his horse on the 3-11 cover, which posed the question "Must It Happen?" Inside, *TE* looks over the monumental economic problems Gorbachev faces, but concludes the only policy that could save him, price reforms (!), is growing increasingly harder to implement as conservative opposition increases. "Russia's economic mess may be too deep to scramble out of." Hailing Gorbachev as "Mikhail The Liberator," 4-8, *TE* praises him for his willingness to loosen the Soviet grip on Eastern Europe, and advises the West to "take time off from being Gorbacharmed to think about recent events in Russia's outer empire and the awkward question they raise: how to undo Europe's post-1945 division without undoing its post-1945 stability." "Wow," 9-16, took Gorbachev off his horse and put him on a surfboard, riding the crest of an incoming wave, having finally realized, *TE* said, the seriousness of his economic situation and the necessity for radical reform.

The Economist's straight news sections — "American Survey," "Asia," "International," "Europe," and "Britain" provides state-of-the-art coverage of breaking events from Berlin to Bora Bora, giving us extra details and perspectives that we don't get elsewhere, often of a government intelligence briefing quality. And, just like an intelligence service, *TE* produced the occasional clunker. "Schweik's Way," 11-4, decides the political upheaval sweeping other Eastern European nations was unlikely to spread to Czechoslovakia, despite that country's tolerant and highly educated people with a democratic tradition: "But the Czechs (unlike the Poles, for example) are not an impatient people anyway. The caricature in Jaroslav Hasek's 'Good Soldier Schweik' — long on wily timidity, short on initiative and nerve — still rings true. . . .Czechs are better at grumbling than agitating."

Stand-outs include Japanese coverage; reflecting *TE*'s growing awareness of the importance of Asia, many of it's best correspondents now seemed to be stationed there. In "What Sort of Peace In Heisei?" 1-14, the Tokyo correspondent writes: "The symbol of a new emperor, Japan's 125th, offers the occasion for one of those periodic re-creations of themselves for which the Japanese have become famous." Generally the tone of *TE*'s news coverage remains firmly pro-Western, but relatively clearheaded, even when that results in news that Washington may not like to hear. "Frustrated in their pursuit of the rebel fighters," the Central American correspondent writes in "Bloodstained El Salvador," 11-25, "Salvadoran soldiers flailed out at softer targets, picking on those they have long suspected of aiding and abetting the rebels." Coming from *TE*, it cannot be dismissed as liberal boilerplate.

"Science and Technology," was good again this year, debating subjects in a language that addressed both the scientist and the layman. "Books And Arts," keeps us abreast of the latest developments in literature, theatre, opera, classical music, and the arts in the Western world, with growing attention paid to the Communist and Third World as well. "The Critic Imprisoned," 11-25, for example, profiled Liu Xiaobo, a Chinese literary critic and hunger striker during the May demonstrations who is facing 15 years at hard labor in Qincheng prison.

After the editorials *The Economist* sometimes includes a longer 3-page piece that doesn't seem to fit anywhere else. Sometimes these articles are indeed misfits, for example, "Homage to a Liberal," 3-25, a historical tribute to free-trader John Bright who died 100 years ago. "Visitors are Good for You," 3-11, is good on the economics of tourism in developing countries. Also good: "A Singular Prime Minister," 4-29, a 10th anniversary piece on Prime Minister Margaret Thatcher; "The Slow Road To Doi Moi," 7-29, on Vietnam's economy, "It Doesn't Have To Be Like This," 9-2, a well-argued case for the legalization of drugs in America, timed to pre-empt President Bush's much ballyhooed "War on Drugs;" and "There's One Born Every Minute," 5-27, an irreverent look at the soaring market for contemporary art.

To have survived as long as it has, *The Economist* can not be hidebound very long. It has been known to shift gears suddenly over the centuries, and we have been sniffing change on the horizon. Besides, Editor Rupert Pennant-Rea promises us he will review his newspaper's analytical framework on international money in the coming year. Scanning the distance from the eastern shore of the colonies, this is a bottle we eagerly await.

Editor: Rupert Pennant-Rea

Address: 25 St. James Street
               London SW1A 1HG
               United Kingdom
               (In the U.S.) (212) 541-5730

Circulation: 161,166 North America
               380,920 Worldwide

Forbes

We said of *Forbes* last year that to describe it as "contrarian" wasn't just quite right, but as close as we could come to pegging the philosophy at the biweekly. "At the very least, it means no margin for 'knee-jerk' journalism at the business biweekly and when combined with the expertise and audacity of *Forbes* reporters, it's what helps give *Forbes* a vigor and vitality not so evident among its competition." It's because of this dynamism in the periodical that we have been reaching for *Forbes* above any other business magazine. Its closest competition, *BusinessWeek,* which has boom years and busts, got "boomy" this year and came very close to even with Malcolm's biweekly in our esteem. We love the competition, but so do the Forbes's.

The 1990s promise great shoot-outs between these two, especially testing the skills and strategems of Malcolm Jr., known universally as Steve. The old order is ending with Dad already retired from the day-to-day operations. A bigger question involves the eventual departure of editor James W. Michaels, one of the great editors of the era, getting close to his gold watch or Faberge egg, or whatever Malcolm is handing out these days. The deck is already shuffling. Sheldon Zalaznick retired as managing editor, succeeded by his deputy, Lawrence Minard. Edwin A. Finn Jr., 35, moved from senior editor to the post of assistant managing editor, following Christopher Byron's defection to *New York* to become "The Bottom Line" columnist. Jean A. Briggs also moves into an assistant managing editor position. Joe Queenan, lately of *Barron's,* came aboard as a senior editor.

Consistently sharp and trenchant, the articles by the contract players well illustrate the magazine's *modis operandi*. It demonstrates *Forbes'* willingness to bring fresh opinions from different sources to flavor its pages. George Gilder, under a second year of a 2-year contract, is probably mismatched, not happy harnessed to deadlines, but we appreciated "IBM-TV?" 2-20. A 10 Best selection, his tough questioning of high-definition technology as the wave of the future is insightful and keenly honed, dramatically altering thinking in Washington and Silicon Valley. An end-of-year cover by Warren Brookes, "The Global Warming Panic: A Classic Case of Overreaction," 12-25, is an adept debunking of the greenhouse effect, an important follow-up to our 10 Best selection for his acid rain series. Languishing at *Fortune* for several months before Marshall Loeb passed it up, Brookes' treatise swooshed to the *Forbes* cover as soon as Steve Forbes got his hands on it.

The outside contributors are only the tip of the iceberg of talent Michaels has assembled at the magazine. Although only Gilder scored with a 10 Best selection, *Forbes* had as many nominations as any magazine reviewed, an indication of the consistent quality of the work there. Both our editors and theirs cite Laura Saunders for her tax column on home mortgages, provocative and informative with "House-Hunting? Read This First," 3-20: "People shopping for a house assume there will always be a home mortgage interest deduction. . .because there always has been one. That could be a big mistake." Jerry Flint goes into overdrive in covering the auto industry. Gretchen Morgenson pens deft analyses of companies and industries, particularly sharp in the cover "How Different Can a $17 Lipstick Be From a $3 Version?" 9-18, on the changing face of the cosmetic industry. She offers unadorned explanations for sluggish growth: The consumer is simply getting smarter and better informed as the FDA is involved in debunking much of the miracle creams that promise youthful skin, and the industry is ignoring the demographic situation, playing to youth rather than the aging female population, a market that would benefit.

Peter Brimelow, a longtime veteran of financial journalism, is happiest when he is advancing startling, provocative ideas or innovations, or profiling those who do. His "How Do You Cure Injelitance?" 8-7, is a very lively sojourn with C. Northcote Parkinson of Parkinson's Law fame, earning a 10 Best nomination from his editors. Howard Rudnitsky, a 25-year career man at *Forbes,* constantly commands our attention with his flexibility and workmanlike dispatch. He sorts out how struggling S&Ls may ruin what little is left of themselves by offering low "teaser-rate" adjustable rate mortgages, in "Digging Their Own Graves?" 5-29, skillfully arguing that all the best ideas for saving these sick institutions always backfire simply because, as his last sentence, "Heads [S&Ls] win, tails the government pays."

From the bureaus, Lisa Gubernick continues to provide solid coverage of the entertainment industry, choosing topics we might not see in other business periodicals, such as her look at Freddy Krueger's parent company, New Line Cinema, and its founder Robert Shaye, " 'It's Great for a Date,' " 2-6. Her boss, West Coast bureau manager Marc Beauchamp, handles the environmental topics, more of an odd-job craftsman. Steve Weiner in Chicago is adept at making a story come to life, but this year there seemed to be less vitality from him than we'd seen before. Smart in listing the problems Mark & Spencer Plc. faces in the U.S. market, purchasing Brooks Brothers and New Jersey's Kings Supermarkets chain, "Low Marks, Few Sparks," 9-18 he offers few solutions, although he details the company's history well enough. Washington bureau manager Howard Banks served up the usual statistics and usually harmless observations through the smoke, evincing only modest daring for *Forbes,* though with as much boldness as we saw from some of the other Washington correspondents.

The periodical also assigns its reporters to more idiosyncratic beats. Richard L. Stern is the only detective-reporter we know of; we picture him in Humphrey Bogart garb, consistently on the lookout for corporate and stock fraud deals, frequently fingering dastardly crooks. A wise warning to Wall Street and investors, he and co-author Marc Beauchamp relate the story of Traditional Industries, which sells camera packages of questionable value while sporting impressive numbers due to creative accounting measures, "The Facts Behind the Figures," 8-21.

James Cook, executive editor, deals almost exclusively with energy and environmentally-related companies, the beat of the '90s in the '80s. Dyan Machan, who knocked us out last year with a piece about a McDonald's restaurant inspector, "Great Hash Browns, But Watch Those Biscuits," 9-19-88, was ever-so-slightly-off in her "Careers" beat this year, fluffy in spots. "Pepperidge Farm's Doughboy," 3-20, a human interest piece about the middle manager who oversees cookie development at Pepperidge Farm, isn't very nutritional to the brain but it does provide filler. She's more substantive in "On a Roll with the Man from G.E." 4-17, detailing the professional background of Robert Wright, President of NBC, and the challenges he faces at the network. Deirdre Fanning's "On the Dockets" reports are credible enough, one of the few business magazine reporters to deal exclusively with corporate law, written for the layman, not the lawyer.

The magazine pumped up a much-heralded technology section last year, but it is still in a shake-down stage. So far it has produced here and there ahead of the pack, but mostly seems to have gotten the juices running of the *Business Week* high-tech team, which really ginned up this year. We do love competition. Esther Dyson, "Random Access" columnist, who publishes her own newsletter *Release 1.0* for computer junkies, read less like analytics and more like computer program reviews more readily available in *PC Magazine.* A good idea, but one that hasn't yet borne fruit.

The capable staff at *Forbes* is broadly based, spread all over the planet, and although they don't have a great number of foreign bureaus, and don't yet have a Moscow bureau, as *Business Week* does, they manage to cover the globe adequately. Esther Dyson ponders the question of Soviet computer know-how and compatibility and the potential effect on *perestroika* in "Three Weeks That Shook My World," cover 6-12. After a slow start around some dubious pop sociology about hunter-gatherers, she shows the early progress that is being made and the mindboggling obstacles to be overcome, but the interesting material is buried in a less than world-shaking presentation.

London-based Peter Fuhrman keeps the Soviet Union in his sights from his Europe bureau on a regular basis. "Moscow's Debt Crisis," 5-29, paints a dire picture of the East Bloc's own Third World debt plight. Soviet clients have chalked up huge debts, buying from the Bloc on credit not hard currency, with little intention of repayment. Fuhrman divides the specific situations, noting that the U.S.S.R. retains some leverage since these countries remain dependent on it as their major arms supplier. Also in London, bureau manager John Marcom Jr. racks up an impressive year, his smart and savvy "Welcome to Hauppauge, the World's Next Financial Capital," 10-30, everything we wanted to know about Reuters, the news and financial information business, as the electronic financial information biz booms, a 10 Best nomination from his editors. On the other side of the earth, Andrew Tanzer works the East Asia beat, putting Taiwan into focus during the year. He works the theme of authoritarian government being undermined by economic success in "Taiwan's Long March To Democracy," 4-3. There is a fair amount of new economic detail here, and Tanzer brings out Taiwan's disposition to accommodate U.S. pressure, even to the point of a 45% revaluation of their currency over the last three years when U.S. trade negotiators leaned on the country.

The infrequent misfire does occur, particularly with the acerbic Joe Queenan, whose wickedly irreverent wit seems misplaced in the biweekly, and may be more appropriate in *The American Spectator,* where he contributes. It was the misfortunate Queenan who penned "Straight Talk About AIDS," 6-26, an efficient update on Michael Fumento's theses on the spread of the disease in the heterosexual community. Despite the cynical tone that is Queenan's trademark, AIDS activists took the article to mean that the reporter, and *Forbes,* agreed with Fumento, and began to picket the Forbes Building in Manhattan in protest. A flustered Malcolm Forbes Sr. not only apologized in the next "Fact and Comment," he also presented information from the Center for Disease Control and different studies which contradict the theorems put forth in Fumento's book, *The Politics of AIDS,* the only time we'd ever seen him debunk an article in one of his own publications. We were also unimpressed by Phyllis Berman's "The Man Behind Chanel," cover 4-3, which we found dry and overbearing.

The columns peppered throughout the magazine add variety and flavor. Michael Novak, conservative philosopher and theologian, pens an unlikely column that fits in surprisingly well, covering "The Larger Context." Consistent in his efforts to bring other dimensions to bear into what are often treated as one-dimensional issues, we get an insightful distinction from Novak between European and American attitudes regarding capitalism's moral worth in "How About Obscene Losses?" 3-6. We all assumed publisher Caspar Weinberger's "Commentary on Events at Home and Abroad" would be boilerplate. But Reagan's Pentagon chief was a newspaperman back in his salad days, and his material ain't bad, covering a broad spectrum of topics. Advising Reaganite caution he delightfully opens "Can We Trust This Nice Mr. Gorbachev?" 1-9, with sagacious counsel: "Is it ungracious, churlish, unwarranted or any of the above to examine very carefully, perhaps even in the mouth, Mr. Gorbachev's recent gift horse? Possibly. But since much of the security of the U.S., and indeed the West, could depend on our attitude and response to the Gorbachev proposal, let us risk being all of the above."

Let there be no doubt about it, though. The success of the magazine in the last decade especially has been the combination of Malcolm Sr. and editor Michaels, together brewing just the right mix for the tastes of this new entrepreneurial age, value added for the investment community in every issue. The bread and butter at *Forbes* are the two-page quick-and-dirty business stories, public companies large and small examined for random information that will hit the bottom line sooner or later. Will Steve Forbes and Michaels' successor brew the right mix? Will there be a clean passing of the baton? Will *Business Week* keep on booming? And what of *Fortune,* the rechristened *Financial World,* and *Barron's*? My, oh my, how we do love competition.

Editor: James W. Michaels

Address: 60 Fifth Avenue
               New York, NY 10011
               (212) 620-2200

Circulation: 741,731

Foreign Affairs

Although there continues to be a rigorous sense of history at *Foreign Affairs,* the question remains: Which period of history is the venerable foreign policy journal attempting to address? There's a serious imbalance with the way in which *FA* attempts to shape elite opinion and views on major issues of political economy. The journal produced one of the 10 Best reports this year, Robert Kaiser's "The U.S.S.R. in Decline," Winter 1988/89, but it also produced some the year's worst articles. We begin with *FA*'s treatment of economic policy, because here we are most starkly presented with another question — how has the publication become so woefully bogged down in a view of political economy that has been rendered obsolete by real events? *FA* began the year still looking backward, its contributions regarding economic policy still waging battles the outcomes of which had already been decided. *FA*'s outlook regarding the framework for discussion of economic policy seemed to be heavily weighed down by, among other things, an attachment to the thesis of America's decline as purported by Professor Paul Kennedy in 1988. The contributions were stale, tendentious litanies on behalf of tiresome themes.

What, we are compelled to ask, is the fresh, insightful information or perspective in Felix Rohatyn's "America's Economic Dependence," which appeared in the "America And The World, 1988/89" issue of *Foreign Affairs*? The senior partner in the investment firm of Lazard Freres & Company displays the limits of a global model heavily shaped by and dependent upon the outlook of a financier when he inveighs that ". . .the real power in the world is coming to consist of surplus capital combined with national self-discipline, advanced technology and superior education." Yet, that, in and of itself, is tolerable. What isn't, though, is the cavalier disregard of the evidence when it contradicts his thesis. In procrustean fashion, Mr. Rohatyn attempts some sleight of hand, albeit clumsily, when he advises that "This [U.S.] addiction to debt, fueled in the 1980s by financial deregulation, supply-side economics and stock market speculation, has occurred in the government sector as well as in the private sector. . ." It was, he continues, "Sky-high interest rates in the early 1980s, driven by the Federal Reserve's fight against inflation, [that] pushed the dollar up by fifty percent and caused a recession." But his model compels him to contradict what he's just acknowledged, so he adds that "The resulting budget deficit, *caused* [our italics] by tax cuts and high defense spending, resulted in a typical 'Keynesian' recovery which, because of the high dollar, sucked in huge amounts of imports, creating an ever larger trade deficit."

This scenario still enjoys some popularity, among critics of the Reagan recovery, but little credibility. So why did the editors find Mr. Rohatyn's account of utility? We also noted that his bugaboo regarding "foreign ownership of U.S. business" as another area for major concern overtly alarmist and distorted. For a well-honed rebuttal of this thesis, see "The New Bogeyman: Foreign Direct Investment," by Jahangir Amuzegar in *SAIS Review,* Summer/Fall, 1989.

Mr. Rohatyn has to present a view of global economy at variance with the real state of things in order to advance his prescriptions. And here we discover an identity between his statist approach and the global model with which *FA* appears most comfortable, which appears thusly: The U.S. won't be shaping global policy in the 21st century *unless* it reorganizes its domestic economic affairs along the national planning strategies.

In case we missed Mr. Rohatyn's message about making hard economic choices, *FA* discharges the other barrel of the scattergun in its lead feature for the Winter 1988/89 issue, "The Economy After Reagan," by C. Michael Aho, Director of Economic Studies at the Council of Foreign Relations and Marc Levinson, editorial director of *The Journal of Commerce.* These authors advise that "due largely to U.S. *domestic* economic policies, the world economy remains seriously out of balance." Incredibly, they assert that "Much of the prosperity of the past six years. . .is due to the federal government's persistently spending more than it was taking in by a very wide margin." Of course, the solution lies along the road of "a sustained program of budget reductions and tax increases over a four-year period." And, "the pain of deficit-cutting will have to be spread equitably among the American people." Reduce consumption, raise "productive" investment, and combine deficit reduction with a less restrictive monetary policy. Certainly not reticent in doling out painful medicine, they add "an increase of one or two percent in marginal personal income tax rates may be unavoidable. Or, alternately, the indexing of personal income taxes could be postponed."

Additionally, "moving to a formal system designed to keep exchange rates within specified levels is neither a realistic nor a desirable step during the next few years." These "agreements. . .unfortunately have kept the U.S. currency from falling further despite the continued large U.S. trade deficit." In fact, they advise, "The value of the dollar is not and should not be the U.S. government's principal economic concern." If Democratic presidential contenders continue to read *FA* for inspiration, why should we be surprised that the White House eludes them. These "dead scrolls" are reminiscent of GOP national platforms during the Roosevelt years, which repeated calls for strict adherence to the Smoot-Hawley Tariff Act.

"Must We Retrench?" by Francis M. Bator, Spring, also addresses the "mistaken sense of economic weakness" in the U.S. "The hypothesis that the American economy is so over-stretched that we must curtail our commitments abroad or suffer economic decline at home. . .is odd even on its face." He goes on to comment that "By reducing its transfer payments and raising taxes, and thereby reducing personal disposable income, it [the federal government] can make personal consumption go down. By adopting the right mix of taxes and transfers the government can make sure that it squeezes the consumption share of the non-poor. Even relative to ambitious targets for domestic investment and net exports, we are far from having reached the technical limits of taxable capacity."

But, "the right question in a prescriptive analysis is not whether we will reduce the consumption share, but whether we *should*." "Failing a dramatic breakthrough in arms control, most of the cuts to make room for the investment [in defense areas] will have to come from personal consumption." After sin, energy and pollution taxes, Bator "would start by raising personal income taxes, but also, perhaps by 1992-93, phase in some kind of national sales tax, taking care to avoid damage to the poor. When thinking about the total tax burden we should remember that, in relation to national income, we are taxed much less than any other Western industrial nation."

In the lead feature of the "America And The World, 1988/89" issue, "Reagan's Foreign Policy," Robert W. Tucker concludes with a similarly sour theme: "Thus the principal Reagan legacy in foreign policy may well have been just this: that the nation's 40th president transformed what had been a disposition not to pay for the American position in the world into something close to a fixed resolve not to do so. If there is a consensus today in foreign policy, this must be regarded as its central tenet. A disposition to want more than the nation was willing to pay for has of course characterized American policy since the beginning of the postwar period. It may be seen, for example, in the recurring assumption that economic growth rather than increased taxation would provide the means for meeting increased military expenditures. . ..The most unfortunate feature of the Reagan presidency, as it relates to foreign policy, has been the president's persistent refusal — or perhaps his inability — to confront the public with the simple truths governing the nation's position."

The imbalance is dramatic when the above-mentioned analyses are compared to the whole of the efforts *FA* put into getting its arms around developments in the Communist bloc. Here the publication excelled. The best political perspective we saw as the year opened on whither Gorbachev's *perestroika* was "The U.S.S.R. in Decline," by former *Washington Post* Moscow bureau chief and then-*Post* assistant managing editor Robert Kaiser, Winter 1988-89. A 10 Best selection, the essay was both gloomy and upbeat, fearful of the difficulties Gorbachev faces in attempting reform, but then, "the entire Gorbachev phenomenon was hard to imagine before it happened. The most dramatic political experiment of the century is collapsing before our eyes — slowly, but certainly."

The "America and the World, 1988/89" issue was particularly weighty with contributions regarding the Communist bloc. Charles Gati's "Eastern Europe" still posed the relationship of forces there as one in which some progress will continue in Hungary and Poland while East Germany, Czechoslovakia, Bulgaria, and Romania resist any movement for reform. Gorbachev is portrayed as relatively impotent to effect any difference here. Gati's proposals for U.S. policy direction are very similar to those made by Former President Richard Nixon in "American Foreign Policy: The Bush Agenda," in the same issue, among them: continue the policy of differentiation and put Eastern Europe on the U.S.-Soviet agenda. "Gorbachev's New Thinking" by David Halloway and "The Revolution In Soviet Foreign Policy" by Robert Legvold, both from the "America and the World" issue, draw similar conclusions about the opportunities for a new relationship between the superpowers, making the case that Gorbachev's U.S.S.R. is undergoing a conceptual revolution in its attitudes toward the non-communist world.

The editors also deserve credit for providing a forum to former U.S. Ambassador to Japan, Mike Mansfield. His "The U.S. and Japan: Sharing Our Destinies," Spring, was an important and timely response to the worsening Japan-U.S. relationship: "The most important bilateral relationship in the world today is that between the United States and Japan. . .I am concerned that emotional responses will erode the goodwill in both Japan and the United States." Mansfield argues that the impressive progress being made in Japan on the issue of market access is not being sufficiently acknowledged by the United States.

FA can always rely on heavy guns to appear among its contributors. In addition to former President Nixon, there were contributions from Valery Giscard d'Estaing and Henry Kissinger, all on East-West relations which was the focus of the Summer issue. Some perspectives here were rendered obsolete by the astounding and fast-moving developments this year in the East Bloc. This was certainly the case with "Central European Security" by Henry Owen and Edward C. Meyer, Summer, in which their discussion on changing security relationships, the tasks and perspectives of NATO, and the existence still in Central Europe of the threat of war, all have to be re-examined in light of the transformations. We're not faulting *FA* on this. After all, even weekly publications had their share of obsolete or moot analytical features given the rapid pace of developments this year.

"China's Big Chill," Fall, by former U.S. Ambassador Winston Lord, is a sober, thoughtful assessment of the post-Tiananmen Square relationship between the U.S. and China. Lord takes the broad view, putting Sino-American relations into strategic and bilateral context, and he strongly disagrees with conventional wisdom's assertion that strategic factors in the Sino-American relationship are dwindling in importance. Without in any way backing off from a critical appraisal of the regime's behavior, he nonetheless counsels against any rupture in the U.S.-China relationship.

Among the smaller caliber material, we found "El Salvador's Forgotten War" by James LeMoyne, Summer, of interest only to the degree that it confirmed the uncontrolled bias he harbored against the ARENA party when he was *The New York Times* San Salvador bureau chief.

The recent events in Eastern and Central Europe have shaken world views everywhere, certainly including that of the Council of Foreign Relations which publishes *Foreign Affairs*. Pleased overall with its assessments of developments in the U.S.S.R. this year, we're eager to see how *FA* responds next year to the developments in Central Europe.

Editor:	William G. Hyland
Address:	58 East 68th Street
	New York, NY 10021
	(212) 734-0400
Circulation:	107,500

Foreign Policy

"Does the United States need a new foreign policy? The answer is yes." Thusly, *Foreign Affairs* editor William G. Hyland opens his contribution in *Foreign Policy* magazine, "Setting Global Priorities," Winter 1988-89. This was one of the more thoughtful efforts on foreign policy we saw during the year. Hyland makes a reasonable case that, even though the foundation of U.S. policy is solid, "the threat to American national security is changing and the superstructure of U.S. policy, which was erected over the past 40 years in response to that threat, is collapsing."

Hyland's perspective is essentially a call for retrenchment. Still, he clouds some of the focus by asserting a bit too easily what hasn't been verified, but what seems to be an article of faith at *FP* as well as at the journal he edits, *FA*: "the public's obvious concern over America's waning economic influence and what this portends for the well-being of the average citizen." While *The National Interest* was establishing Francis Fukuyama's thesis on "The End of History" as the most important topic within foreign policy circles, *FP* and *FA* were still absorbed with the 1988 thesis of Prof. Paul Kennedy — the decline of America.

FP editor Charles William Maynes weaves elements of Kennedy's thesis into his contribution, "Coping With the '90s," Spring. Kennedy and others did help open up an important debate in the U.S. — "Can America afford the international costs of its traditional postwar foreign policy?" — and Maynes attempts to outline the challenges to the future this presents. The effort is extremely uneven, though, especially as Maynes moves onto an assessment of what economic policies the U.S. ought to advance (since "in the 1990s...economic issues will rival political issues as America's number one diplomatic priority"). He importantly locates, as one of the pillars upon which U.S. strength was based, the Bretton Woods system of fixed exchange rates. But he confuses what the embrace of the regime of floating exchange rates meant, advancing it as meaning that "the marketplace rather than senior American officials began to dominate the world's monetary system." The essay isn't a revival of Club of Rome "limits to growth" perspectives, but it does share with them a narrow view of options and no appreciation of the global applicability of the dynamics at the heart of America's sustained, continued economic expansion.

The same issue was probably *FP*'s weakest all year. "America's High-Tech Decline," by Charles H. Ferguson suggests that the "United States is being gradually but pervasively eclipsed by Japan." Frankly, there was little in this essay we haven't seen presented elsewhere. The "details" of the alleged high-tech decline are less important than the general thesis — Japan is a menacing threat, but the U.S. can remain a superpower in the face of Japan's ascendancy if it adopts a variation of industrial policy. Old stuff.

FP also provided a forum for unverified alarms about "Our Endangered Earth" in this issue. "Climate Chaos," by David A. Wirth, asserts the apocalyptical view on global warming. "The international community," Wirth advises, "cannot afford to continue to delay elevating the greenhouse effect to the top of the foreign-policy agenda." It's a shame that *FP*'s editors decided to take as given that debate on this issue is closed, thereby giving us only one point of view, when the reality is that an intense debate continues over the validity of the greenhouse effect. They also need to be faulted for the other unsatisfying essay in this section, "Environment and Security" by Norman Myers. Again, our criticism here is that *FP* employs such narrow, constricted, and frequently discredited conventional views on issues. For example, maldistribution of land, unjust distribution of economic and political power, and population growth are trotted out by Myers as reasons for El Salvador's increasing inability to feed itself. This sounds too much like the U.S. formula for Saigon in 1961.

This was also the issue in which *FP* provided a forum for Farabundo Marti National Liberation Front *commandante* Joaquin Villalobos. That the guerrilla leader so desired to have his article "A Democratic Revolution For El Salvador" appear in an American journal was naively cited as a sign of the ferment that is taking place within the communist world. No response from the democratically elected government of El Salvador appeared in *FP*. But *FP* seemed not to appreciate either scholarship or unbiased journalism when it came to El Salvador. Sam Dillon's "Dateline El Salvador: Crisis Renewed," Winter 1988-89, is an hysterical warning about the likelihood that ARENA will win the presidency. ARENA is characterized as having "terrorists tendencies," and the party's founder, Roberto D'Aubuisson, is identified as having "a clear terrorist record." Dillon, incidentally, is the *Miami Herald*'s Central America bureau chief.

Still, we did find some very stimulating and important essays in *FP*. "Crossing The European Divide," Summer, by Corneliu Bogdan a retired Romanian diplomat, was especially provocative. The lead itself immediately arrests our attention: "Eastern Europe today. . . .is the region undergoing the fastest social change on the Continent." Bogdan argues that the bi-polar approach to Eastern Europe (which he means to include Central Europe and the Balkans) that has marked the post-war years has to be replaced by a multi-polar approach, now that the post-war era is drawing to a close. Bogdan suggests that the real question is not how far reforms in the Soviet Union will go nor whether the West should help Gorbachev. Instead he asks "Can the new situation be used to strengthen the structure of peace, cooperation, and freedom in the world, or in Europe, so as to move more forcefully toward dissolving the Continent's division?" His answer is "yes," a deft mixture of vision and pragmatism. This is an example of what *FP* excels at — bringing to our attention the elevated analytic of a central issue in foreign policy, an analytic the premise of which we may not accept, but which nonetheless challenges our view and at least forces us to rethink the perspective.

John Fincher's "Zhao's Fall, China's Loss," Fall, was one of the best analytics we read on the events in China. Fincher, an Australian university professor, writes authoritatively on both the behind-the-scenes maneuvering and the larger social and political forces that culminated in last spring's democracy movement and resulting crackdown by the regime. Noting that China's economic reforms over the past 12 years have added to the urban population while also creating a "'circulating' population" that moves between city and farm Fincher writes: "Thus it seems that China has evolved into a tripartite society run by a tripartite party-state-army political system, a fact that foreign policy makers and observers will have to bear in mind." A shortcoming, though, was the insufficient development of the role inflation played in exacerbating crises throughout the country.

"Nouveau Law And Foreign Policy," by David J. Scheffer Fall, was another provocative article: "The Bush administration remains perched atop a legal time bomb that has been ticking away since the end of the Reagan era: the practice of justifying foreign policy by reinterpreting treaties and national security laws." Scheffer, a former staff consultant for the House Foreign Affairs Committee, savages the "Sofaer Doctrine" of reinterpretation that was created during the SDI debate. While Scheffer appears to be operating from the mindset that occasionally romanticizes the "Rule of Law" (especially the rule of international law), the picture he draws of political opportunism, legal cynicism, and Catch-22 logic is powerful. It could even grab the attention of the Bush administration, giving it reason to rethink the "reinterpretation policy" before submitting a future START or conventional arms reduction treaty to the Senate.

Richard H. Ullman's "The Covert French Connection," Summer, created considerable stir, both here and abroad. Ullman traces twenty years of covert American assistance to the French nuclear weapons program, assistance which contradicted the public policy of both nations but which was agreed upon and carried out by the highest levels of government. Ullman touches on the political and strategic considerations which drove both sides, through administrations of the left and right, along with the logistics of the cooperation itself. Since this article is apparently extracted from a forthcoming book on the relationship between American, British, and French nuclear forces some points are underdeveloped and others are not touched on at all, but the article stands on its own as a valuable lesson in power politics.

FP's weakest material on geopolitical strategy continues to be its economic analytics. "Selling Off America," Fall, by *FP* associate editor Thomas Olmstead, is Old Guardist moaning and groaning about an America that lives beyond its means. The flow of foreign investment is reduced simply to Americans being willing to trade ownership of assets for that privilege. The article reeks of misinformation.

Editor:	Charles William Maynes
Address:	11 DuPont Circle, NW
	Washington, DC 20036
	(202) 797-6420
Circulation:	29,000

Fortune

Fortune suffered through a disappointing year in 1989, made all the more painful because of the encouraging signs we applauded in last year's *MediaGuide*. After spending the better part of the decade trying to regain its sense of mission, *Fortune* seemed posed for a comeback in 1989. We had high expectations for a milestone year. Instead, it was a year of sliding backwards, as a journalistic Gresham's Law took hold and the bad *Fortune* chased out the good. Overshadowing everything was the Time-Warner merger and Paramount's takeover bid, which put *Fortune* Editor Marshall Loeb in the uncomfortable position of trying to cover his parent company in the biggest business story of the summer. But even allowing for this conflict, *Fortune*'s coverage of the takeover battle fell far short of objective standards.

Fortune was cheering for the home team, from its opening salvo at Paramount's CEO (Bill Saporito opens "First Salvos in the Fight for Time," 7-3, with "Martin S. Davis knows a good business strategy when he steals one") to its piece celebrating the decisive Delaware court ruling in August (Saporito's "A Legal Victory For The Long Term," 8-24). Later came an "Other Voices" opinion piece written by a sympathetic investment banker, 8-28, that endorsed the position of Time-Warner management — a glaring error, since the magazine should have been bending over backwards to print an opposing point of view. *Fortune*'s partisanship was made even more shameless by its haughty, holier-than-thou First Amendment stance: "As the country's largest magazine publisher, Time [Inc.] considers its editorial independence a national trust not to be trifled with for mere coin."

In November, the magazine tried to make belated amends for its biased coverage with a 16-page opus, "The Inside Story of Time Warner," 11-20, that was ostensibly an evenhanded account of the deal. "Inside Story" did contain material that was unflattering to Time-Warner management, but the article was gratuitous, so long after the fact, it appeared to have been done as a sop to *Fortune*'s editorial conscience. The November article was flawed, too, because Paramount's Davis declined to be interviewed for it — an understandable decision on Davis' part, given *Fortune*'s behavior over the summer. We can only imagine Davis' reaction when reading this pyromanaical description of himself in the second paragraph of "Inside Story:" "What he [Davis] did was waltz by Time's dream house with a pail of gasoline and a flame thrower, torching the company's long-planned merger with Warner."

Yet another embarrassment occurred at *Fortune* late in the year when *Forbes* led its 12-25 cover with "The Global Warming Panic: A Classic Case of Overreaction," by Warren T. Brookes. The piece had originally been written for *Fortune,* which had called Brookes during the summer, after his debunking an ABC News acid-rain hoax in *The Washington Times,* and asked him to do an article for the magazine. Brookes delivered the "Global Warming Panic" to *Fortune* by Labor Day. In November, it still had not appeared and was not scheduled. The editors apparently had forgotten that *Time*'s "Man of the Year" cover story of the previous January had been the Planet Earth, a no-holds-barred celebration of the environmental agenda, including a medium panic over global warming. It would not do for *Fortune* to debunk *Time*. The piece, already paid for, was returned to Brookes, who was soon admiring it on the cover of *Forbes*. Editor Loeb, a good company man, hunkered down a bit more.

The takeover dust had barely settled when *Fortune* lobbed out the worst cover story of the year by a major business publication: "CEO's Second Wives," 8-28. Written by Julie Connelly and edited by Walter Kiechel, the article was a trashy wallow which pondered, among other things, whether young wives ("hot tomatoes") were more sexually pleasing to their CEO husbands than older wives. So bizarre was this cover, and such a lapse in judgment did it represent, that we pondered for a moment if a lampoon issue of the magazine had been foisted on us. It was the real thing. Kiechel continues to tackle some of the lighter topics, touting conventional management techniques, although his yuppie treatise "The Workaholic Generation," 4-10, was nominated for our 10 Best by his editors.

In its less salacious business coverage, the magazine continued writing gushy tributes to big company CEOs, a failing we complained about last year. Typical in 1989 was a fawning sidebar on the new chairman of Pacific Telesis, Nancy J. Perry's "Pacific Telesis: 'Noon on a Sunny Day,' " as she tells us "Whether he is trying to sink a putt, return a volley, or close a customer account, he hates to lose." Or this description of John Young, "Hewlett-Packard's Whip Cracker," 2-13: "He reminds many of a fighter pilot — cool, competent, confident. He's cheerful and wants to be liked; new parents at Hewlett-Packard receive a baby blanket from him."

A strange Stratford Sherman cover story on General Electric's Jack Welch dwelled on the man's close relationship with his mother and attempted to interpret GE's strategy in that maternal light, "Inside the Mind of Jack Welch," 3-27. The profiles of cities were much better. Myron Magnet turns in "How Business Bosses Saved a Sick City," 3-27, on Cleveland's turnaround, that's sharp on the problems and solutions. Kenneth Labich's "The Best Cities for Business," 10-23, a 10 Best nomination from the eds at the biweekly, is surprisingly well rounded, going far beyond the standard business list we'd expected. A companion, "Fortune's Top Ten Cities," by David Kirkpatrick, was also suggested.

We still welcomed the bylines of old reliables like Carol Loomis on corporate finance and Gene Bylinsky on science. Dan Seligman's irrepressible "Keeping Up" column continued to inform and entertain, although he was lighter this year than ever before. The other bright spots of the year mostly came from newcomers. Carla Rapoport, who joined in late 1988 from the Tokyo bureau of London's *Financial Times,* contributed even-handed and assured pieces on Japan that refreshingly countered the "Japan Invasion!" tone that *Fortune* often strikes. Rapoport's work earned our highest rating this year, the magazine's first four-star reporter in the five years we have been compiling these guides. She also earned a 10 Best selection for "Ready, Set, Sell — Japan is Buying," 9-11, on the revolution in retailing there.

Two *Wall Street Journal* reporters arrived during 1989 with welcome results. Brenton Schlender, of the *Journal*'s San Francisco bureau, had gems in consecutive issues on the logjam in software programming, "How to Break the Software Logjam," 9-25, and the IBM-Microsoft-Next computer rivalry, "How Steve Jobs Linked Up with IBM," cover 10-9. John Huey, a witty veteran of the *Journal*'s Atlanta bureau, stopped by long enough to write an outstanding cover story on Sam Walton and the Wal-Mart empire, "Wal-Mart: Will It Take Over the World," 1-30, a 10 Best nomination from both the *Fortune* editors and our own selection. It set the pace for the other newsmagazines that picked up on the beat, before Huey was whisked off to edit another Time Inc. publication.

Last year we thought that *Fortune* was challenging *BusinessWeek* and *Forbes* in the competition for our reading time. In 1989, with *BusinessWeek* on one of its occasional surges, and with *Fortune* repeatedly tangling its feet in Time, Inc. haywire, Marshall Loeb's fortnightly fell back into a distant third place. But then, into every life a little acid rain must fall.

Editor:	Marshall Loeb
Address:	Time-Life Building
	Rockefeller Center
	New York, NY 10020
	(212) 586-1212
Circulation:	672,134 National
	782,990 Worldwide

FW

The big event at FW this year was its remodeling, beginning with the 11-14 issue. The business weekly, founded in 1902, has jazzed-up with a new logo, new format, a whole new look. We're not sure why they think they needed a new dress-up, except that the world is moving on, especially in print business journalism. As we did a year ago when *The Wall Street Journal* went to a third section, we'll allow our readers time to adjust before we point with praise or view with alarm. But our first reaction is on the negative side — the new typeface especially less attractive and the boxes around the columns hemming us in. But we know that any change in format is a gamble with the readers, who instinctively abhor it, and we'll give it a chance.

We wondered in 1988 if *FW* would really be able to distinguish itself from the competition. Fewer lists in 1989, and more "Global Reports" on Telecommunications, 4-18, the Pharmeceutical Industry, 5-30, Defense, 9-19, and Computers, 11-28, among others, got *FW* on its way. The "Global Reports" are sweeping views of the topic written in a number of single-bylined articles by a series of reporters and vary in quality; the three just mentioned are sterling examples, with solid reporting and interpretation within a clear analytic framework. The Defense Report, "Showdown at the World's Arms Bazaar" by Robert Wrubel 9-19, was submitted to us by the editors at *FW* as a 10 Best nomination. But the Ethics Report, 6-27, is alphabet soup, employing the talents of nearly every reporter on the masthead, and with no clear focus on a nebulous topic, we're lost. Although the magazine continues to publish multiple lists, they're normally on the inside, and then well within the parameters of the "Selected Issues" column. The editors appear to have discontinued the reams of financial information that went on for twenty pages at a clip on various issues in favor of the aforementioned shorter column, but we rather liked having all that information in one place, with the detail that went with it.

The covers, except for the "Global Reports," are a mixed bag. There's little original, with editor and *Forbes* veteran Geoffrey Smith playing it safe with business magazine fare. We're not impressed by the difference between "CEO of the Decade," 4-4, and "Man of the Year," (who's also a CEO) 12-12. We've already read about Sharon Reier's "CEO," Sam Walton, in John Huey's *Fortune* piece, 1-30, and Sana Siwolop's "Man" should really be "CEO," a competent profile of the management and management style of Xerox chairman and CEO David T. Kearns. Nice profiles, but not deserving of the hyperbolic headlines.

Former TV correspondent Dan Cordtz provides some new insights in "World War II: The Economic Aftermath," 10-17, garnering a nomination from his editors at *FW* for our 10 Best section, informative to the baby boom generation, and perceptive in evaluating the socio-economic consequences of the war, asserting that going overseas may have helped a generation of businessmen to prepare for international trade and a global economy. We learned this in college, though. Also nominated by the editors was the perfectly awful Ellen Benoit cover "A Case for Legalization," 10-3, simple blather and bald assertion about crime diminishing. "A Case for Legalization" simply should not have been run as is, so cursory is the reporting, logic and analysis. Anthony Lewis of *The New York Times,* in his "Investing in Disaster" column, 9-24, is where the action is on legalization. We wonder what could have possessed the editors to run such an important cover in a page and a half worth of column space. We were not surprised that the article generated much hostile mail, one letter from a prison counselor running a full page, a 3-column annihilation of Benoit's arguments.

Two of the stars at the biweekly are Southwest bureau chief Sharon Reier and West Coast bureau chief Robert Wrubel. Both earned three-star ratings and each a 10 Best nomination. Replacing the frenzy of New York and Washington with the laid-back attitudes of St. Augustine, Florida, and Los Angeles has given both the room to maneuver. Reier files a spectacular "The Last Tango," 5-30, a timely economic profile of Argentina that hit the stands coincident with protestors hitting the street in that country. Wrubel's "Le Defi Mickey Mouse," 10-17, bullish on Disney's prospects, provides all the needed detail for us to agree on "the mouse that soared." Washington bureau chief James Srodes seemed much too flippant a year ago, but has gotten this under control, filing more than adequate, timely, material, including a 10 Best selection for the magazine, "How the Fed Sees 1989," 12-28-88. But Lauren Chambliss, who covered the capital gains issue for the magazine, was sorely in need of guidance, superficial at best.

FW has a long tradition and a respectable circulation base, a distant fourth from the other business magazines, but trying to keep its elbows at the table in this increasingly competitive world. We don't exactly see where they are trying to go with this souped-up format, but perhaps they should think about the name the founders gave them in '02, combining "finance" and "world." We saw an inkling of something in Sharon Reier's "Last Tango" in Argentina. The magazine needs something more than redesign if it is to be in good health in 2002, celebrating its centennial.

Editor: Geoffrey Smith

Address: 1450 Broadway
              New York, NY 10018
              (212) 869-1616

Circulation: 400,223

Harper's

"Damn it, Harper's, I love you — you cruel, beautiful magazine you." Ahem. Well, ah, er, um, okay. We imagine that there are indeed among the monthly's subscribers, individuals who write love letters to the magazine along the lines of the intimacy from which the above excerpt is taken. (That excerpt, by the way, in bold print, graces many of *Harper's* ads.) Ah, love is such a wondrous thing. Yes, it is. We hear that *Harper's* readers have a love affair with their magazine every month. We hear that *Harper's,* like love, is a "jolt of recognition," that it's "a clearinghouse of ideas," even "a delicious romp through life's more relevant questions." But somehow Cupid's arrow misses us every time we pick up an issue of this monthly. Is it a matter of "Lookin' for love in all the wrong places?" We think not. It's more a case of "Different strokes for different folks." And we're reconciled to the fact that *Harper's* appeals to very different folks.

Editor Lewis Lapham and publisher John R. MacArthur have revolutionized this 139-year-old magazine. The result? "The search for meaning is what the new *Harper's* magazine is all about." Hmmm. The meaning of some of its "Readings" selections are very, very deep. We're still grappling with a 1-89 selection, "Ultimate Nudity," from an interview with film director John Waters, conducted by E. J. Kahn III:

INTERVIEWER: Is there anything that shocks you?

WATERS: Yes — ultimate nudity. I heard about it in L.A. It's when you have the skin of your testicles removed and replaced with clear skin. The thinking being that it's more erotic to see how your body works inside. Think what will eventually happen: we'll all walk around with clear bodies, like high-school science projects. "Oh, I can tell that person doesn't love me. His heart isn't beating fast." Or, "I don't want to date that person. She drinks too much. Look at her liver." It's the ultimate voyeurism. I was shocked. But maybe that's the nineties.

The 4-89 cover story, "He's Back!!!" a "Forum" section contribution on packaging Christ's second coming is intended as a parody of the state of public relations art. Senior editor Jack Hitt came up with the idea of asking expert consultants to "offer Jesus advice on six tasks critical to winning over American public opinion: developing a media strategy, writing a monologue for a guest-host appearance on 'Saturday Night Live,' redesigning the cover of *The New Testament* and writing the jacket-flap copy, designing a contemporary wardrobe, and developing a story line for a one-minute television commercial." From the new jacket-copy for *The New Testament*: "At the age of 30 Jesus was an obscure carpenter in a backwater province of the Roman Empire. . . .today, countless millions in every corner of the world call Him Savior. In an age devoted to the creation and near-worship of celebrity, His name recognition worldwide is uncontested." *The New Testament* retells "the compelling personal saga of Jesus, a breathtaking rags-to-heavenly-riches story of struggles and triumphs, of faith and betrayal, of suffering and death — and Eternal Life." The use of religion as the vehicle for satire isn't offensive, but the level of satire here is sophomoric at best.

"All The Congressmen's Men: How Capitol Hill Controls the Press," 7-89, by contributing editor Walter Karp, was provocative enough to enjoy a circulation well beyond *Harper's* itself. The *Utne Reader* reprinted it in its 11/12-89 issue, and the editors of both magazines regard it as one of the 10 Best reports for 1989. Karp's thesis is that "The myth of media power is nothing more than a political orthodoxy that conveniently masks the purloined truth: the professional politicians of Washington quietly shape our national news to suit their interests." Karp attempts to replace the "myth" of the power of the press with what he sees as the real truth — the power of Congress — telling us that "congressional leaders make and unmake the nation's news."

The Washington press corps, little more than parrots, forced to follow the party line or else face "the rule of the whip," which Congress and presidents crack unmercifully. Oh, yes, Karp works presidents (Nixon, Reagan) into his governmental "oligarchy" as well, which brings up one of the biggest complaints we have about conspiracy theories — the way they can stretch, bend, or shrink the facts to fit the thesis, so much so that it becomes possible to prove anything they want, while it's nearly impossible to disprove the theory itself. But, Karp is right in his criticism that too often Washington journalists simply rely on government sources for their stories, and we're sure that the press has been leaned on from time to time to kill a story.

One of July's "Readings" is an excerpt from a letter written in 1985 by Bruce Amero, a former Exxon navigation officer, to Daniel Paul, then fleet services manager for Exxon. The letter complains about an Exxon captain under whom Amero served, charging that between 1980 and 1982 the individual falsified records and apparently was an alcohol abuser. The individual was Joseph J. Hazelwood, who later became captain of the Exxon *Valdez.*

"The Quiet Coup — U.S. v. Morison: A Victory For Secret Government," 9-89, by contributing editor Philip Weiss, was one of *Harper's* better reports this year. In a searing indictment of both the press and the federal government, Weiss presents the story of Samuel Morison. He is the right-wing bureaucrat in Naval Intelligence who swiped two KH-11 satellite photographs of a Soviet carrier off a desk and sent the pictures to *Jane's Defence Weekly,* for whom he was working on a part-time basis. Because of the circumstances (especially his politics and his murky motivations, which pretty much excluded any support from the press) Weiss explains, Morison became the perfect vehicle for the Reagan administration to test the vague Espionage Act of 1917 in court, and establish a precedent of making the leaking of classified material a criminal offense. "In the dark of night, with little check or balance and scarcely a growl from the watchdogs, the executive has seized a weapon. Who knew when it would prove useful." A sobering report.

Certainly, the article for which *Harper's* 1989 performance will be best remembered is Tom Wolfe's "Stalking The Billion-Footed Beast," 11-89. This 10 Best nomination turns his prediction of 16 years ago into an exhortation: "If fiction writers do not start facing the obvious, the literary history of the second half of the twentieth century will record that journalists not only took over the richness of American life as their domain but also seized the high ground of literature itself." In a breathtaking tour-de-force, Wolfe, the High Priest of New Journalism and the author of the Dickensian *The Bonfire of the Vanities,* looks at post-war American literature and discovers that just as American life was becoming more "chaotic, fragmented, random, discontinuous, in a word, *absurd,*" American fiction was either disdaining all connection with realism or else placing real situations in "lonely Rustic Septic Tank Rural settings." Wolfe argues that the breakthroughs in realistic style of the 19th century novelists who placed characters in their social *milieu* represent the best way for novelists to capture life in America at the end of the 20th century. Brilliant, sure to be argued over in editorial offices and creative writing programs across the country and the subject of English Lit theses for years to come, this issue of *Harper's* was swooped up all over the place by the "penthouse intellectuals."

Editor:	Lewis Lapham
Address:	666 Broadway New York, NY 10022 (212) 614-6500
Circulation:	186,000

Harvard Business Review

Although it was a year of solid accomplishment for *Harvard Business Review,* 1989 will be remembered as "The Year of the Mommy Track." In a loony turn of events, an article in this scholarly periodical became fodder for talk show comedians, editorial cartoonists, mainstream magazines, and the usual gang of social pundits.

What caused the blizzard was a lead article in the 1/2-89 issue by business consultant Felice Schwartz entitled, "Management Women and the New Facts of Life." In retrospect, it was a sober, rather dull article that used consultant-ese phrases like "plateauing" and "counterproductive expectations" to make an obvious observation: Some females were mostly interested in their jobs ("career-primary women") while others wanted a balanced life ("career-and-family life"). While this might seem about as controversial as cookies and milk, it hit a media nerve in the slow news weeks following the Bush inauguration. *BusinessWeek* devoted a 3-27 cover to "The Mommy Track" (a phrase Schwartz never used) and op-ed pages at the big dailies were full of wrath and fury. *HBR* itself printed a special section of letters on the subject and called Ms. Schwartz back for an encore to defend herself. Was it all silly? Of course, but we tip our hat to Ted Levitt, then *HBR*'s editor, for a shrewd bit of marketing and attention-getting publicity.

Fortunately, there was plenty else to applaud during the year. *HBR* has become the number one forum in the U.S. for Japanese business leaders to present their point of view — an enormously important development during a year of worsening trade relations. The 7/8-89 issue, for example, had a superb interview with Yoshihisa Tabuchi, head of Nomura Securities, the world's largest and most profitable financial institution. The interview was expertly handled by Michael Schrage, a former *Washington Post* reporter now at MIT. In contrast to the news magazines, who would have confined Tabuchi's comments to a sidebar, *HBR* gave seven pages to the Q&A. In addition, *HBR* printed several chapters in consecutive issues from a new book by McKinsey & Co.'s Kenichi Ohmae, Japan's foremost thinker on corporate management and strategy, in which Ohmae urged businessmen to recognize the realities of an integrated global economy. And the 3/4-89 issue contained an interview with former Prime Minister Yasuhiro Nakasone.

There were also smaller but valuable surprises during the year. A piece on Pacific Bell's policy towards employees with AIDS was informative and moving; the article would have been entirely comfortable in *Harper's* or *Atlantic Monthly*. An almost hidden article in the 5/6-89 issue, "Learning from Losing a Customer" and written by the head of a small video business, was lively and useful. There was balance, too. A gloom-and-doomer by a Harvard professor about the alleged U.S. inability to compete was balanced in the same issue by a piece by Yale's Marshall Robinson, "America's Not-So-Troubling Debts and Deficits," a sharply-reasoned retort to deficitmania. Meanwhile, *HBR* had a prominent influence on the mainstream business press, two examples being *Fortune*'s 2-13 cover story on speed as a strategic advantage, and *BusinessWeek*'s cover "Is Your Company Too Big?" 3-27, both of which drew from earlier *HBR* articles.

HBR is less effective when it wallows in a big public policy story. A killer 5/6-89 issue on the meaning of Europe 1992 tossed up thumbsucking pieces that were only marginally useful and which merely matched what is available in plenty of other magazines. It reminded us of how *HBR* closed out 1988 with a top-heavy and largely ignored "Advice to the New President" issue that drew from the likes of Ralph Nader, Martin Feldstein and Clyde Prestowitz.

There are some improvements we'd like to see at *HBR* during 1990. Too many disappointing articles seem to be printed solely because of the author's eminent byline — a retired CEO here, an ex-Harvard department chairman there. So thin were some of these pieces that they made *HBR* look like a vanity press for the well-connected. The editors should rely less on the Cambridge-Manhattan-Washington DC axis and discover more provocative and daring thinkers in the hinterlands. Also, the magazine ought to speed up its article approval process, which moves at a glacial pace and frustrates many potential contributors. A new editor, Rosabeth Moss Kanter, comes on board for the new decade, and perhaps this will further freshen the bimonthly.

Overall, though, *HBR* made a strong claim on our reading time during 1989. We're spending more time with it than a few years ago, highlighting more passages to send to business colleagues, recommending more articles to friends and clipping more selections for our reference files. All appearances are that 1990 will be an excellent year for *HBR* — even without another ride on the Mommy Track.

Editor:	Rosabeth Moss Kanter
Address:	Soldiers Field
	Boston, MA 02163
	(617) 495-6182
Circulation:	204,757

Human Events

We had wondered in last year's *MediaGuide* how *Human Events* would deal with the new Bush administration. *HE,* of course, enjoyed a special relationship with President Reagan, a long-time faithful and enthusiastic subscriber of the conservative national weekly. But Bush is cut from a different mold than his predecessor, and his appreciation of the publication isn't as intense. Still, *HE* circulates within the White House. Its impact on policy varies, of course, just as reaction to it varies. It runs from the estimable appreciation given it by Vice President Dan Quayle to the grudging respect it receives from others who happen to be the target of a *HE* intervention on a policy that appears to be egregiously straying from conservative moorings.

It issued "a warning to George Bush" with "Who Will Run U.S. Foreign Policy," 1-7 by Ralph Kinney Bennett, senior staff editor of *Reader's Digest.* This front-pager was provocative on the tension between the State Department careerists and the White House, drawing heavily from Constantine Menges' book *Inside the National Security Council.* Take back foreign policy from the establishment elites, Mr. President, is the message here. In "Some Conservative Thoughts For the New President," 1-28, the editors advance the "roll back the Soviet Union" perspective, outlining areas where ouster rather than containment ought to be employed by the administration. An especially thoughtful "How Good Is Baker's Latin America Appointment," 2-11, examines the divided attitudes toward Elliott Abrams' designated replacement, liberal Democrat Bernard Aronson. There's no rush to judge him, as *HE* instead examined dispassionately the pros and cons of his appointment. We found this approach very useful, as it helped clear up for us the issues over which his opposition and supporters had drawn demarcating lines within conservative circles.

HE again deserves note for being the most committed defenders of the Nicaraguan resistance fighters, the contras. Throughout the year, it kept a steady focus on the erosion of their support, issuing warning after warning, as with "Bush and Baker Must Make Contras Their Top Priority," 2-25 and "Last Rites for the Contras?" 4-8. It was particularly forceful in rapping the administration's knuckles over its decision to support demobilization of the contras, "Bush Bankrupt Diplomacy Sinking Central America," 8-19.

Foreign policy remained an area in which *HE* found itself firing off front-page critiques and warnings on the direction coming out of the White House: "Bush Must Force Noriega's Ouster" ("through the 82nd Airborne, if necessary"), 5-20; "President Falters at the Summit" ("the President. . .[has] committed this nation to a treaty that will be 'neither global nor verifiable' "), 12-16; "Scowcroft Mission Sends Wrong Signal to Beijing — and Moscow" ("we have not only forgiven China's murdering leaders for the Tiananmen Square massacre, but Gorbachev and Co. now know that if they feel inclined toward a brutal crackdown to preserve their power, the United States government will come crawling back to renew the friendship in short order"), 12-23.

At the same time *HE* was there backing up the President on a host of other issues, as for example with "Bush's Drug Plan On the Right Track," 9-16. "Who are the Democrats to criticize?" the paper asks, and the "Inside Washington" column carries a revealing "How the Democrats Dealt with Drugs," detailing the Carter administration's attitudes, with a particular focus on Dr. Peter Bourne, Carter's chief of the Office of Drug Abuse Policy.

"Inside Washington" is one of the publication's strongest features. Subjects included in "Inside Washington" are diverse and usually provide information or a perspective not found elsewhere. In addition, there are frequently key stories here that the rest of the press only gets around to much later. "Environmental Activist To Head EPA," 1-14 on William Reilly, was particularly informative and insightful. The article reported on Reilly's history as an advocate of federally mandated land-use controls, raising a question about the endangerment of property rights. The article on Mayor Barry's problems, 1-7, was well done, tracing his alleged drug involvement and administrative corruption. However the 1-14 article on Mayor Barry seemed to uncover little new and seemed unnecessary so soon after the previous article. One of the best articles was "Coach Thompson Wrong on Rule 42," 1-28, an interview with Arthur Ashe who supports proposition 42 and the maintenance of academic standards for all student athletes.

There was a steady supply of very informative, revealing reports on a wide range of policy issues. The analysis of Voice of America, "The VOA Made Gains Under Reagan," 2-11, is one example. In its analysis of the different sections of VOA, *HE* probed the role of the foreign service, and came up with recommendations which called for doing everything possible to "encourage well-motivated liberals, conservatives, and moderates who want a distinguished VOA." "Why Private Care Is Far Superior to Public," 2-4, enlightened on how private shelters in DC are providing better quality service at less cost than public shelters. The interview on the merits of deregulation with former Secretary of Transportation Burnley, 2-25, was substantive. "Will Congress Pass *Anything* In the Name of 'Handicapped'?" was another particularly informative effort.

Of course, not all the cover stories held up this year. "A Fond Farewell To The Gipper," 1-21, and "Democrats Relish Bi-Partisan Strategy," 1-14, were mediocre. "Ollie North Deserves a Pardon," 7-15, was gritty and tough, and perfectly acceptable, but "Tokyo Rose Was Pardoned — So Why Not Ollie?" a week later, 7-22, doesn't quite work with its comparisons of Ollie's transgressions against a rogues' gallery of traitors, perverts, and scoundrels who were pardoned. And the headline just doesn't work the way it must have been intended. But, these were relatively minor departures from *HE*'s solid norm.

Another outstanding feature of *HE*, "Politics 89" can amaze you with the information it puts together on power shifts from all 50 states, as well as on important elections, issues on ballots, political activities and political trends at state and local levels. We constantly find information here that we don't see anywhere else. Lee Atwater should make "Politics 89" required reading at the RNC. We're sure the Democratic National Committee closely monitors it.

HE has one of the most extensive ranges of conservative columnists appearing in print. There's a fair amount of rotation, new talent also appearing now and then, but we're pleased to see certain bylines appearing regularly. Warren Brookes, for example, *The Detroit News* and syndicated economic columnist who has received a four star rating in the *MediaGuide* every year, appears frequently in *HE*. Patrick Buchanan and James J. Kilpatrick are two others whose commentary is frequently carried in the weekly.

HE's book reviews are always very useful, though the quality of course varies with the reviewer. We find especially well-done those by Allan C. Brownfeld. Similarly, "Focus on the Media," handled by Cliff Kincaid, is a very worthwhile column. Kincaid watchdogs the press for egregious sins of liberal bias, and, although himself ideologically biased toward conservatism, the case he makes when criticizing an instance of media bias is based on real evidence. *HE* also carries articles on media bias by others from time to time. The major press has failed miserably in its coverage of El Salvador with its unrestrained partisan reporting, so we appreciated seeing "Fact and (Media) Fiction About El Salvador," 7-22 by H. Joachim Maitre, foreign affairs editor of *Strategic Review*.

HE's role as conservative tribune is enhanced even more so with George Bush in the White House. An important voice for the "grunts," the activists in the conservative movement, it's had to do more shouting this year than it had to in the past Reagan ones. But it has managed to keep shrillness out of its voice — so far. As the post-Cold War era expands, moving the administration into testing new conceptions that take it further from the traditional conservative policy consensus on East-West relations, we'll watch to see if *HE* changes either its message or tone of voice next year.

Editor:	Thomas S. Winter
Address:	422 First Street, SE
	Washington, DC 20003
	(202) 546-0856
Circulation:	39,000

Insight

A year ago, we expressed more disappointment about this slim, offbeat newsweekly on its fourth birthday than just about any other publication we review. Designed to be less trendy than its competitors, it had impressed us with its depth, the vitality of its youthful staff and the consistent strength of its cover stories. All of these elements seemed to sag in 1988, partly because *Insight* seemed so out of it during Campaign '88.

Nothing pleases us more than to have our expectations exceeded, and this is what happened in '89, the magazine bouncing back to the fast track it had been on. Its cover stories received thirteen 10 Best nominations from our readers in our 5 categories; 4 of these were final selections. This number of selections was exceeded only by the *The New York Times* with 13 and *Wall Street Journal* with 10, and matched the 4 of *The Washington Post.* Managing editor Kirk Oberfeld, who advised us during the year that he thought us correct in last year's assessment of his periodical, may have cracked the whip or turned on the charm to achieve these results. We have no idea what went on to so dramatically turn up the inventiveness of the cover stories, the tighter relevance of the inside book, and the snap in the writing, but we wound up spending more time with it this year, its fifth, than in previous years. It's still pitifully slim in advertising, heavily subsidized by the Washington Times Company and its Korean owners, but at long last major advertisers are appearing with some regularity, including autos and hotels.

Insight's "cover packages," unique to the magazine when Oberfeld began the practice of running three or four stories off the same cover theme, are now seen elsewhere, *Business Week* and *USN&WR* doing so occasionally. The *Insight* covers this year were still riskier, with imaginative themes that could easily have failed, but more often than not paid off. Carolyn Lochhead's "No Way Out: The Brutal Snare of Poverty," 4-3, does a better job of probing methodically at the roots of the underclass than any we'd seen, maintaining an ideological detachment throughout. Daniel Kagan's "Fast Food Kids," 8-28, dug into the drug- and crime-infested inner city of the nation's capital and found its promising side, teenagers who have their noses to the grindstone, turning down fast money and the fast lane for fast-food jobs and the minimum wage. Both are 10 Best selections, as is Holman Jenkins, Jr.'s "Truly Talking Shop at the Kremlin," 1-2, a timely year-opener on Soviet commercial overtures to the West. The fourth 10 Best selection was Bill Whalen's cover package on "The Democrats," 3-27, another timely reconnaissance that showed up just when we were ready for it.

With Oberfeld, 45, the only managing editor the magazine has had, it by now has his distinctive stamp, the covers a "look" we can spot a mile away: the red logo and red strip setting off the right "ear;" white, stacked headlines in inch-high type; creative and colorful arrangements of people, posters, or man-made things. An exception was the 7-17 cover, a silly cartoon depicting the "Battle over Funding the Arts," which did not work at all, and we assumed Oberfeld was on vacation.

Other cover stories we thought exceptional and engaging were "Drug Money Soils Cleanest Hands," by Stephen Brookes 8-21, comprehensive, wide and deep, on money laundering, four months before *Time* put the story on its cover, 12-18. Brookes looks ahead to Europe '92, which the launderers await eagerly as currency controls will end and "They can all park their money in Germany, which is particularly obsessed with not touching the banks." Daniel Kagan, who did "Fast Food Kids," also did an illuminating, offbeat cover on "The Forgotten History of the First Drug War," 11-20, quirky and confusing in spots, but where else had we read of earlier bouts the United States has had with drug epidemics? Richard Lipkin tailed off in quality later in the year with his science pieces, but he got us twice early, with material we didn't think we'd read at first, "Greener Pastures in Deep Blue Sea," 12-26-88, skillfully written on undersea exploration, and "Cracking Weather's Secrets," 1-9, a ho-hum topic written with excitement and life. Bill Whalen, *Insight*'s political bigfoot, who is almost always a pleasure to read, is great in an early characterization of House Speaker Jim Wright and the various pickles he finds himself in, "Wright Hits Ground Running as a Speaker With an Agenda," 12-26-88. With a little extra reporting kick and smoother opening, Whalen could have scored big with "Bush's Smooth and Lucky Stride," 7-17, an otherwise fine effort on maneuvering around capital gains.

With a tiny staff compared to the competition, *Insight* has demonstrated during its brief life how much can be accomplished with relatively young reporters flooded with responsibility and given seasoned direction. It usually succeeded very well this year in the coverage of foreign affairs, with only a few hands to scoot around the globe. David Brock's finely honed piece on El Salvador, "An Embattled Nation Back Atop Policy Agenda," 5-15, gives all sides fair representation as we observe close up the handoff from the Christian Democrats to the ARENA party. Brock's cover, "Dueling in Peru," 1-30, was nominated by his editors as a 10 Best foreign dispatch, but while we had read it thoroughly for detail on this deeply troubled country, a major source of cocaine, the economics was missing, except for some broad-brush observations from one expert or another. Brock's cover on the mechanisms of the Japanese press corps, "Gentlemanly Press Gets Gloves Dirty," 12-4, is broad and shallow, but we'd never seen anything like it, so we appreciated greatly what we got.

Richard Martin produced an excellent cover on "The Wave," 1-16, pieces on Asian immigration, the Vietnamese, Khmer, and Hmong, masterfully written, with balanced sensitivity and warmth, a 10 Best nomination that misses only because of patches of confusion in spots. Richard Mackenzie, again a three star foreign correspondent, provided fine coverage all year of events in Afghanistan, although clearly from a perspective that sometimes led him into an overestimation of the *mujaheddin*'s strategic situation. He also developed two insightful reports on political developments in the subcontinent's two major powers. "Rajiv Gandhi's Bloody Inheritance," 2-13, on political currents in India and "Jolts for New Democracy End Prime Minister's Honeymoon," 3-13, updating on the tasks and perspectives of PM Benazir Bhutto as her opposition in Pakistan grows stronger. We saw too little of Africa from *Insight* this year. Jonas Bernstein did a cover on "A Freedom Fight Deep in Africa," 12-19-88, on the Angola war, but it wandered around, with little solid sense of what it's all about or why we should care. Holman Jenkins, Jr., did a welcome piece on the business of South Africa, "What Counts is Color of Money," 7-31, which gave us a different angle on the new developments taking place there. If there was anything significant on sub-Sahara Africa, which we would have liked to see, we didn't.

Soviet and East Bloc developments should have been an *Insight* strength this year, with the estimable Henrik Bering-Jensen on duty. He has been one of our top rated foreign correspondents for years, and this is his beat. His material was just not up to the fast-breaking developments, though. A cover story on Germany, "Struggling Against Bonds of History," 3-20, gave us a series of snapshots, but should at some point have been assessing the hairline fractures in the Brezhnev Doctrine and what this would mean in the dynamics of the Germanys. His "Blocbusters" cover package on Poland, East Germany and Hungary, 11-13, is competent and professional, but too far from the action, the material almost surely developed out of whatever he could lay his hands on wherever he was, but not at the scene. *Insight*'s weakness on its bench shows up with tight lead times, as here. Bering-Jensen's cover on "France: Two Centuries After the Guillotine," 7-10, which he had time to work on, was the best we saw on the bicentennial celebration.

The other political reporter at the weekly, besides Bill Whalen, is young Daniel Wattenberg. He's also developing rapidly, and could be snapped up by another outfit at the rate he's going. His 8-7 cover on how the GOP aims to make inroads in Dixie, "How Atwater Plays Rhythm and Blues," was nominated by his editors for 10 Best, and seemed awfully good by our lights too, our reader noting: "Funny fascinating insight on 'the guy who could drive Mother Theresa's negatives over 40 percent.' Sound political analysis with a writing style that is breezy, chic." The magazine's law and justice reporter, Charlotte Low Allen, a three-star entry for the third year and getting better, is another talent that has developed at the magazine. Oberfeld seems to push her into new fields, thinking he may have a big star on his hands, and he may. Her cover story on "The Mouse That Ate Orlando," 10-30, Mickey of course, is superlative, albeit a mite long for the subject. Her cover on urban architecture, "Radiant City's Dull Legacy," 8-14, is also remarkably impressive, especially for the first time we see her approach this subject.

Business, as usual, is pretty choppy. *Insight* has a New York bureau, staffed with Christopher Elias, a solid veteran who would be a credit to any business page, and Carolyn Lochhead, the up-and-coming young woman who delivered the 10 Best on the underclass. There's still too much of a tendency to squeeze the small staff for business news every week, however insignificant. Oberfeld would be much better off mobilizing this talent totally on significant stuff, which is something none of the competitors would dare try, or even contemplate, but which we think would work for *Insight*. It's inefficient to have Elias, who could produce a three star cover story on Michael Milken, "The Man with the High-Yield Vision," 6-12, also produce "Rare Posters Worth a Pretty Penny," 1-16. Just because *Time* and *Newsweek* think they have to feed their readers such trivia each week does not mean the new kid on the block has to play that way. Oberfeld should think of adding *Fortune* to his list of competitors.

Each year we add gratuitous complaints about "The Last Word" column on the back page. The back page, we think, is the most important page in the magazine, after the cover and the table of contents. It should not be thrown away as most periodicals do, out of some misguided notion that because it's at the end of the book it is of lesser significance. Last, but not least. *Newsweek,* of all periodicals, is correct in putting big guns on its back page, George Will and Meg Greenfield. *Time* is smart in putting Michael Kinsley on its back page, when it can get him. *Insight* continues to throw away its back page with utility infielders, not one of whom we will mention here, but not one of whom batted higher than .115, about the average of all *pitchers* in the Three-I league. Yet the Washington Times Company has available to it Warren T. Brookes and Richard Grenier, back-page sluggers the likes of Ruth and Gehrig. We are baffled at the lineup Oberfeld selects in this regard. Otherwise, he's doing beautifully, back on track.

Editor:	Arnaud de Borchgrave
Address:	3600 New York Avenue, NE Washington, DC 20002 (202) 636-8800
Circulation:	525,000

Manhattan, inc.

In past years we've fretted about *Manhattan, inc.*'s penchant for serving us enormously long articles that do not stick to the ribs, and an overly cutesy writing style. In 1989, we got both length and cute in abundance. *Manhattan, inc.* is still a relative newcomer next to the established business magazines, but already even younger up-and-comers are nipping at its heels, such as

Business Month, formerly *Dun's Business Monthly.* Editor Clay Felker and his monthly no longer have the room to maneuver in the marketplace they once did. We noted last year that "Felker has announced plans to reshape the magazine, hoping to broaden the audience and give *Manhattan, inc.* a range beyond the metropolis." This wasn't the year. Although it bills itself as carrying "The Business of New York," *Manhattan, inc.* is more on a par with *The Washingtonian,* about as pertinent to money matters on Wall Street as *The Washingtonian* is to politics inside the Beltway. Not much.

Felker lost one of his key writers this year, Edward Jay Epstein, off to greener pastures to write another book, not appearing in the monthly past March of '89. Epstein had served as an anchor to a writing team that tends to float off into the ether, given the editor's insouciance on such matters as crispness and efficiency.

Having said this, Epstein's three pieces for the magazine this year were less than breathtaking. Perhaps he simply unloaded the bottom of his bag knowing he was going. "The Win-Win Game," 1-89, is an expose on how corporate raiders or "wanna-be" raiders use an SEC loophole to make profits on takeover clients that would be illegal for any other investor. "Capital Punishment," 2-89, continues his crusade against federal prosecutors of Wall Street capitalists, but now sounding more like an apologist. In "SEC's French Revolution," 3-89, he dissects the Triangle Industries/ Nelson Peltz deal with Pechiney SA of France, following the same trail as the SEC to figure out that this deal has a certain aroma to it. Still, we miss him in the monthly. His best work appeared in the June issue of *Vanity Fair,* of all places, penning an investigative report on the death of General Zia of Pakistan. "Was General Zia Murdered?" is a heck of a mystery, only half explored here, leaving many unanswered questions in typical Epstein fashion; we're not even sure Epstein went to Pakistan.

Otherwise, we are not unhappy with the writing stable, Felker grabbing the occasional Rita Koselka from *Forbes* or Isadore Barmash from *The New York Times* to do sometime freelance work on this and that. But the cover material he came up with this year suggests he has to explore a broader cocktail circuit. The *People* of business magazines, *Manhattan, inc.* sported covers that had to scream for our attention: "Talent Moguls," on literary agents Lynn Nesbit and Mort Janklow by Jennet Conant 1-89; "Best Friends at War," on the Bill Fugazy-John Kluge feud by Mary Billard and Patricia O'Toole 4-89; "How a Tokyo Earthquake Could Devastate Wall Street," on how buildings falling in Tokyo might affect the markets here by Michael Lewis 6-89; and "Have I Got a Painting for You," on dealer Richard Feigen by Mary Marx Better 11-89. We get cheesecake on Donna Karan, after a *Newsweek* profile, among others, in "The New Queen of New York," cover 10-89. And, naturally, there's the requisite Ralph Lauren accolade in "From Ralph's House to Our House," cover 7-89. Two covers on the Time-Warner merger leave us yawning, "And the Winner Is. . .Steve Ross," by Jennet Conant 5-89, a long, long profile of Warner's CEO that comes complete with glossy pictures of Ross with Dustin Hoffman and lovely ex- and current wives, and "Greed and Ego in Gotham City," by Robert Sam Anson 8-89, an indictment for the editors and publishers at Time Inc., both brightly promoted, too tough to slog through. Loads of gloss and glitter, gossipy and semi-fun, which can be hard work.

Inside material is little better. Typically idiosyncratic to New York, *Manhattan, inc.* specializes in matters particular to the borough it's named for. But it's mostly trivial stuff, and even important matters sometimes get trivial treatment, cutesy and just utterly too-too. We get updated on NBC in Jennet Conant's "Michael Gartner: What's Behind the Bow Tie," 3-89, very long and insidey on the new NBC news chief, and "The Norville Affair," again by Conant 12-89 on the turnover at "Today," as blonde Deborah Norville replaces blonde Jane Pauley, commendable in pitting the ladies against the bosses instead of against each other. This last article is heralded on the cover trailer as "Broadcast Bimbos on Parade: The Real Story of the Jane Pauley Blunder."

Edward Klein plugs into nippophobia in "The Shadow Warriors," 5-89, stuffy and dramatic on the Japanese in New York, and their purchases. Klein, deposed editor of *The New York Times Magazine,* gave us the following gem: "He was unaware he was being observed, because he was sitting at the mahogany desk, thirty feet away, with his chair swiveled completely around so that his back was to the door. It must have been a rare experience for a Japanese like Hisao Kondo, who bears such weighty responsibilities, to be exposed and yet feel as though he was unseen and unjudged. And so, for this brief moment, the president of Mitsui USA, the American subsidiary of the oldest of Japan's fabled trading companies, let down his guard and began to stumble over a speech he was rehearsing out loud." We feel queasy at this voyeurism, but are at least thankful that Klein does not follow him into the loo.

Other NYC-indigenous pieces covered varied ground. Late after *The Wall Street Journal*'s Stephen J. Adler's profile of Lisa Ann Jones, Rachel Abramowitz's rehashing his story in "Why Won't the Caged Bird Sing?" 6-89, adds little. We get a dense inside look at the management of the New York Mets, "The Big Blue Machine," by Loren Feldman 5-89, right in mid-season, but only a die-hard fan could get through this, witty wordsmithing, but little payoff. Oddly, there was little on the hottest mayoral race in the country, won by the borough president of Manhattan. What's-his-name. Did Felker go to any cocktail parties where this was discussed? At least we got Gerald Austin, Jesse Jackson's campaign manager in '88, taking a peripheral tack with "Running with the Reverend," 9-89, looking at the Big Apple's mayoralty race by reviewing the history of Jesse Jackson's campaigns in New York.

Editor: Clay Felker

Address: 420 Lexington Avenue
New York, NY 10170
(212) 697-2100

Circulation: 110,000

Mother Jones

What used to be the star magazine of the left is quickly becoming the *Star* magazine of the left, taking on the trappings of a Socialist *People* or populist *Vanity Fair.* Every issue contains at least one celebrity story, usually on the cover, be it U2, Susan Sarandon, Spike Lee or Casey Kasem. While some are intelligent profiles, too often they are skin-deep. There is still occasional sharp public policy analysis of the kind the portside San Francisco magazine has been reviled and praised for. But less than we've come to expect. *MJ*'s respectability has worked against it, leaving "The New *Mother Jones*: People, Politics and Other Passions" approaching the bland and ordinary.

But it's not there yet. *Mother Jones* will still reach beyond the conventional to find the story. Elizabeth Farnsworth's explosive profile of then-Peruvian presidential candidate Mario Vargas Llosa, "The Temptation of Mario," 1-89, is broad and sweeping, Farnsworth travelling the campaign trail with him. In "New Believers," 4-89, Bill McKibben looks at the new generation of labor leaders, some of whom use quite different assumptions and tactics than their predecessors. John Kirch's "Culture Crash," 10-89, a fascinating article on mental illness among Indonesian refugees and how some clinics are responding, lets the story proceed without forcing it into categories. Kirch writes about the people, their experiences, and about different views of mental illness and approaches to it with a sympathy for Far Eastern views and a skepticism toward psychoanalysis, something rarely covered elsewhere. "The Era of Bad Feelings," 11-89, by AIDS chronicler Randy Shilts, sensitively details the chaotic AIDS conference in Montreal, hitting activists for their many disruptions without belittling their many frustrations with researchers, and evaluating the highs and lows of the event. These are pieces that are serious, going beyond the expected, giving that extra bit of research or analysis that brings them importance in the grand scheme of things.

But too often the remainder of the material in *Mother Jones* takes the easy way out. Instead of hell raising, we get ho-humming. "The Morning After," by Brett Harvey 5-89, postures as an analytic against overturning *Roe v. Wade,* but is really a dirty emotional appeal, overwrought and badly structured: "It's hard for today's young women to imagine abortions in dark, dirty rooms that smelled of Clorox, done by doctors who breathed bourbon fumes and copped a feel before they got to work, and warned you not to scream or they'd walk out and leave you alone in the middle of nowhere. Or self-aborting alone in your college dorm room, scared to tell anyone, watching your metal wastebasket fill up with blood, flushing the fetus down the toilet, terrified that it would clog the plumbing and you'd be found out." Ick.

Katy Butler's "The Great Boomer Bust," 6-89, is nicer, but is a thinly disguised advertisement for communal sharing, an All You Need Is Love and a Good Neighbor mentality that's not supported by the hard economic data needed to make her case that the Boomers really aren't ever going to be able to live in the middle class like their parents. "Untrue Confessions," by Philip Weiss 9-89, begins as an indictment of the justice system, and winds up a muddled argument against capital punishment, arguing the potential for mistakes in capital cases without deciding the guilt of the test case Weiss presents. In "Where Did Randy Go Wrong?" 11-89, Susan Faludi argues that Operation Rescue's Randall Terry takes the tactics he does due to a bad childhood reaction to a feminist family. Huh?

With the popular press pushing the environment so hard this year of *Time*'s Planet Earth, *Mother Jones* sat back a good part of the year, but did weigh in with an "ozone expose," in "Highest Disregard," by Dennis Hayes 12-89, all about how the original ozone wiz, F. Sherwood Rowland, has long warned Silicon Valley that the electronics industry was doing bad stuff to the old ozone layer, yet "it actively blocks our best chance to save the planet's atmosphere." Hayes is at least good enough to note that the American Economics Association clings tenaciously to the concept of "scientific uncertainty" as its defense, getting that word in edgewise. In the same issue we get a "Mother Jones Forum," several Chinese students talking with Orville Schell on "The Hopes of China," moderately interesting, but we'd rather read a Schell essay on the same subject. The liveliest piece in the 12-89 issue, "Is TV the Coolest Invention Ever Invented?" by Sean Elder, with a slow start, but we eventually get a good look at Matt Groening (rhymes with "raining," we're told), one of our most favorite cartoonists this year, the guy who draws the little rabbits, you know.

And then there are the ever-present profiles. "Witch Craft," by Camille Peri 4-89, is standard feminist hype on best-selling Canadian author Margaret Atwood, solid, but conventional. In "Spike's Riot," 9-89, Peggy Ornstein gives us a *People*-quality glimpse into the filmmaker, dutifully chronicling his childhood and interviewing his siblings and friends, but like *People,* we don't get any sense of Lee himself, just what everybody thinks of him. "Master of Disaster," 10-89, David Beers' damning profile of House Minority Whip Newt Gingrich can't decide whether to indict Gingrich or the entire conservative movement. Beers writes about mean young conservatives, Newt out of touch with his district, the hypocrisy of running as a family man while cheating on a hospitalized wife, a nasty guy to his staff, and skirting the law on book deals. It's a roundup of mostly familiar materials, and by sticking to the *People* rules of journalism, Beers loses the story. This is one weakness of *People*-centered journalism: without something new or conclusive in the investigation, the story falls flat. The magazine gives up the radical analysis it could be doing. An exception to this is Bernard Ohanian's "Casey Kasem's Flip Side," 10-89, a superb profile of the Top 40 king who devotes most of his time to supporting Arab causes and working for Middle East peace, well researched and compellingly written.

The regular columns are often poorly done. Barbara Ehrenreich's arguments are too muddled to be useful, and Lynda Barry's back-pagers read like post-adolescent ramblings, often sexually ambiguous and hostile, that were once rejected by an eleventh grade English teacher. The "Thinking" column varies, due to different authors. The best we saw was an adaptation of a Dixon Terry speech outlining his farm policy philosophy, a fitting testament. "Outfront," however, catches quirky glimpses of the best of the left, including the Robert Mapplethorpe flap, tastefully reprinting two of his less explicit efforts, "Jesse Helms, Art Critic," 9-89, and Martin Delaney's renegade AIDS diagnostics tests, "Life Underground," 10-89.

Once the premiere magazine for the left, *Mother Jones* now runs third to the other alternative press, behind the *Utne Reader* and *In These Times*. Not enough intelligent commentary this year to hold the magazine afloat, we look for hell raising elsewhere.

Editor: Douglas Foster

Address: 1663 Mission Street, 2nd Floor
San Francisco, CA 94103
(415) 558-8881

Circulation: 200,000

The Nation

"There has not been a political debate in the United States since the one that ended with the Japanese attack on Pearl Harbor." *The Nation* usually isn't quite as strident as it would seem to be from this lead for "Cue The Green God, Ted," 8-7/14 by contributing editor Gore Vidal. But hyperbolic polemics frequently appear on the pages of this weekly magazine. *TN* is the alternative for those who don't trust what the media tell them. After all, from *TN*'s perspective, not only do most in the media speak for "the big money/power cartels," they are in fact *owned* by them. The theme of Vidal's article is not a novel one for the magazine — the elite opinion-shapers manipulate the public by exposing them to only a narrow range of opinions on the political spectrum, excluding real dissenting views from the media, television in this case.

Alexander Cockburn keeps a regular watch on the work of other journalists, catching them when they stray from professional objectivity and lambasting them in his "Beat the Devil" column. Ben H. Bagdikian, author of *The Media Monopoly,* produced a cover story on the ascending domination of the world's mass media by a handful of mammoth private organizations, "The Lords of the Global Village," 6-12. Variations of this theme are regular grist at the weekly. In "Four Titans Carve up European TV," 1-9 by William Fisher and Mark Shapiro, the authors are succinct in their examination of Euro Television, where the rules can't keep pace with technological development. They cast a critical eye at bureaucrats; rules are written by lawyers who don't understand the complexity of a television studio. And they warn that a mass programming onslaught, controlled by four kingpins — Robert Maxwell, Rupert Murdoch, Leo Kirch and Silvio Berlusconi — will have deleterious effects on national cultures. The story is provocative, and the authors do explore an angle here we haven't seen anyone else touching upon.

TN's contributors often write from the presumption that theirs is not simply a unique point of view, but that it's a point of view deliberately excluded from assertion within the mainstream media. This can work sometimes to give *TN* articles an aggressive liveliness not seen elsewhere, but it can also lead to a lot of tendentious, sometimes shrill writing. The editors, though, handle this problem with reasonable balance on the whole, and we do get novel insights as a result. "Gorbaphobes in The U.S. Media," 12-26-88, by contributor Michael Massing, is a good example of a report along those lines that is effective. Massing examines the media response to Mikhail Gorbachev, noting that "Gorbachev's rise has created a serious dilemma for die-hard cold warriors, who over the years have loudly declared Soviet totalitarianism to be immutable." He cites reactions from many who seem to "view Gorbachev's turn toward diplomacy as posing *more* of a threat to the United States, not less." His salient point is persuasive: "to maintain that nothing has changed in Moscow — to see no difference between the use of diplomacy and the dispatching of troops — seems a singular exercise in ideological mindlessness."

In the past year, there had been some tension among the views of *TN* reporters and columnists regarding Gorbachev's reforms and the changes in Eastern Europe, but it was in much less evidence this year. Alexander Cockburn posed the "big question" in his "Beat the Devil" column, 2-20: If capitalism has 'won,' even pro term, then what is the definition of victory, what sort of capitalism has done the winning, and how does it go about its business round the world? Cockburn has generally stayed aloof of any support for the transformations in the Communist world, keeping a resolute watch instead on the transgressions of global capitalism and colonialism. Cockburn still has fun throwing barbs at other *TN* correspondents whom he sees sometimes transfixed by fear of being seen as somehow too left-wing. Who else today but Cockburn would even dare attempt to raise as a defense of Joseph Stalin's pact with Adolf Hitler as a necessity forced upon him by the failure of the Western powers to offer any security arrangement to the U.S.S.R.? Cockburn does so within his 9-18 column.

Among those reporting on the transformations in the East Bloc, *TN*'s Europe bureau chief, Daniel Singer, produced a very informative two-part series on the developments in Poland, "Looking For A Historic Compromise," 12-19-88 and "The Market Is The New Religion," 12-26-88. Once again, we get dimensions explored or revealed here that don't appear elsewhere. Among other things, for example, we learn that the nomination of Mieczyslaw Rakowski as Prime Minister is regarded as a gloomy sign for many Solidarity leaders. Although Rakowski is still viewed as a "liberal" in the West, in Poland he's seen as an enemy of Solidarity.

Singer, as with some of the other *TN* correspondents, is so much better when his report is based on real contact with flesh-and-blood people involved in real day-to-day life. In "Dancing On The Graves of Revolution," 2-6, an analytical effort on a French variant of the Francis Fukuyama "The End of History" thesis ("The End of Revolution"), Singer suggests this theme is precisely the message the establishment media is looking for. *TN* indulges a lot of wasted space, and his affirmation of the revolutionary message in response to "The End of Revolution" thesis was but one instance of wasted space this year: "You stupid lackeys, your order is built on sand. Tomorrow the Revolution will raise its head again and proclaim to your sorrow amid a brass of trumpets: I was, I am, I shall always be. . ."

We're slowing coming around to better appreciate *TN*'s economic stories, but only because they're slowly starting to improve. There's always the sterile, jargon-ridden screed that is totally without reward, but mixed in now and then we get something like "The Austerity Agenda: Have We Really Been Bingeing?" 1-9 by Doug Henwood, editor of the *Left Business Observer*. Henwood ably debunks the idea that the U.S. has been on a consumption spree "throughout the Reagan boom," or that trade deficits are caused by budget deficits, and forcefully makes the case that the austerian solution to the non-problems could push the economy off the cliff. So far so good, and *TN* ought to be appreciated for its effort on this issue. But then Henwood slips into stale leftist jargon and produces an argument that isn't simply old-fashioned but deeply flawed: "An economic program to redistribute income from rich to nonrich would act as a wondrous antidote to these deflationary risks, but hardly anyone makes such Keynesian arguments anymore."

TN's political reporting was off a bit this year, it being an "off year" for elections. We missed seeing the usually more frequent reports by Andrew Kopkind, an associate editor at *TN* and certainly one of the sharper political reporter/analysts when it comes to perceptions or approaches from the less-traversed angle. His "Strategies for Now — And Next Time," 9-25, is one of the year's best reports on the role Jesse Jackson plays in U.S. politics.

But it was foreign correspondence that had the edge as the most impressive cover stories in the magazine this year. "An Armenian Journal: Faucet Sales And Crush Syndrome," 4-24, by Michael Arlen, is strong reporting on the aftermath of the earthquake in Armenia. A devastating account of the ineptitude, he depicts the U.S.S.R. as a rather dumpy Third World nation in many respects. An account of his travels through Armenia, where he finds, among other things, completely demolished villages, political demonstrations, children undergoing therapy, Armenians cynical both about their current condition and reform, and Bud, an American faucet salesman discovering the limits of *perestroika*. While the article has its faults (some dates would have been appreciated) they are outweighed by its strengths, including Arlen's refusal to draw any grand conclusions or force his observations to take on more metaphorical baggage than they can carry. Arlen keeps to short descriptions of the people, events, and conditions he comes across, presenting a grim, gray vision of life in the Soviet Union which may be beyond the ability of anyone to reform.

Also outstanding reporting, "Defenders Of The Amazon," 5-22, by Alexander Cockburn and Susanna Hecht, is a striking story on the Brazilian rain forest — without tears, earning a 10 Best nomination from our readers. Cockburn and Hecht avoid the apocalyptic tones usually associated with this issue and instead calmly (and even humorously) illuminate the real issue at ground level in the Amazon: the economic survival of the Indians and rubber tappers (small farmers) who live in the rain forests. We learn that after having developed a system of "extractive reserves" that both protects the environment and provides for economic growth, they find themselves literally in a life-and-death struggle with wealthy land barons, with the Brazilian government running for cover. Cockburn and Hecht touch on larger issues here (Third World debt, the uneasy relationship between First World activists and Third World social movements) but in the end this is the story of the people of the rain forest, one that simply is not being told and certainly not with such gripping power as this account.

"Scapegoating the Black Family" is an impressive special issue taken up in *TN* in which the underlying theme of race, class and gender discrimination in America is plumbed. Among the articles in this forum, "Teen-Age Pregnancy: The Case For National Action," 7-24/31, by Faye Wattleton, president of Planned Parenthood Federation of America, makes a provocative case for greater national will in combating teen-age pregnancy. Wattleton cites poll materials to establish that 95% of Americans view the issue as a serious problem, "up 11 percent from 1985." While Wattleton at times slides into the 'if all the other Western nations can do it America should be able to do it too' argument that is not persuasive (it is not the United States of Europe over there on the other side of the Atlantic, and Canada is not the 51st state, after all), she's trenchant in her observation that in America "We exploit sex, and at the same time we try to repress it."

Among the changes this year at the magazine, the "Beltway Bandits" team of Jefferson Morley and David Corn broke up, Morley off on other assignments. Morley, we see, explained his article for *The New Republic,* in which he described his experiences smoking crack, in "Aftermath of a Crack Article," 11-20. It's a vitriolic blast at the government and the media on the drug war, with other journalists coming in for some nasty swipes for their alleged failure to question what the government says and does about drugs and the drug war. We'd always found the "Beltway Bandits" column a very mixed effort, sometimes enlightening with good reporting, sometimes low level. We don't know if both columnists contributed to the unevenness or not, but with each now going solo we'll soon find out.

Editor: Victor Navasky

Address: 72 Fifth Avenue
             New York, NY 10011
             (212) 242-8400

Circulation: 175,000

The National Interest

Just four years old, this remarkable foreign policy quarterly, published by Irving Kristol and co-edited by Owen Harries and Robert W. Tucker, is clearly here for the long haul, decisively moving up to the top of the pile of such journals this year. No foreign policy magazine has received as much publicity and attention since the days of "Mr. X" as this neoconservative publication. It was publication of Francis Fukuyama's "The End of History" thesis in the Summer issue that galvanized the attention. A 10 Best selection, no other article this year has stirred so much response as the one by this State Department deputy director. A major news event itself, Fukuyama's thesis has sparked global debate. Practically every single columnist has had at least one column devoted to the subject, and few publications can be found that haven't also added their voices to the discussion. Fukuyama's thesis is provocative: "What we may be witnessing is not just the end of the cold war, or the passing of a particular period of postwar history as such, but the end of history as such: that is, the end point of mankind's ideological evolution and the universalization of Western liberal democracy as the final form of human government."

As much as it's "The End of History" thesis that is now identified with *TNI,* the magazine has been a forum for a number of especially provocative and stimulating new views on issues of strategic policy. "Do We Need A New Grand Strategy?" Spring, by Edward Luttwak, caused a major shakeout in the way in which defense policy was debated and discussed. *The Washington Post* "Outlook" section, the editors of which have a honed sense for picking up critical new shifts in strategic ideas, carried an adaptation of Luttwak's *TNI* article, helping to stir up the otherwise lethargic thinking on the issue.

The spring issue also contains an excellent examination of the relationships between terrorism and Syria's President Assad, "The Syrian Connection," by Daniel Pipes. The details are riveting, the case against Syria extremely powerful. Pipes is very persuasive on how Assad's Syria has become the most successful sponsor of terrorism, managing to avoid the consequences of their action. The involvement of Syria, he also demonstrates, makes untenable arguments that injustice and political frustration are at the heart of terrorist violence.

"Answering Fukuyama" is ongoing, having begun with the forum of responses that appeared in the same issue as Fukuyama's essay, and continuing throughout the year. We skimmed the contributions on that theme in the Fall issue, but found far more important "The Theory and Practice of Japan-Bashing," by *Insight* senior editor David Brock. This was the best article we saw this year on the phenomenon, with Brock appreciative of the new information the new Japan critics provide us while at the same time resolute in cornering them on their disastrous prescriptions for policy. With the new Japan critics getting so much unrestrained access to the pages of the press this year, it was refreshing to see this important departure from the norm.

Josef Joffe's "The Revisionists," Fall, and "A Political Culture in Crisis," Fall, by Jeffrey Herf, were important contributions to new thinking about policy regarding Germany. Joffe, foreign editor of *Suddeutsche Zeitung* provides an insightful perspective on the policy implications of the waning bi-polar relationship in Europe as the status quo rapidly devolves. Herf looks at trends that ought to elevate the political and moral importance of the conservative-liberal coalition of the 1980s in Germany as the Social Democrats drift away from any defense of Atlanticism.

TNI ended the year with "A Reply to My Critics," by Francis Fukuyama, Winter 1989/90. A good part of the article is spent simply setting the record straight, i.e., reaffirming what he said as opposed to what his critics said he said, many of whom responded obviously without having read the full text of his thesis. The issue arrived just as U.S. troops were moving into Panama, providing a dramatic background in which to read Robert Bork's "The Limits of 'International Law.'" Bork's ability to maintain a clear focus through complex issues into the heart and essence of a problem comes through here. His premise is forceful: "The major difficulty with international law is that it converts what are essentially problems of international morality, as defined by a particular political community, into arguments about law that are largely drained of morality." His conclusion is even more forceful: "As currently defined, then, international law about the use of force is not even a piety; it is a net loss for Western democracies."

We don't know yet what impact this journal will have on the other foreign policy publications. These magazines have been lumbering along it seems, but now hopefully, the level of debate and discussion will be raised overall. *TNI*'s performance this year has certainly raised the standards.

Editor: Owen Harries
             Robert W. Tucker

Address: 1112 16th Street, NW
             Suite 540
             Washington, DC 20036
             (202) 467-4884

Circulation: 6,500

National Journal

National Journal really is "The Weekly on Politics and Government," as the subtitle claims. For more than 20 years, president and publisher John Fox Sullivan has upheld the highest journalistic standards to rank *NJ* as the premier Washington-insider weekly. Its no-frills, black & white professionalism leaves little room for humor, other than the regularly featured "Between the Lines" political cartoons. (And some of these are more true to life than comic relief!) All in all, *NJ* wants to be taken seriously, and is selected only by the serious reader.

No other periodical has yet matched *NJ*'s style of going beyond just the facts to provide context and analysis in an inviting presentation and coherent format. Still, long-time rival *Congressional Quarterly,* known as a "nuts and bolts" journal, recently announced plans to enhance its image. We kept an eye out for competitive conversions, thinking *NJ* might try to keep up with *CQ*'s jazzy, fast-paced format. We weren't disappointed; the 9-23 issue featured a dazzling hot pink headline screaming "Auto Glut." We expect *NJ* will not take its image too lightly; serious isn't necessarily boring.

Few have equaled *NJ*'s annual subscription price either, as it is now up to a cozy $589.00 per annum. To increase the number of subscribers, *NJ* has incorporated a special package of three copies for the price of one weekly for government subscriptions. Among the piles of literature assigned congressional staffers and government middle management, you can bet on finding *NJ*'s familiar maroon and white (and sometimes pink) cover. Used by many such subscribers as a reference guide, *NJ* even provides a two-hole punch through its slim pages and offers a set of binders for just $30 extra. But *NJ* is also meant for those outside the Beltway who wish to better assimilate the issues at hand and the minds of the decision-makers. It is already a popular item among academicians and resource centers.

In the wake of the presidential election, 1989 commenced with familiar litany on what has been and what will be. Burt Solomon's first few "White House Notebooks" previewed the Bush appointees and who's who in the White House. "The President's Peer," 1-7, profiled Secretary of State James A. Baker, III; the people in power were presented in "For Now, At Least, Collegiality Reigns Supreme Among Bush Staff," 2-4, and his article "Bush Works The Phones. . .To Stave Off White House Isolation," 4-1, was a great idea, listing thirty people with whom Bush keeps in constant contact. But the tide quickly turned to the other end of the Mall where House Speaker Jim Wright was under wraps from his own colleagues and Majority Whip Tony Coelho stepped down to avoid similar scrutiny. This truly became a year focused on the conscience of Congress and the future of the Democratic Party. Richard E. Cohen's "Fall From Power," 8-19, spoke candidly of Wright's downfall, the limits of leadership and long-term implications for the House, and his "Dispirited Democrats Try To Regroup," 9-9, was a good follow-up.

A subtle shift in *NJ* this year was its close ties to the week's news and the timeliness of its lengthy analytical updates. Health reports, with Julie Kosterlitz on the beat, presented an opportune portfolio. Her two-part mini-series on Canada's universal health care system, "Taking Care Of Canada," 7-15, and "But Not For Us," 7-22, was an excellent critique of U.S. ability to adopt such a plan. *NJ*'s look inside the Pentagon with David C. Morrison proved he is undoubtedly among the best defense correspondents for one reason — he does his homework. His "Defense Focus," a weekly column, concisely cut through to an issue's core. "The MITIgating Factor," 2-4; "After The Bombs Drop," 2-18; and "The Part-Time Military," 3-4, all reveal his ability to provide a sense of the complex to the reader while imposing logic and coherence to the various views without confusing his audience in the process. W. John Moore's special report, "Hands Off," 7-1, raised key questions on the efficacy of recusals, but he is better off writing brief columns. Moore's best work came outside of his legal eagle beat: "The Alumni Lobby," 9-9, adroitly addresses pertinent questions, raising a few of his own, as ex-Congresspeople pursue "new careers along the Potomac. . .when congressional service ends."

The magazine uses outside help for its political commentary, and this has worked well in recent years. Political bigdome William Schneider writes a full-page analytic each week, and so does the veteran duo, Jack Germond & Jules Witcover. The columns were not especially zippy this year, however, with almost nothing in them we couldn't find in *The Washington Post,* which still sells for 25 cents per copy, not the $10 per the *NJ* works out to. Ronald Brownstein, the best political reporter on the staff, is still working on a book in Los Angeles, but took time out to scribble "Facing West Nervously," 10-28, a 10 Best selection on the Pacific view from the Coast.

NJ's economic beat suffered from inconsistency. Jonathan Rauch roused himself for the best early roundup we saw on the economic horizon facing the new President, "Bush's Economic Headaches," 1-21, which presented the first serious questioning of business cycle assumptions in the popular press, a 10 Best selection. Rauch departed *NJ* in the fall for a think tank, probably with a book in mind. Lawrence Haas' budget reports still lack any focus on monetary policies, but he got a big break on "Now Or Later," 8-5, a satirical piece on Darman's now-nowism, and he picked up better than most on the capital gains issue. Bruce Stokes distressed us last year with some flip mercantilism, but this year improved his trade coverage, with a superb analysis "Beat 'Em Or Join 'Em," 2-25. He adds good economic insight on the future of U.S.-Mexican relations in "Boom At The Border," 7-29.

We were very impressed with a newcomer to the foreign policy beat, Rochelle Stanfield, who dug into the Third World in "So That's How It Works," 6-24, on a Latin American ambassador's influence-peddling. "Window Of Opportunity," 8-5, was an excellent effort to explain the Mid-East hostage crisis as part of a "super story." But *NJ* missed the boat this year on the minimum wage and coverage of China's communist controversy.

Room for improvement: *NJ*'s incredibly posed photo poses and "At A Glance," a checklist of major issues, always worth reading, but whose tightly-spaced paragraphs make it somewhat tedious. We still flip straight to "People," featuring Washington's movers and shakers and rely on "Opinion Outlook" as a credible poll. Quotes are appropriate and interviews really tell it like it is. Overall, *NJ* still rates high on our list.

Editor:	Richard S. Frank
Address:	1730 M Street, NW
	Washington, DC 20036
	(202) 857-1400
Circulation:	6,800

National Review

A new editor, John O'Sullivan came aboard at *National Review* in August, 1988, followed by a new publisher, Wick Allison, in January, 1989. The big question was, of course, what would happen to *NR* with O'Sullivan at the helm. It's clear now that in one year, O'Sullivan has transformed the magazine, strengthening it to the point where it's the best we've seen since we began this guide. One indication of its renaissance is the rate at which its circulation has soared since January, 1989 — up 17% to 140,000, the highest in *NR*'s thirty-four year history.

Among the new correspondents brought in this year, three in particular stand out. William McGurn, former deputy editorial page editor of *The Asian Wall Street Journal,* is the new Washington editor. Susan Mandel is the new congressional reporter. Both have had singular accomplishments this year, and they work well when teamed together. *NR*'s reorganized Washington operation is off to a good start this year, and its political reporting from the capital is certainly much better focused as a result. *NR* is strengthening its foreign dispatch with roving correspondent Radek Sikorski. Reporting from Qarga Dam, Afghanistan, on the siege of Kabul, from Warsaw on the daily disappearance of some vestige of the old regime, or from Windhoek, South West Africa on the future of Namibia, Sikorski's first year was impressive. His most cited report, one which created controversial reactions on the right, was "The Mystique of Savimbi," 8-18. Excerpts from Sikorski's critical assessment of the UNITA leader were run in advertisements by the Marxist government of Angola and its supporters. Although the spin put on them was along the lines of *"even* the conservative *National Review* is critical of Jonas Savimbi," the excerpts were out of context, and Sikorski in no way let the MPLA off the hook for the disasters it has put Angola through.

We had long ago stopped reading the "Letters to the Editor" in *NR,* too many of them cutesy exchanges with editor-in-chief William F. Buckley, Jr., on etymology. But the new "Letters" column is quickly becoming a forum for provocative comment and debate, and we're now eagerly turning to it each issue.

NR also devoted more attention to debates and events on the cultural front. Chilton Williamson departed as editor of the "Books" section to sign up with the conservative cultural monthly *Chronicles.* His successor as literary editor, Brad Miner, is working an attractive vibrancy into the "Books, Arts & Manners" department. The magazine had whetted our appetite for this with "The Patron Saint Of The Painted World," 12-8-88, a fiery "exchange" between Roger Scruton, editor of *Salisbury Review,* and Arianna Stassinopoulos Huffington, the author of *Picasso: Creator and Destroyer.* We ended up reading more from this section this year than we have in ages. Aram Bakshian, Jr.'s review of *Goldwyn,* 9-1, was absolutely delightful, for one. Among the other gems: "The Old Pretender When Young," by John O'Sullivan 4-21, a well-focused, richly informative review of Alistair Horne's *Harold Macmillan;* "Having It All: Uncritical Critics In Today's Art World," by James Gardner 5-19, one of the most refreshing and stimulating criticisms of criticism we've seen this year; "All Against All," by Charles R. Kessler 8-18, an examination of the libertarian-traditionalist debate in the context of a review *The Rebirth of Classical Political Economy: An Introduction to the Thought of Leo Strauss;* "When Bad Things Happen to Good Religion," by John Richard Neuhaus 11-10, a critique of "harmonial religion" based on a review of Harold Kushner's *Who Needs God?* We cite these because in their variety they point out a new excitement with ideas that is percolating again at *NR.*

Its attention to economic policy continues to develop. *NR* doesn't do reporting here so much as it solicits analytical contributions which help to raise important angles or perspectives on issues in the debate. "The Great Deficit Debate," 1-27, is an example. *NR*'s selection of economists for responses on the subject was a much more varied one than usually seen in the press, giving us a range of options beyond the predictable and conventional ones.

There's a new daring at *NR* that's refreshing. Imagine Mick Jagger of the Rolling Stones on the cover of *NR!* A caricature of an aged, bald, liver-spotted Mick Jagger sporting a hearing aid on the front of the conservative magazine generated strong protests from readers. The accompanying cover story, "That Old Devil Music," by Stuart Goldman 2-24, was especially provocative. Goldman pronounced 1977 as the year in which rock music died, and he developed the thesis that it has lost every shred of creativity since, with only a cheap imitation of the original model existing now. This provoked a far heavier than normal volume of mail from *National Review* readers who strongly disagreed. But the editors deserve credit for so soundly moving away from those previous cover stories so full of conservative boilerplate that we'd nod off to sleep scarcely halfway through them.

NR's commentary pieces remain a strong suit, as its regulars seem to have undergone some reinvigoration. Joseph Sobran, for instance, had a particularly fine year. "How to Win an Election," by Wick Allison 10-13, was especially muscular, with the *NR* publisher taking well-aimed shots at the Republican National Committee for its role in the GOP defeats taking place in House special elections. Also very strong this year, *NR*'s coverage of the environmental debate was among the best in the press. Fred S. Singer's "My Adventures In the Ozone Layer," 6-30, was only one of the excellently timed selections, appearing just as President Bush was swinging behind the environmentalists' agenda.

Other new features were initiated this year, which are still too new for full evaluation — a "From the Editor" column by John O'Sullivan; "Random Notes," useful items not necessarily organized around a central theme; "Off the Record" by Cato on the last page and "On the Scene" reports. *NR* was still ringing in the changes at the end of the year, yet what's happening shouldn't be described necessarily as a "new" *National Review* so much as a renaissance of the former *National Review* that commanded the field among conservative publications. O'Sullivan, Allison, and crew deserve a strong round of applause this year, as does William F. Buckley, Jr., for his role in giving this team the leeway needed to reassert the magazine's strengths.

Editor:	John O'Sullivan
Address:	150 East 35th Street
	New York, NY 10016
	(212) 679-7330
Circulation:	140,000

The New Republic

For years *The New Republic* has been our political periodical of choice, so far ahead of the competition, liberal and conservative, that we annually strained to find new superlatives. It's still on top this year, but for the first time we advise that it look over its shoulder. Even the Dallas Cowboys didn't win forever, and *TNR* this year did not win as often as we have come to expect. On its neoliberal side, *The Washington Monthly* gained ground over '89. On its right, *National Review* has come to life with new leadership and fresh faces. *TNR* did not sizzle this year.

It occurs to us that it was the passing of the editorial baton from Michael Kinsley to Hendrik Hertzberg that caused the slippage. Perhaps not, but there are not many like Kinsley in the American press corps, and when he departed in January to spend six months editing the American pages of the London *Economist* and scribbling off marvelous essays for *Time,* there was bound to be something of a deflation at the magazine's offices in Washington. Kinsley has been a diamond, earning four stars in every year but this one in our annual guides, with a new surprising facet at every intellectual angle. He abhors the mainstream and hugs the shores and rapids, in the white water where the action can be found, tangling hand to hand with his adversaries whatever the odds against him. Hertzberg is a mainstream liberal, with as many facets as a brick, who is cozy where it is most comfortable, among his friends.

The second big change at *TNR* was its look. Celebrating the 75th anniversary of the magazine, *TNR* did another turn that diminished it, redesigning a format that we had grown most comfortable with, to one that not one of our readers enjoys. And we had to read how management went googly-woogly over this change in the magazine's 3-20 "Notebook," a celebration of the wonderful guys who did the redesign, Drenttel Doyle Partners: "The cover format they have created is at once classical and contemporary. It harks back to the magazine's first covers of 1914 in reducing the size and therefore the weight of the word 'the' in our name, an apt modification. At the same time, the new logo opens the cover to more complex illustration and, when required, more sheer information." La de da.

The premier issue features a cover for Kathleen Day's "S&L Hell," with George Bush, Jim Wright and Donald Regan stuck in a rather gothic vision of you-know-where. Other memorably bad covers include two movie photos: "Special Futurism Issue," 7-17/24, featuring a B-movie-ish future scene that's so tacky we didn't want to look inside, and a shot of Anthony Perkins recoiling from the results of Janet Leigh's shower in "Psycho" graces the 4-17 cover for "The Alibi Industry." More user-friendly photographs included a graveyard on a rainy day, "The Last Yuppie Status Symbol," 9-11, and semi-nude Salvadoran guerrillas covered with mud aiming a gun at the camera, "Salvador," 10-16. Very little "sheer information" here this year. We are happy to say the cover caricature cartoons are still inviting.

Another stumbling block at *TNR* was the magazine's doing the "TRB from Washington" shuffle. The six-month loss of Kinsley had Hertzberg doing the column, then again when Kinsley came back to "TRB" and then to CNN's "Crossfire." Hendrick Hertzberg, now relieved of "TRB" duty, has to grow some on the job to get things sizzling again. Hertzberg's "TRB" columns while Kinsley was gadding about, casting his pearls before *Time*, just didn't have the same consistently wicked insouciance, and some were outright flops. "Gub Control," 4-10, is messy, Hertzberg firing at the assault rifle ban with an AK-47, and getting the same splattery results, obviously aiming straight into the Oval Office: ". . .George Bush, widely rumored to be president of the United States (though this could not be confirmed at press time)." We were pleased, though, that Hertzberg produced a 10 Best nomination, "The Iceman Goeth," 1-30, hilariously reconfronting the fantasy of a Dukakis 1992 campaign: *"You are growing sleepy, sleepy. . ."* With a little seasoning, perhaps helped by some vociferous editorial arguments with publisher Martin Peretz, Hertzberg might develop.

The cast of regulars changed somewhat too, adding a more constantly appearing economics editor in Robert Kuttner, and reducing Pulitzer winner Charles Krauthammer to a contributing, rather than senior, editor. Kuttner is sometimes off-center, doing much better in a political framework than dealing with the straight numbers. "The Fudge Factor," 6-19, is solid on the politics of sequestration, noting that the process "takes effect only if the estimates, not the final numbers, miss the target. This is, of course, an open invitation to cook the estimates." Krauthammer, sadly, hardly appears at all.

Fred Barnes, a four star columnist in last year's guide, also slipped a half-notch, his material not as consistently in the white water, leaving us to wonder if Kinsley's departure was felt here too. He can still produce in his "White House Watch," as we see with "Dick Darman, Wild and Crazy Guy," 1-2, a wild and crazy, ultrasharp political profile of the new OMB director, "the brains behind the Bush administration." Morton Kondracke had the best year we'd seen from him on national security issues, mostly centered around foreign policy, the only *TNR* correspondent to improve this year, much more confident, less a strain to prove himself. "The Two Black Americas," 2-6, a progress report on what Kondracke considers the administration's most urgent policy problem, the growing gap between the middle and underclasses, is detailed, fresh and valuable, as we found a great portion of his material. Like Kondracke, Mickey Kaus returned to *TNR* after a stint at *Newsweek,* but produced little this year.

The topical articles varied in quality, most quite good. Michael Massing's "Coke Dusters," 1-30, is persuasive in criticizing the State Department's next round in the war on drugs, which involves the destruction of Peruvian coca fields with herbicides dumped from specially equipped planes. Massing, a 1989 Alicia Patterson fellow, covers the environmental concerns without being specious, but weaves in a host of other policy objections. Kathleen Day, S&L reporter at *The Washington Post,* turned in a respectable overview of the key players in "S&L Hell," 3-10, despite the Dante-like cover illustration. Henry Fairlie, the resident Brit contributor, shines with "Let Them Eat Hot Dogs," 7-31, telling us the French revolution wasn't so bad, which would have packed a real punch if he'd put his conclusion first: "But we should not permit timorous conservatism to deny that *together* America and France made the Age of Revolution which, for all its fearful atrocities in Europe, improved the lot that most men and women could expect in this world." Michael Lewis does a devastatingly thorough job on the costs and benefits of American Express v. Visa or MasterCard, "Leave Home Without It: The Absurdity of the American Express Card," 9-4.

But when they were bad they were awful. "Old Bland-Dad," by Timothy Noah 4-3, makes Noah look foolish as he tries (and fails) to prove that George Bush's father was really an underwhelming figure because his jobs came from Yale connections and, even though he was a captain in WWI in the field artillery and saw action in the Meuse-Argonne offensive: "he was no Sergeant York. . ..Books about the Eisenhower and Kennedy years, when Prescott served his two Senate terms, scarcely mention him." Arrrrgh.

Jefferson Morley's "What Crack Is Like," 10-2, probably ruined *TNR* forever for Drug Czar Bill Bennett, a truly dopey piece that should never have run, Morley doing us the favor of trying crack so he could report on his high, an unintentional advertisement for crack that reads like a 1968 LSD apologia from a zonked-out flower child. Fortunately some of the drug coverage from *TNR* was superlative, and appeared prior to Morley's quick smoke. "Crackdown," by James Q. Wilson and John J. DiIulio Jr. 7-10, is a sterling effort to move along the policy debate, a discussion of the grave social problems that cause addiction and an excellent outline of perspectives that take the war on drugs to a new level of polemics. The editors themselves can take credit for "Crackmire," 9-11, an equally thoughtful and startling examination of Bush's drug plan, impressively evaluating its chances of success on the margin.

Editor: Hendrik Hertzberg

Address: 1220 19th Street, NW
                      Washington, DC 20036
                      (202) 331-7494

Circulation: 100,000

Newsweek

Two and three years ago we were decidedly unhappy with the screechy, socially conscious path the No. 2 newsweekly decided to race down, screaming "Impact!" which was the byword at the time. Most unpleasant journalism, we thought, souped-up news dispatches and blood-and-gore photos. We asked, in the '87 guide, "Is this what publisher Katharine Graham wants to be remembered for?" Simultaneously we were patting *Time* on the back for maintaining a measure of restraint in the pursuit of evanescent circulation numbers at the high cost of integrity.

What's happened in the years since we could not have predicted. *Time*'s new editor, Henry Muller, has turned loose the masthead into a do-your-own-thing experiment, seeming to believe that untrammeled individuality will produce quality and distinction. At least that's what we think he has in mind. The upside is that some of the vitality he sought has appeared, with individual voices spinning individual tales. The downside is editorial excess, *Time*'s equivalent of "Impact!" Meanwhile, at *Newsweek*, where the souping up did not produce circulation gains, the horns have been pulled in. We were more comfortable with it last year, and this year thought it positively responsible. We no longer don combat gear and keep defensive weapons at hand when we sink into our armchair with a copy. And yet, we're still not quite happy, suspecting Editors Richard M. Smith, Maynard Parker, and Stephen Smith may have shifted too far in the other direction, swinging from an anarchy of individual voices to a thick soup of many.

This commitment to consistency, while an admirable ideal, sometimes produces less than stimulating reportage, and walking such a fine line tends to squelch the initiative to dig that a reporter otherwise might have taken and run with. It also gives reporters more incentive to skim, or to report fluff. We're most pleased that *Time* has moved to many single byline stories, which strengthens accountability and is more likely to produce excellence. *Newsweek* will reward Andrew Nagorski or Bill Powell or Gregg Easterbrook occasionally with top billing. We think every piece should have a single byline, with the stars getting bigger type sizes, if that is the reward system.

Staff changes were held to a minimum, with few additions or deletions. Adam Platt, an *Insight* veteran we regard highly, came aboard, but had too few bylines to make much of a difference. Timothy Noah left the Washington bureau for the staff of *The New Republic.*

Political coverage was solid and informative this year, with just about the right balance of analytics in its news columns without noticeable pursuit of personal agendas. Chief political correspondent Howard Fineman headed the team, along with Eleanor Clift and Tom Morganthau, reporting on the administration's various ethics flaps. The trio delivered an in-depth, analytical account of "Tower's Troubles," 3-6, that was far superior to *Time*'s similar coverage of the defeated nomination.

"The World of Congress," by Jonathan Alter with Fineman and Clift 4-24, was another clear and civilized winner over the screech in *Time*: "Foul air is not a new product of Capitol Hill. Thomas Reed described colleagues who 'never opened their mouths without subtracting from the sum of human knowledge.' As a group, today's congressmen are less venal and better educated than many of their predecessors." The analysis goes a bit deeper, still without breaching an editorial wall: "Congressmen hear a lot: from lobbyists, voters, colleagues. But can they see? Like the sightless fish found in caves, they move to the vibrations of their environment with little ability to break from the school, much less peer ahead." A memorable metaphor.

In what seemed a ploy for sympathy, *Newsweek* was the only one of the weeklies to give cover prominence to "Barney Frank's Story," 9-25, told compassionately, yet pointedly by Morganthau, again with Fineman, Clift, Mark Starr and Bill Turque: ". . .these days, it can be very risky to act like a jerk. There is no question that Barney Frank did so." Clift's accompanying interview, with Frank pleading that his emotional vulnerability and "protracted adolescence" contributed to his errors in judgement, was a questionable damage-control effort on Frank's part, further reinforcing the contention that he did, indeed, act like a jerk. There may have been some dissent within *Newsweek* about putting this on the cover, but the magazine has been high on the Massachusetts legislator, and did not simply desert him. It was an important story in the wider realm of the ethics issue. And we wanted to read a sympathetic account from some source, to weigh the issues, and *Newsweek* did so with taste and sobriety.

Moving from federal to local and state politics, Fineman's "Pro-Choice Politicking," with Michael Reese, Daniel Glick and Patricia King 10-9, offered some perceptive insights on how different candidates used the abortion issue in recent elections. In his solo reports on the politics of this off-year, Fineman was a standout in the press corps, the best year he's had since we have been reviewing his work, ahead of the curve for the most part on the racial politics, and the abortion and ethics issues.

The magazine produced less impressive material on the other major social issues that were on all our minds, drugs, crime and America's underclass. There were plenty of stories, but too much at the level of the police blotter, focusing on spot, regional crimes, and failing to deliver a whole-picture analysis. "Deaths in the Name of Life," 5-8, and "I Told Them I'd Be Back," 9-25, are just two examples of what we thought to be less significant regional crimes touted in the "National Affairs" section. A better cover story "Can the Children Be Saved?" 9-11, intimately examines a crack-infested neighborhood in north Philadelphia, offering a poignant, discouraging glimpse at the scarred lives of the people, particularly the children, involved in the everyday battles of the drug war.

The business section is often useful, as well as enlightening. Jane Bryant Quinn's column offers clear, sound financial advice, alternating on the business commentary page with Robert Samuelson. They have both improved by staying within their limitations, trying swan dives instead of triple economic back flips, although Samuelson had us groaning over his corporate elite arguments against capital gains, "Bribery Is Bad Policy," 3-6, a belly flop. In "The Battle Over Time, Inc.," by John Schwartz with Carolyn Friday, Peter McKillop and Karen Springen cover 6-26, gives a clear, complete summary of the Time-Warner-Paramount merger, showing up the competition at *Time,* who noticeably provided less prominent coverage of their own takeover troubles.

Mark Miller, David Pauly and Rich Thomas tackle the heavier topics, with Annetta Miller, Dody Tsiantar and John Schwartz filling out the coverage. The lighter topics too, some reading more like human interest stories with a business twist, often contained solid information, packaged entertainingly. Drenched beneath Tom Mathews' salivations over *Vanity Fair* editor Tina Brown, "High Gloss News" 5-1, is a nice profile of this smart, capable (and very beautiful) woman who has taken the magazine by storm and cornered the talent market, but we wish Mathews had cooled off before sitting down to gush over Brown's "scarlet dress. . ..her nails polished tooth-and-claw red, her ankles sculpted into drop-dead stiletto heels, her silvery voice. . .."

Gregg Easterbrook's special report "Cleaning Up Our Mess," 7-24, was among the better reports on the environment this year. But Easterbrook echoes the consensus reported in the press of late that "there simply are no respectable anti-environment positions left," where he could have dug just a bit deeper to challenge *Time*'s blatant advocacy position on the Endangered Earth. We sense the editors are so aware of young adults having been spoon-fed on the environment as kids that they think it's better to cater to established tastes than present serious discourse. Still and all, *Newsweek* was superior to *Time* in this regard. Easterbrook's report debunks several misconceptions on both sides of the issue. A perceptive sidebar "A White House Chill on Global Warming," 11-13, notes that "what Ronald Reagan was to acid rain, George Bush may be to global warming," essentially blocking action on the issue, due to lack of significant proof and worry about endangering the economy. Expanding on that topic in the same issue, "E Pluribus, Plures," by Sharon Begley *et al.,* explores arguments for and against how states are responding to Bush's inaction by imposing their own legislation, so that they, in effect, are "no longer merely implementing federal standards but are setting the environmental agenda."

Most of the major foreign developments received cover treatment, but we got little here we hadn't already consumed in the newspaper and television accounts, except for some fresh analysis here and there. "The Party's Over: Communism Crumbles in Poland," cover 8-28, and a eulogy for "The Wall," cover 11-20, were adequate fare for those who take the magazine as the only source of print news. The weekly's special team of China correspondents, Melinda Liu, Carroll Bogert, Tony Clifton, Rod Nordland and Russell Watson, provided good coverage 6-12 and 6-19, but with no fresh angles or insights. The "Amateur Hour" cover 10-16, with an exultant General Noriega grinning at us after the Panama fiasco, probably helped crystallize opinion for the December invasion, but the report itself, with bylines galore, was choppy patchwork. From more of a human-interest perspective, Andrew Nagorski's "The Winter of Their Discontent," 4-3, nicely captures the growing spirit of nationalism in the Soviet provinces. He expertly uses quotes from Soviet citizens to illustrate "a country — an empire, to be more accurate — threatened by the belief that it is beginning to crumble." Nagorski also scored rather well with "A Double Standard," 12-18, mulling Gorbachev's move to allow Eastern Europe to end one-party rule, while drawing the line at the Soviet border.

Newsweek this year continued its attempts to draw readers with faddish cover stories, soft stuff. Some went down with us okay, but there was nothing in the portfolio that was especially impressive. "California, American Dream, American Nightmare," 7-31, gave it a chance to display photos of a surf girl, a smoggy city, and autos bumping on a freeway. We get sappy statistics here: "By the year 2000 the state's average house price could reach $470,000." And, "by the year 2010, a commute that now takes an average of 45 minutes could increase to more than two hours." We liked the cover "All About Alzheimer's," 12-18, especially the piece by Barbara Kantrowitz, "Trapped Inside Her Own World," which took us through the early symptoms on up. The "Medical Mystery Tour" by Geoffrey Cowley, on the science side, would have lost us entirely except for an explanatory graphic. "In an Alzheimer's brain, vast numbers of these cholingeric cells, along with many cells from other neurotransmitter systems, show two telltale abnormalities. . .." Whew.

"Lyme Disease," 5-22, offered more alarming details about this summer's hottest health scare, failing to mention until the second-to-last paragraph that "some physicians are skeptical about Lyme anxiety and claim the disease is actually being *over*-diagnosed in certain cases." Charles Leerhsen's "How Disney Does It," 4-3, didn't warrant the cover attention it received, reading too much like a travel guide to the new Disney theme park. The business section should have handled this seriously and it would have meant more to us. "Hot Cities: America's Best Places to Live and Work," 2-6, "The Summer of '69," 7-3, and "How Kids Learn," 4-17, all managed to inform and entertain, although the topics were not very newsworthy. "The Blue Planet," 9-4, fascinated with an up-close, detailed look at Neptune, courtesy of Voyager 2.

The magazine ran a slew of people-profiles on its covers, peeking into the lives of spy novelist John le Carre, 6-5, actress Michelle Pfeiffer, 11-6, and drug czar William Bennett, 4-19. "The Innovators: 25 Americans on the Cutting Edge," 10-2, delivered 25 mini-profiles of people on the forefront of new developments in science, business, education, the arts and "fun & games." *Newsweek* lost marks for stepping into the Leona-bashing ring with an unnecessarily snide and tacky cover, "Rhymes With Rich," 8-21. Sure, her own defense lawyer called her a "bitch" — and that well-worn excuse is faithfully given in the accompanying article — but this glaring headline was a cheap shot, delivered with obvious, wicked delight. The cover, as well as the article, prompted angry mail from readers, as the editors noted several readers doubted that "had the story concerned a male we would have said, 'Rhymes With Dastard.'"

Dancing the fine line between "Impact!" journalism and outright sensationalism, the weeklies have been succumbing to the use of graphic, even grisly visual images of blood-and-guts gore that we suspect would be censored from prime-time TV newscasts. We noticed a foreshadow of the trend in the 4-17 coverage of Namibia, which featured a short, one page article entitled "A Bloody Road to Peace," accompanied by a small picture that was vividly described in the first graph for all those who might have missed it, "One young guerilla had his head and shoulders crushed. Another sprawled next to a corpse with a head but no face." We'd hoped this venture into sensationalism wouldn't continue, but when events in Panama and China offered prime photo-ops, how could *Newsweek* resist?

We continue to prefer the magazine's back page essay, alternating between George Will and Meg Greenfield, to the various approaches of the other newsweeklies. Will's columns wowed us a year ago, with plenty of meaty information slabbed into his philosophical sandwiches. But man does not live by bread alone, and Will wowed us a little bit less this year. "The Winds of Words," 5-22, was the right metaphor for too much of his material, this one on General Noriega. But to get to him we have to chew through Napoleon, Beethoven, the Duke of Norfolk, and Sir Thomas More. On the same subject, after the October fiasco in Panama, Meg Greenfield offered "When Fury Turns to Foolishness," 10-16, warning against taking hasty action against Noriega, sound advice: "This is the danger zone we are entering if history is any guide — the moment when an embarrassed irate American government must guard against being tempted or pressured into truly foolish actions it will eventually regret."

Editor:	Richard M. Smith
Address:	444 Madison Avenue
	New York, NY 10022
	(212) 350-4000
Circulation:	3,288,453

New York

On the cutting edge of issues in the Big Apple, *New York* covered much ground in '89. A heated mayoral race, violent racial crimes, crack and homelessness helped to set the agenda at the weekly. At the same time, *NY* manages to sing the praises of the five boroughs with its intelligent film, theatre and art reviews and various features on life in Manhattan. Above all else, *NY* keeps its wry sense of humor about life in the city, its denizens and its problems.

The regulars at *New York* continue to be consistently impressive and professional. Off the national campaign trail, contributing editor Joe Klein picked up the local campaigns, no small potatoes when you're talking about New York. Klein covered the mayoral primaries and campaign with the same humor and savvy we saw in the nationals and earned our highest rating in this guide, along with a 10 Best selection for political reporting, "Race: The Issue," 5-29, and "Race: Still the Issue," 11-13. Klein looks squarely at the racial polarization sweeping New York in 1989, with the mayoralty race in the foreground. In "Ghandi vs. Gumby," 11-6, he sharply critiques the New York mayoral candidates, Rudolph Giuliani and David Dinkins, capturing the mood of the voters and campaigns. Klein vividly illustrates the dichotomy the voters face, some of whom probably yearn for the days of Ed Koch, bringing his national expertise to the heart of the city.

Ed Diamond's media coverage is steady and reliable, as he himself is a careful reporter. We thought his material could have been closer to the frontiers than it was this year, however. "The New (Land) Lords of the Press," 2-27, contains quick-mini profiles of the new press scions in New York, who started out doing something else, mostly real estate. But the *New York Post's* Peter Kalikow and *U.S.News & World Report's* Mort Zuckerman are old stuff, at least as presented here.

The lighter side of business is all that concerns *New York,* content to leave international issues and the nuts and bolts to *The Wall Street Journal.* Bernice Kanner sells Madison Avenue to the rest of us, her columns decisive and competitive with the big hitters in the dailies. "A Store is Born," 9-18, on A&S's move to Manhattan after years in the boroughs, sparkles with anticipation and stratagems without sugar coating the problems the retailer will face, a sterling effort. John Crudele was succeeded as "Bottom Line" columnist by Christopher Byron, former assistant managing editor at *Forbes,* giving the magazine some extra expertise. Byron's columns work better than his predecessor's simply because he tends to stick to one subject, rather than giving us little bits and pieces of different stories. "The RICO Squeeze," 7-17, clearly explains the complicated RICO history and forfeiture provisions, as six defendants, 5 Princeton/Newport partners and a former trader at Drexel are charged with RICO violations, organized and complete. Bryon avoids the profiles that are so prevalent at *Forbes,* preferring to stick to the issues.

New York's cover stories this year were thoughtful and thought-provoking, examining much deeper concerns than were bounded by the Hudson and East Rivers. Though most are frivolous covers, mostly confined to holiday entertaining, the Malcolm Forbes birthday bash, seasonal fashions, weekend retreats, etc., *NY* wasn't necessarily meant to be a *serious* digest of political or social commentary, but to be a barometer of events in and around the city. A good number of these covers are serious, and surprisingly well executed. Eric Pooley's "Fighting Back Against Crack," 1-23, is solid on neighborhood associations forming within New York City to beat back the waves of crackheads. "Central Park: What Really Happened," by Michael Stone 8-14, gives a comprehensive bird's eye view of the so-called "wilding" case. *NY's* abortion cover of 9-18 by Jeane Kasindorf is reflective enough, but ultimately inconclusive, which we actually did not mind, as this reflects the complexity of the subject and the emotion involved. In "What Really Happened in Bensonhurst," 11-6, Michael Stone looks into some of the underlying factors that may have been a part of the case, as well as examining the stories of the principals, a powerful overview.

We continue to appreciate *New York's* team of crackerjack reviewers: David Denby, John Simon, John Leonard and Kay Larson, among them. Their reviews of the art show, the new play, the latest film craze, sparkle and are among the best-written criticisms in print, much preferred to *The New York Times'* Sunday "Arts & Leisure" section. Simon got into hot water for his suggesting the performers in Joseph Papp's production of William Shakespeare's "The Winter's Tale" are too Jewish and too black: Mandy Patinkin looks like a cartoon Jew; actress Alfre Woodward resembles the Topsy of *Uncle Tom's Cabin.* Ed Kosner defended Simon against the slings and arrows of outraged readers, and while we wouldn't defend Simon's review, we didn't see "Tale" either.

Then, of course, there are the columns in *New York,* the delicious "Intelligencer," "Fast Track," "Fun City" (which is made still brighter on city life occasionally by the effervescent William Geist), the idiosyncratic "Sales & Bargains," and, of course, the New York theater and movie and personal listings. An enjoyable must for residents and the traveler in and out of Manhattan, and a fun read for those who like to visit and might like to live there, *New York* easily remains our favorite weekly for the metropolitan area, generally unstuffy and happy to be alive and well and in the Big Apple.

Editor: Edward Kosner

Address: 755 Second Avenue
               New York, NY 10017
               (212) 880-0700

Circulation: 433,246

The New Yorker

For the past decade, *The New Yorker*'s future rested on the answer to one question — would *The New Yorker* become more like *The New York Review of Books* or more like *Vanity Fair*? Would *The New Yorker* become more of a journal devoted to analyzing political and economic questions, or would it become a magazine devoted to trends and glitz?

Under editor Robert Gottlieb, *The New Yorker* has managed to avoid the dangers of over-trendiness and over-tendentiousness. It still doesn't sing the way it did when we were in knickers, but at least it is making sounds like it wants to try. Circulation is up a bit and so is the advertising. Gottlieb has changed *The New Yorker* in two fundamental ways. First, he has brought in many new staff writers and bylines. Second, he has largely replaced the three-part exhaustive public policy discussions so pervasive in William Shawn's last years. We now get lots of foreign affairs instead, but too often of postage stamp countries. Why not a long look at Buffalo?

The only major series purely devoted to public policy in the first six months of 1989 was Paul Brodeur's exhaustive (and exhausting!) series on radiation, 6-12/6-26. Brodeur's piece (written by a survivor of the Shawn era) was atypical. The only regular political coverage was Elizabeth Drew's "Letter From Washington" column. Gottlieb tried out a variety of writers to see if they would sink or swim. Most sank, particularly Francis Fitzgerald's "Memories of the Reagan Era," 1-16, easily one of the ten worst political pieces of 1989.

Washington coverage was provided by Elizabeth Drew and John Newhouse. Drew's problem for some of us is that she writes as if the reader would see *nothing* else out of Washington; she tries to be magisterial, but frequently ends up tendentious, her four-to-five page dispatches too often long hikes. Still, a minority here appreciates her seriatim style. placing one foot after another, and we always look for her byline in the table of contents. Newhouse started out badly with a dull two-parter on arms control, but his profile of Tom Foley, 4-10, was thorough, although a bit whiskery, and his analysis of the current state of terrorism, 7-10, was quite meaty and informative.

Robert Heilbroner's "The Triumph of Capitalism," 1-23, was among the best pieces of economic analysis we read during the year, earning a 10 Best nomination. The two pieces of press criticism were Janet Malcolm's controversial series on Jeffrey MacDonald and Joe McGuinness, 3-13 and 3-20, which was overlong and confused, even to someone familiar with *Fatal Vision,* and Leonard Garment's curious history of Richard Nixon's one attempt at being a Supreme Court lawyer, 4-17.

Foreign coverage was extensive and of wildly varying quality. The two best pieces were Raymond Bonner's reportage on the Sudanese civil war, 3-13, and H.D.S. Greenway's look at the current state of foreign affairs in Cambodia, 7-17, both of which were at the three-star level.

We were less taken with William Finnegan's report on Mozambique, 5-13 and 5-20, and Lawrence Wechsler's history of military torture in Uruguay, 4-3 and 4-10, partly because of the spin, but mostly because of *The New Yorker* method of compiling trivia for no apparent reason. The worst piece was Robert Coram's look at Antigua, 2-6, which dumps 20,000 finely-crafted *New Yorker* words on a tiny Caribbean island; the island barely survives.

Non-political writing in *The New Yorker* continued its high standards. Particularly notable were Sallie Tisdale on elephants, 1-23, Ian Frazier on the Great Plains, 2-20, 2-27, and 3-6; Sue Hubble on pie, 3-27; Israel Shenker on the second edition of the Oxford English Dictionary, 4-3; John Seabrook on gold mining, 4-24; William Pfaff on T. E. Lawrence, 5-8; William Murray on the battle of Monte Cassino, 5-15; Israel Shenker on Sotheby's buyer of medieval manuscripts, 5-29; and Lis Harris on the horse race in Siena, Italy, 6-5. These continued *The New Yorker* tradition of lively writing on general-interest topics.

Editor: Robert Gottlieb

Address: 25 West 43rd Street
                     New York, NY 10036
                     (212) 840-3800

Circulation: 608,138

The New York Review of Books

The strength of this publication continues to be the standard it sets for what good book reviews should be — "probing essays on the real issues raised by the most important books being published." The editors work a respectable variety of voices into each issue, attempting to provide readers with authoritative judgment on a wide range of subjects. On the whole, the writing and the intellectual stimulation is appreciable.

TNYRB was an important source of debate, discussion, and dispatches on the China story this year. Early it provided a forum for Fang Lizhi, the former vice president of the University of Science and Technology, Anhui China, and critic of the Chinese regime. "China's Despair and China's Hope," 2-2, assesses the road to democracy in China, against a growing democratic consciousness. This leaves little room for pundits who've been asserting that "democracy" is an alien concept in China. Lizhi is crystal clear that that assertion is baseless. "Keeping Up With the New China," 3-16 by John K. Fairbank gives a rich sense of the Chinese modernization effort, which is of so titanic a scale that he deserves special credit for being able to grasp it all.

Orville Schell's "China's Spring," 6-29, is a magnificent account of the student democracy movement's takeover of Tiananmen Square and the hunger strikes. Schell details with intensity the swirling, heady excitement, while keeping a firm grasp of the reality of limits and constraints on how far the movement would be able to go. In the same issue, Perry Link's "The Chinese Intellectual and the Revolt" provides rich accounts of how the "Beijing Revolt" of 1989 matured, and the depths of its influence throughout Chinese society. Both were pre-crackdown reports, but aside from perhaps an optimism about the direction of immediate events the information and insights are abundant.

The 7-20 issue contains a package of absorbing articles about China. "The End of the Chinese Revolution," by Roderick MacFarquhar, is a very substantive assessment of the post-Tiananmen situation in China. First, however, MacFarquhar effectively traces the attempts of Deng Xiaoping to carry forward China's modernization and locates the ground over which he stumbled in attempting to revamp the political system. It's this perspective that is the best part of his article. Fang Lizhi received tens of thousands of letters from sympathizers all across China for his continued championing of human rights in China. Orville Schell introduces a selection of these in "Letter from the Other China." We discover that Fang Lizhi is hardly a peculiarity, as the letters make clear how widespread are the sentiments he expresses. Simon Ley's "The Curse of the Man Who Could See the Little Fish at the Bottom of the Ocean," mixes harsh reality with cynicism: "Exactly how long should a 'decent interval' last before we can resume business-as-usual with the butchers of Beijing." The senile and ferocious despots who decided to slaughter the youth, the hope and intelligence of China, may have made many miscalculations — still, on one count they were not mistaken: they shrewdly assessed that our capacity to sustain our indignation would be very limited indeed."

TNYRB's coverage of reform in the Communist world also provided readers with a combination of reports containing details and analysis that were impressive. "Moscow: the Struggle for Reform," 3-30, by Abraham Brumberg and "In Gorbachev's Courts," 5-18, by George P. Fletcher, were both very informative pictures of the current state of *perestroika* and *glasnost*. Peter Reddaway provided a excellent appraisal of the current status of Mikhail Gorbachev's political fortunes in "The Threat to Gorbachev," 8-17, and Timothy Garton Ash updated his report on the transformations in the East Bloc with "Revolution in Hungary and Poland," 8-17.

The foreign affairs focus of this publication has always been sharp, and on the major stories the editors kept us well-informed. The political reporting was less intense this year, but Thomas B. Edsall produced one of the best analyses we saw on the erosion of political legitimacy among the Democrats, "Democrats on the Take," 4-13. A bit partisan perhaps, although not unacceptably biased, in his views regarding GOP motives for campaign finance reform, he's sharp on what ails the Democrats: "the party has yet to develop the general economic policies that would appeal to middle-class voters and attract their contributions."

The best of all the articles carried this year in *TNYRB* is unquestionably "Castro's Purge Trials," 12-7 by Julia Preston. The former San Salvador bureau chief for *The Washington Post* goes over every angle and then some in the trial of Cuban military hero Arnaldo Ochoa Sanchez for drug trafficking. Preston unwinds the many, many complexities involved in this trial, tracing webs back to other figures in the regime, and explores the trial in the lights of several critical contexts. One is the general crisis within the Castro regime, and the commitment Fidel Castro has to preventing any attempts to liberalize the country's communism. The report is a 10 Best selection for the year in foreign correspondence. We learn more about the current situation in Cuba in this single report than we would from all the accumulated dispatches for the year on the country. Editors Silvers and Epstein deserve applause for getting this story into print.

Editors:	Robert B. Silvers and Barbara Epstein
Address:	250 West 57th Street New York, NY 10107 (212) 757-8070
Circulation:	130,000

Policy Review

A fortress of not conservative, but progressive conservative thinking, the respected quarterly of the Heritage Foundation addresses policy issues of the day. Foreign or domestic, strategic or religious, social or political, there are few pertinent questions left unasked, though some are left unanswered. Going on seventeen, *Policy Review* exemplifies the Heritage credo, "dedicated to the principles of free competitive enterprise, limited government, individual liberty, and a strong national defense," a posture perfectly acceptable for this opinion journal, edited with youthful enthusiasm by Adam Meyerson.

A special Spring issue on the Reagan legacy, though, reminds us that *PR* is a devoted cheering section for the GOP. For $3 we get a not especially impressive memorium that reads like a long after-dinner speech. As a commemorative edition, it catalogs "the best" snippets of the Reagan speeches plus several pages of brief tributes to RR and his tenure. The question is posed: "How Great Was Ronald Reagan?" Answers come from Karl O'Lessker, James Nuechterlein, Stephen E. Ambrose, and George H. Nash. All four said: "Pretty Great." Associate publisher Burton Yale Pines pens "The Ten Legacies of Ronald Reagan," which reads like Kremlin boilerplate.

Editor Meyerson provides a chronology of "One Hundred Conservative Victories," a listing of milestones by Reagan and the conservative movement over the course of the eight years of RR's presidency. It gets pretty thin in spots, however. In 1986, for example, the victory count begins with "January 25. **CBS Sees Light on Poverty.** Conservative wisdom on poverty becomes conventional wisdom as Bill Moyers' report on CBS, 'The Vanishing Family: Crisis in Black America,' blames breakdown of families for persistence of poverty in inner cities." So where's the conservative "victory"? Moyers, we're sure, will argue that the families broke down because the rich didn't help the poor.

The four regular issues of *PR* contain generally high-quality material from myriad sources. As with other think periodicals, most articles are policy analytics written by those who make the policy or by think-tank veterans. "SDI and Its Enemies," Fall, expands on a speech Vice President Dan Quayle had given to SDI partisans, not especially easy reading for a broader audience, but useful in letting the faithful know where things stand on strategic defense. Rep. Mickey Edwards (R-Okla.) takes a sweeping look at the constitutional powers granted to Congress and the President with regard to checks and balances and the line-item veto, "Of Conservatives and Kings," Spring. Conservative intellectuals make a significant contribution to the journal: Alan Keyes tells us about his failed Maryland Senate race, a thoughtful retrospective useful for future African-American people, "My Race for the Senate," Spring, but otherwise of limited utility.

In the same issue, Linda Chavez's exploration of the progress of Hispanic Americans, "Tequila Sunrise," disintegrates many misconceptions, and she openly advocates no handouts: "Hispanic leaders who call for ever more government intervention in the lives of Hispanics should consider the law of unintended consequences. Too often the helping hand of government becomes a vise of dependency." An excerpt from former Democrat Gov. Dixy Lee Ray's coming book, "The Greenhouse Blues," Summer, calmly accounts for the various CO_2 emissions and suggests that high sunspot activity may account for much of the warm weather, citing historical data to support the idea. One paragraph is worth the whole article: "The quantity of air-polluting materials produced by man during his entire existence on Earth does not begin to equal the quantities of toxic gases and particulates spewed forth into the atmosphere from just three volcanic eruptions: Krakatau in Indonesia in 1883, Mount Katmai in Alaska in 1912, and Hekla in Iceland in 1947. Mt. St. Helens pumped out 910,000 metric tons of carbon dioxide during six months in 1982, not including the eruption." We thought the point worth developing, though.

William Tucker, who so impressed us two years ago with his "Where Do the Homeless Come From?" *National Review* 9-25-87, expands his thesis of fingering rent control as responsible for much of the homeless crisis, regulation preventing the marketplace from natural turnover and self-improvement, in "Home Economics: The Housing Crisis that Overregulation Built," Fall, concluding "The housing crisis of the 1980s, then, is like the energy crisis of the 1970s. It is a problem of overregulation. Municipalities zone out new housing and then try to undo the effects with rent control and inclusionary schemes that provide housing only for the well-informed and politically connected." A contribution from *Insight*'s Charlotte Low Allen, "Special Delivery," Summer, is a comprehensive, readable examination of the barriers to adoption, cultural and political, and the mountains of red tape involved.

In addition to domestic policy, there's at least one article per issue reviewing foreign affairs. Sen. Robert Kasten (R-Wis.) is trenchant on Central America, "Capitalism from the Ashes," Spring. Publisher Pines defines a strategy for "Waiting for Mr. X," Summer, putting together the pieces of a post-Cold War Europe. After Tiananmen Square, an excellent trio of China articles appeared in the Fall issue, which, taken together, form a contiguous whole on the failure of communism in the People's Republic: "Chiang Kai-shek's Second Chance," by Leonard Unger; "Let a Dozen Flowers Bloom," by Karl Zinsmeister; and "Gullible's Travels," by Steven W. Mosher. The latter piece, on the "Inaccurate Art of China Watching," recounts some of the silly things American China "experts" have said about its Communist revolution since 1949. Harvard provided two of the best. John K. Fairbank in 1972 wrote in *Foreign Affairs* that the Maoist Revolution is "on the whole the best thing that has happened to the Chinese people in many centuries." John K. Galbraith wrote: "Dissidents are brought firmly into line in China, but, one suspects, with great politeness." Harrison Salisbury of *The New York Times* in '72 wrote that "In a magnificent way, it has healed the sick, fed the hungry and given security to the ordinary man," ignoring reports that the 1960-62 period held a black famine in which at least ten million perished.

Editor Adam Meyerson, trained at the editorial knee of *The Wall Street Journal*'s Robert L. Bartley, conducts policymaker interviews in each issue, revealing little about himself, but much about his subjects: Elliott Abrams on RR's Latin America policy, "Foggy Bottom Freedom Fighter," Winter; James Miller, formerly of OMB, "The Man Who Brought the Deficit Down," Spring; Fred C. Ikle, ex-Undersecretary of Defense for Policy 1981-87 on national security issues, "The Ever-Present Danger," Summer; and Sen. Phil Gramm on conservatism, "The Genius of Ordinary People," Fall. Each was moderately engaging, Meyerson better than most in his ability to cull pertinent answers from his subject. We'd rather Meyerson tackle tough issues himself and put together his reported material in highly provocative and engaging essays. His "Adam Smith's Welfare Government," Fall, is not what we mean, however. This short essay underscores the "progressive" conservativism in *Policy Review,* quoting from Adam Smith's 18th century writings to show that the supply-sider from Scotland believed in limited welfare. But it really is not pushing on any frontiers.

We get a bit more of that from Assistant Editor Ben Wildavsky, who scores with "McJobs," Summer, a 10 Best nomination. A standout from among his other creditable efforts, "McJobs" reveals McDonald's to be America's largest job training program, replete with salient facts and pertinent, compelling examples. In "Blackboard Jungle," Fall, Wildavsky pens a similar treatise on the school system, focused on discipline as a too-often missing ingredient. Still, we don't get any sense the quarterly is exploring unexplored terrain, especially on domestic issues, but rather consolidating opinion, bringing up the ranks from the Reagan years. As a result there were no real breakthroughs this year at the policy journal. Still and all, there's no quarterly other than *Policy Review* that explores such a wide spectrum of domestic and foreign questions from a Main Street conservative perspective. Perhaps it will see 1990 as a time to pull up stakes and head off to new horizons.

Editor: Adam Meyerson

Address: 214 Massachusetts Avenue, NE
               Washington, DC 20002
               (202) 546-4400

Circulation: 13,679

Reader's Digest

Still mostly prepackaged material, *Reader's Digest* appeals to supermarket-going housewives and policymakers alike. A clever combination, month after month, of selected articles previously published in other sources and original pieces by well known thinkers and journalists, for the most part conservative, plus staff writers of the same hue, makes for a mix that enlightens and entertains. The selection of digested material, though, is what makes up the bulk of the pocketbook, and the editors keep their fingers on enough of the 29 million subscribers to do a good job of selecting what they think will be found useful.

The recycled material is mostly mainstream or conservative, the editors seldom venturing into left-of-center territory. A. M. Rosenthal's three articles on the gulag, one a 10 Best selection from *The 1989 MediaGuide,* were reconstituted by the *RD* editors into "Into the Heart of the Gulag," 4-89, a powerful reconstruction that brings the infamous Soviet prison camps into the heartland a million miles away in position and politics. "Crime and Responsibility," 8-89, brings together a pair of articles by Charles Krauthammer and Ken Ringle from *The Washington Post* on the plight of the victims, respectively Bonnie Garland, murdered in her own bed by her minority Yale boyfriend, and Pamela Small, attacked in a hardware store by John Paul Mack, who would become Rep. Jim Wright's right-hand man. The duo is a powerful punch for the rights of victims, who too often are forgotten in the process, brought to small towns courtesy again of *RD.* John Barnes' expose of cable TV, "Cable TV's Costly Monopoly," 10-89, from *The Washington Monthly,* provides a free-market parable with something for nearly everyone, as it seems that the whole world is wired for cable. The powers that be at *RD* seldom get more radical than a Rosenthal, or a *Post* piece, but we're encouraged by their willingness to venture further than already charted territory.

The original material in *RD* is creative and often quite good. *RD* maintains quite a masthead of contributing and roving editors, most of whom keep a day job but obviously devote energy to the articles they do for the monthly. Evans and Novak's "Congressmen For Life: The Incumbency Scandal," 6-89, is a tightly packaged indictment of a Democratic Congress rigging the rules to maintain a 99% re-election security; although only an overview of the various methods by which Congressional privileges are abused, this is well executed. Covering education, Trevor Armbrister offers "Scandal In Our Trade Schools," 1-89, grass-roots work against training center rip-offs, and "New Jersey's Battle For Better Schools," 11-89, proposing practical, proven solutions to a seemingly intractable social problem, but without mentioning who or how to pay for it. Fred Barnes exposes Washington's ills in "National Capital, National Shame," 11-89, although he doesn't target Mayor Barry as much as might be needed. Rachel Flick also appears on different issues, but her focus on health ("Why We Can't Get the Medicine We Need," 8-89) and drugs ("Why We're Losing the War on Drugs," 10-89) makes us wonder why Ms. Flick can't be satisfied, knowing that if anything goes wrong with either the FDA or the war on drugs we'll get a story asking "Why can't we get the protection we deserve?"

On national security, veteran staff writer Ralph Kinney Bennett gives us "The Growing Menace of Chemical Weapons," 7-89, leading off with "This is the way death came to Halabjah," the Kurdish city that Iraq bombed with mustard gas in March 1988. The bombing and subsequent nearly nonexistent international reaction pushed the world across a dangerous new threshold that serves as the subject of this article: the increasing spread and acceptance of chemical weapons in the hands of "countries whose scruples do not match ours" as one former Pentagon official is quoted as saying. Bennett uses quotes and facts effectively, but the only solution he offers, besides increased international vigilance, is legislation pending in the Senate in which the U.S. would cut off all credit, aid, and technology transfers to any nation stockpiling chemical weapons or helping others acquire them, which means that other nations would pretend not to be doing all that, and we would pretend to believe them. Bennett also shines in his "Brilliant Pebbles: The Amazing New Missile Killer," 9-89, detailing the origins and the progress of the project. David Satter's report from the front lines of the *perestroika* battlefield, "Why Russia Can't Feed Itself," 10-89, is a vivid, comprehensive overview, but he might have mentioned that Mikhail Gorbachev is a former Minister of Agriculture.

The impact of *RD* on political Washington and financial New York is peripheral given the massive amount of policy papers and newspapers accessible to the movers and shakers, but in and among the "Dramas in Real Life," the political and economic messages it carries reach the largest audience of any periodical in circulation, published in 15 languages. For the first time since it was founded in 1922 by the late DeWitt Wallace, the Reader's Digest Association at year's end announced it will sell 25 million of its non-voting shares, about 10 percent, to the public. A good buy? Let's just say if the transformation of the communist bloc into one of democratic socialism continues, a process *RD* has been vigilant in seeking, we expect its circulation by the 21st century will extend everywhere short of the moon.

Editor: Kenneth Y. Tomlinson

Address: Pleasantville, NY 10570
                 (914) 238-8585

Circulation: 16,250,000

Reason

This "think" magazine has been around for 21 years, espousing the cause of those who believe in the libertarian philosophy of individual freedom and opposition to big government. The publication has had impact on policy in the past, most notably on the issue of deregulation, but it's only been recently that the Santa Monica-based magazine has seriously moved into the national mainstream of discussion on ideas. Publisher Robert W. Poole, Jr. envisions a doubling of the publication's circulation as it more forcefully moves to reach out to a natural audience that falls somewhere between, say, *The New Republic* and *National Review,* an audience that's economically conservative, yet socially liberal and tolerant. His perspective is to "create a large tent and allow a number of acts to go on within that tent." Following new changes in personnel and positions at the monthly this year, we were impressed enough with its performance to include it in the *MediaGuide* for evaluation.

Virginia Postrel, who came to *Reason* as an assistant editor from *INC.* and *The Wall Street Journal* in 1986, became editor this year, the only woman editor of a national think magazine. The young woman (let's just say she's the same age as Buckley when he started *NR,* and as Kinsley or Podhoretz when they started respectively at *Harper's* and *Commentary*) is punching out tough editorials. "What Wimp," July, is unsparing on the President — "when it comes to policy, Bush is a wimp" — although she clearly misjudges his commitment to a capital gains tax rate cut in this critique of an agenda-less George Bush. She gets points for style not substance with this editorial. Her best commentary effort, though, occurred outside *Reason.* "How Our High Court Came to be Libertarian," 7-2, *The Washington Post* "Outlook" section, was one of the best assessments we saw of the libertarian streak in the high court and earned her a 10 Best nomination. "Reconsidering Roe," May, was an especially provocative editorial, condemning the absolutism of pro-choice advocates. Interestingly, the majority of letters to the editor generated by her editorial turn out to be non-supportive of her point of view (and letters on this editorial continued to come in for the rest of the year). Of course, there's the obligatory editorial in favor of a libertarian approach to the war on drugs, and *Reason* no longer stood so singularly alone on that point of view this year.

Reason moved to California from Boston some time ago, and it's shed as much as it can any tendency to look at the world from the perspective of the U.S. eastern starboard. Most of its personnel are California-based, although the magazine maintains a Washington editor, Martin Morse Wooster assuming that position this year. *Reason* is definitely bullish on California and the Pacific Rim. Its Aug/Sept. issue was its best for the year. A collection of insightful articles, primarily on southern California in the context of the future of American cities, it leads with a look at Los Angeles as a model city — for better or worse, "City of Dreams" by Virginia

Postrel. The contributions collectively add up to a very persuasive critique of the disasters of government planning. "The Seduction of Planning," by Lynn Scarlett, for example, is a very thoughtful examination of the issue, her thesis wonderfully provocative: "Much of the chaos that planners fail to mold into order is precisely the dynamism and diversity that drive economic prosperity. The vitality of cities depends on disorder."

The editors have been selecting among their contributing editors well enough that lately there is always at least one article among the magazine's "Features" section that is very satisfying. Occasionally, we get a bases-loaded home run month, as with the October issue. The lead story, "The China Syndrome," by Steven W. Mosher, raises serious questions about U.S. policy toward China in the wake of the Tiananmen Square atrocities and the regime's crackdown. We are ultimately not persuaded by Mosher, but he puts up a strong argument for his perspective. "Plowing Under Subsidies," by Karl Zinsmeister, assesses the distortions caused for American agriculture by subsidized farming. This isn't a dry abstract written in some windowless office. Zinsmeister is writing this from the farms and we get a full, rich picture of how the farmers view these issues. We learn a lot here we didn't know before. "What's Wrong with Latin American Economies?" by Hernando De Soto provides a very insightful assessment of the dilemmas: elections without democracy, regulations without law, a private sector without capitalism.

Among other features that caught our attention "Beware the Pork-Hawk," June, by Robert Higgs, was cleverly written. This is a subtly hard-hitting article on how the congressional pork-barrel takes its toll on the defense budget. Many of Higgs' examples are old ones, but his overall synthesis of the problem livens them up. "Kemp's Opportunity," April, by Rita McWilliams and Richard E. Messick, is a competent outline of the opportunity new HUD Secretary Jack Kemp has for changing in a positive manner the way in which poverty programs work and for revitalizing the nation's inner cities. The authors outline perspectives on combining self-reliance, individual initiative and private enterprise, and they assemble the details, data and examples.

Whereas we used to skim the magazine, occasionally finding an article arresting enough for us to stop and read, we now add *Reason* to our regular reading pile. There's something now in every issue that we want to read. The magazine's off to a lovely "rebirth" under new editor Postrel, having chalked up a very respectable performance this year.

Editor:	Virginia I. Postrel
Address:	2716 Ocean Park Blvd., #1062
	Santa Monica, CA 90405
	(213) 392-0443
Circulation:	35,000

The Spectator

The Spectator sailed through 1989 with few major changes. As before, steady as she goes for media baron Conrad Black's recent acquisition. We peruse the weekly for all its offerings, but it is in foreign coverage that we get *The Spectator*'s best presentations. Timothy Garton Ash, *The Spectator*'s premiere reporter, continued to perform at a very high level of quality in eastern Europe and West Germany, which of course was the biggest story of the year. Ash is among the few correspondents capable of both reporting on events and analyzing long-term trends in the region, an intellectual with a pencil, notebook and press card, equally comfortable at home in a Gdansk union hall or among political philosophers in a Berlin think tank.

As a result, *The Spectator* provided consistently incisive coverage of the changes in the East Bloc and Soviet Union, making it the periodical of choice for this particular area of coverage. Ash was one of the first journalists to spot the hairline cracks in the Iron Curtain and Berlin Wall that would widen into fissures, toppling governments and ideologies. "Safe Exit From

Yalta," 1-14, poses the question of western Europe's course as the Soviet empire in eastern Europe continues to disintegrate, and Ash argues that western Europe should continue to integrate, to ensure that West Germany remains West and to provide a more secure harbor for any central European states that, someday, may leave the Soviet orbit. "Knocking on the Wall," 1-28, solid at the time — the Berlin Wall isn't going to disappear because it's not in the interest of the East German government to let it topple. But more important is the fresh information Ash provided as to what indeed did happen when East Germany eased travel restrictions — 1.6 million East Germans under age sixty-five went to the West last year; most returned. He cuts a sharp profile of East Germany's Egon Krenz in "Yesterday's Man," 10-28, persuasive on how short the tenure of this Honecker clone will be. "After the Party," 11-18, unfolds as three stories, the Berlin one flowing into the German one which flows into the European one. Ash does a splendid job here making the case that Europe's map will be redrawn in the wake of the dramatic changes in Berlin.

Ambrose Evans-Pritchard's Washington reportage is somewhat uneven. It's always useful, though, to look at ourselves through the eyes of a sharp non-U.S. observer, and this British journalist now and then turns a novel insight from that perspective. "My Fellow Americans. . ." 1-21, an overview of the Reagan administration, concludes that Reagan's popularity "has moved in lockstep with the employment figures in the past eight years," but Europeans don't know this because newsmagazines and reporters all "share the secular Democratic outlook." "Buddy, Can You Spare a Room?" 3-4, on the homeless, puts the issue into perspective with a distinct European appreciation: "some of the DC homeless are probably refugees from conditions that are routine for the vast majority of people in the Soviet Union." His best pieces, though, were as a Central American analyst; in his best effort, "Mexico by Moonlight," 5-6, he's bullish on it as a place for investment.

Other noteworthy foreign reporters included Robert Cottrell on the European Community, Richard West on Yugoslavia, Edward Theberton on Nigeria, and Diana Geddes on France. Geddes is consistently thorough and interesting, appearing quite regularly. Her "La Dame de Fer," 4-29, looks at how the French view Margaret Thatcher; five years ago, French polls rated Thatcher the third most disliked leader in the world (more disliked than Castro!) but today the French people admire her strength of character, while the intellectuals think her "too banal." Although *The Spectator* has no Moscow correspondent *per se*, Stephen Handelman, Moscow bureau chief of *The Toronto Star*, is a frequent contributor, but rarely picks up material we had not seen elsewhere. "The Breaking of the Icons," 3-4, simply wonders if Gorbachev repudiates the personality cult of the past, can he survive without creating one of his own? The only real hole in the foreign coverage remains the Middle East, where the insufferable Charles Glass still reigns. In "My Querencia in Lebanon," 5-13, Glass returns to Lebanon for the first time since his kidnapping, courtesy of former strongman Suleiman Franjieh and his mob; "I felt a little like Michael Corleone," Glass says, as Franjieh's army keeps Glass safe. Arrgh.

The columns are not nearly as good as they should be. Paul Johnson steadily improved over the past six months, while Auberon Waugh declined slightly. The popular historian, Johnson's weekly column on the British news media usually contains dispassionate commentary, with a fair mix of straight reporting, at times half-baked. He's gradually transformed his media column into something else, using his space to comment on history and general topics. In "When Jesus 'Blasphemed,'" 3-25, he uses the Salman Rushdie affair for a discussion of what indeed is blasphemy.

Waugh's consistent problem is his danger of ranting without result, tiresome at best; too often his humor degenerated into irritating visceral tirades. In "Let Us Pray for Those in Peril On the Sea, the Chinese and the Hislops," 6-10, he compares the slaughter in China with, of all things, Wilson's support of the Nigerians during their civil war; despite spending a month in China, Waugh bleats about China's "hideousness," but fails to provide fresh insight. He's more comfortable closer to home, as with "Mrs. Thatcher Should Privatize, Close Down or Blow Up the BBC," 3-11. Turning press critic, looking at new guidelines for BBC producers and a near-total ban on smoking, causes Waugh to explode, saying that "more BBC means more Health Education and left-wing indoctrination." But does Waugh really believe that people are "prevented from going to the cinema" by no-smoking policies, or is he just being irritating?

Taki, the irreverent Greek who majored in tennis, can be viciously tacky in his "High Life" column, greatly amusing to those who like to watch wings pulled from flies. In a savaging of *The Washington Post*'s Richard Cohen over his commentary on the Salman Rushdie flap, "Phony War," 2-25, this is Taki: "However hard I have tried, I've been unable to come up with a more fitting word to describe one Richard Cohen than asshole. Cohen is a bearded jerk and wimp who writes for the mendacious *Washington Post.* Needless to say, he is a bleeding-heart liberal, and as great a phony as one can find in the city of phonies that's called Washington. The reason I am writing about such an inelegant man. . .is because Cohen last week attacked Mrs. Thatcher. . .for not threatening to go to war if 'one hair on Rushdie's head is touched by someone working for Iran or seeking to claim the bounty.' This came from a man who was not only against the war in Vietnam but also a great respecter of the rights of muggers, murderers and drug dealers."

The editorials are hit and miss, and like Waugh and Taki, sometimes overwrought, with little of the restraint we still, for some reason, expect of the Brits. The editorial board took the events in China personally, particularly with regard to Hong Kong. "Breaking Eastern Promise," 5-13, calls for the British to admit more Hong Kong residents, saying that "many talented and industrious individuals" in Hong Kong would prefer to remain British rather than acquire Australian, Canadian or French passports. We get more on the subject for our two pence in "Our Titanic Betrayal," 6-10, a special double-long editorial about how Britain should take responsibility for the citizens of Hong Kong; by abandoning these people to the communists, "for the first time in history, we have forced Britons to be slaves." Still more, "What Are Leaders For?" 6-17, further examines the Hong Kong question, suggesting that the failure to support Hong Kong is proof of a lack of moral fibre and spinelessness." The last for the stormy month of June, "Practicalities," 6-24, is still another leader about Hong Kong, this time suggesting that Britain institute democracy so that Hong Kong "would become an entity in the eyes of the free world" worthy of protection. British Empire, anyone?

Editor:	Charles Moore
Address:	56 Dougherty Street
	London WC1 2LL
	United Kingdom
	011-01-405-1706
Circulation:	40,389

Time

Henry Luce, founder of the nation's foremost newsweekly, surely would be unhappy at what *Time* wrought this year. *Time*style has always been a bit quirky, with a single hip voice that gave it distinctiveness in a black and white news media. This year, though, the magazine experimented with an open practice of advocacy journalism, the only one of the three weeklies to allow, even encourage, its correspondents to insert their own opinions in their reports. Not that all of them do, of course. There remains a commitment to accepted standards of journalistic excellence by most of the staff. But by encouraging the staff to try out their own "voices," which is the buzzword at the magazine, the editors have given us the feel not of a newsweekly, but of a pamphlet for different agendas.

A year ago we were intrigued by the changes in format, hoping to see a new and improved *Time.* We did take note of managing editor Henry Muller's thinking that "TIME's responsibility more than ever is to deliver understanding," heralding the introduction of "some new voices in

TIME, along with a broader spectrum of points of view," 10-17-88. But we did not realize he was going to turn the masthead into a Montessori classroom. The free-spirit approach might work at a *New Republic* or *National Review,* although we doubt it, but it is just plain laughable at *Time.* The powers that be at Time, Inc. are going to have to decide what kind of magazine they want their namesake to be. Fancy graphics and startling pictures alone will not sustain readers over the long haul. The editors want us to hear voices emerging from the pages of their magazine, but what we hear too often is personal propaganda, the kind of one-sided boilerplate that *glasnost* is now stamping out in Moscow.

A year ago we gave *Time*'s "Man of the Year" cover story a 10 Best citation in general reporting for its profile of Mikhail Gorbachev. This year the magazine selected "Planet Earth" as its traditional "Man of the Year," 1-2, which the editors of *Time* thought worthy of a 10 Best nomination. The idea is worthy enough, but this time the magazine simply put forward the environmental agenda as its own, as if it was now beyond debate. The material did not have much hard empirical scientific support to justify turning theory into fact. Yet we thought the magazine would address these matters as the year unfolded. Instead, the "Planet Earth" cover set the tone for much of the environmental reporting done over the course of the year, not only for *Time,* but for the press in general.

The magazine's science editor, Charles A. Alexander, acknowledged as much in a Washington seminar reported by *The Wall Street Journal*'s David Brooks. A running logo, "Endangered Earth," appeared in *Time*'s Environment section, as in its "Fishing for Leadership," 5-22, goading President Bush to get with the program: "Several signals, including Bush's slow response to the Alaska oil spill and his refusal to consider an increase in the gasoline tax, have raised concern that he is not the kind of forceful, decisive leader the country needs to deal with the growing environmental crisis. That fear intensified last week as the administration appeared to be in a muddle over one of the most pressing ecological issues: global warming." When late in the year *Time*'s sister publication *Fortune* was about to run a piece it had commissioned from Warren T. Brookes on global warming, it was reportedly a decision from Time, Inc. that killed the piece, which ran as a *Forbes* cover, "The Global Warming Panic," 12-25.

The Washington bureau provided a chorus of voices under its new bureau chief, Stanley W. Cloud. We have for some time suggested Strobe Talbott, who Cloud replaced, would be better advocating his strong viewpoints in a column than as bureau chief. Cloud, though, seemed to have even less effect on the ratio of reporting to editorializing. Throughout much, but not all, of the bureau's reportage, liberties are taken in pushing analytical observations into editorial asides. The most blatant screeches we get are from Margaret Carlson, a onetime screechwriter for President Carter. Ms. Carlson seems still in the grip of unremitting malaise. We were astonished at the moral high dudgeon she was permitted in her coverage of the Jim Wright story. She warmed up in "A Case of Wright and Wrong," 4-17, predicting the Speaker would survive: "No matter how unseemly Wright's dealing may appear to ordinary citizens, they are probably not unseemly enough to violate the shabby standards that apply on Capitol Hill." When Wright did throw in the towel, Carlson went bonkers in "How Many Will Fall?" 6-5, beside herself with indignation: "Simply getting rid of a few powerful members is not going to remove the stench that hangs over Capitol Hill." The editors at the weekly ought to ask themselves the same question of "Have We Gone Too Far?" 6-12, in permitting Carlson's pamphleteering in the news columns.

Strobe Talbott continues to report from the Washington bureau, although no longer as its chief. His "America Abroad" columns at times seem less editorial than his earlier reports, although he was definitely part of the Planet Earth team. His report on "The Road to Malta," 12-4, a curtain-raiser on the summit, was superior, restrained analysis that was as good as we saw anywhere. We also thought it interesting that Talbott, who has been a relative softliner on strategic arms and East-West issues, produced an excellent interview with Zbigniew Brzezinski, entitled "Vindication of a Hard-Liner," with Robert T. Zintl 12-18. The best journalists are those who are not quite sure they are right in their softline or hardline personal views. George Church, who we thought pushed his views too casually into his material in earlier years, also seemed somewhat more restrained. His "The Big Spill," 4-10, afforded him plenty of opportunity for high dudgeon, and instead he delivered one of the more impressively assembled accounts of the Exxon Valdez oil spill. Laurence I. Barrett still can't resist slipping his own editorial asides in closing paragraphs. "Going Home a Winner," 1-23, is terribly belittling on Ronald Reagan, and but for the headline you'd never know that Barrett thought him a winner.

Time did score a coup at the foreign desk in '89. Robert Ajemian, in a series of interviews with George Koskotas, a major player in the five year saga of corruption in the Papandreou government, effectively put the PM in the hot seat in "The Looting of Greece," 3-13. Well researched, very detailed and highly revealing, the story helped to topple Andreas Papandreou, spawning a host of investigative follow-ups. The Moscow team, Ann Blackman and John Kohan, is too green to be effective at this point, left behind in the dust of more seasoned reporters from the competition. Johanna McGeary showed promise in the Middle East, her dispatches snappy and without spin, a notable accomplishment given the difficulty in reporting news from that beat, leaving us to wonder why she's been relocated to New York. Ross Monro is also good, but seldom appears, vanishing for months at a time in Southeast Asia. Jill Smolowe continues to be adequate, but unexceptional, as is longtime *Time* writer on foreign events, William Doerner. Bruce Van Voorst, covering foreign affairs out of the Washington bureau, is hit or miss, and his dispatches must be examined with a fine-tooth comb, as his information tends to be thin at times.

Editor Muller also promised us "compelling photography," and the magazine did provide plenty of visual snap. Here again, we thought the editors pushed to far, getting into bloody photographic terrain we had become used to seeing in *Newsweek*. We were most bothered by *Time*'s use of photos coming out of events in Panama and China. *Time* proudly displayed the bloodied Panamanian opposition leader Guillermo Ford fending off his attackers on its cover, 5-22. The 6-12 China cover was possibly repelling, not compelling, showing a dead Chinese student sprawled on the ground, his brains spilling out from his head.

There's a reason why the daily newspaper does not expect its photographers to bring back color photos of traffic fatalities or violent crime victims. *Time* seems oblivious in that regard, as if its editors rationalize that if it is not against the law, they are protected by the First Amendment, and besides, the grotesque scenes are of *foreigners.* Why would taste preclude running color photos of mangled, bloodied bodies of auto victims on the front pages and not the shot of this dead Chinese? This doesn't inform. It's a portent, perhaps, of a growing tendency within the print media to tolerate and indulge the erosion of standards of decency. We don't get it. If this is the kind of compelling photography Muller promised us, we cringe to think what's next.

The new business editor, Stephen Koepp, stayed competitive with the other newsweeklies in providing reasonable compendiums of developments in the business and financial world. There was not much imagination, but we don't really expect it from the newsweekly quarters, with their limited resources and a world to cover. Janice Castro and Barbara Rudolph handle business news and economic outlooks smartly, thankfully keeping their own voices to an acceptable murmur and drawing opinions and viewpoints from a range broader than the always quoted. Jonathan Beaty and Richard Hornik produced an interesting cover on "Money Laundering," 12-18, which most of *Time*'s readers should have appreciated. We'd read most of it before in *Insight,* where Stephen Brookes did a cover "Dirty Money Soils Clean Hands," 8-21, earning a 10 Best nomination. Charles Alexander, in charge of science covers, takes his brand of advocacy journalism into areas other than the environment. We find quite a bit of editorializing on the more controversial scientific matters. Philip Elmer-DeWitt warns of "The Perils of Treading on Heredity," 3-20: "Once it becomes possible to eradicate a gene that causes a fatal disorder, and thus keep it from passing to future generations, it will be criminal not to do so."

The most successful change at *Time* in the last year resulted from the departure of Roger Rosenblatt as its regular essayist. Rosenblatt certainly could write, but the modern newsweekly reader needs to get information, insight and entertainment in the same package. The back-page essay is now circulated to a wider group, Hugh Sidey, Strobe Talbott and Richard Hornik occasionally taking a Washington turn. Walter Shapiro and Lance Morrow provide nostalgia. Pico Iyer, Michael Kinsley and Charles Krauthammer appear, but all too infrequently. Indeed, Kinsley's essay "In Defense of Congress," 4-17, earned a 10 Best selection for commentary. We're not quite sure, but some of our readers think a regular rotation, a la *Newsweek*'s George Will and Meg Greenfield, whether in-house or not, would improve the back page. Perhaps when their reporters perfect their editorial technique in the news columns, they can promote a few to "Essay." They should also be permitted to attack the ozone layer if they feel so inclined.

Our fervent expectation is that Editor Muller will now do a turn on Mao Tse-tung, who, after asking for a thousand flowers to bloom, cut down those who bloomed too much. We really have liked the idea of getting more distinctive voices into the magazine, and we're thrilled to see most of the writers given their own bylines, each professional taking *full* responsibility for the material under his or her name. The policy simply needs a haircut. Muller really doesn't have to decapitate anyone on the staff to achieve this. Even Margaret Carlson, our *bete noire* this year, impressed us with her obvious writing skills and can be taught or edited into a more sophisticated screech. This, and a little less blood and brain in the photos, and Mr. Luce will once again look happily on his baby, and so will we.

Editor-in-Chief:	Jason McManus
Address:	Time-Life Building
	Rockefeller Center
	New York, NY 10020-1393
	(212) 586-1212
Circulation:	4,300,000

U.S.News & World Report

It seems like the same old story at *U.S.News.* In the *1986 MediaGuide* we noted a shift of editors from Marvin Stone to Shelby Coffey III. In '87 the helm went to David Gergen. A year ago we began our comments on the No. 3 newsweekly: "Yet another major editorial change at *U.S.News* in 1988." Publisher Mortimer Zuckerman sent Gergen down the chute and Roger Rosenblatt, earlier plucked from the pages of *Time* to teach the staff how to write, was given the helm. We wondered about Rosenblatt: "Can the intrepid Washington essayist save the weekly in search of its identity for so long?"

No he could not, and down the chute went Rosenblatt. Like George Steinbrenner, Zuckerman can't seem to keep a manager for more than one season. His new choice for 1990 is Mike Ruby, who has been on the masthead for the last three years, more or less running the magazine anyway with too much kibbitzing. Ruby had been wooed from *Newsweek* in 1986 with the better half of the new editorial team, Merrill McLoughlin, his wife and co-editor.

Zuckerman, the real-estate tycoon turned journalist, thought he could turn the nag he bought into a sleek race horse by now. But with the weekly subject to so many shifting sands, it's no wonder *U.S.News* looks more like a camel. The editors appear to have settled on not one identity, but several, at times apparantly competing not only with the other newsweeklies, but with every magazine in the business. We assembled a display of this year's dromedaries on the office floor and were surprised ourselves at the week by week split personalities.

By a narrow margin, the magazine's primary identity is still that of a newsweekly. About half its covers focus on major news events. And *USN&WR* is certainly far more subdued than its counterparts, *Time* and *Newsweek,* which are clearly out to grab the young and the upscale. Much of the material inside is solid, well-balanced and informative, with respectable analytics. Yet there is an unappetizing feel to the periodical that we get from its facial expression, the cover it shows to us. There are virtually no personalities here, no life, except for the animals that show up now and then. "Endangered Species: Can They Be Saved?" 10-2, gives us an elephant look. "The First Humans," 2-27, a bit of nostalgia for the good old days, 1 Million B.C., gives us a "Homo habilis" simian look. "How Animals Tamed People: What Science Tells Us About the Bonds Between Man and Beast," 3-20, gives us a quartet of faces: a pony, a young lady, a cat and a dog.

Or we are served big color headlines: "DRUGS," 9-11 and "JOBS," 9-25, or "BUILDING YOUR FORTUNE," 7-17, which are fine. We are not saying we could not get used to this approach if the editors decided to go this route and stick to it. But as it changes from week to week, from headlines to dogs and cats to spot news, *USN&WR* doesn't have a "look." If we always got headlines, we'd soon learn (in the Pavlovian way that readers have about these things) that the magazine had more inside than "JOBS," which we don't need at the moment. *Reader's Digest,* after all, sells 29 million copies per month, with the table of contents on its cover, for gosh sakes. But it has a "look" that we have become comfortable with over the decades, a reassuring look. *USN&WR* gives us schizophrenia, which demands our heads have to make a wrenching readjustment every week to get into what's happening.

When we do get into it, we find the foreign reporting on a par with the other newsweeklies, at times superior to them. Here we find more depth, less of the tendency to merely summarize daily news accounts, and occasionally a particularly good insight or analysis. With less staff at home to rewrite and meddle and nitpick, the material generally seems to have a clearer voice and realistic perspective. Moscow bureau chief Jeff Trimble provided strong, reliable coverage of the Soviet Union. "The Soviet Agony over States' Rights," 4-24, gave a first-rate overview of the ethnic unrest in Soviet Georgia and other non-Russian areas in the U.S.S.R., with a nice analysis of Moscow's reactions to these problems, noting that the "absence of a broad policy is nonetheless consistent with the Soviet inability to manage dissent."

Reporting from Asia, Dusko Doder, Jim Impoco and James Wallace offered good analysis of the situation in China, "Behind China's Anger," 6-5: "With a phrase, 'It is glorious to get rich,' Deng Xiaoping turned Mao Tse-tung's egalitarian economics on its head and launched a decade of development that made China the wonder of the Third World. But along with progress came inflation, envy, shortages, regional distortions and a national loss of economic direction." An occasional piece by James Fallows "Bright Lights Fade in China's Big City," 6-21, and "South Korea Only Wants a Little Respect," 8-14, rounded out Asia coverage with distinctiveness.

Domestic coverage was adequate, although it frequently took a back seat to the magazine's various self-help and financial guides. Gloria Borger handled the Jim Wright ethics mess well, with particularly good insight into the rumor of Tom Foley's alleged homosexuality, "Anatomy of a Smear," 6-19. She totally missed it in her profile of Defense Secretary Cheney with this puff: "Conservatives who were looking to Quayle as their conscience in the White House have found a better friend in Cheney." Borger could not have had her finger close to the pulse and have written this. Covering the judiciary beat, Ted Gest stayed on top of the Supreme Court abortion debate, "New Abortion Fights," 4-24, and "The Abortion Furor," 7-17, with good analyses, placing the issue in historical perspective. We got foggy coverage of the capital gains fight on Capitol Hill, though, "The Capitol Gains of the Well-to-Do," 10-2, by Michael Barone, predicts "the rich" will win this one, totally out of synch with the newsweekly's Middle America.

Chief diplomatic correspondent Henry Trewhitt retired, disappearing from the masthead during the editorial shuffle, but he did do some impressive work earlier in the year. "What's Unusable — and Indispensable?" 1-9, a composite of a conversation with McGeorge Bundy on nuclear deterrence and related issues, is mildly interesting, but skippable, with a bit of historical value. In "Help Out the Latins, Por Favor," 4-10, Trewhitt ruminates on Soviet and American interests in Latin America, in the wake of Gorbachev's trip to Cuba, but with not much we didn't get by ruminating on our own.

USN&WR dabbled in the realm of science/health magazines this year. In addition to the dogs and cats and homo habilis covers, it delivered "The Truth About Cholesterol," 11-27 (late, after *The Atlantic*'s 9-89 cover), trumpeting new treatments for "Allergies," 2-20, and exploring the pros and cons of "Plastic Surgery," 5-1. Other cover stories probed the "Secrets of the Sea," 8-21, and offered advice on what to do "When Mental Illness Hits Home," 4-24. The "DRUGS" cover, 9-11, presented as "a family guide," started slowly and chopped throughout, but was authoritative and useful nevertheless. There is absolutely no smell of drug legalization about the magazine. If there was, Zuckerman's editorial "The Enemy Within," 9-11, closed that internal debate. David Gergen, who still columnizes for the magazine and does a better job than when he was also editing, got more worked up in "Remember the Drug War?," 12-18, than we've seen him: "America must fight drugs the same way we have fought Communism: With a consuming moral passion." With this fervor at the top, the newsweekly could be crusading reportorially into the social origins of the drug problem as a means of building distinctiveness, but we don't expect much more than helpful hints and huffing and puffing.

By far, the magazine's favorite identity is that of helpful advisor. Continuing last year's utility theme, more and more frequently, "News You Can Use" items, although well written and informative, squeezed more newsworthy topics off the cover. This year, the magazine seemed to fancy itself the answer to the prayers of a misguided Middle America. Extending a helping hand, the editors updated last year's fitness and college guides ("Shaping Up," 5-29, "America's Best Colleges," 10-16), and included a career guide 9-25, two business guides 10-9 and 10-23, a money guide 7-17, an investment guide, 12-4, and the previously mentioned family guide for beating drugs.

The magazine seems to favor giving financial advice over any other kind, sometimes encroaching on *Consumer Reports* or *Money* territory. Its business staff has a fair degree of professional competence, Mary Lord editing. Susan Dentzer, Pamela Sherrid and Kenneth R. Sheets can assemble news in presentable fashion, which we appreciate. Their material they're asked to assemble, though, is too often pedestrian, not unexpected. We got a full page from Sheets, the energy writer, headlined "Would You Believe $16.67 an Hour to Scrub Rocks?" on the nitty gritty of the Valdez cleanup, worth a paragraph or two unless you have a readership into nitty gritty. The cover stories on "The Best Mutual Funds for 1989," 2-6, "Best Ways to Cut Your Taxes," 3-27, "How to Afford Retirement," 8-14, and "What's Your Home Worth," 4-17, seem distressingly targeted at the segment of middle class America that is worried about its finances but can't afford professional advice, and surely can't afford to buy upscale products that might be advertised in *U.S.News.*

The weekly's economic columnist, Monroe W. Karmin, who has a .189 batting average in that game, should be writing business news, where he can hit occasional homers. Editor Ruby should not be writing columns at all. The most promising fresh look we have at the magazine is that of John Leo, whose column on social issues in the "Horizons" section is getting our attention. Instead of mulling things over, *a la* the editorial brass, Leo puts some hard reporting work into his essays and if he keeps it up could break out soon with some important material. "Stop Blaming the Tests," 3-20, on the SATs, lets us know that while blacks still score low, they "are up 21 points on the verbal and 30 on the math since 1978, the highest of any group," with an emphasis on equal educational opportunity, not complaints that tests are biased. "Homeless Rights, Community Wrongs," 7-24, presses on the margin: "The homeless deserve food and shelter. Certainly, a country as rich as this can afford it. But the homeless should not be allowed to destabilize the live communities still left in our cities." Zuckerman should turn the back page over to this fellow and we would have an "opener."

By that, we mean some compelling reason to snatch *USN&WR* off the airport newsstand for $1.95 when the cover screams "JOBS" and we have one. We will know that we might get our money's worth with the back page essay, if nothing else. For Zuckerman to put himself on the back page is like George Steinbrenner announcing that he will pitch the second game. As it is, we are not happy to say, there is no reason for serious consumers of news to read this magazine regularly. As harsh as we are this year on *Time,* it is still a publication we cannot ignore. *USN&WR* can safely be ignored these days, as it has in recent dromedary years. Oddly enough, with all the schizophrenia we observe, we are more optimistic about the newsweekly than we've been from our first *MediaGuide.* Something tells us Ruby and McLoughlin, and managing editors Peter Bernstein and Christopher Ma, are close to turning off the mixmaster. They are not minor-leaguers but real pros in the news business. We eagerly await the look and the identity.

Co-Editors:	Merrill McLoughlin, Michael Ruby
Address:	2400 N Street NW
	Washington, DC 20037-1196
	(202) 955-2111
Circulation:	2,419,000

Utne Reader

The flip side of *Reader's Digest,* the *Utne Reader* calls itself a digest of "the best of the alternative press." And it is. Published and edited by Eric Utne since 1984, the *Reader* brings together a substantive mix of articles and commentary on the political and social issues of the times. It is reviewed here for the first time. By way of explanation, the magazine tells us in the masthead periodically that " 'Utne' rhymes with 'chutney' and means 'far out' in Norwegian."

Well, not all that far out. While the *Utne Reader* does sport articles from such diverse sources as *Mother Earth News* and *New Age Journal,* it also runs material from *Spy* and *Business Week.* What fascinates us about the bi-monthly is that it runs articles from a wide range of publications under the same banner as the cover story and it works. More useful than *Reader's Digest* in this respect, we get differing perspectives on related issues, and sometimes surprisingly similar perspectives from dissimilar sources. The 3/4-89 cover on "Singleness" included articles from *The Washington Post Magazine, Sojourner,* and *Tikkun,* with sidebars from *Psychology Today, American Demographics, Princeton Alumni Weekly, New Woman, East Bay Express,* and *Vanguard Press,* a wonderful compendium on the pros and cons of unwedded bliss.

The section's introduction probes the question of why "our culture dismisses" the fundamental need to sustain a relationship with someone, be it a friend, lover, or spouse. Some articles date back a few years, but this works well too, giving the reader a better sense of how an idea or trend works and evolves over time. "Postmodernism and Beyond. . ." cover 7/8-89, takes itself very seriously in some regards, wryly on other points, but the dichotomy works to an extent: "But the more we got into it the more we realized postmodernism isn't anything in particular, it's really everything after modernism. But since modernism hasn't really come to an end, and continues to this day, just as industrialism lingers on concurrently with post-industrialism. . .we got confused" and offered the selections which followed as the best explanation, a credible job.

Uncommonly thoughtful and thought-provoking, *UR*'s selections are sensitive toward the environment and people, promoting a better, healthier world for everybody. A far more diligent approach than, say, *Time*'s making "Planet Earth" thing of the year, 1-2, there's at least one environmental topic covered per issue, moving from "Apocalypse Now? Ecology and the Peril of Doomsday Visions," Eric Zencey *North American Review,* 1/2-89 to Helen Cordes' "Water: Unsafe in Any Form?" 9/10-89. This culminates in the 11/12-89 cover story, "How the Environmental Crisis Can Improve Our Lives." In addition to an intelligent collection of articles ranging from a King Features R. Emmett Tyrrell column to Pat Stone's "Christian Ecology: A Growing Force in the Environmental Movement" from *Mother Earth News, UR* suggests "133 Ways to Save the Earth and Improve Your Life at the Same Time!" While some recommendations tend toward the wacky ("Be concerned about the situation of Third and Fourth World people and attempt to avoid a standard of living too much higher than them") others are sensible and informative ("Avoid purchasing clothes that require dry cleaning, because it uses toxic chlorinated solvents; dry clean only when necessary"; "Plant deciduous shade trees that protect west windows from summer sun but allow it in during the winter").

The different departments and reviews vary from issue to issue, but for the most part, are enjoyable. Each *UR* begins with an "Editor's Note" from Eric Utne detailing the reason for selecting the cover story, and usually finishes with a "Zeitgeist" column by Executive Editor Jay Walljasper. There's also an "U.N.C.L.E." letters section (that's the "Utne Network for Communications, Letters & Epistles"), cartoons, smaller excerpts and information from various sources mixed together by staff members found in the "In Brief" section, and useful listings of subscription information for the publications that the issue excerpts.

Unreservedly unobjective, the *Utne Reader* is quickly gaining respect among the liberals and the left, cited as a reference more and more. The formula works, and works well, because Utne and Co. are ultimately pragmatists, and certainly entertain enough of a variety of ideas and publications to be balanced in content despite the agenda. Not too bad for a digest only five years old.

Publisher/Editor: Eric Utne

Address: Box 1974
            Marion, OH 43305
            1-800-669-1002

Circulation: 175,000

The Washingtonian

Formerly the *New York* magazine equivalent for the District of Columbia, *The Washingtonian* is fast becoming more of a *Ladies Home Journal* for bored Congressional wives than a monthly both Congressmen, bureaucrats and their spouses can enjoy and use. Going from fun and sassy in the Beltway to gossipy and frivolous, there's little here that's worthwhile reading, either inside the District lines or beyond the Washington-Baltimore corridor.

Like the rubberneckers at Washington cocktail parties, editor John A. Limpert always seems to be looking over his shoulder, ready to bolt to any old moth-eaten VIP instead of looking us straight in the eye. In previous years, we used to be able to find at least one serious item per issue on policy or political personality, such as the in-depth profile of Oliver North that we got best from Neil Livingstone and David Halevy bothered to do, "The Ollie We Knew," 7-87, a 10 Best selection from our '88 edition. This year, far too much material in *The Washingtonian* glosses over the real topics of conversation in the capital that turn on essence of power, not simply its trappings. The most gripping material in the 12-89 issue was "Divorce, Washington Style," by John Sansing, the magazine's executive editor, and "Sunny Side Up," an interview with moth-eaten Mike Deaver. We were not gripped for long, however. We don't expect heavy-duty analytics on the capital gains tax, for goodness sakes. But there's got to be more than foo-foo in the federal triangle. There was not one political piece to match any of a dozen written by *New York* magazine's Joe Klein, for example. "The Education of Dan Quayle," in *The New York Times Magazine* by Maureen Dowd 6-25, was certainly not too heavy for the IQ level of *Washingtonian* readers, we don't imagine. But there was nothing like it in the magazine. Money is not at issue, after all. *The Washingtonian* is fat and rich with upscale advertising.

Which is not to say Limpert does not run some worthwhile reading, but too often we've already seen the material already developed elsewhere, or its pitch is carefully superficial. Barbara Matusow produced a good analytic of Mayor Marion Barry and his troubles with the media, "Marion Barry Under Fire," 4-89, but even here she dealt exclusively with Barry's PR problem rather than his substantive difficulties. Vic Gold's "The Blunder Years," 11-89, is the first of all the looks back at the '80s, witty, although some items won't be recognized or applicable outside the Beltway. "Is It Really Safe to Fly?" by Halevy and Livingstone 5-89, is a solid investigative report from the duo on airport security. Livingstone teams with Terrell E. Arnold to expose the hustlers exploiting the hostages in Lebanon, a sad and sordid business,

"The Hostage Racket," 1-89. Coverage of some social issues is handled with sensitivity. "When They're 64," by Randy Rieland 1-89, deals with the complications of the rising number of elderly parents, and "Barra and Me," 8-89, a personal story by *Los Angeles Times* reporter Marlene Cimons and her adoption of an Indian toddler that moves without being maudlin and makes no bones about the paperwork and difficulties involved.

The real Washington-stuff was often late and then not up to snuff. Fred Barnes, who writes his best for *The New Republic,* gives us second best in "25 Who Make a Difference," 3-89, about the various power brokers and leaders in town, doling out observations, mostly trite and obvious ("Being well liked is an asset"). Martin Schram's "Towering Inferno," 5-89, is a postmortem on John Tower after the body was long buried. "Do Bush's People Have It?" by Owen Ullman 6-89, is obvious stuff, but useful in breaking down all Bush's cabinet and subcabinet members, graded, with strengths and weaknesses and predictions for success. "Mr. Nice Guy," 11-89 on Bob Novak by Eric Alterman nicely updates, but we've heard much of this before in different profiles. The best of the lists was "New Kids on the Block," by Morton Kondracke 12-89, a network of the best and brightest on the foreign-policy circuit, which we skimmed, but filed away where we know we can find it as needed.

Too much of the Washington news we got was better suited to different magazines. Diana McLellan's "My Foreign Valentine," 2-89, dissects the problems with foreign affairs, telling us "these affairs are doomed." What a great way to start the third graph; now we needn't read further. We also got the detailed story of McLellan's facial surgery, "Young Again!" 9-89, a lead-off for a plastic surgery advertisement masquerading as a cover story. The "52 Weekends" is useful, cover 6-89, if you're looking to go on vacation, and not one, but two lists (one cheap, 5-89, one not so cheap, 1-89) of the "Best Restaurants in Washington" are great if you're hungry and within eating distance of Adams Morgan.

Then there's "In Search of Love," 3-89, so you can find someone to eat and go on vacation with. To complete your life, there's work and a *Glamour*-like treatment of stress, 2-89, complete with a *Glamour*-ish cover girl ready to snap her pencil. The fashion layouts are professional, and there's a photographic section every few issues, filled with political out-takes and pictures that tell the whole story, such as the photo of Michael Dukakis giving a speech with a little girl behind him with her fingers in her ears, 5-89. We hear about the beefs Washington Redskins quarterback Doug Williams' ex-wife has with the player, complete with allegedly X-rated Polaroids in Rudy Maxa's "Sacking the Quarterback," 9-89. But the cross between *Cosmo* and *LIFE* just doesn't quite click.

Even the departments seem old and gossipy. The tidbits from "Capitol Comment," edited by John Sansing, are fresh, but Liz Smith-like, and more centered on personalities rather than getting behind-the-scenes grit on policymakers. We even get the dirt on Maureen Reagan and Elvis, 3-89, in response to a query. The column goes on for four full pages, far too long, much longer than the comparable "Intelligencer" in *New York*. We'd have liked instead a survey of congressional wives of all political flavors, asking for suggestions on how to remove the street people who are sleeping all over the city's sidewalks, day and night, or whether they like them there. Plus a list of the best places to sleep.

Editor:	John A. Limpert
Address:	1828 L Street NW, Suite 200 Washington, DC 20036 (202) 296-3600
Circulation:	166,891

The Washington Monthly

Celebrating twenty years of liberal commentary, editor Charles Peters and company have much to crow about. Surviving two decades is itself an achievement for a periodical of such narrow, cerebral appeal, with a natural audience that advertisers have not much interest in reaching. There is no sign yet that *WM* is about to have a circulation breakthrough that might bring it abreast of *The New Republic,* which has three times the readers. But we wouldn't be surprised if it happened soon, the magazine finally coming of age along with its neoliberal platform. Instead of spending the year wondering where the movement went wrong or stalled, Peters and his deft crew at *The Washington Monthly* took time out at the beginning of the year to thoughtfully explore the value of this platform, and where it's going. The balance of the year was devoted to the kind of investigative big government-busting we've come to expect and respect from the pamphlet-like monthly.

Neoliberalism, as expounded by Peters, pivots on the idea that government must be constantly monitored by something or someone. Though *WM* doesn't necessarily pride itself on mere agency-bashing, it does more meticulous adversarial coverage of bureaucratic Washington than any other publication in print; indeed, this is it's credo. It is to Peters' credit that he believes the same thing about ideology, even when it's his own, that it must be constantly refined to remain fresh. In February, we get a look at some of the original work which gave impetus to neoliberalism, "Who We Are," 2-89. The 3-89 issue impressed even more, taking a long hard look at the movement Peters helped to found, with articles by such liberal luminaries and *WM* alumni as Michael Kinsley, Nicholas Lemann, Jonathan Rowe, Gregg Easterbrook and James Fallows, examining such issues as defense, elections, etc., all running under the banner, "The Gospel Reconsidered." A reflective exercise, this is nowhere akin to airing the *WM*'s dirty laundry in public; instead this is a constructive criticism of what's right and wrong about neoliberalism.

Whether you agree with the ideology or not, you have to respect the method and the diligence that Peters and his magazine exhibit in digging for malfeasance in DC. Editor Jason DeParle, who left at year's end to join *The New York Times* Washington bureau, seemed a pit bull in training at *WM,* pulling apart issues and bureaucracy and whatever he can sink his teeth into, month by month. "The Worst City Government in America," 1-89, details, of course, the *Monthly*'s namesake, focusing not on Mayor Marion Barry, but instead on the victims of the city's inadequacies, the poor and the residents of the district, whom the city fathers are supposed to protect and serve, a potent indictment of all involved in DC governing. "Beyond the Legal Right," 4-89, is a sensitive examination of what's right with the Right to Life movement, probing and serious. "Warning: Sports Stars May Be Hazardous to Your Health," 9-89, is exhaustive and relentless on cigarette sponsorship of sports events, and a Congressional bill prohibiting such sponsorship was introduced later in the fall. DeParle's "What the Smartest Man in Washington Doesn't Understand. And Why It Will Hurt You," 11-89, disappoints, though, a laboring and disorganized denunciation of OMB which doesn't amount to much more than DeParle's huffing and puffing.

Co-editor Matthew Cooper appears with less frequency, and much less bite. "A Pension for Trouble," 7/8-89, on "the next S&L crisis," i.e., government pension funds, isn't very smart or informed. Other contributors are usually credible, however. Joseph Nocera's "The Case Against Joe Nocera," 2-89, lays the blame for the decay of the public-school systems at white, middle-class America, like Joe Nocera, persuasive, and intense, but not definitive. In "Down and Out in Washington on $89,500 a Year," 7/8-89, Jonathan Rowe argues somewhat convincingly that Congressmen aren't paid too little, lobbyists are paid too much, making DC a very pricey town; the best comparison: Michael Eisner, president of Walt Disney, Inc. at $40.1 million in 1988, and his deputy, at $32.1 million, got $24 million more than all 535 congressional salaried combined!!

Not to be thoroughly down on government, Scott Shuger's "How to Revolutionize Washington with 140 People," 6-89, celebrates the success of Congress' Office of Technology Assessment and the methods OTA uses, but is not terribly persuasive. "Lessons From the Poverty Front," 12-89, by Nicholas Lemann, is what the magazine does best, looking back critically on LBJ's 25-year-old "war on poverty," and the mythology that has grown up around the expired Office of Economic Opportunity: "In retrospect, it seems obvious that everybody should have been focusing on the question of whether or not the OEO's programs were helping poor people."

The departments are strong. Charles Peters column, "Tilting at Windmills," is one of the most comfortable columns of opinion in the business, with not a trace of pretentiousness or smugness, a maybe-I'm-right-but-maybe-I'm-not casualness that is so disarming we want him to be right. Wise and witty, we find Peters seriously at odds with much of the liberal community in his 7/8-89 column, breaking with the consensus that the criminal is the victim: "Let's distinguish between Jean Valjean and John Paul Mack." He tweaks "my friend, Michael Kinsley," 12-89, for permitting himself to be cast in the role of "house liberal" on CNN's "Crossfire," observing: "His intellectual distinction is based on a willingness to seek truth outside the well-trodden paths of conventional liberalism and conservatism. But the show's current closing lines — 'from the Left I'm Mike Kinsley; from the Right I'm Pat Buchanan' — do not seem promising."

The "Memo of the Month" lets the bureaucracy speak for itself, in all its craziness, reprinting actual memos from different departments. The book reviews continue to be a staple. Timothy Noah's review of Russell Baker's latest, *The Good Times,* 7/8-89, contains very sharp, controlled observations, highly complimentary to Baker and his contributions to American journalism without losing our attention and respect. And Patricia Cohen's "Sex, Lies and the Underclass," 11-89, is superlative on Michael Fumento's *The Myth of Heterosexual AIDS,* giving Fumento a fair shake on the pluses of his book, without glossing over the holes in his theory, a credible and intelligent review.

With the loss of editor Jason DeParle to *The New York Times,* we're not sure that *WM* can continue the pace it set for itself; DeParle has no visible successor, though undoubtedly Charles Peters has something up his sleeve. The spirit of Peters' monthly is best summed up in Nicholas Lemann's recollections of his first experiences at *WM,* recounted in "Act II, Winning an Election," 3-89: "In order to restore the vitality and intellectual honesty to liberalism, much of the psychic energy of the magazine in those days was devoted to raising all the points that liberals felt shouldn't be discussed because it would give the conservatives more ammunition. . .We were trying to make liberalism even better and stronger than it already was." Even the conservatives have to take note.

Editor:	Charles Peters
Address:	1611 Connecticut Avenue NW Washington, DC 20009 (202) 462-0128
Circulation:	30,000

THE RATING GUIDE

We have further refined the ratings for this fifth edition of the *MediaGuide*, toughening the standards for inclusion and evaluation. We have virtually eliminated the (-) rating, except in cases where the correspondent has fallen from a star or above, unlikely as that may be. Anyone ranked below a full star in a previous edition has been deleted, unless his work has shown improvement. We consider all journalists reviewed to be at the top of the profession, the big leagues of print journalism. Inclusion in the *MediaGuide*, regardless of the stars received, is indication of the journalist's prominence, his or her position above the ordinary and routine.

All ratings are based on work written in 1989, but in order to review a full year's work we include material from December of 1988 because of the constraints of production deadlines, our newsyear. Quantity means very little; it's quality we seek. We cite at least three pieces in each writeup; we read and evaluate countless more. The reader may notice journalists with the same rating may have accompanying positive or negative remarks within the entry, but this invariably indicates that one has moved up to that rating, the other down. Dozens of journalists have been dropped from the 1990 edition; some have become editors, some changed professions or retired, some because we saw no need to continue commenting negatively on their work. We find the system to be biased toward the center. It's harder to lose ground at the very top because we tend to read most of the output there for the rewards of doing so. It's also harder for those at the bottom to move up, especially if the trend is downward, as we tend to pass over them and miss potentially good material. As with many things, past reputations have a ripple effect.

The standard for reporters are the three basic criteria for the wire-services: fairness, accuracy, and balance (objectivity); plus three additional measures which elevate the material toward excellence: depth of reporting, writing skills and consistency. For commentators, the basic criteria are content reliability and a minimum level of interesting material presented on a regular basis; plus three more: depth of insight and information, presentation (persuasive ability), and consistency. In order to give a single rating rather than address each point individually, we merge the ratings during a series of discussions, reviews and edits.

(−) Failing the basic criteria on one or more counts.

(¹/₂ ★) Failing the secondary criteria on one or more counts.

(★) Good. Reporters: professional. Commentators: worth trying.

(★ ¹/₂) Good/very good. Very good inconsistently.

(★ ★) Very good. In reporters, above average reporting and writing, average analytical skills. In commentators, generally interesting content and presentation.

(★ ★ ¹/₂) Very good/excellent. Above average in consistency.

(★ ★ ★) Excellent. In reporters, superior reporting and writing, above average in analytical skills. In commentators, superior content and presentation, frequent important information and insight.

(★ ★ ★ ¹/₂) Excellent/exceptional. Approaching the very best.

(★ ★ ★ ★) Exceptional. In reporters, loftily objective, pacesetters for the profession in reporting and writing, penetrating analytical skills, always worth reading. In commentators, pacesetters for the profession in journalistic integrity and independence, must reading for insights and information, a consistently well-defined point of view.

(NR) Not rated. Insufficient sampling; material cited has promise. In the case of consistent multiple bylines, but quality work, this is the rating assigned by default.

THE HIGHEST RATED JOURNALISTS OF 1989

Bartlett, Sarah	*The New York Times*	Financial Dispatch	★ ★ ★ ★
Brittan, Samuel	*Financial Times*	Financial Dispatch	★ ★ ★ ★
Brookes, Warren	Creators Syndicate	Financial Dispatch	★ ★ ★ ★
Burns, John F.	*The New York Times*	Foreign Dispatch	★ ★ ★ ★
Evans & Novak	North America Syndicate	Commentary	★ ★ ★ ★
Keller, Bill	*The New York Times*	Foreign Dispatch	★ ★ ★ ★
Kempe, Frederick	*The Wall Street Journal*	Diplomatic Reports	★ ★ ★ ★
Klein, Joe	*New York*	Domestic Reports	★ ★ ★ ★
Lewis, Anthony	*The New York Times*	Commentary	★ ★ ★ ★
Peel, Quentin	*Financial Times*	Foreign Dispatch	★ ★ ★ ★
Rapoport, Carla	*Fortune*	Foreign Dispatch	★ ★ ★ ★
Ash, Timothy Garton	*The Spectator*	Foreign Dispatch	★ ★ ★ ½
Barnes, Fred	*The New Republic*	Commentary	★ ★ ★ ½
Dowd, Maureen	*The New York Times*	Domestic Reports	★ ★ ★ ½
Easterbrook, Gregg	*Newsweek*	Domestic Reports	★ ★ ★ ½
Friedman, Thomas L.	*The New York Times*	Diplomatic Reports	★ ★ ★ ½
Grenier, Richard	*The Washington Times*	Commentary	★ ★ ★ ½
Kamm, Henry	*The New York Times*	Foreign Dispatch	★ ★ ★ ½
Kinsley, Michael	*The New Republic*	Commentary	★ ★ ★ ½
MacDougall, Colina	*Financial Times*	Foreign Dispatch	★ ★ ★ ½
Mortimer, Edward	*Financial Times*	Commentary	★ ★ ★ ½
Safire, William	*The New York Times*	Commentary	★ ★ ★ ½
Tanner, James	*The Wall Street Journal*	Financial Dispatch	★ ★ ★ ½
Adams, Peter	*Defense News*	Diplomatic Reports	★ ★ ★
Adler, Stephen J.	*The Wall Street Journal*	Financial Dispatch	★ ★ ★
Allen, Charlotte Low	*Insight*	Domestic Reports	★ ★ ★
Allen, Henry	*The Washington Post*	Domestic Reports	★ ★ ★
Alsop, Ronald	*The Wall Street Journal*	Financial Dispatch	★ ★ ★
Archibald, George	*The Washington Times*	Domestic Reports	★ ★ ★
Asman, David	*The Wall Street Journal*	Foreign Dispatch	★ ★ ★
Baker, Russell	*The New York Times*	Commentary	★ ★ ★
Bangsberg, P. T.	*The Journal of Commerce*	Foreign Dispatch	★ ★ ★
Borowiec, Andrew	*The Washington Times*	Foreign Dispatch	★ ★ ★
Buchanan, Patrick	Tribune Media Services	Commentary	★ ★ ★
Byrne, John	*BusinessWeek*	Financial Dispatch	★ ★ ★
Carley, William M.	*The Wall Street Journal*	Financial Dispatch	★ ★ ★
Christian, Shirley	*The New York Times*	Foreign Dispatch	★ ★ ★
Cockburn, Alexander	*The Nation*	Commentary	★ ★ ★

Colitt, Leslie	*Financial Times*	Foreign Dispatch	★ ★ ★
Couvalt, Craig	*Aviation Week & Space Technology*	Diplomatic Reports	★ ★ ★
Cullison, A. E.	*The Journal of Commerce*	Foreign Dispatch	★ ★ ★
Davidson, Ian	*Financial Times*	Foreign Dispatch	★ ★ ★
Diehl, Jackson	*The Washington Post*	Foreign Dispatch	★ ★ ★
Dionne, E. J. Jr.	*The Washington Post*	Domestic Reports	★ ★ ★
Dobbs, Michael	*The Washington Post*	Foreign Dispatch	★ ★ ★
Donohoe, Cathryn	*The Washington Times*	Domestic Reports	★ ★ ★
Edsall, Thomas B.	*The Washington Post*	Domestic Reports	★ ★ ★
Elliott, John	*Financial Times*	Foreign Dispatch	★ ★ ★
Engelberg, Stephen	*The New York Times*	Diplomatic Reports	★ ★ ★
Fisher, Dan	*Los Angeles Times*	Foreign Dispatch	★ ★ ★
Forbes, Malcolm S. Jr.	*Forbes*	Financial Dispatch	★ ★ ★
Gigot, Paul	*The Wall Street Journal*	Commentary	★ ★ ★
Gilmartin, Patricia	*Aviation Week & Space Technology*	Diplomatic Reports	★ ★ ★
Harwood, Richard	*The Washington Post*	Domestic Reports	★ ★ ★
Hoffman, David	*The Washington Post*	Domestic Reports	★ ★ ★
Holley, David	*Los Angeles Times*	Foreign Dispatch	★ ★ ★
Ibrahim, Youssef	*The New York Times*	Foreign Dispatch	★ ★ ★
Ingersoll, Bruce	*The Wall Street Journal*	Financial Dispatch	★ ★ ★
Ivey, Mark	*BusinessWeek*	Financial Dispatch	★ ★ ★
Jenkins, Holman Jr.	*Insight*	Financial Dispatch	★ ★ ★
Kamen, Al	*The Washington Post*	Domestic Reports	★ ★ ★
Kneale, Dennis	*The Wall Street Journal*	Financial Dispatch	★ ★ ★
Kondracke, Morton	*The New Republic*	Commentary	★ ★ ★
Krauthammer, Charles	Washington Post Writer's Group	Commentary	★ ★ ★
Kristof, Nicholas D.	*The New York Times*	Foreign Dispatch	★ ★ ★
Kristol, Irving	*The Wall Street Journal*	Commentary	★ ★ ★
Lemann, Nicholas	*The Atlantic*	Domestic Reports	★ ★ ★
Lloyd, John	*Financial Times*	Foreign Dispatch	★ ★ ★
Lowenstein, Roger	*The Wall Street Journal*	Financial Dispatch	★ ★ ★
Mackenzie, Richard	*Insight*	Foreign Dispatch	★ ★ ★
Malcolm, Andrew	*The New York Times*	Financial Dispatch	★ ★ ★
Marsh, David	*Financial Times*	Foreign Dispatch	★ ★ ★
Norris, Floyd	*The New York Times*	Financial Dispatch	★ ★ ★
O'Brian, Bridget	*The Wall Street Journal*	Financial Dispatch	★ ★ ★
Ostling, Richard	*Time*	Domestic Reports	★ ★ ★
Polsky, Debra Lynn	*Defense News*	Diplomatic Reports	★ ★ ★
Preston, Julia	*The Washington Post*	Foreign Dispatch	★ ★ ★
Redburn, Tom	*Los Angeles Times*	Financial Dispatch	★ ★ ★
Reier, Sharon	*Financial World*	Financial Dispatch	★ ★ ★
Remnick, David	*The Washington Post*	Foreign Dispatch	★ ★ ★
Rosett, Claudia	*The Wall Street Journal*	Foreign Dispatch	★ ★ ★
Sanger, David E.	*The New York Times*	Foreign Dispatch	★ ★ ★
Sawyer, Kathy	*The Washington Post*	Diplomatic Reports	★ ★ ★
Schlesinger, Jacob M.	*The Wall Street Journal*	Foreign Dispatch	★ ★ ★

Shales, Tom	*The Washington Post*	Domestic Reports	★ ★ ★
Shribman, David	*The Wall Street Journal*	Domestic Reports	★ ★ ★
Silverberg, David	*Defense News*	Diplomatic Reports	★ ★ ★
Sowell, Thomas	Scripps-Howard News Service	Commentary	★ ★ ★
Truell, Peter	*The Wall Street Journal*	Financial Dispatch	★ ★ ★
Wermiel, Stephen	*The Wall Street Journal*	Domestic Reports	★ ★ ★
Whalen, Bill	*Insight*	Domestic Reports	★ ★ ★
White, David	*Financial Times*	Diplomatic Reports	★ ★ ★
Wilford, John Noble	*The New York Times*	Financial Dispatch	★ ★ ★
Wrubel, Robert	*Financial World*	Financial Dispatch	★ ★ ★

JOURNALISTS

COMMENTATORS

Adelman, Kenneth. Tribune Media Services. (★ ½)
Former director of the U.S. Arms Control and Disarmament Agency and adviser to former President Reagan on the INF negotiations, Adelman's serious, honest commentary in *The Washington Times* is still erratic in his second year. Sometimes playing out soft ideas, at other times he can reward with muscular and poignant analysis. "Carlucci's Ways Will Be Missed," 1-2, though, is perishable — obligatory kudos to the ex-boss, better left perhaps for a funeral oration. "When Our Diplomacy Whispers," 3-6, strongly argues against quiet diplomacy when it comes to human rights, with appropriate examples cited, though the effort is a bit flat, persuasive rhetoric lacking. His weaker side comes through in "Dusting Off, Stepping Ahead," 3-10, tiresome and trivial, telling us in the fashion of puffy punditry what Bush should do in the wake of the Tower defeat. "Baker's Opportunity in East Europe," 4-3, addresses an important strategic issue — Henry Kissinger's proposal that the U.S. and U.S.S.R. strike a deal to manage change in East Europe — but Adelman doesn't establish a sufficiently coherent critique. "Awaiting Bush in Hungary," 5-10, a preview of what President Bush will find when he visits Hungary in July, sparkles. Well-arranged anecdotes underscore the breathtaking change of pace and exhilarating tempo. "Global Threat Soars on Wings of Agni," 5-29, identifies India's recent test of a mid-range ballistic missile as a curse not being seriously addressed or redressed, offering a provocative argument on behalf of U.S.-Soviet cooperation to stop missile proliferation. "Can the Joint Chiefs Ice SDI?" 6-14, is Adelman working from his strengths. Tightly focused and well-argued, he lambastes the Joint Chiefs for hesitancy regarding SDI: "They caught a bad case of cold feet...the military traditionally resist innovation." His "Turning on Quayle Like Fighting Fish," 7-19, goes for the jugular on those Quayle-bashers who, like Siamese fighting fish, "reserve their best efforts for killing or maiming their own species rather than taking on the enemy." Among the bad-mouths, Edward J. Rollins comes in for trenchant treatment, Adelman asking how this consultant, who now makes a whopping six-figure salary as head of the staff of the National Republican Congressional Committee, can be seriously viewed as a GOP supporter when he so blasts the No. 2 Republican in the land. "Where Playing Tough Pays," 7-31, tightly and efficiently draws the proper conclusions from Thomas L. Friedman's *From Beirut to Jerusalem* regarding a U.S. policy perspective for the Middle East — play hardball.

Baker, Russell. *The New York Times.* (★ ★ ★)
"Observer" columnist. Gathering steam rather than dust from the publication of his latest book, *The Good Times,* Baker's columns seem fresher and more gleeful than ever. "Dancing At The Bottom," 1-18, is a whimsical look at the inauguration, chuckling all the way through: "Going to an Inaugural Ball is not the worst assignment possible on Jan. 20. That distinction goes to the job of covering the inaugural parade...for months afterward you wake up screaming from nightmares starring John Philip Sousa." "The Easiest Money," 2-2, contains some very funny advice on what Reagan should do in his retirement. "Fidget and Scratch," 3-1, is delightfully frothy on the Bush cabinet and their addictions, which they had to ditch to get in the front door: Bennett's cigarettes, Baker's bank stocks, and Vice President Quayle's annual pledge to read Plato's *Republic.* And in "Now That's a Payday," 4-5, Baker cheers on the rich and famous and boos those who can't stand to see others succeed. Using Michael Milken's $10 million weekly

paycheck as an example, he wonders just what the heck you could do with all that money if you had it. "Blades and Pants," 5-31, is an amusing comparison of the Jim Wright mess to the French Revolution. "[Simone de Beauvoir] says once Americans realize that ethical rot has infested the House of Representatives, they will rise up and replace a tyranny of rotten ethic Democrats with a reign of pure-living beaucoup-de-culottes." "The Last, Swish, Certainty," 6-7, is charming on the changes in the world, all old standards and sure things falling by the wayside as Poland holds elections, China explodes, Speakers resign and Ayatollahs go — but basketball, swish, is forever. Sure seems that way. In "Attic Of Failed Miracles," 9-23, we find Baker sitting in front of a now-defunct Compaq hard disk, bought in 1985, then delightedly watch him entomb it in the attic, along with two cordless telephones and a CD player: "Neither cajolery nor brutal kicking could make it do more than beep and write 'Code 1701' on its screen. It turned out that Code 1701 meant 'I shall never work again, hah hah hah.' " "So Down On Wall Street," 10-18, is witty satire on the Wall Street plunge, Baker admittedly reveling in the bad news: "One reason is my suspicion that people who get mixed up with Wall Street are the kind of people who think you can get rich without doing honest work." And he hits the bullseye with "Scrap Iron and Rockettes," 11-4, a 10 Best selection, writing on "the American fear of being the eternal rube," re the sale of Rockefellar Center to the Japanese: "The idea that wily Americans might be capable of putting something over on the Japanese apparently occurs to no one, except Rockefellers."

Barnes, Fred. *The New Republic.* (★ ★ ★ ½)
TNR's "White House Watch" columnist has lost none of his knack for identifying first what later becomes conventional wisdom within the Beltway, but there was a falling off this year of those singular insights that come from his penchant for offbeat angles, costing him half a star. "Dick Darman, Wild and Crazy Guy," 1-2, ultrasharp on the new OMB director, "the brains behind the Bush administration" for so much of the President's agenda, exemplifies Barnes at his best. His uncanny skill at locating the key players on the margin within the Beltway's power relationships comes through clearly. He demonstrates similarly acute insight into key political issues on the margin with "The Poverty Thing," 1-30, recounting how Jack Kemp got to HUD, even over Bush's misgivings, with great detail on the (pre-scandal) perspective for the capitalist war on poverty Kemp will try to wage: "If fighting poverty isn't a top concern, Bush and Kemp won't have any credibility in creating a 'kindlier, gentler' America. They'd be brushed off as conventional Republicans who talk big, but do little." "The Big Schmooze," 3-13, is game analysis of how Bush's actions to extend a friendly hand towards Democrats in Congress will help him with his budget proposal in contrast to the strategy of Ronald Reagan who "thought of folks in Congress as impediments to be overpowered, normally by appealing over their heads to the entire nation on television." "Bennett The Drug Czar: An Agenda," in *The American Spectator* 4-89, keenly proceeds from the fact that the swing in elite opinion on drug abuse hasn't affected the underclass, drugs instead strengthening their grip on inner cities. Barnes outlines bold steps to be added on to current efforts, maintaining that the war is winnable, though "a real war has [yet] to be fought." "Pebbles Go Bam-Bam," 4-17, is a grand wrapup, getting it all in perspective on the SDI "Brilliant Pebbles" concept and Dick Cheney. "Newtered," 4-24, is a careful, accurate assessment of how Bush, "the good cop," looks to bomb-throwing Newt Gingrich, "the bad cop," to help reverse roles from the Reagan years. "The Wright Stuff," 5-15, steps back from the moaning over Jim Wright's ethics woes to appreciate the Speaker as precisely the leader Democrats needed to hold the line against Ronald Reagan, acknowledging his considerable success in advancing the party's agenda against a tremendously popular president. A rare misstep, "Musical Chairs," 6-12, about the future of the Democratic House leadership after Wright, predicts Tony Coelho will never leave and that it is "all but certain" that he will be the next majority leader. "Teflon II," 7-10, effectively uses different policy issues to contrast Bush's management style to Reagan's, making the case that in order to succeed, successors to Reagan do not have to have "a strong presence on TV, a dash of ideology, and a flair of political rhetoric." "Patriots And Traders," 9-4, is a super analysis of the Bush administration's trade policy: "Bush wants to grab trade policy-making from Congress and bring it back to the White

House, and he wants to deny Democrats the trade issue." "The By-The-Numbers Presidency," 11-6, methodically examines Bush's formula of happy talk and timidity and pronounces it a "success" — public opinion polls, not tangible achievement, apparently the administration's criterion for judgment. The analysis, though, seems atypically two-dimensional for Barnes, in step with the new conventionality.

Beichman, Arnold. *The Washington Times.* (★ ½)
Beichman, a tenacious critic of "easy treatment" by the media and policymakers regarding the transformations in the communist world, sleeps with one eye open. Always vigilant, his observations this year, when not tendentious, presented solid reasons for keeping euphorical embraces of the East Bloc in abeyance, his rating moving up consequently. "Reading History's Tea Leaves," 2-6, may be appreciated only as a forum for Historian-Sovietologist Richard Pipes to present his views on the crisis of communism. In "Stories Waiting to be Told," 3-29, Beichman opens a can of worms, spinning out some of the implications of the news that "the Soviet Union is planning to investigate what may have been unprofessional relationships between Western correspondents in Moscow and the Stalin regime." Which journalists lied to us during those years? "The Terrorist Trio's Champ of Charmed Existence," 4-20, effectively and with salutary effect, expresses disgust at the privileged status of immunity from criticism extended to Syria's terror-master, President Hafez Assad: "Western diplomats are always on their knees before him as they beseech his help in bringing peace to the Middle East and his help in freeing the hostages of Lebanon, seized by Syrian proxies and allies in the first place." In "What Isn't Getting Lost in the Shuffle," 4-28, we get Beichman at his best, leaning heavily on Robert M. Gates, once CIA, now NSC deputy director, warning (with bite) about softness toward Gorbachev. We appreciate his shot at those critics and opponents of the Chinese regime who identify it as "fascist." One of the few commentators to address this, Beichman makes the case in "Fascist Fantasies and Munchkin Memories," 6-14, that the opponents grant the Party and communism an absolution they do not deserve. "Taking the World's Temperature," *The Wall Street Journal,* 7-10, incisively and economically devastates William Pfaff's *Barbarian Sentiments: How the American Century Ends*: "Mr. Pfaff has adopted a device whereby he judges the U.S. by sociology and the rest of the world by history." "Confronting Hypocrisy On Terrorism," 8-9, an unabashed defense of Israel's anti-terror policy, is somewhat two-dimensional, but the thrust sharply compels: "For years the civilized world has been clamoring for action against terrorism. Yet whenever action was taken, the doer of the deed was condemned — not, mind you, the killers, the assassins, the kidnappers, the torturers. The doer." " 'Active Measures' Questions To Raise," 9-20, a well-documented broadside against Gorbachev's assertion that "we certainly do not need an 'enemy image' of America," tells us "either Mr. Gorbachev is a liar or else he does not know what is going on in his own Communist Party."

Bethell, Tom. *The American Spectator.* (★ ½)
We'd come to expect a fresh, punchy delivery from *TAS* "Capitol Ideas" columnist, but in the last few years he seems distracted. He still raises interesting ideas, but they're rarely provocative. He develops some thoughtful perspectives on old questions in "Guideline for President Bush," 1-89, advising that Bush is at a crossroads — either capitulate to the Democrats or take control in a way Reagan never did — but there's not much originality here. He's analytically shallow in "Steady As She Goes, on Course to Disaster?" *Los Angeles Times* 1-20, formulaic on Bush's placating conservatives rather than viewing them as "the source of a philosophy that is perilous to ignore." With Bethell scoring points as Dan Quayle answers questions, the awkward structure detracts from this interview with the Vice President in "The Interview Ace," *The Wall Street Journal* 3-31. Effectively useless, "Jim Baker's Politics: Meet The Press," *National Review* 5-5, a mere rewrite of James Baker news clips, shows no sign that Bethell's done any reporting on this cover story. He needs a bit of fresh air in his political economy. In "The Mexican Kleptocracy," 7-89, he makes valid observations on the connections between bankrupt policy and bankrupt socio-economic conditions in Mexico. And, yes, his critique of the ritualized relationship between U.S. banks and the Mexican government is sound. But the final result is

an unjustifiable cynicism because a concrete examination of real changes being effected by the Salinas government today is absent from his analysis. He does take an issue of perhaps limited interest to non-Catholics — the decision by the black Roman Catholic priest Fr. G. Augustus Stallings to establish his own African-Imani rite despite non-approval from his bishop — and accurately informs us of the issues and personalities involved in "Heretic As Hero," 9-89. He dive-bombs U.S. defense policy with "Divided Over Defense," 10-89: "our so-called defense spending is little more than an elaborately disguised public works and middle class welfare program." Bush's strategy to build mobile missiles and then negotiate them away is "the Pentagon equivalent of the Keynesian public-works remedy for a depression: dig holes in the ground and fill them up again." Still fighting the ABM and INF treaties, he's persuasive that the U.S. military mind-set is still stuck in World War II. His effort to celebrate George Gilder and his new book *Microcosm* in "Mind Over Matter," 11-89, spends too much time ineffectively reviewing quantum physics, and too little on the effects of the high-tech revolution on the global political economy.

Bovard, James. Freelance. (★ ★)
Adjunct analyst for the Competitive Enterprise Institute, Bovard finds administrative and government waste repugnant, making uncovering and exposing it a personal crusade. His tightly written exposes appear frequently on the op-ed pages of *The Wall Street Journal.* "Some Waste Cleanup Rules Are a Waste of Resources," 2-15, reveals Bovard the environmentalist, arguing for a reexamination of the EPA's Resource Conservation and Recovery Act, because the continual relegislation and loss of direction have actually impeded environmental cleanups: "Before beginning. . .the company must also get an RCRA permit, which takes two to four years, and the paper work can easily cost between $500,000 and $1 million, according to several industry experts. Mobile waste-treatment units are one of the best hopes for speedy responses to threats from hazardous wastes; yet, their potential is unfulfilled because of the EPA's lethargic permitting process." Yikes. "The Sacred Cows That Keep Milk Prices Up," 5-9, begins arrestingly — "Since 1980, federal dairy policy has cost the average American family enough to buy its own cow" — pinpointing absurdities in the federal milk price support system. "Lester, the Sky Hasn't Fallen," 6-26, is one of his infrequent attacks on the analysis of a particular person, in this case Lester Brown, head of Worldwatch Institute and "reverse Cassandra: His prophesies are wrong, but influential people believe them," Bovard going on to make his case with hard data. He assembles a mound of data, much of it from the World Bank's internal documents, persuasive on the abysmal record of the institution as it uses U.S. taxpayers' money to prop up dubious regimes, "Inside the World Bank," *Reason* 4-89. "Perpetual Milking Machine," *The Washington Times* 10-20, alerts us to the provision in the Senate Budget Reconciliation Bill that nullifies a price cut in dairy price supports set to take effect next year with raised milk prices the result. Strident but effective.

Broder, David. *The Washington Post.* (★ ★)
The dean of the Washington press corps set the pace for political reporting in 1987 and 1988, during the overture and several acts of the presidential race. His skills in understanding the mechanisms of American politics earned our highest ratings. But with the race over, he leaned on his laurels, not quite as adept at keeping up with the dynamics of government itself. Typical was "Next Time — Why the '92 Race Will Be a Corker," 1-22, a thumbsucker about a coming economic downturn. He gives it cosmic proportions in an overdone "The Self-Interest Decade Is Over," 1-29, advising the social contract needs to be renewed. He bounced back with a sharp assessment on the Democrat dilemma, "Ron Brown: Part of the Answer," 2-5: "Democrats run their presidential races on the left. They lose. And then. . .they say there's no need to debate policy." Acute and perceptive with "The Democrats Don't Want to Raise Taxes Either," 2-19, he notes that raising taxes to pay for various Democratic proposals is conspicuously absent as an option in discussions among congressional Dems. He's out of his depth, though, with "Challenges to the S&L Bailout," 3-19, a fairly useless discourse raising questions about off-budget S&L funds. He's sharper on the distortions of bi-partisanship, categorizing the

Democratic effort on Nicaragua as a blow to presidential authority, "The High Cost of 'Coalition Government,' " 4-9. A revealing "Texas Ethics," 4-18, puts Jim Wright in the context of Texas politics, quoting Neal Peirce, circa 1972: "Texas' monied establishment has its own Achilles heel — ethics. . ..There is not even in theory a line between private interest and public responsibility, as the establishment sees it." He's unrestrained with praise in "Mikhail Gorbachev, Embodiment of Change," 5-21, more accolades than analysis, but off-target with "Remember the Things That Dictators Do," 6-11, a patronizing sermon on American sentimentality toward events in China. Broder was off to the U.K. in the spring, but the change of scenery wasn't that helpful. Too many of his London dispatches reeked of stuffy patrician preaching about the Americans' loathsome self-indulgences. He gurgles about the superior wit of British politicians, as he follows Laborite Neil Kinnock on the political trail, "A British Lesson in Wit," 6-14, but he's super serious in "British Leader Buffeted By Political Setbacks," 6-17, which deftly examines the source and nature of Margaret Thatcher's woes. He sternly indicts "Queen Maggie I," 7-23, on her mania for secrecy and enforcement of the Official Secrets Act of 1911 to allegedly squelch parliamentary opposition. "Will the Democrats Ever Learn to Play Hardball?" 8-13, adequately reviews Germond and Witcover's *On Whose Broad Stripes?* presenting as one theme the failure of the Democrats to strike harshly at Bush — to "laugh" at him. Formula writing at its worst, "Eisenhower Lives," 9-13, puts us to sleep with: "Slowly the truth is beginning to dawn on Washington. People and policies are starting to fall into a familiar pattern. And the realization is growing that George Bush has not found a formula for extending the Reagan revolution. Instead, he has re-created the Eisenhower presidency."

Buchanan, Patrick. Tribune Media Services. (★ ★ ★)
Favoring the sledgehammer over the rapier, Buchanan would rather flatten his targets than delicately dispatch them. No other conservative *qua* conservative columnist produced as much carnage in battles with elitists and their apologists, as did Buchanan this year. His "Canon of New Morality," *The Washington Times* 9-4, gives no quarter to the hypocrisy of the liberal establishment's defense of Rep. Barney Frank (D-Mass.). asking the right rhetorical questions: What if it were Newt Gingrich involved in a comparable scenario; how long would his career last? In "Dusting Off 'Messianic Globaloney,' " *WAT* 9-18, he advises long, cold showers for those urging the U.S. go abroad in search of monsters to destroy with democratic idealism. The column provoked widespread response from neo-conservatives the rest of the year. His "Holding the Big Debt Bag," *WAT* 9-27, is a scathing account of the annual World Bank meeting, smartly tying Morgan Bank's covering of Third World loans to the end game at the IMF. He misfires with "GOP Drifting Away From Reality?" *WAT* 1-30, aimed at silent Republicans and a complacent Bush, huffing and puffing about the pay raise. "Where Liberals Have Had Their Way," *WAT* 3-22, with persuasive evidence in hand, focuses the origins of the capital's social crises: "liberalism has proved itself, at best, a costly failure in its showcase city." His "Mirror of Western Weakness," *WAT* 4-26, is powerful and evocative, fusing strategic and moral content into an ennobling plea for Lebanon's cause against the torpor of world opinion. "Next to Be Burned?" *WAT* 5-24, rises above the Gorbymania at the time of the Soviet leader's trip to China with thoughtful, prescient insight: "Unless strong barriers are erected, the roads marked *glasnost* and *perestroika* will one day take him, too, into Tiananmen Square." In "Casualties of Our Own Revolution," *WAT* 6-12, Buchanan lashes out like an *Old Testament* prophet against America's own "sexual revolution," whipping us with sobering statistics: "54,000 Americans are dead of AIDS" every year — "more than 10 million new cases of sexually transmitted diseases" — gonorrhea "the most common reportable disease in school-age children." Perceptive and compelling, he concludes "We have burned off our 'moral ozone.' " He's out in front with "The Shrinking of Ronald Reagan," *WAT* 7-24, forcefully challenging the newly emergent vogue that seeks to write Ronald Reagan out of the center of his revolution, as exemplified with Bob Schieffer's The Acting *President.* "Will the Losers Go Quietly?" *WAT* 8-23, is free of ideological cant, acutely describing precisely what Poland means for the crisis of communism, as he notes that "we have ringside seats at one of the truly epochal events of history."

Buchwald, Art. Los Angeles Times Syndicate. (★ ½)
Perched on the front page of the "Style" section of *The Washington Post* twice a week, Buchwald's humor columns are a Washington institution. "The President's Little Deuce Coupe," 1-26, delivers inside-the-Beltway humor on Bush's new limo, with all the trimmings that James Bond would envy. His gentle methods of poking fun are nice to read, even when they sometimes take on the tougher issues. "Have Gun, Will Cavil," 3-28, is sardonic on gun ownership, giving us a list of rationales tongue-in-cheek as to why the NRA and guns are A-OK: "Gun owners who are heavily armed feel very threatened by all the hysteria on guns. If stirred up, they might use their weapons to make their point" and "The main source of food in the country is provided by hunters. If you took their guns away, the people of America would starve to death." "Democracy's Potholes," 4-27, is poignant on the problems of democracy, and the demonstrations for it all over the world, Buchwald noting the "worst thing a totalitarian government can do is to give its people a *little* democracy. . .it's like making them a little pregnant." "The Excuse-Me Man," 5-30, concept has been used many times by Buchwald, but is still appropriate for downtown DC. "Counter Offers at the Breakfast Buyout," 6-8, is shopworn on international conglomerates buying out Mom & Pops, without his usual zest. "Giving Your All for an Alma Mater," 8-31, pointedly blasts tuition hikes, imagining a conversation with a "Regis Professor of Matriculation at Ivy League Normal" who wants a better class of students: "We're tired of the grungy, unkempt, badly mannered student of the past, and the only way to get rid of them is to raise the rates."

Buckley, William F., Jr. *National Review,* Universal Press Syndicate. (★ ★)
Perhaps breezing around the world on the Concorde reinvigorated Buckley; his commentary seemed fresher, livelier and more insightful than we've seen for a while. He moves beyond the rote litanies suggested by the title in "Government Is the Root of High Medical Cost," *Conservative Chronicle* 1-25, to lightly touch on efforts to deal with the rising cost of medicine, pursuing suggestions of a New York doctor who focuses on malpractice suits and huge sums awarded by juries. "On The Fitness of Tower" *National Review* 4-7, is sharp on some of the reasons why Tower's confirmation as secretary of defense was being held up, but we're surprised an old pro like Buckley didn't take up the executive vs. Congress implications of the battle here. Restrained and sober in his reaction to the Tiananmen Square massacre, he points out in "So What Do We Do Now?" *NR* 7-14, that we've been through this type of thing before with communist regimes, and most likely will be again. Yet the observation isn't cynical, and there's a good deal of serious geopolitical analysis in the commentary. He zings the failure of "our Sinological cadre" who failed to predict anything that occurred in China this year. The right's most prominent advocate of drug decriminalization rambles, though, in "A Lost Cause Is A Lost Cause," *NR* 9-29, advising conservatives it is their duty to "declaim against lost causes when the ancillary results of pursuing them are tens of thousands of innocent victims and a gradual corruption of the machinery of the state." More an attempt to show interdiction doesn't work, he suggests that cutting demand may be an answer, but without any perspective on how to do it. Ever a gentleman, he's poignantly evocative in "Remembering Sidney Hook," *NR* 9-1: "On my television program he insisted he was still a socialist, but he agreed that dogmatic socialism was unappealing. On the other hand if you take from socialism its dogma, you are left with this or that form of the welfare state and by such standards Ronald Reagan is a socialist." The Buckley wit serves for a ridiculing of President Bush's Man-on-Mars mission in "Mars? What Are the Alternatives?" *NR* 9-1 — "For all we know, Mars has on it the greatest of mysteries, the key to political duplicity. Perhaps our astronauts could stuff some of it in a canister, release it in Washington, and cause every political hypocrite to flee its noxious fumes, leaving Washington empty." — but most of the commentary merely scatters thoughts on why we should build nuclear power plants.

Carter, Hodding III. *The Wall Street Journal.* (★ ½)
We'd just about given up on this Mississippi liberal's tired, cranky commentaries on the *Journal*'s op-ed page. But he pleasantly surprised us this year with more energetic, offbeat offerings, *sans*

his patented smugness, and it's no longer a chore to read him. He produced one of the better commentaries on the Bush honeymoon. "Honeymoon's Sweet For George, But Crises Loom," 1-5: "It has been so long since the nation had a normal transition between presidents of the same party that no one was prepared for how much easier it made the process." He raises some valid questions as to who institutionally is in charge of foreign policy in "Too Many First Officers Can Wreck the Ship of State," 2-16. But he could have noted that each administration has really had one foreign policy pro, though seldom in the same job. While a bit sanctimonious on the media's presentation of perception instead of reality in "Alar Scare: Case Study in Media's Skewed Reality," 4-20, he uses the Alar scare quite effectively as a case in point. "Right Showcases a Baneful Big Government," 6-22, moans about absolute power corrupting the Right (conservatives at HUD, Energy), not Wright (House leadership), noisy and meandering instead of focused and punchy. He's aggressive in "We're Losing the Drug War Because Prohibition Never Works," 7-13, conceding that while drug use might increase *at first,* legalization of drugs is appropriate policy. But without any supportive data, the exercise is merely assertive. He's in high gear with "The Perils of Stealth Is an Old-Time Melodrama," 8-3, an engaging metaphor backed by sharp analysis on the likely fate of the B-2 bomber: "that heroine (aka Stealth) will be tied down to the tracks several times, only to be saved at the last minute on each occasion," though "it won't have a mission that would justify even a tenth of its costs."

Chapman, Stephen. Tribune Media Services. (★)
Chicago Tribune editorialist who we see in *The Washington Times,* Chapman's writing can be crisp and charged as he zings and zaps the virtues of Big Government, but too often we're getting responses from rote, his commentary predictably visceral rather than cerebral. A libertarian bent frequently appears, as in "Fleecing for Fun and Profit," 4-26, about state lotteries. There's insufficient backup for his complaints and a conclusion, "my view is that gambling, like other forms of peaceable activity, ought to be up to the free choice of consenting adults," that leaves us wondering why he bothered to waste the time and space. "Too Retarded For the Death Penalty," 1-30, on the other hand, is persuasive and well argued with details of the mental incompetance of Johnny Paul Penry, and opposes the death penalty for rapist-murderers who are severely mentally retarded. "Policies Crazier Than the Killer," 3-3, highlights Dr. E. Fuller Torrey's study on the homeless mentally ill, arguing effectively that it's the sane people who make poor decisions that we need to worry about. "NFL vs. Oregon's Picks," 7-25, is somewhat vague in its support for Oregon's legalization of a lottery on NFL games, but he projects a wider trend. "A Blip on the Detector Screen," 9-15, makes the case against new X-Ray machines being installed in airports: "Saving lives is a noble task, but it's not clear the new FAA rule will do that. More likely it will create some favorable publicity for the agency, a huge nuisance for airlines, a hefty expense for travelers and a modest inconvenience for terrorists." We are unpersuaded. "Health Care Bill's Demise Is No Accident," *Conservative Chronicle* 10-8, is crankily conventional, two-dimensional in its analysis of what the reversal of catastrophic health care signals.

Cockburn, Alexander. *The Nation.* (★ ★ ★)
Unquestionably, the best leftist columnist in the country, Cockburn always provides a high energy level to his commentary, an aggressive ferocity in his reporting, and the street fighter's tendency to go for the most vulnerable spot of an opponent other than the jugular. *The Nation's* "Beat the Devil" commentator also appears on the op-ed pages of *The Wall Street Journal,* in a mildly sanitized version (Cockburn's not one to fret over offending the sensibilities of his readers). He's also a mainstay at the *LA Weekly.* "Secret Life of Radical Journalist Pure Milquetoast," *WSJ* 2-9, delivers an incensed blast at Kent MacDougall, the U. of Cal. professor who revealed that he was a closet socialist for years while a journalist at the *WSJ* and other publications. Cockburn won't let MacDougall explain away why he didn't go public with his politics until after he moved from journalism to academia. Cockburn was grumpy all year on the great transformations occurring within the communist bloc and with its relations *vis-a-vis* the West, inquiring in his *Nation* column, 2-20, with taunting bite, "So the big question for 'Beat

the Devil' this year: If capitalism has 'won,' even pro tem, then what is the definition of victory, what sort of capitalism has done the winning, and how does it go about its business round the world?" No slouch when it comes to political economy, "Brazil's Poor Get Hungrier on Bare Bones IMF Menu," *WSJ* 3-23, paints the stark picture facing Brazil as it's squeezed by the IMF on debt payment. Cockburn's 4-3 column in *The Nation,* is a forceful observation on the decrepitude into which organized labor has fallen, sardonically noting that " 'Organized labor' actually amounts to about 17 million men and women, whose hopes and deeds receive attention sometime when they strike, always when the A.F.L.-C.I.O. musters for its annual meeting in Florida or when an election year raises questions about the union vote. . ..The only other way union members get noticed is if they are in Poland or belong to the Teamsters." "Waiting for the Fall: U.S. Media Ignored Afghan Realities," *WSJ* 5-4, slaps silly purveyors of a conventional wisdom that Najibullah's government would fall to the Afghan resistance after the Soviet withdrawal. However, his assertion that Najibullah's democratic, progressive policies are what enable it to withstand lacks the supportive evidence. "Defenders of the Amazon," with Susanna Hecht *The Nation* 5-22, a 10 Best nomination for political reporting, is a very impressive socio-political-ecological examination of deforestation in Brazil with a detailed focus on relations between the rubber tappers and Indians, and it underscores his reportorial skills. "Millions in Tiananmen Square, But Not of One Mind," *WSJ* 5-25, maddening in its logic that the Chinese don't *all* want democracy. Can he acknowledge they all want *change*? "Shamir, Sharon, What's the Difference?" *WSJ* 7-27, is smart, persuasive analysis on Israel's maneuvers to avoid a serious effort at political negotiations with Arabs and its managing of the U.S. press corps along the way. In "The Killeagh Fields: An Irish War Against Chemical Pollution," *WSJ* 8-17, we find nobody can explain an environmental debate with as much detail, clarity, flow and power and with so few words as Cockburn, a topic he expounds upon in his new book *The Fate of the Forest: Developers, Destroyers and Defenders of the Amazon.*

Cohen, Richard. *The Washington Post.* (★ ½)
Our favorite liberal columnist just a few years ago, Cohen continues to slide, his material rarely a match for his writing skills. Erratic, sour, dyspeptic in '88, Cohen began this year deciding that the future belongs to Franz Kafka's vision of it as laid out in *The Trial,* an ugly divination from the Sunday *Magazine,* "Kafka's 'Trial' Is Ours," 1-15. A new variation on "victimology" had us rolling our eyeballs with "Don't Blame It All on the Mayor," 3-21, Cohen advising us that we ought not put any responsibility on DC Mayor Marion Barry, who should not be blamed for the drug-and-crime crisis in his city because "The guns that do the killing and the drugs that are sold are hardly manufactured within the District." Next he's whining about fellow journalists who get big speaking fees, while he gets peanuts, "A Dose of Our Own Medicine," 4-18. The story's been done over and over. We get a flash of the Cohen of yore with an argument that the selection of William Bennett to head the war against drugs is ill-advised in "Wrong Man for the Drug War," 1-17. Cohen doesn't persuade us ultimately that the war's already been lost, but his presentation is powerful. He's also delightfully original with "Oh, Yes, I'm a Great Pretender," *Magazine* 1-29, "Should the term 'arbitrageur' pass the lips of someone at a party, I will nod knowingly — and then get a mental picture of a place where they slaughter animals. As for 'debenture,' I see false teeth." In "McAmerica the Beautiful," *Magazine* 4-30, we still appreciate his version of "see America this year." Cohen's much vaunted "sensitivity" is missing in "Europe's Secret Fear: The Return of One Germany," 5-7, which generalizes about Germans' lack of spontaneity and Poles' talent for chaos. He backs Jim Baker's plea that Israel disengage from the West Bank and cut a deal with the PLO, but there are no new perceptions in "Blunt and Right About Israel," 5-25. Focusing on Germany this year, Cohen's a bit worrisome in "Bonn Looks to the East," 7-14, that "West Germany intends to use its money to reestablish what used to be its sphere of interest in Eastern Europe." Again, on the theme that "the coming problem is Germany," "Where the Curtain Is Still Iron," 7-18, delivers angst instead of analysis. But he reaches the pinnacle of silliness with "Fakin' It," *Magazine* 8-13, as women fake orgasms *a la* "When Harry Met Sally. . ." men fake attention, a column which caused so much flak among *Post* readers, he felt the need to explain, "What I Meant," 10-15, but doesn't quite excuse

himself. Cohen throws a few zingers at astrology and the Reagans in "Quigley and the Quake," 10-23, taking advantage of a constellation of events — the California earthquake, the publication of Nancy Reagan's autobiography, and the fact that Joan Quigley, the former First Astrologer, lives in Frisco.

Crozier, Brian. *National Review.* (★ ½)
Ever skeptical that the communist bloc can be unhinged from its totalitarian moorings, the "Protracted Conflict" columnist takes a no-nonsense approach to geopolitical analysis. We appreciate his scholarship, but there's still a pedantic predictablity to his columns. He casts the wary eye over the South Pacific, informing us of fretful developments for U.S. influence there, as events in Fiji, New Caledonia, and Vanuatu open the door for Soviet penetration, "The Unpacified Pacific," 1-27. He's very good on the failure of the Iranian revolution in "Islamic Wasteland," 3-24, though a bit stolid on the Islamic calendar. Grand strategy is outlined in "Under Eastern Eyes," 6-2: "The Soviets never forget that Germany is the key to Europe." They want to pull West Germany out of NATO, neutralize it, and then use it as the engine to pull *perestroika,* and Crozier reminds us of a similar Soviet tactic in the '70s. But it's very unsatisfying, too many questions from the current situation left unaddressed and unanswered by his model. How much better, though, with a very impressive post-Tiananmen analytic, "China: The Party Wins," 6-30, where he gets his arms around the key questions and does provide substantial answers. We get an impressive display of Crozier's knowledge of "inside-baseball," Italian division, with "In Andreotti's Tent," 8-18. New geostrategic problems emerge as the Soviet menace fades, this one involving worries about millions of unemployed North African youths, engaged in "a 'war of the poor' against the rich Europeans." We're left wondering, though, if PM Giulio Andreotti's "plan to absorb the poverty of Arab North Africa through shared EC prosperity" is a cover for European protection money to North African leaders who are threatening to let loose those millions of unemployed youths on a Europe-1992 with open borders. "Japan: From 'Inc.' To Superpower?" 9-15, begins as a useful primer on Japan's domestic politics, but Crozier can't resist puffing on Soviet strategy in the Pacific, presenting Gorbachev as a master of duplicity who sacrifices short-term interests to outmaneuver the West in the long run.

Evans, M. Stanton. *Human Events.* (★ ½)
A veteran hard-line conservative, Evans is well past his peak of influence in punditry. He doesn't engage any universe with more than two dimensions, which sometimes leads him into disdain toward a world of broader geopolitical magnitude. It's "bombs away" with "Qaddaffi-Bashing No Substitute For Terrorism Policy," 1-21, as Evans makes the case that the U.S. obsession with the Libyan dictator clouds the fact that we don't have a strategic policy for controlling international terrorism. "Beating up on Qaddaffi is what we do best," but the U.S. really ought to go after the state-sponsors of terrorism the way it went after the Colonel, he advises. Tower's rejection weakens the President and "gives a wholly new dimension to the idea of 'advise and consent,' " he observes in "Tower Debacle: A Political Watershed," 3-18. The insights aren't unique, but the argument is strongly focused. Evans claims vindication of the right wing's opposition of ten years ago in "It's Time To Renounce Panama Canal Treaties," 5-20, stopping short of a call for sending in the Marines. He doesn't give two hoots for adverse "Latin opinion" if the U.S. renounces the treaties, but this so ignores the larger picture that it's little more than splenetic venting. With a quote from Ralph Waldo Emerson, he wonderfully concentrates a skeptical image of Speaker Jim Wright and his farewell address ("The louder he spoke of his honor, the faster we counted our spoons") in "Demise Of Wright, Coelho, Just The Beginning," 6-10. But when he describes Democrats' complaints "as roughly comparable to Adolf Hitler's complaining that the Allies had broken the peace of Europe by daring to land at Normandy Beach," he becomes a top contender for the Worst Analogy Of The Year Award. It's an old theme — when the president defines the debate the opposition has been on the defensive, and *vice versa* — and Evans somewhat mechanically applies it to Bush and the Democrats in an uncharitable critique of the administration, "Dukakis Agenda Prevails In Washington," 7-22.

Looking around inside the Beltway, he sees "the policy agenda of the establishment" being discussed everywhere. With "Liberal Rhetoric On Drugs A Hollow Mockery," 9-16, he's like a hunter in a duckblind the first day of the season — firing at everything that flies overhead, and though it's scattershot, he does bag some hits: the President's do "a bit more of what we are already doing" drug policy; the Democrats' response, "treating the crisis as a pretext for their favorite nostrum — raising taxes," and a national capital that's "a sinkhole of scandal, corruption, rampant drug use and a murder rate that is a national disgrace."

Evans, Rowland & Novak, Robert. *Chicago Sun Times,* North American Syndicate. (★ ★ ★ ★)
In their 26th year as a writing team, the dynamic duo bounced back from a subpar '88 to produce a marvelous string of columns, almost always ahead of the competition in spotting critical turns in policy developments at home and abroad. We catch them in *The Washington Post.* "The Democrats' Confusion Over Taxes," 1-9, is savvy on Democratic division and uncertainty over tax hike prospects, clearly identifying OMB's Richard Darman as key defender of Bush's no-tax-hike pledge. "Playing Chicken on the Budget," 2-10, though murky regarding budget strategy, is persuasive on chances Congress may blink first. "The Baker-Arias Connection," 3-17, gives advance warning that State Secretary Baker's Central America policy review will side with the proposals of Costa Rican President Oscar Arias. "The Fed and Inflation," 3-27, knowledgeable and precise, provides against-the-grain analytics on Fed policy: "The seven governors of the central bank, no monolith today, are wary and uncertain in dealing with a puzzling economy. They are unsure whether they already have tightened too much." "Darman's Dealing," 4-14, is fine inside insight on Darman's handling of the capital gains tax proposal at this early stage. "Pressure On the Fed," 5-26, is sharp, timely and accurate on blossoming pressures in the White House, Congress and foreign central banks for the Fed to ease on short-term interest rates. Very astute, "How Bush Triumphed," 6-5, clearly illuminates the President's skill and decisive role in wresting the initiative back from Gorbachev during his *tour de force* at the NATO summit. "Quayle's Ambitious Space Program," 7-12, is way ahead of everyone on the VP's critical role in moving this ball down the road, with an accurate picture of what the administration will propose on space policy. "Tampering With The Tax Code," 8-25, is definitive, affirming that there will be *no* trade off of new marginal rates for a capgains rate cut. "Bush Sustains Gorbachev," 9-28, a 10 Best selection for political reporting, produces in distilled essence what came out of the Baker-Shevardnadze summit in Wyoming, with the appropriate focus on the administration's decision to help Gorbachev keep the U.S.S.R. from flying apart amidst his reforms.

Fairlie, Henry. *The New Republic.* (★ ½)
A British political essayist who spends a good deal of his time in the colonies, Fairlie has always attracted our attention over the years because of his unusual and arch perspectives on the American scene. In recent years, though, perhaps because he's become part of the background, the unusual has become usual and the arch has sagged, the crisp writing picking up a drone. A satire on the Tower nomination, "A Modest Proposal," 3-27, is a difficult read, written in colonial English, but amusing in spots, suggesting "a system of Eunuch Rule" after Tower. "Hushed Puppies," 4-24, a "Washington Diarist" column, uses Daylight Savings Time as a vehicle to attack government interference, a fine point, but the nasty, nasty ending on Barbara Bush and the White House puppies is unnecessary, bite without wit. "Spurious George," 5-8, is cumbersome, Fairlie comparing Washington and Bush, not quite connecting or contrasting the two in any significant way. "Air Sickness," 6-5, a scathing critique of Frank Lorenzo in the context of his acquisition and, in Fairlie's view, the destruction of Eastern Airlines, is well documented and well argued: "Eastern, the fifth-largest airline in the country, with over $4 billion in revenues, was sold to Texas Air for $640 million — $10 a share." His "Let Them Eat Hot Dogs," 7-31, has great potential as commentary on the French Revolution, but Fairlie tiptoes through it to the last graph: "We are a little crabbed in spirit to deny the intimate connections between the two revolutions. It is proper that good French and American historians have been at work, prompted by the two bicentennials, to reexamine the different courses of the

revolutions. But we should not permit timorous conservatism to deny that *together* America and France made the Age of Revolution which, for all its fearful atrocities in Europe, improved the lot that most men and women could expect in this world." In "Holding Ourselves Hostage," 8-28, he succeeds in putting the execution of Col. Higgins into perspective without belittling it: "It would be going too far to say that soldiers were meant to die. But they are likely to die. They are expected to die. They are employed to be ready to die."

Fields, Suzanne. Los Angeles Times Syndicate. (★ ★ ½)
There's no columnist around better at elevating traditional values by tromping on the foibles and shams of new-age liberalism, with feminists her special prey. To some tastes, overwrought sentimentality pervades her thinking, making many of her columns mushier than need be. But to those who like overwrought sentimentality, she's right on. Just when everyone agreed that nobody should like Nancy Reagan, Fields gave us "Her Turn, With No Apologies," *The Washington Times* 10-24: "Feminists ought to respect Nancy Reagan, even when she disagrees with their agenda. She's everything they say a woman can be: tough, outspoken, someone who gives as good as she gets and who advises every woman to speak her opinion." In "Reflecting Our Own Moral Yearnings," *WAT* 3-14, she argues, plausibly, but obviously, that "at the edges of the Tower controversy," there lurks a revived national "craving for disciplined behavior." "Putting Out the Prime-Time Toms," *WAT* 4-13, is excellently written, a soothing palliative for chastised middle-aged white males, from a lady who doesn't like what Betty Friedan and her friends in the media have done to manhood's image. "Signing On the Dotted Love-In Line," *WAT* 6-13, is well-written commentary on the proliferation of laws to give legal status to "unmarried live-in partners, both hetero- and homo-." She says, with bitter mockery: "The rules for a 'domestic partnership' are fairly simple. The couple has to declare that each wants 'to share one another's lives in an intimate and committed relationship,' be jointly responsible for fundamental living expenses and swear not to be married to anyone else. (Adulterers and part-time fornicators will have to lobby for a law of their own.)" But we hear it all again in "Redefining the Family," *WAT* 7-13, asking how unrelated roommates of the same sex can be considered family. "Yearning For His and Her Friends," *WAT* 8-8, predicts the theme for the '90s will be friendship, a good if maudlin bit of philosophizing occasioned by "When Harry Met Sally." In "Pulling Pricey Sheepskins Over Our Eyes," *WAT* 9-19, Fields draws attention to the Justice Department investigation of 20 elite private colleges for tuition price-fixing schemes.

Gergen, David. *U.S.News & World Report.* (★ ★)
Editor-at-large. Among the best when it comes to identifying, distilling and reflecting upon conventional consensus, Gergen's work improved noticeably this year as he was freed of management chores. He works with an easy, readable style, as in "NATO in Disarray? This Time, Reality," 1-23, which provides a fine overview of complex issues facing the Atlantic Alliance. We appreciate his use of good detail, good sources, good analyses. A lead Sunday "Opinion" feature in the *Los Angeles Times,* "Tower Besieged. . .as Bush Team Bungles," 3-5, is typical Gergen, precisely mainstream conventional observations: "There is a gathering consensus in both parties that the country needs an effective leader." "Baker, Cheney, Scowcroft; Government Between Friends," *LAT* 4-2 is a well-woven and organized "insider" analysis, bringing in interesting tidbits and his own personal knowledge. In "Looking Back From 2000," 5-1, Gergen uses environmental, education, and trade issues to illustrate how Bush's presidency may not be preparing us for the year 2000. Using a much better frame of reference than the first 100 days, Gergen's criticisms are well-founded and deserve attention. "Communism's Final Days," 6-19, reads more like an article than a column on U.S. response to China's actions, with too much on policies (is Bush's policy good or bad?) and not enough on issues (what do the Chinese government's actions say about communism?). "More Choice, More Life," 7-17, is reflective on the abortion issue, with some effective political analysis of *Roe v. Wade:* "Women and children might have received more enlightened treatment had the issue been left in the political arena in 1973 and the process of reconciliation continued." A singular insight we didn't see anywhere else, "The Lessons of the HUD Scandal," 8-7, makes the impressive connection

that the GOP should be happy Thurgood Marshall has hung in at the Supreme Court: "Otherwise, the man probably occupying his seat today would be one Samuel R. Pierce Jr." In "Drugs And White America," 9-18, using the evidence effectively, Gergen begins by arguing that while blacks are disproportionately affected by the drug problem, that is no justification for letting white users off the hook.

Germond, Jack & Witcover, Jules. *National Journal.* (★ ★)
This durable team of political reporters and analysts had an excellent '88 on the campaign trail, but like Broder of *The Washington Post* they aren't as quick off the mark covering issues as candidates. "New Right Comes Up Short in Bush Presidency," 12-31-88, is solid reporting on the diminished influence of movement conservatives, but with no surprises. "Atwater Hopes to Widen Parties' Talent Gap," 1-28, is very informative on "warehousing" political operatives between campaigns, giving a big edge to GOP. "Exaggerating the Import of Wyoming's Election," 4-29, has nice details on the special election for Cheney's House seat, won by the Republicans, but the analysis is a bit too flippant. "President Bush Seems Paralyzed By Indecision," 5-13, is a tepid effort, more of the usual litany that Bush is indecisive. Though expressed cogently, there's nothing here to indicate the dangers of go-slow, except to say it is "dangerous." "Is Dan Quayle More Than a Laughing Matter?" 7-22, is shallow, though there's some liveliness on Quayle's readiness for the Oval Office. However, the column hinges on one anonymous quote of a Quayle "friend" who says the Veep isn't ready. In "Democrats Seem Disheartened and Rudderless," 8-19, G&W take up an appropriate theme — "Bush is riding a wave of popular approval that seems to have intimidated Democrats" — but there are no new clues on how the Party can crawl out of the slough. "Bush Needs More Than Good P.R. For Long Haul," 9-30, is sophomoric at best. Bush must be popular because of "style and gimmickry," they write, a refrain from the Reagan years.

Geyelin, Philip. *The Washington Post.* (★ ★)
A veteran commentator on international affairs, Geyelin doesn't produce many striking insights, but he is astute and possesses a strong working familiarity with the various corridors of thinking in the foreign policy establishment. He's quick to defend "Washington Insiders" against charges they're too elitist and too well-represented in the Bush administration. In "The New 'Establishment' Myth," 1-24, Geyelin makes a point that this group isn't the same as the Eastern Seaboard establishment that ran things after WWII, but he's not altogether convincing in posing the options as if they were between old pros versus faceless outsiders with no experience. Pressuring the administration to lean on Yitzhak Shamir when the Israeli PM comes to Washington in April, "Bush's Improvised Middle East Policy," 3-27, contains only one element of novelty — junior British Foreign Office minister William Waldegrave's call for Israel to enter direct talks with the PLO — but the implication Waldegrave speaks for Margaret Thatcher is unwarranted. "Testing Linkage in Nicaragua," 4-4, is hardly treading into new territory, *The Wall Street Journal's* Greenberger already over this terrain a month earlier. Geyelin scores the shortcomings of the Bush-Congress "compromise, but doesn't venture any new initiative. We can envision NSC's Scowcroft dismissing the column as facile carping without any solution, yet we appreciate Geyelin's refreshing critique of cynical hypocrisy on the issue. The analytics on Bush's Panama policy following the May election crisis are reasonably astute in "A Promising Panama Policy," 5-16. Geyelin places both the "good" elements — reliance on diplomacy — and the "not-so-good" — "a bracing swig of Old Jingo" — in the diplomatic-political context. However, he loses points for moving Sen. Al D'Amato across the aisle into the Democratic camp so that he can pull on a D'Amato quote critical of the administration's Panama policy to illustrate the low "level of bipartisanship" a year ago. Beneath the banal title, "Bush Put The Ball In Gorbachev's Court," 6-3, Geyelin delivers *realpolitik* assessment of President Bush's first major arms control proposal, delivered at the end of NATO's 40th anniversary celebration. Though he doesn't pursue questions raised by the "end of the Cold War," he provides a coherent picture of relations among the U.S., U.K. and West Germany. Very insightful and very informative, ' "Glasnost' In Jordan," 10-3, is adept on the political-economy of King Hussein's

country, where the first national elections in 22 years are to be held. The myriad pressures on the country's stability are clearly outlined, and the approach of the royal office is underscored with a quote from a significant political figure who believes the king should dole out *glasnost* "in little doses." We nodded off with "Foreign Policy Isn't Football," 10-14, a space-filler.

Geyer, Georgie Anne. Universal Press Syndicate. (★ ★)
She gets high marks for the passion of her commentaries, but it's really for an improved insight into political economy that we up her rating this year. "Damage Fed By Desperation," *The Washington Times* 1-18, effectively reveals that, although Marxism is dead, its practitioners still cling to power, as Cuba's Fidel Castro tries to knit together anti-Gorbachev forces in Afghanistan, Cambodia, the Caribbean, and North Korea. The analysis is too thin in "From a Stronger Position," *WAT* 2-28, an interview with Puerto Rico Governor Rafael Hernandez Colon, on his call for a plebescite on statehood as the *final* statement on the island's status. She skims over too much, focusing mostly on how good the island is doing relative to Cuba. Her best work, and her enriched insights into political economy, is exemplified by the powerfully-argued "Trigger Finger Itching Over Debt," *WAT* 3-10: "There are triggering mechanisms in various stages of effectiveness, or non-effectiveness, poised all across the hemisphere and as in Venezuela, it is 'the debt' that will pull that trigger on all of us." Her "Illegal Immigration's Risky Impact," *WAT* 5-26, fulminates against illegal aliens from Mexico and the devaluation of U.S. citizenship. Passionate, though polemical, it does introduce some new information on overcrowding of San Diego and Los Angeles hospitals by illegals. Passion appears again (with a bit of the high pitch shrill) in "Where Disintegration Looms," *WAT* 6-20, which is filled with substantive admonitions about the horrors awaiting Peru: "Sendero [Luminoso] has killed the mayors, the teachers, the best people of the land; and now fully half the Peruvians live in military controlled 'emergency zones.'" "Intent Clear From the Start," *WAT* 7-25, is an effective arrangement of evidence against the Sandinista regime in Nicaragua: "No food. No water. No free investment. No democratic opposition. No free newspapers. An economy so disastrous that Nicaragua will have a 40,000% inflation this year and is now poorer than Haiti. And Tomas Borge presides over an Orwellian Ministry of the Interior building with a chillling sign in front of it: 'Sentinel of the Happiness of the People.'" "Choking On Victimhood Politics," *WAT* 8-4, aimed against the self-serving compassion industry, is solidly argued and documented.

Gigot, Paul. *The Wall Street Journal.* (★ ★ ★)
An editorial writer, Gigot surfaces on Friday's editpage as the *Journal*'s only regular political columnist, his "Potomac Watch" taking up some of the slack of the Washington Bureau. A Treasury official in the early Reagan years, the relatively young Gigot has the supply-side, neoconservative bent that is a hallmark of the editpage, also good contacts inside the administration and among pro-growth Democrats. His columns are always newsy, generally lucid and insightful, an up-and-coming star. He's superb with the handling of James Baker's State Dept. team, "Crafting of State Under Baker Is Not So Diplomatic," 2-3, establishing the good news on the diplomatic front, with an alert over a worrisome ceding of international economic policy to Treasury. Gigot produced the best overall commentary on the John Tower nomination, consistently focusing it in the context of a struggle between presidential authority and congressional resistance. A 10 Best nomination, he nails Sen. Sam Nunn (D-Ga.) in "Statesman Sam: Cracking the Whip, Twisting Arms," 3-3, calling into question Nunn's much vaunted statesmanship — If the senator were "genuinely torn" over the Tower nomination, why didn't he let Armed Services Committee members vote their individual consciences? "Democrats: Please, Sam, Don't Do Us Any More Favors," 3-10, among the best wrap-ups on the defeat of the Tower nomination is astute and quick. Bob Dole's star is up and "simply for having fought, George Bush has won," and, against conventional wisdom, Nunn's "Towerplay leaves him weaker than if he'd remained a totem of bipartisanship." A Gigot weakness shows up in "Bush Must Beat Odds to Make His Tenure Work," 1-20. The basic point is fresh and insightful — "Though he takes office with pomp and media flourish, Mr. Bush today becomes the leader of the weakest of the three branches" — but thoughts in support of the headline are

too scattered. "Anatomy of a Congressional Smear," 3-24, a provocative case history of Rep. John Dingell's (D-Mich.) transgressions, is Gigot still not overcoming his weakness. The column has to be read through twice to untangle the skein of events. He works with see-saw angles, opening new insights where others see only a single dimension, in "Is Jack Kemp, Happy Warrior, Switching Sides?" 5-19. The analysis properly catches the HUD Secretary's non-ideological approach for breaking constraints on new social policy. "After Wright's Fall: Perhaps A Balance of Ethical Terror," 6-2, is definitive: "...the past week has witnessed one of the great mass conversions of modern times: the Washington political community suddenly concluding that its prescriptions with ethics has gone too far." Perfect material amidst the year's preoccupation with "endism," "After Cold War: Bring Back the Gunboat," 8-11, is well-argued and thought-provoking: "The need to resort to force will become more likely, not less, if the Cold War ebbs." "General Gephardt Loses A Battle In The Class War," 9-29, is pungent comment on GOP victory in the House on capital gains tax, though Gigot hammers Rep. Richard Gephardt (D-Mo.) into the ground with a bit too much relish. A bit confusing on details, "Child Care: George Bush's Domestic Panama," 10-13, is nonetheless the best spotlight we've seen on the child-care bill before Congress, a bill "that amounts to the greatest expansion of government power in at least a decade."

Goodman, Ellen. *The Boston Globe,* Washington Post Writers Group. (★ ½)
Post-feminist on "This Week with David Brinkley" from time to time as well as in print, Goodman sometimes takes the message too far, promoting it in inappropriate places. "The Post-Feminist Message of 'Working Girl,'" *The Washington Post* 1-10, sounds like post-Milk Duds ravings, failing because the movie isn't necessarily social commentary in the sense Spike Lee's films are, and Goodman misses that point, reading too much into it: "The woman who has gotten ahead is expected — often expects herself — to be more sensitive to the women who work for her and tougher than the men who work beside her. To be twice as good in every way." "Justice O'Connor's Question," *WAPO* 4-29, is muddled on abortion, losing steam after a promising start by claiming that women can be "pregnant against their will." Only in cases of rape or incest, Ellen; otherwise there are other birth control methods. "Curtains for 'The-Bitch-Deserved-It' Defense," *Los Angeles Times* 5-23, an unapologetically feminist diatribe on light sentences for murderous husbands, lovers and exes who crack under stress, is exceptionally good. Goodman uses a case in Michigan to look at the broader picture, with a punchy use of details and tightly presented information. "James Worden's Solar Cars," *WAPO* 6-3, informative on the solar car prototype, pushes her environmental agenda, with solid reporting though, which we don't always get from Goodman. "I Dreamed I Was On the Cover of *Life* — But In My Bra?" *LAT* 6-8, debates the hidden meaning of *Life* magazine's celebration of the bra, on its cover no less. Silly stuff, but Goodman makes some valid points. However, "Silicone, Suction, and Miss America," *WAPO* 9-19, is too convoluted on the cosmetics of beauty pageants: "Any sporting event has to draw lines and rules, and any pageant worth its image would draw them at the cosmetic knife."

Greenberg, Paul. Freelance Syndicate. (★ ★)
A syndicated columnist in addition to editorial page editing duties at the *Pine Bluff* (AK) *Commercial,* Greenberg's mid-America viewpoint holds up well next to the Washington-New York pundits. When he keeps his sermonizing in check, he really cooks. "Tyranny of the News in Our Time," *The Washington Times* 2-24, bewails the unreal state of news, so distorted as to be parody, quick and poetic without being preachy. "Reflections in the Mirror of History," *WAT* 5-26, sizzles on George Kennan receiving the Arnold Toynbee Prize, concluding they deserve each other: "The unique character of the American experiment has been lost on George Kennan. The theory, or rather faith, of American exceptionalism makes no more sense to him than it would to Arnold Toynbee, who clearly resented any people so perverse as to violate his rules and refuse to decline and disappear on schedule." His "What Huck Could Tell the Glibs," *WAT* 8-11, seethes with sarcasm, but still well-reasoned, on the obsessive anti-religious ostentation of "glib" liberal education. "Feverish Fed Bashing?" *WAT* 9-8, staunchly defends

the current arrangement and powers of the Federal Reserve Board against Rep. Lee Hamilton's assault: "Let's be fair: the politicians aren't asking for control of the Fed; then they might have to take responsibility for it and lose a convenient scapegoat in the process." Ouch. "Livability Ratings Game," *WAT* 10-20, is a delightful rebuttal of the *Places Rated Almanac,* which ranks Greenberg's hometown dead last: "Berlin in 1936, a model city, would have topped out on this numerical scale. By 1946, it was a collection of rubble. And all because one or two intangible values were missing — like freedom and decency."

Greenfield, Meg. *Newsweek, The Washington Post.* (★ ★ ½)
The editorial-page editor at the *Post,* Greenfield's bylined columns in *Newsweek* continue to draw close to three-star status, but just miss on consistency grounds. Neither stunning nor complex, her comments on the passing political culture are deft, neat, often wise, but sometimes mechanical. Lately there's more brio, less of the sophisticate's pretentious whine in her columns. She smothers her efforts with reasonable calm in "Deep in the Ethics Bog," 2-6. The thought is interesting, but mushy, not definitve, and not followed through: "The sad thing is that for all the talk of corruption, often as not we don't know it when we see it." She discharges both barrels at the invocation of "constitutional authority" in the battle between Congress and the administration in "Hamilton Made Me Do It," 3-20, making the long overdue distinction between "whether these Senators were entitled to vote down Tower" and "whether they should." She's Pollyanna with "Don't Bet on a Sure Thing," 4-3, a column uplifting on what we take for granted. Lovely with indignation, she castigates the specious defense of sleaze in "Everybody *Doesn't* Do It," 5-1: to "say we can't do anything about ethical temporizing and downright sleaze on the Hill because it is so widespread, thus making it impossible to single out any individual, seems to me defeatist and feeble." She asks key questions in "Misled by the 'Facts,' " 6-26, — how people in an open society like ours who know so much, could not have predicted the crackdown in China — and provides a respectable answer: "We are misled by our own information, knowing much more than we understand." But her argument that we lack the necessary cultural and historical knowledge to put events in context takes too long to crystallize, and remains questionable. She puts some fire into her ire with "Indignation on Demand," 7-10, angry about feigned indignation in the Beltway. She picks up on Steven Brill's critique of the decomposing criminal justice system in "Scandal In the Courts," 8-21, expressing her sense of how far from reality is society's perception of the system. We found her banal regarding the controversy over the Mapplethorpe exhibit, "Summer Storm," 9-4, observing that "the artists are raising hell about the repression, the patron — government in this case — was raising hell about the artists, and the public was thronging in unprecedented numbers to avail itself of the denounced works of art."

Grenier, Richard. *The Washington Times.* (★ ★ ★ ½)
If you don't like Grenier's idiosyncratic jingoism, his puckish erudition, his leering insouciance, you just won't like him at all. No, you won't. But if you can imagine Harpo Marx with a Harvard degree in comparative religion, a flag and a gun and a way with words, you might find yourself among his adoring fans. Yes, you will. We swoon over the likes of "Two Hits For New Women," 8-30, a dual movie review of "When Harry Met Sally. . ." and "sex, lies and videotape," and a 10 Best nomination, where Richard asks: "Are you ready now for the 'Year of the Orgasmic Woman'? Because it's arrived. Oh, yes it has." His appreciable knowledge of East European history and politics comes through in "The Coming Crack-Up of Communism: And In the Ukraine," *National Review* 1-27, an excellent background and reference when turmoil swept the Ukraine later in the year. Also in *NR,* "Have Typewriter, Will Run," 3-24, approvingly profiles Peru's capitalist revolutionary and presidential candidate, Mario Vargas Llosa, as "nothing less than a Latin American Margaret Thatcher." He's nothing if not graphic in "Stepping Through Fidel's Looking Glass," *WAT* 3-24, visiting Havana and finding "Even in the public facilities of Havana's best restaurants and hotels for foreign tourists, there are no toilet seats, usually no paper, no soap, no water, no locks on stall doors, often no doors. Toilets rarely flush." And "Getting a Back-Home Flossing on Fidel," 4-19, careens hilariously through a political debate

on the worker's paradise in Cuba between two unequals: a drill-wielding "progressive" dentist and his patient (anti-Castro Grenier) strapped on the chair. In "Clinic For Socialist Survival," 5-26, we get a spoof on a Warsaw clinic for U.S. liberals "who want to believe in socialism." "Markers In Our Channel," 6-9, is Grenier responding from his gut, grabbing the lapels and shaking those "ratty little intellectuals [who] tell you America is a terrible place." "Revisionist Bastille Day," 7-14, is deliciously entertaining, sprinkled with wit and irony on how Frenchmen don't adulate the French or any other revolution though naive tourists do. He's sober and thought-provoking on the Middle East in "Deadly Barrage of the Rubble-Makers," 8-25. With "Anniversary Worthy Of Red Banners," 9-4, he's tweaking noses and poking fun at Marx's *Communist Manifesto* on the 141st anniversary of its publication: "It's a stirring text. It has sweep. Freeman and slave, patrician and plebian, lord and serf, oppressor and oppressed, all at each other's throats since time immemorial. And then along comes the bourgeoisie, the greatest oppressor of them all! But doomed by its own success!. . .but I think my copy of the Communist Manifesto is a cute antique and I'm going to keep it." Occasionally he'll hold up and shake the head of someone he's just decapitated, simply to show us there's nothing inside, as with "Triumph Of the Patti Doctrine In Panama," 10-10. Vintage Grenier, Reagan daughter Patti Davis' new book, *Dead Fall,* is examined against the Panama coup backdrop: "The Patti Doctrine in a nutshell. . ..Never barrel into a small, weak country. And God forbid we should barrel into a big, strong country." In defense of Martin Luther King, "Prying Has Its Precedent," 11-6, a wonderfully humorous and engaging column and a 10 Best selection, enumerates the human weaknesses of the original Martin Luther: "So I don't care if Dr. Martin Luther King dallied with three, six or 10 women on the eve of his assassination. Or indeed none. I don't care if he played pinochle."

Hentoff, Nat. *The Village Voice, The Washington Post.* (★ ★ ½)
"Sweet Land of Liberty" columnist for the *Post,* Hentoff is marvelously clear and focused, bulldog-like on first amendment and related legal issues. In "Can't They Mention Lent?" 3-26, pointed on CBS radio's cancellation of the Lenten message of Chicago's Joseph Cardinal Bernadin because of codes restricting "religious advertising," lets the Lenten messages and the codes speak for themselves. Working in quotes from CBS executives, he effectively demonstrates how ridiculous the decision was. In "Not a 'Hopeless Case' After All," 4-29, we get a wonderfully written, clear and witty story of Carrie Coons, 86, whom the court, using medical testimony from "a nationally recognized expert in geriatric medicine," declared to be in an irreversible noncognitive vegetative state, ordering the plug be pulled on her life support system. The court and the expert were wrong, the woman survived, largely because the hospital staff fought to keep her alive. "The RICO Dragnet," 5-13, is vivid on broad misuse of the RICO law, citing examples and historical pre-passage heebie-jeebies by the American Civil Liberties Union. Hentoff doesn't suggest specifics for reform, but is persuasive that it's needed. He underscores how absurdly the "separation of church and state" idea is misused with "James Gierke's Right to Read His Bible," 6-10. The case involved a 10-year-old's attempt to read his *own* Bible on his *own* time in school, a case of landmark potentials that was eventually settled out of court, and we appreciate having it brought to our attention. He's very lucid in "Secularizing the Sacred From the Bench," 8-12, disagreeing with the libertarian approach on the creche-menorah-Christmas tree ruling, and quoting from Justice Kennedy's dissent to give us the parameters.

Hertzberg, Hendrik. *The New Republic.* (★ ½)
Now full-time editor at the weekly, Hertzberg also pulled part-time duty as replacement for Michael Kinsley on the "TRB" column. It wasn't all damp ashes in the column, but the customary sparkle and fiery wit wasn't as frequent. Our favorite was "The Iceman Goeth," 1-30, a multi-chuckle column in which he confronts a fantasy of Michael Dukakis running again in 1992. After running through a typical Dukakis promo mentioning the appropriate virtues and values, he concludes "*You are growing sleepy, sleepy. . ..*" Not so quick on the draw, he fires off a pop at the President's vacuous inaugural speech, with trivial impact, in "The Nice Age," 2-13, tacking on the customarily partisan assertion that George Bush "hasn't got a mandate."

He seems oddly against the grain on the John Tower nomination, moving toward his defense in "Tower Play," 3-27, but coming after the Senate vote, the scattered insights weren't enough to distinguish this from Monday morning quarterbacking. He fires off a cutesy shot at George Bush — "widely rumored to be President of the United States (though this could not be confirmed at press time)" — in "Gub Control," 4-10. The title comes from "Take the Money and Run," but that's the only coherent thing we find in this disorganized mess on gun control. "Late Returns," 4-17, is an election returns account, heavily laden with statistics, not a column. He breaks no new ground with "Wright, Writer," 5-15, though it's useful as a review of Jim Wright's *Reflections of a Public Man.* Hertzberg categorizes it as "no worse, certainly, than the sort of thing that turns up as filler material in *Reader's Digest.*" Pointed on the virtues of former President Jimmy Carter in "Mr. Ex-President," 6-5, he compares him to other members of the club, like Gerald Ford, who "has grown rich using the prestige of his former office to hawk everything from commemorative coins to shopping malls." His language is strong, but the argument itself is routine against the proposed flag-burning amendment in "Flagellation," 7-17: the flag can't be destroyed because it's only a physical manifestation of a symbol. He's hilarious with "You Had to Be There," 8-28, on Woodstock, by someone who was there, and who went home to watch it on television.

Hitchens, Christopher. *The Nation.* (★ ½)
"Minority Report" columnist. A writing stylist with a gift for imagery, Hitchens' drawback is careless reporting. With a world view that sees the Reagan years as "grotesque," and the prospects no better with President Bush, his leftist ideological drive too often inclines him to mix fact with fiction. In the Reagan years, he advises in his column of 1-9/16, we witnessed "a panic or collective hallucination that arose spontaneously to seize and stricken the masses." Among them: "terrorism," the "Evil Empire," the KGB plot to kill the Pope, "Yellow Rain," KAL Flight 007, and the Sandinistas' export of revolution, all Reagan-invented and managed. In his 1-30 column he rhapsodizes over Sweden, though not fixating on its socialized-everything system. Gushing about its diplomatic contributions to world stability, (e.g. "a Swede. . .brokered the Israeli withdrawal from Sinai, thereby saving the stupid Eisenhower's bacon"), Hitchens ignores Sweden's substantial arms industry that contributes to its influence in world affairs. An engaging 2-27 column on the political renaissance of the Baltic states compares that situation to Poland eight years ago: "You get the same sensation. . .that of watching a fire burn under water and wondering how long such an offense to the given laws can possibly continue." He finds in these impressions the basis for condemning the West's entire strategy for conducting the Cold War — illuminating imagery submerged in cant. Strongly assertive, he charges that John Tower got the Secretary of Defense nomination in return for having gotten Bush off the hook on Iran-contra. The story enjoyed considerable circulation, Hitchens' column helping to give it some added life, but the evidence is definitely not there. Hitchens launches a scathing personal attack on Paul Johnson, [London] *Spectator* columnist, in his 4-10 column — wife-beater, dog-kicker, drunken bigot, etc. — unconvincingly attempting to justify this egregious excess as permissible because Johnson's book *The Intellectuals* also disparages the personal lives of its subjects. His 7-3 tribute to C. L. R. James, the Jamaican-born black Marxist historian, revolutionary figure, poet and international authority on cricket, is an evocative testimonial to a singular figure in the history of 20th century revolutionary activity. Hitchens recalled that when he last saw James prior to his death "He was already old by then, with a nimbus of silver surrounding his anthracite features." Francis Fukuyama's "End of History" thesis is a "crackpot hypothesis" and "self-congratulation raised to the status of philosophy," Hitchens inveighs in his spirited 9-25 column: "The end of history. . .has ignited a saturnalia among the intellectuals," and raises some points worth considering. But he's as guilty of misreading Fukuyama as he accuses Fukuyama of having misread Marx.

Johnson, Paul. *The Spectator.* (★ ½)
The popular historian, Johnson's weekly column on the British news media usually contains dispassionate commentary, with a fair mix of straight reporting, at times half-baked. He's not

at all dispassionate, though, in "Eggheads and the Big Lie," 2-4, with almost an Auberon Waugh-like ranting against notions that Britain is becoming a police state. In "The War Of Rushdie's Sneer," 3-4 he questions if the author would have still received so much support from Britain's literary establishment if he weren't non-white and left-wing, indulging a lapse into some moral equivalency with "one of the great irrational dogmas of our times, the Divine Right of Writers. . . .do not differ, in principle, from the old-style religious triumphalism of the Ayatollah." He's more preachy than perceptive in "Feeling Synergetic," 3-11, arguing that "synergy" among media corporations, *a la* Time-Warner, is nothing new, then advising Rupert Murdoch and Robert Maxwell to curb their empire-building tendencies. He's also thoroughly unpersuasive with a warning about ominous Japanese "penetration" of Western media. Better with cultural-historical critiques than as a media critic, Johnson produces a better than average column with "When Jesus 'Blasphemed,' " 3-25, using the Salman Rushdie affair for a discussion of what indeed is blasphemy. He's out of a topic for serious thought in "Any Good Faxes Lately?" 5-25, writing about the mechanics of his writing. He's effective with the umbrage he takes toward Labour's plans to regulate "sexual and racial stereotyping" in fiction, castigating the party in "The Return of Big Brother," 5-27, for "the compulsion to peer into and correct every aspect of our behavior by those who know best what is good for us." The best we saw this year is "The Television Multiplier Effect," 6-24, in which he plays a gutsy devil's advocate, advancing an argument to restrict coverage of events such as riots on the theory that TV coverage encourages others to join in. We are not persuaded, but appreciate the passion with which he promotes the view. Borrowing an analytic mold from the U.S., Johnson's "Number Ten: Time For Silence," 8-5, looks at the bad reactions Margaret Thatcher's getting in the polls and begins toying with style rather than substance as a way to reverse them. With "Will You Let Me Finish?" 9-30, Johnson uses the publication of a television journalist's autobiography to ruminate on the nature of set-piece television interviews, delightfully revealing some of the tricks interviewers and interviewees use to maneuver with one another.

Kilpatrick, James J. Universal Press Syndicate. (★ ½)
He's been hammering away for half a century, but Kilpo still surprises us now and then with a youthful sprint. "Gun Control: An Exercise in Futility," *Human Events* 12-31-88, takes on a topic about which it seems nothing new can be said, but we enjoy his clever formulation: "The [Washington, DC gun control] law doesn't catch criminals. It catches Carl Rowan." Constitutional issues his *forte,* Kilpatrick brings a common sense lucidity to the questions involved. Following up on the peculiar ruling affecting Georgetown University in which a U.S. District court upheld the Washington, DC, council's noncompliance with legislation exempting religious organizations from having to accommodate groups promoting homosexuality, he's trenchant on the central question: "Where stands religious liberty if a local council may interpret liberty to mean whatever it says?" "Humpty-Dumpty Rules From The Bench," *Conservative Chronicle* 1-25. With an economy of language and proficient insight, he provides a fine measure of ex-Secretary of the Navy John Lehman in "Lehman Book Promotes Defense Excellence," *HE* 2-11: "Lehman's waves flattened out on the bureaucratic beach. He accomplished a great deal as secretary; he revitalized the office and got things done, but many of his reforms never left port." Forcefully and with the necessary details there, he makes a persuasive case for ending the astonishingly high marginal tax rates that are a major disincentive to older Americans who choose, or need, to keep working after retirement age, "Why the Elderly Lose By Earning More — Part II," *HE* 5-6. Kilpatrick lives by the First Amendment and goes a long way in defending its rights, often taking on his conservative peers, which is why his commentary in "An Enormous Insult to Art And the Art World," *HE* 7-8, rings so true. Regarding the photographs of Robert Mapplethorpe, the exhibition of which was cancelled by the Corcoran Gallery of Art, he states bluntly: "this is not art in any rational view. It is prurient junk, intended to shock the decent sensibilities of those who would come to a public museum." "Puerto Rico Faces Future of Unpleasant Political Options," *HE* 9-16, touches on the various shortcomings of the various options facing the island in its 1991 referendum. Though each will probably be resolved as the plebiscite bill moves along, Kilpatrick leaves a disconcerting thought in our heads: "Suppose the option for statehood carries by a mere handful of votes?"

Kinsley, Michael. *The New Republic.* (★ ★ ★ ½)
"TRB from Washington" columnist. A superstar journalist with an off year, the first time since the *MediaGuide* began that he doesn't get the highest rating. But he was off the screen for the first half of the year, sojourning in London as editor of the "American Survey" column of *The Economist,* and then distracted by his "Crossfire" TV obligations later. His logic and lucidity were still there on his return, but except in the war he waged against capital gains, the incandescence was missing. As one of the high priests of liberal theology, he was ferocious in counseling the Democrats to fight Bush and the GOP on the capital gains issue in "Where Are the Democrats?" 9-18. In "Talking Chop," 10-23, he's savagely brilliant and satirical in urging class warfare over the issue! "For all the talk of 'class warfare' around Washington and in the press, you would think that the Democrats had erected a guillotine on the mall and were chopping off the heads of plutocrats as they stepped out of the Willard Hotel." He takes on with clear logic Charles Peters' argument in defense of a military draft with "The Rich Don't Serve — So What?" *The Washington Monthly* 3-88: "But to snatch two years from just a small fraction of the population against their will, and to make room for them by reducing opportunity for people who want it, all in the name of 'fairness,' seems insane." We were not surprised to see Kinsley playing devil's advocate for Congress, arguing on behalf of the system that produces it (In 1988, he denounced democracy for having produced President George Bush!), with a 10 Best selection, "In Defense of Congress," *Time* 4-17: "In the Executive Branch, George Bush got 54% of the votes and all the seats." Kinsley is in typical high form with "Thatcher for President," 5-15, offering praise for Margaret Thatcher and contempt for Ronald Reagan and George on the issue of leadership: "Thatcher has taught the British people self-discipline. Reagan and Bush have taught Americans self-indulgence." He's gutsy and passionate in his critique of efforts to free Dr. Elizabeth Morgan in "Morgantic Marriage," 7-31. He advances the liberal case for altering the FDA drug "efficacy law" to permit faster licensing of new drugs in "Conflicting Prescriptions," 8-28: "Let's even relax our standards of safety a bit, so drugs can get to market quicker and cheaper." "It's Your Party," 9-11, screams about the possibility of Malcolm Forbes deducting his $2 million birthday party from his taxes as a business expense, jumping on the Forbes bashwagon that derailed just as this was published. Ever the contrarian, his facile "In Defense Of RICO," 10-16, defends criminal prosecution on insider information trading, simply because of an assumption that the information in these cases really must be "inside" info.

Kirkpatrick, Jeane. Los Angeles Times Syndicate. (★ ½)
The baleful former UN Ambassador, acknowledged as author of the thesis that no totalitarian system ever reformed itself into democracy, Kirkpatrick had an interesting year in which to focus that premise. For the most part, she stayed behind the curve. She does provide a very thoughtful look at whether the reforms in China, Hungary, and the U.S.S.R., are seriously undermining prevailing assumptions that totalitarian communism is incapable of reform from within, "The Dismantling of Totalitarian Society," *New Perspectives Quarterly* winter 1988-89. Less profound, though, "Above All, Human Rights," *The Washington Post* 1-23, is banal on the East-West Accord on human rights. She's cautious with "Is the Brezhnev Doctrine Dead?" *WAPO* 3-20, not venturing much beyond the obvious: "No one knows how much freedom or independence Soviet leaders will tolerate." Soft material in "Wright and North: Only in America," *WAPO* 4-25, the headline makes the entire point. Ponderous on an integrated Europe, she gives us clumsy imagery and little else in "A New Europe. . ." *WAPO* 5-18: "The new Europe emerging from its long gestation will be as different as a butterfly is from a crawling caterpillar." We expected a strong column with "The Cold War Isn't Over," *WAPO* 6-7, but were disappointed with the litany of uncharacteristically weak warnings. But she's excellent on tracing historically "How The PLO Was Legitimized," *Commentary* 7-89. The evidence is compelling on how the UN was co-opted over the years to identify the struggle against colonialism, racism, Zionism, with the plight of the PLO, with even terrorism being excused as a "necessary" weapon of Palestinian liberationists. We're still left wondering whether or not half a loaf is better than none, a question she never addresses in "A Bad Bargain in Poland," *WAPO* 9-11, arguing merely that the Communist party retains too much control.

Kondracke, Morton. *The New Republic.* (★ ★ ★)
Senior editor with a primary focus on foreign affairs, Kondracke has the potential for
superstardom, getting there with time as he piles up experience and confidence, more relaxed
on a lofty perch. He has just the right tone in "The Democracy Gang," 11-6, expertly surveying
the field of the new democracy movement in arguing that it needs a leader who will make it his
chief political activity. He has the essence of it: "This is not just a moral crusade, but a matter
of America's self-interest. Democracies don't go to war with one another." He introduces a fresh
intensity to an urgent policy problem, the details poignant and useful in "The Two Black
Americas," 2-6. One of Kondracke's best for the year, this "progress report" was a timely
message to the administration. Complaining that Bush "hasn't decided the big questions yet"
in the arena of foreign policy, he states the obvious in "Blind Men's Bluff," 3-6 — the world
has changed. The examination of the record of State's James Baker and Brent Scowcroft and
the NSC, as background for the "lack of vision" case simply dismisses as acceptable that the
administration take some time to evaluate the global changes before it sets policy. His pitch is
strong on behalf of open borders in "Lottery to Get Through Our Gates," 3-28, though he
doesn't satisfy us on the implications of free immigration policy. More on the debate over
immigration policy, "Borderline Cases," 4-10, summarizes with fairness and balance the
arguments of the inclusionists and the restrictionists and the proposals currently on the table.
Never hidebound, in "One Day At a Time," 5-8, he defends Bush's cautious approach to foreign
policy during his first 100 days. Then bemoaning Bush's inability to beat Gorbachev in the
international PR game, he advises "Get Me Re-Write," 6-12. We get a respectful profile of Rep.
Richard Gephardt, the new House Majority Leader, in "Man for All Seasons," 7-3: "He
acknowledges that Japanese trade barriers represent only a small part of the reason for the trade
deficit between the two countries, but he devotes most of his speech to attacking them."
Meticulously fair to the pro-life, pro-choice viewpoints, Kondrake is deeply thoughtful on how
the nation feels about abortion in the wake of the *Webster* decison in "The New Abortion Wars,"
8-28, the presentation is messy, littered with scattershot observations. He's loose, and
freewheeling in "Bright Ideas," 8-28, a Diarist column on a variety of topics. Among them, Spike
Lee's movie *Do the Right Thing,* which Kondracke sees as quite the opposite the racist film
neoconservatives are buzzing about. Medium depth with "The World Turned Upside Down,"
9-18, declaring that the nothing-can-change model of totalitarianism the right has been working
on for 40 years is wrong, but he could be more rigorous in stating the thesis.

Krauthammer, Charles. Washington Post Writer's Group. (★ ★ ★)
Particularly bold, taking aim at a variety of moving targets this year, Krauthammer's clarity of
intellect distinguishes his commentary. His not so subtle ironic wit is effective regarding the rush
to Rushdie in the West with "Fearless Self-Inflation," *The Washington Post* 3-10: "Poor Salman
Rushdie. His enemies are out to kill him and his friends, those who profess to be, are out to ride
him. For awhile Rushdie was a cause. Now he is just a platform on which writers can fight their
own little battles in Salman's holy name." As George Kennan testifies before Congress
promoting the thesis that the time has passed for viewing the U.S.S.R. as a military threat,
Krauthammer reminds us in "Kennan: Cold Realist," *WAPO* 4-14, to take Kennan's vision with
a grain of salt, recalling his grotesque euphemism describing the Soviet invasion of 1968 —
"increased troop movements into Czechoslovakia." In "Losing the Mandate of Heaven,"
WAPO 5-26, we get fresh comments from Krauthammer on China's unrest: "After several
centuries of experimentation, the West has solved the mandate problem. Popular elections, even
communists are now learning, are the only enduring source of political legitimacy since the
demise of the theory of the divine right of kings." "Communist Imperative," *WAPO* 6-23, cuts
through much of the sentimental effluvia of public reactions to Chinese events: "The reign of
terror is not uniquely Chinese but characteristically communist. . .Now that Soviet communism
has adopted a human face, the baby boom generation has a hard time recalling what the Cold
War was about. A popular revisionism holds that the Cold War, fed on a mutual paranoia, was
a cherished project of the American right. In fact, China today has clarified the issue. It has
dramatically recreated precisely the kind of forces America fought during 40 years of the great

twilight struggle." "A Failed Revolution," *WAPO* 7-14, is a critical obituary years after the French Revolution. "Stealth: The Weapon For Going It Alone," *WAPO* 7-21, beats George Will's defense by two days and with a more sophisticated, comprehensive case for the B-2's utility. Krauthammer did some of the most forward thinking on the strategic implications involved with the "End of the Cold War" thesis, and links Stealth to a post-Cold War multi-polar world in which the U.S. has fewer friends and fewer bases. Appreciative of the candor and moral seriousness in William Bennett's anti-drug plan, he underscores the modest yet positive role government can play in "Stigmatize Drug Use," *WAPO* 9-8, with persuasive arguments that law enforcement will have effects on demand. A 39-year-old baby boomer, Krauthammer is delightfully satiric in his reflective, "Grumpy at the Movies," *WAPO* 10-20, in which he discovers he's out of sorts with his generation.

Kristol, Irving. *The Wall Street Journal.* (★ ★ ★)
Co-editor of *The Public Interest* and publisher of *The National Interest,* the godfather of neo-conservatism has enjoyed a rebirth of sorts in moving to Washington after a lifetime in Manhattan. Always cleverly offbeat in his social and political commentary, his standing as an intellectual and a humanist permits him to march where angels would not tread. He produced a novel examination into academia's hostility toward corporate governance in "The War Against the Corporation," 1-24, locating the center of the attitudes in the faculties of law schools, where pressure for removal of judicial rules against "derivative litigation" builds. In a 10 Best nomination, "Cries of 'Racism' Cow Crime Fighters," 2-28, "Almost nothing can be done to help the law-abiding majority of the ghetto unless and until crime and the drug trade are brought under control. Can we do it? Of course we can. . .[by] inconveniencing criminals. So why don't we do it?. . .[Because] any attempt at such a remedy immediately would be denounced as 'racism' by a flock of politicians (black and white) and by the media. The fact that such an objection is crazy will count for nothing." The Atlantic Alliance has always been an area of special concern and expertise for Kristol, and he warns that NATO's myopia regarding West Germany's anxieties is producing a major strategic crisis for the Alliance, "A Smug NATO Is Letting Germany Secede," 5-2. Kristol's wisdom is apparent in a delightfully reflective antidote to the current, mushy, sentimental approach to child-rearing in "Some Kindergarten Remediation," 6-22, in which he recalls and reasserts all those age-old truths that constitute the world's wisdom, as for example: "Marry in leisure, repent in haste: This revised version is directed at those young people who live together for years, then get engaged, then have an expensive wedding, and soon get divorced." There's a pugnacity to his contentions, but he's not merely polemicizing. The arguments are subtle and sophisticated in "Education Reforms That Do and Don't Work," 10-24, in which he answers the question "why can't we teach our children to read, write and reckon?"

Leo, John. *U.S.News & World Report.* (★ ★ ½)
Leo is the most promising young commentator at the weekly, new to us this year. Leo frequently pursues the obvious arguments, so there's both an easy pace and an easy content to his columns. There's nothing tepid, though, in "Baby Boys, To Order," 1-9, on "designer-abortions" because a child of the female gender isn't desired. It's but a short step from this to "getting rid of a fetus. . .for insufficiently high intelligence or the wrong ultimate height." He strives to make the case for tolerance of Salman Rushdie's *Satanic Verses,* with "In Search of the Middle Ground," 3-6, drawing a parallel to derogatory books about Martin Luther King, Jr. and Anne Marie Frank, but the effort is weakly argued and unconvincing. "A Lesson From the Deep, Dark '60s," 5-15, a standard press release obituary of Abbie Hoffman is immediately perishable. If George Will can write one column a year about baseball, then Leo can do one on bird watching, "A Lark of a Way to See the World," 6-12. He's effective on the issue of codes regulating appropriate "sensitivity" on campuses and the erosion of civil liberties as a consequence in "Chipping Away At Civil Liberties," 6-26: "I myself have violated most of the new antitalk laws, including those sternly prohibiting insults about marital status (my little jokes about Liz Taylor), religion (lack of respect for Jim Bakker, and Al Sharpton), sexual orientation (scornful views about

sadomasochism), and Vietnam-era status (furtive one-liners about Dan Quayle)." It's on these kinds of topics that Leo did his best work this year, picking up on the trend toward the extreme with anti-discrimination codes (no more "Ladies' Night" at the movies, suits being filed against airlines for not allowing a blind person to sit next to the emergency door, etc.). "Let's Try Discriminating For Once", 8-7, is funny and incisive. In response to the New York City decision that two homosexuals living together constitutes a family, he argues effectively that if you have "two gays, two straights, four flight attendants or a fraternity, you have a household, not a family." His best for '89 is "When The Feds Turned Drug Dealers," 11-13, a grim, yet witty, projection of the consequences of surrender in the war on drugs that is totally prescient. A fellow to watch.

Lerner, Max. *New York Post,* Los Angeles Times Syndicate. (★ ★)
Nearing his ninth decade without any obvious loss of pace, clarity of intellect, or acuity of insight, Lerner's columns this year seemed a bit more reflective, more philosoph:cal. Drawing broader visions, projecting major geopolitical shifts on the grand scale, he opened the year with "Awaiting a Moral Order," in *The Washington Times* 1-2. Well-written and lofty in outlook, he sizes up 1988, yet there's no single, penetrating insight or observation there. Again, we come away from "Whose Century Will It Be?" *WAT* 2-9, with a collection of interesting but scattered thoughts on the shape of the next century, as the unifying thread is too feeble and thin: "America's role must more strongly center on shaping a moral world community in which terrorism is abolished, the rights of the person become central, and the creative imagination can take flight everywhere." There's a touch of eloquence in his call for "the moral equivalent of war," as he backs the idea of declaring Washington, DC, a drug disaster area in "A Wise Target for His Opening Salvo," *WAT* 3-20, although the idea we need something morally right to distract users and sellers away from their habits isn't as elegantly advanced. Lerner's been around for a long, long time, and has the proper disdain for the chorus of those who, impressed by Gorbachev's PR victories of the moment, moan and groan about Bush's lesser rating. "On the Stage of History," *WAT* 5-22, trenchantly observes that there is "a curious delusion of the thunderers in the media that they are both theater critics and stage managers." He's thoughtful on the corruption of the Democratic House, from whence it flowed, what nourishes it, and how it can be excised, "Ethics and the Monopoly of Power," *WAT* 6-5. "When the Truth Emerges," *WAT* 7-24, examines the French, Russian, and Chinese Revolutions, and the Terror they unleashed, counterpoising the end of their careers against the continuation of America's. His observation regarding the video-taped display of the hanged U.S. Col. Higgins is poignant in "More Than A Visage Of Terrorism," *WAT* 8-3: "more than the outward visage of terrorism. It is the reality of evil." His lively philosophizing includes projections on the season's favorite subject — Gorbachev's predicament — and, though there are no new insights or information in "Going West . . .." *WAT* 9-14, the column is creatively penned.

Lewis, Anthony. *The New York Times.* (★ ★ ★ ★)
"Abroad at Home" columnist. Another fine year for the nation's premiere liberal pundit, who can only be found at the margin, where all change occurs. A few years back, we docked him for submitting inadmissible evidence and hyperbole, but in recent years he rarely slips from relentless lawyer-like logic in making his case. The foremost critic of South African apartheid among American journalists, Lewis this year began cashing in as the tide finally turned in Johannesburg. "Starting on the Road," 10-15, is a remarkably frank acknowledgement of the significant political changes for the better there under PM de Klerk. Now Lewis shifts his fierce pen to question Israeli apartheid, slashing at Tel Aviv's hard-nosed non-negotiating position with Egypt and the *intifada,* forecasting a dire picture of an Israel 10 to 20 years down the road, "Time for Straight Talk," 10-8. Wayward Democrats continue to feel his sting as well. He zaps House Speaker Jim Wright in "But We Are Going To Pay," 2-9, a concise history of the S&L crisis, its folly and greed, a 10 Best nomination. Lewis got another 10 Best nomination for his lucid "World Upside Down," 4-2, on the Soviet elections: Gorbachev "is not just tinkering in his program of restructuring, *perestroika,* and *glasnost.* He is not just responding to economic

necessity. He is seeking a new basis for political legitimacy in that society." Lewis had high appreciation for Gorbachev's initiatives most of the year, advising in "Missing the Big One," 4-23, that despite different starting points on global security, there is a common good in the Soviet perspective that Bush may be missing. He's superb again, scoring yet another 10 Best nomination, with "Investing in Disaster," 9-24, using libertarian arguments to challenge prohibitionist drug views, going after William Bennett for rejecting the call of Prof. Milton Friedman and others for drug decriminalization. He's always devoted special attention to sub-Saharan Africa, getting off to a sputtering start with "Shadow on the Future," 1-15, advising that "Zimbabwe is the success story of black Africa" and never accounting why. He's honest and thoughtful in his assessment of the difficulties posed by Jonas Savimbi's future relationship with the Marxist government in "An Angola Proposal," 1-19. In "The Price of Reagan," 2-2, Lewis stretches our patience by tacking the ineptitude of the U.S. Attorney in Boston onto Ronald Reagan: "The damage done to the country's institutions in the Reagan years will be a long time in the reckoning." But he's in bounds regarding the decline of public services in the U.K., quoting Prof. J. K. Galbraith in "Is It Thatcher's Britain?" 3-23: "It is increasingly. . .a land of private affluence and public squalor." In "The Slime Slinger," 6-8, he's positively sulphuric with Lee Atwater for the RNC's innuendo about Tom Foley: "I do not know that we have ever had a major party chairman who raises viciousness and cowardice to as professional a level as does Lee Atwater."

Lindberg, Tod. *Insight.* (★)
An *Insight* editor, Lindberg rotates with others on "The Last Word" page, improving to the point where we now read him. But he's still erratic, at times serving up soggy commentary that drips with schmaltz. Zapped by the romantic muse, for example, he's molasses sweet in a farewell to Reagan, "Exemplary in the Extraordinary," 2-13. We imagine Lindberg's eyes misting with tears, as he sees the ex-actor President walking off stage proudly, the "long, dark overcoat in stark contrast to a brilliant white scarf, the hair going gray at last." Zippy, witty, and riotously funny, his retrospective on Jimmy Carter's last year, "1979 Makes 1989 Look Good," 4-10, reminds us of all the malaise and misery back then, an appropriate but not overbearing response to the moaning and groaning about the Reagan years. He's unsatisfying in his analytic effort regarding the "End of History" thesis of Francis Fukuyama in "World Verging on Democracy?" 6-26, and we nod off. Lindberg is aghast at the awarding of the Medal of Freedom to George Kennan in "Medal of Irony and Obfuscation," 7-24, and uses the occasion to assert that Kennan possesses an "overwhelming desire to diminish the absolute magnitude of American military power." We need more incisive complaint for this to be useful. He conveys outrage over John Hinckley's bid to overturn St. E's rule on no talking to the press (without ever mentioning Hinckley by name), but he is too petulant with the broader point in "Keep Him Out of the Public Eye," 9-4: "One of the underappreciated merits of the death penalty is that it causes the executed to shut up already. It is a final rebuke to the proposition that anyone with a barbarous disposition and a gun has a right to enjoy the fruit of ill-gotten fame." In "A Story of Lives Saved," 11-6, he opens with a 200-word quote from Machiavelli's *Prince,* somehow relevant to the San Francisco earthquake. Zzzzzzz.

McCarthy, Colman. Washington Post Writers Group. (★)
A fine wordsmith, McCarthy eloquently champions the cause of the most wretched and hopeless among society's underlayers, but without differentiation, with no cutting edge. How often does he expect us to weep with him? He maintains the same kind of moral equivalency between the U.S. and its downtrodden adversaries, suggesting Libya has as much right to chemical weapons as does America. In fact, America's the hypocrite, he pens in "Our Libyan Double Standard," 1-22. Though the U.S. said the Libyan jets were engaged in hostile maneuvers, McCarthy advises "no, no," they were merely "curious." Moralizing we expect, but "Bluster on Drugs, But That's No Solution," *Los Angeles Times* 3-21, is simplistic drivel about drug abuse as a consequence of poverty, unemployment, poor housing, etc. Everyone is to blame but the druggie. Light, easy, and warm, "News From Flickeville Mountain," *WAPO* 4-29, tunes us in on the retirement to

a farm of fellow *Post* journalist Ward Sinclair. We get a throw-the-book-at-'em admonishment in "Inflicting Corporate Punishment," *WAPO* 5-7, arguing in favor of punitive jury awards against corporations that cross the line. Sweet and well-written, "The Day Pepper's Car Stalled," *WAPO* 6-3, relates two lovely stories on Rep. Claude Pepper in tribute to his character and devotion to duty. "The Unusual Trial of the D.C. Seven," *WAPO* 6-18, is a surprising paean to Judge Mildred Edwards of DC Superior Court, one of the last Reagan appointees who appears to be socially conscious, as shown in her handling of 7 DC protesters on behalf of the homeless. Colman leaves us to ask why there aren't more like her, and obviously feels the same. "Saving Elephants: This Year's Cause," *WAPO* 8-19, advocates a wider range of environmental reform, beyond the latest media-pressured abhorrence over the slaughter of elephants. McCarthy reminds us the seal hunts are now back, for example, and lays out the bottom line: "Stopping the slaughter means stopping the buying at home."

McGrory, Mary. *The Washington Post.* (★ ★)
The Republicans have been in the White House almost a decade now, and this more than anything grates on Mother McGrory in a way that too often renders her acid commentary grumpy and splenetic. "It. . .[is] as if a Democrat running for President is not just presumptuous, it is a crime," she moans in "For Liberals, A Day of Dirges," 5-30. A year of headaches for the Democrats, McGrory was more morose than menacing. She raises a worthy point — that the "shelter mentality" — has replaced "housing" in HUD's mentality with "Think Housing," 1-12, but then loses control by trying, without recourse to facts, to explain why some projects didn't get a HUD grant. Early on, while it still seems that John Tower was safely home at DoD, McGrory raised an eyebrow in "Sweet Tower of Babble," 1-29, throwing in an informative quote from the nominee: "I am not such a mindless hawk that I would come and ask you for increased expenditure when I know it is not going to happen." She lets loose with pure, effective rage over the Central Park rape with "Horror In the Park," 4-30: "We are conditioned to looking for deprivation when we are confronted with depravity. It is not here; nor is the other contemporary all-purpose alibi: drugs." Treading water as Jim Wright sinks, she produces idle observations on the Speaker's hearings in "Brilliance All In Vain," 5-25. She shudders and chokes with angry resentment over the reception given Bush on his visits to Poland and Hungary, noting in "Bush's Hungarian Rhapsody," 7-13: "He adjusted a slicker over his shoulder and they applauded. He smiled and they waved and waggled the V-sign at him." She sees "opposition to capital gains tax cuts. . .such a surefire issue," that she can't understand why Democrats were tearing themselves apart on it. Apparently misinformed, she advises in "A Sticky Situation," 9-21, that "it even served Michael S. Dukakis well in last year's presidential campaign." McGrory's happy as a puppy with a new toy in "A Scrappy Star Is Born," 10-5, heralding Sen. John Kerry (D-Mass.) as the latest in the line of party knights who might at last challenge the GOP franchise on the White House. She's ineffective in "Panama: Where Was George?" 10-8, which, while taking pains to note that "not that we should have intervened militarily," wonders why Bush didn't attempt an "Entebbe-type" raid, sending a U.S. helicopter to drop down "to extract the vile beast [Noriega] and. . .[fly] him here for trial."

McGurn, William. *National Review.* (★ ★ ½)
Washington bureau chief. The former deputy editorial page editor of *The Asian Wall Street Journal,* McGurn is part of *NR*'s new forward-looking vitality. He had Beijing seething because of the constant critical focus he kept on China's policies in Tibet, and Britain's foreign office fuming because of piercing criticism of their vapid Hong Kong policy, but it's a bit early to see how deeply he's getting under the skin of Beltway blusterers in his new post. The best report anywhere on the current situation in Tibet and the challenges facing the Dalai Lama was "Dalai Lama Seeks Middle Way on Tibet," *The Wall Street Journal* 3-8. McGurn provides a rich portrait of the Tibetan religious and political leader and his search for a way to prevent China from destroying one of the world's most ancient cultures. We get no fresh insights in "Exit Stage Wright," 6-30, but he's right in calling to attention that the scandals are "symptoms of a House of Representatives grown arrogant through the lack of accountability." He quickly picks up on

the flip slide of Jim Wright's woes in "High Noon For Newt," 8-18, in which he brings us speedily up to date on the campaign to go after GOP Minority Whip Newt Gingrich who started the successful challenge to liberal hegemony in the House. He's unforgiving with the failure of the administration's strategy to secure the appointment of William Lucas as assistant attorney general for civil rights. McGurn makes a persuasive argument in "Guess Who's (Not) Coming to Dinner," 9-1, that the GOP muffed this one because it doesn't appreciate how much it threatens the Democratic and black-establishment agenda. And McGurn is full of wrath over the Sandinista triumph against the contras, though it doesn't cloud his acute perception of what led to the situation, as "The Dodd Doctrine," 9-15 lambastes the administration for essentially giving anti-contra Democrats veto power over its Central American policy.

Meyer, Cord. News America Syndicate. (★ ½)
As befits his many years of service with the Central Intelligence Agency, Meyer's columns often read like intelligence briefings —but given the remarkable changes underway on the planet this year, his material seemed thinner than we would have expected. We get a first-rate briefing on the military situation in Ethiopia with good operational detail in "Tottering Toward the Ropes?" *The Washington Times* 3-17, Meyer reporting on the fast declining fortunes of Mengistu Haile Mariam. There are no surprises in "Historic Turning Point for Soviets?" *WAT* 4-7, a survey of conclusions drawn by U.S. institutional watchers of the U.S.S.R. after the Soviet elections. As Gorbachev's *glasnost* spurs nationalism, "Delicate Balancing Actions," *WAT* 4-21, Meyer picks up on Zbigniew Brzezinski's perspective that the U.S.S.R. may be forced into "genuine confederation," acknowledging Gorbachev's quick reaction to the Georgia S.S.R.'s disturbances, replacing party leaders and promising dialogue with the activists. "China Exploding Into the Modern World," *WAT* 5-26, is skimpy stuff, recapping news from Beijing, offering an opinion or two, but not much here is worth the effort. In "What Will Be the Outcome?" *WAT* 6-9, he disappoints us by anchoring his arguments on reports that "commanders of rival armies jockey for position on the outskirts of Beijing" almost two days after this particular rumor was determined baseless by Western intelligence agencies. He gets the bead on the contras' fortunes in "Uncertain Grip for the Contras," *WAT* 7-28: "The Bush administration faces the danger of a serious setback in the meeting of the five Central American presidents scheduled for Honduras on August 5-7. A majority of the Central American presidents seems prepared to go forward with a plan calling for the demobilization or relocation of the Nicaraguan resistance." "Afghan War Can Be Won," *WAT* 8-11, contains good analysis of the weaknesses of the Afghan anti-communist guerrilla opposition, but this isn't strategic analysis. In "Staying A Tricky Course," *WAT* 9-22, there's little depth in his assessment of Salvadoran President Alfredo Cristiani's first semester in power, the perspective conventional and fogged: "The events to date suggest that with continuing American assistance Mr. Cristiani's administration will be able to handle the danger on the far left, but there is new evidence of an incipient threat from the hard right." A look at Italian attitudes regarding Gorbachev as the Soviet leader prepares to visit the once-imperial city, "Warily Watching and Hoping," 10-13, doesn't tell us much beyond they're "watching with a mixture of hope and apprehension."

Mortimer, Edward. *Financial Times.* (★ ★ ★ ½)
"Foreign Affairs" columnist. As fast as the world was turning in 1989, Mortimer stayed at the edge of the horizon, providing us a lofty London vantage point. We always look for his byline in the *FT* as he rarely disappoints with his wise, deep reflections, strengthened by a secure grasp of history. He paints a bold, broad overview of changing superpower relations in "A Time of Hope, a Hint of Peace," 12-19-88, very perceptive on the progress in regional conflicts during this "watershed year." He poses exactly the right question for the continent this year in a 10 Best selection, "The Dog That Failed to Bark," 1-10 — whether Eastern Europe will test limits of *perestroika*. Presciently, he projects an East Bloc putting the Brezhnev doctrine to the test to find out if U.S.S.R. has really renounced the right to intervene militarily outside its frontiers in defense of socialism. "If it has not, that will be the end of the new detente and probably of *perestroika* too." He combines superb analysis and appropriate historical background with wry

wit to put complex issues into an understandable context in "Bringing Down the Wall," 1-24. A similar effort also serves to develop our insights with regard to the situation of Lebanon's Maronite Christians and France's particular concern in "A Divided Stand in Lebanon," 4-11. He presents a well-written, sophisticated analysis of the short-range nuclear modernization issue in "Why All This Fuss About the SNF," 5-16. We couldn't help but recall this column when we saw NATO leaders accepting perspectives Mortimer had advanced here. Some straight reporting with "Iraq Troops Begin Forcibly Resettling 300,000 Kurds," 6-4, alerts the world that "Iraq's Bathist regime began this week a mass displacement and forcible resettlement of the Kurdish population in northeastern Iraq, moving it to areas outside 'Kurdistan' and to areas more susceptible to government control." (This in the same week that a *Wall Street Journal* correspondent was reporting that Iraq was on a new course of toleration of minorities!) We get very informative insights into shifts of elite opinion regarding Gorbachev's "Common European Home" in "Why Europe May Become a Region," 9-19, but he's a bit too partisan here, urging haste and hurry in backing the proposal without really producing convincing or compelling reasons. On a trip to Leningrad, he finds "For Soviet Democrats, the Danger is Despair," 10-3, a tightly focused picture of anxiety among intellectuals about the degeneration of the economy and its threat to political stability, plus his usual superior analytics.

Novak, Michael. *Forbes.* (★ ★)
"The Larger Context" columnist. Author, philosopher, journalist, ex-ambassador, Novak had been most appreciated by us as an informed observer on developments within the Roman Catholic Church. We saw less analysis of that situation in his commentary this year, as he shifted into broader topics with a new column in *Forbes.* Novak is consistent in his efforts to bring other dimensions to bear into what are often treated as one-dimensional issues. For example, we get an insightful distinction between European and American attitudes regarding capitalism's moral worth in "How About Obscene Losses?" 3-6. "The Two Americas, as Viewed from Rome," *The Washington Times* 3-20, is accurate and insightful on what transpired between the Pontiff and U.S. Bishops in their recent meeting, Novak combining his expertise of Vatican affairs with sensible, well-tuned social observation. "The Abortion Debate, Close Up," *WAT* 4-14, is a beautifully written, sensitive rendition of the pro-lifers' latest argument: "Reason itself does not allow some of us to infer that the embryonic infant — with its own individual genetic code, its human shape, its sex already determined (in a majority of instances female) — is anything but an individual human being, who will develop normally unless brutally terminated. . .it seems to me 'progressive' to take the most inclusive view of rights and, among the bearers of inalienable rights, to side with the most vulnerable." He's fairly solid in "Why Latin America is Poor," 4-17, blaming the traditional Latin aristocratic feudal systems for the prevalent poverty in the region, but there's no treatment of how past policies of the capitalist colossus to the north also helped deform their economies. "Business Should Speak Up," 5-1, argues that the corporation as set between the individual and the state has a responsibility to "protect, nourish and fertilize the soil from which they spring" and to get involved in political matters, making credible points, but we'd have liked to see some examples of how this works in actual practice. "Egalityranny," 5-15, flows nicely, introducing interesting sources to support his argument that as socialism fails, we must make the victor, capitalism, ever more humane. He's eloquent, on respectable grounds constitutionally and historically, and very persuasive in "The New 'Secular' Orthodoxy," *The Washington Post* 7-10, reacting to the Supreme Court's opinion *Allegheny County v. ACLU*: "Our faith is an inalienable dimension of our citizenship. A citizen divided against himself, half religious and half secular, cannot stand. We expect wise and generous accommodation, not niggling mutual hostility." "To Honor Auschwitz's Catholic Dead — Move the Nuns," *The Wall Street Journal* 9-12, takes a different tack on Auschwitz's Carmelites, suggesting the place be left desolate as a testament to the hell it was. He clears away the misinformation fogging up the issue of income differentials, illustrating in "Is the Income Gap Widening?" 10-2, that age, education, marital status and *work* itself play the key roles as opposed to the false notion tax cuts do: "A full 64% of those in the bottom quintile did not work at all in 1987."

O'Leary, Jeremiah. *The Washington Times.* (★ ½)
Ending almost half a century as a Washington scribe, O'Leary now turns his hand to commentary and we're not surprised to find that he can be entertaining, peppering his commentaries with illustrative vignettes drawn from his rich experience. We especially appreciated one of his first, "Rumor Mongers," 6-2, imperceptibly tongue-in-cheek, taking to task the "current spate of rumors of homosexual activity and pedophilia in the House and the Senate," noting "There may or may not be pedophiles and undiscovered homosexuals in Congress. If there are, I do not look forward to reading the sordid details." O'Leary's newspaper, of course, was providing the details. "One Use for the Death Penalty," 7-4, is heart-wrenching, despite his unconvincing argument favoring the death penalty. It's a gripping narrative that takes us back to a day in 1948, "just five days before Christmas," to the execution of three convicted murderers at which O'Leary had served as official witness. "Agonies And Challenges That Endure," 8-7, is sweetly nostalgic, and optimistic: "Eight years ago today that best of all newspapers, the Washington Star, perished from the Earth and I for one still have the taste of bitter gall in my mouth. . .But for seven years now there has been the Washington Times. The Post tries to ignore us, as the Star once ignored the Post. But it is good to have an arrogant foe. It makes all of us work harder and, by God, we'll get 'em yet." He reaches down the memory hole to recall how Lyndon Johnson handled Santo Domingo back in 1965, advising Bush he could learn a lesson about Panama in "Coat-Holding. . ." 10-9. In "Crossing the Sex Divide in Culottes," is a marvelous reflective on how far women have come in the newsroom in 52 years, with several charming lines: "The newsroom of the Star was, figuratively speaking, knee deep in women."

Perle, Richard. *U.S.News & World Report.* (★ ★)
The brilliant former assistant secretary of defense's strength is an ability to pointedly ask the right questions at the right time. But when he's determined to simply pronounce the right answers, we get mediocre pontification. He did better keeping the latter under control this year. There's not a lot new being said in "Why Military Spending Pays Off," 1-16, but this exposition on the Reagan approach to military and foreign affairs is well-argued, logical and clever. Perle is particularly strong in defense of John Tower's nomination, hitting "the malicious campaign against him of rumor, hearsay and unsubstantiated allegations," with "Tower: Worth The Fight," *The New York Times* 2-21. He argues against the U.S. policy dialogue with the PLO, charging that it's destabilizing because it "has raised expectations among the PLO leadership that the U.S. somehow will 'deliver' Israel into the arms of the Palestinian state." We're not totally persuaded, but he assembles a strong body of evidence in "What America Should Say to Arafat," 3-20, for the case that Yasir Arafat's renunciation of terrorism and recognition of Israel's right to exist is dubious. Certainly one of his best columns, "Defending People by Defending Rockets," 6-26, asks the right questions about limits to passive defense, laying out a persuasive case for the cost-effectiveness of a strategic defense: "What now makes cheap missiles so expensive is the immense cost of making them mobile — putting them on rail cars or specially designed vehicles or submarines. . .Mobility is really a form of 'passive' defense." He's scathing on the West German policy of subordinating "Western security. . .to the commercial interests of German exporters" by allowing merchants legally and illegally to sell high tech weapons to North Korea, Libya, and Iran. The indictment seems harsh, but he documents the case in "Selling Security for Deutschmarks," 7-31. He amuses with an imaginary Politburo discussion in "Figuring Out The Cost In Rubles," *The Washington Times* 9-26, a Gorbachev exclaiming "If the Americans throw their money away on weapons, how are we going to get them to finance *perestroika*? I'm counting on them to bankroll us, not some midget missiles."

Peirce, Neal R. *National Journal.* (★ ½)
"State of the States" columnist. A veteran "urbanologist," Peirce still seems trapped in the sociology textbooks of the '60s, his material too often coming across as ponderous, bureaucratic boilerplate. In "Bush Should Champion Neighborhood Cops," 2-4, he does argue vigorously for

socially-conscious neighborhood beat cops who are preventing crime, using the example of NYC's Ronald MacGregor, but it still strikes us he's shoveling against the tide with such marginal topics. In "State Budgets: Calm Now, Stormy Seas Ahead," 3-4, he offers a sketchy outlook on state finances, with no linkage to the national economy, no mention of aggregate budget surpluses at the state level. "Almost-For-Life Mayors Keep Hanging Onto Office," *Los Angeles Times* 3-28, is very bold for Peirce. Leading with "Marion Barry, resign. Ed Koch, abdicate. Tom Bradley, retire. Coleman Young, go." The oldtimers-are-burned-out thesis is well done, but there's no clear idea on who should take over the reins and why. He's better on an overview of the major mayoralty races in "The Writing's on the Wall for Burned-Out Mayors," 4-15, with a startling fact: "In 1988, not a single new home was built in all of Detroit." He's lively again in "Bush's Bold HUD Choice: Good News For Cities?" 1-7, on the selection of Jack Kemp: "For the first time in years, no one will have to wonder whether HUD is brain dead, or its Secretary retired in place." He pumps up one of the sillier ideas of the year with "Removing the Poison of Campaign Attack Ads," 6-24, proposed legislation "that anytime an opposition candidate for federal office is attacked or even mentioned in a television ad, the candidate buying the spot has to be on screen, in person, to deliver the blow." Hmmm. In "Can Young Volunteers Make a Difference?" 7-8, he's back in the sociology texts of the '50s.

Pfaff, William. Los Angeles Times Syndicate. (★)
We readily acknowledge Pfaff's graceful, literary style, but there's an unpleasant pretentiousness that creeps into his columns, as he preaches from his Paris pulpit about morally inferior Americans. There is some new information on West Germany's role in East Europe's disintegration in his *New Yorker* feature "Where the Wars Came From," 12-26-88, but this is mostly familiar ground, repeating what Timothy Garton Ash covered in *The New York Review of Books* earlier in '88. He intervenes into the debate over the values of Western civilization taking place on campuses with "In Their Crisis, Universities Can't Shove Truth Down Memory Hole," *Los Angeles Times* 12-30-88, advancing thoughtful, persuasive arguments against cultural relativism and the post-modernist assertion that there are no credible universal truths. The Paris expatriate reflects upon the loss of America's moral and civic identity (a consequence of both liberal and conservative sins), and issues forth with an indictment of her "morally isolated people, no longer connected to a culture deeper or more responsible than that provided by the mass entertainment industry," in an extremely pompous bit of commentary, " 'Wilding' in New York, Moral Void in America," *LAT* 5-7. In "The Fallen Hero," *The New Yorker,* 5-8, Pfaff delivers a sterling, vivid dissection of the life of T. E. Lawrence, and its meaning, a wonderful, sweeping portrait of Lawrence of Arabia. He handles the complex issue of East-West relations with some sophistication in "Bidding War on Arms Cuts Should Stop Short of Zero," *LAT* 6-1, the writing thankfully lucid.

Price, Raymond. New York Times Syndication Sales. (½ ★)
A speechwriter for President Nixon, there's no question about Price's ability to put words to paper. But unlike William Safire, who also ghosted for RMN, Price does no noticeable reporting in his columns, preferring armchair analysis. This might work if he were incredibly passionate or witty or both, but he's neither, and is thus predictable, with observations that tend toward the innocuous. His engaging presentation often redeems him, but he really has to come up with more to keep our interest for another year. Routine stuff in "Sizing Up President Bush: Effective, Not a Daredevil," *Los Angeles Times* 1-20, — Bush will be pragmatic and thus will make better policy. He's entertaining with "Like Jellyfish. . ." 2-9, making a case for a Congressional pay raise, though suggesting they cut their $2.5 billion operating budget for mail and TV (thats $4.7 million per member). Price has trouble handling more than one moving target, as a fuzzy "Singed by Their Own Fire," *WAT* 4-20, sights but never quite fires on Jim Wright, ethics, Congress. He's off on a tangent about a scandal-minded public that thinks well of Congress but can't name its congressmen in "Congress After the Fall," *WAT* 6-22. He comes to the President's defense against the carping critics with "Fooling the Know-it-All Brigade," *WAT* 7-20, — "Overall, Mr. Bush gives every indication of knowing what he's doing and why; of

thinking before he acts and then acting in a precisely calibrated, often subtly calculated way that combines a large measure of refreshing directness with a substantial dollop of artful indirection. It has been a good six months." — and we agree, but his case would be more convincing if salient evidence were there alongside faith. "Wiser to Watch. . ." *WAT* 9-2, an overview of Gorbachev's situation, advises Bush to wait longer before acting on policy and not much else. "Defining Life and the Living," *WAT* 10-6, attempts to do both, and really does neither, and Price doesn't conclusively communicate to us the generational circumstance that compels him to write on the subject: the abortion and right-to-die cases about to come before the Supreme Court.

Pruden, Wesley. *The Washington Times.* (★ ★ ½)
The *Times*' managing editor, Pruden decided years ago that he does not have the luxury of being able to drink tea and eat cookies while contemplating competition with *The Washington Post.* His "Pruden on Politics" column, which he scribbles with hot pen, bare knuckles and in bare feet, is not for society matrons or small children, but remains one of the best features of the newspaper. "Grandma Grundy and Mr. Tower," 2-26, remarks on John Tower and the bedsheet brigade: "Soldiers are already known to consort on occasion with women not their wives, in inebriated condition. Even if it were possible to recruit an army composed entirely of teetotaling virgins and celibates, it's not at all clear that the Joint Chiefs of Staff would know what to do with it." We laughed through "An Honest Woman to Greet Raisa," 3-29, on Gorbachev and Raisa's pending visit to Cuba, while Fidel is without a first lady or a feminine fourth for dinner: "There's never a lady, gorgeous, chic or otherwise, close enough to him to get an accurate count of the fleas in his beard." Prudent misfires with "Finding An Agent For An Assassin," 4-21, an inconsequential commentary on John Hinckley retaining Mark Lane as his lawyer. "Three Convictions to Take Pride In," 5-5, is acerbic, contrasting the just-convicted Oliver North and Congress, arguing that North's $8,000 security fence is "chickenfeed to the likes of Jim Wright and others who will take anything that is not nailed down." In "A Gallows Built of the Wright Stuff," 5-26, he exults in the lack of sympathy for Jim Wright: "If the leadership Democrats fancy themselves victims of a lynch mob, they should remember who built the gallows." He sticks the needle in deeper in "How to Devastate a Dinner Party," 6-5, chortling over Sally Quinn's "This Isn't Fun Anymore" *Post* op-ed of 6-4, reminding us that while Ms. Quinn is up-chucking in adverse reaction to the virulence of the congressional ethics issue, she once had a much stronger stomach when she dished out her own brand of acid. "In Hot Pursuit of a Corpse," 7-19, takes malicious pleasure in noting how the columnists and talk show hosts have taken to reviling Mike Dukakis, only a year after they swooned over his presidential nomination. In "A Little Outrage For the Children?" 8-25, he tears into the *Post* for ignoring the continuing sex scandals exposed by the *Times*: "O.K. you guys over there on 15th Street, if you sleep through this one, you ought to go back to Dubuque to sell shoes." "The Sweet Times in the Low House," 9-1, is vintage Pruden, spiteful and vicious on the "lacy scandal" between Steve Gobie, "the tireless hooker whose personal services ad in a homosexual newspaper first caught the eye of Rep. Barney Frank. 'Sweet'n Low' is what Gobie called the congressman — 'a sweet guy, low on cash' — late at night when they turned out the lights." In "A Wake-Up Call For The Entities," 9-20, Pruden again gloats justifiably for having forced the competition to listen to the *Times*-initiated Barney Frank scandal, as different media pick it up. Among his best was "The Magic Works for Rogues, Too," 6-23, supporting the Supreme Court's flag-burning decision: "The First Amendment is the safe harbor guaranteed to rogues by true Americans, and the only thing 'wrong' with it is that it belongs to everybody."

Raspberry, William. *The Washington Post.* (★ ★)
One of the top-rated columnists in recent years, Raspberry slipped a bit this year, his material a bit too soft, too far from the action. We've come to expect his commentary on black America to be close to definitive, but this year it was peripheral. He can still get passionately engaged without being strident, however. He dabbles with an interesting topic — 54% of the DC police force is black, but not yet a part of the community — and advances Houston as a role model in "Policed by Strangers," 3-6, but the direction needs further development. "Once You Put

Your Mind To It," 3-29, is a graceful way of stealing an idea from a letter written on the simple thought: "Some people work with their hands; some people work with their mouths. Everyone works with his head." Drugs and crime are consistent subjects, but his themes are never shopworn. He wrestles with the issue, sometimes coming up with a novel angle, as in ". . .to Here," 3-17, urging anti-drug demonstrations in the style of the "civil rights era." They won't end the drug problem anymore than civil rights demonstrations ended Jim Crow, but now as then, they could be the necessary trigger. He sees the "nonaddict users — ordinary middle class people who are looking for a little fun" — as appropriate targets as well in the war on drugs, "Get Tough on Drug Users Too," 3-31, an effective arguing of that perspective. Prescient perhaps, but delightful in any case, he reports words of wisdom from a DC cabbie on prospects of Jesse Jackson as mayor of the city in "Be Careful What You Pray For," 5-10: "You put Jesse Jackson in city hall, and what have you got? Another mayor for life, is what." Focusing again on drugs, "Don't Legalize Drugs," 5-26, is a somewhat uneven, bumpy critique of a new CATO Institute study that recommends legalized drugs. "Thoughts On Ending Racial Discrimination," 6-30, is cumbersome on proposed liberal social engineering designed to counteract the Supreme Court's rollback on affirmative action: consensus building, fashioned remedies, measuring competency and measuring progress. Raspberry's interview with HUD Secretary Jack Kemp, "Reaching Out to Blacks," 7-14, has a fine focus and appreciative judgment on potentials for political realignments: "Kemp believes the Republican Party can make serious inroads into the black electorate without abandoning its basic conservatism. Indeed, he has taken it as one of his key missions." In "Abernathy's Betrayal Of King," 10-18, Raspberry raises more questions than he answers as he ponders Ralph Abernathy's motives for revealing seamy details of Martin Luther King Jr.'s last night on earth in a controversial new book; but even racist diehards could agree with Raspberry that Rev. King deserved better treatment from a man whom he trusted like a brother.

Roberts, Paul Craig. *The Washington Times.* (★ ★)
A former *Wall Street Journal* editorialist, Treasury official in the early Reagan years, with a Ph.D. in economics, Roberts pushes national security themes as often as he does supply-side economics. His columns, in *Business Week* as well as in *The Washington Times,* continue to improve as he relies less on simple assertion. In "Presidential Power Slipping Through His Fingers?" 2-9, he admonishes the administration for letting itself take a direct hit on the John Tower nomination. The judgment is hardline, but of the "cold-water-in-the-face" kind that gets its target to sit up and take notice: "lacking any real agenda, they don't need any power." He's weaker in "The Subtle Consequences of Terrorist Attacks," 1-3, heavy going just to tell us that terrorism is terrible. "Supply-side Survives the Kangaroo Trial," 3-15, declares a victory, noting that "The failure of the National Economic Commission to damn Reaganomics and advocate higher taxes is powerful evidence that the visible success of the supply-side policy has outlived the eight-year effort to smear it and its architects." "Ditch the Capital Gains Tax Once and For All," *BW* 4-3, makes solid arguments for eliminating the capital gains tax, levied as "envy crowds out logic, and the economy suffers," using as an example a middle-class businessman who retires and sells his business. "That year the capital gain swells his income to several hundred thousand dollars and he is 'rich' for the year." Warning of a potentially "recessionary policy being charted by the Federal Reserve Board," Roberts makes a case for Fed easing in "Tight-Fisted Fed Replaying 1981?" 5-30. His analysis is not especially persuasive, but the argument is intensely focused: "Much more of this and the Carter administration will begin to look competent by comparison." Most of Roberts' writing is in high dudgeon, as in "Misguided Justice Becoming Institutionalized?" 6-16, on "our liberal criminal justice system [which] cannot keep insane criminals off the streets," building the column around the recent case of the rape and mutilation of a 7-year-old boy by a released pedophile and murderer. "Supply-Side Is Alive and Well — In Moscow," *BW* 7-24, fascinates with inside stuff from his trip to the Soviet Union, reporting that Soviet economic reformers understand supply-side economics better than its critics in the West. One Soviet official, he reports, told him "you must promise not to send your [John Kenneth] Galbraiths. They are not helpful. They don't believe in freedom." "Departing

Casualty of Stanford's War," 8-23, is trenchant, albeit overly emotional, on the war between Stanford and its Hoover Institution on the occasion of W. Glenn Campbell's removal from its directorship: "Most of the motivation was ideological, but some was purely opportunism on the part of Stanford administrators with an eye on Hoover's large endowment." His "Fiscal Policy Myopia," 9-6, is Roberts doing what he does best, poking at the internal inconsistencies of his Keynesian adversaries.

Rosenfeld, Stephen S. *The Washington Post.* (★)
Just when we'd been warming up to the columns of this *Post* editorialist, he retreated to safe, familiar ground, advancing the foreign policy views of the liberal establishment, the conventional and the predictable overwhelming his commentary. In "Bush Can Go Back To Basics," 1-27, Rosenfeld argues that events ranging from *perestroika* in the Soviet Union to crisis in America's nuclear production facilities give Bush the chance to totally rethink America's nuclear strategy. As to what this new strategy might be, Rosenfeld ventures no ideas. Wishy-washy on the "whither Eastern Europe" theme, "Partners With Moscow?" 2-24, turns off with a cognitive breakdown: "The judgment of opportunity and risk cannot rest just on a reading of one's particular hopes or fears." Huh? "Drug Store Diplomacy," 5-19, is the worst kind of on-the-one-hand-on-the-other-hand analysis, with Rosenfeld qualifying Washington's positions, Moscow's positions, even his own positions. Consequently financier George Soros' mushy paean to *glasnost* sounds less shallow than it otherwise should. Not only is the proposal in "Time to Retrench," 7-14, vacuous, but Rosenfeld's argument is shoddy. Ebullient over the Soviet miners' strikes, Rosenfeld sees them as the equivalent of the Russian Army's disintegration in WWI, and in "Moscow at the Point of No Return," 7-28, he howls at "our conservatives" to do something. What, aside from sharing his enthusiasm, is left unclear, as he limply observes that "Increasingly, the burden on us is not to predict what may come in the future but to grasp what has already taken place." Rosenfeld opens "An Afrikaner Example For Israel," 10-13, by putting words into the mouth of Yitzhak Shamir, then goes on to say that Shamir should possess the "statesmanlike vision" of South African President F. W. de Klerk and follow his policies of reform by reaching out to his government's enemies. Without sharper analysis, the idea is simply glib.

Rosenthal, A. M. *The New York Times.* (★ ★ ½)
"On My Mind" column. The former executive editor of *The Times,* Abe's columns always command our attention when they appear. His best material this year focused on the national drug problem, Rosenthal insistent that every angle be explored in search of a solution. He's especially provocative and challenging in "The Drug Train," 2-3, which helps shift opinion among liberal elites on the drug war: "Strangely, American intellectuals who would suffer most from a repressive attitude toward civil liberties, and who almost instinctively get involved in social causes, edge away from the national drug problem. The country hears about drugs from its leading writers, academics and artists occasionally but almost never with real passion and only until they turn again to issues that obviously mean more to them: abortion, feminism, national security, foreign affairs, politics." He challenges arguments for drug legalization in "Tale of Two Mayors," 3-14, disputing the glib suggestion that drug gangs would disappear with legalization: "Did repeal of prohibition eliminate organized crime like the Mafia? Or did it simply turn to new and more profitable lines of work?" He continually worked the issue all year, constantly examining and re-examining it, and turning up new angles and insights. A 10 Best nomination for commentary, "The Japanese Mystery," 4-7, is strong stuff on what the U.S. might learn from Japan, which has no significant drug problem because it has zero tolerance for drug pushers or users. "The Guilty Verdict," 5-5, reminds us that despite the hateful nature of the crimes involved in the Central Park "wilding," the accused are still innocent until proven guilty, took some guts to produce. There's nothing wishy-washy about it, and the point had to be made. Off the drug issue, he was less effective. "Do-It-Yourself-Journalism," 1-24, rambles along with only mildly interesting self-questioning about press coverage of the election year. He inveighs against the hypocrisy of liberal intellectuals and writers coming to the defense of Salman Rushdie, while silent on AP correspondent Terry Anderson in "Four Years of Captivity," 2-28:

"They liked Mr. Rushdie's own sharp criticism of Britain and the United States, so the terrorist threat to his life shook them." In "Now It Is Our Turn," 6-13, he preaches about Chinese communists, and we should do this and that and this and that. A dud. More huffing in "Inciting Eastern Europe", 7-11, he critiques Bush's cautious speech to the Poles: "Do we really believe that Eastern Europeans who have fought so long for freedom at such cost, while we vulgarly took ours for granted, can only grasp the meaning of democracy if a visiting President cautiously ladles it out in infant spoonfuls?" "Soldier in the Wall," 9-29, starts out sharply enough urging full U.S. support for Poland's Solidarity, but Rosenthal jars us with a harsh attack on Jozef Cardinal Glemp that simply isn't supported by any material in the column.

Rusher, William A. Newspaper Enterprise Association. (★)
Appearing regularly on the "Commentary" pages of *The Washington Times*, the former publisher of *National Review* is relatively easy to pigeonhole. An old-time conservative, he sticks to almost pure armchair commentary in his columns, evidencing no reporting efforts. Rusher backs up his premise well enough in a routine advocation that doesn't explore much beyond the headline in "Rescuing Pay Hikes for Judges," 2-21. Rusher's been through all the battles and can draw out the broader strategic assessments, as in "Why SDI Refuses to Die," 5-2: "The fundamental problem, of course, is that SDI's foes are not merely bucking a new weapons system; they are resisting the whole progress of science as manifested in war." He's a bit supercilious in "Whose Money Anyway?" 6-28, going after *The New York Times*' Anthony Lewis for already having spent the money that is projected to flow from cuts in defense spending. The sentiment is appropriate, but he doesn't provide much beyond sentimentality with "In Hong Kong, Questions," 7-4. Suggesting that Great Britain has a moral obligation to protect Hong Kong from Communist China now that the latter's assurance of tolerance is in question, he projects no real course of action and merely asks the British to remember how great an empire they once were and act upon that. He's rather eloquent in a credible commentary on Francis Fukuyama's "End of History" thesis. In "Mankind Seeking a New Road," 9-22, Rusher hones the perspective more narrowly as the closing of the Age of Enlightenment, the ending of "the confidence we misplaced, two centuries ago, in science and our own good natures." He examines the contrary positions of the *NYT*'s Abe Rosenthal and old buddy Bill Buckley in "Who Is Right on Drugs?" 10-6. Rusher doesn't take a position himself except to say that they're both right to some extent, which seems to be uncharacteristic fence-straddling by him.

Safire, William. *The New York Times*. (★ ★ ★ ½)
"Essay" columnist. Three consecutive years among the highest-ranked columnists, *The New York Times*' in-house conservative political analyst always keeps one eye askance on the current emerging wisdom while the other searches for prey among the players in the corridors of power, which is why friend and foe alike always keep an eye on him. Mighty reverberations flow from his blockbuster "The German Problem," 1-2, a 10 Best selection for commentary, as he mercilessly excoriates West German collaboration with Libya's "Auschwitz-in-the-sand" poison gas project. It puts the FDR in a frenzy, *Der Spiegel*'s Rudolf Augstein huffing "Come on William. You must have lost your marbles," as we learn in his update "Stop the Todeskramer," 1-16. But Safire comes out on top, his column in fact prodding Bonn into confessing something is indeed amiss. He piques the administration with "Bush's Emperor of Ethics Is Wearing No Clothes," 2-6, going after C. Boyden Gray, after he's tipped off by an anonymous letter that the special counsel to the president has some unethical skeletons in the closet. The column and story by *NYT* reporter Jeff Gerth provoke *The Wall Street Journal* editors into taking a swipe at them ("Gerth, Safire and Anonymous," 2-6), but Safire gets in the last word with "Media Manipulated!" 2-9, the *WSJ* silent this time on his elaboration of how Gray pulled media strings to dodge heat over his financial records. Safire isn't the first to focus the Tower nomination fight as "a struggle for Constitutional power," but his "Nunn vs. Bush," 2-27, is one of the most forceful arguments on behalf of that assessment. "Not Mad, But Even," 3-13, on post-John Tower consequences, locates a special importance in the replacement of Richard Cheney as House Minority Whip — it opens the way for "a scrap of philosophy and style" in the House

GOP between the "go-along, get-along" group and the activists under Newt Gingrich. He soars like an eagle with "Madness of Crowds," 3-23, parlaying the incident around the two poisoned Chilean grapes into a call for deployment of a "rudimentary space shield." Introducing the surprise conclusion in the penultimate paragraph yields maximum impact. He parades like a peacock, though, in "Sununu's Different Template," 4-3, all fluff and no new material from the chief of staff, a mere reminder of Safire's days in the White House. Tough and timely on behalf of continuing the harvest wrought by "the swooshing scythe of ethics" investigations, he takes a "damn the torpedoes" approach with "Beware the Schmethicist," 5-29. He's honest and accurate in his appraisal of the fine leadership role President Bush played at the NATO summit, "Raise and Call," 6-1, but Safire is shallow on Margaret Thatcher, ranting about her resistance to a common currency and the EMS, without any analysis, in "Maggie on the Beach," 6-28. He's properly concerned with the President's statement that the U.S. is not trying to "drive wedges between the Soviet Union and Eastern Europe," responding in "The George & Gorby Show," 7-10: "Wedge-driving, that nefarious practice condemned by all is precisely what 1989 diplomacy is all about," with reminders about Gorbachev's efforts to split Western Europe from the U.S. While giving no sympathy to the convoluted criticism coming from the doves on the failed Panama coup, Safire pulls no punches with his assessment of the fiasco in "The Man With No Plan," 10-9: "Mr. Bush's Joe Cool can also be Joe Frozen." Yet it's not all invective, Safire drawing a "blessing in disguise" moral from the affair.

Samuelson, Robert J. *Newsweek,* Washington Post Writers Group. (★ ★)
He can effectively mix light, breezy social-political commentary with thoughtful and contemplative themes, though his columns with a heavier focus on economics are still hit and miss. An example of the former, "The Irony of Capitalism," 1-9, keeps speculation under control in a thoughtful look at potential for capitalistic reform in communist countries. He misses with a dismal "Bush Must Take Off His Blinders on Inflation," *Los Angeles Times* 2-23: "Perhaps only a recession can reverse rising inflation" with very little logic or evidence behind it. "Bush's Bow to Japan," 2-6, contains meritorious suggestions on how to improve relations with Japan, dispelling current myth with clearly presented information. Conventional misinformation abounds in a pathetic argument against a capital gains tax rate cut, "Bribery is Bad Policy," 3-6. A bit too breezy and light, he takes us through "The Daddy Track," 4-3, noting that people don't know at 26 what they want to be at 36 or 46, without stirring up much to chew on. Critical of the minimum wage hike and subsidized day care proposals, he assembles appropriate data and argues effectively in "Help the Working Poor," 5-1, that "Government programs don't pull people out of poverty; people pull themselves out of poverty." With the issue of forthcoming recession voguish among some economic circles, Samuelson takes a try at the question in "A Soft Landing?" 6-14, looking Hamlet-like at various courses. In the end, he pulls his conclusion out of a black box: "for now, faith in a soft landing strikes me as soft thinking." He knocks "redistribute-the-wealth" assumptions about the effects of defense spending cuts in "The Peace Dividend," 6-26, illustrating how much more wealthy America becomes from increases in productivity. Mushy moralizing about America's "spending spree" in "The Binge Is Over," 7-10, Samuelson substitutes sermonizing for analytics. The topic is novel and interesting — will moral issues rather than economic ones dominate the 1990s — in "The End of Economics," 7-19, but it's front-porch, rocking-chair philosophizing, Samuelson wistfully noting "there's still interest in economic news but my stuff is being pushed from the top of the political agenda." He's focused in "Highbrow Pork Barrel," 8-21, favoring the end of agencies like the National Endowment for the Arts. After all, "Art consumers benefit from the NEA because their ticket prices are indirectly subsidized." He does his homework with "American Sports Mania," 9-4, providing the data on how much money Americans spend on sports, (about $7.4 billion or "a bit more than 1% of our gross national product") which roughly equals the total GNP of Yugoslavia or Algeria, but if there is any other point here we miss it.

Schneider, William. *National Journal.* Los Angeles Times Syndicate. (★ ½)
Schneider, who pulled a four-star rating in the '88 *MediaGuide,* hasn't been able to get his batting average back up into superstar categories, popping up frequently with limp analysis. His one grand slam for the year was not in the bite size columns he pens for *National Journal,* but in the magazine length "JFK's Children: The Class of '74," *The Atlantic* 3-89. A 10 Best nomination for political reporting, this is a long look at the new Democrats who came into office in 1974 (Hart, Dukakis, Wirth, Downey, *et al.*) and how they changed their party. Far richer than the usual "rise of the neo-liberals" story, Schneider strives for an overview that posits political history as a tug-of-war between big-hearted populist and technocratic progressive tendencies within both parties. In *NJ,* "Read Voters' Lips: Spending Is OK," 12-31-88, plays voter hesitancy about big domestic cuts as a strength for a Democrat Congress, but the premise rests a bit too much on wobbly public opinion polls. Schneider's analysis is murky and not really supported with any evidence in "Symbols, Values May Not Be Enough," *NJ* 1-28: "The Bush agenda is beginning to look like a clean-up operation. His administration is dominated by reformers and incrementalists, people like Bush, who see their jobs as cleaning up the problems Reagan created." He's woefully out of focus in "Caving In to Pressure From the Public," *NJ* 2-11, advancing nonsense disguised as analysis: "It was a failure of leadership," not lack of public support that killed the savings deposit fee and pay raise proposals. "Bush's Stubbornness Lacks Conviction," *NJ* 3-18, on Bush's approach toward the Eastern Airline strike, never gets off the ground. Minor league material in "Bush Pays Price For Unheroic Approach," *NJ* 4-29, Schneider is feeble on the first 100 days: "It was pretty good for us. But it wasn't so good for him." "Welcome to the Greening of America," *NJ* 5-27, is pure bluster, chastising Bush for dragging his feet on global warming without a hint there's any deep division over the scientific validity of the issue. "Will Bush Give Caution A Bad Name?" *NJ* 6-3, gets to the edge of an insight, but it gets away from him: "Bush usually says sensible things, but he is so easily rattled that he makes people nervous. He seems to be paralyzed by two fears — the fear of being called a wimp and the fear of creating a controversy." "Bush too 'Professional' about China?" *NJ* 7-1, trails off onto flag burning and Dukakis. Among his best *NJ* columns was "Populist Rhetoric, Public Indifference," 9-30, on why Democrats are having a tough time getting the electorate unhappy with Bush's proposed capital gains tax cut. "But a contest between interests and party loyalty may be much closer," which turned out to be right on.

Shields, Mark. *The Washington Post.* (★ ★)
There's a specter haunting many of the liberal commentators — the fear that the party of their persuasion is entering into a permanent electoral lockout from the White House. Shields manages to deal with it while not succumbing to hysteria or desperation, but he's rattled by it, as a less-than-deadly aim in his commentary reflects. Usually a keen political observer, the acuity is missing in "Another Brief Honeymoon?" 1-19, a little too distant generalization on the transformation of George Bush that takes place in just two months "from hack political candidate to leader of the Western world." The gleeful side of Shields comes through in a light but ironic "Limit Everybody's Term! (Except Mine)," 3-17, a very amusing examination of "unintended consequences" involved in limiting Congressional terms. Lobbyists would end up on top, for one. A good Democrat, Shields can't sit back and not advise his party. "Democratic Couch Potatoes," 4-5, takes the Democrats to task for not seizing the initiative on three policy issues already discarded by Bush — the Eastern strike, gun control and technology exchange — but he confounds real strategic perspectives with mere tactical jabs. "Volunteer Service Is A Fair Idea," 5-20, is muddled on the McCurdy-Nunn bill to encourage volunteerism, not specific enough as to how this would work to be useful. "The Golden State Has Lost Its Glitter," 7-6, is an informative cataloguing of California's emerging woes, early and eloquently: ". . .1989, California optimism is a casualty to traffic, the high prices of housing, crime and pollution. If California, the national center of bullishness, sustains a loss of confidence, the nation will suffer the consequences." In "Anger About Privilege," 7-30, he springs forth with more advice about great, seething movements ready to be tapped by the politically astute, noting from conversations at coffee stops and gas stations across the land there are unmistakable signs that "a popular

insurgent revolt against Privilege is. . .waiting to be galvanized for 1990." Opening with "I have liked Barney Frank for 20 years," but. . ., "Barney Frank: Burden on His Party," *Weekly* 9-25/10-1, is a substantial news item in and of itself, as he gently but firmly advises that it's time for the congressman to leave office. He echoes some FDR era sounds about "economic royalists" in "Two Cheers For House Democrats," 10-10, congratulating Foley and Co. for their "good public policy and good politics" in opposing the capital gains tax rate cut: "a two-year attic and garage sale for the most affluent Americans, an undeserved chance to sell off appreciated assets for those few on Easy Street at the inevitable expense of most Americans on Main Street."

Sidey, Hugh. *Time.* (★ ½)
"The Presidency" columnist. Wistful as the Ronald Reagan years wore down, Sidey hasn't bounced back on the presidency watch during Bush's first year. Anecdotal, and little else, "The Gipper Says Goodbye," 1-30, provides brief glimpses into Reagan's last moments as president. In a column written from far outside the Beltway, "The Real Deficit Is Water," 2-27, Sidey's vividly empathic on the scourge of drought on frustrated but unbowed farmers. He's been around Washington a long, long time, and can pluck an appropriate anecdotal story out of the barrel from time to time. In " 'Dead Soldiers' Along the Potomac," 3-13, he recalls, as John Tower's nomination is defeated, that "Lyndon Johnson, as Senate Majority Leader and early on as President, could polish off a dozen or so scotch-and-sodas in an afternoon and evening." There's not a lot of high octane in his columns, as even a forcefully titled "The Speaker Should Step Down," 4-24, merely settles for an easy point: the Speaker has to be judged by a higher standard because of the nature of his job, and therefore Jim Wright ought to relinquish his post though not his congressional seat. "A Busy Thursday," 5-22, is pure, but enjoyable, fluff, following Bush and the photographers around the White House, accessed to impress. "The Warm Reverie of Reagan's Retirement," 6-26, skims several topics, from the 22nd Amendment to the high-priced speeches the ex-president is "cashing in on," but they're too scattered to add up to much of a larger picture. He pulls another striking anecdote out of his memory for graphic effect in "Giving Honor to Old Glory," 7-3: "Lyndon Johnson quite literally ground his teeth when he looked out his White House window and saw the Vietnam protestors desecrate flags." Sometimes the historical analogies work, and though they aren't perfect he pulls some insights out of a comparison of the war against drugs with America's fervor in fighting WWII vs. the losing mentality in the Vietnam War, "The Struggle With Ourselves," 9-18.

Snow, Tony. *The Washington Times.* (★ ★ ½)
Editorial page editor. He plays a big role in the improvement of the daily's editorials, but, as with all journalists rated in the *MediaGuide,* only the bylined material counts. He can be muscular and trenchant in one commentary while delicately poignant and intensely moving in another. He's totally unsympathetic to the fears being generated about the use of Alar in apples, in "Ban Bread!" 3-16. Leaning heavily on the alarm, he's critical of its manipulation, noting that "The worst thing about the Alar debate is that it begins with the assumption that eating an apple is equivalent to guzzling Drano." A delightfully argued, unconventional "Let's Party!" 4-20, wickedly celebrates the end of bipartisanship. Snow welcomes Newt Gingrich's selection as GOP House Whip precisely because it will makes politics fun again, whereas today's "bipartisanship is a sham" describing only "the tributes exchanged between a party without power and a party without ideas." His "Something Real," 5-18, on the slow death of a young child, is poignant without being sentimental or maudlin. He's scalding on the recipes for disaster being cooked up by the cooperation of environmentalists and government with "Lysenko Lives," 6-23, zapping the administration for emulating goofball recommendations. Snow presents a balanced, appreciative acknowledgment in "The Monthly Turns 20!" 6-29, a tribute to the neoliberal *Washington Monthly,* despite whatever disagreements he may have with the monthly's neoliberal faith in Big Government, because "they pale in comparison to my gratitude that they're around to expose the impolite truths that others would rather ignore." Drawing broader perspectives from the Barney Frank scandal in "Barney Frank and 'Privacy,' " 8-31, Snow notes that "As weird as Congress' internal standards of 'ethics' seem, its standards for the rest of us

may be stranger. It has tried to impose new morals on America by making it impossible to maintain an old-fashioned nuclear family. . .Barney Frank's plea for privacy may well set off a public sick of hypocrisy and hungry for a little private freedom. After all, why should voters protect politicians' 'privacy' when politicians won't honor theirs?''

Sobran, Joseph. *National Review,* Universal Press Syndicate. (★ ★ ½)
An unyielding, hard-line conservative, Sobran sometimes approaches every single issue as if it were Custer's last stand, but this year a bit more detachment allows a bit more wisdom to work its way into his columns. There is no dearth of commentary on the Reagan legacy, but Sobran's "Is There a Reagan Legacy?" *National Review* 1-3, is analysis clearly on the margin, rebuking a somewhat fashionable dismissal of the former President's years as sleepy and mediocre ones: "In the world before Mr. Reagan, a liberal was a guy who was open-minded about the left, always ready to see the Soviet point of view, and always available to be nudged toward socialism. That's no longer true. Liberals have ceased to believe that bigger government is automatically better government, and though few of them would go so far as to call the Soviet Union an 'evil empire,' they pay Mr. Reagan's common sense the subtle deference of acting as if his phrase was apt." He's quick to the cut in his review of Paul Johnson's *Intellectuals,* a "book for people for whom 'intellectuals' is already a dirty word." Though Johnson details how sordid and rotten to the core 12 "progressive" intellectuals were, there's no evidence to connect that to their lives, Sobran advises in "Bad Guys," *NR* 4-21. "Barney Frank: Restoring the Symbiosis," *Conservative Chronicle* 6-28, gets it on the record that the homosexual smear of Tom Foley actually originated with the Democrats themselves. However, Sobran spins his wheels trying to make a case that Barney Frank's clever judoing of the issue of his homosexuality adroitly restores a harmony between Congressional Democrats and the media. Sobran replies to a *Wall Street Journal* article which predicted the pro-life movement would splinter apart "once the issue is taken off the agenda," in "Variety Is Pro-Life's Movement's Strength," *CC* 8-30, developing a perception that even pro-choicers would share — a political movement is a means to an end, not an end in itself. A fine writer, he displays the talent with a gently mocking look back at Woodstock in "A Nation of Losers," *NR* 9-1: "Losers have a way of finding each other. What Woodstock proves is that when their numbers reach critical mass, they become a market, and you can herd them together and tell them things they desperately want to hear from someone else: that they're winners, that they hold the hope of the world, and all their unresolved personal problems are only one big political problem that can be solved instantaneously." "Socialism In One Country," *The Wanderer* 10-12, is coloring book commentary. Color everything socialist bad. Color everything "free market" good. Color all Democrats socialists, etc. He provides a chance to relive Ronald Reagan's greatest domestic setback "In Ted Kennedy's America," *NR* 10-13, a review of *Battle for Justice: How the Bork Nomination Shook Justice,* by Ethan Bonner, adding a modicum of historical perspective: "It's easier now to see the contours of the affair. As long as the court was their reliable ally, liberals protectively insulated it from the pressure of politics and publicity. Now that its membership is predominantly conservative, the rules have changed." We wonder, though, if Sobran ever marched to protest a Warren Court decision.

Sowell, Thomas. Scripps-Howard News Service. (★ ★ ★)
We always look for this Hoover Institution scholar's byline in *The Washington Times* "Commentary" section. His writing is tough, hard and tight, as Sowell can use his mind the way a boxer uses his fists. He lays a solid punch on the Federal Trade Commission for its case against publishers who charge book chains less than the mom and pop bookstores. There aren't enough monopolies around to keep bureaucrats busy prosecuting them, he advises in "FTC's Federal Book Case," 1-23, but "The devil finds work for idle hands, especially if they are bureaucrats who have to justify their jobs and power." He uses irony to deliciously pointed effect in "The Economics of Academia," 3-10, noting that the Federal government pours billions into colleges and universities, many of which prohibit ROTC courses and indulge openly anti-American biases. The knockout: "There are colleges from coast to coast where anyone can get a degree without bothering to get an education." He delivers, without any fancy footwork or new hooks,

a defense of nuclear power in "Nuclear Power Risks and Realities," 6-19, effectively comparing risks in that form of electrical power generation with a variety of other activities. Academia is a favorite topic, with Sowell attentive all year to any ominous trends or developments. In "Academe's Double Standards," 7-28, he furiously indicts left-radical bias in academia which results in new rules gagging students who speak out on the wrong side of what is currently in favor among the ideologically committed. For example, "Both at Yale and the University of Chicago, students have been suspended for [putting up] posters criticizing homosexuality — even though homosexuals are free to put up posters all over campus saying how wonderful their 'lifestyle' is." "Theories Vs. The Children," 8-1, is heartbreaking on the bureaucratic tangles involved in adoption, as children wait the world over: "The number of childless couples wishing to adopt children is 40 times as great as the number of children actually adopted." Back to campus again with "Fences Around Parents," 8-22, he broadsides academic slicksters, with a warning to parents that sounds more like Orwell than Sowell: "If you have done an especially good job and gotten your young man or young woman ready for a highly rated college, you may feel entitled to a feeling of a job well done." However, "At many of the leading colleges in the country, 'imposing your values' is the name of the game, whether these are the sexual values or the ideological values of the faculty and administrators. Parents are gotten out of the picture so they will not interfere with the brainwashing or browbeating of those who wish to retain the values with which they were raised."

Starr, Richard. *Insight.* (★ ½)
Rotating as one of the weekly "Last Word" columnists, Starr's efforts are as erratic as the others. The fine delivery or solid punch we sometimes see in his columns is too infrequent. He's too cynical on the issue of doing away with agricultural farm subsidies, suggesting in "Farm Subsidies for Icons Only," 12-19-88, that Uncle Sam ought to just give the nation's 500,000 "family farmers" a cash grant of $20,000 a year. Starr builds a nice set of legal ironies on the effort to bring discipline and order back into the classroom in "The Drug Dealing is Disruptive," 1-9, but we're left frustrated as he shies from presenting any solutions. We enjoy the fine writing in "A Greenhouse-Grown Agenda," 2-20, though the effort seems a bit credulous. Certainly his best, he packs a solid punch in "Scourge of the Demon Experts," 3-20, awarding the prize for dishonorable behavior among the sideshows regarding the John Tower nomination to the so-called experts on alcoholism. Starr quotes the remarks of these experts in which they call Tower a drunk and a liar, and we are more than sufficiently persuaded they do deserve that prize. He's provocative, stoking the fire, on the way in which the American Civil Liberties Union and some "tenants' rights" groups make it difficult to evict drug traffickers from public housing, in "No Home for Drug Traffickers," 4-17: "It would be enlightening to conduct a referendum of public housing tenants, asking them if they feel they have been well-represented by those who speak on their behalf." "The Veto With Flying Colors," 7-3, flows well on Bush's veto of the minimum wage bill — "the first faxed veto in history" — capturing the dismay of the Democrats left empty-handed at their own press conference. In "Big Brother, Keeping Me Safe," 8-7, Starr uses his real life big brother as an analogy for the federal government and its pure food regulations. The gimmick doesn't work, though, and even after two readings we couldn't tell whether he's for or against government regulation in this situation.

Summers, Col. H. G., Jr. (Harry). Los Angeles Times Syndicate. (★ ★)
This retired career officer often mixes his own experiences and an institutional memory for a perception on defense and strategic issues that we don't see elsewhere. He's artful in making arcane principles of war intelligible and immediate, as he does with an adroit "Kicking the Wind," *Los Angeles Times* 1-9, on the issue of retaliation against terrorists following the Pan Am 103 bombing. Piqued by Bush's inaugural reference to a "statute of limitations" on the debate over Vietnam, he suggests the President is premature in "Do We Want the Memory to Fade?" *The Washington Times* 1-30, and while the point's worth considering the column isn't that persuasive. More cogent, though, in "Afghanistan and Vietnam," *WAT* 2-16, he does persuade that "Not only are such comparisons invidious, they also reveal how little is

remembered about what really happened in Vietnam." Almost Churchillian in tone, "Cheney's Chinese Fire Drill," *WAT* 5-4, remonstrates about the costs of past defense budget finagling and warns that the Defense Secretary might just be cutting the wrong programs given the changing state of warfare. "A Bankrupt Military Strategy," his contribution to the series on the defense cover story in *The Atlantic* 6-89 is a standout, Summers combing strong analytics with appropriately deployed personal insights. He makes a case that our military strategy is obsolete, refuting short-war strategies and forward basing: "It is not that we have too few military forces; it is that we have too many jobs for them to do."

Talbott, Strobe. *Time.* (★ ½)
Editor-at-large and "America Abroad" columnist. His work is smoother than it's been in ages, but there's still a bumpiness when he ventures into areas armed only with partisan conviction and no evidence. He misses the threat of protectionism to global stability in "Of Deficits and Diplomacy," 3-6. In this examination of how "American economic problems have become a national security and foreign policy issue," he spins too much off of the conventional bias on the deficit issue. Terse and to the point in "Real Weapons, High Hopes," 3-20, on the conventional forces in Europe (CFE) talks. Talbott's angle is interesting, and he blends past and present developments to help make his case. He develops an appreciable overview of Israeli-PLO diplomatic problems in "How to Move the Immovable," 4-3, but we're still left without much of a bead on the question raised in the title. He's persuasive on reasons for excluding the Khmer Rouge from any U.S. aid package to the Cambodian resistance coalition in "The Killing Fields Revisited," 5-1, but then, who isn't persuasive with that position? His analysis is easy to follow, yet not facile, in "Fighting the Founders," 6-5, in which he compares and contrasts the changes occurring in the U.S.S.R. and China. He nicely sums up Gorbachev as "simultaneously the leader of the entrenched power structure and the leader of the opposition." "Happy Campers, For a Change," 8-28, takes the reader behind the scenes to discover, gasp, that Defense Secretary Cheney and James Baker actually get along. He's not sympathetic to the "End of History" thesis of Francis Fukuyama, though his discussion of the premises is spongy in "The Beginning Of Nonsense," 9-11.

Thomas, Cal. Los Angeles Times Syndicate. (★ ½)
Unabashed about the religious foundation and perspective for his commentary, Thomas is one of the few columnists in this category who handles it with aplomb. His strictly political material is generally lightweight, as with "Sununu's Humble Catechism," *The Washington Times* 1-2, an interview with the president's chief of staff in which we learn nothing more than John Sununu says Bush has evolved out of Rockefeller Republicanism. "What Used to Hold Marriages Together," *WAT* 1-30, effectively spins off of Judith S. Wallerstein's book, *Second Chances: Men, Women and Children A Decade After Divorce,* adding to her thesis: "This voice from the right has some solutions. They go by such names as reconciliation, forgiveness, commitment and love. These are not ideals of the right or left. They are what held marriages together before traditional values fell out of fashion." Persuasive on the appointment of the first female Episcopal bishop being a bad call, practically and theologically, in " 'Thus Saith the Pollsters. . .' " *WAT* 2-6, he goes on to make the case as to why non-Episcopalians or the non-religious ought to care about the issue: "Because bishops are called to teach pastors, who then teach lay people, who then take these teachings into the political and sociological marketplace where they ultimately affect us all." There isn't a lot in his interview with the Vice President, "Candid, Confident Quayle," *WAT* 7-18, though few others would have drawn the VP out on his praying and the content of his petitions to the Almighty. "Decisions Based on Whimsy," *WAT* 7-5, is forceful commentary on abortion as a constitutional issue, Thomas focusing the danger of replacing the *Constitution* as the source of law with whatever a majority of the Court thinks about the *Constitution* at any given moment. Delicious commentary, "The Henry Higgins Defense," *WAT* 8-31, disposes of Rep. Barney Frank's contention that he was attempting to reform Stephen Gobie. Thomas is thoughtful on the deteriorating relationship between the church leadership and the black community in "Worshiping At What Altar?" *WAT* 9-4.

Tyrrell, R. Emmett Jr. *The American Spectator,* King Features Syndicate. (★ ½)
The irreverent monthly's irreverent editor-in-chief is having one of his better years. Wicked and unsparing, his columns continue to drip with caustic sarcasm, though in some cases the targets seem just too trivial for all the ridicule. "*Yesterday* Show Strolls Down Memory Lane," *Conservative Chronicle* 1-25, aptly renames NBC's "Today" show "Yesterday," — since it simply doesn't cover the 1980's: "Watching the *Yesterday* show is like watching the *Today* show, say, in the spring of 1975 — except for one thing: recent history has demonstrated that radicalism's infantile sneer at the American way of life is no improvement on reality." He has a quirky streak, though, sometimes taking delight in flogging dead horses, as with "The Duke Did His Best," *TAS* 1-89. He consoles Michael Dukakis over his electoral loss, by telling him his successor will do worse in 1992 "if the cads in your party continue to avoid their critics and to blame the fortunes of their party on bad breaks and Republican skullduggery." He's sophisticated in his critical treatment of the high-yield bond market in "Junk Dangers," *TAS* 1-89, acknowledging it as economically sound and socially beneficent when initially developed by Michael Milken. He returns to this issue again with an equally sophisticated "The Bizarre Spectacle of Takeovers," *CC* 6-21, in which he sees a lot of assets being saddled with debt and raises questions about shaky prospects for their repayment. With "The Junk Bond Frenzy Is Sure to End," *CC* 8-23, he goes after leveraged buyout wizards Kohlberg Kravis Roberts & Company, but we aren't sure he really knows what he's talking about. "Students Are Being Defrauded," *CC* 2-17, scores a point in favor of the view that universities are not merely lax in the teaching of humanities, but lack even a civilized conception of them: "At Stanford, Plato's *Republic* is read as an example of 'anti-assimilationist movements.' " He's flat in the "Continuing Crisis" column 3-89, devoting too much attention to "the puissance and malign influence of the animal rights militants." "Dream Come True or Nightmare on Gorki Street?" *The Washington Post* 8-12, is concise on Gorbachev's struggle with Ligachev on political reforms, Tyrrell hoping the U.S. press is right that Gorbachev is winning, but believing the British press is more correct with its skepticism. However, "The End of What?" *TAS* 11-89, on Francis Fukuyama's "End of History" thesis, is popped off the top of his head without much thought.

Wattenberg, Ben. Newspaper Enterprise Association. (★ ½)
A neoconservative of the Democratic persuasion, Wattenberg is always looking for the early signs of those broad new contours of changing socio-political-economic relationships. We know we'll always get at least one column from Wattenberg that springs from his book of a few years back, *The Birth Dearth.* He comes through on that with "No Growth Future By Default," *The Washington Times* 2-9, telling us census projections show that the U.S. population in decline and advising a national "debate" on whether or not we ought to have higher birth rate. "A Boom Amid Gunfire," 3-23, is a tough, almost nasty assault against "Washington's weirdo Mayor Marion Barry," with an effective deployment of facts. He's weaker in "With a Little Bit of Luck," 6-29, almost cynical, and certainly on shaky ground, in his explanation of America's success at blending ethnic, religious, and racial differences: "Call it luck. And if luck is involved, maybe we're not as much of a universal model as we like to think." A somewhat soggy "Courting the Neo-Moderate Liberals," 7-12, attempts to phylogenetically pigeonhole our present Supreme Court: "The recent Supreme Court decisions, typically denounced as 'conservative' have shown again that in America today most conservatism can be described more accurately as Neo-Moderate Liberalism." "Showdown at the Nuclear Power Corral," 7-26, is standard commentary, neither the language nor the arguments zippy. He's terse and crisp with "The Attitudes Behind American Exceptionalism," *U.S.News & World Report* 8-7, a one-page analysis of polling data on why Americans are different: "America is the most religious [perhaps] because religion has been wholly voluntary, separated from the state." The questions raised in "Does Less Equal More Bias?" 9-21, are interesting. Why do polls show over 90% of whites claim to have no racial prejudice and 60% of blacks claim to feel discriminated against: "It's a mystery. All those nice unprejudiced whites, and all those blacks being discriminated against. Who is doing it? There is an answer. The other person, that's who."

Weinberger, Caspar. *Forbes.* (★ ½)
Turning up as publisher at the business biweekly, Reagan's former secretary of defense gets a column as well and we're pleasantly surprised that it is not boilerplate. "Commentary on Events at Home and Abroad" is just that, the topics wide-ranging enough that we get a positive impression of Cap's thinking and insight on a variety of issues. Advising Reaganite caution he delightfully opens "Can We Trust This Nice Mr. Gorbachev?" 1-9, with sagacious counsel: "Is it ungracious, churlish, unwarranted or any of the above to examine very carefully, perhaps even in the mouth, Mr. Gorbachev's recent gift horse? Possibly. But since much of the security of the U.S., and indeed the West, could depend on our attitude and response to the Gorbachev proposal, let us risk being all of the above." "We Must Not Give Up Strategic Defense," 2-6, is forcefully argued, without being strident, Weinberger letting his years of experience at DoD do the talking for him. "The Common Market — Friend or Foe," 3-6, is somewhat muddled on predictions for American opportunities in Europe come 1992, but his bottom line is clear, though conventional: plan for the future. Weinberger pulls success out of the hat in his unconventional assessment of the National Economic Commission (of which he was a member),"The NEC: A Success, Not A Failure," 4-3: no united call for new taxes came out of the commission, therefore, it was a success. He's surprisingly adroit with his argument for the Stealth bomber in "The B-2 — A Low Cost-Insurance Policy," 8-21. He especially focuses on true incremental cost, only 20% above B-1, not $500 million per plane, but $274 million, minus sunk costs. He takes shots at Tip O'Neill for the scant U.S. support to the contras and at Robert McFarlane's "stupidity" for the Iran-Contra scandal in a vituperative "A Slim Hope for Freedom in Nicaragua," 9-18, but it's excess vim and vinegar. " 'Swift Responses' Usually Mean Bad Agreements," 10-23, persuasive rewording of "Haste Makes Waste" in the defense department, is nothing new, but works nicely.

Wicker, Tom. *The New York Times.* (★)
"In the Nation" columnist. It must be the "another-GOP-presidential-victory" syndrome, because Wicker exhibits all the symptoms, dragging through a miserable performance this year. Grumbly, sour-pussed, down-right nasty, nothing seems to be going right for him. Whining a one-note dirge, his arguments are disheveled and his columns creak with cranky contempt. "Democracy at Its Worst," 2-7, is Wicker at his worst, exuding ugly disgust with a "blind" public for its "irrational opposition" to Congressional pay hikes. "Looking for the Lumina," 3-17, is a Russell Baker-ish look at Tom's memories of a beach resort that beats his usual stuff, but it's lightweight. "Baker's Nice Try," 3-28, is muddled on James Baker's deal with Congress on contra aid. "Fair or Fowl?" 4-18, three mini-op-eds on Jim Wright, Marion Barry and Michael Milken, is mushy all around. "Bennett Boots It," 5-12, harshly critical of Bennett's proposed "boot camp" punishment for drug offenders loses impact with a resort to a "Users are often victims" appeal. "Making Things Worse," 5-2, on the Central Park "wilding" is out of focus, Wicker's reaction to the incident a prediction that it will be exploited by the NYC mayoral candidates. Wicker hits bottom again with an indecent "Art and Indecency," 7-28, running amok and exposing his worst side with one *ad hominem* attack after another on Sen. Jesse Helms. He begins "Plight of the Planet," 8-18, with an incredible quote from the *White River Valley Herald* in Rochester, Vermont — "Every species of fish in waters used for food is now fished at, or above, its capacity to replace itself" — but it remains a soft environmental column, a lazy effort.

Will, George. *Newsweek,* Washington Post Writers Group. (★ ★)
The master pundit seemed more pontifical this year, his thinking less rigorous and more cantankerously Tory, his columns wielding less influence as he harps on economics, which he knows little about. With campaign '88 behind him, he's again fixated on the budget deficit, beating this horse repeatedly during the year. An uninformed "Inflation Can't Be Tolerated," *The Washington Post* 3-9, is an old whine about the "twin deficits," recycling his old pal David Stockman's characterization of the Reagan economic expansion as "gluttony." He's Pavlovian in responding to the "ethics" issue by dismissing Jim Wright's "nickel-and-dime scams" as petty

compared to "Bush's determination to continue running huge deficits which rob the voiceless, voteless rising generations," in "The Pastel President," *Newsweek* 4-24. Will asserts his moral superiority to Bush's on the issue by calling for more taxes. The deficit also weighs down his *Newsweek* cover story, "How Reagan Changed America," 1-9, but we were surprised to see just plain inanities in this appraisal of Ronald Reagan's tenure. For example, "Reagan recently said that he sometimes wonders how presidents who have *not* been actors have been able to function. I don't know precisely what he meant, and he probably doesn't either, but he was on to something." He sees more reason for the GOP to back off from its nearly categorical opposition to abortion if *Roe* is reversed than if it's upheld in "Splitting Differences," *NSWK* 2-13, suggesting that it'll lose in state races otherwise. The analysis is thoughtful, but also two-dimensional. Going after the NRA's opposition to a ban on assault rifles in "Playing With Guns," *NSWK* 3-27, Will delivers a well-aimed shot to the gut: "Surely any hunter who needs 30 or even five shots to kill his quarry is an antisportsman deriving sick delight from slaughtering something immobile enough to be riddled that way." He updates us with new data on an old issue in "Disintegration of the Family Is the Major Cause of Poverty Welfare Dollars Can't Cure," *Los Angeles Times* 4-9. More moral musings from Will with "In the Grip of Gambling," *NSWK* 5-8, making the case that lottery hype erodes the work ethic. He suffers no dearth of wit, as we see in "Jokes as Tiny Revolutions," *NSWK* 6-5, on a novel approach for evaluating Soviet reform. He's at his best with the tightly-presented "Hands Off Madison's Document," *WAPO* 6-30, opposing any "piddling-fiddling amendment about the flag." Likewise with "B-2, The Question of Soviet Intentions," *WAPO* 7-23, certainly one of the best defenses of the Stealth bomber at the time. He gives us the standard stereotype, though it's well-developed in "Gorbachev And The '1946 Rules,' " *NSWK* 9-25. He provides a wry celebration of Mick Jagger and the Rolling Stones, who "please kids by horrifying parents," and are now holding their middle-aged fans too in "Childhood's Private Church," *WAPO* 9-28: "Since the mid-1950s, rock music has been the signature of the baby boomers. They comprise a generation large enough and with enough leisure time and discretionary wealth to be a market for its own expensive culture."

Yoder, Edwin. Washington Post Writers Group. (★)
More preachy than perceptive, Yoder produces conventional sound and fury, but without any panache. Though he loses steam with a digression towards the end, "A Message to John Thompson," *The Washington Post* 1-26, is forthright commentary on proposition 42 (no basketball freebies for less than 700 on the SAT's) and the issue of "culturally biased" tests: "This isn't a question of quadratic equations or Shakespeare, only the elementary ability to read, grasp and follow a set of directions." He's aghast over the Vice President's theme that "hatred of God" in the U.S.S.R. accounts for the failure of their revolution. Yoder produces one of the most pathetically myopic observations of the year in "Quayle Is Sliding on the Slippery Slope of Agnewism," *WAPO* 2-3: "Quayle chose an odd time to poke and probe at the well-known sensitivity of the Soviet leaders." He's on surer ground with "The Hundred Days Relic," *Los Angeles Times* 3-10, taking on the Bush administration's critics to make a strong case that the "Hundred Days Syndrome" is a "stale relic." There's a debilitating pretentious streak that seizes him a little too frequently. In "New Boys: Gingrich and Brown," *WAPO* 3-28, he pontificates from on high that "Powerlessness can be as corrupting as the excess of power — distorting the vision, souring moods and manner, dimming memories of the responsibilities of office, tempting people to squander their energy on small-bone fights like Gingrich's long-running vendetta against Speaker Jim Wright." He's particularly mushy with " 'He Broke the Mold,' " 4-30, praising George Washington's decision to proclaim neutrality at the outbreak of the French revolution. He's better with "Where Does 'Symbolic Speech' End?" 6-23, raising questions about inconsistencies in the application of first amendment rights. "Too Long in the Wilderness, Democrats Grope for Power," 10-10, has no special insights in predicting the Democrats may go the way of the "Whigs — and dinosaurs."

Zuckerman, Mortimer. *U.S.News & World Report.* (★ ½)
We see his columns reprinted now and then in the *Congressional Record,* which is some indication of the seriousness with which his commentary is treated. We still find him out of focus on economics, but he's developing strengths in other directions. He gets off to a good start with "The Key to the Alliance," 1-30, pulling us in with a fine lead on West Germany and NATO. Zuckerman combines perceptive historical insights with current developments in the column and concludes with a punch. Zuckerman's economic sophistication is minimal, and he's woefully confused in "The Real Bottom Line," 3-20, dismissing a perspective of lower interest rates and higher economic growth as "unrealistic." "Can Moscow Play Defense?" 3-13, tries to cover too much in an analysis of Soviet military strategy in Western Europe in the context of arms negotiations, and winds up somewhat befuddled. He counsels patience by the U.S. on changes in the U.S.S.R. in "Big Brother to Big Mac," 4-3, not at all unconvincingly, but there are no new insights or angles here. He sees a connection between the war on drugs and the spread of AIDS, and makes a case for the distribution of free, clean needles to addicts in "Addicted to Life," 4-24. While we aren't persuaded, the data and arguments he assembles have a compelling attraction. He identifies the Central Park "wilding" incident as a consequence of the breakdown in family values, but "Meltdown in Our Cities," 5-29, is mostly a call for spending more money on social problems. "The Illiteracy Epidemic," 6-12, has some interesting ideas: higher standards, national "cultural literacy tests," more preschool, though Zuckerman chooses a non-offensive consensus approach. "Vive La France," 7-24, reflections on how French politics have moderated, doesn't hold together. "To Honor the Colonel's Memory," 8-14, expresses forcefully his outrage both at the murder of Col. Higgins by terrorists and the U.S. government's rebuke of Israel for kidnapping Sheik Obeid: "No wonder the terrorists did not announce the execution of Israelis — only of Americans." Zuckerman displays forceful logic in his arguments against drug decriminalization in "The Enemy Within," 9-11, though the alternative policy recommendations are thin.

FINANCIAL REPORTERS & COLUMNISTS

Abelson, Alan. *Barron's.* (★ ½)
Editor. Abelson continues his patented front page "Up and Down Wall Street" formula of wiseguy wit on the passing political parade and sassy digs at Wall Street flyers, but he seems to be putting less effort into it and we get less return for our investment. His 1-2 column opened the year on the wrong foot with an unfunny lead that segued into a soggy prediction that the economy will do well in the first quarter, which will drive up interest rates, ultimately sinking the economy. Hmmmm. A review of Houston Biomedical at the back of the column didn't seem very useful either. A survey of IBM, 3-27, is useful for some tech stock analytics, and his introduction on the FDA's fruit guidelines is hilarious, defending Marie Antoinette: "For when she uttered her famous injunction for the people to eat cake, she was not, as legend has it, showing her contempt for the masses. Rather she was merely warning them of the dangers of grapes and apples, to name two ferocious killers." The 4-3 column has some good lines to wrap up events that took place during the just finished first quarter: "Treasury Secretary Brady single-handedly reversed a substantial flow of funds into the S&Ls. . .democratic refusenikism. . .Mike Milken got indicted in the waning days of the quarter, assuring himself a place in history as the only man threatened with 520 years in prison for parking violations. . .." In his 5-22 column, we get little but a wry sense of humor on the effects of death on stock prices: "Even Warren Buffett, a justly renowned observer of investment mores, speculated at the recent annual meeting of his company, Berkshire Hathaway, that were he to die, his stock would go up. He neglected to disclose whether he had any immediate plans to test his thesis." On 7-24, Abelson offers capricious commentary on Dennis Levine and other current gossip: "Mr. Levine is an alumnus of two great institutions, Drexel Burnham and Lewisburg, which differ in, among other ways, the facts that executions are performed only at the first. There is a certain collegiality between the two, and, indeed, indirectly Drexel was Lewisburg's benefactor by recently contributing $650 million to the latter's parent organization." Abelson's column of 9-11 careens madly through the issues of the week, SciMed Life Systems, S&Ls and Donald Trump, but the funny stuff doesn't connect. It does 10-30, with Abelson at the top of his form. "The public, everyone knows, isn't in the market. But just how much he isn't in the market, as Mr. Berra might say, is truly amazing." Commenting on the earnings of Rollins, parent of Orkin Exterminating: "We should note that although 1989 has proved a blah termite year, it was a very decent flea year, and that provided some additional scratch for Rollins." He's widely read for his impact on stock prices, but clearly down from his heyday.

Adler, Stephen J. *The Wall Street Journal.* (★ ★ ★)
New York, law reporter. Assigned the Drexel case, Adler worked hard to find angles and stories other publications just weren't covering. His grasp of the legal issues involved is good; his styling professional. "Heated Argument: Are RICO Seizures A Violation of Rights, As Critics Contend?" 2-15, tells us the issue, in legal terms, has been decided by the Supreme Court, which upheld such seizures, but the philosophical case remains. "Former Runaway Hit Big Time at Drexel But Now Faces Prison," 3-21, captures the tragedy and humanity of the huge government-Drexel fight better than anything else we'd seen as a low-level assistant trader gets squeezed by over-zealous prosecutors on one side and their ultimate prey, the big-money man at Drexel, on the other. A 10 Best selection, this trader's assistant may spend more time in jail than the big fish. "The Other Shoe: Indicting Milken, U.S. Demands $1.2 Billion of Financier's Assets," co-written by Laurie P. Cohen 3-30, sets the stage as we prepare to watch one of the greatest battles in the legal-financial era in history. Teamed again with Cohen, "Clearance of RICO Suits Proposed," 5-9, reports on an idea to reform RICO that flopped, a requirement of Justice Department approval for all civil RICO cases tried, interesting, but not quite newsworthy. In "Name of This Game Is Trade-Offs," 8-25, Adler and co-author Ellen Joan Pollock intelligently probe the price of settling out of court with regard to Pete Rose's gambling and the Major League Baseball settlement, Union Carbide's settlement after the Bhopal chemical

221

explosion, and the SEC's settlements of some major insider-trading suits: "The case is resolved, but the facts remain uncertain and blame is never fully assigned." "Litigation Science: Consultants Dope Out The Mysteries of Jurors For Clients Being Sued," 10-24, is a fascinating look at Litigation Science, a subsidiary of ad giant Saatchi & Saatchi PLC and its "legal consulting firm, which is helping corporate America prepare for high-stakes litigation by predicting and shaping jurors' reactions." In addition to examining the history of sociology and psychology in jury selection, Adler also takes us behind the scenes at LS, and evaluates the pros and cons of such service (it "doesn't make moral decisions") as it provides "pre-trial opinion polls, creates profiles of 'ideal' jurors, sets up mock trials and 'shadow' juries, coaches lawyers and witnesses, and designs courtroom graphics."

Alsop, Ronald. *The Wall Street Journal.* (★ ★ ★)
News Editor, marketing and media page. Now the brains behind the page, we cite Alsop for some superior work he did prior to going behind the scenes, and for selected special "Centennial" efforts that appeared after he moved upstairs. "Giving Fading Brands a Second Chance," 1-24, is excellent on the repositioning or promotion of old brands, like Cheez Whiz, Geritol, Dippity Do, and V8, to a new segment of the market. Alsop provides specific examples of successes and failures, as well as the numbers on cost and risks of introducing new brands versus upping promotion on old brands. Cheez Whiz, often the butt of jokes, is being promoted as a microwave cheese sauce. "More Ads Bombard Airplane Passengers After Takeoff, Until Landing: Commercials," 2-14, details the latest in advertising schemes: ads on airline movie screens, audio programs and lavatory doors. (What better way to capture a consumer's attention than by blitzing him at 32,000 feet, where there's no hope of escape?) "In '88, There Were No Ads Like Old Ads," 2-23, is a light, but informative article noting that of 1988's top commercials, as rated by Video Storyboard Tests, Inc., most are either holdovers of previous themes or revivals of old slogans and characters. "A Centennial View: Products That Last — Enduring Brands Hold Their Allure By Sticking Close to Their Roots," 6-23, is a superlative look at products, like Coca Cola, that last and the marketing that helps them along, beginning strong and keeping our attention: "To a supermarket shopper, a package of Oreo cookies, a jar of Planters nuts and a box of Nabisco Shredded Wheat are worth about $7.75. To Kohlberg Kravis Roberts & Co., they are worth a fortune." "The American Way of Buying: Brand Loyalty Is Rarely Blind Loyalty," 10-19, part of the *Journal*'s centennial survey, while far-reaching and done well, seems like a thankless assignment, as we all know most loyalty to consumer products is contingent on the price tag.

Altman, Lawrence K., M.D. *The New York Times.* (★ ★)
A "Science Times" reporter for 20 years, Altman's "Doctor's World" column and his reports are detailed and authoritative. His presentation sometimes tends toward the clinical, as befits his degree, but the emergence of his lukewarm bedside manner leaves us cold; it probably works better in person, as we see when he has specifically peopled examples. Altman relates a peripheral topic well to the average Joe in "When an Exotic Virus Strikes: A Deadly Case of Lassa Fever," 2-28, warning that anyone who travels overseas is subject to foreign germs, a vivid story of one traveller's journey to the funeral of his parents in Nigeria ending in his own death outside Chicago, detailed and instructive to both doctor and patient. "U.S. To Ease Methadone Rules In Bid to Curb AIDS in Addicts," 3-3, is fuzzy on the actual before-and-after shots of guidelines, but okay on implications and hopes that change will bring. "For Those With Tattoo Regret, Here's Hope," 4-28, is delightful, informing those who'd like to get rid of Agatha, or remove her in favor of Virginia, there's a treatment to make this possible, complete with possible side effects and details on the process, but no costs. "Medical Advances Brighten Jogger's Prognosis," 5-21, provides an overview of "brain-injured" individuals prognoses that is interesting in light of the Central Park jogger's recovery to this point, but Altman doesn't address whether all this therapy does any good. "Scientists Fear That A Parasite Will Spread in Transfusions," 5-23, tells us of yet another thing to worry about, given to us this time by the Vice President of the U. of TX Med School in Galveston, but an expert at the Center for Disease

Control Altman consulted said he does not favor national testing now because of the expense involved and the rarity of the disease in this country (two cases in three years, one of whom recovered and one, who had a transfusion from his father, died). "New Study Is Easing Fears on AIDS and Mental Illness," 6-3, is dry but informative, providing the latest data on AIDS, and the first we saw on psychological impact of the disease itself due to neurons rather than trauma. "In Battling Dengue Fever Mosquitos, Expert Enlists Public's Assistance," 8-22, Altman has difficulty going beyond the data and relating it to his audience; what we get is interesting, but dry, and somewhat alarmist: "Unless more people clean up their yards to prevent dengue-carrying mosquitos from breeding around their homes, additional devastating epidemics will occur." But where? The bugs are found all over the U.S., but the disease has not yet moved north of Texas. A worthy topic and treatment deserving of front-page placement, "Europe Supplying Blood for the U.S." 9-5, is an eye-opener on blood donations, with officials around the country telling Altman it's easier to buy blood from various sources than to try and beat the American public into donating a pint or two.

Ansberry, Clare. *The Wall Street Journal.* (★ ★ ½)
Pittsburgh. Solid dispatches from the industrial city, Ansberry's material is unadorned in her spot news, as we like it, but breezy and confident in her front-page business leders. We've come to respect her byline. A deeper look at how companies in Pittsburgh might be affected by outside events, or *vice versa,* would give her work a broader perspective that would be valuable. "Allegheny International Retains Right On Reorganization Plan in Court Ruling," 1-16, is thorough on Allegheny's filing, but doesn't look at wider implications for the industry or the legal options involved in a continuing bankruptcy action. "Creditors Seek to Reorganize Consumer Firm," 2-23, gets detail into a short amount of space, as the unsecured creditors of Allegheny file a reorganization plan of their own that would force the company into selling its profitable Sunbeam/Oster appliance line, as well as other subsidiaries. "Allegheny International Inc. Posts Quarter Loss," 4-28, is well rounded on Allegheny's losses, comparing this quarter to previous quarters and other years, including stock prices, but not much on analytics. In "West Virginia Weighs Lawsuit Against Brokers," 6-6, Ansberry takes a peek at the state considering suing a firm retained to handle the state's consolidated investment fund, losing $279 million, mostly in 1987, a bare-bones view that gets all the relevant data, without any frills. A "Who's News" profile, "Banc One's Hoaglin Seeks to Transfer His Ohio Success to Struggling Texas," 7-3, is quick but substantial on Thomas Hoaglin, new president and CEO of Banc One, which just purchased the struggling MCorp bank in Texas, containing a telling quote from one discouraged employee: "It's nice to have someone want us." "USX Planning To Sell Reserves Of Oil, Gas Unit," 10-3, is improved, examining some of the implications of the proposed sale of USX's Texas Oil & Gas unit. Her front page "Kodak Chief is Trying, For the Fourth Time, to Cut Costs," with Carol Hymowitz 9-19, sparkles with imagery: "Kodak watchers are shaking their heads, wondering why he needs four tries to accomplish essentially one job: cut costs. 'Is he simply the leader of a gang that can't shoot straight?' they ask."

Armbruster, William. *The Journal of Commerce.* (★ ★)
Senior correspondent, covering international trade. Compact, dependable reports are what we see from Armbruster. Though he's sometimes light on analytics, Armbruster gets bonus points for covering stories others miss, and angles others don't think of. "Namibia Pact Silent On Port's Fate," 12-27-88, describes the peculiar history and potential fate of Africa's fifth largest port, Walvis Bay, located in Namibia, that will remain under direct control of South Africa even after Namibia's independence. "Business Contends GATT Is Still Alive," 1-31, resoundingly refutes Lester Thurow's suggestion to abandon the Uruguay Round of trade liberalization talks by going to business and taking an impartial survey; the result is overwhelming support for a "very active corpse" of the General Agreement on Tariffs and Trade despite its imperfections. "U.S. Urged to Strengthen China Ties," 2-8, pre-Tiananmen Square, is nicely detailed on U. of WA China expert Nicholas Lardy's report, with supporters and detractors cited. "Maritime Interests Fight Trade Talk Inclusion," 3-30, is a sweeping overview of the fight over inclusion of maritime

services under GATT, looking at the history of the struggle and future prospects, with some great quotes from Carla Hills and her staff, and industry bigwigs. In "Top Polish Officials Tour U.S." 4-6, he deserves credit for his coverage of the event, but there are no analytics here. "Business Expects Hard Bargaining at Trade Talks," 4-11, is merely a roundup of opinions of business groups, interesting, but not terribly useful. "Court Ruling Could Save Importers Millions," 6-15, doesn't address the legal implications of the ruling, but is thorough on the impact on importers, though we would have liked to see more specific estimates on savings to importers and costs to customs as they lose the authority "to assess duty on quota charges paid by importers in certain cases." "Taiwan Seeks Role in Global Groups," 10-24, is well structured, down to the last detail over the feud over Taiwan's name, but there's little analysis here of what acceptance into GATT and other multilateral bodies would mean for the country except in terms of debt relief.

Auerbach, Stuart. *The Washington Post.* (★)
Financial correspondent, covering international trade and semiconductors. While adequate in most respects, Auerbach just doesn't have the broad perspective to move him beyond the conventional on his beat. "Why The Trade Deficit Won't Improve," 1-29, is a narrow, superficial, Sunday business lead that doesn't support its headline and is lopsided to boot, quoting several "experts," all from the same school: "It's a technical impossibility to lower the trade deficit more than 10 percent below current levels," said David Hale of Kemper Financial. "U.S.-Japan Collaboration on Jet Draws Fire," 3-15, gives a reasonable overview of the FSX controversy, the co-production deal between U.S. and Japan on the new jet fighter, but is marred by an inclination to give greater space to opponents of the deal. In an attempt to show how the FSX flap has broader implications for the economic elements of national security, Auerbach offers extensive views of Commerce Secretary Mosbacher, a foe of the FSX, and three private sector specialists who echo the line that the Soviets are less of a threat than they used to be, Japan more of a threat, and we wonder of his biases. In "For New Japan Envoy, Economics Is Key," 5-2, we get a sketchy profile of new U.S. Ambassador to Japan, Michael Armacost, telling us how he sees his job: " 'The American ambassador has to regard himself as the first commercial officer of the embassy,' " Armacost tells the Senate Foreign Relations Committee. But the subject is much too big for this cursory job. "Global Stakes High As Decision on Japan Trade Nears," 5-25, gets the stakes right, but this is a rehash of familiar material, sparse on detail or illuminations that bear on the growing tensions here on trade and capital flows. "U.S.-Japan Telecommunications Pact Sours," 6-16, details the dispute between Motorola and Japan's Ministry of Post and Telegraph, involving possible Japanese violation of a three and a half-year-old agreement, which "poses the question of whether the Japanese system is so conditioned against foreign competition, especially in areas of technology such as telecommunications, that it is impossible for negotiations to succeed." "U.S. Offers Plan to Ease Trade Dispute," 7-13, is clear and succinct on a new proposal to reduce barriers to agricultural imports, but the larger backdrop of Japanese sensitivities is largely missing.

Bailey, Jeff. *The Wall Street Journal.* (★ ★)
Chicago. A strong reporter who should be left to craft his own material, Bailey's byline too often appears layered with others in joint efforts that almost always sag under the weight. "Moody's Lowers Sears Rating Two Notches," 1-11, accurately covers Moody's lowering of Sears' rating, not optimistic at all on the Chicago retailer's ability to turn its business around by reducing prices and eliminating sales as a strategy. As part of a "Small Business" special report, Bailey files "Tightening the Rules: New Court Decisions Are Making It Tougher For Borrowers to Win Liability Suits," 2-24, beginning with a vivid illustration in 1986 and following through with the case of Jon Ginder as he sues the bank that backed out on a handshake deal; the case still isn't settled. "How a Chicago Investor Lived the Good Life On Other People's Cash," with Barbara Marsh 5-17, an interesting P. 1 scandal story of William J. Stoecker, 32, who borrowed $390 million from banks, with $250 million now missing, leaves too many questions unanswered on how he pulled it off. "Traders Are Indicted for Running the Pits by Their Own Rules," 8-3, is

an exceptional lead that not only explores what the government is alleging these traders did wrong, but also takes note of the power struggle going on between traders and government lawyers on who gets the upper hand. "Birth of a Haven: In the British Virgin Islands, Dummy Corporations Are Becoming as Prevalent as Tourists," part of "World Business: Investing" special report 9-22, is a delightful, feature-ish look at the new tax haven in the Virgin Islands, deftly and professionally executed, even covering some of the legal aspects. "Eagleton Accuses Chicago Merc's Leaders and Quits," 11-8, is standard stuff on former Sen. Thomas Eagleton resigning from the Chicago Mercantile Exchange after accusing its leadership of butting into a federal regulatory suit, Bailey not getting us much beneath the surface.

Banks, Howard. *Forbes.* (★ ½)
Washington bureau chief and "What's Ahead for Business" columnist. It was a tough year for most economic columnists and Banks was no exception, serving up the usual statistics and usually harmless observations through the smoke. "Attention Mr. Greenspan," 2-6, is moderately daring in advising that consumers are "much calmer about the recent relatively moderate uptick in inflation" than the Fed chairman, and that he shouldn't boost interest rates. "De Facto Industrial Policymaking," 2-20, is a rather poor presentation on an important subject, scattershot material that yielded little on three readings. "Science Fiction," 3-6, about the weightlessness problem disclosed by Oleg Atkov, resulting in the National Academy of Sciences and the National Academy of Engineering sharply criticizing NASA's plans, already agreed to by the President, for construction of a space station and a trip to Mars, both of which present grave human endurance problems, contains a good description of the Russian experience. Banks takes us from "Denver to Seoul, Nonstop," 5-29, a concise update on the Pratt & Whitney Airbus, but we get lost in his descriptions of turbines and rotors. "Rivets and Revelation," 6-12, is an interesting tidbit that tips off the reader to follow an obscure case before the Federal Trade Commission that may give any indication of a possible change in direction from Reagan's *laissez-faire*. In the 8-21 cover "Why George Bush Wants to Bring IRAs Back," Banks' conclusions are hampered by poor organization and mediocre analysis, vague on the distinctions between IRAs and a capital gains differential in promoting growth, instead harping on what an increased savings rate means for the U.S. economy, promoting CEA Chairman Michael Boskin's personal *bete noire.*

Barber, Lionel. *Financial Times.* (★ ★)
Washington correspondent. His first year in DC, Barber does well enough keeping up with his general assignment beat, with emphasis on trade and monetary matters. We expected sharper analytics from him, but this will no doubt change as he gets better acquainted with the colonies. "Hills Appointment Puts a Premium on Competence," 1-5, questions why Bush chose novice Carla Hills as his top trade official. Barber doesn't really give an answer, but he does provide background on the new U.S. Trade Rep nominee, with emphasis on her skills as an administrator over her trade expertise, suggesting she will not be a policymaker. "Greenspan Says Fed Ready to Provide Funds for Ailing S&Ls," 2-24, is solid on the politics behind the economics of the S&L bailout, but would benefit from greater use of direct quotes. "Completion of Start Nuclear Treaty 'At Least' Two Years," 3-25, a report on the Labour Party defense delegation meeting with Bush, provides a sampling of analysis, broad scope, repercussions, but is not in-depth enough. "U.S. Makes Plans for Possible Intervention in Panama," 4-27, gets early rumblings of different possibilities due to Noriega's probable rigging of the election: "An aide to Senator Lugar was concerned that the administration was not preparing U.S. public opinion for trouble ahead." "Baker Calls on Israel to Hold Serious Talks with Palestinians," 5-23, solidly reports on JBIII's tough-talk speech to the American-Israel Public Affairs committee, vividly relating the remarks, which included calling "on Israel to forswear annexation, stop the expansion of Jewish settlements, reopen schools in the territories and to lay aside what he called 'the unrealistic expectation of a greater Israel' " and the reaction: "His speech was greeted with silence." While Barber tells us this policy speech will have "international" repercussions, we don't get any sense of what he thinks they might be. "White House Warns Fed Caution Could

Trigger U.S. Recession," 8-14, reports clearly on statements made by OMB's Richard Darman on a Sunday news show warning the Fed that high interest rates and tight money risk tipping the U.S. economy into recession.

Bartlett, Sarah. *The New York Times.* (★ ★ ★ ★)
Banking reporter. A prime example of how a richly-talented reporter can flourish with a bit of freedom, Bartlett has a marvelous year at the *Times* after being weaned from the constraints of *BusinessWeek.* Firmly established as the star of the beat, she is consistently on-target in reporting and analytics, if not always dead center. A 10 Best selection, "John Reed Bumps Into Reality," 2-5, is timely and irreverent, thoroughly devoid of hype as Bartlett interviews Citicorp's Reed, musses his hair, and generally roughs him up for dreaming more about the bank's globalization than executing on the current nuts-and-bolts. "Plan or No Plan, Debt Relief Is Not Around the Corner," 4-9, a P. 1 "Week in Review" piece, reveals that the Emperor of the Brady Plan has no clothes: "The debate has subtly shifted to what role public entities like the IMF and the World Bank — not to mention the world's taxpayers, who stand behind them — should play in helping to soften the blow to the banks." "Why Wall Street's So Topsy-Turvy: Tough Times Are Forcing Firms to Amputate Business or Cut Pay," 5-7, uses good statistics and many interesting quotes to back an analysis of the consolidation on Wall Street. In the *Times*'s special Sunday addition, *Business World,* we get "Where the Ace Is King," 6-11, a fast-paced, enjoyable profile of Alan "Ace" Greenberg of Bear Stearns, the most productive firm on Wall Street, no doubt due to Ace's single-minded dedication to the business and his management style. "In Media Giants' Takeover Battle, Power of Debt Is Starkly Revealed," 6-18, gives a marvelous overview of the Time-Warner-Paramount financial maneuvers that is at once clear, sharp and persuasive: Warner's initial bid of Time was too low, an invitation to Paramount's hostile tender. "U.S. Efforts to Aid Debtor Nations Bring 'Profound Disappointment,' " 7-24, provides a comprehensive review of Brady Plan shortcomings after the initial euphoria, but contains no new insights. There are plenty in "Cracks in House That Debt Built," 8-17, informs us how some of KKR's junk bond deals are going sour — a major turning point in the handling of Henry Kravis, who no longer seems invincible. The editors, we gather, trimmed back an even more scathing report. "The Third World Debt Crisis Reshapes American Banks," 9-24, is a crisp analytical report on the Manufacturers Hanover deal with Dai-Ichi Kango, Japan's largest bank, to shore up its capital base, and J. P. Morgan getting reserves to 100% on its Third World portfolio, very smart in seeing implications for the Brady Plan, weakness of the Citicorp position. There's only the rarest misfire, when she tries to bite off more than she can chew. "Vicious Circle Keeps Latin America in Debt," 1-15, is ambitious, but out of Bartlett's depth, producing a scrambled history of debt crisis and helplessness except for debt relief.

Beauchamp, Marc. *Forbes.* (★)
West Coast bureau manager. Quirky stuff on the Pacific coast, Beauchamp's topics ranging from water rights to diapers. Although his style is lively enough, in keeping with convention at *Forbes,* the material he gets his teeth into is too often floss. In "Mistaken Identity?" 2-6, Beauchamp gives a superficial view on Pope & Talbott, Inc., and Peter Pope's management strategy; we come away with some interesting tidbits, but no sense of how Pope & Talbott fits into the industry or the world at large. "Fishy Arguments," 3-20, tells how Japanese fishing ships poaching on U.S. territorial (200 miles) waters combined with, or causing, lower fish prices have Seattle fishermen looking for ways to curb foreign competition. Political clout as well as economic muscle is used to keep profits up and supplies down, but we're thrown as Beauchamp begins moralizing with anti-business arguments. Beauchamp draws an interesting parallel in concluding "Changing Orbits," 5-29, the story of the struggle between optical fiber and communications satellites: "Radio and television managed to coexist. So too with optical fiber and satellites." Telling the story of mismanagement at Hawaiian Airlines in "What's Hawaiian For 'Rotten Management?' " 6-26, Beauchamp, deposits blame at the door of Chairman John Magoon Jr. for the airline's troubles, supporting his case with relevant information, but he gets a bit carried away with the *Forbes* hotshot style: "How do you flirt with bankruptcy in a business that is

indispensable during an unprecedented economic boom? You get swell-headed, expand stupidly, manage poorly, neglect maintenance, delay and cancel flights and then plunge into a ruinous price war trying to gain market share." Taking his title from a Mark Twain quip, " 'Whiskey's for Drinking, Water's for Fighting Over,' " 7-24, Beauchamp explores some of the consequences of the Central Arizona Project, which will export water from Southern California, an admirable enough effort, but Beauchamp only reports one side of the story, relying on Arizona engineer Frank Welsh's expertise, with Welsh and Beauchamp fingering local water subsidies for farmers and government as part of the problem in Southern California water shortages: "Charge farmers the true cost of the water and they would use it more efficiently, and fears of a shortage would vanish." In "The Sewers of Malibu," 8-7, Beauchamp reviews the fight for developmental control of Malibu, "a 27-mile divot of Pacific coastline and rugged chapparal-covered mountains." Nicely done as far as it goes, but we have a strong feeling there's more going on in Southern California than we saw from Beauchamp.

Bennett, Amanda. *The Wall Street Journal.* (★ ½)
New York management reporter. Bennett seemed to be well on the way last year to picking up the pace at this beat after a slow start on her return from a Beijing posting. The material we caught this year was not up to the '88 pace, though. Solid enough, but not enough sparkling detail or angles for this critical *WSJ* assignment. A good topic hits a stone wall in "Going Global: The Chief Executives in Year 2000 Will Be Experienced Abroad," 2-27, as Bennett explores some recent twists in the path up the corporate ladder as different factors change the face of the boardroom; new trends helping to expedite this are the increasing globalization of markets, technological changes and the importance of "multienvironment, multicountry, multifunctional, maybe even multicompany, multi-industry experience." Mffff. In "At Contract Talks, Union Leaders Reach for COLA," 3-7, Bennett examines how cost-of-living adjustments are creeping back into union contract talks this year as inflation increases, making good use of specific examples to make the point. "Critics Fault Chief Executive of Exxon on Handling of Recent Alaskan Oil Spill," with Allanna Sullivan 3-31, combines Sullivan, the oil beat reporter, and Bennett's management focus, contrasting the low profile Exxon's CEO kept during the crisis vs. crisis management at Johnson & Johnson and Union Carbide, who certainly had bigger PR problems and came off much better than the oil company. Among the amazing facts: Exxon's PR for the U.S. was handled by one man and an answering machine; and Exxon's decentralization led to a lapse of authority for responding to the oil spill. "Firms Debate Hard Line on Alcoholics," with Jolie Solomon and Allanna Sullivan 4-13, reads like a newsmagazine piece, and no wonder, with the three bylines; all over the map, the trio simply tries to cover too much in canvassing what firms do with alcoholic employees. "Move Over You Type-A People, Here Come the Type ZZZZZZs," 5-5, is written as a fun article, but contains some serious and interesting information on a recently released report by Northwestern Mutual Life Insurance Co., based in Milwaukee, which contends that quiet in the workplace improves productivity by allowing concentration. "Company School: As Pool of Skilled Help Tightens, Firms Move to Broaden Their Role," 5-8, is full of company programs and quotes to illustrate changing attitudes, but this latest entry in the *WSJ*'s interminable anniversary "Second Century" is dull and hard to slog through, the issue of business having to get more involved in education and training, due to woeful schools, has been covered endlessly by *BusinessWeek* and *Fortune*. Relying on her experience in Beijing, "China Syndrome: Beijing's Economic IOUs Pose a New Threat of Social Upheaval," with Adi Ignatius 8-3, gives a host of anecdotes depicting China's economic slide, as the last of foreign currency from tourists passes on and foreign companies pull out. "Business Takes Out Its Trimming Shears," 10-5, is a routine wrap-up of downsizing at big companies, quoting all the usual suspects.

Berg, Eric N. *The New York Times.* (★ ½)
Chicago. General assignment on the Windy City's business beat, Berg handles his material with steady professionalism, but after spotting his early work on New York's banking beat a few years ago we had expected he might be a superstar by this time, not riding the bus in the minors. "U.S.

Promises More Enforcement," 1-23, based on the U.S. Attorney General's promise to beef-up enforcement of securities and commodity trading laws in light of the various scandals, is a credible overview, but only contains a limited attempt to explain how the commodity pits really work and why they are subject to manipulation. On the Chicago retailing giant, Berg files "Sears Cutting Prices By as Much as 50% In a Shift of Strategy," 2-24, a sharp dispatch on Sears' new strategy, getting different opinions on all sides on the chances of success for the 102-year-old firm, but with little of his own analysis. "Sears Shifts Management, Sets Jobs Cuts," 3-31, updates, Berg giving a detailed overview of the second step in Sears' makeover, with this change occurring behind the counter. "An Electronics Chain's Sharp Slide," 4-29, explores some of Highland Superstores' problems, ones that are typical of the industry, good descriptions but no solutions or analytic. "A Peculiar Twist Arises in Complex NWA Battle," 5-11, an account of the cross ties of numerous raiders chasing the same target with the same money, offers real-life commentary on the 80's financial highwire act. "At Fuller Brush, New Ways to Get Foot in the Door," 5-18, is a nice, but not in-depth, update on Fuller Brush's new marketing strategy — catalog, showroom, door-to-door — that offers an insider's detailed peek at what they're doing to make all three work effectively together, but not much on future plans. "Fight on Quick Pizza Delivery Grows," 8-29, looks into the current problems associated with the Domino's Pizza chain's guarantee of 30-minute delivery: personal safety experts, as well as other chains and smaller operators, are hysterical over a slew of accidents that have occurred recently as a result of the guarantee, but the article doesn't give details, Berg unable to decide whether to write about Domino's, personal safety or pizza industry.

Bernstein, Aaron. *BusinessWeek.* (★ ★)
Labor editor. Adding panache to his dispatch, Bernstein's work was brighter, zippier than we'd seen previously. He's meticulous about keeping himself balanced between management and labor, no mean feat. Bernstein informs in "The Feds Drive a Wedge into the Teamsters," 2-6, on how the two factions on the union's executive board are negotiating separately with the Feds concerning an agreement on "reform," with some nice analysis of the potential effects of the settlement on the board and the union in general. In "Eastern's Labor Mess May Land in Bush's Lap," 3-6, Bernstein works the slippery street of scenarios in the Eastern Airlines labor-management dispute and does a good job of laying out a major selection of "if...then" possibilities, including the pending Bush decision on whether to appoint a mediation board. Solid in "Overhauling the Teamsters," 3-27, Bernstein provides good analysis of the implications of the recent Justice Dept./Teamsters settlement agreement in the government's racketeering suit, giving us some interesting details of the Fed's reported negotiations strategy, concluding that the union officials alleged to have mob ties were the losers. With Susan Garland, Bernstein discusses the pertinent issues in the AT&T-union talks, "Almost Everyone Is Listening in on the Telephone Talks," 4-10, well organized, smoothly flowing, telling us that apparently neither side wants a strike. In a useful, behind-the-scenes look at how the deal developed, "Why Mike Milken Was So Eager to Help Peter Ueberroth," 5-1, Bernstein notes that Drexel was putting up the cash behind Uebie's buyout offer for Eastern Airlines because Drexel wanted to help protect the value of $1 billion of paper it sold for Texas Air and its subs. But "Why More Mothers Are Not Getting Married," 5-29, disappoints, hard to follow in spots, Bernstein contending that economic factors may discourage *men* from getting married. The article notes that young, little-educated white men in low-paying jobs feel they can't afford it, and women "tend to marry less as their income rises." In "The Boeing Strike: Both Sides Are Flying Blind," with Leslie Helm and Maria Shao 11-6, we get a good feel for the walkout from labor's side, but no sense of why Boeing is so hard-nosed when it seems to have room for give, possibly a side-effect of the teamwork journalism.

Berry, John M. *The Washington Post.* (★ ½)
Economics correspondent. When he's of a mind, Berry can assemble worthy reports on Washington macro-policymaking, but he seldom gets far enough above the debate. He confuses in "The Tricky Feat of Balancing the Budget," 1-15, correctly asserting that the Fed is indeed

walking a fine line between growth and inflation, but not quoting any direct sources until the 15th graph, and then citing only three after that; early in the piece he makes sweeping assertions that go unsupported by specifics. In "Behind the Rise in Gasoline," 4-20, Berry has the right numbers, but his Alaska oil spill theory, trumpeted in the second graph, is discredited at the end of the piece; so little of the oil dumped was earmarked for gasoline. The underlying causes for the price rise are skimmed over. Berry provides no answer to the question in the headline, "How Long Can Japan's Trade Surplus Go On?" 4-30, instead lining up the parameters that must be considered around his central thesis: the surplus is due to the uniqueness of the Japanese distribution system and "the Japanese consumers and their odd willingness to pay too much for everything, whether made here or abroad." In "Bush Aides Worrying About Rates," 5-17, is no doubt an authentic report from *some* anonymous insider worried that Greenspan's Fed was flirting with recession. In "The Lender of Last Resort," 5-21, Berry replies to critics who had opposed the Fed's decision to lend money to bankrupt S&Ls, developing the case of historic precedents in the context of ". . .the Fed's ultimate responsibility is to keep the entire financial system safe." "Farm Credit System: Back From the Brink," 6-18, reports on the reorganization and recovery of the Farm Credit System, filled with useful information: "like the S&Ls, the Farm Credit System plunged into turmoil in the mid-1980s. . .but [unlike the S&Ls, it] has survived through infusion of nearly $1 billion worth of federal help in the past year and by making sweeping changes in its structure and ways of doing business. . ." Berry argues the bottom line of the restructuring: "As bad loans have been foreclosed and many more creditworthy borrowers paid off their loans, the system's total loan volume plummeted from more than $800 billion at the end of 1983 to $50.7 billion at the end of the first quarter of this year." Berry maintains a straight balance in "Brady Predicts Economy Headed For 'Soft Landing,' " 7-7, noting that "many private economists agree with Brady that the U.S. economy is likely to grow through next year." In the autumn clash between the Fed and Treasury over exchange-rate intervention, Berry was impressive in his detachment, laying out the arguments with good quotes from several expert observers in "Picking Policy Over Dollar Intervention," 10-8, but he needed to identify Treasury players and also offer a sense of where the White House stood.

Bishop, Jerry E. *The Wall Street Journal.* (★ ★)
Science beat. It sometimes gets hard when you're on a beat as long as Bishop has been to remember who your audience is, in this case the business and financial community, not the subscribers to *The New England Journal of Medicine*. Still, we appreciate his byline, as hard as the going gets at times. We especially liked his balanced work on cold fusion, a science controversy that tests a reporter's detachment. In "Taming H-Bombs? Utah Scientists Claim Breakthrough in Quest For Fusion Energy," 3-24, we get a good review with a detailed explanation of the science behind it and excellent information on other work being done in the field. In a followup, "Scientist Sticks to Claimed Test-Tube Fusion Advance: But Utah's Pons Concede Other Reactions May Also Be At Work," 3-27, Bishop is balanced on B. Stanley Pons, the Utah chemist who claims to have achieved cold fusion, while conflicting claims and skepticism abounds. "Heat Source in Fusion Find May Be Mystery Reaction," 4-3, is one of the first looks at Pons' actual research, a copy handily obtained by the *WSJ*. Bishop avoided being swept away by the scorn heaped upon the announcement at the physicists' meeting. He further reports the growing controversy, "Physicists Outline Possible Errors That Led to Claims of Cold Fusion," 5-3, as scientists at the annual meeting of the American Physical Society attacked the cold fusion claims of Univ. of Utah chemists B. Stanley Pons and Martin Fleischmann. Bishop's account is superior to others, "Fusion Brouhaha May Be Settled Soon By Helium Test," 5-10, as Pons and Fleischmann agree to helium tests at the Electrochemical Society meeting in L.A. In another realm, we get crisp detail in "Hostility, Distrust May Put Type A's at Coronary Risk," 1-17, on Duke researchers unraveling the controversy over Type A personalities and risk of heart disease by subclassifying the workaholic Type A's. "Test That Measures Left Ventricle's Mass Can Predict Healthy Person's Heart Risk," 1-24, on the findings that an enlarged left ventricle, detected by echocardiography, is a better indicator of cardiovascular risk than such factors as obesity, high cholesterol, and smoking, but we needed some comment on the

economics. In "Genetics Flaw Leads to High Cholesterol," 2-7, he reports discovery of a genetic defect in a poliprotein B100 that causes high blood cholesterol levels. We can handle a decent amount of technical lingo, but he whips us here. He's clear enough and emphatic in "Cholesterol Connection in Heart Disease Is Incontestable, 2 Health Groups Say," 11-15, but no word from the opposition. In "Researchers Collect 'Bottle' of Antimatter," 3-2, Bishop sounds like a Trekkie as he tells how researchers at AT&T Bell Labs collected a magnetic "bottle" of a few hundred thousand antimatter positrons, the antimatter equivalent of electrons: "Positrons are identical to electrons except they carry a positive charge, while electrons are negatively charged."

Bleiberg, Robert M. *Barron's.* (★ ½)
Publisher and editorial director. Bleiberg's page-length editorial commentaries are a fixture at the weekly, and there's no use our trying to browbeat him into shortening them. We urge him as he approaches his 70s to go easy on lengthy "I-told-you-so openings," that cause his younger readers to lose heart. History will reward him for his unflagging confidence in the capitalist idea. He blasts Jamaica's Michael Manley, "Down With Manley," 1-23, rooting for Edward Seaga in advance of the Feb. 9 election, with probably the most thorough account of the island's economic history under Manley and Seaga we've seen. But it's a distant view, hardly examining why Seaga is behind in polls, eventually going down to defeat. In "Animal Workshop," 2-13, Bleiberg is strong and fairly early on the animal research flap. "Whither the LBO? To Judge By the Sorry Congressional Record, the Market Will Decide," 3-6, is a parade of examples of times Congress did the wrong thing at the right time and/or *vice versa,* used to forecast either mistakes or inaction on the LBO front; similar to predicting the sunrise on the morrow, but fun. Though Bleiberg is top-heavy in "McNamara to Clausen to Conable," 4-10, reminiscing about "Robert Strange McNamara," there's good material here we didn't see elsewhere questioning the Brady Plan and the World Bank role in Third World debt write-down, quoting Moody's. We give up after two columns in "Back to the Horse and Buggy?" 5-1, Bleiberg's ponderous carping at EPA's William Reilly for regulatory excesses. "Back to the Future?" 7-24, offers a rare critique of the U.S. manned space program as a waste of money, Bleiberg arguing that private funds should seek return on investment, not public pie-in-the-sky: "As Barron's time and again has pointed out, private enterprise should be mobilized whenever possible to do the job. Bureaucracy works no better in space than it does on Earth." He told you so.

Blustein, Paul. *The Washington Post.* (★)
Washington. Given a broad portfolio on international economics and finance at the *Post* after an unhappy time at *The Wall Street Journal's* Washington bureau, the talented Blustein disappoints us with his insistence on hanging on to preconceived angles instead of letting his experience follow stories where they want to go. In "Is the Budget Deficit Really So Bad? You Bet Your Future It Is," 1-25, Blustein tells us Robert Eisner of Northwestern says we shouldn't worry about the twin deficits, as Eisner "uses complicated mathematical calculations to show that adjusted for inflation and other factors, the deficit is really a trivial sum." Blustein dismisses the thesis with a wave of his wand: "trust your good old American instincts. Keep worrying." Unacceptable — this is not analysis. In "Putting the Tax Code Back on the Table," 2-26, Blustein is at his professional best, laying out the pros and cons on the economics and politics of the Bush capital gains proposal. He's early with "Treasury Developing Program to Address Third World Debt," 3-7, a timely report on Brady's debt relief approach, but with less detail than we looked for. Minimalist himself in "Justifying the 'Minimalist' Budget Pact," 4-16, we get a fair account of what happened at the White House Rose Garden bipartisan budget agreement ceremony, presenting it as, basically, little ado about not very much. Blustein's at his professional worst in "Bush Urged to Accept Tax 'Trade,'" 4-28, on a Camp David bull session, taking his sources out of context and thus coloring their perspectives. A column, "The Coming Capital Gains Compromise: Indexing Taxes to Inflation," 5-17, showcases Blustein's talent, nicely blending politics and economics, predicting that Congress and the White House will compromise on indexing capital gains for inflation rather than a lower tax rate. Blustein is frankly opinionated here, perfectly acceptable in a column, but not when it sneaks into Blustein's

news reports. "Compromise on Capital Gains Could Produce Some Pretty Weird Tax Policy," 6-14, follows the *WSJ*'s Alan Murray by a day in shilling for a one-year cut in the capgains tax. Travelling to the Orient, Blustein files "Japan's Old Guard Stops Front-Runner for Premier," 8-1, a very colorful rendition of a non-story, Blustein reporting on an event that did not happen: "With swift, ruthless finesse reminiscent of the shoguns, a small group of power brokers in Japan's ruling party today killed a bid by a relatively young politician to become the country's next prime minister." In an opinion column, "Waging the Argument for a Capital Gains Tax Cut on Its Merits," 10-4, Blustein makes a commendable run at challenging the administration arguments, point by point.

Boyd, John. *The Journal of Commerce.* (★ ½)
Domestic economy reporter. Boyd's analytics need some work, but we appreciate his willingness to dig beneath the surface of a story. We sometimes get data from him we don't find elsewhere, his facts alerting us to different trends in the economy, but it's rare we get a discussion of pros and cons of different policy prescriptions. Boyd effectively debunks the conventional picture of a slow-moving administration in "Bush Moves on Plan for the Economy," 1-30, but he skips over some pertinent details of Bush's "trial balloon," leaving us reassured that Bush is doing something, but a little hazy on what. "Programs Survive But May Face Cuts," 2-13, has Boyd seemingly wishing for a one-handed economist, as the administration and Congress jockey for position over the budget, a nice solid overview, but little more. In the "Economic Beat," 3-27, Boyd summarizes the week's monetary rumors and opinions, adequate and non-judgemental. With Keith Rockwell, Boyd interviews G-7 participants in "Test Case Sought for U.S. Debt Plan," 4-6, on their reading of Brady Plan possibilities, a good effort, with details we didn't see elsewhere. The 4-10 "Economic Beat" is also above average, with Boyd getting to Michael Boskin, who tells the *JofC* that "it would be foolish" to try to shrink the trade deficit by slowing the economy to cut imports. In "Fed Banks Call Economy Healthy," 5-2, Boyd alerts us to conditions suggesting a need for Fed ease, showing that he has some sense of what criteria may be appropriate. Detailed on debt restructuring in "Mexico Warns of Disruption in Bank Debt," 6-15, Boyd offers no source with a solution or information on the ultimate problem: how to stimulate the Mexican economy so it won't have to continually restructure foreign debt. We have a tough time caring about "CFTC Faces Fight Over 'Delisting' of Peoria," 8-25, on the Commodity Futures Trading Commission's consideration of dropping Peoria, IL, "as a point for the delivery of live cattle to satisfy futures contracts from Chicago," but Boyd makes it work, giving us a sense of the wrangling going on: "Illinois Rep. Edward Madigan has thrown his weight behind keeping Peoria at this time. He is the ranking GOP member of the House Agriculture Committee, the oversight panel for the CFTC."

Brimelow, Peter. *Forbes.* (★ ★ ½)
Senior editor. A Canadian who came to *Forbes* via Toronto's *Financial Post, The Wall Street Journal,* and *Barron's,* Brimelow is happiest when he is advancing startling, provocative ideas or innovations, a trumpeter of supply-side economics when it was most unfashionable. As one would expect, he frequently misses the mark, but in never knowing when, we always look him over. In "Tower or Trickle," 12-26-88, Brimelow's commentary and *Forbes*' graphics put the issue of debt burdens as a percentage of GNP into sharp perspective: "Today's interest burden actually represents about the same share of federal receipts as in the immediate pre-World War II years. . . .." But he includes questionable assertions about how the U.S. managed low interest rates in WWII, which were "an unconscionable rape of the people who saved and invested." He provides no great revelations after a trip to Moscow in "Empire of the Will," 1-9, describing the U.S.S.R. as a Third World economy that through sheer political will has become a superpower, reporting on the endemic shambles and scarcity, a standard overview. We get from him an offbeat profile of Murray Rothbard, a leader of the "Austrian" school of economics, in " 'No Water' Economics," 3-6, a smart presentation, putting Austrians in context relative to Keynesians and monetarists, but no word about supply-siders, although Rothbard seems to share some of their policy views. In "An End to Monetary Instability?" 4-3, Brimelow debates

an unorthodox idea, the privatization of the currency, looking at all kinds of different schemes (including a design by Richard Rahn, chief economist at the U.S. Chamber of Commerce), and goes on to explain how such a step might be both feasible and beneficial: "Banks could simply be freed from reserve requirements and other regulations, allowing them to make loans — in effect, to create money — according to their own judgement of risk." Delightfully insightful in talking to Lemuel R. Boulware, GE's labor negotiator in the '50s, Brimelow zips merrily along, cataloguing different "Boulwarism" anecdotes and giving a good sense of the 94-year-old gent's one-time management style, in "A Look Back at 'Boulwarism,' " 5-29: "He would not bargain, labor leaders complained. He would simply make whatever offer he had determined was in 'the balanced best interest' of company, work force, and consumer — and thereafter refused to budge." "How Do You Cure Intelligence?" 8-7, is a very lively sojourn with C. Northcote Parkinson of Parkinson's Law fame.

Brittan, Samuel. *Financial Times.* (★ ★ ★ ★)

The *FT*'s chief commentator on the world political economy. Brittan is consistently splendid in his analysis, remarkably flexible and inquisitive, moving among the array of economic models as easily as a fickle Lothario at a fancy ball. "Monetarism's Second Coming," 1-19, is a pragmatist's look at money in the U.K., encouragingly "applying common sense and one's knowledge of history" to the problems at hand, with Brittan cheerfully defining his own position at the outset: "It is quite possible to be a critic of post-war, so-called Keynesian, demand management and believe that inflation has monetary roots not amenable to wage or price controls or other treatment of symptoms. . .this is my own position, which can be described as classical, counter-revolutionary, 'low church monetarist' or by any other words which convey the flavour." Brittan's insight is appreciated in "Don't Count on a Soft Landing," 2-16, concerned but not alarmist, with the best categorizations of Nigel Lawson and counterpart Alan Greenspan we saw: "Mr. Lawson is perfectly entitled to be a growth optimist and Mr. Greenspan a growth pessimist. What is expected from both of them and others is to suppress their private hunches as much as humanly possible and concentrate on the movement of demand in nominal terms and its distribution between countries." Applicable to U.S. trade too, Brittan's analytics shine in "Teenager's Guide to UK Trade," 4-27, in which he demolishes mercantilist doctrine. "There will always be a flow of funds from countries with savings surpluses to others where the rate of return on new equipment exceeds the real rate of interest.─." and this is a healthy trend that ought to be appreciated as such. His "A Realistic Target for Price Stability," 5-11, is both esoteric and, at least to the initiated, lucid, predicting that U.K. inflation will fluctuate at 5 or 6 percent, "that attempts to keep it even as low as that will be painful in terms of lost output and employment, and that an attempt will be made to blame everyone for this outcome except those really responsible." Sharp political economics from Brittan in "Central Banks Come in From the Cold," 7-24, we get a superb historical overview from multiple countries, as New Zealand moves to give more power to set its central bank free, *a la* the Fed or Bundesbank, "as a more promising route to price stability than lobbying governments to adhere to one or other fashionable monetary rule." Brittan's informed and informative on the exodus from Eastern Europe, "Impact of Migration," 9-14, persuasively making the case that the flight of human capital away from Socialism is a net plus. Brittan just happens to be at the Fed when the stock drop occurred, "Fed Well Prepared for Wall Street Crash," 10-16, predicting Fed easing and strongly hinting his information comes from highest authority — Greenspan or confidants.

Broad, William J. *The New York Times.* (★ ★)

Science reporter. One of the mainstays at the "Science Times," Broad is capable of the finest reporting and presentation, careful and qualitative, and he usually delivers. He's less satisfying in drawing his material toward conclusiveness, at times leaving us wondering if he's worked the ground thoroughly. At his best, exacting digging pays off in "Pentagon Leaves the Shuttle Program," 8-7, an excellent report on a bonafide waste-in-government story on how the Air Force basically walked away from the manned shuttle program, preferring to rely on unmanned launch vehicles for spy satellites as a result of the Challenger disaster, with a price tag of $5 billion. An elaborately documented history of the military's relationship with NASA, which was calculating at best and frigid at worst, is complemented by a wide array of quotes, including Air Force types explaining why the service abandoned a nationwide complex of bases and programs to piggyback on the nation's manned space effort. In "Vital Gas for Nuclear Weapons Lies Untapped at Reactor Sites," 2-28, eventually tells us the government can build a plant for $90 million, but over what period and at what operating cost is not specified, unclear on just how much tritium can be recovered as well. His bias shows. In "Private Rocket Industry In Giant Step Skyward," 3-30, about the launch of a 630-lb. payload of "scientific experiments" developed at the U. of AL, Broad reports that the nation's aerospace giants are building mammoth vehicles for twenty private launches for more than $1 billion, yet provides no other details, reserving technical data for the last two paragraphs. He gives a marvelous look inside the politics of scientific grantsmanship in "House Panel Hears Debate on Fusion," 4-27, as scientists seek research grants for fusion. Despite the "strongly negative" consensus, Broad is careful to report on exceptions at the Santa Fe conference, leaving us with some hope for the Utah scientists in "At Conference on Cold Fusion, The Verdict Is Negative," 5-30. Broad misses an opportunity for an analysis of realistic prospects for success, in "U.S. Losing Ground In Worldwide Race For 'Hot' Fusion," 6-20, as the news is that the National Research Council, an advisory body to the government, said the U.S. has given the R&D lead to the Europeans, by a 50% cut in funds over the past decade, to only $350 million a year. In the laser fusion area ($164 million) the U.S. is still ahead, yet hampered by secrecy, the wisdom of building these big toys not dealt with. "Diverse Factors Propel Bush's Space Proposal," 7-30, is hampered by poor writing, and filled with anonymous quotes on a Bush speech in July supporting a stretched out plan to build a space station on the Moon followed by a trip to Mars. "A 30-Year Feud Divides Experts on Meteorology," 10-24, is engrossing on a clash of methodology re the greenhouse effect between two Wisconsin academics, but Broad never does tell us what they conclude.

Brookes, Stephen. *Insight.* (★ ½)
The *Insight* editors seem to be assigning Brookes to random topics trying to plumb his capabilities. For some reason he's able to deliver on the politics of Greece and scores with a report on international drug money laundering. Otherwise, he's feeling his way along, always at least readable without being pretentious or fuzzy. In "Trying to Stay Above Water as the Oil Market Slips Under," 12-19-88, he starts slowly, getting to the subject midway through, and there's little enough there. Then he provides solid, first-rate coverage of the GATT meeting in Montreal and the failure to negotiate the elimination of agricultural supports, "Free Trade on the Farm Reaps No Consensus From GATT," 1-9, touching all the bases, fairly impressive. He whets our appetite for things to come in "Papandreou's Tempestuous Voyage," 1-16, an intriguing look at scandals in Greek politics. In "Two New Blocs and Shifting Sands," 3-13, a feature on two Arab economic blocs that were evidently organized to counter "Fortress Europe" in 1992, we get a strong start, but he seems to lose his enthusiasm for the subject halfway through. "Greeks Fear Chaos if Papandreou Regime Collapses," *The Washington Times* 3-16, is an accurate, timely portrayal of a wobbling political culture entering a period of crisis, an informative composition of unfamiliar issues, personalities and features that make up the Greek political canvas. Brookes examines Third World debt and the Brady Plan in "Another Plan to Mop Up the Mess," 4-10, which makes a stab at spotting bank attempts to get at Western taxpayers for relief, quoting from John Makin of AEI, Jeffrey Sachs of Harvard, and Larry Sjaastad of Chicago, but he's struggling. In his "Europe: Birth of a Supernation" cover, 6-19, we get a well structured assessment of '92 integration, adequate for the casual reader, but he's clearly pulling this out of the general assignment bag. Perhaps reporting here laid the groundwork for "Drug Money Soils the Cleanest Hands," 8-21, a 10 Best nomination, with Brookes comprehensive on the heart of the drug operation — money laundering — as the launderers salivate over Europe's 1992 integration and the removal of currency controls: "They can all park their money in Germany, which is particularly obsessed with not touching the banks." In "Digging For Clues to the Revolution," 9-4, Brookes presents lots of detail on the excavation of Fort Independence in Vermont, but a quote that reads like an advertisement for the state tourism industry is jarring.

Brookes, Warren. *The Detroit News,* Creators Syndicate. (★ ★ ★ ★)
Now the only journalist who has gotten our top rating for all five editions of the *MediaGuide,*
Brookes continues to astonish us with his relentless determination to get to the bottom of things.
In '88, with the presidential campaign the big story of the year, Brookes almost single-handedly
defrocked the Democratic nominee on issues that determined the election. This year, with the
press corps looking sheepish on the environment, Brookes is again practically alone looking at
the flip side of acid rain and global warming. His acid rain series, *The Washington Times* 8-10,
8-13, and 8-17, is outstanding work, Brookes challenging this bogeyman with an onslaught of
facts, a 10 Best selection. We get another barrage in " 'Greenhouse Glasnost' at Sundance,"
WAT 8-24: "There must be something in the Utah air that makes people jump to premature
conclusions. Last March a pair of Utah scientists told us they had produced nuclear fusion with
cold water. Today Robert Redford, the Meryl Streep of climatology, kicks off a three-day
conference at Sundance, Utah, to warn the world about 'global warming' which many top
climatologists now worry could turn out to be the 'cold fusion' of meteorology." Brookes shows
a sharply genuine appreciation of Sen. Bill Bradley (D-NJ) as the outstanding Democratic
spokesman for the international pro-growth agenda, "Bill Bradley to the Rescue," *WAT* 1-5,
on open trade, stable exchange rates, and LDC debt relief. He blasts away in "Golden Parachutes
for Beltway Bandits," *WAT* 1-30, firing at a new congressional pay raise, including painful
statistics on pension payouts for former members of Congress who left under a cloud or served
time. Sharply critical, "The Rising Consumer Cost of Protectionism," *WAT* 4-24, Brookes
skewers U.S. Trade Rep. Carla Hills and Commerce Secretary Mosbacher. "Feeding sharks
tidbits only makes them more frenzied. Now Super 301 promises to be their main course."
Ferocious on trade, in "Treacherous Trade Move?" *WAT* 5-30, Brookes attacks with solid
information the protectionist "Super 301 trade retaliation list," warning that "if the economy
is to survive the high interest drubbing from the Federal Reserve, it must keep the export boom
going," reiterating Boskin's reasonable warning: ". . .the greatest threat to continued economic
expansion is a protectionist trade war." In "Pacific Rim Rising, Including the U.S." *WAT* 6-8,
he presents a provocative analysis from the Rand Corp., suggesting the U.S. focus on Pacific
strategic alliances in the '90s and let Europe "assume more of its own security concerns."
Excellent economic commentary, "Has the Fed's Recession Begun?" *WAT* 7-6, Brookes using
impressive, statistics-based arguments to warn that it is not the case that ". . .the Fed's planned
'soft landing' for the economy is going 'exactly according to plan.' If so, this will be the first time
in postwar history it ever was." In a meaty effort to draw conclusions on the impact of tax rate
reforms and vigor of entrepreneurial capitalists, "The Rise of Venture Capitalists," *WAT* 10-12,
Brookes looks at data compiled in a major study and persuasively extracts the trend.

Browne, Malcolm W. *The New York Times.* (★ ★ ½)
"Science Times" reporter. We were thrilled last year by Browne's report, 9-4-88, elevating
scientists skeptical of the greenhouse effect, and thought we might have finally found a science
reporter willing to take the guff that goes with challenging environmentalist theology. But for
some reason this year he steered clear of the hot political stuff. "In Protecting the Atmosphere,
Choices Are Costly and Complex," 3-7, he does present a close-to-comprehensive update on
CFCs, the kind of item that can be clipped and filed away for later reference, a 10 Best selection.
Our readers chide him for a common weakness of science reporters, using a secondary source
as a primary one, in "Diamond Coatings Grown on Silicon Chips," 2-28, citing the finding as
reported in *Science;* although we get a good overview of the uses of the coating written in
understandable terms, it doesn't look like Browne did much legwork on this one, besides
consulting his magazine. In "Chemists Create A New State of Matter: One Molecule Inside
Another," 3-21; based on an interview with a Nobel Prize chemist at UCLA about a nice piece
of pure stereo-chemistry, we appreciate Browne attempting to suggest practical applications,
even though this might detract a bit from the pure joy of the achievement. "Radar Could Have
Tracked Tanker," 4-5, is flawed by the omission of any discussion of what traffic control system
is in place, and how the system might be changed, using radar or not. Browne culls a key
observation from Dr. Howard P. Furth that other reporters seem to have overlooked on fusion,

"7,000 Scientists Cheer Fusion-in-Jar Experiment," 4-13: "There is no point in trying to learn the truth by polling scientists. What's needed is a great deal more scientific work." In "Researchers Enlist Bacteria To Do Battle With Oil Spill," 5-23, we get some new methods of using microbes against toxic chemicals, but failing to mention a time scale to indicate how artificial methods compare with a clean-up by nature. Browne trumpets the use of new materials in the manufacture of tanks, "Plastics and Ceramics Replace Steel as the Sinews of War," 7-18, fascinates on what works and is plainly stated. We wish he would have examined the utility of tank warfare as well, but perhaps that's not his turf (though he does tell us the nature of tank warfare has changed since WWI). Eminently readable, Browne catches and transmits the gee-whiz nature of his topic in "Radio System Uses Fiery Meteor Trails to Transmit Data," 8-22, but we're somewhat disappointed to find this technology is most useful in remote wilderness areas for battlefield communications in a nuclear war after all conventional radio satellites and communications are off the air.

Bulkeley, William M. *The Wall Street Journal.* (★ ½)
Boston. Less and less able to keep up with some of the hotshots on the computer beat, Bulkeley is adequate, informative, but too seldom breaking new ground. His dispatches on the finances of the computer giants and small fries just don't inspire; the necessary elements are usually present and accounted for, however. Bulkeley's cursory analytics in "Digital to Unveil Workstations, Personal Computers Next Week," 1-3, offers a smattering of perceptions on the chances of success for Digital's venture, with some industry repercussions, but there's no overall sense of where these new products will fit in. "Shane Riding Into Sunset as Troubles Hit Leading Edge," 2-2, is pretty mysterious and we get few answers from Bulkeley as Michael Shane sells Leading Edge Products to PC Systems for a mere $921,000 amid a cash crunch. Bulkeley's confusing, without enough background, in "Prime Computer Upheld in Request For Data on Drexel," 3-30; we don't even get a read on how far-reaching the federal appeals court decision concerning Drexel's disclosure of additional financial information before a subsidiary can acquire Prime Computer. Standard in "Xylogics Estimates Profit Fell 40% For Its Second Period," 5-15, Bulkeley gets all the right pieces, but the pieces don't add up to much, as he relies only on interviews with the CEO, Bruce Bergman, and CFO, Vincent Salvi, with no feedback from the computer makers who buy the boards made by Xylogics. His P. 1 leder, "Long a U.S. Province, Supercomputer Market Feels a Japanese Threat," 5-24, offers move and countermove at Cray Research Inc., a difficult subject well handled. "In Its Liquidity Crisis, Wang Labs Could Face Loss of Independence," 7-14, Bulkeley covers Wang's precarious finances, reviewing growth and stumbles, good graphs in this well-researched piece. A profile of Wang's new COO, Richard W. Miller, "Wang Labs Names Computer Novice President and Chief Operating Officer," 8-24, doesn't compute; Bulkeley gives us little idea of what Miller is like, or what he is likely to do specifically, instead telling us what other Wang personnel think of him. Bulkeley adequately tracks the performance of selected software manufacturers, "Results Mixed for Software, Computer Firms," 10-9, getting most of the numbers, but he's not evaluative at all, leaving us to figure out whether the plus and minus numbers are due to good or bad products or good or bad marketing, with only the citation of Ashton-Tate's dBase IV an exception.

Burgess, John. *The Washington Post.* (★ ★)
Computers and telecommunications. Burgess' international experience gives an added zing to his reports. Interrupted briefly on the business beat by events in Tiananmen Square, Burgess didn't miss a step. He's timely in "Japanese Securities Firms Hit Bumps on Wall Street," 1-29, offering broad detail on how the Big Four have fared since the crash, but focusing too much on how many bodies have been cut, and not much on why there is such a considerable loss. In a potentially explosive story about West German computer hackers who may have passed on data to Moscow, "Race to Secure Computers Threatens Free Exchange of Data," 3-4, Burgess notes this "could prove to be the first confirmed instance of Soviet computer espionage." He does a nice job updating a tired journalistic dilemma, i.e., the needs of an open society versus national security concerns. He points out that computer safeguards are being devised, becoming a high-

growth industry, but this piece deserved better placement than a Saturday Business section. In "Growth Stirs East Asia's Winds of Change," 5-24, former Tokyo correspondent Burgess offers excellent analysis early on of the brewing political trends: "Remarkable as [the Chinese demonstrators'] revolt may be, it is not taking place in isolation, but is part of a general push toward greater political freedom over most East Asia. . .in most cases, a common force can be found reinforcing the push for new political freedoms: rapid economic growth, or, in a few cases, the lack of it." From Beijing, Burgess files "China Says Hundreds of Protesters Held," 6-11, collected morsels of information in the midst of the press blackout, to weave an informative picture of how the government's repression campaign is methodically unfolding. Burgess continues in "Climate of Fear Grips China," 6-16, solid reporting on the unfolding Chinese government campaign of intimidation, including a poignant selection of sad vignettes from everyday life. Burgess examines the yin and yang of the transaction, "Japan's Phone Company To Buy AT&T Equipment," 7-11, the good news that Japan's phone company plans to buy $154 million worth of advanced telephone equipment from AT&T, the bad that the sale "will facilitate putting calls, video images, fax messages and computer data on one national 'digital' network, could help Japan move ahead of the United States in modernizing its telecommunications system." "FCC Presses 'Indecency' Fight," 10-27, zips merrily along, citing different radio stations fined, and the legislation that lead up to FCC action, for once propelled along by someone other than Sen. Jesse Helms or Sen. Albert Gore, whose wife, Tipper, heads up the PMRC. Burgess looks at how Japanese-owned banks are winning customers in California, "New Wave in California," 11-12, a well-structured, comprehensive management piece.

Bylinsky, Gene. *Fortune.* (★ ★ ½)
More than 25 years on this beat, Bylinsky keeps grappling with complex issues on the frontiers of science and bringing them home in simple language. Steady and confident, he doesn't get splashy play in *Fortune,* but he is a dependable resource. His workmanlike, thorough hand shows in "A Quantum Leap in Electronics," 1-30, as he explores the development of a new theory of electron behavior that "is about to set off a transformation of everyday electronics as profound as the one begun forty years ago when the transistor replaced the vacuum tube." Bylinsky's imaginative in "Managing with Electronic Maps," 4-24, showing how industries from paper to caribou tracking are using graphic imaging to make huge increases in efficiency; the excellent photos of the electronic images by Robert Holmgren round out the coverage and make the story shine. In "Fusion's Future: It Ain't Dead Yet," 6-5, the veteran science writer brings a calm and assured touch to the fusion controversy, aided by good graphics and sidebars. He frequently takes the contrarian role, so it is no surprise to see him bullish on the Utah discoveries at just about the same time that the press is pulling back and the science establishment is debunking the startling discoveries. Held back by poor presentation, "What A Way to Start A Company!" 6-19, disappoints on Smith-Kline's investment of $70 million into Nova Pharmaceutical on a concept. "Where Japan Will Strike Next," 9-25, opens strongly: "If you think you have seen surprises from Japan, stick around. Responding to fire-breathing challenges from Korea and other growing Asian dragons, the folks who brought you the Walkman, the VCR, and the Honda are readying a new assault. Primed with an arsenal of high-tech products from filmless cameras to mid-engine sports cars, they are also preparing to branch out across the globe in services from credit cards to construction." Bylinsky then goes on to tell us all about it without miring us in technical jargon or being overly protectionist.

Byrne, John. *BusinessWeek.* (★ ★ ★)
Associate editor. Byrne last year scored with one of the 10 Best business pieces, "The Best B-Schools," 11-28-88, and then spent most of this year on leave, turning it into a book we await. The fellow has considerable talent, as he showed again before departure, on the management beat. We cite him for three superlative covers he did early in the year. Byrne continues to find new twists and angles in his coverage of executive recruiters (he wrote a book on the subject in 1987) in "The New Headhunters," cover 2-6. Here his catchy lead-in is the high-powered search for a CEO at the newly LBO'd RJR Nabisco, which he compares to seeking the actress to play

Scarlett O'Hara. Byrne catches some great color with Henry Kravis and the man he's commissioned to find the new executive, Thomas Neff of Spencer Stuart & Associates, bringing the reader inside this small and arcane business of "top gun" searches and demonstrates Byrne's insider understanding of this topic. He's breezy in "Is Your Company Too Big?" cover 3-27, as he extols the benefits of smaller, more nimble corporations, a counterpoint to the merger boom. Of sixty-seven industries ranked by *Business Week,* Byrne notes, only four were both the biggest and most profitable, as measured by return on equity, catching the overflow from the *Harvard Business Review* debate between pro-small George Gilder and MIT's anti-small Charles Ferguson cited in the '89 *MediaGuide.* Byrne's article is a fresh and lively treatment of an old chestnut topic that has become pertinent again. In "Is the Boss Getting Paid Too Much?" 5-1 cover, Byrne avoids cliched answers in *BW*'s 39th annual survey of executive compensation, adequately addressing the question at hand, but not really answering it, leaving the reader to draw his own conclusions.

Byron, Christopher. *New York.* (★ ★)
"The Bottom Line" columnist. Formerly an assistant managing editor at *Forbes,* Byron came aboard midyear, an improvement over predecessors John Crudele and Dan Dorfman. He takes one subject and runs with it, rather than chopping up his columns as Crudele did. Byron is also able to dissect complicated financial and legal issues, paring them down to their parts and putting them in perspective. Byron's report on the 1985 failure of the Bowery Savings Bank and its subsequent bailout is timely both due to the S&L crisis and the mayoral race, as primary candidate Richard Ravitch "pocketed somewhere between $3 and $10 million" for putting the deal together, "Bowery Follies," 5-29, an admirable effort, clearly presented. Byron's less organized in "Is Getting Rich Quick Becoming A Crime?" 6-12, although he makes a game go at trying to sort out the case of Paul Bilzerian, arrested for allegedly "setting out to fleece some investors, even though he made them richer instead." He gets his act together in "The RICO Squeeze," 7-17, putting together a complicated story of five Princeton/Newport partners and former Drexel trader Bruce Newberg charged with RICO violations, *and* explaining RICO history and forfeiture provisions, all in plain English. Byron sniffs out new information on the IRS, amid new allegations that the agency is a fish rotting from the midsection, if not the head, "The IRS Follies," 8-7.

Carley, William M. *The Wall Street Journal.* (★ ★ ★)
New York. Bracing the world against terror in the air, we get more from Carley's dispatches on airline safety and terrorist tactics than anyone else. As much detective as reporter, Carley is a bloodhound when it comes to his subjects, but he appears too infrequently. We'd like to see more from him, perhaps on different safety features, as the year has shown there's more than one way for a jet to go down. We appreciate this expert look in "Wing Flap: Contractor's Mishaps in New Technology Made the Navy Seethe," 1-11, Carley taking us through the story of wing problems due to metal fatigue in the Navy's A-6s made by Boeing, without losing us in technical jargon. He sleuths in "Terrorist Blueprint: Sophisticated Bombs Like One in Lockerbie Prove Hard to Detect," 2-22, meticulously tracing the steps of Mohammed Rashid and his pursuers, culminating ultimately in his 1988 arrest for a 1982 bombing, carefully documenting all his evidence and relating his tale to the Lockerbie bombing as the explosives used in both cases were similar. He follows the debate over alerting passengers to potential terrorist attacks, "Terrorism Alerts: The FAA's Dilemma," 4-3, vividly capturing the quandary of FAA and airline officials, and compellingly describing the consequences of a tragic mistake over Lockerbie: "When the bomb exploded, at 31,000 feet, it blew a hole in the left side just big enough so that the plane's nose canted slightly to the right. Caught by the wind rushing by at about 500 miles an hour the nose swung violently to the right as if on a giant hinge. Then the nose, containing the cockpit and forward passenger cabin, snapped off completely. Pieces of the plane began plummeting toward earth." Marvelous reporting in "Airline Security Offers Only Weak Protection Against Bombs On Jets," 5-10, Carley's troubled only by a few bumps in this presentation on the state-of-the-art in preventing terrorists from smuggling bombs aboard

aircraft. Sympathetic in "Legacy of Terror: Lockerbie Bombing Of Pan Am Flight 103 Bred Anger and Fear," 7-7, Carley takes moving snapshots of the survivors, and the different ways they are coping with grief. Carley updates the latest terrorist bomb tactics in "Keeping Terrorist's Bombs Off Airplanes," 7-28, reviewing the safety measures implemented by carriers, including a ban on Halawi candy as explosives can be fashioned to fit inside the tin. Carley retains his sense of humor, pointing out that bans on certain objects that can be imitated by a plastic explosive device might be impractical by quoting one security official: "Have you ever tried to take a hair dryer or curling iron away from a woman?" Putting his fedora and trenchcoat back on for "Study in Terror: How Asian Schoolgirl Tutored in Espionage Became Bomber of Jet," 10-12, Carley probes the saga of Kim Hyon-hui, responsible for the 1987 bombing of KAL flight 858, filled with inside tidbits and information on Kim's life, motivations, and the bombing itself.

Carroll, Paul B. *The Wall Street Journal.* (★ ★ ½)
New York, computers, especially Big Blue. Substantial work this year, Carroll's able to turn the most mundane product release announcements into effective reports by his consistent digging. He's timely in "The Data Game: Unisys Chief Is Facing Hard Job as Company and Industry Falter," 3-31, a leder detailing the problems at Unisys and the general lethargy of the computer industry, profiling Unisys CEO Mike Blumenthal, a Shanghai ex-patriot and ex-Treasury chief. Carroll handles a spot news item extremely well, "IBM Names Kuehler President, Recognizing His Role in Technology," 5-31, putting the appointment of a new IBM president in a broader context and showing that Kuehler is not a likely successor as CEO, but is a likeable guy with a firm grasp of technology and manufacturing issues. "Smart Cards Are Getting A Lot Smarter," 6-26, is a tasty and useful overview of the move towards charge cards in a host of new applications — movie theatres, highway toll booths, railroad yards; while there's little new here, Carroll compacts the story admirably into a quick readable format, with lots of leads for the reader who wants to dig deeper. A routine financial story, takes on a sharper focus in Carroll's hands, "Xerox Says it Plans to Buy Back 11% of its Stock and Set Up an ESOP," 7-11, as he shrewdly points out that this is an anti-takeover move in the long-running saga of Xerox to avoid raiders. Carroll gives us the background on what strategists see in Xerox's break-up value. In "IBM Agrees to Purchase a 19.8% Stake in Policy Management for $116.5 Million," 7-27, Carroll takes the reader beyond a routine news story. On the surface, IBM is making a routine acquisition of a software firm for a tiny price, but he shows how IBM is wheeling and dealing to take positions in all sorts of companies, and he brings in testimony from third-party vendors. "Calculated Move: Computer Firms Find Service is What Sells, Not Fancier Hardware," co-written by John R. Wilke 8-15, presents some good examples of companies specializing in what they do best and contracting out things like their computer operations. Carroll's savvy shows in "IBM Unveils Products To Speed Writing of Mainframe Software," 9-20, reporting on a big move by IBM to standardize mainframe software programming and a terrible bottleneck in corporate development, and with depth and clarity pinpointing the problem: most programming is done with languages that are 31 years old, and programmers average just ten lines of code per day. An A-hed, "Dear Dad: At Last, Your Boy's Become a Real Professional," 4-12, is a classic, Carroll going to training camp for professional wrestlers and taking his lumps as the "Wall Street Warrior," dazzled when kids ask him for an autograph after a match: "It occurs to me that this never happened following any of the stories I've written as part of my day job covering the computer industry." He's the first *WSJ* reporter pictured bare-chested on page one.

Charlier, Marj. *The Wall Street Journal.* (★ ★ ½)
Dallas. Charlier is a good storyteller, weaving together information with insight. At times light on the numbers, her dispatches sometimes lack specifics that we'd like to see. She's interesting but not persuasive in "Outflanked Steak: The U.S. Beef Industry Just Can't Seem To Get the Hang of Marketing," 1-4, lacking quotes from cattlemen or pros and cons from economists, but with otherwise okay details. She clearly lays things out in "Patient Money, United States Firms Find Asian Investors Are Willing To Wait for Returns," 2-24, explaining that foreign investment

helps U.S. create new jobs, new technologies and new entrepreneurs, timely as the Bryant bill, H.R. 5, to require filing of statements by foreign investors not required by U.S. companies circulates in Congress. Charlier brings us into "At Least It's Better Than Debating Which Has the Fewest Jobs," 3-14, with a strong opening: "You'd think Texas and Louisiana, what with the oil bust and economic despair, would be humbled enough to quit bragging for a while. Think again." She then goes on to detail the rivalry between the states over their quality of respective crawfish, a delightful feature, with many figures wittily reported: Louisiana "sells 100 million pounds of crawfish a year, making Texas' output of 10 million pounds look shrimpy." More serious in "Court Sides With Penny Stock Broker," 4-14, Charlier draws her lines carefully around the legal and financial aspects of the SEC case, neatly tying up the loose ends as much as she can at the close. "Proposed Denver Airport: Essential or Extravagant?" 5-16, is sharp in debating the new airport, pointing out that traffic is down 14% from last year and 25% of the current airport's 110 gates are vacant, tough on all the problems, but there's little coverage of the benefits here. Her best we saw this year, a P. 1 leder, "Labor of Love: How A Mine in Arizona Wooed Workers Away From Union Loyalties," 8-8, is an incredible story, indicative of an important trend in labor-management relations, as these workers, unionized 50 years, reject union representation in response to the company's new approach to labor relations. Management's motivation: "We wanted to get communications going better so we could find ways to running the mine better" and "miners saw their unions as big businesses themselves, more interested in self-preservation than in helping the little guy."

Chase, Marilyn. *The Wall Street Journal.* (★ ★)
San Francisco, covering health issues and Silicon Valley. Chase nails down her dispatches, keeping incendiary information to a minimum, particularly important on her beat as she deals with AIDS so frequently. Her style is still upbeat, but we're finding a dryness we didn't notice before. She's brief but provides adequate detail with "Genentech Enters Venture for Drugs To Prevent Clots," 1-11, as Genentech announces a joint venture with Mitsubishi to develop a drug for the prevention and treatment of deep vein thrombosis. "Businessland Inc., To Enter Computer Rental Business," 1-24, is crisp, thorough, the firm getting its plans for expansion and defining the competition; the computer rental market has already been developed by Computerland and Computer Factory. In "Bad Chemistry: Mixing Science, Stocks Raise Question of Bias In the Testing of Drugs," 1-26, is an excellent front-pager, documenting plenty of cases plus comments pro and con, enough quotes to give life to her story on different kinds of conflicts of interest in the scientific fields. Chase is solid in "Miscues Prevent Drug for Blindness Tied to AIDS From Being Cleared," 2-10, without being too technical in explaining how a Syntex drug is believed to prevent a blinding retinal infection related to a type of herpes virus. Syntex had hoped for FDA approval under a compassionate NDA, but was turned down in October 1987 because the agency considered the trials sloppy. Chase files a good roundup on research of AIDS drugs in "Homing In: Science Edges Closer to Designing Drugs to Defeat AIDS Virus," 3-3, placing the emphasis on rational design, and relating new information. A 10 Best nominee, "Paradise Lost: Heartbreaking Scenes Of Beauty Disfigured Follow Alaska Oil Spill," co-authored by Ken Wells 3-31, is everything we looked for, told in compelling detail: at Eleanor Island, thirty miles from where the Exxon supertanker ran aground and spilled crude oil into Prince William Sound, oil carried by the tides has produced a 12-ft. brown ring along the beach; and that despite assurances by Alyeska Pipeline Service Co., "the black tide of oil is now out of control." In "AIDS Agency Asks Risk Groups to Get Tests Voluntarily," 4-21, she gets views from all sides, giving a brief history of diagnosis, treatment, and prevalence, as the San Francisco AIDS Foundation launches a campaign appealing to everyone at risk to be tested. She makes good use of statistics with "Up To One-Third of IV Drug Users Carry AIDS Virus," 5-12, but there's little extra here. "Shock Troops: Activists Risk-Takers May Gain Legitimacy In The War on AIDS," 7-28, is compelling reading, as the terminal nature of AIDS coupled with the sluggishness and small scale of clinical trials has led grass roots groups to start unapproved treatments on their own, containing interviews with participants as well as NIH officials and researchers in approved clinicals. Simply reporting on the NIH study, "Big AZT Study Says Drug Slows Onset of AIDS," 8-4, Chase does a credible job, clearly reporting the news with comments from all sides of the equation.

Commins, Kevin. *The Journal of Commerce.* (★ ★)
A utility reporter, Commins seems reliable and competent on nearly every subject *The Journal of Commerce* covers. He's shy on analytics, though, rarely trying his hand at putting the pieces together for us. Commins' wit comes through in the lead of "Barge Lines Dispute IC Low River Report," 1-5, a serious discussion of the possibility of long term weather trends which "threaten to undermine the viability" of the Mississippi river transport system: "After decades of skirmishes over antitrust issues and waterway maintenance, barge lines and railroads have something new to argue about — the weather." He provides relevant facts, but little analysis of the effects of the measure he describes in "Wis. Bill Aims To Limit Rating by Territory," 2-10, as the state legislature prepares to vote on a bill prohibiting the inclusion of residency as a factor in determining auto insurance rates. In "Currency Traders Ready to Test Central Banks," 3-30, he ventures tentatively into analysis, tiptoeing through the various actions of the different G-7 banks and checking potential moves on the chessboard, but doesn't make any predictions as to cause and effect. He describes the rush for internal reform at the Chicago Mercantile Exchange before the Feds force the CME into it, "CME Recommends Floor Trading Reforms," 4-20, in the wake of allegations of impropriety and a Federal investigation, allowing his source, CME Special Counsel Lee Melamed, to make the story for him: "There's a perception that we're too clubby. That the public doesn't know what goes on in our disciplinary committees." A quirky, entrepreneurial germ pays off with "Insurers Plan Computer Virus Coverage," 6-8, Commins' humorous side showing again, without detracting from the quality or amount of information he presents, a delightful feature. Commins gets beyond the press release with "Hungarian Glass Expands Exports With Joint Venture Inked in U.S.," 7-21, hinting at further capitalist ventures to come.

Cook, James. *Forbes.* (★ ½)
Executive editor. Cook is a company man through and through, both for *Forbes* and the subjects he covers, mostly companies that deal in environmental equipment or technology. He's quick and accurate, but avoids most of the traps connected with this kind of beat by going easy on the scientific side, focusing instead on the business. As a result, we at times come away feeling we've only read half the story. In "Warming Trend," 2-20, a promising business piece, Cook doesn't suggest solar power for more than "peaking" power usage, but fails to address whether or not this is competitive. Catching gambling fever early, Cook examines the pluses and minuses in state-run lotteries, "Lottomania," 3-6, a sweeping perspective with insight we didn't find in the wake of the Pete Rose episode, Cook pointing out that small businesses who sell lottery tickets are as much winners as the states, and the trickle-down effects are good for everybody. Cook details the strategies of Transcanada Pipeline with "Back From the Dead," 4-3, which has benefited from firmer conditions in the gas supply, bringing Alberta gas into the industrial Midwest. The company tried to become an integrated producer-transporter, but the pipeline business now looks better than production, so again a reversal of strategy. Cook makes an effort to justify cogeneration in technical terms in "The Profits In Hot Water," 4-17, but he skims over the fact that it is heavily based on legislation that forces the utilities to buy the power and he skips entirely a technical explanation of land-fill methane except to cite an O'Brien Energy Systems statement. An obvious analytic ending to " 'We're Still Harnessing Power,' " 5-29, a quick snapshot of Stewart & Stevenson, which went from horses to horsepower in products and services, has us smirking: "You could, of course, say that Stewart & Stevenson was lucky to have the right products at the right time. But there has to be more than good luck in moving logically from horseshoes to power cogeneration. It's called good management." Cook skims the technical end of S&S as well, although he does get a quick peek at their balance sheet. He begins solidly on the natural gas bubble, "Unrealistic Expectations," 6-12, but he segues into a commercial for natural gas and never quite recovers his footing: "Gas is cleaner and easier to handle than coal, cheaper and more abundant than oil, and given that it's a combustible fuel, it's virtually pollution free. Low nitrogen oxide, lower sulfur dioxide, not even much carbon dioxide. So if you're worried about acid rain, the greenhouse effect, nuclear waste or the Valdez oil spill, gas is the fuel for you." In "From Coal to Water," 8-7, he investigates the management and turnaround of Eastern Enterprises, which had more difficulty dealing with obsolescence than his earlier subject, Stewart & Stevenson, avoiding cliches and easy answers and telling his story clearly.

Cooper, James C. & Madigan, Kathleen. *Business Week.* (★)
"Business Outlook" columnists. The information from the team is solid, and we often mine the column for the little nuggets of information they provide that we don't necessarily see elsewhere. The perspective, however, tends to be ever-so-slightly off-kilter, in need of finer tuning from an editor somewhere, especially important since the team doesn't have an analytic framework in which to work. For a week-to-week short range look at the numbers, though, this is the column to be reading. In "Is a Distant Early Warning of Inflation Flashing," 1-30, the pair gives a cautious account of the discordant signals on inflation, presenting numbers without forecasting. Similarly in "Inflation Is Lurking — But Greenspan Is on the Case," 2-6, sorts through the statistics, reporting on Fed chairman Alan Greenspan's testimony before the House Banking Committee, talking tough, but the duo is still clearly worried, the view clouding some predictions on construction that follow. The twosome is okay in assembling official stats, "With the Economy Gathering Steam, Prices Are in a Pressure Cooker," 3-6, but working without a clear matrix, they can't support the headline: "The economy may begin to show signs of slower growth in the second half of the year. And that could become even more pronounced as inflation pressures force the Fed to raise interest rates further." "Slower Growth? The Jury Still Can't Reach a Verdict," 5-15, is more numbers, mishmashed together, the pair not knowing what the heck is going on. In "The Fed May Stop Tinkering for a While," 8-28, Cooper & Madigan tell us consumers are at it again, showing a "willingness to keep spending" they didn't have earlier in the year, obviously relieved at the upturn. Even happier, "The Sleigh Ride Should Last Clear Through Christmas," 9-18, we get a happy Christmas early, with numbers and analysis slightly off-center, but still okay, the pair never attributing the slowdown and pick-up in consumer spending to the much-hyped yuppie pay-back and spend-off.

Cordtz, Dan. *Financial World.* (★ ½)
Chief correspondent. Switching from television to print when most journalists are heading in the other direction, Cordtz is still measuring his words in sound bites. Often too cursory, he flounders in some of his longer pieces; he also tends to go for the lowest common denominator, making his analysis, where it appears, conventional. In "The Gravy Drain," cover 1-24, Cordtz says "too many Americans are retiring too early." The question is how much longer the nation can afford it," but we waited in vain for him to put his finger on any flaw in the present system. A pleasant surprise, "Dropouts Retrieving America's Labor Lost," 4-4, showcasing his ability to ferret out new information on alternative education programs, was appreciated. There's a broad range of programs boasting a measure of success, sponsored by business, etc., examined within, credibly treated, before the topic got hot. Expanding on his 4-4 dispatch, he takes a closer look at business-sponsored training programs to make up for what employees have missed in school, taking Motorola as a case in point, but he never asks how the students feel. "Detroit's Catch-22," 6-27, gives the history of Detroit's safety record and fight against self-improvement, containing some detail, but he comes to no conclusions as to industry progress: it "seems, in many respects, to have improved." His editors nominate his "World War II: The Economic Aftermath," cover 10-17, for our 10 Best section. The material celebrates some of the socioeconomic benefits of the war, asserting that going overseas may have helped a generation of businessmen to prepare for international trade and a global economy, the "pent-up demand" that sparked the post-war economy, the Marshall Plan for Europe. But this is all rather superficial, relying on 40-year-old reminiscences of oldtimers who were up-and-comers in the late '40s. Not a word of the most important underlying changes: the Bretton Woods agreements on postwar money and trade, reciprocal trade agreements, Ludwig Erhard's German miracle, postwar tax cuts.

Cowan, Alison Leigh. *The New York Times.* (★ ★ ½)
"Business Day" reporter, management. Sparkling treatments of interesting topics carries her sometimes slender material a long way. We're always entertained, but frequently think it both tastes great and is less filling. In "Trend In Pregnancies Challenges Employers," 4-17, Cowan offers an enlightening look at the differing ways management deals with maternity, but never

mentions male leave, which is beginning to become part of the landscape. Very good for what's there. "Favorite Things: Timesavers All," 5-10, is a wonderful fluff piece on the things we can't do without and why, like microwaves and VCRs; silly and frothy, she does a good job of it. Buoyant in "Meek and Mumblers Learn Ways of Getting a Word In," 5-29, Cowan outlines the different courses offered for those who wish to overcome a fear of interaction or public speaking. Cowan reports that *Harvard Business Review* lost circulation and ad revenues as Theodore Levitt almost doubled the subscription rates, but the net is a profit increase, "Harvard's Shrewd 'Blunder,' " 7-30. She needs a bit more from editors on the shifting philosophy of the magazine, content as well as style. Cowan turns to more weighty business matters later in the year, "Accounting's Era of Change Brings Growing Conflicts," 11-13, a comprehensive look at the effects different conflicts of interest have on the accounting field, with some delicious anecdotes and cynical observations.

Crossen, Cynthia. *The Wall Street Journal.* (★ ★)
New York, publishing. A mainstay on the Marketing & Media pages, Crossen rarely suffers from writer's block. She covers diverse angles, frequently scoring with them. In "First Books Were Books, Then Tapes; Now Disks?" 1-18, she describes how SoftServ Publishing will publish original fiction on computer, with customers buying software to decode the encoded text, sent by modem, and display it on a computer screen, taking it on the road. Standard but thorough on "Magazines Use Free Copies to Attract Readers," 2-13, as general interest periodicals are using targeted lists of different demographic characteristics to attract readers and, thusly, advertisers. Going beyond the standard, "Reader's Digest Will Sell Shares to the Public," 5-26, Crossen nails down some pertinent facts: "the company had been sitting on a time bomb. Because of tax laws, the two Wallace funds [trusts established by the late founders] must reduce their holdings to 50% or less of the voting stock by the year 2000." Frothy in an A-hed, "A Craze of the '20s Makes a Comeback, Even in Manhattan," 8-4, she zips merrily along, playing through this congenial feature on miniature golf by taking us over the greens and through the rough of Manhattan's first course, financed, naturally, by Donald Trump. (She warns prospective players in advance that they are expected to return the pencils provided.) "Hard Choices: In Today's Adoptions, The Biological Parents Are Calling the Shots," 9-14, is a brisk, clear-cut guide to the business of adoption in the '80s, with some inkling of what things will be like in the '90s, but Crossen doesn't examine other alternatives to couples seeking to adopt, such as overseas adoptions.

Cushman, John H., Jr. *The New York Times.* (★ ½)
Washington. Moving from the national security beat to business regulation, Cushman uses his experience to ferret out obtuse issues, but loses half a step in transition. An ideal story for him would have been to give him exclusive rights to the Pentagon procurement scandal, but instead his editors assigned him odds and ends. He begins "Piedmont Jet Loses Engine in Chicago," 1-20, with a quick perusal of the events at O'Hare, broadening his view to examine other incidents, linking a crash in England to the Chicago incident by model and make similarities and differences. Terse in "U.S. Voices Dismay on Release of Hijacking Warning," 3-24, he walks a fine line as he reports the leak of a hijack tip released by the British press, his sentiments expressed by the parent of one of the Lockerbie victims: "They either protect us or they warn us. Right now, they're doing neither." "Tougher Fuel Economy Rules Planned, in Shift From Reagan," 4-15, is given P. 1 play, but he offers rather sparse comment and detail considering the importance of the issue. Nor does he adequately illustrate how the traffic control system works in "Coast Guard Officer Defends Traffic Controllers in Oil Spill," 5-21, except to say that the controllers don't instruct skippers on their course and speed, just the presence of hazards, leaving us with many questions. Adding together more pieces from the United Sioux City crash, "In Iowa's Corn and Bean Fields, Clues to Jet Crash," 7-25, Cushman intrigues, keeping our interest in the detail without bogging down in technical jargon. Cushman is on the mark, analytic, without being editorial in "Opposition Is Slowing Drug Testing Programs for Transport Workers," 8-21. Adequately reviewing concerns attending proposed takeovers of Northwest and United, Cushman only gives half the story in "Airline Debt, Foreign Investors Worry Washington," 9-24, his analysis light, missing a recession scenario for example.

Dentzer, Susan. *U.S.News & World Report.* (★ ★)
Senior editor, economics. Dentzer stays away from tough policy analytics preferring to do solid, but compacted articles. Even so, she periodically comes up with an insight we appreciate. "Medicare's Sickbed," 2-6, cautions that there are real costs to deficit reduction as far as cutting Medicare is concerned, without being biased. In a profile of Treasury Secretary Nicholas Brady, "The Pick-and-Shovel Work of Nick Brady," 3-20, Dentzer's quick-witted, noting presciently that Brady's "abilities as a policymaker will clearly be overshadowed by Bush's budget director, Richard Darman, who holds the purse strings." Timely, Dentzer does a nice job with "The People Tax Reform Left Behind," 4-17, on the unintended problems caused by tax reform, especially for the elderly, with good use of quotes by experts, though she's skewed in some of her assertions ("the prospect of still higher taxes later will deter today's workers from saving for their retirement") and passes over the budget deficit. "Trade's Most Wanted List," with Mike Tharp 5-22, examines the Super 301 list of free trade violators which was due to be released on May 30 and the implications of Japan and South Korea being on that list; the process and policy are nicely explained, but violators' retaliations aren't discussed. Stories of the afflicted add to "The Network of Life and Death," 6-19, as she focuses on the politics involved in providing health care to AIDS patients, interesting, but we've heard much of this before. Poorly presented, "How Soft a 'Soft Landing?' " 8-14, she loses us halfway through on the possibility of a recession, with some backwards theories on how some sections of the economy might actually benefit from a recession. Back to Medicare with "Rx For Rising Costs," 9-11, we get the reasons for and against the planned Medicare drug reimbursement system and its national computerized prescription network. Her explanation of the program, the reasons behind it, and its possible effects is easy to follow and informative, using quotes well.

Deutsch, Claudia. *The New York Times.* (★ ★)
Sunday "Business" reporter. Deutsch's lively style snaps with enthusiasm, from root beer to RJR, and we enjoy seeing her byline atop the Sunday business section, knowing we'll get a good read. She doesn't produce many heavyweight pieces, though, and might think of setting her subjects on broader canvases. She's vivid in "A&W: Prospering by Avoiding the Big Boys," 1-15, well written and with good angles and numbers, but were thirsty for more on the cream-soda story, and the potential for the business. "Whirlpool Is Gathering a Global Momentum," 4-23, lightly skims the changes and challenges facing the world's largest major appliance maker as it goes global. Deutsch's investigation of products which combat Lyme disease, "Turning Tick Bites Into Dollars," 6-4, is readable, informative on the health side, but short on the science of the disease, its potential for damage and treatment, and what researchers are looking for to be truly effective. We do get a satisfying, broader emphasis to varying strategic approaches in "The Image Polishers Go Global," 6-25, noting that big PR firms are opening offices everywhere, because "even when the profits aren't there, nobody wants to be seen as pulling back." In "Colgate's Next Trick: Controlling the Chaos," 8-6, she reports that Reuben Mark, Colgate's hands-on CEO, wakes up formerly sleepy Colgate by taking "the handcuffs off our people," but the article needs more anecdotal material on how he's doing it. "RJR's Brave New World," 9-17, offers fine detail, efficiently presented, on Louis V. Gerstner Jr., new CEO, who is trying to get RJR under control, so far so good, as Gerstner slashes overhead, perks, and corporate fat. But "Has Kellogg Lost Its Snap?" 9-24, is little more than an interesting skim over the details of some mysterious doings in Battle Creek, MI, where the most likely successor to Kellogg's chairman has suddenly resigned, Kellogg losing ground to General Mills' oat-based cereals. Commendably objective in a 10 Best selection, "The Giant With a Black Eye," 4-2, Deutsch provides an inside look at Exxon that's undistracted by the oil spill, nicely formulated on Lawrence G. Rawl, who "has made a science out of the low profile."

Dobrzynski, Judith. *BusinessWeek.* (★ ★)
Senior writer. Dobrzynski is the resident enthusiast in the world of art and its business, and that's where we appreciate her work the most. Most of her time is spent on more prosaic business-finance stories on Wall Street, where she holds up well enough, but with less confidence and

style. In "Art Dealers Are Puttin' on the Glitz," 2-27, about how art galleries are fighting to compete against newly resurgent auction houses in a hot art market, she's snappy, with good quotes from top people in the field. Though she doesn't shine as Anthony Bianco did a few years back in a look at Salomon, "Is John Gutfreund Dreaming an Impossible Dream?" 2-27, she's still solid on analysis, with a raft of interviews with current and former execs, strategically placing the firm against future and past goals and describing its new push toward merchant banking and M&A. We note former *BW* staffer Sarah Bartlett following her lead, picking up the theme in the *NYT* Business section, "Salomon's Risky New Frontier," 3-7. Redundant in "Giant Steps Toward the Global Village — Or an Ego Trip?" 3-20, Dobrzynski follows David Lieberman's preceding superior news article giving the pros and cons of the merger between Time, Inc. and Warner Communications, adding almost nothing. She informs in "The Hell with Glamour. Give Me Groceries," 5-1, on quiet buyout man, Gary Hirsch, who now owns supermarket chains with revenues totaling $6 billion. Taking Time-Warner as a test case, Dobrzynski makes a proposal to save shareholders $$$ in merchant bank and lawyers' fees in cases of "serial" bidding for a company, and while there are usually other axes grinding on M&As, she holds our interest in "Why Doesn't Time Inc. Just Put Itself on the Block?" 6-26. The 7-3 cover, "Taking Charge: Corporate Directors Start to Flex Their Muscle," with Michael Schroeder, Gregory Miles, and Joseph Weber, details on how outside directors in some big companies are starting to get tough on management which is not producing for shareholders. She offers information on the action at several companies, focusing on ideas that have been implemented and work, as well as ideas that haven't been tried yet but may be useful. There's no compelling storyline in "Running the Biggest LBO," 10-2, but Dobrzynski competently reviews the actions taken by new RJR CEO Gerstner, including some tasty anecdotes, such as how he increases his charm the lower he is in an organization, how he couldn't get a messenger after 3 p.m. because the company was on "summer hours," and losing the company limo.

Donlan, Thomas G. *Barron's.* (★)
Washington editor. There's no question Donlan can report, skimming information with a vacuum. Getting through his material is another matter; it's too often like trying to cut concrete with scissors, his reports so densely packed with data that they're tough to read. We need a chisel in "Read His Lips," 1-9, Donlan laying out the changes in the tax code for 1989, but the information is solid. You need a strong interest in the government's tendency to bookkeep by moving things off-budget to get through "Cooking the Books," 2-13, with incredible amounts of information and a veritable forest of government acronyms making it a toughie to slog through. Reviewing the progress of Chrysler, "Still A Lousy Idea," 3-6, Donlan is again overloaded with information as the carmaker pays for its error of disconnecting odometers, finding Chrysler's action wanting. In "Capital Idea," 5-15, he updates prospects for a tax rate cut on long-term capital gains, reporting there's a strong force building that could push the plan ahead and notes that "one school of economists — the school President Bush sides with — sees a preferential gains rate as a revenue raiser." Here's where he could have gone through some numbers and didn't. Donlan's well organized on the budget and the debates occurring in "Smoke and Mirrors," 7-10, a good overview that informs. Donlan doesn't explain in clear terms what it is exactly that Ginnie Mae does that gets it into trouble, "Poor Ginnie," 8-9; there are pieces here, but they're not put together. *Barron's* needs stronger editing throughout to cull repetition, smooth out wrinkles, and be more user friendly, especially with this writer's otherwise sound material.

Dyson, Esther. *Forbes.* (★)
"Random Access" columnist. Rather conventional commentary on PCs and other computer matters, Dyson's columns can always be understood by the average reader, rarely sliding into hacker jargon. Her material is much slower in developing than the *Forbes* formula, however. Also editor of *Release 1.0,* a computer newsletter, she covers different innovations in the industry, some we've heard of, some not; her treatments are interesting, but rarely engrossing. Dyson never quite captures the WOW of the technology she reports on that gives life to the

dispatches of others on the beat. Dyson's clear with "Repairman in a Box," 1-9, telling us of the advent of artificial intelligence to diagnose equipment failure, not new, but nicely treated, with some examples. In "Ma and Pa Engineering," 2-6, Dyson raves about a software program for producing concrete, forwarded to her by a reader, giving a nice overview of program and industry, but she stretches trying to draw a broader meaning to mixing. Encouraging the entrepreneurial spirit, Dyson writes "Letters to a Young Software Company," 4-3, giving a state-of-the-industry look at how the companies interact in a delightful format. In "Three Weeks That Shook My World," cover 6-12, she tells of her visit to the Soviet Union, meeting with their computer people in cooperatives and government. After a slow start around some dubious pop sociology about hunter-gatherers, she shows the early progress that is being made and the mindboggling obstacles to be overcome, but the interesting material is buried in a less than world-shaking presentation. She examines the new techniques of customer service, "Computers, Customers and Hand Holding," 8-7, which include complex software for service reps to both solve problems and manage databases of questions. In "Physics for Economists," 10-16, she kills some of our time meandering around the Santa Fe Institute's incipient work on chaos theory, "which understands that a small change may not have small results, because it may be magnified in a series of cascading events. 'For want of a nail, the kingdom was lost,' " etc. This is Walrasian general-equilibrium theory in economics, going back well over a century, which is not mentioned here.

Elias, Christopher. *Insight.* (★ ★)
New York. A veteran of business journalism, Elias is able to skillfully collect and structure his information and he has a detachment from the conventional drift we appreciate. If he's not enthusiastic about his assignment, though, he can be pedantic, tending to textbook presentations. He's fine in "Thrifts Face Uncertain Future as Buoy-Up Costs Keep Rising," 12-26-88, Elias providing a feast of information that not only explains the cause of this S&L mess but revealing the reasons we're not getting solutions. He clearly enjoys his interview with Michael Milken, "The Man with the High-Yield Vision," cover 6-12, which needs more on the 98-count indictment, but as a personality profile it's among the best we've seen on the man, eliciting a persuasive Milken defense of high-yield borrowers as "the best risk on any list of debtors. The savings and loan industry doesn't lose money by investing in such borrowers. They lost it by blindly investing in commercial real estate." Elias' keen sense of detail is appreciated in "Ruble May Need the Midas Touch," 10-23, Elias relating a broader picture in Fed Gov. Wayne Angell's recommendation to Moscow of a gold-convertible Soviet ruble, the best account we saw. But then in "Rare Posters Worth a Pretty Penny," 1-16, we have the feeling Elias could care less about the popularity of poster art, plodding a bit and closing abruptly, and, as a result, we can't get excited about it either. "Fed Blasts a Large Loophole in Ban on Bank Underwriting," 2-13, opens like a text entry with a long, dry, historical lead, leaving the news item hanging until the 4th graph, collecting a hodgepodge of statistics in the middle. Elias doesn't even define the abuses in securities underwriting that threaten bank solvency three-quarters of the way through, and we can't tell whether he's talking about 1933's Glass-Steagall Act, or today's headlines. Elias is sharp with "Neighbor's Taxes Reform Relations," 4-17, a crisp, fact-filled piece on the "war" between NYC and NJ as NYC residents and businesses leave Manhattan for cheaper rents and lower taxes the other side of the Hudson. There's no kick to "The Hiatus That Can Cause Havoc," 7-24, on the excessive delays in clearing securities for sale and the recommendations by a panel of experts that would set an international standard, mired in technical jargon. Elias repeatedly has to define his terms, which he does without examples, the result being that this reads like a how-to manual. His cover story on AT&T, five years after the breakup of its monopoly, "Brushing Off the Ash of Divestiture's Pyre," 4-17, is competent in reviewing the subsequent history. We get more detail on tariff skirmishing than we need, however. There was no interview with CEO Robert E. Allen, and not enough from AT&T's competitors, MCI and U.S. Sprint.

Elmer-DeWitt, Philip. *Time.* (★ ½)

Staff writer, almost exclusively on science and technology, he assembles the information his team collects well enough, but in *Time*'s current fashion of letting writers do their own thing, he sometimes can't keep his hands off his subjects, at times crossing the line from analysis to advocacy, either in his leads or his closings. Part of *Time*'s "Planet of the Year" cover 1-2, "Preparing for the Worst," with J. Madeleine Nash, is a jumble, speculating about responses to natural disasters and occurrences, covering Africa, China, plant genetics, tap water fouled from sewage in four columns. He's xenophobic in "Battle for the Future," with Scott Brown and Richard Woodbury 1-16, a typical "The Japanese Are Coming!" article, favoring increased cooperation between American companies as the answer to the problem, bemoaning "Japan's rapid advances" in superconductors, Japan's "decisive lead" in x-ray steppers and "daunting head start" in HDTV. Whew. Elmer-DeWitt is exhaustive on the pros and cons of genetic engineering and gene therapy without bogging down in terminology, "The Perils of Treading on Heredity," with Nash and Andrea Dorfman 3-20, but obviously comes down on the con side of the equation: "To speak in terms of eliminating genetic defects is to tread on slippery scientific and ethical ground. As any biologist will testify, genetic variety is the spice of life, a necessary ingredient to survival of the species. . ...Even to label genes as defective can be dangerous" as, he points out, this "misguided pseudo science" fueled the Nazi eugenics movement, and drive towards a master race. Sharp and factual, he's balanced on the fusion furor, "Trying to Tame H-Bomb Power," with David Bjerklie and Nash 4-17, accurately calling the energy-yielding fusion reaction "a Holy Grail of physics for nearly 40 years." He's down on the new phone technology that requests a caller push a button on a touch tone phone for specific services in "Hello! This Is Voice Mail Speaking," with Thomas McCarroll 5-22, though he retains his humor amidst his complaints: everyone ". . .can sympathize with the California man who pressed the wrong button and sent a private love message to an entire department." He waxes rhapsodic, closing with T. S. Eliot, in "Postcards from a Distant World," with Edwin Reingold 9-11, an effective summary, but little more. In "A Trinity of Families," 10-23, he is somewhat confusing on the family of subatomic particles and their definitions, but the information we can sift out is neat. Now we know there are particles called neutrinos, billions passing through our bodies per second. Paging Stephen Hawkings.

Fabrikant, Geraldine. *The New York Times.* (★ ½)

"Business Day" reporter, specializing in media. There's a comfortable roundup feel to Fabrikant's dispatches, nicely flavored with anecdotes and light analysis. She manages to treat her sometimes dry subjects in a lively, stylish vein, but with only modest reportage. Fabrikant covers considerable ground in "Time Inc.'s Magazine Drought May Be Ending," 2-6, on the moderate success of *Cooking Light,* Time's new healthy cooking bimonthly, but she doesn't go very deep into any points she raises. In "Fox Broadcaster's Successful Gambles," 4-3, she offers light fare on Fox Network's successes and shortcomings, but really just updates on what they're doing to the schedule and who's got a piece of what market; there's no analysis or explanation of why Fox isn't a "regular" network or bound by same FCC rules as NBC, ABC and CBS, something we're curious about. She takes an interesting peek at "A Cold Spell for CBS Records," 5-17, with some light analysis and a recounting of CBS' difficulties, but she doesn't offer much in way of solutions. Fabrikant also goofs on the title of one of CBS' heaviest heavy hitters: the title of Guns 'N' Roses' first album is *not* "Every Rose Has Its Thorn," (a Poison single from "Open Up and Say Ahh. . .") but "Appetite for Destruction." In "Behind a Corporate Courtship," 8-13, Fabrikant shifts through Time-Warner court documents for another angle on the corporate triangle with Paramount, but her fuzzy presentation lacks a unifying theme. Fuzzy again with "Cable Giant Hungry for Programs," 11-16, she's credible enough in using John Malone's Tele-Communications Inc. as a starting point, describing the jockeying for position among cable networks in the wake of the Time-Warner merger. The piece loses focus, though, unable to decide whether to write about the cable industry, its plans or Tele-Communications.

Fanning, Deirdre. *Forbes.* (★ ½)

Associate editor, "On the Docket" reporter. Corporate law is Fanning's specialty, examining different legal issues relating to business internally and externally. What she does, she does competently enough, but our readers who specialize in corporate law feel her work is "once over easy" — skimming the surface, but nicely. In "Beware the Boomerang," 2-6, she's disorganized somewhat, muddled in her explanation of corporations using outside firms to conduct internal investigations, clearing up the fog in her concluding graphs. She skimps with "Lawsuits, Ahoy!" 3-6, telling us many municipalities are enacting local restrictions to give favorable treatment to residents in boat docking and other related fees and regulations, quoting a prominent lawyer as saying due process requires everybody be treated alike, but the cases she cites lead to the opposite conclusion. Joining a growing debate, Fanning examines the merits of taxing mail-order customers, "Tax By Mail," 4-3, getting into a discussion on the constitutionality of the issue, and including a nice selection of business reaction and problems with the idea, a well-balanced view. Sharp in "A Stacked Deck?" 6-12, she neatly fuses business and recent legal decisions designed to protect small investors and creditors in bankruptcy claims trading, using an example of the Allegheny bankruptcy filing as a case in point. Seeming especially familiar with her topic, Fanning finds the first chink in the armor of the latest Wall Street wunderkind, Bruce Wasserstein, in "Bid-em-up Bruce," cover 8-7, a 10 Best nomination from *Forbes*' editors, planting seeds of doubt on his motives and on the savviness of his deals with hard information. This was the best we saw of her this year.

Farnsworth, Clyde. *The New York Times.* (★ ★)

Global trade reporter. A veteran who has been on this beat for ages, Farnsworth has practically become part of the trade establishment, his posture bending from free trade to mercantilism as the winds shift around him. We found him more productive this year, but his vision is too narrow to encompass the field, behind the curve as he remains comfortably conventional. Still, he is a competent enough reporter, always worth reading if only to get that important perspective. In an important Saturday piece, for example, he gives us a "Warning by Europe on Trade," 5-20, reporting the EEC might challenge the new U.S. trade law if DC accuses the community of unfair trading practices, quoting Frans Andriessen, EEC chief trade negotiator: "We have made crystal clear that the unilateral way of dealing with trade matters is not what we are ready to accept." But in a lamentable "Why Trade Remains a Jumble," 1-29, he deplores the fact that we let minor issues such as foreign policy get in the way of a "tough" trade policy. He meanders about in "World Bank and IMF Approve Plan to Cut Debt of Poorer Lands," 4-5, confusing on the IMF meeting, mixing the Philippines with Mexico and Zimbabwe, leaving us without a clear sense of the issues. Late, "U.S. Feeling Pressures to Cite Japan on Trade," 4-24, Farnsworth tells us that Democrats insist Bush exercise Super 301 and "list Japan as a country engaging in unfair trade practices or it will render new trade legislation 'virtually useless.' " His "Washington's Hard Line On Trade," 6-25, is a timely interview with S. Linn Williams, deputy USTR, dancing around contradictions on Super 301 and GATT provisions. In "The Bush Team Has Competing Ideas on Competing With Japan," 6-25, he outlines the struggle between interventionists and free-traders, reporting that the idea of a managed economy has gained ground in the administration, but overstates the case: "The tougher line on trade and technology transfer already being taken with Japan could be a sign that interventionists will prevail." Hardly. Farnsworth offers fairly good economic analysis in "Industrial Nations Discussing Dollar," 9-24, covering the options available to G-7 on the eve of the IMF meeting in Washington. He maintains his balance in " 'Revisionist' Influence Seen in Japan Talks," 11-6, a disquieting report on the preponderance of "managed trade" advocates among USTR Carla Hills' circle of advisers. Farnsworth includes her disclaimer that she finds those policies repugnant, but keeps the focus solidly on how policy is bending in the direction pushed by those advisers.

Farrell, Christopher. *Business Week.* (★ ★)
Associate department editor, economics. The acronym expert at the weekly, Farrell's specialties in '89 were LBOs and ESOPs. His coverage of the markets and different business trends is good, but not often on the cutting edge. On the effect of LBOs, "Bondholders Are Mad as Hell — and They're Not Going To Take It Anymore," with Leah Nathans, Joan O'C. Hamilton and Leslie Helon 2-6, he pulls together a lot of useful details pertaining to particular companies, and shows evidence of good background interviews with company execs and money managers. In "Suddenly, Blue Chips Are Red-Hot for ESOPs," with Tim Smart and Keith Hammonds 3-20, he looks at the growing corporate interest in ESOPs, using them as defense weapons against takeovers and to reap tax advantages delivered by Congress in 1986. The piece includes good explanations of those factors plus benefits to lenders who provide money to the corporations buying stock for employees. Farrell surveys the future of home prices, "This House Party Is Winding Down," 3-27, clearly-written, but dull, concluding that home sale prices nationally will do no worse than track inflation and that the "major regional markets will move closer together over time." A new angle on ESOPs in "Stuffing Nest Eggs with ESOPs," with Tim Smart and Zachary Schiller 4-24, he explores how ESOPs are being used increasingly by companies to fund retirement plans, lowering costs significantly in the process. "ESOPs: Are They Good for You?" 5-15, is a clear, comprehensive survey of the pros and cons for companies and employees of the popular employee stock-ownership plans, including an interesting discussion of the "worker participation" issue; in part a reworking of Farrell's 4-24 article on ESOPs and pension plans, but this is longer, meatier, and explores some broader aspects of the program. Farrell offers a so-so assessment of the bond market with "The Next Best Thing to Bond Market Nirvana," 6-26, his writing zipping along although the ideas could be sharper. "Insurers Under Siege," co-written by Chris Welles cover 8-21, is a bit melodramatic on the insurance industry, recounting tales of woe, seeing current weakness extended out indefinitely and the advent of socialized insurance. "The Bills Are Coming Due," with Nathans 9-11, takes us on an informative, though not compelling, tour through the realm of high debt financing, advising the junk market is still seen as "highly viable." Farrell escapes *BW*'s tendency to hyperbole, giving a balanced view. He discusses those companies in trouble, such as Campeau, but also gives credit to several companies where LBOs have produced increased productivity, such as Wilson and Holiday Corp.

Feder, Barnaby J. *The New York Times.* (★ ½)
New York. A general assignment reporter on the Sunday business staff, Feder produced some reasonable material on the Valdez spill and covered selected environmental issues midyear. He's steady and workmanlike, but we do not expect anything earthshaking when we settle down under his byline. He gets as an assignment "The Miniatures Industry Grows — By Inches, Naturally," 1-1, a story on dollhouse furniture that does not belong in the *NYT* Sunday Business section. Feder needs some specific anecdotes to round out "A 'Ticking Bomb' But No Explosion," 3-19, one of the first of scattered reports on the new law requiring early warning on plant closings: "Early warnings on plant closings produce no dire effects, at least so far." Hey, there's been no recession yet. He's thorough in "Turning On the Research Switch," 5-14, a carefully-written look at the 17 year operation of the Electric Power Research Institute, owned by electric utilities, and atypical because it contracts out almost all research, but accounts for about half of all industry research. "Getting the Electronics Just Right," 6-4, focuses on Wells Fargo & Company, "exploiting the information revolution," with good material. In "Wringing Profits From Clean Air," 6-18, Feder offers scattered ideas on how money can be made or lost as the Bush administration revives environmentalism, missing the details of Bush's Clean-Air proposal, but getting a great quote: " 'The environment is definitely a boom business for lawyers an lobbyists at the moment,' says Anthony Montrone, a waste management expert. . .." Tedious with "Who Will Subscribe to the Valdez Principles," 9-10, Feder reviews a new environmental code of ethics for businesses designed by environmental groups, too unfocused to be of real interest. "Exxon Valdez's Sea of Litigation," 11-19, amounts to little more than a list of who's suing who, Feder noting Exxon has already forked over $130 million to 10,000 Alaskans directly

affected, like the fishermen, for example. He doesn't address questions of legitimacy of some claims — like "California drivers who had to pay sharply higher gasoline prices after the Valdez grounding temporarily closed the port of Valdez and interrupted the flow of North Shore oil to California refineries."

Flanigan, James. *Los Angeles Times.* (★)
Business columnist. Pleasant middle-of-the-road reads are Flanigan's trademark, but for the prominence of his column, he doesn't deliver for the newspaper. Very *status quo,* he's suspicious of any new trend in the markets and usually has an idea how the government can stamp it out. In "The Real Cost of Fraud: Jobs of Average Worker," 12-22-88, he lays out a rationale for the reasons white collar crime cannot be dismissed, as it undermines the capitalist system by portraying all financiers as dishonest and greedy as well as hurting the ordinary worker who gets laid off to pay the debt and exorbitant fees. Along the same line in "Futures Pits Too Important Not To Reform," 1-20, he advocates a cleanup, saying it's in our best interest to regulate them a little more to make sure, as much as possible, that the markets aren't rigged. In "Dusk Falling on the Day of the Raider," 2-1, he notes the disappearance of corporate raiders from the magazine covers and news columns, offering several not-too-convincing explanations for the dearth of cover boys. Flanigan takes a cursory look at the changes in the labor market with "Work Force Is on Its Own as the Rules Shift," 3-5, and, while it's not exactly cutting edge material, it is probably worth the two minutes it takes to read. Short but insightful in "Information to Give Airlines Added Thrust," 3-12, he examines the reasons why airline computerized reservations systems have become so important and expensive. "Lockheed Has Powerful New Weapon: ESOP," 4-5, is useful on Lockheed's use of an ESOP for a takeover defense against raider Harold Simmons. In "World Economy Feels Impact of Perestroika," 5-7, he offers solid, sprightly analysis, questioning "Will Gorbachev survive, and does it matter anyway?" and adding "There's a lot of truth in President Bush's remarks last week that 'the United States should hope that economic reform succeeds everywhere in the world.' " Describing the Australian as "a classic entrepreneur" in "Murdoch Again Gambles to Add Building Block to Vast Empire," 9-15, Flanigan is cautionary on Murdoch's highly-leveraged holdings, stressing the "gamble" in the title, but striking paydirt on the payoff as Murdoch's media empire will, in the long run, be worth more than the sum of its parts. Flanigan clings to the bewhiskered "crowding out" idea, and it shows up repeatedly in his material, as in "No New Taxes Means More Borrowing," 10-29, muddled on taxes, public works, and public and private debt.

Flint, Jerry. *Forbes.* (★ ★)
Senior editor. Among the most experienced reporters on the auto beat, Flint usually dazzles us with a provocative projection or insight two or three times a year. This year there was more meat and potatoes, little that was adventurous. He takes an adversarial look at leasing, "When the Payments Never Stop," 3-6, providing insightful, cautionary advice on different leasing agreements, a good primer, covering actual cost evaluations to insurance, for those who might consider the option. He blames the weak dollar for VW's U.S. sales problems, "Can Volkswagen Stop Its U.S. Decline?" 4-3, sharply quoting a VW official who pegs the origin of the problem to the 1971 freeing of the dollar, but we'd have liked a more questioning look at VW's marketing and management in this country, instead of reminiscences about the Beetle. He comes up with an obvious explanation in "Habit Dies Hard," 5-29, as to why we keep buying foreign cars, habit and performance, but he includes some useful market sales figures. Dire in "With Friends Like This. . ." 6-26, he foresees no end in sight to DC regulation of Detroit, while the rules remain oddly skewed as Detroit's compact cars made abroad are the most fuel-efficient, but may not be included in their MPG accounting to the government and now, "amid the near panic over global warming, the Exxon spill, and pollution, Washington is talking about pushing the fuel average requirement to anywhere from 33 mpg to 45 mpg. In a broadly focused "An Urge to Service," with William Heuslein 9-18, Flint lists a multitude of examples as American businesses set their sights on better customer relations and service, delectably done and quick:

"Competition is behind this service craze." Rosy on Roger Smith and GM, ' "1990 Will Be the Year of the General,'" 11-27, is a bit of the daring Flint of yore. He supports his happy scenario with credible projections and figures, and revealing quotes from the outgoing Chairman of the Board.

Forbes, Malcolm S., Jr. *Forbes.* (★ ★ ★)

"Fact & Comment II" columnist and deputy editor-in-chief. "Steve," as he's known to all, is not at all facile in his writing, so don't expect to be entertained. Instead, he has his family's instinct for spotting value in ideas, a deep sense of history, and an intellectual daring that rivals his father's athletic audacity. And the bite we missed last year is back. A terrific forecaster of political trends and markets, his column is becoming more adventurous than the magazine. While advising the Fed of dangers ahead due to its own error in "1989 *Should* Be a Good Year," 1-9, Steve offers a sensible perspective on the trade deficit: "The trade deficit is not a moral equivalent of a company losing money. It is, on the contrary, a result of our strength. The bulk of the growth in imports in recent years has not been cameras and VCRs but investment-oriented items such as parts and machine tools. In restructuring our economy during the 1980s, we have mobilized not only our own capital but that of other nations as well." Jumping off Hernando de Soto's *The Other Path,* "Self-Made Crisis," 2-20, is succinct in stating the Third World debt problem: "We tell debtors to cut politically popular food and fuel subsidies, to balance their budgets, to increase their trade surpluses, to devalue their money. The results are predictable: Taxes are raised, particularly on the salary-earning middle class; the economy thus stagnates. The money is debased, fueling ruinous inflation." He sides with Ben Wattenberg, "America's Looming Shortage," 3-20, effectively arguing that an aging population won't necessarily stagnate an economy, but that society as a whole won't be as "vibrant." Covering NATO and the budget deficit, 5-29, he offers solid advice to Bush. Although he facetiously suggests moving the entire deficit off-budget to meet Gramm-Rudman targets, he seriously ponders the viability of Bush pushing German reunification, months before anyone else. A believable review *cum* analytic of Gregory Fossedal's *The Democratic Imperative,* "The Chinese Massacres," 8-7, doesn't gloss over the volume's shortcomings, Forbes reaching for the bottom line in promoting the American Revolution. In "The Next Few Years Will Be The Most Momentous," 9-18, an important analytic on the sweeping changes of reform in Eastern Europe, he's trenchant and insightful, effectively relating the developments to the goals of NATO. But his 11-27 column doesn't work, his advice on program trading and comparison of SC Gov. Caroll Campbell and Frisco mayor Art Agnos skewed, reading like he talked to some sources for five minutes, and put the column together in ten.

Forsyth, Randall W. *Barron's.* (★ ★ ½)

"Current Yield" columnist. For the first year in our annuals, Forsyth slips a notch. Not that we're not still happy with his clear, competent reviews of the credit markets, but he really has taken to recycling the week, with rarely a surprise from him. There's no longer a sense that he's contemplating the intersection of fiscal policies with money or in other ways exploring scenarios outside the conventional. In "Junk is King," 1-23, Forsyth reports exceptionally high returns by junk funds in 1988 with new money pouring in, but he doesn't try to analyze. His "The People's Choice," 2-6, contains an excellent overview of the credit markets, yet it doesn't have a sense of the strength in bonds that's ahead. Our impression was of Forsyth bearishness early in the year. He's thorough in "An Unkind, Rough Market," 2-13, a blow-by-blow of all the events that help to drive interest rates up during the previous week that we appreciated. With another review, "Junk Defaults: Nothing New," 4-17, he competently surveys all the information critical to the bond market over the last week. We don't agree with the analysis in his "Sunny or Stormy? A Bond Fund Weathervane," 8-14, believing he too easily buys the rationale for Fed tightening at this point, but he gets plenty of credit for the timely identification of the market's dip with the Fed decision that no recession is likely and therefore further easing is unnecessary. With "Current Yield: Like a Spring, Market Tightens," 9-25, we like Forsyth's strong overview of credit markets, especially the balanced approach taken towards last week's junk debacle followed by a comeback. "Another Fed Easing?" 11-20, simply suggests we look at whether the trading desk adds reserves when fed funds are at 8 1/2% to see if it is aiming to get to 8 1/4%. Nor does he mention the continuing negative influence of the Treasury's David Mulford in talking down the dollar in the week preceding.

Freedman, Alix M. *The Wall Street Journal.* (★ ★ ½)
New York, food and beverage industry. Freedman's beat is a lively one. She does it justice with sparkling writing and offbeat topics that serve as launching pads for a wider information flow. With another push on analytics of corporate trends, she'd be even better. She's delectably gossipy in "White-Collar Chic: Studio 54 Partners Are Even More Successful As New York Hoteliers," 1-19, undiscerning on the rehabilitation of Steve Rubell and Ian Schrager, but nice touches on their new hotel venture, down to descriptions of the too-small-for-tubs bathrooms, despite the $200 per room tab. Getting comments from all sides in "FTC Alleges Campbell Ad Is Deceptive," 1-27, she details the complaint against a misleading Campbell Soup ad which touted the soup as low in fat and cholesterol and helping to fight heart disease, but didn't mention its counterproductive high sodium content. She maintains an excellent balance in the debate between natural and artificial sweeteners, *and* between competing artificial products in the broad "New Sweeteners Head for the Sugar Bowl: But One Entry Already Raises Safety Concerns," 2-6. She's excellent on the war over the baby market, "Bad Reaction: Nestle's Bid to Crash Baby Formula Market in the U.S. Stirs a Row," 2-16, as the Nestle entry is plagued by bad reactions to a "hypoallergenic" tag on the label, and as a result of complaints, the FDA is investigating all hypoallergenic formulas. A follow-up, "Nestle to Drop Claim on Label of Its Formula," 3-13, updates on Nestle's dropping the use of "hypoallergenic," due to customer misconception that it means nonallergenic rather than reduced allergy potential. She's on the ball with "Never Have So Few Intimidated So Many," 3-20, citing multiple examples of consumer protests that work, including the Kimberly-Clark "Married. . .With Children" flap, questioning if an ad that will offend no one can be created. With Frank Allen, "Family Misfortune: John Dorrance's Death Leaves Campbell Soup With a Cloudy Future," 4-19, Freedman intriguingly details how the heirs are being tempted to sell off the family dynasty for huge profit. She makes good use of industry experts in "Stroh Brewing Attracts Several Foreign Suitors," 5-5, as Stroh invites companies to the dance. In " 'De-Nicotined' Next Gets Pitched By Philip Morris Just Like Decaf," 8-4, she's complete on the marketing of the Next cigarette. Freedman doesn't miss a beat in telling this story of Helena Amram, a high-priced matchmaker with big plans to franchise, "Beautiful Women Don't Go to Bars, But Helena Does," 9-26. With a deadly eye for detail, Freedman shows us all the wonder that is Helena: "She began her career by finding husbands for widowed friends after the Six Day War. . .she decamped to New York, however, in 1979, after a client had claimed on TV that Helena had fixed her up with three guys she didn't hit it off with — an Arab, a criminal and a married man."

Friedman, Jon. *Business Week.* (★)
Investment banking department editor. A selection of interesting banking topics helps keep us reading Friedman's material. For the most part, he offers competent overviews, rarely ahead of the game. He provides a nice sketch of Japanese investments in U.S. investment banking firms, "Japanese Dealmakers Yearn to Play QB," 1-16, exchanging capital for experience, but he doesn't plumb the most interesting part, the cultural differences in personality between self-effacing Japanese and their swashbuckling U.S. teachers, which could stand in the way of the Japanese becoming M&A experts on their own. He talks to a number of experts, culling a few good quotes in "Can Shearson Regain That Old Midas Touch?" 1-23, a dense review of Shearson's past and future. He's not terribly timely with "The Greatest Invention Since. . .Burnt Toast?" 3-6, a report on the unfavorable investor reaction to Shearson's unbundled stock units, since the reaction was known a couple of months ago, but is still a useful summary. "For Peter Cohen, It's Even Lonelier at the Top," 4-3, is troubled by a "hearsay" quality, since Shearson Chairman Cohen was away and couldn't do an interview for this story. In "Fidelity Fights Back: Can CEO Johnson Revive the Behemoth of the Mutual Fund Industry?" co-written by Leslie

Helm and Gary Weiss cover 4-17, Friedman offers thorough coverage on Ned Johnson's attempt to breathe life into Fidelity. He gets little new in "Wall Street Runs Scared," with Chris Welles and Eric Schine 5-1, reporting that Wall Street's troubles have not ended and further layoffs can be expected; the most interesting comment is that "bottom-fisher" Sandy Weill is "on the prowl" again for acquisitions (Drexel's retail business), and that Weill only fishes when waters are troubled to get cheap prices. An above average overview of Merrill Lynch and its future, "The Remaking of Merrill Lynch," 7-17, Friedman does a good job explaining the ins and outs of stock-lending from brokerage accounts, wondering if this is the next Wall Street scandal as federal investigations continue, but doesn't quite connect with " 'The Business Nobody Wants To Talk About,' " 9-25. Co-authored by John Meehan, "Can AmEx Win the Masses — And Keep Its Class?" 10-9, is a good analytic on AmEx's move to broaden its coverage to less upscale businesses and cardholders than it's been known for, in the face of stiff worldwide competition.

Fuerbringer, Jonathan. *The New York Times.* (★ ½)
New York, currency markets. Fuerbringer is standard in reporting the facts and figures, more professional here than on his earlier budget beat in Washington. Very bright, aggressive and enterprising, he still has a basic ground-level, conventional view of the action and needs to climb to a higher platform. In "Future of Debt Plan," 4-10, a readout from the thinktanks, he's still less interesting than the material the *The Wall Street Journal* had two weeks earlier, or Leonard Silk had previously in *The New York Times* itself. Caught in the rut of the conventional with "Dollar's Puzzling Rise Continues; 30 Month High Against the Mark," 5-16, he mentions many reasons why the dollar may be high, save the most obvious: U.S. monetary policy is tight against a steadily expanding economy. In "Dollar Up Again Defying Efforts of Central Banks," 5-23, he gives a fair assessment of the exchange market, though he's still quoting confused economists, also referring to Kilborn's incorrect story of 5-22 that White House is backing away from stabilized currency even as he quotes White House officials to the contrary. A quick update with "Chairman of Banks Discuss Mexican Debt," 7-17, is harmless enough, wire-service quality, hastily perusing the proposals, but not telling us who the participants are. He makes a gallant effort to get a handle on the privatization of Mexicana Airlines, "Chase Group Gets Stake in Mexican Airline," 8-24, but Fuerbringer can't quite grasp it, the article a little confusing, because the deal is. He doesn't bother to analyze or comment on "Foreign Exchange Trading Rising, Central Banks Say," 9-14, a review of data released by central banks showing the explosive growth in foreign exchange trading, though the facts do imply a lot of speculative trades. He's got a real beef in "Accuracy in Short Supply In Flood of U.S. Statistics," 10-30, pegging the importance of figures released to the markets and policymakers, but he attributes the problem to "a combination of budget cuts and deregulation — begun in the Reagan era — is eroding important yardsticks" and advocates Bush throw more money at his statisticians without ever evaluating the relevance of different measures offered. Boo. He doesn't quite understand the correlation, but it's enterprising that he's established that there is one, "Dollar Takes Its Cues From Stocks," 10-31. He shines in "Venezuela's Offer for Citgo Gives Banks Indigestion," 11-24, with nice background, detail and quotes on Venezuela's $675 million bid for the 50% of Citgo Petroleum it doesn't own already, its bankers, having just loaned the country $600 million, "stunned" by the deal. Fuerbringer might find his nitch in Third World debt.

Gilder, George. *Forbes.* **(NR)**
The principal chronicler of the computer age, a visionary philosopher as well, Gilder is the author of *Wealth and Poverty, The Spirit of Enterprise,* and now *Microcosm.* He's in a class by himself and probably doesn't belong tied to the magazine's staff. Under contract with *Forbes* for several articles over two years, Gilder scored a 10 Best selection and a 10 Best nomination with two major pieces. But only one was for *Forbes* early in the year, and thereafter he seemed out of place, sent off on routine assignments. Directly confronting the near hysteria over Japan's beating the U.S. in high-definition television, accompanied by calls for government aid and intervention, "IBM-TV?" 2-20, Gilder competently, calmly and persuasively displays why it really doesn't much matter, that the U.S. would soon leapfrog HDTV technology, a 10 Best

selection. Journalism students preparing for science reporting could not do better than to study this excellent exposition. It dramatically altered thinking about this issue, in DC and Silicon Valley, a clear victory for entrepreneurial capitalism over state corporativism. In his 10 Best nominee, "The Victim of His Virtues," *The Wall Street Journal* 4-18, Gilder produces the most compelling, supportive commentary we've seen to date on Michael Milken, the financial wizard and junk-bond maverick who now faces a 98-count federal indictment for various technical violations in securities trading. We also appreciate *Fortune*'s excerpting, a few weeks prior to the publication of *Microcosm,* Gilder's awesome chronicle of the semiconductor industry and its future, "The World's Next Source of Wealth," *Fortune* 8-28, a tremendous effort at visionary thinking, whetting our appetite for the book itself.

Gladwell, Malcolm. *The Washington Post.* (★ ★)
Biotech, medicine and healthcare reporter. Gladwell does an excellent job of ferreting out information and presenting it clearly. He's been on this beat two years, though, and probably should be bolder in sharing his own analytical insights, which should be considerable. In "The Judge, the Lawyers and the Dalkon Shield," 1-22, he details the latest flap as contingency fee lawyers handling the Dalkon Shield cases rack up big bucks, exploring various sides of the issue, but presenting no alternatives. He briskly identifies barriers for the biotech industry, "Risk, Regulation, and Biotechnology," *The American Spectator* 1-89, making it clear: "Biotech's regulatory problem is the product of the extraordinary expectations that have been swirling around the industry since the first human gene was synthesized and cloned more than a decade ago." A review of the Union Carbide case, "The Costly Outcome Of Bhopal," 2-19, is the best we've seen, but could have used more than just guesswork as to how the $470 million settlement will be divided. Gladwell's even-handed and informative on the first fetal alcohol suit to go to trial, "Trial Against Liquor Maker to Test Limits of Liability," 4-26, asking the pertinent question: Is the liquor company liable for damages if it doesn't provide labels or other warnings to pregnant women who drink? Straightforward in "Plastics Manufacturers Speed the Search for New Ways To Recycle Disposable Products," 5-2, on the economics and progress of plastics recycling, a creditable effort. Again, his legwork shows in "U.S. Expected To Lift Ban on Cyclamate," 5-16. "Wonder Drug Battle: Whose Price Is Right?" 6-11, is instructive on how product pricing in the pharmaceutical industry is influenced by the government. We get an interesting, if not terribly useful, insight on Asian bees and their propensity to defecate *en masse,* "Bees: An Explanation for 'Yellow Rain,' " 9-25. Gladwell's alarmist though, in "Makers of Medical Devices Faulted: FDA Often Informed of Problems Late, GAO Finds," 11-4, breathlessly spouting current law, but not fingering the lawbreakers. There's far too little information in "Immunology: Side Effects of Ozone Loss," 11-13, a P. 1, four-graph screamer telling us "even minimal doses of ultraviolet light — only enough to cause mild sunburn — are sufficient to suppress the cellular immune response of mice to mycobacteria by 50 percent," citing only one study.

Gleckman, Howard. *BusinessWeek.* (★ ★)
Washington. A talented reporter on *BusinessWeek*'s economic bench, Gleckman has our respect over the years for keeping his distance in the ideological wars. We see flashes of brilliance at times, leading us to wonder if he's being held back by the magazine's institutional barnacles and teamwork journalism. In "Brady's Long-Term Plans Will Collide With the Deficit," 1-23, Gleckman identifies early Treasury weaknesses on policy initiatives, and we learn that one of the ideas being kicked around Treasury is to exhort corporations to tie executive compensation to long-term performance. He misses Darman's plans for Bush's pledge to cut the capital gains tax in "The Trillion Dollar Man: Can Richard Darman Tame the Deficit," with Lee Walczak cover 3-13, but he's very fair and acutely observant with this timely focus on a key Bush player, the "inveterate schemer...who approaches negotiations by 'multiple-contingency planning,' " a great line. Conventional with "The Bush Presidency: Cautious to a Fault," co-authored by Richard Fly 5-8, his commentary on Bush's first 100 days is fairly insightful, focusing on an ordinary catalogue of "missed opportunities," such as the capgains tax cut, but with no mention

of White House tactical wins on the budget and minimum wage. With "Why Budget-By-Crisis May Be for the Best," 7-17, he offers a fairly smart thumbnail analysis: "Welcome to Budgetland, where spending increases reduce the deficit, tax cuts raise money, and nothing is quite what it seems." He's no-frills solid in "A Bout of Fed Bashing," with Mike McNamee 8-28, on Darman's shot across the Fed's bow, warning 8-13 on TV that the Fed should "be more attentive to the need to avoid tipping this economy into recession." His cover, "The Quiet Crusader," with McNamee, Jon Friedman, Victoria English and Ted Holden 9-18, is way below par for him, surely better done solo. The profile of the Treasury Secretary is very puffy, as if *BW* is determined to throw its arms around him. The "crusader" baloney refers to Brady's three-quarter-baked ideas on how to shape the business culture toward long-term investing. There's almost no critical examination of their economic or political viability by Gleckman's team or through quotes from interested observers; the picture we get of Brady the personality is two-dimensional. In a solo commentary piece, Gleckman warns of the dangers inherent in "Tinkering With Tax Reform: A Bad Idea That Will Just Get Worse," 11-6, staunchly supporting his thesis with pertinent information and quotes from congressmen, better commentary than most.

Greenwald, John. *Time.* (★ ½)
Senior writer. Greenwald's business pieces are frequently roundups, and we're generally appreciative that the pros and cons of boom or bust are buttressed with authoritative quotes. The economics are conventional budget-deficits-cause-high-interest-rates, though, which tells us the analytics are ankle deep. So it is in "Look Out Below!" with Bernard Baumohl and Jerome Cramer 5-22, Greenwald mapping out the dangers below the economic tightrope Fed Chair Alan Greenspan is walking, the springtime discussion of a "soft landing." Balanced in presenting differing opinions on the chances of impending recession. This is analytically of little use; we don't need interviews with "Wendy and Brian," a Phoenix truckdriver and bookkeeper on how tough things are, but we blame the editors for this fluff, not Greenwald. In "Let's Make a Deal," with Frederick Ungeheuer 1-2, he summarizes the current strategies and takes a guess at the likely outcome of the Government/Drexel/Milken battle, a complex topic compactly explained. He's clear and concise with "You Scratch My Back," with Kumiko Makihara 1-9, noting that the Recruit scandal that's helping to bring down high-powered officials on corruption and bribery charges, focuses scrutiny on Japan's *kinken-seiji,* or "money politics." "Feeling the Heat," 3-6, is a straight rewrite of the daily press accounts on Alan Greenspan and the discount rate hike to 7%. He assesses the results of leveraged buyouts, using anecdotes and quotes from experts well to further his case in "LBOs: Let's Bail Out," with Thomas McCarroll 8-14, but he misses the question of who will foot the bill for failed LBOs. Too short, "Will Everybody Get On Board?" with Gavin Scott 9-18, competently explains and analyzes the recent moves in the high stakes battle for United Airlines. He's sharp and clean on auto emissions and the push to raise standards in Congress, as well as exploring relatively new technologies being tested in spite of Detroit's opposition, but there's no examination of the actual severity of the pollution problem caused by emissions, "Yearning to Breathe Free," 10-16.

Grover, Ronald. *Business Week.* (★ ★)
Los Angeles bureau manager. Feature topics in quirky California style are Grover's forte. He manages to get a smattering of numbers in his reports without losing the buoyant feel. He takes a good financial snapshot of Fox and its chairman, Barry Diller, "Fox Elbows Into the Network's Big Picture," with David Lieberman 2-20, with solid numbers on viewer share and demographic delineations, but we'd have liked to see some of the creative side, too. Capturing producer Spelling on the downswing, "Is Aaron Spelling Still in His Prime Time," 4-17, is vivid on the slide, but there's too little on the recent merger of his production company or what he's going to do with the two companies he acquired. "Now Sonny Bono Is Singing 'I Got You, Babe,'" 5-8, is a cute feature on Palm Springs mayor earning 15K, Sonny Bono "selling glamour," trying to attract tourists and cut the $2.5 million budget deficit. "Fighting Back," 5-22, skims the issue of consumer and grassroots activism resurfacing, missing some pertinent examples, such as Kimberly-Clark's advertising pullout of Fox's "Married. . .With Children,"

due to consumer pressure and threatened boycotts. He reconstructs the battle for Northwest Airlines, "Landing Northwest," with Russell Mitchell and Seth Payne 7-3, getting some delectable insider information, and including some projections for the future success of NWA and Al Checchi. Grover lays out the potential for Pauley Petroleum as former Arco head Robert O. Anderson takes on new oil ventures, "Pauley Hits More Red Ink Than Black Gold," 9-11. "*When Columbia Met Sony. . .A Love Story*," 10-9, never succumbs to the protectionist ranting that went with some of the other news items on Sony's purchase of Columbia, Grover providing a neat overview of events leading up to the buy, and why Sony did it.

Gubernick, Lisa. *Forbes.* (★ ★)
West Coast bureau reporter, covering entertainment. A little polish this year helped to brighten her work, Gubernick finding more interesting angles on Tinseltown and TV-land. " 'It's Great for a Date,' " 2-6, is wonderfully anecdotal on Robert Shaye, founder of New Line Cinema and former Fulbright scholar, who began his distribution with an accidental hit, "Reefer Madness," and ended up with Freddy Kreuger. Quietly heralding the second (or third) coming of Fred Silverman, " 'I'm Not Rumpled Anymore,' " 3-6, she brings us up-to-date on his latest productions, including NBC's hit "Matlock," and cataloging briefly Silverman's many ups and downs. "Through the Looking Glass," 4-3, is a close-up valuation of Columbia Pictures' stock, and prospective buyout requirements, picking up Sony rumblings early on. Gubernick's quick glimpse of Stephen Cohen, "As Long as the Price Is Right," 5-29, is cursory on the entrepreneur who went from phones to film. "Living Off the Past," 6-12, reads like an obituary for the William Morris Agency, reeling off a long list of names defecting to other agencies; Gubernick plumbs some interesting anecdotes from Morris' history, like how Clint Eastwood got his first Dirty Harry role, but there's far too little on Morris' chances of recovery. Unfocused on the boom in comedy as entertainment, "The Comedian Gets the Girl," 9-4, she meanders about mediums, without ever coming to any conclusions. Her lead and a startling photo of the brothers Weinstein grab our attention in " 'We Don't Want to be Walt Disney,' " 10-16: "Bob and Harvey Weinstein, co-chairmen of Miramax Films, look like they belong on a loading dock, not distributing tony arthouse films." It's a gem of a business feature on the Queens, N.Y., boys, throwbacks to the oldtime movie moguls, and how they got the *Palme d'Or* at Cannes this year with "sex, lies and videotapes."

Haas, Lawrence J. *National Journal.* (★)
Budget and tax beat. Despite coming from *The Bond Buyer* as its DC correspondent, Haas seems terribly naive of the ways Washington political economics work. We get the occasionally useful survey, the sometime glimpse of insight, but inconsistently. Haas examines likely budget debate scenarios in "Budget Challenges," 1-21, suggesting less conflict over taxes than generally assumed, but missing key variables in the equation such as monetary policy and interest rates, far too long an endeavor for such little return. He isn't analytic in "Slippery Slope," 3-11, focusing on tax issues facing Bush and Congress, Haas wondering if the capgains cut will "unravel" the 1986 tax reform, quoting from economists and lobbyists pro and con. Long and puffy on Rep. Dan Rostenkowski, "Rostenkowski's Way," cover 7-22, Haas offers almost nothing of value except a quote here and there, a sophomoric effort that glances too late at capital gains, the big, big issue of '89. "Loading the Last Train," 8-5, contains salient facts on the debt-limit raises, 66 since 1940, giving us the procedural poop and a balanced look at both the Democratic and Republican sides, but Haas doesn't tell us whether Congress will actually raise the debt ceiling from $2 to 3 trillion, predicting incorrectly there will be a long hard fight. He tells us in "Gaining Political Capital," 9-2, a broad, somewhat unfocused, overview, that "if the mail flowing into Capitol Hill offices is any indication, plenty of Americans are not buying the message of class envy" on the capital gains tax cut, but never examines why the Democrats aren't buying that. "Temptations of Automatic Cuts," 10-21, shows Haas' potential we noted in 1988, a clear review of Richard Darman's plans to maneuver a capital gains tax cut through Congress: "But Darman doesn't hold all the cards," saying Dems will push revenue-losing arguments on the debt limit. His "Budget Carving Season," 11-4, is a bread-and-butter *National Journal* piece on how the departments are circling OMB as it begins to mix the fiscal '91 pie, with almost nothing on the Pentagon slice as the Cold War melts down in the background.

Hamilton, Martha A. *The Washington Post.* (★ ½)
Airline industry reporter. Not as fact-filled as the *Journal*'s William Carley or as well-connected as *The New York Times*' Agis Salpukas, Hamilton still manages to stay close to the two veterans of this beat. We don't expect to see the big trend piece from her, though, perhaps because she has her hands full of spot news. Hamilton's cursory, non-analytic, in "Bund Capital Partners Hope to Recamp Cabinet Business," 1-7, as Whirlpool sells its cabinet division to the company; we don't need to read much beyond the title as she writes it here. She foreshadows the debate to come over airline reservation systems with "Way Cleared for Trial on Airline Dispute," 2-24, a quick look at the antitrust suit aimed at United and American Airlines, as between the two companies reservations systems, they control a whopping 70% of the market. Examining the history of deregulation, she offers little analysis, but it's nice to have all the information we find in "Eastern Strike Raises Fears of Higher Fares," 3-13, all in one place. Nicely reported, Hamilton's clear with "Eastern Begins Sales Pitch for Leaner Airline," 4-25, as Frank Lorenzo meets with lawyers and creditors to try and get the airline flying again, although we'd like more specifics. "Eastern Strikers Offer Aid to Ritchie Group," 6-2, tells us the latest on the strike detail, a quick update. She gets all the numbers as "Pan Am Posts Quarterly Loss Despite Sale of Subsidiary," 8-5, but only takes a snapshot of what may or may not happen to the carrier. A little more in-depth with more bad news for Pan Am on the Lockerbie bombing, she tells us that upon origin in Frankfurt, "Pan Am security identified five passengers on Flight 103 for additional screening, but that none was referred to security personnel for scrutiny and further searches" as the FAA fines the airline $643,000 in civil penalities, "Pan Am Was Lax on Security For Fatal Flight," 9-21. With some detail, "Braniff Ends Passenger Air Flights," 11-8, is a concise overview of the carrier's demise, though the actual events on the glide slope aren't really explored.

Harris, Anthony. *Financial Times.* (★ ½)
Washington economic columnist. Harris' crankiness is sometimes offset by his sharp analysis, but not often enough. He was a good gauge of conventional wisdom, often tapping into it early, but rarely rising above it. "Confrontations That Are Waiting To Happen," 1-3, analytically outlines all the economic fights Bush is likely to face, warning early that "backsliding" on the 1986 tax reform would be troublesome, particularly the capital gains cut. He touts higher taxes in a pessimistic evaluation of Bush's first 50 days, "Adding Up the Costs of Political Evasion," 2-27, beginning by incorrectly asserting that the right is "incensed" with Bush over John Tower, when it was Paul Weyrich, not "his own right wing, which has provided much of the evidence against Mr. Tower." "Mr. Brady's Radical-Sounding Presentation," 3-13, delivers hard-hitting, well-deserved criticism of Treasury Secretary Nicholas Brady's proposals on LDC debt, finding it lacking necessary detail, far too vague, and noting, perceptively, that it was premature, an unfortunate consequence of the Secretary's believing "he had to say something." He rambles in "Policy Under a Political Stalemate," 4-18, to little purpose, concluding that the Bush administration may be on "automatic pilot, which ran the Exxon Valdez onto a reef." "Why the U.S. Is a Magnet for Capital," 5-15, is a strong buy recommendation for the dollar, cleanly analytic of the different factors that contribute to the boon. In "The Real Test of President Bush's Ability to Lead," 6-2, he is sharply disparaging of the Brady plan again, as varying events, such as the IRS ruling that "U.S. banks will not be allowed to offset any losses incurred in international debt reduction against the profits of their domestic operations," reduce the "Brady initiative to the Brady evasion," alertly defining possible scenarios. Harris is insouciant with different acronyms, but obviously unhappy with Bush's S&L bailout, "Bankrupt Thrifts Take the RAAP," 8-25, making gloomy evaluations of the situation. In an interview with Fed Gov. Wayne Angell, Harris is professional, not drowning Angell out on his Moscow proposal for a gold-convertible ruble, "Maverick Who Touted the Gold Standard to Moscow," 10-9. Harris is a very smart veteran who has survived the ideological wars. He still needs to get out of his armchair more often, see some people, make some phone calls, add another dimension to his analytics.

Hayes, Thomas C. *The New York Times.* (★ ½)
Dallas. Western economic correspondent. Solid work from Hayes as some of the S&L mess fell under his jurisdiction. He's always been thorough, though non-analytic at times, sharp on the microcosm, but fuzzy on the macro. Broad in "Savings Units Might Get Fed Loans," 2-17, as he examines statewide implications for Texas as the Federal Home Loan Bank system gets pressed for cash, but doesn't address broader questions on the margin. "MCorp Says It May Seek Chapter 11," 3-28, is sharp even in retrospect, reporting on MCorp's announced plan to file for Chapter 11 protection as Hayes states that such a bankruptcy would make a bail-out more difficult. While he's balanced and fairly complete on J. C. Penney's rebound and marketing plans in "New Shine On A Tarnished Penney," 4-23, he doesn't relate much of his information to the entire industry, or bring in consumer trends that forced Bonwit Tellers and B.Altman's to file for Chapter 11 later in the year. "Lomas to Sell Credit Card Bank Operation," 6-9, is a clear, well-rounded snapshot of the sale for Lomas, with related information all present, and even including some industry data and projections. He's solid on the advent of new technologies in "New Tools Aid Oil Hunt in U.S.," 8-16, but he doesn't ask if these techniques will effect the price or demand for oil, and doesn't touch the early debate on clean fuels. Covering all the bases in "Deal in Advanced TV by Texas Instruments," 9-14, Hayes gives this dispatch a news release feel on TI's acquisition of HDTV technology, with little in-depth. Much better in "Japan Grip Still Seen on Patents," 11-24, where we get an abundance of background to Japan's drawn out patent system, following its breakthrough granting of a 12-year patent to Texas Instruments for its computer chip application, filed Feb. 6, 1960! But what other U.S. patents are pending in Tokyo? Hayes gets the Sunday business lead with "The N.F.L.'s Painful Profit Crunch," 10-29, with a slow start on a relatively unimportant story about the football business.

Herman, Tom. *The Wall Street Journal.* (★ ½)
New York. A veteran of over twenty years at the paper, Herman's able to be more diverse with "Your Money Matters" than with the "Credit Markets" column, which simply related yesterday's market moves. His focus on advising investors takes on many topics, some useful, some not, but the broader base has made him slightly more readable, and more interesting. He gets out some important information on "U.S. Bond Dealers Incensed About Threat to Price-Data Control," 3-2, as RMJ Securities Corp. begins to offer its trading screen to a wider group than its brokers, perhaps even considering its transmission to a news service. But in a later dispatch, "Big Dealers Keep Monopoly on Bond Data," 4-11, we find out RMJ buckled under pressure, and is keeping things pretty much *status quo.* Doing the "Credit Markets" column, 5-8, he's fairly temperate in relating inflation to the bond markets, "Concern About Inflation, Interest Rates Remains Strong Despite Indications of Slowing Economy," but it's too short-sighted to be useful in a big way. With "Small Investors Can Lose Way in Muni Maze," 7-31, Herman offers some prudent advice for municipal bond investors, some of which is rather obvious ("get professional help"), but nice for the beginner. Also cautionary, "Bailout Bonds: Will Investors Like the Yields?" 9-29, looks at the bonds to be issued by Resolution Funding part of the S&L bailout, with a nice perspective on previous issues in similar situations, carefully touting a buy recommendation. A guide to investment newsletters is cursory, Herman not emphasizing the benefits to the investor, as he focuses appropriately on the bottom line of market performance, measured against the Dow and the S&P indices, "Scoop on Newsletters May Be Bad News," 11-13.

Hershey, Robert D., Jr. *The New York Times.* (★ ★)
Washington. A utility reporter, Hershey is the conduit between government and business, covering most issues where Congress sees a dollar sign. He spent much of the year on the tug-of-war over capgains, doing his usual competent job, no more, no less. In an advance on Bush's capital gains proposal, "Bush Plan for Gains Likely," 2-9, he provides adequate detail, though not much on the arguments separating the warring parties. With "Whip Denies Converting Campaign Money for Personal Use," 4-14, following up after the *The Washington Post* story on Rep. Tony Coelho's alleged use of campaign funds to purchase $100,000 of junk bonds via

Drexel Burnham Lambert, Hershey focuses on his denial of allegations, whereas *The Wall Street Journal* focuses on his profitting from purchase. He doesn't ask where the money's coming from, or examine long-term effects in "U.S. May Revamp Its Salary Set-Up," 5-11, a good overview of potential pay-to-scale economic regional adjustments in government positions, but still a reasonable job on how a system reflecting the cost of living in different regions would be better than across the board salary standards. Above average, "Slack Job Growth Seen as Evidence of Slow Economy," 6-3, reviews the accumulating evidence that the economy is slowing down, correctly forecasting the Fed would be forced to ease because of it. With a P. 1 lead, "Rostenkowski Is Reconsidering Opposition to Capital-Gains Cut," 6-8, Hershey's much better than *WSJ*'s same day account, communicating the sense that Rep. Dan Rostenkowski may actually see the potentials of a capgains rate cut as a revenue raiser, quoting Rosty: "If my Democrats or Republicans can offer me a way to raise revenue without a capital-gains cut, I'll jump at it. . .But so far I haven't see a way." Hershey adds ". . .some of the money that might be raised by a cut in the capital-gains rate could pay for child-care programs and other Democratic initiatives that otherwise might not get financing," as *The New York Times* plays Rostenkowski reversal on opposition as major move that will enhance the Bush administration's efforts to get a rate-cut this year. Puffy, "Capitol Hill's High-Tech Tutor," 7-16, he's entirely uncritical of the Office of Technology Assessment and its director, John H. Gibbons, showing evidence of very little legwork here. "Congress Gets Serious on the Capital Gains Tax," 9-10, is a nice, concise collection of arguments, quotes, pro and con, on the cap gains issue on the eve of House Ways and Means voting: "White House. . .sees the center of gravity on the capital gains issue finally moving its way." Hershey gives us a very nice business feature in "A 'Prime Mover' in U.S. Banking," 11-23, on the 90-year-old head of Southwest Bank of St. Louis, I.A. Long, who still has an uncanny knack of knowing when to lead the nation's big banks in a prime-rate cut.

Hilts, Philip J. *The New York Times.* (★ ½)
Switching from *The Washington Post* to the *Times,* Hilts' writing is lively, and he's sometimes skeptical enough to be credible. Surprising the greenhousers with "No Global Warming Seen in 96 Years of U.S. Data," 1-27, he quotes one co-author of the study in question: the averages "don't say anything about man's effect and global warming except that we don't see it in this [96 year] period." He buries his news item in announcing that chlorine chemicals were found in the circle, in "Arctic Ozone Also Imperiled," 2-18, the real news being that the scientists went to the Arctic looking for a hole and after six weeks hadn't found one yet. "An Underwater Window on the Changing Earth," 4-1, is a nicely written feature about studies of coral in Saint Croix, given additional weight by the possibility that coral reefs may give early indication "if the world warms and the seas rise over the next 50 years as the 'greenhouse effect' theory predicts." He's intriguing with "10 Days Beneath the Caribbean: An Experiment Within Itself," 4-1, a study of the behavior of marine biology researchers living together for ten days at the bottom of the ocean inside Aquarius, the underwater "spacelab." "An Energized Quest for Nuclear Fusion," 4-13, is a beautifully written summary of the first three weeks of activity on this story. He's alarmist in "A Sinister Bias: New Studies Cite Perils for Lefties," 8-29, with regard to left-handed people, who, scientists caution, may or may not have a shorter life span; he makes all sorts of quirky observations about biological characteristics related to left-handedness, but never tells us that it's a southpaw currently sitting in the Oval Office. He lists different companies that offend in "F.D.A. Considering New Rules to Curb Health Food-Label Claims," 9-31, to limit the claims that cereals and other foods can make on their labels and advertising, including a history of regulation and litigation, but this is as dry as Wheaties without milk and sugar. He confirms what we've always suspected, that a little exercise is good for you, "Exercise and Longevity: A Little Goes a Long Way," 11-3, giving us all the details on the latest study.

Holusha, John. *The New York Times.* (★ ★ ½)
Getting out of Detroit did Holusha a world of good, his horizons extended beyond the nuts and bolts of the automakers. He gives us "Emhart Plans Merger With Black & Decker," 3-21, a birds-eye view of the ins-and-outs of the proposed merger, Holusha cautionary on the massive amount, 80%, debt incurred. He catalogues the goofs Exxon and company chairman Lawrence G. Rawl made in the Valdez incident, "Exxon's Public Relations Problem," 4-21, balanced and somewhat analytic, just right for P. 1 "Business Day" with regard to management. Only slightly unpolished in "Canadians Open 9-Mile Rail Tunnel," 5-5, he reports on the longest rail tunnel in the Western hemisphere opening to Canada's west coast, seen as a sign of an economic turning to the Far East, interesting, informative, and historical. In "Overcoming Limits to Rail Tunnels," 5-10, he gives an interesting description of the CP's new 9.2 mile Mount MacDonald Tunnel in British Columbia, which had to deal with venting exhaust and providing oxygen for six locomotives per train, mostly westbound and uphill (eastbound trains use another tunnel). The solution was a series of massive fans and gates. Holusha furnishes great detail in "Taking Natural Gas for Test Drive," 5-31, very clearly presented, on a British Columbia experiment with cars and vans converted to burn natural gas, answering almost all our questions. He's amazingly complete and interesting on newspaper recycling, "Old Newspapers Hit a Logjam," 9-10, with all the pros and problems of recycling newspaper. But "McDonald Acts to Recycle Plastic," 10-27, is a routine account that compares unfavorably to David Stipp's *WSJ* same-day report. His "$10 Billion G.E. Stock Buyback," 11-18, is smart, though, getting high up the positive reaction from the investment community, which "had feared the company would make an unsuitable acquisition as its cash reserves grew."

Holzman, David. *Insight.* (★)
Writer, science and health beat. Holzman lacks any sort of panache, his reports sometimes dense, though densely packed. A bit more style would take him into the big leagues. Pedestrian in "Back to School for Aching Backs," 1-9, on a "school," run by an insurance firm, that helps workers with back injuries return to the workforce, Holzman never clearly states what exactly they hope to accomplish. He does tell us that the administrators of this school don't know if some of their methods work, don't know if they're getting the workers back on the job any faster, and don't know if they're saving a dime, making us wonder why this article was written at all. He discusses spontaneous remission from Lourdes to medical miracles, "Chasing Answers to Miracle Cures," 2-20, with different examples of the phenomenon, also called spontaneous regression, as doctors begin to feel that these remissions are an important part in the study of disease. He plods a bit through "Working Designs Lighten the Load," 3-13, an interesting piece on redesigning manufacturing and office equipment in order to lessen work-related injuries, but we'd have liked to have seen the survey in progress of stats showing that workman's comp dollars had been saved. Multidimensional in "To Find a Way to Age in Health," cover 4-10, Holtzman's up-to-date in providing assessments of various findings on relevant issues, and we're relieved to find that it's no longer necessarily true that if you live long enough you lose your sex drive and your mind. He comes to some intriguing conclusions in "Elusive Culprits in Workplace Ills," 6-26, on "sick building syndrome," looking at possible causes for increases in employee illnesses related to the workplace: ventilation, lighting, building maintenance. Holzman handles "A Better Ride Around the World," 7-3, well, effective about the design of improved, lightweight, low-cost wheelchairs for the disabled in Third World countries. We're intrigued by the title in "Rationalizing Thoughtless Emotions," 9-18, but Holzman quickly loses us in a jargon-riddled discussion of experiments with lab rats. We looked to *Insight* for a cover takeout on global warming, but it would need a higher caliber reporter than Holzman to handle it.

Horowitz, Rose. *The Journal of Commerce.* (★ ½)
International trade reporter. Horowitz runs one of the tighter ships in the business, clear and accurate, but usually only roundup quality. We'd like to see more digging from her. In a summary *cum* assessment of the Soviet Union's first major trade show in the U.S., "Soviets Proclaim Trade Show Success," 12-21-88, Horowitz offers the conclusion that it was a partial

success despite criticism from some Western observers, presenting pro and con views well. She includes all pertinent information in "U.S. Importers, Exporters Eye Grace-Period Accord," 1-9, a quickie piece, with some insights as to the purpose and intent of grace-period accord to make it worthwhile. "FDA to Hold Fruit From Chile at Docks," 3-15, shows evidence of some legwork, but she, like many other reporters, takes for granted that the grapes were tampered with in Chile, which we found later might not have been the case. In "Lawsuit Claimed Hazelwood Abusive," 4-5, Horowitz reveals further alleged mismanagement by Exxon and the captain of the Valdez. She presents a competent, fast look at the Bush administration's decision to export wheat to Russia in "U.S.S.R. Gets U.S. Assistance in Buying Grain," 5-3, nicely based, covering some good angles, including the zig-zag on commodity markets. Co-authored by Howard S. Abramson, in "Dean of Agents Says Avoid Conflicts," 6-19, Horowitz gets some good quotes from Harry J. Smith Jr. as well as presenting a clear overview of his management of St. John International, a food aid shipping business, not skimping on the questions of his possible involvement in the Tongsun Park affair. She holds our interest in "Calif. Hopes To Weave Big Profits From Pima," 9-22, on pima cotton, info-packed and beginning with a nice lead: "When farmers in California saw a selling price for long, silky pima cotton that was nearly triple the price for common upland cotton earlier this year, they went for the profits."

Ingersoll, Bruce. *The Wall Street Journal.* (★ ★ ★)
Washington, covering agricultural and food issues. Ingersoll has worked this beat into one of investigative reporting, rather than merely recycling press releases. His reports are like mini-bombs, well-packed and explosive, although sometimes he can be off in his timing and delivery. He was the talk of the town with his most startling exposition of the year, "In Chilean Grape Case, New Data Raise Doubt as to What Happened," 11-16, a breathtaking review of the evidence of the almost forgotten Chilean grape scare, with Ingersoll uncovering facts that make the State Department and the FDA's arguments look mighty fishy on the finding of those two contaminated grapes, a gripping story and 10 Best selection. Reminiscent of Upton Sinclair, he's relentless in "Slicing It Thin: Meat Inspection Cuts Proposed by Reagan Are Hot Issue for Bush," 1-2, a well-documented account of conditions in some parts of the meat packing industry, a 10 Best nomination. In a followup, "Inspection Cuts At Meat Plants Placed on Hold," 4-5, he reports that the "Agriculture Department, yielding to a consumer uproar, withdrew its plan to cut its force of food-safety inspectors and reduce the frequency of inspection at most meat and poultry processing plants." We wonder how much his earlier account had to do with this. Loaded with grisly detail, he doesn't make his case with hard information in "New Beef Inspection Would Be So Cursory Even Packers Are Wary," 5-16, a dubious account of beef slaughterhouses, with little credibility in suggestions that new Agriculture Dept. "Streamlined Inspection System" is inadequate. Vivid with "Perilous Profession: Farming is Dangerous, But Fatalistic Farmers Oppose Safety Laws," 7-20, Ingersoll tells some gruesome stories of lost limbs and other accidents as a result of carelessness on farms, but provides few solutions. In a good overview co-authored by Gregory Stricharchuk, "Generic-Drug Scandal At The FDA Is Linked To Deregulation Drive," 9-13, he tells us much of what we need to know about the generic drug scandal, peppering the piece with liberal quotes.

Ivey, Mark. *Business Week.* (★ ★ ★)
Houston bureau manager. Pithy and sharp on issues in the Sunbelt, Ivey's dispatches are lively and well informed; often striking, his material jumped out at us this year. Anyone in the country interested in oil has to read "The Man Who Strikes Fear in the Heart of the Oil Patch," 11-6, Oscar S. Wyatt, Coastal Corp. chairman and "one of the toughest, shrewdest, most successful men to set foot in the oil patch," also "one of the most despised," a "bully" and "pariah," with a beautiful wife who throws barbecues in Monaco. We'd compare Wyatt to J.R. Ewing, but are afraid he'd sue us. (Really, Oscar, you're our kind of guy!) Ivey's also refreshing in "Houston's Sick Economy Is Taking a Little Nourishment," 1-16, on how battered Houston is coming back, at least somewhat, based on non-oil sectors such as biotech, aerospace, and chemicals. "I Feel Like a Dentist Pulling Teeth," 2-27, is useful and interesting on Gov. Roemer's attempts to solve

some of Louisiana's economic problems, including cutting above-average taxes on business, forcing more homeowners to pay property tax (90% are now exempt), and improving a poor education system, based on an interview with Buddy. He skims in spots, weak on the individual income tax system, which goes undescribed, except that Roemer would like to raise rates, and he doesn't interview Roemer's opponents on these measures. In a sparkling profile of the heart surgeon, "Will Denton Cooley Make Medical History Again?" 3-27, Ivey details his comeback from personal bankruptcy and his struggle to stay competitive in the heart surgery field: "Cooley's comeback strategy is a lot like Sears Roebuck's: everyday low prices," going beyond profile depth to report that Medicare is interested in a pilot test of these flat fees at Cooley's Institute, and discussing the possible implications for national health care regarding Medicare's desire to save money. "Jim Kinnear Is Pumping New Life into Texaco," 4-17, is a progress report on Texaco since bankruptcy, including a good analysis of CEO Kinnear's strategy. He's spirited with "What's Pumping Up Gasoline Prices?" with Ronald Grover 5-8, smoothly organized on refiners, who are doing very well lately, with tight supplies of crude oil and stretched U.S. refining capacity. He offers a nice analytic in "How Compaq gets there Firstest with the Mostest," with Geoff Lewis 6-26, on — how the company became a computer industry leader and how its management sets product strategy, offering little new, but tautly presented. He's well rounded in "Why Natural Gas Is Burning Brighter," with Grover 8-28, abundant information on the outlook for natural gas production, distribution and price, without venturing into advocacy. In "Methanol May Be Clean, But It's a Dirty Word to Big Oil," 9-4, he notes the growing groundswell in the grassroots sector for cleaner air, advising big oil to get it in gear.

Jenkins, Holman, Jr. *Insight.* (★ ★ ★)
Writer. His clear-eyed, smart looks at countries are definitive, often setting the tone as to what we look for in followup coverage from the press. Jenkins is best when his editors give him free rein and enough space to cover his topics thoroughly; otherwise he ends up either skimming or cramming too much into a smaller space. He makes a sharp identification here of a crisis brewing for the 40-year-old alliance in the cover "Truly Talking Shop at the Kremlin," 12-26-88/1-9-89, a three-parter on Soviet commercial overtures to the West and prospects for reform. This 10 Best selection provides a detached look at Gorbachev's attempts to finance *perestroika* with Western credits and subsidized loans, with a great quote from Richard Perle: "The West can't insure the success of *perestroika.* But we can screw it up with misguided generosity." Snappy in "Fight to Open Skies Grounded by Red Tape, National Pride," 1-16, on deregulating international airline routes, Jenkins moves smoothly from one thought to another, opening and closing strongly, taking us through a dry topic with ease and flair. "Fast Ride for the Jet Set Turns 20," 3-27, reads like a gushing brochure on the Concorde, as the planes celebrate their 20th anniversary in service, completely omitting the flap over the U.S. SSTs and how environmentalists claimed a fleet of them would destroy the ozone layer. Eye-opening and replete with examples and information in "Uncle Sam Counts on Airlines to Carry Forces to Battlefront," 4-17, he tells us about the Civil Reserve Air Fleet, in which most major carriers are participants and would carry a whopping 95% of the soldiers and 25% of the equipment to a war in Europe, should one ever break out; meanwhile, the carriers make $1.4 billion in shuttling various military personnel and equipment now, making the Pentagon their biggest customer. "The Nation's Figures Indicate a Number of Deficiencies," 5-1, throws a spotlight on the clumsy way the government compiles economic stats, with a great example showing the country gets $21.1 billion more from its foreign investments than it pays out, even though the Commerce Dept. says we're a debtor nation. He gets a 10 Best nomination with "Doing Business in South Africa," 7-31, the first detailed look at the black informal economy in South Africa, divided into two parts: "What Counts Is the Color of Money," on black hawkers turned entrepreneurs; and "A Market as Oppressed as the Black Majority," a credible examination of the shrinking white economy, burdened by shrinking tax base. He gets a new angle on the S&L crisis and Resolution Trust Corp., as entrepreneurs begin to put out advisory newsletters and investors put in big bucks, "Thrift Bailout Boon to Some, Possible Burden to Uncle Sam," 10-16, nicely rounded and equitably handled.

Johnson, Robert. *The Wall Street Journal.* (★ ★)
Chicago. Slipping a bit as he begins to stick to somewhat more conventional topics, Johnson seemed in a rut, unable to get the in-depth evaluative looks on quirky subjects we prized in previous years. A quick glimpse of Buffalo Bill and questions about his legacy, "Mr. Cody's Public-Relations Aide Couldn't Be Reached for Comment," 2-22, is cute, but not terribly useful. In an optimistic look at the Manpower Employment Outlook, "Firms' Hiring Plans for Second Quarter Look Bright, Manpower Survey Shows," 3-6, he extends the forecast to rebut economists' predictions of an upcoming recession. Compactly analytic in "Shaw Publishing To Acquire Control of American City," 5-22, he offers a quick view of the ins and outs of the deal, as well as peripheral offers for the two companies involved with an overview of the history of the players. In "Haunting Melodies Make Zamfir a Star of Cable-TV Ads," 8-9, he uncovers the misery behind the pan flautist fondly known to anyone who has stayed up late watching CNN Headline News, where advertisements for his haunting serenades frequently air: "Without benefit of even one hit song played by radio disc jockeys to bolster sales in record stores, the 48-year-old Romanian is peddling enough albums on cable TV to keep him in Rolls-Royces, $200-a-bottle wines and the Italian fashion he loves." But there's an underside too: Zamfir, it turns out, is pretty fed up playing "Somewhere My Love," and he lives in fear of Soviet secret agents. Now that's a riveting story. Standard stuff in "Holder Boosts Cummins Stake; Stock Up $1.625," 9-20, though there's evidence he did a little digging, and the piece is nicely rounded. A riveting expose of charity fundraising is flavored by a *caveat emptor* mentality, as Johnson comes up with hard evidence that while there are many legitimate charities (he lists some), there are also many scams, "Give and Take: Many Fundraisers Think Charity Begins at Home — Their Home," 10-20: "Without a microscope and a subpoena, it's often hard to sort out worthwhile causes from ripoffs if all you've got to go on is the solicitation itself."

Johnston, Oswald. *Los Angeles Times.* (★ ½)
Washington, economics/labor beat. Most of what we see from Johnston is stock rewrites of the various administration bureaus responsible for vital economic statistics. He crunches these numbers well enough, but seldom adds things up to a level that adds useful perspectives. In "Bush, the Insider, Will Forgo Usual Kitchen Cabinet," 1-20, he provides further proof that the Bush administration could be one of the most difficult administrations in recent memory to predict, as Bush doesn't have just a couple of close friends he relies on for advice, but the ones he does have are in Cabinet positions, so he could go in many different directions. On the inflationary numbers beat, "Retail Price Rise Is Highest in 2 Years," 2-23, he continues to avoid the hysteria that can be generated by stats, staying calm and reasonable, but he's non-analytic. He provides alternate viewpoints in the balanced "Low Savings Rate Seen as Perilous to Sound Economy," 3-9, based largely on a study by a special interest group, but he still needs a wider net to get this in perspective. In "Stocks Surge on Wholesale Prices Post Only 0.4% Gain," 5-13, he catalogues all the reasons by economists as to why they've been so wrong on inflation and the markets, without making the article into an apologia. Taking an obvious, but new, tact in "Few Worry as Wholesale Prices Spurt 0.9%," 6-10, he talks about the fact that there is no inflationary psychology that accounts for a buying spurt. Written with the layman in mind, "Democrats Seen Blocking Vote on Capital Gains," 7-24, he does a good, balanced job of defining the terms of the proposed cut in capital gains taxes and of explaining the projected benefits or flaws — depending on which side one listens to. "Choice for SEC Sails Through Hearing," 9-15, is non-analytic on Richard C. Breeden's confirmation hearing, taking us through it step-by-step, a useful exercise.

Jones, Alex S. *The New York Times.* (★ ★)
Press reporter. We listed Jones as a Social/Political Reporter in the last *MediaGuide,* but he's really a business reporter, covering the business side of the news media, and we wonder why the *Times* doesn't shift him to that department. "Disposal of Old Newspapers Worrying Publishers," 4-26, is timely and fairly complete on what to do with old newspapers and how suddenly it's the paper's responsibility, covering the intricate relationships involved and what

avenues they can pursue; Jones segues into ad revenues towards the end of the piece though, and the connection doesn't seem quite clear. "Will Profits Still Grow?" 8-27, a lead Sunday business story on Gannett's *USA Today,* now run by Gannett CEO John J. Curley as Allen Neuharth retires, is disappointing, lacking any sense of Curley's or Gannett's horizons, but scattered detail kept us reading to the end. "Gannett's Former Chief Tells Why He Did It," 9-14, evidences a light touch on Al Neuharth, with not enough on his real management style, although vignettes in here are supposed to do it. "New York's *Daily News* Prepares for a War With Its Unions," 9-25, almost gets it all in the flap over Jim Hoge's preparations for a strike at New York's Hometown Paper, but not enough from the labor side. Although we get a lot on the "posturing" of both sides, there's too little on what either the union or management really wants in the contract when it expires 3-30-90. He writes sympathetically, yet without unacceptable bias, in "New York Post's Owner Is Optimistic," 11-13, as Peter Kalikow takes some knocks learning about publishing the hard way.

Kagan, Daniel. *Insight.* (★ ½)
Science and business coverage from this *Insight* reporter who is innovative and enterprising in the material he develops, although he is sometimes a bit disorganized. His cover "Fast-Food Kids," 8-28, was among the most notable in the magazine this year, cited in *The Wall Street Journal* for its insights. Kagan reports on the poor inner-city kids of DC who *don't* peddle drugs, why they are happy enough at the minimum wage flipping hamburgers, how they've made their decisions, etc., a timely and enterprising piece that earned a 10 Best selection. Kagan lets "Getting a Jump on the Trailblazers," 12-26-88, wander off, and this "Experts" version of astrologers' forecasts for 1989 needed a humorous lead so we wouldn't take it too seriously. In a brief history of shortwave radio, "A New Wave in the World of Radio," 2-20, he finds the medium resurgent, and is successful in conveying the breathless excitement of a radio junkie hearing Radio Moscow or Voice of America for the first time. Taking a different angle on the same subject, he turns shortwave into a cover story, "Shortwave Signals a Competitive Era," 4-24, looking at the actual broadcasts of different countries, and how it's used as a representation of countries. While he repeats much of the information of the earlier piece for those who might have missed the first broadcast, he presents enough that's new to keep the story fresh, though his use of overly technical terms on "bouncing" signals gets annoying. Despite some occasionally heavy-handed historical parallels in "How America Lost Its First Drug War," 11-20, Kagan presents an overview of the history of the first drug war of the 19th century, how frustration can lead to exaggeration and sometimes to efforts to ban all mention of drugs, which leads to ignorance in the next generation. He shows how fear-mongering and the State Dept have used drug campaigns for their own ends, how statistics have been inflated or made up and quotes experts warning against letting frustration drive our policies in directions that have failed before.

Kaletsky, Anatole. *Financial Times.* (★ ★ ½)
New York. More thoughtful and analytic than over the last few years, we find Kaletsky to be as stimulating as we've ever seen him, without the sarcasm we found irritating in some of his earlier work. Consistency in his depth of analysis is all he needs to take him higher. He's limited in "Polaroid in $1.1bn Share Purchase," 1-31, a report on Polaroid's stock repurchase to avoid a takeover by Shamrock partners. Organized in "Ford Advances Strongly for Third Year Running," 2-17, he lays out all the mind-boggling numbers in a good rundown of the immense strides Ford is making on profitability. He impresses with "Monument to Media 'Synergy,' " 4-22, a discussion of the rush to create "global" communications groups, conglomeration towards "global reach" and other media cliches, a real debate with several ideas tossed about. In "Puzzle on Rising Equity Prices," 6-26, he offers sharp analysis, comparing PE ratios and divided yields to the Dow Jones peak in '87, also to the peaks of '81, '77 and '73: "In each of those years. . .the stock market seemed to offer even better value than it does today. Yet stock prices fell by an average of 31 percent in the three bear markets which followed those cyclical peaks." "A Mood of Caution," 6-26, surveys Wall Street's "medium-term prospects, noting they are, if anything, less favorable today than they were two years ago" as the current bull market

"has been a profitless one for most financial businesses." But we need more on "medium-term prospects." "The Economic Recovery Continues," 6-26, is also smart, concise, weaving in the importance of continued growth to Bush and the GOP in 1990. He takes a quick, but important, peek at a British Airways and Morgan Stanley leveraged takeover proposal for UAL, "UAL Vetoed Buy-Out Plan in June," 8-22, just as the story got hot. On Cummins Engine, "Strategy Before Profits," 10-12, Kaletsky presents a complete picture of both, a sterling account.

Kanner, Bernice. *New York.* (★ ★ ½)
"On Madison Avenue" columnist. Not burdened by the grind of daily coverage of the Manhattan ad business, Kanner is free to pick and choose among her subjects. Her topics are always readable and interesting, although not always as important or informative as we'd like them to be. In "The War of the Hoses," 1-2, she delightfully details the advertising plans of the major hosiery makers, from Hanes to Round the Clock, all getting *very* sexy, but not particularly sexist, although the Round the Clock ads had some people steamed. A delicious "Hot Potatoes," 2-6, looks at different food campaigns and their varying success. We've heard much of "Color Schemes," 4-3, before, although it's nicely presented on the art of colors: what they mean, and how to use them to your advantage in all sorts of interesting ways. Kanner puts a name, Jan Leighton, to the man we see as all kinds of historical figures, from Harpo Marx to Ben Franklin, in advertising, a neat industry insider's look, "Man of a Thousand Faces," 5-29. More offbeat with "Dear John," 7-17, she examines ad campaigns for bathrooms, looking at the trends that led up to increased importance of the commode in the house, arguing persuasively that some people spend more time relaxing in the bathroom than the living room. Taking a new tack on the new technology, "I Want My HDTV," 9-11, she catalogues the advent of ads and programming in the new medium, interesting, but light.

Karmin, Monroe W. *U.S.News & World Report.* (★)
"Economic Outlook" columnist. A veteran who probably has this assignment because he once won a Pulitzer at *The Wall Street Journal,* Karmin is simply misplaced. He should be covering business news, not economics, his material usually bits and pieces of conventional wisdom lightly strung together. He's not as dour as he used to be or as some of his predecessors were, and his insights are sometimes useful, but come too few and far between. He does go against the grain a bit in reckoning there will be no new taxes in '89, sharp early on Brady and Bush, "A Championship Season for Bush?" 1-16. But he falls prey to conventional wisdom, fretting over Bush's plan for the deficit, "Bush's Stealth Budget," 2-27, backing his worries up with few numbers and examples of "fiscal conundrums." In "We Ain't Got a Barrel of Money," 4-3, he gives an interesting comparison of the economic conditions today with those of a decade ago, but again he gets hung up on the deficit, telling us that it would make it impossible for the government "to find the money needed for jobs programs to help a recovery." Scattershot with "Shadowboxing Over Fair Trade," 6-5, he writes entirely on trade from the perspective of bureaucrats at the office of the U.S. Trade Rep. "The Fed's Hot Seat at Darman's Breakfast Table," 8-28/9-4, focuses on OMB Director Darman's recent Fed bashing and call for lower interest rates, taking a look at the economic climate and implications of Darman's goal being realized: lower rates mean more tax revenues without a tax increase, lower national debt payments, and a greater chance of meeting the 1991 Gramm-Rudman requirements without new taxes. The newsweekly simply needs a stronger entry in this slot to provide the occasional insight or surprise.

Kehoe, Louise. *Financial Times.* (★ ½)
San Francisco. The *FT*'s Silicon Valley reporter, Kehoe spends her time between computer chips and trade policy, keeping us up with able handling of the routine. We didn't see a great deal to lift her above the ordinary, but now and then she sparkled. One such, "A Sudden Blemish on Quick-Growing Apple," 1-30, she's clear and understandable, telling how Apple misjudged the DRAM chip market and took a hit on earnings earlier this year. She interviews CEO John Sculley and, in a nice bit of craftsmanship, alternates between the chat with him and an account

of what Apple did six months previously. In "U.S. Switches On TV of the Future," 1-24, Kehoe faithfully retells the industry story, but nothing on the other side, quoting Congressmen who favor government investment in HDTV: "There is a growing consensus that HDTV is vital to our national economy and security. . .the U.S. Congress is not going to want to see America left out of the creative origination of the next generation of computer technology." She also quotes the enthusiasm of William Verity, the outgoing Commerce Secretary who presided over the decline of Armco Steel and who has referred to our trading partners as "Japs," calling for repeal of anti-trust provisions to support HDTV. A solid recap, "Memories Will Be Made of This," 2-24, is dense reading in spots, but a good clip-and-save piece on the next generation of semiconductors. She's undiscerning again in "Chipmakers Fan Flames of U.S. Rows With Japan," 3-7, a wrap-up of the complaint U.S. chipmakers have with Japan, making the protectionist case without challenge and dutifully reporting that Carla Hills "has expressed concern." She gets good detail on the reaction of Japan to U.S. Japan-bashing, "Japan Threatens to End Pact on U.S. Chips Trade," 4-28. In "Tremor at the Heart of U.S. Chip Industry," 5-31, she cautiously recounts U.S. chipmakers' woes and how they are now affecting makers of semiconductor manufacturing equipment, but Kehoe's overly respectful to Robert Noyce, the industry's leading protectionist, and she reports the industry's case for tariffs and "tough new approaches to Japanese trade disputes" with little or no challenge. Too close to the industry line in "Where the Fog Hangs Thickest in San Francisco," 6-1, she gives an innovative financial idea — a market for chip futures — the cold shoulder, as she "examines the reaction" to the idea by quoting people in the electronics industry, who don't like it; a Dataquest analyst gets in a careful statement that "the idea deserves due consideration," but you come away from this article thinking that it doesn't stand a chance. She's brief but intriguing with "Schools in Soviet Union May Get U.S. Computers," 9-13, on the new venture, Samcom, between the U.S.S.R. and the Phoenix Group International, that will provide computers.

Kiechel, Walter, III. *Fortune.* (★ ½)
Management column. Kiechel's "Office Hours" column is a very important forum for the magazine. It should inspire a fan club the way Dan Seligman's "Keeping Up" column has. Kiechel hovers on the edge, but somehow just doesn't deliver. He can be on the margin in picking a topic, but too often its development falls flat. "A Hard Look At Executive Vision," 10-23, is a case in point, a great idea spinning off President Bush's "vision thing," but Kiechel sanitizes it with quotes from several "experts" on vision instead of pondering visionaries. Another nifty idea, "How to Spot an Empty Suit," 11-20, tackles the flip side of visionary, but with the same sterile approach, quoting human resources consultants who sound like empty suits themselves: "Often he wants to make everybody feel good, so he goes around agreeing with what everybody says." His "How Important Is Morale, Really?" 2-13, has a snide tone that works against it, and he doesn't answer his own question, even in the most peripheral sense. In a 10 Best nomination from his editors, "The Workaholic Generation," cover 4-10, Kiechel does well to try to give us an understanding of this group, but it's difficult to get through the self-absorbed, narrow-minded and canned phrases from this sampling of yuppie managers. "When A Headhunter Calls," 5-8, contains straightforward and practical advice, but nothing your mother didn't tell you before that first post-college interview; the bottom line is do your homework, just like everything else, but Kiechel hasn't. "Workaholics Anonymous," 8-14, proffers some obvious, but well-written advice for those of us who never see their friends or get home except to sleep.

Kilborn, Peter T. *The New York Times.* (★ ★)
Washington. A new "workplace" beat for Kilborn at midyear after several years covering Treasury/Fed economics. He now reports on new trends and problems of Americans at work, not quite "labor" or "management," but potentially interesting. "Milwaukee Helps Pace U.S. As Innovator for Workplace," 10-12, has splendid material on how both city and county government there accommodate workers with "jobsharing" and such to keep productivity high, but could have benefited with a lively quote or example near the top. His "Drugs and Debt: Shackles of Migrant Workers," 10-31, is so-so, turning on a "wine book" discovered by feds,

migrant worker crew leaders keeping their crews in "debt servitude" by selling them tobacco, alcohol and drugs on credit. He broadens a feature on coping with the quake, "Quake Gives an Impetus to Commuting by Phone," 11-15, to wonder if telecommuting might be a wave of the future. While still at Treasury, he's timely and forthright with "Brady Avoiding Critics as Groups of 7 Gather," 2-2, noting that "Nicholas F. Brady seems to be off to a rocky start as Secretary of the Treasury." "Debt-Policy Shift Set on 3rd World," 3-11, reports on a speech by Treasury Secretary Nicholas Brady on Baker plan variation, that includes almost no substance or detail on exactly what this plan is all about, except to introduce the concept of debt relief. "Administration Seeking to Explain Debt Policy," 3-15, tells us "Amid signs of internal discord and hurried conferences over the reversal in its developing country debt policy, the Bush administration appeared to be redoubling its efforts today to refine the shift." Sensitive to the global debate, "Rate Caution By Fed Seen," 3-22, he's precise in focusing on the Fed's evaluation of various signals of inflation and in noting that members "are not inclined" to "slam the economy" with much higher interest rates to stop inflation. "Tight White House Control Marks Bush Economic Policy," 3-26, is an important, insightful report on Bush's departure from the looser Reagan approach: "President Bush has built a sizable economic policy apparatus within the White House to supplement and second-guess the policy-making work of the Treasury and other departments, and sometimes to take the initiative." Useful with "Debt Reduction: Ways To Do It," 4-6, he surveys technical means for debt reduction supporting the conclusion that "debt reduction" as such won't do very much. "New Strategy on the Dollar," 5-22, is terribly misleading, suggesting Boskin and Darman are trying to persuade Treasury to revert to the practices of the 70s and early 80s, "when countries left the fate of their currencies largely to the marketplace." "The Dollar Defies Those Who Would Rein It In," 6-4, is gibberish, Kilborn arguing that to keep the dollar from rising "means a substantially lower budget deficit." And "The deficit, it is generally accepted, contributes to the hardness of the dollar rising by increasing Washington's need to borrow money from foreigners." Hmmmm. The change of beats did him good.

Kleinfield, N. R. *The New York Times.* (★ ★)
Sunday "Business" section. There's no question that Kleinfield is in the top ranks of business feature writers, his writing and presentation almost always enough to pull us through. He doesn't tackle many of the big, complex business stories, though, which sometimes leaves us with a sense that we're reading less for information than for amusement. "The Video News Release: Let the Viewer Beware," 1-2, has Kleinfield exploring whether it's right or wrong to have companies sending out video cassettes as TV press releases. The only example he uses, though, is Drexel's reaction to its settlement over Fed securities laws. "In Search of the Next Medium," 3-19, is up his alley, and he gives us a well-crafted, provocative piece on Christopher Whittle of Whittle Communications and his innovative products, including special reports for doctors' offices and Channel One for high school students. We appreciate Kleinfield digging into communication theory along the way. In "Keeping Hotels On Their Toes," 6-25, he follows a quality-control inspector for a few days at the Sheraton Stamford. Reminiscent of Dyan Machan's piece on quality control at McDonald's last year in *Forbes,* "Great Hash Browns, But Watch Those Biscuits," 9-19-88, this piece has value both for its interest to a business traveler and as a real world study for hotel management students. "A Double Whammy for the Insurers," 10-22, grapples with the problems of the insurance industry after being hit by Hurricane Hugo and the California earthquake, and we learn a great deal about these at a surface level, but Kleinfield doesn't dig into the second-order effects, so we never do get a sense of why the market bid *up* insurance shares after the earthquake. Similarly, we learn a great deal about the decline in the $5 billion coffee industry in "A Cold War Over Coffee," 10-29, but he never delves into the likely connection with the decline in cigarette smoking, which would have added a broader perspective. We're offered a long feature on the business of TV wrestling, "This Is Not Real," 11-26, but before we let Kleinfield get us into a hammerlock with his fancy writing, we simply cry "uncle!"

Kneale, Dennis. *The Wall Street Journal.* (★ ★ ★)
New York, covering the networks. The chief chronicler of CBS's troubles since Lawrence Tisch took over, Kneale is sharp on other matters dealing with the Big Three. He's a good example of a reporter who can improve his performance markedly by changing beats, Kneale coming off computers two years ago. His "Distress Signals: CBS Frantically Woos Hollywood to Help It Win Back Viewers," 2-9, is an informative, readable piece on CBS's costly programming errors, detailing the problems and perils of an aging product and waiting too long to attempt a turnaround. Witty in "How to Shun Friends and Influence Shows; Notes From a Week as a Nielsen Household," 3-3, Kneale offers a sprightly feature as he clocks a week watching the tube as a Nielsen rater, raising serious doubts about the validity and accuracy of the Nielsen system, whose immutable numbers provide the basis for decisions in the TV and advertising industries. He's slow in developing a P. 1 leder, "TV Networks Suffer Lasting Ill Effects of the Writers Strike," 1-5, and might have fared better with a harder news lead. In "Time-Warner Pact Raises Ante in TV-Rule Dispute," 3-8, he catches an important side issue to the blockbuster media merger — the jousting between the three networks and big movie studios over deregulation of network TV, including some snappy one-liners between the movie's Jack Valenti and Robert Wright of NBC, putting the Time merger into the larger context of the broadcast industry. He demonstrates with wit and precision how TV networks throw money at pilot episodes, "Reshaping the Irrational TV-Pilot Game," 4-14. Aggressive and smart in "Time Inc. Urges States and Cities to Sue Paramount Over Local Cable-TV Rights," 6-30, he shows how Time is trying to use local governments to harass the Paramount bid, perceptive in finding the faulty arguments in the Time position. Good color in " 'Big Play' Seeking Ratings Gains, CBS Pays Huge Sums for Sports Contracts," 10-10, but he's a little short on new information or analysis as CBS's big investment in sports programming has been well covered, and we don't learn much new about the major players or their motivation. "TV Networks Seek Way Around Rules," 10-16, is an ambitious overview of the dense thicket of regulation limiting TV networks, with the Japanese influence now mixing the pot even more. Not an easy read, as the "tangled web" of regulation and provisions is like "eating sawdust without butter," but Kneale takes a good run at it, and this is a good reference piece of what the regulatory outlook is for the TV networks.

Kosterlitz, Julie. *National Journal.* (★ ★)
Staff correspondent, covering health. More in-depth work from Kosterlitz boosts her rating, going beyond the conventional to dig out creative angles and insights. She's clear in "Unhappy Season for Employers," 1-7, as the new tax code takes effect and employers must deal with Section 89, which "applies so-called nondiscrimination rules to employer-sponsored health, term life and accident insurance plans" and, although she doesn't look forward to the implications of the law, such as increased employer costs and insurance revenue gains, she gets the Beltway debate well enough. In "Random Rationing," 4-22, she's muddled in debating the pros and cons of state-sponsored health care, trying to take on too much in covering this, plus the tug-of-war between insurers, pharmacists, doctors, hospitals and consumers. A potent profile on David S. Liederman, CEO of the Child Welfare League of America, "A Commuting Advocate for Throwaway Children," 6-24, is timely, coming at the height of the debate over the juveniles involved in the Central Park rape case, with Liederman taking the part of the children without sounding like a bleeding heart. She's deep in a two-part series on Canada's universal health care system: "Taking Care of Canada," 7-15, clearly illustrates the themes of Canadian health care reforms, but is mostly pro-Canada, not mentioning that they do not provide *any* health care for AIDS patients; "But Not For Us?" 7-22, deals with whether elements of Canada's health care program might be adopted by the U.S., concluding that the two countries are too different, politically, demographically, and philosophically, and it won't happen. She's up-close and personal with Sen. Orrin Hatch, "Tough to Typecast," 8-19, with plentiful quotes and Capitol Hill insight. She takes a good look at businesses' desperate cry for relief from corporate health care costs in "Bottom-Line Pain," 9-9, focusing on the regional phone companies as a test case as she tells us how corporate tactics are changing to employee cost-sharing and even an embryonic consideration of national health insurance programs.

Kriz, Margaret E. *National Journal.* (★)
Regulatory beat. Kriz surprises us once in a blue moon with a satisfying piece that tells us she has potential, but for the third year since we've been critiquing her we have to note that she is, on balance, pedestrian. "Politics in the Air," 5-6, puzzled us, perhaps because it seemed designed as a guide for Washingtonians about to become involved in Clean Air legislation after an extended trip to the antipodes. On the one hand, on the other; space filled with names and pictures of participants, names that probably carry weight in DC. The characterization of the technical questions is just the recital of the usual suspects; the quality of prediction poor. "Ozone and Evidence," 11-11, is not good either, advising us immediately about "the dangerous global warming trend" without presenting the "evidence." The lengthy piece is sophomoric, quoting every available hand-wringer, with no sense of debate. Then we get "The Fight for Access," 7-8, a sweeping look at regulation and deregulation of the telecommunications industry, well presented and tightly packaged, raising some interesting questions regarding cable TV, and the right to information of the average viewer. "Saving the S&Ls," 1-14, is an early curtain-raiser, dry as dust, ironically leading with a photo and quote from Senate Banking Chairman Donald Riegle, Jr. (D-Mich.), charging the GOP with burying the S&L issue in '88 "for fear of its effect on the presidential election," with Riegle later in the year snagged on the scandal himself. "An Ounce of Prevention," 8-19, tells us the EPA wants to encourage industry to prevent pollution, not just clean it up when it occurs. But environmental groups don't like that idea for some reason we never quite understand. The writing gets heavy at times. "It's difficult to say that you're forging ahead with the environment if your mantle is pollution prevention." It isn't easy either with "Ringing the Bells," 2-4, on how two regional Bell telephone companies are trying to pry the case from the courts and Judge Harold H. Greene. A very slow start with an awkward metaphor. Still, we get the details eventually.

Kuttner, Robert. *The New Republic.* (★ ½)
Economic correspondent. Kuttner's neo-Keynesian model may be battered and bruised, but he does as good a job as any in pumping up the best of it. We tune in to watch him at work, often marveling at his dexterity. He writes of the generational problem in "The Baby-Boomers' Parents Had It Better," 1-20, solving an alleged "housing shortage" by taxing the dickens out of the "unearned capital gain reaped by longtime home owners, and using the proceeds to help young families afford to buy a first house." If this sounds like social engineering, Kuttner seems to have second thoughts too: "Real generational equity requires expanding public services to help the young, not taking them away from the old." Hmmmm. "Whatever Is Driving Inflation, It's Not Wages and Salaries," *Los Angeles Times* 3-6, opens with the assertion that workers *can* cause inflation if they want to, and the Fed can halt inflation by raising interest rates and punishing workers with unemployment. The idea is quaint, but Kuttner uses it to argue that *in this case* wages are not causing inflation, therefore the Fed shouldn't be tightening. Taxes should be raised to balance the budget, of course. Kuttner does take a whack at the "wrongheaded economics" of his fellow Keynesians, disputing the view that a cheaper dollar is a "painless cure for the trade deficit." In "Bloc That Trade," 4-17, he refutes the idea that bilateral trade negotiations like the one between the U.S. and Canada signal a shift toward a world economy segmented into trading blocs. But how about this for verbosity: "recent history offers a frantic oscillation between the sacred ideological imperative of even freer markets and the profane business of looking with almost equal urgency for practical economic stabilizing devices to offset the chaos that laissez-faire can engender." Whew. He claims that the Voluntary Restraint Agreement works in steel and that it should be renegotiated before it expires 9-30 as with limits of imports "voluntarily" held to 20% of the U.S. market. The U.S. Steel Industry has prospered in "Why Scrap a Steel Policy that Works," *Business Week* 5-22, making a good case for not holding the U.S. to fair trade and open markets unless the rest of the world in willing to play — at least in steel. He argues for re-regulation of the airline industry in "Plane Truth," 7-17/24, a case bound to appeal to frustrated consumers, but he's flawed in missing a discussion of the argument made by pro-deregulators that all these problems are caused by the failure to deregulate airports (e.g., landing fees). Ably recounting John Maynard Keynes' association with

TNR, "Keynes the Able," 11-6, he goes a bit overboard putting words in JMK's mouth: "Were he alive in 1989, Keynes would surely be railing against the austerity cure for Third World debt, the failure of statesmen and the orthodox view that American must deflate its way to budget balance."

Labaton, Stephen. *The New York Times.* (★ ½)
New York, on the legal side of business. With all the SEC indictments and assorted Wall Street trials, Labaton had a good deal of ground to cover. We can rely on him for the routine updates on this motion and that maneuver, but we don't expect to get many flashes of insight from him, his grasp of this particular business not as confident as it should be. But we admire his professional detachment in matters where there's a temptation to take sides. He's impartial in "The Trials and Errors of Boyd Jeffries," 1-15, featuring the Wall Streeter who turned state's evidence to save his firm, but there's no payoff. A quick, adequate update with "Settlement of S.E.C. Charges By Drexel Said to Be Near," 2-21, he skims the edges of the issues, not going below the surface of the Drexel/Milken indictment. A bit deeper in "Preparing for the Milken Battle," 3-31, he examines probable witnesses, testimony, and related cases, intriguing, but inconclusive on a case that was, at the time, a year away. Labaton focuses on the court battle between the IRS, the SEC, and shareholders to decide who gets what in the Dennis Levine case in "IRS vs. SEC On Inside Funds," 4-3, an unusual ruling that could put a real bite on the pocketbooks of people convicted of insider trading. Some insights in "High Court Helps Assure Drexel Pact," 6-6, but he's disorganized, and we must work to find them. A cursory dispatch, "Wall Street Trader Admits He Is Guilty In Stock Price Case," 8-31, isn't worthy of front-page treatment, as Labaton provides little beyond the headline. He gives us a nice package of information and background in "S.E.C. Files Fraud Case On Retailer," 9-7, on insider trading charges against Eddie Antar, "the reclusive entrepreneur who at Crazy Eddie Inc. brought widespread discounting to retail electronics." Labaton's "Rainmaker: Mario Baezo Of Debecoise," *Business World* 9-24, is a zippy profile of a black superstar at the white-shoe law firm, via his ties to Louis Kelso, the titan of ESOP buyouts, but contains almost no supporting evidence on why the fellow is brilliant, seeming puffy as a result. We wondered about the accuracy of some of the minor detail as well, and it's clear from this that Labaton doesn't quite understand investment banking.

Labich, Kenneth. *Fortune.* (★ ★)
Board of editors member. His unusual angles are hit-or-miss, but we generally appreciate his attempts to investigate different aspects of American and international business. He analyzes favorably Herman Miller and his success with "new" management techniques in "Hot Company, Warm Culture," 2-27: "The folks who run Herman Miller Inc., the fast-growing office furniture maker, credit much of their success to treating their workers right — even when times are tough." In "Making Over Middle Managers," 5-8, he's insightful, taking success stories from different industries as roles change, supporting his assertions with plenty of anecdotes. He takes off very quickly in "Should Airlines Be Reregulated," 6-19, with fresh information jammed into opening graphs, covering surprising angles, and coming up with a clear "no" as an answer to his title. We're extremely disappointed that *Fortune* would run his "Let's Let the Asians In," 7-17, apparently advocating screening in talented Asians, screening out everyone else, most blatant, quoting a sociologist: "There is no reason to believe this population will ever become part of the underclass." He applies some healthy skepticism to the euphoria over the UAL takeover with "Can United Afford To Be Taken Over?" 9-11, nicely balanced and presented as the shares trade at $257, a month before the deal falls apart. In "The Best Cities for Business," the 10-23 cover, Labich manages to get his arms around the subject in credible fashion, lifting the piece above the usual biz mag list story. The criteria seem reasonable, starting with a big pool of skilled labor, and Dallas/Fort Worth comes in first even as the Cowboys hit bottom in the NFL. The piece is solid and well rounded, even in its treatment of city politics, and it gets a 10 Best nomination from his editors for his effort. We thought there should have been a bit more on the downside, however. 100515

Laderman, Jeffrey. *Business Week.* (★ ½)
Associate editor. We've complained for years about Laderman's assignment as Markets & Investments Editor, on the grounds that he doesn't understand markets. Laderman's peromotion may or may not mean he's been kicked upstairs, but the move has improved his outlook; his arguments are more moderate, his reports more descriptive. He's fair in depicting "Why the Bulls Are Running Wild on Three Continents," 1-30, telling us markets are up despite high interest rates, because investors see continued economic growth and control over inflation, and making the point that institutional investors have large cash holdings, based on recession fears, that could go into stocks if interest rates dropped a bit. He argues reasonably that, although it may be premature to scrap the open outcry system, perhaps a new electronic system could be introduced for small orders, as at the stock exchanges in "How to Clean Up the Mess in the Commodities Pits," 2-6, adding other insights into practices questioned in the ongoing probe. In "The Business That Brokers Would Love to Ditch," with Jon Friedman 3-27, he takes off from a Morgan Stanley decision to do block trading only for its most profitable institutional clients because of low commissions, suggesting that in the future, brokers may abandon commissions altogether and trade Big Board stocks by marking up their inventories. He hits all the high points introducing the quarterly mutual fund scoreboard, "Big Returns in Small Packages," 4-17. "Wall Street Falls in Love with 'Soft Dollars,'" with Tim Smart 4-24, an interesting piece on the $1 billion per year and growing soft-dollar market, has nothing hard and fast, but he reports that a money manager asked if he could rent office space with soft dollars. There's good analysis in "Does Junk Have Lasting Value? Probably," 5-1, on the outlook for junk bonds in the wake of the Milken indictment and the Asquith study on junk default rates, as he points out that on a diversified basis, junk bonds have been holding their value, and the overall default rate is still low, even though the default rate on older bonds is high. In a well-organized summary, "In a Soaring Market, There's Still Room at the Top," 6-26, he reviews conditions supporting demand for U.S. equities, led by the strong dollar encouraging foreign investors strongly. He's sketchy in "Sans Fred, the Fur Vault May Be Ready to Fly," 7-3, on the death and resurrection of Fred the Furrier. He opens with a good lead, speaking to an investor who bought a stock mutual fund during the highs before the '87 crash, and reassuring him and others that many funds have now reached new heights and made the investment worthwhile, "How Mutual Funds Have Battled Back," 9-19, organized, with some interesting analysis.

Landro, Laura. *The Wall Street Journal.* (★ ★)
New York, covering the entertainment industry. Consistent year in and year out in the quality of her material, Landro's light, deft touch does not detract from her ability to present information clearly and cleanly. She doesn't often dig deeply, but her material remains enjoyable even when she skims. Quick and sure in "It Was Such a Flop, the Plaintiffs Don't Even Name It in Their Suit," 3-16, she tells us that Warren Beatty, Elaine May and Dustin Hoffman have had to sue Columbia to get their dough for "Ishtar," one of the big-time flops: "They don't claim the film made money, but they say in their suit filed in Los Angeles Superior Court, that they didn't receive their promised shares and that Columbia didn't do enough to promote the film. They want at least $8 million in back fees, expenses, damages and interest." Ouch. "Cashing In: Gulf & Western Plans to Sell Finance Firm, Build a Media Giant," 4-10, explores the market and accounting motives for G&W's acquisitions and sales, somewhat interesting, but a chore to finish. Nicely rounded with "Viacom Is Said To Be Talking To G&W, MCA," 5-5, she's even-handed in looking at the producer/distributor's desire to merge in order to give it breathing room for expansion, and the different residual effects from such a move. Teamed with David Hilder, she's solid with "Time, Warner Slated to Study Strategy Today," 6-15, compactly analytic and good with the numbers, but somewhat short-sighted, not really examining the broader picture. A fast update, "Viacom Forms Unit to Produce Movies for Its Showtime," 7-18, contains all the necessary information, but few extras. She gives a brief history of Columbia under Coca-Cola and a description of its strengths and weaknesses for a new owner, Sony, nicely presented in "Hollywood Ending: Columbia Pictures Racked by Losses is a Crown Jewel Now," 9-26. She's

also organized in "MGM/UA Bid Being Considered by Cable Group," 11-14, investigating different angles and bids, and probing the industry assumption that a network must be able to produce and distribute, as well as to air, to be an effective competitor in broadcasting today.

Lawrence, Richard. *The Journal of Commerce.* (★ ½)
Trade reporter. Admittedly we were less attentive to the trade issue this year than last, when Lawrence impressed us much more. But our sampling of his material throughout the year turned up a spottier performance, at times firm, energetic, at others late and lackadaisical. "Bush Aims to Cut Third World Debt," 3-9, could have been summarized out of the previous day's *Wall Street Journal,* for example. "A Landmark Economic Year," provides a useful summary of major changes for global economic policy, with Lawrence concluding that, overall, performance is good, even in Africa which may exceed 3% growth, but Latin America is on a skid — and "this is where much of the action may turn in 1989, in both finance and trade." Dull in "Hills Optimistic Uruguay Round Will be Successful," 4-12, he sounds like he's reading notes of an interview with Trade Representative Carla Hills, showing little evidence of independent work. With Keith M. Rockwell, "Hills Seeks to Soothe Fears About Trade List," 5-15, he gives us details of what the USTR can do with Super 301, reaction and anxieties abroad, and the potential for diffusing the threat. On it first, and with the best details, he submits "U.S. Offers Novel Idea To Open Farm Trade," 7-13, a quick report on Agriculture Secretary Clayton Yeutter's proposal for nations to convert their non-tariff agriculture trade barriers to equivalent tariffs, an important policy proposal. There's little journalism in "Bush, Kaitu Likely to Reaffirm Ties Between U.S. and Japan," 8-31, reading like he copied a White House and Japanese foreign office press release. "Bill Requires Banks to Boost Loan Reserves on 3rd World," 9-15, is standard stuff. "U.S., Canada May Hasten Tariff Cuts, Officials Say," 10-5, could be clearer. On the one hand the piece says things are going quickly and smoothly on the U.S.-Canada trade agreement, then it notes complaints by politicians of foot-dragging.

Levin, Doron P. *The New York Times.* (★ ★)
Detroit. Levin probes unusual angles in the auto industry, getting us the technical side as well as the business. We're steadily coming to appreciate his byline on mid-depth material. Even when he runs with the pack, he's often insightful. He still has a way to travel to confidently handle the big overview pieces, the way the *WSJ*'s young Jacob Schlesinger can. In "As Credit Comes More Easily, More Car Buyers Default," 2-17, Levin provides almost everything we could ask for, but focuses only on Ford and GM defaulters, leaving us dissatisfied, not knowing what the experience is at Honda and Nissan. He examines how European carmakers are losing sales a bit in "Luxury Cars Lose Some Status," 2-27, but doesn't really address the coming Japanese ventures into the luxury market, nor all the European makers (Lamborghini for example), concentrating only on the yuppie cars, like Porsche and BMW. He's also too narrow with "Exhaust of Gasoline Engines May Be as Clean as It Can Get," not investigating why this might be so, and leaving the debate of alternative fuels until the close, skimming the problems therein. Ultimately inconclusive in "Bronco II Performance Criticized," 5-18, he still may have the start of a bigger story as he lays out the Consumer's Union warnings on the Ford Bronco; Ford naturally, disputes the findings, despite a Consumer's Union report of 19 fatal rollovers (per 100,000 vehicles) for the Bronco for 1987, "while the Samurai was involved in 6." In an exceptional report and analysis of how Nissan improves on the function of the UAW and keeps it out, "Nissan Workers in U.S. Test Union and Industry," 8-12, he gets at the obvious value-added that must threaten all of industrial organized labor: "The union, careful to avoid internal backlash from its conservative wing, has avoided crossing an important ideological line by declaring that its goals and the companies will never be identical." His very satisfying "Olds Offers Full Credit To Unhappy Buyers," 9-8, shoehorns facts galore about the company and industry along with details of the innovative return program. In "Detroit Is Honoring Honda, the Man and the Car," 10-9, on Shoichiro Honda, the Henry Ford of Honda, Levin's inclusion of colorful anecdotes and brief history brilliantly illustrate his personality and management style as he is inducted into the Automotive Hall of Fame. We learn a lot in "Antilock Brakes, Once

Rare, Emerge as Prime Auto Option," 11-18, Levin covering technical detail with perfect clarity. He's also careful to note that the new system "may imbue drivers with an undue sense of invulnerability when driving on wet or icy pavement," when in fact it still takes longer to stop a car on wet pavement than on dry.

Light, Larry. *Business Week.* (★ ★ ½)
Corporate Finance department editor. Light came to the weekly mid-year, rising quickly from the bottom of the multiple bylines at *BW.* He and co-author Laura Jereski tackle the dangers of real estate limited partnerships, "Real Estate Partnerships Are Sinking With No Lifeboats in Sight," 7-3, a morality play that begins compellingly as a retiree loses her savings; the duo ably covers the ins-and-outs of this particular deal gone sour, and makes the case that this may be indicative of the entire industry. Sharp on Drexel, he demonstrates another of the many ways the company has made money with junk, this time by saving "a client's hide," in "Drexel Rushes in To Save a Fallen Disciple," 7-17. He compactly sizes up the junk situation in "Corporate America Wants Out From Under Its Junk Pile," 8-21, carefully detached, pegging the circumstances precisely as companies begin to move away from junk debt: "Towering interest rates aren't the only reason junk wears out its welcome with issuers. It's also a matter of image." Light smartly examines the changing role of real estate in the corporate realm, as increasing numbers of corporations discover its value, both in cash and as a bargaining chip, "From Backwater to Blockbuster," co-authored by David Zigas 9-11. He waffles in "Mitsubishi's Gamble on a Manhattan Jewel," with Ted Holden 11-13, a bit mercantilist and ironic, attributing Japan's ability to buy to its trade surplus, rather than relative profit opportunities and good business sense; it's still cheaper to buy Manhattan jewels like Rockefeller Center than a small building in downtown Tokyo, especially as the world continues to become a global marketplace. But it was a sterling "The Power of Pension Funds," cover 11-6, that really caught our eye, a broad reconnaissance of the "$2.6 trillion stash" that everyone — management, labor, government — has its eyes on. Light misses some of the cross-currents in this lallapalooza of a story, which can take on the dimensions of greed in "Treasure of Sierra Madre," but not many. A 10 Best selection.

Lipkin, Richard. *Insight.* (★ ★)
A science and technology reporter, Lipkin puts great effort into his stories, sweating out each word, and it shows. He's good at infusing his accounts with his enthusiasm, but he does sometimes try to get too much into his pieces, losing spark and adding clutter. Skillful in "Greener Pastures in Deep Blue Sea," 12-26-88, with an attention-getting lead on undersea exploration is fascinating and packed with detail. Masterful in "Cracking Weather's Secrets," 1-9, he's effective in his use of quotes and stories, breathtaking in its visual imagery. There's not enough space to cover the technical advances in microscopy in "Great Magnification in Microscopy," 2-27, requiring a thorough explanation of both the new technology and its application, opening with a fuzzy lead and just skimming the surface. He does his usual good job of explaining technical material to hold the story together, "Testing Heavy Rain's Role in Flying," 3-13, as he informs on NASA efforts to test effects of heavy rain on airplane performance, no reassurance for white-knuckle flyers. He's gushy in "A Buggy With a Mission in Space," 3-27, his lead a rendition of man's vision of space and the potential there for making quantum leaps in research, exploring new worlds and bettering life as we now know it, but then the focus abruptly narrows to a snoozy, technical look at NASA's development of a new moon buggy. He gives "Math Set Succeeding Exponentially," 4-17, a good go, but this article on research mathematics just doesn't work, opening with cliches about the field entering a "golden age" and how there are more mathematicians alive today than there have been in the last 5,000 years combined. In "To Return to Space and Stay There," 7-24, an overview of the successful re-launch of the U.S. space program includes information on planned missions, research capabilities, the space station, and the cost for the whole package, he effectively captures the renewed sense of excitement and discovery, and the intangible benefits of manned missions. A wonderful lead is wasted in "A Little Glue Makes the Difference," 8-28, on the kind of silk that

spiders use in making their webs, as he flops around, giving a little on spider webs, a little on synthetic silk, and not a whole lot on what synthetic spider silk would be used for. We get too much science and not enough business on the "opening of commercial launched industry," in "Pint-size Pegasus Trots into Space," 9-18, containing much of interest on its design, but skimming the "industry" that's supposedly been spawned.

Lochhead, Carolyn. *Insight.* (★ ★ ½)
New York writer. Business from the social side, Lochhead covers some quirky, innovative topics, providing much information, putting her stories together with considerable skill. "Good Time to Pound the Pavement," 12-26-88, is fast-paced on the manpower shortage in the workforce, using quotes well, but she exits a bit too abruptly. "No Way Out: The Brutal Snare of Poverty," 4-3, is super, a timely, ambitious review of the welfare underclass, replete with salient facts, and identifying the critical shifts regarding social policy that have taken place. A 10 Best selection, this ought to be required reading by all relevant policymakers; a bit less than we'd hoped for in terms of perspectives for stripping away the bonds of failure among the underclass, though the central focus on restoring confidence in people's ability to govern themselves is certainly there. In "A Fight with Foreign Petal Pushers," 4-10, Lochhead can't resist the temptation to use floral metaphors in this piece on imports taking over the U.S. cut flower market, but all in all she does a competent job of putting it together. "Fire Ants Are Nipping at Our Heels," 5-8, is eminently readable on the indestructible fire ant from South America, marching westward from Dixie, but we don't get anything on how it's doing in South America. "Corralling Urban Cowboy Market," 7-24, is a smooth feature on a Greenwich Village merchant selling "used" cowboy boots to free-spending Manhattanites, finely presented. *The Wall Street Journal's* Francine Schwadel had the story first, earlier in August, but Lochhead builds on it beautifully in "Retailer's Charm Kills Competition," 8-28, rapid-fire, fact-filled on retailing giant Nordstrom's: "Critics, if any exist, are in hiding. Mall developers and clothing makers court the company. Analysts rave. The Harvard Business School does a case study. Consultants tell their clients: Nordstromize." She gets a 10 Best nomination from her editors in "Firms See Financial Handicap in Disabled Civil Rights Bill," 10-30, and it is indeed splendid journalism, all sides presented with scrupulous detachment, fine detail, statistics and quotes.

Loomis, Carol J. *Fortune.* (★ ½)
Board of editors. Loomis continues to collect awards for her distinguished career in business journalism, this year adding a second Gerald Loeb Award, plus laurels from the New York Society for CPAs and the Elliot Bell Award for financial reporting. She has frankly disappointed us in recent years, the pitching in this league getting faster all the time while her knuckleball loses some speed. Still, she handles "Will 'Fasbee' Pinch Your Bottom Line?" 12-19-88, well, writing an important and, surprisingly, interesting story on the Financial Accounting Standards Board, FASB, which is charged by the SEC with setting up uniform accounting practices for public companies; she describes, with as light a touch as she can muster, how FASB wants health care liabilities acknowledged in financial statements, and financial instruments booked at market, not historic cost. The CPA Award-winner, "The Killer Cost Stalking Business," 2-27, doesn't add much to what we know about the problem of corporate health care liabilities, having already seen much of this in *The Wall Street Journal.* Snappy in "Secrets of the Superstars," 4-24, she screens 21 high-performing companies in the *Fortune* 500 briskly, with common themes and differences highlighted. "Stars of the Service 500," 6-5, is another standard piece by the veteran Loomis, an overview of the star performers in the Service 500 whose ROI is better than 20 percent. Her reporting skills are evident in "The $600 Million Cigarette Scam," 12-4, telling us that through a process called trade loading, RJR Nabisco is creating megabucks of bogus profits by shipping increased amounts of cigarettes to wholesalers, even though customers aren't buying more, but she takes an awfully long time getting her points across.

Lowenstein, Roger. *The Wall Street Journal.* (★ ★ ★)
New York. "Heard on the Street" columnist after an excellent tour on the real estate beat, Lowenstein is always snappy and sharp, just the right combo for this column — which we like seeing more on the first "Money & Investing" page. He dishes out different advice and investment options in "Savants, Asked Their Investment Preferences for Four Years with Bush, See Stocks Rising," 1-19, effectively capturing the optimism of Wall Street on the eve of Bush's inauguration. He's very careful in a book review, "Hizzoner's Fall From Grace," 2-1, evaluating *City for Sale: Ed Koch and the Betrayal of New York,* by Jack Newfield and Wayne Barrett, precisely fair in casting shadings and nuance in putting Koch exactly where he should be on permissiveness to political bosses. He begins fluffily on "Micro Technology Gets Novel 'Boost' From Potato King," 3-2, but gets serious quickly in discussing J. R. Simplot's "encouraging" workers at his company to buy shares of Micron Technology, where he is a director, a delicate, tensile treatment. He also gives very careful treatment of a skeptical analyst's report, "an arrow at the company's heart," in "Analysts Bashing Rocks Blockbuster Entertainment," 5-10, with thorough, balanced quotes pro and con, lively writing: "Other analysts who have been recommending the Fort Lauderdale, Fla.-based company stood fast." He's smart with relevant examples in "Amstar-Essex Deal Sparks Criticism of Merrill Lynch," 7-21, on potential conflicts of interest over buyouts. An "OTC Focus," "Buy-Out Signs Are Discerned at BMA, But Some Like the Stock for Other Reasons," 10-9, gives an accounting of BMA's viability and potential, nicely structured and supported on the combination broadcasting-labtest-real estate business. Intelligent in "Salomon's Shopkorn Says Instability in Stocks Is Due in Part to Non-Fundamental Trading," 11-13, Lowenstein and Stanley Shopkorn, Salomon's vice-chairman, apply a little common sense to stock volatility, recommending traders look at the bottom line rather than following the pack. "Kemper's Junk-Fund Star Picks Lemons in Bad Year," 11-22, squeezes Ken Urbaszewski for angles and advice. "This leads to an Urbaszewski axiom: It's better to hold good cash than bad bonds."

Machan, Dyan. *Forbes.* (★ ½)
"Careers" columnist. Machan knocked us out last year with a piece about a McDonald's restaurant inspector, "Great Hash Browns, But Watch Those Biscuits," 9-19-88. This year she landed a few punches, but too much of her "Careers" work was fluffy, focusing on soft targets. She takes a look at the succession process for a new chairman, as well as the successor, at the consulting firm Booz, Allen & Hamilton, "Gladiators' Ball," 12-26-88, and declares it a big mistake. She puts all the substance in the concluding paragraph of "The Charisma Merchants," 1-27, filler if we've ever seen it. More pap, "Pepperidge Farm's Doughboy," 3-20, a human interest piece about the middle manager who oversees cookie development at Pepperidge Farm, isn't very nutritional to the brain but it does provide filler. She's more substantive in "On a Roll with the Man from G.E." 4-17, detailing the professional background of Robert Wright, President of NBC, and the challenges he faces at the network. Making a good point in a short space, "Cut the Fluff," 6-26, she tells us corporate recruitment pamphlets are running way behind the curves, as business-bound students have access these days to more useful information in libraries and news retrieval systems. "The Clients Are Restless," 7-10, takes a look at the big-time executive search business and concludes they are headed for a fall due to excessive fees and conflicts of interest; she could be right, but this is too thinly-documented to work as a cover story. She's good on the policy of hiring senior citizens as seen through the eyes of Days' Inn's manager of recruitment and employment, "Cultivating the Gray," 9-4, mentioning other companies who do the same thing, but the real insight is from the Days' Inn practice of hiring the homeless, with the executive concluding there are two types: "the ones who are victims of bad breaks, and the street people." He feels the street people can't be helped.

Magnet, Myron. *Fortune.* (NR)
Very little on the social side of business from Magnet this year. We're compelled to mention his two articles, solid and informative, covering intriguing topics. He tells us "How Business Bosses Saved a Sick City," 3-27, an expansively detailed accounting of Cleveland's turnaround that

neither scrimps on the solutions nor whitewashes the problems. He asks "Can Your Kid Become President?" 6-5, filled with anecdotes, and a surprisingly optimistic answer about America's open door to ability in non-WASP types, but he doesn't address the problem of the underclass. We especially like his ability to put together the most pointed and amusing stories to make his point: "American society wasn't always this open. Remember Groucho Marx's funny but wistful plea to the swim club that refused membership to his children: Since they were only half Jewish, he wondered, perhaps they could be allowed in up to their navels?"

Malcolm, Andrew. *The New York Times.* (★ ★ ★)
National news correspondent. His strongest work is on social issues related to his beat, particularly powerful on the drug story. He reveals that significant suspicions remain in the areas of trade and military defense, in "U.S. and Japanese: Closer Ties Found" 2-23, despite simultaneous opinion polls in both countries, taken on the eve of Emperor Hirohito's funeral, finding that both now take a more positive view of the ties between them. In "FBI Opening Door to Wide Use of Genetic Tests in Solving Crime," 6-12, we learn that "Although defense lawyers in one New York murder case are challenging the technique and interpretation of a DNA profile by a private laboratory two years ago, the basic science has gone virtually unquestioned in more than 80 court cases in the last two years as prosecutors seek to construct a framework of legal precedents." But we think he should have been more skeptical of the FBI case. "Drunken Drivers Pay Own Way in Innovative Jail," 8-13, outlines a marvelous, innovative idea, now being implemented in Akron, Ohio: Drunk drivers, as an option to longer prison terms, are put into rehab units and made to pay overhead on release. He cites powerful statistics in "Capital Punishment Is Popular, But So Are Its Alternatives," 9-10, a concise, informative, unbiased review of life without parole as a death penalty alternative, telling us there have been 117 executions over the last 13 years and "In the same period there have been 259,800 murders that did not result in an execution." He presents trenchant stories and data on new crack addicts, "Crack, Bane of Inner City, Is Now Gripping Suburbs," the first of two 10-1, so strongly documented and presented it ought to kill the legalization debate for awhile. The second of the two, "Affluent Addicts' Road Back Begins in a Climb Past Denial," 10-2, loses some steam, as we're left wondering what treatment sessions are like; an okay followup, with nice statistics, quotes. Another sweeping piece, "In Making Drug Strategy, No Accord on Treatment," 11-19, offers good background on the controversy over treatment, and gets behind the numbers on waiting lists with professionals who discuss how soft those numbers can be. His Sunday "Week in Review" piece, "More and More, Prison is America's Answer to Crime," 11-26, is mostly a string of dismaying stats, 673,565 prisoners in state and federal systems, but also crisp analysis on a toughening public attitude and willingness so pay for more and longer incarcerations.

Markoff, John. *The New York Times.* (★ ★)
Computers. We admit to being spoiled by David E. Sanger on this beat, before he was dispatched to Tokyo. As competent as Markoff is, he'd have trouble following Sanger's act in any case. In fact, he could be more consistently clear, punchier, more thorough, more detached when politics intersect with high-tech. Compact and precise in "Compaq to End Dealings With Businessland," 2-20, he does present a clear picture as the computer maker pulls out of its deal with the retailer, a respectable overview. With a P. 1 mainframe to microprocessor story, "In an Age Where Tiny Is All, Big Computers Are Hurting," 4-4, he makes the broader trend clear, but there's very little analysis of what's happening on the margin. He's cursory in "The Big News In Tiny Computers," 5-14, on the promise of tomorrow, very short on technical details and price, and there's no discussion of the merits of a book-sized portable. He reviews the state-of-the-art in computer chip design, notable for its focus on "fabless" chip designers, farming out designs to chip foundries, with a lead Sunday business piece, "Silicon Valley's Design Renaissance," 8-6, but he needs a little more sense of direction about where business and profits are headed. There's a big story in "Personal Computers May Combine Brain with Beauty of TV," 9-12, but he only covers half of it, outlining which company is doing what, with some bits of how new technology will work, with little on its applications other than games and better graphics and entertainment,

leaving us wondering what this multimedia computing will do for business applications other than training. Hitting all the bases with "New Digital Software Links Various Products," 10-11, he skims the surface of the implications of All-in-1 software application products for the industry and the business world, imparting all the necessary information. A Sunday business lead, "Here Comes the Fiber-Optic Home," 11-5, has good up-to-date costs on conversion to fiber-optic from copper cable, but first we have to slog through concerns that because it will be expensive, rich people will be able to convert faster than poor people. He's somewhat sloppy in "Cuts Are Expected for U.S. Financing in High-Tech Area," 11-16, with many unattributed generalizations: "Such programs, which have both military and civilian uses, are viewed by many as vital to American competitiveness," he says on HDTV, never mentioning there are scientists who think HDTV will be obsolete before it's produced because of fiber optics. "Need for Re-Evaluation Is Seen on Cutting High-Tech Aid," 11-17, is also heavy-handed in weighing in for the taxpayer-backed Sematech consortium, which might a good thing, but Markoff should be doing pros and cons in depth.

McDowell, Edwin. *The New York Times.* (★ ★ ½)
Publishing. The most important reporter on this beat, also the best, a very careful reporter, McDowell writes easily about business, politics, literature and history. He seemed to lose a little of his edge this year, though, his material just a bit lighter, not quite the weighty portfolio he compiled a year ago. He asks no questions and provides no answers in "And They All Said It Wouldn't Sell," 2-6, an amusing tongue-in-cheek look at some publishing no-no's that proved to be wrong, such as never put a green cover on a book because it won't sell. *Bolt* and *Reflex* by Dick Francis both had green covers and were best sellers. He's calm on " 'Satanic Verses' Is Removed From Shelves by Book Chain," 2-17, on the threats of reprisals by outraged Muslims over Salman Rushdie's "blasphemous" book, but captures the tensions at Viking and at bookstore chains — mostly Waldenbooks — who had it removed from their shelves. "First Novelists With Six Figure Contracts," 4-10, is well formulated and conclusive, with a lot of angles converged from the editors' end, but little from the authors. He latches on to a growing trend, "Book Clubs Are Developing More Titles on Their Own," 8-21, a sweeping overview of how different book clubs are publishing their own titles, accurately accounting part of the phenomenon to corporate takeovers (The Book-of-the-Month Club and Little, Brown are both owned by Gulf & Western, for instance), but accounting for most of it in the increased competitiveness in the hardback and softcover markets. In a followup on the resignation of Random House's Robert L. Bernstein, "Random House Swept By a Rash of Rumors," 11-6, McDowell catalogues the rumors running rampant at the publishing giant, giving more credence to some than others, and although he's ultimately inconclusive, it's a useful insider's view.

Melloan, George. *The Wall Street Journal.* (★ ½)
Deputy editor of the *Journal's* editorial page for well over a decade, Melloan is now off to edit the European edition's editorial pages. Gone with him is his Tuesday "Business World" column, a sober mixture of business and political themes of a most timely nature, usually smart material but with absolutely no razzle-dazzle. "Ponzi Was A Piker Compared to 'Troubled Thrifts,' " 1-10, is a well-done, clear analysis of the S&L financial crisis, setting the stage for the congressional bailout. Melloan at times has trouble getting off the ground, though, and "How Johns Hopkins Bridges the Lab-to-Market Gap," 1-24, is a prime example, offering very slow going for very little payoff. He's almost talking to himself in "Technology Transfer in Weapons Is a Two-Way Street," 11-14, which plods on and on around the FSX fighter plane. "Japan's Bid for a Bigger Monetary Role," 2-21, is much more interesting, tackling the notion of "Mercantile Imperialism," which is what critics of Japan assert the country is doing with the foreign exchange it has earned, mainly dollars, managing international accounts in a way that threatens U.S. influence. "Why America Rules the World's Software Markets," 2-28, contains a good interview with Fred M. Gibbons of Software Publishing Inc., but he doesn't offer much to support the headline. Interviewing Citicorp's Reed, "John Reed's Reservations About the Mexican Debt Plan," 5-30, Melloan offers little useful analysis, but the information and attitude

he elicits in his questioning of Reed is well worth the effort. "Doing Badly Trying To Do Good on Capital Hill," 7-18, is a solid analysis of how Congress screws up the general welfare on pension funds by adjusting the ban to benefits in special class. A feature-like treatment of the management of Jervis B. Webb Co., "a world-wide enterprise engaged in engineering, fabricating and installing materials handling equipment," propels "Keeping Things Simple in a Big Family Enterprise," 8-29.

Miller, Annetta. *Newsweek.* (★ ½)
Senior writer. Light dispatches on quirky topics are Miller's specialty, leaving the policy matters to Rich Thomas. She offers good newsweekly reading, spotlighting the new and trendy. She gets a look at the new laundromats, complete with video, in "Beautiful Laundrettes," with Judy Howard 1-3, that are opening around the country, with a good estimation of their management, marketing and chances for success. She's deliciously skeptical in "Psyching Out Consumers," co-authored by Dody Tsiantar 2-27, describing ad agencies' turning to social sciences testing to better market product lines: "Good morning ladies and gentlemen. We've called you here for a little consumer research. Now, lie down on the couch, toss your inhibitions out the window and let's try a little free association. First, think about brands as if they were your *friends.* Imagine you could talk to your TV dinner. What would he say? And what would you say to him?" Her sense of humor shows in "A Pitched Battle for Baby's Bottom," 3-6, beginning "Diapers have become a down-and-dirty business," going on to detail why and what new innovations in the industry are making it more competitive, including the new demand for biodegradable diapers. In "Tuning Out TV Ads," co-written by Tsiantar, 4-17, the pair is poorly focused, opening with a look at "glitz" in TV ads and the problems of using celebrity endorsements, then shifting to an examination of the overall effectiveness of TV advertising, and it just doesn't flow well. In their analysis of advertisers' attempts to recapture viewer attention, the authors do not mention that some companies have even resorted to advertising on home videos. She's late with "Seeking an Rx for Nurses," with Elizabeth Bradburn and Betsy Roberts 7-10, but she presents an interesting collection of anecdotes to tell the tale. A solid "Diets Incorporated," with Karen Springen, Linda Buckley and Elisa Williams 9-11, sweeps the growing industry for weight loss, and although late after Brian O'Reilly's *Fortune* piece, she gives us some interesting data, such as the fact that Weight Watchers, founded in 1963 by Long Island housewife Jean Nidetch, is now run by "the same folks who market such high-calorie fare as Steakumms and Ore-Ida french fries." Pass the ketchup.

Miller, Michael. *The Wall Street Journal.* (★ ★)
New York, covering the computer industry. Teamed on the beat with Paul Carroll and William Bulkeley, he rounds out the trio nicely, combining the hardware and business sides of the industry well. He writes clearly, a must on this beat, but doesn't often get the nuance we appreciate from compatriot Carroll. He spotlights Rodime PLC's side of the story, "Rodime Patent Fight With IBM, Others Stirs Up Disk-Drive Market," 1-6, over the reissuance of the patent for the 3-1/2 inch disk drive, a solid overview, but he makes no guess as to how this will turn out. A quick, but nonanalytic, look, "IBM Holds 40% Of InterACT Corp., A Software Firm," 2-7, gets early rumblings of IBM's purchasing of the stake from Advanced Computer Techniques Corp., in order to develop PCs "with more programs built into microchips, rather than on removable disks." Hmmm. More buying by Big Blue is duly noted by Miller, "IBM, Adding to List of Investments, Buys Stake in Maker of Software For Scientists," 3-2, again buying into a software firm, Polygen Corp., which designs "programs that let researchers simulate three-dimensional molecules for designing new drugs, chemicals and other products," fitting neatly, he tells us, into IBM's plans to expand into the scientific market. He's featurish in "Computer Associates Disarms Its Critics," 4-28, obviously impressed with the success and chutzpah of Computer Associates International Inc.; nicely rounded, he doesn't overlook their shortcomings, including poor service. He's philosophical in "A Centennial View" piece, "Visions of the Future — A Brave New World: Streams of 1s and 0s," 6-23, a nicely crafted view of new possibilities for the computer revolution with regard to the media and information management:

"It could hardly sound more simple or be more complicated: the idea of reducing almost all forms of information to streams of 1s and 0s. And it promises to bring about one of the great leaps forward in the history of humankind." On a lighter subject, but still seriously treated, "A New Picture for Computer Graphics," 7-5, he details the new video technology that's more interactive, a fascinating picture, more vivid than the John Markoff piece on similar technology that followed. An interesting exercise, he takes messages off an electronic bulletin board post-earthquake to get individual reactions up-close and personal, "From the Fault Line, Electronic Tales Of a Quake's Fury," 10-19: "the lawn started rolling like ocean waves."

Mitchell, Constance. *The Wall Street Journal.* (★ ½)
New York, covering credit markets, mutual funds and other financial news. A utility reporter who lets her sources do the talking, Mitchell's material is a cut above the crowd's, relatively solid, a market influence on the front page of the *Journal*'s C section on "Money & Investing." Her Monday morning column, "Economists See Fed Pushing Rates Down," 11-27, was about as off the mark as it could be: "The Federal Reserve will continue to drive down short-term interest rates in the weeks ahead in an effort to reverse the sharp slide in the nation's manufacturing sector, investment managers and economists predict." The ink was barely dry and the Fed was tightening, partly in reaction to Mitchell's pronouncement of a Fed policy that 'twern't. She gets the whole story in "Mutual Funds: Higher Rates Hurt Fund Sales For November," 1-3, as rising interest rates put a cramp on the mutual market, but there's no look ahead as to where rates or mutual funds might be going. She warns of how economists' predictions of inflation affect the bond markets, "Credit Markets: Softness in Bonds May Persist," 6-19, a wide-ranging look that's fair, and ends up advising caution in the markets. Going a bit beneath the surface issue in "Chase Cuts Prime to 10% From 11%, Signaling a Drop in Borrowing Costs," 7-11, correlating the cut to the Fed's loosening and predicting other banks will follow suit, somewhat conventional but nicely structured. In a followup, "Economy: Most Big Banks Cut Prime Rate to 10.5%, In Move That Finally May Aid Consumers," 8-1, she's better rounded, getting peripheral effects of the cut, such as General Motors Acceptance Corp. cuts of the rates it charges to automobile dealers, though a spokesman points out it will take "a while" before the saving is passed on to the consumer "in the way of lower auto financing costs." Taking a new angle in "Unrest May Aid German Bond Issues," 11-20, she applies some long-term analysis as to the effects of the events in East and West Germany to the bond markets, gathering a range of opinion and presenting it concisely.

Morgenson, Gretchen. *Forbes.* (★ ★ ½)
Senior editor. Frequently ahead of the curve, Morgenson is insightful and smart on a fairly wide range of subjects. She also is eminently readable, rarely boring, although some of her material might be. In "Mr. Wu Knows His Customer," 1-23, she profiles the L.A.-based General Bank and its chairman Li-Pei Wu, an early credible view of Asian purchases of California banks; though most of the later somewhat xenophobic reporting focused on the Japanese, Wu is Taiwanese, catering to Taiwan's immigrants in Monterey Park. She's trenchant in a morality play for VP Corp., "Sacrificial Brand," 2-6, describing their classic management mistake, putting their Lee jeans in discount stores, getting complaints from upscale stores for taking away business and prestige from the Lee name, and from the discounters, who can't make the markup with Lee they can with other brands: please all, please none. She's ahead of the pack with "You Bet Your Life," 7-10, on the increasing weakness of many insurance company balance sheets, warning that this may be the next S&L. "The Captains Who Didn't Go Down With the Ship," 8-21, delivers a no-holds-barred journalistic left hook to the top management of Thomson McKinnon Inc., as Morgenson looks at the huge salary and perks of people allegedly destroying this Wall Street firm. Sharp in the cover "How Different Can a $17 Lipstick Be From a $3 Version?" 9-18, on the changing face of the cosmetic industry, she offers unadorned explanations for sluggish growth: the consumer is simply getting smarter and better informed as the FDA is involved in debunking much of the miracle creams that promise youthful skin, and the industry is ignoring the demographic situation, playing to youth rather than the aging female

population, a market that would benefit. "Storm Warning," 12-11, is cautionary on the J. Crew Group, as the mail order business slows with increasing competition and internal wrangling complicates the situation, an insider's profile.

Mossberg, Walter S. *The Wall Street Journal.* (★ ★)
Washington, international economics. He's definitely improved in his second year on this beat, a bit more detached and analytical, not so quick to believe what anyone tells him, no matter how high their rank. He provides an adequate setup of where G-7 is, with the dollar strengthening as the Fed "fights inflation," in "The Group of Seven Faces New Tests," 1-16, but he's insistent the dollar fall has begun "to ease the huge U.S. trade deficit." He's timely and correctly inconclusive in "The Crowbar and the Handshake," 2-13, on Carla Hills, pointing out all sides are watching to see her actual style and substance on trade issues. He sees confusion and dissention within the administration over the Brady plan, including problems of Japanese funding, bank supervision, and U.S. taxpayer liability in "U.S. Will Seek to Slash Debt of Third World," 3-8, putting it together in a coherent fashion. He opens with a vivid lead in "Bush Aides Are Likely to Offer a Plan Soon on Third World Debt," with Peter Truell 3-9, — "While the Bush administration searches for a new U.S. policy on Third World debt, red ink is turning to blood" — then goes on to give an excellent evaluation of the political and economic stakes involved, providing some cold-eyed realism on the administration's response to the challenge. He offers sharp analysis on the Brady plan, calling it "more promise than program," in "U.S. Strategy on World Debt Faces Hurdles," 3-13. His legwork shows in "U.S. Plan May Cut Debt 20% for 39 Nations," 3-16, on hidden assumptions about "market value of the loans, and the willingness to write them down, and the exact use of the special support funds to be allocated by the World Bank and IMF," which will "be challenged by skeptics who are already complaining that the new policy isn't likely to have a big impact." He's clear in "Officials at IMF World Bank Meeting Express Optimism," 4-4, a usable presentation of the lineup at the IMF meeting regarding the Brady proposals, including European reluctance, Latin skepticism, that's well-rounded and well-written. "U.S. Talking With Palestinian Official It Previously Branded as Key Terrorist," 7-10, is less a "Washington Insight" analytic than a straight report, but still informative as the individual involved, Sala Khalaf, provided guns to Italy's Red Brigades. He's rightfully concerned in "Security Aides Expect Terrorist Attacks Against U.S. by Colombian Drug Cartels," 9-21, providing a razor-edged view of the situation that's supported well. In an admirable update, "Purge of Hardliners in East Germany Stirs Unification Hopes, Fear," co-authored by Terence Roth 11-9, he tries to get a handle on the fascinating events cascading out of East Germany, but even a day later this is outdated. But in a P. 1 leder, "Policy Void: Upheaval in Europe Tests Bush's Capacity for Leadership of West," with Robert S. Greenberger 11-14, the headline gives away the Beltway burbles in the article, adding nothing new to an already worn perspective.

Murray, Alan. *The Wall Street Journal.* (½ ★)
Washington. If Murray were not so talented a reporter, his economic biases would disqualify him from this guide altogether. But he does have access to the folks in Washington who share his biases, and we have to acknowledge the combination makes for interesting reading as he follows his own agenda. He is on his toes in "Bush S&L Bailout Creates Illusion Of Deficit Cut," 2-22, finding OMB's Richard Darman at his creative best in juggling the books, observing that Congress will go along because it's all part of the same Gramm-Rudman charade. He's out of ideas, however, in "Many Americans Fear U.S. Living Standards Have Stopped Rising," 5-1, wondering if "manufacturing technology" is helping *manufacturing* productivity, but then claiming overall productivity (including services) "slowed to a crawl. . .in the past decade." Murray also confuses average hourly wages with the income of average workers, apparently not realizing that there has been a sharp increase in the number of students able to find part-time jobs (which dilutes the average wage). "Fed Postpones Decision on Rates Amid Heated Debate on Policy," with David Wessel 6-1, is a sharp, accurate report on divisions between 7 Fed Governors and regional presidents, hinting at a breakout toward marginal ease. In "Congress,

Treasury Study 1-Year Cut in Capital Gains to Raise Revenue," 6-14, he presents total misinformation, with not a single person quoted by name to support the story, and several top figures quoted with "no deal," Rostenkowski and Brady among them. Cliches abound in " 'Soft Landing' Could Prove Painful, Hurt Administration," 7-31, the "wisdom" provided here good for about 10 minutes. While he scoops the *Times* with "Officials in the White House Say They Like Rostenkowski's Proposal on Gains Tax," 8-4, on a deal in the works, Murray misses the revenue implication of the plan's failure to "unlock" capital gains. In "Capital Gains Tax Bill Would Spur Asset Sales More Than Investment," 9-29, a heavily biased P. 1 leder, he almost thoroughly discounts the positive effects of even a permanent capital gains differential: "Even proponents of the proposal admit that such a temporary tax, while helping constituents, does little to help the economy." He then quotes Lawrence Summers of Harvard, an opponent of the proposal. In "Is Fed's Greenspan Cautious to a Fault," 10-30, there's no sign Murray knows what the debate at the Fed is all about: "The Fed's reluctance to ease credit now could be laying the groundwork for a new recession."

Nasar, Sylvia. *Fortune.* (★)
Associate editor. Improved somewhat, we much prefer Nasar's pieces on corporate strategy to her work on macroeconomic policy, which tends to be predictably erratic. She provides a useful and sensible overview of the car insurance industry, including good information on the interaction of regulators and the industry, "Hard Road Ahead for Auto Insurers," 5-8, with especially interesting references to several niche competitors within the monolithic world of automobile insurance. "America Still Reigns in Services," 6-5, suffers from a nationalistic, flag-waving tone, but is an okay overview of how the U.S. service sector has been revitalized by deregulation, computerization, and the pursuit of worldwide consumers. She wraps up ways to make money if the dollar goes down, which she suggests is bound to happen in "Currency Strategies that Will Pay Off Big if the Dollar Drops," 7-3. She suggests foreign currency futures and options, a good angle for the "Personal Investing" column. But then, while the dollar fell against the DM, it stayed put against the yen. Among the best work we've seen by Nasar, "The Foolish Rush to ESOPS," 9-25, raises provocative questions about the wisdom of employee stock plans and points out that often they are a self-serving management dodge that penalizes shareholders, a tough-minded, against-the-flow piece that has zip and bite.

Nash, Nathaniel C. *The New York Times.* (★ ★)
Washington. The S&L crisis ripened this year, and this was supposed to be Nash's forte. The banking beat also got competitive and complicated in '89, and while the talented Nash kept up, we were rather surprised he rarely got ahead of the game. More utilitarian than analytic, we found ourselves turning to other sources for breakouts and the bigger picture. "Bush Aides' Plan on Savings Units Is Said to Place Cost on Industry," 2-4, is a straight news report with good detail. Straight again, "U.S. Takes Over 20 Texas Banks; High Cost Seen," 3-30, without depth or analysis, he focuses on how the takeover came to stop heavy withdrawal of deposits from 20 Texas Banks owned by MCorp of Dallas, Texas' second largest banking concern, and the last major Texas bank which hadn't needed government protection. Uninsightful in "No. 1 Whistle Blower Derides Deficit Figures," 4-24, on Comptroller General Charles A. Bowsher's (who heads the General Accounting Office) challenge to the administration's "rosy projections" on the budget deficit, he presents no opposing views on the dispute over figures and accounting, but includes some Congressional criticism of GAO's overstepping the line from being a technical expert adviser to Congress to acting in a political, more partisan way. He's more discriminating in "Savings-Unit Withdrawals Shrink," 6-8, more thoughtful on what continued withdrawals will mean to an ailing S&L industry, but he's ultimately inconclusive. He reviews the politicking over Lincoln Savings and Loan Association of Irvine, CA, in "Showdown Time for Danny Wall," 7-9, but doesn't provide enough detail on Wall's culpability or ineptness; a good backdrop, nonetheless, as Congress weighs his reappointment as chairman of Home Loan Bank Board. Nash is confusing in "Wall Street Measures Are Facing Congress," 9-5, trying to cover the S&L bailout, Danny Wall's confirmation hearings, upcoming Senate banking committee

debates, and predicting future wrangling between Congress and the administration over continuing deregulation, in far too small a space. On the lighter side, "Silver Lining For Business Chiefs," 10-16, is cursory on the meeting of 150 past and present CEOs at the Business Council, interesting, but skimming. In "A Savings Failure That Illustrates Everything Wrong With the Industry," 11-12, he summarizes the Lincoln S&L debacle in able "Weekly Reader" fashion, and we're reminded that Nash spent the year looking over his shoulder.

Norris, Floyd. *The New York Times.* (★ ★ ★)
Moving to the *Times* in late '88 from *Barron's,* where he'd written the weekly "Trader" wrap-up column, Norris suddenly could spread his wings and write "Market Place" analysis and commentary on the spot. His column is quickly rivaling the *WSJ*'s patented "Heard on the Street," consistently fresh, smart and adept at adding up his numbers. He takes a fresh and able look at the likelihood that cyclicals are underpriced, "Cyclical Stocks Seem Depressed," 1-13. In an outline of a rare market corner at Chase Medical, "The Case of the Curious Corner," 1-22, he provides a clear explanation of what's going on, although several big questions remain on Moore and Schley, who got the corner. In "Enserch's Plan To Shed a Unit," 2-23, he opens with a forceful lead — "Getting rid of an unwanted subsidiary isn't easy" — then lays out simply the complex arrangements on the dumping of its oil-service operation by this energy pipeline company. "Time Inc. and Warner to Merge, Creating Largest Media Company," 3-5, is a crisp account of the megamerger. As the Dow is at 2,418.99 and climbing, Norris interviews various bears in "Surge In Stock Has Its Doubters," 4-28, Federated Investors of Pittsburgh, Raymond Dalio of Bridgewater Associates, etc., a nice exercise. Norris details analyst's accounting complaints, shedding light on potential business weaknesses, in "Behind the Plunge at Video Chain," 5-10, a bit better than Roger Lowenstein's same-day treatment of Blockbuster Entertainment's stock slide. In a morality tale, "A Tale of Woe for Bondholders," 7-28, Norris tells us how AP Industries used junk financing for the wrong reasons and now may seek Chapter 11. In "Why Is Buffett Raising Money?" 9-22, Norris displays his knack for finding the margin of financial thinking, quoting Warren Buffett: "The best time to buy single assets may be when it is hardest to raise money." He's interesting on the psychology of the markets in "Market Place: When the Panic Failed to Happen," 10-23, zeroing in particularly on how market plunges no longer worry investors: they have come to accept them as opportunities. He was the first of the financial journalists to link the stock market rally with the likelihood of a capital gains tax cut, in "Tax-Cut Outlook and the July Rally," 8-2: "As it happens, it was in mid-April, just about the time that a capital gains cut began to seem possible that stock prices broke out of their recent trading range and began to climb." Inexplicably, when the market crashed October 13 as the White House pulled the rug from under its capgains strategy, dooming it for the year, Norris watched silently, not a word.

Nulty, Peter. *Fortune.* (★)
Associate editor. Rarely giving us news, Nulty's updates are competent, if unexciting. In another sidebar to the "Fortune 500" issue, "Growing Fast on the Fringe," 4-24, he touches the bases of a few smaller companies, done okay, but this is *Inc.* magazine turf, and they've already discussed these outfits, so there's little new here. He wraps up the state of the oil industry after the Big Spill, with "The Future of Big Oil," 5-8, including a few cutesy lines that must make Alaska residents grit their teeth: "The least credible worry is the danger to caribou. Most Alaskans thumb their antlers at the thought." But given the deluge of media coverage of the Valdez incident, this one doesn't really stand out. "Get Ready for Power Brownouts," 6-5, is a difficult, muddled read, caused by Nulty's alarmist tone about imminent electricity shortages and his anxiety to convey all points of view. He puts us to sleep with "Big Oil Faces a Big Squeeze," 10-9, a snoozer on the woes of the big oil companies, with not much to pick at here, nor in the shrunken-down sidebar Q&A with the head of Arco. Like Woody Allen said of a Catskill resort, "The food is terrible, and the portions are so small!"

O'Brian, Bridget. *The Wall Street Journal.* (★ ★ ★)
Airlines. O'Brian did much of the Eastern coverage at the paper, setting the pace for the rest of the press, constantly pushing at the envelope and impressing with sharp, taut writing. She minces no words in "Bad News for Travelers: Airlines Raise Maxsaver Fares," 1-27, offering diverse angles on price, restrictions and motive as selected carriers bump up fares: "Airlines today will begin sticking vacation travelers with the same kind of fare increases that have been hitting business travelers in recent months." In "Feud Between Borman, Lorenzo Explains Much, But Not All," 3-6, a sharp, tight thumbnail review of the Eastern Airlines saga, Frank Borman and Frank Lorenzo, she pens a provocative last graph, suggesting Lorenzo is in a win-win situation, "bankruptcy bringing a sizeable breakup price or the end of the strike." A followup makes her point as she interviews Frank Lorenzo, "Lorenzo Denies Intention to Dismantle Eastern," 3-13, timely, telling us Lorenzo feels bankruptcy "a lot cleaner and clearer in many respects than what we've had to deal with." A smart view of Eastern's suitors, co-authored by Christi Harlan, "Eastern Air Has Offers From 2 Groups, But Creditors Unlikely to Back Either Bid," 5-15, is broadly focused and tightly organized, leaving no questions in our mind as to the viability of these offers. She's snappily detailed in "Eastern Airlines Presents Plan to Reorganize," 7-24, on both the carrier's troubles and plans to remedy them. O'Brian combines material from creditors and the Frank Lorenzo press conference for a superior report on both in "Eastern Air's Creditors Ask Experts To Present Options for Reorganization," 10-18. A solid update, "Arbitrator Awards Back Pay to Pilots Of Eastern Airlines," 11-1, defines the complications engendered by the court's decision with regard to the carrier's bankruptcy filing, getting a good view of the ripple effect of the ruling.

O'Reilly, Brian. *Fortune.* (★)
Associate editor, Los Angeles. Less on the Pacific Rim from O'Reilly, he spent the year running around California, covering gadgets and doodads. Some of his technical coverage was snappy, but most of it was just soggy. He tries to convince us that Californians are becoming greater activists in the fight against housing and highways, in "The War Against Growth Heats Up," 12-5, but this is just another chapter in an ongoing battle that goes back to the '60's between developers and an alliance of militant homesteaders, environmentalists, and opportunistic politicians. Nifty in "Computers That Think Like People," 2-27, he touts the potential of a new technology called neural networks, which simulate human brain cells, while still acknowledging how tedious and difficult it is, including good profiles of several start-ups that are trying to cash in on logical systems for insurance companies and banks. He's silly in a love letter to "John Sculley on Sabbatical," 3-27, telling us what John did on his summer vacation, O'Reilly not mentioning that while Sculley was taking photography courses up in Maine, Apple made a serious error about the prices of computer chips, spending lots of money to corner a large supply, only to have chip prices fall. Apple stock got severely punished and there were ripples through the organization; the effect was that no one was in charge. In yet another Sculley story, "Apple Computer's Risky Revolution," 5-8, O'Reilly rehashes the latest factional fighting at Apple, this time between the two guys under Sculley. "Diet Centers Are Really In Fat City," 6-5, is a sprightly and refreshing change, well-done and entertaining on weight-loss centers, which are big business. He's flimsy in "Gadgets For Executives," 9-11, on laptops, fancy calculators, mobile phones, etc., reading like a puff piece for advertisers. "New Truths About Staying Healthy," 9-25, is a grim and occasionally graphic account of what kills people, including smoking, heart disease, diet and the like, but we've seen this before, and done better, in other places, such as Thomas Moore's *Atlantic* article debunking the cholesterol scare. In "America's Place in World Competition," 11-6, he gives us a remarkably upbeat set up stats on how far ahead the average American is to everyone else, handling his material very well. The same issue carries "The Captains See a Tilted Field," 11-6, various Fortune 500 CEOs making random complaints about foreign competitors, O'Reilly simply letting them huff and puff.

Ott, James. *Aviation Week & Space Technology.* (★ ½)
Senior Transport Editor. Standard fare from Ott, although with all the airline stories this year he ought to have done better. His best: "Northeast Asian Airlines Bracing for Fast Growth," 5-8, a mammoth, comprehensive special report, comprised of 14 individual articles, which together give a detailed picture of the commercial aviation industry in Japan, Taiwan and South Korea, the fastest growing of the sixteen regions of the International Air Transport Association. "NTSB Raps Aloha, Aviation System for Fuselage Failure," 5-29, is credible on the National Transportation Safety Board's finding of a "breakdown in the nation's aviation maintenance system;" occasioned by the disintegration in flight of an Aloha Airlines Boeing 737, the study "found fault with the airline, the manufacturer and the FAA...." "Investigators Find Reconstructed Tail of DC-10 Riddled With Damage," 8-7, updates the investigation of the United Airlines Sioux City Crash, now focusing on the forging and machining process of the General Electric engine that blew up, very detailed on the hardware. "Lack of U.S. Interest Derails International HSCT Consortium," 9-11, is a good evaluation of the reasons behind the collapse of the commercial effort to develop a high-speed civil transport. But a "let the flyer beware" mentality pervades "20-Inch Crack Spurs FAA to Order 727-100 Checks," 7-10: "Discovery of a 20 in. fatigue crack at a lap splice below the window line of a United Airlines Boeing 727-100 has prompted a new set of FAA-ordered inspections of early 727s. An emergency airworthiness directive issued four days after the crack was discovered on June 26, requires by mid-July a visual inspection from the inside of fuselage lap joints at Stringers 14 Right and Left of the first 47 727-100s. The aircraft are owned by United, American, Continental and Trans World Airlines and the Trump Shuttle." With little followup from Ott on this, we're going Amtrak. Equally chilling, "10 Fatal Crashes Spark Call For New Safety Measures," 10-9, he continues in the tradition of *A WST*'s vigilant concern over airline safety: "Safety experts, unable to find a common link in a recent series of fatal U.S. airline accidents, are expressing concern that pilot inexperience, the fallout of growth in the industry, and a mercenary legacy of deregulation's intense competition are among the root causes."

Paltrow, Scot J. *Los Angeles Times.* (★ ★)
New York. The business side of law, Paltrow ended up covering the Drexel/Milken indictments for much of the year, pausing now and then to handle other high-powered cases. We were generally impressed with his openness, curiosity and fairness, and he occasionally turned up information we didn't see elsewhere. His "Drexel to Enter Plea of Guilty in Fraud," 12-22-88, seemed endless, but even so missed information and relied heavily on unnamed sources, but for those with the patience to stick with the story, he eventually pulls together all the pieces he has. He appears to have sources others don't, garnering information we didn't see any place else in "Drexel-SEC Deal May Cost Milken His Job, Most of '88 Earnings," 1-6, a P. 1 biz piece on the terms of the SEC agreement with Drexel and how it will affect Michael Milken. He takes an inside look from the jurors point of view in "Jurors at GAF Trial Distrusted Chief Witness for Government," 1-12, at what went on in the GAF trial that eventually was declared a mistrial, a good report on this case in particular and a reminder of how the smallest detail may swing a jury one way or the other. He picks up on *The Wall Street Journal*'s Stephen Adler's newsbeat in "First Conviction in Drexel Probe: Aide at Beverly Hills Office Is Guilty of Perjury," 3-23, reporting the first conviction in the Drexel case, that of a 26-year-old assistant trader; though this pales next to Adler's, it does competently cover what happened to this young woman. "A Pall at the 'Predators' Ball,' " 4-6, is merely a human interest story on who attended and who said what about Milken. He presents all we looked for in "Milken Resigns Drexel Post, Will Open Southland Consulting Firm," 6-16, on the Milken press conference announcing his new business venture. He is gossipy in "Hotel 'Queen' Helmsley Convicted of Tax Fraud," 8-31, satisfactory on Leona Helmsley's conviction, recounting the trial, but not getting to her claim that she actually overpaid taxes by a half million until the last few graphs. He gets a bit beneath the surface in "U.S. to Allow Milken to Collect His 1988 Pay," 9-7, on Milken's payday, nicely presenting the legal mire to come up with an explanation as to why the government dropped the Drexel requirement not to pay MM: to clear the way for the company's filing of a guilty plea.

Passell, Peter. *The New York Times.* (★ ★)
"Economic Scene" columnist. Heir apparent to Leonard Silk, PhD. at the *Times,* young Dr. Passell is in the process of finding his footing in this important assignment after some years scribbling economic editorials at the paper. A shaky Keynesian, he's not afraid to break new ground and often gets a particular angle we appreciate. His willingness to try out new stuff produces quite a few misfires, mostly on international debt, but most of his material is credible and trenchant. He provides good detail in "A No-Losers Deal for Busy Airports," 12-28-88, explaining a move by big airports to cut delays by raising landing fees for single-prop planes, the first we saw on the issue. In an interesting, though unpersuasive, "Ad Ban Might Help Cigarette Makers," 1-2, he gives a micro-analysis on how the tobacco industry would benefit if it ceased its total $2.4 billion annual expenditure on ads and promotion. He goes in circles with "Inflation Is Looking Like It Is Going to Last," 3-5: "With fiscal policy in stalemate, the only way to reduce inflationary demand pressure is to tighten credit. But the resulting increase in United States interest rates would attract more foreign capital, bidding up the value of the dollar and making American products less competitive in global markets." But you can see he's trying. He puts the current debate into sharp focus in "Minimum Wage: A Reality Test," 3-15, a fine presentation of the pros and cons: "The battle, long stylized as one of jobs versus incomes, is over. What has yet to be decided is how far the Democrats will go to save face" in caving in to a teenage minimum. He has nothing to add in "Michael Milken is Other Accusers," 4-12, summarizing Milken's impact on corporate America. He is against the curve with "Frank Lorenzo Strikes Back," 5-10, outlining advantages of Eastern selling off used planes and slimming to a "Piedmont-sized, Atlanta-based carrier." At his worst, pure neo-Keynesian, "Fed Fiddles, Dollar Booms," 5-31, is moth-eaten and mind-numbing. In "The Long Road to Argentina's Financial Disaster," 6-18, he disappoints as we look for some new insight, Passell baffled on the hyperinflation, quoting Jeffrey Sachs of Harvard saying the creditors did it! He gets it right in "The Morning Line On the Next Nobel," 10-18, listing possible future candidates for the economic prize, saying laureates are chosen in much the same way as Oscar winners, sentimentality eclipsing merit at times, as "economists are a gossipy, competitive lot," compiling his candidates from an informal survey. In "Trade Law is Tangled Web," 11-8, he lucidly explains the complex dispute with Japan on the omnibus trade act of '88. An important Sunday P. 1 "Curing the Greenhouse Effect Could Run Into Trillions," 11-19, is only flawed in taking the science totally for granted in this look at the economics, although he's probably on target with a prediction that in another 100 years the climate will be far less important in how people live than what the technology will be.

Pauly, David. *Newsweek.* (★)
Senior writer. Frequently paired with old pro Rich Thomas, Pauly is not as satisfying in this winning pair as going solo. Now that he is doing harder economic policy pieces, he is green and it shows. He and Thomas do a good job of sorting through the Brady Plan for Third World debt in "The New Spelling of Relief," 3-20, but the duo is skewed in asserting Brady's plan can only solve part of the problem because "debtor countries must promote investment in their local economies" by getting "the upper classes to return their own capital from havens abroad." In "Is Inflation Getting Better or Worse?" with Thomas 4-3, he devotes much of his space to explaining the relationship of the PPI to the CPI, muddled, he never really answers the question posed in the title, except to suggest that if the current upswings in the PPI and CPI continue, "the economy is headed for trouble." He digs, but only shallowly, in "Deathwatch Investments," with Cecilia Slaber 4-24, as death, or the rumor thereof, of corporate chiefs fuel rumors that the company will be in play, taking the 20% rise over two days in Campbell Soup stock when chairman John Dorrance died as a case in point. He is easy to follow in "Wall Street's New Muscle Men," 6-5, on the growing power of pension fund managers and their significance in the finance markets, but his analysis is facile: "Now pension funds own such a big stake in some companies that they would drive down the share price by starting to sell, reducing the value of the stock they still owned." In "The Fairy-Tale Economy," with Thomas 9-11, Pauly discusses the reasons why the economy has broken out of the traditional boom and bust business cycle. He notes that in an international economy "strong export sales can ease the effect of slumping domestic orders."

Pennar, Karen. *Business Week,* (½ ★)
Economics editor. Slipping below par again, Pennar is confused, terminally overheated on economics. Her macro articles are all over the place, and she didn't do enough on the micro to be useful. In an apologia for protectionist academes, "The Gospel of Free Trade Is Losing Apostles," 2-27, she is ineffective, taking many quotes from these people, but her arguments go unsupported by pertinent facts, and she only gives a brief nod to potential trade-war effects. She is muddled in "The Wolf at the Door Doesn't Look so Scary," 3-27, a house of cards, defining the problem as overheated resources causing wage/price pressure causing Fed higher interest rates causing recession. But on the other hand, many say it won't. But on the third hand, if recession happens, it will be mild, because, to quote Allen Sinai: "The Fed simply won't tighten enough to propel us into a deep recession." There follows some speculation about the recession that takes no account of the Fed's reasoning in its actions or of prospective world monetary developments. Arrgh. A hodgepodge, "Inflation Stages a Comeback: But It Is a Different Breed - So It May Not Spiral Out of Control," with Howard Gleckman, Michael Schroeder, and Mark Ivey 4-3, makes grand pronouncements about commodity prices, confused analysis, concluding we should probably worry a *little*. She is dull as dishwater on the overworked subject, how the future of the U.S. depends on a higher savings rate, "Have You Hugged Your Bankbook Today?" 5-29. "Fewer Guns Could Mean A Whole Lot More Butter," 6-12, is filled with strictly theoretical, pie-in-the-sky calculations on the "dividend" from potential deep defense cuts based on arms control negotiations with the Soviets, perfectly conventional. The problem — if such cuts do indeed happen — lies in assuming that Congress will use the "savings" to cut the budget deficit, instead of spending it somewhere else. She is better than usual in part of "The New America" cover, "Economic Prospects For The Year 2000," 9-25, questioning "conventional analysis" of slow growth in the 90s, opting for a scenario of prosperity and strong growth, intelligently done, reviewing key economic sector outlooks: workers, technology, managers, markets and information, government. But it is getting so we shrink at seeing Pennar's byline. She definitely belongs on business news, not macro-economics.

Pine, Art. *Los Angeles Times.* (★ ★)
Washington, international economics and trade. Throughout the year Pine gave solid rundowns of international trade, economics and LDC debt. A veteran on this beat for more than 20 years, he's reliable in the facts and quotes he presents, continues to grow as an analyst, and has our attention when we spot his byline. He does a sound job of explaining the issues and analyzing the potential impact of U.S. retaliatory measures, "Some European Foods Face 100% U.S. Tariff," 12-28-88, good reporting on the latest round in the U.S.-European food fight. He takes on a good theme with "Variable Mortgages Weaken Inflation Fears for Many," 1-29, telling us debtors don't welcome inflation as they did in the 1970s with a spread of variable rates. He explains foreign investing, including a section on how foreign purchases of U.S. securities helps to cover the budget deficit, "Bush Hits Fears of Foreign Investing," 2-22, but in the second half of the article, he veers off in a discussion of trade with South Korea and the EC, losing direction in the process. In "New Trade Law Has The Makings of a Monster," 3-26, an exploration of the workings of the 1988 Trade Bill, he chronicles the law's unintended consequences. In a P. 1 lead, "Senate OKs Hike in Minimum Pay," 4-12, he spends an inordinate amount of time explaining the House proposal, the Senate proposal, the White House proposal and the politicking behind each, addressing the most obvious question in the last paragraph: "Economists contend that. . .with the unemployment rate now so low and only a few million workers currently earning the minimum wage, the actual economic impact is likely to be modest." He sounds the alarm in " 'Nippophobia' Affects Making of Trade Policy," 4-24, on growing protectionism in Washington: "At least two well-known business groups — including Hills' own Advisory Council on Trade Policy and Negotiations, a committee of top corporate executives enlisted to help drum up support for free-trade policies — have declared that free trade will not work in the case of Japan." Puffy with "Bush Vows to Seek Agreement on Mexico Debt," 7-15, on the opening of the Economic Summit, rehashes old news. Part of the "Economic Nationalism" series, he is tough on trade in "Much of Trade Deficit May Be Made in the

U.S.A.," 8-9, effectively arguing that flawed policy is only part of the problem: "U.S. business can no longer dominate by default. Now it must compete." He's late after *Defense News*' David Silverberg's coverage of CFIUS, but still effective with "Plans to Fortify Foreign Investment Panel Earn Praise, Scorn," 8-29, bringing the story to a broader audience.

Platt, Gordon. *The Journal of Commerce.* (★)
Financial editor. Tentative in his analysis and reporting, Platt is adequate, but bland. He takes far too much at face value, and while the information he presents can be valuable, Platt has a one-track mind, and it's rare that we get more than one angle on a story. He tells the tale in "Italian Banking System Modernizing for 1992," 12-22-88, as the President of the Italian Banker Association acknowledges there is no backing down from a unified European market, despite cold feet in some quarters, but it could take anywhere from five to twenty years before Europe gets a single central bank and a common currency. He's ludicrous in "Currency Traders Ready To Give Bush a Chance," 1-3, naive in thinking currency traders can fix the dollar's value any more than traders can fix stock prices: "Currency traders said...they want to see specific proposals on spending cuts or they will begin selling dollars again." He relates growing concern over LDC debt, taking an interview with David Novick, vice chairman and CEO of Bank Leumi Trust Co. of New York, in "Latin America's Debt Harms Trade With U.S.," 2-24, making good suggestions in the micro, arguing for no devaluations, but his ultimate prescription of writing off the debt is counterproductive. Xenophobic, he duly reports Swedish banker Jacob Palmstierna is advising countries not to lend to the U.S.S.R., "Lending to the Soviets Termed Too Risky," 4-14, but he never presents an alternative view. He doesn't do enough homework in "Economists Pessimistic On Further Trade Gains," 7-27, relying on "analysts" at Drexel and Salomon, and Gerald Anderson, a Fed Bank economist in Cleveland, to conclude that the rate of improvement in the trade deficit will slow, making the good news bad, and implying that a growing U.S. economy might not be such a good thing, as it encourages import purchases. Huh? A nice, but non-analytic overview, "Currency Trading Volume in U.S. More Than Doubles in 3 Years," 9-14, tells us who is buying what and where, but not why.

Pollack, Andrew, *The New York Times.* (★ ½)
Reporter, San Francisco. Periodic forays outside of Silicon Valley drag down his body of work, rattling his powers of observation and gift of organization. While Pollack is able to keep up with the pack on the machines, we didn't see the flashes of insight and flourish we looked forward to a few years back when reading his byline. In a typical business piece, "Another Silicon Valley Tailspin," 1-6, he's superficial on the decline in the fortunes of Wyse, 40% of whose volume is in personal computers, the decline blamed on its delay in producing a 80386 machine, never telling us why Wyse was so successful to begin with. His story barely comes through, so disorganized is "First Interstate's Turn to Squirm," 2-12, as Joseph Pinola, First Interstate's chairman, struggling with Bank of America, which he tried to absorb in 1986, flourishes again. He's scattered in "America's Answer to Japan is MITI," 3-5, burying his best material at the end of this profile of the Defense Advanced Research Projects Agency, a Pentagon "technological sandbox for bright scientists who can fund projects in accordance with their vision," further hampering the piece by starting slowly. Rehash and speculation abound in "Beating A Path To Fusion's Door," 4-28, Pollack providing only the news that 80 companies have called the University of Utah, and 30 have signed non-disclosure agreements, of which three are named. He is more balanced with "Wells Sets Venture with Nikko," 6-28, as Wells Fargo & Company spins off its investment management subsidiary, said to be the largest single investor in the stock market, into a jointly owned money management venture with Nikko Securities Company, allowing Wells to expand into Japan. He files "An Avalanche of Information Is Coming to Video Screens," 7-25, an enticing preview of what the age of hypermedia offers. Mushy and in a chicken-or-egg frame of mind, he appears to argue both for and against government regulation simultaneously in "Innovators and Investors Hindered In the Business of Pollution Control," 8-29, telling us that "barriers arise because polluters see little reason to spend on new and better technology unless the Government makes them do so" but that "the

need to obtain permits from several levels of government greatly slows the introduction of technology" though this seems to be more an organizational problem than anything else. Against the grain, he files "Imported TV Sets Face Test in Japan," 9-6, as Philip's Consumer Electronics Company begins exporting color TV sets from Tennessee to Japan, a test case, and he finds that quality and distribution are problems for U.S. companies, along with non-tariff barriers.

Power, William. *The Wall Street Journal.* (★ ★)
Wall Street. Power's reporting on the markets is coming more and more to anchor the *Journal*'s section on "Money & Investing." He impresses us this year with his confidence in maneuvering through the complex mechanisms of the marketplace, the way Floyd Norris of *The New York Times* does so well. Power takes analysts' opinion in "Battered High-Tech Stocks Show Signs of New Life," 1-3, and runs with it, putting all the pieces together as he examines what this will mean for the markets, the companies, and the stockholders; we're also impressed he's not afraid to name names, Motorola and Texas Instruments among them. He explains the "buy-minus" and "sell-plus" variation on program trading with clarity and depth in "Wall Street's Kinder, Gentler Program Trades," 5-1, probing possible market reaction and giving examples to show the system in action. He and co-author Matthew Winkler cull candid quotes in "New Hierarchy: Along Wall Street, Once-Mighty Traders Are Reduced to Pawns," 7-20, a worthwhile piece on the winds of change blowing through Wall Street since deregulation. He is one of the few reporters to tell us that the "Stock Market Rally May Be for 'Real,' New Data Suggest," 8-4, as more investors buckle down for the long haul, but midway through the piece Power falls into a circular cash-flow trap that leads nowhere: "why isn't this development good news? Because it chips away at conventional wisdom that there are a host of big and medium-sized institutional investors 'on the sidelines' still refusing to buy stocks. Conventional wisdom holds that these investors can be counted on one day to flood back in and carry the market even higher." He disappoints moderately with "Limited Partnerships Are Often Faltering, To Investor's Dismay," co-written by Jill Bettner 8-17, opening strongly on this expose of problems in the huge Limited Partnership investment arena, but the pair begins to ramble and what we end up with is the tale of woe of one particular LP that is hurting, for unknown reasons. Power is light again, offering little more than a summary of the American Stock Exchange survey on program trading, "Guess What's 'Ruining' the Stock Market," 10-6, no analysis, no prescriptive. His "Firms Bypass Big Board Floor to Execute Many Program Trades," 11-9, was an eye-opener on off-exchange trading. But we should have known, right? Grim on Merrill Lynch and its cost-cutting measures, "Streets Woes Spread as Merrill Plans Layoffs," 11-22, he's effective enough in accounting for their troubles, relating them to cutbacks on the Street, but we looked for a little more helpful analysis here. His "Lane, 15 Others to Be Reassigned in Shearson Shake-up," 11-29, is an important piece, but underplayed and underdeveloped, plenty of great material that Power could have improved upon with clearer presentation.

Price, Joyce. *The Washington Times.* (★ ½)
Health reporter, and sometime "Your Health" columnist. Steady as she goes, Price does bread-and-butter reporting, basic and reliable. We'd like to see her venture into analytical asides that would elevate her dispatches, or at least discriminate better in choosing from the vast body of material on her beat, to avoid sounding like a public service announcement from time to time. She doesn't treat important findings in depth in "Study Downplays Need for a Complete Physical," 2-1, as this *Annals of Internal Medicine* study says healthy people don't necessarily need complete physicals, just relating the pertinent data. She doesn't dig in "Tension, Kidney Damage a Black Problem," 3-20, either, citing another study from *The New England Journal of Medicine,* and while it's good to report this, the dispatch is not much above wire service copy. In "Cuba's Quarantine System Works in Combatting AIDS," 4-17, she contrasts other countries' ineffective public health policies to Cuba, although their methods seem somewhat crude and unsympathetic: "the only nation in the world which quarantines citizens found to be infected with the AIDS virus — is breathing easily." A useful "Your Health" column, "Medical Groups Endorse Mammograms After 40," 6-28, delivers little beyond the headline. She is

modestly thoughtful on a growing trend, "Women Waiting Longer to Have Babies," 7-6, although this isn't exactly fresh news. In "Officials Disbelieve Africa's Report of 24,000 AIDS Cases," 7-20, she explores the growing controversy over the grisly AIDS body count: "Although only 24,000 AIDS cases have been reported in Africa, world health officials believe the actual figure is closer to 300,000." Additionally, in "CDC Doubts AIDS Figures," 8-8, balanced and statistically sound, she offers the most recent AIDS estimates from Public Health Service officials, with the bottom line effectively doubling due to an underestimation of the infection rate: "current CDC estimates of 1 million to 1.5 million HIV-infected people are based on an estimated 0.4 percent to 0.6 percent infection rate in the general population. But. . .data from six large urban hospitals have shown an infection range of 0.12 percent to 0.80 percent, with a median of 0.24 percent." She breaks a repulsive story, but one that must be told on high-tech sleaze in "Pedophiles Are Making Use of Computer Bulletin Boards," 8-29, as child molesters go high-tech to solicit services. Price's editors let her stray into *National Enquirer* turf with a grisly and off-the-beaten-path "Former Cult Follower Describes Human Sacrifice At Satanic Rite," 9-14, where she presents a close look at an apparently growing phenomenon, as "Regina, a Denver mother of two, says she watched in horror while a 17-year-old girl, high on drugs, stood grinning as a knife was plunged into her heart during a satanic ritual five years ago." Now really, Arnaud.

Queenan, Joe. *Forbes.* (½ ★)
A talented, all-around, general utility, conservative satirist, Queenan arrived from *Barron's* at the beginning of the year. His sharp wit denigrates into snideness more often than not, and, while he is generally informative with bits we don't see elsewhere, we find ourselves gritting our teeth to get to them as he dances around the lines of discretion and civility. He goes way beyond debunking Peter Peterson's balance-the-budget economic philosophy in "Cadillac Cassandra," *Barron's* 1-16, spending much of the article smearing him, his associates at the Blackstone Group, and friends, using innuendo and quotes from his biggest detractors. With less of a heavy hand, he's sharper in "Different Slant: A Look At the Left Business Observer," *Barron's* 2-6, a review of a left-wing newsletter. He succeeds with "G. Robert Blakey versus Michael Milken," 5-1, a hatchet job on the author of the Rico Act that works by hacking up the law first. The "Scam Capital of the World," 5-29, is Vancouver of all places, more serious in describing the Vancouver Stock Exchange (VSE) as a vacuum cleaner sucking money from legitimate deals and putting money into VSE frauds, well substantiated. Queenan unintentionally drops a bomb with "Straight Talk About Aids," 6-26, an efficient update on Michael Fumento's perspective that the disease is not epidemic. The tone here is wrong, however, too cynical, and the article itself generated a storm of controversy over the reporter's apparent endorsement of Fumento's theories, bringing picketers to 60 Fifth Avenue. Malcolm Forbes himself not only retracted, but *rebutted* some of the information Queenan presented. He uses irony well in "Bringing It All Back Home," 9-2, a witty, cynical survey of the social critic rock bands and the piles of money they make. He is obviously angry about a couple of self-proclaimed hippies making tons of money selling ice cream in "Purveying Yuppie Porn," 11-13, a no-holds-barred hatchet job on Ben & Jerry's that leaves out relevant information and launches nasty attacks on these longhairs. Queenan's unquestioned writing talents aren't enough to carry him, and we suspect he needs more editorial guidance to prevent him from making himself look foolish. Moonlighting at *The New Republic,* Queenan writes "Dead and Breakfast," 3-20, perfectly awful and downright nasty, as he uses his family's sightseeing tour of England as a framework in which he reveals the less well-known atrocities committed during Britain's history. "Japun, Inc," *TNR* 10-16, has a dumb title plus incredibly silly filler on Japanese satire.

Quinn, Jane Bryant. *Newsweek.* (★ ★)
We find solid, utilitarian advice from Quinn's columns, for the investor, the taxpayer, the saver; there is generally something useful for everyone. There's rarely a question on policy debate that's treated in the macro or theoretical framework, for which we are grateful as she gets in over her head when she does. Quinn relates all her topics to the man-on-the-street. She offers some

options for "Financing Long-Term Care," 1-30, bringing up good points about insurance, but only cursorily admitting her own bias towards the end: "But in my view, old age costs are the thing that we're all supposed to be saving money *for*." She wraps up the problems with no-fault insurance, obvious in "Car Drivers in Revolt," 2-13, but it's useful to have all this in one place. She provides free, sound tax advice for those of us who haven't filed yet, "Tax Guide for 1989," 3-20. She warns potential investors of the dangers of investing in one of these new offerings, but doesn't present alternative opportunities, in "The War on Penny Stocks," 4-10. A guide to life insurance is a little difficult to follow in spots, but informative, "The Money on Your Life," 5-8. We get lost in "Know-Nothing Investments," 6-5, her explanation of productivity for your limited partnership investment, thorough, but tough to get through. She does a nice job illustrating how tax-deferred "[a]nnuities never beat an equivalent investment in a no-fee-tax-deferred savings plan offered by your employer. They can't even do better than a nondeductible Individual Retirement Account" in "Annuities Reconsidered," 7-17, with good use of quotes by experts and a six-point criteria checklist to see if these annuities are a good buy. She argues rightly there's no such thing as a safe investment in "What Can Go Wrong," 8-14, obvious, but solid. "A Word To The Muni-Mad," 9-25, on how to decide what kind of a municipal bond to buy is not only informative but also easy to follow: "So sullen have Americans grown about income taxes that sometimes they choose tax-exempts even if it costs them money." Her "Saying the Big Goodbye," 10-9, does a nice job of illustrating the brain drain being caused by early retirement packages that more employees took advantage of than expected by management. This again provides one of Quinn's useful checklists of questions you should ask.

Quint, Michael. *The New York Times.* (★ ★)
"Business Day" reporter. Breaking away from the daily job of wrapping up the credit markets, Quint is developing into a solid business reporter, adept at making some of his dryer topics readable simply through good organization. At times, when he gets into tougher subjects he can still get lost in the finer points, taking us with him. Deftly analytic in "Texaco and Icahn End Feud," 1-30, he details the war from start to finish, gathering together pertinent facts and numbers as Carl Icahn and Texaco cut a deal: Icahn won't buy more Texaco stock or mount a takeover while Texaco shells out over $2 billion to the shareholders and stock repurchases. Quint is organized, but standard in reporting all the requisite numbers, "Leading Indicators Down 0.3%," 3-30, nicely rounded in collecting various opinions as to what the numbers mean, although he comes to no conclusion. In "Brady Plan Lifts Bank Stocks," 4-12, he seems thorough enough, but hard to follow, and we wondered how many readers could. He could be clearer too in "After Citizens Rejection, NCNB Turns to MCorp," 4-27, as he tries to inform on NCNB's proposed merger with the Citizens and Southern Corp. of Atlanta. But we appreciated Quint in explaining the complexities of late 80's finance as embodied in the RJR debt being floated in "Nabisco Bonds Coming to Market," 5-8. He tries valiantly to explain interest rate saps and the new aggressive marketing, relatively well done theoretically, but giving confusing examples, "Eliminating Risk of Rising Rates," 7-3. "Investors Wary of Utility's Bonds," 8-30, lays out the pros and cons for investors looking at a new issue of bonds by WPPS, a well-balanced view. In "New Bank to Emphasize Aid to Small Borrowers," 9-18, Quint reports on a local new bank in Brooklyn that looks to lend to community and local projects, a sympathetic portrayal. His straight news account, "Primerica To Buy Unit Of Barclays," 11-25, steps us through the deal crisply, lucidly, much better than *The Wall Street Journal* account two days later. "While the Barclays unit has been operating at a break-even level recently, profits will come quickly once it is combined with Commercial Credit," he writes confidently.

Ramirez, Anthony. *The New York Times.* (★ ★)
"Business Day" reporter. Ramirez spent most of the year at *Fortune* on the science and technology beat, moving to *The New York Times* in November. Always diligent, Ramirez tended to be more introspective and reflective than some of his colleagues at the magazine, preferring solid workmanlike stories to some of the jazzy profiles we see there. He is thoughtful with "Making Better Use Of Older Workers," 1-30, on the demographics of the aging workforce,

finding a fresh group of examples among retirees and seniors without using the tired McDonald's "Masters" program, with the best line from a hiring manager in Southern California, who's confronted with a mysterious malady that strikes only youths on sunny days: "With older workers we don't get surfer's throat." In a words-and-photo essay that is the most interesting of the stories that accompany the *Fortune* 500 list, "Factories That Shine," 4-24, he spotlights Timken, Milliken, Worthington, AT&T and Hoover, which have upgraded certain factories to world-class status. This is the sort of meat-and-potatoes coverage *Fortune* should do more of. He's more serious, and downright dull in an expansive "Boeing's Happy, Harrowing Times," 7-17, touching all the right aerospace bases, but a chore to read, Ramirez's usually taut writing laborious in this one, and we suspect heavy editing and re-writes, making the overall effect choppy and flat. Ramirez ventures into policy and management prescriptives in "EPA Should Clean Up Its Own Act," 11-6, pinning the chances for the EPA's success on its new administrator William Reilly. He seems naive in reporting that environmentalists fault Reilly for being "too willing to work out solutions with industry. Reilly believes that it simply makes sense to bring all parties to the bargaining table." Reilly is nothing if he is not an environmentalist from head to toe. At the *Times,* Ramirez serves up, "Now, From Brazil, 'Light' Water," 11-25, a marvelous little piece that tells us in a few hundred words, plus graphics, all we want to know about the world of bottled water. "High Stakes for Product Managers," 12-4, also has several dimensions — the war for market share and supermarket shelves with a focus on laundry detergent. "Even manufacturers concede that many products really are pretty much alike, which means there are few lasting competitive advantages with which they can dominate the markets."

Redburn, Tom. *Los Angeles Times.* (★ ★ ★)
Washington economic correspondent. Redburn is one of the pillars of the *Los Angeles Time*'s Washington bureau, smart, alert, inquisitive. The general high quality of his material was not as consistent as we would have liked in delivering on the S&L and budget stories. But he's still stronger than his competitors at the other major dailies, never afraid to cut against the grain, with no sign of him pushing his own agenda. We liked seeing him forceful in "Bush May Use Gramm-Rudman as Club," 12-21-88, on the possibility the Bush administration strategy to curb spending and reduce the deficit may take a riskier, confrontational approach to dealing with Congress. Redburn talks to Richard Breeden, the assistant to the President for issue analysis (eventually named by Bush to chair the SEC), about the S&L bailout plan in "Manhattan Beach Native Helping Bush Through S&L Minefield," 1-27, good on-the-margin information about what the plans may be. He explains in relatively easy-to-understand terms how the government is going to bail out the S&Ls, "Fiscal Wizardry Figuring Into the Complex Proposal," 2-7, incisively laying out the "Rube Goldberg inspired" scheme that makes a relatively complex issue hopelessly complex. His Q&A "Real Cost of S&L Bailout Depends on 'What If?' " 2-28, is well done, confident in handling megabillions, fairly clear. Redburn gets inside Rosty's head in "Rostenkowski May Be Ready to Deal on Tax Cut for Capital Gains," 5-26, getting Rosty's wavering on the issue days before anyone else, but he cites no named sources in this piece, a habit some in the DC bureau can't seem to break, relying on "tax experts," a "congressional tax specialist," a "White House official," and "a spokesman for the Ways and Means committee" to make his case. He zips along in "Wholesale Prices Fall, Sales Climb," 8-12, as the economy rebounds, crediting Greenspan's machinations at the Fed for putting the brakes on inflation yet — so far — steering clear of a recession. Are we recessing or not? Part of the paper's "Economic Nationalism" series, "Difference Between 'Us' and 'Them' Blurs in a Global Economy," 8-8, is pretty soft for Redburn, about U.S. competitiveness in HDTV, how we must "gain a foothold" in the industry, although he's open-minded about open markets, and on-target in his assertion that "global markets have thrown policymakers in Washington into disarray." He adroitly gets the behind-the-scenes politicking in "New Effort to Revive IRA Tax Breaks," 9-13, on Sen. Lloyd Bentsen's (D-Tex.) IRA proposal. In "House Panel Rejects Faster Refunds for Utility Customers," 10-12, he presents a satisfying report on the Ways and Means refusal to prod utility companies to refund windfalls garnered in the 1986 tax reform, after the utilities collected $19 billion from customers to pay future federal taxes at the old rate of 46%.

Reier, Sharon. *FW.* (★ ★ ★)
Southeast bureau reporter. Clearly the superstar at the weekly, Reier holds down the fort capably. She writes with grace, compellingly, and never skimps on pertinent information, solidly analytic. She fascinates with "Credibility Gulch," 2-7, a complete corporate profile of mortgage banker Lomas Financial and its CEO, Jess Hay, whose defensive diversification of the company saved it and whose too-optimistic earning predictions for '88 and '89 might have crippled it, a fact-filled effort. She's biting on the possible sale of military bases, "Mission Impossible," 3-21, and rightfully so, providing bunches of examples to state her case, including the "virtual giveaway" of 1,416 acres at the Presidio in San Francisco, "without maximizing values that may well be worth billions." In the case of the Presidio (estimated value — $1 billion), the entire area, excepting 36.5 acres available to developers in 10 years, will be a historical landmark: "When the military tries to act like a business, the 'Army way' translates to buying dear and selling cheap." Her "CEO of the Decade," cover 4-4, on Sam Walton of Wal-Mart follows John Huey's *Fortune* piece, an incisively prepared update that even adds a little. Very timely, on the margin with "The Last Tango," 5-30, she profiles Argentina, which once had the sixth largest GNP in the world, on the verge of collapse, appearing at the eruption of the country's economic crisis: "No matter who wins the election, the victor will have to deal with a bankrupt government." Part of the mushy "Ethics" cover, Reier files a scathing attack on the S&L crowd, all the finagling going on in the industry and in the government, catching the Lincoln Savings aspect of the scandal decisively, "Let's Make a Deal," 6-27. Her "Real Crude," 9-5, gets her points across on energy LPs, although we have to slog through some sandy stuff to finish this.

Rich, Spencer. *The Washington Post.* (★)
National desk writer, covering health issues. Rich is a competent professional, a veteran of social-issue reporting at the *Post* now into his fourth decade. He does not make many splashes, but few mistakes either. He is uncritical in "Overhauling the Social Safety Net With Standardization and Savings," 1-10, on Robert Haveman of the U. of Wisconsin, who proposes doing away with Social Security in favor of a uniform monthly retirement benefit equal to the poverty line. He gets the debate adequately in "Aiding Needle Exchange is Illegal, Rangel Says," 3-10, Rep. Charles Rangel criticizing HHS Sec. Louis W. Sullivan for saying that the government would be "supportive" of local communities who want to use a needle exchange program, arguing such programs are illegal, while other "experts" disagree with Rangel, but overall this leaves us blank. He takes the example of Maryland's McCready Memorial Hospital and applies it painlessly to other rural hospitals in difficulty, in "Resuscitating a Rural Hospital," 3-18, a sparkling job with pertinent facts and figures, with human examples to bring them to life, but we'd have liked to see another hospital success story as a case in point. He doesn't go far enough in "Studies Question Insurance, Hospital Care of Elderly," 4-5, on the GAO Medicare study, and, given the rise in the senior population, this is important stuff. Compact, he barely breaks the surface in "Plan May Benefit More Mentally Disabled Children," 8-15, never relating specifics on the HHS proposal. Perfectly clear in "Law Helps Spouses of Nursing Home Residents," 10-30, he explains the change in the Medicare law that gives spouses more breathing room financially, opening with a powerful example to draw us in: "When Roland Davis, a former electrical engineer at Walter Reed Army Medical Hospital, entered a nursing home with Alzheimer's disease 15 months ago, the $1,100-a-month cost threw his 71-year-old wife, Margaret, into poverty, with only a few hundred dollars a month to live on. Her situation was typical of the financial crisis faced by thousands of elderly people, usually women who find that most of the family assets and income are in the husband's name." In a Thanksgiving offering, "Despite U.S. Prosperity, 1 in 5 Youths in Poverty," 11-23, he updates us on the most recent findings on children in poverty, appropriate for the season, but, while he quotes civic and congressional leaders as saying something must be done, we get little insight as to what that something must be.

Richter, Paul. *Los Angeles Times.* (★ ★)
A utility reporter at the *Times,* Richter impresses us with his easy handling of M&A and SEC topics, knitting together bits and pieces of information into a satisfying whole. He seems to have all the details in "Corporate Raider Bilzerian Charged With Stock Fraud," 12-22-88, on the federal investigation of Wall Street corruption, focused now on Paul Bilzerian, and we hear no axes grinding in the background. We get an excellent look at what's happening post-Murdoch at the *New York Post,* a respectful overview of the daily in "Shocker! Tabloid Wants Respect," 12-28-88. Against the grain with "Some Question Advantage of Time-Warner Deal," 3-7, he provides a counterpoint to the PR line given out on this business happening, lining up a few skeptics to review the Time and Warner merger to look at whether or not this really makes sense. More colorful and smartly readable with a P. 1 feature on the day of Michael Milken's indictment, "Those Touched By Milken Knew Success or Ruin," 3-30, he offers wonderful anecdotes of those who gained and lost in the M&A junk bond period. Innovative, but not quite persuasive in "Victory for Time Also May be a Strategic Victory For Paramount," 7-18, he argues that by losing, the debt-laden Time-Warner won't be a threat, while Paramount spent millions of dollars on white-collar hired help trying to become debt-laden. Whew. In a short, but solid, look, he implies the easy part is over as Time-Warner will have new worries due to the done deal, "Time, Warner Start Ironing Out Details of $14 Billion Deal," 7-26. Organized with "Top Wall Street Speculator Pleads Guilty to 3 Counts," 8-31, he relates how Salim B. (Sandy) Lewis pleaded guilty to 3 federal felony counts stemming from a 1986 scheme to drive up the price of Fireman's Fund Corp. stock, a standard dispatch raised by some minor insight. But he doesn't get behind the scenes, giving no drama to "Drexel Pleads Guilty to 6 Federal Felony Counts," 9-12, as Drexel paid $523 million of its $673 million of fines and penalties because of Ivan F. Boesky's testimony; and although the government had requested that Drexel not pay over $100 million in 1988 compensation to the Milken brothers as part of the settlement, that part was left out. Ho hum.

Ricklefs, Roger. *The Wall Street Journal.* (★ ★)
New York. A senior scribe at the financial daily, Ricklefs was also one of the earliest advocates *within* the national press corps of gay rights. He's been a great asset to *The Wall Street Journal* in recent years in reporting on the AIDS crisis in all its dimensions. This year Ricklefs is back pounding the business beat, with his usual care and precision, but we wonder why he's been moved off the health beat. "Little Firms Hiring Guns to Fight Their Tax Battles," 1-10, tells of a growing army of consultants offering legal services to small businesses in challenging property tax assessments, often on a contingency basis, promising more casework for the courts. He reports on courses in entrepreneurial thinking, a new hot field, in "Schools Increase Courses to Help Entrepreneurs," 2-6, but he doesn't ask if entrepreneurship can be taught, nor does he offer examples of business success after taking a course. Quirky, he pens an ad for small businesses, examining specifically the class reunion biz, taking an example of Reunion Times in Tinton Falls, NJ, which can locate up to 90% of a class, compared to the 65% the class secretary might be able to find, in "Pros Dare to Go Where Amateurs No Longer Bother," 3-31. He presents substantial information to argue that "This Old House May Not Be Worth Fixing These Days," 4-13, as the renovation business is no longer as profitable, due to the rise in property tax and the '86 tax reform, which eliminated many deductions on real estate investments, raised capital gains, and lowered tax incentives for historic preservation. In "Traumas of a New Entrepreneur," with Udayan Gupta 5-10, first in "The Entrepreneurial Cycle" series, he's mildly interesting on how many hours the entrepreneur works, especially in a start-up year, but there's too little of value to the prospective entrepreneur. Anecdotal, but interesting in "Success Comes Too Late for Small Firm," 6-12, Ricklefs details the start-up, rise and fall of a small entrepreneur, a Red Bank, NJ, concrete drilling concern that went under even as sales were rising. "Road to Success Becomes Less Littered with Failures," 10-10, is an interesting survey of 2,994 new businesses done by AmEx and the National Federation of Independent Businesses, finding 77% survive three years, that's quite readable despite the bunches of numbers he presents.

Riley, Barry. *Financial Times.* (½ ★)
"The Long View" columnist. We wonder sometimes if the "Long View" doesn't refer more to the labyrinthine paths he takes us down in his columns, rather than the sweeping perspective he's supposed to present. There are sometime insights, but it's progressively more difficult to get to them, and we're now addressing his material only at gunpoint. He gets mired in Keynesian twaddle in "Lawson Buries His Budget Treasure," 3-11, filled with twisted logic on why the U.K.'s economy is running a budget surplus. In "Cutting Out the Piggy in the Middle," 5-20, he takes a narrow, dense perspective, rambling on creative disintermediation, unpersuasive that pension advantage over individuals is in marketing, not taxation. Very tricky, "The Foreigners Trickle Back to Tokyo," 5-6/7, is cleverly written as foreigners are coming back to the Japanese equity market, even though they don't understand it, according to Riley, who argues the market in Tokyo has to be viewed the Japanese way. Tangled up with "Inflation as Both Friend and Enemy," 7-1, he struggles to figure out the pros and cons of an inflationaary blip on corporate profits, handing off the problem to the "accountancy profession." In an interesting schoolbook exercise, Riley wanders in circles and dictionary definitions, attempting to distinguish between income and capital, "When the Arithmetic Does Not Add Up," 9-16. Mind-numbing, "Support Your Neighborhood Regulator," 10-7, gives microscopic detail as to how many angels can dance on the head of a unit trust. "Making Good Use of a Scapegoat," 10-28, is the correct diagnosis on the British economy, but prescribes the wrong medicine, advising policymakers to manipulate a recession to attract long-term capital! We're frustrated trying to get what's in his obviously fertile mind.

Riley, Karen. *The Washington Times.* (★ ★)
Washington economic correspondent. Riley's dispatches are comfortably facile, dependable and detailed, understandable by the layman, but with too few forays into the broader news analytics that she does increasingly well. A nice survey of bank response to the S&L bailout plan, "S&L Rescue Posse Gallops into Action: Banks May Raise Service Charges," 2-8, compactly gathers analyst opinion, government regulation and proposals to speculate on long-term implications for the thrift industry. Her "Debtor Plan to Face Foreign Scrutiny," 3-31, is properly skeptical of the Brady Plan: "Commercial banks may well balk at lending out new money to a debt-burdened country at the same time they're recovering only a portion of their stake in an old loan." In a feature look at Martha Seger, "Fed's Seger 'Speaks The Truth' Whether Board Likes It Or Not," 4-12, Riley offers some good detail on how Martha looks at regional economics, but glosses over her model, pegging Seger as a "self-described 'garbage collector' who refuses to adopt any one economic theory or focus on any given set of business indicators." An excellent survey of the Polish economy is hampered by her austerity view, "Poland Hides Its Economic Strengths," 7-12, telling us rightly that despite its $39 billion debt and 100% inflation, ". . . the Polish economy has enough underlying strengths so that it could be turned around in two to five years, provided the people and the government have the political will to make the sacrifices." She surveys the state of two-handed economics in "Dismal Science Keeps Searching For the Perfect Economic Model," 8-18, sorting out econometricians' proliferating and frustrating efforts to develop reliable predictive models of an economy that continues to mock pessimistic forecasts: "Like investors charting every tick of the Dow or gamblers toting up blackjack odds, economists keep striving to develop a fail-safe system for predicting economic trends. But the daunting task of forecasting the ups and downs of the $5 trillion economy has eluded even the most eminent members of the dismal science for decades." Standard in relating the debate over capital gains, "Bentsen Wields 2-edged Sword in Gains Tax Battle, Dole Warns," 10-5, she weighs little of the economic benefit of either side's proposal. But she hits pay dirt with "Corporate Capital Gains May Get Next Tax Break," 10-6, the best report we saw anywhere on the background to Senator Packwood's capgains proposal extending to timber: "Tax reform was a blow to the nation's 65,000 tree farmers, especially those who were preparing to harvest a crop after a 25-year growing period and claim a hefty capital gain." An early warning, "U.S. Plans to Boost Soviet Trade Status," 11-17, is well substantiated on plans to make a major move toward improving U.S.-Soviet trade relations and ground rules, hinting the move will come at Malta.

Rockwell, Keith M. *The Journal of Commerce.* (★ ★)
An off-year for the normally stellar Rockwell, he didn't seem to be able to pull together his sources, analysis and information as he's done in previous years. His major work, on the Brady Plan, followed the curve for the most part, although what he did was competent enough. In "Bush Team Vows Much Higher Priority for Trade," co-authored by Richard Lawrence 2-16, the team interviews new Commerce Sec. Robert Mosbacher as to his views on trade, particularly with regard to the Japanese, providing some salient insights as Mosbacher pledges to avoid "Japan bashing." In "Brady Plan on Debt Hot Topic for Parley," 3-30, he covers the bases, but presents nothing new. "U.S.-EC Row Dominates Trade Talks," 3-31, shows the results of Rockwell's hard work interviewing administration and Congressional figures, offering some insight from those quips and quotes. Competent in "Brady Debt Plan Stirs Some Fears," 4-5, his information is far inferior to earlier stories in the *Journal* and elsewhere. He and John Boyd take the trouble to interview several G-7 participants on their reading of the Brady Plan in "Test Case Sought for U.S. Debt Plan," 4-6, a useful exercise that gets a viewpoint we didn't see much of in other journals. Again teamed with Lawrence, "Hills Seeks to Soothe Fears About Trade List," 5-15, is well done, giving us the details of what the USTR can do with Super 301, the reaction and anxieties abroad, and the potential for diffusing the threat. He tries unsuccessfully to get to the heart of the problem in "U.S., Japan Take New Trade Tack," 9-1, as negotiators sit down to talk about some of the underlying causes of the trade imbalance, but here Rockwell only looks at what the Japanese need to do to correct the problem: "Many Japanese consumers, for example, prefer to shop in less efficient and more costly 'mom and pop' stores. Likewise, many businesses prefer to deal with customers and suppliers of long standing even if the goods are more expensive." He doesn't take into account different factors that influence both sides and are important in trade, like service, availability and quality of the merchandise.

Rosenbaum, David E. *The New York Times.* (★ ★ ½)
Washington. Writing almost exclusively on taxes over the years, Rosenbaum regained some of the lustre he lost on the campaign trail, now that he's back on his home territory. There's still the sometime backfire, particularly when reporting on the budget deficit, but for the most part he's true to his old form. In a P. 1 lead, "Experts on Budget Voicing Optimism on Goal of Deficits," 1-26, perfectly balanced, he concludes there's no need for new taxes in 1989, but there may be an effort to force a vote this year with taxes taking effect in 1990, an election year. Timely with "Darman Balances Hard Decisions and Hard Numbers," 2-12, he provides an insider's look at Darman's style and fervor in grappling with the first Bush budget. In a lead "Week in Review," "Budget Nears the Point of No Pretense," 3-26, he fails to offer credible scenarios, imbalanced in assuming everybody agrees with him on taxes and spending. "A Politician Outside the Mold," 6-2, is a sterling Man-in-the-News profile of Tom Foley, with good anecdotes we haven't seen before, underscoring Foley's flexibility and affability, although Rosenbaum just skims the issues the new Speaker must confront. He gathers all the talk of more campaign reform in a satisfying "Week in Review" summation, "For Congress, Money Is the Root of Evil and Reelection," 6-4, evaluating the merits of the push for public financing, balanced by opposing ideas. In "No New Taxes, But Plenty of New Plans," 9-10, a lead "Week in Review," on how the Bush drug war and other spending initiatives are bumping against Bush's "read my lips" pledge against tax increases, he crisply reports on the fiscal status on Capitol Hill. Clearly detailed, Rosenbaum takes us through, step-by-step, the minefield of tension between Congress and the administration over raising money for the drug war, and how to spend it, "Debate on Drug War Focuses on Financing It," 9-15. In a superior account, "House, 239 to 190, Votes Bill To Cut Capital Gains Tax," 9-29, he offers more detail on the likelihood of Senate passage, also citing GOP supporters who argue revenue effects will be more positive than official estimates. He blames Bush for wanting to cut capgains, thereby "unraveling" tax reform, by his definition in "The Tax Breaks America Couldn't Give Up," "Week in Review" 10-8. We were irked with his "Fresh Look Is Taken at the State of the Economy," 10-17, which slighted U.S. Chamber of Commerce economist Richard Rahn's interpretation of the 10-13 stock market drop as relating to the setback to the capgains cut. One-sided, "U.S. Agencies Twist as Budget

Cutbacks Linger," 11-2, he just doesn't dig when he reports the FAA says cutbacks will mean fewer air traffic controllers and safety inspectors, and the FBI says it will reduce drug enforcement. Rosenbaum never hints there may be some bureaucratic games being played here, he may not have had time to investigate, but surely he could have found someone to suggest an alternate view.

Rothenberg, Randall. *The New York Times.* (★ ★ ½)
Advertising. One of the great talents in American journalism, Rothenberg for some reason is devoting a chunk of his life to chronicling the marvels, foibles and shams of Madison Avenue. His ad features of course appear regularly on the front page, in the *Magazine* and "Week in Review" section, but he's still operating on two cylinders. He fascinates with "Read This And Win $10 Million!!" 1-31, a report on the Publisher Clearing House sweepstakes and the oddities of mass mailings; it's here we learn manila envelopes do better than white envelopes, but nobody knows why. A day late on Saatchi & Saatchi's annual London meeting, "Saatchi's Strategy Hits a Snag," 3-23, he adds a new angle to the *Journal* story of 3-22, that of the company's "lack of attention to shareholders." Despite the background and fair detail he presents here, we're still puzzled by the sharp, surprising tailspin in earnings. In "Brits Buy Up the Ad Business," *Magazine* cover 7-2, he focuses on Martin Sorrell, financial wiz of WPP Group, relating interesting anecdotes, but this is a financial story and it strikes us that Rothenberg never investigates the British tax advantage in owning global ad agencies, among other things. A clever feature on three ads appearing almost simultaneously with almost identical themes and graphics, "Sometimes Lightning Strikes Thrice," 10-18, is a bit confusing at first, but he handles the material deftly. He explores the expansion of paid messages into previously strictly editorial spaces, including *Esquire* and books, via Chris Whittle, in "Message from Sponsors Become Harder to Detect," "Week in Review" 11-19, culling information from a variety of sources, although we would have liked to have heard from John Kenneth Galbraith and William Greider, both of whom have written for Whittle, to get the author's point of view. Time to move on, RR.

Rowen, Hobart. *The Washington Post.* (★ ★)
Economic commentator. Wobbling on LDC debt and trade, Rowen took too much at face value during the year, skimming the issues. We find shallow analysis in "An Early Warning From Greenspan on Inflation," 1-29, Rowen assuming the chairman speaks for the entire Fed, with no critical look at the indicators that are supposed to be scaring Greenspan. "After the Baker Plan," 3-16, is a useful roadmap of issues, institutions and persons involved in the continuing debate over Treasury Secretary Brady's Third World debt plan. While he focuses on the rising star of David Mulford in "Treasury's Key Man on Third World Debt," 3-30, he also provides a guide to the issues and players in Treasury. He takes care to present all sides in "Fumbling for a Way to Deal With Japan," 4-23, but he fumbles himself in this survey of clashing views of policymakers and economists, and we wind up confused. "Surprising Solidarity on the Trade Front," 4-30, provides excellent comment on the apparent convergence of trade policy views between Secretary of Commerce Mosbacher and Democrats, with Mosbacher coming down on the retaliatory side. With a weakness among economics writers, he offers an "almost everyone agrees" solution in "How to Stop the Rising Dollar," 5-25: "Almost everyone agrees that the most effective way of bringing the dollar down is to make investments in the United States less attractive." We don't. He keeps his own perspective out of "Open Up Trade With Moscow," 6-29, providing satisfying detail on the view of Sen. Bill Bradley (D-N.J.) who believes that "the best service the West could perform for the Soviets is to abandon the German-style offer of government credits, which could create a Soviet debt crisis in the 1990s — somewhere between Poland and Latin America." There's little of use in "The Market's Split Psyche," 7-2, as Rowen ponders the question of the ages: Is bad news good news or is it really just bad? More Democrat than economist at times, Rowen tries to make a case in "Cutting Capital Gains Tax: A Popular, But Bad, Idea," 8-13, but isn't very persuasive, and we suspect he really does like the idea. "The IMF and McGonigle's Bar," 9-28, is a cagey defense of the IMF and its request for increased funding: "There is a need for a combination of public and private monies during the next couple

of decades to restore growth in Latin America and to jump-start Eastern Europe." "Rubles and Reform," *Weekly* 11-13/19, is a mixed effort, some insights, some confusion on the issue of a convertible ruble. Rowen tends to side heavily with "American experts" who argue against convertibility as a prime necessity now, though he does report that a close economic advisor of Gorbachev is inclined toward using gold or a hard currency as an "anchor" for the Soviet currency, never wondering about the sovereignty questions that would attend Moscow pegging to the dollar or D-mark.

Rudnitsky, Howard. *Forbes.* (★ ½)
Senior editor. A veteran of 20-plus years at *Forbes,* Rudnitsky's dispatches are crisp, leaving little room for frills or frivolity. We appreciate his seriousness, but a little brevity is appropriate sometimes too. No-nonsense in "Creativity, With Discipline," 3-6, he takes a solid look at Disney, but he skimps on the company's future plans for movie-making, and we feel we must remind him they are more than holders of choice real estate. Minutely describing a fight over prime casino real estate in a questionable Atlantic City deal, with Trump stealing the land out from under the nose of the competition, he gets our attention with his lead in "How Trump Plays Monopoly," 4-17: "If you're looking for solid insight into how Donald Trump makes money in real estate, skip his bestseller *The Art of the Deal* and check out instead the orgy of charges and litigation surrounding Trump, *Penthouse* magazine publisher Bob Guccione and their adversary, Dallas' Pratt Hotel Corp." He sorts out how struggling S&Ls may ruin what little is left of themselves by offering low "teaser-rate" adjustable rate mortgages, in "Digging Their Own Graves?" 5-29, skillfully arguing that all the best ideas for saving these sick institutions always backfire simply because, as his last sentence, "Heads they [S&Ls] win, tails the government pays." He reminds us why an investor should always view insider selling of stock as a good sign to sell his own in "Abandon Ship," 7-10, covering the story of Integrated Resources. "Tiger By the Tail," 8-7, is a creditable look at what Primerica has to try to maintain profitable A.L. Williams while toning them down. He ventures into Disney territory again as management at the Florida theme park squeezes out more business from the locals, offering more nightlife and convention facilities for the grownups, "Mickey Is Eating My Lunch!" 9-18, but this doesn't amount to much more than free press for Disney, the local complaints treated at the end of the article, and then only perfunctorily.

Rudolph, Barbara. *Time.* (★)
Senior writer. Rudolph does a good job rounding up the events of the week, sometimes trendy, sometimes venturing into the policy arena. But she's hampered by the lack of space allotted to business in the weekly, too restricted to do much beyond summaries. She compares the Brady Plan to that of his predecessor, while gauging the reactions of such notables as Sen. Bill Bradley (D-N.J.) and former Fed Chairman Paul Volcker, in "Enter the Brady Plan," co-authored by Richard Hornik 3-20, but they fail to analyze the Brady Plan in the context of the economic problems of the Latin American nations: little investment inflow, high inflation and high unemployment. A post-spill piece, "An Oil Slick Trips Up Exxon," with Stephen Pomper 4-24, is good on how the Valdez accident might have been prevented, Rudolph fingering the company's "reduction of its spill-management staff during cost-cutting in the mid-1980s" as part of the problem. She needs more on the economics of the problem in "Second Life For Styrofoam," 5-22, on recycling plastic bottles to "pea-sized pellets that can be used in wall insulation and industrial repackaging." Plastic is forever. Fluff, she profiles three yuppie catalogue businesses, "The Chic Is in the Mail," 7-17, sounding like an advertisement rather than assessment: "Besides selling a garden-variety pocket T-shirt ($12), J. Crew offers a pre-washed (or 'weathered,' as the catalog puts it) T-shirt for $24 in 15 different colors, including watermelon, tangelo and mango." In "Adrift In The Doldrums," 7-31, she does a nice job of reviewing economic numbers and views, staying controlled and slightly detached from the conventional views. Again, there's too much emphasis on the clothes and too little on the business in this look at Donna Karan, "High Style for the 9-to-5 Set," 10-23.

Salpukas, Agis. *The New York Times.* (★ ½)

Airlines. It was a big, big year for airline news, and while this veteran of the airline beat had his byline always in front of us, he was not the carrier of choice, usually losing out in comparisons with the reporters from *The Wall Street Journal.* Nor was there any outstanding analytics to help us plumb the roots of the turbulence in the industry and how it moved the markets. Still, what we got was professional. Precise in "2nd Offer Is Made For NWA," 3-31, he assembles all the relevant information as Marvin Davis bids for Northwest Airlines, even including some peripheral data on the struggle for Eastern, taking that buyout as a parallel. Anecdotal, he details a travel agent's worst nightmare as the computer booking and reservation system goes kablooie, "Computer Chaos for Air Travelers," 5-13, nicely done, although we wish he'd tell us how the system actually works, except for the obvious fact that it's a mainframe. He argues that "For Lorenzo, Strike Is Harder Than '83 One," 6-28, skillfully weaving together the aspects of each strike to compare and contrast the two: in '83 Lorenzo was able to persuade workers to cross the picket lines, cut fares to bring back customers, and use the bankruptcy laws more to his advantage; in '89, "despite his position of strength," three months later he still hadn't gotten off the ground. We find some good analysis on airplane values in "Looking For Value In Airline Assets," 9-1, as he attempts to interpret the runup of airline stocks, but this could be broader and deeper. His "Decision at UAL May Take Weeks," 9-6, sketches out a few glitches in the takeover contest, but with little sense of how serious any of them are. "Eastern Rebuilding Faster Than Expected," 10-18, is adequate on the Lorenzo press conferences, but Bridget O'Brian's same day *WSJ* report, "Eastern Air's Creditors Ask Experts To Present Options for Reorganization," has better focus and more thorough reporting. Standard stuff, "Eastern Creditors to Study Options," 10-19, is well balanced, Salpukas adequately covering all sides of the equation. His "Delta Order for Boeing, McDonnell," 11-15, one of the biggest in history, 260 planes for $10 billion, is extremely sparse, not approaching the fine detail of the *WSJ* account.

Saporito, Bill. *Fortune.* (★ ★ ½)

Board of editors. A couple of real clunkers on the Time-Warner merger knock Saporito down a notch from his excellent rating a year ago. Swallowed by the conflict of interest, he may have wished some other poor soul had been assigned the story, but a clunker is a clunker. "First Salvos in the Fight For Time," 7-3, is a brief for Time's management against Paramount; from its now infamous opening line ("Martin S. Davis knows a good business strategy when he steals one"), this sounds like it was edited by Time's lawyers. He may have been tossed this assignment because of his excellent coverage of RJR Nabisco, where Paramount's Davis was a director, but the one-sided quality blows his key argument: "As the country's largest magazine publisher, Time considers its editorial independence a national treasure not to be trifled with for mere coin." He only devotes two graphs to the opposing view, dishing up a congratulatory memo for Time's victory in a Delaware chancellory court, "A Legal Victory for the Long Term," 8-24: "In the often brutal war between corporate managers and acquirers, it is definitely a victory for the long-term managers." Saporito is better with more sharply focused profiles of individual companies and retailing trends. Having distinguished himself as a retailing reporter and RJR expert, he shows his depth in this fair-handed and knowledgeable book review of *Sparrows Point,* an opinionated history of Bethlehem Steel written by a former Baltimore *Sun* reporter, "The Steel Saga's Human Side," 12-5, calling the reader's attention to another work on Bethlehem, John Strohmeyer's *Crisis In Bethlehem,* as a better book. A superlative, "How Ross Johnson Blew the Buyout," 4-24, is taut, exciting on the RJR Nabisco deal, making us feel like we are in the Manhattan conference room with Henry Kravis. He rehashes old news in "Companies that Compete Best," 5-22, a big, puffy cover that rounds up an arbitrary grouping of "killer competitors" that is really just the usual suspects: Emerson Electric, McDonald's, Kodak (a dubious choice), and Anheuser-Busch. He demonstrates his unerring touch on the retail beat in the smoothly engrossing "Woolworth to Rule the Malls," 6-5, giving the feel of the business and revitalization on historic F. W. Woolworth, easily the best piece in this big issue of the Service 500. "PPG: Shiny, Not Dull," 7-17, is trademarked Saporito, finding an old company that has recharged itself: PPG's CEO "has shattered the old glass company's culture and helped remold it into a model of modern management."

Saunders, Laura. *Forbes.* (★ ★)
Associate editor, "Taxing Matters" column. Heading up the tax coverage is a thankless job at best, and while she doesn't address policy matters, Saunders is smart in maneuvering us through the ins-and-outs of the tax code. Demerits, however, for her avoidance of the capital gains tax cut issue. She breaks down the early returns on the '86 corporate tax change, telling us who saves and who doesn't by industry, an instructive exercise, clearly and compactly executed; overall, corporate effective rates are up 3.2%, "Who Got Reformed?" 1-9. A 10 Best nomination from her editors, she files a provocative, informative "House-Hunting? Read This First," 3-20, way ahead on the home mortgage interest deduction: "People shopping for a house assume there will always be a home mortgage interest deduction. . .because there always has been one. That could be a big mistake." She details the IRS change in tax law to allow corporate income from interest rate swaps to be spread and taxed over the life of the contract, delightfully written, facetiously muddled on the IRS reasoning in the title, " 'It's The Right Thing to Do,' " 4-17: "Has a kinder, gentler spirit suddenly possessed the folks at 11th and Constitution Avenue? Did the budget deficit disappear? Has the millennium come?" The IRS gets into the LDC debt act, limiting tax advantages for banks writing off foreign loans, "An Offer They Can't Refuse," 5-29, a sharply written dispatch. She takes the long-term view in "All in the Family," 10-9, speculating that a recent court ruling allowing firms with "captive" insurance companies to take the same types of deductions as the companies more conventionally insured might help to overturn *Moline Properties v. Commissioner,* a 1943 ruling which establishes separate taxation for separate subsidiaries. Saunders' evaluation of such an event: "all hell would break loose: Some interest deductions for intercorporate loans, for example could be disallowed for the borrowing subsidiary while the income would still be taxable to the lender."

Schiebla, Shirley Hobbs. *Barron's.* (★ ½)
Senior Washington editor. A column divided against itself cannot stand, and Schiebla ought to stop subdividing her "Potomac Potpourri." She's much more effective when she sticks to one subject, even if she's long-winded at times. There's no cohesive thread in "AT&T's Big Way — Will a Rival Try To Spoil It?" 1-23, a compendium of semi-interesting DC business snips and snatches, beginning with the AT&T FTS 2000 contract, that leaves too many loose ends. She meanders about in "Storm of the Orphans," 3-20, on patents, trials and orphan drugs, presenting a goodly amount of information, but she doesn't organize it effectively. She executes an overlong textbook evaluation of the CPI index, breaking it into its parts, telling us what each is used for, a useful exercise for the layman, maybe, in "The Cost of Living," 5-22. Like everybody else who does business in China, the World Bank is reevaluating after Tiananmen Square, part of the potpourri she gathers for "How an Agency Is Cleaning Up Its Act," 6-19. The last item is of particular interest, as the *Toronto Sun* prepares to take on DC, she quotes the editor of *The Washington Times,* Arnaud de Borchgrave, as saying that "Washington is a tough nut to crack." Insightful on the pluses and minuses, she finds a silver lining in the S&L cloud, "The Banks' Big Victory," 8-21, after a minute examination of the bailout law reveals a provision that will "help banks continue their thrust into the pension-fund market, by selling investment contracts protected by federal deposit insurance." She informs on a new angle in "A Tug of War Over a Failed S&L," 10-16, as investors in Lincoln Savings' parent company, American Continent Corp., sue for their fair share of the kitty when the bank is liquidated.

Schlender, Brenton. *Fortune.* (★ ★)
Associate editor, San Francisco. Schlender moved to *Fortune* from *The Wall Street Journal* in September, bringing technical zip to the magazine it didn't have before. In a P. 1 leder, "Fast Game: Intel Introduces a Chip Packing Huge Power And Wide Ambitions," 2-28, he uses Intel's lead in semiconductors due to the introduction of the 860 chip to provide a backdrop for the ongoing battle between Intel, Motorola, Texas Instruments and the Japanese to win the chip battle, superbly crafted: "Intel's scramble to unveil the 860 is but the latest example of how the microprocessor business is still a horse race even for the company that dominates it." Ready with background material in "Missed Deadline: Its Failure to Deliver on Promised Software Hits

Microsoft Hard," 3-8, he says that the computer industry is at a point of diminishing returns, hitting the wall because of the low productivity of software writers due to the increasing complexity of the hardware. But we think the software bottleneck is the real story here, not the short-term ripples in Microsoft stock that's the real news item. He doesn't provide enough on the HP side in "Hewlett-Packard Agrees to Acquire Apollo Computer," with William Bulkeley 4-13, an okay assessment of the surprise acquisition, dwelling on Apollo's rivalry with Sun Microsystems in the workstation market. He informs with a lively profile of hyper-aggressive Lawrence Ellison, a less known, but still influential force in software, in "Software Tiger: Oracle Corp.'s Ellison Spurs Its Fast Growth With Aggressive Style," 5-31. His first piece for *Fortune* shows promise. "How To Break The Software Logjam," 9-25, is meaty and compelling, with excellent graphics that dramatize the complexity of writing software — how many lines of code compared to the Manhattan telephone book. Astute in "How Steve Jobs Linked Up With IBM," cover 10-9, he demonstrates his savvy on the Silicon Valley software wars, although he falls into the trap of the personality cult fascination with Steve Jobs and overplays the silly feud between Jobs and Microsoft's Bill Gates. But overall Schlender has revved up *Fortune*'s electronics coverage several notches since coming over from the *WSJ*.

Schneider, Keith. *The New York Times.* (★)
Washington, environmental issues and policy. One of the biggest practitioners of advocacy, it's clear from some of his scientific dispatches that Schneider would prefer that we all eat organically, wear only cotton, and travel by horse instead of Honda. When he keeps his nose out of his topic, he can inform, but if it's something he feels strongly about, look out. He was chastised publicly by such diverse bodies as *The Washington Post*'s Eleanor Randolph, 1-9, and the editpages of *The Wall Street Journal,* 2-6, for his anti-nuke campaign. Another prime example is "U.S. Urges Curbs on Deadly Insecticide," 3-21, about an EPA panel of toxicologists recommending aldicarb be eliminated from potatoes and bananas, even though a survey "may substantially underestimate the aldicarb residues to which consumers may be exposed." This comes out in the lead paragraph as: "The EPA's pesticide division has recommended barring using an acutely toxic pesticide on potatoes and imported bananas, presenting an unreasonable risk to infants and children." He uses scare tactics as a rationale for abolition of the use of pesticides in "Food Industry Is Testing for Toxics To Reassure Consumers on Crops," 3-27, telling us we can't really trust either the government or the private sector to test for residue accurately. He blames Alaska for the oil spill, as the state wasn't ever vigilant in requiring the oil companies to have disaster plans, something akin to blaming the fireman for the fire, in "Under Oil's Powerful Spell, Alaska Was Off Guard," 4-2: "One dramatic example was an industry decision in 1981 to disband a 20-member emergency team prepared for round-the-clock response to oil spills in Valdez Harbor and the sound. The reaction from Alaskan officials was modest." He doesn't tell us what all the jumbled figures and tests mean to the consumer in "Tainted Milk and Meat Raise Vigilance," 5-11, and we're left with no idea how many, if any, contaminated products as a result of cows and fowls eating pesticide-treated feed reached the supermarket. Balanced, "The Soviets Show Scars From Nuclear Arms Production," 7-16, he informs fairly on the state of the issue: "In the United States, and to a lesser extent in the Soviet Union, domestic concerns about the dangers people face from the weapons industry have begun to enter the debate about nuclear arms policies." He vividly describes an organic food fair in "Maine Fair Promotes Pure Food and Rural Values," 9-25, but we'd like to know if he bought anything.

Schwadel, Francine. *The Wall Street Journal.* (★)
Chicago, retailing beat. She spent much of '89 occupied with Sears' restructuring and new marketing, filing step-by-step dispatches, but we would have benefitted by more skepticism on her part when confronting her corporate sources. Schwadel's trademark is zippy writing laced with humor, although she occasionally shortchanges us on the core financial or marketing aspects. "Sears Pulls the Rug on Its House Brand In One Area, Stepping Up New Strategy," 1-6, she opens wittily — "Sears, Roebuck & Co. is rolling out new carpet departments that

signals an even broader shift in marketing strategy than the nation's retailer had suggested" — but doesn't get to the hard market analysis until the end of the article on Sears' turn to brand-name carpets, eliminating the house brand. She waits until opening day to file "A Look Behind Sears's New Approach," 3-1, getting some nice insider detail, but we've heard much of this before. More on the reorganization, "Sears to Eliminate 800 Manager Jobs and Streamline," 3-31, is quick and non-analytic, just the facts. She adequately captures the management style of Peter S. Willmott, a "Who's News" profile, but she doesn't tell us much about *him,* more of a corporate portrait, with only one anecdote included to illustrate his personality, "Willmott Faces Buyer Who Wants It All," 4-12. She updates on Sears credibly with "Sears Will Keep Merchandise Group in Chicago Area," 6-27, a compact micro look. In "Courting Shoppers: Nordstrom's Push East Will Test Its Renown For the Best In Service," 8-1, we get her best of the year that we saw as she examines how, by using old principles of pushing decision-making to ground level and treating customers like kings, Nordstrom has become a powerhouse, a subject later picked up by other reporters. She takes a look at the other side of the coin in "The American Way of Buying: Shoppers' Blues — The Thrill Is Gone," 10-13, an anecdote-laden inspection of what's wrong with stores today, never mentioning that this might account for part of the surge in catalogue sales. She finally gets at the numbers in "Sears Projects Only Small Gain In Sales for 1990," 11-3, but then it's just the numbers, and when Sears gets clobbered at Christmas, we're all surprised. We know she's got a definitive profile of Sears in there somewhere, but expect it will take more seasoning and cooking.

Shabecoff, Philip. *The New York Times.* (★)

Washington, environment, on leave writing a book foor the latter half of the year. In a word association, when we're tossed the word "Shabecoff," we still think "environmentalist," not "journalist covering environmental news." But enough balance crept back into his material this year to warrant us bringing him into the *MediaGuide.* His editors are to be congratulated in playing high on P. 1 his "U.S. Data Since 1895 Fail to Show Warming Trend," 2-6, detailing a report that says U.S. weather has been steady over the last hundred years. Shabecoff confuses in noting that the U.S. is only 1.5% of global surface, which was the environmental response, without pushing further into the debate. In a "Week in Review," "An Emergence of Political Will on Acid Rain," 2-19, he balances Bush's Ottawa trip pledge to reduce acid rain, including statements of varying degree on the problem, but he's clearly alarmed: "acid rain is now recognized as destructive to fresh water life in many lakes and streams, particularly in the Northeast and Canada. Acid rain is also believed to contribute to the deterioration of forests and buildings and to threaten human health." The debate is over! His treatment of an EPA statement and congressional subcommittee is even-handed, "U.S. Calls Poisoning of Air Far Worse Than Expected and Threat to Public," 3-23, matching quotes from the greens and industry spokespeople. In "Bush's Call for Leadership in a World Cleanup Puts the Focus on the Mess in America's Backyard," 5-2, he presents a slightly distorted view, but this is also a useful litany of the environmental agenda in the U.S. He's off-center, however, in "Traditional Definitions of National Security Are Shaken by Global Environmental Threats," 5-29, giving no counterweight to his assertions: "Now, with the world threatened by global warming, acid rain, climate changes and the destruction of the ozone shield, environmental matters are seen as a serious threat to the internal political stability of some nations. . .." "A Rising American Impulse to Leave the Land Alone," 6-11, is a pitch for adding another 90 to 100 million acres to the wilderness system, Shabecoff quoting only supporters. He summarizes Bush's proposals in a straightforward manner in "President Urges Steps To Tighten Law On Clean Air," 6-13, with little addition, but this reporter says that Reilly (EPA) "appears to have prevailed largely," contrary to the advance peek that *The Washington Post* was given.

Sheets, Kenneth R. *U.S.News & World Report.* (★)

Senior editor. Adequate in covering the quirky topics he gets assigned to, Sheets rarely touches a policy issue. In "How Wal-Mart Hits Main St," 3-13, he takes up where *Fortune*'s John Huey left off, using the success of Wal-Mart to discuss the larger issue of the erosion and consolidation of mom & pop stores in rural communities, but he relies on evidence from a recent Iowa State study of Wal-Mart's effect on rural business, claiming that Wal-Mart does not cause these problems, it just speeds up the process. He's off in concluding that rising oil prices will contribute to a rise in the trade deficit, "America's Oil-Chill Factor," with Robert Black 3-27, not putting enough emphasis on the fact that the U.S. may benefit from higher oil prices as well. He looks at the bright side of the Valdez incident, in "Would You Believe $16.67 an Hour to Scrub Rocks?" 4-17, an overview of oil cleanup methods. We're dubious, however, about "How to Turn a New Leaf in the Papermaking Business," 5-8, a report on the potential for the new kenaf plant to replace trees as the future source for paper products. He advises us that farmers are again investing in big tractors, "Big Bruisers Come Back to the Farm," 6-19, an important step in the recovery of the farm belt, but there's little investigation of the underlying causes of the rebuilding. In "The Wonder Fuel for the 1990s," 7-31, he asserts that the recent decontrol of natural gas prices could make it the economic and environmental fuel of the coming decade, piquing our interest, particularly in his treatment of cars powered by natural gas, but there's barely any follow-through. He adroitly picks up on the advantages the 1986 tax reform offers to lease, but not to buy, pegging that as a primary factor in a report on the growing industries that lease, "Firms Now Lease Everything But Time," 8-14, but there's little on the downside, unlike Jerry Flint's "When Payments Never Stop," 3-6 in *Forbes,* which deals with car leasing. Expanding an aspect of this in "A Dogfight For Dominance Of The Skies," co-authored by Peter Dworkin 9-11, he does a fine job on airline M&A, bringing leasing into the bargain in terms of debt: "Leases also let airlines convert debt into an operating expense that often does not show up on the balance sheet as a liability."

Sherman, Stratford P. *Fortune.* (★ ½)

Board of editors. The difficulties we chided him for last year haven't disappeared. He can still indulge a weakness for tasteless personal descriptions, but is better at keeping them in check. Still, we puzzle at how Sherman can have slipped from the talent we noted in earlier years, a carelessness creeping into his material we can't explain. We're encouraged by "Who's In Charge At Texaco Now?" 1-16, a perceptive followup on the Texaco-Icahn confrontation, correctly criticizing Texaco for its past arrogance toward shareholders, describing the "surreal series of events," and restrained in depicting Texaco's CEO Kinnear as "a preppy organization man in the George Bush mold." In "Inside the Mind of Jack Welch," 3-27, though, Sherman gets seriously Freudian, spending time with GE Chairman Jack Welch. We get to know Welch a little better, but most of the changes at GE have been documented, and we don't need an interpretation of Welch's relationship with his mother, even if she is terrific. What he doesn't say is that Welch is unhappy with GE's stock price, that he feels that investors don't understand his company; this is no secret, as Welch says as much in the new GE annual report. We also are disconcerted by Sherman's description: "If you are with him long enough, his eyes may lose their grip on yours for an instant and you may see the skull beneath the skin, the animal inside the man, driven and hungry." Would you trust your daughter with this CEO? Perceptive in a book review of James Fallows' *More Like Us,* "How to Beat the Japanese," 4-10, he praises the book's evaluation of the U.S.'s strength, and derides the tedious digression into Fallow's personal life that follows. He makes some astute points in "Smart Ways to Handle the Press," 6-19, advice on corporate PR, but as he doesn't take his own advice with regard to descriptives, we have a hard time taking this seriously. In "Trashing A $150 Billion Business," 8-28, on recycling plastics, he wanders all over and never retains our interest. "How Philip Morris Diversified Right," 10-23, is okay, taking a bird's-eye view of the company, but we have to laugh trying to picture the CEO, who he describes as resembling Charles Laughton, but with a *quiet* voice. Mr. Christian!!

Sherrid, Pamela. *U.S.News & World Report.* (★)

Senior editor. Back on the business beat after a sojourn in London, there's little special about those of her dispatches we reviewed, although she presents her material competently enough. A rather spotty overview of Drexel's history and deal with Rudy Giuliani almost doesn't register on the scale, "The Deal Drexel Could Not Resist," 1-9, considering the amount of ink spilled on the subject. In a look at Sears, "Attention, Discount Shoppers!" with Lynn Adkins 3-13, she rounds things up effectively, her comparison of the retailer to K-Mart a nice touch, but there's little new here. She misses an evaluation of the RICO laws in "Will Michael Milken Go to Jail?" with Jack Egan 4-10, a skimpy, flawed account. No frills in "From Boon to Bust in the Student Loan Business," 5-22, Sherrid focuses on banks' decisions to curtail loans to high-default trade schools which service mostly low-income students, telling us this decision was made due to the profit motive, for which she presents some cursory figures. She relates how industry's reliance on automation has contributed to a decline in labor costs, it is no longer cheaper to make their products in low-wage developing nations, "How to Keep the Home Forges Burning — and Profitable," 7-3, making good use of anecdotal evidence and quotes by experts to support the argument. She lacks balance in "A Realty Firm That Rewards Risk Takers," 10-9, on the Re/Max real estate firm's innovative management techniques, discussion of the firm's high commission policy is good, but she merely skims the downside of the firm.

Silk, Leonard. *The New York Times.* (★)
"Economic Scene" columnist. The dean of economic commentary in American journalism, semi-retired Silk now appears irregularly on P. D2 of the *Times,* gradually releasing the reins to a less-ardent Keynesian, Peter Passell. With his own analytical framework ossified, Silk spends most of his time puzzling over the unfolding scene rather than probing others for explanations. In "The Daunting Job of George Bush," 1-20, he struggles to find out why the stock and bond markets are rising while the trade deficit rises. "We have achieved, by dumb luck, stable international equilibrium." Huh? In "Bush's Campaign on the Budget," 2-17, he's skeptical of the White House budget assumptions, but there's no new analysis. He decries the budget becoming "a form of political rhetoric and partisan maneuver," but that's exactly where Silk himself seems to be. His "Markets Puzzling Over 3 Riddles," 3-24, presents interconnected questions: How high will interest rates go? How serious is the inflation threat? Will rising interest rates produce a recession before the end of '89 or by early '90? Thinking aloud, he's a bit helpful here as we ponder with him. In "Third World Debt: The Brady Plan," 3-31, Silk tries to look beyond Brady's "economics of vagueness" but gets lost in a maze of paper shuffling. "Subscriptions of both creditor and debtor countries would not be paid in, but would be subject to call in event of a default." IMF gold sales are thrown in. Hmmmm. He thinks aloud again in "Debt Reduction, Now the Details," 4-7, the Brady Plan reconsidered, mulling details on guarantees, but getting it all mixed up with concerns about the Fed and recession, an odd but interesting Jeremiad about weaknesses in the Brady Plan. He seems to conclude that monetary policy to avoid recession in the West alone is the solution to the LDC debt problem. The same meandering can be found in the NYT editorial 4-8, "Relief for Foreign Debtors. But When?" His "Growing Worries on Dollar's Rise," 5-19, is a very sharp assessment of monetary cross-currents: "Unless the Bundesbank and the Bank of Japan raise their interest rates soon, the Fed may be forced, by the overstrong dollar, to bring down the discount rate and the fed funds rate." In "Greenspan's View on a Soft Landing," 6-16, we get musings along the old Phillips Curve. Will the economy slow, lowering interest rates, thereby stoking economy and fueling inflation? He rides the Curve again in "The Difficult Task Facing The Fed," 9-1, to ease or not to ease. Advancing the Malta summit, "Aid for East Bloc Expected To Be a Vital Summit Topic," 12-1, frets about the ruble overhang and seems to suggest Soviet budget cuts, via mutual defense cuts, will do wonders for them, and us, but this is demand management, as if shifting guns to butter in the U.S.S.R. will produce a worker's paradise.

Sims, Calvin. *The New York Times.* (★)
Telecommunications. We have much less trouble with Sims' reporting than with his presentation. On any given piece, he gives us 80% of what we want to know, which is about average. We have to wrestle the information out of him, though, our readers too often complaining it takes them two reads. It's tough going in a lead Sunday "Business" piece, "AT&T's New Call to Arms," 1-22, Sims providing no new insights, and too much detail for

so little thematic framework. He includes sketchy background on why FCC Commissioner Dennis R. Patrick has some of his initiatives rejected by the Democratic Congress, but doesn't make clear why it could reject his plan to cap long-distance rates in "Agency to Vote on Capping AT&T Rates," 1-30, this needing two readings to get close. He's muddy in "Let the Dealer Beware: A New Phone Era," 2-12, detailing the April 1 switch permitting long-distance options on pay phones. He leaves to the last graphs an explanation for the significance of the charges in "Ex-Official Admits Guilt on Phone Contract," 5-24, as a former GSA official, Sureshar Lal Soni, admits accepting $400 in lunches from BellSouth, "which was competing for telephone contracts worth $55 million" — the FTS-2000 government contract, no less. We find out how a digital cellular phone works, in "Meeting Mobile Phone Demand," 7-19, an improved dispatch; we only have to re-read parts of this, particularly cloudy when he tells us the analog and digital phones won't be compatible, but doesn't explain how this will be remedied, except to say that phone companies will make sure everyone has access to service. His "Challenging Airfone's Monopoly," 9-5, on GTE's service that allows airline passengers to make calls during flights, has 41 words in the lead sentence. In "Telephone Companies' New Foray," 11-10, he tells of voice processing systems that provide centralized answering machines so subscribers can get a variety of services without buying machines, but never discusses technology or suppliers. His "Not Everyone Applauds New Phone Services," 12-3, is on the privacy debate over customers being able to screen numbers of incoming calls, fairly well done, but with too many questions left unanswered. (Message to Mr. Sims: Tell your editors to be tough on you. A little work and you'll be fine.)

Smith, Geoffrey. *FW.* (★ ½)
"Editor's Page" column. A cut above the standard editor's column that nearly every magazine has, Smith's columns actually take on real issues raised in a story in the magazine, not merely summarizing its high points. He makes a muddled appeal for unity against the Japanese and Germans in "The Samurai Code," 1-10, arguing that companies ought to forget the takeover wars and spend dollars on plants and equipment in order to compete more efficiently. He offers mixed prescriptives in "Long-term Gratification," 2-7, on corporate debt, takeovers and capital gains, to "make it even more attractive for the average investor to invest in long-term objectives." He relies heavily on associate editor Laura Sachar's interview with British Airways CEO Sir Colin Marshall to make his case in "Reciprocity," 4-4, a heal-thyself solution for the airline industry, speaking authoritatively to reduce government intervention, while urging the airlines not to ignore problems created by increased air traffic. A mere survey, he rehashes some of the information found in his ethics cover, culling some more quotes from CEOs on what they find to be most disturbing ethical problem, "Closed-door Decisions," 6-27: Martin Marietta's Norm Augustine thinks it's firing a loyal employee during a business downturn; Mutual Benefit Life's Henry Kates doesn't like having to deal with AIDS in the life insurance industry, interesting, but not terribly useful. Unfocused in "Return to Golconda," 7-11, he can't decide whether to write about S&Ls, home loans, leadership or Gatsby, and we can't find a common thread to pull it all together. Savvy, he effectively shoots a hole into his own cover, "When Realities Clash," 9-5 on the "defense savings dividend," airtight: "The very notion of a 'defense savings dividend,' for example, like the supposed 'peace dividend' after Vietnam, is a political reality. It is not an economic reality, in the sense that money not appropriated by one department is not really money 'saved.' It will be spent by Washington somewhere." A recounting of a James Srodes' conversation with Wendell Wilkie II, general counsel of the Commerce Dept., conjures up powerful images of Soviet attorneys grabbing at copies of the constitution, "The Russian Bar," 11-28, but Smith is off-base in saying the "real barrier" to U.S. investment in the U.S.S.R. is the absence of a legal system, when businessmen have been inventing and circumventing the law for years.

Specter, Michael. *The Washington Post.* (★ ★)
Health reporter. We appreciate this reporter's obvious expertise, examining pertinent issues in health care without getting bogged down in the medical jargon. Authoritative in "Cesarian Birth

Rate Halts Its Sharp Rise," 1-27, he offers a complete and understandable guide to the procedure, its complications and advantages, but he never addresses the turnaround, nor the origin, of the trend that peaked in 1987, when cesarian delivery accounted for 24.4% of births. A quick "Medical Schools Revise Entrance Test," 3-14, relieves us, as medical schools revise qualifications to include communication and writing skills, perhaps resulting in improved bedside manners. He has credible nuance and is nonalarmist in "AIDS Gaining Resistance to AZT Therapy," 3-15, that belies the horror story headline, a first cautionary warning. He uses *Science* as a source for "Test Can Screen Blood For Elusive Form of Hepatitis," 4-21, providing detail beyond what might be expected. An important, but inconclusive, dispatch, "Quality Control of Published Medical Studies Debated," 5-14, gets buried on P. 20, as he and editors and scientists question the quality of reports and research which appear in the medical journals, but you can't always believe what you read; this is of particular relevance to science reporting as many on the beat use these publications as primary sources. He informs, proffering relevant examples in "Pressure From AIDS Activists Has Transformed Drug Testing," 7-2. He clearly relates the results of the study in "Early AIDS Treatment Urged," 8-4, as experts recommend early administration of AZT to combat the disease, not losing us in technical detail. An update, "Early HIV Care May Cost Over $5 Billion a Year," 9-15, puts the breaks on the good news, as the economic cost begins to catch up with the epidemic, and the irony of the health care system begins to cost lives: "Unlike treating AIDS when people are near death, the costs of which are often reimbursed by private insurance or Medicaid, the expense of treating a disease before people get sick is rarely covered by private or public insurance." In *The New Republic*, he's only got half his tongue-in-cheek as yuppies snap up funeral plots, "Hot Tombs," 9-11; he's aptly named anyway. So much for preventative medicine. Inside HHS, "Vacant Health Posts: A Symptom," 10-3, he depicts the lack of management and organization at the department, but offers no solutions.

Srodes, James. *FW.* (★ ★ ½)
Washington bureau chief. A dramatic improvement from Srodes, who has knocked off the wise guy, pretentious approach we complained about last year. We also got more adept, long-range treatments from him during the year, as he frequently got ahead of the pack. Against the grain in a 10 Best selection, "How the Fed Sees 1989," 12-27-88, he leans heavily on the upbeat outlook of Fed Govs. Manuel Johnson and Wayne Angell when the conventional mood is much more pessimistic, the insights of considerable value to institutional investors. He files a treatise of prospects and solutions for the S&L crisis, in which it becomes clear that a reform of deposit insurance is in order, "The Insurance Trap," 1-24, with knowledgeable, long quotes from Angell and S&L expert Bert Ely, as part of "great body of informed opinion that believes the Great American Insured Deposit may, in fact, be one of the pivotal problems facing the banking industry today." His interview with SEC Commissioner Joseph Grundfest, " 'Bundy Solutions,' " 3-7, is flawless in mulling the Socratic question: "How much deterrence and how much enforcement of the securities laws does America want?" The almost straight Q&A style risks dryness and boredom, but the Qs and As are so good on this important theme, packaged so well, that we sense we're getting more out of a five-minute read than if this were a half-hour TV talkie. The "Bundy Solutions," by the way, refers to the serial killer, Grundfest putting that as the extreme in dealing with unscrupulous Wall Streeters. Part of the "Ethics" cover, "Mr. Diogenes, Call Your Office," 6-27, is surprisingly flimsy, disappointing in his retelling what people think about ethics, making the observation that if John Tower "had remained in the Senate or out of the public eye entirely, the personal criticisms of his activities would never have come up." In "And Protect Us From Protectionism," 12-12, he details the USTR Carla Hills/Ag Sec. Clayton Yeutter's proposals to GATT in order to open markets abroad to U.S. farmers, more editorial than report on this "sensible initiative," as going through GATT avoids invoking the "Super 301" clause and possible retaliation.

Stelzer, Irwin M. *The American Spectator.* (★ ★)
"The Business of America" columnist, Stelzer is director of the Energy and Environmental Policy Center at Harvard's JFK School. He continues to impress with his ruminations on the U.S. and global political economy, mainstream, but with clever twists and turns. But he can't squander the luxury of space afforded him in two pages as he sometimes does. A tighter organizational structure would be beneficial, as he frequently gets off on tangents that are too much work to follow. "The Debt Presidency," 1-89, mulls several domestic and debt issues facing George Bush, and we meander with him. He serves up sharp, confident commentary on the pressures gathering on Bush to roll back the reform of the Reagan years, "Save Us From the Reregulators," 2-89, on the grounds that Dukakis was right and the economy is in a mess — when it isn't. A good polemic in "Some Like It Hot," 3-89, on the environment's greenhouse effect, he includes a particularly good analogy from Thomas Schelling of Harvard that, even under the worst estimates on global warming, it won't be as big a change as moving from Boston to Irvine, Calif. Nor does he close off the debate, advocating better research. "Third World Deadbeats," 4-89, is another skim through that problem, mildly interesting, but droning without an occasional quote to break the monotone. Somewhat unfocused, his scattered reasoning in "Corporatism Ousts Reaganomics," 5-89, argues against official U.S. government cooperation on research projects and corporate joint ventures, imitating Japan's MITI, but just doesn't add up. He pins down the trouble in the airline industry early, "Unions Fly High," 7-89, as he warns that the success of deregulation "is now at risk," citing different factors, landing fees, centralized reservations systems and the crucial role of the unions, help to squeeze out small competitors and discourage new entries into the air, thus giving the big carriers the monopoly deregulation was supposed to prevent. He crafts a persuasive case in "Independence Day Blues," 9-89, a late look at what worries "thoughtful" Americans over their barbecues: foreign investment and the Greenhouse effect, effectively debunking the former ("Using stock market data to measure capital appreciation, and adjusting both U.S. and foreign investments accordingly, the Morgan Bank economists reckon that America has some $500 billion *more* invested in foreign assets than foreigners have invested in American assets") and offering sensible solutions for the latter ("A much smaller sum [than to alter U.S. plants and emissions], spent on dirty Third World installations, would produce much greater reductions in noxious wastes").

Stern, Richard L. *Forbes.* (★ ★ ½)
Senior editor. The magazine's designated fraud reporter, a one-man bunco squad, Stern dishes the dirt more often than not. A bit of digging turns up gold as Arnold "Charlie" Kimmes sings to keep himself out of prison for stock fraud, naming names and exhibiting amazing versatility, both at creative wheeling 'n' dealing and keeping one step ahead of the law, "Never, But Never, Give a Sucker an Even Break," co-authored by Matthew Schifrin and Claire Poole 1-9, detailed and clearly written. Investigating another setup, we get a peek at George Bissell and his Palm Beach scamming, "Gentleman Scamster," 2-20, balanced and detailed, with quotes from a selection of all the interested parties. He compels with " 'How Did I Know the Guy Was Calling From Jail?' " 5-29, this time telling the story of the victim of a penny stock scam, Jaime Darder, "broke and crying in front of a restaurant full of people," who ventured into the fold-up razor business with disreputable characters, and paid dearly for it, although he still believes in his product. A wise warning to Wall Street and investors, Bear Stearns in particular, he and co-author Marc Beauchamp relate the story of Traditional Industries, which sells camera packages of questionable value while sporting impressive numbers due to creative accounting measures, "The Facts Behind the Figures," 8-21. He relates all the detail in "Just Smart Stock Pickers," with Claire Poole 9-18, but without his usual flair, just another insider-trading bust, this time of Swiss bank Ellis A.G., whose principals, Claude and George Dreyfuss are admitted "good stock pickers." More advice for Wall Street is offered in "But the Client Is Delighted," co-authored by Charles M. Bartlett Jr. 4-3, this time as brokerage houses don't do their homework and the clients have to take the hit: "The moral of this story shouldn't be plainer. Too often, when an underwriter brings a stock to the public, its chief concern is the company issuing it, not the small investor buying it."

Stevenson, Richard W. *The New York Times.* (★ ★)
Los Angeles. We've been steadily impressed with Stevenson's enterprise, carefulness and reporting skills. He loses a little ground this year as too many of the pieces we looked at in '89 lacked concentration and verve that we'd come to expect of him. He throws us off in "Networks Plan More Moonlighting," 1-30, his depiction of the struggle between the networks and studios over reruns, fairly clear, but in the last graph he reports that the network ownership of the "Moonlighting" series is an "economic disaster," and doesn't explain. Better developed, he spots the trend and covers it adequately in "Debate Grows on Development Fees," 2-16, as California developers are now stuck with paying $10-$20K per new home for the infrastructure, school fees, that were once borne by municipalities. In "Hospital Company's Stock Climbs," 3-28, on the potential buyout and stock rise of American Medical International Inc., he's dusty, and although he gets quotes from the principals, he can't get this one off the ground. Again uncharacteristically heavy, he includes lackluster quotes that help drag down "Hollywood Takes to the Global Stage," 4-16, on the larger trends, important material, as the subhead announces: "Studios are bursting into markets abroad as foreigners snap up U.S. companies." A lead Sunday "Business" is timely, "Not Just Another Charlie Bluhdorn," 6-11, on Paramount's Martin Davis' management style, but Stevenson focuses on his serving shareholders by wringing value out of assets, while he ought to have explored why Davis thinks Time executives are below par, and why he stuck with the media side of Gulf & Western and sold off the finance side. He picks up the newsbeat from the *Journal* in "Watch Out Macy's, Here Comes Nordstrom," *Magazine* 8-19, an engrossing business feature on the retail apparel chain devoted to customer service, forcing other retailers to follow suit. Delightfully humanizing his subject in "Muppets Join Disney Menagerie," 8-29, he gets beyond the paperwork, getting a marvelous quote from Disney head Michael Eisner on the transition and merger of Henson Associates and Disney: "We will bring Miss Piggy into the fold the same careful way Walt Disney brought Winnie the Pooh into the fold." His "Behind the Military Selloff," 11-21, is a smart, quick-and-dirty analytic on the 11-20 plunge in defense-related stocks as Wall Street bets, "from a financial perspective at least, the cold war might be over." He carefully stresses potential over-reaction.

Stipp, David. *The Wall Street Journal.* (★ ★)
Boston. For the most part, Stipp stayed away from the greenhouse paranoia that gripped most of his colleagues during the year. Stalwartly professional, Stipp restrains himself to provide solid, but unimaginative dispatches, rarely asking questions that break new ground. He sounds like Brown's press agent in "Lester Brown's Star Is Rising As His Forecasts About the State of the Globe Seem to Come True," 12-30, and Lester Brown's apocalyptic Worldwatch Institute: "...as chunks of the sky have seemingly begun to fall, Mr. Brown's star is rising." He comes up short on the FDA's view in "Fast AIDS Test May Be Hard For Some Users," 2-8, but is otherwise complete on Cambridge Bioscience's five-minute AIDS test, FDA-approved, which shows high rates of false positives: 10% in a doctor's office study and 15% in an emergency room study. He uses *Nature* to back up his important findings in "Abnormal Cells in Nose May Assist in Diagnosis of Alzheimer's Disease," 2-23, as Boston researchers identify "abnormal proteins and masses of abnormal nerve fibers in the olfactory tissues of people who died from Alzheimer's" disease, which could lead to an definitive outpatient method of diagnosis. He turns in "Fusion Findings in Utah May Take Months to Verify," co-authored by Jerry Bishop 4-7, taking a minuscule look at the discrepancies and questions on the Pons and Fleischmann cold fusion reaction. Among the variables confronting these researchers are the voltage of electricity used and the question of the reaction vessel being sealed or unsealed. Also scientists feel that a control experiment should be conducted with ordinary water as well as the experiment with deuterated or heavy water that is purported to have caused the fusion. He smartly summarizes the theoretical explanations advanced, "Theories on Cold Fusion Abound," 4-13, if the Pons phenomenon actually exists. In "Groups of Physicists, Releasing Reams of Data, Despite Claims of Cold Fusion," 5-2, Pons-Fleischmann claims refuted by physicists, but Stipp carefully quotes views indicating controversy will remain alive. His "McDonald's Offers Recycling Program," 10-27, on plastic trash recycling, is far better than John Holusha's account in the *Times,* crisply

written, good numbers, content and quotes. "A Two-Edged Sword," 11-13, in the "Technology" insert, steps quickly into a timely review of the "health-care inflation monster," which will soon devour 12.5% of GNP in paying for the miracles of medical science. A good chart on the costs of high-tech medicine adds utility to the hand-wringing.

Stokes, Bruce. *National Journal.* (★ ★)
International trade beat. Although he can be pedestrian in his analytics, a mercantilist at heart, Stokes does his homework, and is more discriminating than we'd seen in past years. His profile of Treasury's assistant secretary for international affairs Charles Dallara is the first we've seen and was welcome, "Senior Treasury Aide Didn't Start at the Top," 2-4, although not telling us his proclivity for a weak dollar. Stokes' piece on the controversy over whether the U.S. should co-produce the Fighter Support Experimental (FSX) with Japan was the best piece on the topic that appeared at the time, "Beat 'Em or Join 'Em," 2-25, well researched, interesting, and a superb analysis of the many dimensions involved. In "Something's Wrong," 4-22, a commentary on James Fallows' new book, *More Like Us,* he's thoughtful and balanced in treating its thesis that the U.S. need only nurture its cultural roots to stay on top. But he's mushy in citing the trade deficit — which is, after all, a capital inflow—as a sign something is "radically wrong" with the U.S. He doesn't do enough homework, superficial, on the Brady Plan in "Revving Up Mexico's Growth Engine," 5-27: "A way to increase exports would be to further devalue the peso, whose worth has been dropping steadily for months," failing to note that devaluations have been coming regularly since 1976, producing only inflation and capital flight. He questions the feasibility of U.S. negotiations with Japan in "Talking With Tokyo Worthwhile?" 6-3, particularly in light of "Super 301," exploring many unanswered and possibly unanswerable questions in U.S.-Japan trade dealings. A good preliminary "Boom At the Border," 7-29, on a building U.S.-Mexico economic boom creating interdependence faster than the governments can keep pace. On the positive side, opportunities for Bush are vast and exciting. The downside is air traffic control problems in San Diego and Tijuana, environmental concerns and illegal immigration. In a special report, "Auto Glut," 9-23, he develops the point: auto competitiveness will be increasingly determined by national social and economic policy.

Sullivan, Allanna. *The Wall Street Journal.* (★ ★)
New York, oil industry. Batting cleanup on the Valdez spill, Sullivan saw less of OPEC this year than oil-soaked rocks in Prince William Sound. In "For the Petroleum Industry, Pouring Oil Is in Fact the Cause of Troubled Waters," 3-31, she and co-author Caleb Solomon take an excellent look at the repercussions of the Valdez spill, which could cripple further exploration in the area, using as a case in point an off shore installation which 20 years ago spewed 3 million gallons of oil into the Santa Barbara Channel, and today, oil industry officials view doing business in California in the same way they view doing business in an unstable foreign country. The same day she files "Critics Fault Chief Executive of Exxon On Handling of Recent Alaskan Oil Spill," co-authored by Amanda Bennett 3-31, a good look at crisis management, or lack thereof, at Exxon, compactly relating the long list of mistakes and problems: the PR effort was limited to one man and an answering machine in Houston, and overloaded lines in Alaska; Exxon's decentralized structure may be a major factor, but Mr. Rawl received his information secondhand; and the president of Exxon U.S.A. didn't leave for Valdez until President Bush decided to send three representatives to assess the situation. She and Ken Wells depict the problems, environmental and economic, of the cleanup effort, "Stuck in Alaska: Exxon's Army Scrubs the Beaches, but They Don't Stay Clean," 7-27, an effective catalogue, but little else. In a quick update with a facetious title, "Now the Big Search Is On to Find Sea Otters That Use Styling Gel," 8-23, Sullivan points out something that other reporters missed, that some of the rocks on Alaska's beaches aren't oil-soaked, just black, made from volcanic rock, and now Exxon is using this information as a PR tool: "Exxon says its comments aren't an exercise in defensive public relations, but an effort to educate the uninitiated about the area, which was only partly slimed." "The Spoiler: How Kuwait's Holdout From OPEC Quotas May Reform the Cartel," co-authored by James Tanner 6-12, is half profile of oil minister Ali Khalifa Al-Sabah and

Kuwait, half analytic of the inner mechanisms and arguments of the Organization of Petroleum Exporting Countries, an intricate tale of struggle that may lead to more wrangling as NJ-sized Kuwait demands a bigger piece of the action. More dissention in OPEC is detailed in "Cartel Ministers Face Daunting Task Of Revamping Production Quota System," 11-22, well rounded, Sullivan giving us a good idea of how and why OPEC countries are haggling so vociferously over "decimals."

Swardson, Anne. *The Washington Post.* (★)
District of Columbia economics. She's new at this, moving from federal taxes to the local economy midyear, and eventually we expect the change of scene will be good for her. While she's feeling her way around, the material is soft, okay bits and pieces, but we expect broader sweeps. Anyway, Swardson ought to have more fun on this job. A quickie on "The Tax Menu: Plenty of Choices, Little Appetite," is superfluous on the arguments over taxes, nice to read, but perfectly forgettable, beginning: "If talk of new taxes raised money, the current level of discussion would eliminate the budget deficit by spring" and going nowhere, saying little else. Startling detail in "Cash Crisis Hobbles the IRS As Agency Workload Doubles," 3-16, as the IRS struggles to get its act together in the wake of budget cuts, but she offers no solutions or analysis, just straightforward reporting, with nicely illustrative anecdotes. "Rostenkowski Offers Tax Hike Package," 7-12, is solidly reported on the House Ways and Means Chairman's plan to raise $5.3 billion on tax revenues, accurately getting the real story: "More notable. . .was what Rostenkowski's tax bill would not do: lower taxes on capital gains, extend numerous popular tax benefits expiring at the end of this year and reduce a surtax on older Americans to finance health insurance for catastrophic illnesses." She covers the ripple economic effects of the big Bethesda storm, "Toppled Trees a Windfall For Contractors, Hotels," 6-18, as hotels fill up and contractors and tree removal people jack up prices, okay, but unexceptional. Experts aren't sure of the reason that "DC Income Growth Is Tops in U.S." 8-24, topping at a rate of a 9.4% rise in personal income per capita, and neither is she, really only reporting the numbers with regard to DC and a few states. She takes an informal survey, and comes up negative, in "Voices Rise Above a Whisper With a Dirty Word: Slowdown," 10-30. She admits this "slowdown" doesn't show up in the numbers "yet," sharply executed and precautionary, although we're unsure how definitive her sampling is, and thus we don't quite buy it: "Cause and effect are hard to separate in an entity as complex as the Washington economy, but the federal-spending bust comes as other once-booming industries are softening." "Report Says DC Wine Industry in Grape Shape," 11-15, isn't serious on either the "importance" of the wine industry to the District's economy or the growing trend of studies commissioned by lobbyists and consultants to push a product, and we come away with little but the hiccoughs.

Symonds, William C. *BusinessWeek.* (★ ★)
Covering the business side of sports, Symonds is the only reporter we know of consistently on this beat. Although he sometimes tackles telecommunication topics, he can mostly be found checking balance sheets on the baseball diamond or the golf course. He files an interesting profile on the cable TV pioneer, " 'Wild Bill' Daniels Tries One More Comeback," 1-30, whose gutsiness has carried him into cable sports programming. He adds a third dimension by using good quotes from the competition in "People Aren't Laughing at U.S. Sprint Anymore," with John J. Keller and Tim Smart 7-31, focusing on the dynamism of United Telecom CEO William T. Esrey, whose company stock has doubled in the last year on the turnaround. He presents a strategic overview, "American Cable is Lassoing Foreign Markets," with Richard Melcher 8-14, of U.S. cable companies and Baby Bells in cable markets abroad, and the competition they face. "The Boom in Golf as Baby Boomers Hit the Links," with Brenton Welling 3-27, is a thorough, serious dispatch detailing the golf boom, the shortage of courses, the demographics and appeal of the sport, and the corporations producing golf equipment, a booming industry with a "phenomenal" growth rate. He digs out another angle in "Driving to Become the IBM of Golf," 6-19, as ClubCorp, "the world's largest manager of private clubs," moves into public golf courses, golf resorts, and foreign clubs, a well-written "niche" story. He combines the sprightly

written history and analysis on the Senior PGA tour in "Golf's Old Greats Are Really Swinging Again," 6-26, and in "Will Europe Take A Divot Out Of The PGA Golf Tour?" 9-25, he provides a lucid explanation of how the European golf tour competes with the U.S. PGA tour and what the issues are in trying to lure foreign players to compete here. On the new baseball commissioner, "Professor Hardball," co-authored by Welling, with Aaron Bernstein and Ron Stodghill II cover 4-3, is just in time for opening day, a broad overview of what A. Bartlett Giamatti will face, notably labor-management relations and franchise expansion, with a good selection of quotes from Giamatti and other key players. Looking to the future in "If The Mariners Don't Shape Up, They May Get Shipped Out," 9-11, Symonds credibly analyzes factors that could lead the new, savvy owner of Mariners to success, or could lead him and his partners to move the team from Seattle. "A Crucial Inning for Baseball," 10-23, is well-crafted on the baseball owners' plans to try to kill salary arbitration, particularly good on Milwaukee Brewers' owner Bud Selig and his prominent role in upcoming negotiations.

Tanner, James. *The Wall Street Journal.* (★ ★ ★ ½)
New York, oil industry. The most experienced and knowledgeable petro-reporter in the U.S., probably the world, Tanner still works this beat with the energy of a cub. The Byzantine world of OPEC is his specialty, although he knows the U.S. oil patch as well as anyone in the press, serving up consistently professional and informative reports. Much of his work by necessity is of roundup quality, but when we see him working the broader picture, we know it will be definitive. His front-page "Energy Assurance: OPEC Adds Capacity, Easing Risk That Cost of Oil Will Soar in '90s," 11-22, comes precisely as specialists in the industry worry about the long lead times involved in avoiding a supply shortage and rising prices by '92 or so. Tanner writes: "At the root of this scramble is OPEC's desire to become known as a reliable global supplier of petroleum. In other words, a contentious economic environment with soaring oil prices — what many oil experts have been predicting — is just what OPEC seeks to avoid." He's not as sharp in "Oil Market's Price Rally Is Stoked by Indication of Further Cuts by Saudis and Qatar," 3-15, fine on the oil end of it, but his numerical analysis on other commodities is muddled. His "Saudis Appeal to Other OPEC Members to Maintain Oil-Production Discipline," 5-5, demonstrates how loose lips can sink a cartel, as King Fahd's unclear remarks on production quotas and oil prices stir up the Middle East, a compact, precise analytic. "The Spoiler: How Kuwait's Holdout From OPEC Quotas May Reform the Cartel," co-authored by Allanna Sullivan 6-12, is half profile of oil minister Ali Khalifa Al-Sabah and Kuwait, half analytic of the inner mechanisms and arguments of the Organization of Petroleum Exporting Countries, an intricate tale of struggle that may lead to more wrangling as NJ-sized Kuwait demands a bigger piece of the action. A mid-meeting dispatch, "Iran Proposes OPEC Overhaul of Quotas," 9-27, brings us up to date, complete with nuance and detail. "OPEC's Unused Capacity Boosts Need to Adopt New Quota System," 10-23, is admirably reported and organized, with authoritative quotes and no-nonsense asides from Tanner: "The United Arab Emirates, a chronic quota cheater, refused to give any guarantees it would change its ways." His "Saudis Find Greatly Prized, Low-Sulfer Oil," 11-7, reads like he was in his own backyard, confident and precise on the economics and technical facts and figures.

Taylor, Alex, III. *Fortune.* (★ ★)
Detroit. Our auto-industry reporter of choice a few years back, Taylor continues a glacial slide in our evaluations. He hasn't *lost* his talent for squirreling away interesting nuts and bolts about carmaking itself, but the recent dynamics of the industry have been calling for deeper business and financial insights and Taylor has been struggling here. A 10 Best nomination from his editors, "Fords for the Future," 1-16, his profile on how Henry Ford's great-grandsons want to run Ford in the future, is nice enough, but skirts industry analysis and may be more appropriate for the profile section of *People.* He doesn't get much in "The U.S. Gets Back in Fighting Shape," 4-24, a celebration of a cheaper dollar as the cause of the increased competitiveness of the U.S., sophomoric at best. He tags along with Bob Lutz, Chrysler's number one operating executive, in "How a Top Boss Manages His Day," 6-19, very interesting,

informative, insider stuff, Taylor keeping a focus on the wheels at work. Yet the deep problems at Chrysler are mostly side-stepped. Hampered by a poor headline, "A Tale Dow Jones Won't Tell," 7-3, Taylor still files an excellent reconnaissance of the company, the circulation decline of *The Wall Street Journal* being offset by the great success of its electronic information business. In "Here Come Japan's New Luxury Cars," 8-14, he makes a very convincing argument that the Japanese are better and cheaper than their German competitors. A book review, "What Hath Roger Smith Wrought," 9-25, lets auto-analyst author Maryann Keller tromp over GM's Smith, with little complaint from Taylor about the larger forces at work. A major effort, "Why U.S. Carmakers Are Losing Ground," 10-23, is interesting for minor details collected at ground level, i.e., "Some 30 automakers, including nine Japanese and 19 European, sell 600 models to American buyers." Taylor doesn't see the macro picture, though. He again cites the cheap dollar as a U.S. advantage, then notes Japanese firms can borrow at 2% while GM and Ford pay 9%, but he never thinks to explore the connection between the devalued dollar and 9% rates, or equate the economic trade-offs of falling labor costs and rising capital costs.

Thomas, Paulette. *The Wall Street Journal.* (★ ★)
Washington. Credible spot reporting on the S&L crisis and bailout from Thomas, her second year working this labyrinth. She stays within her capabilities, careful and professional in handling complex deals and personalities, leaving the investigative stuff and grand themes to others. "Wall Defends Year-End Rush on Sales Of Thrifts Against Mounting Criticism," 1-3, a fine summary of various transactions with the corresponding amounts and government guarantees, provides little information to help us decide if the FSLIC is giving away the store. Well covered, "Deposits Flowing From Thrifts in '89 at Near Record Pace, Congress Is Told," 3-2, Thomas collects various opinions on the hemorrhaging and various predictions of when and if it will stop, but to no conclusion. In "Senate Overwhelmingly Passes S&L Bill Containing $50 Billion in Rescue Money," 4-20, she hints at coming conflict-of-interest troubles for Sen. Riegle, but only hints. In "Shaky Reserve: As S&L Bailout Plan Draws Nearer Passage, Flaws Become Clearer," 7-21, she takes the longer-term view of some of the problems inherent in the plan and in the industry. She offers clean, concise detail in "Thrift-Bailout Financing Plan May Reduce S&L Deposit Rates Faster Than Expected," 8-7, a Monday-morning review of Friday's S&L action in Congress, particularly good on all the legislative maneuvering going on. A broader view filed the same day, "Big Thrift-Rescue Bill Is Likely to Realign the Financial System" with G. Christian Hill, is a mind-numbing, mammoth look at what Congress has wrought and Bush will sign to "rescue" the thrift industry. The material is developed well, with startling revelations about the changes ahead, emphatic in that taxpayers have only just begun to pay. "Over Half of Lincoln S&Ls Reported Net Since '84 Said To Be From Sham Deals," 11-15, is a sound account of the new information that has been added to this story, more fraud by Arizona bankers.

Thomas, Rich. *Newsweek.* (★ ★)
Chief economic correspondent, Washington. The best known of the newsweekly reporters on this beat, Thomas has a nice swagger and bravado in his enterprise that we've always liked, *usually* uncomfortable running with the sheep. As a matter of course, he offers prescriptives more often than his *Time* and *USN&WR* competitors. In "Return of the Untouchables," 3-6, he submits to the taxpayer yet another list of programs that waste the taxpayers' money and ought to be cut, but he's obvious here, offering no perspective. Co-authored by David Pauly, "The New Spelling of Relief," 3-20, ably sorts through the Brady Plan for Third World debt but the duo steps into sheep dip in asserting Brady's plan can only solve part of the problem because "debtor countries must promote investment in their local economies" by getting "the upper classes to return their own capital from havens abroad," this week's pat Beltway nostrum. He and Eleanor Clift smartly debate the merits of raising the minimum wage, "It's Sacred — But Is It Smart?" 4-17, offering the choice of the Earned-Income Tax Credit (EITC) as a better alternative to raising the minimum wage. He offers nothing new in "In 'Hip-Deep' Water," with Clift 5-1, a straightforward outline of the charges facing House Speaker Jim Wright, including

brief, encapsulated summaries of each. He sounds a solid warning in "The Second S&L Scandal," 6-12, prophesying that unless tough legislation is passed to reform the industry, thrift managers may continue to take risks in investing, expecting Washington to bail them out, thus "this may not be the last time that billions of taxpayer dollars are needed to fund a huge S&L bailout." In "What You Won't Hear in Paris," 7-17, occasioned by the upcoming G-7 summit, he addresses what he thinks are the root causes of the world trade imbalance, America's declining influence and a warming of the cold war. Unhappily, Thomas falls prey to the mercantilist bent that pervades the weekly, including a discussion of how Bush could use the IMF constitution to punish those who have a continuous trade surplus with the U.S. He reports on the fiscal mismanagement of the Farmer's Home Administration, in "Harvest Of Red Ink," 9-18, detailing how the original purpose of the organization was subverted, after big farmers began to cash in.

Tolchin, Martin. *The New York Times.* (★ ★)
Washington. A pro we've always admired for his carefulness, his double-checking method, his absence of partisan bias on a beat where this is an exception, Tolchin delivers on health, housing and welfare, more consistent this year than last. He's more thorough than his competition in "Kemp Vows To Oust Tenants On Drugs," 3-8, on HUD Secretary Jack Kemp's pledge to crack down on drug dealers and abusers in public housing projects, including Kemp's response to American Civil Liberties Union objections that his plan might undermine constitutional rights, succinct and to the point: "In some cases, the A.C.L.U. is part of the problem." We get a cutesy angle overblown in "How Bentsen Steered the Lightning to Bush On Medicare Surtax," 5-3, on how Bentsen and Rostenkowski delivered "a political karate chop" to Bush, with Tolchin including too little of the real impact on the elderly lobby. He offers a nice wrapup of the problems of workfare, a term that isn't mentioned but about what it comes down to, in "Welfare Changes Endangered, Governors Say," 5-21, putting it all in perspective, with information on outlines. He provides no framework in which you can estimate the potential success, however. He takes us through the tax and Medicare mess, in "Senate Reweighs Extra Medicare," 6-2, which could have been clearer, though this may be demonstrative of the way the government does things. He's out of his element in "Retreating on Pledge, White House Hints at Tax Increase to Aid Elderly," 7-18, taking a mile where he's got only an inch, as he has Darman caving in on Social Security taxes when Darman merely answered a hypothetical question on an option paper. In a "Week in Review," "Sudden Support For National Healthcare," 9-24, he asserts a trend, but doesn't substantiate his claim: "Employees are changing their minds about national health insurance because they are losing the advantage in international competition by having to pay for healthcare, instead of having the Government pay." The quote is from a labor lobbyist.

Trachtenberg, Jeffrey A. *The Wall Street Journal.* (★ ½)
Retail, New York. Trachtenberg moves from the "Marketing" column in *Forbes* for the rush of a daily paper's deadlines. He loses nothing in the transition, though, having cut his teeth on the retail circuit at *Women's Wear Daily.* He captures the major flaw in Fur Vault's marketing, astute in "R.I.P. Fred the Furrier," *Forbes* 2-20, as Fred Schwartz is forced out: "Fred Schwartz had failed to realize that his Fred the Furrier persona had created a powerful brand image: the warm, friendly person your cousin would feel comfortable with, ready to answer questions sensibly and willing to provide good values and easy credit terms. Without that familiar, consistent image, the Fur Vault was just another retailer." He's microscopic with the numbers, "New Customers at $50 a Head, Not $2,500," 3-6, but there's nothing to hold them together in this piece on Continental Cable Systems (2.2% disconnects per month, 2.35 million subscribers who take 2.6 million take "pay units," etc.), and we wind up on the wrong side of the balance sheet. His first article for the *Journal,* "Can Liz Claiborne Continue to Thrive When She Is Gone?" co-authored by Teri Agins 2-28, doesn't answer the question in the title, unsatisfying as Liz Claiborne and husband Arther Ortenberg step down from running the fashion house. Although the duo assembles quite a bit of industry opinion, plus a decisive history of the company, this really doesn't amount to much, vascillating between a "yes" and "no"

answer. His savvy pays off in "Ann Taylor Plans Expansion to Pay $37 Million in Interest from Buy-Out," 5-11, compactly evaluating the risks of the LBO and the proposed expansion of stores as the market softens. He makes the best of what might be a standard report in someone's else's hands, in "Big Retailers Had Mixed Gains for July With Apparel Sales Leading Durables," 8-4, compiling estimates and explanations of different analysts, but not proffering his own explanation given his information. "Hooker Corp. Chief Seeking to Speed the Sale of B. Altman," 10-6, a taut, quick update, is adequate, complete with pertinent data, but no predictions or prescriptions. In another look at Hooker, Trachtenberg provides more information, "L. J. Hooker Planning to Sell Bonwit Teller," 12-7. We get the feeling from these little updates that there's a story here just dying to be told, but Trachtenberg is missing it.

Truell, Peter. *The Wall Street Journal.* (★ ★ ★)
New York, international banking. Truell has the potential of being one of the great financial reporters of the era, one who got our highest rating in the '88 *Guide.* He has a demonstrated capacity to work on the broadest canvas, but we see too few such efforts in recent years as he works the equivalent of a daily police blotter on Third World debt. His "IMF Reluctance Blocks Progress By Argentina," 2-2, on the conflict between the IMF and World Bank over a lead role, offers only sketchy detail. Back on track with co-author Mossberg in "Bush Aides Are Likely to offer a Plan Soon on Third World Debt," 3-9, he submits an excellent evaluation of the political and economic stakes involved, and cold-eyed realism on the administration's response to the challenge, with one of the year's best leads: "While the Bush administration searches for a new U.S. policy on Third World debt, red ink is turning to blood." His "Japanese Banks Increase Role in Debt Talks," 3-17, provides the best detail we saw on Japanese banks' attitudes toward Latin American lending, but he concentrates on the surface issue of bankers squabbling over share of new loans; with bigger policy issues at work, we had the feeling Truell missed an even bigger story. Timely in "Bush To Back Efforts to Cut World Debt," co-written by Walter Mossberg 3-18, the duo covers well the reaction in Latin capitals as well as Japanese attitudes on the Brady proposal. He makes it clear in "Crucial Talks on Latin Debt Bog Down, Dimming Outlook for Brady's Strategy," 5-3, that the Brady Plan just isn't going anywhere now. Though he's cloudy on potential weaknesses, he gets rather good details in a timely dispatch, "The Brady Plan for Third World Debt Gets Off to a Bad Start in Latin America," 5-10. A 10 Best nomination, "Hills Will Wield 'Super 301' as Lever for Exports, But Some Warn It May Trigger Protectionist Wars," 5-17, is the best review of the trade decision facing Carla Hills and the Bush administration we saw, the partial Q&A format effective. From DC, "Bush Economic Advisors to Ponder Renewal of Steel Import Limits as Anti-Quota Lobby Grows," 6-14, we get his usual razor-sharp focus and detail on anti-quota lobbyists including Caterpillar and General Motors. His fine presentation and clear explanation in "Mexican Pact Shows U.S. Has Refocused its Strategy Away From Debt Reduction," 7-25, on small but important shifts in the Brady Plan impresses, and he presents numbers showing Mexican debt *won't* be reduced by the announced agreement. "Funding Clouds World Bank, IMF Parleys," 9-29, is clear-sighted and thorough on IMF/World Bank difficulties in getting more resources out of Congress: "The U.S. contends that a strong case hasn't been made for an increase."

Uchitelle, Louis. *The New York Times.* (½ ★)
New York. An economics reporter who is almost always against the grain, but as we said last year, he's "too often impaled on it," burdened by a helter-skelter analytical framework. We always give him a look, but more and more it's to see what mischief he's up to with his offbeat themes. In a *Times Magazine* profile of Alan Greenspan, almost entirely personality with unusual focus on bachelor Greenspan's love life, "Caution at the Fed," 1-15, Uchitelle is useless in conveying an understanding of the cross-currents of Fed policies, except to say that Greenspan doesn't want a recession. Skimming in "Just Another Quick Fix," 1-15, we get reactions from several CFOs to Bush administration ideas on getting businessmen to focus on the long term, learning they don't want to cut the capital gains tax. Huh? "Weak Dollar Seen as Main Factor In Inflation Rise in Recent Months," 3-1, is innovative on price rises following dollar

devaluation, but Uchitelle has no clear analytical framework. His mish-mash anti-competitive theme is contradicted halfway through "Trade Barriers And Dollar Swings Raise Appeal of Factories Abroad," 3-26: "While American companies invested $42 billion abroad in 1988, foreign concerns put a similar amount into their American operations." A "Week in Review" piece, "In Search of the Rates That Bring Borrowers," 7-16, is dominated by a Phillip's curve framework on the decline in short-term rates and when the fall will invite an increase in home and auto loans : "The Fed pushed up interest rates from March 1988 until this spring, out of concern that people were borrowing and buying too much — in fact, buying more than the economy could supply." Says who? He offers analysis from an odd angle in "Ripples From a Bailout," 8-13, as the nation "has lost more than $100 billion in wealth in the S&L bailout, perhaps forever," but no big deal, the earnings lost "only pennies for a nation generating $5 trillion in annual income," collecting interesting data and quotes along the way. "Government Spreading Net to Break Market Free Falls," 10-30, is typical, a survey of opinions with no overall conclusion on an unsettling topic, this time the government's increasing attempts to limit stock market crashes. In the first mainstream piece to deviate from the "soft landing" theory, "Data Are Signaling Bad Slump," 11-20, he interprets the data and the economists as predicting a bad slump. This is a wholly unacceptable, misleading report, Uchitelle selecting his data to support his conclusion, including a decline in housing when, in fact, housing starts were reported up 11-17. "Small Companies Going Global," 11-27, has the makings of a good story, but Uchitelle doesn't deliver, with a few skimpy anecdotes to support his thesis, not one hard statistic showing a directional trend.

Verity, John. *Business Week.* **(NR)**
Computers. The department editor for Information Processing, Verity scores with a 10 Best selection for "A Bold Move in Mainframes," 5-29, almost everything we ever wanted to know about IBM (in early May). This dissertation on Big Blue includes an evaluation of its strategy that impressed market analysts, highlighting the major paradox: as IBM makes its software proprietary, it may be passed by as customers look for open systems, a la UNIX. Not puffy in any sense, his piece is a hard look at a bold strategy and its implications for IBM, its competitors and its customers. We didn't see major material from Verity frequently; he handles concise one-page updates on the industry. He adds up all the evidence after the fact in "If It Looks Like a Slump and Crawls Like a Slump. . ." 5-1, as IBM spokesmen try to put a happy face on things, but Verity isn't fooled and neither are we. Very smart in explaining IBM's difficulties in getting the 3390 off the ground, in "Back in the Driver's Seat in Disk Drives," 11-27, ("Imagine flying a Boeing 747 at 500 mph just inches off the ground. That's an analogy IBM uses to describe the microscopic tolerances required in computer disk drives.") Verity's also savvy in getting IBM's marketing Catch-22 down: "IBM will need to stay a few technological steps ahead of competitors to keep its prices up. Then, once they catch up, IBM's costs will be largely covered, and it can cut prices. With the 3390, Big Blue has stolen the march." More run-of-the-mill, "A Double Whammy Spooks Investors," 4-3, is nice on the technical double whammies of IBM and DEC as chip problems hit stock prices, his background nicely structured, predicting no slump, although we find several weeks later, that's just what he's got.

Vise, David. *The Washington Post.* **(★)**
More on Milken-Drexel from Vise, he was hard-pressed to keep up with Stephen Adler of the *Journal,* particularly after partner Steve Coll went on overseas assignment. He's much better on the straight business beat. We get wire service quality stuff in "Drexel Agrees to Admit Fraud Schemes by Milken," co-authored by Steve Coll 1-25, solid and straightforward, but nothing special. He makes a good assessment, in "RICO Goes to Wall St," 7-30, of the impact that the application of the anti-racketeering law on the Princeton/Newport case is having on other pending cases such as Drexel and Goldman, Sachs as the lawyers "contend that prosecutors were counting on the threatening shadow of RICO to force the defendants into plea bargain agreements that would include significant cooperation as witnesses against [Drexel's] Milken and Goldman, Sachs partner Robert Freeman." He adequately details the Redskins' owner's sale

of his cable TV outlet, "Jack Kent Cooke Selling His Cable TV Operations," 1-10, but a paragraph on Drexel is jarring, relevant as Drexel is handling the deal, but awkwardly structured: "For the investment firm of Drexel Burnham Lambert Inc., which recently agreed to plead guilty to six felony counts and to pay $650 million in a plea bargain agreement, the deal is expected to mean millions of dollars in fees. In a cable financing for Cooke in 1987, Drexel earned between $15 million and $20 million." A lengthy, in-depth profile away from RICO and the SEC does Vise good, "Bear Stearns's Old Hand at Bridge, Brokerage," 10-29, giving us a sense of Jimmy Cayne the man and the manager, who is passionate about B&B (bridge and brokerage). Too short, "In Silver Spring, a Takeover Turns Sour," 11-20, doesn't amount to much more than an anti-takeover treatise, Vise skimming pertinent information that might have made his case as to how and why the BancTec takeover of Computer Entry Systems Corp. went bad.

Wald, Matthew L. *The New York Times.* (★ ½)
Energy beat. Less of value from Wald drops him a full star. He manages pretty well in keeping his own biases out of his reports, but he can be disorganized to the point where his dispatches are effectively useless. He provides extensive detail on safety regulations in "10 Years After Three Mile Island," 1-23, but only mentions in passing the costs and finances of the nuclear industry, which should have been near the top, not the last graph. He shills for solar energy subsidies in "U.S. Companies Losing Interest in Solar Energy," 3-6, very poor material and effort: "Some of the nation's biggest backers of solar energy are losing interest just as the technology to transform sunlight into electricity is getting closer to being economically competitive with some competitive power sources." Instead of being sixteen times the competitive price, they're now "only" three times the price! Uncritical in "Exxon Head Seeks Environmentalist To Serve On Board," 5-12, he describes efforts of institutional investors, through an institute started with the California Funds and a union, to gain a greater say in corporate governance. He tours the Indian Point plant in "Russians Talk of Nuclear Aid by U.S." 5-23, with the guests of Bechtel, the Chairman of the Soviet State Committee for Supervision of Nuclear Safety and three other officials, getting for the record that the U.S.S.R. "might turn to an American company for help in designing reactors." But a spokesman at Bechtel Headquarters said "I don't see us playing a role in their construction program, but we have some management techniques we can help them with." Straightforward in "Voters, In A First, Shut Down Nuclear Reactor," 6-8, about the first successful referendum in 15 tries in 13 years, with extensive quotes from Tom Hayden who led the fight, he makes no comment on the fact that municipal power systems like this one have poor operating records, nor that municipal systems have an advantage buying Grand Coulee and other public power by law. Timely, "That 'Cleaner Fuel' May Be Gasoline," 8-23, on how gasoline can be made "cleaner" thereby avoiding costly alternatives, could lose the reader in the middle with all the technical mumbo-jumbo. A "Week in Review" feature, "An Energy Glut in the Ground Imperils Ecological Hopes," 10-15, effectively makes the case that incentives for reduction of fuel costs will not come from the marketplace, but only from the government. His "Finding a Burial Place For Nuclear Wastes Grows More Difficult," 12-5, is hopelessly disorganized, but we do struggle to an amazing closing quote from the Natural Resources Defense Council lawyer: "We simply can't rely on distant generations to have the same sort of institutional controls over this very dangerous material that current society does." My, what good boys we are!

Waldholz, Michael. *The Wall Street Journal.* (★ ★ ½)
Pharmaceutical industry. A very good trade reporter, Waldholz at times seems to drift with the FDA bureaucracy in the always controversial issues surrounding drug-approvals, but he usually manages to rise above the debate and present top-drawer material. More than the average company report, he provides many tidbits on the company's R&D and new drugs in "Squibb Estimates Its Per-Share Profit Rose 25% In 1988, Led by Heart Drug," 1-10. Timely and authoritative, "Tracking a Killer: Merck Scientists Find a Chink in the Armor of the Aids Virus," 2-16, he gets the inside story of the research at the firm leading up to the discovery. A

10 Best nomination, co-authored by Walt Bogdanich, "Warm Bodies: Hospitals That Need Patients Pay Bounties for Doctors' Referrals," 2-27, is superlative, relating how patients have become the hot commodity as hospitals suffer from cost containment, resulting in more outpatient treatment and faster discharge for those admitted as inpatients. In a followup, also with Bogdanich, "Warm Bodies: Doctor-Owned Labs Earn Lavish Profits In a Captive Market," 3-1, the team investigates the growing trend of physicians starting radiology centers, diagnostic laboratories and other services as joint ventures, at quite handsome profit levels. "Physicians Sending Patients to Test Labs That They Own Sparks Unusual Debate," 7-21, expands on his theme, a credible exercise which projects there will be legislation of some sort to regulate this trend. "Gene Linked to Colon Cancer Identified," 4-14, is a quietly effective followup to last year's 10 Best selection, Waldholz getting more evidence out of Johns Hopkins and U. of Utah on the identity of the gene that triggers the cancer, stellar work on a story that continues to have huge medical implications. More troubles for J&J are detailed in "Tylenol Overuse Tied to Kidney Disease," 5-11, thoroughly covered, down to market shares of different brands. He loses sight of his subject, confusing in "New Drug May Slow Parkinson's Disease," 8-4, on Deprenyl, a anti-depressant drug from Hungary, that's effective in postponing the onset of severe symptoms of Parkinson's disease. "Squibb Corp. Acquires Marketing Rights to Drugs for Acne, Wrinkling, Baldness," 9-21, has nice detail on Squibb's purchase of marketing rights to a family of drugs tested by Chantl Pharmaceutical in L.A. He's timely with "Bad Blood: Fight Between Generic And Major Drug Firms Heats Up as Stakes Rise," with Gregory Stricharchuk 10-4, wrapping up the battle between large R&D drug houses and feisty generics. "A Death in the Family," 11-13 special "Technology" section, he tells of his 93-year-old grandmother's death, without an attempt to resuscitate as per her wishes, and how relieved he felt later of the family decision upon learning how pitifully few patients over 70 could return home after resuscitation, eight of 503.

Wallace, Anise C. *The New York Times.* (★ ½)
New York "Business Day" reporter, New York. After catching our attention with a splashy 1988, several nifty pieces on the takeover frenzy, Wallace seemed subdued this year, certainly not approaching her three-star rating of a year ago. Actually a freelancer who appears in the *Times* almost exclusively, her status perhaps inhibits her range from time to time. She files a good primer, explaining the inverted yield curve in "A Warning Signal Is Flashing," 1-22, nicely analytic and smart. On the trail of the bond bulls, "Bond Bulls Expect Rally to Continue," 7-17, she notes how many investors were caught unaware by the rally and the belief that yields on long bonds will drop to 7% by year's end, importantly calling attention to the very bad performance in the high yield, or "junk" bond mutual funds, with their total return of 4.6% for the first half of the year. In "Time for the Jitters in Junk Bonds," 8-6, she vacillates, "This may be the year that some of the roof falls in," but there's not enough analysis on how government action is causing problems for high-yield bonds, especially on the S&Ls, which she only mentions in passing. Wallace reports on a new equity fund at Forstmann, Little & Co. in "Leveraged Buyout Leader Shifts Attention," 11-3, but she equates Forstmann's approach incorrectly with that of Kravis Kohlberg & Roberts, and all buyouts done with "subordinated" debt are not the same. Our reader notes that Forstmann's firm deals with subordinated debt, but has never used junk debt, and the new fund will be buying companies that Kravis piled with debt, and then stripped out the equity. "Fidelity Is Freeing Its Funds to be Assertive Investors," 12-5, is confused and clumsy in trying to explain what's up as Fidelity Investment, whose mutual funds own shares worth $46 billion, is removing investment limitations from those funds. We don't understand how they could initiate takeovers when, she points out, U.S. law prohibits such funds from buying securities for the purpose of seeking control of a company.

Wayne, Leslie. *The New York Times.* (★ ★)
Sunday Business. We generally enjoy the Sunday business section for the writing as much as the substance, the staffers getting more freedom to maneuver than they might elsewhere. Wayne is among the cluster we're especially appreciative of on this score, superior on marketing angles we want to read to the end. In an excellent review of the problems faced by the companies in

the Kidder Peabody-GE merger, "Remaking Kidder in G.E.'s Image," 1-29, she looks at the clash of cultures and other problems, some resolved, some not. "With Futures Under Fire, A Watchdog Feels the Heat," 3-26, is slightly disappointing; although Wayne covers the issues well, we expected more somehow from this piece on Wendy Gramm and the CFTC. An engaging look at how Charles Schwab stays the largest discount broker even in slow times, "For Charles Schwab, A Time To Tinker," 5-7, is colorful in relating how they really are quite shrewd and well managed. A look from the darkside of the S&L crisis, "Digging Out From The Savings Crisis," 6-25, predicts potentially more fraud in the selling of assets of insolvent thrifts; Wayne, while pessimistic, isn't panicky, and she's balanced in her presentation. She mixes detailed reporting and analytical effort in "Rewriting the Rules of Retailing," 10-5, a Sunday "Business" lead and 10 Best nomination that's skillfully presented on who's surviving and *why,* amid retailing's most dire times since the depression. Her piece on the A.G. Edwards brokerage firm, "Where the Brokers Are Still Smiling," 11-26, takes awhile to get going, repeating several times that it avoids Wall Street's latest trend on the way to the industry's highest profit margins. But it finally develops with plenty of support for the theme. "Edwards prefers to do little with its capital other than count it." Wayne is totally lost, tromping onto Jonathan Fuerbringer's turf with "Driving Down The Dollar," 9-17, showing almost no understanding of the issues, simply rounding up the usual suspects, a collection of two-armed economists, and offering a scramble of quotes. We will try to forget she wrote this.

Weiner, Steve. *Forbes.* (★ ★ ½)
Midwest bureau manager, Chicago. He left the Sears story alone, delegating it to other reporters, providing a more quirky look in and around the Loop. Weiner is generally adept at making a story come to life, but this year there seemed to be less vitality from him than we'd seen before. He and co-author Charles Siler catalogue the different ways companies and states work together to provide training for employes to better the economy of the state as part of the incentive for building, "Trained to Order," 6-26, but the pair doesn't address the central problem of why up to 20% of the training is remedial. Smart in listing the problems Mark & Spencer Plc. faces in the U.S. market, purchasing Brookes Brothers and New Jersey's Kings Supermarkets chain, "Low Marks, Few Sparks," 9-18 he offers few solutions, although he details the company's history well enough. In "Price Is the Object," 2-20, he provides keen business reporting on the new marketing bandwagon among retail stores, identifying the conceptual background for the sharp shift in marketing strategy *via* a quote from a Target Stores vice president: "Lifestyles have changed and people don't have time to chase after sales." A real success story is compellingly detailed in "Poor Customers, Rich Profits," 3-6, served with a twist as Goldblatt's Department Stores bounce back after bankruptcy under the able eye of William Hellman, returning to the original goal of serving those in the lower-income brackets with inexpensive merchandise that's priced cheaply, while turning a profit: " 'The prices are right and everything is satisfactory,' says Eugene Ziarko, a retiree, as he selects a $14.99 dresser lamp, its green shade stamped with the name of a famous cognac. 'Most stores don't think about people like us.' " His piece on debt-laden Tonka Corp., "Keep on Truckin'," 10-16, could have been better organized, not reporting until the end that the toy company struggled into the black in the second quarter, but he makes a reasonable case that CEO Steve Shank's risk management may continue profitability. In the same issue, he serves up "Phone Bill Detective," 10-16, on software programs that enable companies to sort through their monthly bills and spot long-distance personal calls, which account for about 4% of the total. This can save big money, but Weiner doesn't cover the costs as well as he might. He sees the future and its name might be Wal-Mart, in "Golf Balls, Motor Oil and Tomatoes," 10-30, as the chain prepares the "Hypermart USA" which, admittedly, needs work before becoming the place where you can shop for everything, a sharp critical evaluation of the company's foray into the grocery business, garnering a 10 Best nomination from his editors.

Weiss, Gary. *BusinessWeek.* (★ ★)
Markets & Investments department editor. Less planning ahead from Weiss, he spent the year looking back at what the markets did, rather than estimating their future performance. He does retrospectives well enough, but we didn't see the healthy skepticism of the conventional that peppered his earlier work. Certainly not a novel subject, he covers the bases of brokers and relevant indicators in "The Market Rally Is Getting No Respect," 2-13, as he explains the small investor is waiting for a sign before reentering the market, although he adeptly picks up on some indications of a "falloff in hostility to equities," meaning more interest in looking that could be followed by more money later. He informs in a sidebar to Jeff Laderman's bond fund article, outlining the '88 results and projecting believable scenarios for '89, in "Closed-End Bond Funds: Great in '88, But Keep an Eye on Rates," 2-27. An investigative report, "The Sad Saga of a Penny-Stock Company," 5-15, on Sequential Information Systems, the peddling of whose stock earlier in the '80s led to convictions of Rooney, Pace for SEC violations, is clearly researched, detailing alleged rottenness in "the business practices and finances of Sequential itself." We enjoy "The Marv Throneberrys of Mutual Funds Get a Hit," 7-17, on the transformation of the 44 Wall Street mutual funds by new management into a moneymaker, after resting in the dungeons of mutual funds ratings for years. Weiss provides more information on the still-cautious small investor, an informative survey of the equity mutual funds' sales and redemption pattern during 1989, in "Small Investors Tiptoe Back to Wall Street," 8-14, opening wittily, comparing the scarce "homo investicus, or small investor" with the rare "short-nosed sturgeon in the Hudson River." He offers a new perspective on Warren Buffett's Berkshire Hathaway in "Would You Believe A $10,000 Stock?" 9-4: its "razor-thin float" discourages institutional investors, but buyers of one share (at record-high $8,100 per share or higher) would only pay about 1% in brokers' commissions. With co-author David Greisling, he gets the dirt in "Is Program Trading The Target of a 'Witch Hunt'?" 11-13, as Congress toys again with regulations that are likely to have adverse effects on the markets.

Weisskopf, Michael. *The Washington Post.* (★)
Environment, science topics. Weisskopf is a capable reporter, as he showed once again in his midyear dispatches from China. But when it comes to his regular beat, he's more environmentalist than journalist. A jumbled "U.S. Seeking To Expand Ban On Ozone-Depleting Chemicals," 4-25, confuses on an EPA notice that the Helsinki meeting was likely to propose methyl chloroform and carbon tetrachloride be included in the Montreal Protocol, which calls for a 50% reduction in chlorofluorocarbon use by 1998, beginning with a mind-numbing discussion of ppb levels. He offers an insider view with "Bush Panel Agrees on Options To Reduce Air Pollutants," 5-5, but shows his colors, telling us "none of the proposals requires the most advanced technological controls advocated by environmentalists regardless of cost." His "Under EPA a Regulatory Breakdown," 6-2, makes it clear, that, once again, it's all Reagan's fault, this time for interfering with the objectives of the Clean Air Act, which is perfect in every way. More jumbling in "Administration Split On Clean Air Plan," 6-10, anticipating the Bush speech, with unnamed officials giving various reviews, and stating that the reduction of ozone (in cities, not the stratosphere) "is considered a key test of Bush's promise of environmental reform" because it will hurt the automobile and oil companies. He swallows the global warming theory as fact, unquestioning in "U.S. Commits To Talks Of 'Greenhouse,' " 6-13, as the EPA's Reilly announces a global workshop schedule, quoting an environmentalist as complaining that Reilly's timetable is too slow. "U.S. Willing to Speed Talks on Global Warming," 11-21, is a perfunctory update. His work from China was far better. "Chinese Entrepreneurs Expect Customers to Return," 6-18, details the quick-fix optimism on China's entrepreneurial side after the crackdown: " 'There are too many of us to change policy now,' said Xiao Liu, 26, who owns a small restaurant at the foot of Beijing's historic Front Gate." Arresting, "Student Leaders Elude Police In New Chinese Underground," 6-24, he paints a vivid portrait, with on-the-run detail, as the students stay a step ahead of their hunters. "The Crackdown's Cost," 7-9, is lively on Western business prospects in Shanghai: "No one is planning to walk away from investments here. Foreign firms have sunk $2 billion here in the past decade and have no choice but to

nervously protect their equity and continue operations. But foreign companies are reevaluating plans to expand ongoing ventures. . .and with billions of dollars in credit lines dried up, projects in the pipeline are in limbo."

Welles, Chris. *BusinessWeek.* (★ ★)
Senior writer. When he can keep his dramatic flamboyance under control, Welles is quite palatable, providing reliably steady coverage on the Street, and related issues. He's much better than the portfolio we saw from him this year, though, and should have taken up the slack left by Anthony Bianco, still off writing his Wall Street opus. A smart, compact overview, "Just How Corrupt Is Wall Street?" 1-9, doesn't quite answer the question, but offers insights calmly and reasonably in the wake of SEC indictments, and one then-pending for Drexel's Michael Milken. "Drexel's Deal With the Feds: How Much Will It Hurt?" 2-6, is well written but cold potatoes — nothing much but a rehash of old info and analysis. He pens a workmanlike summary on the Milken situation, "The U.S. vs. Milken: Now the Last Act Begins," 4-10, particularly notable for his assessment of the strength of the SEC's case, concluding that a "hard-fought trial" is fitting and, more than likely, to follow. He explores the burgeoning gambling activities in the U.S. — mostly legal — and some of the mind-boggling electronic fun and games in store for the future, in an in-depth, nicely-written cover, "America's Gambling Fever," 4-24, his best line quoting an expert on compulsive gambling imagining a Cincinnati kid saying, "Bet my allowance on the Bengals." He captures the scaling back of Rupert Murdoch, "Even Rupert Murdoch Has His Limits," with Ronald Grover and Richard Melcher 10-2, cautionary, but compactly analytic, not writing off the media giant by any means. But it's back to doom and gloom in "Insurers Under Siege," co-authored by Christopher Farrell cover 8-21, as the team relates dramatic tales of woe from the insurance industry, projecting that the current weakness will be extended out indefinitely, socialized insurance is on the way, etc.

Wessel, David. *The Wall Street Journal.* (★)
Washington. Adequate in rewriting press releases on the economy, Wessel needs some heavy-duty seasoning to catch up with the pack on the national economic beat. In "Economy Rose 0.3% Last Month; Strong Production of Cars, Trucks Cited," 1-9, he gets the relevant figures, pulling them together with not-so-great analysis, giving little indication as to where the economy will go. He mildly amuses in an A-hed, "At Present Rate, 'Meaner, Tougher' Would Be a Relief," 1-19, on the adoption of Peggy Noonan's/George Bush's "kinder, gentler" phrase into the popular culture, that's neither very funny nor substantive, an opportunity for real satire blown. "Treasury Department Calls About-Face On Capital Gains 'Generally Consistent,' " 2-13, adequately reports the differences inside Treasury over revenue feedback. He may know something in "Bush Takes Aim At Tax Breaks For Companies," 7-11, but he doesn't tell us here, a cursory look on what specifically Bush and Ways & Means would close up, but still spouting all kinds of figures as to how much closing these holes would bring in. More detailed, "Debate on IRA's Centers on Whether Tax Break Should Be Immediate of Put Off Till Retirement," 10-27, he gets most of the pros and cons, but lacks tidy organization, with important material on back-loaded IRAs coming very late in article. "Seeking Better Prices, Firms Haggle A Lot, Affect Inflation Rate," 4-14, is a dumb market story that could be written any day or year: "Such haggling between supplier and buyer, repeated countless times a day across the country, will help determine whether the annual rate bumps along at today's 4 1/2% to 5% or zooms back toward the double-digit misery of the early 1980s.." Nonsense. A "man the lifeboats" mentality is evident in an "Outlook" column, "If a Recession Hits, Is the U.S. Prepared for It?" 4-17, Wessel displaying classic *Journal* DC bureau thinking: half of fifty economists say mild recession is possible so therefore we have a half empty glass, beginning dramatically with "The U.S. may be about as well prepared for the next recession as Exxon was for the Valdez oil spill. It's none too soon to begin reviewing economic contingency plans. . .The betting is the downturn will be mild. But economists' track record in forecasting the severity of oncoming recessions hardly inspires confidence." All ashore that's going ashore. His "Counting the Homeless Will Tax the Ingenuity of 1990 Census Takers," 11-14, is trivial stuff, unworthy of the P. 1 slot. We do learn the census cost will be $2.6 billion, up 70% over 1980's enumeration even after an inflation adjustment, but Wessel doesn't tell us why.

White, Joseph B. *The Wall Street Journal.* (★ ½)
Detroit. Following Jacob Schlesinger's hard act on the auto beat, White is competent, smart, but doesn't yet have Schlesinger's consistency in dealing with several dimensions of a story at once. He does cover several angles in "Maker of Yugos Aims at New Tack With Plan to Buy Part of Importer," 1-10, effectively detailing the ins-and-outs of Zavodi Cverna Zastava's struggles to retain its opening in the U.S. market, but misses the drama, as buyers tend to equate the Yugo with the Edsel. He tells his story well in "Highway Wreck: Fruehauf, Overloaded with Buy-Out Debt, Will Be Dismembered," 3-29, an example of excess in an LBO deal. Teamed with Paul Ingrassia in "Auto Anxiety: Debate over Pollution and Global Warming Has Detroit Sweating," 5-4, the pair provides solid coverage, culling good quotes from both sides on the current emission standards debate. He misses the point in "Car Wars: After a Brief Pause, Japanese Auto Makers Gain on Detroit Again," 5-23, sliding over the crucial distinction between cars made in Japan and cars made by "Japanese car companies" inside the U.S., usually in joint ventures with U.S. car companies. "Auto Makers Drive Into a Mess as Plants Expand and Sales Fall," co-authored by Bradley A. Stertz 7-28, is good piece that provides a snapshot of where the auto industry stands after seven years of expansion, pointing to what appears to be a turn for the worse for the industry. Standard, "Oldsmobile Plans Buy-Back Program For 1990 Models," 9-8, on Olds' return policy, sounds like a rewritten press release on the newest GM sales gimmick, not up to Doron P. Levin's same day account in the *NYT.* His "Detroit's Misery May Have No Company," 11-29, is superior business journalism, with a riveting lead that goes on to briskly explain why the Big 3 are slumping while the economy is not.

Wilford, John Noble. *The New York Times.* (★ ★ ★)
Science. The veteran Pulitzer winner, Wilford impressed us with his range this year, able to produce pieces on widely difficult subjects overnight, doing so in a plain American accent we can understand, rarely getting tangled in technical jargon. He summarizes the developments admirably in "Fusion Furor: Science's Human Face," 4-24, after the Pons-Fleischmann announcement, and contains little gems like the fact that Jones says his notebooks confirm that he was working in the field before he heard Pons was, that Pons' acclamation at the American Chemical Society meeting reflected the fact that "one of their own had made good, it seemed. . ." and that the 1927 Swedish patent application that seems to anticipate the Pons-Fleischmann experiment had been distributed by Brigham Young officials. He provides exquisite detail in "U.S. And Soviets Quietly Team Up To Explore Space," 5-8, a P. 1 story about the cooperation accomplished and projected due to "the new openness in Soviet society and warmer political relations between the two superpowers." He expends considerable effort in "New Clues Emerge in Mystery of Planetary Rings," 6-27, an enjoyable "get ready for Neptune" piece. In "The New Priorities: Closer Looks at Venus, Mars and Jupiter," 8-27, we get a general survey of plans and prospects for planetary science, deftly penned. He's straightforward in his reporting but rhapsodic in his prose in "Shuttle Launched After Delay and Galileo is Sent to Jupiter," 10-19, on another shuttle launch, a nice touch: "It was last seen a hundred miles out over the Atlantic as a tiny sparkling crystal vanishing in the blue." But he's blah in "Space Failure: U.S. Partnership Fades," 3-30, a non-"News Analysis" based on failure of Russian unmanned probes to a Martian moon, no more than a review of Soviet failures in the past, padded out with statements from a most unlikely cast of experts. Richard Kerr of *Science* did this better.

Wrubel, Robert. *FW.* (★ ★ ★)
West Coast bureau chief, Los Angeles. Another of the standouts at the weekly, Wrubel evinces a healthy skepticism in his reports, asking pertinent and sharp questions that add zest. He presents a good roundup on GM's success in Europe, "No Pain, No Gain," 1-24, very well conceived on how the car company did it, although we'd like to have known where they need to go from here as Japan invades the market, or an analysis of how they could do it stateside. In "Silver Lining," 3-21, he's smartly bullish on James Morgan and Applied Materials if not necessarily the semiconductor industry, asking, after explaining Morgan's gung-ho attitude in the face of a downturn, "Is he nuts?" Wrubel then presents all the relevant figures and

interpretations to show that he's not. Part of the "Ethics" cover, he's astute in pinning down the problems inherent in creating an ethical defense industry, "Addicted to Fraud?" 6-27: "The underlying problem, though, is the economics of the business. The defense industry is a one-customer market in which the customer spends money in chunks ranging from a few hundred dollars to tens of billions. Competition has been contrived, at best. The same handful of major defense suppliers has been around for years, with certain contractors being given a *de facto* monopoly on specific technologies and weapons, such as General Dynamics and its M-1 tank, or Northrop and its B-1 bomber." In a breezy, confident snapshot, "Cliff Function," 8-8, he predicts Rockwell International's CEO Don Beall is one to watch, as he proves Wall Street critics wrong, there is life after the B-1B bomber. More on the defense industry, "Showdown at the World's Arms Bazaar," 9-19, a 10 Best nomination from his editors, details the worldwide shiftings and restructurings in the global defense market, as subject to laws of supply and demand as any other product, a complete and insightful presentation. A 10 Best nomination from our editors, "Le Defi Mickey Mouse," 10-17, is bullish on prospects for the European Disneyland, and Wrubel provides all the detail we need to agree with that assessment, appropriately concluding that the European deal is "Another coup for the mouse that soared."

Zachary, G. Pascal. *The Wall Street Journal.* (★ ★)
San Francisco. Off to a flying start in the shoes Brenton Schlender left behind, Zachary seems very promising, displaying a nice touch for sorting out the gossip from the relevant information that enlivens his reports. "Next Inc. to Receive Canon Financing, Marketing Help," 6-9, is quick but sharp on the new Steve Jobs pairing to sell Next in Japan. He recaps the recent troubles at Sun in "Sun Microsystems Slump Has Endurance," 8-11, well developed, but he needs some positive analysis to lift credibility. "Toshiba Agrees to Buy Diasonic's Imaging Division," 8-24, would have been a routine acquisition story in other hands, but Zachary uses his knowledge of Silicon Valley to enhance this into an intriguing little piece about Japanese investment. One point he catches is that the executive running Toshiba U.S. is an alumnus of Diasonic, the company he is buying a division from. Perceptive, he pulls many Valley opinions to give perspective to the long-awaited introduction of Apple's latest, "Apple To Unveil Portable MacIntosh That Already Gets Mixed Reviews," 9-13, that isn't a laptop, too bulky to sit on a lap or airplane tray table, and the price is bulky too (starting at $5,800). "At Apple Computer Proper Attire Includes A Muzzle," 10-6, is a zesty zinger that was sure to cause furrowed brows and frantic phone calls at Apple. It's been reported plenty of other places that Apple is imposing secrecy standards, including funny posters and videos. But Zachary goes further and blasts the results: "Apple's campaign may win awards for cuteness, but probably not for effectiveness. Some suspect the program may even be backfiring." Zachary's move from the San Jose *Mercury-News* has been an important addition for the *WSJ.*

FOREIGN CORRESPONDENTS

Anderson, Harry. *Newsweek.* (★)
This veteran journalist takes responsibility for assembling reports from the field, sharing bylines with the various foreign correspondents at the weekly, but the editors give him primary responsibility for the final product and so do we. "And Now, It's George's Turn," 4-17, is one of those multiple-bylined efforts that diffuses the sense of which reporter deserves praise and which does not. Anderson's byline appears at the top, so he gets some credit for putting together, in a coherent manner, the varied bureau reports on the administration's emerging perspective for a new approach on conventional arms control. Khomeini's rise to power and rule is summarized in "The End of the Khomeini Era," 6-12, without much of a forward look as to what is ahead in Iran. "Gorbomania in Germany," with Fred Coleman 6-26, is succinct on Gorbachev's visit to West Germany: "longer on symbolism than substance," the Soviet leader "presented no new initiative on arms control," and "offered no new hope for reunification of the two Germanys." "The Shock Wave Has Come From Below," with Carroll Bogert 7-31, maintains clear focus on the causes and possible effects of a strike by Soviet coal miners for better working conditions. A picture of the economic and political problems facing Gorbachev is sketched in "Crises Around The Clock," with Carroll Bogert 8-7, but the vista is so broad we don't get sufficient, specific detail. The struggle of various competing political forces in Poland is put into the context of growing economic crisis in "Poland Pays the Price," with Anne Applebaum 8-14, a good mix of analysis and reporting.

Ash, Timothy Garton. *The Spectator.* (★ ★ ★ ½)
Foreign editor. One of the most astute observers of the East European scene, even Ash had to rush to keep up with the pace and depth of the transformations on this beat. He's sound with his analysis on the current state of the Iron Curtain in "Safe Exit From Yalta," 1-14, as the Soviet empire in Eastern Europe continues to disintegrate. Noting that "The frontier between Austria and Hungary is less of an iron curtain than that between Czechoslovakia and Poland," he builds a case for using West Germany as an attraction for any Central European states that, some day, may leave the Soviet orbit. "Knocking on the Wall," 1-28, seemed solid at the time — the Berlin Wall isn't going to disappear because it's not in the interest of the East German government to let it topple. But more important is the fresh information Ash provided here that helped provide some clues as to what indeed would happen when East Germany did ease travel restrictions — 1.6 million East Germans under age sixty-five went to the West last year; most returned. On West Germany's fortieth anniversary, he puts German *angst* in context with "The Restless Republic," 4-1: "Germany without worry would be like France without wine: unthinkable." He's persuasive that the resurgence of German nationalism is less ominous than many assert it to be. "Sold Down the Danube," 4-29, is clever on how communism in Hungary is becoming "capitalism" as "communist bosses become capitalist bosses." He provided one of the most intelligent reports on the elections in Poland with "Poland: The First Campaign," 5-13, giving attention to nuances initially overlooked by others: it's not Solidarity vs. the government, but all sorts of opposition groups vs. the government; the Church is *not* backing Solidarity, but supporting rival "Christian Democratic" candidates. In "Communism Gives Up the Ghost," 5-27, he takes on the question "Why is communism failing *everywhere* in the world — and why aren't people talking about 'the third way' anymore?" — with sweeping, persuasive analytics and a firm conclusion: "There can be few, if any, moments in history when one set of ideas (i.e., democracy and capitalism) has so thoroughly routed its rivals across so vast a field." He updates the outcome of Poland's elections in "The Shock of Victory," 6-10, with an intimate picture of the voters' delight in repealing the past fifty years: "It would require a poet to describe the deep, almost sensual satisfaction on people's faces as they crossed out name after name on the long, complicated ballot papers." He cuts a sharp profile of East Germany's Egon Krenz in "Yesterday's Man," 10-28, that is persuasive on how short the tenure of this Honecker clone will be. "After the Party," 11-18, unfolds as three stories, the Berlin one flowing into the German one which flows into the European one. Ash does a splendid job here making the case that Europe's map will be redrawn in the wake of the dramatic changes in Berlin.

Asman, David. *The Wall Street Journal.* (★ ★ ★)
"Americas" column editor. Asman's column is an outstanding feature of the *WSJ*, with the contributors always well-selected for the timeliness and acute perceptions of their reports. Asman's contributions are also similarly rich. A fine dispatch from San Salvador, "U.S. Policy Costs Salvadorans Dearly," 3-17, reports the American embassy is rooting for the Christian Democrats, although their corruption and inefficient socialism points to an ARENA victory as this party pledges free-market reforms. "Nicaragua's Second-in-Command Dishes Out First-Class PR," 3-24, reads lively with Asman's meeting with *commandante* Sergio Ramirez, whose newfound faith in the marketplace "doesn't square with well-publicized Sandinista attacks on retailers and wholesalers who have tried to sell goods outside the government's well-controlled outlets." Asman gives a fairly good picture of how producers there view economic conditions. "Central American Peace Initiative: What Has Arias Wrought?" 3-31, contains some information on tax reforms in Costa Rica (a cut in marginal rates from 50% to 30%). "Man in the Middle of Drug Trafficking," 9-25, makes a reasonable case that Castro's drug trials in Cuba may be an attempt to isolate the country's involvement in trafficking to the one area where the U.S. already has irrefutable evidence of Cuban involvement. "Chile's Prosperity Doesn't Translate Into Votes," 11-17, updates us on the flagging campaign of free-marketer Hernan Buchi despite the solid economic health of the country, Asman laying out the context for reasons why. "Carnival '89: Brazil's Elections," 11-15, has a wealth of information on a wealth of issues — the pressure on the parties to represent more than corporate-statist interests, tax policies, a strong disposition against protectionism by the chief economic thinker in a major leftist party, new thinking against price controls and the protected status of Brazilian auto production. And we learn that the new constitution enfranchised 16-year-olds, hiking the number of eligible voters from 82 million to 140 million. We had to read a dozen different dispatches from other journalists here to come across all the info packed into this report. No reporting trip to Mexico by Asman, though, left us disappointed.

Baker, Stephen. *BusinessWeek.* (★ ½)
Mexico. No one really got deeply inside the Mexican economy in this year of *Salinastroika,* but Baker's dispatches more often than not contained accurate reports on the transformations taking place there. While keeping abreast of these developments, he didn't display much resourcefulness by digging into unexplored areas of the country's economic policies. He adeptly summarizes the "to-the-death" struggle between Mexico's President Carlos Salinas de Gortari and the Godfather of the oil workers' union in "Salinas Declares War on 'The Maximum Chief' of Oil," 1-23. He reports Salinas' intent to use a softer approach with the telephone workers' union, having sharpened his teeth on the oil workers' leadership, advancing his plans to privatize chunks of the state telephone monopoly in "Salinas Goes After Another Monster: The Phone System," 3-6. "One Tough Hombre," with Elizabeth Weiner 4-3, an effort by the Mexico bureau that produces a starkly drawn outlook piece on whether Salinas can remake Mexico, with an effective cross section of opinion within Mexico and the U.S. "Why Salinas Must Tame the Teachers," 5-15, is a decent outline, but in its brevity leaves a lot out of an obviously complicated situation, wildcat teachers' strikes showing dissatisfaction with wages and Salinas. Baker tries hard in "Down and Out in Latin America," 7-10, but the subject is larger than he can handle: why Latin American economies are in a shambles and what needs to be done. Its mostly old sombrero, relating to the need to spur private foreign investment. "Charlie Crowder Sees Utopia, and It's a Border Town," 7-31, is fascinating on the developer who wants to create a new "*maquiladora* metropolis" straddling the Mexico-U.S. border, where he owns a total of more than 50,000 acres, with good analysis of what will make or break the project. "And in this Corner Coin Box: An All-Sports Daily," with David Lieberman 8-21, describes Mexican media mogul Emilio Azcarraga's plans for an all-sports tabloid in the U.S., with a decent look at the competition — and the willfulness of "the domineering 58-year-old, known as El Tigre." "Now Mexico Looks Like a Fiesta For Investors," 8-28, respectably summarizes the outlook and the obstacles to foreign investment in Mexico, with a focus on dilapidated infrastructure and its energy-system monopoly. "Salinas Strikes Before the Miners Can," with Adrienne Bard 9-4, is competent on

Salinas' shutdown of the huge Cananea copper mine and what benefits accrue from the action, with a fine observation on the President added in: Salinas "has a knack for beating his enemies to the punch." A pithy "Free-For-All for Carmakers South of the Border," 10-16, covers another dramatic move in Mexico — the elimination of local-content rules for auto production and the opening of the Mexican market to imports.

Bangsberg, P. T. *The Journal of Commerce.* (★ ★ ★)
Hong Kong correspondent. We've been identifying him every year as the best business reporter in Southeast Asia, and there's no reason to suggest otherwise this year. Bangsberg is way ahead of the pack with "Asean Renews Bid For Economic Clout," 12-30-88, reporting that these countries, discussing the need for closer coordination in the wake of burgeoning economic relations with the U.S., are finding Japan as the catalyst for closer economic ties: "This is a supreme irony considering that is in effect what Japan sought to do by force of arms in the 1940s with its visions of a Greater East Asian Co-prosperity Sphere." He picks up signs of a rebound in Asian electronics sectors in "S. Korea, Singapore Forecast Recovery in Computer Sector," 2-9, with details on the plans for heavy investment by the industries. "Malaysia to Require Foreign-Owned Banks To Incorporate There," 3-31, describes the intention of this important legislation, including some background on the country's New Economic Policy which had frightened off many investors. He is constantly working the region for economic news, and provides a steady stream of reports that come off corporate or government press releases. Yet he generally folds appropriate background, context or other critical details into the dispatch, as with "Second Philippines Mine for Sale," 4-21, expanding on the government's attempt to sell off assets acquired when previous owners failed to meet debt obligations. In the wake of turmoil in China, Bangsberg fills us in on the consequences for HK's economy with "Hong Kong Reaction to Upheaval in China May Hit U.S. Importers," 6-12. The key information is packed up front, and Bangsberg then provides a broader picture of HK's economic problems. "Cabinet Changes In Taiwan Stun World Observers," 7-21, is crisp reporting on the reshuffle, with Bangsberg clueing us into future policy as he delivers up mini-profiles of the new ministers. He rounds up informed reaction from analysts and businessmen in the region to Deng Xiaoping's departure in "Power Struggle Feared in China," 11-10, carefully working his own analysis into the report. Bangsberg reports no one faction has consolidated control, which leads to wildly contradictory decisions on the economy.

Barnard, Bruce. *The Journal of Commerce.* (★ ★ ½)
Brussels correspondent. Barnard provides fine reports on the European Economic Community, staying especially alert for trends that provide clues as to what may emerge on the continent in 1992. He's quick on catching the shifts that portend movement away from free trade. He's appropriately skeptical on the EC's pledge that a single market in 1992 won't create "Fortress Europe" in "EC Trading Partners Are Wary Despite a Pledge of Openness," 1-3. Barnard reports that as the EC "dismisses talk of fears of Fortress Europe as completely groundless and mere scaremongering, it is tightening its anti-dumping rules, toying with suspect reciprocal trade deals and mulling tougher local content regulations for foreign-owned plants in Europe." He provides straight reporting on the new "local content" rules in "EC Announces New Chip Rules to Gain Plants," 2-7, making it clear that Japan and U.S. chip suppliers will have to build new plants in the community to ensure free market access. "Asian Exporters Face Wrath of EC Traders," 4-10, is an information-rich news analysis on problems arising from the Asian NIC's attempts to divert exports from the U.S. market to Europe. Information is also packed into "Rails Poised to Recapture Glory," 6-6, where we learn that Europe's railways, all state-owned and in dire financial straits, are now very attractive to investors as the 1992 single-market perspective reinvigorates their prospects. An analytical "EC to Ask Japan To Curb Car Sales," 9-29, provides one of the best overviews we saw on the issue of Japanese car imports into Europe. Barnard gives the EC credit for a determination to create a level playing field in the post-92 car market, but reports that in any case the winners aren't likely to be domestic manufacturers, but their hard-charging Japanese rivals. "Mega-Carriers Could Derail EC Air Deregulation

Efforts," 10-10, gives sharp reconnaissance on the EC's plan to dislodge the airline cartel that has dominated Europe's skies and the subsequent shakeouts and new structures emerging as deregulation looms.

Battiata, Mary. *The Washington Post.* (★)
Warsaw, moving midyear from Nairobi. Nothing really distinguishing coming off her pen while in Africa the first part of the year, she had the advantage of being posted to Poland in the midst of that nation's tumultuous times where she's quickly getting her footing. "African Nations Cold-Shoulder Exiled Idi Amin," 1-15, updates us on the former Ugandan dictator, with details on what his trip from Saudi Arabia to Zaire was all about. Becoming a *persona non grata* in Saudi Arabia, no other country is eager to receive Amin, she reports, but this news was not worth the front-page placement it received. "Somalia Fights Charges of Human Rights Abuse," 1-25, is satisfactory as an adequate roundup, providing sufficient background and enough of the big picture there. She provides a one-dimensional report on a complicated issue, merely rewriting press releases in "3 Cardinals Tell Poles to Honor Pact," 9-4, in which a statement by the archbishops of Lyons, Paris, and Brussels directly challenges Poland's primate, Josef Cardinal Glemp, to move a Carmelite convent from the grounds of Auschwitz. We get some nice inside flavor in a report on the extraordinary proceedings of the new Polish parliament in "Solidarity Tells How It Will Cure Poland," 9-12: "Like surgeons contemplating a nasty case of gangrene, leaders of Poland's proposed Solidarity-dominated government have spent the past few days explaining how they intend to cut out the rot without killing the patient....Under the new government's plan, everything from behemoth, state-owned steel mills to the drab, government-run corner drugstore will be auctioned off to private owners." Returning again to the Auschwitz controversy, she doesn't get below the surface with "Glemp Concedes Mistakes," 9-25, the information inferior to what some wire service reports contained. We get better depth in an importantly selected topic — how fares the old Polish Trotskyist Jacek Kuron in his new job as Labor and Social Security Minister — in "TV Talks Try to Reconcile Poles to Pains of Transition," 10-25. Battiata persuades us that his may be the most difficult job in the new government, as "the abstract longings for democracy and prosperity that produced Solidarity's landslide in the June elections meet the difficult reality of overhauling a collapsing, overextended, centrally planned economy."

Bering-Jensen, Henrik. *Insight.* (★ ★ ½)
After a few fumbles early in the year, this top-notch analyst recouped, but not quite back up to the outstanding level of past years. Surely one of the magazine's most likely candidates for production of a definitive cover story on the great transformations in the Soviet Bloc, he composed no such picture this year. He frustrates us with "Palme Assassination Still Smolders," 12-19-88, as it seems he can't decide whether he's taking an in-depth look at the Olaf Palme assassination and the investigation surrounding it or just summarizing a book on the subject. There's a story somewhere in "Becoming Smarter on Intelligence," 12-26-88, but Bering-Jensen doesn't produce it in this weak report, keying off a single study by an obscure group. He doesn't have a lot to hang a story on with "Paper Trail of Tyrants' Bootprints," 1-9, but he does provide a fascinating look — via a recently surfaced letter and interview — at the inner workings of the Polish government prior to the imposition of martial law in 1981. He's back on the track, with a reinvigorated style and tight writing in "Kohl's Prestige First Casualty of Qaddafi's Pharmaceutical," 2-13, on the political fallout over the sale of military weapons and technology by West German firms to communist and terrorist governments. A first-rate job, Bering-Jensen packs in much information on the depth of German involvement and the damage to Helmut Kohl's prestige. His analytical powers reappear in a sharp "An Election Adds Up to Red Faces," 4-17, a wrap-up on the Soviet elections that saw surprising opposition to Old Guard candidates emerge. Bering-Jensen underscores the pickle Gorbachev has gotten himself into by underestimating the democratic fervor in many of the SSRs. Among his better efforts is the cover story "Revolution That Lost its Head," 7-10, a terrific idea melded into a well-written, concise history of the French revolution and Terror in which he interjects interpretations and arguments

by historians. He delivers smart, compact news analysis in "Thatcher Takes Labor Party Punch", 7-24, an analytic of Margaret Thatcher and EC maneuvering. Though deficient on monetary disputes, he shines with a great closing graph: "Asked at the post-summit news conference what it felt to be described by President Francois Mitterrand of France as the Brake of Europe, Thatcher shot back that 'this was a bit rich' coming from someone who 'has scarcely got into the car yet.' That handbag still packs a mean punch." "A Turning Point," 9-11, on the victory of Solidarity adviser Tadeusz Mazowiecki in becoming Poland's prime minister, handily outlines the road to his confirmation and the obstacles he faces, a compact summary. "Freedom Chain," 9-11, is also a good summary of rapidly moving events within the East Bloc, a focus on the tremors in the Baltic states, with fine detail on Estonia.

Bernstein, Jonas. *Insight.* (★)
A second full year under his belt, Bernstein still isn't using all cylinders, his reporting a mixture of sputtering misfires and smooth-running stories. "A Freedom Fight Deep in Africa," 12-19-88, is just such a mixed effort. Within this cover story, "The New Game in Angola" section provides intelligent analysis of weaponry, tactics, diplomatic initiatives involved in the country's civil war, and we learn also that there are many Cubans with dual Angolan-Cuban citizenship who aren't being counted among the numbers of Cubans stationed in Angola. But the story wanders, with information on Jonas Savimbi's UNITA somewhat jumbled. The reporting on relations between Namibia and Angola in this feature is better. He leaves too many questions unasked and unanswered in "Rival Factions Pave the Way to Unity Under One Umbrella," 1-9, on the current situation in Zimbabwe. Economic problems are not addressed until late in the report. There's no information on the situation of the country's 5,000 white farmers, and we never get a clear picture of what the grievances of the dissidents are. We get solid foreign correspondence under a blah headline in "A Party to the Destruction: Unsound Building Practices," 1-16, a nicely organized report on construction that contributed to loss of life in the recent earthquake in the Soviet Union, with Bernstein ferreting out the details. He paints too sanguine a picture on Venezuela in a superficial "President's Pragmatism Eases Fears," 3-13. Bernstein clings to regional policy experts who offer no observations about the country's economy. There's no insight here, riots sweeping Caracas almost simultaneously with this rosy report. There's nice attention to detail in "Readying Against the Odds for a Showdown over Noriega," 4-10, on the upcoming Panamanian elections. The report flows smoothly from one thought to another, with Bernstein effectively capturing the emotion of the situation. Routine summarizing on China, "A Pro-Democracy Uprising Uncovers Mass Discontent," 6-12, does go an extra step in at least rounding up observations from area specialists who challenge a budding conventionality that democracy is somehow alien to the Chinese. He has trouble finding a focus in "A Haven for Immigrants Opens Its Borders to Its Own," 8-7, employing a long historical lead and taking forever to get to the point in this story about Turks fleeing repression in Bulgaria. "The Treaty that Tore People Apart," 8-28, is confused and muddled on the 50th anniversary of the German-Soviet Non-Aggression Treaty. He begins with an overview of several books on the topic, throws in a couple of anecdotes of Communists betrayed to the Nazis, then ends with more on *glasnost.* It sounds as if it should hold together somehow, but it doesn't.

Bobinski, Christopher. *Financial Times.* (★ ★ ½)
Warsaw correspondent. Bobinski is a very reliable and thorough reporter, but more than that, a very sensible one, keeping speculation in restraint and able to work in the most tumultuous currents without losing focus. He gets his arms around several important angles in "Poland to Cut Forces by 'Tens of Thousands,' " 1-4, a fine strategic report on the country's plan to shed "tens of thousands" of personnel in an effort to reduce defense spending and increase efficiency. Although, this is on top of a 15,000 troop cut, the reductions are not expected to make any difference in the country's combat strength. We appreciated his calm assessment of Poland's political situation following the government-Solidarity arrangement as reported in "Now, Solidarity's Difficulties Begin," 4-6. While not necessarily sanguine, Bobinski seemed to better tap the popular reaction and sentiment in the country than other, more alarmist accounts we

saw. We get an insider's look at Solidarity's electoral strategy in a refreshing "Poland's Free Vote," 4-13, with Bobinski sorting out the issues and writing this up as a report on a party campaign. The analytic is sharp in "A Political Void Opens," 6-10, on the road ahead in Poland, as Bobinski reports that worsening economic conditions combined with Solidarity's electoral triumph will feed intense pressures for radical solutions. "Man Spurred by Challenge of Solving Poland's Debt," 9-13, is a very informative profile of new Finance Minister Leszek Balcerowicz, a "pragmatist" in the face of an economy that is over 70% state-owned. Bobinski fills us in on the outline of plans Balcerowicz and others in the economic leadership are working with. "Polish PM Talks With Gorbachev at Kremlin," 11-25, covers the essentials of the meeting, highlighting the fact that Gorbachev broke a long tradition of allegiance to communist parties in the Soviet Bloc when he met for an hour and forty minutes with Polish PM Mazowiecki.

Borowiec, Andrew. *The Washington Times.* (★ ★ ★)
Chief European correspondent. What we most appreciate in his reporting is the off-beat angle he comes up with, often clueing us into a fissure that others overlook. Borowiec picks up on the emerging political tone in France with "Mitterand Breaks Silence, Urges Reforms," 1-3, as French socialists seem no longer to believe in socialism. Borowiec displays skillful analytics in "Experts See Signs that Gorbachev Is Phasing Out Brezhnev Doctrine," 4-6 tying together numerous fascinating developments of political self-assertion in Eastern Europe with the reasonable speculation that Gorbachev may renounce the right to military intervention if he gets "something" from the United States. He identifies a new Soviet approach to the Middle East, stressing moderation rather than confrontation following Jim Baker's trip to Moscow, with "Soviets Turn New Face Toward Middle East," 5-16. Borowiec writes with a deep knowledge of Eastern Europe in his background, but he seems too pessimistic on the prognosis for Poland in "Bleeding From Ballot Wounds, Polish System Slow to Die," 6-12. We get good reporting with appropriate attention to background and context in "Gorbachev Snubs Bush Proposal, Lauds Dialogue," 7-6, on the Soviet leader's Paris visit where he "spoke of reforms in the Soviet Union as 'positive but complex, fragile and subject to risks,' claimed that communism was not in crisis but being revitalized and reiterated the freedom of action for Poland and Hungary." The assessment is sober, with sufficient detail in "Pole's Journey Full of Pits and Traps," 8-21, on the challenges for Poland's Prime Minister-designate Tadeusz Mazowiecki, though nothing above most of the accounts on the same theme. Though not conclusive, "Communist Sabotage May Jeopardize Polish Experiment," 8-31, offers a skeptical perspective of an uncertain atmosphere: "We are witnessing creation of two Polands — one represented by Solidarity and its supporters, and the other consisting of 1,200,000 members of the Communist nomenklatura which still controls the administration and economy." In "At a Perilous Time, Solidarity Breaks Into Factions," 9-5, Borowiec is again alert to ominous developments in Poland, although the evidence again isn't sufficiently conclusive. Reporting on the inner tensions within Solidarity, Borowiec gives voice to alarms that it's in the grip of a major rift that is destroying the pro-Catholic, anti-communist appeal that attracted its first supporters in 1980.

Borrus, Amy. *BusinessWeek.* (★ ½)
Tokyo correspondent. Her reporting is decent, respectable but not penetrating, as she's only beginning to approach the power curve here. "Takeshita Talks Political Reform — But Doesn't Sound Convincing," 1-23, is an interesting summary, as far as it goes, on the roots of corruption in the Japanese political system coming off the Recruit Co. scandal. She incorporates potential effects of this scandal into a good report on what the subsidiaries of giant Nippon Telegraph and Telephone are up to in developing international business lines with "Japan's Telephone Colossus Takes Its First Baby Steps Overseas," 3-13, although the facts and figures are slightly dizzying in places. Borrus' sketch of the latest developments in the scandal is decent, with a focus on the growing political threats to former PM Nakasone and current PM Takeshita, in "The Recruit Scandal Bubbles to the Top," 3-20. Profiles of entrepreneurs can be dull, but Borrus injects this strategic look at Harunori Takakashi with lively zip, "Meet the World's Busiest Man — Oops, You Missed Him," with Dori Jones Yang, Stephen Hutcheon and Peter Finch 4-17. This whiz

does three deals (at three tables) in one restaurant in three hours, and has amassed property all over the world, $7 billion worth. Despite reductions of import restrictions and increased purchases of U.S.-made goods, East Asian trading nations believe they will be targeted for unfair trade practices on April 30 by the U.S. Trade Representative. Borrus gives a merely adequate summary of this issue in "The Asians Are Bracing for a Trade Shoot-Out," with Laxmi Nakarmi, Dirk Bennett and Paul Magnusson 5-1. She's unconvincing in "For Japan, the Day of Reckoning On Trade Has Finally Arrived," 5-22, projecting that Japan's bilateral relationship with the U.S. won't suffer if Super 301 provisions of the U.S. trade bill are enacted against the country. She kept up a steady watch on Japanese politics and in "Will the Recruit Scandal Just Go Away," 6-12, profiles the short-tenured PM Sosuke Uno, and the disagreeable tasks he faces in upcoming elections and trade negotiations with the U.S. "Japan Inc. Hangs Out a Help Wanted Sign," 7-24, is a detailed eye-opener on Japan's here-and-now labor shortage. The writing is dull, but she does pick up a good, forward-looking theme in "You Know Who Is Flooring It Again," with James Treece 10-9, indicating a Japanese auto export drive may come off their "investment binge in new design technology and capacity." "The Book That's Creating a Firestorm," with Magnusson 10-23, is a once-over-quickly report on the controversial book by Shintaro Ishihara calling upon Japan to assume superpower status and to say "No!" to the U.S.

Boudreaux, Richard. *Los Angeles Times.* (★ ★ ½)
Managua bureau chief. Totally straight, objective reporting from this area of the world was harder to come by this year, but Boudreaux seemed less biased than most others we read. He impressed us with his inclination to get out of the regional capital cities to look for the stories behind the disinformation mills run by the various partisans here. He has a lot of trouble in "Ortega Rejects Talks on 2 Rival Contra Truce Plans," 1-1, with confusing opening paragraphs and the questionable assumption that all of Nicaragua's economic problems can be blamed on the U.S. and its support for the contras. Even if Boudreaux can't put all the pieces together, "The Puzzling Life, Death of Gen. Alvarez," 2-25, is still a worthwhile story as he profiles Gen. Gustavo Alvarez Martinez, former Honduran strongman turned missionary zealot who was killed in a hail of gunfire. The opening is straight out of Gabriel Garcia Marquez: "The day he died, Gustavo Alvarez Martinez awoke before dawn, entered his study and opened a Bible. Spreading his hands over a map of Honduras, he prayed for his people: 'Blessed is the nation whose God is Jehovah.' " There didn't seem to be a whole lot of basis for "Freed Somoza Guards Describe Life in Prison," 3-21, a story on the release from Sandinista prisons of former Somoza guards, whose description of their time behind bars sounded remarkably similar to prison conditions in the U.S. Journalistic scoop or propaganda coup? "Nicaragua Telling Contras Their Chiefs Are Quitting; U.S., Rebel Aides Deny It," 8-12, offers competent coverage of the war of nerves in Nicaragua as the contra leaders struggle to hold their troops together, but lacked a response from the rank and file. "War Shadows Campaigning In Nicaragua," 11-9, was the first story we saw written from a contested area as the pre-election fighting heated up, with Boudreaux doing a fine job of portraying the pressure the political opposition is under, squeezed between two armed forces, and contrasting the political situation today with 1984, the last time that country went to the polls. "So heavy was the crush in some rural precincts this time that two small children standing in line with their mothers died of suffocation." "Security Forces Abused Them, 2 Americans Say," 11-20, a dispatch from San Salvador, never once refers to the FMLN as being Marxist.

Boustany, Nora. *The Washington Post.* (★ ★)
Beirut bureau chief. An evocative writer, Boustany can summon empathy with her lucid and poignant style. But there's strong substance in her reports, and she was acutely perceptive on the critical political shifts within Lebanon all year, particularly attentive to the changes affecting Syria's role. A timely "Radical Palestinians Deny Bomb Role," 1-9, makes a persuasive case that Syrian involvement in the Pan Am 103 atrocity is unlikely. With "Truce Between Rival Shiite Factions Collapses," 1-26, she highlights the dilemma Syria faces in attempting to maintain a

tenuous balance between commitment to its closest Lebanese ally, Amal, and regional affiliation and indebtedness to Iran, the sponsor of Hezbollah. "Syria Works to Mend Ties With Moderate Arab States," 1-18, well-organized analytically, further elaborates on the diplomatic maneuvering as Syria bends and twists to out-flank the PLO's Yasir Arafat and Iraq's Saddam Hussein on the Middle East chessboard. Boustany deserves credit for her effort to counter "world fatigue with the everlasting spectacle of Lebanon's convulsions" with "Fifty Shells a Minute," 4-2, a riveting report on the ordeal of imperiled Lebanese Christians. "An Old War Claims new Victims," 4-12, is an excellently written account of how the Lebanese Christian minority, among whom "there are few who doubt that more apocalyptic days lie ahead for Lebanon," is being galvanized by Lebanese Army chief General Michel Aoun. "Beirut at War: Life Among the Ruins," 4-22, is simply a heart-rending, gripping narrative of sheer human suffering in the war-gutted capital. Boustany surveys the gamut of various factional differences among Christian deputies at the Taif meeting, giving as good as possible a sketch of the specific differences in "Lebanese Christians Debate New Concessions by Syria," 10-22. "President Elected in Lebanon: Aoun Rejects Decision," 11-6, is clear on the weak backing Rene Moawad had as new president in Lebanon, despite support from Syria and its Muslim and Druse allies.

Branigan, William. *The Washington Post.* (★ ★)
Mexico City bureau chief. His reporting on the political side of Mexico's story this year is as sound as ever, but so much of the country's story was located in its economy, where Branigan comes up deficient. "Mexicans Await 'Brady Plan' on Debt, See It Fall Short." 3-28, updates on the attempts of the Salinas government to politicize the debt issue amid the background of Mexico's social and economic pressure cooker, but subsequent economic transformations never received sufficient detail from Branigan. He examined closely the drug-corruption network in the region, beginning with "Mexican Drug Kingpins Recovering From Crackdown After DEA Killing," 12-21-88, which reports on the entrenchment of Colombian drug traffickers in the Mexican state of Jalisco. His reports on the corruption scandals revolving around the 1984 assassination of Manuel Buendia, the country's most widely syndicated columnist, and the indictment of Mexico's former secret police chief for the murder, locate perceptively the potential for this to become a Pandora's box for the administration of President Carlos Salinas de Gortari. "Mexican Writer's Death Linked to Ex-Police Chief," 6-13, provides a very competent account of the details of the case and "New Corruption Charges Emerge In Mexican Case," 6-26, stays abreast of the expanding scandal. He keeps the drug cartels in focus also with his reporting from Panama. "Noriega Opens Banks, Perhaps For Laundering," with Michael Isikoff 1-27, develops the view that the newly-opened Banco Institutional Patria, with Panamanian Defense Forces chief General Manuel Antonio Noriega as president of the board of directors, functions as both a money-laundering operation and as a move to consolidate greater control over the Panamanian economy in Noriega's hands. Juicy with facts "Panamanians Arrest 5 Accused in Drug Ring," 4-2, highlights several quirks and ironies in the current stormy relationship between the United States and the Noriega regime. "Opponents of Noriega Warn of Electoral Fraud," 4-19, surveys pre-election activities in Panama, making the case that an honest election is out of the question. We get a dramatic account of the post-election atrocities in "Panama Invalidates Election; Opposition Leaders Attacked," 5-11, and he draws some somber conclusions in an analytical "After 9 Days of Upheaval, Panama Is Back to Square One," 5-17: "President Bush has explicitly called on Panamanians to overthrow Noriega, but, as was the case last year, Panamanians are still looking to Washington to do the job." Still on the drug trail he offended the government of Belize with a story on drug trafficking there, but "Jungles vs. Jobs In Belize," 10-19, and "Belize's New Leader," 10-19, provide very fine details on where the country's economy is headed amid growing signs that Belize has pulled in the reins on rapid development.

Brauchli, Marcus W. *The Wall Street Journal.* (★ ★)
Tokyo correspondent. With Damon Darlin now heading up the Seoul office, there's a hole in the *Journal*'s Japan coverage. Brauchli seems to be just the man to fill it, turning in an impressive

328

first year here. His reporting holds up well in "Shopping Spree," 4-10, on the new attraction to credit in Japan as a consequence of rising prosperity and more free time, Brauchli working in a colorful sketch of the local loan sharks (*sarakin*). The analytical side, though, is impaired by exclusion of the impact Japan's closed market on affordable housing has in diverting spending into other areas. He is enterprising with an important "Japan Prepares For New Financial Leaders," 5-26, shining the spotlight on three up-and-coming Tokyo finance ministry bureaucrats and what they think about the world. Regarding Koji Kashiwaya, who's about to join the World Bank as vice chairman in charge of debt strategy, we learn that "He is optimistic that the debt crisis can be resolved, and he's fond of pointing out that when he joined the Finance Ministry in 1961, Japan was the world's second-most heavily-indebted country, after India: 'If the total size of the country can expand farther than debt, we don't have to worry about debt.' " We need more of this kind of reporting from Tokyo, direct quotes on what people are thinking. There's colorful flavor in "Japanese Companies Keep Employees Together — Even the Dearly Departed," 7-10, a fascinating report on how Japanese corporate loyalty to the worker extends past his death. "Trading in Tokyo: U.S. Brokerage Firms Operating in Japan Have Mixed Results," 8-16, is adequate, although there isn't a lot of pushing for new information beyond the PR statements made by the heads of these Japanese divisions. "Japanese Seek Low Profile in U.S. Deals," 11-10, is very informative and timely on the fears Japanese investors have about anti-Japanese backlash after a spate of U.S. acquisitions and on the steps they're undertaking to mitigate it.

Brinkley, Joel. *The New York Times.* (★ ½)
Jerusalem bureau chief. Brinkley is obliged by his editors to chronicle and file dispatches on every stone tossed by an Arab at an Israeli every day — or so it seems from the endless stories of that nature on the *intifada* this year. As a consequence there is sometimes a disconcerting mechanical side to his writing. In between the stone-throwing stories, though, we see some marginal improvement from Brinkley this year. "Arafat's Faction Is Said to Refrain From Terrorism," 1-16, handles with balance the shifts in thinking within the Israeli military, and Brinkley is careful not to overplay the implications of the report by the Israeli army that Yasir Arafat's wing of the PLO has not planned or carried out any guerrilla actions in more than two months. We get some useful seesaw angles on the frustration and despair that is appearing among the Israeli officer corps, as in "Israel Reviews Military Tactics, and Sees Only Defiance," 1-29, and "Israel: Mired in the West Bank: The Soldiers," *Magazine* 5-7, which works somewhat on a shock level. However, both lack a special thread around which they're organized. Later in the year, he's in the *Magazine* again, once more on the theme of routine violence between Jew and Palestinian in "Inside the Intifada," 10-29, but no new dimensions are brought out on the brutal cycle. "Israeli Minister Meets Soviet Aide in Cairo This Week," 2-20, satisfies with the basic details plus appropriate, non-speculative treatment of what the trip will involve and what is likely not to occur. Brinkley's best, "Debts Make Israelis Rethink an Ideal: The Kibbutz," 3-5, a penetrating examination on "the end of socialism" in Israel, is splendid foreign correspondence, evocative and insightfully adept. "For West Bank Arabs, Education Has Been Deemed a Criminal Act," 5-8, steers clear of bias or preaching on the Israeli policy of keeping West Bank schools and universities closed to Arabs (excluding 320,000 elementary and high school students and 18,000 college students from almost 2 full academic years). "Pride and Resentment Rising Among Israeli Arabs," 6-18, assembles a fairly good sampling of quotes, set against a "nonsense scenario" by Yitzhak Shamir's Arab affairs advisor, but for such an important topic Brinkley ought to have developed more dimensions.

Brock, David. *Insight.* (★ ★ ½)
Senior editor. On balance, Brock had quite a good year, getting his arms around a couple of the major stories for foreign correspondence. But he bites off too much in "Success Story May Have a Sad End," 12-26-88, an unsuccessful attempt to look at the fate of Latin American democracies. There's not enough information on each country to really illuminate the problem. He provides a well-paced, convincing on-the-surface report on the failures and successes of the

Reagan doctrine in "Consistency Keeps a Policy Alive," 3-13, using observations from a number of commentators on the issue, but an ideological bias seems to intrude, and we're not satisfied overall. We looked high and low all year for reporting on El Salvador that was simply informative and unbiased, and Brock is one of the very few who accomplished that. "An Embattled Nation Back Atop Policy Agenda," 5-15, is a finely honed report on the country as the Arena Party takes over from the Christian Democrats, with all sides getting fair representation. He successfully captures the tension and confusion in Peru with "Impulsive Novelist Rewrites Script for a Queasy Coalition," 7-17, a story on political maneuverings in Peruvian elections. But we're still left wondering what all of this may mean, post-election, in a country with 40 percent inflation per month. Brock masters some solid political economy with "The Theory and Practice of Japan-Bashing," *The National Interest,* Fall. A superb, rigorous examination of the subject, he acknowledges that the picture of Japan being presented by the current "bashers" is far more realistic than past ones, then strongly makes the case their prescriptions for U.S.-Japan relations are disastrously off course.

Brooke, James. *The New York Times.* (★ ★)
Rio de Janeiro bureau chief. A major disappointment for us this year, as we'd looked forward to Brooke taking this post. Former Abidjan bureau chief, Brooke handled all of sub-Saharan Africa north of the RSA as if it were his backyard (four stars in 1988), but Brazil is proving to be more complex, his reporting here moving with abrupt spurts and jagged gyrations. A perceptible, unacceptable bias, for which we criticized him in the 1989 *MediaGuide,* still intruded in his reporting from Africa, as "Angola Inches Toward Capitalism," 2-20, reveals. This report on signs of changes in one of the last strongholds of socialism in Africa includes a disparaging *non sequitur* on UNITA. "Rapid Spread of AIDS Alarms Residents of the Ivory Coast," 3-1, reports that "In busy maternity hospitals, one syringe is used for 30 people." Though we want to know more than he tells us, Brooke at least produces a lot of statistics we haven't seen anywhere else. There is no insight in "For Argentina, Inflation and Rage Rise in Tandem," 6-4, to distinguish this report from the conventional efforts. He's insufficient on the economic policies that brought on a 12,000% annual inflation, quoting a social scientist that Argentina needs "a shock program, increasing government taxes and cutting government spending." We felt satiated with stories telling us how Argentine families cope with hyperinflation, but "A Weary Buenos Aires Family Wonders How to Keep Afloat," 6-18, manages to communicate a feel for the changing numbers. There is new detail in "Peru's Guerrillas Become a Threat to the Capital," 6-12, which reports that the Shining Path guerrillas have control in the cocaine-producing valleys and are now threatening coastal cities with terror, leading to potential civil war. More satisfying detail is worked into "Peruvian Farmers Razing Rain Forest to Sow Drug Crops," 8-13. But this report really needs a forward look to be complete, as we were left uninformed on the intentions of the Peruvian and U.S. governments here. "Cariocas Live for Carnival, but Live With Crime," 10-26, puts Rio's crime problems into the electoral context, providing startling details on the problems. Brooke uses Brazil's debt service demands as a backdrop, but the case is developed strongly. Leading into the election, "inflation leads the list of voter concerns" (100,000% a year, 1% every 20 hours), he reports in "Trying to Outwit Brazil's Inflation," 11-14, although we don't get a word on how the candidates propose to deal with it.

Brooks, Geraldine. *The Wall Street Journal.* (★)
Middle East correspondent. No heavy-duty reporting from Brooks this year, light work predominating in her coverage of the region. There's often a colorful assembly of anecdotal material in her dispatches, but this year she worked in some inexcusable misinformation. She gives us a full-flavored report on the divisive debate in Israel in an A-hed feature, "Israelis Are Divided Over the Meetings Between U.S., P.L.O.," 1-19, employing a wide selection of quotes. Many Israelis, she reports, are troubled about the lack of opposition by some American Jews to U.S.-PLO meeting. Another A-hed feature, "This Iraqi Sect Has a Devilish Time Explaining Itself," 2-2, on the Yezidis, a religious sect in Iraq that worships Malek-Taus (a restored Lucifer),

is a so-so curiosity item. However, Brooks makes the following incredible assertion —"Trying to fuse a state out of the plethora of minority sects, Iraqi President Saddam Hussein has enforced equal rights for the country's minorities, including formerly persecuted groups such as the Yezidis and Jews" — about a regime that gassed its own Kurdish citizens! A refreshing counterpoint to the plentitude of dismal news from the Middle East, "Hardy Israeli Chicks Help an Egyptian, and Cause of Peace," 3-27, is uplifting on a doughty Egyptian entrepreneur and his Israeli suppliers, although it's not clear if he's an anomaly. "Mubarak Seeks a Role in Palestinian Elections," 9-19, is a relaxed, compact report on the Egyptian President's initiatives for Israeli-Palestinian peace negotiations. The larger picture on the future of the anachronism escapes Brookes, but she presents very interesting anecdotes in "The Israeli Kibbutz Takes a Capitalist Tack to Keep Socialist Ideals," 9-21. The Israeli communal farms stagger under debt burdens, inherent inefficiencies, and are making allowances for the profit motive, she reports. "Riddle of Riyadh: Islamic Law Thrives Amid Modernity," 11-9, on the role of women in Saudi Arabia, seems to bristle with a bit too much resentment.

Browning, E. S. *The Wall Street Journal.* (★ ★)
Paris. We certainly get more on France's political economy from him than from most in the U.S. press. As much as we appreciate his material, though, he could be much better. We note gaps at times in the quality of his reports that he could plug with another phone call. The insight is crisp in "Arnault Gets Moet Vuitton Chairmanship and Wastes No Time in Making His Mark," 1-16, Browning reporting that the 39-year-old financier Bernard Arnault, after a furious fight to acquire the highly profitable luxury giant is sending a message that, although a newcomer, he intends to run Moet Vuitton with a strong hand. The details and forward look at what this might mean weren't developed, however. "French Concern Faces Charge in Exports Bid," 2-1, is a straight report on the charges that a subsidiary of one of France's largest banks (Societe Generale) attempted to export high-tech equipment to the U.S.S.R. A very nicely presented "High Death Toll on French Roads Leads to Efforts to Quell 'Monstrous Savagery,'" 4-3, totally absorbed us. Browning cites experts here who suspect good living in France is linked to its high rate of road deaths — 10,000 deaths a year, a per capita rate second only to that of the U.S. "French drivers today are 50% more likely to kill one another than are the West Germans, despite West Germany's speed-limitless autobahns." Opening with a great lead, Browning goes on to deliver a wealth of information on the anxieties in France's defense establishment in "Dassault Family Has Maintained Grip Despite Hard Times and Slipping Clout," 6-21. He disappoints us, simply failing to ask appropriate questions in "France Plans Cut in Taxes on Business," 8-31. The material is contradictory or confused, as when he reports that personal income taxes won't be changed, but the government "plans to reduce taxes on investment income" — which presumably means the personal tax on interest, dividends and/or capital gains. The story is cast as a contest between "the rich and the poor," without showing why the poor would be hurt by, say, lowering the VAT on automobiles from twenty-eight percent to twenty-five percent. Wouldn't there be more jobs in the auto factories?

Bruce, James. *The Journal of Commerce.* (★ ★)
Sao Paolo correspondent. We renewed our appreciation of his coverage from Brazil, finding a steady stream of key detail and information in his reports that we just aren't getting elsewhere. Bruce is trenchant in his critique of the "debt-for-ecology" chic in "Brazil's Ecological Face-Off," 2-3. Without downplaying the international concern over the Amazon, he strips the glamour from this political theater. He competently handles the key technical details involved in Brazil's decision to exclude remittances of profits and dividends on foreign investments from the extension of its floating exchange rate system in "Brazil Limits Its Freeing of Currency Trading Rates," 3-31. He has a sharper feel than many others in the press corps for Brazil's economy, as is illustrated by "Cleaning Up Brazilian Banking," 4-3, a fine report on plans to close "special lines of subsidized credit" to banks with a high rate of failure that "have increasingly served as conduits between the federal treasury and the political machinery of their respective governments," with a high rate of failure. What he does is to pinpoint a political-

economic problem that shows "Brazil's debt is not the sole cause of this country's current economic ills." He updates us on the country's ambitious industrial integration project in "Brazil's President Finally Inaugurates 'Steel Railway,'" 6-6, reporting that after running quadruple its original $743.5 million budget and 11 years late, service will open on 334 of the originally intended 1,100 kilometers. We get good news on a move away from protectionism in "Brazil Cuts Import Duties to Foster Competition," 7-12, and Bruce was the only journalist we read who reported this. "U.S., Brazil Near Accord on Steel Trade," 11-13, gives us Brazilian reaction and perspective on preliminary agreements for an increase of its steel exports to the U.S., citing the belief of the country's chief trade negotiator that chilly trade relations with the U.S. are now thawing, especially since the White House won't open an investigation into some alleged Brazilian violations under section 301 U.S. Trade Law.

Burns, John F. *The New York Times.* (★ ★ ★ ★)
Toronto bureau chief. An outstanding foreign correspondent, Burns gets better intelligence handles on some situations than does the CIA. Spending as much time in and around Afghanistan as in Canada, Burns efficiently put together the big picture there, way ahead of everyone (including various intelligence operations) in reporting that the "imminent" collapse of the Najibullah regime was anything but imminent. Reporting from Canada early in the year, he filed a delightful review of the famed Ottawa photographer at 80, "Yousuf Karsh and the Art of Friendly Persuasion," 1-1, "Arts and Leisure" section, in which Burns relates Karsh's photo of Winston Churchill in the Canadian House of Commons, December 30, 1941, as "the slingshot that launched Mr. Karsh's international career." From Moscow, "A Rude Dose of Reality for Gorbachev," 2-21, on Mikhail Gorbachev's trip to Kiev, Ukraine, is richly spiced with vivid quotes of people expressing widespread dissatisfaction, interrupting the President repeatedly. Conventional wisdom held that with the departure of Soviet troops from Afghanistan, the country would fall to the Afghan resistance. Burns distinguished himself from the pack very quickly with the timely "Soviets Gone, Najibullah Boasts and Life in Kabul Changes Little," 3-12, simply reporting evidence that the perspective was highly questionable. He quickly followed up with "Kabul Troops Scoff at Notion They Are on Their Last Legs," 3-13, in which he interviewed soldiers who reflect the confident tone from Afghanistan's Marxist government, again calling attention to the unlikelihood of a victory by the *mujahedeen*. There's excellent strategic intelligence in "With Soviet Weapons to Lean On, Kabul Is No Pushover," 3-19. Efficiently organized, it includes critical new information on Pres. Najibullah who is now "exploiting the ethnic and religious complexities. . .His government has been stripped of almost all the outward trappings of Marxism, and he has become a regular Friday visitor to Kabul's mosques." In a rebel bunker, reporting under fire from government troops, Burns gives us crisp, comprehensive material in "Afghan Rebels, Divided But Resolute, Fight on From Peak Above Jalalabad," 8-12. Presented with precise focus, this is reporting at its best, citing the fractious politics of rebel groups, yet the high morale and determination to oust President Najibullah. These last two are a 10 Best selection. "Quebec Separatists Surge but Fail to Oust Liberals," 9-27, is a tight wrap-up on the landslide re-election of Premier Robert Bourassa's Liberal government over the separatist Parti Quebecois, with Burns importantly including an analysis of the unlikely prospects for ratification of the Meech Lake accord.

Carrington, Tim. *The Wall Street Journal.* (★ ★)
London. This former Pentagon scribe isn't producing at his new posting on the same level as when he worked the national security beat, his U.K. stories still a bit foggy. But he's a skilled journalist, and with this year under his belt we expect he'll be scoring soon. Carrington wastes our time with "Economists Offer More Pessimistic View of Global Outlook Than Group of Seven," 4-14, providing space for Fred Bergsten to issue yet another call for devaluation of the dollar. Although the framework is Keynesian, Carrington presents a rather good recap of the global economic picture on the eve of the Paris summit in "'Soft Landing' Welcome News for Summit," 7-13, supplying good quotes and reporting everyone is happy that the U.S. economy has slowed. The story is a bit puffy, with no quotes from Sir Alan Walters' critics, but this

thumbnail sketch of him in "Thatcher Aide Becomes a Powerful Force," 8-29 is useful in identifying the influence of a figure who already has Thatcher's ear in opposing a British link to the EMS. Carrington rounds up an array of views from West German economists and analysts on the reshaping of the political-economic landscape as thousands of East Germans move westward into Europe with "German Emigration Echoes Across World," 9-14. He reports some fear that a "consumption boom" could provoke inflation, with the Bundesbank likely to raise interest rates, thereby provoking serious problems for other countries, especially Britain where an increase in base rates could set off a recession. There's a lot of undeveloped, and unchallenged assertions here, but we find the report useful on attitudes that could affect policy there. A routine "Recession Fears in U.K. Grow; Trade Improves," 10-25, ascribes partial culpability for Britain's inflation to tax cuts, without any elaboration. "Hungary Savoring Goulash Capitalism," 11-17, is a decent report on the flock of western investors drawn to the country by its liberalization, with some details of the players involved.

Chesnoff, Richard. *U.S.News & World Report.* (★ ★)
Senior correspondent. Chesnoff works the Middle East beat with a respectable facility, the mix of information and insight appreciable. "Diplomacy in the Dark," with Douglas Stanglin 3-6, examines options open to the U.S. and Iran in their relations, pulling on area specialists for insights. One insight is that the need to rebuild war-torn Iran puts a boundary around some of the nation's foreign policy options. Chesnoff maintains estimable balance in "The Intifada's Surreal Effect," 3-20, an information-rich report on the current situation in the Israeli West Bank. In addition to discussing the prospects of negotiations, he examines the factions within both the Israeli and the PLO camps along with their different agendas. He's persuasive on Syria's role in support for policies of destabilization in "Spoilers of Peace in the Middle East," 7-10, backing it up with documentation and effective quotes from terrorists. The content was a bit thinner than the title suggested, though, with Syria's role in Lebanon excluded from the report. Chesnoff handily folds political, strategic and economic policy issues into a compact report on Iraq and its leader, Saddam Hussein, in "Alas, Babylon — Can Saddam Rebuild It?" 9-25.

Christian, Shirley. *The New York Times.* (★ ★ ★)
Buenos Aires bureau chief. At a critical time for Argentina, with its economy imploding as a new president and party assume the helm, Christian kept abreast of the events in the southern cone with reliable, solid reporting, evidencing more effort at economic detail. Although much of the report was based on the conclusions of a study by the Institute for Contemporary Studies, we appreciate the data and detail in "Argentina's Dollar-Based Economy," 1-23. Christian helps put in context the puzzling anomaly of Argentina's relatively low unemployment rate (5.5% at the time) and perpetual sense of economic bustle even when so many statistics look grim. "Oh What a Campaign That Was," 5-14, with little vignettes from the electoral race, is smoothly done, celebrating the bottom line: the first democratic exchange of power in 60 years in Argentina. "Argentine Departs, Democracy Hardly Bankrupt," 7-8, is insightful on the triumphs and tribulations of outgoing President Raul Alfonsin's administration, with a cogent general observation: "Every few months a new monetary or credit policy emerged. New taxes were created, but as people quickly learned to evade them, they were forgotten and others invented only to be evaded as well." There's a sharp focus in "Bolivia to Seek Anti-Cocaine Money," 8-13. This notable dispatch reports the country's new president, Jaime Paz Zamora, insists the U.S. shift its war against drugs to economic aid, to give cocoa farmers a cash-crop alternative, quoting him: "We are willing to make a frontal fight against drug trafficking as long as it does not make us poorer than we are now." "Chile Plans to Create Strong Central Bank," 10-23, is an important dispatch that fills us in on the significant debate in Chile over the direction of economic policy. She draws up a somber assessment of what lies ahead in "Uruguay's Mixed Election Result May Lead to Conflict," 11-28, after national elections in which the Broad Front took control in the capital. A bloc of Communists, Socialists, former Tupamaro guerrillas and various Marxists, the Broad Front, she reports, eschews the transformations sweeping eastern Europe and predicts the failure of economic liberalism in Latin America.

Claiborne, William. *The Washington Post.* (★ ★)
Johannesburg bureau chief. There were dramatic changes in southern Africa this year, and Claiborne managed to stay well abreast of the swirling transformations. We get important details in "A Free Namibia May Still Have to Rely on S. Africa," 12-23-88, on the Southwest Africa People's Organization's (SWAPO) post-independence plans to implement socialist economic policies, with Claiborne passing on the views of "many political scientists and economic experts" that "a free Namibia will be so economically dependent on South Africa for survival that...change in day-to-day life will be scarcely noticeable." A timely, informed "Namibian Agreement Threatened," 4-2, reports serious alarm that the Namibian independence plan may be aborted at the very instant of its implementation. Claiborne sheds light, and some humor, onto the tragi-comic bunglings of guerrillas and U.N. bureaucrats, attending Namibia's birthpangs, in "SWAPO Incursion Into Namibia Seen as Major Blunder by Nujoma," 4-7. "Alleged Arms Deal Attempts Sets Off Furor in London, Pretoria," 4-25, is a fascinating, very well-written tale of international intrigue involving both the arms trade and diplomacy, reminiscent of pre-WWI Balkan plots; a South African diplomat offers to give weapons to Northern Ireland terrorists in exchange for a stolen British high-tech missile, and a French magistrate exposes the deal that sets off a domestic political storm against Margaret Thatcher, who wanted to protect South Africa from an economic embargo. "Majority Rule 'Unjust,' Says Botha's Heir," 5-13, is an estimable presentation of policy options available in S. Africa, on the occasion of a major speech by National Party leader and "heir" to South African President Pieter W. Botha, Frederik W. de Klerk. The information a little too dense, "South African Negotiations Opposed," 6-6, falls short on informing us about the growing role of a recently founded South African tribal chief's organization, the Congress of Traditional Leaders of South Africa, in opposing Botha's "power sharing" negotiations. "Angola Pact's Unanswered Question: Savimbi," 6-25, works nicely as an analytical effort on the Angolan cease-fire agreement. Claiborne's account lends credence to the key role played by Zaire's President Sese Seko Mobutu in effecting the accord. "Ruling Party Victory Indicated in South Africa," 9-7, provides a rounded perspective on what the pace of change may be like in South Africa as Pres. de Klerk and his party win a reduced but still comfortable majority.

Clines, Francis X. *The New York Times.* (★ ★ ½)
Moscow bureau correspondent. The former London bureau correspondent was appropriately selected by the American Society of Newspaper Editors as a recipient of its Distinguished Writing Award in the deadline category for his '88 coverage of Northern Ireland. But one of the most sparkling wordsmiths in the profession, Clines gets off to a slow start on his new beat with a surprisingly cumbersome lead in "From Space, a Voice Vote Has to Suffice," 3-27. This sidebar feature on the Soviet deputies' election focuses on the election bureaucracy, but lacks the characteristic Clines color. The Clines touch is back in "Bells Are Ringing as Soviets Return Churches to Faithful," 4-16, a Sunday P. 1 feature. He presents some nice detail about the government's return of 937 churches to the people, as compared with only 10 the previous year, but doesn't pursue the authorities for an explanation why. A great topic, he should have developed it more. "Moscow Represses Freud's Slip Into Print," 5-2, tells the story of a cagey Moscow entrepreneur who gets 100,000 copies of Freud printed on state presses, only to have them held up at the eleventh hour. We find new insights into the co-op movement in this report. Watching TV with average Soviet citizens in an appliance store, "It's Moscow's Line: New Faces, New Ideas and Impertinence," 5-26, is the best close-up of how the new Supreme Soviet plays with Moscow's equivalent of "Joe Six-Pack." Says one of them, it's "the first lesson in the first grade of the school of democracy." He puts Gorbachev into context with "Gorbachev Mutes His Voice Over China," 6-13, as *glasnost* at home "only underscored his own painstaking, uncritical view of China's violent repression of its pro-democracy demonstrations." Clines delivers both new information and insightful detail with "In Poland's Wary Farm Belt, a Sobering Wait for Change," 8-27, reporting on a visit to a Zenbok farm community where farmers operate private farms, but have to contend with an inefficient state distribution system and price controls. Celebration of the non-Communist Prime Minister, thus, is *muted.* In the

events surrounding the yearend political dynamics, Clines was professional in his filings throughout, but with no especially impressive analytics. As East Germans poured into West Berlin, he did a Moscow man-in-the-street reaction, "Russians See an Omen of Their Own Progress," 11-12, finding an "It's about time" attitude, spiced with complaints that their own border is still closed. "Gorbachev Welcomes Polish Premier," 11-25, was routine on Tadeusz Mazowiecki's visit to Moscow, when we expected some new angles or asides.

Cody, Edward. *The Washington Post.* (★ ½)
The Paris bureau chief was all over the map, filing dispatches from Europe and the Middle East, and even occasionally from France. One consequence, of course, is that we don't get the depth we ought to on the important political economy of this G-7 nation. "Panel Says Mitterrand Friend Benefitted From Stock Deal," 2-1, updates on the latest developments of the insider trading scandal as it becomes a major embarrassment for France's Socialist government, but Cody doesn't take us beyond the details provided in the investigative report of the Market Operations Commission. We get some insights and forward-looking analysis in "Unions in Spain Seek Greater Share," 2-3, on the disenchantment of the unions with Socialist Prime Minister Felipe Gonzalez, Cody noting that "beneath the fight over money lies a deeper struggle over the definition of Spain's socialist movement and the spirit of its young leaders as they seek to prolong the economic boom." "Rise in Islamic Fundamentalism Challenges Turkey's Secular State," 4-4, although timely on the issue, is another report that isn't followed up; the criticism applies to the *Post*'s foreign editors. Cody provides accurate information on Israel's first "hard-line" action after PM Shamir's U.S. visit with "Israeli Troops Raid Village; At Least 4 Palestinians Killed," 4-14, but so did the wires. And "Israelis Contrast 'Hour of Greatness,' Intifada," 5-1, a very well written comparison and contrast between the kibbutz-soldiers' morale in the aftermath of the June War, and now, really tells us nothing new. "AIDS and Addicts in the Land of Heidi," 5-29, a depressing account of a visit to Platzpromenade park, "Zurich's Needle Park," a free-fire zone for addicts instituted by city fathers in an experimental effort to control the spread of AIDS, never quite delivers a conclusive picture. Cody fills us in competently on Greece's political scene with "Scandals, Premier's Affair Dominate Greek Election," 6-16, in between a couple of reports from France. "A First Lady's Prickly Diplomacy," 6-10, on Danielle Mitterrand, the vociferous political activist wife of the French President, whose espousal of controversial topics often causes serious problems for his official diplomats, gives a vacuous treatment to what otherwise could have been a terrific story. The best we saw: "Liberte, Egalite. . .Blase," 7-9, a rare, keen dissection of France's national mood, written with verve, poignancy.

Coleman, Fred. *Newsweek.* (★)
Moscow. Decent reporting, so-so analysis, Coleman's dispatches were solid enough most of the year. There's a mix of convention and insight in his analytic look at upcoming Soviet elections in "Gorbachev Gets Out the Vote," 3-27, although the bottom line isn't new: The Party "ultimately settles every issue," and therefore Gorbachev's success depends "on politicking within the party, not at the polling booth." A nicely flowing contrast of the situations in China and the U.S.S.R., "The China Syndrome," 6-5, points persuasively to nationalistic tensions and food shortages as two areas within the Soviet Union that could lead to a version of Tiananmen Square. He reminds us that "More than a third of the food now produced in the Soviet Union gets lost between farm and family table because of poor transport, storage, and processing." He's not completely clear on the democratic shift in his report on the Congress of People's Deputies, "The Kremlin's Talkathon," 6-12, the picture undeveloped on the power of the new Supreme Soviet and its relations with Gorbachev. "Gorbomania in Germany," with Harry Anderson 6-26, on Gorbachev's visit to West Germany, is efficient reporting and analysis. "Longer on symbolism than substance," Gorbachev "presented no new initiative on arms control. . .[and] offered no new hope for reunification of the two Germanys." There isn't any new information in "Until We Are Free Again," 9-4, on the growing momentum for economic and political reform in the Baltic countries, but the report is an appropriate update for the weekly's readers. Although we didn't find the effort to compare Gorbachev's chances for political survival with Nikita Khrushchev's satisfying, we appreciate Coleman's initiative in trying to play out the idea in "Nikita Gorbachev," 9-11.

Colitt, Leslie. *Financial Times.* (★ ★ ★)
Berlin. A stringer for the *FT,* Colitt has an intimate knowledge of the Germanies and Central Europe and was indispensable in keeping us ahead of the fast-breaking news this year. One of the most alert journalists on this beat, Colitt picked up early the increasing radicalization of Czech youth who see the regime on its last legs, incapable of reforming, with even Gorbachev unable to nudge it in "Angry Young Czechs Shed Parents' Fears," 1-18, a fine mix of solid reporting and ahead-of-the-curve analysis. In "Gorbachev Pledge on E. Europe Creates Stir," 3-31, we get an interesting picture of East Bloc leaders pondering whether Moscow would still intervene to stop political reform although the Soviet leader has repudiated the Brezhnev Doctrine. He finds deep public skepticism about political reform in Hungary in "Hungarians Wary of Another False Dawn," 4-14, reporting that cynicism is deep at all levels: "Ordinary Hungarians, too, suspect that they will be losers in a free market system." Colitt's pipeline into the East German party is impressive. The first word that the Honecker regime was considering a cancellation of relaxation of travel controls between East and West Germany was reported by Colitt in "East Germany Considering 'Much Tougher' Policies," 9-18, with an alert that Egon Krenz could succeed Honecker very soon. Colitt reports the first signs of dissent within the party leadership In "Honecker Says Communism Must Survive," 10-10, calling attention to growing pressure from rank-and-file Party members for reforms. We get some picture of the potentially dangerous rebellion Krenz faces within the Party with "E. German Government Quits," 11-8, as Colitt reports on the calls from a leading Party institute for all members of the Politburo to personally account for their responsibility for the "crisis in society and the party."

Coll, Steve. *The Washington Post.* (★ ½)
New Delhi bureau chief. A former business reporter at the daily for part of this year, Coll jumped energetically into the reporting for the subcontinent once reassigned there. "U.S. Cuts Mujaheddin Parties Out of Afghan Arms Pipeline," 8-3, is an excellent report and analysis on one of the most important developments of the Afghan War since the Soviet withdrawal — the cutting of stipends and military supplies to the seven Pakistan-based Afghan rebel parties by the U.S. and Pakistan, who now are attempting to deliver guns and money directly to guerrilla commanders and tribal leaders inside Afghanistan. There's a superficiality to "Indian Ballot May Turn on Issue of Corruption," 8-4, Coll reporting the problems for Rajiv Gandhi with the anti-corruption campaign, but missing its potential to become an anti-establishment campaign. We get some perspective on the complications of U.S. policy from the role of Afghan Muslim fundamentalist commander Hekmatyar in "U.S. Facing a Dilemma in Arming Afghan Rebels," 8-13, as the U.S. attempts to channel new and more sophisticated weapons to resistance groups for use in an anticipated late summer offensive. "Murder for Hire, High Finance and a Big Dose Of Family Feud," 8-17, is lively and humorous on an exotic feud between Indian business magnates that has embarrassed PM Gandhi and threatened the stability of his government. Coll turns this into an informative snapshot of the habits and practices of Indian power circles: "Here in Bombay, a city that wealthy Indians like to describe as a cross between Hollywood and Manhattan, corporate life increasingly resembles a prime-time soap opera fantasy — with the difference that even the most outlandish plots are true." There's no real field intelligence in "Afghan Guerrillas Sustain Fighting Near 3 Cities," 9-11, although it serves as an adequate spot report on the renewed offensive by the Afghan resistance. A graphic account, "Riots Between Hindus and Moslems Touch Off Political Alarm in India," 9-23, locates the reshaping of India's politics that's beginning to emerge from an upsurge in religious fundamentalism. "Indian Voters Frustrated by Pace of Change," 11-18, is a sharp political reading based on the story of a small village Indian family. While having grown richer from their work on the land than in shops, they're frustrated by the rate at which inflation is eating up the new wealth. This frustration will be directed at all office-holders come election day.

Cowell, Alan. *The New York Times.* (★ ½)
Cairo bureau chief. Cowell never really digs deeply into the political economy of Egypt, and it's this side of his work that most disappoints. He's ramshackle in his attempts to capture the

mechanisms and atmosphere of Egyptian society, although he started the year off promisingly. "Finance and Islam Mix, Igniting a Mighty Scandal," 1-5, is an excellent first approach to the many dimensions of a scandal in which thousands of middle-class Egyptians have seen their modest wealth disappear in the hands of fund managers accused of dubious dealings. Cowell alerts us to the serious political overtones of the scandal, makes the striking observation that it is also a chronicle of an era in which boom times have turned into national penury, helping in turn foster an Islamic revival. There are many stories here, but we never see them further developed. An awkwardly structured "Israeli Army Sergeant and 3 Arabs Die in Gunfight," 6-5, throws all the things occurring in Israel during the *intifada* into one loose package, mixing three separate reports into one and the integration doesn't work. He is successful in using a specific event to provide broader insight into the diversity of Jewish Israeli attitudes toward Arab neighbors in "An Israeli Mayor Is Under Scrutiny; Badges for the Arab Workers Bring an Investigation of Incitement to Racism," 6-6. The reporting is straightforward in "Israel Issues ID's to Arabs in Gaza: Aim Is to Punish Fomenters of Uprising by Prohibiting Travel From Territory," 6-7, with nothing much added to official communiques on the event. He offers plausible analysis of Cairo's intentions in "Egypt and Libya Begin a Reconciliation," 6-8: to secure the diplomatic isolation of Syria, "which had counted Libya as one of its few remaining allies in rejecting overtures toward Israel." Some context for Tripoli's overtures would have better rounded this out. "Egyptian Population Growth Strains Resources and Society," 7-8, is a lazy effort recycling the tiresome, standard "population-causes-poverty" story. Almost an assertion, Cowell gives us *nothing* on current policy planning or pros and cons from Egyptian opinion leaders. "Egypt's Pain: Wives Killing Husbands," 9-23, reports on the changing status of women as urbanization increases. Marital laws heavily biased toward men leave Egyptian women no choice but murder to escape the brutality of husbands, he reports, although citing only three cases and no statistics, so we're left without perspective.

Crossette, Barbara. *The New York Times.* (★ ★ ½)
New Delhi bureau chief. Having turned in an excellent year as Bangkok bureau chief (three-and-a-half stars in 1989), we were dismayed at how little she was reporting from the subcontinent after her posting there. India's economy and politics were undergoing important changes all year, but it wasn't until later in the year, as critical national elections loomed, that Crossette began filing reports of the quantity and quality that so distinguished her the previous year. And while back in stride, she didn't satisfy us with details on India's economy. She has a fair perspective in "Soviets Negotiate to Avert Violence in Afghan Pullout," 2-5, reporting only one thousand Soviet troops remain in Afghanistan, almost all around Kabul airport. A timely "The Depth of the Anger in Pakistan Tests Bhutto," 2-19, asks appropriate questions as to why did the most violent demonstration Islamabad has known in a decade occur just now, and provides an overview of problems faced by Benazir Bhutto and what a resurgence of Islamic fundamentalism could lead to for Pakistan. "Shiny Tomorrow Meets Ragged, Hungry Today," 7-3, is a fascinating report on attempts to make technology "down to earth, rural, very docile, and user-friendly" in India, focusing on the efforts of Maheshwar Dayal, a pioneer in nuclear technology. "India's Parliamentary Ways Are Yielding to Other Forces," 10-15, piques interest with a perspective on the decline in importance of India's legislature, as the five years of Rajiv Gandhi's government are described by a social scientist as "institutionally, the worst in Indian history." But her treatment isn't as deep or satisfying as hoped for. Her reporting is very focused in "India's Low Castes Turn the Tables," 11-10, as she examines the growing importance of the pivotal role the country's disadvantaged groups will play in the elections. "Coalition Talks Begin as Gandhi Loses a Majority," 11-28, is a fine post-election wrap-up, with a rundown the important political changes in key Indian states. Crossette's immediate assessment is to the point: "The voters bashed incumbents of all stripes."

Cullison, A. E. *The Journal of Commerce.* (★ ★ ★)
Tokyo correspondent. In a year when no journalists mastered this year's story of the Japanese political-economy, the steady supply of fine detail and fresh news from Cullison was substantial.

We don't see anywhere else useful reports like "Japanese Bankers Seek LDC Lending Initiative," 3-17, quoting the views of Japanese bankers at length, though Cullison could have made it more usable with some evaluation. More on the larger implications would have also been useful in "Japan Defense Minister Slams U.S. on FSX Deal," 4-3, although it's a fine report on Japanese outrage over the trouble in the FSX deal, with good Japanese source material. "Insurance Opens Doors in Japan," 4-6, is a worm's-eye view of the Japanese savings pattern via a profile of insurance sales, but it contains the kind of detail we rarely see elsewhere. Cullison does the kind of top-notch business reporting that provides a steady stream of updates and profiles on many Japanese companies, large and small. We get a fine reading on the president of Japan's largest tramper-tanker operations, Shozo Magoshi, with "Navix Chief Guides Specialized Line Through First 6 Months to Profit," 9-26, Cullison going considerably beyond the rewrite of company press releases. We learn that with 60% of Navix's expenses and 80% of its income in dollars, Mr. Magoshi appreciates a stronger dollar. A well-organized summation of global trade talks in Tokyo, "U.S. Formula for Tariffs Gets No Support," 11-14, points up the lack of support for the U.S. principle of bilateral tariff agreements, with the Japanese strongly supporting the current GATT formula. He's very alert to signs that major changes in the Soviet attitude may be under way in "Island Dispute Fades Away," 11-29. This careful, knowledgeable assessment of the visit to Japan by top Gorbachev aide Aleksandr Yakolev is the best we saw anywhere.

Darlin, Damon. *The Wall Street Journal.* (★ ★ ½)
Seoul. Darlin was off somewhat this year, but moving from Tokyo to set up a bureau in Seoul had a lot to do with it. The *Asian WSJ* has had a reporter in Korea for more than ten years, but midyear Darlin became the first resident correspondent for the U.S. paper. A very skilled, hard-working journalist, we expect he'll set a heady pace on coverage of Korea and Taiwan. "New U.S. Ambassador's Aggressive Tack Reflects Change in Approach to Japan," 5-31, reports on a speech by new U.S. Ambassador to Japan, Michael H. Armacost, that echoes language frequently used by Japan-bashers. Darlin picks up on the new situation: "Many U.S. officials here have noted a dramatic change in mood, morale and method at the embassy since Mr. Armacost arrived." There is a modicum of insight in "Trade Threats Against Japanese Work Despite Hand-Wringing of Free Traders," 5-23, although it lists to the side of "constructive conflict." *Defense News* best covered the implications of the FSX story for Korea-U.S. aerospace co-projects, but "Korea Feels the Heat from Japan FSX Furor," 6-7, is a fine report on the Korean project. He joins Karen Elliott House in "South Korea's Roh to Downplay Focus on Shared Interests in U.S. Visit," 10-13, to establish some picture as to the agenda for talks between the administration and ROK Pres. Roh Tae Woo. With the U.S. troop presence high on the list of topics, Roh, we learn, warns that tensions are rising, not falling in Asia, as "the clock has been turned back in China." Reporting on a shift away from the government's protective climate for Korea's giant conglomerates, the *chaebol,* the top five of which make up 51% of the country's GNP, Darlin only touches on the government shift to help middle entrepreneurs in "Korea's Goldstar Faces a Harsh New World Under Democracy," 11-8.

Davidson, Ian. *Financial Times.* (★ ★ ★)
Paris. His analytics lofty, his reporting rigorous, Davidson was the most satisfying among the foreign corps with overall coverage of France. "If there is one issue which really gets the French going, it is education," he informs us in "Education Goes to the Barricades," 1-16, which is comprehensive on the debate over plans for French school reforms. He keeps the issue in focus all year (Mitterrand made it the highest priority of the current legislature), returning to it again with an especially well-done, multi-dimensional "Jospin's Reforms Face Age-Old Force of Vested Interests," 6-28, as the tension between an elitist model and what the French call the "massification" of education pushes the system toward its breaking point. He overturns conventional assumptions about the French political condition in what was the most outstanding analytical report we saw on France from anyone all year, "Vulnerable in Theory," 6-28. He's persuasive, clearly writing as a partisan of the West, but obviously critical of Bush's and PM Thatcher's visions, in "West Fails to Meet Gorbachev Challenge," 5-18, and "A Time for

Greatness of Vision in the West," 6-15. Clever, lively, and trenchant "Snatching a Reprieve From the Jaws of Defeat," 6-1, cuts through the conventional wisdom in this analytic of current problems with NATO "orthodoxy." Davidson displays keen-eyed insight into fratricidal politics among French conservatives, and in "French Star Suffers a Political Eclipse," 9-27, puts the nasty fall of rising young conservative star Francois Leotard into context. While the consensus among pundits is that the Republican Party leader has suffered a serious blow in the battle over control of conservative forces, Davidson makes the point that opponent Giscard D'Estaing has yet to win a real victory.

Dawnay, Ivo. *Financial Times.* (★ ★)
Rio de Janeiro. A solid reporter, Dawnay keeps us up-to-date on the Brazilian political economy, but he really needs to sharpen a forward look for this beat. He uses a report on the case of the tourist ship that sank off the Rio coast with heavy loss of life to effectively illustrate the massive decomposition of Brazil's criminal justice system, "Disaster Puts Spotlight on Failure of Justice," 1-13. We get some detail on Brazil's monthly inflation rates creeping back toward double digits with "Summer Plan Loses Its Bloom," 4-21, but it's not clear enough on policy detail. From Asuncion, "Rodriguez Wins in Paraguay," 5-3, is a standard report, although Dawnay cites the conclusions of independent observers that the many electoral irregularities were attributable to leftover practices from the Stroessner regime rather than any deliberate government action. We get some sense of the tensions between embattled Finance Minister Mailson da Nobrega and Brazil's business leaders in "Brazil Fights to Stem Inflation," 7-21, with da Nobrega trying to convince the business community that Brazil isn't heading into an Argentine-style hyperinflation: "Only you people can drive us into hyper-inflation, and if you do, you will end up the losers." He picks up a measure of the lack of Brazilian familiarity with the privatization process in "Sarney Sends Proposals for Privatisation to Congress," 8-18, quoting the banner headline of the liberal *Folha de Sao Paolo* newspaper: "Sarney Wants to Privatise Even Profitable Companies." Dawnay's "Brazil Investigates $360m Foreign Exchange Fraud," 11-11, doesn't settle for the Justice Minister's allegation that the transfers are the work of "an organized gang of fake importers with the objective of laundering money from drug-trafficking." Instead, he reports that "others believe, however, that the motive behind the alleged fraud might well be the more prosaic flight of capital from Brazil's inflation-racked economy."

Dempsey, Judy. *Financial Times.* (★ ½)
Vienna. This *FT* stringer is our preferred source for political-economic news on Austria, but it was her coverage of the turbulent developments in Central and Eastern Europe that we most appreciated this year. "Red Vienna's Child Celebrates a Troubled Centenary," 1-19, is nicely analytic on Austria's Chancellor Franz Vranitzky, who faces problems reminiscent of those in the 1920s. Dempsey poses the dilemma well: he's torn between maintaining a strong, paternalistic state on one hand versus modernizing the socialist party that will give greater scope to private enterprise at the expense of the state's role. She's very informative with "Major Players Square Off on Yugoslavia's Chess Board," 3-29, on the complications posed for economic reform because of the country's ethnic and political problems: "Tito believed that age-old rivalry between Serbs and Croats could only be checked by a decentralized system of decision-making. In the event it made rational decisions unattainable." The best we saw on Yugoslavia all year was the *FT* "Survey," 6-29, the majority of which was written by Dempsey: "Medicine for Nationalism" reports PM Ante Markovic has a perspective for orienting the economy toward the market, but the war of polemics and vitriol has brought nationalism to a boiling point, threatening the fragile unity of the country and undermining economic reform efforts. Her reporting is concise, the key information well-focused, on the agreement to introduce a multi-party system in Hungary, "Fudging in Hungarian Poll Deal," 9-20. "Hungarian Party Faithful Search for the Recipe for Survival," 10-6, is an excellent reporting job, comprehensive on the splits in the Hungarian Socialist Workers' Party [Communist] as it meets for its last congress. A flavorful "Czech Spirit Blooms in the Prague Winter," 11-27, while not reporting anything we weren't getting elsewhere, is at least lively, quoting Party leaders, demonstrators, policemen and opposition figures, as crowds begin to take power into their own hands.

Dickson, Tim. *Financial Times.* (★ ★)
Brussels-based, but Belgium is only part of his beat, the EC really the focus of his reporting. Dickson provides important intelligence on EC policies, and early on he was filing alerts on the growing trade policy tensions between the U.S. and the EC. He shines the spotlight on Jacques Delor, EC Commission President and a leading hawk for counter-retaliation against the U.S. ban on EC food products, who urges no compromise with the U.S., "U.S.-EC Battle Over Hormones Set to Escalate," 1-4. Delors is put under the light again in "Britain and Denmark Urge Lull in Trade Hostilities with U.S.," 1-5. Britain and France want a pause for reflection on trade war hostilities with U.S., he reports, but Jacques Delors is anxious to send more aggressive signals to the U.S. to avoid any impression EC resolve is weakening. We also learn that one in four Belgian butchers is selling meat treated with hormones. Protectionist forces in Europe would love an excuse to retaliate, and the Super 301 section of the 1988 U.S. trade bill could just set them in motion, as is made clear by information in "EC Steps Up War of Words Over Trade With U.S..," 5-4. "Car Emission Issue Moves Out of Europe's Political Slow Lane," 6-12, establishes that the EC's acceptance of emission standards as a reflection of growing impact Greens are having on the continent's politics. He reports 85% of the cost of the catalytic converters will be subsidized. "EC Urged to Toughen Pollution Codes for 1992 Market," 11-15, updates us on the tougher environmental policies that are being proposed for the Community. We get a very good report on Belgium from him, "Fitter and Running Faster," 6-19, which describes the structural changes the approach of Europe-1992 is imposing on the country.

Diehl, Jackson. *The Washington Post.* (★ ★ ★)
Jerusalem, moving there midyear from Warsaw. Diehl picked up right where he left off last year, keeping his readers on top of historic events in Eastern Europe, making us feel like we were being treated to a government intelligence briefing at our breakfast table. In "Poland Eases Curbs on Private Sector," 12-24-88, and "As Economy Worsens, Polish Leader May Yield on Solidarity," 12-26-88, Diehl sets the stage for the historic events to come, writing about the new laws that represent a major step toward dilution of Poland's socialist system and the growing economic disorder and mounting strength of Solidarity pressing in on the communist regime. "Dismantling Communism: Rough Roads in Workers' Paradise," 4-17, part two of a three-part series on Eastern Europe, combines a wealth of information on economic and political developments in Poland and Hungary at ground level with a breath of vision approaching a historian's horizon: "Over the next few years, the new partnerships between the ruling Communists and opposition forces in Poland and Hungary seem destined to free tumultuous forces that will rend both sides to pieces while encouraging dangerous currents of populism and nationalism." Diehl's "Polish Party Acknowledges Stunning Defeat by Solidarity," 6-6, is an excellent political assessment of the paradoxical outcome of *Solidarnosc*'s landslide election victory, "that might touch off a serious political crisis. . .the election results frustrated the political elite [both Party and *Solidarnosc*] in several respects. . .unexpectedly low voter turnout — 62 percent — suggested that many Poles failed to heed the efforts of both Solidarity and the party to stir them." "Polish Vote Leaves Wins and Losers in Political and Economic Quandary," 6-7, is a pacesetter in clarifying and explaining the Polish electoral result's paradox, although the fifty word lead turned some of our readers off. "33 Years After Revolt, Hungary Buries a Hero," 6-17, captures the solemnity of that historic moment. Diehl was reassigned to the Middle East during the summer, and two of his first reports, "Labor Moves to Leave Israeli Coalition," 7-11, and "Israel Plagued by Recession," 7-24, dealt with familiar topics — political troubles in a failed socialist economy.

Dobbs, Michael. *The Washington Post.* (★ ★ ★)
Moscow bureau chief. A smart reporter, Dobbs has a sense for the broader dynamics of events. He provides splendid coverage and analysis of the unfolding new political world in the U.S.S.R., although missing several key shifts on the margin in economic policy here. In "Strained Soviet Citizens Debate Costly Burden of Empire," 1-15, we get a peek at the torrent of letters to Soviet publications from citizens questioning the way the Kremlin allocates its resources. A familiar

complaint: "Why must we help everybody else. . .when we don't have enough for ourselves?" We were generally impressed by Dobb's coverage of the March elections. "Yeltsin Given Solid Support in His Opponent's Stronghold," 3-22, is a lively, old-fashioned election campaign report from the hustings, building up the legend of maverick Boris Yeltsin. "Soviet Science Group Rejects Election Slate," 3-23, points out that defeat of the official slate of congressional candidates from the Academy of Sciences opens up the possibility that both dissident Sakharov and ex-space program chief and detente enthusiast Sagdeyev may be elected to the Congress of People's Deputies. In "Soviet General Faces Challenge," 3-24, and "Politics on the Front Lines of Perestroika," 3-26, Dobbs zeroes in on the contest in Yaroslavl, where a lieutenant colonel is running against the commander-in-chief of Soviet forces in Germany. His election day write-up "Soviet Vote Trend Shows Support for Reformers," 3-27, provides informative vignettes and good insights. Our readers judged it superior to *The New York Times* coverage. "Soviet Voters' Revolt Carries Hidden Dangers for Gorbachev," 3-29, offers sensible early evaluation of Soviet election results: "The emergence of a group of radical reformists in the People's Congress and the Supreme Soviet. . .will allow Gorbachev, in effect, to occupy the middle ground of Soviet politics." In "Gorbachev Purges Central Committee," 4-26, Dobbs soberly reports that Gorbachev just purged 25% of his Central Committee, and the event "underlines the political skills of the 58-year-old Kremlin Chief at a time when his perestroika program has run into major difficulties. . .it will now be much more difficult — although not impossible — for conservatives to organize a political coup. . . ." "Juggling Gorbachev Fails to Impress French," 7-8, provides first-rate news analysis, purged of the "Gorbymania" still afflicting other correspondents.

Doerner, William. *Time.* (★)
Associate editor. Another of the weekly's scribes whose byline appears along with those from *Time*'s various foreign correspondents, we can't help but feel that Doerner simply can't assemble several news flows into one without losing the spirit or essence of a foreign event. A follow-up report on the scandal surrounding Greek PM Papandreou, "No Mud Touches Me," with Mirka Gondicas 3-20, gives some space to the PM's response on the allegations, but Doerner never explains why he concludes Papandreou will keep his post until June. Reporting on the cease-fire breakdown in Namibia, "Botching the Peace," with Peter Hawthorne 4-17, Doerner omits mentioning that SWAPO never signed the cease-fire agreement. The fact that one of the "local players" refuses to sign on is an important context for assessing how good is an agreement between the super powers. There are plenty of factual items in "The Face of Repression," with William Stewart 7-3, on the execution of student dissidents by the Chinese government, but as the replacement of General Secretary Zhao Ziyang with Jiang Zemin is reported, there's no accompanying forward projection nor underlying analysis. "The Language of Unrest," with John Kohan 9-11, reports on the nationalist stirrings in the Soviet republic of Moldavia. However, Moldavia is just grouped with more news of unrest in the Baltics, when we wanted more specific information about the Moldavian situation.

Ellingsen, Peter. *Financial Times.* (NR)
This Australian journalist was an eyewitness to the events in Tiananmen Square in May, and appeared on ABC's "The [Ted] Koppel Report" on Tiananmen, 6-27. We caught some of his dispatches from China, mostly in the *Financial Times,* and, although not enough to rate his work, we were very impressed by his insights into the China story. Ellingsen was distancing himself very early from what left so much of the press corps unprepared for the Old Guard's resurgence, discounting the activity and high profile of the liberal Chinese intellectuals, as "False Forecast Of 'Peking Spring,' " 3-30. He cast their efforts to set the stage for more measured and successful assaults on state despotism as already doomed, and reported signs of ominous Old Guard activities that would lead to a serious clash: "China is struggling through an economic crisis with raging inflation forcing an ever-widening split between the reformers and the conservatives." The reporting is straightforward and professional in "University Elite Join the Student Strike for Democracy in China," 4-25, and he steered clear of any shortsighted euphoria,

soberly reiterating that "the students have embarked on a collision course with both the party and Government, which, although relatively restrained in their response up to now, have shown no interest in liberal reform." He doesn't do much beyond merely summarizing a paper issued by Australia's largest company, Broken Hill Proprietary, that relates the tricky and difficult undertakings involved in doing business with China, "Trade with China Is Still a Disorienting Experience," 5-5. Ellingsen produces a compact assessment of the unsuccessful efforts to enforce a return to communist orthodoxy in China with "Unrepentant Peking Edges Back Toward Normality," 8-16: "Like the two gold-coloured Rolls Royce limousines outside the hotel, only a few blocks from Tiananmen Square the [reappearance in China of Hong Kong] newspapers testify to the paradox facing China's leaders. How do you enforce Marxist conformity while embracing Western capital, economic ideas and goods?"

Elliott, Dorinda. *Newsweek.* (★)
Beijing. No advance over her past year's effort, but in a year when many journalists here had trouble keeping their heads above water, Elliott negotiated the currents respectably enough. She picks up on an interesting theme in "We're All Gold Diggers Here," 2-20, on the generation gap in relation to diverse political ideas in China. There is a good use of quotes from prominent Chinese dissidents like Fang Lizhi and Su Shaozhi in "Intellectuals Are Waking Up," 3-6, and, in this report on the newly emerging combative streak among China's intellectuals, Elliott astutely observes that the "Chinese have absorbed so many new ideas from the outside world that almost nobody has the kind of unquestioning faith in the party that was once so common." "China Puts on the Brakes," with Lenore Magida 4-3, on the change of course plotted at the opening session of the National People's Congress, isn't that perceptive on the roots of the country's current economic instability, but she gives us an early sign of tensions between Chinese Communist Party Leader Zhao Ziyang and Premier Li Peng. A personality profile of student leader Wuer Kaixi in " 'We Have Enthusiasm and Daring,' " 5-8, is filler, adding nothing to what we'd already learned. A contrast of the economic shortcomings of Soviet reform efforts with the political shortcomings of China's modernization frames a useful focus in "At Least Now We Have the Will to Fight," 5-22, although the theme is conventional. " 'We Shouldn't Be So Afraid,' " 10-9, attempts to make the case that the Communist regime in China really doesn't represent a break with the country's past, but instead is merely a variation of a tradition that gives deference to hierarchy, rote education, and the cult of the emperor. The thesis is respectable, although the presentation isn't convincing.

Elliott, John. *Financial Times.* (★ ★ ★)
Hong Kong. Reporting for a British publication, he's more focused than others on the effect that Hong Kong's planned return to China in 1997 is having on the colony. The issue is not exclusive, as he turns in some high-level reports from elsewhere in the region. Elliott weaves a mound of data and details with analysis and sharp perspective in "Booming Taiwan Prepares to Pay the Social Price of Growth," 1-17, putting the burst of the economic bubble from the previous autumn into context. Because Taiwan is successfully grappling with financial and industrial change, it's the social integument that is vulnerable. Elliott plays on the irony of Hong Kong's major, twin problems — an annual brain drain of 45,000 people concurrent with a steady influx of Vietnamese boat people, both because of fears and experiences with Communist regimes — to provide a framework for "Hong Kong Anger Surprises MPs," 4-24, a report on the reaction of the British House of Commons Foreign Affairs Committee to the "extent of bitterness" against the U.K. for not helping more. He reports a former Minister's poignant observation: "This is the first time in Britain's history of decolonisation that we have handed over a territory, not to its people and independence, but to another sovereign power." The worries about Hong Kong, after Tiananmen Square permanently changed the view of 1997, are excellently developed in "A New Set of Fears," 6-29. Elliott picked up again on the diminishing hope and ascending cynicism in Hong Kong with "Peking Steps Up War of Nerves With Hong Kong Liberals," 7-22, identifying China's attacks on two prominent democratic leaders of the colony as a new phase in the war of nerves between HK and China. There's evidence, he reports, that Beijing is

mobilizing supporters in Hong Kong to oppose demands for faster democratic development before and after 1997. "The Other China's New Confidence," 8-14, is loaded with detail on Taiwan's stock market and economy, with Elliott developing several insightful angles on the country's future. More on the tense relations between China and Hong Kong is provided by "China Refuses to Accept Return of Illegal Immigrants," 10-10, a short report that puts China's decision in that context. At the same time, he reports on China's efforts to try to boost confidence in the British colony and other parts of the region with "Three Airports To Be Built in Hong Kong Region," 10-10, citing a very significant approval by the Bank of China for the Hong Kong government's proposal that some of the airport financing could come from a special fund now being built up to help finance the first post-1997 administration.

Erlanger, Steven. *The New York Times.* (★ ★ ½)
Bangkok bureau chief. He's proving to be a very hardworking foreign correspondent, crisscrossing South East Asia in hot pursuit of the region's major stories. In "Daughter of Burma, but Can She Be a Symbol?" 1-11, he interviews Aung San Suu Kyi, the daughter of the founder of Burmese independence and foremost symbol of the country's hopes for democracy. She impresses Erlanger as "a sensible politician, articulate and straightforward, who understands above all that Burma's military must be preserved as a united institution if the country is to achieve democracy of a sort." His "Cambodia Impasse: Patrons of the War Are Absent," 2-23, provides good info on the progress being made on some of the elements needed for a comprehensive solution for a Cambodia settlement, noting that troop withdrawal remains unresolved and that the fundamental flaw of the talks has been the absence of the U.S.S.R. and China. "China and Vietnam Try Some Trade Diplomacy," 4-15, datelined Hanoi, includes important news on economic liberalization in Vietnam: "in mid-February after the Lunar New Year, or Tet, when Prime Minister Du Muoi delivered a much-discussed and well-received speech encouraging private enterprise, promising that private capital would be safe and saying, 'I wish you to become rich.' " He gives us an update on the Philippine "communist insurgency" in "In War's Changing Strategy, the Civilians Count," 6-13, taking us on a tour of a southern island with Defense Secretary Fidel Ramos, but there's precious little on the dynamics of the conflict. "For Asia, the Strain Is Showing," 7-16, looks at the grave doubts about what's next in SE Asia as the Vietnamese depart Cambodia. A good snapshot, but it's a bit muddy on where this is likely to lead.

Fallows, James. *The Atlantic.* (★ ★ ½)
Still listed as Washington editor on the monthly's masthead, Fallows has long been sending missives from East Asia, overturning what he views as the instinctive stifling of outright complaints about Japan from the "American fraternity of Japan-handlers," and establishing himself as a most provocative purveyor of "Yellow Peril" concerns. We have to acknowledge that Fallows is providing a better picture of Japan than we've seen elsewhere, but it's all too often views through a prism that rearranges the colors according to his policy perspectives. "The Hard Life," 3-89, takes on the conventional questions — if the Japanese are so wealthy, why do they live in cramped housing and commute on cramped trains? — and delivers a too familiar answer: the Japanese just don't want to change. However, there are mountains of sharp detail in every paragraph of this long report. He furnishes the Japanese viewpoint on defense spending, with emphasis on the FSX controversy in "Let Them Defend Themselves," 4-89. This works well, showing how unpopular the *jieitai* (self-defense force) is, and sharply poses the question of what, exactly, an expanded Japanese defense would do. If we could excise his policy proposals and his tendentious analytics from the exhaustive 5-89 cover, it would be an outstanding report, the wealth of detail, data, and insights into Japan so impressive. But his agenda is metastasized throughout the report, beginning with the title itself, "Containing Japan," which conjures up an image previously reserved only for the Communist menace. He puts Shanghai's historic uniqueness within China's economic landscape into a current context with "Bright Lights Fade in China's Big City," *U.S.News & World Report* 6-21, and in "South Korea Only Wants a Little Respect," *USN&WR* 8-14, he reports on the strained relations between the U.S. and the R.O.C.

However, the general cultural point he makes isn't really sufficient as a basis for the issue addressed: "As a small country in a region where large powers contend, Korea is used to seeing itself as an *innocent* victim whose pure Confucian virtues become polluted only when outsiders interfere." With the thesis that "Japan's rise has changed the rules of international trade," Fallows counsels an end to the U.S. negotiating strategy in "Getting Along with Japan," 12-89. Reviewing various strategies for U.S.-Japan trade relations, Fallows rejects most (though he ends up supportive of shock treatments like tariffs) and settles for the use of blunt instruments against Japan.

Farah, Douglas. *The Washington Post.* (★)
El Salvador stringer. We could read his dispatches from this tortured nation without having to grit our teeth in frustration this year, as Farah has cleaned up some of the more egregious biases in his reporting. "War, Poor Coffee Crop Afflicting Salvadorans," 12-28-88, reports on the potential for a swelling in the ranks of the country's Marxist guerrillas as a consequence of a poor coffee harvest, but this is really pure conjecture. One-third of the country is without local, elected civilian authority, we learn in "El Salvador's Mayors Quit in Droves," 1-8, as mayors whose lives have been threatened by the guerrillas continue resigning. Farah reports that although Christian Democrat mayors have also been threatened, the majority targeted are associated with ARENA. He's relatively accurate, but timid, in "Salvadoran Leftist's Campaign Comes Under Guns of Guerrillas," 3-17, on the uneasy relations between the leftist Democratic Convergence party running in the elections and the Farabundo Marti guerrillas who are violently opposing national elections. There is an informative focus on Cuban and Sandinista mischief here. Farah, as almost every other correspondent on this beat, draws the same question out of ARENA's electoral victory in "Key Salvadoran Case Thrown Out of Court," 4-3: Can President-Elect Cristiani "control right-wing elements in his own party." "Salvadoran Rightist Sworn In as President," 6-2, is a straightforward report on the transfer of power to Alfredo Cristiani that includes a good summary of his basic 5-point plan for talks with leftist rebels and proposals to allow peasants individual title to property rather than collective ownership. The usual pejorative descriptions of ARENA are absent in this report. "El Salvador Civil War — New Tactics Old Stalemates," 7-23, is skewed in the images it presents: From the government side, "the gunner in the helicopter gripped his twin machine guns *nervously*," while on the guerrilla side, "they *feel confident* that their new Soviet-Bloc weapons can now partially neutralize the army's." "3 Salvadoran Politicians Found Dead," 11-8, cites sources from Ruben Zamora's Popular Social Christian Movement that the murder of three of its members was carried out by soldiers of the 6th Military Detachment, and quotes U.S. officials on the incident and its consequences for the administration of Pres. Cristiani, but Farah never gives any response from the government.

Fein, Esther B. *The New York Times.* (★ ★ ½)
Moscow. The *Times* enjoys its lofty reputation largely because of its substantial resources. More often than not those resources are journalists like Fein, skilled, feature-oriented reporters posted to foreign bureaus who can go after human-interest and other non-earthshaking news stories, leaving the more celebrated correspondents free to shmooze with their sources and to write 10,000 word articles that win Pulitzers. Stories like "A Day in (Basketball) Court for Soviet-Israeli Diplomacy," 1-13, and "It's a Disgrace! Moscow's Warmest January in 100 Years," 1-18, are typical Fein fare, colorful featurettes about topics that may not be as vitally important as START negotiations, but are very helpful in giving us a more well-rounded view of Soviet society. "Soviet Openness Brings Poverty Out of the Shadows," 1-29, has officials admitting the existence of poverty, conceding that 20 percent of the population lives in poverty, with pensioners living on fixed incomes the hardest hit. "Full of Fight, Yeltsin Feels He's the One," 2-23, describes Gorbachev's chief foil as a "burly man with a wave of white hair and a lip that often seems curled on the verge of a defiant sneer, [who] sees. . .[the election] as a vehicle of bitter popular discontent, as if he were a Soviet George Wallace or Huey Long." A sharp image, but the report lacks any evidence to support this. "Soviet Conservatives Try to Turn Back the Clock

on Gorbachev's Policies," 2-27, is somewhat disorganized in telling how Soviet "conservatives" yearning for the old ways are using liberalized policies to restore them. "Loss of a Soviet Mars Spacecraft Shakes Project to Explore Planet," 3-30, contained news we hadn't seen elsewhere, that the main transmitter on Phobos 2 had failed in December and they were relying on a backup. "In Lenin's Classless Society, It Hurts to Be Old and Poor," 5-10, is a remarkable feature on Leningrad's first private, free soup-kitchen for the elderly poor. An important development, "Estonia Approves Law on Residency," 8-9, the Baltic state blatantly discriminating against native Russians, Fein satisfies except in failing to provide Moscow's thoughts on mechanisms to prevent this. "Read Their Lips! Soviet Legislators Vote No to Proposal for New Sin Taxes," 11-1, is a frothy headline, but quite good on the economic discussions at the Supreme Soviet. "The Kremlin Reacts Calmly, But Says Border Must Stay," 11-11, provides surface reaction on the opening of the Berlin wall, not much more. In Prague for the big day of Alexander Dubcek's return, she catches the spirit nicely, "In Wenceslas Square, a Shout: Freedom!" 11-25 P. 1: "Word surged through the crowd like a current, and it seemed that within seconds every one of the hundreds of thousands of people in Wenceslas Square learned that the entire Czechoslovak Communist Party leadership had resigned." *Svabodu!* Freedom!

Fineman, Mark B. *Los Angeles Times.* (★ ★)
New Delhi bureau chief. Fineman turned in another year of reliable, albeit unspectacular, reporting. Although he doesn't break many stories, we appreciate his ability to contribute to our understanding of events which are superficially covered elsewhere. His reports on Vietnamese refugees in Hong Kong is a strong case in point. "Soviets Try to Keep Afghan Lifeline Open," 2-3, datelined Kabul, reports on the tactical and strategic significance of the Salang Tunnel, "the final battleground for the Soviet Union in its long and bloody struggle in Afghanistan." It's solid stuff, although Fineman doesn't bring up Western diplomatic charges of a Soviet "scorched-earth policy" until six paragraphs into the article. "Spiraling Wave of Terror Washes Once-Idyllic Isle," 4-11, offers a chilling account of the situation in Sri Lanka where 2,000 people have been killed in random attacks by both government and rebel groups. Fineman captures fully the sense of fear among the people, with vivid imagery and personal interviews. "Bhutto's Visit to U.S. May Set Off 'Benazir Mania,' " 6-4, offers a favorable profile of the Pakistani leader on the eve of her visit, with Fineman giving PM Bhutto the benefit of the doubt on her domestic and international headaches. The interview yields no real news, though, and he quotes a criticism from a member of the opposition of her policy of borrowing abroad — "I would rather eat grass than borrow money" — without picking up on the reference to her father, Zulfikar Ali Bhutto, who claimed Pakistanis would eat grass if that's what it took to finance a nuclear arms program. "Hong Kong's Pent-Up Refugee Crisis Erupts," 9-3, does a good job of acquainting American readers with the horrible conditions Vietnamese refugees live under in Hong Kong, and the problems they present for the small British colony. His description of the recent refugee phenomenon as a "largely economic exodus" seems to play into the official Hong Kong government policy of granting legitimate refugee status only to those Vietnamese who can claim political persecution. "Battle of Gandhis Heats Up in Heartland," 11-20, is the sort of Indian election story that Paul Scott might have written, with Fineman profiling the race between Rajiv Gandhi, grandson of Jawaharlal Nehru, and Rajmohan Gandhi, grandson of Mohandas K. Gandhi. Fineman offers us some wonderful vignettes of modern campaign techniques being plied in remote impoverished villages, but he never cites even one opinion poll, which might have let us know how well or how poorly the beleaguered Prime Minister is really doing in his home district.

Fisher, Dan. *Los Angeles Times.* (★ ★ ★)
London. This outstanding pro in the *LA Times* stable of foreign correspondents picked right up on his new beat after turning in a three-star performance in the Jerusalem bureau. "At Least 258 Dead in Scotland Crash of N.Y-Bound 747," 12-22-88, crackles like a rapid-fire, on-the-scene radio broadcast, and we found Fisher's subsequent coverage of the Pan Am disaster to be

first-rate. Each report carefully recapped all that had happened and all that had been learned up to that point, leaving us feeling like we knew everything there was to know about this incident. Reporting from Moscow in January, Fisher filed "Back-Room Maneuvers Mar Soviet Vote Drive," 1-25, an informative look behind the scene at the Soviet Union's first-ever multi-candidate national elections, casting a more discerning eye on the subject than others did at the time: "the results of elections scheduled March 26 for a new national parliament are already being manipulated in the Soviet equivalent of smoke-filled rooms. But even this carefully controlled exercise in Soviet-style democracy has encouraged the beginnings of grass-roots political expectations that could have important influence on the shape of life here for years to come." His "Soviets Disclose They Had Warheads in Cuba," 1-29, is a sharp account of a Moscow seminar on the Cuban Missile Crisis, the clearest on the story of one participant who reported Castro urged Khrushchev to fire missiles at the U.S. "Multicultural Concept Takes a Beating in Britain," 3-1, was disappointing, with Fisher giving us a long, dry lead and then a rehash of old British newspaper editorials. Too bad, because he was writing about what was actually an interesting topic: inexcusable journalism. "$21 Billion Bid for Huge British Conglomerate," 7-12, on the bid to take over BAT Industries, is an example of superior reporting, Fisher using interesting bits of background information and a multitude of details to make high drama out of what could have been another LBO story. In "Popular Political Loner Emerges as Most Likely Successor to Thatcher," 8-12, Fisher produced another one of his occasional clunkers, a profile of British politician Michael Heseltine that isn't fleshed-out. Fisher spends far too much time before getting to the personal side and when he does he doesn't reveal enough. Just as important, there's no analysis of what the U.S. could expect from a Prime Minister Heseltine.

Ford, Maggie. *Financial Times.* (★ ½)
Seoul. For steady, consistent reporting on the political economy of this bustling country, we turn to Ford, although this year *The Wall Street Journal* moved up as a strong competitor. Ford is upbeat on potentials for a thaw in relations between the two Koreas in "Korea Trades Away Its Divisions," 1-17, noting that "Perhaps the best hope for progress between the two Koreas will be in economic links, where propaganda and ideology are less important than hard financial facts and mutual economic interest." She puts industrial relations into a context for projection as to whether the future is to be one of confrontation or negotiation, with "Labour Relations Poser for Seoul," 4-25. Ford makes no unnecessary conclusions, but does provide enough details and background in this report for us to have a decent reference point for the questions she poses. Developing the lead article for the *Financial Times* "Survey" on South Korea, she delivers an empathetic appreciation of the country's transition from authoritarianism, intelligently relating a series of recent political and economic events that bear on the efforts to restructure South Korea's economy, "Difficult Transitions," 6-15. Among the triumph's of foreign policy, she cites the country's achievement in persuading the U.S. not to include S. Korea on its Super 301 list of targets. We get additional information and details on the country's local car industry in "Volvo Joint Deal Sets Pace for S. Korea Carmakers," 9-20, which has a very bullish spin to it. "S Korean Business Under Fire for Investment Failure," 10-11, is an important report on the debate within the country over strategies for economic growth. Ford gives us more information on this than we see elsewhere, but even here the treatment is one-dimensional. "Snakes Alive in Korea's Cinemas," 10-5, updates us on the ultimately successful battle to distribute foreign films in the country. Ford reports that the initially hostile reaction (in which live snakes were released in cinemas showing foreign films) based on fears of a further invasion of American culture, is giving way to the popularity of quality films.

Frankel, Glenn. *The Washington Post.* (★ ★ ½)
Frankel started '89 in Jerusalem, but mid-year, the '88 Pulitzer Prize recipient transferred to London, exchanging Yitzhak Shamir, Yasir Arafat, and the Israeli censors for Margaret Thatcher, the I.R.A., and the Official Secrets Act. "West Bank Mayor Drops Truce Call," 1-4, provides a clear-eyed look at PLO tactics in the West Bank: "[Bethlehem Mayor Elias] Freij's

quick, submissive response [to Arafat's warning that anyone proposing an end to the Palestinian uprising "exposes himself to the bullets of his own people"] suggested to some observers here that despite recent professions of moderation and renunciations of terrorism, the threat of assassination remains an important weapon in the PLO's arsenal for controlling local Arab leaders." His "Israeli Intelligence Agencies Link Peace to Talks With PLO," 3-21, is a well rounded, informative report on the hottest leak yet out of the Shamir cabinet. "Intifada Proves Durable," 3-25, offers an in-depth look at the fifteen-month-old Palestinian uprising's secret underground war with Israeli authorities. In "Vote Plan Approved in Israel," 5-15, we get a good survey of th eissues and political maneuvers which led to the Israeli coalition cabinet's decision to provide for election of Palestinian reps in the occupied territories: "The plan marks the first time that Israel's two major political parties, the right-of-center Likud and the left-leaning Labor, have been able to agree on a joint peace program," and Frankel judges that it was neither easy nor enough. "Palestinians Divide on Use of Arms and Israeli Vote Initiative," 6-15, is a vintage Frankel report, an insightful look both at how the Palestinian leadership ranks are beginning to splinter "over the future of the uprising and the use of firearms against soldiers and Jewish settlers. . .[and] Arafat's calls for continued restraint," and the Israeli policy to hound moderate Palestinian leaders in order to tilt the scales in favor of radicals who oppose the election plan. "Thatcher Style, Judgment Reevaluated," 10-28, an analysis of the political fallout of the Lawson resignation, does a good job of showing how the present crisis, like so many of Mrs. Thatcher's political crises in the past, stemmed from a volatile mixture of policy and personality — the strong-willed Mrs. Thatcher insisting on her own policy. Frankel quotes British insiders to bring home the point that for the Thatcher government, this may be the beginning of the end.

Freed, Kenneth. *Los Angeles Times.* (★ ½)
San Salvador bureau chief. We suspect Freed shares the bias against ARENA and its leaders that so many of the other journalists here exhibit, but he at least keeps it in check sufficiently enough to report important information we aren't seeing elsewhere. Doing duty elsewhere in Central America, his "Panama's Delvalle Pay Dearly for Brief Reign as President," 12-22-88, spends far too much time discussing President Delvalle's personal problems, and not enough on the upcoming elections. In "Rebels Target U.S.-Aided Program in Rural El Salvador," 1-13, Freed reports on leftist guerrillas effectively disrupting civic leadership in rural areas by killing mayors and other officials, primarily ARENA members. Freed makes a point we rarely saw from his *New York Times* counterpart: "The rebels have little in the way of a substitute program, so they have chosen to terrorize rather than convert." In "Salvador Winner: False Face for D'Aubuisson?" 3-21, he raises many questions but provides few answers about the political situation in El Salvador. But Freed importantly notes what other journalists here omit — that the Salvadoran working class regards ARENA and its leader D'Aubuisson with almost messianic adoration, despite their history and opposition to populist programs such as land reform — but he's not able to sort this out nor satisfactorily explain the Christian Democrat Party's defeat. "Gunman Opens Fire at Medellin Airport; 2 Die," 9-5, is flat, wire-service quality writing, perhaps reflecting the fact Freed was writing from Bogota, and relying on official police accounts. "U.S. Aid Called Unsuitable for Colombia Task," 9-10, is better, with Freed using unnamed U.S. and Colombian officials to criticize Bush's military aid package to Colombia, with the "key officials" pointing out that the package consists of hardware suitable for conventional warfare, not the radios and communication equipment needed by Colombian law enforcement officials. He gives us a trenchant observation from one U.S. critic there: "It would have been better to have had a shopping list for Radio Shack." Unlike most reports of this type, which simply say the President's tactics for waging the War on Drugs won't work, this gives us some idea of why they won't work.

Fuhrman, Peter. *Forbes.* (★ ★)
Europe. *Forbes* doesn't have a bureau in Moscow — yet — but Fuhrman kept the U.S.S.R. a steady focus of his reporting for the year. "Another Stake Through Stalin's Heart," 12-26-88, reports the rehabilitation of N.D. Kondratieff (originator of the Kondratieff long-wave theory

of economics), putting it in context; it's not the content of his ideas that are key, but the fact that reformists can publicize this Russian's criticism of state planning in agriculture to justify the loosening of controls. A novel angle, but there's not much meat. "Governing Legacy," 1-23, details the huge burden for an otherwise thriving Austria of OAIG, a huge, state-owned holding company, and the inertia around its reform as politicians insist economic restructuring must be accomplished without adding to unemployment. "Herr Reuter Takes to the Skies," 3-20, gets a good forward look at the perspectives of Edzard Reuter, Daimler-Benz board chairman, for "unifying splintered parts of German industry to make Daimler-Benz nothing less than the cornerstone of the economically united Europe promised for 1992." Fuhrman does note that some politicians worry that Daimler is growing too large to be effectively regulated, but we would have appreciated a bit more on the potentials for a clash here. He's persuasive on Bulgaria's partnerships with world drug dealers, carefully following the evidence out in "The Bulgarian Connection," 4-17. "Moscow's Debt Crisis," 5-29, paints a dire picture of the East Bloc's own Third World debt plight. Soviet clients have chalked up huge debts, buying from the Bloc on credit not hard currency, and have little intention of repayment. Fuhrman divides the specific situations, noting that the U.S.S.R. retains some leverage since these countries remain dependent on it as their major arms supplier. Fuhrman attempts to answer questions as to "what's up with the Soviet gold industry?" Although we get some new information out of this, and interesting guesses, we still come away with unanswered questions from "The Man with the Golden Headache," 9-18.

Galuszka, Peter. *Business Week.* (★ ½)
Moscow bureau chief. There was unevenness from Galuszka, with important topics given too little attention or detail this year, although he is edging into the economics of *perestroika*. "And You Think Western Capitalists Have Problems," 1-30, outlines the problems faced by Soviet cooperatives — hoodlums, bureaucrats, jealous citizens — but there's nothing new here. An incredibly important story gets very skimpy treatment from Galuszka *et al,* in "The Vote Heard Round the World," 4-10, only two pages of text and photos devoted to the Soviet elections. Excellent, though, is "Gorbachev's Reforms: Will They Work?" with Rose Brady in Moscow, Robert J. Dowling in Leningrad, 6-5. The intersection of politics and economics is attended to, with first an analysis of Gorbachev's next moves ("He is preparing to dump the blame for the failure of *perestroika* on the government"). This is followed by a look at the economy, which includes information on the attitudes of workers and factory managers and on the progress of attempts to lease businesses to workers. The consequences of having no banking system are addressed and there's exploration into the implications of lifting price controls, devaluing the ruble, and letting the currency trade on foreign markets. "A Talk With Nikolai Ryzhkov, Economic Czar," 6-5, is interesting and useful on the Soviet official's frank strategic outlook and his worried concern over potentials for avoiding "social unrest" that could be a consequence of going too far too fast (e.g., dumping price controls). "Farming For Dollars: Gorbachev's Latest Gamble," 8-28, is a coherent report on the latest move to boost Soviet grain production: paying grain farmers in U.S. dollars or other hard currency, and it includes the outlook for grain purchases from the U.S.

Goodhart, David. *Financial Times.* (★ ★)
Bonn. A satisfying reporter, Goodhart is dutiful in providing the necessary amount of data and background in his reports. We often pick up a detail here not seen elsewhere. There are sufficient details in "German Steelmakers Forge Strongly Ahead," 1-4, to provide an informative report on the steel industry, pushing aside gloomy forecasts and on the perspective for increased production. Goodhart provides some new angles on the issue of German laxity regarding sensitive exports in "Obsession with Exports Blinds West Germany to the Rules," 1-6. Reporting that while critics argue that the government is unaware of what murkier parts of the private sector may be up to, feeble application of tough export control is now an integral part of the country's export-obsessed national culture. Goodhart employs a good range of different views to make his analysis interesting and somewhat comprehensive in "Missiles Represent Wider

Debate on German Interests," 1-24, a very good overview of the short-range nuclear missile issue and how it divides West Germany from the United States in terms of NATO policy. However, he unaccountably fails to identify most of his sources; "analysts," "supporters," and "observers" do not normally require anonymity. Essential detail on West Germany's corporate taxes, among the highest in the world, are supplied as important background for a concise report on the Economic Minister's announcement that the '92 corporate tax reductions should not be paid for by higher consumer taxes nor involve a fundamental change in the corporate tax paid by municipal authorities, "Haussman Revises Stand on Changes in W German Tax," 3-23. "The New Mood Picks Up The Fortunes of West German Greens," 4-11, works very well as a summary of the Green Party's growing influence in West German politics, Goodhart not discounting the possibility of their involvement as a coalition partner in a new government down the line. "W German Parties Continue to Squabble," and " 'Now We Can Be a Single Family — Together Again,' " 11-13, are both colorfully written reports. In the first, we can feel the pique both Chancellor Kohl and West Berlin's SPD mayor Walter Momper feel with each other, the personal annoyances overlaid by political differences. Goodhart works background and some analysis into two reports on the perspectives for the Germanies from the West German government, rounding the stories out with a fine reporting of responses from officials from both sides of the wall: "Genscher Stresses That Europe Should Not Fear the Open Door," 11-11, and "Kohl's Vision of German Unity," 11-29.

Graven, Kathryn. *The Wall Street Journal.* (★ ½)
Tokyo. It was somewhat difficult deciding what rating to give this correspondent, as she so often shares bylines. We did find her reports on proposals for regulation of Japan's financial markets basically informative. "If Japan Is So Hot, How Come Its Yen Ain't Worth a Cent?" 1-19, is a light feature about concern in Japan (where it takes 10,000 yen to buy a silk necktie) over proposals to lop zeros off their currency. "Japan Sets Insider-Trading Curbs, But Critics Say Rules Lack Punch," 1-25, is straight reporting on the guidelines proposed: prohibiting company insiders from trading shares until twelve hours after material information has been disclosed to two or more news agencies. The media, of course, becomes as critical as some companies. "Japanese Regulators Want to Hold Down Volatility Caused by Stock-Index Futures," 1-26, alerts us to restrictive proposals now circulating among regulators who are worried that Japan's new stock-index futures are too volatile. Graven reports that the Finance Ministry hasn't any evidence of increased active arbitrage trading causing the increased volatility. "As Coffee Supplants Tea Ritual, Japanese Smell Opportunity Abroad," 7-17, is a rich report. The details are fresh, and strongly brewed as we learn that since 1986 Japan has been drinking more coffee than green tea, and is now the world's fourth largest coffee consumer. However, Graven reports, Japanese favor a stronger flavor than exists in U.S. coffee, and think they've got a winner in their brew. Yep, they're embarking on a campaign to market their canned coffee in the U.S. "Shareholder Rights Idea Grows in Japan," 8-28, is a zippy post-T. Boone Pickens assessment of an issue that has rocked Japan's establishment. Graven reports on the emergence of home-grown advocates of individual investors there. "JAL, Lufthansa and Air France Discuss Venture," 10-19, can't confirm plans to form an international air freight company that will further consolidate the industry, but Graven at least makes a serious effort.

Greenhouse, Steven. *The New York Times.* (★ ★)
Paris. After steadily advancing the past several years Greenhouse seemed to stall out in '89. We frequently would finish one of his articles and find we still had many questions. "Nestle's Time to Swagger," 1-1, was one of the best stories we saw all year from Greenhouse, as he profiled Helmut Naucher, the first German to run Swiss Nestle, including great data on the rejuvenation of the biggest food company in the world. Much as we liked the article we would have appreciated an explanation as to why Naucher's decision to sell voting shares to foreigners caused so much turmoil in the market. "Spain, Losing Backward Image, Booms as It Lures Foreign Money," 1-15, gives no explanation why unemployment is 20% in a "boom." There's no statistical comparisons and no info on fiscal or monetary policy, although we do learn at least

that there is growth. We learn where Giovanni Agnelli and Fiat are these days in "Fighting to Stay on Top in Europe," 2-5, a snapshot which places too much emphasis on a two-man power struggle that Agnelli already decided. One intriguing line, that Italians are "patriotic" in buying their own cars, is never really explained. "European Fighter: Cost vs. Pride," 2-21, gives us the flip side of the FSX flap, with four West European countries chipping in to create the new European Fighter Aircraft and the U.S. claiming that the aircraft is too expensive, too duplicative and too prone to technology leakage. Greenhouse, based in Munich, does a nice job of presenting the European case, less concerned with U.S. (or French) objections. He also fails to tell us why Congress isn't in a panic about occidentals who refuse to buy our planes. "Europe's Economic Split," 4-24, provides fairly good background on U.K.'s resistance to a European currency and central bank, but Greenhouse doesn't understand monetary fundamentals and doesn't grasp the nature of the sovereignty issue. "The Television Europeans Love, And Love to Hate," 8-13, captures the growing battle of cultural influence vs. the economics of the entertainment industry as France pushes for quotas on U.S. television productions, with Britain and Germany resisting: "American producers assert — and many European broadcasters agree — that American programs are as good as, if not better than, European shows because of Hollywood's larger budget and wealth of talent." Greenhouse does very well, shipped to Prague in a hurry to cover the big news there, "Prague Premier Sees Top Foes, Shares Platform With Dubcek, Party Calls Special Congress," 11-27 P. 1, giving us a mixture of detail and informed speculation on what's up with the Politburo shuffle.

Gruson, Lindsey. *The New York Times.* (—)
San Salvador bureau chief. There's nothing we hate worse than having to flunk a journalist, as we did Gruson's predecessor here last year. However, the reporting out of this bureau is the least credible from all the foreign corps, and Gruson's dispatches simply violate professional standards of journalism. *Times*' editors certainly share culpability, but Gruson isn't a novice. "Besieged San Salvador Feels Realities of War," 1-23, tells us nothing about the goal of the country's Marxist guerrillas, sticking simply to their short-range tactic: turn the capital into a war zone and target all Americans living there. Gruson reads tea leaves — "Is Alfredo Cristiani, ARENA presidential candidate, too close to Roberto D'Aubuisson?" — and doesn't tell us what the campaign is all about in "As Salvador Vote Nears, Which Way for the Right?" 3-12. He recirculates a stale old story about ARENA and death squads in "Likely Rightist Victory in El Salvador Poses Major Policy Challenge for U.S.," 3-19, quoting former U.S. Ambassador Robert White, but no officials from ARENA. He makes no attempt to discover why the party is so popular, instead contemptuously dismissing the electorate of El Salvador, "a country that tunes into the emotional pitch of a stump speech rather than its content." Slim material, "The New Faces of the Right," 3-21, presents Alfredo Cristiani as a pasteboard character with one saving grace, the ability to listen to complaints. Gruson doesn't supply even one quote from Cristiani to distinguish him. Gruson's at his worst with "Rightists Take Control Today in El Salvador," 6-1, producing one of the most blatantly biased dispatches we saw anywhere in the press all year. There's no perspective whatsoever, as ARENA is mentioned in connection to "right-wing death squads" throughout, with a pejorative "fascist" quote thrown in. We get a better snapshot from him as the ARENA party takes over in El Salvador in "Deeper Fractures in Central America," 6-4, but his designation of Jose Duarte's defeated party as "center right" is wacky. "Salvadoran Government Proposes Laws to Crackdown on Dissent," 7-4, is a barely acceptable account of new proposals strengthening language and penalties on civil dissent, needing some comparisons in order to evaluate its accuracy. Gruson does very little reporting in "Priests Killed In A Campus Raid In San Salvador," 11-17, much of the article devoted to his standard recirculation of old allegations about Roberto D'Aubuisson and ARENA.

Gumbel, Peter. *The Wall Street Journal.* (★ ★)
Moscow bureau chief. We found less static and more detail in his reporting this year. Though still keeping the wary eye on *perestroika,* the cynicism that sometimes intruded in the past was kept locked away. We get an enlightening A-hed feature on Soviet environmentalism in "Save

the Reindeer: Siberian Gas Drillers Feel Activist's Wrath," 12-23-88. "Over Pepsi and Cigars in Moscow, Ex-Officials Dissect '62 Cuban Crisis," 1-30, is a sketchy report hitting the high spots, but giving us nothing on reports that Castro urged nuclear attack on the U.S. in 1962, which was reported in *The Washington Post* 1-29 and *The New York Times* 1-30. "Critics Doubt Soviet Psychiatry Reformed," 2-2, is persuasive on the reasons to question reports affirming the end of psychiatric abuse in the U.S.S.R., Gumbel using good quotes in one interview. The wary eye falls upon Gorbachev's plans for agricultural reform and the resistance he's encountering in "Moscow Tackles No. 1 Domestic Problem," 3-10, and, although it still left us with questions, the details were basically satisfying. But Gumbel let the story get away from him, producing a skimpy "Gorbachev Asks Restructuring of Farm System," 3-16, buried on P. 13, while the *NYT*'s Bill Keller gets a P. 1 lead. He improves with better detail in "Plan to Let Soviet Farmers Lease Land Gains Approval in Boost to Gorbachev," 3-17, including a fine observation: "As so often with economic reforms [Gorbachev] announces with a flourish, the fine point of the legislation is as important as the vision." "Election of Yeltsin, Other Radicals Could Mean Trouble For Kremlin," 3-28, is a solid account and analysis of Soviet elections. "Moscow Spring. A Wide-Open Debate Helps Soviets Avoid The China Syndrome," 6-7, reports the "democracy" movement has strengthened Gorbachev's legitimacy, but the analysis, while not facile, is too quick, with no angle on how a serious economic downturn could change this. "Gorbachev's Style and Good Advance Man Make Him a Hot Ticket in West Germany," 6-14, illuminating Gorbachev's Bonn trip by focusing on his advance man, Nikola Portugalov, contains absorbing detail and angles, and is among the best we've seen from Gumbel. "Red Square Scare: As Coup Talk Sweeps Moscow, How Firm is Gorbachev's Grip?" 9-13, is the report for which he'll be long remembered, as it was one of the most hotly discussed reports on the U.S.S.R. this year. Gumbel produces many details, angles and anecdotes on the problems battering the head of the U.S.S.R., but there really isn't the evidence here to support any notion of an anti-Gorbachev coup.

Haberman, Clyde. *The New York Times.* (★ ★)
Rome bureau chief. Unlike his counterpart at *The Washington Post,* Haberman doesn't work the Italian political economy intensively, and we feel cheated on his coverage of this G-7 nation. Bustling about the region, Haberman often covers other countries in the eastern Mediterranean and the Balkans. We get some perspective on the political uncertainty that may be ahead in Turkey as inflation emerges among other problems to challenge PM Turgut Ozal, "Favor Fading, Premier Faces Turkish Vote," 1-11. "As Islam is Revived, Secular Turks Wince," 3-26, a good report on Islamic revival, isn't clear on implications for the course of the Turkish state. "Italy Embarks on Bold Efforts to Save Fabled City of Venice From Threatening Tides," 1-31, although a well-done feature for P. 1 of "Science Times," adds nothing we haven't already read elsewhere on the topic. There's a bit of new info in "Life With Glamorous Venice Isn't All Romance," 6-14, but his choice of stories leaves something to be desired. Haberman works fresh information into "Abortion Law in Italy Draws Growing Fire," 2-19, and we learn some 70% of the gynecologists in Italy declare themselves conscientious objectors and refuse to perform abortions. "Pope Addressing Syrians, Labels the Shelling of Beirut 'Genocide,' " 8-16, selects sufficiently from the Pontiff's appeal to convey its dramatic tone, Haberman providing further details on Pope John Paul II's concern for Lebanon with comments from his aides and a Vatican spokesman. From Sofia, "Bulgarian Chief Quits After 35 Years of Rigid Rule," 11-11, is the best report we saw on the resignation of Todor I. Zhivkov and the new breed of dissidents in a country that seemed the rear guard of the Communist World. Haberman reports on an important advantage secured by the country's dissidents (who have an interesting connection to environmentalism) with "Bulgarian Hearing Heartens Illegal Dissidents," 11-14, putting into context the question as to how fast Bulgaria will change.

Hamilton, Masha. *Los Angeles Times.* (★ ★)
Moscow. "Promising" may be the best way to describe Hamilton's work, as she broke out of the pack with her foreign correspondence this year. An able addition to this hardworking bureau,

she led off the year with "Gorbachev Calls for Gumption in Reform Push," 1-1, giving us sound, objective reporting on Gorbachev's New Year's Eve speech in Moscow. Hamilton worked-in recent events in the Soviet Union, particularly the televised confrontations between Gorbachev and Soviet consumers, to provide a richer context. "Don't Forget Us, Fasting Women Refuseniks Plead," 3-10, has Hamilton interviewing a group of 46 Jewish women on a three-day fast in hopes of getting enough attention to convince the Soviet government to let them emigrate. But she doesn't tell enough about these women to provoke a sympathetic response. "Kremlin Aide Sent to Calm Riotous Area," 4-11, is a fast-paced news piece on riots in Soviet Georgia. Though unable to report from the scene because of restrictions on foreign journalists, Hamilton makes the most of official reports and interviews by phone, conveying the tension and drama. Articles like "Soviet A-Tests Blamed for Deaths, Illness in Siberia," 8-17, made us wonder if Hamilton got the job of reading Soviet newspapers this year, this piece on high death rates in a Soviet region near the Bering Strait is a rehash from *Moscow News* and TASS. "Khrushchev Put Back on the Pedestal," 9-15, looks at the most recent example of "the Soviet process of remaking history" — a Khrushchev exhibit at Moscow's Youth Palace. Hamilton does a top-drawer job of placing the rehabilitation of Khrushchev in the context of current Soviet political dynamics, but there's little mention of what the exhibit did and didn't say about his role during some of the worst crises of the Cold War, and no mention of what the Khrushchev revival may portend for Gorbachev's foreign policy. In "Muscovites Hoard Goods as Consumer Crisis Grows," 10-23, Hamilton brings home to American readers the physical and psychological impact of the growing consumer crunch in the U.S.S.R. — "It was fear that drove Valentina Gregenschikov to stand in line to buy two packages of imported razor blades for which she had no use, the same anxiety that made her, for the first time in memory, salt away in her cupboards extra sacks of flour and rice against Moscow's long winter" — but she allows the experts she talks with to lay the blame for the crisis at everyone's door from the Czars to Gorbachev, without raising the possibility that the fault may be in the communist system itself.

Harden, Blaine. *The Washington Post.* (★ ★)
Warsaw bureau chief. We saw little of the former Nairobi bureau chief's byline for much of the year as he was preparing for his new posting. More than just a change of clime and customs, the assignment to Warsaw is demanding, and we chalk up a year less impressive than the last one, when he racked up a three-and-a-half star rating, to Harden still getting his footing here. Harden includes a nice amount of detail and data in "African Nations on Long, Miserable Road to Economic Reform," 1-15, contrasting Zambia and Ghana's experiences with economic reform. There's a dependence here on the IMF's perspectives of hardship and pain as the road to reform; Harden is too easily persuaded by the IMF view. "Refugees Face New Obstacle," 9-5, contains newsy details and vivid imagery on the saga of East Germans once again fleeing to freedom in West Germany, but the composition is a bit immature. Only towards the end is there an attempt to unify these vignettes with a theme. "Polish 'Vacations' Highlight Plight," 9-15, is his version of a story we saw all year in the press — impoverished, highly-qualified Polish specialists taking their vacations to work as menials in West Germany. In this one Harden tells us of an anesthesiologist who "by working for just two months as an illegal and untaxed employee of the H-L Market in the fashionable Schwabing quarter of Munich. . .earned the hard-currency equivalent of 16 years' salary in Poland." He's alert on important shifts in Czechoslovakia in "Czechoslovakia Awaits A Thaw," 9-29, reporting that "party members are beginning to hedge their bets," noting "the reluctance of mid-level Communist officials to demand that their subordinates and non-party members toe the party line." Harden's evocative skills come out in "Warsaw Rite Recalls Terrors of Stalin Era," 10-31, which is a moving account of the sad, sobering ceremony in Warsaw. He's deliberative and thoughtful in an analytical "Strong Influence Suspected in Sudden Departure of Bulgarian Leader," 11-12, although he never provides detail on the Soviet role in Zhivkov's retirement. A flabby "Unaccustomed to Protest, Bulgarians Try to Learn," 11-13, struck us as pretentious and contrived on a meeting of 20 Bulgarian ecologists, the hard news on the dissidents not there.

Hazarika, Sanjoy. *The New York Times.* (★)
India. India's role and influence throughout the subcontinent was an important theme in his work all year. We get as much basic information here as anywhere else on India's "experimental" project, "India Is Reportedly Ready to Test Missile With Range of 1,500 Miles," 4-3, with Hazarika concluding that "the move is seen as an effort to assert India's military dominance in the region and to show its determination to play a more prominent role in the world." Nepal has been accusing India of bullying all year, and Hazarika gives us the story in "India Presses And Nepalese Feel the Pinch," 5-10, persuading us that the Nepalese are being squeezed. More details come out on India's extension into the other countries of the subcontinent with "Bangladeshi Insurgents Say India Is Supporting Them," 6-11, Hazarika detailing the history of this and reporting that an Indian senior security official has confirmed the assistance. A terse "Hindus Rally at Disputed Shrine in Show of Power," 11-10, gives us basic details on this focus of growing Hindu-Moslem confrontation with a bit of a sense on the assertion of power by Hindu militants. "Two Famous Names Face Off In India," 11-14, lightly fills us in on Rajmohan Gandhi, the Mahatma's grandson who's challenging Rajiv Gandhi for his Parliament seat. Hazarika's quote from an old man touched by the memory of Mohandas Gandhi is telling, not so much about his grandson, but about the electorate's attitude toward the incumbent elites: "Your grandfather sacrificed his life for the country. Yet your family did not take advantage of his name and profit from it. Other politicians have taken advantage of their lineage. So the least we can do is vote for you."

Hiatt, Fred. *The Washington Post.* (★ ½)
Tokyo bureau chief. Straightforward, reliable, even displaying a flash of daring and imagination at times, Hiatt still has problems in sighting the intersection of politics and economics here. He teamed with Young Ho Lee to produce "South Korea May Cut Joint U.S. Exercises," 1-6, putting into context press reports of possible cutbacks; they see it as a gesture to North Korea. "Stock Scandal Seen as Threat to Takeshita," 1-28, brings us up-to-date on the Recruit scandal, with the third resignation from the cabinet over insider stock deals prompting the first serious speculation that the "Recruit affair" may bring down the government of PM Noboru Takeshita. "Japan in Search of Fresh Thinking," 5-21, is a good characterization of Japan's greatest problem in the aftermath of the Recruit scandal: "embarrassing poverty of political leadership just as this economic powerhouse is being pressed to play a more active role in the world." "Envoy Warns Japanese on Trade," 5-31, reports and characterizes the tough "new tone" that the new U.S. Ambassador to Japan, Michael Armacost, set in his first major speech, "when he bluntly warned Japan today that the world no longer will accept excuses of delays in opening the Japanese economy to outside competition." In "For Some Japanese, It's Business as Usual in China," 6-16, we get an informative report on "Japanese businessmen streaming back to Beijing," which creates concerns that Japan's eagerness will allow China to play a "Japan card" as well as a "Soviet card." "Voters Deserting Japan's LDP," with Margaret Shapiro 6-25, is a conventional, if articulate, analysis of the unraveling of Japan's ruling Democratic Liberal Party a month before upper house elections. He created a stir in some policymaking quarters in the U.S. with "Putting Their Country on the Block: Baby Bankers Sell U.S. Firms to the Japanese," *Weekly* 7-10/16, on young U.S. investment bankers who are "pioneers of a new world order." These recent U.S. college grads, still in their early 20s, "are the flip side of the U.S. trade deficit with Japan. . .While some Americans at home buy Nissans and Sonys, the growing corps of 'baby bankers'. . .helps Japan channel its dollars back into U.S. skyscrapers, factories, and other assets."

Hiltzik, Michael A. *Los Angeles Times.* (★ ★ ½)
Nairobi bureau chief. Although events in sub-Saharan Africa north of the southern tier may not rank as being among the major stories of the year, Hiltzik produced a number of memorable reports. Whether it was acquainting readers with the religious customs of Madagascar (where people exhume corpses of loved ones and wheel them around the streets) in "Pope Hints He May Visit South Africa," 4-29, or analyzing the collectivization policies of Ethiopia's President

Mengistu in "Hoping to Leave the Famine Rut," 10-23, Hiltzik covered the continent admirably. "Zaire's Veneer of Affluence Undermined by Reality of Power," 1-2, while a well-written report on Mobutu's economic problems could use some comments from the ruling elites on where the country is going and the plans for reforms, if any. "Issue of Islamic Law Fuels Political Strife in Sudan," 2-26, is a chilling account of a nation under the rule of fundamentalists, opening with the story of one young thief being punished under Islamic law — "His right wrist and left knee were injected with a painkiller, and an antique ceremonial sword imported from Saudi Arabia was brought down sharply on numbed joints" but Hiltzik never tells us if the Muslims in Sudan are Shi'ites or Sunnis, nor does he compare the country with other Islamic states in the region. "Just for Once, Corruption's a Real Scandal," 4-20, is first-rate, the essence of foreign reporting. The story is not earth-shaking. No government will fall, nor will war break out, yet this account of public officials involved in a car selling racket in automobile-starved Zimbabwe holds the reader to the end, as Hiltzik offers a penetrating look at Zimbabwean society and an object lesson in greed and the universal quest for justice. "Cocoa Turns Bitter for Ivory Coast," 7-12, is an absorbing article on attempts by the Ivory Coast to manipulate the cocoa market — and the disastrous results. With good, meaty quotes and rich on-site detail this is one international trade story that shows the human impact. "Fruitless Leads a Blow to Leland Plane Search," 8-12, is a disappointing piece on efforts to find Rep. Mickey Leland. Hiltzik recounts some of the obstacles, but his dry and matter-of-fact tone fails to capture the sense of mission and misses the drama. Readers suffering from an Ethiopia overload may have skipped "Hoping to Leave the Famine Rut," 10-23, missing an insightful look at current efforts to lift that country out of its cycle of drought and famine, a cycle brought about by "a decade of inept agricultural planning, much of it based on Marxist-Leninist principles already abandoned by the rest of the communist world."

Hoagland, Jim. *The Washington Post.* (★ ★ ½)
"Uneven" may be the best way to describe the output of the *Post*'s associate editor and chief foreign correspondent this year, who more often than not buried his provocative analysis in prose that often struck us as being murky or pompous. The never-ending presidential election lives in "Labels and the Politics of Race," 1-19, where Hoagland reports from Zambia that "[Jesse] Jackson's performance here erases any doubt that he has begun his 1992 presidential campaign." Staying slightly ahead of the curve with "Europe's New Romance With Ecology," 3-28, Hoagland alerts us to a new issue beginning to shape European politics: "Will this new burst of interest in environmental politics...bring some shifts in the European political landscape where new issues are needed by mainstream parties as traditional left-right differences continue to blur?" We'd like to see somebody tackle the question of what happens if Western Europe goes "Green" at the same time Eastern Europe wants to go all out for economic development. "Perestroika at a Crawl," 4-6, offers shrewd diagnosis of the screw-ups of *perestroika* planners, with an original comparison: "Gorbachev resembles no one so much as Jimmy Carter after four years in power. He has met severe economic problems at home with moralizing and constantly changing policies." "Time For A Little Heresy On China?" 6-22, takes an unsentimental look at Western policy towards the Middle Kingdom: "A trip into deep isolation by China is not something to be wished for or provoked by outside powers. But it is time for Washington, London and other Western capitals to think the unthinkable: that Deng, his bloodstained army and cowed bureaucracy will not be available or particularly useful to the West in the next few years." "The Terrorists' Edge," 8-2, probed a little deeper than most articles on the fallout of the Sheik Obeid affair, with Hoagland arguing that the Israeli's action was "worse than a crime: a blunder," resulting in the Israeli secret services now possibly becoming factionalized. "All Aboard the European Express," 9-28, on 1992 which "looks to Americans and many West Europeans like a skittering of crabs on the beach. But from behind the Iron Curtain, Western Europe looks like a train building up steam and pulling out of the station." We've seen the train metaphor a thousand times before, but the crabs are new to us. Nice touch.

Holden, Ted. *BusinessWeek.* (★ ★)
We were impressed with the work out of *BW*'s Tokyo bureau this year, Holden one of its stronger reporters on the beat. A well-written summary of the serious political problems faced by the Japanese PM and his party, "Now Takeshita Really Feels the Flames of Scandal," 2-27, paints a bleak picture, although it does conclude that "For now, it appears likely that Takeshita can ride it out." Holden beat a similar *NYT* story by close to two weeks with this. A densely-packed survey, "An Onslaught from the West," 3-20, informs us on the effects of foreign traders on Japanese financial markets and the tension between foreign traders and government regulators, who are worried about keeping control and preserving certain local traditions. He forecasts Takeshita's resignation in "Why Time May Be Running Out for Takeshita," 4-24, with some analysis as to why that course now seems sensible. "Real Reform in Japan? Don't Hold Your Breath," 5-29, is a workaday review of corruption in Japan. There's not much new, except for the interesting statistic that a Diet member's expected contribution of $400 for each of 200 weddings and funerals a year push his average spending to $1.2 million, compared with $580,000 allocated by Congress to each member for staff/office expense. "Salomon Just Can't Lose — in Tokyo," 6-12, piques our interest about the "substantial local clout" of Salomon as Tokyo's biggest and most profitable foreign brokerage. Though rivals cry tokenism, Holden reports, it does seem to have influence with the government. Holden begins this informative article on Japan's Norinchukin Bank with a good lead, and follows through with a satisfying picture, "There's No Keeping This Bank Down on the Farm," 7-24. "The Birth Of A Behemoth," 9-11, an "In the News" portrait of a big bank merger, delivers a compact outline of why corporation-oriented Mitsui's earnings were lagging as cash-rich companies didn't need to borrow as much anymore. Well-written on the Dai-Ichi/Kangyo merger and what it faces in Japanese competition, "Dai-Ichi's Move On CIT: It's Bold — And About Time," 9-25, develops a picture of the outlook for "stodgy DKB."

Holley, David. *Los Angeles Times.* (★ ★ ★)
A busy year for the Beijing bureau chief, Holley impressed us with his level-headed reporting in the midst of rapidly swirling events. As the demonstrations swelled in the late spring he was producing both hard news stories such as "Protesters Retain Control of Square," 5-22, where he wrote about a "trainload of about 1,500 soldiers armed with AK-47 automatic rifles" sitting at the train station, along with sidebar human interest stories such as "For Tourists in Square, A Brush With History," 5-24, where he referred to a "bus filled with foreign tourists," prevented by the demonstrators from reaching Mao's mausoleum. But he always struck the right note while conveying the awesome spectacle and contradictions of Beijing's spring of democracy, capturing the joy and the tension while giving prominent play to the political intrigue going on behind the scenes. Marshalling at times what seems to be superhuman effort, he managed to stay on top of the burgeoning story, always tying developments into what had gone before, whether it was seven days or 70 years. "China Police Break Up Pro-Democracy Protest," 4-19, covers "the most dramatic display of anti-government sentiment in the Chinese capital in more than a decade" but then probes beneath the tip of the iceberg, Holley talking with one student. "The student said that even the liberal reformer Hu — in whose memory, nominally, the march was being made — would be seen as a target for criticism by the students were he still alive." His "Chinese Trained in Moscow Take Key Roles as Relations Improve," 5-17, a sidebar story in the *LA Times'* Sino-Soviet summit coverage, was the only article we saw anywhere that dealt with the Chinese who had studied in the Soviet Union before the split — and the important positions they occupy in China now, including the premiership: "As a group, they tend to be organization people, comfortable with planning, central control and a search for technological solutions to problems." Teamed with Jim Mann for "Troops Fire on Beijing Crowds," and "Lights Go Out — Then the Shooting Starts," 6-4, Holley produces two of the best dispatches we saw out of Beijing immediately following the bloodbath in Tiananmen Square. This includes the best account we saw of the events of Saturday June 3rd, leading up to the retaking of the Square, from troops being pushed back by demonstrators earlier that morning, to a 10 p.m. speech on the environment given by Premier Li Peng: "In a manner virtually unprecedented for Chinese television, Li was shown reading his speech alone, with no Chinese leaders alongside him and no audience listening to him."

Housego, David. *Financial Times.* (★ ★ ½)
New Delhi. Having come to depend on his reports for the best picture of political economy here, we were surprised that in a year in which so much occurred in India, Housego's pen was less prolific than usual. In the previous year, India's central bank required foreign banks to raise their lending to priority sectors to 10% of their net lendable assets, with plans for raising it to 15% and higher. Housego brings us up to date on efforts of the foreign banks to resist the regulations with "Foreign Bankers Seek Review of Indian Loan Rules," 1-18. He effectively reports their case, but there's no forward look as what success they might attain. "Gandhi Makes Changes in Party," 3-6, assesses changes among provincial leaders and central government ministers as the PM begins to reassert leadership of his divided Congress (I) Party. Housego combines those moves with budget concessions recently announced to conclude that Gandhi will enter the national elections fighting "from a populist, left-oriented platform," while making maximum use of the Congress Party advantage in funds and patronage. We didn't see these kinds of early analyses elsewhere in the press, yet we also didn't see enough of them subsequently carried throughout the year by Housego. "India's Public Sector in a Dickens of a Muddle," 6-15, delivers numbing details on the steady draining of government resources by the bureaucratic lack of accountability — "the cumulative delays in the 303 government-funded projects costing more than Rs200m...amounted to 515 years." Among the early, pre-election reports on India's political economy, the best in all the press was Housego's "Ready to Confound the Critics," 10-11. A lay of the land survey, he provided the broad picture without sacrificing the important, specific detail. With simple narrative Housego conveys the picture of Gandhi's decline in "Gandhi Sees Campaign Turn Sour," 11-14, as Gandhi, four hours late, enters a village in his home district for a rally in a 10,000 person capacity stadium where only 1,000 are present.

Ibrahim, Youssef. *The New York Times.* (★ ★ ★)
Paris. France-based Ibrahim works the Middle East with as much ease as if it were his backyard. Knowledgeable and very alert to the key nuances that escape others on this beat, he handled some special stories with fine depth this year. "At Persepolis, Shadows of Two Pasts," 2-21, items from this "Reporter's Notebook" aren't not strong enough for a major story, but each is a satisfying vignette. "Egypt Urges Arab Lands to Join to Build Vision of Peace," 5-24, is tightly efficient with essential details and includes a forward-looking analytical perspective as Egypt formally returns to the Arab fold. A concise "Arab Conference Is Split by Syria: Refusal to Withdraw Troops Is Divisive," 5-26, identifies Syrian intransigence regarding withdrawal of troops in Lebanon as the surprise spoiler of the Casablanca Arab League Summit, and Ibrahim is among the first to point to the recent intensification of Iraqi military involvement in Lebanon as a major new obstacle to Syrian withdrawal. The best *immediate* post-Khomeini analytic report, "Iran Quickly Appoints Successor To Khomeini," 6-5, projects increasing marginalization of Iranian clergy exhibited by "politicians wearing turbans rather than clergymen conducting politics." There's an appropriate focus on Rafsanjani's pragmatic side in "Iranian Parliament Speaker Favored in Presidential Vote," 7-29, Ibrahim reminding us that unlike Iran's more radical clerics who care little for economics, Rafsanjani "has never abandoned his ties to the bazaar and businessmen." A very important dispatch, "Abu Nidal Is Reportedly Placed Under House Arrest by Libyans," 11-28, contains a comprehensive picture on the global operations of this terrorist. Ibrahim reports the event is a consequence of Arab and Palestinian pressure to end Abu Nidal's activities, which were becoming an obstacle to Arab diplomacy, but left unanswered why Qaddafi has finally bent to this pressure.

Ignatius, Adi. *The Wall Street Journal.* (★ ½)
Beijing. With so much demanded of him, given the powerful events here this year, Ignatius's efforts weren't as strong as required, although his reporting has improved overall. The details on China's plans to cope with unemployment are sketchy in "Millions More Are Expected to Lose Jobs As China Implements Its Austerity Plan," 1-27, but Ignatius presents a compact picture of superfluous labor: "Fully automated elevators are manned by operators around the clock. At state-run stores, buying a simple item can require three attendants: one to hand over

the product, another to write the receipt and a third to take payment." "Moscow and Beijing Sharing the Lesson of Revisionism," with Peter Gumbel 5-12, doesn't touch Kristof's same-day *NYT*'s advance of the Sino-Soviet summit, but it's a helpful review of the pace of political and economic changes in the two countries. Ignatius secures some good quotes from student leaders and includes colorful detail on Gorbachev's visit in "Beijing Protestors Increasingly Aim Their Criticism at Deng Xiaoping," 5-17, although he's stingy on the political dynamics and prospects for Deng's successor. "China's Hard-Liner Li Struggles for Political Survival As Standoff With Pro-Democracy Protestors Continues," with Julia Leung 5-23, mixes information, speculation and simply unconfirmed material, without any identification of sources. The key information was buried far too deeply, whereas it should have been the lead: "Among the most dramatic defections is a group of seven prominent retired generals who wrote an open letter to the Central Military Commission, headed by Mr. Deng, and the martial law troops commander, set up by Mr. Li's martial law decree. The generals urged that troops not be brought into the capital." We get an important update in "For Hong Kong, All Bets On China Are Off," 6-8, which reports that the argument of HK legislator Martin Lee, that events in China have made the Sino-British Declaration worthless and that renegotiations ought to take place too, is becoming a consensus in the colony. Ignatius provides good detail on Western companies pulling back investment, but almost nothing on what the leadership plans to do about the economy in "Beijing's Economic Ills Pose a New Threat of Social Upheaval," with Amanda Bennett 8-3. The analytic side is very poor, though, with Ignatius ascribing urban inflation to rapid economic growth, not currency devaluation.

Kamm, Henry. *The New York Times.* (★ ★ ★ ½)
Budapest bureau chief. Some of the finest material we saw all year on Eastern Europe was under his byline. While other correspondents often seemed to resemble ice cream cone eaters in July, Kamm was covering the historical developments with a cool professionalism that captured both the passion and the irony. In "No Communist Slogans This Election," 6-5, Kamm travels to the Polish village of Radom on election day and visits Communist and Solidarity headquarters, catching the country in microcosm as he paints a picture of Communists awaiting defeat and an opposition torn between two factions. "Communists Concede Victory by Solidarity and Urge a Coalition," 6-6, is informative but seems truncated. Kamm touches all the bases, from the hard numbers to the government's reactions to the question of where Poland goes from here, but nothing is fully developed. Did the *Times* catch a *USA Today* cold here? "300,000 Reported to March in Largest East German Protest," 10-24, and "East German Catholic Bishop Adds to the Cry," 10-29, sketch the rising tide in East Germany on the eve of the tidal wave, with Kamm writing in the 10-24 piece: "Until earlier this month, demonstrators were vilified as minions of West German manipulation, calls for an end of censorship never reached the public and few deficiencies in the Government's performances in any sector were admitted." His "Hungarians Reject Election Timetable of the Ruling Party," 11-28, manages to make Hungary's Kafkaesque referendum on the timetable for a presidential election comprehensible, with Kamm expertly leading readers through the Byzantine strategies of the Communist government and the opposition forces. It was perhaps a sign of the times in 1989 that, by December, demonstrations in Eastern Europe were becoming standard news stories, but Kamm managed to put a fresh and memorable spin in "Protest Rallies in Prague in Effort to Oust New Government," 12-4, capturing the "passionate dialogue" between a Civic Forum spokesman, Radim Palous, and the crowd. " 'Jakes,' he began, referring to the deposed Communist chief, Milos Jakes. The crowd responded, 'Throw him out immediately.' " And, "At Mr. Palous's next listing of deputies, the crowd roared, 'Give them a shovel.' 'They have lost the right to be deputies,' the speaker said. 'Mafia,' the crowd responded. 'You no longer have our mandate,' the speaker said of the deputies. 'They don't have it,' the chorus crowed.' " Breathtaking story. Breathtaking coverage.

Kandell, Jonathan. *The Wall Street Journal.* (★ ★ ½)
We wish his byline appeared more frequently because Kandell possesses a fresh eye and pen for Latin America's stories, one of the best foreign correspondents on the *Journal*'s bench. Kandell is refreshing with "Property Rights," 3-22, a dispassionate, informed, credible account of policy changes likely in El Salvador following Arena's electoral victories. A disappointing "What Crisis? Argentines, as Usual, See Country Averting Plunge Into Poverty," 6-22, goes from a slow lead into what new President Carlos Saul Menem faces in Argentina, where wistful thinking takes precedence over real substance. We get outlines of the shock treatment perspective of Menem's advisers, which Kandall accepts as being able to bring hyperinflation down, albeit with a thud. We don't see anything that's new here and most of the data and details of the economic crisis are bunched into the second half, with no fix on tax policies at all. "Peruvians Find a Better Bank on Sidewalk," 7-24, is crisp with fresh details on the *cambianistas,* the underground money-changers without whom the country's economy would come to a sudden halt. We also learn that Peru is the most "dollarized" of South American countries, Peruvians holding between 880 million and one billion of them — of course coming in via the cocaine trade. "Brazil's Costly Mix: Autos and Alcohol," 9-28, is the best report in the press this year on the screwy economics of ethanol in Brazil, where consumers buy ethanol that costs twice as much to produce as gasoline. Kandell's review of the background to this is most useful as a reminder to ethanol fans in the U.S.

Keller, Bill. *The New York Times.* (★ ★ ★ ★)
Moscow bureau chief. One of the top correspondents in the foreign corps, Keller worked this assignment diligently, producing a steady stream of reports that were full of tightly-wrapped analyses, superb detail, and sturdy insights. He was a bit off this year, ever so slightly, though, on catching some critical shifts on economic policy that Peel at the *FT* didn't miss. We get a grim picture of the shriveled fruits of *perestroika,* with shortages in Moscow the worst in memory, in "For Grim Soviet Consumers, The New Year of Discontent," 1-1, with all the ingredients of the annual new year's feast unavailable. In "Waiting For The New Soviet Economy," 3-19, we learn of the new law on cooperatives permitting the private employment of labor. The detail is great in "Soviet Voters Deal a Mortifying Blow To Party Officials," 3-28, a report on Soviet elections. An excellent news analytic, "Soviets and China Renew Normal Ties After 30 Years," 5-17, draws the very insightful bead: "While Mr. Gorbachev and China's leaders learn to like each other better, the citizens of the two giant neighbors are beginning to envy each other. Russia is getting freer, China is getting richer, and at the human level far below the meeting of the leaders, the people of each country are demanding more of what the other has." The best account of the new experiment in parliamentary politics was "Moscow Congress Grills Gorbachev, Then Elevates Him," 5-26, Keller feeding us fine detail on Boris Yeltsin's intentions. His focus is precise in "At the Soviet Congress, Watching Big Brother Squirm," 6-4, on Supreme Soviet and Congress of People's Deputies: "Is this the birth of something like democratic government, or is it just a big political sauna, where the country sweats out its poisons before lapsing back into apathetic languor?" Without overdoing it, he identifies key changes in the relationships of power in the U.S.S.R. — Gorbachev, we learn, prefers to rule by consensus and compromise — "Kremlin Deputies Bask in New Role," 8-6. He re-examines the thesis in light of new shifts in attitudes among the reformist elites toward liberties and democratic reforms in "Even Gorbachev's Friends Want a Little Order," 10-8, alert on the ominous tendencies emerging. "Bush Will Meet Gorbachev To Get 'Better Acquainted' in Talks at Sea Next Month," 11-1, is crisply efficient analysis: "Even if the shipboard meeting does not produce tangible agreements, Mr. Gorbachev can expect to profit from the atmospherics. The comforting imagery of the two men using warships for a friendly get-together, the language and gestures of mutual understanding, may make the helter-skelter transformations in Eastern Europe seem more manageable." Keller's pre-summit opener, "Gorbachev's Hope for Future: 'A Common European Home,' " 11-30, spells out the "huge exchange" Moscow has in mind: surrendering its "costly ambitions of expansionism" for "admission to the club of Western industrial countries."

Knight, Robin. *U.S.News & World Report.* (★ ½)
The London-based European senior editor generally offered conventional examinations of political and social trends, written mostly in newsweeklyese. "A New German Nationalism in the Age of Gorbachev," 1-23, focuses on the national infatuation with Gorbachev in West Germany and the increase in negative attitudes towards the U.S. "Restless, confused, a bit anxious, 61 million West Germans today are in a mood for change. Pacifism, rather than militarism, is giving a new edge to German nationalism...At the same time, a go-it-alone impulse is coursing through West German foreign policy." "Cracks in the Bloc," 3-27, focuses on reform movements in Poland and Hungary, with Knight observing that Communism "has not delivered the prosperity it promised." Instead, Eastern Europeans see "chronic shortages of starchy food and substandard housing." So what else is new? "Just You Move Over, 'Enry 'Iggins," 4-24, examines the decline of class distinctions in England, with Knight noting that income, "taste and education, rather than birthright, now set Britons apart from each other." Interesting, including Knight's observation of the negative impact that this phenomenon has had on the Labor Party, which draws its legitimacy from class conflict, but we question the wisdom of running it the same week as the soccer stadium deaths in Liverpool. "The Perilous Trek of Helmut Kohl," 6-5, examines the dynamics of West German politics which led Helmut Kohl to change his position on nuclear weapons, and features above average looks at Germany's different political parties and the causes behind their changing popularity, along with observations on how Kohl has managed to survive for so long. "Hungary's Heir Apparent Gambles on Radical Change," 7-17, and "New Hopes, Old Grudges, Great Dangers," 7-31, swing the spotlight onto the eastern Bloc, with Knight profiling Hungarian reformer Imre Pozsgay in the 7-17 article and reporting on growing ethnic unrest in the 7-31 piece. Both pack a lot of information, but some historical perspective would have helped. In "Has Britain's Iron Lady Begun to Rust?" 8-28/9-4, Knight tries to explain the recent decline in Thatcher's popularity, observing that in Thatcher's recent cabinet reshuffling the PM "managed to alienate senior colleagues, perplex voters with clumsy backstage maneuvering and lay herself open to charges of political incompetence."

Kohan, John. *Time.* (★ ½)
Moscow bureau chief. With good reporting, respectable analysis, and decent insights, Kohan's coverage of the U.S.S.R. was very satisfying this year. Arriving in Armenia on the first private American relief plane, Kohan gives us an intimate report on the country's earthquake survivors in "A Journey into Misery," 12-26-88. In "Go Faster! No! Go Slower!" 4-10, we get a good sense of how far Estonians want to go with reforms, with quotes from members of an Estonian popular front group to underscore the theme. "A Volcano of Words and Wishes," 6-12, is a fine summary on the first meeting of the Congress of People's Deputies in Moscow, Kohan reporting on the issues which were addressed, the speeches, and the personality clashes. "The Boss of Smolensky Square," with Ann Blackman and William Marder 5-15, is certainly one of the most informative report/profiles of Soviet Foreign Minister Eduard Shevardnadze we saw in the press. "Cry Independence," 8-21, is first-rate on the pace and content of changes in the Baltic Republics, with Kohan keeping the future of *perestroika* a central question as these countries push for sovereignty.

Kraft, Scott. *Los Angeles Times.* (★ ★)
Johannesburg bureau chief. He seemed to be getting his sea legs this year, and we noticed a marked improvement in his R.S.A. coverage. Hopefully we'll see more analysis in his work in 1990. "S. Africa Woos Black Nations in Wake of Namibia Accord," 12-27-88, is a good roundup of attitudes among various African leaders as they rethink their position *vis-a-vis* South Africa in the wake of that country's willingness to grant independence to Namibia, Kraft capturing the trend toward "pragmatism over ideology." His "3 Reportedly Accuse Mandela of Beatings," 2-28, is an evenly-paced account of the alleged attack on four black activists by Winnie Mandela and her bodyguards, with good use of detail to document Mandela's erratic, often bizarre behavior. In "His Party Turns Its Back on Botha," 3-14, Kraft does an outstanding job in

covering the National Party vote endorsing Frederik W. de Klerk over Pik Botha as South Africa's president. Our readers found that Kraft was masterful in weaving together the details, capturing both the drama and the trauma of this political shake-up. But in "South African Detainees Flee Hospital," 3-21, Kraft's structure is distracting, and he leaves some questions unanswered on the four anti-apartheid activists who escape detention and take refuge in the West German embassy, never identifying the activists by name and organization until the last paragraph, leaving us wondering "who are these people?" More illuminating was "S. Africa Blacks, Students Protest on Eve of Vote," 9-6, a write-up of election-eve violence along with a look at the various political parties and where they stood regarding reform, from the liberal left to the hard right, Kraft notes that the National Party may be forced to form a coalition but does not speculate on what that may mean for its own moderate policies. "Trapped Between 2 Worlds," 10-25, profiles Gideon Skhosana, sales manager for a South African brewery, and one of the "one million black men and women [who] have ascended into the middle class and beyond in recent years only to become even more embittered than their poorer neighbors by the system that dictates where they may live and denies them a vote on their own future." Kraft works well in bringing home the humiliations, large and small, that this proud, articulate man has to suffer in his day-to-day routines, but he never tells us how far those "one million black men and women" are willing to go to bring about change in their country, nor if they share the Marxist beliefs of the ANC.

Kristof, Nicholas D. *The New York Times.* (★ ★ ★)
Beijing bureau chief. We'd recommended in our '88 *MediaGuide* that this smart young reporter be reassigned to Beijing from his posting then in Hong Kong. His re-assignment as new bureau chief here bore out all we suspected it would, as Kristof was the journalist who best reported from China accurate accounts of the country's turmoil during May and June. He begins the year with a snappy summary of the revolutionary changes in "China Celebrates 10 Years Along the Capitalist Road," 1-1. "Taiwan Desire For Mainland Is Dwindling," 2-5, reports that prosperous Taiwanese now worry that the mainland is "too poor and has too many problems. We don't want it back." Kristof is on to a good angle here, but it needed more depth. He calls what appears to be an important shift on the margin with "In China, Democracy Makes Yet Another Big Comeback," 2-21, on the "sprouting" of democracy in China: "the calls for a more democratic system are coming not just from students and intellectuals but from the Communist Party itself," and he stayed involved with this theme, providing welcome updates and analyses of power shifts, as in "For China's Congress, How Much Democracy?" 3-19, "Power War, Chinese Way," 3-23, and "Privately, More & More Chinese Say It's Past Time For Deng to Go," 4-17. Each provided fresh information, but each also neglected to sufficiently grid the reaction or thinking within the Old Guard elite on these developments. He does go after that angle in "Why Deng Trembles," 6-1, a crisp news analysis, as Deng's fear of a China returned to "chaos and division" overtakes his longer run goal of "modernization." To the Old Guard "there was a deep-seated alarm at the possibility that the Communist Party would crumble the way that Chinese dynasties have fallen." A *Magazine* cover, "China Erupts: Reasons Why," 6-4, presents new material on economic bottlenecks, but Kristof doesn't get high enough and we lose a chance for lofty perspective on the economic/political intersection. In the midst of the Tiananmen Square events, he's cool under fire, his reporting under control in "Troops Attack and Crush Beijing Protest; Thousands Fight Back, Scores Killed," 6-4, Kristof weaving fine detail into a larger tapestry, resulting in a 10 Best nomination for the dispatch. The best on-the-spot report, he avoided reporting what couldn't be confirmed by sight or highly reliable sources, something many of his fellow professionals didn't treat with the same rigor. "China Ousts Zhao: New Team Likely to Curb Dissent," 6-25, contains brilliant detail on political shifts in the Politburo, as Shanghai Mayor Jiang Zemin is elevated to Communist Party General Secretary. In "China Is Planning 2 Years of Labor For Its Graduates," 8-13, Kristof sees that it could lead to great unrest among students. But he doesn't note the prospects that exile to the countryside could have the opposite effect, radicalizing the peasantry *via* student instigation, a 10 Best nomination.

Lee, Dinah. *Business Week.* (★ ★)
Hong Kong. Generally good to very good, although inconsistently, Lee displayed a real flash of critical insight, producing one of the 10 Best foreign reports this year. It was Lee, who two weeks before Gorbachev's visit to Beijing, was prescient in seeing a hardline crackdown with "China's Next Great Leap Could Be Backward," 5-8: "Inflation has reached levels not seen since before the 1949 Communist takeover....Even if the student protests are stamped out, the underlying crisis can only deepen." "U.S. Importers Aren't Jumping Ship — Yet," with Pete Engardio and Amy Dunkin 6-26, is coherent on the thesis that so long as the Deng Government doesn't do anything rash there is little possibility of foreign companies shutting down factories anytime soon, because they are dependent on Chinese production. "Who's Minding the Store in China?" with Jasper Becker 8-14, is a satisfactory, although depressing, chronicle of Chinese economic policy adrift with foreign investors cutting back. While there isn't a lot new here, Lee is keeping her finger on the country's pulse. A lot of good, tightly packed information appears in "How Bad Will China's Debt Crunch Get?" with Ted Holden and Mike McNamee 9-25, on the country's dire situation with foreign banks since the repression.

Lehner, Urban C. *The Wall Street Journal.* (★ ½)
Tokyo bureau chief. Although we're getting more information out of his reports, Lehner is still too hit-and-miss. The quality of his reporting varies according to the intensity of his drive to dig for the heart of the story. He outlines some worrisome trends, putting them into perspective, in "After Hirohito, the Big Question Remains," 1-9, a thoughtful outlook on Japan as the new year opens: "As disturbing as anything happening in Japan today is the tendency on the part of some politicians and intellectuals in the U.S. to assume that Japan wants to push the U.S. around. But to mistake Japan's challenge to U.S. economic leadership for enmity, to confuse Japan's desire for a bigger role in the world with imperialist lust, is to risk creating self-fulfilling prophesies." "Divine Rite: Japan's Plan to Include Shinto in its Ceremony for Hirohito Stirs Flap," 2-23, is an informed picture on the relationship between the state and Shintoism, as the inscrutable is made less so. "Japan's Uno, Lacking Clout at Home, Could Balk at Major Trade Concessions," 6-5, closely supports the theme with analysis and delivers details on the LDP's political status, although there remains some room for maneuver on Super 301 trade issues. "Disparities in Wealth Affront Japan's Vision of Itself As Classless," 6-20, a P. 1 leder, is extremely superficial, with no mention of traditional classes, samurai, education, etc. Lehner strings together quotes from people on their reactions to corruption and the Recruit scandal, and we suspect this may even be misinformation. "New Front-Runner for Japan Premier is Relatively Young and Little Known," 8-3, is really bare bones, with Lehner copping-out in this almost information-less profile: "What is less clear is what Mr. Kaifu stands for, if anything." We find that hard to believe about this figure who at 58 years of age has ten terms in the Diet! An improvement, "New Japanese Premier Steps to Plate But He's Not Viewed as a Power Hitter," 8-9, works in fairly good political detail on Toshiki Kaifu's meeting with intellectuals to discuss policy: "By Japanese standards it was a remarkable performance: A *typical* candidate for the LDP Presidency wouldn't have had so deep an interest in policy." Lehner starts slow, with the best material in the second half of "For North Koreans, 'Mass Games' Are Sport — And Indoctrination," 8-15, a rare view of life in Pyongyang with its numbing regimentation and Orwellian loudspeakers in every room blaring slogans of the Great Leader.

Lerner, Marc. *The Washington Times.* (★)
Foreign Editor. Lerner spent most of the year posted to Manila, brought back in October to manage the foreign desk. He's adept on picking up various angles on political, economic and strategic developments throughout the region, but we found two aspects of his reporting disconcerting — a not infrequent lack of unifying themes and a tendency toward sketchiness. He's sketchy, for example, with the picture of Hanoi's version of *perestroika* in "Vietnam Tries More Open Market to Relieve Stagnation," 1-19, Lerner focusing on Madame Nguyen Thi Thi, who complains taxes are too high and are discouraging enterprise. He's generally balanced with "Aquino Unmoved by Marcos' Illness," 2-6, although there isn't much new here. The writing

is far better and we do get fresh information in "Aquino Overcomes Scruples to Accept Gambling Revenues," 6-1, in which he reports that "Three years after President Corazon Aquino campaigned for office promising to outlaw casino gambling, government owned casinos are expanding and now constitute the third-largest contributor to the national treasury." He pokes into rumors of Aquino family members getting payoffs from casino operators, turning up nothing substantive. Although its demonstrations rivaled those of Beijing in size and intensity, the situation in Chengdu was under-reported by the media, but Lerner gives thoughtful and informative material on the political climate in the capital of China's most populous and industrialized province in "Chengdu Snuffed Much Like Beijing," 6-19. "Foes of U.S. Bases in Singapore Reconsidering Their Opposition," 8-17, picks up a story out of the regional geopolitical eddies and we learn that "Singapore's offer to play host to U.S. military facilities has...raised a chorus of protests from Indonesia, Malaysia and other neighboring states alarmed by the prospect of a U.S. military presence in the already well fortified U.S. ally." Lehner cites that as basis for signs that "Southeast Asian leaders are exerting pressures to ensure that the Philippines keep the bases." He never gives us the full measure of the former Philippine president in "Ferdinand Marcos Dies In Exile; Aquino Rules Out Philippine Burial," 9-29, no achievements cited among the review of his failures and excesses.

Leung, Julia. *The Wall Street Journal.* (★ ★)
We watch for the byline of this *Asian Wall Street Journal* correspondent to percolate through to the U.S. publication. We called her work "promising" last year, and she came through with richly detailed reports on the burdens and barriers to China's economic modernization this year. Her *AWSJ* reports are underutilized by the U.S. editors. Early into the year, she's detailing the near chaotic economic pressures as the worst of two worlds prevails in China's economic policy, "Energy Crisis Shuts Factories in China," 1-6. Central planner directives are ineffective, but free market avenues are distorted by all sorts of restrictions, with China's coal production slipping into the danger zones. She reports that there's appreciable sentiment among Chinese economists to deal with the crisis not by repressing coal demand, but rather by stimulating supply with deregulation of freight rates and coal prices. She paints the year's best picture of China's struggling auto industry, and we empathize with the hapless manager she interviews. "Socialism Burdens a Chinese Car Venture," 4-13, informs us that "about 60,000 employes — 80% of the...workforce [at First Automobile Works] — have jobs completely unrelated to car production. They include barbers, sales assistants, even policemen, and they are on the payroll to ensure that the factory meets its welfare responsibilities." Another case study on the theme, "Chinese Modernization Drive Flagging," 8-14, this one on the waning foreign confidence in the showcase province of Jiangsu and its massive Meishan Metallurgical Corporation projects, notes worries among foreign investors than sanctions could drive China back into the arms of the Soviets. However, this muddy aspect is left undeveloped. Japan's biggest investment in China is going nowhere, Leung reports in "Ambitious Project for China Hits Snag," 11-24, as "hardliners view the modern industrial complex plan with suspicion," finding its smacks too much of capitalism.

Lewis, Flora. *The New York Times.* (★ ½)
"Foreign Affairs" columnist. Lewis continued her professorial ways this year, offering routine and predictable advice to world leaders and policymakers, a sometimes weary tone intruding. " 'Darkness' Was in Our Vision," 1-18, was typical pedantic lecturing from Lewis, without any insight or originality on Africa's dilemma of "development-environment-population." In "Opportunity for Bush," 1-29, she writes about "how much was blocked by the taut barriers [between U.S.-U.S.S.R.]...how easy it is to open up once the political leadership wills it." One reader thought Lewis was somewhat naive as to the keystone to improvement of U.S.-Soviet relations. "Salvador at Crossroads," 2-19, gives a simplistic view of what's happening in El Salvador: "The U.S. should encourage more self reliance." Among her better efforts for the year were "Soviets Buy American," 5-10, where she deftly explains Soviet problems in getting Western credits — both Japan and West Germany are only interested in upscale markets that

pay cash, and "Revolution Builds an Impasse," 6-11, where Lewis observes "The problem for totalitarian leaders now is how to get out of the dead end they constructed," since they have no model to go by. "The power of the people, mouthed by revolutionaries who by their nature become totalitarians, is a delusion. They don't know how to give people the power taken in their name. That is the hardest part. It brings disorder." "Summitry's Purpose," 7-16, dispenses obvious comments on the Paris economic summit, where problems include: "how to help Hungary and Poland through a painful transformation to market economics," and: "the global ecology depends on developing countries not repeating the old practices which made industrial countries rich." "Gorbachev's Great Test," 7-23, offers conventional reflections on the tough job of "changing society" in the East Bloc, but one line stood out: "Now that there is real stirring out there in the industrial lands, he has courageously kept open public communications, which enable the process to spread, take root, and create representatives." Her " 'General Winter,' " 11-29, has nice touches in dwelling on the effect the severity of this winter will have on the politics of the East Bloc. She recollects living in Warsaw in the winter of 1946-47, "one of the coldest in a century. . .working mostly by candlelight and, as much as possible, in bed under an eiderdown." The point: "Historically, 'General Winter' has been a Russian ally, helping to defeat the armies of Napoleon and Hitler. But this year he threatens to be a foe of the hopeful forces for change throughout the East. The West should not dither as he approaches."

Liu, Melinda. *Newsweek.* (★)
Hong Kong bureau chief. Liu shared bylines on most reports coming out of China during its period of upheaval, but we saw enough from her solo to appreciate how her reporting has improved this year as well as the sophistication of her analytic efforts. From Afghanistan, Liu files a field report on conditions in the country after the Soviet withdrawal of troops, "Inside A Frightened City," 3-13. She efectively conveys the sense of anxiety and foreboding within Kabul, with very effective use of quotes, but she overdoes somewhat the picture of weak support for the government of President Najibullah. We also don't get a real sense of how the government's troops view the future here. Liu profiles Burmese drug lord, Gen. Khun Sa, guerila leader of the Mong Tai Revolutionary Army, in "Burma's 'Money Tree,' " 5-15, illustrating quite well the connection between drug trafficking and insurgency there. From Khun Sa, she quotes a potent portent: "Our people grow opium to barter for food and clothes; they don't even know what heroin looks like. It is up to you in the West to cut down demand. Otherwise your babies will still be addicted." "Upheaval in China," co-written by Russell Watson with Carroll Bogert and Douglas Waller 5-29, is a fast-moving account of the swirling events, capturing all the emotions, anxieties and euphoria, fear and anger of the drama. An intense picture, it suffers by an exclusion of economic problems in its background on the lead up to the events. "Reign of Terror," co-authored by Russell Watson with Carroll Bogert, Tony Clifton and Rod Nordland and Douglas Waller 6-19, is one of those efforts in which the bylines are multiple; thus, we can't tell how much or what part is Liu's reporting. A mix of reporting and analysis on the hardliners' crackdown, we get a bit of excess, as in "For the moment, at least, the butchers were firmly in control." "Bad Days in Beijing," 7-31, places China's recent events in a historical context, drawing out their similarities to the Anti-Rightist Campaign, the Cultural Revolution, and the fall of Hua Guofeng. This is a nice example of a second-look journalism that worked well, with Liu waiting until the dust had settled and then putting events in a big picture context.

Lloyd, John. *Financial Times.* (★ ★ ★)
Soviet affairs. Lloyd has an incredibly sharp eye for key detail here, and was one of the main sources of information in the press with news about critically important shifts in fiscal policies. A first hand report from Armenia immediately after its December, 1988 earthquake, "The Coming Crack-Up of Communism: From the Rubble," *National Review* 1-27 offers a strong overview: "My own impressions, possibly overdetermined by the Soviet press, were that the rescue efforts suffered from the same problem that self-confessedly afflicts much of the Soviet economy and society: that of habitually looking to the top for every direction." His "The Search

for an Acceptable Balance," 3-3, was the best we saw on Poland's struggle at the time. Economic and political detail is well integrated and presented, although the report is flawed by insufficient treatment of the Roman Catholic Church's role. A concise "Moscow Decree Strengthens Farmers' Rights to Land," 4-10, is important news on a decree of the Supreme Soviet permitting Soviet farmers to pass their land on to their children. We don't get a lot of details, but Lloyd focuses the essence: "The decree appears largely to satisfy those who called for freedom for farmers to take over their own plots." From Trotskyites to Thatcherites, the political groupings in Hungary are setting out their stalls, and Lloyd takes us on an informed tour, examining what each has to offer in "Hungary: The Political Pulse Quickens," 4-15. This is an excellent political map of Hungary's political factions and new parties. "Soviet Tax Remains Progressive," 4-17, gives us a key detail we couldn't find elsewhere in the press that the 50% tax kicks in at 1500 rubles. More singular detail appears in "Wide Change in Soviet Taxes Foreshadowed," 4-18, a short but critical report on a significant move to restructure the Soviet tax system. Progressive rates will kick in at over 700 rubles, with a 50% top rate. He quotes Financial Minister Boris Gostev on an ominous outlook for economic growth: "All our experience now indicates that taxation of private income is an important mechanism in the distribution of wages." His "Soviet Call to Scrap 5-Year Plan," 4-20, gives us quickies on key items in the new Soviet journal *Moscow Business* in which a member of the Politburo, Aleksandr Yakolev, suggests the centerpiece of the Soviet economy since the 1920s might be dispensed with. However, we really wanted to know about the journal itself. "A Rush of Events Whose Sequels Are Not Yet Clear," 11-11, is speculative on where reform might lead in Eastern Europe, but the perspective is sharp.

Lohr, Steve. *The New York Times.* (★ ★ ½)
London. A particular strength of this veteran is his drive to come up with new angles. He zooms in on a flip side to Soviet reforms with an insightful "Perestroika Enters Finland, a Bit Bumpily," 1-16, noting that "the decentralization of [Soviet] decision making has brought a period of uncertainty in which Western business executives are hard pressed to find those with real authority. . .The result, in many cases, is to intensify the very stagnation the restructuring was intended to cure." The reporting and presentation are very well-done in " 'Pygmalion' Update: Henry Higgins Was Right," 1-31, an enjoyable report on the debate in Britain over whether British accents do make a difference in class standing. Lohr can organize material clearly, as with "Free-Market Health System: New Thatcher Goal for Britain," 2-1, a very informative description of government proposals for a market-oriented philosophy for health care and reactions. In "European TV's Vast Growth: Cultural Effect Stirs Concern," 3-16, Lohr astutely points out that restricting European purchases of American programs because of cultural" reasons is protectionism, however "artfully packaged." The report is somewhat dry, however. "Sheffield Knife Maker Beats the Odds," 4-15, is an outstanding report on Richardson Sheffield Ltd., world competitive in a declining industry. Lohr approaches this story from several angles — internal management, ideas from abroad, product development — his best for the year that we reviewed, it's a rich, three-dimensional feature. "In Umbrella Land, Sunshine Gets Mixed Reviews," 8-28, is a delightful perception of how England's sunniest summer this century is affecting the country. He uses wry quotes to good effect, as this from a BBC weatherman: ' "It's all those depressions that come across the British isles. . .so if you got rid of America, we would have sunny weather all the time.'" At year's end, Lohr returned to New York to become an Assistant Business Editor.

MacDougall, Colina. *Financial Times.* (★ ★ ★ ½)
Among the correspondents covering China, none has quite the feel of intimacy that MacDougall displays in her reports. She knows precisely when to stand back and refocus and when to jump in aggressively to play out an insight that opens entirely new dimensions. She clears away the fuzzy edges around the perspectives of PM Li Peng and party General Secretary Zhao Ziyang in "Hunger Rumbles Under China's Search for Viable Reform," 12-31-88, a taut assessment of efforts to restore central control of the economy and improve efficiency. Clear in the report is that China is going into 1989 with potential for serious instability because of its economic

problems. "Chinese Racism Surfaces Violently," 1-5, looks at the sordid reality behind the decades of Chinese propaganda about Third World solidarity. There's no recognition in China that Africans might have a culture of their own, she reports: "This kind of arrogance is obvious also in China's treatment of its own minorities, notably the Tibetans." "Peking Keeps the Dalai Waiting," 1-26, is timely, as China's agreement to hold discussions with Tibet's exiled spiritual leader, the Dalai Lama, wanes. "Industrial Output in China Falls 11% in January," 2-9, reports stagflation is now a serious risk. MacDougall is sober on the "democratic stirrings" among China's intellectuals, producing the best perspective at the time with "Insoluble Problems at the Gate," 4-21: "The [student] demonstrations could hardly have come at a worse moment. Clouds are gathering around Peking in a manner unseen since the last days of the Chiang Kai-shek regime in 1949. In the past 40 years, China has faced several catastrophes but a solution was always at hand awaiting only the political will to apply it. Now a divided leadership is faced with new and explosive problems which it does not know how to fix." "Deng Xiaoping: Determined to Hold on to Power Dearly Won," 5-20, an insightful, timely analysis as the political crisis mounts, notes that "There is much in Deng's past to account for his grim determination to cling to power." She holds back from the pack on writing off economic liberalization in China, reminding us with "Economic Inequalities Test Power of Centre," 6-8, that even the hardliners want a rich and prosperous China. "Family Dynasties Take China on a Long March to Feudalism," 11-29, is estimable reporting and analysis, with MacDougall charting the webs that link the Old Guard aristocracy as a new dynasty comes on the scene in China.

MacFarquhar, Emily. *U.S.News & World Report.* (★ ½)
Contributing editor. MacFarquhar's reporting on China, which is straight enough, helped round out the weekly's coverage, adding in an analytic bent that wasn't always on the mark. "Can Pakistan's Superwoman Survive?" 4-17, a report and analysis of the major foreign and domestic policy issues confronting Pakistani PM Benazir Bhutto is superior. She employs quotes effectively and develops some insights into Bhutto's internal political problems. "Deng's Hard Liners and Their Enemies," 6-5, examines the options available to China's Old Guard and the role of the military in the new power situation. The "threat of withdrawal of foreign capital may well have a greater moderating effect on China's new leadership than mildly regretful statements from foreign governments," but there's nothing to indicate that is being seriously considered. "China Prepares for a Bitter Harvest," 7-10, stumbles on economic policy, mislocating the sources of inflation in agricultural policy rather than in the country's monetary policies. "Outside Agitators for Democracy," with Susan Lawrence 8-7, details the activities of Chinese student dissidents since their arrival in the U.S. There is some historical comparison between them and the problems of their predecessors of the 1911 revolution, who split into various factions. "Will the Last One to Leave Please Turn Out the Lights?" 8-21, covers territory already well-worked by others and doesn't add anything new, although it is a clear summary of the current situation in Hong Kong.

Mackenzie, Richard. *Insight.* (★ ★ ★)
After the Soviet withdrawal from Afghanistan, the intensity of media coverage also receded, especially once the "imminent" fall of Kabul never occurred. Mackenzie, though, continued to provide fine coverage all year, although clearly from a perspective that sometimes led him into an overestimation of the *mujahedeen*'s strategic situation. "Enemies Amid America's Afghans," 1-23, contains great detail about high-level defectors from Kabul's communist regime who are seeking asylum in the U.S. and the reactions of *mujahedeen* to the "11th-hour" decisions. Mackenzie developed two insightful reports on political developments in the subcontinent's two major powers. "Rajiv Gandhi's Bloody Inheritance," 2-13, examines with balance and objectivity the culture of violence that appears to be spreading throughout India's Punjab. He acknowledges that the PM inherited the problem, but introduces criticisms from others that blame Gandhi for failing to defuse the conflict. "Jolts for New Democracy End Prime Minister's Honeymoon," 3-13, brings us up-to-date on the tasks and perspectives of PM Benazir Bhutto as her opposition in Pakistan grows stronger. Mackenzie edges toward the perspective of a

resistance victory as Soviet troops leave Kabul (an expectation that was widespread among U.S. intelligence agencies) in "Amid Bombs and Rockets, the Gestation of a Government," 2-20, although it's useful with a picture of what the *mujahedeen*'s picture of a new Afghanistan was at the time. "Using Tears to Stem the Fears," 4-17, is entertaining in spots on the perils of Australian Prime Minister Bob Hawke, but it's simply too dependent on crude and sometimes shocking commentary by a single Australian author and columnist. We have no way to judge his capacity for a fair assessment. There's a good amount of field intelligence in "The Guerrillas' Conventional Woes," 5-1, as Mackenzie details the resistance's switch from guerrilla to conventional tactics, as the fighting over Jalalabad intensifies. Mackenzie remains disposed toward seeing a *mujahedeen* victory there, and then "on to Kabul." The best reporting we saw anywhere on the assassination by another *mujahedeen* faction of top commanders and officers of an elite Afghan resistance corps "30 Key Afghan Rebels Killed," 7-17. His two-part cover story, "Afghan Dance," 9-11, is a comprehensive summing up of this story thus far for the year.

Mallett, Victor. *Financial Times.* (★ ★ ½)
Middle East. The wealth of fresh information we got from him when he was covering East Africa for *Financial Times* readers didn't appear in his reporting from this region. He can still pack in the details, but we ended up with more unanswered questions than we expected. "Syria Reverses Decline with Oil and Economic Reform," 1-4, positions fine background on the huge problems of bureaucratism and inefficiency here and on efforts to revive the economy. The customary Mallett knack for packing information into concise reports is here. Syria spends more than half its budget on defense, but the country's ruling Baath socialist party has a strong aversion to free enterprise and little enthusiasm for Soviet's *perestroika.* "Towards the Post-Oil Era," 3-29, on Dubai, briskly explores new opportunities for the United Arab Emirates' traders in the wake of the Gulf War ceasefire, with Mallett persuasively bullish on further economic growth in Dubai. "Israel Revives Controversial Plan for Refugees," 7-26, is spot news, with nothing the wires didn't tell us. "Dodging the Arab Blacklist," 7-27, is a commendable evaluation of the firmness of the Arab League economic boycott against Israeli and U.S. anti-compliance legislation, with a glimpse at recent corporate attempts to break through Arab blacklisting. Mallet is more cautious on the significance of Coca Cola's successful entrance into the Arabian peninsula despite two decades on the blacklist, reminding us that the "great strength" of the boycott is its "vagueness" plus "the haphazard way in which it is enforced." "Tehran Hints at Better UK Ties," 8-23, is straightforward on signs of this moderation, and British caution. "Iraqi Ministers Fired as Strains Show in Economy," 10-10, is somewhat cloudy on the reasons for the sackings, and introduces too much that simply isn't expanded upon — for example, we learn Iraqis are complaining bitterly about the high prices accompanying farm privatization and economic liberalization, but there's no description of the content of these reforms.

Marcom, John, Jr. *Forbes.* (★ ★ ½)
London bureau manager. Smart corporate profiles and a zippy style are two of the rewards in his reporting. As European television goes private, he files "Le Defi Disney," 2-20, heralding the new market (and revenues) for Hollywood in Europe, but he gets no inkling of the rumblings of the quota system that came later in the year, as countries moved to keep themselves safe from more episodes of "Dallas." In "Britain's Mixed Blessing," 3-6, he points out that the U.K.'s balanced budget won't solve everything, as Maggie and then-Chancellor of the Exchequer, Nigel Lawson struggle with inflation, a deteriorating trade balance and falling savings rate, presented as a morality play for Washington. Neatly focused on Parker Pen Plc., moving to England from Wisconsin after the European head Jacques G. Margry's leveraged buyout, Marcom provides insightful detail on the rededication of the company, due to Margry's return to the founder's original vision that plays up the pen as a status item, "Penmanship With a Flourish," 4-3. A quickie profile of Michael Green, "Is This One for Real?" 7-24, offers a complete, compact look at his Carlton Communications Plc., but we get little sense of Green himself. How did he go from an "obscure" publishing market tip sheet job to the head of a multi-billion dollar company?

A snappy comparison of U.S. and U.K. cellular systems, "Operator, Can You Connect Me to the Real World?" 9-18, neatly informs, although he's short here on the changing technology, with phones and phone systems going from analog to digital. Smart and savvy, he tells us everything we wanted to know about Reuters, the news and financial information business, as the electronic financial information biz booms, "Welcome to Hauppauge, the World's Next Financial Capital," 10-30, a 10 Best nomination from his editors.

Maremont, Mark. *BusinessWeek.* (★ ½)
London. We find this correspondent's reporting to be engaging, his style lively, the information density appreciable. "The Lofty Dreams of Upstart Air Europe," 4-17, is a lively look on another "big-time dreamer," Harry Goodman, and his Air Europe, which is becoming a serious competitor all over the continent. Maremont delivers a delicious quote from a former officer: "The essence of Harry is that he's a professional opportunist." "Banned in Britain: A New Chapter in the Harrods Saga," 4-17, on a business vendetta between two tycoons — all because one snatched away famous Harrods department store from the other, is decently written on a not overly exciting subject. "A Sky-High Bet on the Plane-Leasing Business," 5-1, is startling on a cleverly run Irish leasing company that has somewhat of a lock on the aircraft leasing market. The firm, GPA, not only leases, but sets up fee-generating deals as well. There's ample, concise information well-organized here. "Has LBO Fever Struck Europe?" with Richard Melcher and Stanley Reed 7-3, is short but meaty on the significance of the recent LBO of Gateway Corp., Britain's third-largest supermarket chain, and the implications for future LBOs and the creation of a European junk bond market. "Is Consgold 'Just an Appetizer' for Hanson?" with Chuck Hawkins 7-10, is another brief, but information-packed report, this one on Hanson's effort to make Europe's biggest acquisition yet. "Unilever is all Made Up, With Everywhere to Go," with Stewart Toy and Andrea Rothman 7-31, well-written on Unilever's new role in the prestige cosmetics market, treats us to a series of perfumed puns ("And the margins are a thing of beauty"). "British Telecom is Getting Less British All the Time," 8-14, a review of British Telecom's aggressive expansion drive, adequately sketches its strategy and advantages in Europe. The headline is kind of a slam at the Brits, though, with the clear suggestion that aggressive business strategy is unusual in the UK! "Meet Asil Nadir, the Billion-Dollar Fruit King," with Judith H. Dobrzynski 9-19, about the Turkish Cypriot who has quickly become a power in the fresh fruit business, has a nice flow.

Marsh, David. *Financial Times.* (★ ★ ★)
Bonn. He now has competition as "perhaps the best correspondent covering West Germany," as we described him in last year's *Guide.* Still, he satisfied us again this important news year, not letting the stories here get away from him. "West German Communists Face Perestroika Poser," 1-6, reports the ebbing support for the DKP (West German Communist Party) in the wake of Mikhail Gorbachev's reforms. Marsh quotes party chairman Herbert Mies as to one reason for the slide: "We used to have the monopoly of peace efforts," but now some of those policies have been taken over by other parties. "Profiting From Perestroika." 3-7, is a typical Marsh blending of fine reporting and analysis, updating us on the increasingly closer commercial between the U.S.S.R. and West Germany, the Soviet Union's leading trade partner in the West: "More than any other country in the West, the Federal Republic understands and sympathizes with the objectives of Soviet economic reform." "Testing the Strength of the Ties That Bind," 4-4, contains adept analysis on the changing relations between France and West Germany on the eve of the meeting between Helmut Kohl and Francois Mitterrand in southern Germany, Marsh very satisfying with this picture of the anxieties and disquiet involved. His "Companions for the March to 1990," 4-14, on the West German April cabinet reshuffle, is very informative on the current turmoil plaguing Helmut Kohl's administration. There's some sophisticated analysis in "Germany as a World Financier," 5-15, with Marsh pursing a geopolitical theme. The U.S., he suggests, "will be progressively reluctant to keep 200,000 troops in a country which has become the second-ranking creditor — and which is turning a more attentive ear to Moscow." Marsh is balanced with "Bonn Rail-Link Plan Turns Country Folk Green with

Outrage," 9-27, avoiding advocacy and spin in this report on obstacles to the government's plans for a high-speed track across the idyllic Rhineland landscape. It's the conservative farmers rather than the archetypical Greens who are up in arms, he reports. "Police Keep Dresden's Mood of Confrontation Firmly Under Control," 10-9, locates important detail on the intentions of young protestors in this second round of Dresden demonstrations: they want reform, but have no intention of leaving East Germany.

McCartney, Robert J. *The Washington Post.* (★ ½)
Bonn bureau chief. The events in Germany later in the year seemed to overwhelm McCartney, although his earlier reporting was respectable. "Bonn Rebuffs U.S. on Libyan Factory," 1-3, gives us the German reaction to the Libyan chemical plant imbroglio, with a quote from the president of Imhausen-Chemie, the company said to have played a central role: " 'We don't have the know how to build chemical weapons and we wouldn't do so anyway. . .My firm has been the object of a smear campaign from U.S. rivals.' " "Bonn Leadership Pressed to Move to Right," 2-2, discusses the arch-conservative Republican Party with no supporting material for the assertion that the ruling parties fear defections to the Republicans. "Thousands From East Bloc Drawn by Westward Hopes," 3-31, is a fact-filled report foreshadowing the tumultuous autumn to come: "Drawn by the twin beacons of political liberty and economic prosperity, tens of thousands of Poles, Soviets, East Germans and other East Europeans are flooding into western countries." In "Austria Buries the Last Hapsburg Empress," 4-2, McCartney files a poignant report of the "lavish funeral" of Europe's last crowned empress, Zita, whose death sealed a 640 year period of history in which the Hapsburgs reigned. "Cabinet Reshuffled in Bonn," 4-14, is a passable account of the West German political dynamics which led to an unscheduled government shift in Bonn, but we would have appreciated more info on Genscher's role in the shake-up. "Bonn Seeks More Independent NATO Role," 5-2, offers accurate if conventional analysis of West Germany's challenge to the United States over the alliance policy respecting short-range nuclear arms. "West German officials and some allied diplomats said that the United States and other NATO allies, notably Britain, would have to adjust to Bonn's growing independence or risk a permanent split within the alliance." In "U.S.-Bonn Accord Laid to One Word," 5-31, McCartney provides behind the scenes insights into the tortuous dealings between Genscher and the rest of the Alliance foreign ministers, with a quote from a U.S. official that the agreement was delayed because " 'Genscher was very blockheaded.' " "German Unity a Topic Anew," 7-16, was a bit historically uninformed, but provided a useful scene-setter for events to come: "The 'German question,' a hardy perennial of European diplomacy for more than three centuries, has blossomed again, principally because current reforms in Eastern Europe are arousing hopes for historic changes that could transform East-West relations and ties between the two Germanys. . ."

Miller, Marjorie. *Los Angeles Times.* (★ ★)
Mexico City bureau chief. Miller skidded last year, but in '89 she recovered some of her zip and resourcefulness, if not her objectivity. "Mexico Arrests Powerful Boss of Pemex Union," 1-11, provides no critical treatment of charges by the Pemex union that the arrest of its leader Joaquin Hernandez Galicia was because of a personal vendetta by Mexico President Salinas. Miller got her bearings on this important story five days later in "La Quina Ran Mexico Oil Union as a Feudal Lord," 1-16, giving us background on Galicia, playing up his arrest as enhancing the aura of Mexico's President Carlos Salinas de Gortari, and reporting that Fidel Velasquez, chief of the workers congress of Mexico, is supporting Salinas and the PRI over Hernandez. "Controversial Mexico Police Official Quits," 2-25, is a disjointed piece where Miller tries to link two topics — the resignation of a police chief and the pardon of political prisoners — but only succeeds in missing the real news angle on each. "Mexico Claims Progress Against Drug Traffic," 3-1, offers solid reporting on Mexico's claims of progress in the drug war. "Cocaine Cuts New Route to the North," 4-13, is a lengthy article, the first of two parts, on drug trafficking and new efforts by the Mexican government to stem the flow to the U.S, but it held our attention as Miller provided engrossing detail on the creativity — and in some cases boldness — of the drug

smugglers, who pack cocaine in everything from canned beans to live tropical fish. In the news analysis piece "Salvador Rebel Peace Plan Crafted to Win U.S. Favor," 9-16, Miller argues that the FMLN is adopting a more conciliatory stand in the peace talks, "seeing the unhappy alliance between ARENA and the United States as providing them with a chance to pursue negotiations with a U.S. blessing." But Miller never addresses the question if the rebels' moderate stance is genuine, or just a tactical retreat. In "Battle Rages in Salvador Capital," 11-13, Miller covers the first twenty-four hours of fighting, concentrating on public statements issued by the government and the rebels, and if she doesn't provide the kind of details we saw in other print accounts, from dead dogs in the streets to the caliber of bullets being fired, she doesn't quote army statements that the fighting is under control, which we also saw in other print accounts.

Moffett, Matt. *The Wall Street Journal.* (★ ★)
Mexico City. An energetic young correspondent at an important posting, Moffett is diving in a little more, his reporting on Mexico's economic restructuring at least at a respectable waist-deep level. He is not quite ready for deeper waters yet, badly handling a story on the country's capital flows that should have been assigned to Peter Truell. "Mexico City's Subsidies Present Stiff Challenge to President Salinas," 1-10, gives us what we're looking for — a picture of the debate within Mexico over a policy to control inflation. "Mexican Strike Severely Tests Salinas' Reforms," 4-25, focuses on the risks to Pres. Carlos Salinas de Gortari's thus-far successful campaign to modernize Mexico's economic and political system by toppling pillars of the ruling Institutional Revolutionary Party. "Monterrey Sides With Mexican President," 5-22, reports that Mexico's industrial north, which produces one- third of Mexico's manufactured exports, expresses support for Salinas' stance against creditor banks in NYC. The report is useful as far as it goes, simply showing Salinas' political popularity. "Mexico Pins Hopes on Debt Agreement, Such as It Is, For a Boost in Confidence," 7-25, contains excellent detail on crosscurrents in Mexico's economy — declining short term interest rates, pressure on the formal economy from the growing off-the-books economy. "Back in Business: Mexican Conglomerate Cuts Costs and Learns There's Life After Debt," 7-26, is useful as a success story of how Mexico's biggest private company crawled out from under a crushing debt load and other problems. "Mexico Debates Liberalizing Car Market," 8-8, is good reporting, with appropriate quotes, detail and arguments on how free traders hope to end the 1962 ban on auto imports, giving domestic industry relief on domestic content rules. In over his head, too much is askew in a P. 1 leder, especially embarrassing on the eve of Salinas' visit to Washington. "Crippling Export: Mexico's Capital Flight Still Wracks Economy, Despite the Brady Plan," 9-25, Moffett suggesting capital flight continues when there is already an inflow. To be fair to Moffett, the editors helped mess this up with the headline, the story being more about how capital that previously flew is already invested abroad. "In Catholic Mexico, A Priest's Power Is Limited to Prayer," 12-6, is an astonishing A-hed on "the most astonishingly aggressive anti-clerical laws in the non-Communist world," but no hint from Moffett on how these laws may change under *Salinastroika.*

Morrison, James. *The Washington Times.* (★ ½)
London. The analytical side has a tendency to be underdone in his reports, although the information is generally fresh. "Miss India Has Tabloids Toiling Overtime," 3-20, is a disorganized report on what British papers have to say about the sexploits of a beauty queen. "Thatcher Marks a Decade in Power," 5-4, is a nicely appreciative perspective on the British PM's last ten years: "During that decade, Mrs. Thatcher, the longest-serving British leader of the 20th century, has led Britain with a single-minded determination to revive a nation that was suffering from exhaustion after its loss of empire." His "All Sides Claim Victory at NATO Summit," 5-31, is a sturdy, upbeat report that focuses on the key details of Bush's proposed compromise on the short-range nuclear modernization issue. Morrison succeeds in effectively using a short space to identify the different, previously conflicting concerns of allied government which were successfully harmonized. "European Parliament Swinging to Left," 6-20, is a solid round-up on the European Parliament election, although he could have developed more of an

analysis as to why the vote swung to the left with socialists, communists and greens capturing a majority. Morrison sorts out the confusion around U.S. policy toward UNITA with "Rebel Hands Bush New Peace Plan for Angolan War," 10-6, an informative account of the meeting between the President and Jonas Savimbi. The UNITA leader, he reports, "criticized the Bush administration for refusing to believe the Angolan Army has used Soviet-supplied chemical weapons against his rebels." Morrison carries off a broad summary of the sweeping changes behind the Iron Curtain in "Freedom's Call Reaches Deeper Into East Bloc," 11-20, with some perceptions on the transformations by Zbig Brzezinski, Rep. Tom Lantos (D-Calif.) and a former Czech diplomat.

Neilan, Edward. *The Washington Times.* (★ ★)
Tokyo, NE Asia. This veteran China watcher may be having his best year ever on this beat, especially quick to handle the China story competently. An interesting "Eager Japanese Palms Reveal Fortunetellers' Bright Future," 1-2, informs us that the Japanese (including all the top politicians) spend $6 billion a year on fortunetellers and supernaturalism. "Takeshita Totters Toward Ouster as Scandal, Tax Take Toll," 4-4, tries to get economic policy into focus, linking indecision on policy with the current political crisis in Japan. There's decent historical perspective in "China's Student's Fed Up With Party's Free Lunch," 5-2, drawing parallels with the student revolt of 70 years ago, in this focused report on the grievances of Chinese students with the elite's official perks, emoluments and corruption. "Protest Rocks Beijing Before Summit," 5-15, is terse reporting on China's growing domestic turmoil and the first Sino-Soviet summit in 30 years. "Million Protesters Dwarf Summit," 5-18, is lively and focused on the demonstrations and their impact. "Chinese Students Undergo Power Struggle of Their Own," 5-25, is keen-eyed on fractional differences within the student protest leadership. "Deng Seen as Out of Touch With China's Youth," 6-5, could have been so much better if Neilan would have played out his insights into the re-emergence of gerontocracy instead of reporting rumor and gossip. "Chicken's Back, But China Is In the Pan," 6-15, is an informative report on where things stand with the international business and financial communities in the wake of the repression. "Japan's Leader to Limp onto the World Stage," 7-7, contains a good mix of news, gloom-and-doom, *schadenfreude* about Japan's fumbling economic elite, all in lugubrious garb: "Japan goes into the 15th economic summit of developed nations this week a deeply troubled nation, led by a lame-duck prime minister whose party is under fire. . ..the state of affairs in the ruling party is rapidly assuming the character of hemorrhage." "Japan Has Split Personality In Diplomacy With Chinese," 9-28, contains useful, oblique observations on Japan's diplomacy toward China, bending toward "business and volleyball as usual" even as it pays lip service to Western condemnations of Beijing.

Newman, Barry. *The Wall Street Journal.* (★ ½)
Eastern Europe. In one of the most important assignments Newman is likely to have in his career, given the political avalanche on this beat this year, he was largely disappointing. His spot reports were handled professionally enough, but when he reached for the big story it drifted away with themes not fully developed and presentations that were garbled. "In a Freer-Speech Era, Poles at Last Confront Ghosts of the Ghetto," 1-4, a P. 1 story on Poland, once a cradle of Jewish culture, exploring its guilt about Holocaust victims, is very heavily weighted on the side of Polish responsibility or culpability in the holocaust. The presentation is unbalanced, without even a perspective on what more Poles could have done under the Nazi occupation. Newman provides a studied picture of East German retrenchment in the wake of Gorbachev's reforms, as hardliners control the helm, have no sympathy for reform, and for whom talk of reunification sets off alarm bells, in "East Berlin Leaders Recoil From Glasnost," 1-31: "A neutralized, non-nuclear Germany, generous with aid and trade, may well be Soviet leader Mikhail Gorbachev's secret desire. But it makes the East Germans quake." "Solidarity Offers an Olive Branch to Humbled Polish Communists," 6-7, is richly informative on Solidarity's devastating victory over the Communists in Poland's 6-4 election, where "With one eye on China, however, Solidarity volunteered not to capitalize on this cataclysm." Newman's quotes from defeated Communist

Party candidate for Senate, Mieczyslaw Wilczek, Minister of Industry are excellent: "Nobody wants to rule. The opposition should be given power and be able to show what it can do. . .I don't want to deprecate my opponent. . .but I would have lost against an ape. It's another victory of an idea over common sense. It's a different idea this time, quite different. . .I think the Communist Party will fall apart." Still, we fault the report for its lack of information on the activity and perspectives of party hardliners, an omission not permissible after the experience in China. "The Privatizer: Polish Entrepreneur, Now Industry Minister, Takes a Capitalist Line," 7-19, a breezy sketch of Mieczyslaw Wilczek, self-made bone meal industrialist, is not a very clear picture of what his strategy is on transforming the Polish economy. "As East Europe Opens to the West, Comecon Seeks a Market Niche," 9-28, a P. 1 leder, contains interesting material scattered in this long, long piece, but it's poorly presented, a scrambled stream of consciousness here and there, leaving us dismayed.

Owen, David. *Financial Times.* (★ ½)
Canada. We depend on Owen for the steady stream of reports on the political and economic doings of our northern neighbor. No journalist in the U.S. press is as comprehensive in what he tries to cover here. Although a somewhat conventional assessment of the issues facing PM Brian Mulroney, "Canada. Uncomfortable Trade-offs," 12-15-88, is an accurate depiction of how the Canadian government, business and political factions view the road ahead. "A Tough Second-Term Ahead," 12-15-88, is a rounded overview on the Tories' election victory in Canada and the new political relationships among Conservatives, Liberals and the New Democratic Party. "Ice Cream Row Jolts Canada Free Trade Pact," 1-19, is an important dispatch, locating potentially serious ramifications for Canada's agricultural marketing board system of what otherwise appears as a minor trade complaint. "A Committed Creator," 4-17, analyzes International Thomson Organization (ITO) and its acquisitive nature (60 purchases of U.S. specialty publishing properties since 1979 as well as others and over $100,000,000 spent on new product development in the last fiscal year). But Owen gives us only management's point of view. "Tax Reforms That Can Damage a Government's Health," 8-23, is an excellent report, with all the details on the tax policies of the conservative government. From the evidence assembled it seems as if Canada's economy is poised for decline.

Parks, Michael. *Los Angeles Times.* (★ ★ ½)
Another strong year for the Moscow bureau chief, and if he didn't hit any home runs, his pop-ups were few and far between. "Quake Aid Influx Gave Soviets New Self-Image," 12-24-88, is a stirring account of international relief efforts in Armenia and how this collaborative effort has changed the Soviet's image in the West as well as the Soviet's image of Americans and of themselves, with Parks getting some good quotes. "Soviets Plan to Review Cases of Lost Citizenship," 2-25, is a sound story on attempts by the Soviet government to lure back members of the intelligentsia previously stripped of citizenship and deported for alleged anti-government activity, though Parks wrongly assumes at times that all of these dissidents are household names in the West. We get an enthusiastic assessment of the forthcoming elections in the U.S.S.R. in "New Style Election Altering Soviet Political Landscape," 3-6, which features a fine mixture of reporting, analysis, and use of quotes to convey a sense of world historic events in the making. "Soviets Reform Legal Code to Soften Curbs on Dissent," 4-12, offers a tightly written, informative piece on reforms in the Soviet legal codes, underscoring the fine line Gorbachev is treading trying to maintain order and at the same time relax restrictions on political dissent. And he works in good background on the Stalinist regime. In "Gorbachev Offers More Arms Cuts," 7-7, Parks writes on Gorbachev's proposal to make further unilateral reductions of tactical nuclear weapons. Maintaining his objectivity, he avoids any gush and rightly pegs the proposal as a challenge to NATO unity. Back in the field for "As Rebuilding Lags, Armenia Quake Victims Are Losing Hope," 9-5, Parks discovers that both physically and psychologically, much work needs to be done. The streets have taken on the "look and smell of a refugee settlement" and the people possess "The querulous temper and soul-destroying malaise, typical of long-term refugees." Informative, but lacks the impact one would expect, the fact that it appeared on page

six of a newspaper based in earthquake conscious Los Angeles tells you something. "Soviet Party May Lose Its Reserved Legislative Seats," 10-25, is a dry account of a vote in the Supreme Soviet defeating an amendment to reserve a number of seats for Party representatives, though more quotes from the amendment's opponents may have made the article more accessible to non-political science readers.

Parmelee, Jennifer. *The Washington Post.* (★ ★)
Rome. With so many of the correspondents of the U.S. press based here reporting so little from Italy itself, flying off instead throughout the eastern Mediterranean, this *Post* stringer delighted us by filling the holes on coverage of this G-7 nation. "Italian Communist Chief Reshaping Party Image," 5-16, is an excellent, appropriately humorous report of really changing times: Italian Communist leader Achille Occhetto, the "head of the West's largest Communist party. . .talks of using American democracy as a model for Italian reform. . .even contemplating dropping 'Communist' from his party's name." Parmelee writes with gusto, as in "European Unity: an Offer the Mafia Can't Refuse?" 5-19, an absorbing report on the double-breasted suited Mafiosi getting ready for Europe 1992. "Rome's Grit Stables Marcus Aurelius," 6-19, is vivid on Romans trying to save their city's historical riches from pollution and vandalism. "Sicily's Modernization Aggravates Mafia's Avarice," 9-25, an observant journal of a visit to southern Sicily, reports the sudden and shocking escalation of murders and attempted homicides in regions where control over public money and drug trafficking has absorbed all the energies of the areas Mafiosi. The intersection of the global drug trade and the Mafia was a frequent focus of her reports. "Colombian Cartels, Mafia in Italy Working Together," 10-21, defines the link of what seems to be a perfect partnership —Italian organized crime has the world's best distribution network; the cartels have a lock on raw cocaine.

Peel, Quentin. *Financial Times.* (★ ★ ★ ★)
Moscow. Peel was the best correspondent covering the U.S.S.R. this year, picking up critical key details overlooked by others, including even *The New York Times*' Keller. Key is his sense of precisely where to look for that piece of news that on the margin defines a whole new process. The fate of the co-operative movement in the U.S.S.R. was a good indicator all year as to the depth and direction of Soviet reform. "Moscow's Limit on Co-operation," 1-6, is an important report on the backlash against private enterprise, as a whole range of new restrictions are imposed on the movement. Peel gives exactly the right reading on this, noting the Council of Ministers decree was published without public debate, and that leaders of the co-op movement are alarmed and despondent. We get an indication as to what degree state officials take into account public opinion with "Soviet Price Reforms 'Are Being Slowed,' " 1-17, Peel quoting the first vice-chairman of Gosplan, the state planning committee: "people are against any increase in prices. . .Price reform is inevitable," but "many decisions at the top are being taken under the influence of certain articles in the press. People are dissatisfied." "When the People Said 'Enough,' " 3-29, was our selection for the best of the press wrap-ups on the historic Easter elections in the U.S.S.R., the details, perspective and analysis all on target. "Moscow May Introduce Second Currency," 4-4, while thin, is the best of all reports on the prospects that the Soviets are seriously debating a convertible ruble. Peel reports information we didn't find in other reports on the disturbances in Soviet central Asia, as in "Kazakhstan Hit by Riots Over Food Rationing," 6-19, where he informs us that among policy changes being called for by rioting youths is the closure of co-operatives, which were blamed for food shortages and rising prices. "Soviet Tax, Investment Rules 'Will Be Radically Reformed,' " 7-13, is concise and timely on the new Finance Minister Dr. Valentin Pavlov, outlining what appears to be a dramatically new set of positive changes in the Soviet tax system and investment rules. Again, here's a development that only Peel among the Moscow corps seems to have caught. He efficiently updates us on the new restrictions imposed on the Soviet's fledgling private sector with "Moscow Acts on Co-operatives," 10-17. Peel is comprehensive in a masterful report and analysis on the radical new plan to reform the Soviet economy with "The Battle Lines Are Drawn," 11-20, a 10 Best selection. Deputy prime minister Leonid Abalkin envisions the reforms leading to a social democratic U.S.S.R., and the reformists' radical document on where *perestroika* ought to take the U.S.S.R. has Gorbachev's blessings, he reports.

Perlez, Jane. *The New York Times.* (★ ½)
Nairobi bureau chief. Slow-paced, but not sluggish, Perlez's coverage of East Africa (with occasional forays elsewhere on the continent) is a respectable mixture of topical reporting and feature material. She isn't clear enough on economic policy in "Zambia's on Its Uppers (Just Try Buying Shoes)," 1-23, reporting that as copper reserves run out and production slows because of the scarcity of foreign exchange to buy spare parts for the mining equipment, President Kenneth Kaunda, who had denounced the IMF for its harsh terms, now wants it back in Zambia. "Early Exodus Portends Sudan Famine," 3-12, is an critical alert that large numbers of Sudanese refugees are likely to die of starvation without large-scale food deliveries within the next few weeks. "Kenya to Press for Worldwide Ban on Ivory Trade," 5-12, is straight reporting on this effort to preserve the fast dwindling elephant herds. Perlez covers the various points of view in the debate, noting that some conservationists oppose the ban, believing it will drive the ivory trade underground, making it impossible to control and with the same disastrous results for the elephant population as occurred with the black rhinoceros when rhino horn trading was banned. "Coup in Ethiopia Seems To Be a Failure, Diplomats Say," 5-18, is adequate, based on sources among the Western diplomatic community, but it totally misses the intense drama of the attempted coup and President Mengistu Haile Mariam's bloody counterstrike. "Where Elephants Roam, a Plea for Understanding," 8-9, reports that Zimbabwe elephant herds increase under good management, but legal ivory traders are suffering from President Bush's ban on all ivory imports. This is a good feature from Harare noting differences among black African countries on the ban. "Birth Control Making Inroads in Populous Kenya," 9-10, is unbalanced and unsatisfying, Perlez either too partisan here or simply sloppy, with the report reading as if it were a ZPG promo.

Pletka, Danielle. *Insight.* (★ ★ ½)
After a satisfactory but not stunning first year at the newsweekly, Pletka switched to high octane this year, globe-trotting to story centers and assembling her fact-filled notebooks into appealing articles. An intelligent journalist, Pletka competently works a new angle on a running topic in "The Lower Profile for Rising Terror," 12-26-88, examining the potentials for a more sophisticated and deadlier form of terrorism, including the use of chemical and biological weapons. Her close could have been better, but she cites appropriate sources and organizes the piece well. "Old Allies Tie a New One On," 1-9, tries to provide some perspectives as to where North Korea may be heading in the context of spreading *perestroika* and South Korea's booming development. Pletka takes this as far as she can, but we're looking forward to a reprise that will look anew at the question against the backdrop of changes in Eastern and Central Europe. "Beijing Gunfire Jolts the Jewel of the Crown," 6-26, on the shockwaves the Communist crackdown in Tiananmen Square send through Hong Kong, slated to rejoin China in 1997, displays a solid grasp of the issues. Again, Pletka keeps the writing tight, the organization clear and utilizes a full array of substantive quotes. Fact-filled and entertaining, "The Colonel's Bourgeois Conversion," 7-24, on a "new" pragmatic Qaddafi, flows with breezy prose and wry humor. Pletka provides good background on Libya's recent events in this sound analysis of what the Colonel is up to. We were getting a little jaded with the media coverage of Israel, most reporters rearranging the same information without really finding new angles or insights. Pletka, though, carried us through an *Insight* cover on Israel, 9-18, with decent analysis, although the second part of the effort, "Socialist Dreams Die Hard," was the meatier section. "Tangle of Conflicting Interests Locked in Perplexing Puzzle," 11-6, breaks down the specific policy perspectives of the various players in the Middle East in the Arab-Israeli conflict, nicely uncomplicating what otherwise seems complicated. A good year!

Porter, Janet. *The Journal of Commerce.* (★ ★)
Our first year rating this London-based head of *The Journal Of Commerce*'s European bureaus, we're won over by her byline. Porter provides a continuous stream of important details on the U.K. economy that we just don't find anywhere else in the U.S. press. "U.K.'s January Sales Arrive Early as Economy Cools Off," 12-20-88, reports that although the retail industry is in

a slump, Chancellor of the Exchequer Nigel Lawson isn't unhappy: "So far all the signs are that the economy is slowing down just the way that I hoped it would." Of course, some clues as to his glee are appropriate. "Transportation at the Breaking Point," 12-20-88, has nice detail on Britain's transportation infrastructure, now reaching a breaking point. The analytic end, though, doesn't hold together that well as Porter reduces it to a question of whether the government's "good housekeeping" drive has allowed cost savings to be given priority over meeting capacity needs and safety requirements. She establishes a better case for infrastructure spending in "Thatcherism Faces Fiscal Test," 3-28, suggesting the PM is mistaken in wanting to instead pile up a budget surplus: "Britain is no longer the sick man of Europe but a rich nation growing richer all the time. . .Shabby public transport networks, run-down hospitals and litter-strewn streets contrast sharply with the image of squeaky clean West Germany, Switzerland, or Sweden." Her "Soviet Bank Hires Western Experts," 3-30, is a good inside view of Soviet attempts to gain Western expertise through Moscow Narodny Bank. We get useful detail here not available elsewhere, but the report would have been even better with an evaluative effort by Porter. "Geneva's Crucial Trade Talks," 4-5, is admonitory, although appropriately so, advising the U.S. to maintain "the sort of behavior expected from a world power," while reminding us that "the EC is just as much to blame for the present crisis." "Optimistic Talk Masks Rifts at Trade Round," 4-6, is solid, insightful digging around the Geneva meeting, and "GATT Chief 'Uncomfortable' About Talks," 4-7, a clear, focused review of the delegations' positions, was the best available on GATT's situation. Porter's "Privatization Is Under Attack," 10-13, focuses on the convergence of the government's plan to privatize the water industry and the controversy and anger over the poor quality of the country's drinking water. Although most of Thatcher's efforts to sell government enterprises have been successful, this one is in trouble.

Powell, Bill. *Newsweek.* (★ ½)
Tokyo. It was a smart move to beef up this bureau, and Powell, who has solid credentials as a fine business reporter, can add a lot to the coverage here. Unfortunately, so far he's working his way through the political economy as if he were armed with a copy of James Fallow's book for standard reference. It's clear from some of his work that he's none too optimistic about America's ability to meet the "Asian Challenge." Pre-Tokyo, he files a lightweight, somewhat gossipy look at the Ford Motor Co. dynasty, "Ford: The Family Strikes Back," with Ginny Carroll 1-16, running concurrently with Alex Taylor's more comprehensive look in *Fortune.* We get more of a half-shut door in "Still Only a Half-Open Door," 2-13, a "deeper" look at the causes of why Americans still have trouble cracking the Japanese market; we already know the story, the trade gap, buy U.S., etc. as Japan's entrenched business practices, layered distribution systems and joint ventures are blamed. This is a soft-hitting article which warms over the huge pile already written on this subject. He reviews James Fallows' book in "To Our Own Selves Be True," 4-3, fitting right in with the *More Like Us* crowd. In "We Simply Can't Go Rushing Back In," 7-3, he writes about the uncertainties faced by American firms deciding to re-enter China, including many quotes from businessmen, but he fails to bring them together with coherent analysis. Sharper in "Bailing Out Bangladesh," with Hassan Shahriar 8-28, he gives a good sense of the internal geopolitical wrangling over flood relief aid to Bangladesh, and although some might take offense at his wit, we found it refreshing: "President Francois Mitterrand's wife, Danielle, was stuck in Dhaka during the flooding of 1988 — 'literally got her feet wet,' says one U.S. source, 'and her husband has taken quite a personal interest in the subject ever since.' " He extends "The Asian Challenge" to Europe in "The Japanese Invade Europe," with Daniel Pedersen, Meggan Dissly and Theresa Waldrop 10-9, carefully negotiating the political minefield here, picking up some ominous sentiment from the continent — "For Europe, the concern is that the Japanese challenge will turn out to be real" — but never properly weighing and assessing it.

Powers, Charles T. *Los Angeles Times.* (★ ★)
Warsaw. As with *The Wall Street Journal*'s reporter here, Barry Newman, we were disappointed this year in the work we saw from Powers, a three-star correspondent a year ago. Too often he

seemed caught up in details, losing sight of the bigger picture, and when he did try to expand his canvas all we got were broad brush strokes. "Warsaw Tries to Define New Role for Solidarity," 1-19, offers not much detail on the party's stand, but gives some information on internal debate over the proposal to legalize Solidarity, as Powers attempts to fill in as many holes as he can here. "Voters Backing Opposition in Polish Election," 6-5, is a disjointed affair with Powers mixing in human interest material with the deadly serious political news. The result is that both sides of the story are shortchanged. We don't even learn the exit poll figures until the bottom third of the story, and there's little speculation on the post-election political landscape. We do learn about 48 nuns in Warsaw who received special permission to leave their convent and vote. "Poland Confronts Crucial Issue as It Hosts President," 7-10, an analytical piece written on the eve of the Bush visit, notes Adam Michnik's proposal that the country ease its political deadlock by having "Solidarity give its support for a communist president in exchange for running the government — that is, choosing the prime minister and the Cabinet in charge of the day-to-day management of the state." An idea "first regarded as extreme and described by other Solidarity leaders as 'one man's opinion' " has "gained currency in recent days." His "2 Parties Support Solidarity Regime," 8-17, and "Polish President Endorses Plan for Solidarity Cabinet," 8-18, give solid coverage of rapidly changing events in Poland as Solidarity pulls political support away from the Communists and engineers a historic change in government. Powers was one of the few journalists covering this story to use the label "indecision" to characterize Lech Walesa's actions in the week leading up to this in the 8-18 article. With "Stop Threats, Walesa Tells Communists," 8-22, and "Communists in Poland Get Boost," 8-24, Powers keeps us up-to-date on the public statements the communists and Solidarity are issuing back and forth — Walesa warning the communists they will "lose everything," 8-22, the Communists publicizing a message from Gorbachev saying the Communists must remain in the government, 8-24, but other than characterizing Walesa's statements as "barbed," 8-22, there's little analysis on Powers' part, nor much indication that he's done much digging to get the stories behind the public bromides.

Preston, Julia. *The Washington Post.* (★ ★ ★)
Another strong year for this Central America correspondent, Preston kept her readers on top of breaking stories from Port-au-Prince to Panama City. She filed multi-layered reports reflecting a degree of understanding that transcended the ideological perceptions that seemed to color 90% of the correspondence we saw from datelines south of the border this year. *Post* readers got an extra Christmas present in "8 Years Later: Reagan, Central American Leftists Discover Their Limits," 12-25-88, an outstanding retrospective on Central America at the end of the Reagan years, featuring articles on El Salvador: "After Years of Anarchy, A Nation Is Transformed" and "Sorrows of the Past Haunt El Salvador's 'Model Town,' " and Nicaragua: "Despite 'Visible Scars' Sandinistas Endure," and "In Jalapa, a Grim Wait for a Long War to End." "Today while they have supporters, it is hard to find anyone in Central America who describes the [Farabundo Marti National Liberation Front] FMLN or the Sandinistas as heroes. . .Second, the myth of invincible Yankee might foundered." Though 1989 may have been the end of an era, it was not the end of the Central America story. "Cristiani Gets Mandate to Govern El Salvador, but Not His Party," 3-21, aptly focuses on the central issue which emerged from the Salvadoran election: "whether the overwhelming victory will allow him [Cristiani] to govern his own party." In "Havana Summit: Forum for Gorbachev, Castro to Air Differences," 4-6, she delivers a sober analysis of the actual status of Soviet-Cuban relations away from the cheering crowds: Castro's bombastic bravado "did not stop Gorbachev from implicitly playing down Cuba's importance in the Soviets' overall picture." In "Full-Scale Fighting Erupts Outside Presidential Palace in Haiti," 4-8, Preston files a crisp battle report of a fast-breaking situation, dropping in a subtle hint that the U.S. Embassy and Roman Catholic Church in Haiti may not be on the same wavelength in the confrontation between General Avril and the rebel troops. "Nicaragua Sends Arms To Panama," 6-9, is a solidly documented, first-rate scoop: "Nicaragua's army sent several planeloads of Soviet-bloc weapons to Panama in recent months [which are] being used to equip the Dignity Batallions, a militia of about 1,500 civilians that

Noriega formed last year as part of preparations against a U.S. attack." A 10 Best selection for foreign correspondence, "Castro's Purge Trial," *The New York Review of Books* 12-7, is excellent reporting and analysis on the trials of top Cuban military figures on charges of drug trafficking. Preston addresses the question: "What did Fidel Castro know and when did he know it?"

Randal, Jonathan C. *The Washington Post.* (★)
Middle East. Randal is one of the more enigmatic foreign correspondents we read. At times he has a hard-hitting cynical style that makes us sit up and take notice, at other times he just seems to coast, taking assertions from various sources at face value. "PLO Offers Full Cooperation in Probe of Pan Am Bombing," 1-4, reads at times like a press release for the PLO, with Randal tossing out assertions such as: "For many years, the PLO has shared intelligence on terrorism with several Western European governments on the assumption that much of the information would be passed on to the United States, according to PLO sources." In "Rushdie's Book Burned in Britain," 1-18, Randal writes that "The book burning [of Salman Rushdie's *Satanic Verses*] — and subsequent events — have focused Establishment attention on the more intolerant side of sections of Britain's two million-strong Moslem community. . ." without giving any clear picture of why the book is regarded as so offensive by Moslems. "French Effort to Play Peace-Keeping Role in Mideast Misfires," 4-14, combines a lucid report of how French domestic politics are affected by Lebanese fortunes with inadequate inferences about how the major power Middle East policies actually are worked out. In "Thatcher, Opposing Kohl, Seeks to Block New Weapons Talks with Soviets," 4-27, one of his better efforts of the year, Randal places Margaret Thatcher in the power equation which shapes Western Europe's posture in world affairs: "Already unpopular in many West European countries for opposing greater integration in the European Community, Thatcher has displayed little warmth or sympathy for Kohl. In this dispute, she has not flinched from provoking Bonn's wrath in opposing a new set of arms talks that she believes could jeopardize the balance of power in Europe." His "French Visit Polishes Arafat's New Image," 5-5, a news analysis of Yasir Arafat's visit to Paris, struck one of our readers as being cynical about French diplomatic intentions in the Middle East, but this may be a topic where a little cynicism is called for. "PLO Finding It Hard to Adapt to Mundane Existence," 6-3, offers tongue-in-cheek analysis: "The PLO leadership is finding it hard to adapt its survival tactics of secrecy and subterfuge to the more prosaic demands of the diplomatic world." His "Economic Debate Continues in Iran," 6-18, provided a surprisingly balanced assessment of the relationship between Iran's theological politics and that country's shattered economy.

Rapoport, Carla. *Fortune.* (★ ★ ★ ★)
Tokyo. Rapoport was our reporter of choice in Japan in the first *MediaGuide,* with our highest rating in 1986 when she was covering business news out of Tokyo for the *Financial Times.* In her first full year back after maternity leave, she's a major asset at *Fortune,* her sensitivity to Japanese matters better than anyone else we see in the English language press. She writes the lead piece in the magazine's special Autumn "Pacific Rim 1989" issue, "Understanding How Japan Works," that puts Nippon into a few pages as nobody else we know could manage, with a last graph worth writing on your sleeve if you're planning to do business there: "In sum, don't let the golf, the McDonald's franchises, the just-like-ours office towers and the Western business suits fool you. Japan is and will remain very foreign." Her "Ready, Set, Sell — Japan Is Buying," 9-11, a 10 Best selection, swirls and eddies this way and that to give an almost palpable sense of the dynamics of retailing in Japan today, the traditional mom-and-pop stores cascading into gigantic hypermarkets. We learn more on the subject in this little feature from Rapoport than we have in hundreds of news clips combined, and we know she's right about the changes coming: "This is the break U.S. and European companies have been waiting for." In "Japan's Big Knack for Coming Back," 11-6, we also get several dimensions, marveling at how Rapoport can get her arms around a story so quickly, this one the renaissance of several "sunset" industries. "One of the sources of Japan's strength is that old industries never die. They don't even fade away.

The Japanese textile, shipbuilding, and steel industries — once presumed doomed — suddenly look more alive than ever. They not only are profitable but are also once again setting the pace worldwide." A secondary theme on triangular trade with Latin America excites us too. In "Great Japanese Mistakes," 2-13, Rapoport nicely demonstrates that the MITI planners can be just as myopic as anyone else: "One of the paranoid fantasies Westerners have about Japan is that Japanese can see the future." She gives us a nice, thumbnail sketch of the current state of Tokyo's military producers, which demolishes the case of those who fear the Rising Sun's big electronic concerns. "Japan's Rising Defense Industry," 4-24, reports that Japan's defense contractors are dwarfed by U.S. firms, and their main contribution to foreign arms makers is in the area of electronic and computer subcomponents. Rapoport also describes the pressures on the Japanese government to grant waivers on existing restrictions on arms exports. We only wish she had commented on the rising nationalist tendencies in Japan and the current Japanese bestseller, *A Japan Which Can Say No,* a xenophobic diatribe in which they write: "The heart of the world's defense power is in the hands of Japanese high technology." Welcome back, Carla!

Remnick, David. *The Washington Post.* (★ ★ ★)
Another strong year for Remnick, who we were delighted to see was a recipient of the American Society of Newspaper Editors Distinguished Writing Award in the deadline writing category for his reports on the earthquake in Soviet Armenia in December, 1988. His analysis is often of award caliber as well, as in "Gorbachev: One Leader Can Make a Difference," 12-31-88, where Remnick sums up 1988 as "a year short on groceries, but long on ideas, permissions, proposals and gestures." Many reporters would have taken three paragraphs to say the same thing. "Picking Out the People's Choices," 3-27, offers effective coverage of the "human interest" side of the Soviet election, our reader found it more "meaty" and less flowery than the same day *The New York Times* "human interest" dispatch from Moscow. In "Ethnic Winds Buffet Kremlin," 4-11, Remnick upgrades the growing outburst of nationalist protests to the status of a "threat to the Soviet Empire," and notes the Kremlin has no effective policy to handle this challenge: "Even Gorbachev, who is ordinarily the master of his own emotions and public performances, has some times become hot-headed and muddled." "Glasnost Shines on Party Brass," 4-27, and "Soviet Party Chiefs' Speeches Show Anxieties," 4-28, offered fine coverage and analysis of the 4-25 proceedings where Gorbachev purged 25 of the Central Committee, with Remnick pointing out in the 4-27 piece that the purge is "a prime example of how Gorbachev has mastered the mechanisms of Soviet power," and he notes: ". . .the fact that the leadership has chosen to bring its own internal debates more into the open is a striking new development." In "Ligachev Losing Power in Moscow as Yelstin Gains," 6-20, he updates where Gorbachev's opponents stand in the Soviet Union's new political universe: "Yegor Ligachev, the politician once thought to be the most serious conservative threat to Mikhail Gorbachev's radical changes, has lost much of his power and almost all of his ability to send a chill through pro-reform forces." We get a somewhat existential mood piece about Leningrad in "White Nights in a Grey Land," 7-3. "Leningrad, city of Pushkin, Gogol and Dostoyevsky, city of Mandelstam, Akhmatova and Brodsky, is on these white nights a brilliant embodiment of all verse and prose that has been written about its eternal qualities." In "Perestroika Has to Move Forward," 7-22, Remnick takes us into the homes, villages, markets, and workplaces of striking coal miners and gets a three-dimensional sense of it all.

Revzin, Philip. *The Wall Street Journal.* (★ ½)
Paris. We'd hoped he'd venture into the French economy for more of his stories this year, an area the U.S. press seems to think American readers care less about. He disappointed us there, although the rest of his work continues to hold up. Reporting from Brussels, with the ink barely dry on the great NATO Summit, Revzin makes clear that European unity is perhaps a bit exaggerated, "As Bush Leaves Europe, Elbows Fly Again," with Thomas F. O'Boyle 6-2. The report crackles with perspective on the remaining, very entrenched disagreements over how to proceed with the unification deal of 1992, Revzin quick on the attitudes of various countries, as with one official's interpretation of British feeling toward Germany: "The British still have

this occupation mentality. . .Although they don't tell the Germans directly, they clearly feel that the Germans should rightly carry more of the defense burden because they lost the war." His "Europe's 'Mr. 1992' Is a Tireless Crusader," 6-14, gave us the best picture of newly appointed EEC President Jacques Delors. Revzin using great quotes putting Delors' squabble with Thatcher in context, but a slow start hobbles the piece: "Jacques Delors, the closest thing to a Pan-European president, is on the road again." Snappier with "Not All Are Waving Tricolor as France Begins Bicentennial," 7-14, an A-hed on the relative lack of interest in the Bastille Day bicentennial: "Today is Bastille Day — the best of times or the worst of times, depending on your tastes, to begin the bicentennial of the French Revolution." In "The Road to European Unity — 1992: Unity Drive Feeds EC Bureaucrats' Power," 7-27, he's bullish on the integration, reports businessmen moving at rapid rates, already completing the preparation game in some industries. Revzin also notes the unresolved areas of controversy. From Warsaw he fills us in on Poland's newspaper "war," as Solidarity and communists share the same building, "Two Warsaw Dailies, Poles Apart, Labor Side by Side," 9-7. He uses the differences in work habits between the two to illustrate critical changes percolating throughout the country. "United We Stand," 9-22, part of a special section on world business, struck us as more irreverent than informative in sections. Although steady on how some countries are more free market than others, and on how trade-offs are inevitable, the underlying reasons for this aren't developed.

Riding, Alan. *The New York Times.* (★ ½)
We thought his move from Rio to Rome would have positive benefits, his reporting from South America starting to slip into two-dimensional ruts, but the change in bureaus hasn't turned out that way yet. "Paraguay Coup: Battle for Succession," 2-4, reports some background on the coup against Pres. General Alfredo Stroessner. Riding cites "Latin American experts" who say the coup came about not so much because of a desire to end the authoritarian style of government, but more because of a desire to oust the faction that placed itself in a position to succeed Stroessner, but we don't get any internal reading to know one way or the other. "Italy's Battered Communists Reinvent Themselves Again," 3-25, is a nicely efficient report on the party's attempts to change its image in the wake of the economic growth and social changes that have taken place in Italy. The juxtaposition of remarks by PCI head Occeheto and Socialist Craxi liven up the report. "Peru Fights to Overcome Its Past," 5-14, is a big disappointment from the former Rio bureau chief, Riding developing no new angles or information on Peru in this plodding effort. Too much of a naked eyeball account of poverty, simple chronology of political turmoil, "Shining Path" and insurrection, there's nothing on what impedes economic development. "Women to the Fore! (What Would Franco Say?)," 5-30, gives a glimpse at the burgeoning women's movement in Spain, but without much exploration of where it's going next. Riding peddles disinformation in "Casting Off a Cloak, Opus Dei Carries On the Work," 10-25, putting on a definite spin here so as to conjure up an image of the spiritual, religious Roman Catholic organization as a shadowy, elitist cult-like operation. Riding quotes an unidentified American Jesuit who's only too willing to disparage the organization and the late Penny Lernoux, whom he identifies not as a *Nation* correspondent but as an "expert on the Catholic Church." In "The Spanish Victory: A Mandate for the Socialists," 10-31, we get a post-election wrapup, somewhat thin, but Riding gives us a forward look, suggesting everything in the campaign points to a resumption of focus on rapid economic growth by PM Felipe Gonzalez.

Riemer, Blanca. *Business Week.* (★ ½)
Paris. One of our favorite writers on economics and finance when she was located in the Washington bureau, who could imagine Riemer could catch the blahs in Paris? As the bureau chief, though, perhaps there are constraints on her talents as a financial writer. If so, the editors should remove her as bureau chief, give her a raise, and turn her loose in Europe, where great stories are waiting to be written. "Insider-Trading Shocks Rocks the Elysee," 1-23, a skeptical look at the insider trading scandal that may involve a top finance ministry assistant, has Riemer guessing on the political fallout. "Europe's Press Isn't Taking 'No Comment' for an Answer Any More," with John Templeman 2-6, is an interesting new angle on how the press in France and

Germany has started changing character and is now into muckraking. We don't get new details here, but she holds our interest with the different slant. She does produce good detail in "The Socialist Dodge One Bullet — But the Next?" with Frank J. Comes 2-13, on the Pechiney purchase of Triangle Industries and its continuing damage there to the Mitterrand administration. But it's so difficult to follow the main point that we learn little. "In Europe, Inflation Is No Longer Distant Thunder," with Mark Maremont, Templeman *et al* 3-20, is unenlightening. We don't know who came up with the wage-price-spiral analysis here, illustrated (literally) with flying demon-monsters representing the products of "overheated" economies worldwide, but this effort is a bust. We find it hard to believe Riemer would be so simplistic as to write that "Price pressures mean interest rates have only one way to go. Up." But her byline is on the report. "A Marriage of Giants to Defend French Finance," 4-10, is a straightforward account of how powerful French financier Jean Peyrelevade has brought together his insurance company with Europe's biggest commercial bank for joint operations, looking toward 1992. "Europe's Smart Money Heads Back to Wall Street," 5-22, is crisp on how foreign investors are back again buying big and small stocks in the U.S.for the first time since the '87 crash. Riemer gives us a sense of European thinking on the U.S. economy, "The European Parliament Gets Its Act Together," with Richard Melcher 6-12, an interesting introduction to this institution. But it's all too positive, with just passing reference to the sovereignty questions or other divisive issues. "The Group of Seven Won't be Singing Harmony," with Richard Fly 7-17, is a decent attempt to preview actions at the G-7 parley in Paris. Riemer notes a shift in the attitude of foreign central bankers' away from intervening heavily in currency markets to limit another upsurge of the dollar.

Robbins, Carla Anne. *U.S.News & World Report.* (★ ★ ½)
Latin America. We were disappointed we didn't see more from Robbins, her work this year reflected a degree of sophistication on this beat not normally found in American newsweeklies. "The Graying of a Revolution," 1-9, reports from Havana on the Cuban revolution after thirty years, capturing the demoralization and anomie afflicting Cuban society. "Not one of the young Cubans mentions politics as a priority. All seem turned off by years of indoctrination in the schools. The young men say they would willingly fight against an American invasion. Three out of four, however, admit they would go live in the U.S. if given the chance. And not one knows the meaning of the word *perestroika*." In "The Power Politics of Carlos Salinas," 3-20, Robbins presents a mixed view of Mexican President Carlos Salinas' first three months in office, documenting the benefits of deregulation and privatization while also noting that things are still bad. We were impressed by her ability to integrate her material on Mexico's economy with the new Third World debt plan proposed by Treasury Secretary Nicholas Brady, and her observation on Salinas' political reforms stood out: "The PRI's idea of democratization seems to mean choosing better candidates for the ruling party, not sharing power with rival parties." Her "Taking Aim at Noriega," 5-1, examines U.S. strategies in the upcoming Panamanian elections to unseat General Noriega along with summarizing the conditions in Panama and the opposition's chances of winning. "Noriega has made no efforts to disguise his clout with the Electoral Tribunal administering the vote." We get first-rate political and economic analysis in "Cocaine, Communism, and Crisis in Peru," 9-18, with Robbins surveying that beleaguered South American country in light of its role in Bush's drug strategy. About all that was missing was a discussion of Peru's major industries and their relationship to the drug trade. Teamed with Janette Staubus in Buenos Aires for "Should Anyone Cry for Argentina?" 10-30, Robbins attempts to trace the problems afflicting that country to their historical sources, while showing the magnitude of the economic crisis facing the new president, Carlos Menem from succeeding: ". . .an entire nation, everyone from blue-collar workers to pampered industrialists, must be weaned from a deeply rooted habit of dining at the public trough and from a pervasive belief that all of them are entitled to dine well simply because they are Argentines."

Robinson, Eugene. *The Washington Post.* (★ ½)
South America. While his work is usually more informative than imaginative, readers can usually count on sound, objective reporting. "Land Wars Caught Up Ecologist," 1-17, reviews events leading up to the murder of Brazilian ecologist Francisco (Chico) Mendes, no new information here. " 'Peron's Heir' Pulls Movement Together," 3-30, provides a lively and informative update report on the changing character and fortunes of the Peronist movement as the May elections approach. "Argentine Vote Keyed to Inflation," 4-16, is a good roundup of how the domestic economic mess has driven the middle class to capture the Peronist presidential candidate, who now calls for privatization of state enterprises — the very ones created by "founding father" Juan Peron. "Peronist Leads, But in What Direction?" 4-24, profiles Argentina's Peronist presidential candidate Carlos Menem and his campaign, while "Argentina Heads for Crucial Election," 5-13, pinpoints the possibility of Argentina's electoral college upsetting the popular vote. "Peronist Wins Presidency in Argentina," 5-15, conveys Argentina's democratic election and its clear-cut result that has left many uneasy and cautious: Peronism is back with a clear and unambiguous electoral sweep. "Argentine Crisis Reflects Region's Malaise," 6-4, succeeds in placing the Argentine food riots in their wider economic policy context. "...governments throughout Latin America are watching the week's events in Argentina closely for signs that the 'social explosion' long predicted to flow from the region's worsening economic crisis is indeed in progress." "Gen. Rodriguez Displays Unexpected Political Skill in Paraguay," 6-25, was one of the few follow-ups we saw on Paraguay's Gen. Andres Rodriguez, who ousted dictator Stroessner by force of arms and who appears to be sticking to his promise of democracy: "Opposition leaders and foreign observers have watched carefully for signs that he is wavering in his promised commitment to an open, democratic society, but so far those signs have not come." In "Chile Vote Will Pit Experience vs. Youth," 7-22, Robinson surveys political party lineups in preparation for Chile's December elections, focusing on the leader of the anti-Pinochet coalition, conservative Patricio Aylwin, who has united the opposition "behind a moderate platform that appeals to the left with promises that more attention will be paid to the needs of the poor, while reassuring the more conservative factions that the economic progress of the Pinochet years will not be undermined."

Rodger, Ian. *Financial Times.* (★ ★ ½)
Tokyo correspondent. The *Financial Times* has always had strong reporters on this beat, and Rodger carries on the tradition. He doesn't make many mistakes in his reporting, and his analysis is generally of high caliber. "Strategic Islands Obstruct Soviet-Japan Accord," 12-17-88, is a concise description of issues facing Soviet Foreign Minister Eduard Shevardnadze on the eve of his Tokyo visit. "Tokyo May Spread Investment More Widely Across Europe," 3-14, discovers hints in a speech by Toyota's President Shoichiro Toyoda, that although the U.K. is the most likely host country for Japanese plants, the corporation is sensitive to EC complaints that the British are getting too much of the investments. "Japan Rides the Profits Express," 6-6, reports Japanese industry looks "more invincible" after posting 25% increases in pre-tax profits, a well rounded look at financial results. "Pressures on the System," 7-10, a lofty analytical survey on the succession of internal and external shocks this year, draws a positive forward look for what may emerge out of the political crises. Rodger extends the analysis into foreign policy with "The Line of Least Resistance," 7-10, while appreciative of Japan's complex and delicate relationship with China, still effectively makes the case that confusion reigns, although policy is beginning to focus around questions of *Pax Americana* vs. *Pax consortia.* "Spectre of Sanctions Haunts Talks," 9-4, does a splendid job of counterposing "what Washington says" vs. "what Tokyo says." Rodger notes that it really is difficult for the Japanese, and many others, to see what the U.S. wants or expects from the talks. "A Chance to Clean Up," 11-23, is a fact-filled survey of Japan's "last frontier," the island of Hokkaido which, having missed out on much of the country's economic success is now the scene of an ambitious economic program.

Rohter, Larry. *The New York Times.* (★ ½)
Mexico City. We mildly chastised Rohter last year for his insufficient attention to Mexico's economic story. This part of his reporting is still deficient and our complaint is louder. "Mexico Puts Signs From Bush in the Worst Light," 2-19, conveys how the fumblings of the Bush administration on Mexico are going down in that country: ". . .a sense of alarm, even hysteria, has developed among the press, political opposition and intellectuals here — segments of Mexican society always inclined to suspect the worst of the United States." "Mexican Teachers Win Raises and End Strike," 5-21, is basically solid reporting, with some insight as to Salinas' options, but it lacks the depth we associate with dispatches of the *Times.* And Rohter never specifies if the teachers out on strike are elementary, secondary, or university teachers. Rohter was entertaining and informative in "For Refugees From U.S. Prices, Haven in Mexico," 6-1, reporting on the recent rise in the number of American citizens applying for permanent residency in Baja California to take advantage of cheap housing rates. But this is only one brick in the structure of the Mexican economy, and Rohter makes no attempt to see the others against this one. "Mexico Feels Squeeze of Years of Austerity," 7-25, is a long takeout on the state of Mexico's economy as a deal is struck with creditor banks, weakened by Rohter's total focus on government statistics of the formal economy, which overstates the general level of poverty, making per capita numbers look awful. "U.S. Athletes Advised: Get Your Steroids Here!" 9-25, a "Tijuana Journal" story, is written in the stilted, awkward style that seems to afflict *Times* correspondents when they try their hand at a "lighter" story. Try fighting your way through this sentence: "But the openness with which the kind of drug that led to Ben Johnson's downfall at the Seoul Olympics is hawked here demonstrates the dimensions of a problem that increasingly worries authorities on both sides of the border: the production, sale and smuggling of anabolic steroids in Mexico, largely for consumption by Americans intent on beefing up their bodies." And, if you're only going to read one story this year on U.S. plans to renovate the All-American Canal in Imperial County, California, to provide a new water supply for Los Angeles and Mexico, over Mexican objections that the project would endanger the water supply of Tijuana and Mexicali, then "Canal Project Sets Off U.S.-Mexico Clash Over Water For Border Regions," 10-1, is that story. Please, Larry, *Salinastroika!*

Rosett, Claudia. *The Wall Street Journal.* (★ ★ ★)
Editorial page editor of *The Asian Wall Street Journal.* An editor who does some of the best overview reporting we see coming out of Asia, Rosett's coverage of the events in China contained some routine material, but her insight into Japan's major story this year was extraordinary. "Woe to Those Who Try to Slow Asia 1989," 1-4, is a broad, satisfying analytical assessment of the peace developments throughout Asia and its move away from authoritarian rule. Rosett sets a perspective by noting that the most serious threat to Asia's gains is Western protectionism. "Japan's Recruit Scandal in Context," 4-10, a 10 Best selection in foreign correspondence, is excellent and singularly insightful on the significance of the scandal that rocked Japan this year. Rosett peels away with ease layers that baffled so many others on this affair to reveal what it's all about. "Gorbachev Wary as Chinese Students March," 5-10, with Rosett in Beijing on the eve of Gorby's visit notes that "It's an open question who might lead a sprint for further reform. The 84-year-old Mr. Deng is still hesitating." She also reports that much of the funding for the student movement is coming from China's growing class of private businessmen. "Anything Could Happen Next in Tiananmen," 6-7, is a waste of time and space. "A kaleidoscope of uncertainty and terror," she reports rumors and more rumors. "Self-Preservation in Shanghai," 6-16, is a fine "mood" feature, Rosett reporting on her farewell with an opponent of the regime: "He asked that his name not be used. He said good-bye with a fierce handshake and a phrase that in China right now is more than small talk: 'I hope I will see you again.'" Her "Lost in the Chinese Gulag," 8-8, provides details on the arrests and executions, with Rosett presenting brief bios of several Chinese democrats now missing. She gives a rich report on the Federation for a Democratic China conference in "China Exiles Launch Their Democracy Drive From Paris," 9-27. The commitment of the delegates to strong democratic and capitalist aims (upholding private property rights among other ones) is clear. Also made clear is just how vague is the delegate's plan of where they're going from here.

Roth, Terence. *The Wall Street Journal.* (★ ½)
Frankfurt correspondent for the Europe edition of *The Wall Street Journal,* but Roth's byline appears with sufficient frequency in the U.S. paper that we've established a serious appreciation for his political coverage, although we acknowledge some routine and fumbling reports during the year. West Germans are paid the highest wages and work the shortest hours in the European community, raising industry concerns of eroded competitiveness, and Roth reports on fears now among West German labor that industry may move production to other, lower-cost countries in 1992 in "Schism Forms Within German Unions About Extending Workweek to Sundays," 12-29-88. Roth focuses the rift among leading West German labor unions over whether to work on Sunday, as hardliners oppose any weekend work while other labor leaders favor conciliation in preparation for Europe 1992. "New Assertions About West German Role in Libyan Plant Taints Kohl Government," 1-16, updates on the growing controversy over how much and when the West German government knew about aid by West German companies in Libya's construction of a suspected chemical weapons plant. Roth draws on a report in the West German news magazine *Der Spiegel* that the country's intelligence service had alerted the government about this in 1986. "German Firm Involved in Libyan Probe Never Let Awkward Questions Bother It," 1-23, leaves many questions unexplored, and it's hard to accept his treatment of Imhausen-Chemie. We did learn here that Arthur Imhausen, founder of Imhausen-Chemie G.m.b.H., who had one Jewish parent, was so important to the Third Reich that the Nazis "Arayanized" him, expunging the Jewish link from his official records. There's not too much beyond the headline in "Election Advances by Berlin's Far Right Unlikely to Set Trend for West Germany," 2-2, on the Republican Party victory in West Berlin. Roth's assessment is interesting, but the reporting isn't strong enough to necessarily support it: "With its disproportionately large population of immigrants, students, the young and the old Berlin tends not to reflect the rest of Germany." In "As One German Far-Right Party Gloats, Another One Is Banned From Elections," 2-10, we get an excellent analysis on the use of far-right splinter groups in Germany, following the October 1988 death of Franz Strauss. Although West German banks have weathered efforts to impose new regulations on them in the past, proposals to "reduce the banks' concentration of power" are being taken as a new threat, and Roth gives us details on a growing consensus to reduce the direct ties between industry and banks with "West German Banks Face Threat of Reduced Influence in Industry," 7-18. "East German Refugees Face the Reality of Life as Familiar Strangers," with Thomas F. O'Boyle 10-4, is an informative picture of how the refugees are rebuilding their lives in the West, and we learn here that "finding work isn't a problem," but finding housing is a major difficulty.

Rubinfein, Elisabeth. *The Wall Street Journal.* (★ ★)
Tokyo. New to the *MediaGuide* this year, her byline already throws off positive vibes. She combines good detail in her reports with crisp, tight writing, and we sense she has a sense of her subject. Japan's policies on drugs and crime are often held up for emulation, but Rubinfein sheds light from another angle on this with "U.S. Police Seek Lessons on How to Keep City Streets Crime-Free," 1-11. We learn the first and foremost advice: policing the racially and culturally homogeneous Japanese population has little in common with U.S. problems. The writing is sharp in this colorful culture picture of satire and other forms of comic relief following the Recruit scandal, "Did You Hear the Thigh-Slapper About Takeshita?" 5-18. "Sex Scandal Rocking Japan's Premier Shows Traditional Attitudes Changing," 6-20, is fairly late, with little new here not seen elsewhere, and it certainly needs a line or two on where the opposition party can take this scandal. "Japan May Face a New Political Equation," 7-19, a prelude to the upper-house parliamentary elections, contains great depth of detail on parties, issues, scenarios of likely LDP defeat, and coalition government. She notes tersely that "Much of the opposition support feeds on anti-LDP anger, however, and as such may be short-lived." In "New Japanese Leader's Political Frailty Likely to Encumber Him on U.S. Trip," 8-30, she previews PM Toshiki Kaifu's diplomatic tour of North America, suggesting he'll find it difficult to make even token pledges regarding trade initiatives or concessions with the LDP just recovering from its electoral defeats. "U.S. Slice of Japan Beef Market Grows, But Doesn't Sizzle, Amid Quota Accord," 11-16, is the best of the reports we saw summing up the status this year of the U.S.-Japan agreement to eliminate beef import quotas within three years.

Ryan, Leo. *The Journal of Commerce.* (★ ½)

Canada. Some solid broader efforts mixed in with the steady reporting on business and trade north of the border this year, Ryan's dispatches continue to satisfy. "Free Trade Era Poses Challenges for Canada," 12-15-88, the lead story of 16 page special on Canada is an informative survey. Ryan is sharp on sensitive Canadian apprehensions about "a mouse getting into bed with an elephant." "Free Trade Accord: Winners and Losers," 12-15-88, goes through categories (manufacturing, energy, auto, agriculture, etc.) with a knowledgeable reading on how various sectors benefit or face hardships as a result of U.S.-Canada trade pact, with winners outnumbering losers. This is the best we saw anywhere on this. "Canada Plans Sanctions against U.S.," 3-31, is a basic news report, which we appreciate at least seeing reported in the U.S. press, but more analysis would have been welcome. "U.S., Canadian Firms Act to Speed Tariff Cuts," 7-14, reports both governments taken by surprise as sweeping requests to eliminate tariffs come from U.S. and Canadian companies more rapidly than even stipulated under the U.S.-Canada Free Trade Agreement. Ryan reports the Canadian government's assessment: "This demonstrates that business is anxious to get on with expanded trade between Canada and the U.S." "Waste Cargo Returns to Montreal From UK," 8-17, is a tight update on the return of a Soviet freighter with a cargo of Canadian toxic waste to Quebec Province after it was refused discharge in the U.K. With another freighter carrying PCB waste expected to be also returning unloaded from the U.K. to Quebec, the province now has a serious toxic waste problem. "U.S.-Canadian Trade Pact Helps Spark Buffalo's Revival," 12-7, is bullish on prospects for this U.S. point of entry, freer trade combining richly with other features of the city's recovery.

Sanger, David E. *The New York Times.* (★ ★ ★)

Tokyo. This young man broke into the big league news business at the *Times* a few years back the way DiMaggio did with the Yankees, collecting four-baggers (in this guide) for his coverage of the computer industry out of New York. We'd hope his posting here last year would advance the *NYT*'s Japan reporting far ahead of the competition, but he isn't leading the pack, yet. We can't *complain* about his work: Japan's political economy was one of the more difficult stories to cover in his rookie year of foreign dispatch. Sanger excelled both at covering breaking news stories (Recruit, FSX) and, spotting newly emerging trends, as with "Seeing a Dependent and Declining U.S., More Japanese Adopt a Nationalistic Spirit," 8-4, capturing the shifting relationship between Japan and the U.S., which in 1989 was a very big story indeed. "Technology Pact for Fighter Creates Dispute With Japan," 2-20, is a page D-1 story that would soon move to page A-1, with Sanger smoking out the two sides in the Bush administration on the FSX deal, injecting clarity into a muddled affair by detailing the genesis of the controversial arrangement. "Takeshita Undone by System That He for So Long Lived By," 4-26, offers excellent presentation of smart observations on the Recruit scandal impact, and is completely fair to Takeshita in every nuance. In "Tokyo, Unsure of U.S., Talks of Developing Its Own Arms," 6-28, Sanger, reporting from the Misawa Air Base in northern Japan, delivers a sound account of how the FSX aircraft controversy has resonated among officers and pilots of the Japanese military. We get some nice colorful details as "troops drive around military bases here in American-style jeeps made by Mitsubishi," etc., but we would have appreciated a little more on the military missions the Japanese see themselves doing in the future. "Mighty MITI Loses Its Grip," 7-9, has little focus, and leaves us with little beyond the headline. "Japan's Voters Rise Up," 7-25, delivers one strong point analyzing Socialist gains: "For many, what has changed was that Japan became prosperous enough to afford some anger and confident enough to take some risks. An electorate previously known for its docility bet that the Socialist Party, and the woman who became its symbol, Tohako Doi, would abandon its anti-military and pro-welfare state language as the party moved closer to power." "Tokyo's Top Official for Overseas Trade is Critic of the U.S.," 8-8, profiles Makoto Utsumi. Who is Makoto Utsumi? "As Japan's politicians raced around Tokyo jockeying for power in the wake of the biggest electoral upset here in decades, Makoto Utsumi walked slowly around Japan's financial ministry, meeting old colleagues, smiling and bowing a lot, and modestly demurring when people suggested that in some ways he is now running the government." This is an important story on Japan's vice minister of finance for international affairs that we saw nowhere else.

Schlesinger, Jacob M. *The Wall Street Journal.* (★ ★ ★)
Tokyo. Covering autos in Detroit last year, this young man barely out of college impressed us as one of the top U.S. business reporters (three-and-a-half stars, plus a 10 Best selection), and he is now off to a promising start on his business reporting from Japan. He has a gift for learning the whole story before he sits down to report it, then writes so we will learn, as he has. "Zen and the Art of Auto Sales," 3-13, is lively on Nissan hawking the Infiniti Q45 with mystical flare, observing that with the "difference in quality narrowing" companies are going beyond "outrageous" to "flaky" in selling their image. The U.S. Trade Representative singled out the Japanese satellite market on the Super 301 list of trade barriers, despite the fact the three major U.S. companies that sell space equipment in Japan didn't request such action, he reports in "U.S. Looks Skyward and Sees Satellites Bearing Japan's Imprint, Not Its Own," 6-15. Good quotes move this well. "Motorola Finds in Dealing With Japan It Needs Brickbats as Well as Bouquets," 6-16, provides a good sense of the strategy being employed by Motorola to secure a larger share of Japan's telecommunications business, with the U.S. threatening to impose sanctions if the company doesn't get its way in Japan. "From the beginning," Schlesinger reports, "Motorola has played the governments in both countries masterfully." We appreciate his fresh outlook and ability to quickly move beyond conventional wisdom on issues as with "One High Tech Race Where U.S. Leads: Personal Computers," 10-31. Reported from Tokyo, where office workers use old-fashioned abacus and calculators, it's a flawless presentation, carefully structured with a logical flow of information and analysis. But we still would like to know — how did computers make such progress in manufacturing? His "Fantastic Voyage," 11-13, in a special "Technology" section, introduces *The Wall Street Journal* audience to a Star Trek of "micro machines" being developed in Japan, as well as the U.S. and Europe, to navigate inside the human body to perform a variety of medical miracles: "A rotary blade smaller than a vein could travel through the bloodstream, scraping cholesterol buildup from vessel walls." Didn't we see this in a Woody Allen movie?

Schmemann, Serge. *The New York Times.* (★ ★ ½)
Bonn. Some consider Schmemann's work to be staid and uninspired, but in a year when history was literally being made day after day, Schmemann's solid professionalism saw him and his readers through. In "Angst and Anger in Bonn," 1-16, Schmemann writes that the U.S. disclosure of the Libyan chemical plant raises hackles and questions about NATO and that Bonn shows "the complex anxieties of a nation whose economic and military power has outstripped the revival of its self-confidence." In "Polls Say Kohl Is in Trouble," 3-30, Schmemann disdains the alarmist tone taken by others on the "flight from the center" taking place in West Germany, saying that between the lines it's clear that the vote reflects a necessary "message to Bonn" from the electorate and isn't as troubling as often played. In "Look at the New Germans, Rich and Living It Up," 4-11, he discovers that the German nouveau-riche exist. While there's nothing on the effect of the new wealth on traditional values, the piece is still valuable in bringing us up-to-date on the West German *Wirtschaftwunder.* In "For Bonn and Moscow, Affinity and Suspicion," 6-11, a "This Week In Review" essay, Schmemann provides a brief but informative history of West German-Russian relations, setting the scene for Gorbachev's visit. "Succession Watch in East Germany," 7-24, offers background on the potential successors to ailing East German leader Erich Honecker, with Schmemann zeroing in on Egon Krenz. "Whether a succession was imminent or not, Berlin-watchers from both West and East agreed that Mr. Krenz, a 52-year-old hardliner, was probably first in line to succeed Mr. Honecker." "Watch Conservative Klaus Get Racy," 7-29, and "A European Unconfined, Even by His Own Views," 9-2, on West Germany's autobahns and a leading German poet, demonstrate that Schmemann still has difficulties in writing good feature stories. "Hungary's Defiance and Europe's Future: Journey Without Maps," 9-17, is typical Schmemann, giving us a solid bread and butter analysis of the E. German refugee flow *via* Hungary. In "East Germany Opens Frontier to the West for Migration or Travel; Thousands Cross," 11-10, Schmemann is covering history and he knows it, taking us from the Wall "where celebrating Berliners, East and West, had filled the celebrated Kurfurstendamm, blowing on trumpets, dancing, laughing and absorbing a glittering scene they had only glimpsed before on television," to government chancelleries in East Berlin and Bonn.

Schoenberger, Karl. *Los Angeles Times.* (★ ★ ½)

Toyko. Schoenberger, one of the new breed of Tokyo correspondents who can handle the Japanese language, gave us more multi-layered coverage than we saw from most other Western correspondents reporting from Tokyo. In a year of upheaval in Japan, his studied knowledge of the country carried him through. "For Japan, Gilded Age of Riches," 1-30, is a vivid account of the effect of the money boom on Japan's values and way of life. "Scandal Shakes Japan, Won't Topple Party," 3-26, is a serviceable summation of the Recruit scandal, with Schoenberger providing details of both the scandal itself and the inner workings of Japanese politics. He mentions Recruit as different from past scandals because this time the "sacrosanct" bureaucracy is involved, but he fails to note the role the traditionally passive Japanese press played in breaking the story. Disdaining speculation that the LDP will be driven from office, he writes: "The Japanese public tends toward malaise rather than electoral revolt, partly out of a sense of resignation that although the ruling party may be flawed, the alternative is a sanctimonious opposition that is hardly fit to govern." Of course, the LDP's trade policies which protect its rural constituency may have something to do with it too. Dostoevsky once said we could learn a lot about a society by entering one of its prisons, and in " 'Bird Cages': Legal Trap for Japanese," 4-28, Schoenberger takes us inside Japan's prisons and police stations, and shows us the sort of human rights violations that causes Congress to cut off aid to less developed countries. If he could have dug a little deeper into the reasons why practices such as torturing prisoners to extract confessions persist in these presumably enlightened times, rather than just attributing it all to "Japanese custom," this article would have been 10 Best material. In "Self-Denial Wears Thin for Japanese," 7-7, we learn that the average Japanese "salary man" commutes 90 minutes each way, pays high prices for everything and likes to complain, but does nothing about it. Why? *Gaman* translated as perseverance or self-denial is Schoenberger's contribution to the growing 'Sure, the Japanese are Number One economically but are they really happy?' storyline developed in the American press this year. "Key Japan Cabinet Member Resigns in New Sex Scandal," 8-25, a write-up of the latest Japanese politician forced to fall on his sword, has a weary tone to it.

Shapiro, Margaret. *The Washington Post.* (★ ½)

The Tokyo correspondent once again combined solid journalistic skills with a flair for feature writing, helping her maintain an objective middle ground that many other American reporters in Japan are forsaking these days. "Takeshita Plunges to Historic Low in Japan Polls," 3-18, is a conscientious report of Takeshita woes at the polls and in the Diet, but Shapiro leaves us tantalized with the assertion: "many commentators believe that Takeshita's crisis augurs a basic change," as she fails to reach behind the fact and figures of polls and headlines leaving us asking "What's up in Japan?" Her "Pressure Seen Mounting on Takeshita to Resign," 4-8, updates the growing Japanese political crisis, focusing on the emergence of "a group of about 40 junior LDP members. . .[who] will push for what would amount to a purge of the top echelon of the party that ruled Japan for the last 34 years." "Entering Business, Japan-Style," 4-10, is a lively and humorous account of Japan's spring ritual of mass induction of new corporate employees. ". . .With military precision [the young inductees] jumped to the command barked at them by a company personnel officer — 'Stand! Bow! Sit!' — then stiffly listened as their new boss exhorted them to work hard, pay attention. . .and become good company men." Teamed with Fred Hiatt on "Japanese Politics Shaken," 4-26, Shapiro provides an excellent evaluation of what Takeshita's resignation involves: "Japan is headed for a Watergate-style upheaval in its political system," which will determine whether it will remain a "first rate economic power with a second rate standard of living and third rate politics." "Japan Warns of Backlash Over Action on Trade," 5-27, gives no real sense of intensity of reaction, perhaps because quotes from government, business and finance people were missing. "Uno Becomes Japanese Leader," 6-3, is a cautiously balanced report and evaluation of Sosuke Uno's elevation to prime ministership in Japan: ". . .his selection was criticized both within and outside the ruling party as LDP backroom politics as usual. Party members who attempted to propose an alternative candidate were squashed by their leadership." Teamed once again with Hiatt, in "Voters Deserting Japan's LDP," 6-25, Shapiro analyzes the unraveling of Japan's ruling Liberal Democratic Party, a month before the upper house elections.

Sieff, Martin. *The Washington Times.* (★ ★)
Eastern Europe. A top-rated correspondent a year ago, Sieff offered nothing that dazzled this year, as we know he can, and we thought we detected an anti-Gorbachev bias at times that clouded his judgment. In "Hard-Line Communists Are Marching Anew in Hungary," 1-3, Sieff provides details we didn't see elsewhere on party members fighting back against political reform in Hungary. "The Reagan Legacy: He Contained, Revised Kremlin," 1-19, is strong on what Reagan accomplished in eight years, but weak on how or why. "Religious Passions Rumble In Ukraine," 2-9, and "Gorbachev's Church Ploy In Trouble," 5-19, update us on the surging expression of religious belief in the Ukraine and Gorbachev's attempt to harness that sentiment in favor of *perestroika,* with Sieff noting in the 5-19 article that the beneficiaries of the new Kremlin policy toward religion "contend that even if implemented, it is flawed by loopholes that will continue to limit the independence of Soviet churches." His "Minister Flexes His Muscle In W. German Foreign Policy," 6-22, was Sieff's contribution to the growing literature on Hans Dietrich Genscher, looking at the West German Foreign Minister in the context of shifting electoral alignments. Although at present triumphant, "Mr. Genscher and his liberal Free Democrats could find themselves on the defensive, facing strong domestic pressure to deliver new foreign policy coups as more powerful expressions of neutralism challenge them from left to right." In "Warsaw Pact Allies Reeling from Whiff of Soviet Reforms," 7-7, Sieff delivers compact analysis of the state of disrepair in the Warsaw Pact, as "the annual summit of the military alliance. . .finds Moscow's once-pliant European allies confused, uncertain and at odds over Mr. Gorbachev's domestic reforms." In "More Extremist Parties Chip Away at West German Kingmakers," 8-17, he goes overboard in analysis of the changed political landscape of West Germany: "The Free Democrats and the Christian Social Union, pressed by younger, more energetic and more extreme political movements, may be headed for oblivion." Speaking of overboard, in "Yeltsin, In Travels Across U.S., Baled Plenty Of Political Fodder," 9-18, Sieff sums up Yeltsin's visit to the land of capitalist decadence. "Soviet maverick Boris Yeltsin's barnstorming tour of America drew to a close here yesterday after providing the former Communist Party Moscow boss with a glimpse of American life unseen by any Soviet leader since the 1917 revolution." Didn't Sieff ever see the T-shirt from Khruschev's '59 tour? And since when is Yeltsin a "Soviet leader"?

Simons, Marlise. *The New York Times.* (★)
Rome. Simons could almost have been listed as *The New York Times*' "Amazon correspondent," as that was a major focus of her reporting until moving here this year from Rio. While not into advocacy journalism, on the issue of the environment, she danced close to it at times. "A Latin AIDS Meeting Opens Its Ears to What Was Once Unmentionable," 1-16, is an intelligible overview of a regional conference on AIDS in Latin America. Simons reports on the different habits and attitudes regarding AIDS here, and that policies go by assumption, not research. "Brazilians Tell of the Forest and the Fears," 1-22, is fairly balanced as five members of the U.S. Congress tour the Amazon on environmental concerns: "Brazilian officials have also argued that the industrialized nations have no right to criticize Brazil because they have destroyed so much of their own environment and are responsible for most of the world's pollution." Her "Brazilian Is Looking to Japan To Link Amazon to the Pacific," 2-19, is a P. 1 story that had serious impact on Japanese plans for the Amazon. Simons reports that Japan's heavy demand for Amazonian timber is prompting interest in the construction of a highway to move goods to Pacific ports. The protests from environmentalists escalated intensely after this news broke, with the Japanese easing away from the prospective project. "Ecologists Rush For Seats on European Parliament," 5-31, is a rather rosy view of how "greens" are advancing with agendas of limited growth. Simons reports no views of anti-greens or a credible perspective. "Abortion Fight Has New Front in Western Europe," 6-28, surveys the attitudes on this issue in various European countries, providing some look forward as to where changes in prevailing laws may take place and what impact Court rulings could have on either side. Simons never really examines from where this new pro-life sentiment in Europe has come, however. "Rising Heroin Use and Addict Deaths Alarm Italy, Where Drug Use Is Legal," 10-8, is an important story, but Simons takes forever to establish a connection between worsening drug abuse and its legalization.

Southerland, Daniel. *The Washington Post.* (★ ★)
Beijing. China presented Southerland with a large canvas this year, and he filled it with vivid material, capturing and re-creating the turbulence in his dispatches with the flair of a dramatic artist. But getting his story wrong at a critical point hurt his credibility, and rating. "China's Congress Ends Session With Leadership Doubts Unresolved," 4-5, "150,000 Chinese March to Demand Democracy," 4-22, and "Chinese Students Seek to Uphold Protest Tradition," 4-22, combine ground-level coverage of the rising tide of events with on-target analysis of what it all means, with Southerland noting in "Chinese Students," that "an aging leadership not in the habit of making concessions" is being confronted by a mass of students who "share a powerful sense that they are upholding a historical tradition of student protests in China." His "Protest Leaders Share Commitments, Goals," 5-7, profiles two of the Chinese student movement's leaders he clearly admires. In "Chinese Politburo Said To Favor Ousting Liberal Party Chief," 5-25, and "Chinese Premier Li Emerges, Hard-Liners Seen Ascendant," 5-26, he tries to get ahead of the curve, seeing Deng and his successor "building a majority position against Zhao." In "Deng Intensifies Chinese Campaign Against Enemies," 5-27, and "Chinese in Struggle for Raw Power," 5-31, he attempts to take readers behind the scenes where the power struggles are going on. Southerland covers Deng's delicate relation with the military establishment in the 5-27 piece, throwing in a piece of hard intelligence: "The military is divided right up to the military commission." and writes in the 5-31 article: "The struggle is not about ideology but about raw power." With "Troops Roll Through Beijing to Crush Protesters; Scores Reported Killed As Chinese Fight Back," 6-4, he provides a comprehensive account of events on that grim day, with some historical perspective thrown in: "While the People's Liberation Army was warmly welcomed 40 years ago when it triumphantly entered Beijing without a shot, today it met resistance every step of the way from a citizenry that has lost faith in the Communist Party and its leaders." His "Chinese President Gains New Power," 6-9, looks at Beijing's new power equation from a slightly different angle, noting that Gen. Yang Shangkun controls tens of thousands of soldiers in Beijing, Yang Baibing, his younger brother, is head of the political department of the PLA, and Yang Jianhua, Yang Baibing's son, commands the 27th Field Army. "Chinese Army Seen Near Conflict," 6-6, however, represents one of the egregious sins of many of the foreign corps covering the events in China, reporting what couldn't be confirmed, with misinformation the result, as in his lead: "Opposing armies maneuvered to confront each other Monday night and early today in a power struggle here that raised the prospect of a civil war beginning in this capital."

Stanglin, Douglas. *U.S.News & World Report.* (★ ★)
As much as we enjoy reading the work of this associate editor, we are always thrown off when virtually all his reports are multiple byline affairs, featuring Stanglin as the lead in a cast of thousands. But his editors reward him often enough with a solo byline to enable us to rate him. "The Baltics: The Old Flags are Unfurled," 4-3, a report on the independence movements in the three Baltic republics, was informative but could have used both a discussion of Moscow's reactions to these developments and an attempt to draw subtle contrasts to illustrate the differences among the three republics' movements. "Commanding Mao's Gun," 6-5, profiles the Chinese Army (PLA) from a new angle, emphasizing the PLA's dabbling in economic activities: "The PLA also produces wine and runs an airline that competes with the national carrier." Although we don't get a lot of discussion of the PLA's role in politics or military capabilities, we're satisfied with the fresh look. In "How to Understand the Unthinkable," 6-12, Stanglin does an outstanding job of identifying both the issues involved in nuclear arms reduction talks and the sticking points between U.S. and the U.S.S.R. The analysis is sound, the explanation easy to follow, and the accompanying charts and graphs are excellent.

Sterngold, James. *The New York Times.* (★ ★)
Tokyo. Another top correspondent out of the *Times*' stable of business reporters to be posted in Tokyo, it's still too early to determine what strengths Sterngold will ultimately bring to this bureau. He has begun by looking into stories where Wall Street and Japan intersect. "Tutoring

Japanese on Takeovers," 5-23, despite some valid information, basically borders on the hysterical view that Japan plans to capture U.S. patents. "Japan's Washout on Wall Street," 6-11, on Tokyo's Big Four regrouping after five frustrating years, reports losses still continue at Nomura, Yamaichi, Daiwa and Nikko. It's a very interesting report, with good detail and anecdotes, but Sterngold doesn't put his finger on the problem. "Fed to Report on Japan Bond Market," 8-21, is clear, concise and raises appropriate questions about Congress and Wall Street firms backing away from trying to open Japan's securities markets. "Japan Leading U.S. In Raising Capital For Corporations," 10-27, a P. 1 report on the boom in raising capital for Japan, presents a fair amount of detail, draws several conclusions, and offers analyses of the advantages Japan has and is accruing from this situation. Curiously, he never mentions anything about how capital gains tax rate reforms might alter conditions for the U.S.

Tagliabue, John. *The New York Times.* (★ ★)
Another respectable year for the *Times* man in Warsaw, whose dispatches were usually informative if at times uninspired. Late in the year he began reporting from Czechoslovakia, the change of scenery rejuvenating his writing. "Polish Union Says Yes To Discussing Its Legal Status," 1-23, includes necessary background on Solidarity's acceptance of a government offer to discuss restoration of its legal status as a union. "K. Makes His Way Into The Castle," 4-12, we learn that Franz Kafka, banned in his native Czechoslovakia during the 1960s, will be published there once again. Good material on a signpost of Changing Times in Eastern Europe, but we would have appreciated more on why he was in disfavor, along with an explanation of the statement Tagliabue makes near the end of the article, that libraries carried Kafka's books throughout despite the ban. "Jaruzelski Quits As Party Leader; Premier gets Post," 7-30. A P. 1 Sunday lead on an obviously important development that we were dissatisfied with. Prime Minister Rokowski gets top party post, which "appears to indicate that the party leadership favors more political and economic change." We wanted to see this developed further. "Poland's Foreign Fix," 8-13, provides an okay review of the debt situation and foreign investment, but is a little too confusing in exposition now and then, leaving us feeling unsure that we've learned very much after slogging through all the detail. Tagliabue is essentially running in place in "Two Sides In Warsaw Seem Near Cabinet Pact," 9-4, which has nothing really newsworthy in it. Perhaps he should have used the lull in the Government-Solidarity talks to produce a news analysis piece. But he draws on his experiences in Poland for "New Prague Opposition To Enter Free Elections," 12-5, as he writes about the Civic Forum's movement towards becoming a political party, seeing the parallels between Civic Forum and Solidarity without over-emphasizing them. "Leaders of Civic Forum compare the organization they have developed to a spider, with the command post at the center and the arms reaching out."

Tanzer, Andrew. *Forbes.* (★ ★)
Pacific bureau. Working the East Asian beat, Tanzer kept Taiwan in particular focus this year, chronicling and analyzing the myriad changes there. "The Right Kind of Problem," 3-20, pulls together sharp detail and data in a swift, bullish profile of the aggressive Hong Kong-based Cathay Pacific airlines, projecting a shakeout for transPacific carriers. Tanzer works the theme of authoritarian government being undermined by economic success in "Taiwan's Long March To Democracy," 4-3. There is a fair amount of new economic detail here, and Tanzer brings out Taiwan's disposition to accommodate U.S. pressure, even to the point of a 45% revaluation of their currency over the last three years when U.S. trade negotiators leaned on the country. "Brain Drain in Reverse," 4-17, reports on the shift of talent back into Taiwan as the country moves high gear into high tech. Tanzer gives a good picture of the potential here and of the ROC's perspective for competing in the market. Unlike the Republic of Korea, which tends to compete head on with Japan, Taiwan's strategy is to look for weaknesses and find niches. "His Father's Son," 5-29, profiles the impressive Kim Suk-Won, who was 29 when his father, the head of one of Korea's largest family-run conglomerates, died. In the fifteen years since, the son increased sales 50 times, to $6 billion. In "The Bank," 12-11, Tanzer gives us a timely close-up of the Hong Kong & Shanghai Banking Corp., one of the world's biggest and most profitable banks, but whose shares are cheap, and how it is betting the 1997 reunification with China will be okay, but now it seems to be hedging that bet.

Tempest, Rone. *Los Angeles Times.* (★ ½)
Perhaps it was because of the relative domestic tranquility in France, that most of the work we saw of the Paris bureau chief tended to be lighter, more feature-oriented stories. "Once-Chic Avenue Goes Democratic," 1-10, is an absorbing, colorful feature on the great debate provoked by the coming of fast-food restaurants to the Avenue des Champs-Elysees, is it "degradation" or "democratization?" Your move. Tempest opens and closes "French Ecologist Party Benefits From Ozone Effect," 3-14, with information on the emergence of the Ecologist Party as a political force, but he gets bogged down in the middle, talking about French politicians that by and large we neither know nor care about. In a year when a big political story in Western Europe was the emergence of "Green" parties everywhere, this piece was dissatisfying. "Fewer Words of Wisdom Are French," 4-12, is a superb piece on the spread of English in France, despite government efforts to preserve the language, with Tempest pointing out that one impact of Europe 1992 will likely be the spread of English within business and scientific circles throughout the twelve European countries. Great closing quote from a French business consultant: " 'there is only one true European language, English, perhaps the only major contribution by the British to Europe.' " His "70 Nations Act to Stem Flow of 'Boat People,' " 6-15, is a report from Geneva on the International Conference on Indochinese Refugees, written in diplomatese. In "Nothing Subtle on Eiffel Tower 100th Birthday," 6-17, he wisely stands back and lets the facts — "Soviet officials objected to [the] idea of having Kremlin guards goose-stepping down the street to African music while a ballerina danced with a bear" — speak for themselves. "Minitel: Miracle Or Monster?" 10-24, is a "Column One" feature on a French network of telephone-linked home computers caught up in a controversy over pornographic services allegedly being offered over its lines. Tempest loses the storyline as he pads the article out, but then we've seen this happen in other "Column One" stories as well. "Bulgarians Celebrate Freedom Of Speech," 11-20, is a nice, short story on the winds of *glasnost* now blowing through Bulgaria. "In the bright sunlight Sunday afternoon, the clumps of orators and political polemicists were more evocative of London's Hyde Park or Berkeley's Sproul Plaza than they were of the sullen, silent, secret society that existed under most of Zhivkov's reign."

Thurow, Roger. *The Wall Street Journal.* (★ ½)
Johannesburg. Steady reporting, without any dash or novel angles for the most part, Thurow's work is edging toward the routine on this beat. "Potent Weapon," 1-16, on the South African government's use of detention without trial as the most devastating weapon in its state-of-emergency arsenal, cites more than 30,000 government opponents having been so detained since declaration of the emergency in mid-1986. The report is balanced, and Thurow does include a response from the Law and Order Ministry that detention at the time was necessary to counter the revolutionary onslaught. "Zambia's Go-It-Alone Recovery Collapses," 1-25, is fair in its assessment of the country's attempt to reform its economy without the harsh IMF program: "Good intentions, poor execution, disastrous results. So it goes under Zambia's quixotic economic recovery plan, a concoction of home-brewed reforms called 'economic adjustment with a human face.' " He provides useful details on the economy and prospects as Zambia's copper deposits will be nearing exhaustion. A very insightful "Development Bank in Africa Transcends the Region's Despair," 5-16, reports on the African bank in the Ivory Coast that is solvent in a sea of insolvency: "The bank is championing new lending strategies that cater to the basics of African life, such as farming, rather than the grandiose schemes of Western planners." "In South Africa, Home Life Can Be Just as Bad as Jail," 7-5, is a feature on the torment of house arrest for activists that is poignantly told. "Debt Crisis Locks Africa Into a Whirlpool of Despair," 9-19, has a bit of detail on Kenya (which is pushing ahead to meet its debt obligations) and some data on the continent's indebtedness, but the overall perspective is grim and we wonder what the point of the article is. From Germany, Thurow is perhaps adjusting to the new beat, as "Culture Clash: East German Tourists Leave Brethren in West with Second Thoughts," 11-16, is routine on the downside of the exodus from East to West, despite a fine opening.

Toman, Barbara. *The Wall Street Journal.* (★ ½)
London. Toman has a way of beguiling us into reading reports on subjects we'd otherwise put at the bottom of our pile of priorities. The experience is rewarding, though. "Will the Telly Turn Britain's Feisty MPs Into Milquetoasts?" 11-21, opens with a colorful lead, and we end up reading through a report we might have otherwise skipped: "The honorable member of parliament for Shrewsbury and Atcham, Conservative Derk Conway, is angered by jeering from Labor Party hecklers in the House of Commons. 'You rabble!' Mr. Conway snaps. 'Disgrace! Withdraw!' the aggrieved Laborites shout. 'Order!' roars the bewigged speaker of the house. 'Mr. Speaker,' says member Conway. 'If you could hear what this lot are muttering you would throw them out of the Chamber.' It is marvelous theater. But will television cameras turn it deadly dull?" The analysis seems somewhat rushed and mechanical in "Britain's Thatcher Faces a Shaky Future After Big Setback in European Elections," 6-20, an analytic following the European parliamentary elections. Toman draws a critical assessment of Britain's ability to shape the EC's future as a main point. She also suggests that as the Republican Party draws votes from the ruling Christian-Democrat center-right government in Germany, the party is creating a prospect of a deadlock in the country's politics, with neither right nor left holding an outright majority. She assembles excellent detail for "Now Comes the Hard Part: Marketing," 9-22, which appeared in a special report on world business, "The Uncommon Market." Toman is succinct: "When it comes to marketing, the Pan-European view evaporates." Her "Britain's Newly Confident Labor Party Lays Plans For Dislodging Thatcherism," 9-29, is a very tight, fact-filled report on Labor's policy review, revamping its agenda to win public support. Says one: "We've now got a set of policies that are radical, but sensible and realistic. They are more in tune with the times." The review calls for a maximum income tax rate of 50% — "above the current 40%, but well below the 83% ceiling of the previous Labor government." This is the kind of detail we love!

Toy, Stewart. *Business Week.* (★ ★)
Paris bureau manager. Toy took care of our appetites for news on how Europe 1992 will affect countries across the Mediterranean, an added bonus to his respectable reporting from the continent. "Avant le Deluge at Moet Hennessy Louis Vuitton," with William Holstein and Mark Maremont 4-24, is a clear presentation on the battle royale for ownership of LVMH, including the role of Britain's Guinness PLC. Toy gives us a looks at the motivations of the different parties. "Algeria Tries Untying the Knots of Socialism," 7-31, is a small but very meaty analytic on the moves away from socialism in Algeria, with Toy providing a startling quote from the Finance Minister: "I hope two or three state-owned companies will go broke." There's some information of a new North African common market to offer *maquiladora*-type manufacturing to the EC. "The Race to Stock Europe's Common Super Market," co-authored by Richard Melcher, with Lois Therrien 6-26, is a readable report on M&A fever among European food producers preparing for 1992, a question of "eat or be eaten." We get good background on BSN and other food giants. The 1992 unity will also affect the travel industry as cross-border barriers are lowered and competition increased. "Kicking Sand in Club Med's Face," with Mark Maremont and Heike Schneider 8-14, is adequate on merger activity in Europe and the recent problems of travel pioneer Club Med. "Is Renault's New Engine Built For The Long Haul?" 8-21, is a good profile of French automaker Renault and its fiery chief and chief renovator, Raymond Levy. The analysis is sound and Toy uses lively quotes from an interview with Levy, who, by the way, got a master's in nuclear physics from MIT.

Treaster, Joseph B. *The New York Times.* (★ ★)
Caribbean. We always enjoy raising a reporter's rating, and are happy to give Treaster his highest in our five annuals. One word that stood out in our readers's evaluations on Treaster's work this year was "balanced," which we saw time and again. This counts! "A Nice Place to Live (Just Ask the Drug Barons)," 5-23, offers a slice of life from Cochabamba, Bolivia, but nothing more than that. A promising piece that's half finished. "In Bolivia, U.S. Pumps Money Into the Cocaine War, But Victory Is Elusive," 6-11, provides a good overview of Bolivia's cocaine

problem and U.S. efforts against it, with Treaster going into how economics, law enforcement and political stability, are all affected by the trade. A bit of work on what it does to the social fabric and this would have been four-star material. "Move (Slowly) to Beat of a City With 1/3 Less Air," 6-21, is a delightful feature on life in La Paz, almost 12,000 ft. above sea level, that we would recommend in full to *Reader's Digest*: "Planes take longer to take off and land. Food cooks slower and recipes have to be doctored. Fires have to be coaxed into flame and cars have less power. Digestion is slower and cocktails have more kick. Tooth paste packed at sea level squirts out of the tube." In "The President With The Biggest War On Drugs," 9-10, Treaster looks at President Virgilio Barco Vargas' war on drug lords in Colombia, producing a well-written article that could have used a few quotes to give it depth. "U.S. Sending Wrong Equipment to Fight Drugs, Colombians Say," 9-12, offers constructive criticism of U.S. policy in the drug war, capturing the bureaucracy thesis that if you spend enough, it doesn't matter how. Treaster misses only one thing here — who's in charge, specifically, of sending enough stuff. "In U.S. Exile, A Colombian Is Tearful Still," 9-29, profiles former Colombian Justice Minister, Monica de Grieff, who resigned and is now under Federal protection in Florida, providing the flip-side to stories of courage, though hers is one of prudence not cowardice — her three year old son received a death threat. "Colombians Weary of the Strain, Are Losing Heart in the Drug War," 10-2, gives a look at the man in the battle-strewn street, Treaster painting a vivid picture of the discouragements of living in a country under siege and remaining realistic about chances for success.

Trimble, Jeff. *U.S.News & World Report.* (★ ½)
Moscow bureau chief. Trimble fits in comfortably with *USN&WR*'s foreign correspondents. His work is sturdy, reliable, and, if without frills, also without the silliness that sometimes afflicts American newsweekly journalists. In "The Kremlin's New Crackdown," 2-20, we learn, yep, they're having a drug crisis there too. "After decades of a head-in-the-sand approach toward narcotics Soviet officials are going all out now to dam the flow of drugs into the country and slow the pace of an even worsening domestic drug crisis. But they may have awakened too late." His "The Ukraine: The Critical Republic," 4-3, is an informative and well-defined article on the Ukraine, with Trimble going back to the Stalin era to provide historical perspective. The piece is a little weak analytically, we thought. "Power to the People," 4-10, a wrap-up of the Soviet elections, is uneven. We liked the explanation of the new pyramid-like electoral structure, but he failed to discuss any issue other than corruption, and devoted too much space to Boris Yeltsin. "The Soviet Agony over States' Rights," 4-24, provides a first-rate overview of the ethnic unrest in Soviet Georgia and other non-Russian areas in the U.S.S.R., with sound analysis of Moscow's reactions to these events, noting that the "absence of a broad policy is nonetheless consistent with the Soviet inability to manage dissent." Trimble also makes a good case for placing most of the blame for the Soviet response squarely on Gorbachev's shoulders instead of party hardliners. In "Watermelon Diplomacy on the Border," 5-15, he focuses on the relationship between the Soviet town of Blagoveshchensk and the Chinese town of Aihui since the 1950s as a barometer of Sino-Soviet relations. The historical background is particularly good, but the piece is lacking in any broader analysis. In "Reform is a Risky Business," 6-19, Trimble's summary of the events which have transpired at the recent meeting of the Congress of People's Deputies is quite good, but again he's light on analysis. He tells us who will probably be named to head both the Defense and Security Oversight Committee and the Foreign Affairs Committee, but he fails to tell us what to expect from these people. "Where Perestroika Makes Strange Bedfellows," 8-28/9-4, is disappointing, with Trimble writing about two different breeds of people's deputies on the Soviet island of Sakhalin but failing to probe the two men profiled in the article very deeply.

Tuohy, William. *Los Angeles Times.* (★ ★ ½)
Bonn bureau chief. In this tumultuous year Tuohy did a better job of providing his readers with hard information than analysis. "Libya Plant Poisons U.S.-Bonn Ties," 1-18, provides quotes and reactions from diplomats, political observers, and editorialists in West Germany on the row

over West German companies' involvement in that Libyan chemical plant. Not surprisingly, it's clearly seen as seriously souring U.S.-West German relations. "Bonn Jolted as Rightists Gain in W. Berlin Vote," 1-30, is somewhat stingy on why the Republicans made such a strong showing in West Berlin elections. "Like France's far-right party, the Republicans campaigned for law and order and against drug abuse and foreign workers. . .Strong Republican support came from West Berlin's working class districts. . .where unemployment is high and competition for jobs stiff." This information was left until the concluding paragraphs. "Calls of 'Kohl Should Go' Haunt Beleaguered Bonn Chancellor," 3-21, a look at Kohl's battered coalition government opens with a lot of zip, then fails to deliver, Tuohy getting bogged down in describing the machinations of various obscure German political parties, but only skimming the surface when it comes to discussing the political, social and economic issues they're griping about, leaving us shaking our heads at the end. In "Cold War Over, Bonn Foreign Minister Says," 5-8, Tuohy quotes West German Foreign Minister Hans-Dietrich Genscher: " 'The Cold War is at an end. The Iron Curtain is getting brittle. It's crumbling. This is the historic moment in which we're making policy,' " but doesn't offer much in the way of analysis. "Thousands of E. Germans Push Efforts to Emigrate," 8-17, is a tightly-written piece on the stream of East Germans trying to get to the West via Hungary, with Tuohy capturing the tension of the moment and the total lack of a diplomatic solution. "A solution must be found urgently or the queue will never end." "Krenz Goes From Hated to Wait-And-See," 10-25, a canvass of Western diplomats and East German dissidents on the new communist leader, contains this line: ". . .Krenz's predecessor as national leader, Erich Honecker, was viewed as misguided but well-meaning." Huh? "E. Germany Gets a New Politburo," 11-9, does a good job of capturing the mood in East Berlin. It's clear that something is about to give, and he goes out on a limb — not in predicting that the Wall is about to fall, but in labeling new PM Hans Modrow East Germany's Gorbachev.

Tyler, Patrick E. *The Washington Post.* (★ ★)
Cairo. A veteran Middle East correspondent, Tyler maintained a particularly steady focus on events in Iran. The political economy of the region's other major player, Egypt, never received the depth it ought to from him. "Arafat Vows to 'Do Best' Against Terrorism," 12-18-88, is balanced and thorough on PLO Chairman Yasir Arafat's pledge to "do all our best" to stop Palestinian terrorism, Tyler making clear that the pledge does not apply to resistance in the occupied territories. "Khomeini: Father or Avenger?" 2-2, is an insightful analysis of the Ayatollah Ruhollah Khomeini's vision of a benevolent Islamic nation "where the government focused its attention on the 'downtrodden,' the 'disinherited' and the 'poor' and 'oppressed' was the populist vision that drew the illiterate and disenfranchised Iranian masses to Khomeini's call. . .at the same time, it also drew the intellectuals, the students and the political leftists who were seeking to piggyback on the revolution their own utopian visions." His "Jordan Grapples with Political, Economic Woes," 3-14, is a timely report on King Hussein's priority focus on tackling his domestic problems, but the critical economic detail is thin. "Iraq Pursues Politics of Pragmatism," 5-13, is a good, informative sketch of the kind of foreign policy orientation being sought by Iraq in the aftermath of the Gulf War, as the priority national task has become to rebuild the country. President Saddam Hussein is "pursuing a more pragmatic political agenda that emphasizes stronger alliances with moderate Arab states, fresh appeals for Western technology and a less bellicose relationship with Israel." The Syrian relationship, of course, is key and needs more examination. "Discontent With Revolution Emerges in Post-Khomeini Iran," 7-16, only skims the surface: "While there are no reliable figures on how many of Iran's 50 million people have become disillusioned with the clergy-led revolution that overthrew Shah Mohammed Reza Pahlavi in 1979, there appear to be more and more Iranians willing to express openly their grievances with the government."

Uhlig, Mark A. *The New York Times.* (★)
Managua bureau chief. His reporting from Nicaragua varies. Sometimes straight, sometimes naive, he's not immune to being used for disinformation purposes by the Sandinistas, who have become expert at bagging our scribes. It says something that we look forward to seeing him spell

Lindsey Gruson in San Salvador from time to time. Uhlig is strong on assertion, weak on evidence in "Sandinista's Medicine," 2-1, a skewed analysis of the Sandinista's austerity program in which he rationalizes the measures rather than examining them. "Manager Acts to Revive Businesses," 2-2, is an inadequate follow-up report on Nicaragua's new program of economic austerity. He brings attention to government officials asserting their determination to implement a "mixed economy" and to help the private sector, quoting Jaime Wheelock, Agrarian Reform Minister, but omits any mention of Sandinista intentions to crack down with taxes on the private sector. "While Washington Reorganizes The Sandinistas Are Talking Fast," 2-19, provides succinct analysis of a Sandinista *fait accompli* on winning agreement from four other Central American presidents on a plan to disband the contras in return for guarantees of free elections inside Nicaragua: "Nicaragua has succeeded in forcing its own agenda on its relations with Washington." "Nicaraguan Study Reports Economy In Drastic Decline," 6-26, is focused and clear on the details in a confidential study, prepared at the request of the Sandinista government, that positions Nicaragua alongside Haiti in poverty among Latin American countries. The report calls for a sweeping reversal of Sandinista priorities as the only means to recovery. Uhlig is detached in a solid "The Contras: Last Chance?" 8-10, a P. 1 news analysis on the push for agreement to demobilize the contras by five Central American presidents while the Bush administration clings on as "the logic seems to have gone out of the fight." However, it does need a few words on East-West, Soviet relationships. Uhlig reports that there may be severe hunger in Nicaragua prior to the February elections in "Nicaragua Facing Shortage of Food," 8-13. He attributes the crisis to drought, followed by heavy rains, which devastated crops, but we don't get a word about the crop conditions in the rest of Central America. From San Salvador, "Americans Told to Seek Refuge In Salvador War," 11-30, is straight reporting, and refreshingly free of pejoratives.

Walsh, Mary Williams. *Los Angeles Times.* **(NR)**
Canada. An impressive foreign correspondent when with *The Wall Street Journal,* we haven't seen enough of her *Los Angeles Times* byline out of Canada to give her a rating. Her *WSJ* dispatches earlier in the year from the sub-continent and Afghanistan included some strong reports. "Baluchistan Threatens Pakistan's Stability," 12-20-88, is very informative on a secessionist-leaning province where U.S. aid seems to have had little effect: "Yet for all the tractors, Tang and temptation of the West, Islamic Baluchistan still has one foot planted in the fourteenth century, and its gaze locked on Moscow. Despite an economic boom it remains one of the sub-continent's most backward places." The report is very well detailed on this province, but we would have appreciated some perspective as to how PM Benazir Bhutto approaches issues there. From Kabul, "Afghan Leader Dismisses View He'll Be Ousted," 12-22-88, is straightforward on President Najibullah's interview in which he insists his People's Democratic Party of Afghanistan will and must play a central role in any future coalition. "The Veil Descends Again on Afghanistan," 1-19, is an inconclusive look on what may happen to the women's movement and its achievements in Afghanistan. Practically every correspondent with a posting in the vicinity has written up the good work of Abdul Saltar Edhi, and Walsh joins in with a "The Samaritan: One Man's Mission Helps Ease the Pain of Pakistan's Poor," 1-25. Mildly interesting, its P. 1 placement seems overdone for so narrow a subject. A report from Samarkhel, Afghanistan, "Afghan Tragedy: On the Jalalabad Plain, Mujahedeen Now Fight Among Themselves," 3-27, is a very credible analytic, with information on the military situation in the field. This was one of the few early reports in the year that clearly established how far the resistance was from taking Jalalabad, let alone Kabul.

Weisman, Steven R. *The New York Times.* **(★ ★)**
Tokyo. Weisman's first year in Japan after his three-year tour in New Delhi turned out well, as he was quickly tested by fast moving events. He's ripening into an able correspondent, not as sure of himself as when he landed from almighty Washington and his White House beat, and the better for it. "Japanese Scandal: Stark Parable of the Country's Postwar Transformation," 4-15, arrests us with thoughtful analysis: "Experts agree that none of the revelations would have

had such shock value if Japan's middle class had not begun to feel a bit beleaguered itself, a fact that may seem strange to people overseas reading about Japan's booming economy." His "Japan Scandal Prosecutors End Inquiry Without Charging Major Politicians," 5-30, wistfully reports that insufficient evidence was found in the Recruit scandal to charge now former Prime Minister Takeshita or any other major political leader with criminal activity. "Tokyo's Politician of Both Pen and Sword," 6-3, a profile of Sousuke Uno, Japan's 18th postwar PM, explains how he got the job — he doesn't have a network, and hence wasn't involved in the Recruit scandal. Several facets to the man are delineated, but Weisman needs to give us more of his career accomplishments before we can understand him. Weisman's alert with "U.S. and Japan Report a Stalemate on Trade-Talk Format," 6-16, giving us good, pertinent information on the beginning talks over Super 301 issues. "A Front Runner Emerges in Japan," 8-3, doesn't have much about Kaifu's views, but Weisman does have good insights into the overall LDP strategy for coming national elections. "Japan's Troubled Successor," 8-9, is one of the first decent profiles of Tashiki Kaifu, with a memorable lead that purports Kaifu predicted to friends twenty-nine years ago that he would be Prime Minister in twenty-nine years. Weisman's "Japan Weary of Barbs on Trade, Tells Americans Why They Trail," 11-20, picks up on the increasing assertiveness of Japan and the unusual unity on policy toward the U.S. among the country's Foreign, Finance, and International Trade and Industry ministries. He details their critique of U.S. management, but for the most part it's already been well-circulated.

Williams, Daniel. *Los Angeles Times.* (★ ½)
Jerusalem. Williams appears to have a broad understanding of the Israeli political situation. His emphasis on stories from the occupied territories may be due to his coming in new to this bureau, as he handles the *intifada* as if it were a new story to him, if not to his readers. In "Labor Party Approves Israeli Coalition; New Government to Take Office Today," 12-22-88, he presents the motivations behind the coalition objectively, and touches on the economic problems the country is facing due to a system of paternalistic socialism as well. "Israel Approves Consumer Price Boost as Part of Austerity Plan to Aid Economy," 1-2, provides better detail on what's been done, but asserts in the second paragraph "Many observers felt the action was long overdue..." with nothing to the contrary. "As Intifada Goes On, Dreams of a United Jerusalem Fade," 2-27, is an outstanding presentation of the political subtleties of life in Jerusalem since the *intifada,* with Williams supplying quotes from all sides but avoiding inflammatory rhetoric. In "Israeli Troops' West Bank Undercover Role Told," 3-14, he maintains an objective stance but provides devastating details about IDF undercover activity on the West Bank. In first-rate behind-the-scenes reporting he creates a powerful vision of Israel as it seemingly self-destructs. "Israeli Intelligence Said to View PLO as a Talks Partner," 3-21, details leaked information from an Israeli intelligence report on the PLO, Williams structures the piece well and examines the possible effects of this report in Washington and in the Israeli government, but neglects to examine the reaction of the Israeli public, leaving us wondering what the Israeli man-on-the-street thought. In "Palestinian Causes Bus Crash; 14 Israelis Die," 7-7, Williams does a good job of presenting all sides in an initial report on a controversial incident, but somehow fails to convey the national mood in Israel, making us feel as though we're expected to judge the situation there on the basis of inflammatory quotes from a handful of people. Where's the tide of public opinion? What's the trend? "A Life of Betrayal: Danger Stalks Arab Collaborators," 8-12, an article on Arab collaborators working for the Shin Beth is interesting but doesn't quite gel, with Williams essentially portraying them, in general, as traitors. The one he profiles, however, comes across as a man of some personal character and conviction who truly identifies with Israel. The images clash.

Williams, Nick B. Jr. *Los Angeles Times.* (★)
Cyprus. Posted in Nicosia, where he covered events in Lebanon, Williams' reports too often had a second-hand quality to them. "Islamic Captors Claim To Have Killed Higgins," 8-1, for instance, was written without Williams even having viewed the videotape released by the terrorists. He could have turned in a first rate wrap-up of news dispatches, radio broadcasts, and

official communiques and "diplomatic" statements — such as in "Syrian Forces Launch Ground Attack In Beirut," 8-14. He only needed to give readers a broader picture than they would have received from a reporter at the eye of the storm. But too often his stories were wire-service quality. "Hostage Spared; Role of Iran Seen As Pivotal," 8-4, is a good example. The one piece of real news in this was the use by the U.S. of the Algerian ambassador in Beirut, the same man who helped negotiate the end of the 1979-81 hostage crisis — to intercede with Hezbollah to save Joseph Cicippio. Yet this bit came from Reuters. Williams's first hand reports in '89 were generally on the same level as a year ago, when he was Bangkok bureau chief (which we rated at one-and-a-half stars). "Indonesia — A Potential Powerhouse Is Gearing Up," 12-29-88, provides a somewhat satisfactory overview of Indonesia, with some information on emergence of challenges to President Suharto's "New Order" by impatient military officers seeking a more open system. "Jamu: It's a Way of Life in Indonesia," 1-2, is a moderately well presented feature on *jamu,* an all-purpose tonic and herbal potion sold by five thousand lady peddlers on the streets of Jakarta. But Williams is a little confusing on the business aspects. "Aiming for Big Leagues," 1-16, provides good economic data and details on the growing pains of Thailand, East Asia's next newly industrialized country. "Iraqi Leader Basks In Glow Of Victory, Arabs' Respect," 4-10, contains nothing we haven't seen before on Iraq and its strongman president, and Williams never presents a clear picture of Saddam Hussein's future intentions, both domestically and regionally. We can understand the reluctance of the *LA Times* to send a correspondent into the Lebanese cauldron, but perhaps the paper should consider using an Arab stringer for news from Lebanon, as other U.S. publications are now doing, and transfer Williams out of the Nicosia bureau, where right now his talents are withering.

Worthy, Ford S. *Fortune.* (★)
Hong Kong. We appreciated Worthy's reporting out of Chicago, much of it "don't miss" quality, and had been allowing a readjustment period as he gets settled in Asia. But he's simply not connecting with this beat. "Tightwad Taiwan Starts to Spend," 12-5-88, is a cautious wrap-up that breaks little new ground, although it is workmanlike on the trend towards consumerism in Taiwan. Worthy is too dependent on the easy, obvious metaphor: "After decades as hoarders, the people of Taiwan are throwing money around like sailors on shore leave. . .Here the sentiment is not 'Yankee go home, but Yankee, you're welcome.' " (the last line was a quote from a Bechtel executive.) There's sparse attention to the mom-and-pop entrepreneurism and small-scale business lobby that is so powerful, both financially and economically, in Taiwan. "Why There's Still Promise in China," 2-27, is dutiful, dull and ultimately disappointing. This piece is a hedge-filled reprise of how Western companies are doing in China, with two examples of bummers and a matching set of more successful companies. The result is bound only to be of interest to unsophisticated readers, as we see with Worthy's clanky-sounding conclusion: "The China road is now strewn with boulders and pitted with potholes. But for those with the right products, as well as deep pockets, patience — and heavy-duty shock absorbers — it's still a ride worth taking." His "Asia's Reluctant Growth Champs," 4-24, is careful, measured and rather dull as Worthy touches all the conventional bases in this regional roundup. "Perils of Getting Tough on Korea," 6-5, is an earnest slog through the diplomatic trade quagmire, heavily dependent on establishment sources on both sides of the Pacific. "What's Next for Business In China?" 7-17, is pedestrian — the short-term looks shaky, but many Western companies are banking on the long term. Worthy advises that inflation is, of course, something to watch very closely, but has absolutely no understanding of what set it off in China. After Tiananmen, his "Doing Business in China Now," Pacific Rim 1989 edition, advises that "both foreign and local business folk must operate under a cloud of uncertainty. Nor does this cloud carry a silver lining." And more, like that.

Wren, Christopher. *The New York Times.* (★)
Johannesburg bureau chief. In a year in which South Africa set out on what seem to be dramatic changes, Wren seemed rather pedestrian in his coverage. "Blacks Battle Fellow Blacks in Natal," 1-29, is balanced reporting on the mounting violence, with youths between fifteen and twenty-

five committing 90% of violence in the townships. The analytical side is a bit loose, though, as he describes the situation as not simply a power struggle between black political groups, but also a reflection of "rage turned inward among apartheid's victims." Wren tries to stay objective, presenting views of Inkatham (the Zulu movement) and the UDF (United Democratic Front) of the black against black violence in South Africa's Natal townships. "Anti-Apartheid Groups Cast Out Winnie Mandela, Citing Terror," 2-17, reasonably details the decision by the UDF to effectively cast Winnie Mandela out of the anti-apartheid movement, and Wren includes strong quotes from a UDF spokesman on her abuse of trust and confidence. "Winnie Mandela, as a Symbol, Is Dismantled," 2-20, is somewhat soggy, as he compares the circumstances of her rise from poverty to prominence to that of Argentina's Evita Peron or Imelda Marcos of the Philippines. Buried at the end is his citing of worries that "Mrs. Mandela, who has been popular with [the ANC's]. . .military wing, retains enough influence to split the anti-apartheid movement and this could lead to internal bloodshed." His "Apartheid Divides 2 Brothers of the White Tribe," 3-23, would be just another skippable feature, except that the brothers happen to be Willem and Frederik de Klerk (new National Party leader in the R.S.A.). But we really wanted to know how Willem and Frederik came to hold antagonistic positions. With "Pretoria Leader And Mandela Meet In Hint Of Release," 7-9, Wren does the best he can to draw conclusions out of the unprecedented meeting, but it's guesswork. As Namibia approaches independence, "the diamond industry, like everything else in the territory, is being buffeted by the winds of change," and Wren draws some perspective on its arrangement post-independence in "SWAPO and De Beers: Are They Engaged to Wed?" 10-10. Although not sanguine, the outlook is pragmatic.

WuDunn, Sheryl. *The New York Times.* (★ ★)
Beijing. Reporting from the capital during the student demonstrations and the government's crackdown, WuDunn's coverage of the events there were respectable. Her reports on what's happening in China since then have been even better. "Civil Warfare as a Spectator Sport," 6-8, vignettes from the reporter's notebook, is a colorful, absorbing canvas of details on how Beijing residents are learning to deal with chaos. "An Urbane Technocrat," 6-25, a "Man in the News" profile of Jiang Zemin, the new General Secretary of the Communist Party, employs second-hand quotes from anonymous sources who depict him as either incompetent or brilliant. "Business in China Adjust to the Party Line," 9-25, is perhaps too focused on one example, albeit involving China's biggest investment company, but there are some general insights that may be drawn from it. "An American Singer Dazzles the Chinese With Sequins and Sex," 10-24, reports on the highly successful tour of rock star Fei Xiang, an American who has sold more cassette tapes than any other singer in China, in the midst of a campaign against "bourgeois liberalism" and foreign influence. We get a sense of why the regime permits his tour, but almost nothing on the singer's thinking. "China Cracks Down on Private Work," 11-8, is detailed on the measures and scope of the economic retrenchment program (that began more than a year before), and notes how mixed are the policy signals the government is sending to private enterprises and rural collectives. More of this at the grassroots, please.

Yang, Dori Jones. *Business Week.* (★ ½)
Manager of *Business Week*'s Hong Kong bureau, Yang handled most of the stories here with an ability that's from fair to middling good. We don't get fully satisfactory economic reporting from her, though. "China's Economy Is Careening Out of Control" 4-3, is confused on the spring mechanisms of China's inflation and without a solid sense of where the economy is going to end up. Written around the time of Gorbachev;s visit, "Genie Is Out of Beijing Bottle," co-authored by Dinah Lee 5-29, is steady analysis, without losing sight of the ball here: "China aging rulers are likely to concede minimally and grudgingly" to student demands, and instead will be tempted to jail key activists." "The liberal Zhao's policy of restraint toward the students may have deepened his troubles." "China Begins A New Long March," with Dinah Lee, Robert Neff, and William J. Holstein 6-5 is perceptive and information packed on the "other" new challenging force in China: the capitalist economic elements concentrated along the coast vs. inland

provinces like Hunan and Guizhou, which are anti-business, backward, and aligned with the Beijing bureaucracy. A nice sidebar by Yang, based on a trip to Guangdong and Hunan, details the contrasting lifestyles. "Foreign Investors Are Wary — But They're Not Running," co-written by William Glasgall 6-5, is an adequate survey measured against the unsettled climate in China. The early line is, the big foreign companies are battle-hardened and not likely to pull out. But "some U.S. executives fret that Beijing will be less hospitable to foreign investment if government hardliners somehow manage to reassert their authority. "The Outside World Puts China on Hold," co-written by Bill Javetski, with William J. Holstein 7-10, is repetitive of a longer 6-26 article. The new information is the assessment that Congress will not revoke China's most-favored-nation status, and the revelation that Richard Nixon is "Bush's personal envoy to China's leaders" (denied by Nixon). "Taiwan Isn't Cloning Anymore," 9-25, contains good statistics and uses good quotes on Taiwan leap ahead in the computer industry as a producer of clones.

Younghusband, Peter. *The Washington Times.* (★ ½)
Johannesburg. Overall we saw little improvement in the quality of his straight news dispatches, which were rarely more than a step or two above wire copy. He seemed at times to be overly optimistic about F.W. de Klerk and future reforms. "De Klerk Represents New Moderate Force in Divided S. Africa," 3-20, adequately captures the nuance of de Klerk's position, although he doesn't go into much depth as the headline would suggest on de Klerk's politics. "Namibian Independence in Peril, Botha Reminds Marxist Monitors," 4-28, offers a crisp news report of President Botha's meeting with Soviet, Cuban and Angolan negotiators, laying down the rules for the withdrawal from Namibia of SWAPO intruder units. "S. Africa Faces Massive Government Upheaval After Vote," 6-12, surveys the impending "biggest government shake-up in South Africa since. . .1948," which will "amount to the sweeping out of the old-guard Afrikaner leaders and, apparently, the ascent of younger men more amenable to political change — loosing segregation laws." In "Mandela Meeting Points to Release," 7-10, Younghusband's writing doesn't seem to be quite up to the occasion: a dramatic, historic 45-minute meeting between President Botha and Nelson Mandela in South Africa's presidential residence. But he does provide a modest sampling of the political reactions it elicited. "Apartheid Party Faces Loss in Upcoming Vote," 7-24, analyzes the coming election: "South African politics might be on the threshold of breaking out of its rigid, traditional two-party mold. . .[as] support for the National Party. . .is draining away on both flanks — to the right and the left." Younghusband draws a colorful character sketch of the departing South African president in "Unpopular Botha Leaves S. Africa Still Divided In Turmoil," 8-15. ". . .the 'Great Crocodile,' as he was known to his Afrikaner associates [was] tough, unscrupulous and ugly-tempered. . .he will probably be judged by history as South Africa's least loved and most feared leader." His "Namibian Capital Has Gold-Rush Air," 9-20, is a first-rate foreign dispatch: "As Namibia moves closer to independence after more than 100 years of colonial rule, Windhoek, its capital, has assumed the air of a gold-rush town. . .The gold-rush flavor comes from the influx of people who sense that there is money to be made in the new scheme of things in the huge, sprawling territory on Africa's southwest coast. This is a diamond-rich, copper-rich, fishing-rich and ranching-rich country." Perhaps Younghusband should do more of these.

NATIONAL SECURITY/DIPLOMATIC CORRESPONDENTS

Adams, Peter. *Defense News.* (★ ★ ★)
With the departure of Trish Gilmartin to the glossier pages of *Aviation Week,* Peter Adams, now in his third year as a staff writer, has become the resident *Defense News* superstar. Writing on arms control, SDI, and particularly Soviet military affairs, Adams surpassed his 1988 output in both sheer byline numbers and analytical strength. Knowing Russian history and language certainly helps, as in "Soviet Forces Lack Skill, Top Military Official Says," 1-30, a review of an otherwise ignored article in a Soviet military journal, "Military Resisted Gorbachev's Arms Cuts," 3-13's coverage of Soviet official Andrei Kokoshin, from the U.S.A./Canada Institute in Moscow, complaining about military resistance to Gorbachev, and one of the better pieces on Soviet Marshal Sergei Akhromeyev, "Akhromeyev: Major Weapons Cuts by 1990," 7-24. No one-trick pony, Adams delivered the goods on the Lance missile debate with "U.S. Wants New Lance, Despite Soviet Vow on Missiles," a 1-23 state-of-the-debate piece and "NATO's Altenberg Says Lance Issue Is No 'Litmus Test' for Atlantic Alliance Survival," 5-1, a classy profile of West German General Wolfgang Altenburg. He also came through on the politics of SDI, telling us "Proponents Argue SDI Is Affordable," 6-12, and updating us on U.S.-Soviet negotiations on Star Wars, "U.S., Soviets Edge Closer to Rewritten ABM Treaty at Defense and Space Talks," 8-21. We also saw several winners on the Asia/Pacific region, such as "Longstanding Kurile Dispute Clouds Japanese-Soviet Relationship," 4-10, on how Tokyo remains a stalwart cold warrior even as trade strains with the U.S. could trigger softness, and "Emerging 'Asian Tigers' Become Power Brokers in Pacific Basin," 8-28. While all *Defense News* staffers admirably pull double and triple shifts, Adams seems to handle the load with greater substantive breadth, without showing off stylistically. And who else, anywhere, showed the insight and hustle to produce in-depth "10 Countries Now Have Biological Weapons," 2-20, or "Economy Hurts Soviet Ability to Improve Air Defense Shield," 9-4, a synthesis of the economic/strategic dichotomy facing Moscow? He coasts on automatic pilot only occasionally, as in "Aspin Says M Missile Can Be Put on Ice for a Few Years," 1-16, a rehash of a Les Aspin statement on the Midgetman, but overall, he deserves the extra boost, and we hope *Defense News* can keep him for '90.

Almond, Peter. *The Washington Times.* (★ ★)
Pentagon correspondent. His facility with this assignment continues to improve. A very reliable correspondent, the efficiency and liveliness of his reporting combines nicely with a solid professionalism. "With the Military, He Stuck to His Guns," 1-18, quickly and efficiently reviews Ronald Reagan's military legacy, Almond's judgments appropriately professional. "Future of Euromissiles Splits U.S., W. Germany," with Thomas J. Breen 4-25, establishes clear context with an uncluttered account of the U.S.-West German differences over short-range nuclear arms in the upcoming NATO summit. Though choppy in spots, "Hill Will Invite Soviet Advice on Arms Cuts," 5-2, provides intelligible detail on Rep. Les Aspin's move to have Soviet officials appear before the House Armed Services Committee. Almond's professionalism is evident in "7,000 Were Killed In Beijing, NATO Believes," 6-9, an admirable attempt to sort out fact from fiction in the Beijing massacre. He assiduously compares and weighs the partial reports of his numerous official intelligence sources and is among the first to refute reports that the Chinese Army was torn by dissension. "Ethnic Turks Fleeing Bulgaria Describe Brutality," 6-21, highlights an event deserving of greater world attention, the forced mass deportation of ethnic Turks from Bulgaria. "According to Turkish and U.S. officials the forced emigrations are the final stage of a five-year effort to assimilate Turks, the remnants of the old Ottoman Empire, into officially atheistic Bulgaria." "Low Flying at Heart of Nato's Fragility," 8-1, explains NATO's Follow-On Force Attack strategy, "which largely ignores the swirling, fast-moving battle and concentrates on follow-on, second echelon enemy troop concentrations, airfields, key rail and road bridges, supply dumps and communications centers," but Almond stretches it when he argues that FOFA is in jeopardy because West Germans are mad about the noise.

Amouyal, Barbara. *Defense News.* (★ ★ ½)
Covering the air warfare beat, Amouyal is a newer face at *Defense News,* having been a
Jerusalem Post reporter and a former director of media relations for AIPAC, a pro-Israel lobby
in Washington. Amouyal is a solid professional, with above average savvy on aircraft production
and air tactics, all delivered in the straightforward *DN* manner. We like her work on defense
electronics issues, such as "General: Defense Electronics Industry an 'Achilles' Heal,' " 2-13,
an interview with a pessimistic Air Force General Bernard Randolph, saying the U.S. industrial
base is failing to produce hi-tech, cost-effective avionics. She's a trooper on the Stealth bomber
issue with "Air Force May Need to Reduce B-2 Secrecy to Secure Funds, Sources Say," 3-13,
looking for new angles on the B-2's travails on program secrecy, "Air Force Will Buy Before
B-2 Bomber is Ready to Buy," 5-8, on the Air Force B-2 purchasing plan, and "Air Force
Supporters of the B-2 Fear Stealthy Tactics Have Lured Budget Ax," 7-24, an analytic on Stealth
budget woes. Of course, aviation is still the true forte of *AWST,* where one still must go for the
last word on Air Force questions. Amouyal did out-hustle her competition, though, with
"Soviets in Paris Say Su-27 Fighter Will Incorporate Stealth Materials," 6-12, a report from the
Paris air show on the sincerest form of flattery for our Stealth manufacturers. She needs a wider
scope of assignments to move up, but what we saw in '89 was promising.

Baker, Caleb. *Defense News.* (★ ★)
Staff writer on Army issues, Asia and Central America, plus more specialized industry concerns
such as helicopters and unmanned aerial vehicles. In his first full year at *Defense News,* Baker
is no neophyte, having published a book on NATO's command structure, and he shows promise
on a host of land warfare topics. Though an army buff, Baker did not slight the Navy, conducting
colorful interviews with John Lehman and James Webb in "Pentagon's Land-Warfare Mentality
Thwarts Navy Goals, 2 Former Secretaries Complain," 1-16, and covering a U.S. Naval Institute
conference at which several old admirals and naval officials jumped all over Defense Secretary
Cheney's plan to streamline DoD procurement, "Former U.S. Navy Officials Criticize Cheney's
Management Review," 9-11. His strongest suit is unconventional warfare, or special operations,
with two knowledgeable dispatches standing out: "Special Operations Budget Directive Ends
Two-Year Battle," 2-6, on the granting of budgetary autonomy to the Special Forces Operations
Command; and "Special Forces Need More Funding, Study Says," 7-24, a perceptive account
of a government report calling for enhanced bureaucratic clout for special operators. Baker puts
in three or four articles per issue, however, and his coverage of drones and helicopters may not
be as authoritative as the output of his *Aviation Week* competitors. He knows his army
hardware, though, as evidenced in "Army Plans New Weapon to Complement Stinger," 3-27,
and "Army Long-Range Training Plans to Rely Heavily on Simulation," 8-7, spins on the
heavily-covered topic of training simulation at Army facilities. Finally, Baker did well on the
Army reserve beat, a subject that will increase in importance as pressures rise for active force
cuts, with a fine and farsighted "Reserve Forces Examine Larger Role in U.S. Military," 8-21.
An up-and-comer, who needs seasoning on aerial issues if he is not to become typecast as an
Army scribe.

Bedard, Paul. *The Washington Times.* (★ ½)
White House correspondent. A *Defense Week* veteran, Bedard's one of *WAT*'s utility reporters
who fills in the holes on the paper's national security/defense coverage. Reliable on the basics
and displaying a competency for distinguishing salient information from conventional, we think
his editors ought to give him a freer hand with some analytical pieces. "Bush to Route Arms
Talks Away from Nuclear Weapons," 4-12, surveys Bush's preparations for the NATO summit.
He notes "the shifting emphasis [to conventional arms cuts] emerging from the State
Department and the National Security Council does not differ with ongoing strategic reviews
of foreign policy and arms control that recommended the President make no major changes in
Ronald Reagan's policies," but clearly an analysis of the implications for policy was in order
here. "Bush Asking European Leaders to Halt Nicaraguan Aid," 5-10, neatly and substantially
covers the broad array of Bush administration measures for continued international pressure on

Managua to keep to the Central American peace plan. "Bush Talks Softly of China Turmoil," with Chris Harvey 5-23, looks at Bush's cautious handling of the events in China despite pressure from both Democrats and Republicans to take bolder steps in support of the students' demonstration, but is sufficient only as an outline of the relationships. "Quayle Sees Cuba-Nicaragua-Panama Axis Developing," 6-13, comes across very well as an informative account of the Veep's tour of Central America, built on the theme that "The axis of Cuba, Nicaragua and Panama threatens peace and democracy in this hemisphere." "Bush Offers Concession If Missiles Are Approved," 6-21, on Bush's bridge-building style as he combines arms control talks with domestic politics to win over Senate support for his nuclear missile program, but here again further analysis is appropriate. "Bush: Soviets 'Long Way' From Joining Group of 7," 7-17, is basic material, covering the discussions at the Paris Summit provoked by Gorbachev's request for Soviet presence at the Group of Seven meetings. "White House to Press for Return of Higgins' Body," 8-9, displays professional handling of a story, Bedard's selection of the pained, dignified public remarks of Lt. Col. William Higgins' widow, respectfully and tastefully accomplished.

Broder, John. *Los Angeles Times.* (★ ½)
Pentagon correspondent. Though generally straightforward, the analytical side of his reporting is somewhat slack, and while not characteristic he lets a sloppiness with regard to accuracy occasionally intrude. "Move by Libya Led to Heightened U.S. Alert," 1-6, is well-written and balanced on the aerial clash between Libyan MiG-23s and U.S. Navy F-14s which resulted in the downing of the two Libyan fighters, but with nothing to distinguish it from the accounts by others we reviewed. "Panel to Begin Hearings Today on Cheney Nomination," 3-14, begins with a garbled, overly-long lead and though it manages to proceed in a basically straightforward and organized manner, Broder's reference to John Tower's "drinking and womanizing" is sloppy work and should never have appeared without the qualifying "alleged." " 'Star Wars' Was Oversold, Cheney Says," 3-29, solid, basic coverage of Cheney's early remarks on SDI, adds new information with an examination of the military's ulterior motives for opposing SDI. "Pentagon Quickly Learns That Cheney Is in Charge," 4-5, a review of the first signs of Cheney's emerging management style at the Pentagon is standard Broder: concise and interesting reporting, the facts appropriately organized, but analytical depth only knee-deep. "It's Still 'Business as Usual,' Despite Defense Fraud Probe," 6-15, sufficiently updates us on procurement scandals, but suffers by a lack of analysis of legislation pending regarding the procurement process. "Iraqis Seeking to Neutralize Kurds, U.S. Says," 7-12, on the forced resettlement of 50,000 Kurds that had lived in villages along the northern Iraqi border, informs sufficiently, despite it not being an on-the-site report. Broder provides enough background on Saddam Hussein's policy toward the Kurds to make the most of this story.

Covault, Craig. *Aviation Week & Space Technology.* (★ ★ ★)
Senior space editor. Still on the cutting edge of new developments, Covault's forte is his ability to lure his readers with interesting angles and hook them with his straightforward handling of technical topics. In "Magellan Mission to Venus Requires Precise Shuttle Launch Operations," 4-24, Covault gives a fascinating description of past quandaries and potential problems facing the upcoming launching of the Magellan probe to Venus. "Manned Soviet Shuttle Flight Delayed Until 1992 for Systems Installation," 5-8, an absorbing assessment of the current status of the Soviet space program, evaluates information brought by Soviet astronauts and program managers visiting the U.S.A. He points out that primitive computer technology is the biggest drawback of their shuttle, but notes they are working toward turning the rocket into a reusable launch vehicle. On the same subject, "Soviet Space Program Strife Threatens Mars Mission Plans," 5-22, is excellent, a well-documented, insightful report of the managerial "incompetence and irresponsibility" of the Soviet space program. Based on information from senior Soviet officials, we get a convincing argument for *glasnost* and *perestroika* in the Soviet aerospace industry: "These policies keep the Soviet aerospace industry so compartmentalized that scientists and other space mission planners are excluded from participation in critical spacecraft

development." We get a good look at the internal wrangling over the National Aero-Space Plane, currently under review by the National Space Council, in "Bush Administration Speeds NASP Review Spurred by Soviet, German Competition," 6-5, Covault assembling alternate and supporting views to the CIA view that the Soviet Union and West Germany pose a near-term competitive threat in hypersonic technology. "Sanger Aero-Space Plane Gains Increased Support in Europe," 7-10, is comprehensive on the work-in-progress of the European multinational program for development of hypersonic aircraft technology and horizontal takeoff space launch vehicles being formed around the West German Sanger aero-space plane concept. "Manned Lunar Base, Mars Initiative Raised in Secret White House Review," 7-17, lays out in detail the sub-surface political struggles to relaunch America's space effort in Kennedy-like style, virtually a manual of the factional lineup over the nation's future space policy. And "U.S., U.S.S.R. Test New Strategic Satellites; Soviet Intelligence Spacecraft Explodes," 8-14, is a superlative intelligence summary of the current status of the Soviet Union's satellite program, containing important new details.

de Briganti, Giovanni. *Defense News.* (★ ★ ½)
His third year as Paris-based European editor, de Briganti couldn't have been too pleased about the addition of a new bureau in Brussels, which cribbed some of his column inches and bylines. While still in charge of the "coordination" of *DN*'s European coverage, de Briganti's byline is not as prominent, and the range of his topics seems more constrained. Not altogether bad, since his concentration on NATO arms cooperation and interviews with bigwigs insures tighter, if less frequent, coverage of key concerns. A London-based report, "British Officials Explore Possibility of Other Light Attack Helicopter," 1-30, and "Germany Questions Cooperative Programs," 10-2, were fine examples of the former focus, while a top-notch session with Soviet arms negotiator Victor Karpov, "Soviet Disputes U.S. Aircraft Plan, Flexible on Deeper Cuts in Troops," 6-12, gets the official to show some old-fashioned intransigence. His "Analysis" on Europe 1992, "Trying to Dispel 'Fortress Europe' Perception," 2-6, is a less than inspiring account of the potential cartelization of NATO Europe. And we wonder about his op-ed entry, "NATO Gropes With Midlife Identity Crisis," 4-10, since it told us little new, and we don't think a bureau chief's reportorial objectivity is enhanced by doing op-ed pieces.

Dornheim, Michael. *Aviation Week & Space Technology.* (★ ½)
A utility reporter at the weekly, Dornheim combines adept analysis and interpretation with keen observations on developments within military aviation. Sometimes, though, the lay reader may get lost when he starts revving up the technical side of his reports. "Galileo Thrusters Approved for Flight but Mission Plan May Be Abbreviated," 4-10, handily updates us on the status of the maneuvering thrusters for the NASA Galileo probe to Jupiter. Approved for flight, they are being reattached at the cost of degrading mission standards, he discloses, as "the thrusters are restricted to operating only a few seconds at a time, instead of the 7-8 minute maximum planned." In "USAF/Lockheed F-117A Has High Wing Sweep But Low Wing Loading," 5-1, Dornheim plays technological sleuth, delving into a speculative analysis of the Stealth fighter's weight and engineering characteristics. It's interesting but too specialized. ' Contractors Grapple With Low Stock Prices, Peak Cash Needs," 5-29, is better, a clear and succinct account of one problem facing defense contractors: the effect of the budget on the stock market, and in turn, the contractors. In "USAF Continues to Increase Daytime Flights of F-117A Stealth Aircraft," 7-3, Dornheim keeps his vigil over the fortunes of the Stealth fighter, still in its operational testing phase. Though not as dramatic as his 5-1 report, it's still refreshing to see how he garners information from private "observers in the desert area surrounding Edwards AFB, Calif.," presumably residents. "Initial Taxi Runs Highlight B-2s Advanced Design Details," 7-17, gives us an expert's sharp observations of the B-2 Stealth bomber's 7-10 taxi tests, so clearly done a Soviet spy would give this article five stars. More off his beat, "Latest Soviet Planetary Mission Plans Reflect Shift to Conservative Outlook," 8-28, is a solid, revealing assessment of the Soviet planet exploration program.

Dorsey, James M. *The Washington Times.* (★ ½)

Diplomatic correspondent. Primarily assigned the Middle East, where he's generally judicious and discerning, his trouble-shooting on Central America suggests a tendency to indulge a questionable spin on some stories. In "U.S. Envoy, PLO Discuss Pan Am Air Crash," 1-3, we get good material deep within the article, but most readers won't get past the slow lead. "Beirut Christian Begs for U.S. Help," 3-31, details the plight of General Michel Aoun, military commander of Beirut's besieged Christian ghetto (who made a desperate appeal to the *WAT* by transatlantic phone after Syrian artillery razed the sector), and one can't help but appreciate the effort to challenge complacency on this tragedy. "Baker's Nominee House Cleaning at State Bureau," 4-26, is a juicy inside story of wholesale head-chopping at the State Department's Bureau of Near Eastern and South Asian Affairs by the not yet confirmed Assistant Secretary of State-designate John Kelly. "Latin States, Europe Denounce Panama's Election," 5-11, rounds up international reactions to Noriega's fraud, but there's a spin here that results in a not necessarily supportable conclusion that "Growing international condemnation. . .would appear to strengthen the Bush administration's hand in crafting a strategy for dealing with the Noriega regime." "Church Turns on Noriega, Blasts Fraud," 5-15, on the mounting political, military, domestic and foreign pressure confronting Noriega is informative but the suggestion that the general is about overwhelmed by it is unwarranted. "Inflation 435% in Nicaragua as Unemployment Hits 40%," 6-1, though not new information, is a solidly presented firsthand account from Managua on how the dismal economic situation is shaping adverse public attitudes toward the Sandinistas. "Baker Rejects Israeli Position on PLO Talks," 7-17, keeps the information clear on the respective views of the U.S. and Israeli governments on the role of the PLO, and the resultant conflict. "White House, State Fume Over Kidnapping by Israel," 8-2, is a sharp characterization of U.S.-Israeli frictions over the Obeid/Higgins affair. "Colombians Not Confident of Triumph Over Cartel," 9-6, isn't new on the corruption angle but is a credible investigation into the infiltration of the government at so many levels by the drug cartel.

Engelberg, Stephen. *The New York Times.* (★ ★ ★)

National security, investigative correspondent. A top pro on this beat, the hard-working Engelberg (with Michael Gordon) produced one of the year's major intelligence stories with the expose on the West German-assisted construction of a poison gas plant in Libya, a 10 Best selection in general reporting. "Germans Accused of Helping Libya Build Nerve Gas Plant," with Michael R. Gordon 1-1, was a blockbuster with global reverberations, persuasive on Imhausen-Chemie being at the center of a web of western companies that have built a poison gas plant in Rabta, Libya. In a followup, "U.S. Sees Gains in Efforts to Stop West German Aid to Libya Chemical Plant," 1-14, Engelberg remains icily detached with this excellent report on U.S. intelligence confronting Bonn with evidence of West German companies supplying East Bloc and Third World countries with weapons of mass destruction. "Poison Gas Fears Lead U.S. to Plan New Export Curbs," with Michael Gordon 3-26, is an extensive early warning examination of the weak controls on U.S. companies dealing in chemical technology exports to the Third World. Complete with a survey of current laws, he reveals that, excepting Iran, Iraq, Syria, and Libya, anything goes with American firms selling or building "dual use" chemical facilities that could be used for military production. Although it's stylistically dry, this could be the kind of piece we look back on as prescient. "Soviets Sold Libya Advanced Bomber, U.S. Officials Say," with Bernard E. Trainor 4-5, details how, in the midst of Gorbachev's less than spectacular trip to Cuba, the U.S. played the global propaganda game too, with a shrewd leak of intelligence/military data that embarrassed the Soviets: apparently not only have the Soviets sold Sukhoi-24D bombers, comparable to the F-111s that bombed Tripoli in 1986, but they also trained pilots and detailed airborne refueling capabilities. In "Document in North Trial Suggests Stronger Bush Role in Contra Aid," 4-7, Engelberg casts a more sober light on the phantom memo, which purports to reveal a 1985 plot to pressure the Honduran government to assist the contras in return for U.S. aid, putting up front the fact that this document was "a summary of information from still-classified material that the North defense was not allowed to introduce at the trial," and that then VP Bush was not identified explicitly as the messenger to Tegucigalpa.

"On Helping Defectors to Stay in From the Cold," 7-14, reviews some spectacular failures at keeping East bloc defectors happy, Engelberg scoring on a *Washington Times* specialty for non-*WAT* readers.

Fialka, John J. *The Wall Street Journal.* (★ ★ ½)
Pentagon correspondent. Credible, competent, this seasoned professional seemed a bit frayed at the edges more often than customary. No complaints on his factual assembly, but his usually rigorous analyses appeared soggy at times, and, though not enough to pull his rating down this year, it needs correction. "Downing of 2 Libyan MiGs Comes as U.S. Steps Up Pressure Against Chemical Site," 1-5, begins the year nicely enough. It's standard Fialka, substantial and well-organized, as he makes up for the *WSJ*'s failure to stay abreast of the story earlier. His strengths shine in "Tricky Targets: 'Smart' Arms Failure to Distinguish Decoys Has Pentagon Alarmed," 2-17. Reporting on the down side of advanced technology utilized on the modern battlefield and effectively quoting a wide range of military and civilian experts, he credibly shows that relatively cheap methods of camouflage and deception can obviate the effectiveness of high-priced enhanced technology artillery. Trying to form the conventional wisdom before it solidifies, Fialka with Gerald Seib in "Advise and Reject: Tower Fiasco Hurts Bush, but Also Puts Congress on Defensive," 3-10, reviews the Tower fiasco as a parable for the halting initiation of the supposedly seasoned Bush administration. "Anxious Allies — Race to Demilitarize Poses Fresh Challenge for a Divided NATO," 5-31, is another "end of NATO" yawner, but this one shows more ingenuity than most. Looking at the malaise caused by a fear of the unknown in Germany, with the role of nuclear weapons at the center, Fialka examines the breakdown of old verities while no new structures are yet in place for a cohesive political community. An interesting A-hed, "New War Games Try to Give G.I.s Taste of Real Battle," 6-27, is okay, but we've heard this before from various sources. Showing his extensive knowledge of the Third World arms industry in "Space Research Fuels Arms Proliferation," 7-6, he gives us the scoop on the big security challenge of the 1990s: utilization of space research for missile proliferation. Surprisingly, "Attacking the Drug Menace: The Bush Plan," 9-6, is unfocused, less interested in Bush's policy than in making comparisons between military advisors in Colombia and the early years of U.S. involvement in Vietnam.

Foley, Theresa. *Aviation Week & Space Technology.* (★ ★)
Moving on to become Editor of *Space News* later in the year, Foley continues to impress us with her able handling of complex, technical issues. She is especially adept at making these issues of interest and import to the non-specialist reader, an ability that clearly comes across in "U.S. Prepares for First Test of Neutral Particle Beam in Space," 5-15, an intelligible update on the progress of SDI particle beam work. She stumbles a bit with "Quayle Denounces U.S. Reliance on Foreign Space Launch Vehicles," 4-10, a less-than-thorough report on the overall orientation of the newly-formed National Space Council that mistakenly identifies federal support for private space launching enterprises as top priority issue for the Council. "Space Station Faces Possible Delay or Cancellation," 5-1, is a fine presentation of the political and scientific policy issues defining the fight to secure funding for the space station. We get a tight, clear focus on a wide range of technical and budget issues in "NASA Space Station Faces Scale-Down as Budget, Technical Realities Emerge," 5-29. "SDI Phase One System Will Meet Joint Chiefs' Minimum Defense Levels," 6-26, efficient and concise, gives us what we need to know of the Senate testimonies by Defense Undersecretary for Policy Paul D. Wolfowitz and of U.S. Space Command Chief Gen. John Piotrowski.

Friedman, Thomas L. *The New York Times.* (★ ★ ★ ½)
State Department correspondent. A former Beirut and Jerusalem bureau chief (Pulitzers on both assignments), Friedman is able to draw on particularly deep insights and experiences to enhance his already significant reporting and analytical abilities. With Robert Pear, he gives the *NYT* the edge over all competition on State Department coverage. "Israel: Mired in the West Bank: The Politicians," 5-7, is by far the best single piece on the sources of tension and political

stagnation in Israel this year, a 10 Best selection for foreign dispatch. With Friedman having been away long enough for the scene to crystallize, his piece is rich with appropriate historical detail, background, and razor-sharp insights. "Baker's Pace for Mideast — Experience Tells Him Gradual Approach Puts Onus on Warring Parties to Plan Peace," 3-16, puts together the reasons behind the new administration's reluctance to offer a broad Middle East peace plan early in the administration, despite all the criticism, and here Friedman displays his analytical finesse. Friedman is always focused on substance, yet he never neglects the salient movement within the shadows, as we see with "Baker Brings an Inner Circle of Outsiders to State Dept," 3-27. Written after the Bush-Congress accord on Central America but before the President's highly-touted conventional arms control offer, he authoritatively profiles the Secretary of State's inner sanctum. "For Palestinians, Washington Is Losing Promise as a Peacemaker," 6-25, is a rare effort to sum up the present state of Middle East affairs, deciphering the deadlocked dialogue between the Bush administration and the Palestinian Liberation Organization, and concluding that this relationship has become hostage to the "dialogue of deeds" between Israeli Jews and Palestinian Arabs. Contrary to those who have argued that recent violence would lead to policy momentum, Friedman is far more persuasive in contending that the current diplomatic paralysis is the product of the developing "intercommunal war" which effectively blockades all restraint and concession. "U.S. May Tell Soviets: Let's Share Some Secrets," 4-21, on Baker's taking a Bush plan on data-swapping to Moscow, skillfully explores the overall question of trusting what was once the "Evil Empire." It's an important preface of the administration's general approach to the Soviet Union, "clearly torn between a 'don't-rock-the-boat' and a 'don't-miss-the-boat' instinct." "Baker and Shevardnadze Finish Talks With Accords," 9-24, on the Wyoming talks, presents clear detail: "For the first time ever, Robert Zoellick, Mr. Baker's counselor and an expert on international economics, led a discussion Friday between Soviet and American officials about the state of Soviet economic changes." His late year accounts of tricky U.S.-Soviet relations set the pace for the profession.

Gertz, Bill. *The Washington Times.* (★ ★ ½)
National security, intelligence correspondent. An improved effort to expand the density of facts in his reports, plus a less hurried construction to his dispatches, worked well for him this year. "Pentagon Claims Hackers Failed to Penetrate Secret Files," 3-17, rewards with fresh and credible material on authorities' effort to conduct damage assessment of the first case of computer espionage by the KGB against the U.S. military in Germany. "Soviet Radar Site Remains Treaty Violation, U.S. Says," 4-13, tight and concise on the technical and legal issues involved in a potential violation of the ABM treaty by the Soviet Union, displays his ability to secure critical, inside information. Compact and well-researched on the controversial issue of technology transfer, "Britain to Defy U.S. in High-Tech Export to Soviets," 4-27, provides a coherent analysis of a case in which Britain decides not to go through CoCom (Coordinating Committee on Multilateral Export Controls). "Ever Vulnerable, Canal Is More So Now," 5-10, excellently presents the raw military realities emerging out of the U.S. relationship with Panama. "Communism's Most Recent Crisis Called A Prelude to Era of Danger," with Peter LaBarbera 6-7, is lively on the proceedings of the Atlantic Council seminar on East-West relations, focusing the consensus outlook that "Political reform within the Soviet Union, election victory for the opposition in Poland and near civil war in China are clear signs of communism's failure and the ultimate dissolution of Marxist regimes." "Bloch Had Large Role in Drafting Strategic Review on East Bloc," 7-31, though choppy in spots, still serves well to inform us on Felix Bloch's involvement in shaping the administration's strategic review. "Chinese Economy Faces Grim Future," 8-9, is a well-composed report on an extract from the CIA report on China's economy, Gertz locating the major role inflation and shortages contribute to continued political unrest. Supplying hard data to support the thrust of this story, "Glasnost Hides Soviet Threat, Experts Say," 9-11, he does substantive reporting on the discussions at the Sovietologists conference sponsored by the National Strategy Information Center. He has good instincts for ferreting out scoops on intelligence matters, as with "Soviets Sneaking Arms to Managua," 9-18. Gertz was the first with this report that U.S. intelligence agencies had photographed a Nicaraguan ship at

a Cuban port being loaded with Soviet patrol boats and helicopters, in "apparent violation of a pledge by Soviet leader Mikhail Gorbachev to stop supplying arms to the Marxist Sandinista regime."

Gilmartin, Patricia A. *Aviation Week & Space Technology.* (★ ★ ★)
Still among the most competent of correspondents covering defense, she did less ground-breaking reporting this year. Part of the exodus from *Defense News* to *Aviation Week,* the switch coincides with a bit of a loss of the bloom off her work. "Cheney Hoists 'Red Flag' Against B-2, Orders Cost and Technical Review," 5-1, is very efficient reporting, competently summarizing the major issues involved in defense budget/defense policy now being negotiated between the administration and Congress. "House Defense Leader Attacks Air Force Plan to Add $1.4 Billion to B-1B Program," 5-29, updates the latest turn in the defense budget fight on the Hill. With "Administration Officials Say Defense Cuts Will Not Endanger Industrial Base," 6-19, Gilmartin selects highlights of testimonies at the ongoing congressional defense budget hearings, all of which serve to persuade us that "lawmakers pushing to reinstate funding for aircraft programs targeted for elimination by the Bush Administration may have a tough time arguing that the terminations will jeopardize the industrial base." Some perspective regarding the Democrats' action on big spending items is developed in "Panel Boosts Conventional Weapons Spending, Cuts Strategic Bomber Funds," 7-10, and "B-2 Clears First Crucial Votes in Congress; Restrictions Loom," with Michael Mecham 7-31, masterfully analyzes the current status of the defense budget in Congress, with a special focus on the B-2 and other strategic acquisitions. "Airborne Optical Adjunct Program Threatened with Cancellation," 8-21, updates the work-in-progress on this key SDI technology and all the politics that go with it. "SDI Experiments Set for Launch in January," 9-11, is big strategic news, informative and exciting on "the most ambitious directed energy weapons-related research to date into laser targeting and atmospheric perturbation with application to a future ground-based laser weapon."

Gold, Philip. *Insight.* (★ ½)
He's well-informed, with a broad knowledge of military history, but sometimes careless, on occasion overlooking or omitting critical information. "Battle for the Command of the Guard," 1-16, nicely balanced, clear and concise on the importance of the National Guard and the battle between state and federal government for control, is troubled by a soft lead that makes it seem too much like a brochure for the National Guard. "Private Virtues a Public Business?" 3-6, a report on the Tower confirmation flap, asserts that "despite all the titillating potential, the public seems uninterested. Or perhaps it might be more accurate to say that no one has bothered to ask the public." Gold is less than thorough, failing to note a number of public opinion polls and letters to congressmen on the issue. "Ex-Marine Provides Security to Vital U.S. Energy System," 4-10, is a decent effort at building up a story that really doesn't seem to have much substance to it. Gold is better with "Virtue Gets Vicious," 5-8, a three-part cover story on "special interest Puritanism," but it falls short because he offers no special insights or themes. "Contractors on Alert as 1992 Nears," 7-17, is a well-structured examination into how 1992 European integration will affect efforts by the U.S. defense industry and defense contractors to enter European markets, utilizing substantive quotes which are skillfully woven throughout. However, Gold neglects to mention a *widely* publicized CSIS report showing that 80,000 U.S. firms have gotten out of the defense business since 1982 — 2/3 of the total, shedding some doubt on his conclusions. "Newly Lean, Newly Mean, Still Marine," 9-25, is an outstanding, comprehensive report on the changes taking place with the U.S. Marine Corps as Commandant Alfred M. Grey moves toward a complete makeover of the corps. Gold notes that major cuts may be forthcoming in other services and, with budget constraints already guaranteeing gradual erosion, as the other services shrink "the Marine Corps, as the nation's force in readiness, becomes even more vital than ever."

Gordon, Michael R. *The New York Times.* (★ ½)
Defense correspondent. He's inconsistent. When he flexes his muscles, he can be very good, pushing hard on sources, hustling and getting the real information we need. However, he can be mediocre, producing superficial reports and analyses with dubious conclusions. Two stories from the beginning of the year illustrate this. "How a Vital Nuclear Material Came To Be in Short Supply," 1-1, is a slack effort, giving us the background on the Savannah River tritium plant, but nothing really from those who still oppose a new reactor. However, a 10 Best selection in general reporting, "Germans Accused of Helping Libya Build Nerve Gas Plant," with Stephen Engelberg, 1-1, making the case that Imhausen-Chemie is at the center of a web of western companies that have built a poison gas plant in Rabta, Libya, was the global intelligence story of the year. "Poison Gas Fears Lead U.S. to Plan New Export Curbs," with Engelberg 3-26, is comprehensive on the controls on U.S. companies dealing in chemical technology exports to the Third World states, underscored with a telling quote from an unnamed State Department official: "I live in fear of the day when the German Ambassador may come in here and say that Bonn has found an American company selling chemical weapons material to the Middle East." "Bush Plans to Cut Reagan Requests for Key Weapons," 4-24, is a superior overview of the underpinnings of the Bush-Cheney defense budget, hitting all the key points. "Reagan Arms Adviser Says Bush is Wrong on Short-Range Missiles," 5-3, relates how Paul Nitze, the "silver hawk," has become Mr. Softie of the '80s, but then Gordon does a rehash of this the following day, "Bush is Criticized on Capitol Hill Over NATO Crisis," 5-4, a make-news piece if we ever saw one. "Arms Pact on Fast Track," 5-30, is a solid, well-conceived once-over of the impact of the Bush conventional arms proposal, with good background and analysis. In "U.S. Weighs New Ideas for Geneva Arms Talks," 6-13, Gordon flexes his muscles and ability to get sources to leak, detailing a possible offer to limit silo-based multiple warhead missiles and Mirved mobile weapons. However, "In Shift, U.S. Eases Computer Exports to Eastern Bloc," 7-18, seems to consist of the Commerce Department press release and telephoned comments from Mosbacher and two trade associations. He's not clear exactly what types of computers can now be sold, possibly computers with a clock speed of 8 Mhz, but if so, that is a relatively meaningless specification. The real story, that the barn door is being closed too late, or that Soviet citizens who can travel in the West have been bringing them back in checked baggage for sale in the U.S.S.R. at enormous prices (see *The Economist,* 8-5, p. 44) is missed.

Goshko, John M. *The Washington Post.* (★)
State Department. A relaxed year for this veteran, so much so as to have been almost sluggish, the information in his reports is sometimes too scant to be worth the effort of wading through them. "Baker, Hill Discuss Renewing Nonlethal U.S. Aid to Contras," 3-2, which previews the Bush-Congress deal on Central America, is simply boring, and is additionally weakened by the use of "congressional sources," "many sources" and "administration officials" who don't say much of anything. "Nicaraguan Plan Shifts U.S. Emphasis to Diplomacy — and Compromise," 3-25, is blase "News Analysis" on the bipartisan accord on Central America. There's no treatment of the delegation to congressional committees of legislative "veto" power over the entire policy, and there's no support provided for the assertion that many "regional specialists" view the Sandinistas "the likely victors in a free and fair election." "Bonn Given U.S. Rebuff on Missiles," 4-24, is better, a clear account of U.S. clobbering West German Foreign and Defense Ministers over their proposal to negotiate away short-range nuclear weapons in Europe. In "U.S. Faults Israel on Territories," 5-23, on Jim Baker's provocative speech before the American Israel Public Affairs Committee (AIPAC), Goshko is accurate in intimating the increasing Arabism in the State Dept.'s higher circles. "U.S. Mutes Anger Over New Israeli Terms," 7-7, is just okay on Bush's balancing act. A front-pager, "U.S. Denies Recognition to Panama," 9-2, is standard, just a report on the usual State Department briefings, with little digging.

Greenberger, Robert S. *The Wall Street Journal.* (★ ★)
International relations correspondent. Two years ago, we applauded him for his first-string State Department coverage, noting his "knack for the subtle gradations of meaning in diplomatic subject matter." Though still consistent and reliable, the rigor of his reporting is becoming less than exacting. "Bush Waits For Concrete Gorbachev Acts Before Rewarding Soviets For Openness," 1-30, contains nothing new, but has a good compilation of laws and regulations that the U.S.S.R. would liked removed. "Baker Is Pressing 'Linkage' With Soviets, Even Though Policy Has Its Limitations," 3-6, is standard fare, done briskly, Greenberger breezing through the multifarious strains of the Washington-Moscow relationship. "Hussein to Back Bush in Seeking Mideast Peace," 4-20, gives us a cursory yet satisfactory sense of the intricate weaving of interests and politics in the region. However, "Missed Opportunity in Panama Election Opens Hornet's Nest for the White House," 5-1, doesn't go far enough. He captures adequately the Canal Treaty debate and Bush administration wavering, but misses too much of the underpinnings. Greenberger points out there have been 679 incidents of harassment of U.S. personnel by Panamanian troops in 15 months, including one rape, and we're left wondering what the administration is going to do about this. "Momentum Gathers to Give Special Trade Status to the Soviets as a Reward for Jewish Emigration," 6-27, neatly structured and interesting on the Jackson-Vanik amendment pegging certain U.S. trade benefits to the ability of Soviet citizens to emigrate from the U.S.S.R., covers the debate on lifting it with appropriate caution as to where it may lead. "New Soviet Moderation in Middle East Raises Prospect of Partnership With U.S.," 8-7, probing the possibilities of U.S.-Soviet cooperation for peace in the Middle East, is an interesting update, though without much analysis.

Griffiths, Dave. *BusinessWeek.* (★ ½)
Dealing with the nuts and bolts as well as the dollars and cents on the Pentagon beat, Griffiths is rarely dull. He does well with packing the necessary information and appreciable analysis into a few column inches. Occasionally, his editors ought to indulge him a little more space in order to expand the analytics when appropriate. Not a consistent slugger, though, he strikes out with "Defense: Tower Won't Have Much Room to Maneuver," 2-13, a short, but deadly four-paragraph squib in "Washington Outlook" which gives no recognition to the already developing clash around Tower's nomination. "Does Cheney Have Enough Artillery to Scrap With the Brass?" 3-27, provides food for thought in predicting that Defense Secretary Cheney may cross swords with the armed services chiefs in trying to make cuts in the military spending budget. "Why the Stealth Bomber Should Really Become Invisible," 4-17, is a well-ordered argument for using "stealth" technology for an unmanned cruise missile instead of the costly B-1B and B-2 manned bombers. Griffiths takes aim at the electronics in the B-1B bomber and other new weapons systems in "High-Tech Weapons Are Coming Under Friendly Fire," 5-22, a tightly written, persuasive commentary peppered with some juicy quotes from Air Force weapons brass who question the complex software. "Congress May Ram a Chopper Down the Pentagon's Throat," 6-5, gets right to the point on the battle of Defense chief Cheney to kill the Osprey tilt-rotor plane/helicopter. And punchily expressed commentary in "Defense Spending: It's Time for a Showdown with the Brass," 8-7, gives us a sense of the strategic and political sides in Washington defense matters, even though Griffiths takes a couple of rhetorical swipes at the B-2 without explaining. "Now, About Those Defense Savings You Were Expecting. . ." 9-4, warns that all the dollars saved in the DoD budget cuts in U.S. troops in Europe are likely to be spent by the DoD on other things, like upgrading those U.S. troops returning to Europe, packing information and analysis into a small space.

Halloran, Richard. *The New York Times.* (★ ★ ½)
Pentagon correspondent. This top pro among the profession still turns out fine-tuned "big picture" reports, but was off a bit on both pace and range this year. "New Helicopter Deaths Spur Debate," 2-21, describes a fatal crash in South Korea involving a new Marine Corps helicopter, yet we're at a loss to see who is spurring the "debate" from this story. Newer helicopters can do more, and new missions are more demanding on craft and crew, but aside

from the good bit on night goggles (amazing, but with limited peripheral vision) used by pilots, there's not much to chew on here from a policy or procurement point of view. A "Week in Review" feature, "Calling for a Redesign of National Security," 4-2, hinges on the long-awaited Bush "strategy review" of East-West policy and deftly reviews the postwar history of high-level U.S. documents, from the famous "containment" report, NSC-68, to the largely excellent, and ignored, "Discriminate Deterrence" report of 1987. In the process Halloran discusses how such review can augur real policy change, or merely codify the status quo in a political or budgetary exercise, a worthy topic for a fuller treatment. "U.S. Considers the Once Unthinkable on Korea," 7-13, is a solid look at a story that should get more headlines during the Bush era, that of U.S. troop withdrawal from Korea, with revealing quotes and numbers from all levels of the military. "Scramble On to Succeed Chairman of Joint Chiefs," 8-7, a splendid, informative overview, is enjoyable to read, Halloran writing and structuring it skillfully. "U.S. Is Sending Military Specialists to Train the Colombians," 9-1, fills in many of the holes around the still undecided upon advisory role for U.S. servicemen in Colombia.

Healy, Melissa. *Los Angeles Times.* (★ ★)
Pentagon correspondent. More seasoned, she's handling the important news on this beat with increasing aplomb. Still the range of her efforts needs expansion, and we'd like to see more imagination demonstrated in her stories. "Texan Faces Superhuman Pentagon Task," 12-17-88, is constructed as an interesting profile piece on the then-defense secretary-designate, John Tower; it reads well, providing good background information that develops our insights into the man. "Tower Pledges to Forgo Drinking," 2-27, effectively paced and well-organized is full of meaty quotes and good detail. "Relief, Concern for New Delays Expressed at Pentagon," 3-10, reads well, Healy having a knack for organization and good writing, but she just skims the surface, failing to convey more than a general feeling of malaise at the Pentagon as its members look forward to a few more weeks without a cabinet secretary. In "Panel Backs Basing of MX on Rail Cars," 4-13, on a proposal by the Defense Science Board to keep armed MX missiles moving over U.S. commercial railways at all times, Healy does a conscientious job covering the concerns and issues on all sides, adeptly handling much technical detail. She's carried away on a tangent in "U.S. Troop Cut Would Save Relatively Little, Experts Say," 6-1, focusing on the level of savings involved in Bush's proposed troop cut rather than the overall policy implications. "Panel Cuts $800 Million in Stealth Bomber Funds," 6-29, is straightforward, stand-alone reporting on the political winners and losers in the defense budget process. "Air Force Officials to Fight START Pact if B-2 is Killed," 7-22, competently presents the Air Force arguments for hanging on to the B-2, but she shortchanges us on the underlying political issues in the call by Congress to kill the plane. "Powell Charts the Middle Course," 8-11, gets us the background on Colin Powell, nominated by Bush as chairman of the Joint Chiefs of Staff. It's zippy and uplifting, good quotes strategically utilized, but it's a bit too brief, Healy terminating just as things get interesting.

Hitchens, Theresa. *Defense News.* (★ ★)
In their advertising campaign this year, *Defense News* marketers made a big deal of the new editorial bureau in Brussels, repeatedly promoting the young Hitchens as bureau chief. We think they could have placed a more seasoned hand in this post, particularly if *DN* is planning to highlight the bureau, but we are impressed with her efforts to impart a strategic angle on many hardware stories. She warms up in Washington with a few arms sales/technology transfer pieces, such as "Congressional Opponents of FSX Fear Technology Trade Benefits to Japan," 2-6, with plenty of inside-baseball industry data, and "Israeli Supporters Less Volatile Over Arms Sales," 2-6, a dog that did not bark piece. In Brussels, focusing on the defense implications of the 1992 European Community, NATO weapons, and SHAPE, Hitchens seems to have taken over some of the coveted high diplomacy stories once filed by Giovanni de Briganti. Two spring pieces pegged on President Bush's European trips stood out: "Western Leaders Fear New U.S.-Soviet 'Yalta' Pact on East Europe," 4-10, with revealing excerpts from Zbigniew Brzezinski's speech on a Bush-Gorbachev "deal" regarding the Warsaw Pact, and "Allies Ask if Bush Has Vision

to Lead NATO," 5-15, part of the continuing "vision-thing" problem Bush had with Europe as a result of his foot-dragging "review" of strategic policy. It's not a novel angle, but few others gave us a fair reading of European perceptions on the current White House. The other big Euro-issue this year was the flap over modernization of short-range nukes, Hitchens starting off slowly with "Belgium Joins W. Germany in Plea for Lance Missile Upgrade Delay," 4-17, a mere codification of conventional wisdom on Brussels, but coming back strongly with "NATO Shifts Philosophy on Short-Range Weapons," 6-12, a page one "analysis" that demonstrated the doctrinal "shift" on nukes from warfighting to deterrence only. She shows a nice grasp of budgetary legerdemain with "W. German Defense Budget: More Is Really Less," 7-31, and "NATO Naval Commanders Find Communication Is the Biggest Hurdle," 9-25, demonstrates her reach on sea power. But we're still not convinced that there's enough good work to go around for two European bureaus, Paris plus Brussels, though Hitchens appears to be carving a nice niche, having been given the opportunity.

Hughes, David. *Aviation Week & Space Technology.* (★ ★)
Hughes' quirky writing style keeps us entertained as well as informed. There's just enough jargon to appeal to the techies, but enough English for the armchair engineer. "Defense Electronic Industry Expects Little Sales Growth," 5-29, is a fascinating report which ought to draw the attention of economists and economic analysts in general, as it fixes attention on the rapidly growing economic role of "mental capital," brought on by excessive Defense spending on computer software. "Soviet Attempts to Buy U.S. Computers Continue Despite Customs Crackdown," 6-12, is an excellent, fun to read, police-blotter-type report on Soviet computer smuggling and spying efforts, and the Customs Service's countermeasures. "Airlines Evaluate Boron/Epoxy for Repair of Aircraft Structures," 7-10, is technically adept on the application potential of boron/epoxy in repairing aircraft. Hughes's "Quebec Will Upgrade CL-215 Waterbomber Fleet," 8-21, is a sprightly look at how Canada fights forest fires with air water bombardment: "The Canadair CL-215 waterbomber is the first line of defense in Canada, France, Spain, Greece, and other countries, many of which are fighting a record number of fires this year. The amphibian waterbomber fleet in the province of Quebec is part of a military-style organization designed to combat forest fires. . .Since the waterbomber was introduced in 1972, Quebec has cut its forest-fire losses in half." Are you listening, Smokey the Bear?

Kempe, Frederick. *The Wall Street Journal.* (★ ★ ★ ★)
On leave for most of the year, writing a book on Panama, Kempe scored high every time he did appear, the mix of reporting and analysis still of the high caliber he's demonstrated in the past. We cited him last year as the reporter of choice in Panama, and he beat everyone with his report from Panama City on what went wrong with the attempted coup against Noriega in October. His "Panama Tragedy: How the Inexperience of American Officials Helped Doom Coup," 10-6, was the best single piece written during the Panama debacle, with such an inside, intimate feel for the event that we want to at once take it as authoritative, a 10 Best selection in the foreign dispatch category. It was Kempe who first reported that the wife of coup leader Maj. Moises Giroldi relayed a message to U.S. officials in Panama City three weeks prior to the coup attempt that her husband and several other Panamanian military officers wanted help in deposing Gen. Manuel Noriega. To appreciate his report, compare it with the *NYT* effort of 10-8, a front-pager, written by four of its top national security/defense correspondents that still adds very little to the effort of the *Journal*'s lone Fred Kempe. "Noriega, With Fewer Cards, Buying Time," 5-17, is great reporting on the situation at the moment and the possible scenario for bringing down Noriega. Kempe catches the critical shifts in attitude there: ". . .the country waits, confident that change is near but bewildered about how it can come about." However, he quotes a citizen, "People are conscious of their impotence, but they are no longer resigned. The moment will come when they will no longer care about the danger." His "Rocky Relations: West Germany's Ties With U.S. Become Increasingly Testy," 3-13, one of the best pieces on the state of U.S.-German relations seen anywhere this year, grabs us with a very strong opening presentation and develops a perceptive analysis of Germany's eastward tilt, though Kempe disappointingly tails off for a

weak closing: "Its people have been long threatened by Soviet missiles and protected by American tanks, but they increasingly regard the threat as friends and the protection as threatening." Shades of Chamberlain and appeasement. Kempe demonstrates an instinctive grasp of German political culture, current European politics, and even cultural sensitivities.

Kempster, Norman. *Los Angeles Times.* (★ ½)
National security correspondent. Assigned to covering Europe and the Middle East, Kempster's extended his purview globally. New to this year's *MediaGuide,* Kempster impressed us with the range of his efforts and his ability to handle a wide order of strategic issues. "U.S. Lists Demands for Ties With Hanoi," 12-21-88, is competent on the withdrawal of Vietnamese troops from Cambodia, providing reliable background on the current situation there and an overview of possible U.S. diplomatic strategy. "U.S. Seeks to Bar Libya Plant Help," 1-4, is thorough on U.S. contingency plans for attacking the suspected Libyan chemical plant near Tripoli. He sticks to the bottom line in "U.S. to Stand by Contras, Bush Vows," 2-17, and delivers a fine report on Bush administration contra policy. Though somewhat repetitive in spots, "Baker Challenges Soviet Latin Policy," 3-31, is satisfying, basic reporting on Baker's speech; Kempster skillfully assembles appropriate quotes and melds the significant aspects of Baker's remarks with related developments. "High Number of Ambassadorships Go to Bush Friends, Contributors," 7-22, well-written, is thinly veiled Bush-bashing. "Repression in China Called Economic Blow," 8-9, on the findings of a CIA report, is tightly organized and okay as far as it goes, but fails to elaborate on the economic factors leading to China's inflation and balance of payment problems.

LaBarbera, Peter. *The Washington Times.* (★)
Diplomatic correspondent. Quick, in-and-out, reporting that properly locates and establishes the salient developments involved, but he's not a digger. There's so little expansion into analytics or new angles in these reports that LaBarbera is less satisfying than the competition. "Solarz Says U.S. Arms Needed in Cambodia," 6-13, is respectable reporting on the debate over U.S. military aid to Cambodian resistance, an issue likely to become geopolitically hot, telling us Democrat Solarz of the House Foreign Affairs Committee agrees with the White House and favors "military deliveries to non-Communist forces" in Cambodia, while Democrat Cranston of the Senate Foreign Relations Committee does not. "House Demands China Sanctions," 6-30, covering the overwhelming House vote to impose new sanctions against China over the objections of Secretary of State James Baker III, who defended the Bush administration's more cautious approach toward Beijing, is a story begging for analytical development, but he doesn't produce it. "As Sandinistas Exult, Poll Finds Majority Favoring Opposition," 7-20, is confusing; we are confounded to discover that a "scientific poll" conducted in Nicaragua, found that "Nicaraguans' first choice for president is Mr. Ortega, whom 13% chose. . ." How Ortega retains the status of "first choice" while at the same time the "poll showed 49% of Nicaraguans supporting a UNO presidential candidate," we are never told. "Democrats Poised to Cut All Aid to Contras," 8-9, is good, straight reportage, unadorned yet useful

Lewis, Paul. *The New York Times.* (★ ★)
U.N. correspondent. Down a bit in his rating, Lewis lost none of his professionalism, the salient details always clearly presented in his carefully reported dispatches. However, the analytical exploration we expected wasn't in evidence, though his editors may share culpability for this fault. Quick, neat and efficient reporting is a Lewis hallmark, and we get just that with "U.N. Tries to Streamline Inquiries on Poison Gas," 1-13, and "U.S. Vetoes U.N. Measure on Arab Uprising," 2-20, neither of which wastes space nor our time. His ability to tersely organize information comes across in "The War Over, Iraq's Ruler Announces Plan for Liberalization," 3-31. Lewis tightly works background and context into the report, but we were left unsatisfied with the sparse analytical treatment of Pres. Saddam Hussein's apparent shift toward "liberalization." "New Aid Strategy for Latin Refugees," 5-29, handles with solid professionalism an issue onto which other correspondents sometimes tack a biased spin. Lewis handles the reasons for the increased numbers of Central American refugees objectively and

competently fills us in on the "model" strategy for moving these refugees from the camps and off of aid. However, "Donors Urge Self-Help by Latin Governments in Refugee Plan," 6-4, an update on the refugee "crisis" in Central America, is a bare bones report. "China Is Said to Execute Some in Secret," 8-31, builds off an Amnesty International report of secret directives issued by the Party Central Committee ordering death sentences for the "counter-revolutionaries" who "committed the most serious crimes. . ..in order to make examples," but avoids any examination of the directive's authenticity. "U.N. Panel Puts China on List Of Human Rights Defendants," 9-1, is standard, basic reporting that unfortunately reads a little too much like the minutes of this subcommission's meeting. "Soviets, Welcoming Bush's Plan On Chemical Arms, Go Further," 9-27, accurate, well-organized and developed, reads with all the authority and professionalism we expect of Lewis. We keep looking for a broader analytic from him, but it obviously won't come without some prodding.

Mann, Jim. *Los Angeles Times.* (★ ★)
National security correspondent, covering Asia. An old, reliable China hand, this was certainly the year for him to utilize his experience and talents. We have a problem rating him on his China reporting, though, since he was so often double-bylined that we couldn't tell whether the work was primarily his or his co-author's. "U.S.-China Strains Surface; Basis of Relationship Shifts," 1-1, relies heavily on scholars, and the information is neither new nor compelling. "Journey Will Help Revise Geopolitics: Triangle now a Quadrangle," 2-19, is useful and informative on the current dynamics of power relationships among East Asian powers. "U.S. Curbs Travel of U.N. Chinese Aides," 3-10, is appreciated for the density of facts Mann produces, but we left looking for better explanation of why the U.S. is restricting the movement of Chinese diplomats. Mann can work credible sources effectively, as with a productive "U.S. Asia Policy Places Top Priority on Ties With Japan," 5-21, a comprehensive, engaging report on the complex nature of U.S.-Japanese relations in the context of U.S. policy toward Asia. A front-pager on the military action against the crowds in Tiananmen Square, "A Turning Point Seen in China," has the analytical touch and careful reporting of Mann, but we can't be certain about it since he shares the byline with David Holley. "U.S., Soviets Plan New Afghan Talks," 7-22, on a U.S. reevaluation of the Afghanistan situation, fails to provide sufficient analysis, being too distant from the Afghan issues. "Quayle Lobbied Foreign Nations for U.S. Firms," 7-30, attempts to catch Quayle committing an impropriety that falls flat, given the realities of the world market and the fact that lobbying for U.S. firms competing with foreign firms for foreign contracts is a common practice among other heads of state.

Mauthner, Robert. *Financial Times.* (★ ★)
Deputy Foreign Editor, he's on the lookout for NATO and Europe's security issues from his London perch, but his vision is never parochial. "In Search of a Concept for NATO," 12-20-88, is an early warning that West Germany is sending out signs that "a groundswell of opinion is building there for a radical reassessment of Western policy." "Hoisting Gorbachev on His Own Petard," 4-18, provides good, basic analysis on why the West needs to consider overall strategic goals before it finalizes any position on short-range nuclear arms. "Applying the Logic of Alice in Wonderland," 5-23, is well-argued, but unexceptional on whether the media are excluded from the tit-for-tat spy expulsions that take place between the British and Soviet governments. "UK, W. Germany Soften Positions on SNF," 5-30, is straightforward reporting on movement by the British and German governments on the short-range nuclear modernization issue. Saddled with a misleading headline, "Alliance Sets Goal of Promoting Warsaw Pact Glasnost," 6-2, turns competently into a discussion of current NATO strategy, with only a concluding reference to the promotion of democracy in Eastern Europe. In "Enter the EC Builders," 7-25, Mauthner combines historical perspective with a logical analytic framework exploring the role of the EC in bridging the East-West political and economic divide in Europe, a fresh angle few others picked up on. "A Baptism of Fire for Mr. Major," 8-1, hard-hitting analysis of Britain's allergy to 1992 integration, focuses on the then newly-appointed foreign minister, now Chancellor of the Exchequer, Mr. John Major, clarifying where he may steer policy.

McManus, Doyle. *Los Angeles Times.* (★ ½)
National security correspondent. Covering Latin America with frequent attention elsewhere, he's generally reliable and thorough, but still too often disappointing, his reporting a mixture of gems and duds. "Baker's Hectic NATO Trip Helps Set Up Personal Ties," 2-17, is crisply written, purposely focusing on personality more than on issues, an interesting account of the Secretary of State's whirlwind European tour that's useful and insightful. McManus falls short in "Administration to Seek Funds to Keep Contras Going," 3-14, using the space to detail who said what as the contras lobbied for more money. Opening with the statement that non-military contra aid has surprisingly strong support in the Senate and at least a majority in the House, we're left in the dark as to what brought this about. "U.S. to Focus on Salvador Rights Issue," 3-21, is unacceptable, McManus laxly citing "sources familiar with the President's *thinking* [our italics]," and simply fails to explain why in free elections Salvadorans voted in the ARENA candidate by a large margin. "Document Tells of Bush Contra Role: Was Reportedly Involved in '85 Honduran Deal," 4-7, comes across as a balanced examination on the issue of Bush's possible involvement in a quid-pro-quo deal with Honduran leaders during the Iran-contra affair. "Smiling Soviets Upset Baker's Game Plan in Moscow," 5-16, is prime McManus, discussing Baker's first trip to Moscow, digging below the surface and looking for evidence regarding motives. "Bush Faces Tough New Challenges," 6-4, well-organized analysis of the troop-cut initiative by Bush, outlines how the plan was conceived around the bureaucracy. "President Comes Away From Eastern Europe With 'Bush Doctrine' Taking Form," 7-14, an overview of the "post-containment" vision, distills for us the essence of the "Bush Doctrine," the cautious weaning of Poland and Hungary from communism's grip by promotion of Western free-market options.

Mecham, Michael. *Aviation Week & Space Technology.* (★ ★)
Congressional Editor. He's doing a fine job producing the survey-like scope on the congressional terrain affecting defense issues. The summaries work well, pulling the relevant data together, though we'd appreciate a bit more daring from him on the analytical side. "Soviet Sale of SU-24 Deepens Concern about Mideast Weapons Proliferation," 4-10, is a valuable survey of the status of ballistic missile technology proliferation in Third World nations, though poorly organized with important details buried. "Contractors Charge That Proposed Rules Threaten Procurement System," 4-24, supplies a careful rundown of the complaints of industry officials against the Pentagon's "strict new procurement regulations." An outstanding report, "Bush Includes Combat Aircraft Cuts in NATO Arms Proposal," 6-5, comes through with appreciable analysis of the President's NATO proposal to reduce conventional forces. "U.S. Suspends Military Sales In Wake of Massacre in China," 6-12, comprehensively summarizes the status of business relations between China and its major U.S. civilian and military aerospace partners. "Threatened Job Losses Fuel Congressional Opposition to FAA's Foreign Repair Rules," 7-3, productively reviews the controversial flight-safety vs. job-security issue. "House Panel Proposes $1 Billion Cut for NASA," 7-17, is itemized, informative on the House Appropriations Committee action proposing that "NASA take a cut of more than $1 billion in its proposed Fiscal 1990 budget, including a $400 million reduction in space station funding." Along the same lines, "Industry Slow to Comply With FAA Drug Testing Rule," 9-18, rips into the industry's soft-on-drugs attitude, with only one-quarter of the U.S. regional and national air carriers meeting the FAA deadline for submission of mandatory employee drug-testing plans.

Moore, Molly. *The Washington Post.* (★)
Military correspondent. More careless than usual, her efforts seemed softer this year with less hard data and accurate information turning up in her reports. She seriously botches up a report on new weapons systems likely to be closely scrutinized for potential savings as the Pentagon's new $315 billion budget request plays out against a backdrop of renewed concern for spending restraint. In "Hard Times Ahead Over Hardware," 1-24, she exaggerates costs, determining unit costs in a way no one else does. She's built up some key sources as "Pentagon May Lose Weapons," 4-15, reveals, listing Dick Cheney's classified internal recommendations for $10

million worth of budget cuts, garnished with reaction from an unnamed Pentagon official: "There are some generals here down on their knees." "B2 Bomber Cancellation is Urged," 5-19, lacks balance, focusing only on the perspective of former Defense Undersecretary Robert Costello, who dislikes the B2 because of cost overruns and its principal contractor, Northrop. "Defense Firms Restive at Funding Shift," 7-3, is better on the House Armed Services Committee deliberations, which "signaled what could be the beginning of a major shift in the way Congress funds the nation's military in the coming years of declining budgets." " 'Stealth' Bomber Called Success in First Flight," 7-18, is an acceptable effort to put the maiden flight of the B-2 Stealth bomber into political context. "Women in the Military," *Weekly* 10-2, a two-part series, is the best we've seen on the frustrations of females in military service and the trauma of a male institution being quickly transformed into a coed one.

Morrison, David C. *National Journal.* (★ ★ ½)
Defense correspondent. Since we first evaluated and rated him four years ago with a single star, we have seen him improve every single year since. He's always been among the hardest working of journalists on this beat, and is decisively on our list of must-read defense correspondents. He still needs, however, to work on smoother delivery. In "Undersight," 1-7, Morrison attributes the Energy Department's snafus regarding nuclear weapons production to a lack of Congressional or even executive oversight, making a decent case, but the reading is tough going over the bureaucratic acronym field. He's efficient with "The MITIgating Factor," 2-4, the writing tight in this "Defense Focus" column examining the issue of Pentagon support for private ventures aimed at maintaining certain key technologies. "After the Bombs Drop," 2-18, shows Morrison does his homework; this piece on Command, Control and Communications (C3) is logical, coherent and balanced by quotes from those on all sides of the issue. "The Part-Time Military," 3-4, is superb analysis, well-researched and well-written, this time on the question of active versus reserve strength in the military. "Missile Mania," 4-15, encapsulates the land-based missile modernization debate and is particularly prescient: "A prominent straw in the wind, however, would have Bush opt for deployment of both systems. Such a compromise might make sense politically, but not fiscally." A compromise was indeed struck. Moonlighting in *The Atlantic,* "The Build-Down," 6-89, is a nuts-and-bolts guide to cutting the defense budget, with a nice analysis of how the Pentagon spends its money. "Vice President for Space," 7-29, offers an enlightening comparison between Bush's Space Council and Reagan's SIG Space, though the interview with VP Dan Quayle is weak. He speaks of vision and boldness, but Morrison doesn't press him for substantiation. A *NJ* cover, "Only the Beginning," 8-19, has much information scattered over several pages, but there's no unifying theme, and is hampered by occasionally clumsy writing. His best for the year is "Spy Stalkers," 9-9, a super-thorough look at the counterintelligence business in the U.S., the bottom line being that despite additional money, the U.S. still has no coherent trans-agency approach to protect national security secrets.

Oberdorfer, Don. *The Washington Post.* (★ ★ ½)
State Department correspondent. He's able to handle just about everything, his access to knowledgeable sources apparent and nicely balanced with his own acumen. But like many veterans on a beat, he still sleepwalks occasionally, going through the motions and missing pieces he would not have missed in earlier years. "Europe Awaits U.S. Moves on Security and Economy, Baker Finds," 2-20, a snapshot analysis of James Baker III's maiden voyage to NATO states as Secretary of State, lacks any new insight. His strength is the politics of foreign policy/defense decisions, as we see in "Soviet Military Cuts Proposal Parallels West's," 3-7, a skilled dissection of Soviet Foreign Minister Shevardnadze's conventional arms proposal which identifies and weighs all the issues. "Contra Talks Were Intense, Personal and Secret," 3-26, displays real savvy as to what details are important in the 22 days of "confidential, intense and sometimes contentious negotiations" between Secretary Baker and congressional Democrats that led to bipartisan accord on Nicaragua policy. "Snags Hit Gorbachev Economics," 4-23, is a competent account of the contents and significance of the current CIA-DIA evaluation of Gorbachev's growing economic troubles, though it would not have been inappropriate for him

to have introduced his own critical evaluation of the agencies' report. "Eased East-West Tension Offers Chances, Dangers," 5-7, is a well-composed collage of the emerging long-term world strategic vistas opening up as a result of the changes in Soviet society, as seen by some of America's senior foreign policy thinkers. He brings to our attention their concurrence that we're witnessing the end of a historic era which had once been defined by communism as a political phenomenon. "Bush Proposes Cutback in U.S. Troops in Europe," 5-30, covers all the bases on Bush's proposal for NATO conventional arms control negotiations, but "House China Vote Shows Power of Domestic Politics," 7-1, is analytical pablum on the House vote for sanctions against China, a big yawner from Oberdorfer. "Underestimating Soviet Resolve in Afghanistan," *Weekly* 9-24, comes across the story late, yet Oberdorfer makes it worth reading, establishing that a debate brews within the administration and U.S. intelligence community over the reasons for the strategic miscalculation.

Ottaway, David B. *The Washington Post.* (★ ★)
State Department. A former Middle East correspondent, Ottaway's feel for the strategic nuances of political developments in that region is one of his strengths. He didn't break much new ground this year, though his harvesting of critical information made up for it. "Foreign Aid: Sweeping Change Debated," 2-27, a "Federal page" filing on State Department-AID-House Appropriations Committee negotiations on structural changes in foreign assistance is of limited interest to the non-professional, but does remind us of the dimensions of foreign assistance to Egypt and Israel ($8.4 billion per year between them). "Strike on Iraq No Longer an Easy Option for Israel, Analysts Say," 3-31, is the kind of Ottaway report we appreciate — digging beneath the surface, he usefully gives background shape to upcoming U.S.-Israeli talks, the focus low key, on "a rapid change in the Arab-Israel strategic military equation. . .not yet fully absorbed by Israeli political leaders." "Angolan Rebels Ask Rise in U.S. Aid," 4-25, an update on the status of UNITA policy debate, works better than others we saw because of its insights into the attitudes of various departments. "Bush's Soviet Trade Stance Hailed," 5-13, is a fine, early full treatment of the brewing reconsideration regarding Jackson-Vanik Amendment. "Kabul Forces Gain Combat Edge," 6-27, delivers a satisfactory evaluation of the tactical situation of the Afghan war, noting that "Soviet military experts and Afghan government forces have gained a surprise battlefield edge over the mujahedeen resistance and its 1980s vintage weapon of choice: the U.S.-made Stinger antiaircraft missile." "Administration May Switch and Support Angola's Admission to the IMF," 7-10, alerts us to the imminent "first step toward U.S. diplomatic recognition of the Marxist Angolan government," namely, "the Bush administration. . . switching its vote against admitting Angola to the International Monetary Fund." He still puts out perishable products at times as with "Senior U.S. Diplomat Investigated by FBI as Possible Soviet Spy," 7-22, a rambling, disorganized and overblown story on middle level diplomat, Felix S. Bloch, under investigation for espionage for the KGB.

Pasztor, Andy. *The Wall Street Journal.* (★ ★)
Defense, Pentagon correspondent. Picking up where Fred Kempe (on leave writing a book) and Tim Carrington (reassigned to London) left off, some of his bigger efforts have been under a shared byline, but he's not wet behind the ears as his solo efforts reveal. He does reasonably well on coverage of the procurement issue, appearing to have been given that assignment for the year. He brings us up-to-date informatively and without any spin in "Northrop Contacts With 2 Consultants Cited in Affidavit," 1-5. "Lengthy Controversy Over Tower's Nomination Is Leaving the Pentagon Somewhat Defenseless," with Gerald Seib 2-15, is sharp on how the Tower imbroglio threw a monkey wrench into Pentagon planning, actually focusing on the future of land-based missiles, but we get little exploration of budgetary and program areas. "Attempts to Streamline Pentagon Procurement Soften Amid Resistance of a Jealous Bureaucracy," 6-6, a respectable overview of Cheney's emerging plans for rejiggering the procurement apparatus in "the Building," establishes how difficult it is for any civilian Secretary to get a handle on all the levers in this most complex of government agencies. Pasztor persuades us that Cheney has the right ideas, but he'll need political help from Bush and good luck. "Stealth Bomber Comes Under

Fire in Congress as its Price Mounts," with Rick Wartzman 7-13, holds together as an informative consideration into the future of the ultra-expensive new plane. "Senate Votes to Raise Northrop's Liability for Fixing Problems With Stealth Bomber," 8-1, tightly written, gets us through the information quickly and efficiently. "Defense Contractors Seek to Strengthen Ethics Codes to Avoid New U.S. Controls," 8-31, handily outlines voluntary support for ethical behavior, but the added feature is the way Pasztor captures the debate on sanctions for violations within the administration as well.

Pear, Robert. *The New York Times.* (★ ★ ½)
State Department correspondent. A *NYT* big foot on the foreign policy beat, Pear turns out another year of solid work. A problem that bears correction, though, is his tendency to rush with his material. He's quick in getting us critical news the moment he finds it, but we saw an increase this year of reports that drop off precisely where they should have shifted to higher gear. For example, "U.S. Experts Doubt General's Democracy Vow," 2-4, reports that in 1985, the DEA received a document produced by the Paraguayan narcotics police identifying General Andres Rodriguez, Paraguay's new leader, as a drug trafficker, but doesn't follow-up or expand on the information. "Rightist Surge Complicates Decisions For U.S.," 3-20, is more back and forth on El Salvador's new government. Pear does report some democratic expressions from the State Department, but doesn't work the story properly, leaving out consideration of why Salvadorans chose ARENA Party candidates. A terrific "Pact Challenged By Bush Counsel," 3-26, shows what Pear can really do, laying bare the conflict of White House counsel C. Boyden Gray and Jim Baker over Baker's "preclearance" deal with congressional Democrats on contra policy: "Such a congressional check on Presidential power would be unconstitutional if it appeared in a law." "The PLO's Many Voices Differ About its Commitments to the U.S.," 5-2, promises more than it delivers, but does convey a sense of the critical significance of diplomatic linguistics and nicely gives us the flavor of PLO hard and soft sides. We find insightful "Why the U.S. Is Urged to Think Again About Afghanistan," 6-11, an informative portrayal of President Najibullah, who "has shown more staying power that most American officials had expected from a 'puppet,'" yet the larger picture remains opaque. "Now, the U.S. Looks at Cambodia Differently," 7-16, is superlative coverage on shifting U.S. policy, Pear chronicling the perspective *vis-a-vis* Cambodia as a Vietnamese depot, with the Khmer Rouge now a threat.

Pincus, Walter. *The Washington Post.* (½ ★)
National security. An off-year for this veteran investigative reporter. Stuck with following a non-story, his attempts to massage something out of it were blatantly obvious all year. "A Chance to Fill in Iran-Contra Blanks," 2-23, though styled "news analysis," is really mediocre speculation on a half-dozen Bush appointees who may have had some knowledge of the Reagan administration's darkest hour. "Nominee Denies Knowing of Iranian Arms Deal," 4-18, develops some smooth reading on Reginald Bartholemew, but little else. "Verdict Opens New Options for Investigators," 5-5, with Dan Morgan, ostensibly delves into the implications of Oliver North's conviction, asserting that it "strengthens the hand of investigators and could increase the likelihood of further disclosures." However, it's not supported. "Bush Given Ultimatum on Gregg Nomination," with Joe Pichirallo 5-17, on the nomination of Bush's old national security crony, Donald Gregg, for ambassador to South Korea, is basically a platform for Alan Cranston to rehash Iran-contra, demanding new documents. "Secret Reagan File Found by Senate Intelligence Panel," 6-24, is dense, convoluted and confusing. Presumably an attempt to demonstrate the complex web of government operations, Pincus exposes a "heads of state" file from the NSC that was overlooked by the Iran-contra panel, but this goes nowhere, Pincus not even telling us the contents. Better, "CIA Chief Fights Congress on Access to Documents," 7-14, is a good, juicy story of CIA Chief Webster trying to ward off the House Intelligence Committee's prurient curiosity about his agency. "$82 Million for Missives to 'Occupant'?" 9-19, is but one of several reports Pincus produced later in the year on costs to the taxpayers of abuse by government of various privileges. Informative, they contain more thunder than appropriate for the subject.

Polsky, Debra Lynn. *Defense News.* (★ ★ ★)
Staff writer covering special assignments. A relatively new pen at the weekly, Polsky joined the editorial staff in 1987 to cover land warfare. She is no novice when it comes to handling procurement policy, defense funding or a variety of weapons programs, and this year she merits hearty applause for her stories appearing on 4-3 and 4-10 on the DoD's weapons laboratories — outstanding work earning a 10 Best nomination for general reporting: 4-3, "Experts Decry DoD Laboratory Efforts," "Defense Contractors Compete With DoD for Big Lab Dollars," and "Researchers Lost in Paper Chase"; and 4-10, "Officials Offer Several Solutions to Solve Research Doldrums," "Scientists, Officers Struggle to Improve Work of Labs," and "Given Their Evolution, What Is Expected of Laboratories in the '90s?" Industrious and hardworking, she drew on interviews with 78 experts in government and industry to come up with a picture of why the weapons acquisition system doesn't work. (The Pentagon's 68 military labs spend $8 billion per year and still fail to develop the basic technologies for more capable weapons.) There's added value to this story we saw nowhere else — the effects of Polsky's publicizing the labs' failure to perform. (In early October, 1989, the Secretary of the Army proposed a major restructuring of the Army laboratories to make them more responsive to the needs of the service's combat units.) With "Large Firms Maneuver For Trainer Market," 7-17, she quickly focuses the effect of the rising demand for training packages that include equipment, maintenance and instruction — a trend toward domination of the U.S. military simulation and trainers market by a handful of corporate giants. "Industry Is Wary of DCAA Plan to Ease Rift Over Auditing," 9-25, on the unexpected heavy criticism the Contractor Risk Assessment Guide is drawing from defense contractors, identifies the invective being slung back and forth with terse, to-the-point precision as symptomatic of a larger problem: "Many industry financial managers and auditors despise each other." The report is splendid, Polsky assembling the pros and cons, the gripes and complaints in a way that can only help industry and the Defense Contract Audit Agency improve their relations. Reporting what is appropriately critical of the audit force, she maintains thorough balance, adding in the perception that CRAG still appears to be the only way to reduce auditing. "Industry, Navy Oceans Apart on View of Problems at Service Labs," 10-9, assessing responses from aerospace and electronics industry representatives as well as laboratory technical directors on competition and cooperation between Navy labs and industry, is another well-balanced effort at locating the essentials involved, Polsky never ever tipping her hand as to where she might line up on the dispute. An impressive virtuoso among the *DN* stable of professionals.

Rosenthal, Andrew. *The New York Times.* (★ ½)
Pentagon correspondent. New to the defense beat, Rosenthal got his feet respectably wet, but he needs more seasoning and some work at building up his rolodex. His early efforts were marred by a tendency to be slightly out of focus. A profile on the Secretary of Defense, "Cheney, a Conservative, Is Also a Compromiser," 3-12, covers a lot of territory, noting Richard Cheney's House floor fights for aid to the Nicaraguan, Angolan and Afghan rebels, noting his extensive background in intelligence, little recent involvement in military policy and no experience in managing a bureaucracy the size of DoD. But it's flawed by too heavy an emphasis on the "compromise" angle. "The Military Prepares for (Relative) Austerity," 3-19, also points up the need for more experience. A good outline of the situation Cheney faces at the Pentagon, Rosenthal stumbles by suggesting "[the] time pressures on Mr. Cheney are acute," since many of these issues remained unresolved into midsummer. "Missile Shield Must Be Balanced Against Other Goals, Cheney Says," 3-29, simply misses the mark, reading into the Secretary's remarks a policy perspective that isn't there. "Pentagon May Spend More on Plane It Plans to Cancel," 5-5, reveals steadier work and concisely makes the point that "The debate over the Osprey graphically illustrates the legal, financial, strategic and political maze involved in cutting the $300 billion military budget." "It's Loneliest at the Top of the Bureaucracy," 7-23, on how it's harder than ever to recruit top scientists and executives for top government jobs, underscores the point with a quote from Norman Augustine, 53-year-old chairman of Martin Marietta and one-time potential defense secretary: "It is not possible for a person my age and my profession

to serve in the government anymore." However, this is old news. "House Backs Cut in Bomber Project of $1 Billion in '90," 7-27, effectively shows the 257-160 vote as symptomatic of the Democratic approach to national defense: cutting the budget request for the B-2 by 20%, placing restrictions on the program and ignoring for all practical purposes Defense Secretary Dick Cheney's plea not to "nickel and dime" the Stealth bomber to death. "Senators, at Odds with House, Pass Military Measure," 8-3, is thorough but without flash on the Senate vote on the 1990 defense budget, complete with an inside look at the rancorous debate.

Sawyer, Kathy. *The Washington Post.* (★ ★ ★)
One of the few space reporters who captures all the exciting developments on the subject while still keeping her feet on the ground and her eyes attuned to the sometimes mundane but critical details. "Crossroads in Space: Orbiting Lab Raises Questions of Mission, Need," 4-20, an is excellent presentation on the fight over the future of the space station which could be operational by 1996. "Crossroads in Space: Mission to Moon, or Mars?" 4-21, an outstanding motivational effort to get the space program going again, is aimed at prodding the White House committing itself to a long-range objective. Her enthusiasm is evident in "Slower, Cheaper Approach Proposed to Save Aerospace Plane Project," 6-29, which details the technological issues involved in the National Aero-Space Program (NASP) to build the X-30, able to take off from a runway in a single bound, and whose "goal is to work its way gradually to Mach 25, the velocity required to go into Earth orbit." "Shuttle Starts Magellan Probe On Way to Venus," 5-5, is terse, well-focused on our first interplanetary mission in 11 years. "Space Council Gives Boost to Experimental Jet Craft," 7-1, is a tightly written report on the National Space Council's decision to "recommend to President Bush that the proposed aerospace plane be developed at a reduced pace and cost, with the focus on pure research rather than any practical application." "New Titan IV Rocket Orbits Secret Satellite," 6-15, details the first Titan IV rocket, the new "Defense Department's workhorse launch vehicle," and its secret military payload, an advanced early warning satellite of the Strategic Air Command. "Moon Missions' Physical Legacy Still Holds Many Mysteries," 7-20, sentimental, but rewarding on Apollo 11's twentieth, that unfortunately is troubled by a rambling lead.

Sciolino, Elaine. *The New York Times.* (★ ★)
Washington bureau, covering foreign relations. On leave part of the year, the occasional reporting she did then holds up well as professionally reliable and solid. She's best when diligent, as with her focus, near year's end, on the failed Panama coup. "Bush Selections Signal Focus on Foreign Policy." 1-17, assesses the appointment of James Baker III as Secretary of State with the suggestion that foreign policy will become a centerpiece of the administration's efforts, even over domestic policy. However, asserting her point of view, she clouds the analysis — President Bush and Secretary Baker "face an impossible challenge: they must protect American strategic interests while seizing what may well be a once-in-a-century opportunity to reshape East-West relations." "What Was Lost in Afghanistan?" 2-5, a concise presentation on the eve of final Soviet pullout, works well as an analytical effort that doesn't stray from the evidence at hand. "Montazeri, Khomeini's Designated Successor in Iran, Quits Under Pressure," 3-29, on more rumblings of change in Iran as Ayatollah Montazeri is forced out, nicely gathers nuance against appropriate background information and provides respectable exploration of implications. "Independent Labs Play Key Role in Aerospace Testing, Verification," 5-22, a look at how major defense contractors seek outside help in testing, demonstrates her versatility. "Once Again, A Survivor," 10-4, is far too weak for its front page display. We get little concrete information regarding the attempted coup in Panama, and the observation that Noriega "has been able to stay in power because, despite much anti-Noriega language, Washington was reluctant to take the kind of brutal military action that would have overthrown him," is common-place, with no new dimension explored. "What Should Washington Do About Noriega?" 10-8, satisfactorily reviews the pros and cons of various options, raising the possibility that President "Bush will simply beat the Noriega drum loudly while marching in place." Sciolino reports that none of his advisers seem to have a clear idea where to turn next, and that

despite reports of tensions between some administration officials over policy there, none of the parties is advocating a shift in basic policy. "U.S. Says Leaders Of Panama Revolt Were In Disarray," 10-11, is really very good reporting, with Sciolino taking the material way beyond the limited headline. While accurately informing on the Pentagon's portrayal of an inept and divided Panamanian coup leadership, she also gives appropriate play to the assertion of an escaped rebel leader that the U.S. bears onus for the failed coup by its failure to deliver on promises of assistance.

Scott, William B. *Aviation Week & Space Technology.* (★ ½)
Balanced between an A in engineering and a C+ in journalism, Scott needs to restrain the excessively technical jargon. When he does, he's readable and informative; otherwise, his dispatches tend to be intelligible only to a specialized audience. "Falcon Eye Flier, GEC Helmet Aid F-16 Mission Flexibility," 4-17, would have been terrific, with Scott's own flight experience coming through, but we get sentences like "The Falcon Eye system was designed specifically for CAS/BAI and reconnaissance applications, while Lantirn is tailored for high-precision strikes and deep interdiction missions." CAS/BAI is an acronym for close air support/battlefield air interdiction, but nowhere is this ever deciphered, much less explained. A word to those in the balcony would be much appreciated. He does splendid work with "F-117A Crash Reports Cite Pilot Fatigue, Disorientation," 5-15, an outstanding summation and evaluation of the sanitized version of the otherwise classified 300-page accident reports of the crashes of the F-117A Stealth fighter in 1986 and 1987. Scott displays sophisticated insight into how the Air Force tests the outer limits of new technologies, how it explores and develops their potential for new combat tactics, how it trains on the new tactics and its questionable response to blunders that cost lives. "NASA Adds to Understanding of High Angle of Attack Regime," 5-22, covers a fascinating subject (how a NASA project is producing an invaluable wealth of data for aeronautical designing), but Scott's shortcoming — excessive technicalese — is splattered all over the piece. "Ball Develops Multi-Anode Microchannel Array for Space Telescope, Defense Uses," 6-12, a super description of a new, second-generation photo-intensifier device capable of magnifying one single captured photon into one million electrons, draws the appropriate conclusions on its potential for SDI-related deployment. "USAF, Northrop Counter Congressional Critics With Positive B-2 Test Data," 7-17, focuses clearly another side on the effort to save the B-2 from congressional budget cuts. His best for the year exemplifies a real strength, reports written off his own personal experiences. "AT3 Demonstrates Feasibility of Cargo STOL With Long Range," 9-4, in which Scott co-pilots the experimental advanced technology tactical transport, gives a readable and conscientious report on its capabilities.

Silverberg, David. *Defense News.* (★ ★ ★)
International defense trade, technology transfer and the intense (and therefore intriguing) bureaucratic wrangling over economic security issues are the specialties of this prodigious, widely-published reporter. Silverberg churned out numerous updates on the Commerce-State-Defense turf standoff over international arms sales and technology exports to friends such as Japan and Europe, and semi-foes like the U.S.S.R., as in "State Department Prepared to Wrest Control of Export Policy," 2-20, and two FSX pieces, "FSX Controversy: Harbinger of Tougher Defense Trade Agreements," 3-20, and "FSX Plan Walks Shaky Ground as Crucial Senate Vote Nears," 5-15. The distinguishing characteristic of Silverberg's coverage, notably absent from most entries on bureaucratic politics, is his command of the substance behind the political-power maneuverings. It is a pleasure to read someone who actually knows about the aircraft, or sub-components, that are the items debated in these fights. We look forward to Silverberg's analytical pieces with great expectation and anticipation, as he and Peter Adams are the best "trend" story writers. Two must reads: "U.S. Analysts Examine Soviet Budget Cuts," 1-30, on numbers-crunching in the age of Gorbachev; and "Mosbacher Forges National Security Role for Commerce," a 4-17 profile of the Commerce Secretary whose stature is enhanced by his close friendship with the Texan in the White House. Given the presence of several *DN* European correspondents, we see a bit of staff overlap, such as "European Commission Chief Urges

Caution in Trade with East Bloc," 6-19, covering Jacques Delors's trip to Washington with an admirable go-slow recommendation on Eastward investments. Silverberg was way ahead of everyone all year on following and breaking the story of CFIUS investigations, beginning with "Wafer Firm Sale Causes Commerce, DoD Jitters," 12-19-88, on the sale of Monsanto's electronics materials division to a West German company, and following up with excellent analytic reporting in "Defense Industry Comes to Know, Often Dread, Power of CFIUS," 9-18, and "Proxy Boards Frustrate Foreign Investment in U.S. Defense Firms," 10-9. Silverberg is someone to watch closely, as his prime issues — East-West trade, West-West technology cooperation — are sure to crystallize in the next year or two.

Smith, R. Jeffrey. *The Washington Post.* (★)
Weapons correspondent. His reporting would be better appreciated if he could keep his own agenda out of it. Smith's predilection for providing partisan circles a forum via his dispatches makes his reliability questionable. "Army Poison Gas Stockpile Raises Worries in Kentucky," 1-22, provides good maps and data on a typical damned-if-you-do, damned-if-you-don't situation, but we question why he hardly gave the Army any benefit of doubt here. "Groups Urge Nuclear Arms Control by Limiting Production of Materials," 2-26, gets "the-cart-before-the-horse" award, and it highlights Smith's shortcomings. Emphasizing a familiar arms control clique's call for a nuclear freeze in disguise, Smith is on top of this issue. But it's clear that he is promoting this ad hoc group of environmentalists and disarmers, such as John Isaacs of the Council for a Livable World: "It is the coming hot issue for environmental and arms-control groups." "Bush Advised to Hold Steady on Nation's Foreign Policy," 4-9, is the first substantive report we saw on Bush administration's policy review process. "Arms Cuts Gain Favor as Anxieties Ebb," 5-8, is an informative sketch of U.S. voters' shifting mood about the Soviets, but Smith's treatment is too facile. As with any analysis of poll results, the questions not asked are as important as the answers. "Alliance Caught in Superpower Squeeze," 5-14, is a good attempt to analyze a highly complex, shifting strategic situation, Smith making a decent attempt to locate the short-range nuclear missile issue within the larger context. "New U.S.-Soviet Accord Entails Philosophical Shift," 6-8, is adequate as an evaluation of a pending pact to reduce risk of conflict from accidental military encounters, seen as "a basic philosophical shift for armed forces historically trained to expect the worst from one another." His "Intelligence Ties Endure Despite U.S.-China Strain," co-written by George Lardner Jr. 6-25, is a respectable example of hard-nosed research and reporting on the evolution and history of the U.S.-China strategic intelligence-sharing relationship from 1971 to date. He's sloppy, though, with "House Panel Hears Top Soviet Military Officer," 7-22, on the appearance of Soviet Marshal Sergei Akhromeyev before the House Armed Services Committee, failing to convey the thrust of the testimony and indulging minor inaccuracies.

Stanfield, Rochelle L. *National Journal.* (★ ★ ½)
Diplomatic correspondent. The *NJ* editors did well in moving Stanfield to this beat, exactly when foreign policy dynamics call for fresh thinking and no encumbered alliances with hackneyed sources. Last year, we noted approvingly Stanfield's careful work on environmental stories. She rarely disappointed us this year, pushing on the fast-moving frontiers of foreign policy, but again, carefully. "The New Establishment," 1-21, compares President Truman's foreign policy to what President Bush may do, a fast-paced scholarly piece that's very interesting to the history buffs, but not necessarily illuminating as to Bush's choices. "Offbase," 2-11, is a nicely organized, effective roundup of U.S. bases abroad and debate over which ones to keep open, structured well with many intricacies covered admirably. Stanfield relates this only lightly to the broader defense picture, however. In "So That's How it Works," 6-24, we find Latin American ambassadors are learning that real influence on U.S. policies come from lobbying, not traditional diplomacy, complete with fitting examples. She might have mentioned the inactive role of the Organization of American States. "Window of Opportunity," 8-5, is superlative analysis and reporting, telling us that despite the threat to U.S. hostages and the hanging of Col. Higgins, the Mid-East peacekeeping efforts remain alive, but depend on U.S. diplomatic agility, and, important to any

Mid-East analysis, Stanfield raises the history/religion element and deals with it effectively, noting "Emotion dominates conflict." Her "Beyond the Cold War," 9-16, is astonishingly clear-eyed for a rookie on this beat, methodically examining near-term scenarios suggested by Soviet and East Europe specialists. Again clear and methodical in "Nicaragua's Rattling the White House," 9-30, Stanfield charts out options keyed to the coming elections in a crisp, one-page brief. "Back in Fashion," 11-4, is a very timely look at the United Nations and what might realistically lie ahead in this new world of potential U.S./Soviet cooperation.

Strobel, Warren. *The Washington Times.* (★ ★)
State Department correspondent with an appreciable background covering defense issues, Strobel moved across a wide range of stories this year, his instincts for issues better than his efforts at analysis. Though we don't get many scoops, he's still consistent and reliable. He did score a coup with "Error Made Missile Impotent During '86," 3-20, on a story that has been filtering about the defense intelligentsia for the past few years, but really moving beyond those circles: the questionable shape of the U.S. command and control system for nuclear forces. "Commercial Launch Takes Momentous Step in Space," 3-29, is a spiffy look at the effort to involve private industry in space business, focusing on the first-ever American private rocket launch, by Space Services Inc. of Texas. "Bush Aides Take Notice of Fusion's Big 'If,' " 4-11, is a quick and timely alert that the White House and Department of Energy are taking serious interest in the intriguing, maverick "chemical fusion" experiment recently reported at the University of Utah. In "Cheney Predicts Germany Will Unify If Policy Succeeds," 5-8, Strobel makes a good attempt to provide the proper diplomatic context for an intriguing statement by Defense Secretary Cheney: "While any unification of East and West Germany appears years away, that's a natural outcome if we're successful in our other efforts." "Chinese Official's Visit Here Put Off as Ties Unravel Rapidly," 6-8, covers the deterioration of U.S.-China relations as the U.S. studies further options, including a ban on all technology transfers to China, the suspension of insurances against political risk for U.S. companies by the Overseas Private Investment Corp. and the opposing of new loans to China by international financial institutions. "U.S. Worries China May Renege on Vow Not to Aid Khmer Rouge," 6-20, gives a forward look at what might prove to be a foreign policy litmus test for the new Beijing power equation — Cambodia policy. "Afghan Killings Could Affect How Rebels Fare in Fighting," 7-18, is straightforward, tightly updating developments that affect U.S. policy toward the Afghan rebels, with an informed focus on the assassination of several key Afghan resistance leaders and their aides by a rival faction. "Tools Center of New Export Control Fuss," 9-13, timely and informative, does a fine job reporting on the internal administration debate over future U.S.-Soviet trade policy.

Toth, Robert C. *Los Angeles Times.* (★ ★ ½)
National security, covering the U.S.S.R. and arms control. With good instincts developed over the many years he's been on this beat, Toth handles big picture material with aplomb while keeping sharp attention to salient detail in the straight news stories. A rare misfire, though, with "CIA's Gates Picked as National Security Aide," 12-29-88, which skims over the fact that Gates was the personal choice of Brent Scowcroft and considered by many to be highly competent and a Soviet expert. Instead Toth wastes a lot of space on Gate's possible Iran-contra connection, dredging up all of the old allegations about George Bush *ad nauseam.* "Iraqi Use of Gas Spurred U.S. Action on Issue," 1-5, is a tightly-written examination of the underestimated effects the Iraqi use of poison gas had on Iranian forces in the war, with a deft elaboration on the implications of this successful use of chemical warfare. "Planners Split on How to Meet Nuclear Threat," 2-24, begins with a dramatic opening, but turns into little more than a lengthy overview of the defense debate — from the Eisenhower administration to the present — over the strategy of preemptive strikes or retaliation. While interesting, it's only moderately useful. "Paul Nitze: Last of the 'Wise Men,' " 3-22, is an excellent profile piece — well-written, insightful and organized — in which Toth explores Nitze's influence on presidents over the years, providing good background and interesting anecdotes that bring some of recent history alive. "Plan Is a

P.R. Hit for Bush but Hard Work Remains," 5-30, is your good, basic news analysis. Toth's fairly comprehensive, but could go farther on the implications of where Bush must go from here. Following Bush's troop-cut initiative, "Bush Faces Tough New Challenges," 6-4, illuminates with a well-organized picture of how the initiative was conceived by going around the bureaucracy. Toth maintains balance and is characteristically thoughtful on strategic arms control in "Proposed Arms Pact Launches Strategy Debate," 7-25. Competency is a real staple of Toth's reporting and he handles nicely the significance of Soviet proposals to the U.S., how they affect key obstacles to a broad new agreement in the Strategic Arms Reduction Talks, and initial U.S. response with "Shevardnadze Gives Bush New Arms Proposals," 9-22.

Trainor, Bernard E. *The New York Times.* (★ ★)
Military correspondent. Down considerably from his previous rating, Trainor astounded us with a terrible sloppiness on attribution of sources and an unacceptable abnegation of the responsibility for analysis. "City Under Siege: Afghan Rebels Foiled, for Now," 3-16, precisely because it is written from Washington, D.C. and not Kabul, begs for military analysis. Instead we get a string of "American military experts say. . .," or ". . .an American official said. . .," plus "Logistic experts say. . ." More of the same appears in "Afghan Insurgent Siege: Planning Appears Weak," 3-22, with not a single observation attributed to a specifically named source. Trainor doesn't produce any firsthand information here, utilizing solely the speculations of Pentagon-bound officials. However, with years of military service under his helmet, Trainor has the advantage of substantial connections into the defense and military community, and he's able to put that to good use from time to time. "Soviet Tale of Survival at Sea: Rescue Sphere Saves Only 1," 5-4, shows how he can outclass the competition. While everybody got the Soviet sub accident story, no one else had the contacts to piece together how a rescue sphere malfunctioned, or how one Soviet sailor miraculously survived. "Bush's Latin Gamble: Hoping Panamanian Armed Forces Will Oust Noriega," 5-17, delivers an informative picture of the structure and power relationships within the Panamanian Defense Forces, the combination here of analysis and background information working well. However, though we don't fault Trainor for being unable to unravel the alleged enigma of the armies at the time, "Beijing's Lessons: Loyalty to Whom?" 6-7, is another "analysis" that strings together estimates and observations from "officials," "specialists," and "experts," none of whom is ever identified by name. "Pentagon Worried by Use of Reserves," 7-16, sets a standard Trainor ought to employ consistently. This report on how heavy reliance on reserve units is posing a readiness question, is extremely well done precisely because Trainor specifically identifies by name and position major parties in this discussion. He's strong also with "Risky Military Cards," 8-3, a model for a concise options package, skillfully identifying and critiquing three plausible military options available to Bush for dealing with the Lebanese hostage-takers.

White, David. *Financial Times.* (★ ★ ★)
Defense correspondent. Deft reporting on all sides, from NATO to London to DC, White is versatile and innovative. He makes the most of his vantage point, developing an angle or side to a problem skimmed over by U.S. correspondents. He caught our attention in "Army Kept Waiting for Its Christmas Gift," 12-22-88, an excellent analysis of the tank competition between the British Vickers Defence Systems and U.S.'s General Dynamics, providing background material and capturing the nuance of the British government's dilemma. "Shevardnadze Makes Life More Difficult for NATO," 1-20, examines concisely and with steady, solid analysis, the implications of the Soviet Union's announcement that it would withdraw some nuclear weapons as part of its planned troop and equipment cuts in Europe. "Re-Grouping for Battles to Come," 3-17, provides a nice sample of White's added edge as a defense reporter, particularly because he provides good international business coverage involving defense that's too often lacking among American defense correspondents. "The Dilemma of New Arms for Old," 4-15, is a truly superb, innovative and entertaining overview of the short-range nuclear modernization question. Using a question-and-answer format, White is incisive, analytical, and straightforward. "Indian Missile Test Raises Fears of Arms Proliferation," 5-25, tight and comprehensive, delivers

informatively on the threat of missiles that could be used for chemical weapons delivery by Third World countries. "Lingering Problems Cloud East-West Hopes for Arms Control," 6-2, is a deft overview of the various talks taking place and some particular sticking points. We find thorough and articulate analysis in "Between Cuts and Burden-sharing," 7-7, examining how the withdrawal of U.S. troops from Europe is connected to other outstanding NATO issues. "Superpowers Set Pace Over Chemical Arms," 9-28, coherently summarizes the principles and initiatives for the destruction of lethal chemical weapons stockpiles, without neglecting the dimension of the problem involving the proliferation of chemical arsenals in the Third World.

Wilson, George C. *The Washington Post.* (★ ★ ½)
Military correspondent. Certainly still one of the top pros in the field, this veteran lagged a bit behind the pace he's set for himself in the past. The material in his reports is almost always solid, but this year we saw less of the refreshing originality that set him apart from others handling the stories in and around the Pentagon. "U.S. Answer to Soviet Military Cuts Weighed," 1-3, on the ideas regarding reassessments among NATO experts, is Wilson in high gear — excellent quotes deployed effectively, a style of presentation that moves us along smoothly, a very competent and reliable grasp of the material he's working. Wilson wasn't in the cockpit having to make the split-second decision, but we have to appreciate "Admiral Messaged F14s, But Too Late," 1-10, which reports that Navy jets involved in the dog fight with Libyans were in a cautionary "warning yellow" situation rather than the "red" condition reserved for fire-at-will encounters when they fired. "Flat Budget Would Weaken Pentagon, CBO Says," 3-31, is a straightforward report on the Congressional Budget Office report regarding the implications of a five-year freeze on the defense budget, a not-unlikely proposition. "Armed Forces' Civilian Chiefs Are Selected," 4-4, on the naming of three service secretaries by Defense Secretary Cheney, is the height of lazy reportage; Wilson presents raw, undigested information, cribbed directly from the DoD press release, on Army Secretary-designate Richard Armitage, Navy designate Lawrence Garrett, and Air Force designate Donald Rice. "Ex-Chief Warns Army to Prepare for World of Next Century," 6-3, is an excellent presentation of issues facing the U.S. military in the post-Cold War universe, but we don't know whom retired Army Chief of Staff General Edward C. Meyer is addressing, nor where, nor when. "Pentagon Shifts Policy on Arms Development Costs," 6-20, is a fine evaluation of an important policy change at Defense: The new Pentagon team has decided that the DoD will pay the full cost of bringing weapons to production rather than continue to require contractors to help finance the expensive development phase. Ouch. "U.S. Advisers Allowed to Leave Latin Bases," with Michael Isikoff 9-13, takes us as far as it can on fleshing out the Pentagon's perspective for an expanded military role by the U.S. on the drug wars in Latin America.

Wright, Robin. *Los Angeles Times.* (★)
National security, covering the CIA and the Middle East. Given Wright's considerable experience covering the Middle East and her respectable knowledge regarding Iran and terrorism, we expected more from her than she delivered this year. Perhaps lax editors don't recognize her ability to do better, too much weak material sliding past them. "Pinpointing Guilt Seen as Hardest Task," 12-29-88, does little to illuminate on responsibility for the bombing of Pan Am flight 103. Please. Do we really need "a State Department expert" to tell us the Iranians might want to retaliate for the downing of *their* airliner!? "Khomeini's War on Book Seen as Bid to Unify Iran," 2-22, is too speculative, and not very unconventional at that, spinning around on the notion that the Salman Rushdie flap is a ploy enabling Khomeini to divert attention from his domestic problems, but with nothing about how this may fit in with his foreign affairs agenda. "U.S. Protests to Syria Over Envoy Incident," 3-10, is squeaky thin informationally on the detention of two U.S. military attaches by the Popular Front for the Liberation of Palestine after they were caught checking out a PFLP camp in Syria. "Iran Faces Key Challenges at Home, Abroad," 6-5, isn't new nor are there fresh insights, but it is a competent and very well-written analysis of the problems facing post-Khomeini Iran. In "U.S. Probe Focuses on Alleged Spy Payments to Bloch," 7-29, covering the ongoing federal investigation of Felix Bloch, the

evidence of his guilt is ephemeral, but Wright tries to fluff it out. However, nothing still remains nothing. On a bigger-picture effort, she's better. "Counterspy Effort: Gaps in the Net," 7-27, uses sources from different angles on the issue, and proves informative on the problems with U.S. counterintelligence capabilities. "Chemical Arms Pact Called Near," 9-13, handles the attempts at preparing the way for a global ban on chemical warfare quite well, Wright working various aspects of the story for a satisfying report on the potential for a superpower agreement. "Chemical Makers Back Efforts on Arms," 9-21, nicely follows up, informing on a major initiative by the world's chemical makers to help achieve a ban on deadly poison and nerve gases.

SOCIAL/POLITICAL REPORTERS

Adler, Jerry. *Newsweek.* (★ ★)
Senior writer. Adler's work has a characteristic mark: a witty, spirited style that makes otherwise mundane topics a pleasure to read. "Jocks With Books," with Karen Springen and Howard Manly 1-9, looks at the practice of Duke and Notre Dame demanding academic quality from their athletes, not giving them any special treatment. "The Fanciest Dive," with Nina Darnton and Todd Barrett 2-13, takes a humorous look at *Sports Illustrated's* 25th anniversary swimsuit edition and the influence it has had on other sports magazines: "It took *Sport* a few years to get the right formula. Its previous swimsuit issue, in March 1986, used pictures of female athletes, including a real swimmer. Never again; this year's 'Hot Swimsuit Issue' features the athletes of Elite Model Management." "A Case of Morning Sickness," with Sue Hutchison 3-13, wittily explores "the yin and the yang of morning television: Bryant Gumbel and Willard Scott," and the infamous memo in which Gumbel skewers many of his co-workers, most notably the unpredictable weatherman. In "The Final Days of Howard Simons," 5-22, we get a respectful, sensitive portrayal of the former *Washington Post* managing editor as he deals with his impending death from pancreatic cancer: " 'I have no regrets, no apologies,' [Simons] added; 'I am completely at ease with myself.'. . .Perhaps if he had led a less exemplary life, he would not face death with such confidence." Another profile, "The Temples of Lapidus," 6-26, is detailed and clever on architect Alan Lapidus and his unique designs. "Les Jours de Gloire," with Christopher Dickey 7-24, describes the international parade held in France in honor of Bastille Day; peppered with French phrases, the article provides the flavor of a whirlwind, spectacular celebration. "Bran Ferren: Truly Special Effects," 10-2, a short profile of an innovative designer, effectively captures the unique distinction of his creations, but in the short amount of space allotted, tells too little about the man behind the designs. But his environmental coverage is thin in spots. "Alaska After Exxon," reported by Harry Hurt III, Lynda Wright and Pamela Abramson 9-18, attempts to make sense of the "Babel effect" surrounding the spill, "in which the din has become an issue itself." And "Where Will the Cranes Go?" with Karen Springen 4-3, about a dispute between the Audubon Society and the Denver Water Board which wants to build a new dam on the Platte, twenty-four miles out of town, raises many questions and answers almost none, lacking technical data on the question, just talking about lawns vs. birds, a million Denverites vs. Audubon Society bird-watchers.

Allen, Charlotte Low. *Insight.* (★ ★ ★)
Law reporter. The magazine's law expert, Allen's coverage of legal issues is consistently clear and informative, and we're drawn to her material because of its vitality. We know she's going to hold our attention. In "Interagency Fight on Insider Funds," 4-10, she deftly weaves in stats and commentary to produce a firmly-grounded look at the tug of war between the IRS and the SEC to see who gets control of money obtained illegally by insider traders. "When Awards Become Too Punitive," 4-17, on the practice of awarding excessive punitive damages and the test case now before the Supreme Court, presents the issues lucidly, leaving the reader with an I-can't-wait-to-see-what-happens-next feeling. She's clear, concise and intelligent with an often obtuse subject in "Bondholders the Losers in a Buyout," 5-1. In "Stepping on the Dotted Line. . ." 6-26, Allen fascinates, despite the esoteric topic, with an informative, well-written piece on the extension of tort claims to breach of contract cases and how some judges are starting to throw these cases out of court. "Flag Ruling Unfurls Patriotic Fury," 7-10, very well-written, reads like an insider's guide to the Supreme Court decision. "When the Gavel Fails to Compel," 8-28, is lively on proposals to put a 12-month cap on jail sentences for civil contempt. "Special Delivery," *Policy Review* Summer, is sweeping on barriers to adoption, calling for specific policy reforms which include tax incentives for adoption, interracial adoption and tapping prospective adoptees outside the mainstream, including people over 40, single parents, etc. The article abounds with her creativity.

Allen, Henry. *The Washington Post.* (★ ★ ★)
"Style" reporter. With the departure of Stephanie Mansfield for *Vogue* and various book-writing chores, Allen has become the preeminent wordsmith in the section. Alternately humorous and stoic, Allen's ability to draw us in impresses. In "This Is 1953 Without Air Raid Drills," 1-29, his pleasant insights about this "harmonious era" flow graciously, evoking all the guiltless pleasures the American century once promised. Allen takes us on an exhilarating ride up and down the tracks of pop culture in "Fashion, Music, Politics, Inventions. . .Where is the Former Frenzy of Change?" 2-27, a slangy treatise on America's cling to the safe and familiar, supporting his idea with a mix of quotes ranging from *Spy* to Daniel Webster, and of course, author Alvin Toffler, whose famous book inspires Allen's lead: "What future? What shock? These are dog days in America. Nothing seems to be happening." But his comic touch is heavy-handed in "Meryl Streep, From Turnpike to Causeway," 3-17, going too far on celebrities who take up causes. He is sarcastic, taking cliched swipes at Meryl Streep's New Jersey roots, and trivializing himself and his story instead of Streep. "What Is This Thing Called Spring?" 4-2, refreshes, telling us all the things spring means to Allen. Though versatile, technology isn't Allen's forte, we find, in "At the Geographic, Life, Death and Laser Art," 6-16, a two-dimensional report on holograms as art. "The French Revolution in Brief," 7-14, is just that, filled with lesser-known facts: "Children are given names like Dandelion, or Rhubarb, in honor of nature." Well, maybe it sounds better in French. "Woodstock, For What It's Worth," 8-15, one of the best commentaries we saw on the "phenomenon," recognizes the absurdity in much of the commemorative activities and lets it speak for itself. "The End, Or Is It?" 9-27, jests on the fuss created by Francis Fukuyama and his *National Interest* article "The End of History?" but Allen can't decide whether to make the piece clever satire or a serious profile. Despite the occasional bumps, he is Mansfield's heir apparent.

Alter, Jonathan. *Newsweek.* (★ ½)
Senior writer covering the media. We knocked Alter a bit last year for his routine election-year coverage and thought he'd get back on track this year. His is still a byline we look for, but his writing remains less compelling than it has been in the past. "The Art of the Deals," 1-9, questions the practice of the "cooperation" that takes place between news organizations and the celebrities to whom they give exposure: "The unspoken essence of most deals is access in exchange for favorable coverage. . ..It's a slippery slope from quote clearance [repeating quotes back to sources before publication] to manipulation. In fact, that courtesy was extended three times during the course of reporting this article. It probably shouldn't have been." "The President and the Press," 2-6, a look at some of the problems that reporters face in covering the White House, contains little new information. "Karl Marx, Meet Marshall McLuhan," 5-29, is a bland exploration of the impact television coverage has on authoritarian regimes. Concluding that "TV simply won't provide extended coverage to a story without pictures," we're left feeling TV is the same the world over. In "Unwilling Informants?" 6-26, Alter's thoughtful in reporting the Chinese government's use of U.S. media film footage to identify and track down student dissidents, suggesting "Perhaps the China experience can reinforce the idea that 'protecting sources' should take on more resonance when one is shielding them from torture and prison than from political accountability." "When Anchors Meet Actors," 7-24, focuses on the "news" show combining live footage with actors "reenacting" a news event, sounding the warning bell early on this trend. In "Gays in Washington: Voters Aren't as Alarmed as Politicians Think," 9-25, Alter cites past sex scandals to support his argument that "when harnessed to the overwhelming power of incumbency, candor can save even gay politicians who solicit minors," but conspicuously missing is a discussion of the contributions made by the gay politicians whom he identifies in the piece. "The Intellectual Hula Hoop," 10-9, is a rehash, though a well-written one, of Henry Allen's *Washington Post* piece on Francis Fukuyama, adding only the history of the media blitz on "The End of History" thesis.

Apple, R. W., Jr. *The New York Times.* (★ ★)
Chief Washington correspondent. Apple is the designated bigfoot of the *Times* political coverage, but he's edging over the hill as a reporter and not yet confident as a pundit. He can still get his arms around some of the big issues, of course, but on others grass grows under his feet. He wonderfully captures the spirit of the new Secretary of State with "In Senate Forum, All Hail Baker!" 1-18, on James Baker III's Senate confirmation hearings: "Every word floated out, in his soft Texas drawl, as if it were borne on a little pillow of reasonableness and courtesy." "An Effort To Recover," 3-11, supplies the pros and cons of the aftermath of the Tower vote, Bush seeking to end the rift, with a limp conclusion: "Which is the greatest political peril: being labeled a wimp, or losing momentum so early in the game." Apple misses the essence of the James Baker deal in "A Balance of Bush, The Congress and The Contras," 4-2, a slim analysis that fails to mention the Gorbachev factor at all. As far as it goes, "Budget Agreement Finesses Tough Questions," 4-16, offers fairly good analysis of where the budget agreement works and where it doesn't, noting that, "It will be harder now for Wall Street and foreign governments as well as ordinary American voters to say, as they have grown used to saying, that no one is doing anything," but Apple assumes the deal hinges on Richard Darman "giving up" capital gains. Apple's "Capital" column, 5-3, is mere Beltway baloney, a typical "Everybody Knows" story about the necessity to raise taxes. "They" admit this at cocktail parties, but assume a different pose in public, he advises. Hmmmm. "Measured Judgement," 5-5, submits some very sharp analysis of the North verdict, noting that, "where the jury was the hardest on Mr. North was where he seemed to have behaved like the loose cannon that he often denied being." They "did not want him to take the fall for the higher-ups, and it seems a safe bet that the country as a whole, however much people may have tired of soldierly glamour, will sense a certain fairness in that." We see the Apple of yore, flexing his analytic muscles as he assesses "Bush's New Direction," 5-29. The analysis from the NATO conference in Brussels opens strongly: "Many here believe that this continent stands on the verge of a political reorganization not unlike the one engendered by Metternich at the Congress of Vienna in 1815." In "A Polish Journey," 7-12, he offers some new analysis, sound stuff at a facile level. Another strong effort from Apple, "Bush and Panama: Chance Lost, Perhaps to Hesitancy," 10-8, pushes a powerful case in this news analysis of fault line in Bush: " 'It's hard to imagine Lyndon Johnson or Ronald Reagan hesitating, especially in the case of a man we've been trying to get rid of for the better part of 10 years,' said a Democrat with long foreign policy experience."

Applebome, Peter. *The New York Times.* (★ ★)
National correspondent. An engaging writer, Applebome pulled hurricane duty in the fall, with work in the Carolinas on Hugo and, surprisingly, the Jim Bakker trial. Before that, though, it was hit-or-miss feature stories that ranged from the sublime to the weird. "Energy vs. Environment: Clash on Carolina Coast," 1-30, about a promising oil and gas leasing proposal off the Atlantic Coast ranging from Long Island to the Outer Banks is designed to give full vent to the anti-development side: "But environmental groups and local residents say that the coastal eddies could bring any pollutants and spills rapidly to shore, imperiling a priceless system of estuaries. And they worry that a major find would encourage industrial growth that the area could not support. The region's fresh water supply and road system are already strained by rapid growth brought by tourism." "Setting the Table For Kids' Cuisine," 3-19, is nice feature journalism that explores how demographics has more families eating out with kids, and consequently restaurant chains are catering to them, but there's nothing on how bratty, crying kids are handled. The central question of how this kind of policy affects adults without children is left to end of the piece, where Applebome hastily notes that restaurants "may have trouble getting the parents to visit on their own." "Leprosy Patients Recall a Pain Beyond Disease," 3-27, is strange on the country's only center for Hansen's Disease or leprosy in Carville, LA, and muddled to boot, but Applebome certainly covers a topic not seen elsewhere. "Atlanta in Accord on Plans for Domed Stadium," 6-7, gets it all on a big issue in the state of Georgia. "After Hurricane Relief Gives Way to Despair," 9-27, is superb, sensitively drawn, with selective human anecdotes bordering the statistics on Hurricane Hugo's long- and short-term effects on

South Carolina. "Bakker Is Convicted on All Counts, First Felon Among TV Evangelists," 10-6, focuses on the legal, rather than the carnival aspects of Jim Bakker's trial, a dignified dispatch after all the hoopla.

Archibald, George. *The Washington Times.* (★ ★ ★)
National correspondent. Always a dependable, hard-working journalist, Archibald had an exceptional year, using his formidable investigative prowess to uncover sleaze and unethical excesses within the Beltway. Archibald, with Paul Rodriguez, uncovered one of the year's major scandals on Capitol Hill, the articles which appeared 8-25 a 10 Best selection. "Sex Sold From Congressman's Apartment," 8-25, a double-barreled expose on the private life of Rep. Barney Frank, an acknowledged homosexual. The story, though, was "Frank's Lover was 'Call Boy,' " 8-25: "A male prostitute provided homosexual and bisexual prostitution services from the apartment of U.S. Rep. Barney Frank on Capitol Hill on a periodic basis from late 1985 through mid-1987." In the companion "School Used as Base for Sex Ring," 8-25, we get background on the male prostitute's drug trafficking and arrests for sexual offenses with a minor. Congressman Frank meets with Archibald and Rodriguez, and spills the beans himself in "Frank Gave Call Boy House Favors," 9-7, conceding that "he used congressional immunity to write off delinquent District parking tickets that his one-time lover, prostitute Stephen L. Gobie, said he received while using the Congressman's car to keep appointments for illicit sex." Elsewhere on Capitol Hill, he knows how to assemble critical detail, providing us information we didn't see explored as thoroughly elsewhere in "Hill Staffers Swept Along on Tide of Rising Salaries," 1-30, on the import of congressional pay raises to staff salaries. Archibald draws blood with "Oakar Aides Given Cushy Jobs with Her Subcommittee," 3-21, as the next day a House Banking Committee probe of the Ohio congresswoman's alleged favoritism is announced. Archibald gives us more juicy details of "payroll abuses" associated with Rep. Mary Oakar (D-OH), in "Banking Chairman to Probe Possible Abuses by Oakar," 3-22. "Cooperation Over, Rumsfeld Tells FBI," 4-5, draws attention to an important side-effect of the Tower nomination hearings: Serious people, like Donald Rumsfeld, will not cooperate with future FBI background investigations of nominees, unless the integrity of the process is restored. "Top Democratic Aide Wields Sharp Probes Against GOP," 6-6, is a must-read expose of the impressive career of major Watergate figure Robert Spenser Oliver: "For the past ten years as a key Democrat operative on Capitol Hill, Mr. Oliver, now chief counsel for the House Foreign Affairs Committee, has waged war-by-investigation against dozens of his political enemies." He continues snooping into questionable relationships, as with "The Unelected: Congress' Silent Power Brokers," 6-6, on illegal influence peddling by congressional aides.

Babcock, Charles. *The Washington Post.* (★ ½)
Among the *Post*'s team of investigative sleuths, Babcock is one of the harder workers, steadily digging into Congressional improprieties this year, although the results were more shadowy than substantive. He outlines a questionable relationship between Sen. Dennis DeConcini and retired Phoenix businessman Earl Katz, who travels under government "official" auspices, in "DeConcini Places Fund-Raiser on Senate Payroll," 1-7. While the report is somewhat garbled, it asks questions about who goes where and who pays for it. "Lobbyists Put Democrats on Track for Posh Trip," 2-3, details the expenditures and payments of this trip before it occurs, but doesn't tell us anything about the legitimacy of the seminar topics or its sponsors. Somebody has to tell us about it, and Babcock does a good job with "Scowcroft's '88 Income Was $500,000," 3-14. He doesn't make a solid case for Rep. Newt Gingrich's book *Window of Opportunity* as being the same kind of unethical arrangement Speaker Jim Wright employed, but "Gingrich Book Venture, Unusual Partnership Gained Tax Benefit," 3-20, is the article cited by Rep. Bill Alexander (D-Ark.) to begin the campaign suggesting Gingrich violated House ethics rules. "Texas Well Deal Boosted Assets of Wright Farm," 4-21, is very specific on Mallightco's Sabine Lake well that so benefited Jim Wright, thanks to partner George Mallick. He presents the facts effectively, but an overview putting it all in perspective is appropriate. "Tobacco Industry Led '88 Hill Honoraria Givers," 7-11, is only half the story, listing who gave

what, but not specifically to whom. "Cranston and 'NonPartisan' Voter Registration," 8-6, is a non-starter implying Sen. Alan Cranston bought votes. He doesn't prove his point, nor is there a great deal of information here.

Balz, Dan. *The Washington Post.* (★ ★)
National editor. Amidst his editorial duties, Balz manages to do a fair amount of reporting, generally going for subjects that lend themselves to broader themes suggestive of political trends. With some of the paper's former heavyweight political reporters absent during the year, Balz had a heavier load than usual. He teamed with Helen Dewar on "Tracing The Steps In Tower's Downfall," 3-29, a 10 Best selection, to provide a behind-the-scenes account of the John Tower fiasco. It's informative, but Sen. Sam Nunn and the Democrats win the spin control here. "Speaker Wright And The Business Of Politics," 4-23, "is a tale of power and money: Jim Wright had one and wanted the other." Balz gets into the gritty details of Wright's book royalties and his ties to Mallightco, and we feel as if we'd gotten a peek at House Ethics Committee counsel Richard J. Phelan's report. "The Public Politics of Rumor," 6-8, is an excellent survey of political rumor-mongering, "a phenomenon that has taken root in this media-intensive era of negative politics: trafficking in rumor and innuendo for political advantage." "Redistricting Transformed by Computers," 6-12, finds an interesting angle on the playing field for 1990: redistricting is being altered by the rapid advances in computer technology. "Republican Party Chiefs Endorse Aggressive Tactics, Rally Behind Atwater," 6-16, on the Republican National Committee's three-day meeting, reports party activists inclined toward more aggressive campaign tactics against the Democrats, which "contrasted sharply with the response of Republican elected officials." However, more analytics were needed. "Governor At Risk On Abortion Issue," 8-1, is one of the very few three-dimensional stories we saw all summer on Florida governor Bob Martinez's call for a special legislative session in the wake of the *Webster* decision. Balz places the issue of abortion in Florida in the context of state's political and judicial history, and allows Martinez to present his views. "New Jersey A Campaign Laboratory For Politics In 1990 And Beyond," 11-5, is a real disappointment, with Balz telling how the national parties and abortion groups are micromanaging New Jersey assembly races. He never interviews any voters, just candidates and campaign consultants, giving the article an insular, inside-baseball tone while missing out on the big picture.

Barnes, James A. *National Journal.* (★ ½)
Chief political reporter. A mixed bag from Barnes this year, a superficial side appears at times. Perhaps tired from the rigors of an election year, Barnes spent part of the year behind the curve. He focuses on what will happen with the institutional relationship between Congress and the President in this administration in "Trying to Be Friends," 2-11, a good start on what does become a substantive question for the year. But "Ron Brown's Fast Start," 5-6, is deadly-dull puffery for Brown on the nuts and bolts at the Democratic National Committee, without a word about issues or the Jesse '92 problem worrying Democrats. "Only Three Years to Go," 7-15, looks forward to 1992, from the Democratic side, interesting, but needless to say, a tad premature. "Mr. Tabor Comes To Washington, Again," 7-29, is weak on the House candidate running for the third time, not zeroing in on the financial factor, but with a $250,000 campaign fund increase plus costs for a consultant, it becomes an obvious element that Barnes misses. "Politics After *Webster*," 8-12, is well-written, but not quite on the mark: The controversy over abortion rights may influence voting decisions of Americans, but overall, it's not likely to affect the political balance of power nationally. He also overlooks New Jersey in discussing the impact on gubernatorial elections. He's at the top of his form, though, with "At His Own Pace," 10-21, a 10 Best nomination, on prospects for Sen. Bill Bradley (D-NJ) running for President in '92. It's an early report, but politically sensitive and three-dimensional, even though Bradley refuses to be interviewed on the subject.

Barol, Bill. *Newsweek.* (★ ★)
Senior writer. Barol's features are breezy, entertaining, a pleasure to read, ultimately escapist. Specializing in Americana and lifestyles, his writing lets the magic of the heartland shine through. "Put On A Happy Face. . .Or Else," 2-27, is a delightfully madcap look at the success of Bobby McFerrin's ditty and the backlash, ". . .consider the possibility that a bad attitude is hazardous to your health. . ..In other words: Don't worry, be happy, or die." "Back to the States, the Long Way," 3-20, warmly profiles 70s pop singer Chris Rea as he makes a slow comeback: "If Rea isn't a kid anymore, neither is he a burned-out crooner coasting through his upper 30s on old glories and beer endorsements. At 37 he's a strong songwriter, a seasoned bandleader and a singer of gruff, plain appeal." "The Stuff of History," 4-24, reminisces about the Smithsonian's National Museum of American History, reminding us that "American history is bigger and broader than just the first ladies' gowns, and in all its million parts it belongs to all of us." "Big Fun in a Small Town," 5-29, about a new computer game that allows "players" to design, plan and build their very own cities, then watch them fall prey to changing property values and tax rates, crime statistics, population shifts, pollution counts and traffic shifts, is deliciously entertaining. "Batmania," 6-26, gets the pulse of how the men behind the movie did it, walking the delicate line of covering the story without being part of the hype or reviewing the film. Less enjoyable was "Saturday Night LIVES!" 9-25, a slow-moving history of the show "that blew apart and redrew the boundaries of television comedy," that over-analyzes the show's fluctuating success rate over the past 15 years. "Oh, Those Darn Kids," 10-2, effectively captures the collective zaniness of a Canadian comedy troupe, The Kids in the Hall, stars of ex-SNL producer Lorne Michaels's latest HBO/CBC series.

Barone, Michael. *U.S.News & World Report.* (★)
Senior writer. We were pleased to see this former *Washington Post* editorial page staffer's byline reappear after some hiatus, as we recalled his former analytic facility. However, the value of his insights this year was less consistently rewarding than in the past. In "Paying the Price For Political Errors," 5-1, Barone delivers a political damage control report for the Iran-Contra scandal as the Oliver North trial comes to an end, taking a big picture approach and analyzing how Bush will walk away virtually undamaged. "Wright, Coelho, and the S&L Fiasco," 6-12, is first rate as Barone uses a special Congressional election in Texas to show how campaign financing and the S&L crisis are intertwined. As usual, Barone makes good use of anecdotal evidence, and provides sharp analysis: "S&L's in Texas and elsewhere continued to make imprudent and sometimes crooked loans, confident that the Bank Board did not have enough money to shut them down." He has a fine question to work with in "The Democrats' Success Formula," 6-26: "Why so many Democrats have been elected consistently in this conservative era and why they enjoy a bigger margin now in the House, 259-175, than when Ronald Reagan became President." However, his answer is simplistic at best: "Operating out of their offices as Congressmen, seeking out community problems they can help solve, they have taken on roles once performed by big-city machines and courthouse-square town leaders." Barone gets into the capital gains tax reform debate in "The Capitol Gains of the Well-To-Do," with Kenneth T. Walsh 10-2, but comes up with a totally unsatisfactory analysis as to why Democratic congressional leaders are having so much difficulty with the issue: "The affluent [defined here as those making more than $50,000] are more numerous than they used to be and disproportionately influential because they are the most politically active." He wrote "The Lessons of the Elections of 1989," 11-13, before the returns had even come in, and he never really sells us on the idea that the "lessons" are part of any national trend: "Voters believe government has work to do"; "Negative advertising doesn't work — in a positive climate"; "Abortion rights is a political winner — if it's handled right."

Barrett, Laurence I. *Time.* (½ ★)
Deputy Washington bureau chief. A lackluster year, Barrett doesn't pose or shape critical questions. He's unquestionably one of the fancier political writers, but he's not as smart as he thinks he is, which is probably true of all of us, but it too often comes through in his work. He's

terribly belittling of Ronald Reagan in "Going Home a Winner," 1-23. The ex-President might be a big winner, but if it weren't for the headline, you'd never know it from this report. He shares the byline with Jerome Cramer and Elaine Lafferty in "Have Weapons, Will Shoot," 2-27, on the controversy over sale and possession of semi-automatic weapons. It opens with a dramatic lead, but beyond that artifice there isn't much. A flawed "Battling an Old Bugaboo," with Gavin Scott 4-17, uses the recent Chicago mayoral election and the upcoming Virginia gubernatorial election to highlight the degree to which race is a factor in politics, but fails to discuss the role of demographics in both elections. "Dan Quayle's Salvage Strategy," 6-26, takes a relatively well-balanced second look at Dan Quayle's vice presidency. In "Neo-Plumbers on the Attack," 9-11, on attempts by Attorney General Thornburgh to stop leaks to the press, Barrett offers routine analysis of why vicious and unsubstantial leaks are often broadcast and printed: "The fastest way to stardom is to produce pizazz early and often; the worst sin is being second. This trend discourages solid investigative work with its prolonged drudgery." Barrett can do splendid work when he stays within himself, as with "Driven to Beat the Budget," 2-27. He's sufficiently detached to produce a masterful, three-dimensional sketch of Richard Darman, "a state-of-the-art public official," that is respectful, without being puffery.

Birnbaum, Jeffrey. *The Wall Street Journal.* (★)
Washington. A congressional correspondent and one of the top rated journalists a few years back, Birnbaum has been getting more personally involved in his material, a partisan player, his biases showing through too often for us not to notice. As a result, he slips a few notches this year. He displays heavy prejudices against Newt Gingrich in "Bitter Fight for Republican Whip Places Divisions in Party Thinking in Stark Contrast," 3-21, on his contest for GOP Whip with Rep. Edward Madigan (R-Ill.): "Gingrich partisans sneer at Mr. Madigan as a lawmaker lacking the imagination and drive necessary to lift the Republicans out of their current condition" with nothing about Gingrich's kinder and gentler agenda. "Well-Respected Panel Moves to Center Stage," 4-18, provides a simple, effective sketch of the House Ethics Committee re the Wright Report: "They are the solid citizens of Congress. They certainly don't seem like the kind of lawmakers who would want to topple a speaker of the House. And that is why the unanimous decision by the House Ethics Committee to charge Rep. James Wright with 69 violations of House rules is likely to carry so much weight." Saddled with a misleading headline, "Merging a Lower Capital Gains Rate with a Rise in Gasoline Tax Would Leave the Poor the Losers," 5-8, is misinformation. Birnbaum tips us to his bias on the capital gains rate cut issue, dismissing facts from the IRS as something that "rate-cut proponents *claim*" or "contend," yet treating fanciful estimates by "a labor-backed group" as factual data. His grudging coverage of the capital gains saga results in Birnbaum barking and snarling at those Democrats who dallied with the administration on it. Rep. Dan Rostenkowski, whom he compared to a tail-wagging "puppy," gets a cold-water treatment for what was a key development. "House Tax-Writer Hints at Possible Capital Gains Cut," 6-8, fails to suggest that Rostenkowski may now be attracted by the potential for revenue-raising via a capital gains tax rate cut, and "Rostenkowski's Tax Package Includes a 50% Cut in Health Insurance Surtax," 7-19, is barebones reporting on the House Ways & Means Committee Chairman, Birnbaum lazily omitting the context of Darman's strategy on cap gains or the sequestration threat. "Rep. Anthony, With Key Vote on Capital Gains, Has Close Ties to Washington Tax Lobbyist," with Brooks Jackson 7-25, reeks heavily of a "Get Anthony" alert for the congressman's support of the capital gains tax cut: "Mr. [Beryl] Anthony intends to side with Ways and Means Republicans, with President Bush and with his duck-hunting companions." On the losing end, Birnbaum's "House Agrees To Cut Capital Gains Tax," 9-29, is a solid account of the larger than expected 239-190 vote. But once again, when the issue went to the Senate, we had to follow Susan Rasky of the *Times* to keep up.

Borger, Gloria. *U.S.News & World Report.* (★ ½)
Assistant Managing Editor at the weekly, Borger handles the Beltway beat with appreciable care. Although her reporting sometimes lacks compelling insights, she generally handles her stories with more meticulous care than the competition at *Time,* for example. "The Short, Unhappy

Life of Tax Reform," 2-13, delivers a smart early warning about potential changes in the 1986 tax codes, but implicit is the Democratic assertion that a capital gains differential is a loophole, not part of the Bush electoral mandate. It's easy going in "Judging Jim Wright," 4-17, Borger relying on anonymous sources to repeat conventional wisdom that Rep. Jim Wright's days as House Speaker are numbered. She's much better with "The Last Stand of Speaker Jim Wright," 4-24, developing angles on Congress' reputation and the impact of Wright's woes on the Democrat party's political clout. However Borger weakens the effort with a less than compelling observation that Jim Wright, "while probably guilty of bad judgment, was not so much guilty of criminal intent as a more common intent to finagle rules as porous as a tennis net." "The Painful Political Trial of Speaker Jim Wright," 5-1, speculates on how the Democrats will vote on the charges facing Wright, but ignores the question of what will happen to Wright's defenders if he fails. In "The Rise of the Accidental Speaker," 6-5, Borger makes good use of quotes and comparisons with Jim Wright to create a striking, in-depth portrait of the next Speaker of the House, Tom Foley. She displays high professional standards in "Anatomy of a Smear," 6-19, examining the rumor of Tom Foley's alleged homosexuality. Whereas other journalists immediately stuck the GOP with authorship of the rumor, Borger's reporting is on the mark: "Democrats probably started it. Republicans gleefully fanned it. And the press ultimately gave it full-blown legitimacy even though from all available evidence, it is entirely unfounded." The analysis is outstanding, the historical perspective to the point in "Oh, Say Can You See An Amendment?" with Sarah Burke 7-10, a successfully executed report on the proposed constitutional amendment to ban flag burning. "Congress's $113 Million Junk-Mail Habit," 8-7, is an adequate report on use of the franking privilege and how it has grown, though she makes no adjustment for the tenfold inflation of the last 20 years. "Why the Catastrophic-Care Fight Will Change Generational Politics," 10-9, is observant on the Democrats' shifting attitude toward the elderly as a special interest group: ". . .those who once fought for senior programs in the best Claude Pepper tradition now admit the focus must turn to a needier clientele — poor children, unwed mothers, drug-ridden neighborhoods, to name a few."

Brownstein, Ronald. *National Journal.* **(NR)**
NJ's West Coast correspondent, Brownstein is one of the best political reporters around. His "Same Old Democratic Message," 4-23-88, was one of the best of Campaign '88. But he's back to writing a book, presumably, and most of his material we saw this year was his freelance work in the *Los Angeles Times,* and most of that seemed done on the fly. "Out of the Boondocks Into Mansions of Power," *LAT* 1-29, brings little new to light, but is well-presented and timely on the importance the 1990 gubernatorial races will have on national policies via congressional redistricting. "The Two Worlds of Maxine Waters," *LAT Magazine* 3-5, is a slow puffy profile of the State Assemblywoman, "perhaps the most influential elected official of her race and sex in the country," in which Brownstein doesn't tell us enough about why we need to read all about Maxine. Once past a slow start, "Zen and the Art of Japan-U.S. Fighter Plane Building," *LAT* 4-9, provides exceptional commentary on the U.S.-Japan trade stance. From the front line of the Pacific Rim, Brownstein produces a superior overview of the conflicts and contradictions involved in U.S.-Japanese economic linkage. "Facing West Nervously," 10-28, a 10 Best selection for the year, is loaded with fresh data, novel insights, solid analysis, and is the most comprehensive reporting we saw on the issue.

Campbell, Linda Ponce. *The Washington Times.* **(★)**
Supreme Court. Mostly standard, but always reliable, Campbell plods through the caseload of the nation's highest court. She sticks to the evidence, but with a distracting style that suggests a less than empathetic connection to her material. She assembles the appropriate information in "Spring May Bring Some Hint of Fate of Roe vs. Wade," 1-23, reviewing the SCOTUS stance on abortion, though without full clarity. "Jury Shouldn't Get Profile of Victim, Justices Told," 3-29, does a fine job giving us the various views regarding limits on how far prosecutors may go to "humanize" victims of crimes in order to get a higher penalty for defendants. You can't get more standard than "Court Hears Arguments on Abortion Regulation," 4-27: "in a case that

could determine the continued validity of 1973's Roe v. Wade, Webster v. Reproductive Health Services is the focal point of the most volatile debate over abortion in years, since the court could use it to alter abortion rights significantly." Her "North Verdict Seen to Boost Independent Counsel's Office," 5-5, is competent on why North's conviction came as a relief to the besieged and much criticized Office of the Independent Council and the statute that created it. "Abortion Activists Gear Up For Court Decision," 6-21, sums up the political implications of the pending ruling on abortion which, if ambiguous, "would send activists scurrying to fight over existing inactive laws never repealed after Roe and new legislation made possible by the justices' decision." A followup, "Court Chips Away at Abortion Rights," 7-4, is level-headed amidst the controversy, no mean feat. There's more life in her stride with "A Life Sentence Means Anything But Life in Prison," 8-29, solid, effective reporting on the mockery of a justice system which systematically fails to enforce the sentences it passes on criminals: ". . . this year state courts convicted about 583,000 people of felonies in 1986 and sent 46% of them to prison — where they can be expected to serve less than half their original sentences." Murderers convicted are "likely to serve an average of seven years and two months in prison, though the average sentence is 18 years and five months." "Supreme Court To Rule On Judicial Power," 9-26, is clear on the national significance of two legal cases now before the Supreme Court that will define the limits of federal judiciary power.

Carlson, Margaret. *Time.* (—)
Senior writer. One of the new "voices," at *Time,* Carlson assembles reports from the field and then does the editorializing from her desk with unrestrained biases. A former Jimmy Carter speechwriter, it shows. Carlson hurt the credibility of *Time*'s Beltway coverage this year. "How Many Will Fall?" with Nancy Traver 6-5, throws out a novel thought in a sidebar — maybe the House ought to reach outside its ranks for a Speaker who's the image of virtue: "Perhaps the Democrat who best personifies this republic of virtue is former President Jimmy Carter. . .Carter would actually bring to the task energy, integrity and his legendary distaste for congressional business as usual." The editors should be horsewhipped for permitting the blatant editorializing in "Have We Gone Too Far?" 6-12: "The real scandal in Congress is not what's illegal; it is what's legal: the blatant, shameless greasing of congressional palms that violate good sense, good taste and good government. Capitol Hill is polluted by money." This, in a *news* account! Again, in "How to Spread A Smear," 6-19, Carlson opens with "Have you no sense of decency, sir?" She smears Lee Atwater and Newt Gingrich as new purveyors of McCarthyism, trying to hang the rumor about Tom Foley's alleged homosexuality on them. Despite colorful writing, there's not much in "Do You Dare To Eat A Peach?" with Gisela Bolte, Dick Thompson, and Andrea Sachs 3-27, on the Alar controversy that skirts its technical side, using colorful writing to disguise this glaring omission. Routine, "A Case of Wright and Wrong," with Hays Gorey 4-17, summarizes the case against House Speaker Jim Wright, with no new angles. Nor do we get much of the dynamics of LA mayor Tom Bradley's administration in "How to Make Boring Beautiful," with Edwin Reingold 4-24: "Bradley is part of a wave of certifiably boring, aggressively bland politicians." "I'm Nobody, Who Are You?" 5-8, uses anecdotes to illustrate the problems facing congressional wives in the wake of the Wright scandal, without examining the qualifications of working wives. "Can Pro-Choicers Prevail?" with Steven Holmes 8-14, competently summarizes and analyzes the political task facing pro-choice activists in the future. "Revenge of the Little People," 9-11, is "Impact!!!" news on Leona Helmsley, totally devoid of any new information or analysis, belonging more to *People* than *Time.* "A Skeleton in Barney's Closet," with Robert Ajemian and Hays Gorey 9-25, is moronic, mushy moralizing on the Barney Frank affair: "On a scale of 1 to HUD, Frank's transgression is a low single digit. . ..One must learn to forgive the sinner while hating the sin — or risk shutting out the daughter who has the abortion, the son with AIDS, the nephew trapped by drugs." Her *Time* screeds belong in *The New Republic,* and in fact a few appeared there this year, where she chops to pieces Jim Wright protege John Mack in "One of the Boys," 6-5, and Tony Coelho in "Fallen Angel," 6-12.

Church, George J. *Time.* (★)
Senior writer. Another from among *Time*'s stable of senior writers whose name appears at the top of multi-bylined reports, Church may be appreciated for his ability to keep editorializing at a minimum and biases under control in his political reports. He does dance on the edge at times, as with "The Education of a Standby: Dan Quayle Gets a Cram Course — Just in Case," with Dan Goodgame 1-30: "the whole nation has a stake in whether the Vice President can gradually make the phrase President Quayle something other than a trigger for laughter — or dismay." "The Other Arms Race," with Jonathan Beatty, Elaine Shannon, and Richard Woodbury 2-6, doesn't inject opinion until the last graph or so, instead letting the statistics on guns speak for themselves, solemn as a funeral bell tolling; while Church doesn't say much we didn't know already, it's good to have it all in one place, and examined from different angles. "Is This Goodbye?" with Michael Duffy, Dan Goodgame and Laurence Barrett 3-6 cover, is a fairly decent rundown on the John Tower fiasco, but there's not a word on the administration belief that this is a Democrat power-play to run defense policy from Capitol Hill. "The Big Spill," with Jay Peterzell, David Seideman, and Paul Witteman 4-10, is an impressively assembled account of the Valdez fiasco; Church avoids purple prose, remaining detached in citing weaknesses in federal, state government, pipeline consortium, and Exxon. "Bombshell in the House," with Hays Gorey 5-1, summarizes the charges made against Speaker Jim Wright by the House Ethics Committee and Wright's defense. "Fighting Back," with Dan Goodgame and Steven Holmes 9-11, realistically explores Bush's proposed drug plan, editorializing that "Bush's program may be all that is politically possible now, and it does contain some worthwhile ideas. But it falls far, far short of what a true war on drugs would require." In "Look Who's Feeling Picked On," with Ann Blackman 9-25, Church reports on formal acts of discrimination against Russians by ethnic minorities in Soviet Republics dominated by those minorities. The focus of the piece splits when Church digresses to write about threats to Gorbachev's power. The result is that he never has a chance to give the discrimination a thorough analysis.

Cimons, Marlene. *Los Angeles Times.* (★ ½)
Washington. Cimons covers the health beat and related issues with a noteworthy resourcefulness and competency. In "Attitude of 'Denial' Perils Major AIDS Drug Project," 1-2, Cimons focuses attention on one of the least covered aspects of the AIDS epidemic — its affect on the hemophiliac population — and does a first-rate job of presenting the psychological problems a nationwide AZT test is creating for hemophiliacs and their doctors. This is health reporting at its finest. However, Cimons comes up with a clunker in "Ex-Press Aide Brady to Help the Disabled," 3-14, turning what could have been a triumph-of-the-human-spirit story into an article that, at best, is merely clanking and unfocused, and, at worst, makes James Brady appear the object of patronizing sympathy. In "Mother, Jailed Since '87, Says Child's Safety Is Key," 5-7, Cimons introduces shades of gray into a heavily-covered story that was mostly presented in black-and-white: the Elizabeth Morgan custody dispute. "Whatever the truth may be about Morgan and Foretich and the judge, their confrontation appears to have produced an impasse in which Hilary's well-being could become the ultimate casualty." "Far-Reaching Bill to Protect Disabled From Discrimination Gains Speed," 7-30, comes across as a one-sided story on pending legislation that would ban discrimination against the handicapped, including as "handicapped" those with contagious diseases and alcohol and drug problems. Appearing in *The Washingtonian,* Cimons gives us a glimpse of her personal life in "Barra and Me," 8-89, the sensitively-told saga of her adoption of an Indian toddler that moves without being maudlin and makes no bones about the paperwork and difficulties involved. "FDA to Lift OK of Last Dyazide Generic Version," 8-29, identifies well the specifics of this particular FDA action, placing it in the context of FDA's escalating "campaign against generic drugs that it believes have been marketed improperly." Still on the generic drug beat, in "Only 2 of 12 Generic Drug Makers Found Free of Problems in FDA Investigation," 9-12, Cimons tells what the problems are that the FDA found, but makes no effort to give the drug company's side of the story. Granted, she was covering a congressional hearing, but even a standard "could not be reached for comment" would have sufficed. "2 Drugs Combined Cut Colon Cancer Fatalities," 10-3, is the type of good news story that makes working the health beat worthwhile, but the writing at times is too clinical.

Clift, Eleanor. *Newsweek.* (★)
Washington correspondent. An avowed liberal Democrat who displays her views on the McLaughlin Group TV talkie, Clift's *Newsweek* reports show how well a reporter can keep a personal bias under control. Her work is respectable and balanced, her major weakness her level of analytical depth. "Politics Under the Palms," 1-9, insignificant fluff, reporting American political advisors go south to advise other countries for the post-campaign winter, makes us wonder if there isn't something more substantial she ought to be covering. Clift really captures taxpayers' outrage in "The Tea-Bag Revolution," 2-6, a well-balanced recap, but nothing more, on the uproar over the congressional pay raise. "Jim Wright on the Ropes," with Larry Martz 4-3, is routine on House Speaker Jim Wright's continuing ethics problems. "In 'Hip-Deep Water,' " co-written with Rich Thomas 5-1, a detailed, highly informative article on the charges against Wright, goes deeper, explaining how he allegedly attempted to "smuggle extra income through the maze of House rules." Clift's stories on the Jim Wright/John Mack affair, "The Protege and the Victim," 5-1, and "Wright's Aide: Too Little, Too Late," 5-22, are overkill on this subject, merely summarizing what had appeared in other news accounts and offering no fresh analysis. In "A Nasty Job for a Nice Guy," 6-12, a short profile of Tom Foley, Clift does a competent job of sizing up his political pluses and minuses. She's adequate with "It's Back! The Return of the Pay Raise," 7-3, outlining Foley's strategy for raising salaries, contrasting his tactics to his predecessor's. "Millions of Dollars on the Ocean Floor," 8-28, on the surplus equipment which the Navy leaves on old ships that are sunk instead of selling them to salvagers, offers no new dimension on the issue, and we wonder what other countries do with their old ships' surplus materials.

Cohen, Richard E. *National Journal.* (★ ½)
Congressional reporter. Cohen had an exceptional '88, we thought, his material zippier than we'd seen in earlier years. This year there's less zip or sparkle, not many big-picture shots, but his reports are thoroughly competent. "Nailing Down Power at Armed Services," 1-21, is interesting, telling us Reps. Les Aspin and Ron Dellums now chair the two most powerful subcommittees of the House Armed Services Committee; Aspin has been chair of the full committee since 1985, however, and the Pentagon still largely gets what it wants so far. He goes out on a limb with a somewhat optimistic "Reasoning Together On Foreign Policy," 2-4, exploring possibilities for a more cooperative foreign policy relationship between the Bush administration and Congress, while not strongly persuasive, he inclines us to consider the prospect. "Many Colleagues, Not Enough Friends?" 3-4, is a thoughtful essay on the vagaries of political/congressional life. "Bush May Miss Boat on Minimum Pay," 4-1, mixes up a variety of issues — the contras, the Tower nomination, the minimum wage — with a garbled perspective: "Republicans may eventually score some tactical points if Bush keeps his politically risky promise to veto the seemingly popular bill." His heavy pen weighs down "Blaming Everything on Speaker Wright," 5-27, with the House stuck on dead center, pointing to Wright's problems; there's not much here beyond a few facts on procedures. In "Business As Usual," 6-3, Cohen quickly disputes House Democrats' ability to put their leadership woes behind them, and under the "soothing nonpartisan" Foley, return to the legislative tasks at hand. He cites important barriers, but loses some consistency at the end, where he drifts into the 1990 campaign. "Foley's Honeymoon," 7-15, is a nicely-written overview of Foley-Gephardt-Gray triumvirate's strengths and weaknesses, what they are likely to win and what course they may steer, taking the short-term view. "When A 'Junket' Becomes Hard Travel," 8-19, uses the deaths in plane crashes of Reps. Mickey Leland (D-Tex.) and Larkin Smith (R-Miss.) as examples of grueling travel and work schedules against notions congressional trips are unnecessary junkets to romantic places. In "Fall from Power," 8-19, we get House Members speaking candidly about Wright's downfall, and what they say about the limits of leadership has important long-term implications for the House, but Cohen doesn't discuss the *need* for outside counsel to bring objectivity, nor necessary changes in Ethics Committee rules. "Deep-Sixing Their Wayward Colleague," 9-30, is a stale review of the Barney Frank story, with no sources quoted directly. Worst line: " '. . .[Expletive deleted], yes, this is a problem for Democrats,' a former House Democrat said."

Davidson, Joe. *The Wall Street Journal.* (½ ★)
Washington. Working the HUD beat, Davidson slips below par with weak reporting and a not-infrequent inability to keep himself out of his stories. Routine with "Black-White Party on Several Fronts By Year 2000 Is Urged By Urban League," 1-25, he provides a standard rehash of the Urban League press release. "Missed Chances: As Homeless Suffer, A Federal Aid Council Focuses on Politics," 3-15, doesn't belong on the front page. Davidson gets the detail on the infighting at the Interagency Council on the Homeless, but interviews only one member, Cassandra Moore. While she says she is "proud" of the council's achievements, Davidson doesn't inform us about them, emphasizing only the negatives. It's tough ploughing to get through "Pride of Ownership: Takeover by Tenants Of Housing Projects Makes Place Liveable," 7-6. He overloads the lead graph with negatives on HUD Secretary Jack Kemp's plan to allow public housing residents to purchase and own their own units, which sounds a false note that pulls us up. The reporting is stronger in an organized and lucid "HUD Aide's Report Says Program Abuse Is More Wide Spread Than Was Thought," 8-3, Davidson naming names on this go 'round, with specific dollar figures awarded for housing contracts. Also accorded undeserved front page display, a convoluted "How U.S. Housing Aid Helped a Biloxi, Miss. Build a Fancy Marina," 9-1, takes forever to get off the ground, Davidson wearing his sentiments on his sleeve, and we wonder about some of the accuracy of the material. He's adequate on the current HUD plans with "Kemp Seeks Tightening of Rules at HUD, Other Officials Look for a New Name," 9-6, working the details of the department's 26-point proposal.

de Cordoba, Jose. *The Wall Street Journal.* (★ ½)
A Miami bureau reporter, who doubles as pinch-hitter on Caribbean-based stories, de Cordoba's reporting was less impressive this year, but his writing and presentation are strong. "Wanted: Good Managers," 2-24, moves off of venture capitalist Michael Chaney's image of a total entrepreneur — the simple connection between an idea-filled brain and business acumen — an interesting, but not startling report. "What OAS Wants Is Not Noreiga's Style," 6-12, updates on thugs in Panama, and contains a smattering of analysis, but no special insights. "Argentine Official Is Facing Charges in Trade Scandal," 7-19, is quick and dirty on Nestor Raparelli, the just-named economics minister presently on the lam for fraud, a polaroid view we didn't see elsewhere. In "The Front Lines: In Colombia, the War On Drugs is Producing Some Real-Life Heroes," 9-7, de Cordoba finds adversity makes for greatness in a few, breathing life into those on the front lines. He moves us with this picture of their grace and dignity.

DeParle, Jason. *The Washington Monthly.* (★ ★)
We appreciated his mix of reporting and analytical efforts, often featured cover stories of the monthly where he's an editor. A rising talent, the young man is moving on to *The New York Times.* DeParle is stinging with his report on the inadequacy of Washington, DC, focusing on victims — the poor and other residents of the District — in "The Worst City Government in America," 1-89. He's persuasive on why it deserves the title ascribed it. He employs a lighter hand with "Spy Anxiety," 3-89, a delightful profile of the New York monthly satire magazine *Spy,* looking at its heritage in city magazines. "Beyond the Legal Right," 4-89, is a sensitive examination of what's right with the Right to Life movement, probing and serious, soundly debunking some of the opposition's more radical posturings. DeParle keeps an intense focus on the moral aspect of the issue, noting that "Beyond questions of abortion's legality, the Left tends to hold values that encourage the acceptance of abortion's morality too." Less successful, "Why America Loves Letter Carriers and Hates Postal Clerks," 7/8-89, takes us behind the counter at the Post Office in an attempt to expose the differences in working conditions between the two halves of the postal workforce, but the anecdotes here are trite. "Warning: Sports Stars May Be Hazardous to Your Health," 9-89, is an exhaustive, relentless critique on cigarette sponsorship of sports. DeParle soundly disappoints us with "What the Smartest Man in Washington Doesn't Understand. And Why It Will Hurt You," 11-89, a lumbering and disorganized denunciation of Richard Darman's OMB. Uncharacteristic for DeParle, neither his reporting, insights, nor analysis offer much. An early effort at the *Times,* "The Bitter Legacy of Yalta: Four Decades

of What-Ifs," 11-26, is a flawless thumbnail history of the 1945 summit, pros and cons: "This week President Bush makes the trip in reverse: on to Malta, with the ghosts of Yalta behind him, perhaps fading at last."

Devroy, Ann. *The Washington Post.* (★ ½)
Deputy national editor/political editor. A hallmark of the paper's political coverage is the step-by-step, who-did-what-when-and-to-whom kind of insider account of Beltway politics. Collecting information is a strength of Devroy's reporting, but she doesn't always know what to do with it, leaving the "big think" coverage to David Hoffman. Devroy still succumbs to weaknesses, though, as with a thoroughly irresponsible "RNC Helped Pay for Quayle Vacation: Party Provided $25,000 Last Month for Colorado Skiing Party," 1-11. This front page "expose" doesn't reveal until the end of the article that *no* RNC money was used to pay any of Vice President Dan Quayle's or his family's personal expenses and that he did not request any such payment. In another Quayle effort, "Quayle, Unlike Predecessor, Speaks Out in Policy Debates," 3-28, we learn the VP has opinions, but little else about his performance. Her best efforts come through with "Bush Plan: Around the Bureaucracy in 7 Days," 5-30, as she peels away the layers around the making of Bush's first major foreign policy initiative. She delivers the goods on how NSC deputy Bob Gates and State Department's Lawrence Eagleberger, among others, basically "junked" the policy reviews of the bureaucratic jungle. "Plane Carrying Rep. Leland Missing In Africa," 8-8, is straightforward with the early information on Mickey Leland (D-Tex.) and the missing plane. "Bush Insists U.S. Troops Have Minimal Drug Role," 9-12, is balanced on the staunch Presidential denial that Colombia will turn into Vietnam of 1990's. She goes beneath the surface on the issue, but not enough to satisfy. "Mr. Smith Comes To Washington — For A Fee," 10-1, is delightfully entertaining on Larry Smith, who took the Republican Senatorial Inner Circle for all it was worth, as the self-styled "federal relations expert" promised ultimate breakfasts with different bigwigs. Devroy makes her point, listing other Lee Atwater fundraising silliness, but we get nothing on the Democrat side.

Dewar, Helen. *The Washington Post.* (★ ★)
Capitol Hill correspondent. We've zinged Dewar in years past for insufficient detachment, and in fact she continues to improve each year, keeping lopsided reports to a minimum and developing her great potential as a journalist who can adroitly handle a "bigger picture" effort now and then. "Tower Says He'd Accept Hill Budget Restraints," 1-26, notes the extended grilling of John Tower as overcompensating for his being questioned by former colleagues, but there's no hint of anything amiss at this point. Her reporting is outstanding in "Tracing the Steps In Tower's Downfall," with Dan Balz 3-29, a 10 Best selection. This dramatic, beautifully reported and organized summary, is lofty and detached, yet intimate in detailing the relevant milestones. A cloud hovers over Senator Sam Nunn, and there is surprising sympathy for Tower as 26 years of public service goes down the drain. "Congress Off to Slowest Start in Years," 5-13, decently characterizes an immediate relationship between Congress and the administration: "Many lawmakers complain that, with the distraction of ethics troubles and without a compelling agenda from either Bush or Democratic leaders, both the administration and Congress are drifting aimlessly from one accommodation to another, nearly all of them circumscribed by deficit-driven budget limits." Dewar is informative on the Senate attitude toward "soft-spoken, serious-minded and upright" Senate Majority Leader George Mitchell in "Mitchell's Orderly, Consultative Style Gets Early Plaudits in Senate," 5-15, where we learn even Republicans compliment him for creating a "kinder, gentler Senate." However, it needs a bit of a forward look as to how short-lived the sweetness might prove to be. She's sharp and into an issue that may get much fuller play in 1990 with "Bush's 'Two-Missile' Proposal Jeopardized," 6-19. Bush's penchant for splitting the difference on policy disputes may end up alienating both sides, and she secures taut salvos from liberal Reps. Les AuCoin (D-Oreg.) and conservative John McCain on this one, though she doesn't dwell enough on the strategic rationale for either land-based missile. "GOP Looking to Move Up in Senate While Democrats Hope to Stay Even," 7-2, provides an excellent survey of the two parties' prospects in the

upcoming Senate races, Dewar quick on GOP potentials: Democrats "already have lost some of their strongest prospects for key races, giving the GOP at least some hope of recapturing control of the Senate — in 1992 if not in 1990." In "Senators, White House Agree to Add Drug-War Funds," 9-26, Dewar quotes only Democrats, the Republican side of the picture opaque. She's clear on the capital gains vote being only delayed in "Senate Approves Deficit Plan," 10-14, a nicely balanced, well-detailed account.

Diamond, Edwin. *New York.* (★ ½)
"Media" columnist. Teaching journalism at NYU for the past five years, Diamond's schedule may be starting to wear on his efforts. He catches us up with solid reporting and respectable analysis, but there is no out-in-front material on the media beat from him this year. "Eleventh-Hour Gamble," 1-9, on PBS's late night 11 o'clock news entry, has a witty opening, a cautionary tale, all the right elements. However, Diamond leaves us hanging on some big questions: what is the show about? will it work? "Behind the Peacock Throne," 2-13, is realistic on Michael Gartner, new president of NBC News, and the "hothouse" at NBC, but it's late to be worrying about the "advent" of "trashavision." "The New (Land) Lords of the Press," 2-27, a collection of mini-quick profiles of New York's new press scions, who started out doing something else (mostly real estate), is worthy though not jazzy, but the *New York Post*'s Peter Kalikow and *U.S.News & World Report*'s Mort Zuckerman are old news. "Lenin Meets Letterman," 4-3, a cautious review of Soviet TV reporting, delivers lots of information, but in a somewhat superior tone that's mildly annoying. "On the Roller Coaster with Diane and Sam," 7-24, gives us ample warning that "Prime Time Live" with Diane Sawyer and Sam Donaldson will be no "60 Minutes," but more of "A Current Affair." Diamond is devilishly delightful here: "Prime-time rules also mean high production values, good music, well-lit sets, and some quickly grasped concept like that of 'L.A. Law' (lawyers and sex) or 'Knots Landing' (sex and sex)." "A Fan's Notes," 8-14, is no-nonsense on *The National,* Peter Price's entry into the sports weekly business, surveying its short history and founding, and evaluating its chances. "Trump Vs. Stern: The Unmaking Of A Documentary," 9-4 cover, on the feud between Donald Trump and Leonard Stern of Hartz Mountain, publisher of *The Village Voice* and *7 Days,* gives an effective blow-by-blow, but much too long, with Diamond saving for the tail end the real reason the documentary on Trump failed — it was two hours long. "Cover Stories," 10-9, follows *Newsweek*'s Jonathan Alter's 1-9 story on magazines of all types in bed with their interview subjects — a concrete rehash, but nothing more.

Diegmuller, Karen. *Insight.* (★ ★)
Social issues. Broadening a bit the range of topics within her portfolio, Diegmuller continues to grow in producing competent, smooth, well-organized reports. She still has room to develop new angles with the material, but she clearly has the potential. "Somber Days for a Creaky Colossus," 3-27, is fast-paced and fact-filled on the issues facing the winner of the April 4th Chicago mayoral election, covering a broad spectrum of problems, abuses and recent attempts at reform. "Higher Minimum Wages at a Price," 4-24, is a fine, balanced account, no soft spots along the way, among the best accounts of minimum wage politics, though she doesn't hint at the trading value for Bush with the AFL-CIO on capital gains. "Nomination For Rights Post Clouds Overture to Minorities," 5-8, is timely, with good detail on the William Lucas nomination as Assistant Attorney General for civil rights, though there's nothing on Jesse Jackson's role or the split in black community. Diegmuller scores in "Its Scandalous Past Can't Stop Kemp From Rousing His HUD," 7-17, an excellent forward-looking review of HUD posture under Kemp amidst the inherited scandal. "The Abortion Debate Drops a Level," 7-24, is sharp on the SCOTUS decision, detail from the state, detached and fair and crisply written; there are no great insights, but we're grateful for a thoroughly professional account. "Extended Definition of Family Fuels Partnership Controversy," 8-7, successfully explains that proposed city ordinances redefining "family" offer additional benefits, but often omit additional legal responsibilities. "Passing a Legacy of Drug Addiction," 9-4, disappoints, muddled and redundant in spots, on pregnancy and drug addiction.

Dionne, E. J., Jr. *The Washington Post.* (★ ★ ★)
Moving to the *Post* in October from his lofty perch at *The New York Times* Washington bureau, where there was not room for him and Political Bigfoot Johnny Apple, Dionne (PhD., PoliSci) can now flap his wings in a more convivial atmosphere. Given this squabbling at the bureau, it was no surprise Dionne was slightly off his feed, but he still had his moments. In "Which Way Does the New Breeze Blow?" 1-22, a "Week in Review" lead, Dionne finds it puzzling that in his inaugural address Bush can praise both "the exercise of free will unhampered by the state" and the "virtues of duty, sacrifice, commitment," perhaps because Dionne does not see that even the Establishment has moved; he quotes a Bush aide: "There are Reaganesque elements in what everyone, including liberal Democrats, is saying." Dionne is at his best in "Looking Past Dukakis, Democrats Mull Defeat," 2-19, a 10 Best nomination, clear on the torment within the Democrat Party as it tussles over moving right via the South, or staying left via the West: "After losing so many Presidential elections, Democrats have become high strategists in the art of interpretation wars." "Quayle Works to Build His Own Base. . ." 3-13, is timely, accurately identifying William Kristol and Carnes Lord as chief links to intellectual conservatives. "Crime in Capital Fuels Assault on Home Rule," 3-24, opens with an effective lead — "Suddenly the unspeakable is being discussed here: Is home rule in the District of Columbia a failure?" — and Dionne follows through with the details. "Pressing For Abortion, in the Name of Family," 4-16, is thoughtful and insightful on the march on Washington by pro-choicers, a "distraction" for feminists who "have to defeat the right-to-lifers to move forward on other issues." "GOP Keeping Up Ethics Pressure on the Democrats," 5-29, reports that Newt Gingrich and Lee Atwater don't want the ethics issue dropped with the departure of Wright and Coelho, but the report needs some discussion of threats to the Bush agenda, with a party debate. "Gingrich, Pursuer of Democrats, Now Finds Himself Pursued," 6-4, is sharp and timely, on the GOP party pressures for Gingrich to pull his punches and cool it, as Democrats gear up for revenge. "Bridge Led to Detour Over 20 Years," 7-18, looks at Ted Kennedy's presidential possibilities without Chappaquiddick, and whether renouncing the office has made him a better Senator, but Dionne can't really make us care about this. He's in over his head with analytically garbled "Spending, Politics, and Darman's Slap at the Profligate American," 7-30. Trying to fathom the OMB director's complaint about "now-nowism," he sees it as a contradiction to Darman's support of Reaganonomics. "Parties Draw Up Plans for Restricting Battle," 8-9, is a dutiful accounting of the coming fight over the census and congressional redistricting.

Donohoe, Cathryn. *The Washington Times.* (★ ★ ★)
One of the best stylists at the *Times,* Donohoe's personality profiles in the "life!" section are almost always winners. She doesn't have the drop-dead dazzle of Stephanie Mansfield, but her subjects are heavier. Her most arresting this year was "To Be Liberal and Pro-Life," 11-6, a marvelous sketch of veteran journalist Nat Hentoff, who is so "cracked" on the First Amendment that at age 64 he has broken with the liberal establishment and has become an anti-abortionist!!! His wife of 30 years is angry, so is her 90-year-old aunt and mother! "I have no doubt why women are against me. I have committed the rank heresy on the left. . ..I am pro-life." In another left-right conversion, "Mort Sahl, Iconoclast of Comedy," 2-1, she traces the comedian's rise and fall, the wrath he incurred from the left, and his current "comeback," Donohoe is tartly vivid, catching an insight and passing it on to us: "The famous wolflike grin widens, then vanishes, as if it were a tic." With images like the "handy little hook that links related scraps of language," she beguiles us into reading material on a subject that otherwise would never appeal to us. Quirky yet practical, "Apostrophes Join the Dispossessed," 4-3: answers all the questions on "whither the apostrophe?" — "The possessive apostrophe is dying, taking with it every sense of possession except that of outright ownership." Ultimately "An Artist's Proud Banner and the Blood of Beijing," 6-5, proves satisfactory, but Donohoe's very slow takeoff on Chinese artist Ling Ling, doesn't tell us soon enough why we should read this. She's colorfully brisk with fine organization and appropriate quotes in "A Historian's Revolution," 6-14, on Simon Schama, the Harvard historian whose *Citizens,* a best selling history of the French Revolution, infuriates his fellow historians because it reads like a

conservative's view of the revolution in popularized form. "On the Brink of Something New," 7-17, a delightful profile of author Daniel Boorstin, who is hard at work on his 19th book, a sequel to *The Discoverers,* is full of her enchanting wit: "Two centuries ago, when a great man appeared, people looked for God's purpose in him; today we look for his press agent." She moves fast in "Whittle Carves Out a Niche in Media," 7-19, a profile of Christopher Whittle, the "insurrectionist" publishing mogul assembling lots of facts, but somewhere buried underneath is his personality. She gets points for bravery with "Eric Foretich: Loser in Dr. Morgan's War," 8-3, telling Foretich's side of the child sex-abuse charges. She handles it deftly, taking no sides, though a bit too complex in parts, her writing could be smoothed out. But really a grand year.

Dowd, Maureen. *The New York Times.* (★ ★ ★ ½)
White House correspondent. It's almost impossible to begin a Dowd report or feature and not finish it. There's a light, pleasant side to her reporting, as she easily settles in with her subjects, no tricks up her sleeve. But don't mistake that for shallowness. She can subtly pluck a telling essence from a story far more skillfully than many on this beat. She moves in for some wonderful closeups of the Bushes on day one as President in "The People, in Thousands, Get a Look at Their House," 1-22, with great quotes of Bush at ease with his grandchildren. Dowd weaves great detail into "How Cheney's Name Came Up Again," 3-12, an account of how the Defense Secretary's nomination surfaced. "Under Siege, NRA Fights the 'Hysteria,' " 3-19, is an extremely fair account of the NRA's response to the semi-automatic weapon controversy. "Journalists Debate the Risks As President Woos the Press," 4-2, marvelously reports on the revived debate among journalists over how close to get to the President, as Bush shamelessly woos them. "Betty Wright Angrily Defends $18,000 Salary," 4-21, is straightforward on Mrs. Wright defending her position with Mallightco Inc.: "Oh, well, they are making me a Nancy Reagan. I felt sorry for her when they did it to her. I don't know why they ever started on me." Not quite, but Dowd treats her equitably. The "White House" column, 5-12, reports that Bush's list of enemies is short, including George Will and Garry Trudeau, but adds: " 'If you come to the end of a long political road and don't have any real enemies,' said one Bush friend, 'you haven't really shown the stuff of leadership.' " With the emphasis on his capable staff, "The Education of Dan Quayle," *Magazine* cover 6-25, was the turning point in press treatment of the VP, with cheerful, graphic subtleties that bring out a third dimension in him. A 10 Best selection, the best line is when he points out he got better grades than his wife in law school, but he won't release them because she might retaliate. " 'Yeah,' says Quayle laughing, 'She might release my college records.' " Her best, "Bush in a Crisis: Casting the Widest Net," 8-6, insightfully recaps Bush's week regarding the hostage crisis, which "provided an opportunity to demonstrate that what he had learned over the years could help him outflank the extremist forces in the Middle East that had toppled Jimmy Carter and ensnared Ronald Reagan." Her "Washington Talk" column, "Remorseless Dozing Gets Presidential Nod," 11-10, is a Dowd classic, citing anecdotes of Presidents and their Cabinet officers and aides who dozed off during meetings. "The only faux pas is snoring. 'It's like a Mafioso code of honor,' explains one Bush adviser. 'We all wake each other up when the snore occurs. We never let things deteriorate to that stage.' "

Drew, Elizabeth. *The New Yorker.* (★ ½)
The magazine's "Letter from Washington" columnist, Drew is capable of much better work than the portfolio she produced this year. She's forced to write with a longer lead time than most political observers, but still her material didn't have to be as stale as it seemed. And yet, amid all the dross, there always surfaces one Drew report that is sparkling and definitive. There is no reporting in her 2-27 armchair look at Bush's cabinet, concluding that Bush is not Reagan and not much of a leader, tendentiously restating the obvious: "Bush's cabinet appointments are largely respectable and unimaginative." Conflict makes Drew a better reporter than usual in her 3-20 column, in which she examines how John Tower's nomination fell apart; she gets more points this time for her analysis of why relying on an FBI report full of dubious rumors did not help the Democrats win. On 5-1, Drew argues that the charges against Jim Wright are

"ambiguous" and that he did nothing particularly awful, but she appears to be writing for an audience that seemingly reads *no* other political coverage. Her 5-15 report covers a melange of topics, including Bush's First Hundred Days, Iran-contra developments, the budget and Jim Wright's troubles, but her best points, on Bush's vagueness, repeat Fred Barnes's *New Republic* piece of two weeks earlier. Drew's cliche generator seems to have gone into overdrive in her analytically lame 6-12 report: "The quietude of the Memorial Day weekend was shattered early" —as she discovers plots in the fall of Jim Wright and Tony Coelho — "The atmosphere in this city is fetid: mean, vengeful, and frightened." Abysmal stuff. Then out of the blue, she soars 6-26 with a sweeping and very thoughtful review of Bush's foreign policy to date. Fairly handled, beautifully crafted, she delivers a precise snapshot of the conventional view. In her 10-30 piece on the Panama fiasco, Drew provides us with the most disjointed sentence of the year: "Whether the United States could have and should have made the coup succeed — as it probably, under the circumstances, could not have, and, for a lot of reasons, should not have — its incoherence both at the time and in the following days gives one pause." But her account of how Washington botched things up, and why, added to our understanding of the affair. With an obvious bias and a slow start, 11-27, she presents an impressive amount of information on the Bush administration's handling of the developments in Europe and the U.S.S.R., assuming she knows better how it should be done. Her presentation, however, is awkward, hard to read, full of dashes, parenthetical phrases and very long sentences.

Easterbrook, Gregg. *Newsweek.* (★ ★ ★ ½)
Contributing Editor. One of the finest in *Newsweek*'s stable of contributing editors, Easterbrook's impressive portfolio is a mix of lively, compelling reports and the broad, close to comprehensive study on special topics. He's skeptical of the Stealth bomber, making a persuasive case against it in "Sticker Shock: The Stealth Is a Bomb," 1-23. Easterbrook disappoints us with "Death and Dogma," a *Washington Post* "Outlook" feature, 2-19. While he convincingly establishes that an enduring Western ignorance of Islam is behind its failure to appreciate the Moslem fury at Salman Rushdie's *Satanic Verses,* he undermines his point with a backhanded slap at Islam: "If some Islamic fanatic assaults Rushdie, it would only go to prove that the derisive tone of 'The Satanic Verses' was justified." "Clearing the Air: Bush's Plan," 6-19, explores Bush's options prior to his introduction of the Clean Air Act, accurately predicting the responses of both industry and environmentalists, and pointing out at least one instance that suggests "industry may be better prepared to carry out the presidential agenda than its lobbyists would ever dream of letting on." His 7-24 *Newsweek* cover "Special Report: Cleaning Up," a 10 Best nomination, is a highly detailed, complete and insightful report on the environment. Easterbrook rarely disappoints those editors who assign him the comprehensive-picture feature reports. Very balanced, he debunks myths and misconceptions on both sides of the issue. "The Sky Is Always Falling," *The New Republic* 8-21, is a delightful romp through the land of Chicken Little financial journalism, a splendid chronicle of the travesty, his analytics only narrowly below standard.

Eaton, William J. *Los Angeles Times.* (★ ½)
Washington. Eaton works the congressional beat, mostly on the House side of the Hill, with a respectable facility, though he's not one to scoop the opposition. Eaton starts off the year with "Business Groups Call Deficit Most Critical Risk," 1-2, a survey of business lobbyists on the pros and cons of the deficit that is above average for this sort of article, although he misses any hints of action on capital gains. He finely captures both the emotional and political tones of the biggest story on his beat this year in "Wright Resigns, Urges End to This 'Mindless Cannibalism,' " 6-1. Eaton let the outgoing Speaker, "dressed in funereal black," have his say while also outlining the allegations against him. He adeptly handles the story involving the allegations and rumors regarding the new Speaker of the House in "GOP Aide Quits in Furor Over Memo on Foley," 6-8, without compounding the damage to Speaker Foley's reputation. It's high drama on the Hill in "Ex-Aide Disputes Pierce Testimony," 7-15, as former HUD officials contradict sworn testimony by Samuel Pierce that he never promoted a housing deal.

With telling, meaty quotes, Eaton produces a tightly structured report that flows well. He doesn't give us a full picture in "Broke Rules to Aid Sen. D'Amato, Ex-HUD Official Says," 7-29, never informing us whether the five rent subsidy projects requested by Sen. Al D'Amato resulted in affordable housing or if the jobs were completed properly and on time. "Bill Against Flag Burning Ok'd by House Panel, 28-6," 7-28, is somewhat wry on partisan flag-waving antics on the Hill, meaty on the underlying issues ("more political guile than patriotic fervor"), but trickles off at the end. Eaton includes a brief history lesson on Teapot Dome in "Pierce Invokes 5th, Says Probers Prejudged Him," 9-27. However, his observation that "Pierce, living up to the 'Silent Sam' nickname that reflected his low-profile Cabinet style, spent less than 45 minutes in the witness chair," is a cheap shot that has no place in a straight P. 1 news story. "Use of Abortion Funds Expanded," 10-12, is a provincial account of the House vote to extend federal funding for abortions to victims of rape and incest, with Eaton more interested in telling us which members of the California delegation switched their positions from a similar vote in 1988 rather than why they switched their positions. Perhaps with his references to the Supreme Court decisions and "galvanized" pro-choice advocates, Eaton is going for analysis through osmosis.

Edsall, Thomas B. *The Washington Post.* (★ ★ ★)
Politics. Penetrating perceptions a hallmark of this pro, Edsall comes through the non-election year with his senses no less dull, although his output slimmed while he worked on a book (which we would recommend sight unseen). "Duke Builds Credibility by Fighting Tax Proposal," 4-27, is a powerful, nonbiased piece on David Duke, his plans and tactics, that goes well beyond the standard. "Moral Issue May Shape 1990's Political Agenda," 5-21, reports that "Both Democratic and Republican strategists are struggling to anticipate two seemingly disparate developments — the epidemic of crack cocaine and criminal violence and the Supreme Court's reconsideration of its landmark 1973 abortion decision — that will change the political landscape in 1990," giving a nice roundup of attitudes and thinking among strategists in the respective camps on the issue. "The Democrats Confront a No-Growth Southern Strategy," 6-25, is an example of solid political reporting, detailing deep strife within the Alabama Democratic Party to symptomatically reveal the partisan erosion and deterioration taking place in much of the Deep South, as white voters move to the GOP in droves. "Abortion's Power at Polls," 7-10, attempts to sort out the political implications of abortion legislation being tossed back to state legislatures, though the focus is a little too pat: "the sudden prominence of the abortion issue will change the structure of political campaigns in ways that strategists are now struggling to predict." In "Democrats on the Take," *The New York Review of Books* 7-20, Edsall is a bit partisan perhaps, although not unacceptably biased, in his views regarding GOP motives for campaign finance reform. But this essay meticulously details the erosion of political legitimacy among the Democrats: "the party has yet to develop the general economic policies that would appeal to middle-class voters and attract their contributions."

Evans-Pritchard, Ambrose. *The Spectator.* (★ ★)
Washington correspondent for the British weekly, his reportage is uneven, with Evans-Pritchard spending much time and energy on foreign policy questions. It's always useful, though, to look at ourselves through the eyes of a sharp non-U.S. observer, and this British journalist now and then turns a novel insight from that perspective. "My Fellow Americans. . ." 1-21, an overview of the Reagan administration, concludes that Reagan's popularity "has moved in lockstep with the employment figures in the past eight years," but Europeans don't know this because newsmagazines and reporters all "share the secular Democratic outlook." He's sophisticated in his debunking of Keynesian orthodoxies on budget deficits in "Voodoo Deficits," *The American Spectator* 2-89, while still fuzzy on the U.S. and U.K. savings rate "problem." "Bush: Slayer of Congress," 2-18, looks at the Congressional pay raise fight and the Tower nomination, restating what are, for American readers, obvious facts, and concluding that if Tower fails to be confirmed, "it would mark the beginning of a Democratic parliament." "Buddy, Can You Spare a Room?" 3-4, on the homeless, puts the issue into perspective with a distinct European appreciation: "some of the DC homeless are probably refugees from conditions that are routine

for the vast majority of people in the Soviet Union." Too loose, and uninformed, with his political characterizations (El Salvador's ARENA is a market-oriented fascist party) in "A Landslide for the Death Squads," 3-25, the post-election report from El Salvador is without serious rigor, or utility. He's witty in "Who Ruined Washington?" 4-8, noting that the District of Columbia "excels at anarchy" because it is "the showcase of the American welfare state," but there is no mention of drugs in this analysis of the Capital's crime problems. He comes away from Mexico deciding that the country has taken a turn for the better and with "Mexico by Moonlight," 5-6, he's bullish on it as a place for investment. He lifts an eyebrow in ominous concern to note that "it is astonishing that Gephardt's mad ideas no longer make much news in Washington," in "The Slow Death of Free Trade," 6-24. He gets in to the NATO debate, worrying about the "tank gap," as the Soviets, despite Gorbachev, still produce 3,400 tanks a year, with a dire warning in "Disarmament?. . .No Tanks," 6-3: "turbulent, declining empires with large armies are exceedingly dangerous." He's been reporting on Latin America since 1983, and produced a substantial story from Buenos Aires, "Argentina Drifts Toward Disaster," 9-89. A review of the sins of Peronism and their legacy, and a competent critique of various economic policy schemes in circulation, he also does very competent reporting on the current situation in the country. Still, there are plenty of jarring notes, as he asserts it's not possible to stop hyperinflation without the shock of a recession.

Farney, Dennis. *The Wall Street Journal.* (★ ★)
Kansas City, MO. Having escaped the Washington bureau after years in chains, Farney is cheerier than we've ever seen him. Colorful, wry, and empathetic, his writing is never as horizontal as the great plains he covers. "From the Heartland: Kansans Are Optimistic About Bush But Say He's No Dwight Eisenhower," 1-20, a survey of what Abilene thinks of George Bush on Inauguration Day is light stuff, redeemed by its nice touch. "A Hot, New Personality for the Democrats, Kerrey Tries to Reconcile Washington and His Nebraska," 5-15, is a press release rewrite, minimally informative on Sen. Robert Kerrey. "Nature Conservancy-led Land Preservation Plan Outperforms and Out-Innovates Federal Program," 5-24, is a short, but appreciated look at the Natural Heritage Program, a scientific conservation effort, that's good on their methods, short on their means. In "A Centennial View: The First Hundred Years — One Newspaper's Century: The Inside Story," 6-23, Farney skips too much to be definitive in this accounting of the people that helped make the *Journal* great on its centennial; though we do get loads of history here with illustrative anecdotes, Farney never mentions that supply-side theory, hallmark of the Reagan revolution, really got its rebirth through Robert Bartley's editorial pages. "To the Stresses Faced by Rural Clergyman, and His Own Isolation," 7-14, a feature on the pressures faced by a small town minister, is well written, solidly reported, earning it P. 1 status, and Farney delivers a delightful observation about Kansas: it is "overwhelmingly horizontal." "Abiding Frontier: On the Great Plains, Life Becomes a Fight for Water and Survival," 8-16, is an above average, but not exceptional, story of life on the Great Plains in the late 20th century, providing a good taste of man's struggle against nature, and the endless onslaught of the elements.

Fineman, Howard. *Newsweek.* (★ ★ ½)
Chief political correspondent. The weekly's political bigfoot has a knack for clear writing and sensible organization, adding several uncommon insights on race and abortion politics this year. We've knocked him before for an unpleasant snideness that creeps into his material, and thankfully it's crept out. Fineman's output was unusually low as he worked on a book, and there were not many incisive big think efforts from him. His best, "Pro-Choice Politicking," with Michael Reese, Daniel Glick and Patricia King 10-9, was prescient in outlining how different candidates are using the abortion issue, keying on polls showing a pro-choice drift. He sees Virginia's Douglas Wilder using it as a "silver bullet" on his way to becoming the nation's first black governor. He can be thought-provoking on racial subtleties, as with "Playing the Politics of Race," 2-6, on the consequences of Ron Brown as new Democratic National Committee Chairman. Again, in " 'It's Like I'm the Invisible Man,' " 10-16, he sees "the heady,

uncomplicated days of 'Run, Jesse Run' are over, and workaday politics intrudes" for the Rev. Jackson as moderate blacks distance themselves from him. In "The Politics of Race," 11-6, he carries the theme another step, observing black candidates competing "to portray themselves to whites as champions of interracial harmony." A sidebar, "For the Son of C-Span, Exposure-Power," 4-3, is a quick, crisp profile of new House Minority Whip Newt Gingrich, which attributes his rise to power to his exposure on C-Span, and summarizes his strategy as playing "video samurai against the Democrats on issues such as drugs, crime, taxes and welfare. Now that baby boomers have become parents, Gingrich believes, they are ready for a hard-line traditionalist message." His "Congress and the Culture of Money," 6-5, is smart in analyzing the footings of the Wright/Coelho ethics problems. He reports that "Democrats are trapped in a machinery they built to protect themselves. The process of collecting cash is time-consuming, hard to police and a continual temptation to step over fuzz lines." The treatment is too cursory in "Playing the Politics of Reform," 7-10, on both parties' attempts to steal the election reform issue, covering everything from franking privileges to gerrymandering, but too quickly.

Fritz, Sara. *Los Angeles Times.* (★ ½)
Senate reporter, Fritz combines straightforward, dependable reporting with an occasionally refreshing analytic, her better work on defense issues. We don't often find subtlety or uncommon angles in her material, however. She writes up the John Tower defeat with a hammer in "53-47 Vote is Humiliating Blow to Bush," 3-10. It's a "smashing blow" to Bush, a "humiliating setback" that saw him, at the 11th hour, "plead" with Democratic senators to cross party lines to vote for confirmation, while afterwards "Nobody credited Bush with persuading them to vote for Tower." Ouch. Not a word to suggest that Bush cheered his partisans by getting into the trenches on behalf of his old friend in this losing cause. "3 Issues Key to Panel's Verdict in Wright Probe," 4-13, is a well-structured, unbiased overview of the charges against House Speaker Jim Wright, a good job of detailing the charges and how the special prosecutor hopes to make his case. "Defense Budget Ok'd but Panel Wants B-2," 7-15, on Senate committee passage of the defense budget starts out routinely, then builds to an interesting debate over who gets what and for how much. Among her more analytical efforts, "Congress Determinedly Meddles In Policy-Making," 8-5, is better on the who and how than the why, but still instructive on congressional "micromanaging" of national security policy. Rampant during the Reagan years, it continues into the Bush administration, despite pledges of better cooperation and consultation between the branches of government. She's on spongier ground with her analysis in "Key Lawmakers Discount Soviet Shift on Arms," 9-26, where Fritz lets us know that even though the Soviets will no longer let SDI stand in the way of a START agreement, congressional Democrats will. "Bank Panel Chief Asks Bush to Fire S&L Regulator," 10-31, is another weekly installment in the ongoing S&L serial. First Fritz tells us that House Banking Committee Chairman Henry B. Gonzalez wants President Bush to fire M. Danny Wall, director of the Office of Thrift Supervision. Then she tells us why, an adequate account by this non-financial scribe.

Gerstenzang, James. *Los Angeles Times.* (★ ½)
Washington. A former Pentagon correspondent with good sources but so-so instincts, Gerstenzang is the *Times*' top honcho on the White House beat. We don't find him making any egregious errors, but, shying away from daring work, he doesn't dazzle either. "Reagan Challenges Soviet Commitment on Pullout of Troops from Afghanistan," 12-28-88, is a solid, thorough and clearly written report on Reagan's no-nonsense view on the Soviet withdrawal from Afghanistan and the likely U.S. response if the Soviets continue to support the Kabul regime with weapons. Once past a garbled, overly long lead, "Asia Trip Gives Bush Chance to Review Policies," 2-22, satisfies with a well-balanced overview of the Bush administration on the eve of Bush's Asian trip. He turns to domestic concerns in "Bush Says Gun Control Answer Is Up to States," 3-21, producing a deficient report, depending on sources with an apparent ability to read minds, relying on someone "familiar with the President's thinking." He makes good use of quotes in "Bush Urges Coup to Topple Noriega," 5-14, on remarks the President

made regarding Noriega's possible ouster. But we get hodgepodge in "Americans Collide With Gallic Indifference," 7-15, on the Economic Summit, opening with inconveniences associated with French conference planners, then brushing over an alarming security lapse around the President, and finally wandering off on descriptions of the dinner menu and Bush's lineage according to Burke's peerage. "Bogota Will Get $65 Million in Emergency Aid," 8-26, is good on the particulars of the Colombian military aid package, but, perhaps because Gerstenzang files this report from Kennebunkport we get only the administration's side of the issue. Covering one of Bush's major foreign policy addresses of the year, "Bush Offers Cut in Chemical Arms," 9-26, he produces a lukewarm front page lead. He delivers some footnotes to the Panama fiasco in "Bush Backs Webster, Aide Says, Amid Report He'll Be Replaced," while giving both Webster supporters and backstabbers equal time.

Gerth, Jeff. *The New York Times.* (★ ★)
The *Times'* top sleuth, Gerth starts the year with a bang, digging into possible improprieties in the office of ethical propriety, but in this year of juicy scandals and exposes, he didn't deliver the big scoop. Working off an anonymous tip, he's hot on the tail of presidential counsel C. Boyden Gray, probing his financial affairs in "Bush Ethics Aide Kept Outside Job," 2-4, and "New Account of Ethics Briefing," 2-5. Gerth's reporting uncovers at least the appearance of ethical violations, and provokes a heated response from *The Wall Street Journal,* an editorial ("Gerth, Safire and Anonymous," 2-6) disputing the thrust of the stories. "For Some Officials, The Revolving Door Turns Smoothly," 3-19, begins with the confirmation hearings on Deputy Secretary of State Lawrence Eagleburger, broadening to survey how some high-level federal appointees have more trouble than others in securing Senate confirmation. While offering a schematic picture of other candidates, such as George Shultz, Treasury's David Mulford, and John Tower, Gerth raises a worthy, thorny question: How can the federal government attract top-flight talent with current byzantine conflict-of interest regulations? "Kissinger and Friends and Revolving Doors," with Sarah Bartlett 4-30, outlines some possibly questionable conflicts of interest at Kissinger Associates that are ultimately inconclusive. We do learn that Henry Kissinger's client presentations interestingly are "mostly oral." Good instincts and dogged reporting show in "Wright, Needing Money, Got Special Treatment in Venture," 5-5, Gerth producing juicy material on the soured Texas nursing home investments by the Speaker of the House, in which Wright received $22,000 from the bankrupt company while other investors got nothing. "Risks to H.U.D. Rose After Its Shift Of Responsibility to Private Sector," 7-31, is detailed and rich with information on the breakdown of oversight within the department, but it overdoes the link between the problems and a dogged pursuit of Reagan's goals. Gerth explains complicated situations with clarity, as in a deftly handled "Loss of $4 Billion Is Found in Audit of Mortgage Fund," 9-28.

Gest, Ted. *U.S.News & World Report.* (★ ½)
Gest focuses primarily on the judiciary, and his reporting on the volatile court issues this year was balanced and informative. He doesn't fully satisfy with "The Bizarre and Troubling Escapades of Mayor Barry," 1-9. We get a rundown of DC Mayor Marion Barry's personal misadventures, but little of his administration. "The Drive To Make America Porn-Free," 2-6, works fairly enough because Gest attempts to maintain balance in this report on the rising opposition to pornography. He adequately updates us in "Bringing the Terrorists to Justice," 3-6, on the trial of captured terrorist Fawaz Younis, including an examination of the loopholes in international law used by terrorists to avoid extradition. Gest contributed to two cover stories on crime this year, "Murder Zones," 4-10, and headlining "Victims Of Crime," 7-31, each effort respectably informative. In "New Abortion Fights," 4-24, Gest projects that the Supreme Court will not overturn *Roe v. Wade* in the upcoming *Webster* decision, and focuses on Justice Sandra Day O'Connor as the pivotal vote. He wisely avoided the usual rhetorical quotes from pro-life and pro-choice advocates that weigh down reports on how the Court may proceed on the issue. Gest was the headliner in "The Abortion Furor," 7-17, an article on the *Webster* decision featuring the usual newsweekly byline of a cast of thousands, but the article rises above the

passions of the moment and provides some historical perspective: "What Rehnquist did not say was that the *Webster* decision did something the Court has done only rarely in its 200-year history: Cut back on a right it had granted, in this case less than a decade earlier." He was also able to discern judicial trends, such as the growing activism of state courts, as in "The Swing to the Left in State Courts," 10-23, where he reports that "The real hot spot for judicial activism these days is state courts, where jurists in increasing numbers are expanding the rights of citizens at the same time the Supreme Court is limiting constitutional protections in such areas as privacy and discrimination." While Gest doesn't go into the subject in depth, we get enough of an overview to come away informed and feel safe in predicting that "radical" state courts will figure prominently in conservative mail fundraising drives in the '90s.

Greenhouse, Linda. *The New York Times.* (★ ★)
Supreme Court. We thought she might be unhappy last year, shifted back to the Court after an interesting sojourn at the Senate. If so, she's adjusted, handling this beat with estimable objectivity, keeping any biases under control. Although Greenhouse popped up in the pro-choice March on Washington (and was called on it by her editors), you'd never know her position on the abortion (or other) issues from her reporting. "Collapse of North Trial: Back to Basics," 1-7, gives the background leading up to Lawrence Walsh's decision to drop the heart of the case against Oliver North: "The administration's stance was inherently suspect for the obvious reason that both the departing President and the incoming one had nothing to gain from a trial that threatened to dissect a mortifying foreign policy debacle." Thorough and balanced, "Court Bars a Plan Set Up to Provide Jobs to Minorities," 1-24, is a fairly satisfying account of the 6-3 vote, but it could have used a little legal background. "Justices Void New York City's Government; Demand an End of 5 Borough's Inequity," 3-23, provides a clear, crisp description of the interwoven constitutional law and political issues for the city; while the one-person, one-vote basis of the ruling could hardly be a surprise, the political fallout may be hard to predict. We get some vignettes and anecdotes not seen elsewhere in "For One Hour, a Look into Abortion's Future," 4-26, with some presentation on the court's workings, but the system by which they hear cases isn't clear. "A Changed Court Revises Rules on Civil Rights," 6-18, on three recent SCOTUS rulings that seem to set up a new tide against civil rights activists on quotas, etc., contains good material and analysis. However, it is rather confusing at the top, requiring careful re-reading to get to the gist. "Supreme Court, 5-4, Narrowing *Roe v. Wade,* Upholds Sharp State Limits on Abortions," 7-4, is firm and objective on the long-awaited decision, containing good analytical material at the end of the piece, which would have been clearer had it appeared earlier in the article. "High Court Facing Fight on Abortion, Privacy and Death," 10-2, is a respectable overview of the SCOTUS caseload for the fall, with some analytics, with everything nicely pulled together. In "Abortion: A New Round," 11-24, she sets the stage for the Court scheduled hearings of Ohio and Michigan cases involving parental notice of teenage abortion and the wider implications for *Roe v. Wade,* alerting us that the administration is gearing its arguments to Justice Sandra Day O'Connor, the swing vote on abortion issues.

Hall, Carla. *The Washington Post.* (★ ½)
"Style" reporter. She can craft finely written stories and profiles, but even given the wide bounds of "Style," there's often more fluff than substance. We *do* need to come away feeling informed as well as entertained by the wordsmithing. In "The Lawyer Who Will Challenge Oliver North," 1-31, despite the fact that her subject refused to speak with her, we got a real sense of John Keker, the cocky lawyer who prosecuted Oliver North. Hall brings him to life in great part through the words of Keker's law partners, and it's not all praise. "AIDS Anxiety: The Message in the Hudson Verdict," 2-20, has plenty of quotes from a variety of knowledgeable sources, but tells little about the far-ranging consequences of the "Hudson Verdict." "Ron Brown, the Practical Politician," 3-14, is a well-written profile of Ron Brown, the first black man to be chairman of the Democratic National Committee, full of information, but not enough analysis, with apparently Hall finding Brown a tough nut to crack: "When you ask Brown's friends about him, they give you his resume. So does Brown." In "The Salvadoran Story," 4-26, we get a moving

tale of a woman whose murdered husband is the focus of her mission to testify on human rights violations in El Salvador, well-told. Nonetheless, Hall has to set the stage better by including a clear, concise summation of the political conflict in El Salvador. Too much emotion, not enough substance mars "Arab Americans & the Voices of the Intifada: A Conference Focuses on Palestine's Uprising," 4-17, as it promises a refreshing American-Arab angle to the *intifada* debate but only repeats familiar abstract images: "Palestinians have come to occupy Israel psychologically as Israel physically occupies Palestine." "Welfare Woes of Hill Wife Mary Davis," 6-8, is just plain silly, a non-story played out in the *Post,* with Mary Davis angry at estranged husband Rep. Robert Davis (R-Mich.) for moving in with a 26-year-old aide. "Bridesmaids Revisited, & A Princess Recalled," 8-21, is fluff on Grace Kelly's bridesmaids, profiling Judith Quine and her book, *The Bridesmaids,* not telling us much of anything, with no sense of what it was like, or what life is like now for these women. One is in a New York shelter — by what tortured paths did she get there?

Hallow, Ralph Z. *The Washington Times.* (★ ½)
Political writer. Hallow impressed us with his Campaign '88 material, but slips a notch this year. His conservatism always sticks out in his idiosyncratic approach, but too often he works only the GOP side of the party fence to produce political pictures that are satisfying or complete. His sources among GOP conservatives are his bread and butter, but he's much less rigorous about getting inside the Democrat operations and mindsets. He picks up the shifting sentiments on the John Tower nomination with "Support From GOP Wanes," 2-9, giving us the mood at least with pro and con quotes from Republicans. Hallow ascribes the right proportions to Newt Gingrich's election as GOP Whip in "Gingrich Ascends to Power as Man with Mission," 3-23, which portends a "sea change" in the posture, status and fortunes of House Republicans. "GOP Quick Study Leaves Wright Twisting in the Wind," 4-14, retraces, step-by-step, the year-old, unobtrusive GOP strategy, in which Gingrich was only a cog, that brought about the Speaker's present unspeakable woes. "Conservatives Split into Warring Camps," 6-2, teases with items on a growing, bitter rift within the conservative movement, but doesn't go in deeper: "Neoconservatives, in the eyes of the so called 'paleoconservatives' of the old right, are the Johnny-come-lately ex-liberals and ex-Marxists who, disgusted by the left's flag-burning and dope-taking, converted to conservativism in the 1960s. . .Paleocons also think U.S. policy tilts too much toward Israel." "Civil Rights Panel Chief Fears GOP Slipping Left," 7-24, outlines the issues and personalities behind the fight to shape the policies of the U.S. Civil Rights Commission whose chairman, William Allen, objects to capitulating to liberal pressure. This is acceptable, but it's still one-side-of-the-street reporting. Hallow comes across as an uncritical conduit for partisan factions at times. For example, "Lucas Vote May Produce a Meaner Bush," 8-2, reports Senate Republican leaders are clamoring for, and mapping out, a tougher partisan stance. But he retails rhetoric: "The hand of friendship President Bush has been extending to the Democrat-controlled Congress may turn into a fist after the Senate Judiciary Committee's rejection of William Lucas, the White House hinted and some Republican lawmakers demanded." His "Embarrassed Leaders Want Frank To Go," 9-8, is rather lax reporting, the conclusion without much depth. "Gephardt, Moderates Dueling as Rift Shows," 10-20, updates us on the Democrats' ideological flux, although to be credible on the Gephardt-Sam Nunn ideological differences we really need more details.

Harrison, Eric. *Los Angeles Times.* (★ ★ ½)
Chicago. Like a great painter, Harrison possesses an immense gift for evoking just the right atmosphere without artifice. He can uncover the natural drama of a story without any sacrifice of detail or information. "Jamaicans: New Faces in U.S. Crime," 1-3, an enterprising and fast-paced report on how Jamaican drug gangs, "Bloods & Crips," invaded Kansas City, immediately caught our attention. "Protesters Absent as Brown Endorses Daley in Chicago," 3-21, crackles with tension, as Harrison combines high drama with effective, forceful quotes to point up the intrigue among black Democrats as Ron Brown zips in and out of Chicago to endorse candidate Richard Daley. "Weeping Father Pulls Gun, Stops Life Support," with Tracy Shryer 4-17, is

a powerful, non-sensational recounting of Rudolfo Linares unplugging his 15-month-old son from a life support system that had kept the child alive for eight months after he choked on a balloon. In an "American Album" column 5-29, he is uncharacteristically businesslike on the centennial celebration of the Johnstown, PA, flood that decimated the town, giving us all the information, but not a real sense of the continued high spirit of the people there. "Did Cocaine Sting Fuel Drug Sales?" 6-14, professionally and clearly done, tells the complicated story of a Cleveland drug sting operation gone awry: the police got their men, and then were tried (and acquitted) for conspiracy to sell drugs. Harrison connects the story's relevance to the mayoral race, as candidates are split between support and condemnation for the police. He keeps himself out of "Exiled Student Sees New Hope for China," 7-29, but there's an engaging empathy in this report on the Chicago speech of China's Student Democracy Movement organizer Wuer Kaixi. He satisfies with an effective overview and analysis of Cleveland's politics in "Fiery Council President Leads Pack for Mayoral Primary in Cleveland," 10-3. Although vivid on black attorney George Forbes, he avoids any unprofessional projections on the electoral outcome.

Harwood, Richard. *The Washington Post.* (★ ★ ★)
"Ombudsman" columnist. A senior editor at the *Post* after a distinguished career as a congressional and political reporter, Harwood opted for this op-ed column that enables him to stand above the internal politics of the paper in helping shape it through gentle critiques. It is now the best regular column of press commentary we see, Harwood not limiting his wise and witty observations to the *Post.* In "A Shilling From the King," 1-22, he comments on ethical questions arising in the Periodical Press Gallery of Congress, of narrow interest, but with a marvelous lead: "Washington has two great obsessions, the Redskins and money. More than a trillion dollars a year pours in for redistribution by the politicians, which accounts for the perepetual porcine glint in our eyes." His "Memo to the Captain," 3-19, is a very entertaining, offbeat column, a memo to *Post* president Richard Simmons regarding a letter from a 79-year-old lady in a local hospital who has asked for the *Post* to alphabetize its obituary list. In "Ads Not Fit to Print," 4-30, Harwood challenges NBC's Mike Gartner's attack on commercial censorship of any kind, with serious pros and cons well developed. A remarkable piece, "A Bloodbath the Media Missed," 7-23, grows out of a call to Harwood complaining that the paper's coverage of the May 16 attempted coup d'etat in Ethiopia was covered poorly. Harwood calls a friend in the intelligence community, who agrees to provide an account of the coup, and we are treated to an excellent, sanitized intelligence report of that fascinating affair. "Unnamed Sources," 6-11, has several news items as examples of stories from anonymous sources that turned out to be wrong, topped with an admission of error in one of his own pieces that had an unidentified source, although "senility has not been ruled out."In "Not Uncommon Conflicts," 9-24, he weighs the dual ethical standard for journalists in receiving honoraria or engaging in political activity, depending upon whether they work for the paper or merely write for it, like Henry Kissinger: "The politician/pundits we have brought into the news business operate in an ethical world of their own making." He anguishes over the fact that fewer young adults are reading newspapers these days, "We're Losing the Boomers," 11-26, citing a Knight-Ridder survey: "Financial and work-related stresses and heightened interest in health, fitness and home have shifted [their] attention from society to self," away from reading to the tube. "It is perhaps the Luddite in me," says Harwood, "but I cannot he is that will survive out of all this. Our newspapers, for all their frailties, have had personalities and — unfashionable thought — souls. If that is lost because of the fickleness of the Boomers and the clutter in their lives, it will be one of the unhappy ironies of the age."

Hedges, Michael. *The Washington Times.* (★)
Investigative reporter. Hedges' work is sometimes written in a style more suited to the *New York Post* than his own paper. While some entries inform and educate, others repel. "Bennett Wants to Make 'Casual Users' Pay," 3-20, rehashes Drug Czar William Bennett's appearance on "Meet the Press." "Feds Debate Plan to Put Bounty on Drug Kings," 6-14, scoops on the ongoing

debate inside federal agencies around a customs service proposal, "Operation Paladin," offering up to a $5 million reward for "information leading to the capture of alleged drug smugglers like Manuel Noriega and the leaders of the Medellin and Cali cocaine cartels. . .." "Drug Trial Testimony Forced Castro's Hand, Officials Believe," 6-26, is interesting on the fallout from the Cuban drug bust of General Ochoa. "Power Broker Served Drugs, Sex at Parties Bugged for Blackmail," co-written by Jerry Seper 6-30, sensationally probes the homosexual prostitution ring of Craig J. Spence, not clearly differentiating between his legitimate business gatherings and blackmail, with no sense that any illegal activity was "alleged," the lead reading: "Craig J. Spence, an enigmatic figure who threw glittery parties for key officials of the Reagan and Bush administrations, media stars and top military officials, bugged the gatherings to compromised guests, provided cocaine, blackmailed some associates and spent up to $20,000 a month on male prostitutes, according to friends, acquaintances and records." His "friends" and "acquaintances" are for the most part quoted anonymously, and "records" are never quoted from directly, leaving us questioning the veracity of the charges, given their seriousness. "White House Access Probed," 7-3, portions out morsels of the scandal, some recycled from the 6-30 article, repeating verbatim the menu of names on Spence's party list, which included: "Eric Severeid, Ted Koppel and William Safire; former CIA director William Casey; [and] the late John Mitchell" but *not* telling us if this list has anything to do with Spence's prostitution activities. "Sex Party Held at Aussie Embassy," with Seper 7-28, is also hot on the trail of Washington perversion, atop the front page, spread across all six columns. The final ignominy for the Hedges-Seper tango is found in "Spence Arrested in N.Y., Released," 8-9, a six-column spread with two articles on one eight-hour interview with Craig J. Spence, a lurid account of Spence's activities, repeating some of the information previously published. We can't call this journalism: " 'How do you think a little faggot like me moved in the circles that I did?' Mr. Spence asked, his hand fondling the razor blade like the flesh of a lover." His repeated suggestions of suicide didn't faze the reporters, who let him slip off into the night, instead putting him on the front page. A post-mortem by the duo is equally repellent; "In Death, Spence Stayed True to Form," 11-3, reprints excerpts from Spence's suicide note. Similar to the Barney Frank story, the Spence story has all the makings of Greek tragedy, but the way it's told here it's not fit to wrap fish in.

Hoffman, David. *The Washington Post.* (★ ★ ★)
White House. The *Post*'s political bigfoot now that Lou Cannon has faded from the scene, Hoffman is making the most out of the extra room. Flexing more analytical muscle and relying on his own instincts, he turns out his best year yet. There is frequently a quality, big-picture aspect to his reports. He produces just that with "Kemp Chosen for HUD; 'Innovative Ideas' Urged," 12-20-88, working the multiple angles and various dimensions of the appointment. He's alert and thoughtful with "Is There a Deal-Maker in the White House?" 3-26. We get succinct, accurate information in "Bush Is Pressed to Kill Japan Jet Deal," with Stuart Auerbach 3-16, on how the dispute between Commerce and the Pentagon over joint production of the FSX jet fighter with Japan split Bush's NSC. Among all the stories looking at the Bush administration after its first three months, none equalled "Bush's Relentless Pragmatism," 4-30, a 10 Best selection. Hoffman is excellent on synthesizing Bush's management style into a short recap of his first 100 days. His fine reportorial instincts come through in "Bush Looking Anew for Ways To Assert U.S. Leadership," 5-26, on White House dismay with its vaunted policy reviews. He has a fine grasp of the broader overall trends and utilizes excellent quotes from appropriate sources for maximum effect. "China Executions Push Bush to Focus on Future," 6-25, is a credible account of the rationale behind Bush's cautious approach to China. A well-written "Affability, Broad Goals Helping Bush to Stretch Out Honeymoon," 7-2, updates us with an evaluation on Bush's performance. "Bush: Making Himself Up As He Goes Along," 8-13, is not a perfect piece, but the theme is useful in this "Outlook" lead, and Hoffman takes us in for an insightful look at the President's executive style seven months into his administration: "He can't wait until it appears that circumstances are nearly spinning out of control, until his advisors are yanking their hair out, and his friends are telephoning and his critics are in full cry." Bush is

evolving as President and "[t]he next evolution is already on its way and may come into full view this fall." Hoffman had one of the year's big scoops in "December Summit Is Possible," 10-31, where he broke the story of the Bush-Gorbachev summit in the Mediterranean. Most of the fun in this type of article is trying to guess who the "administration official" is that acted as the source. Given the statements here ("The administration official said such a meeting could have benefits for Bush, too, primarily in lessening criticism from Democrats that he has been too timid or cautious in responding to the fast-paced changes in the Eastern Bloc"), our guess is somebody close to Jim Baker, maybe even the Secretary himself. Your move. "The Man Gorbachev Will Face Across the Summit Table," *Weekly* 11-27/12-3, is a waste of time, offering no new insights into Bush, while allowing various unnamed sherpas to lower expectations for the upcoming summit and protesting far too much that, unlike Reagan at Reykjavik, Bush won't get his lunch handed to him by Gorbachev. Readers could learn more about the stakes involved in Malta from the accompanying political cartoon.

Ifill, Gwen. *The Washington Post.* (★ ½)
A political writer covering the Department of Housing and Urban Development this year, Ifill's reporting is competent and fair. Although she occasionally covers HUD Secretary Jack Kemp more than the agency (breaking little new ground), her overviews are respectable and her background material generally appropriate and accurate. "Friends of Domestic Spending Knock on White House's Door," 1-20, is an acceptable account, with some wry humor scattered throughout, on different domestic "beggars" — mayors, *et al.* — who come pleading for federal monies for federally approved programs that Bush supported during the campaign. "Bill to Create Housing Aid Home Sales Offered," 3-16, speedily updates on a tax break bill for first-time home buyers, but shortchanges with little evaluation of the bill's merits or chances for passage. "Kemp Cancels 1989 Funds to Fix Low-Income Housing," 4-27, outlines the beginning of difficulties at HUD, with an informing focus on Kemp. "After Years of Obscurity, HUD Emerges in Scandal," 5-30, delivers a respectable broad overview of the agency, but more on HUD's ultimate goals wouldn't have been inappropriate. "HUD Moved Fast on Carmen Project," 6-22, is an accurate account given the information available to Ifill at the time on the Pebble Creek deal. "Foggy Recollections, Contradictions Mark Testimony of 3 in HUD Probe," 7-17, examines the relationship between Black, Manafort, Stone & Kelly and questionable HUD projects, the information still taking shape and Ifill not running off ahead of it. She catches an incisive quote from Sen. Robert Graham (D-Fla.) that efficiently distills a graphic observation on HUD consultants and their tab in "Twenty Consultants Made Millions Lobbying For HUD Projects," 8-4: "In the earlier hearings we identified the rats. Now we're starting to identify the cheese that attracted these rats." Her "Armed Forces Making Strides, Powell Says," 8-18, contains no surprises on Joint Chiefs of Staff Chairman Gen. Colin Powell's speech to the association of black journalists, but is nicely documented. The selection of quotes is sharp in "Balky Witnesses May Limit Houses HUD Inquiry," 9-29, although the reporting is routine on former HUD Secretary Samuel Pierce, Deborah Gore Dean and Lance Wilson taking the fifth.

Innerst, Carol. *The Washington Times.* (★ ½)
Education writer. We found her reporting less engaging this year, perhaps because she didn't have William Bennett for raw material. She simply doesn't catch us quickly enough with a compelling reason why we should read the stories she's filing, especially with education such a hot topic with or without Wild Bill. Off the education track, "Welfare Welcome Mat Is Rolled Up," *Insight* 2-13, displays some energy that goes beyond the routine in this report on Wisconsin's attempt to lower the state's attractiveness to out-of-state poor. There's thought-provoking counterpoint from the position of the poor in this balanced, informative story. However, there isn't much to digest in "Not All Free Speech to Berkeley's Liking," 5-8, on the witch hunt by leftwingers against a recently launched moderate conservative student newspaper on the Berkeley campus. Likewise, the substance is only adequate in "Futrell Tells NEA: No More Apologies," 7-3, on the politicking and rhetoric at the NEA's annual convention, where President Bush, who wants to be known as the "education president" is the National Education

Association's main target. "Financial Aid Softens Impact of High Tuition," 8-10, surveys the ever-burgeoning difficulties of financing a four-year college education, as rates for tuition and room and board jump again. "Shake-Up Hits Hoover Institution," 9-1, accurately captures the politics and economics behind the tug-of-war between Hoover Institution and Stanford University that resulted in W. Glenn Campbell's "forced" retirement: "Ousting the crusty, hard-line conservative who for 30 years has protected Hoover's autonomy has raised new fears of the think tank's academic and financial absorption by Stanford's traditionally liberal faculty and administration." The optimism in "No Quick Fixes Expected From Education Summit," with Frank J. Murray 9-27, is overdone in this preview of Bush's "education summit" with state governors. "Colleges Torn by Racial Violence," 10-26, reports that instances of harassment, intimidation and physical attacks on campuses are being reported to the Justice Department at double the rate of last year. However, there's not much exploring in this report.

Isikoff, Michael. *The Washington Post.* (★)
Covering the drug story for the *Post,* Isikoff's assignment finds him often filing dispatches from abroad. His reporting is a very mixed bag, as some stories suggest he has an axe to grind, although others are professionally handled. We get a balanced overview of the DEA's controversial campaign against South American cocaine traffickers in "U.S. Expands Role in Peru's Drug War," 1-23. He reports important details of "Operation Snowcap" and includes DEA Administrator John C. Lawn's comments in defense of the program and in contradiction to charges the U.S. is "running the ops." "U.S. Sues Nine Banks in Drug Money Laundering," 3-30, gives us too much cops-and-robbers in Central America, too little on the legal and economic implications of the Feds suing banks holding drug money. Isikoff's been on the beat long enough to judge the credibility of certain sources, yet he indulges discredited sources in "Reagan Aides Accused of Hampering Drug War," 4-14, a retelling of Christic Institute and Lyndon LaRouche accusations about the contras' involvement in drug trafficking. The story reads like boilerplate from Sen. John Kerry's office. He's much better with "U.S. Suffering Setbacks In Latin Drug Offensive," 5-27, a critical, if disheartening status report on the "near breakdown of U.S. antidrug policy throughout Latin America," identifying intractable political problems on the ground and the range of options being considered by the NSC. "Top Officer Arrested in Cuba," with Julia Preston 6-17, covers the basic information on the arrest in Cuba of one of the country's most distinguished military commanders and eight other high-level officials on charges of drug trafficking. "'Privatizing' the FBI's Files," 7-24, is informative on OMB's budget-driven order to send certain computerized functions of the FBI to outside contractors. He cites examples of problems and success with such edicts. "Their Man in Washington," *Weekly* 10-9/15-89, on an ex-Justice lawyer and adviser to the Colombia's Cali cartel, Michael Abbell, is a gripping report, the details of which leave us numbed. Abbell, who headed the Justice Dept. office charged with extraditing alleged drug traffickers to the U.S., now has been retained to advise alleged Colombian traffickers on how to avoid extradition to the U.S. Isikoff restrains any bias, letting the facts speak for themselves.

Jackson, Brooks. *The Wall Street Journal.* (★ ★)
Washington. Much of Jackson's work on the Congressional ethics story builds on information previously published in other sources. Nothing wrong with that, but we'd like to see Jackson doing more of his own research, rather than recycling the competition. "Coelho Confirms Profiting in 1986 Drexel Bond Issue," 4-14, follows up on a 4-13 *Washington Post* story that Rep. Tony Coelho allegedly used campaign funds to purchase Drexel junk bond offerings; this one reports Coelho's denial, blaming the discrepancy on a "computer error" by Drexel. "Speaker Wright Faces a Long, Tough Trial by Ethics Committee," with David Rogers 4-18, is a P. 1 leder on the committee report, but tells little about Wright's prospects or politics of the House. "Coelho Stuns Colleagues with Decision to Quit Congress before End of Term," 5-30, gives good detail on Coelho and the press. "Many Additional Charges Could Have Been Lodged," 6-1, reviews the bill of particulars against Wright, plus charges not raised by Ethics Committee. "Rep. Matsui is Finding It Hard to Roll Back Break He Gave Utilities," co-written by Jeffrey

H. Birnbaum 7-13, uses Rep. Robert Matsui (D-Calif.) to stomp the utility industry on $19 billion refund legislation, prosecutorial journalism, barely a nod at utility arguments. But the big disappointment in Jackson's reporting was the multi-billion-dollar scandal at California's Lincoln S&L Association, involving five Senators, and possibly turning into one of the biggest messes of the century. *The Detroit News* got the ball rolling in '88 with a report on Sen. Don Riegle (D-Mich.), Senate banking chair, and his purported involvement. Jackson picked it up this year, but he only really started to dig *after* it got to committee level, blowing a scoop for the *WSJ*. "As Thrift Industry's Troubles and Losses Mounted, Its PAC's Donations to Key Congressmen Surged," 2-7, gets it going with computer correlations, shrewd in noting the new chair of House banking, Rep. Henry Gonzalez (D-Tex.) only got $1,750 over six years from the thrifts and seems eager to dig into the matter. "Common Cause Asks U.S. to Investigate Arizonan Keating's Gifts to 5 Senators," 10-16, is unusual as Common Cause bases its action on a quote from Lincoln's Charles Keating Jr. in an earlier Jackson story: "One question. . .had to do with whether my financial support in any way influenced several political figures to take up my cause. I want to say in the most forceful way I can: I certainly hope so." In "Gonzalez Pushes Forward in Lincoln S&L Probe," 10-24, he lets us know Gonzalez is not treating the S&L five with kid gloves. Covering a riveting day of testimony, "Thrift Examiners Say They Saw Signs of Criminal Wrongdoing at Lincoln," 11-1, Jackson doesn't have the space to cover what he wants, the fragments a jumble of quotes and assertions. And his P. 1 "How Regulatory Error Led to the Disaster at Lincoln Savings," 11-20, downplays the role of the Senators, bringing in peripheral stuff on the role of Donald Regan and Alan Greenspan during his pre-Fed consulting days. But a respectable summation to date: "What has come out so far isn't a pretty sight."

Jacoby, Tamar. *Newsweek.* (★ ½)
Justice. What we saw was certainly competent, but Jacoby's work shows little flair, sometimes making dry topics still more parched. "An End to Judicial Roulette," 1-30, is a cut and dry update of reforms and rules recently upheld by SCOTUS "premised on a simple idea: that similar criminals who commit similar crimes should receive similar sentences." " 'Now We're On Our Own,' " with Howard Manly, Ann McDaniel and Mark Starr 2-6, examines Supreme Court cutbacks on affirmative action, specifically recent legislation targeting local and state set-aside quotas, a thorough introduction to the impending battle. "Cops Above, Crime Below," with Michael A. Lerner 6-5, looks at the increasing use of helicopters by local and state police departments, specifically Los Angeles, Baltimore, and Texas, to do everything from chase down speeders to locate people lost in remote areas. A crisply written "A New Majority Ticks Off the Reagan Agenda," with Ann McDaniel 7-17, does a nice job of demonstrating that the Reagan majority on the Court has been moving judicial precedent in a rightward direction, but Jacoby glosses over fine distinctions, using too many generalizations. "Waking Up the Jury Box," with Tim Padgett 8-7, is a short piece exploring "jury liberation," an experimental process by which jurors are encouraged to take a more active role in proceedings in order to generate more reliable, accurate verdicts. "Asking juries to passively absorb all the testimony they hear is like asking a college student to take a course without any notes and then take a final exam by memory," says one judge.

Jehl, Douglas. *Los Angeles Times.* (★ ½)
Washington. Jehl's reporting beat includes the environment and drugs, both major focuses of the media all year. He stayed abreast of these stories with respectable coverage, although he never really got out ahead on them. "Hip Maverick Takes Over In Nation's War On Drugs," 1-30, is a first-rate backgrounder on William Bennett, as Jehl offers memorable vignettes of the drug czar's college days when the graduate student in philosophy would "down a few Lone Star beers, squash his cigarette and pick up a guitar." Jehl had one of the first interviews with new EPA chief William Reilly in "Clean Air Act Proposal May Ease City Deadlines," 2-22, allowing the administration's top environmentalist to get some spin control over upcoming revisions in the Clean Air Act. "Bennett Plans Drug Offensive in U.S. Capital," 3-14, provides good coverage of Bennett's plan to target the District for special federal assistance in combatting drug

trafficking in the face of opposition from other agencies with their own drug war agendas. "New U.S. Order Eases 'Let-Burn' Policy, Regards Lightning Fires As Dangerous," 6-2, outlines the government's new policies regarding forest fires with environmental reaction. The ecologists are worried that the government will now put out all fires, regardless of how they are caused. Jehl provided some insight in "Crews Use Pitchforks On Oil Globs," 6-27, a report following a weekend when three tanker spills occurred: "The administration's sharp criticism of oil tankers appeared in part to deflect attention from a new congressional attempt to impose a one-year moratorium on offshore oil drilling." "Trail of Alleged Bloch Spymaster Picked Up," 7-29, reporting the attempt by U.S. investigators to link U.S. diplomat Bloch to a Soviet posing as a Finnish businessman reveals little new information. He tries to fluff rumor and innuendo into a story here. Jehl attempted to give equal time to both sides on the issue of gun control in "Louisville Mayhem Seen Spurring Gun Debate," 9-15, but the opening — "With a spray of rifle fire and a trail of blood" — seems more appropriate for a tabloid.

Johnston, David. *The New York Times.* (★ ½)
Justice. The *Times* reporter assigned to the trial of Oliver North, Johnston maintained decent balance in his coverage, which for the most part he handled professionally and competently. He provides a taut, very readable account of former NSC aide Robert McFarlane's testimony at the North trial in "Reagan's Role Aiding Contras Is Told to Court by McFarlane," 3-16, in which McFarlane pegs Ronald Reagan as the instigator of a plan to assist Honduras in return for the country's aid to the contras. On the first day of North's testimony before his own lawyer, "North Takes the Stand to Defend Himself," 4-7, portrays the "calm and defiant" North as basically arguing that he was following orders as a loyal Marine Lt. Colonel. The only new item here is Judge Gesell's ordering North to turn over his private notebooks to prosecutors; Johnston does weaker reporting here than his counterpart at *The Washington Post,* George Lardner. "Ex-Marines Are Enemies: North Faces His Accuser," 4-11, is a rather strained attempt to endow the North trial with *Inherit the Wind* type of drama, playing up the fact that North and Prosecutor John Keker were both Vietnam-era combat heroes. We do learn that North blames William Casey for much of what he did, including the destruction of the secret money ledger. Johnston keeps the reporting flavorful on the continued cross-examination of North in "North Shifts Blame to His Boss for Several Misdeeds," 4-13, the Marine Lt. Col. fingering John Poindexter as another superior ordering him to destroy documents and mislead Congress. The reporting is deficient in "Judge Tells North Jury That No One Had a Right to Break the Law," 4-21, on the first day of jury deliberations in the Oliver North case, the material late and not covering the defense lawyer's rebuttal until the last paragraph. The reporting in "Score in Court is 3-9 and Iran-Contra Team Is Going to Bat Again," 5-17, is smart, Johnston getting inside the prosecuting team, though the analytics are underdone. "Bush Appears Set to Follow Reagan By Putting Conservatives on Bench," 5-31, is a timely review of an important topic, but Johnston doesn't present much of anything new. There's a noticeably objectionable spin in "U.S. Drops Part of its Case Against Iran-Contra Figures," 6-17, as theft, fraud, and conspiracy charges are dropped against Poindexter and Richard Secord, ostensibly to avoid legal infighting about classified documents. Johnston extrapolates that Ronald Reagan and George Bush knew more than they disclosed. We're confused by "Use of Secret Data Barred in Trial; Iran-Contra Prosecution Imperiled," 11-23, as Attorney General Richard Thornburgh takes a minor step in the action against Joseph Fernandez, the ex-CIA station chief in Costa Rica. Way down in this P. 1 piece we learn the problem could easily be solved by coding classified material, but we're not told why Lawrence Walsh, the special prosecutor, objects to this.

Kamen, Al. *The Washington Post.* (★ ★ ★)
Supreme Court. A year in which hotly-contested issues came before the Supreme Court, Kamen stayed coolly objective in his coverage. There's appropriate passion in his reporting, but we never ever guess how he might line up on one issue or another. "A Chance to Deepen Stamp on Court," with Ruth Marcus 1-29, gives good detail and quotes on presidential appointees to federal courts: "Within a few years, liberal judges will be an endangered species," says one professor of political

science. "Court Asked to Prohibit Execution of Juveniles," 3-28, is a short, but interesting and clear account of an oral argument before the Supreme Court, on whether inmates who were under 18 when they murdered their victims should be spared from execution. "Kennedy Moves Court to Right," 4-11, presents a superlative evaluation of Supreme Court Justice Anthony M. Kennedy's performance during the first fourteen months since his appointment, contending that Kennedy has altered the court's balance by proving to be "more conservative" than Robert H. Bork would have been. "Court Hears Oral Arguments in Missouri Antiabortion Case," 4-27, exhibits exemplary handling of arcane legal technicalities for a lay public very much interested in the legally complex *Roe v. Wade* case. "Landmark Rights Decision Narrowed Court Ruling Will Hamper Enforcement of Bias Laws, Opponents Say," 6-16, is clearer than most articles on the subject. "Court Nullifies Flag-Desecration Laws," 6-22, excels, often verging on the dramatic, resolving "an issue that had split the court for 20 years." Kamen's "Supreme Court Restricts Right to Abortion, Giving States Wide Latitude for Regulation," 7-4, is compact and measured on the news, balanced coverage for an emotional issue. Two articles later in the year, "Court Hears Argument on Peyote Use," 11-7, and "Court Hears Jailed Md. Mother's Case," 11-8, are competently done. Kamen acquaints the reader with the issues involved — the use of hallucinogenic drugs in religious ceremonies in "Peyote Use," and the jailing of a mother refusing to reveal the whereabouts of her allegedly abused son in "Mother's Case," without ever really tying the cases into larger social or judicial trends.

Keating, Susan Katz. *Insight.* (½ ★)
Sluggish this year — we don't know why, after a fairly zippy '88 — Keating just couldn't get her material together, her alert eye and facile pen falling away to drudgery. There's less analysis than there ought to be in "Shifting Appeal in Women's Slicks," 1-9, examining the ways women's magazines portray their subjects. She also disappoints by overlooking magazines for black women in this report on the fragmentation of the women's magazine market. "Modern Version of Medieval Gems," 1-16, on facsimiles of medieval illuminated manuscripts, leaves the reader with too many questions. She quotes one scholar saying "There is quite a bit of information you can get from the original that no facsimile can reproduce" but doesn't tell us what the information is. She assembles the facts and produces a solidly-written, interesting "Heading Off a Bogus Paper Chase," 4-17, on "research" firms that sell term papers to college students. Choppy and dry, "A Lesson on Year-Round Schools," 6-26, is an insufficiently fleshed out examination of extending the school year. Keating quotes one educator as saying that there's a lot of opposition because it's hard on working parents and difficult to plan vacations around the schedule. However, she doesn't adequately explain the situation, nor does she provide enough information on the costs and benefits of this type of system. There's little effort in "A Convention That's All Booked Up," 7-3, on the annual American Bookseller's Convention in Washington. Little more than a superficial description of one exhibit after another, there's no why, where, how, when content. A profile of Capt. Jacqueline Parker, the Air Force's first test pilot, "Female Test Pilot on the Fast Track," 11-27, drones: " 'The fighters are all so exotic,' she says, ticking off the F-16, the F-111 and the F-4. She smiles fondly at this last one, the Phantom used heavily during the Vietnam War. 'I like the F-4,' she says. 'The F-4 flies just like an old fighter.' " Zzzzzz.

Kenworthy, Tom. *The Washington Post.* (★ ½)
Capitol Hill. Kenworthy drew the scandal-and-sleaze watch on the Hill, covering this aspect of Congress with relative professional balance. "Intrigue in the House: Leadership Choices Loom," with Don Phillips 3-20, is accurate and informative on the current congressional leadership races, as both parties' choices will set the tone for the next election and beyond. "Texas Businessman Testifies on Wright Oil Profit," 5-4, is crisp, short and *understandable* on Jim Wright's and three others' $9,120 investment in an oil well that returned $440,000 on the same day — a $170,000 profit for the Speaker. Kenworthy's somewhat disorganized in "Wright, New Legal Team Join in Attack on Panel's Counsel," 5-10, on the efforts of House Speaker Jim Wright and his defense team to discredit the House Ethics Committee's special outside counsel,

Richard J. Phelan. There's a story here somewhere, but Kenworthy doesn't uncover it. "Panel Continues Probe of Wright Investment," 5-18, focuses on Wright's and his friends' politics of maneuvering to survive, with little emphasis on details of the charges against the Speaker. "Speaker Wright Said to Be Negotiating Resignation," 5-25, is a fast-paced news feed with the right priorities, focusing on GOP opposition, as well as the committee's nervousness with the idea that Wright would resign if the most serious charge against him were dropped. "Wright to Resign Speaker's Post, House Seat," 6-1, is a balanced and conciliatory account of the House Speaker's resignation, with focus on "the House's weariness with the turmoil of the Wright affair and its bewildered entry into a new era of ethics standards in which few understand the shifting ground rules." "Frank's Chances of Political Survival 'Looking Worse Every Day,' " with Don Phillips 9-19, updates on the "death watch," quoting several "colleagues and friends" of Frank who are urging him to resign. Kenworthy kept up with the November congressional gyrations over the budget. "Budget Bill Stalls as Republicans Charge Cuts Fall Short," 11-20, saves his best quote from a Democratic leadership aide for last: "It's going to get done. It's just a question of screaming at each other for awhile and deciding what's the most painless way to do it." And so it was.

Kirschten, Dick. *National Journal.* (★)
Departing his White House column for an urban/sociology beat, Kirschten can't complain he doesn't have a world of material beckoning. His reports are narrow and stolid, perhaps reflecting his inexperience this first year. As an Oval Office swan song he gave us "Reflections on Chiefs of Staff Who've Produced for the Gipper," 1-14, not very profound observations on several aides, "not known for ideological fervor, who have done the most to advance both the realities and the myths of the Reagan Revolution." Kirschten now produces lengthy sociological tracts that often contain worthy material, but are rarely developed smoothly. "Earning Bread at Home," 2-11, tells of GOP attempts to end New Deal prohibitions against textile "homework," but the topic needs crispness, sharper quotes, better images and analysis. He plods along again in "Leveraged Lobbying," 4-29, as local governments join with private sectors to lobby the feds on key issues. In the 8th graph we learn "the nub of the matter." A fast start in "The Melting Pot Recipe," 3-4: "With a fast-rising tide of international migration lapping against American shores, loud cries are being heard for a new system of levees and floodgates," but we're soon lost in a backwash of pressures and proposals. "Speaking English," 6-17, has excellent material on the debate over bilingual education, but he needs a sharper focus at the top to pull us in and keep our attention. "More Problems, Less Clout," 8-12, examines the problems big-city mayors are having to face, the biggest being cities are losing strength as people flock to the 'burbs, and the federal government and the political parties no longer jump when mayors speak. A cover on how Philadelphia is confronting the drug problem, "Taking Back The Streets," 9-30, is very slow in developing, hackneyed and useless at the top half: "On blocks where drug trafficking prospers, young men, flashing gold jewelry, sit on door stoops socializing with their girlfriends." We knew that. A one-page "Immigration Focus," entitled "Bearing the Burden," 11-4, has the makings of a terrific piece, "a classic example of the unexpected ways in which an immigration grapevine can grow," as Russian Pentecostals flood to Oregon and Hmong tribesman from Laos aim for St. Paul, simply because a tiny group of them got footholds there some years ago.

Klein, Joe. *New York.* (★ ★ ★ ★)
Contributing editor. A slambang year for this political reporter, who set the journalistic pace in the New York City mayoral race, staying fresh and on his toes following Campaign '88, while many others succumbed to lax reporting and insipid analysis. Klein's greatest attribute, aside from intelligence and professional skills, is his audacity in writing at the core of a campaign. "Race: The Issue," 5-29, and "Race: Still the Issue," 11-13, taken together for a 10 Best selection, are an excellent mix of commentary, analysis, and reporting on the topic the competition ignored. Klein's premise is compelling: "There is no question that the problem of the underclass can't be solved unless an ethic of personal responsibility pervades the entire society, from top to bottom." In "The Real Thing," 11-13, he laments that the heated campaign between David

Dinkins and Rudolph Giuliani did not reopen a "political dialog on race relations, especially the core issues that are never discussed: the disintegration of the black family and the growth of a violent, anarchic, alienated welfare-dependent underclass over the past quarter century." The theme continues in his cover on Dinkins, "The New Mayor and the Crisis of New York," 11-20, sensitive, insightful, skeptical and hopeful all at once. About the best on Ed Koch's last hurrah as Hizzoner, "The Lion in Summer," 9-4, with the mayor huffing and puffing on the comeback trail. He's on the mark in "The Restoration," 1-23, with: "In Washington this week, the staff regains control of the asylum. Order is restored. . .The republic has withstood a most grievous threat: government by amateurs." However, a rambling close on the deficit bogeyman detracts from the overall story. "Bush League," 3-13, is deftly probing, sensitive and non-judgmental on the President, John Tower and the sense of an agenda-less administration. "The Last Liberal," 4-3, is a fresh, delightful sketch of New York Liberal Party Leader Raymond B. Harding: "He is an enormous man ('The Graf Zeppelin of New York politics,' David Garth has said), with a fine head for politics, an old-world sense of honor, and a witty, wonderfully, profane mouth." Klein's "Jackson Action," 5-15, speculates on what a Jesse Jackson mayoralty in DC would mean: a Bush vs. Jesse affair, with the media rushing over for Jackson's reaction. He also goes against conventional assessments at the time that Mario Cuomo has lost his luster. In "What Price Freedom?" 6-19, Klein not-too-successfully ventures into macroeconomics, analyzing moves toward democracy in China, Poland and the U.S.S.R., deciding people don't really want the "freedom to fail." In "Winners and Sinners," 10-9, he compares Sen. Alfonse D'Amato (R.-N.Y.) and Barney Frank on ethical grounds. Candid and hard-nosed, he defends Frank and skewers D'Amato, presenting novel and fresh insights.

Kolata, Gina. *The New York Times.* (★ ★ ½)
New York, health and related issues. Kolata spent much of the year covering drugs and homelessness, and exploring the relationship between the two. She also deals with AIDS and other health problems, reporting the latest information or study. Her expertise and contacts keep her byline a front-page regular. A 10 Best selection in general reporting, "AIDS Is Spreading in Teen-Agers, A New Trend Alarming to Experts," 10-8, finally reports what local doctors have been warning about for years, that the teen years, normally a time for experimentation, sexual and otherwise, have deadly pitfalls. She adequately covers a study from *The New England Journal of Medicine* in "Taxes Fail to Cover Drinking's Costs, Study Finds," 3-17, but you don't need to read much beyond the lead: "Taxes on cigarettes cover the costs imposed on society by smoking, but taxes on alcohol do not pay for the costs of drinking." Duly reported, Kolata breaks through with what has always been suspected in "Twins of the Streets: Homelessness and Addiction," 5-22, as homeless advocates finally admit that if a homeless persons' alcohol or drug addiction isn't treated, nothing else will help, though she overuses her stats to make her case. She replays the theme in micro in "Drug Addicts Among the Homeless: Case Studies of Lost Brains," 5-30, a powerful followup profiling McKenna House in DC. A good reminder, she tells us in "AIDS Test May Fail to Detect Virus for Years, Study Finds," 6-1, that "Some people may carry the AIDS virus for up to three years without its being detected by standard AIDS tests, a study has found. The finding raises concern that some people who are infected with the virus may unwittingly pass it on. . ." but we've heard this before, and were well into the article before realizing Kolata was talking about a *new* study, which she doesn't compare with the old until more than halfway through. "Innovative AIDS Drug Plan May Be Undermining Testing," 11-21, reports that 20 times more patients are lining up for the new drug DDI as are volunteering for tests to see if it is safe and useful, thus threatening the government's "bold, new plan" to make promising but unproven AIDS drugs available on a parallel track. Getting some good news, "Experts Finding New Hope On Treating Crack Addicts," 8-24, she tells us that crack addicts must be habilitated before being rehabilitated, with treatment stressing changing environment and social support systems like family and friends over physical dependency aspects. Relating information from another study, "New Study Says Diuretics Raise Heart Attack Risks," 9-28, she's muddled, not conclusively deciding what to do about the troubling conclusions of the study she cites. Not so in "Sharp Cut in Serious Birth Defect is Tied to Vitamins in Pregnancy," 11-24, termed a "landmark" study, showing women who take over-the-counter multivitamins during pregnancy reduce the risk of incurring a serious neural tube defect in their babies.

Kramer, Michael. *Time.* (★ ½)
Special correspondent. His first full year at *Time* after bouncing from *New York* to *U.S.News & World Report,* Kramer still hasn't found his footing, but as young and as talented as he is, we have no doubt it will come together soon for him. He's weak in "A New Breeze Is Blowing," 1-30, gushily reviewing Bush's inaugural address, rehashing the budget problem and providing little insight in this pseudo-Bush profile. "Playing for the Edge," 2-13, is puffy on Baker: There's the Bush-Baker relationship, the Reagan-Baker relationship, the Baker-(Susan) Baker relationship and you still don't quite know what Jim is like. "Smart, Dull and Very Powerful," 3-13, is a balanced and well-written profile of Sam Nunn. "Something else must happen if Nunn is ever to become President. Americans will have to fall out of love with charisma. . ..Thirty-second sound bites are not his forte." His "First Steps Towards A Policy," 3-27, contains nice analysis and solid reportage that are blown by two cracks at the beginning and end of the article. "Only now is the Bush administration beginning to make moves that may allow it to capture some momentum." Only now? He's only been in office two months. Kramer effectively draws on conversations and experiences from his trip to China for "Free to Fly Inside the Cage," which appeared in *Time*'s 10-2 cover story on China. Interestingly, Kramer reports that he never heard "a coherent analysis of the Cultural Revolution, an event that so inverted the natural order that parents were shamed, beaten, and in some instances killed by their own children." He could ask around and he'd get one.

Kurtz, Howard. *The Washington Post.* (★ ★)
New York bureau chief. He handles the northeast U.S. scene with respectable attention, although the major focus is New York City. There's a definite "outsider's" feel to his reports, which isn't at all objectionable, except that Kurtz didn't seem to get as deeply inside the Big Apple this year. He's vividly descriptive in "Across the Nation, Rising Outrage," 4-4, with a chilling compilation of nationwide "battle reports" from the War on Drugs. In this stark portrayal, he reports "that drug abuse and violence have multiplied like a computer virus, spreading to communities large and small," with law enforcement agencies outnumbered, outfinanced and outraged. "Carrying Cocaine from N.Y. to Washington," 4-22, recounts gruesome tales of drug couriers, "mules," dispatched from New York's Port Authority Bus Terminal to Washington to catch up with weekend demand for cocaine, Kurtz telling us who they are and what happens to them. There's a hollow ring to "Wallach Was Paid to Link Wedtech to Meese, U.S. Claims," 4-29, on how federal prosecution claims that E. Bob Wallach "used his friendship" with then Attorney General Edwin Meese III to fraudulently obtain more than $500,000 from Wedtech, a South Bronx defense contractor. The prosecution witnesses were convicted felons whose objectives in testifying were to lighten their sentences. Wallach was convicted, his appeal still pending. "Concord Does Things a Bit Differently," 4-30, is thoroughly entertaining from graph to graph. It's a great subject — small-town, part-time legislators in Concord, NH, who work as truck drivers and hairdressers, people who vote to keep adultery a crime. Kurtz tells the story through the consciousness of Claire Ebel, the lone liberal in town, who single-handedly runs the ACLU's office, which makes her a frequent target for the ultraconservative local newspaper: "Ebel, 46, is talkative and irreverent and takes these assaults in stride, although she objects to the paper's repeated use of an unflattering photograph taken on a day when she had the flu." "Attack in Park Reopens N.Y. Racial Wounds," 5-3, uses better than average quotes on the racial polarization of the city, but this kind of stuff, quoting the unavoidable Rev. Al Sharpton, just makes it worse, especially since there's no analytic here. "HUD: Fertile Ground For Wrongdoing," 6-18, gives some "early explanations" of why things went wrong at HUD, but reads like a lengthy indictment with no defense. Two factors are stressed: 1) Secretary Samuel Pierce was not allowed to even name his own deputy, as the White House filled HUD with Republican loyalists — Pierce made more than 700 speeches in his eight-year term and was often on the road; 2) Budget cuts were savage at HUD: 16,000 staff cut to 11,000 — $26 billion subsidized housing outlays cut to less than $8 billion. Kurtz goes in for psychological profiling with "In Pierce's Past, Seeds of His Failure at HUD," 7-26, an apparently seriously researched examination of the embattled Sam Pierce: ". . .the seeds of his

failure at HUD can be glimpsed at several stages of his career. A private man thrust by white politicians into increasingly public roles, he has climbed the ladder of success even while delegating the details to others." "Dinkins, Giuliani Wind Up Mean-Spirited Campaign," 11-5, is an informative wrapup of New York City's mayoral campaign, Kurtz balanced and non-partisan in his reporting and assessment.

Lambro, Donald. *The Washington Times.* (★ ½)
National Affairs Editor. The paper continues to lack the heavy-hitting political reporter to bat cleanup and anchor the reporting staff. Lambro isn't coming through. There's a rigidity in his analytic efforts and an occasional sloppiness in his reporting that mar his otherwise good, aggressive political instincts. "Vote for Gingrich Was Vote Against Michel," 3-23, contends that House GOP goodwill for new GOP Whip Newt Gingrich had been building for awhile, effectively underscoring the point with a House GOPer's explanation of his vote: "I am not supporting him for his ideology; I am supporting him for his leadership but more importantly for his goal to create a Republican majority in the House." His "Eager to See Bush Score Some Points," 3-27, informs us that the Republican Congressional Committee wants to build congressional majorities by confronting Democrats, and wants to integrate Bush into RCC stratagems, but there's no treatment of the strategies to be employed. Lambro shortchanges with "2 GOP Groups in Congress Fusing to Redefine Party Role," 4-3, reporting on the realignment of two GOP House caucuses, the "92 Group" and the Conservative Opportunity Society and their "Wednesday meetings," but offering no unifying theme or analysis. "Confusion in the Ranks," 5-16, is a hard estimate of the effect of the Jim Wright scandal on the Democratic party in Congress: "possibly the Democrats' Watergate." There's little insight and no new angle in "Both Parties Look to Foley to Bring Peace," 6-7, which surveys the new Speaker's preferred legislative agenda, the problems facing him, and his colleagues' expectations of him. Lambro projects the conventional: "Many Democrats do not see Congress tackling much more than the budget and a handful of other measures this year, including ethics reform." "Putting Democrats on the Defensive," 7-13, and "Democrats Think It's Time to Fight Each Other," 7-17, are both smug on the relationship between Bush and Congress and Democratic disarray. "Dole Criticism Of Israel Draws Public Rebuke From Kemp," 8-7, relays Jack Kemp's pro-Israel stance in the current hostage crisis, as contrasted to Sen. Robert Dole's more critical posture, without sufficient background or analysis included. When Lambro does offer analysis of the issue, it is simplistic at best, as in "Behind the GOP Doors," 8-18: While Sen. Dole and the Bush administration are unhappy with Israel's kidnapping of Sheik Obeid, Kemp and Atwater are looking out for future pro-Israel voter registration. "Democrats Warned: No Tax Talk," 9-12, is well-done on efforts by Democrats to attune themselves to dominant public attitudes. Lambro is less than rigorous with "Kean Faulted by GOP for Weak Role in Race," 10-23, a little too generous in the space he allows for unsubstantiated allegations regarding Gov. Thomas Kean of New Jersey: "Some [advisors of GOP gubernatorial candidate Jim Courter] even go so far as to suggest that the popular governor, who is constitutionally prevented from seeking a third term, may want to see a Democratic victory so that he can run again four years from now." Silly stuff.

Lardner, George, Jr. *The Washington Post.* (★ ★)
National staff reporter. Lardner's major reporting efforts this year focused on the trial of Oliver North. His coverage is sturdy, comprising many fine outlines of the case. He does satisfactory homework, and handled the complicated aspects well. "North Team's Subpoenas Challenged," 1-26, gathers all the relevant facts to back up the headline in a fine roundup. He's a bit too long in "North Trial Judge Rejects Secrecy Deal," 2-15, outlining clearly Gerhard Gesell's refusal to allow the Justice Department to block disclosure of certain materials on a case-by-case basis at the trial of Oliver North. As it turns out Lardner was mistaken, though his reporting here is accurate, since the trial turned out to be halted numerous times due to attempted "disclosure of individual pieces of classified information" by North's defense team. "North Flouted Law, Court Told," 2-22, covers the opening arguments in the trial, standard stuff, with Prosecutor

John Keker focusing on narrow specifics — false statements to Congress, accepting illegal gratuities — while North defense counsel Brendan Sullivan paints the big picture. "Hamilton 'Relied' on North — Assurances on Contra Aid Ban Cited at Trial," 2-23, recounts the testimony of former Chairman of the House Intelligence Committee, Lee Hamilton, who said he believed North and McFarlane in '85 when they told him to discount "unsubstantiated newspaper allegations" about their activities. Lardner provides a nice flavor of the budding drama in the trial: "Staid and unruffled on the witness stand, Hamilton at times made points on cross-examination in even stronger language than he had on direct questioning by independent prosecutor John W. Keker." "North Advised Rebels on Tactics, Supplies, Trial Told," 3-3, is skimpy on a "Cuban-born protege of the Central Intelligence Agency," whatever that means, who testified to collecting over $200K to help set up an airstrip in Costa Rica for the contras. We find in "Reagan Urged Aid Secrecy," 3-11, Lardner may have been the first to have picked up this story, which subsequently became bigger due to the involvement of then-Vice President Bush as a strong arm envoy to Honduras. The gist of the story is that certain material was released in the trial that didn't make it to the Iran-Contra congressional panel. "Defense Closes by Calling North a Government 'Hostage,'" 4-20, judiciously focuses on the issues involved at the Ollie North trial. After the trial, he went on to cover legal issues involving policy. "Intelligence Ties Endure Despite U.S.-China Strain," with Jeffrey R. Smith 6-25, is top-notch, although reference manual quality, on the evolution and history of the U.S.-China strategic intelligence sharing relationship from 1971 to date. "Chappaquiddick, 1989," 7-16, is a fair rehash, but little more, on the unanswered questions regarding the Sen. Ted Kennedy scandal of 20 years ago.

Lauter, David. *Los Angeles Times.* (★)
Washington. Lauter shares the White House beat with James Gerstenzang, and although a zippier writer, has a greater difficulty keeping his bias under restraint. He's formulaic and in fact comes across as antagonistic toward the former quarterback in "Kemp: Man In Motion Is Full Of Ideas," 12-20-88, a snide account on Jack Kemp's nomination as HUD secretary: "He is being called upon to do something he has never had to do before — try to make his theories work in the real world." Five yards for unnecessary roughness. He's much better in "New Obstacles Complicate Last-Ditch Stand for Tower," 2-27, a smooth flowing analytical piece on the behind-the-scenes machinations to get Tower confirmed, marred only by duplicating some quotes used by Melissa Healy in a related story on the same page. Is there an editor in the house? It's hard plodding through "Bush to Present Ethics Reform Package," 4-12, and there's a perceptible anti-Bush bias. Lauter should provide examples to back up some of his assertions. Teamed with Doyle McManus to cover the President's reaction to the death of Lt. Col. William Higgins, "the first major foreign policy crisis of his administration," in "Outraged President Meets Aides, Weighs Alternatives," 8-1, Lauter produces a cut-and-paste job of public quotes from Bush, congressmen, senators, and armchair experts, with few behind the scenes details. The Israeli angle in this major story, played up in many other reports, is skimmed over here, with Sen. Dole's provocative remarks appearing near the end. The cynical tone of "Quayle Tells Alaskans U.S. Government Will Complete Cleanup if Exxon Doesn't," 9-19, is set right in the lead sentence: "Fulfilling one of the duties of a vice president — going where the President does not want to go — Dan Quayle arrived here today en route to a 10-day tour of the Far East." Lauter details Quayle's itinerary, then goes on to say the trip is part of the White House strategy to "use foreign travel to rehabilitate Quayle's political image." Lauder does better covering the biggest travel story of the year, Bush's sojourn to the Mediterranean to meet with Mikhail Gorbachev. "Critics Ignored As President Clung To Secrecy," 11-1, is a first-rate job of analyzing and reporting the events leading up to the President's surprise announcement on Halloween, leaving readers with a clearer understanding of how major foreign policy decisions are arrived at in the Bush presidency, for better or worse.

Lemann, Nicholas. *The Atlantic.* (★ ★ ★)
National correspondent. Another solid year from Lemann, the prototypical "neoliberal" (much as he may dislike that term). One of the talented graduates of *The Washington Monthly,* Lemann produces at least one masterpiece a year. His two-part series, "The Unfinished War," *Atlantic* 12-88/1-89, is a 10 Best nomination, a sweeping history and evaluation of the War on Poverty. Definitive on the subject, and crackling with provocative conclusions, it's filled with insights and data based on authoritative sources. "Act II, Winning An Election," Lemann's contribution to *The Washington Monthly*'s 3-89 cover,"What's Wrong With This Magazine?" is a manifesto for "neoliberals" to tap into a rising national mood for a government that delivers on its basic obligations, and provides the historical example of the successful Progressive movement. The article is self-referential, but fitting in with the tone of this edition. Lemann showed the always welcomed penchant for taking on Conventional Wisdom in "The Underclass Cycle: Making It — Then And Now," *The Washington Post,* 5-21, using America's urban history to argue that "permanent" underclasses with their attendent crises have come and gone, and the current one will too, with some help from the rest of society. This isn't sensible liberalism, but smart liberalism. " 'Gung Ho On O'B,' " *Atlantic* 6-89, was apparently written for no other reason than to give Lemann and his readers their periodic "Nixon fix." His use of recently published White House memos to show that Richard Nixon wanted to dig up dirt on then Democratic National Committee head Larry O'Brien, and that "even if Nixon's interest in O'Brien waned, the idea of using the government as an instrument for punishing political opponents lived on," results in the sort of "dog bites man" yawner prevalent in Watergate "revelations" at this late date. Lemann is thoughtful and deliberative with "Whistling in the Pentagon," *The New York Review of Books* 10-26, using a review of two books (*The Pentagonists* by A. Ernest Fitzgerald and *New Weapons, Old Politics* by Thomas L. McNaugher) to undertake a serious, provocative examination of the military procurement system. The topic isn't at all new, but Lemann's insights are fresh and from new angles. We started off "Stressed Out In Suburbia," *Atlantic* 11-89, with high hopes, figuring that Lemann's profile of Naperville, IL would be the Big Story on America's suburbs that we had been waiting for. While Lemann does a superior job of playing off contemporary Naperville against the stereotypical image of suburban America forged in the 1950s, he lacks the bold thesis that could have shot the story into the stratosphere. "The Organization Man" of the 1990s is still waiting to be written.

MacPherson, Myra. *The Washington Post.* (★ ★ ½)
"Style" writer. MacPherson's snappy and lively profiles fascinate. She lets her subjects speak for themselves, possessing a knack for easily drawing them out and only adding background and descriptions when needed. "The Living Victims of Ted Bundy," 1-23, is chilling to the bone on the survivors of the Chi Omega killings on the eve of Bundy's execution, a compelling composite. "The Fractured Family at Eastern," 3-20, carries us through individual pictures of strikers at Eastern's Miami HQ, catching us with a terrific opening: "Betsie Romano was 20 the first time she ever got on an airplane. She threw up all the way from Pennsylvania to Miami. Now 21 years later, after millions of miles logged, countless announcements of buckling up seat belts and jillions of gallons of coffee, tea or milk served, Eastern flight attendant Romano may have stepped off her last airplane. Every day now she puts on her perky smile and her uniform, with the crisp bow tie, and walks a picket line." There's little from management's angle, but the story isn't about management, or even labor; it's more about what a long-term upheaval in a job can do to a life. "Unexpected Turns On a Turkish Coastal Drive," 5-14, begins as a travelogue (yawn), and ends as striking, still-life snapshots of life in Turkey outside of Istanbul. "The Passion of Barbara Newman," 5-16, is a captivating, quote-filled story about the life of the former TV journalist and the revelations in her book about her affair with assassinated Lebanese president Bashir Gemayel. "Newt Gingrich, Point Man In a House Divided," 6-12, introduces the Republican pit bull to "Style" readers, skillfully letting him have his say and contrasting that with some of his supporters and detractors, beating the *Mother Jones* cover by a month or two. Though it's more of a personal profile than a political one (as *MOJO*'s was), this picture of Gingrich is most revealing. "The Lost Years of the Cuban Dissident," 8-14, tells the story of

Margarita and Elizardo Sanchez, separated due to his crusade for human rights in Cuba, "the major voice of opposition to Castro." You never find out, though, where he stands politically, and while the human side is poignant, powerful, the political side is confused, and confusing. " 'Arrested Art' Returned," 9-21, is light and interesting on art confiscated from Ramon Cernuda that originally came from Cuba and got snagged under jurisdiction of "Trading with the Enemy Act."

Madison, Christopher. *National Journal.* (★ ½)
Staff correspondent. Madison moves from the diplomatic beat to Capitol Hill, but the change hasn't shaken the doldrums out of his reporting. He's fine on attention to detail and appropriate data close to the ground, but the eagle-eyed broad sweep is too infrequent. "Capital Hill's Pay Raise Politicking," 2-4, is clear and concise on the pay raise debacle, with some detail on the wrangling involved, quotes from Congressmen and leadership effectively used. "Congressional Focus/Insider's Game," 4-8, examines why, despite their control of the House and Senate, Democrats have not been able to wield the whip hand: "To assure their own reelections, members of Congress simply avoid voting on tough issues" writes Madison as if he had discovered something. "The Heir Presumptive," 4-29, a cover on nice-guy Tom Foley, the next Speaker, gets off to a slow start. There is some interesting background, but the effort displays little color or anecdotal material, virtually ignoring his relationship with Republicans. "Ethics as Usual," 7-8, clearly shows the problems Congress has as it tries to come to grips with the Ethics issue — again. Honoraria or dishonoraria? Pay raise phase in or fade out? Campaign finance reform or refinanced seats? PAC go packing? "Fat cat protection act?" Madison does a very good overview here. We're left scratching our heads, though, over "Biden's Comeback," 10-14, about how Sen. Joseph Biden Jr. (D-Del.) was down and out after his presidential run and is now up 'n at'em as chairman of Senate Judiciary, with no substance but many kind words from his colleagues on what a nice fellow he is. This is clearly an obligatory puff assuring Madison of access to the senator, but five pages of it? A more interesting, important story gets one page, "Midair Collision," 10-7, the clash over clean air legislation between Rep. John Dingell (D-Mich.) and Rep. Henry Waxman (D-Calif.), which could have provided a focus for a cover takeout on the subject.

Magnuson, Ed. *Time.* (★ ½)
Senior writer. There's no question Magnuson can spin out a readable story, and he has plenty of reporting help to get him the news. Still, too often there's a fly in the soup, an unnecessary comment revealing a bias of one sort or another. It peeps through in "Kluck! Kluck! Kluck!" co-written by Joseph J. Kane 3-6, an analysis of ex-Klansman David Duke's election to the Louisiana state legislature, starting off well but ending up discussing how ironic that the GOP came out against Duke in view of its shabby history on civil rights. (Perhaps he doesn't remember that it was the Democratic Party that harbored the Klan for the first half of the century.) In the same issue, "Collapse of a Confirmation," with Michael Duffy and Hays Gorey 3-6, we braced ourselves for more of same, but he is surprisingly non-editorial, carefully chronicling the unravelling of John Tower's nomination as Defense Secretary. "Pawn Among Giants," with Steven Holmes 4-17, is a well-written synopsis of the defense's case in the North trial, but offers little analysis. "Brace! Brace! Brace!" with Lee Griggs and Elizabeth Taylor 7-31, is a beautifully written account of the United Airlines DC-10 crash, of course, easier to write with so many survivors; enough technical details, no unnecessary indictment of the DC-10 as an airplane, "unprecedented" breakup of the engine. Six weeks later there would be little to add to this story. "A Father Lifts His Burdens," with Linda DiPietro 8-28, a Detroit story about a man who drove his car into a river in order to get rid of his passengers who happened to be his wife and children, chills. "Bright Kids, Bad Business," with Priscilla Painton 9-11, outlines how the drug trade is becoming increasingly attractive to intelligent inner-city kids who see it as their ticket to a better life, struggles with its analysis; Magnuson seems to fear that these kids will get trapped in the drug business, but in the examples he gives, only one does, the rest going on to succeed in other avenues. Magnuson stops short of condoning their actions in the last graph where he notes "For most, the lure of easy money turned out to be a mirage. It did not come easily, and it did not last," but his article doesn't back this contention sufficiently.

Marin, Richard. *The Washington Times.* (★ ★)
Television critic. In addition to his reviewing chores, Marin takes on broader themes within the medium, examining trends and portents in television, new equipment, new faces, etc. He provides solid information, at the same time employing an action-packed style of writing. "Products Stare Camera in the Eye," 1-9, is fast-paced on efforts by advertisers to have their products used in the filming of television programs — "advertainment," as one source called it. Marin does a superior job putting this together, but left us still wondering if this is an effort on the part of advertisers to combat the often talked-about problem of viewers who tape programs and then fast-forward through the commercials on the replay. "What Ted Turner Is Up to Now," 5-26, a "life!" lead, is a screed against "Captain Planet," Turner's courting of show-biz liberal activists with his flower-child political agenda. It's tilted a bit toward heavy editorializing, but Marin saves it with the last graph, which tells us "It's his money." His "3 1/2 Hours of Gigante Advertising," 7-17, is witty, on the Spanish-language TV hit "Sabado Gigantes" and its Chilean-born host, with an eye-catching, effective lead: "It's Saturday night. You're zapping the remote control for something — anything — to watch beside insipid sitcoms, tabloid smut and bad movies. En route through the double-digit channels, you see a man wearing a funny hat handing $100 bills to an elated housewife holding a jug of Liquid Tide. Next time you zap by, he is sitting at a desk interviewing an expert on capital punishment. Three hours later, he is singing a tribute to 'Rodolfo' Valentino." Marin's "The Host Who Rejects the I-Word," 7-24, is a slick, sharp profile of talk show host Dick Cavett that captures the quirks of the interview and the interviewee. Marin moves in and out, now probing for the innermost man, now stepping back for an arm's length view of an American oddity.

Martin, Richard. *Insight.* (★ ★)
Back tromping around Southeast Asia this year from his home base in Southern California, Martin continues to display professional reporting skills and his byline is one we respect. We're having more problems with the presentation of his material in recent years, his stories less complete and not as well organized as they ought to be. More attention to this end would easily get him back to three stars. "The Wave," 1-16 cover story, begins as a *Forbes*-like success story on Asian immigrants, but quickly disintegrates into confusion, Martin trying to cover too much, with too little structure to the material. "A Cloud of Controversy Over L.A." 2-13, on the controversy surrounding a proposed monument in Los Angeles, stumbles from the start with garbled overlong sentences that try to pack in too much information, gradually picking up. He's poorly focused here, trying to be both an art critic and social commentator. "The Debated Truth in Cocteau's Lie," 3-13, reviews the Jean Cocteau festival at the University of California at Irvine, avoiding much of the usual gush to make this an interesting, informative piece, but we're left with many questions. Why was "Beauty and the Beast," Cocteau's most noted work, not shown? Why was he a "pain in the ass?" Did he indeed weasel his way into the lives of his more famous contemporaries? And what about all those affairs with his "proteges?" "Aging Athletes Master Fleet Feats," 4-17, on athletes still competing after age 40, is handled quite well. He resists the temptation to gush like some sportscaster and instead puts together a very solid article that is tightly written, opens and closes on a strong note, and contains much detail. "Illegal Tours of Enemy Territory," 7-17, is fairly good on the U.S. "trading with the enemy" law, which forbids, among other things, the booking of travel tours to Vietnam and Cambodia, telling us about a travel agency that lodged a legal challenge, lost, then violated the law anyway and got fined $75,000. "It's Still Sabotage, For Earth's Sake," 8-7, is well-organized crime coverage of alleged acts of sabotage by extremist environmental groups, particularly a "caught in the act" attempt to cut power lines, with good quotes. In "Economy Contrives to Breathe Fire," 8-7, on the economic boom in Thailand, Martin skillfully weaves together both the big and little pictures with respect, wonder and a little bit of humor, making good use of metaphors. On the Thai-Burma border, he digs into an obscure clash between Burmese troops and rebellious ethnic groups in "Forty Years of Ethnic Strife, and No Negotiations in Sight," 8-28, with too weak an opening for a two-page story we're not sure we want to read about anyway.

Mathews, Jay. *The Washington Post.* (★ ★)
The *Post*'s Los Angeles bureau chief, doing decent work on California and West Coast stories, was called upon to help cover the events set off in China by the Student Democracy Movement, having the advantage of being the *Post*'s former Beijing bureau chief (1979-80). Mathews displays his adeptness in handling a fluid situation that is changing every moment with "Crisis Grows in Shanghai After Train Is Burned," 6-8. He pulls on many sources from varied vantages to fill out the volatile picture of what is brewing in Shanghai, bringing to attention the appearance of young, bored and often underemployed urban workers in the forefront of the Shanghai incidents. "Training Welfare Mothers For Work Proves Tricky," 6-12, is solid reporting on the problems experienced in California's effort to comply with the 1985 federal work-fare requirement applied to 200,000 California recipients of AFDC. Mathews is clear on the provisions and its complications. "Private U.S. Groups Act to Restore China Ties," 7-7, is timely and informative on the state of affairs within the mainland-"China lobby" in the U.S. "China Forcing Workers to Accept Government Bonds as Wages," 7-19, is intelligent on current Chinese economic problems. "U.S. Embassy Still 'Home' for Chinese Dissidents," 8-4, reminds us of the status of Fang Lizhi and Li Shuxuan who have taken refuge in the U.S. Embassy in Beijing: "Some observers suggest they may have to wait several years before the two countries can negotiate their departure." In "Back to School in Beijing," 8-13, Mathews intrepidly interviews students at Beijing U. and finds them poised for more "action." He has fairly good insights on the unrest, but what they want and how the government is responding remains cloudy. In *The Washington Monthly,* "Edgar Snow Told You So," 7/8-89, links Mathews' own expectations of progress in China with Snow's of the 1930s and '40s. Although well-presented, it's a bit thin analytically, the best line being: "We are in for decades of mixed messages, and like Edgar Snow we will probably focus again and again on those we find palatable, leaving the rest to surprise us, probably unpleasantly." His "Trouble for Nancy's Center," 1-25, delivers a good overview on the problems and delays for a Phoenix House outlet, but is stingy on the story of Nancy Reagan's involvement. "Spill Cleanup Expected to Take Months," 3-28, on the Exxon Valdez spill and botched cleanup, is cursory in most respects, skimming all the issues involved, without digging too deep.

Matlack, Carol. *National Journal.* (★ ★)
Staff correspondent. Off the space and bureaucracy beat, Matlack worked with a broader portfolio, sinking her teeth into a variety of topics and issues. "Live From Capitol Hill," 2-18, doesn't explore the journalistic ethics problem of congressmen interviewing themselves for the local news, but still informs on the subject. "Return to Sender," 3-11, examines the law of diminishing returns on direct-mail fundraising, a respectable update, no new angles. "Crossing the Line," 3-25, investigates the crossing of Washington journalists from outsiders to insiders. "Should Some Points of Light Be Taxed?" 4-15, examines in some detail whether some tax-exempt groups ought to be subject to taxation for the commercial activities for which they charge fees from members, clearly done. "Elections You Can Afford," 6-24, offers a broad scope with plenty of examples and quotes from east, west, north, and south relative to campaign finance reform and public financing laws; Matlack's smooth and easy style is appreciated on this somewhat confusing topic, especially the clear distinction made between state and federal procedures. "Mobilizing for the Abortion War," 7-15, takes a balanced look at the abortion groups' response to the Supreme Court decision, with good examples of the importance of the gubernatorial races, namely NJ and VA, to abortion-rights groups. "Byrd's Bombshell," 9-9, is good on Sen. Robert Byrd's (D-W.Va.) initiation of an ethics provision requiring full disclosure of lobbyist activities by anyone seeking contracts or grants from the government, but we can't see what difference this is going to make except to generate additional paperwork, and Matlack doesn't catch on to this. She begins "Coming Unglued," 11-4, on the pressures for reopening tax loopholes closed by the 1986 reform, with the Democrats' assumptions that changes in the tax code will drive up marginal rates on personal income, but then smartly and constructively details arguments for the tax breaks. Her closing quote from a lobbyist is nicely selected: "If you have your cake and eat it too, have no change in the rates and get goodies . . . well, why not?"

Mayer, Jane. *The Wall Street Journal.* (★ ★ ½)
Back to the *Journal* after a long sabbatical, Mayer maintains her talented flair for dramatic writing and seems more comfortable away from her old Washington beat. Her strongest efforts are around the drug issue where she brings a passionate intensity to her reporting. "Agent Provocateur: Publishers Bemoan Brash Style, Big Bucks Of Rushdie's Agent," 3-23, a punchy, sharp profile of Andrew Wylie, doesn't judge, though it sounds like this guy isn't 100% aboveboard. She snags our attention with an arresting lead: "These days, the Ayatollah is the most hated man in publishing. Andrew Wylie may be No.2. . . .His clothes are so dark, and his skin so white, that he looks as if he grew up without benefit of sunlight." Mayer is just as blunt on his style too, using verbs like "wrenched" to describe it, but we don't find out where he goes from here, and maybe it's better not to. "Now You Can Dine Knowing the Entree Lived a Happy Life," 4-6, is only half tongue-in-cheek on the "New Age" way of eating, with useful information on hormone/drug-free edibles and their pros-and-cons, nicely presented. A 10 Best selection, "Spreading Plague: Seaford, Del., Shows How Crack Can Savage Small-Town America," 5-4, is a graphic parable on small town Seaford, a crack haven, containing a early warning sign for the middle class. She's compelling in showing, without a sensationalist spin, that crack is as good a poison for humans as any invented to kill rats. "Surely You've Met My Dear Friend. . .(Fill in Name Here)," 6-7, is silly but eye-opening on examples of celebrities who are paid to go to parties. Neither new, nor important, it's only mildly amusing. "Political Baptism: How Chris Whittle Faltered on the Issue of TV Ads in Schools," 8-8, is a light read, profiling the man behind the struggle to get television and commercials into schools. "Street Urchins: In the War On Drugs, Toughest Foe May Be the Alienated Youth," 9-8, is a revealing story told from the "other side," through a former 17-year-old drug dealer's voice, about why inner-city youths get involved with drugs, and how this one managed to barely save himself.

McGee, Jim. *The Washington Post.* (★)
Investigative reporter. This usually sharp bird dog on the *Post*'s investigative beat didn't flush out any serious game this year. The customary McGee tenacity simply didn't work for mediocre targets. "Campaign Funds to Stuff a Goose," 2-23, is relatively nonpartisan, providing documentation on abuse of campaign fund expenditures. If there is to be reform, the whole system has to be reformed, McGee implies, although offering no solutions. "Speaker's Name Used in Pollster's Pitch," 5-11, is lightweight on the usage of Speaker Jim Wright's name by friend James T. Kitchins for "Information America." "Rep. Gray's Office Staff Said To Be Under Probe By FBI," co-written by Tom Kenworthy 5-31, would be more credible if the sources were named, in that Rep. William Gray's refutation includes a request to Dick Thornburgh to investigate leaks. A followup, "85 Housing Deal With Church Benefits Rep. Gray," with Ruth Marcus 6-29, goes to press too soon on gifts between Gray and his church, implying impropriety without supporting substance. "Rep. Savage, Seeking New Suits, Cut Short Official Visit to China," 8-2, makes a persuasive case that Rep. Gus Savage's (D-Ill.) China trip falls into the category of a "junket," but there aren't enough legs to support McGee's assertion that "the episode illustrates the freewheeling, unregulated nature of congressional foreign travel, and the willingness of diplomats and aides to accommodate the personal desires of members of Congress on foreign trips." "Vienna: Fertile Ground For Espionage," 8-27, contains some information on why Vienna is such a hotbed for spies, but McGee is simply sloppy in labeling Felix Bloch a "counterspy."

McQueen, Michel. *The Wall Street Journal.* (★)
White House. A rookie on this important beat, the inexperience shows around the edges. She can handle the routine stuff well enough, but produced nothing memorable about the rookie in the Oval Office or his team. We don't learn much in the A-hed feature "A Harvard Basher In the Campaign, Bush Now Is Backer," 1-17, which tells us Harvard outweighs Yale in Bush's cabinet. "First Family: The President's Kids Get a Few Perks But Lose All Claims to Privacy," 1-20, is inaugural fluff, a non-story she did little with; the Bush kids aren't as visible as the Nixon girls or Reagan offspring. "Bush's Lag In Filling Top Posts Risks A Loss Of Critical

Momentum," 2-28, is lightweight for a P. 1 leder, simply another review of the slow pace in filling subcabinet slots. "Bush Presents a Package of Proposals to Combat Gun-Related Violent Crime," 5-16, adequately captures the main points, but doesn't explore the repercussions. "Presidential Adviser Faces Complaints That His Idea Menu Offers Leftovers and No Punch," 6-20, is a fairly drawn sketch of Roger Porter, assistant to the President for economic and domestic affairs, quoting Richard Neustadt, his Harvard mentor: "His weakness, if he has any, might be originality, thinking creatively." "Bush's Roster of Top Aides Two-Thirds Filled After Six Months, Is Mostly White and Male," 7-20, contains an unacceptable reporting bias, some journalistic support for affirmative action without any supporting evidence: "Though the Bush record on appointing women and minorities probably isn't as good as Jimmy Carter's, it is probably superior to that of Mr. Reagan." In "Bush Says There Is 'Good Likelihood' Iran Could Free Hostages If It Desired," 8-16, McQueen serves up standard, press release stuff — what Bush said about Iran (and Richard Darman and interest rates) and what Darman said to get Bush to agree with him. A poorly conceptualized and weakly organized "Personal War: Battle Against Drugs Is Chief Issue Facing Nation, Americans Say," with David Shribman 9-22, has an overly excitable lead. Although the quotes in this story come from only Detroit residents, the theme rests upon statistics from a nationally conducted poll. "Barbara Bush Earns Even Higher Ratings Than The President," 10-9, is too disorganized. McQueen does pull quotes from people who once disliked Mrs. Bush but like her now, and from all sorts of socio-historical professors as to why, but we come away with no sense of the lady herself.

Meisler, Stanley. *Los Angeles Times.* (★ ★)
The former Paris bureau chief now covers the social welfare beat, and was off to a promising start early in the year with sharply focused reports on education issues. He provides very fine details on President Bush's plan and the strategies he's considering for giving parents wider freedom to decide which schools their children would attend with "Bush Expected to Endorse Parental Choice of Schools," 1-5. Meisler made one of the most useful contributions to the national debate over education all year with "Schools Left on Doorstep of Academia," 1-18, an approving, in-depth look at the proposed Boston University takeover of the Chelsea, Mass. School District. Conservatives can applaud the concept of privatization being put into action, and liberals can applaud BU's willingness to sink money into educational and social programs. Label it Neo-Pragmatical. He switches to lighter assignments, though, as with "Peary Foes, Backers Still Poles Apart," 4-2, taking no sides in the dispute over whether or not Robert Peary ever actually reached the North Pole. Meisler adopts a tongue-in-cheek tone as he presents both Peary's own story and the accumulating evidence against him. A fun read, but it belonged in the Sunday Magazine section, not on the front page. Meisler travels to Tampa, Florida, for "Black Crime: Taking a Look Inward," 6-17. "Black crime," Meisler informs us, "is one of the most volatile and least openly discussed phenomena in America," and then gives a report that is part profile of a modern urban hero, Wali Shabazz, and part sociological tract. We get a lot of information, but Meisler's examination of factors feeding the phenomenon omits any treatment of the high numbers of the crime-prone age groups in the community. Meisler had a tough assignment with "Chief 'Had to Be in the Field,' U.N. Aide Recalls," 8-1, a side bar story on the crisis over Lt. Col. William Higgins, as he had to straddle between writing a "Man in the News" profile and an obituary. Meisler probably did the best he could, cobbling together quotes, biographical data, and the reaction from one of Higgins' U.N. colleagues in Lebanon, leaving us with a better knowledge of the ill-fated Marine, if not a better understanding of what made him tick. "War Turned Impoverished U.S. Into a Superpower," 8-31, a Meisler contribution to a series on "The War In Europe, A 50-Year Legacy" offers some interesting sociological insights on the effect of the war on America, but too much of the article consists of writing along the lines of: "Yet, once America woke up, it somehow transformed itself in an enormous, engulfing and astounding dynamo that would shake and cow the world." He can handle far more substantial material, and we wonder why he's slotted where he is.

Moore, W. John. *National Journal.* (★ ★ ½)
Staff correspondent, covering law issues. Although Moore doesn't have the special flair of a
Charlotte Low Allen to engage our interest, he compensates handsomely with a consistent clarity
and solid knowledge in his reports. "Washington Update: A Booming Alternative to Suing,"
1-21, explores the growing trends of binding mediation, arbitration and other alternatives to
litigation. In counterpoint, observations that arbitrations can be worse than court cases are cited
in this excellent and mercifully brief report. "Global Reach," 2-11, a report on cooperative
multinational efforts to catch drug dealers and tax cheats is interesting, but we're given only the
Justice Department view here. "Lobbying the Court," 4-15, goes beyond standard Supreme
Court coverage to undertake a sweeping overview of all the groups with a stake in *Webster v.
Reproductive Health Services* actively lobbying public support from both sides, appropriately
also working in a history of the *Roe v. Wade* decision. In "A Law Firm's Path to High
Visibility," 6-17, Moore writes a brief for legal success: "Pinpoint areas for growth in the
capital's legal business. Recruit the best available government lawyers. Eschew fads and
gimmicks. Enjoy the results." "Hands Off," special report 7-1, tells of how many of Bush's
appointees, to avoid conflict-of-interest questions, are using recusals to disqualify themselves on
policy decisions directly affecting their financial holdings, with fine examples on the result of
"ethical zealousness." "The Action's Affirmative," 8-5, effectively balances conservative and
liberal perspectives on the Supreme Court debate over affirmative action, Congressional
involvement, and corporate America's "private peace" gained by avoiding strict quotas and
emphasis on recruitment.

Murray, Frank J. *The Washington Times.* (★ ★ ½)
White House. He's an asset that the *Times* editors aren't fully utilizing, bouncing him around
rather than deploying him where he's strongest. He's solid on the national security and defense
strategy beats, filling holes there when not covering the White House scene. Murray produced
one of the major scoops of the year, beating everyone on what the administration would propose
at the Nato Summit. Murray's profile of Peggy Noonan, "Speechwriter Gets Barbs But Praise
For Her Talent," 1-18, is a quick sketch, without much new, reminding us that she quit the
White House when Don Regan rejected the idea of making her chief speechwriter. "Chirac
Cautions Now Is Not Time to Cut NATO Weapon Defense," 5-9, is timely on the French
opposition leader's lobbying activities in the U.S. His report is insightful on this effort to
galvanize opposition against West Germany's attempt to break NATO ranks on the short-range
nuclear arms issue. "President Suddenly Silent on Tax Boost," 5-17, wittily notes that "Bush's
policy on new taxes changed yesterday from 'read my lips' to 'read my mind,'" but Murray
should have backed off from attempting to read into the President's mind the possibility of new
taxes for fiscal 1991. He pulls off a major scoop on the eve of the President's trip to Europe for
the NATO summit reporting ahead of all the competition that "Bush to Reduce U.S. Troops
in Europe by 10%," 5-26. Murray's handling of Bush's conventional forces initiative at the
NATO summit is very competent in "Elated Bush Proposes Bold Troop Reduction," 5-30,
giving appropriate emphasis to the "revolutionary" potential of the move as the administration
sees it. "Bush May Bash S&L Plan in Veto II," 6-15, is a useful summary, although it breaks
no new ground, on what divides Congress and the White House on the S&L bailout legislation.
Murray alerts us that "President Bush might spike the savings and loan bailout bill," if his
proposal to "force S&L owners to supply $3 of their own money for every $100 in assets" is not
accepted by "lawmakers [who] are under pressure from S&L lobbyists to weaken the provision."
He provides rounded, balanced reporting in "President Targets Frontiers of Space," 7-21, on
Bush's Apollo 11 anniversary speech which announced that the "goal is nothing less than to
establish the United States as the pre-eminent space-faring nation," including the skeptical
Congressional reactions from both sides of the aisle: "While Democrats railed at the Bush space
plan, Republicans were strangely silent." "Irate Bush Plans U.S. Response," 8-1, is routine on
Bush's reactions to the murder of Lt. Col. William Higgins. "Bush Hails Education Goals As
A 'Major Step,'" 9-29, tries to make the most of an item that really hasn't much news in it:
"George Bush gave the nation's governors some presidential promises to take home from the

education summit yesterday in hopes of strengthening his claim to the title of 'education president.' But the political bonanza was diluted by his failure to win support for cuts in federal funding for such popular pre-school programs as Head Start."

Nelson, Jack. *Los Angeles Times.* (★)
Washington bureau chief. As the *Los Angeles Times* strives to become a big kid on the block, it's held back by Nelson running things the way he always has, grabbing off choice stories for himself while trying to run a big staff at the same time. A carelessness intrudes into his dispatches with the result that he delivers no acute perceptions and is less than rigorous in his reporting. "Bush's Personal Touches Promote Bipartisan Spirit," 2-6, reads as if filed for *USA Today.* The information is spooned out in choppy, one-sentence paragraphs, everything repeated at least once, and the analysis never rising above the level of "Few expect the new bipartisanship to last indefinitely or eliminate the all-too-real disagreements that exist on critical national issues." The reporting is shabby at best in "Bush Fights Perception of a Floundering Start," 3-8, a waste of P. 1 space in which Nelson asserts for the credulous that "Several sources compared Bush's first six weeks in office to the beginning of Jimmy Carter's presidency, which never recovered from a rocky start." "Bush Must Move Quickly With New Candidate to Recover, Observers Say," 3-10, gives a fairly balanced account of the potential impact of the vote against John Tower, without offering anything really new. However, he's either indulging a bias or simply sloppy when he asserts that "Republicans took after [Sen. Sam Nunn] personally, even spreading the story about a 1972 auto accident that raised questions about whether Nunn. . .had been driving while drunk." Surely Nelson ought to have recalled that this story was resurrected first by the press itself, *The Wall Street Journal* reprinting it from *The Atlanta Constitution.* "Bush Hailed In Hungary, Lauds Reforms," 7-12, nicely captures the personal warmth Bush conveyed on his arrival in Hungary. The piece gushes a bit, but the vignettes that come through — Bush tearing up his speech and speaking in a folksy way to the people, Bush giving his raincoat to an elderly woman soaked by the rain — sound decent and real. After 15 years at the bureau's helm, and turning 60 last year, Nelson should consider devoting *all* his energies to a regular political column.

Noah, Timothy. *The New Republic.* (★)
Contributing writer. Former Washington correspondent at *Newsweek,* the transition to *TNR* hasn't demonstrated a positive side yet. Noah's *TNR* work lacks an appropriate restraint, as he's too prone to run with a story far beyond the limits set by the evidence. In "Shielding the Whistle-blowers," *Newsweek* 3-27, Noah is somewhat facile in this examination of problems that the Office of Special Counsel (OSC) has in protecting whistle-blowers in the federal government and how new legislation might alleviate these problems. "The OSC finks on people it should protect," he reports without ever establishing the veracity of the allegation. "Old Bland-Dad," *TNR* 4-3, a wasted-space profile of Bush's father, Prescott Bush, reveals him to be an unimpressive politician, but who cares? "Be Happy," *TNR* 7-10, is a decent one-topic "Diarist" item on ethics in Washington, including some astute observations: "After honoraria are banned, members of Congress will (legally) bribe their districts en masse with special interest checks that they are no longer permitted to keep." "The Good Times," *The Washington Monthly* 7/8-89, a review of Russell Baker's latest book, offers very sharp, controlled observations, highly complimentary to Baker and his contributions to American journalism, without losing our attention and respect. "Armey's Aesthetic," *TNR* 9-11, is somewhat ephemeral on the controversy over the Mappelthorpe exhibition, focusing on Rep. Dick Armey's (D-Tex.) concern over tax subsidies for such projects. Noah tries to belittle Armey, but succeeds only in displaying his own biases. He confuses satiric irreverence with snideness, employing the wrong tone in "The End of Everything," 10-16, voiding over everything from Francis Fukuyama's "The End of History" thesis in *The National Interest* to Sam Donaldson and Diane Sawyer's "Prime Time Live."

Oreskes, Michael. *The New York Times.* (★ ★ ½)
National correspondent. A year of solid reporting from this reliable young pro. His instincts increasingly well-honed, Oreskes turned in some of the best coverage on Capitol Hill's headaches and heartaches, his reporting crisp and fast-paced. He comes up with a modest analytic in a "Week in Review" feature 1-22, "Here's a New Man Now, Thanks to the Press," wondering how the press can portray Bush in so many modes — lapdog, pit bull, buoyant winner. He strains credulity, though, with inclusion of ABC's Brit Hume's statement: "We think it is our duty to change the public perception of a politician who is coming off better than we think he is. We feel no comparable responsibility to a politician who is coming off worse than we know him to be." "A Week in the Heat," 2-4, contains very good surface analysis of Jim Wright's loss all around in his handling of the pay issue, but needs a little more depth to be really excellent. "Nunn Asserts Issue Of Tower Drinking Is Still Unresolved," 2-23, is compact and careful, with more detail on the FBI report on Tower's alleged drinking problem. Oreskes cites Sen. J.J. Exon (D-Neb.), the second ranking Democrat on Armed Services, as opposing Tower and accurately predicting a close vote. "Wright Fate May Be Decided by Fine Distinction In the Rules," 3-22, has the right scent very early: "Some of Mr. Wright's supporters concede that in the increasing glare of press and public attention, the Wright case is beginning, as one put it, to 'transcend' the question of House Rules." He's briskly adept with "House Set For Bitter Battle on Wright Ethics Issue," 4-15, a fast-paced setup on the coming debate, delivering great quotes. He reports Rep. Charles Wilson (D-Tex.) saying "about 24 yellow-belly turncoat" Democrats would vote against Wright and "about that many men of principle on the Republican side" would support the Speaker. "Final Rounds or Not, Wright Keeps Punching," 5-7, is a deft presentation on the shifting sand under Jim Wright's defenses, as one negative story follows another like the drip, drip of Chinese water torture. " 'Evil Wind' Felt in House After Wright," 6-1, has exactly the right presentation and quotes to convey the mood in Congress as Wright resigns: "Members say they all ask each other whom the reaper will stalk next." In the "Congress" column, 7-25, Oreskes provides interesting bits and pieces of scattered detail on Rep. Newt Gingrich's troubles with other House GOP leaders, but he's only wading analytically. "So Far, Congress Comes up Short on Ideas," 8-6, a "Week in Review" feature as Congress goes on vacation, has no theme, no serious analysis beyond a recitation of what happened, and not a word about colossal struggles over capital gains and the budget, which will occupy Congress on its return. "Barney Frank's Public And Private Lives: Lonely Struggle For Coexistence," 9-15, reminds that behind the screaming headlines on Barney Frank and his dealings with Stephen Gobie, there's a person in there. Not an easy assignment, Oreskes handles this sensitively, without necessarily being sympathetic.

Ostling, Richard. *Time.* (★ ★ ★)
Associate editor. The best we see anywhere on the theological beat, Ostling has a knack for highlighting the different angles of religious topics and issues in a way that makes those reports interesting as well as informative. "Inside the Bible Beltway," with Alessandra Stanley 2-6, offers a perceptive glimpse into DC political prayer groups, centering mostly on the wives, but still providing nice coverage. "Africa's Artistic Resurrection," with James Wilde 3-27, is fascinating on the Renaissance of African religious art, particularly of Christian themes. He explores their mediums, their problems and even their theological implications, but doesn't offer criticism from an artisan's point of view. "Islam Regains Its Voice," with David Aikman 4-10, looks at the growing tolerance of the Islamic religion in the Soviet Union and how far they still have to go, his analysis of why the Soviets are changing their policies towards Moslems is quite good, noting in particular the "need for cooperation from Muslim countries and for popular support along the potentially troublesome southern Asia flank." "Those Mainline Blues," with Jordan Bonfante, Barbara Dolan and Michael P. Harris 5-22, offers very good material on the reasons for the decline of America's Old Guard Protestant churches. One: "Far too many mainline churches are sorely lacking in the marketing and communications savvy that the Evangelicals employ to win new members." In "Selling Hymns and Hees," 6-12, he explores the rewriting of hymns in Methodist church to establish God as neither male nor female. "Catholics vs. the

Church," with Jerome Cramer and Linda DiPietro 7-10, is simplistic impressionism, mixing DC priest George A. Stallings, Jr.'s plans to inaugurate his own "African-American Catholic Congregation" and the closing of inner city Detroit parishes into a non-story on growing rifts between black Catholics and the Roman Catholic Church. "Secrets of the Dead Sea Scrolls," with Michael P. Harris and Robert Slater, 8-14, fascinates, pulling back the shroud of mystery surrounding the controversy of the publishing of the Dead Sea Scrolls. The 800 ancient Jewish manuscripts dating back to the time of Christ were only discovered between 1947 and 1956, but have yet to be made public because of technical difficulties and squabbling among archeologists and theologians.

Ostrow, Ronald J. *Los Angeles Times.* (★)
Washington. Covering the Justice Department, Ostrow seemed never to have really gotten very far inside of the major stories on that beat this year. He's generally lax with "FBI Would Accept Aid From Arafat," 1-2, an overplayed P. 1 lead, making no attempt to provide commentary from expert opinion on what Arafat is up to regarding Pan Am Flight 103. He begins slowly and thinly with "Thornburgh Picks Black Lawyer to Be Rights Enforcer," 2-25, but gradually builds the report into something more interesting. He assembles good background detail on William Lucas, though he leaves us still wondering why some civil rights activists are so opposed to his nomination. "Independent Counsel Explains Why She Didn't Prosecute Figure in '83 EPA Probe," 3-21, is little more than a tedious listing of the reasons independent counsel Alexia Morrison gave for taking five years to complete an investigation of former Justice Department official Theodore Olson on charges that did not involve "an element of personal gain or actions outside the scope of duty." Ostrow missed most of the story on this one. "U.S. Attack on Terrorism Making Progress — At Last," with Robin Wright 5-19, displays a very solid analysis with an interesting angle, looking at how the United States has succeeded at prosecuting a number of terrorists in the courts. We are supplied with good background material and a lot of credible quotes from named officials. With a bit of clipped prose, and well-used quotes, Ostrow comes close to editorializing in "Lucas Foes Risk Rift, Justice Dept. Warns," 7-22, on efforts to confirm William Lucas as the nation's chief civil rights enforcer. However, Ostrow focuses less on the qualifications of Lucas and more on the attorney general's office and civil rights groups and who can shove the hardest. "Lucas Named to Job Not Requiring Senate's O.K.," 8-12, is sluggish, contains little analysis, little behind the scenes information, all of which would have made it a better story, instead of one that reads like a press release for the most part.

Otten, Alan. *The Wall Street Journal.* (★)
Washington. "People Patterns" writer, Otten's more interesting work revolves around changes in medical technology and technique. Oddly enough, he rarely looks at costs. "Technology: Higher-Income Patients Are More Likely To Get a Kidney Transplant, Study Says," 1-16, merely reports the existence of this gap, but doesn't explain it. We find that "further research" is needed, naturally. "Parental Agony: How Counselors Guide Couples When Science Spots Genetic Risks," 3-8, sensitively drawn on genetic counselors, centering on Virginia Corson of Johns Hopkins, what counseling they can provide, what disorders can be diagnosed *in utero,* is very good, but we're left in the dark on how expenses are handled. "Medical Quandary: Intensive-Care Units Are Rejecting Patients Because of Crowding," 5-23, frustrates. Otten conveys a vivid sense that "There's no room at the inn," on use of triage in ER and overcrowding of ICU's, with some tragic examples, but he's pitifully short on numbers and insurance costs, and the expenses involved with ICU patients. We give him credit, though, for his early, complete warning; "MacNeil/Lehrer" didn't raise this to crisis standards until mid-October. "Attacking America's Drug Menace: The Bush Plan," 9-6, is disconnected, contradicting other information, almost denying a drug problem, barely relating to the Bush plan except at the most superficial level, noting the problem is worsened by the availability of guns.

Perry, James M. *The Wall Street Journal.* (★ ½)
Washington. An entertaining writer who has been reporting on the national political circuit for almost 30 years, Perry can answer the bell in producing spot news. His specialty has always been the effective use of wry counterpoints. He has his fans, and we always take a look, but there wasn't much memorable this year, Perry often helping out on stories written by others. He's simply the wrong guy to have assigned for "Reagan's Last Scene Blaming the 'Iron Triangle' For U.S. Budget Deficit Draws Mixed Reviews," 1-5. Perry doesn't have a clue to RR's message, weakly comparing it to Eisenhower's military-industrial complex warning. He is timely, but rather shallow in "Atwater Plans to Reach Black Votes With Zeal," 2-2, offering little explanation of the strategy beyond throwing federal money at black interests. "GOP Stumbles in Wyoming in Effort to Prevent a Sweep by the Democrats," 4-14, gives an excellent account of GOP troubles as RNC co-chairman Ed Rollins sticks his nose into the Wyoming race. He is thoroughly unpersuasive with "Report Reflects a Shift in Attitude on Ethics," 4-18, which portrays Jim Wright as the "first big victim" of a new era of higher standards. "Speaker's Situation Reminiscent of Political Tradition, Texas Style," 6-1, somewhat amusing, is a bit strained, reminiscent of the David Broder column on John Tower. "Homosexual Lawmakers Face Unclear Standards Over Questions of Ethical and Personal Behavior," 9-1, is an eye-opener on a sensitive subject done delicately, and though there's nothing much new here, we do find out there is a "National Conference of Openly Lesbian and Gay Elected and Appointed Officials," with 46 members, "a growing organization that hopes to shorten its name." It may not be Perry's fault that he's assigned to interview the "*Journal*'s panel of political experts" in "East Bloc Moves Give Bush a Boost, Panel Says, But Republicans Stand to Lose on Defense Policy," 11-17. The effort is a waste of space and readers' time, the "experts" a gaggle of political operatives and moth-eaten pundits, not one of whom didn't two years ago ridicule the idea that George Bush would be President.

Pound, Edward T. *The Wall Street Journal.* (★ ★ ½)
Washington. Pound occasionally shared a byline on national security and defense stories in the past, but it wasn't until he began flying solo this year that we could fully appreciate his reporting. Covering the HUD scandals primarily, Pound turned in one of the better performances in the press corps on this saga. He sticks to the known facts with "McDade Balks at Providing Some Data To Panel, Congressional Privilege Cited," 1-20, not adding much new, although the story about Rep. Joseph McDade (R-Penn.) not revealing information regarding his dealings with the now-defunct defense firm, United Chem-Com, received sparse coverage elsewhere. He's completely detached in a fine investigative report, "Holding Firm's Profit On Oil Well Probed," 4-18, an astonishing and detailed account (despite a bit of murkiness) of Speaker Wright's 1987 oil-well deal with Mallightco, Inc. in which he "received $440,000 for an interest in an oil well that the company had purchased the same day for only $9,120." Pound produced a superlative exposition on the HUD scandal in "Housing Subsidy Plan For the Poor Helped Contributions to GOP," with Kenneth H. Bacon 5-25, casting long shadows over Sen. Alfonse D'Amato's (R-N.Y.) Puerto Rican deals. Less rigorous, "Former HUD Official Refuses to Testify Before Panel Studying Program Scandal," 6-14, is confusing on Deborah Gore Dean and her problems with HUD. A sterling report, "Pierce May Have Kept Hands Off, but Projects of Pals Sailed Through," with Jill Abramson 7-12, ties the HUD scandals for the first time to former Secretary Sam Pierce, with special focus on the secretary's friendship with Lionel Hampton and the Newark rent supplement projects. Pound also includes a fine background of Pierce. "Consultant Says His Fee on HUD Project Was Much Higher Than He'd Realized," 8-28, updates us competently on one facet involving Reagan-Bush campaigner Lou Kitchin, with some cursory details, but this report doesn't hold together well. He's overly long in "Good Connections: How HUD Aide Used Ties to Help Himself, Later Paine Webber," 9-22, which becomes "another story" of influence peddling at HUD, this one tied to Paine Webber.

Radcliffe, Donnie. *The Washington Post.* (★)
"Style" writer. Too much of Radcliffe's ink was consumed by the wardrobe of the First Lady, and her profiles were sketchy, a real surprise after last year's superb piece on Mrs. Bush. In "Helene Von Damm's American Dream," 1-8, we never find out her maiden name or anything about her childhood. After four marriages and Ronald Reagan, Von Damm and Radcliffe focus on Nancy, with Von Damm grousing happily all the way, leaving us little but a picture of a bitter lady who lives well and still stokes the fires of ambition. "The Bushes Bearing Gifts," 2-25, tells us what presents they took to Asia when going to Hirohito's funeral and what they wore on the plane, a gossipy and superficial topic at best. "All The Queen's Horses," 5-29, about Queen Elizabeth's horses and their breeding in this country is a nice look into Kentucky horse farming. Radcliffe strays a bit to ponder if Her Majesty and the Bushes stay in the same room in a Kentucky hotel. "Barbara Bush, Decked Out and Down to Earth," 7-14, is a couture-ologue on what Barbara wore in Europe. This may have been an issue with Nancy Reagan, but not with the down-to-earth Barbara Bush. "Bed & Breakfast a la Bush," 8-15, tells us who gets invited to sleep at the Bush's various Presidential type residences. Zzzzz. "Barbara Bush's 'Old-Fashioned' Views on a Mother's Place," 10-3, updates us on Mrs. Bush's latest thinking, this item broadcast originally over the radio and secondhand at best here.

Randolph, Eleanor. *The Washington Post.* (★ ½)
Media reporter. She mixes straight reporting on the media with splashes of informative "inside dope" from the profession, and regularly enough adds a dollop of insightful analysis. Randolph didn't come up with any "big-story" feature again this year to compare with past achievements (e.g. her outstanding '86 feature on the changes at the *New York Times*), though she had all the makings of a major media story early in the year. She's on to something with "*New York Times* Crusade Focuses Attention on Weapons Plants," 1-9, a weighty look at what seems to be an anti-nuke campaign by *NYT* reporter Keith Schneider and editor Soma Golden. With environmental stories so prominent this year, and the ones in which the profession most dangerously strays back toward advocacy journalism, Randolph's instincts failed here, as she didn't follow up on what she'd begun sniffing out. She engages us empathetically with "Query Makes Reporters Cringe," 1-25, a report on the application form reporters must fill out for access to the periodical press galleries: "The 14,000 members — mostly writers and editors for magazines and newsletters — [are asked] to identify every speech, article or activity that has brought in any outside income in the last twelve months. The form doesn't ask how much the journalist gets for such freelance work — merely who paid for it." We appreciate her gutsy "Should Journalists Report Their Own Honoraria?" 4-14, in which Randolph agrees with Senators Alan Simpson and Ted Kennedy that journalists ought to disclose their own honoraria. She wickedly takes a survey of her *Post* colleagues and reports their responses. "Taking A Glove to Television Violence," 6-22, is a good story about a tame little congressional bill lamely suggesting that television "networks, cable operators and others who control television programming be allowed to meet and discuss ways to decrease violence on television," that's provoking howls about "censorship." Her "Las Vegas Newspapers Seek Joint-Operating Exemption," 8-9, a "Business" section report, is very lightweight on the merger of the *Sun* and *Review-Journal,* only stringing together some figures and quotes from the *Sun*-ny side. After a forty year rivalry with patriarchal overtones and colorful bosses, isn't there more of a story than this? "Lantos Asks to Pull Plug Out Of Witnesses' Hands,' 10-3, provides good detail on former HUD Secretary Sam Pierce's request that recording equipment be shut off during his congressional inquiry and on Rep. Tom Lantos' (D-Calif.) proposal to change House rules regarding that, but more on the pros and cons of the issue was needed.

Rasky, Susan. *The New York Times.* (★ ★ ½)
Congressional correspondent. She's clearly more comfortable reporting on the technical details of legislation moving through Capitol Hill, but what she sometimes lacks on the broad, analytical front is well-compensated by her hard-working professionalism. Her feature on a frustrated Dan Rostenkowski, "For the Chairman of a Powerful Committee, the House is No Longer a Home,"

11-20, displays a gift for the political personality profile, coaxing thoughts and emotions out of the Ways & Means chairman and presenting them with care and vitality, a 10 Best selection. Rasky provided steady, reliable information on the capital gains saga this year, our reporter of choice during the Senate maneuvers. Earlier, a light look at the pros and cons of delegating powers to a "bipartisan commission" in the wake of the pay raise debate, "Congress Says: A Commission Made Us Do It," 1-29, cleverly employs an insightful observation from AEI's William Schneider to underscore the issue: "The rule of commissions is that they work except when they don't work." "After Tower Debacle, Washington Wonders About the Fallout," 3-12, is good advance work on "the judgement of Jim Wright," wondering if he will get snagged by "one of Washington's periodic fits of moralism." She goes an extra mile in "Bush Is Accused of Backing Away From Promise on 1988 Arms Pact," 4-7, an important story, with the Bush team citing budgetary reasons for reneging on a Reagan promise to beef up U.S. satellite capabilities in order to verify compliance with arms treaties. While Rasky serves as a mouthpiece here for Sen. David Boren (D-Okla.), who is taking the White House to task on this, she adds new dimensions by seeking out intelligence scholar Jeffrey Richelson for comment. Her analysis is solid in "The Minimum Wage Fight Isn't Really About Pay," 5-7, on proponents conceding that Bush seems to have little to lose in vetoing the Democratic bill. She takes a good idea and runs with it in "Echo of Kennedy Era: Even Camelot's Cast Argues Capital Gains," 8-8, on former John F. Kennedy aides disputing his commitment to lower capital gains tax. She provides excellent detail on the various scenarios confronting Democrat and GOP negotiators going into the final week before the deadline with "Senators See Some Progress On Cut In Capital Gains Tax," 10-8.

Reid, T. R. *The Washington Post.* (★ ★)
Denver bureau chief. Back to a more locally-focused, Midwest beat, after vigorously covering the presidential campaigns there the year before, Reid's reporting continues to bubble up to our attention. We immediately appreciated "Lawyers, Builders Disagree on Impact of High Court Decision on Set-Asides," 1-29, which describes the rampant confusion among contractors, with Reid helping to clarify the issue with an association official's quote: "What everybody has to do is see what happens when public officials review their local affirmative action plans in the context of this opinion. . .And that's going to happen without litigation." His survey is effective in "Patchwork Pattern of Abortion Rules," 4-17, outlining the legal attitudes toward abortion in various states and how they will be affected by the expected reversal of *Roe v. Wade.* He's thoughtful and rather gutsy with "When the Press Yelled Fire," 7-23, which is critical of journalism's role in fueling the fires of Yellowstone. His article itself was a minor news item for its candid observation that "If the first job of the media is to convey accurate information, then we failed in our job. I offer this assessment not as a j'accuse, but rather as a nostra culpa." His "Navajo Tribe Seems Near Civil War," 7-30, is sturdy reporting, attentive to detail and balanced, on the effects the fraud investigation of Navajo leader Peter MacDonald is having on the 200,000-member sovereign nation. Reid updates us on CARL, the Colorado Alliance of Research Libraries, in "Computer Access System Brings the Library Home," 9-2, clearly presented and enjoyable to read. In "Former Navajo Chairman Charged with Fraud," 10-14, Reid gives a quick, effective overview of the 100-count fraud and conspiracy indictment of Peter MacDonald. An acceptable simplified account, we get the feeling there's still much more to come.

Reinhold, Robert. *The New York Times.* (★ ★)
Los Angeles bureau chief. Now into his second year as bureau chief here, Reinhold has expanded his reporting portfolio, though coverage of Southern California's business side is thin. He injects some colorful detail into "From Bad to Worse," 2-19, on the gridlock problem in L.A. where "Friends and neighbors trade stories about short cuts." "Political Fallout From Smog Blurs Future of Los Angeles," 4-30, is a parable on how revamping life in the fast lane can make you choke. If city leaders can't comply with provisions of the Clean Air Act by April 30, 1990, EPA will enforce it for them. "Las Vegas Transformation: A Sin City Is A Family Town," 5-30, is

a terrific profile of Las Vegas — everything you ever wanted to know and then some, though we were left wanting more treatment as to why Nevada has the highest state rate of teen suicide. He provides a fine overview of L.A.'s big media story in "Soul Searching at *Los Angeles Times*," 8-10, on the killing of a story by the *LA Times* regarding possible conflicts of interest by Mayor Tom Bradley, whom the paper has supported for 20 years, while the *L.A. Herald Examiner* takes the lead in pushing the story: "The [Los Angeles] Times has built itself into a formidable newspaper, widely respected for its foreign, national and Washington coverage. But like other powerful urban papers, it has sometimes found itself criticized for not adequately covering the city, where it sells the vast bulk of its 1.1 million copies daily." "Dozens of Cats Killed, Fears Spread in Suburb," 8-13, is an engrossing feature on bizarre episodes of house cats being mutilated, probably by urban coyotes, in Orange County, CA. "Los Angeles Mayor Faces Suit On Ethics; No Crime Is Charged," 9-14, is fairly and equitably balanced reporting, Reinhold restraining any estimation on Mayor Bradley's guilt. "The Koreans' Big Entry Into Business," 9-24, is a very nice treatment of burgeoning Koreatown in Los Angeles, 300,000 immigrants, how they bank among themselves and how commercial banks are just beginning to realize what good credit risks they are. In "An Old Land Deal Nettles The West," 10-10, Reinhold thoroughly outlines the political maneuverings of western states to resolve the decades-old problem of how to generate more revenue from small, state-owned tracts of land scattered amid federal land. "California Alliance Proposes Vote On Broad Environmental Measure," 10-11, explores all aspects of a broad environmental measure slated for next year's ballot including its potential as a means to skirt strict limits on campaign contributions. Superbly penned, "Fault Lines: California Struggles With The Other Side of Its Dream," 10-22, is the one article we can look back to years from now to remember what the San Francisco quake of '89 was like, multi-dimensional and sensitively drawn.

Roberts, Steven V. *U.S.News & World Report.* (★)
Senior writer. Moving from *The New York Times* to the newsweekly, Roberts enjoys more latitude with his analytic efforts, the reported news event often serving as backdrop for the analytical foray. We seem to get more recycled conventional wisdom than trenchant judgment from him, however. He puts the Oliver North trial into an interesting context with "The Dawning of the Bush Method," 4-17, identifying it as a manifestation of the Reagan Doctrine, making a decent stab at delineating a "Bush Doctrine" along the way. "The Dawn of Karate-Chop Republican Politics," 5-1, uses the Congressional special elections to illustrate the problems facing the GOP as it tries to increase its numbers in the House. This analytic, though, has the flatness of conventionality in its explanation as to why Democrats beat Republicans in state and local elections: "Many voters prefer to see a Democrat on the other side of the glass," and "Americans have a natural instinct to limit the power of the president through their vote for Congress." In "The Battle for Democracy," 5-22, his look at the increased global appeal of democracy is weighed down with an insufferably haughty tone. Roberts too quickly asserts that many who advocate democracy are often ignorant of what it entails, and he presumptuously advises that "Americans seem eager to provide military aid if a country is under military siege, but then they lose interest when the fight shifts to the less glamorous, often more costly, economic arena." "After Wright's Fall," 6-5, sets the Wright scandal aside and focuses on how the new Democratic leadership and the White House will deal with difficult domestic policy issues. Roberts miscalls the forthcoming relationship between Bush and the Democrats under Foley and Mitchell, with a superficial analysis that suggests it will be conciliatory, not confrontational as with Reagan and the Congressional Democrats. "Who Won the Ethics War?" with Gloria Borger 6-12, does a nice job of showcasing possible ethics reforms in the wake of Wright's resignation. "Can Jack Kemp Clean Up the HUD Mess?" with Joseph P. Shapiro 7-3, outlines the task facing the new HUD secretary as he tries to clean up the mess at the department, though it dances close to cynicism in its assessment of the difficulty involved in removing political favoritism from the HUD process: "one man's influence peddling is another man's constituent service." Roberts is far too conventional with "Bush's Shovel Brigade," 8-7, picking up on *Post* columnists, but supplying no context on how the "mess" he addresses is a

public sector mess, as in the U.S.S.R., Eastern Europe and China. "The Howl of Congressional Watchdogs," with Joseph Shapiro 9-11, focuses on Congress's inability to fulfill its oversight functions adequately, but with a weary theme: "Congressmen generally make poor watchdogs because they are easily bored by dull, time-consuming investigations that seldom produce political payoffs."

Rodriguez, Paul M. *The Washington Times.* (★ ★ ½)
He's establishing his investigative prowess at the daily this year, teaming up with George Archibald to break the Barney Frank story. Rodriguez did some digging into the Jim Wright scandal, and although he didn't uncover anything new, the coverage was respectable. "Justice Plans to Review 'Line by Line' in Criminal Probe," 4-18, provides a useful overview of the House ethics panel's charges against House Speaker Jim Wright and an update on the Justice Department's response to the committee's charges. Rodriguez works enough quotes in from varied sources to give an extra lift to this report. He reports some inside information that Wright's "closest and most powerful House colleagues" have told him that unless he knocks down two of the most critical charges in the ethics panel's report, he'll have to step down as House Speaker. Rodriguez doesn't identify the legislators, but there is a ring of veracity to the report in "Key Democrats Give Wright Ultimatum," 5-17. "Wright Seeks Graceful Exit," 5-25, reports on attempts by the House Speaker to work various options, among them resigning as Speaker but retaining his congressional seat. Rodriguez assembles enough responses from various Democrats to indicate that there are no options left and it's only a question of how soon Wright will leave Congress. Rodriguez produces a scoop with "Sex Probe Focuses On House," 5-29, reporting that federal law enforcement officials are conducting a preliminary inquiry into allegations of sexual misconduct involving minors and male prostitutes by at least five members of the House. Rodriguez reports the denial of the allegations by potential targets of the inquiry, and demonstrates professionalism by not identifying the individuals at this stage. With ample, incisive material from interviews, he makes "Nervous Democrats Look Ahead," 6-2, work as an accurate picture of the anxious mood in the House after Wright's resignation. Another investigative scoop, "Homosexual Prostitution Inquiry Ensnares VIPs with Reagan, Bush," with Archibald 6-29, breaks the Craig J. Spence story on the pending investigation by authorities of a homosexual prostitution ring, the clients of which allegedly include, among others, key officials of the Reagan and Bush administrations. The teaming up with George Archibald resulted in another investigative scoop, as "Sex Sold From Congressman's Apartment," 8-25, "Frank's Lover Was 'Call Boy,' " 8-25, and "Frank Gave Call Boy House Favors," with Archibald 9-7, reveal an unsavory relationship between the Massachusetts congressman and homosexual prostitute Stephen Gobie. Rodriguez and Archibald interview Rep. Frank, who remarkably acknowledges the bulk of what they revealed, a 10 Best selection. "Tide Is Rolling Against Frank," with Ralph Z. Hallow 9-19, is a mere drumbeat for Barney Frank's execution.

Rogers, David. *The Wall Street Journal.* (★ ½)
Washington. A steady, reliable reporter, Rogers produced no big splashes while working the ethics angles on Capitol Hill this year. He gives us a rambling news analysis, although it's not identified as such, in "Wright, Seeking Loyalty and Tighter Control, Weighs McCurdy as Head of Intelligence Panel," 12-28-88. There is, though, useful information on Jim Wright's pal, Rep. David McCurdy of Oklahoma, who is due to regain a powerful chair with Wright's intervention. Simplistic and insubstantial, "Bush Could Hit Deficit Target With Few Arts," 1-19, is superficial on what's happening with the administration and the CBO's estimates. Rogers' reporting is solid in "Tower Is Still Facing Hurdles In Senate Panel," 2-23, on Sen. Sam Nunn's concerns about FBI report and questions on John Tower's alleged drinking problem. It lacks the more thorough detail of the *NYT* report of same day, with the role of Sen. J. J. Exon (D-Neb.) coming too late in the story, but it's better on Tower's 1981 oil investment. Skimming the Senate debate over Tower, "Senate Begins Tense Debate on Tower Amid Renewed Pressure for Withdrawal," 3-3, Rogers' good selection and use of quotes gives us the tone on both sides. "Wright Is Dealt a Serious Blow By Voting Within Ethics Panel," with Brooks Jackson 4-12, startles, with no direct

quotes, but confident presentation: "The pattern of votes shows that a bipartisan majority has sided with the arguments of special counsel Richard Phelan." "Speaker Wright Close to Stepping Down As Ethics Panel Rebuffs Talk for Deal," 5-25, is informative, but all from Democratic side, with no perspective from the GOP which seems to be pushing for deeper inquiries. "Wright Hopes to End Bitterness by Quitting," 6-1, is a good surface report on the level of tension in the House: "Much of Mr. Wright's presentation had been heard before in different forums, and, as in the past, he showed a penchant for overstatement." "Bill Would Delay Decision on Banning Food Color That Causes Animal Tumors," 7-17, is balanced on fight over use of Red No. 2. It's nicely done, but there's not enough on chances of the bill's passage. "Smoking Lamp for Fliers About To Flicker Out," 9-8, is a decent little update on pending federal legislation expanding prohibition of non-smoking flights. Rogers packs a lot of information into a relatively short "Fiscal '90 Requests of Over $530 Billion Are Before Congress in Year-End Push," 11-13, relating increased aid to Pakistan because of pressure from liberals to show increased pressure for the Bhutto regime, which is "sure to hamper promised military aid for El Salvador." He dispenses useful background and detail on Tom Foley's plan to hike House pay to $120,489, banning honoraria, in 1991 with "Speaker Foley to Press Ahead With Pay Plan," 11-14, but, a bit too complex, it needs a few quotes to clarify the political maneuvers and problems with the Senate.

Romano, Lois. *The Washington Post.* (★ ★)
"Style" writer. One of the better scribes on the Barbara Bush beat, Romano's adept style helps the reader to know the First Lady as she takes her stories beyond the words and wardrobe features. "One Couple's Inauguration: the Thrills and the Bells," 1-22, thoroughly debunks the mythical inaugural experience, and it sounds disastrous — too much money, too many crowds — although they claim to have had fun. "At Home With the First Lady," 3-30, is a great account of a press lunch with Barbara Bush, at the end of which we feel we just got up from her table. We learn here that the ink from *The New York Times* turns Millie's pups grey. "Barbara Bush's Happy Hundred," 5-2, gives a once-over of her demanding schedule, without the particulars that would clarify what the 63-year-old grandmother has been thrown into. A "day in the life" rundown of the First Lady's schedule would have enriched this piece, but it stands well enough on its own. "The Envoy Who Talked Too Much," 5-26, is a charming story about Peter Secchia of Grand Rapids, MI, Bush's chosen envoy to Italy, having his nomination held up. Romano develops colorful anecdotes about his earthiness, handling it respectfully and good-naturedly, for a very entertaining story. In "Mrs. Bush, In Admiration," 5-30, Romano is hampered by the First Lady's refusal to let the media accompany her in Belgium during the NATO summit, so she writes about it. "When reporters complained to Anna Perez, Barbara Bush's press secretary, that they aren't close enough to the First Lady during the tour, she said 'We don't do it in America either.' " Romano always finds enough human interest material to keep her stories lively and informative. "At 10 Downing Street, a Bush and a Peck," 6-2, is a wonderfully detailed account of the Bush's trip to London. As in the 3-30 press lunch piece, she makes you feel like you're in the middle of the press pack, getting better and better as it goes along, mixing it up: chit-chat from the queen, embarrassing moments, Barbara's snappish asides. "The Tangled Saga of Deborah Gore Dean," 8-7, is a tangled story, Romano trying hard to condemn the lady's management style and history; we know little more about the HUD worker upon finishing than when we started. And "The Senator Didn't Sing," 9-28, is just plain dopey on the two Paul Simons, the Senator and the singer, at a Democratic fundraiser in DC.

Scardino, Albert. *The New York Times.* (★ ★)
Press reporter. Second banana now that Alex Jones is back in town, Scardino measures up respectably, his writing clean and sharp. "Ethics, Reporters and *The New Yorker*," 3-21, explores the flap over Janet Malcolm's article in *The New Yorker* that moans about Joe McGinness's treatment of Jeff McDonald in *Fatal Vision*. While she's done the same thing, pretending to be a friend of subject and then turning on them in print, Scardino opens up the debate, following through nicely. "Big Dailies Think Small in Fight for Suburbs," 4-10, is well

covered, not seen elsewhere on the importance of local news and how big papers are using new technology to sell more papers, with examples galore and understandable explanations of technology that allows it. "The Magazine That Lost Its Way," 6-18, tracks *Venture* magazine's downturn; although we really don't get a clear picture from Scardino on why, he's a facile writer and we read through for the available information. "El Diario Sold To Group Led By Publisher," 9-1, reveals the purchase of the NY Spanish newspaper from Gannett by Carlos Ramirez and Peter W. Davidson, but we don't get a feel for the wrangling behind the scenes, or why Gannett wanted to sell this particular paper, as advertising and circulation are both going up slowly after a decade-long decline. "Gannett Profits Rose 11% in Third Quarter," 10-12, is very cursory, giving us little information, though what's there is useful, and Scardino doesn't have much column space in which to maneuver.

Seib, Gerald. *The Wall Street Journal.* (★ ★ ½)
White House. He skipped a beat this year. We didn't see enough of that characteristic penchant for detecting subtleties and nuances in political relationships that gives him an edge in untangling power politics. "Bush Will Attempt to Trim Powers of Congress, Particularly on National-Security Policy Issues," 2-1, displays his keen political sensors, suggesting the administration is wisely selecting trade policy as an area for buttressing Bush's power. "Lengthy Controversy Over Tower's Nomination Is Leaving the Pentagon Somewhat Defenseless," with Andy Pasztor 2-15, assembles a clear picture on the immediate consequences for the Pentagon of the stalled Tower nomination. "Advise and Reject: Tower Fiasco Hurts Bush, But Also Puts Congress On Defensive," with John Fialka 3-10, tries to form the conventional wisdom before it solidifies, reviewing the Tower fiasco as a parable for the halting initiation of the supposedly seasoned Bush administration, but misses the ball on the next SecDef. "Quayle's Leadership of National Space Council Puts Him on a Risky Orbit With Vast Opportunity," 5-10, is mid-depth reporting and analysis of Quayle at the space council, with the best material at the end, covering his leverage in policymaking, plus cheers by the space community. "Bush's Stance on Soviets Gives Him Political Trouble at Home, Abroad," 5-25, is finely tuned reporting on Bush's caution. Seib maintains professional standards, taking no sides on whether it might be warranted or not, and cuts against the grain with assembled facts: "He is an inherently cautious man who has succeeded in life mostly by taking carefully considered steps rather than risky gambits." "Bush's Initiatives on Arms Cuts, Political Change in Europe Lead Some to Call Trip 'Victory Tour,' " 6-2, locates the underlying reality of the President's European tour, his capture of the diplomatic initiative from Mikhail Gorbachev. Seib rolls over, failing to undertake appropriate critique in "White House Promotes the Environment As a Top Foreign-Policy Consideration," 6-19. He simply accepts as established a Western Europe and Soviet push for more "environmentalism," quoting a Soviet official that "Western industries are trying to get into the Soviet Union that most ecologically damaging production process and to turn the Soviet Union into the garbage dump of the planet." Huh? "Bush Is Making Poland the Centerpiece Of His Attempts to Change East Europe," 7-31, neglects the point that change in the region appears to be relatively independent of the White House, offering instead a rehashing of Bush's 1987 trip. "After Shaky Start, Sununu Comes Into His Own," 8-17, is timely, taking note of Sununu's refusal to play "gatekeeper" of people or ideas at the White House, but misses the nuance of his relationships with other key staffers such as Dan Quayle and Michael Boskin. In the year end congressional budget scramble, Seib is on the mark with "Debate is Raging Within Bush Administration On Whether to Accept Automatic Budget Cuts," with John E. Yang 11-13, DoD's Richard Cheney on the rampage against Pentagon cutbacks.

Shales, Tom. *The Washington Post.* (★ ★ ★)
Television critic. Doing much broader work than a reviewer, Shales examines trends in broadcasting with wit unexcelled. Often the information he presents is not new, but he always adds a twist to it with his phrasing. He's appalled at the onslaught of shows like "A Current Affair" (which he calls "squalid") and "Inside Edition," in "Murder, She Broadcast," 1-26, and his disdainful tone works somewhat against him here, interfering with his presentation of

evidence. He coins here the definitive word for tabloid TV: "trashoid." "Stalking Trash: CBS' '48 Hours' Thumbs Through Tabloid TV," 3-2, is somewhat ordinary on the CBS News magazine's look at a TV industry convention of program buyers and sellers. His comments on the weaknesses of the program's coverage are accurate, but not vivid or precise enough to support all his criticisms. "Maury Povich," he writes, "defends his smarmy monstrosity 'A Current Affair' with empty, rhetorical rationalizations" but Shales fails to supply us with even one. "NBC News, Losing Its Plumage," 3-28, is great stuff on defections there, supposedly because of new News President Michael Gartner, a print journalist, but Shales doesn't mention reacquisition of CNN anchor Mary Beth Williams. "C-SPAN, America's Great Town Hall," 4-3, celebrates C-SPAN on its tenth anniversary: ". . .the traditional networks have used its existence, and that of Cable News Network, as excuses to abridge radically their coverage of conventions and other political rituals." "Jackie Mason & His World of Wit," 6-14, is a serious, set-piece interview/profile that is impressive because Shales keeps himself from intruding and lets Mason work for him. "Beyond Reality: Simulating the News," 7-27, is early on the controversy of extensive use of simulations or reenactments in news, though he misses the most infamous incident in discussing simulations being confused with reality: H. G. Wells/Orson Welles' *War of the Worlds* radio broadcast. "The Emmys," 9-18, is a very funny, fast and pointed review/evaluation of the annually interminable Emmy Awards broadcast, leaving no doubt as to Shales' own choices for individual awards. "TV Previews," 10-2, is an admirable review of "Superchief," an Earl Warren documentary. But his editorializing is heavy and clumsy, as when he praises producers for not editorializing or balancing the piece with dissenters, like "pompous Robert Bork, who came within a dreadful inch of being named to the Supreme Court itself."

Shapiro, Walter. *Time.* (—)
Senior writer. Shapiro's work this year was deficient, both by reportorial and commentary standards. His commentary doesn't persuade, and his research and reporting are slipshod. "Government By the Timid," 2-20, sets forth a useless indictment of Congress, questioning, "Why are Congressmen so chicken?" With little backing, it's just a lot of pseudo-psychobabble on a page that would have served better if used for ad space. "Drawing the Line," co-written by Laurence I. Barrett 3-13, makes some good points, but nothing's new, and this analysis of old information is rather superficial: "If the White House has fallen short of the standards it set during its much ballyhooed 'ethics week,' so too has the Democratic Congress been unwilling to judge itself by the criteria it sets for others." In "Wait Till Next Year," 4-24, he devotes little space to the budget deficit compromise and instead dwells on how the compromise reflects the new relationship between the executive and legislative branches of the government. "Is It Right to Publish Rumors?" 7-10, is annoyingly self-righteous. "Unfinished Business," with Dick Thompson 8-7, reports on the recently released survey on blacks in America, "A Common Destiny," but instead of reporting on the results of the survey and trying to explain some of its conclusions, Shapiro uses it to grind his own ax on racial relations: "Consider what that single sentence reveals about White America's smug belief in the healing virtues of progress and prosperity." In "America's Dubious Export," 9-4, he examines how America leads the world in the export of "the sophisticated techniques of manipulating voters in free elections" to fledgling democracies. But the worst is "Feeling Low Over Old Highs," 9-18, a poorly written, unconvincing diatribe on drugs: "But we are all a product of our life experiences, and I, like so many of my peers, cannot entirely abandon this *Lucy in the Sky with Diamonds* heritage." Ick.

Shenon, Philip. *The New York Times.* (★ ★)
Washington. The most aggressive of the reporters covering the mess at HUD, Shenon was also the most comprehensive. He turns up on stories involving questions of government ethics and does very well in covering all angles without assuming a prosecutorial role. "The Smoke Surrounding John Tower," 2-11, satisfactorily attempts to pull together accounts of Tower's drinking habits, quoting an official: "There's a lot of smoke around Tower, but there's no smoking gun, at least not yet." His "Bush's Guidelines On Ethics: Be Above Suspicion," 2-23,

has okay detail as we are "entering an era where high ranking officials will tend to be judged on appearances as much as reality." Shenon's "Taking Heat When the Boss Is Under Fire," 4-13, is an enjoyable but rather slight examination of those who are spokesmen (no women are mentioned) for controversial personalities, like Ed Meese and Jim Wright. We enjoy his wry reporting of his exchange with Mark Johnson, Speaker Wright's talking head: " 'I don't want to talk about myself,' Mr. Johnson said in a very, very brief interview. 'Thanks anyway.' " In "2 Groups Fault Bush Nominee, Deepening a Civil Rights Split," 5-10, Shenon reports that William Lucas is opposed by civil rights groups as Assistant Attorney General for civil rights, but is backed by Jesse Jackson and the Southern Christian Leadership Conference. "Why HUD Has Been So Inviting to So Many," 6-4, is scathing on HUD's "influence peddling, conflict of interest and political favoritism" as the "Federal effort intended to help the poor can instead channel billions of dollars to others." However, Shenon needs some cost-benefit analysis here as to whether HUD should even remain in business. "Money From H.U.D. Foreclosures Stolen By Contractors, U.S. Says," 6-11, is a clearly laid out picture, helped by a diagram showing the embezzlement process. Working the Lincoln S&L scandal late in the year, Shenon did a useful roundup, "5 Senators Struggle to Avoid Keating Inquiry Fallout," 11-22: "Five senators entangled in a fast-growing savings and loan investigation are struggling to devise a public relations and legal strategy to distance themselves and each other from political fallout — and each other," with a thorough, satisfying account that backs up this lead."

Shribman, David. *The Wall Street Journal.* (★ ★ ★)
Washington. The star political reporter in the bureau, Shribman was supposed to have had a "special projects" portfolio in this off year, but the portfolio he assembled mostly involved the usual scattering of Washington issues and events, all well done, but nothing special. An exception earns a 10 Best selection. "Washington Mayor's Mounting Woes Spotlight Racial Tension, Suspicions Inside The Beltway," 1-11, is a powerful indictment of Marion Barry, but carefully detached, letting assembled facts speak for themselves, good quotes from Washington black leaders pinning it all down. "Strike At Eastern Tests Ability of Big Labor To Re-establish Itself," 3-6, is a broad overview of Eastern's machinist strike, laying out the stakes for labor unions generally and specifically. "With Unions Slipping, Kirkland Needs More Than to Beat Eastern," 4-11, is a sharp snapshot of Lane Kirkland's AFL-CIO: "It is still on the defensive against union-busting tactics like Mr. Lorenzo's, some of its leaders are growing impatient with Mr. Kirkland's Cold War views, and its critics deem it unsuited to the workplace challenges of the next century." His "Tough Litigator Leads the Ethics Offensive," 4-18, is a classy, brief profile of Ethics Committee special counsel Richard Phelan. "For A Lurid Look at D.C.'s Sleaze, Just Hop Aboard," 5-11, whimsically features the hot attraction in Washington, a bus tour of Washington scandal landmarks, such as Gary Hart's townhouse. In "The Anti-Abortionists Agree on One Thing, but not Much Else," 8-7, he makes the point and documents with many quotes that as with many one-issue movements, once the goal of the movement is reached, to any degree, it usually begins to collapse of its own weight in disagreements. In "Bush's Get-Tough Drug Plan Shares Philosophy That Didn't Work for Rockefeller 20 Years Ago," 9-7, Shribman reasonably compares the Bush drug plan and that of the late N.Y. governor, but doesn't examine the problem Rocky had with follow-up and pushing for further reform. On the day of the vote in the House, "Skirmish Over Capital Gains Is Likely to Set Terms of Political Battles of the Bush Years," 9-28, impresses, Shribman capturing the tone of debate and the heart of the issue: "The GOP strategy is to broaden the debate beyond capital gains and to portray the issue as one of U.S. competitiveness and fairness to middle-class voters who want to sell an asset to underwrite college tuition rather than as a sop to the wealthy." His P. 1 analysis of the fall elections, "Black Moderates Win At Polls by Targeting Once-Elusive Whites," with James M. Perry 11-9, has a wealth of good material hastily assembled. Best line from a young, black politician in Virginia is buried: "Here's a signal that we can be elected to any office in the United States — without necessarily running as a civil rights leader."

Simpson, Glenn. *Insight.* (★ ★)

Washington. A general correspondent who often seems to be assigned inherently dry topics on the mechanisms of political life, Simpson's reporting and writing skills are good, but when his subjects aren't interesting, he's sometimes not either. "Absentee Ballot's Growing Presence," 12-19-88, needs something to grab the reader's attention; Simpson starts slow and stumbles along for several paragraphs, with the attention-getting passages buried more than halfway into the article. In "Can You Count on the Vote Count?" 1-9, on the potential for vote fraud by computer, there's no mention of the several tight races in this year's election where such manipulation might have affected the outcome. "Shaping Policy for Policyshapers," 2-13, is an absorbing "insider's" piece on two relatively unknown research organizations: the Democratic Study Group and the Republican Research Committee. He's somewhat weighted on the Republican side, both on goals and impact, in this one at least. "Switching Parties Over Principle," 3-27, is a thought-provoking piece on conservative Democrats in the House switching over, but Simpson skims over the most important point: after the switch they've been re-elected by their constituents. "Gingrich Heralds A House Divided," 4-10, is a crisp one-pager on Gingrich's 87-85 victory for Minority Whip, with sound analysis. His "10 Years Into the Congress Watch," 4-24, is a good one-page summary, but not enough on Brian Lamb and the long-distance future of C-SPAN. "In Quest to Reform Congress, Common Cause Slays Giants," 6-26, is outstanding on Common Cause and its criticism of congressional ethics, a slick, professional job with good, meaty quotes. "New Slate for a Conservative Board," 7-17, on attempts by conservatives to reform the Legal Services Corporation, promises an analysis of Bush's new slate board nominees and then fails to deliver. After hinting that this new group will likely please the liberal Democrats, it focuses entirely on actions being taken by the outgoing group. As a result, the whole piece seems rather moot. In "Disabled See Hope For Civil Rights," 8-28, Simpson does an adequate job covering most of the issues from the side of the disabled, covering new legislation that seeks to end discrimination against the disabled in access to jobs, facilities, and services, but does not reveal the costs to businesses, and, ultimately, the consumer and taxpayer. "Misadventures of the Mayor May Not Cost Him Reelection," 9-4, comes up with new nuggets of information on Mayor Marion Barry: ". . . his no. 1 priority is the lubrication of this machine to ensure his future reelection without any concern for what he's doing to this city's fabric."

Solomon, Burt. *National Journal.* (★ ★ ½)

White House correspondent and "White House Notebook" columnist, Solomon produces a steady stream of informative material that we appreciate, although he clearly has work to do on getting the bigger picture. In two columns early in the administration he provides indispensable detail on the pecking orders. "For Now, At Least, Collegiality Reigns Supreme Among Bush Staff," 2-4, is a terrific rundown on who's who in the Bush White House, down to otherwise unknown lieutenants. "Bush Works the Phones. . .to Stave Off White House Isolation," 4-1, is a great idea we didn't see repeated anywhere else, listing thirty people with whom Bush keeps in constant telephone contact. "Bush's Disdain For Image Making May Come to Plague His Tenure," 3-11, is a very solid theme, prescient in fact, but it too easily drifts into vapid Beltway chatter on drift, no agenda, etc. "The President's Peer," 1-7, has a great introduction to this profile of Jim Baker, but there's not much else to this. "Blue-Blooded Bush is Striving to Appear as Man of the Masses," 1-28, contains an interesting theme that's nicely supported: "Bush, the inaugural showed, has succeeded in making a political virtue of the clutter of subcultures that he embodies; it apparently enables voters of diverse ideology and cultures to see bits of themselves in him." "Being a Good Manager Isn't Enough If You Can't Deliver a Good Speech," 5-27, starts slowly, not very well organized, but we find good material on page two of this analysis of Bush's speechifying. "George Bush's Congressional Crew. . .Has an Oar or Two Out of Sync," 6-24, a collection of interesting insider gossip on Bush's attempts at congressional relations, but the analysis itself seems out of sync. In "Rush to Judgment on Flag-Burning. . .Out of Character for the President," 7-8, Solomon says Bush's decision for a constitutional amendment came "more quickly than for any consequential policy he's fashioned yet," using well the example of Bush taking advantage of Dukakis's unemotional response to the flag as an American symbol. "Bush Talks and Listens and Meets. . .During Lebanese Hostage Crisis," 8-12, is substantial, giving us a vivid picture of how Bush thrives on discussion and debate, "an oral person" who considers it important to understand the environment of a decision that's not necessarily Carter-like. In "Specter of Reykjavik Hangs Over Bush-Gorbachev Maltese Summit," 11-11, is gibberish, a string of quotes from a few dozen "experts" no substitute for analysis, especially when Solomon leans on the usual cliches from former Foggy Bottom diplomat Robert Hormats for the clumsy theme.

Spevacek, Jennifer. *The Washington Times.* (★)
Congress. We get a small sign every now and then that Spevacek may have it in her to become a front-rank congressional reporter, but mostly what we see is wire-service level. We really expect the leading journals to give us more than meat-and-potato accounts of what's going on, reaching for deeper detail and providing an analytical overlay. Her "Economic Panel Expects to Accomplish Little," 2-1, is slim pickings on the National Economic Commission, a lame duck even before it had its first meeting, Spevacek never questioning its viability or listing its goals. "Bush, Congress to 'Put Offers On Table,' " 3-20, has little detail on what exactly is going on the table in budget talks, although the overview is adequate. More evaluative than most of her material, "Budget Conferees Draft a Tentative Accord," 4-14, clearly presents the political jostling backstage. Although she doesn't dig into the unannounced terms of the accord, we get the mood, if not the detail. "FEC's Call For Repayment 'Unfair' du Pont Campaign Manager Says," 6-29, reports on a bizarre case which dramatizes the Federal Election Commission's proclivity to intrude and nitpick: should fundraising phone calls and letters of the du Pont for President campaign originating from the state of Delaware be counted as expenses toward the spending limit established for the primary campaign in the state of Iowa? But she doesn't answer her question. "Tobacco Industry Shells Out Most in Speaking Fees to Congressmen," 7-11, rehashes the Common Cause study of congressional financial disclosures. "Urban League Calls On Bush To Back Up Words With Action," 8-10, is almost amusing, reporting on the Urban League's clumsy attempt to respond to the clumsier GOP's wooing: "President Bush and his aides are saying all the right things in their courtship of black voters but they should put their money where their mouth is, National Urban League leaders and delegates suggested yesterday." "GOP: Coalition Will Result From Tax Cut Victory," 9-29, shows some promise, a relatively solid evaluation of the political significance of the capital gains tax cut vote in the House, but along with most of her press colleagues, she gets it wrong in predicting Senate reaction.

Toner, Robin. *The New York Times.* (★ ★ ½)
Washington. We docked young Toner a few points last year for her soft coverage of the Dukakis campaign. She was plenty alert on her new congressional assignment this year and we had little to complain about. "Tower Vote: Party Power, Deftly Shown," with Michael Oreskes 3-12, is a solid, analytical wrap-up, deserving of its P. 1, Sunday edition placement. "Race for Whip: Hyperspeed vs. Slow Motion," 3-22, a "Reporter's Notebook" feature, compares/contrasts the two candidates for the House Whip spot vacated by future Sec. Def. Dick Cheney: Rep. Newt Gingrich and Rep. Edward Madigan (R-Ill.), categorizing the race with a great line: "Yes, it is only a race for minority whip, but then *Moby Dick* was just a book about a whale. There are trends and themes here, not as transcendent as the relationship between God and man, but pretty transcendent for the House of Representatives." A followup, "House Republicans Elect Gingrich of Georgia as Whip," 3-23, is respectably done, a wrap-up of Newt's election after a close race and fight, with a terrific little bit about Jim Wright's wondering what congratulatory gift to send Gingrich; Toner tell us at the close Wright sent his own book inscribed for the occasion "in part, 'For Newt, who likes books too.' " A lead "Week in Review," "Democrats Weigh the Cost of Defending Their Speaker," 4-16, touches all the bases on the week's developments, but with only okay surface analysis. "Wright to Begin His Defense Today Amid Swirl of Rumors and Turmoil," 5-23, brings up the curtain on the ethics committee hearings, with Toner remaining deftly detached, and drenching the article with foreboding: "Indeed, the

emotional timber of the House is tinged with poignance; amid all the political maneuvering, House members each day watch Mr. Wright struggling for his political life and growing ever more battered in the attempt." There's good balance and savvy in "As Foley Steps In, the House Needs Serious Repairs," 6-11, clearly seeing problems facing Tom Foley as he tries to satisfy legitimate GOP demands and pressures from the Democratic liberal wing. "The Democrats Struggle, But Energetically," 9-24, maintains a clear perspective on the central struggle over capital gains, the Democrats taking another risk in seeming to practice class warfare over tax policy, another super addition to Sunday's "Week in Review." Toner's bread-and-butter reports from Capitol Hill rarely go beyond the essentials. "Congress Grinds Toward Adjournment," 11-19, has nothing we didn't see elsewhere, but it has a few nice writing touches. Early in the year, "Dukakis in Defeat: No Time to Brood," 2-28, on her former campaign assignment, doesn't tell much about what the Duke's doing now, except waxing philosophic about his election loss, and she doesn't look into his future either.

Waldman, Steven. *Newsweek.* (★ ½)
Washington. More conventional work this year from Waldman, losing some of the quirkiness that made his business pieces so much fun, but maintaining the quality of information presented. "The Revolving Door," 2-6, is replete with examples of the high turnover from government to the private sector, and is useful in an appraisal of the severity of the phenomenon, but Waldman offers no analysis or angle we hadn't seen before. "Tippling in Washington," 3-6, lightly reviews forerunners to John Tower in terms of the drinking problem, citing only obvious, recent examples, such as Wilbur Mills, who's spotlighted, and Ted Kennedy, who's mentioned quickly then dropped, noting "Reporters rarely write about alcoholism. . ..If drinking isn't affecting job performance in a documentable way, the journalists reason, it's nobody's business." In "The Battle Ahead: Labor's New Playbook," 3-20, we get a thorough examination of labor's new tactics in the wake of the Eastern strike, acknowledging that unions are still threatened by apparent continued declining membership. "Jockey, Scheme and Pray," 4-3, is an amusing look at schmoozing, a tongue-in-cheek account of Bush's "unfinished business" of filling administrative posts, complete with tips on how to land one of those coveted positions, such as "play racquet sports with a Bush child," or "be an Andover/Yale educated millionaire." "Attacking the Real 'Jane Roe,' " 4-17, begins as a short profile of Norma McCorvey, the "Jane Roe" of Roe v. Wade, who "wants to be a public symbol" for abortion rights, but has met with resistance from women's rights groups, and then sinks into a feminist catfight. "The Prop 103 'Prairie Fire,' " with Jennifer Foote and Elisa Williams 5-15, is a competent overview of the auto insurance industry, and how consumers are rebelling against it through legislation. "The HUD Ripoff," with Bob Cohn and Rich Thomas 8-7, tightly written and effectively told, contains some sharp insights, although peripheral bits of data are erroneous in spots.

Weinraub, Bernard. *The New York Times.* (★ ★)
Washington. One of the press pack running after the President wherever he goes, Weinraub keeps up pretty well. No hard analytics, but his fluff is well done and his more serious reports are thorough and fair. "A Down-To-Earth Tenant For An Exclusive Address," 1-15, is a very nice profile of Barbara Bush, "a role model for many American women," with BB thrilled that "My mail tells me a lot of fat, white-haired, wrinkled ladies are tickled pink." "Next Week Called Crucial on Tower," 2-19, is complete and balanced, stressing the solid White House support for Tower and reports of "dry holes" in the FBI inquiries on his alleged drinking and womanizing. ". . .Bush to Define His Course," 3-13, effectively details the pros and cons of a Bush "drift," the "story of the week." "Gray-Baker Vendetta: A Long-Running Tale of Potomac Intrigue," 3-29, is real pap, gossipy, based on hearsay and conjecture, on the "feud" between C. Boyden Gray and JBIII, without one new observation or idea here. "Cheney Remarks on Soviet Future Ruffle the White House's Feathers," 5-2, is slightly out of focus, pitting Cheney and Bush over whether Gorby should succeed or not, Cheney merely saying he didn't think so, and we're then told "President Bush disassociated himself today from remarks by Defense Secretary Dick Cheney." His "Issues and Decisions to Test Bush Popularity," 7-2, asks whether Bush can raise

taxes and still remain popular; two dimensional, but there are good quotes on the differences between Reagan (ideological) and Bush (case-by-case). "U.S. Says CIA Believes It Is Probable Higgins Was Killed Before Monday," 8-3, advertises a potentially significant CIA suspicion that the murder occurred long before the Israeli abduction of a leading Hezbollah sheik. Unfortunately, Weinraub chooses to abandon the CIA perspective for a loose hodge-podge of everything going on in Washington during Bush's first hostage crisis. The sense of being tantalized and then let down is not assuaged by his remark that the administration does not know "exactly how the CIA reached its conclusion." In "Iran's President Offers U.S. Help in Hostage Crisis," 8-5, Weinraub combines a lengthy summation of crisis activity with a careful evaluation of the Iranian President's vague offer of assistance. While it may be pragmatic to treat such pronouncements from Tehran with skepticism, the effect here is to underplay the possibility that indeed U.S.-Iranian relations have come to a "new phase;" as a crisis management update, this is no-frills, but adequate. "U.S.-Canada Warmth in Maine, Except When Talk Is of Lobsters," 9-1, is a witty, but serious P. 1 effort on the lobster issue, plus some other trade items, covering Canadian PM Brian Mulroney's visit to Kennebunkport, but Weinraub stops abruptly, leaving us looking for the end of the piece.

Wermiel, Stephen. *The Wall Street Journal.* (★ ★ ★)
Supreme Court. The reporter to beat at the High Court, Wermiel continues to combine sharp insights with creditable reporting and lively writing. "Minority Firms Worry High Court Will End Preferences in Contracts," 12-28-88, gives no sense of how widespread affirmative action is on contract letting, but we still appreciate the topic covered as well as it is. "With Liberals Watching Nervously, High Court Takes Conservative Tone Into Backlog of Big Cases," 2-6, is a good overview of emerging developments, with Justice Anthony Kennedy "proving to be a dependable conservative," and liberals wringing their hands as there now appears to be a working conservative majority to put the Reagan social agenda into place. "Rehnquist Emerges As A Skillful Leader of the Court's Majority," 6-29, is a sympathetic portrait of Chief Justice Rehnquist, casting him as an affable and effective head of the Supreme Court. "Justices Curb Religious Displays Exhibited By State, Local Officials," 7-5, is a definitive roundup on the SCOTUS decisions, with detail and implications included, plus a highly original delineation of the 5-4 votes, telling us who votes with whom in the five, and with what frequency, useful in spotting trends in voting records and predicting future outcomes. "High Court to Hear California Challenge to American Stores' Purchase of Chain," 10-17, is thorough on the challenge and on the repercussions of possible rulings, both actual and potential.

Whalen, Bill. *Insight.* (★ ★ ★)
Washington. A year ago we suggested Whalen was being asked to do too much, the mountain of material he produced in Campaign '88 well past a point of diminishing returns. He produced less this year, and as we suspected, snapped back to the Whalen of yore. The piece we remember best is a 10 Best selection. "The Democrats," cover 3-27, on "A Party's Time For Solving Riddles," Sen. Bill Bradley (D-N.J.) and Gov. Mario Cuomo, is a great package, with some weak spots here and there, but generally a timely combination at a time when Democrats are oddly not discussing the 1992 race, as if already conceding Bush a second term. "Wright Hits Ground Running as Speaker with Agenda," 12-26-88, was timely at year's end, an excellent update on Jim Wright's options and problems with the ethics committee and House Republicans. "Sununu's Outside Experiences Boosted By An Insider's Bent," 1-30, has some good material on the White House chief of staff, but it's awkwardly organized, without a strong theme to hold it together. "Ruling the House the Wright Way," 2-6, on Jim Wright's brand of arm twisting in the White House doesn't fully explain the mechanisms being employed; though Whalen introduces interesting examples, he doesn't follow through with the results. In "Foley Is Taking His Time to Get to the Top of the Hill," 5-1, with Jim Wright's exit looking more and more assured, this is a well-timed look at one of his likely successors; no really new data, but the review and background was competent and appreciated. "A Capital Issue That Nags Cuomo," 6-26, is fully fleshed out on Cuomo's opposition to the death penalty in the face of a 72% "aye" from

his electorate: "It's difficult for people who have opposed the death penalty for years to admit they're wrong," says one critic. "Bush's Smooth & Lucky Stride," 7-17, is hindered by a bad headline and lead on an otherwise fine story about maneuvering on the capital gains tax. "More Voters on the Rolls, May Not Mean More at Polls," 8-21, updates on congressional proposals to ease voter registration, "motor voters," automatic registration with driver's license, covering all the political bases. "The Conflicting Images of Bob Dole," 9-4, contrasts the Senator's poor campaign style with his successful maneuverings on the Hill, skillfully woven together with an insider's feel.

Zuckerman, Lawrence. *Time.* (★ ★)
Press reporter. Zuckerman is noted here for his meticulously fair and thoughtful treatment of different issues facing the press. "Covering the Bush White House," 1-30, is a good column on exactly what the title tells you, peppered with a nice balance of quotes and examples and suggestions for betterment of dispatch. "Knocking on Death's Door" with Leslie Whitaker 2-27, is well executed on the press' handling of death, how it's covered, concluding self-examination is definitely the best policy; the succinct debate as covered here is most helpful, although Zuckerman doesn't offer solutions. "The Last Stand of the Tabloids," also with Whitaker 3-13, neatly covers the horserace in New York, with the *New York Daily News, Post* and *Newsday* slugging it out. In "Forgive Us Our Press Passes," 5-8, he reports on the charges that Arabs and Israeli press passes are being used by people to spy on the enemy. His analysis of the credentials issue as it relates to PLO sovereignty is quite good, but he fails to address the issue of those Arab countries which refuse to allow foreign reporters in their countries at all. In "Thrust Onto Center Stage," with Jaime A. FlorCruz and Gayle Ray 6-5, Zuckerman finds that the need for television visuals on the China story sparked the first intentional recreations (CBS), noting it was easier to get information on the Student Democracy Movement from a "popsicle vendor" than from the press corps. "To March or Not To March," with Lynn Emmerman and Whitaker 8-14, thoughtfully examines the dilemma faced by reporters who must objectively cover topics about which they have strong personal opinions, sparked by the *New York Times*' Linda Greenhouse participating in a pro-choice march in violation of the paper's policy against such activities.

BIOGRAPHICS

Abelson, Alan. *Barron's.* Editor. B. 1925, NYC. CCNY, 1946, BS-English & Chemistry; U. of IA, 1947, MA-Creative Writing. Freelance, to 1949. New York Journal-American, copyboy, metro reporter, financial desk, to 1956. Barron's, reporter, to 1965; Managing Editor, 1966; "Up & Down Wall Street" columnist, current, 1981; Editor, current. NBC-TV, "News at Sunrise" business commentator, current.

Abramson, Howard S. *The Journal of Commerce.* Reporter. B. 1947, New Haven, CT. U. of Bridgeport, 1970. *The New Haven Register*, reporter, 1967-70. City of New Haven, public information officer, to 1973. States News Service (co-founder), to 1977. Freelance, to 1983. *The Washington Post*, Asst Financial Editor, to 1987. *The Journal of Commerce*, reporter, current, 1987. Author *National Geographic: Behind America's Lens on the World Crown*, 1987.

Adams, Nathan Miller. *Reader's Digest.* Washington Senior Staff Editor. B. 1934, NYC. Colby College, 1958, Art. US Air Force, 1960-63. *New York Journal-American*, "Logbook of Crime" columnist, feature writer, to 1965. Time Inc, London stringer, to 1968. *Sunday Times*, London, 1967. *Reader's Digest*, Sr Editor, special assgnmts, Europe & Middle East, to 1968; DC Sr Staff Editor, current, 1988. Author *The Fifth Horseman*, 1967.

Adams, Peter. *Defense News.* Writer. Fordham, BA-Communications; U. of GA, MA-Political Science. Harvard Fellow, Russian studies. *The Thomasville* (GA) *Times-Enterprise*, reporter. *Today*, reporter. *USA Today*, reporter, 1983-84. *The Orlando Sentinel*, reporter, to 1987. *Defense News*, writer, current, 1987.

Adelman, Ken. Tribune Media Services. Columnist. B. 1946, Chicago. Grinnell College (IA), 1967, BS-Philosophy & Religion; Georgetown, 1969, MS-Foreign Service; 1975, PhD-Political Theory. US Secretary of Defense, asst, 1976-77. US Arms Control & Disarmament Agency, Director, to 1987. UN, permanent representative, 1981-83. *The Washingtonian*, National Editor, current. Tribune Media Services, columnist, current. Institute for Contemporary Studies, VP & Director, DC, current. Author *African Realities*, 1979.

Ali, Salamat. *Far Eastern Economic Review.* New Delhi Bureau Chief. B. 1939. Government College (Lahore, Pakistan), 1953, BS-Chemistry & Zoology. *Pakistan Times* (Lahore), reporter, 1957-60; political correspondent, Islamabad, 1963-78. *Civil & Military Gazette* (Lahore), political correspondent, 1960-63. *Far Eastern Economic Review*, Pakistan correspondent, 1978-79; New Delhi Bureau Chief, current, 1980. Editor of the Year Award, 1979.

Allen, Charlotte Low. *Insight.* Senior Editor. Law. B. 1943, Pasadena, CA. Stanford, 1965, English/Classics; Harvard, 1967, MA; USC, 1974, JD. *The Los Angeles Daily Journal*, Law Editor, 1980-85. *Insight*, Sr Editor, Law, current, 1985.

Allen, Henry. *The Washington Post.* "Style" Writer. B. 1941, Summit, NJ. Hamilton College, (NY), 1963, English. *The New Haven Register*, 1966. *The New York News*, to 1970. AP Dow Jones, 1970. *The Washington Post*, "Style" writer, current, 1970. Author *Fool's Mercy*, 1982.

Almond, Peter J. *The Washington Times.* Domestic Correspondent. B. 1946, Northampton, UK. Nieman Fellow, 1981. *Northern Echo* (Darlington, UK), 1964. *Yorkshire Evening Press*, to 1969. *Cleveland Press*, reporter, to 1979; investigative, to 1982. *The Washington Times*, State Dept correspondent, to 1985; London correspondent, to 1987; domestic correspondent, current, 1987. Charles Stewart Mott Award, 1976; Heywood Broun Award, 1979; Thomas L. Stokes Award, 1979; Northeast OH Press Club, 1st Place Business Reporting, 1982; OH UPI 1st Place, Series, 1982.

Alpern, David M. *Newsweek.* Senior Editor. B. 1942, NY. Columbia, 1963, History. *New York Post*, copyboy, college stringer, 1960-63. *The Daily Journal* (Elizabeth, NJ), reporter, 1963. UPI, NYC, reporter, to 1966. *Newsweek*, national affairs & media reporter; writer; Sr Editor, current. Newsweek On Air, co-anchor, current. The Newsweek Poll (Gallup), coordinator, current. American Assn of Trial Lawyers Award, 1973; ABA Award, 1975; Aviation & Space Writers Assn, 1976; Freedoms Foundation, 1982.

Alpert, William M. *Barron's.* Staff Writer. B. 1956, Highland Park, IL. Yale, 1978, American Studies; Columbia, 1981, MSJ; Columbia, 1983, JD. *Hudson Dispatch*, correspondent, courts, 1981-82. *Barron's*, staff writer, science, current, 1984.

Alsop, Ronald J. *The Wall Street Journal.* News Editor. B. 1953, Indianapolis. IN U., 1975, *Phi Beta Kappa*. *Bloomington* (IN) *Herald-Telephone*, reporter, 1975-76. *The Wall Street Journal*, reporter, Cleveland, 1977-80; reporter, Philadelphia, to 1984; special writer & marketing columnist, to 1989; News Editor, marketing & media page, current, 1989. Co-author & Editor *The Wall Street Journal on Marketing*, 1986.

Alter, Jonathan. *Newsweek.* Senior Writer & Media Critic. B. 1957, Chicago. Harvard, 1979, History. *The Washington Monthly*, Editor, writer, 1981-83. *Newsweek*, Assoc Editor, news media writer, to 1986; Sr Writer, current, 1986. Lowell Mellett Award for Media Criticism, 1987; Gerald Loeb Award, Business Reporting, 1987.

Altman, Lawrence K. *The New York Times.* "Science Times" Reporter & "Doctor's World" Columnist. B. 1937, Quincy, MA. Harvard, 1958, BA-Government, *cum laude*; Tufts School of Medicine, 1962, MD; U. of WA Affiliated Hospitals, Seattle, resident, internal medicine, 1966-68; Sr Fellow, medical genetics. *The Lampoon*, advertising manager, treasurer. *The Quincy Patriot Ledger*, feature writer, to 1962. Mt. Zion Hospital, San Francisco, intern, to 1963. US Public Health Service, *Morbidity and Mortality Weekly Report*, Editor. World Health Organization, Chief, Epidemiology & Immunization Section's Foreign Quarantine Division, DC. Freelance, current. NYU Medical School, clinical assoc prof. *The New York Times*, "Science Times" reporter, current, 1969; "Doctor's World" columnist, current. George Polk Award, Africa AIDS series, 1986.

Anderson, Jack. United Feature Syndicate. Columnist. B. 1922, Long Beach, CA. U. of UT, 1940-41; Georgetown, 1947-48; GWU, 1948. US Merchant Marine, 1944-45; US Army, 1946-47. *Salt Lake Tribune*, reporter, 1939-41. Church of Jesus Christ of Latter-Day Saints, missionary, to 1944. *Deseret News*, war correspondent, 1945. *Washington Merry-Go-Round*, reporter, 1947-65; partner, to 1969; owner, from 1969. *Parade*, Washington Editor, 1954-68; DC Bureau Chief, from 1968. United Feature Syndicate, columnist, current. Pulitzer Prize, National Reporting, 1972. Author & co-author 12 books.

Andrews, Fred. *The New York Times.* Business & Financial Editor. B. 1938, Roanoke, VA. Duke, 1960, BA-Political Science, *magna cum laude*; Princeton, 1965, MA-Politics. *The Richmond News-Leader*, intern reporter, summers 1958, '60. Union Carbide, copywriter, 1962. Fair Campaign Practices Committee, Inc, NY, research assoc; Research Director, to 1965. U. of MD, Far East Division, Taiwan, instructor, 1966. *The New York Times* & Time-Life News Service, correspondent, Taiwan, to 1968. *The Wall Street Journal*, reporter, "Tax Report" columnist, to 1976. *The New York Times*, reporter; "Taxes and Accounting" columnist; "Management" columnist; Deputy Editor, 1977-85; Business & Financial Editor, current, 1985. Author 3 books, including *Tax Tips and Dodges*; co-editor *The Equity Funding Papers: The Anatomy of a Fraud*.

Apple, R. W. Jr. *The New York Times.* Chief Washington Correspondent. B. 1934, Akron, OH. Columbia, 1961, History, *magna cum laude*. US Army, 1957-59. *The Wall Street Journal*, reporter, to 1961. NBC-TV News, writer & correspondent, to 1963. *The New York Times*, metro staff, to 1965, '68; Saigon Bureau Chief, to 1968; Chief Africa Correspondent, to 1969; national political correspondent; London Bureau Chief, 1976-85; Chief DC Correspondent, current, 1985.

Applebome, Peter Charles. *The New York Times.* National Correspondent. Duke, 1971; Northwestern, MA. *The Ypsilanti* (MI) *Press*, reporter/editor, 1974-76. *The Corpus Christi Caller*, reporter/acting City Editor, 1976-78. *The Dallas Morning News*, reporter; Asst City Editor/columnist. *Texas Monthly*, Sr Editor, to 1986. *The New York Times*, national correspondent, Houston, current, 1986.

Archibald, George. *The Washington Times.* National Correspondent. B. 1944, Newmarket, Suffolk, UK. Old Dominion U. (Norfolk, VA), 1967, BA-Political Science & History. *The Arizona Republic*, editorial writer & columnist, to 1973. Administrative, Capitol Hill, to 1982. *The Washington Times*, national correspondent, current, 1982.

Arenson, Karen W. *The New York Times*. "Business Day" Editor. B. 1949, Long Beach, NY. MIT, 1970, BS-Economics; Harvard, Kennedy School of Govt, 1972, MS-Public Policy. MIT Urban Action Fellow, 1969. Russell Sage Foundation Media Fellow, 1972. The Brookings Institute, computer programmer, research asst, 1968. NYC Budget Bureau, summer intern, 1970. Harvard Business School, researcher, 1971. ECIS Company, Partner, 1970-72. *The Miami Herald*, reporter, 1972. National Affiliation of Concerned Business Students, to 1973. *BusinessWeek*, correspondent, Staff Editor, to 1978. *The New York Times*, reporter, to 1984; Enterprise Editor, "Business Day," to 1986, Sunday Business Editor, to 1989; Editor, current, 1989. *The Washington Monthly* Journalism Award, 1981; NY Women in Communication Matrix Award, 1982. Author *The New York Times Guide to Making the New Tax Law Work for You*.

Arledge, Roone. ABC-TV News & Sports. Group President. B. 1931, Forest Hills, NY. Columbia, 1952, BBA. Dumont TV, 1952-53. NBC-TV, Producer, Director, 1955-60. ABC-TV, Network Producer, to 1961; VP, sports, 1963-68. ABC-TV News, President, to 1985. ABC-TV Sports, Inc, 1977-85. ABC-TV News & Sports, Group President, current, 1985. Emmy Award, 1958, '66-74; 3 Peabody Awards; Broadcast Pioneers Award, 1968.

Armbrister, Trevor. *Reader's Digest*. Washington Senior Editor. B. 1933, Norwalk, CT. Washington & Lee U., 1956, English. *Trailways Magazine*, Editor, 1958-61. *The Saturday Evening Post*, Asst Editor, to 1965; Contributing Editor, to 1965; DC Bureau Chief, to 1969. Freelance, to 1976. *Reader's Digest*, Roving Editor, to 1979; Sr Editor, DC, current, 1979. Author 2 books, including *Act of Vengeance*, 1975; co-author 2 books, including (with Gerald R. Ford) *A Time to Heal: The Memoirs of Gerald R. Ford*.

Armbruster, William. *The Journal of Commerce*. Senior Correspondent. B. 1949, Teaneck, NJ. St. Peter's College Economics; U. of HI, 1973, MA-Asian Studies. Freelance, Taiwan, 1975-76. *The Record* (Hackensack, NJ), reporter, to 1977. *The Dispatch* (Union City, NJ), reporter, to 1978. *The China Business Review*, Asst Editor, DC, to 1979. *The Journal of Commerce*, reporter, to 1984; Maritime Editor, to 1986; World Trade Editor, to 1988; Sr Correspondent, current, 1988.

Armstrong, Larry. *BusinessWeek*. Senior Correspondent. Northwestern, BA-Chemistry; MSJ. *Medical World News*, editorial trainee, 1970. *Electronics*, DC correspondent, to 1972; Dallas Bureau Chief, 1972; Chicago bureau manager, to 1978. *BusinessWeek*, Chicago correspondent, to 1984; Tokyo bureau manager, current, to 1989; Sr Correspondent, LA, current, 1989.

Armstrong, Richard A. *Fortune*. Executive Editor. B. 1929, D'Lo, MS. U. of MO, 1950, BJ; Columbia, 1955, MA-English. US Army, 1951-52, Bronze Star. *Gadsden (AL) Times*, reporter, 1950-54. *Time*, Contributing Editor, 1956-61. *USA-1*. Managing Editor, to 1962. *The Saturday Evening Post*, Contributing Editor, to 1969. *Fortune*, Assoc Editor, to 1971; Board of Editors member, to 1975; Asst Managing Editor, to 1977; Exec Editor, current, 1977.

Arnold, Robert. *BusinessWeek*. Senior Editor. U. of MO, BA, MAJ. *The Wall Street Journal*, *The Washington Post*, *BusinessWeek*, Labor Dept Staff Editor, 1978; Editor, to 1985; Sr Editor, current, 1985.

Asman, David. *The Wall Street Journal*. "Americas" & "Manager's Journal" Columns Editor & Editorial Writer. B. 1954, Hollis, NY. Marlboro College, (VT), 1977, Anthropology. *Prospect*, Editor, 1978-80. *Manhattan Report on Economic Policy*, Editor, to 1982. Freelance, to 1983. *The Wall Street Journal*, Editor, "Americas" & "Manager's Journal" columns, editorial writer, current, 1983. Institute for Educational Analysis Journalism Award, 1980; Inter-American Press Assn Tom Wallace Award, 1986. Co-editor (with Adam Meyerson) *The Wall Street Journal on Management*.

Auchincloss, Kenneth. *Newsweek*. Managing Editor & Overseas Editions Editor. B. 1937, NYC. Harvard, 1959, History. *Newsweek*, Assoc Editor, 1966-72; Sr Editor, 1972; Exec Editor, to 1976; Managing Editor, current, 1976; Overseas Editions Editor, current, 1986.

Auerbach, Stuart. *The Washington Post*. Financial Correspondent. B. 1934, NYC. Williams College, (MA), 1957, BA-Political Science. *The Berkshire Eagle* (Pittsfield, MA), reporter. Suburban Bureau Chief, to 1960. *The Miami Herald*, reporter; columnist, to 1966. *The Washington Post*, reporter, to 1969; national medical & science reporter, campaign political correspondent, Latin America, to 1976; Middle East correspondent, Beirut, to 1977; legal correspondent, columnist, to 1979; South Asia correspondent, New Delhi, to 1982; financial correspondent, current, 1982.

Aufderheide, Patricia. *In These Times*. Senior Editor. B. 1948, Germany. U. of MN, 1969, History; 1976, PhD-History. *American Film*, Sr Editor, 1982-83. United Church of Christ, Office of Communication, policy analyst, 1986-87. American U., asst professor, current, 1989. *In These Times*, from 1978; Sr Editor, current. Project Censored Award, coverage of public television, 1979; World Hunger Year, best periodical, 1988. Author *Anwar Sadat*, 1985. Editor *Latin American Visions*, Neighborhood Film & Video Project, 1989.

Aynesworth, Hugh G. *The Washington Times*. National Correspondent. B. 1931, Clarksburg, WV. Salem College, (WV), 1950, Journalism. *Clarksburg* (WV) *Exponent*, part-time sportswriter, 1948-50. *Ft. Smith* (AR) *Times Record*, Sports Editor, to 1953; Managing Editor, 1954-56. *Arkansas Gazette*, sports columnist, 1953-54. *Wichita* (KS) *Eagle*, Aviation Editor, 1956-57. *Dallas Times Herald*, reporter, photographer, to 1959; investigative & State Editor, 1975-77; special correspondent, 1985-86. UPI, Denver reporter, 1959-60. *Dallas Morning News*, Aerospace & Science Editor, to 1967. *Newsweek*, Houston Bureau Chief, to 1974. ABC-TV News, "20/20" Chief Investigative Reporter, 1979-81. KDFW-TV (Dallas), consultant, to 1984. CBS-TV, consultant, 1984. *The Washington Times*, national correspondent, current, 1986. More than 75 state & national awards including Headliners & Special Achievement Awards. Author *The Only Living Witness*, 1984.

Baig, Edward C. *Fortune*. Associate Editor. B. NY. York College, BA-Political Science; Adelphi U., MBA. *Fortune*, cable desk; reporter/researcher, to 1988; Assoc Editor, current, 1988.

Baker, Russell Wayne. *The New York Times*. "Observer" Columnist. B. 1925, Loudon County, VA. Johns Hopkins, 1947, BA-English Literature. US Navy, to 1945. *The Sun*, reporter; London staff; White House correspondent, to 1954. *The New York Times*, DC staff, to 1962; "Observer" columnist, current, 1962. Frank Sullivan Memorial Award, 1976; George Polk Award, Commentary, 1979; Pulitzer Prize, Distinguished Commentary, 1979; Pulitzer Prize, Biography, 1983. Author 10 books, including *The Good Times*, 1989.

Baldacchino, Joseph F. Jr. *Human Events*. Associate Editor. B. 1948, Detroit. Mt. St. Mary's College (MD), 1970, BA-History, *magna cum laude*; Catholic U., 1983, MA-Political Theory. *Dorchester News* (Cambridge, MD), to 1972. *Human Events*, Asst Editor, to 1972; Assoc Editor, current, 1975. Author *Economics and the Moral Order*, 1985.

Baldwin, William. *Forbes*. Assistant Managing Editor. Harvard, 1973, BA-Linguistics. *News Journal* (Wilmington, DE), to 1980. *Forbes*, Sr Editor, DC, to 1987; Asst Managing Editor, current, 1987.

Balz, Dan. *The Washington Post*. Reporter. B. Austin, TX. U. of IL, BS, MSJ. *National Journal*, reporter, Assoc Editor. *Philadelphia Inquirer*, reporter. *The Washington Post*, part-time Asst Editor, 1974-77; Asst Editor, 1978-79; Deputy National Editor, to 1981; correspondent, to 1985; National Editor, to 1989; reporter, national news desk, current, 1989.

Bandow, Douglas. Copley News Service. Columnist. B. 1957, DC. FL State U., 1976, BS-Economics; Stanford Law, 1979, JD. Reagan for President Committee, Sr Policy Analyst, to 1980. Office of the President-Elect, Sr Policy Analyst, to 1981. Special Asst to the President for Policy Development, to 1982. *Inquiry Magazine*, Editor, to 1984. Copley News Service, columnist, current, 1983. Cato Institute, Sr Fellow, current, 1984. Freedoms Foundation Citation, Journalistic Activities, 1979. Editor *U.S. Aid to the Developing World: A Free Market Agenda*, 1985.

Bangsberg, P.T. *The Journal of Commerce*. East Asia Correspondent. B. 1942, Syracuse, NY. TV/radio (Buffalo, NY), news writer, Sub-Editor, producer, 1959-60. UPI, Sub-Editor, Editor, to 1963. ABC Radio News (NY), Sub-Editor, to 1965. *The New York Times*, Sub-Editor, to 1966. *The Daily Telegraph* (UK), Sub-Editor, to 1969. *The Times* (UK), Asst Night Editor, to 1972. *The Birmingham Post* (UK), Asst Editor, Chief Sub-Editor, to 1974. *Birmingham Evening Mail* (UK), Managing Editor, to 1981. *South China Morning Post* (Hong Kong), Asst Editor, to 1983. *The Journal of Commerce*, East Asia correspondent, current, 1984.

Banks, Howard. *Forbes*. Washington Bureau Manager & "What's Ahead for Business" Columnist. B. 1938, Hatfield, UK. De Havilland Aeronautical Technical School, AB. Aerospace industry. *The Economist*, Industrial Editor, Business Britain Editor, West Coast correspondent, 1970-82. *Forbes*, DC bureau manager, current, 1982; "What's Ahead for Business" columnist, current.

Banta, Kenneth. *Time*. London Correspondent. Amherst College. Rhodes Scholar, 1979. *Time*, stringer; Chicago correspondent; writer (on leave), 1984); Eastern European Bureau Chief, 1985-89; London correspondent, current, 1989.

Barber, Lionel. *Financial Times*. Washington Correspondent. B. 1955, London, UK. St. Edmund Hall, Oxford, German; Modern Languages/Modern History. Lawrence Stern Fellow, 1985. *The Scotsman*, 1979-81. *Sunday Times* (UK), business reporter, to 1985. *Financial Times*, financial correspondent, DC correspondent, current, 1985. British Press Young Journalist of the Year, 1981. Author *The Price of Truth*, 1985.

Barmash, Isadore. *The New York Times*. "Business Day" Reporter. B. 1921, Philadelphia. Charles Morris Price School, 1941, Journalism. *Home Furnishings Daily*, Editor-in-Chief. *Woman's Wear Daily*, Managing Editor. Fairchild Publications, reporter, Bureau Chief; Editorial Copy Chief. *New York Herald Tribune*, financial & business feature writer, to 1965. *The New York Times*, "Business Day" reporter, current, 1965.

Barnard, Richard C. *Defense News*. Editor. B. 1943, Alabama. FL Atlantic U., BA-Political Science; American U., MA-Communications. *The Sun Sentinel* (Ft. Lauderdale, FL), reporter, 1967-69. Defense Intelligence Agency, to 1973. The Times Journal Co, writer, Pentagon correspondent, to 1980; Editor, 1984-85. *Defense Week*, Founding Editor, 1980-84. *Navy Times*, Editor, to 1985; *Defense News*, Editor, current, 1985. National Press Club Award; Education Writers Assn Award.

Barnes, Fred. *The New Republic*. Senior Editor. B. 1943, West Point, NY. U. of VA, 1965, BA-History. Nieman Fellow, 1977-78. *The Charlotte News & Courier*, reporter, to 1967. *The Washington Star*, reporter; Supreme Court reporter; White House correspondent, to 1979. *The Sun*, national political reporter, to 1985. *The New Republic*, Sr Editor, current, 1985. *The American Spectator*, contributor, current. "The McLaughlin Group," occasional panelist, current.

Barnes, James A. *National Journal*. Chief Political Reporter. American Enterprise Institute, policy analyst. *The Christian Science Monitor*, *The Washington Post*, contributor. Chief speechwriter, Treasury Sec. James Baker, to 1987. *National Journal*, chief political reporter, current, 1987.

Barol, Bill. *Newsweek*. Senior Writer. B. 1957, Philadelphia. Harvard, 1979, American History. WNBC-TV, 1980. *City Limits* (Boston), Editor, to 1981. Freelance, 1982. *Newsweek*, Gen Editor, 1984-86; Sr Writer, current, 1987. 1st Prize Education Writers Assn National Awards, 1984.

Barone, Michael. *U.S.News & World Report*. Senior Writer. B. 1944, Highland Park, MI. Harvard, 1966, AB-History; Yale, 1969, LLB. Law Clerk, Judge Wade H. McCree, US Court of Appeals, 1969-71. Peter D. Hart Research Assn Inc, VP, 1974-81. *The Washington Post*, editorial page staff writer, to 1989. *U.S.News & World Report*, Sr Writer, current, 1989. Co-author *The Almanac of American Politics*, 1972-current.

Barrett, Laurence I. *Time*. National Political Correspondent. B. 1935, NYC. NYU, 1956, History; Columbia, 1957, MSJ. *New York Herald Tribune*, reporter, columnist, DC correspondent, 1958-65. *Time*, national affairs writer; Sr Editor, Deputy National Affairs Editor; NY Regional Bureau Chief; Sr White House Correspondent; national political correspondent, current. Author 2 books, including *Gambling with History*, 1983.

Barrett, William P. *Forbes*. Southwest Bureau Manager. Rutgers, 1974, BA-History; Rutgers Law School, 1978, JD. *Courier Post* (Camden, NJ), reporter, summers, 1972-74. AP, reporter, Philadelphia, 1975. *Philadelphia Bulletin*, reporter, to 1980. *Dallas Times Herald*, Houston Bureau Chief, to 1982; Middle East Bureau Chief, Cairo, to 1984; national correspondent, NY, to 1986. *Forbes*, Southwest bureau writer, to 1988; manager, Southwest bureau, current, 1988. NJ Press Assn Award, 1980, 1981.

Barron, John. *Reader's Digest*. Washington Senior Staff Editor. B. 1930, Wichita Falls, TX. U. of MO, 1951, BAJ, 1952, MA. US Navy, to 1957. *The Washington Star*, to 1965. *Reader's Digest*, from 1965; Sr Editor, 1986-88; Sr Staff Editor, DC, current, 1988. George Polk Memorial Award, 1964; Raymond Clapper Award. Distinguished DC Correspondence, 1967; DC Newspaper Guild Front Page Award & Grand Award, 1964; Sir James Goldsmith International Award, 1985. Author 3 books, including *KGB Today*, 1983; co-author *Murder of a Gentle Land*, 1978.

Bartlett, Sarah. *The New York Times*. Banking Reporter. B. 1955, Buffalo, NY. U. of Sussex (UK), 1977, BA-Political Science; 1979, MPhil-Development Studies. *BusinessWeek*, International Money Editor, to 1983; Money & Banking Editor, 1986-88; Assoc Editor, to 1988. *Fortune*, reporter, 1983-86. *The New York Times*, banking reporter, current, 1988. Co-recipient Overseas Press Club Award, Best Magazine Reporting Overseas, 1985.

Bartley, Robert L. *The Wall Street Journal*. Editor & Vice President. B. 1937, Marshall, MN. IA State U., BSJ; U. of WI, MS-Political Science. US Army, 1960. *Grinnell* (IA) *Herald-Register*, reporter, 1959-60. *Iowa State Daily*, Editor-in-Chief. *The Wall Street Journal*, reporter, 1962-64; editorial page staff, to 1972; Editorial Page Editor, to 1979; Editor, current, 1979; VP, current, 1983. Overseas Press Club Citation, Excellence, 1977; Gerald Loeb Award, Editorials, 1979; Pulitzer Prize, Editorial Writing, 1980.

Beatty, Jack. *The Atlantic*. Senior Editor. B. 1945, Cambridge, MA. Poynter Fellow, Yale, 1980. *The New Republic*, Literary Editor, 1978-83. *The Atlantic*, Sr Editor, current, 1983.

Beauchamp, Marc. *Forbes*. West Coast Bureau Manager. U. of CA, Berkeley, 1974, BAJ. Seattle Symphony Orchestra, PR Director, 1975-76. *Journal-American* (Bellevue, WA), News Editor, to 1978. *The Japan Times* (Tokyo), News Editor, to 1980. Kyodo News Service, Tokyo, staff writer, Editor, 1982-85. *Forbes*, reporter, to 1986; staff writer, to 1987; Assoc Editor, to 1987; West Coast bureau manager, current, 1987.

Becker, Don Crandall. *The Journal of Commerce*. Publisher & President. B. 1933, Sacramento. San Jose State U., 1957, BA. US Army, 1954-56. *Santa Cruz Sentinel*, reporter, 1957-58. UPI, reporter, Editor, San Francisco, to 1959; correspondent, Manager, Singapore, to 1962, Manila, to 1967, San Juan, PR, 1969-72, Miami, to 1973. National Professional Soccer League, VP & San Francisco, deputy commissioner, 1967-68. Knight-Ridder Newspapers, Corporate Relations Director, 1973-78. *Gary* (IN) *Post-Tribune*, Publisher & Chairman, to 1979. *Detroit Free Press*, President, to 1984. Detroit Symphony, Marketing VP, 1982-83. *The Journal of Commerce*, Publisher & President, current, 1985.

Bedard, Paul. *The Washington Times*. White House Correspondent. B. 1957, Winchester, MA. GWU, 1980, BA-Political Science & Journalism. *The Sun*, news aide, DC, 1978-80. *The Washington Post*, advertising supervisor, writer, 1976-80. Press secretary for NV Dem Senate nominee, 1980. *The* (Salisbury, MD) *Daily Times*, reporter, 1981-83. States News Service, federal political reporter, to 1984. *Defense Week*, Sr Editor, to 1988. *The Washington Times*, White House correspondent, current, 1988.

Behar, Richard. *Time*. Correspondent. B. 1960, NYC. NYU, 1982, BAJ & History. *The New York Times*, education writer & researcher, 1982. *Forbes*, reporter-researcher, to 1984; reporter, to 1986; staff writer, to 1987; Assoc Editor, to 1989. *Time*, correspondent, current, 1989.

Behr, Peter. *The Washington Post*. Assistant Managing Editor - Business & Finance. *The Washington Post*, reporter; financial columnist, to 1987. Asst Managing Editor, business & finance, current, 1987. *The Washington Post Weekly*. Editor, 1987.

Beichman, Arnold. *The Washington Times*. Columnist. B. 1913, USA. Columbia, 1934, BA; 1969, MA; 1973, PhD, all Political Science. Newspaper PM, City Editor. *Newsday*, reporter. AFL-CIO News, UN correspondent. Freelance, current. *The Washington Times*, columnist, current, 1988. Author 4 books, including *Herman Wouk: The Novelist As Social Historian*.

Belkin, Lisa. *The New York Times*. Houston Reporter. B. 1960, NYC. Princeton, 1982, Politics. *The New York Times*, clerk, to 1984; consumer reporter, to 1985; business reporter, to 1987; television & media reporter, to 1987; Houston reporter, current, 1988.

Benjamin, Evelyn. *Fortune*. Board of Editors Member. Bennington College. Economics. Time, Inc. 1957-60. *Fortune*, research assoc, to 1970; Assoc Editor; Deputy Chief of Research; Board of Editors Member, current, 1988.

Bennett, Amanda. *The Wall Street Journal*. Management Reporter. Harvard, 1975, AB-English Literature. *The Wall Street Journal*, reporter, Toronto, to 1978; Detroit, to 1982; DC, to 1983; Peking, to 1985; management reporter, current, 1985.

Bennett, Ralph Kinney. *Reader's Digest*. Washington Senior Staff Editor. B. 1941, Latrobe, PA. Allegheny College (PA), 1963, English. *The Greenburg* (PA) *Tribune-Review*, part-time reporter, 1960-63. *The New Haven Register*, writer, to 1964. *Philadelphia Inquirer*, writer, to 1966. *The National Observer*, writer, to 1968. *Reader's Digest*, Assoc Editor, DC, to 1976; DC Sr Editor, to 1986; Sr Staff Editor, DC, current, 1986.

Berg, Eric. *The New York Times*. "Business Day" Reporter. B. 1958, NY. U. of PA, 1980, Economics; Stanford, MBA. *Chicago Tribune*, *Cleveland Plain Dealer*, reporter, to 1980. *Dallas Times Herald*, business & financial reporter, to 1982. *The New York Times*, "Business Day" reporter, current, 1984.

Bering-Jensen, Henrik. *Insight.* Writer. B. 1951, Copenhagen, Denmark. Oxford, MA-English Literature. Stanford, International Fellow, 1981-82. Danish newspapers, reviewer, 1977-85. *Insight,* writer, current, 1985.

Bernstein, Aaron. *BusinessWeek.* Labor Editor. U. of CA, Santa Cruz, BA. Attended Oxford. UPI, London correspondent. *Forbes,* reporter. *BusinessWeek,* editorial staff, 1983-85; Labor Editor, current, 1985.

Bernstein, Peter W. *U.S.News & World Report.* Business/Personal Finance Managing Editor. B. 1951, NYC. Brown, BA-American History; Christ's College, Cambridge, MA-History. Samuel T. Arnold Fellowship, Brown, 1973. *The Argus Newspaper,* reporter, South Africa, 1973-84. *The* (NY) *Daily News,* reporter, 1976-77. *Fortune,* Assoc Editor, to 1984; DC Editor, 1983-85; elected to Board of Editors. *U.S.News & World Report,* Managing Editor, business, personal finance, current, 1985. ABA Certificate of Merit, 1979. Editor *Arthur Young Tax Guide.*

Bernstein, Richard. *The New York Times.* Domestic Correspondent. B. 1944, NYC. U. of CT, 1966, BA-History; Harvard, 1970, MA-History & East Asian Languages. *Time,* staff writer, 1973-76; Hong Kong correspondent, to 1979; Beijing Bureau Chief, to 1982. *The New York Times,* metro reporter, to 1983; UN Bureau Chief, to 1984; Paris correspondent, to 1985; Paris Bureau Chief, to 1987; domestic correspondent, current, 1987. Author *From the Center of the Earth,* 1982.

Bethell, Tom. *The American Spectator,* Washington Correspondent. B. London, UK. Oxford, 1962, Philosophy & Psychology. Freelance, current. *The American Spectator,* Contributing Editor; to 1988; DC correspondent, current. *National Review,* Contributing Editor, current. John Hancock Award, Amos Tuck Award, 1980.

Bianco, Anthony. *BusinessWeek.* Senior Writer. B. 1953, Oceanside, CA. U. of MN, 1976, BA-Humanities. *Minneapolis Tribune,* reporter, 1976. *Willamette Week* (Portland, OR), business writer, 1978-80. *BusinessWeek,* correspondent, San Francisco, to 1982; NY correspondent, Sr Writer, current, 1982. Amos Tuck Media Award, 1979.

Bird, Kai. *The Nation.* Contributing Editor. B. 1951, Eugene, OR. Carleton College (MN), 1973, BA-History; Northwestern, 1975, MSJ. Thomas J. Watson Fellow, 1973-74; Alicia Patterson Fellow, 1984; John Simon Guggenheim Fellow, 1985; German Marshall Fellow, 1986-87. Freelance, Far East, to 1976. *Newsweek International,* Assoc Editor, to 1977. *The Nation,* Assoc Editor to 1982; "Capitol Letter" columnist, to 1988; Contributing Editor, current, 1988.

Bishara, Michael Alexander. *Far Eastern Economic Review,* Specialist Contributor. B. 1948, New Zealand. Glendowie C. *Asian Business,* Contributing Editor, 1981-82. *Asiabanking - Trade Finance Asia,* Editor-in-Chief, to 1986. *Far Eastern Economic Review,* Deputy Business Editor, to 1988; Specialist Contributor, current, 1988. *Asian Markets Monitor,* Editor, current, 1988.

Bishop, Jerry E. *The Wall Street Journal.* Science & Medicine Reporter. B. Dalhart, TX. U. of TX, 1952, BAJ. *The Wall Street Journal,* copyreader, 1955-57; reporter to 1959; DC reporter, to 1960; science & medicine reporter, current, 1960.

Bleiberg, Robert M. *Barron's.* Editorial Director & Publisher. B. 1924, Brooklyn, NY. Columbia, 1943, BA-Economics; NYU, 1950, MBA-Business Administration. *Barron's,* Assoc Editor, to 1954; Editor, to 1981; Editor & Publisher, to 1982; Editorial Director & Publisher, current, 1982. Dow Jones & Co, Inc, Magazine Group, VP, current, 1980. NY Financial Writers Assn Elliot V. Bell Award. Significant Long-term Contribution to Financial Journalism, 1985.

Blount, Roy, Jr. *The Atlantic.* Contributing Editor. B. 1941, Indianapolis, IN. Vanderbilt, 1963. English; Harvard, 1964, MA. *Atlanta Journal,* reporter, editorial writer, columnist, 1966-68. *Sports Illustrated,* staff writer, Assoc Editor, to 1975. Freelance, current, 1975. *The Atlantic,* Contributing Editor, current. Author 7 books, including *About Three Bricks Shy of a Load.*

Blumenthal, Sidney. *The Washington Post.* Political Reporter. B. 1948, Chicago. Brandeis, 1969. *The New Republic,* national political correspondent, to 1985. *The Washington Post,* political reporter, current, 1985. Author 2 books, including *The Rise of the Counter-Establishment,* 1986.

Blundell, William. *The Wall Street Journal.* National Correspondent. B. 1934, NJ. Syracuse U., 1956, BS-Psychology; postgrad U. of KS, 1961, Journalism. *The Wall Street Journal,* Dallas reporter, to 1964; NY reporter, to 1965; "Page One" rewrite man, to 1968; LA Bureau Chief, to 1986; national correspondent, LA, current, 1986 (editing duties added 1986). Scripps-Howard Foundation Award, Public Service, 1974; American Society of Newspaper Editors Award, Best Non-dead-

line Feature Writing, 1982; co-recipient Meyer Berger Award, Distinguished Metro Reporting, 1966. Author *Storytelling Step by Step,* 1986.

Boffey, Philip M. *The New York Times.* Science & Health Editor. B. 1936, East Orange, NJ. Harvard, 1958, BA-History, *magna cum laude;* postgrad U. of DE. *The Wilmington* (DE) *News-Journal,* reporter, 1961-64. *The Chicago Daily News,* to 1966. *The Wall Street Journal,* to 1967. *Science,* reporter, to 1971; 1975-77. "Science and Government Report," Managing Editor; "Chronicle of Higher Education," Asst Editor, 1971-75. National Association of Science Writers, president, 1984-86. Council for the Advancement of Science Writing, director, current. *The New York Times,* editorial writer, 1977-81; science reporter to 1982; reporter. DC Bureau, to 1988; Deputy Editor, science & health, to 1989; Editor, science & health, current, 1989. Science in Society Award, co-recipient two Pulitzer Prizes; Robert T. Morse Award; Westinghouse Science Journalism Award; Page 1 Award. Author *The Brain Bank of America,* 1975.

Bonafede, Dom. *National Journal.* Senior Contributing Editor. B. 1933, Buffalo, NY. Rutgers, 1953, English, Journalism. Nieman Fellow, 1959-60. *Havana Herald,* reporter, Asst Editor, 1953. *Miami News,* reporter, to 1957. *The Miami Herald,* Chief Latin America Correspondent, to 1963. *New York Herald Tribune,* DC correspondent, to 1966. *Newsweek,* DC correspondent, Chief Latin American Correspondent, to 1969. *National Journal,* White House correspondent, to 1979; Chief Political Correspondent, to 1984; Sr Contributing Editor, current, 1984. *Washington Journalism Review,* Sr Writer, 1978-82. *The Washingtonian,* Contributing Editor, current, 1974. American U., Asst Prof, Journalism, current, 1985. Overseas Press Club Citation, Cuba & Caribbean coverage, 1960; NY Reporters Assn Award, Congressional ethics series, 1965. Contributor 3 books, including *Studying The Presidency,* 1983.

Borger, Gloria. *U.S.News & World Report.* Assistant Managing Editor. Colgate U. *The Washington Star,* MD & DC political reporter, 1975-78. *Newsweek,* political & Capitol Hill reporter, to 1986. *U.S.News & World Report,* Asst Managing Editor, current, 1986.

Borowiec, Andrew. *The Washington Times.* Chief Foreign Correspondent. B. 1928, Poland. Alliance College (PA), 1951, BA-Social Science; Columbia, 1952, MSJ. AP, rewrite man, reporter, foreign correspondent, Chief of various bureaus, to 1966. *The Washington Star,* roving foreign correspondent, to 1975. Carnegie Endowment, Sr Assoc, to 1977. Freelance, to 1981. *Sun-Times,* foreign correspondent, Middle East, Europe, Africa, to 1984. *The Washington Times,* chief foreign correspondent, current, 1984. Overseas Press Club Best Reporting from Abroad Award, 1963. Citation same category, 1965; 1st Prize Front Page Awards, DC-Baltimore Guild, 1971. Author 2 books, including *The Mediterranean Feud,* 1983.

Boudreaux, Richard. *Los Angeles Times.* Managua Bureau Chief. AP, from 1970; reporter, NY; News Editor, Argentina, 1979-82; from 1982: Mexico City, Chile Bureau Chief, Bolivia Bureau Chief. *Los Angeles Times,* Managua Bureau Chief, current, 1987.

Bovard, James. Freelance. B. 1956, Ames, IA. VA Tech, 1976-78. General Arts & Sciences. Cato Institute & Heritage Foundation, policy studies. *The Wall Street Journal, The New York Times, The New Republic, The Detroit News,* freelance contributor, current.

Bowring, Philip. *Far Eastern Economic Review.* Editor. B. 1942, UK. St. Catharine's College, Cambridge, 1960, History; U. of Khartoum, Sudan, 1964, MA-History. *Envoy* (UK) to 1967. *Investor's Chronicle,* London, to 1971. *Finance Week* (Sydney, Australia). Freelance. *Far Eastern Economic Review,* Business Editor, to 1977; Deputy Editor, 1980-88; Editor, current, 1988. *Asian Wall Street Journal,* Economics Editor, 1978. *Financial Times,* SE Asia correspondent, to 1980. Co-author (with Robert Cottnell) *The Carrian File.*

Boyd, John. *The Journal of Commerce.* Reporter. B. 1953, Chattanooga, TN. Lee College, 1977. Social Science/History. Knight-Ridder Financial News, copy editor, Kansas City, 1983-84; economics reporter, DC, to 1986. *The Journal of Commerce,* domestic economy reporter, current, 1986.

Bradlee, Benjamin Crowninshield. *The Washington Post.* Executive Editor. B. 1921, Boston. Harvard, 1943, AB. US Naval Reserve, to 1945. *Sunday News* (Manchester, NH), reporter, to 1946. *The Washington Post,* reporter, to 1951; press attache, Paris embassy, to 1953; Managing Editor, 1965-68; VP, Exec Editor, current, 1968. *Newsweek,* European correspondent, 1953-57; DC reporter, to 1961; Sr Editor, Bureau Chief, to 1965. Author 2 books, including *Conversations With Kennedy,* 1975.

Bradley, Ed. CBS-TV News. "60 Minutes" Correspondent. B. PA. Cheyney (PA) State College, 1964, BA-Education. WDAS radio (Philadelphia), news reporter, 1963-67. WCBS radio (NYC), news reporter, to 1971. CBS-TV News, Paris stringer, 1971. Saigon, 1972-

74; DC correspondent, to 1978; principal correspondent, 1978; "CBS Reports" principal correspondent, to 1981; "60 Minutes" correspondent, current, 1981. George Polk Award, 1980; Emmy Awards, 1979, '83.

Branigan, William. *The Washington Post.* Southeast Asia Correspondent. B. Weisbaden, W. Germany. Ohio U., BS. McGraw-Hill World News (Brussels, Belguim), student intern, chief Middle East correspondent. UPI, Paris correspondent. *The Washington Post,* special correspondent, 1976-79; Asst Foreign Editor, to 1981; SE Asia correspondent, current, 1981.

Bray, Nicholas. *The Wall Street Journal*/Europe. Madrid Bureau Chief. Magdalen College, Oxford. Languages; SOAS, London, Social Anthropology. Reuters, chief correspondent, Belgium, Luxembourg, NATO & Common Market, 1972-82. *The Wall Street Journal*/Europe. Paris correspondent, to 1984; Paris bureau chief, to 1988; Madrid bureau chief, current, 1989.

Breen, Thomas J. *The Washington Times.* Metropolitan Editor. B. 1946, MA. Temple U., English. *Hartford Times,* suburban bureau chief; Acting Asst Editor, 1968-72. *Courier-Post* (Camden, NJ), reporter, political writer & columnist, Political Affairs Editor, to 1974. *Philadelphia Bulletin,* rewrite man, Acting Asst City Editor, to 1975. *The Washington Star,* sports desk, Night City Editor, to 1978. *U.S.News & World Report,* DC News Desk Editor, to 1979. *Peninsula Times Tribune* (Palo Alto, CA), Sports Editor, City Editor, to 1980. *Arizona Republic,* Copy Editor, asst slot man, Scottsdale bureau chief, Deputy Sports Editor, to 1982. *The Washington Times,* City Editor; national political writer, Sports Editor & columnist; SE Asia bureau chief, Manila, to 1987; political writer, to 1989. Metro Editor, current, 1989. Best AP Story of the Month, 1972; co-recipient Philadelphia Press Assn Award, Best Investigative Story, 1974.

Brimelow, Peter. *Forbes.* Senior Editor. B. 1947, UK. U. of Sussex (UK), 1970, BA-History & Economics; Stanford, 1972, MBA. Richardson Securities, Canada, investment analyst, 1972-73. *Financial Post* (Toronto), to 1976; columnist, Contributing Editor, 1979-80. Toronto Sun Syndicate, columnist, to 1982. *MacLean's,* Business Editor, 1976-78. Senator Orrin G. Hatch, economic counsel, to 1981. *Barron's,* Assoc Editor, to 1983; Contributing Editor, 1984-86. *Fortune,* Assoc Editor, 1983-84. *Chief Executive Magazine* (NY), Contributing Editor, to 1986. *Influence Magazine* (Toronto), Contributing Editor, current, 1984. *The Times* (UK), columnist, current, 1986. *Forbes,* Sr Editor, current, 1986.

Brinkley, David. ABC-TV News. "This Week" Anchor. B. 1920, Wilmington, NC. *Wilmington* (NC) *Star-News,* reporter, 1938-41. UP, reporter, bureau manager, Southern cities, 1941-43. NBC Radio/TV, news writer, broadcaster, from 1943; DC correspondent, 1951-81. ABC-TV News, "This Week" anchor, current, 1981. DuPont Award; Peabody Award.

Brinkley, Joel. *The New York Times.* Jerusalem Correspondent. B. 1952, DC. U. of NC, 1975. AP, reporter, 1975. *Richmond News-Leader,* reporter, to 1978. *The Courier-Journal* (KY), reporter; Editor, to 1983. *The New York Times,* DC reporter, to 1988; Jerusalem correspondent, current, 1988. Pulitzer Prize, International Reporting, 1980.

Brittan, Samuel. *Financial Times.* Principal Economic Commentator & Assistant Editor. B. 1933, London, UK. Jesus College, Cambridge, Economics with honors. Nuffield College, visiting fellow, 1973-74; Visiting Fellow, to 1982. Chicago Law, visiting prof, 1978. *Financial Times,* to 1961; principal economic commentator, current, 1966; Asst Editor, current, 1978. *The Observer,* Economics Editor, 1961-64. Dept of Economic Affairs, advisor, 1965. Sr Wincott Award, Financial Journalists, 1971; George Orwell Prize, Political Journalism, 1981. Author 9 books, including *Jobs, Pay, Unions and the Ownership of Capital,* 1984.

Broad, William J. *The New York Times.* Science Reporter. B. 1951, Milwaukee, WI. Webster College (MO), 1973; U. of WI, 1977, MA. U. of WI, Madison, Industry Research Program, reporter, to 1978; teaching asst, History of Science Dept, research asst, Anesthesiology Dept, to 1978. *Science,* reporter, to 1982. *The New York Times,* science reporter, current, 1983. Science-in-Society Journalism Award, National Assn of Science Writers, 1981.

Broadwater, James E. *Washington Journalism Review.* Publisher. U. of FL, Journalism & Advertising. Young & Rubicam, Inc, account exec. *Texas Monthly,* Assoc Publisher. *Saturday Review,* President & Publisher. Baker Publications, Inc, Regional Publishing Director. Blue Water Press, Inc, Director. *Washington Journalism Review,* Publisher, current, 1987.

Brock, David. *Insight.* Senior Editor. B. 1962. U. of CA, Berkeley, 1985, History. *The Wall Street Journal,* intern, summer 1985. *Insight,* writer, to 1988; Sr Editor, News, current, 1988.

Broder, David S. *The Washington Post.* Reporter & Columnist. B. 1929, Chicago Heights, IL. U. of Chicago, 1947, BA-Political Science; 1951, MA. *The Pantagraph* (Bloomington, IL), reporter, 1953-55. *Congressional Quarterly,* reporter, to 1960. *The Washington Star,* reporter, to 1965. *The New York Times,* DC reporter, to 1966. *The Washington Post,* reporter & columnist, current, 1966. Pulitzer Prize, 1973; National Press Club 4th Estate Award, 1988.

Broder, John. *Los Angeles Times.* Pentagon & Defense Correspondent. *Los Angeles Times,* business writer, to 1987; Pentagon & defense correspondent, current, 1987.

Brokaw, Thomas John. NBC-TV News. "NBC Nightly News" Anchor. B. 1940, Webster, SD. U. of SD, 1962, BA-Political Science. KMTV (Omaha), Morning News Editor, 1962-65. WSB-TV (Atlanta), 11:00 News Editor, anchor, to 1966. KNBC-TV (LA, CA), reporter, correspondent, anchor, to 1973. NBC-TV, White House correspondent, to 1976; Saturday Night News, anchor, 1973-76; "Today," host, to 1982; "NBC Nightly News," anchor, current, 1982.

Brooke, James B. *The New York Times.* Rio de Janiero Bureau Chief. B. 1955, NYC. Yale, 1977, BA-Latin American Studies. *The Berkshire Eagle,* freelancer, reporter, to 1978. *The Washington Star,* reporter, 1980. Various publications, stringer, Brazil, to 1984. *The Miami Herald,* South America correspondent, to 1984. *The New York Times,* metro reporter, to 1986; Africa correspondent, to 1989; Rio de Janiero bureau chief, current, 1989.

Brookes, Warren T. *The Detroit News,* Creator's Syndicate. Columnist. B. 1929, Summit, NJ. Harvard, 1950, Economics. Kimberly Clark, 1952-55. W.P. Grace, to 1958. Kenyan & Ecklamst, to 1963. *The Christian Science Monitor,* Promotion Director, to 1971. *The Boston Herald,* columnist, 1975-84. Heritage Features, syndicated columnist, to 1988. Creator's Syndicate, columnist, currrent, 1989. *The Detroit News,* columnist, current, 1984. UPI New England, 1976; USIC Editorial & Columns Award, 1978-80; UPI MI, 1st Place Editorials, 1987. Author *The Economy In Mind,* 1982.

Brookhiser, Richard. *National Review.* Senior Editor. B. 1955, Rochester, NY. Yale, 1977, English. *National Review,* from 1977; Sr Editor, 1979-85; Managing Editor, to 1987; Sr Editor, current, 1988. *New York Observer,* columnist, current, 1987. Author *The Outside Story,* 1986.

Brophy, Beth. *U.S.News & World Report.* Senior Editor. William Smith College (NY); Northwestern, 1978, MSJ. CBS-TV News. Capitol Publications. Medill News Service. Freelance. *Forbes,* govt & public policy reporter, 1979-82. *USA Today,* business writer & columnist, to 1985. *U.S.News & World Report,* Personal Finance & Workplace Assoc Editor, to 1989. Sr Editor, current, 1989. Author *Everything College Didn't Teach You About Money.*

Browne, Malcolm W. *The New York Times.* Science Reporter. B. 1931, New York. Swarthmore College. Columbia, graduate fellow. AP, reporter, Vietnam bureau chief, to 1965. ABC-TV, chief correspondent, Indochina, to 1966. *The New York Times,* to 1981; science writer, current, 1985. *Discover,* Sr Editor, 1981-85. Pulitzer Prize, 1964; George Polk Memorial Award. Author *The New Face of War,* 1968, 1986.

Brownstein, Ronald. *National Journal.* West Coast Correspondent. B. 1958, NYC. SUNY, Binghamton, 1979, English Literature. Freelance, current. *National Journal,* finance & banking reporter, from 1983; political & White House correspondent, to 1987; West Coast correspondent, current, 1987.

Brownstein, Vivian. *Fortune.* Associate Editor. GWU. Board of Governors, Federal Reserve System, economist. Commission on Money & Credit. Committee for Economic Development, economist. *Fortune,* 1960-68; economist, Assoc Editor, current, 1976.

Buchanan, Patrick Joseph. Tribune Media Services. Columnist. B. 1938, DC. Georgetown, 1961, AB-English, *cum laude;* Columbia, 1962, MSJ. *St. Louis Globe Democrat,* editorial writer, 1962-64; Asst Editorial Editor, to 1966. Executive asst to Richard M. Nixon, to 1969; special asst to Pres. Nixon, to 1973. Consultant to Presidents Nixon & Ford, 1973-74. *New York Times* Special Features, syndicated columnist, 1975-78. *Chicago Tribune* — NY News Syndicate, to 1985. NBC Radio Network, commentator, to 1982. White House director of communications, asst to Pres., 1985-87. "Buchanan-Braden Show," cohost, 1978-83. "Crossfire," 1982-85; current, 1987. "The McLaughlin Group," panelist, 1982-85; current, 1988. Tribune Media Services, columnist, current, 1988. Author 3 books, including *Right From the Beginning,* 1988. President's Comm. White House Fellowships, 1969-73; Vice President American Council of Young Political Leaders, 1974-75, 1976-79.

Buchwald, Art. Los Angeles Times Syndicate. Columnist. B. 1925, Mt. Vernon, NY. USC. *New York Herald Tribune,* columnist. Los Angeles Times Syndicate, columnist, current. Pulitzer Prize. Outstanding Commentary, 1982. American Academy of Arts & Letters member, 1986. Author 26 books, including *I Think I Don't Remember*, 1987.

Buckley, Priscilla L. *National Review.* Senior Editor. B. 1921, NYC. Smith College, 1943, BA. UP, copy girl, sportswriter, 1944; radio rewrite, to 1947; Paris correspondent, 1953-56. WACA (Camden, SC), News Editor, 1947-48. CIA, Reports Editor, to 1953. *National Review*, from 1956; Managing Editor, 1959-86; Sr Editor, to 1988; Editor, to 1989. Sr Editor, current, 1989. One Woman's Voice Syndicate, columnist, 1976-80.

Buckley, William F., Jr. *National Review.* Founder & President. B. 1925, NYC. Yale, 1950, BA-Political Science. Economics & History. *Sigma Delta Chi* Fellow, 1976. *Yale Daily News*, chairman. US Army, 1944-46. Yale, asst instructor, Spanish, 1947-51. *American Mercury*, Assoc Editor, to 1955. Freelance, current, 1955. *National Review*, founder, 1955; Editor, to 1988. National Review, Inc, President, columnist, current, 1962. PBS-TV, "Firing Line" host, current, 1966. US Information Agency, advisory member, US delegation, 28th General Assembly of UN, 1973. Best Columnist of the Year Award, 1967; USC's Distinguished Achievement Award in Journalism, 1968; Bellarmine Medal, 1977; NYU's Creative Leadership Award, 1981; Union League's Lincoln Literary Award, 1985. Author 24 books, including *Racing Through Paradise*, 1987; co-author (with L. Brent Bozell) *McCarthy and His Enemies*, 1954.

Budiansky, Stephen. *U.S.News & World Report.* Assistant Managing Editor. B. 1957, Boston. Yale, 1978, Chemistry. Office of Technology Assessment, Congressional Fellow, 1985-86. *Environmental Science & Technology*, Assoc Editor, 1979-81. "Man and Molecules" (syndicated radio program), writer & Producer, to 1982. *Nature*, DC correspondent, Editor, to 1985. *U.S.News & World Report*, Assoc Editor, to 1988; Asst Managing Editor, "Horizons," current, 1988.

Bulkeley, William M. *The Wall Street Journal.* Boston Reporter. B. 1950, Hartford, CT. Yale, 1972, History. *The Wall Street Journal*, reporter, various bureaus, 1972-78; Boston reporter, current, 1978. Coauthor *American Dynasties Today*.

Burns, Jimmy. *Financial Times.* Foreign Desk Page Editor. B. 1953, Madrid, Spain. Stonyhurst College. University College (UK), BA-Latin American Studies; London School of Economics, MA-Politics. BBC TV, scriptwriter, 1975-77. Yorkshire TV, researcher, 1975-77. *Catholic Herald*, reporter, 1975-77. *The Christian Science Monitor*, Lisbon correspondent, to 1980; Buenos Aires correspondent, 1982-86. *Financial Times*, Lisbon correspondent, to 1980; International Desk Editor, to 1982; Buenos Aires correspondent, to 1986; Foreign Desk Page Editor, Latin America, current, 1986.

Burns, John. *The New York Times.* Toronto Bureau Chief. B. 1944, Nottingham, UK. McGill U.; Harvard, 1980-81, Russian; Cambridge, 1984, Chinese. *The Ottawa Citizen, The Toronto Globe and Mail*, reporter, to 1969; Parliamentary correspondent, to 1971; China correspondent, to 1975. *The New York Times*, metro reporter, 1975; South Africa correspondent, to 1981; Moscow bureau chief, to 1984; Beijing bureau chief, expelled 1986; Toronto bureau chief, current, 1986. Co-recipient George Polk Memorial Award, Foreign Correspondence, 1979.

Bylinsky, Gene. *Fortune.* B. Belgrade, Yugoslavia. LSU, Journalism. US Army. Newhouse papers/*The Wall Street Journal*, science writer, to 1966. *Fortune*, Assoc Editor, current, 1966; Board of Editors member, current, 1985.

Byrne, John A. *BusinessWeek.* Associate Editor. William Paterson College (NJ), 1975, BA-Political Science. *Forbes*, DC correspondent; Assoc Editor, 1981-84. *BusinessWeek*, Dept Editor, management, to 1988; Assoc Editor, current, 1988. Author *The Headhunters*, 1986.

Byron, Christopher. *New York.* "Bottom Line" Columnist. Yale; Columbia Law. *Time*, foreign correspondent, London, Bonn; Editor, NY, to 1983. Time, Inc, Sr Editor, "TV Cable Week," 1983. Citicorp Capital Markets Training Program, 1984. *Forbes*, Asst Managing Editor, law, technology & annual industry survey, to 1985. *New York*, "Bottom Line" columnist, current, 1989. Author *The Fanciest Dive*, 1984.

Cahan, Vicky. *BusinessWeek.* Washington Correspondent. Syracuse U., BA. Bureau of National Affairs, Sr Editor, 1973-79. *BusinessWeek*, DC correspondent, occupational safety & health, to 1986; DC correspondent, financial regulation, current, 1986.

Caminiti, Susan. *Fortune.* Reporter. B. 1962, Brooklyn, NY. Fairleigh Dickinson U. (NJ), 1984, Journalism. *The Record* (Hackensack, NJ), reporter, 1982-84. *Fortune*, reporter, current, 1984.

Campbell, Linda Ponce. *The Washington Times.* Supreme Court/Legal Affairs Reporter. B. 1957, El Paso, TX. U. of TX, Ar-

lington, 1979, English; Yale Law School, 1985, MS. *Fort-Worth* (TX) *Star-Telegram*, Copy Editor, reporter, 1980-81; Arlington bureau reporter, to 1982; education writer, to 1984; reporter, 1985-86. *The Texas Lawyer*, to 1987. *The Washington Times*, Supreme Court/legal affairs reporter, current, 1987.

Cannon, Lou. *The Washington Post.* White House Correspondent. B. NYC. Studied U. of NV, San Francisco State College. *Contra Costa Times* (Walnut Creek, CA), editorial. *San Jose Mercury News*, Editor, reporter. Ridder Newspapers, DC correspondent. *The Washington Post*, political reporter, 1972-77; LA staff, to 1980; White House reporter, current, 1980. American Political Science Assn Award, Distinguished Reporting of Public Affairs, 1969. Author 4 books, including *Reagan*, 1982.

Capano, Edward A. *National Review.* Associate Publisher. B. 1941, Brooklyn, NY. St. John's U., 1964, English. *National Review*, promotion manager, 1964-66; Assoc Publisher, current, 1968. Publication Corp, marketing specialist, current, 1967.

Carrington, Tim. *The Wall Street Journal*/Europe. London Reporter. B. Baltimore. U. of VA, 1973, BA. Information Institute, DC representative, 1974. McGraw-Hill, *Securities Week*, from 1976; Managing Editor. *The Wall Street Journal*, reporter, 1980-83; DC reporter, to 1988. *The Wall Street Journal*/Europe, London reporter, current, 1988. Author *The Year They Sold Wall Street*.

Carter, Hodding, III. *The Wall Street Journal.* Op-Ed Contributor. B. 1935, New Orleans, LA. Princeton, 1957. Nieman Fellow, 1965-66. *Delta Democrat Times* (Greenville, MS), reporter, to 1962; Managing Editor, to 1966; Editor, Assoc Publisher, to 1977. Asst Sec of State. Spokesman for President Carter, to 1980. *The Wall Street Journal*, op-ed contributor, current, 1981. PBS-TV, "Capitol Journal" Editor-in-Chief, Chief Correspondent, current. ABC-TV News, "This Week," occasional discussion panelist, current. 4 Emmy awards; National *Sigma Delta Chi* Award, Editorial Writing 1961; Edward R. Murrow Award, Overseas Press Club, 1983. Author *The South Also Rises*.

Chakravarty, Subrata N. *Forbes.* Senior Editor. B. 1947, Calcutta, India. Yale, 1969, Intensive Political Science; Harvard, 1971, MBA-General Management. Harvard, research asst, case writing, 1971-72. *Forbes*, reporter, staff writer, to 1976; co-founder "The Numbers Game" column, Assoc Editor, Sr Editor, 1980-86; Sr Editor, current, 1987. Goodyear India, Ltd, manager, corporate planning, 1976-79. Institutional Analyst, 1986-87.

Chamberlain, John. King Features Syndicate. "These Days" Columnist. B. 1903, New Haven, CT. Yale, 1925, History. Advertising writer, 1925. *The New York Times*, reporter, to 1929; daily book columnist, 1933-36; contributing daily book columnist, 1941-44. *The New York Times Book Review*, Asst Editor, 1928-33. *Fortune*, writer, 1936-41. *Harper's*, Book Editor, 1939-47. Columbia, journalism lecturer, 1934-35; assoc prof, 1941-44. New School for Social Research, lecturer, 1935. Columbia Summer School, lecturer, 1937. *Life*, writer, 1944-50. *The Freeman*, Editor, to 1952. *Barron's*, writer, to 1960. *The Wall Street Journal*, writer, to 1960. Troy (AL) School of Journalism, Dean, 1972-77. King Features Syndicate, "These Days" columnist, current, 1961. Author 6 books, including *A Life With The Printed Word*, 1982.

Chancellor, John William. NBC-TV News. "NBC Nightly News" Commentator. B. 1927, Chicago. U. of IL. *Chicago Sun-Times*, reporter. NBC-TV News, staff, 1950-53; newswriter, reporter, to 1958; Vienna correspondent, 1958; London staff, to 1960; Moscow correspondent, to 1961; NY staff, to 1961; "Today," communicator, 1961-62; Brussels correspondent, 1963-65; network national affairs correspondent, current, 1967; "NBC Nightly News," anchor, 1970-81; commentator, current, 1981. Sol Toishoff Award, Excellence in Broadcasting, National Press Foundation, 1984.

Chapman, Stephen. Tribune Media Services, Columnist. *Chicago Tribune*, Editorial Writer. B. 1954, Brady, TX. Harvard, 1976, History. Freelance, to 1978. *The New Republic*, writer, Assoc Editor, to 1981. *Chicago Tribune*, editorial writer, columnist, current, 1981. Tribune Media Services, columnist, current, 1982.

Chase, Marilyn Morris. *The Wall Street Journal.* Reporter. B. LA, CA. Stanford, 1971, AB-English; U. of CA, Berkeley, 1973, MSJ. *Arlington* (VA) *News*, reporter, 1974-75. *Arlington* (VA) *Journal*, reporter, to 1976. *The New York Times*, stringer, to 1978. *The Wall Street Journal*, San Francisco reporter, current, 1978.

Cheng, Elizabeth. *Far Eastern Economic Review.* China Trade Report Editor. B. 1951, Singapore. U. of Singapore, 1973, Sociology. *Hong Kong Standard*, part-time business & financial correspondent, 1977-78; business & financial correspondent, to 1981; Business & Financial Editor, to 1983. *Far Eastern Economic Review*, Asst Business

Biographics

& Financial Editor, to 1987; Editor, China Trade Report, current, 1988.

Christian, Shirley. *The New York Times.* Buenos Aires Bureau Chief. B. 1938, Windsor, MO. Pittsburg State U. (KS), 1960, Language & Literature; OH State U., 1966, MA. AP, UN correspondent; Foreign News Editor (NY); Santiago bureau chief, to 1979. *The Miami Herald*, Central America correspondent, to 1984. *The New York Times*, DC staff, to 1986; Buenos Aires bureau chief, current, 1986. Pulitzer Prize, International Reporting, 1981; George Polk Award, International Reporting under Perilous Circumstances, 1981; Maria Moors Cabot Award, 1985.

Clad, James Clovis. *Far Eastern Economic Review.* Specialist Contributor. B. 1946, New Haven, CT. Victoria U. of Wellington (New Zealand), 1969, BA-Political Science & Languages; Auckland Law School, LLB; Osgoode Law School, Toronto, Canada, Honors. Center for International Affairs, Harvard Fellow, 1980-81. New Zealand Ministry of Foreign Affairs, diplomatic officer, 1975-83. *Far Eastern Economic Review*, Kuala Lumpur correspondent, to 1984; Kuala Lumpur bureau chief, 1985; Manila bureau chief, to 1989; specialist contributor, current, 1989. *International Herald Tribune*, Op-Ed contributor, current. BBC World Service, commentary, current. Co-author Time-Life country series book on SE Asia, 1986.

Claiborne, William L. *The Washington Post.* Southern Africa Correspondent. B. 1936, NYC. Hobart College, (NY), 1960, English. *Democrat & Chronicle* (Rochester, NY), reporter, to 1966. *The Suffolk Sun*, City Editor, to 1969. *The Washington Post*, Night City Editor, to 1970; metro reporter, to 1972; national reporter, to 1974; correspondent, to 1977; Jerusalem correspondent, to 1982; New Delhi correspondent, to 1985; Jerusalem correspondent, to 1986; Southern Africa correspondent (Johannesburg-based), current, 1986.

Clark, Charles S. *National Journal.* Managing Editor. B. 1953, DC. McGill U., 1976, History. Time-Life Books, chief researcher, writer, administrator, 1976-82. *Congressional Quarterly*, sr researcher, writer, to 1985. *Worldwide Information Resources*, Assoc Editor, to 1986. *National Journal*, Sr Editor, 1986; Managing Editor, current, 1987. Freelance, current. An original Editor of *Mole*.

Clark, Timothy B. *National Journal.* Contributing Editor. B. 1942, DC. Harvard, 1963, History. *Congressional Quarterly*, writer, Editor, to 1969. *Empire State Report*, founder & Publisher, to 1977. *National Journal*, co-founder, 1969, to 1974; financial reporter, 1978-87; Contributing editor, current, 1987. *Government Executive*, Editor, current, 1987.

Clift, Eleanor. *Newsweek.* Washington Correspondent. B. 1940, Brooklyn, NY. Studied Hofstra College, Hunter College, Philosophy, English. *Newsweek*, researcher, to 1965; Atlanta Office Manager, to 1972; Atlanta correspondent, to 1976; White House correspondent, 1985; News Editor & deputy bureau chief, 1985; DC correspondent, current, 1985. *Los Angeles Times*, White House correspondent, 1985-87. "The McLaughlin Group," occasional panelist, current.

Clines, Francis X. *The New York Times.* Moscow Correspondent. B. 1938, NY. Attended St. Francis College, Fordham & St. John's U. *The New York Times*, 1958-1973; Albany bureau chief, to 1976; City Hall bureau chief, 1976; "About New York" columnist, to 1979; reporter, DC, to 1986; London correspondent, to 1989; Moscow correspondent, current, 1989. Meyer Berger Award, 1979. Author *About New York*, 1980.

Cloud, Stanley W. *Time.* Washington Bureau Chief. B. 1936, Los Angeles. Pepperdine College, BA-English. US Navy, 1958-64. *Time*, correspondent, 1968-70; Bangkok bureau chief, to 1971; Saigon bureau chief, to 1973; political correspondent, to 1977; White House correspondent, to 1978; Deputy DC bureau chief, 1987-89; DC bureau chief, current, 1989. *The Washington Star*, Asst Managing Editor; Managing Editor, 1978-82. *The Los Angeles Herald Examiner*, Executive Editor, to 1987.

Cody, Edward. *The Washington Post.* Europe Correspondent. B. 1943, Portland, OR. Gonzaga U., (WA), 1965; U. of Paris Law, 1966-67; Columbia, 1968, Journalism. *The Charlotte Observer*, reporter to 1969. AP, Editor, to 1973; correspondent, to 1978. *The Washington Post*, Editor, to 1979; Cairo correspondent, to 1980; Paris correspondent, 1981; Beirut correspondent, to 1982; Miami (Central America/Caribbean) correspondent, to 1987; Mexico correspondent, to 1987; Europe correspondent, current, 1987. Overseas Press Club, Best Daily Newspaper or Wire Service Reporting from Abroad, 1976.

Coffey, C. Shelby III. *Los Angeles Times.* Executive Editor. B. 1947, U. of VA, 1968. *The Washington Post*, sports writer, from 1968; Magazine Editor; "Style" Editor; Deputy Managing Editor; Asst Managing Editor, national news, to 1985. *U.S.News & World Report*, Editor, to 1986. *Dallas Times Herald*, Editor, 1986. *Los Angeles Times*, Deputy Assoc Editor, to 1988; Exec Editor, current, 1989.

Cohen, Richard. *The Washington Post.* Columnist. B. 1941, NYC. NYU, 1967, Sociology; Columbia, 1968, MSJ. UPI, NY staff, 1967-68; education & MD legislative correspondent, to 1976. *The Washington Post*, Washington Post Writers Group, columnist, current, 1976. Freelance, current. Co-author (with Jules Witcover) *A Heartbeat Away*.

Cohen, Richard E. *National Journal.* Congressional Reporter. B. 1948, Northampton, MA. Brown, 1969, AB-US History; Georgetown, 1972, JD. *National Journal*, legal & regulatory reporter, 1973-77; Congressional reporter, current, 1977. Author *Congressional Leadership*.

Cohen, Roger. *The Wall Street Journal.* Rio de Janeiro Correspondent. Oxford, 1977, History & French. Reuters, London correspondent, to 1983. *The Wall Street Journal/Europe*, Rome bureau chief, to 1986. *The Wall Street Journal*, Miami correspondent, to 1988; Rio de Janeiro correspondent, current, 1988.

Cohen, Stephen F. *The Nation.* "Sovieticus" Columnist. B. 1938, Indianapolis, IN. U., 1960, MA-Politics & Economics; PhD. Princeton, prof, politics, current, 1968. *The Nation*, "Sovieticus" columnist, current. Newspaper Guild Page 1 Award, 1985. Author 2 books, including *Rethinking the Soviet Experience*.

Coll, Steve. *The Washington Post.* South Asia Bureau Chief. B. DC. Occidental College, 1980, *cum laude, Phi Beta Kappa*; attended Sussex U. (UK). *California Magazine*, Contributing Editor. Freelance writer. *The Washington Post*, reporter, 1985-87; NY financial correspondent, to 1989; South Asia bureau chief, current, 1989. Author 2 books, including *The Taking of Getty Oil*, 1987.

Colvin, Geoffrey. *Fortune.* Board of Editors Member. B. 1953, Vermillion, SD. Harvard, 1975, Economics; NYU, 1983, MBA. William S. Paley & Co., asst ghost writer. *Fortune*, member, Board of Editors, current, 1978. The Advertising Journalism Award, 1985.

Comarow, Avery. *U.S.News & World Report.* Assistant Managing Editor. B. 1945, Macon, GA. U. of MD, 1969, English. *The Wall Street Journal*, regional production desk, 1966-69. *Bloomington (IN) Courier-Tribune*, reporter, to 1972. *Money*, staff writer, to 1979. *Consumer Reports*, DC Editor, to 1982. *Science '86*, Sr Editor, Asst Managing Editor, 1986. *U.S.News & World Report*, Asst Managing Editor, "News You Can Use," current, 1986.

Conine, Ernest. *Los Angeles Times.* Editorial Writer & Columnist. B. 1925, Dallas, TX. Southern Methodist U., 1948. Journalism. US Army Air Corps 1944-46. US Army, Psychological Warfare Division, 1951-52. UPI, Dallas, to 1948-51. *Dallas Times Herald*, DC correspondent to 1955. *BusinessWeek*, DC staff, to 1960; Moscow staff, to 1961; Boston staff, to 1963. *Los Angeles Times*, Vienna staff, 1964; editorial writer & columnist, current, 1964.

Conn, David H. *The Journal of Commerce.* Reporter. B. 1963. Baltimore. U. of VA, 1985, Philosophy. *The (Baltimore) Daily Record*, business reporter, 1985-87; Business Editor, to 1988; Managing Editor, to 1989. *The Journal of Commerce*, insurance reporter, current, 1989.

Conners, Thomas J. *The Journal of Commerce.* Washington Bureau Chief. B. 1934, Stamford, CT. Fairfield U., 1955, History. *The (NY) Journal American*, copy aide, 1955-56. *The New York Times*, news clerk, to 1957. *The Journal of Commerce*, energy & trade reporter, to 1960; DC bureau, various assignments, from 1962; DC bureau chief, current. Newmyer Assoc. PR consultant, 1960-62.

Connolly, William G. *The New York Times.* Senior Editor. B. 1937, Scranton, PA. U. of Scranton, 1959, English & Philosophy; Columbia, 1963, MSJ. *Minneapolis Tribune*, Copy Editor, 1963. *Houston Chronicle*, reporter, to 1965. *Detroit Free Press*, Copy Editor, Telegraph Editor, to 1966. *The New York Times*, Copy Editor; Asst Real Estate Editor; Asst National Editor, to 1979. *Virginian-Pilot* (Norfolk, VA). Managing Editor, to 1983. *The New York Times*, Asst National Editor; Deputy Editor, "The Week in Review;" Sr Editor, current, 1984. Author *The New York Times Guide to Buying or Building a Home*, 1978, '84.

Cook, James. *Forbes.* Executive Editor. B. 1926, Schenectady, NY. Bowdoin College (ME), 1947, AB; Columbia, 1948, AM. Yankton College, ND, instructor, to 1949. OH U., instructor, to 1952. *Popular Publications*, Editor, to 1955. *Railroad*, Managing Editor, to 1955. *Forbes*, Assoc Editor, 1955-76; Reviewer, Restaurant Guide, 1975-76; Arabic Editor, 1975-76; Exec Editor, current, 1976. Champion-Tuck Award, 1982.

Cook, William J. *U.S.News & World Report.* Senior Editor. B. 1936, Fargo, ND. U. of OR, 1958, Journalism; Stanford, 1970, MA-Political Science. *Capital Journal* (Salem, OR), reporter, 1960-62. *Newsweek*,

491

correspondent, Atlanta, to 1965; Saigon, to 1966; San Francisco, to 1977; DC, to 1985; DC Deputy bureau chief, to 1986. *U.S.News & World Report*, Sr Editor, technology, current, 1986. Author *Joy of Computer Communication*, 1984; co-author (with Christopher Ma) *Teleshock*, 1985.

Cooper, Gloria. *Columbia Journalism Review*. Managing Editor. B. 1931, Oak Park, IL. Briarcliff College (NY), 1970, BA-English, *summa cum laude*; Columbia, 1974, MA. *Columbia Journalism Review*, asst to Editor, to 1974; Asst Editor, to 1975; Editor, to 1976; Editor, writer, "Darts & Laurels" & "Briefings" columnist, current, 1976; Managing Editor, current, 1978. Editor 2 books, including *Red Tape Holds Up New Bridge*, 1987.

Corrigan, Richard. *National Journal*. Managing Editor. B. 1937, Glen Ridge, NJ. U. of FL, 1959, Journalism. *St. Petersburg Times*, to 1960. *The Washington Post*, 1962-69. *National Journal*, staff correspondent, to 1987; Managing Editor, current, 1987. President's Commission for a National Agenda for the 1980s, member, 1980.

Corn, David. *The Nation*. Washington Editor. B. 1959, NYC. Brown, 1982, US History. Contributor. *The Nation*, DC bureau, current, 1987; DC Editor, current; "Beltway Bandits" co-columnist (with Jefferson Morley), current.

Cotliar, George J. *Los Angeles Times*. Managing Editor. B. 1932, Bronx, NY. Los Angeles State College, 1961, BA-Journalism & History. *Los Angeles Examiner*, Copy Editor, 1956. *Culver City Star News*, reporter, to 1957. *Los Angeles Times*, editorial positions, to 1968; Exec News Editor, 1968; Asst Managing Editor, 1969; Managing Editor, Orange County, to 1972; Sr Asst Managing Editor, to 1978; Managing Editor, current, 1978. CA State LA Alumnus of the Year, 1984.

Covault, Craig P. *Aviation Week & Space Technology*. Senior Space Editor. B. 1949, Dayton, OH. Bowling Green State U., 1971, Journalism. *The Urbana* (OH) *Citizen*, staff writer, 1971-72. *Aviation Week & Space Technology*, Space Technology Editor, Sr Space Editor, current, 1972. Aviation/Space Writers Assn Ball Memorial Trophy, 1982; Space Writing Excellence Award, 1988; National Space Club National Space Writing Award, 1984; National Space Society Space Pioneer Award, 1988.

Cowell, Alan. *The New York Times*. Athens Bureau Chief. B. 1947, Manchester, UK. St. Edmund Hall, Oxford, School of Modern Languages, 1968, BA. Reuters, foreign correspondent, to 1974; correspondent, Ankara, to 1981. *The New York Times*, foreign correspondent, Nairobi, to 1983; Johannesburg bureau chief, expelled 1986; Athens bureau chief, current, 1986.

Crock, Stan. *BusinessWeek*. Washington News Editor. Columbia, BA-Political Science, JD-Law; Northwestern, MSJ. *The Palm Beach Post*, reporter. AP, reporter. *The Wall Street Journal*, regulatory agency reporter. *BusinessWeek*, Regulatory News Editor (McGraw-Hill World News), 1983; DC News Editor, current.

Crossette, Barbara. *The New York Times*. Bangkok Bureau Chief. B. 1939, Philadelphia. Muhlenberg College (PA), 1963, BA; U. of CO, 1965, MA; U. of London, Institute of Historical Research, research work, 1965. Fulbright Teaching Fellow, 1980. *The Teacher* (UK), Production Editor. *Philadelphia Bulletin*, Copy Editor, to 1970. *The Birmingham Post* (UK), Features Editor, political & features writer, to 1973. *The New York Times*, foreign desk, to 1977; Editor "Westchester Weekly" section, 1977; Asst Metro Editor, 1977; Asst News Editor, to 1979; Weekend News Editor, to 1981; foreign affairs reporter, DC, to 1982; Asst Foreign Editor, to 1983; Deputy Foreign Editor, to 1984; Bangkok bureau chief, current, 1984. Columbia, member adjunct faculty, Journalism, current, 1975. Editor *America's Wonderful Little Hotels and Inns*, annual.

Crovitz, L. Gordon. *The Wall Street Journal*. Assistant Editorial Page Editor & Editorial Board Member. B. 1958, Durham, NC. U. of Chicago, 1980, Politics, Economics, Rhetoric & Law; Wadham College, Oxford, 1982, MA-Law; Yale, 1986, JD. *The Washington Post*, stringer, 1976-78. *Time*, stringer, to 1979. *Chicago Daily News*, to 1978. *The Chicago Journal*, Editor, to 1979. *The Wall Street Journal*, editorial page summer intern, to 1982. *The Wall Street Journal/Europe*, Editorial Page Editor, Brussels, to 1984; Asst Editorial Page Editor, Editorial Board Member, current, 1986. NY State Bar Assn, 1st Place for Legal Issues Relating to Iran-Contra Affair, 1988.

Crozier, Brian. *National Review*. Columnist & Contributing Editor. B. 1918, Kuridala, Queensland, Australia. U. of London, Trinity College of Music, 1935-36. Music & art critic (UK), to 1939. UK Newspapers, reporter, to 1945. Aeronautics inspector, to 1943. Reuters (UK), to 1944. *News Chronicle* (UK), Foreign Sub-Editor, to 1948. *Sydney Morning Herald* (Australia), Sub-Editor & writer, to 1951. Reuters-Australian AP, Day Editor, to 1952; foreign correspondent, SE Asia, 1952. *The New York Times*, stringer, to 1953. *Straits Times*,

Features Editor, Singapore, to 1953. *The Economist's Foreign Report*, Editor, leader writer, correspondent, to 1964. BBC Overseas Services, commentator, 1954-65. Forum World Services (UK), Chairman, to 1974. Institute for the Study of Conflict (UK), Director & Co-founder, 1970-79. *Now!* columnist, 1980-82. *The Times*, columnist, to 1983. *National Review*, columnist, Contributing Editor, current, 1978. Author 15 books, including *The Andropov Deception*, 1986; co-author two books, including *Socialism: The Grand Delusion*, 1986.

Curran, John J. *Fortune*. Associate Editor. Bard College, 1975, BA-Languages & Literature. Freelance, to 1977. *Wall Street Transcript*, weekly stock option columnist, to 1978. *Fortune*, reporter, researcher; Assoc Editor, current.

Cushman, John H. Jr. *The New York Times*. Washington Correspondent. B. 1955, Ft. Leavenworth, KS. Dartmouth, 1976, BA. Fairchild Publications, to 1978. King Publishing Group, to 1986. *The New York Times*, DC correspondent, current, 1986.

Dahl, Jonathan. *The Wall Street Journal*. Reporter. B. 1958, Darien, CT. Columbia, 1980, American History, 1981, MSJ. *Houston Chronicle*, reporter, 1981-83. *The Wall Street Journal*, Dallas reporter, to 1985; Chicago reporter, to 1986; airline reporter, NY, current, 1987.

Davies, Derek. *Far Eastern Economic Review*. Editor-in-Chief. B. 1931, UK. Jesus College, Cambridge, English Literature. Reuters, 1954-56. H.M. Foreign Office (Vice Consul, Hanoi, N. Vietnam; Third Secretary, Commercial, British Embassy, Vienna), to 1961. *Financial Times*, 1961. *Far Eastern Economic Review*, Editor, 1964-88; Editor-in-Chief, 1988.

Davis, Bob. *The Wall Street Journal*. Science & Technology Correspondent. B. 1951, Brooklyn, NY. Queens College, 1972, Political Science. *Dealerscope II* (Waltham, NY), Editor & founder, 1980-82. *The Wall Street Journal*, computer correspondent, Boston, to 1986; FCC correspondent, to 1988; science & technology correspondent, current, 1988.

deBorchgrave, Arnaud. *The Washington Times & Insight*. Editor-in-Chief. B. 1926, Brussels, Belgium. British Royal Navy, to 1946. Independent News Service, freelance, to 1947. UPI, telex operator, correspondent, to 1948; Brussels bureau chief, to 1950. *Newsweek*, Paris bureau chief, European correspondent, to 1954; Deputy Foreign Editor, to 1955; Foreign Editor, 1955; Sr Editor, to 1959; chief European correspondent, to 1961; Foreign Editor, Managing Editor — International Editions, to 1963; chief roving foreign correspondent, to 1980. Center for Strategic & International Studies, Sr Assoc, to 1985. *The Washington Times & Insight*, Editor-in-Chief, current, 1985. 2 Best Magazine Reporting from Abroad Awards; 3 NY Newspaper Guild Page 1 Awards; Best Magazine Interpretations of Foreign Affairs Award; George Washington Medal of Honor, Excellence in Published Works; High Frontier Outstanding Media Coverage Award, 1986. Co-author 2 books, including *Monimbo*, 1983.

deBriganti, Giovanni. *Defense News*. European Editor. *Institute d'Etudes Politiques*. *Time*, *Fortune*, Radio Canada, consultant. *Armed Forces Journal International*, international correspondent. *Defense & Armament*, Editor-in-Chief. *Defense News*, European Editor, Paris, current, 1986.

Delfs, Robert A. *Far Eastern Economic Review*. Beijing Bureau Chief. B. 1948, Long Beach, CA. Stanford, 1970, Chinese; Stanford, 1972; Princeton, 1976, MA-Asian Studies. *China Business Review*, writer, 1981. *Far Eastern Economic Review*, China economic correspondent, to 1986; Beijing bureau chief, current, 1986.

Dentzer, Susan. *U.S.News & World Report*. Senior Editor. B. 1955, Philadelphia. Dartmouth, 1977, AB-English Literature. Nieman Fellow, 1986-87. *The Southampton Press*, reporter, 1977-78. *Hampton Chronicle-News*, reporter, 1977-78. *The Wall Street Transcript*, Editor, options market columnist, 1979. *Newsweek*, Sr Writer, business, to 1987. *U.S.News & World Report*, Sr Editor, current, 1987.

Desmond, Edward W. *Time*. New Delhi Bureau Chief. B. 1958, Seattle, WA. Amherst College, 1980, BA-English; Fletcher School of Law & Diplomacy, 1982, MA. Freelance, to 1984. *Time*, reporter & researcher, to 1985; writer, to 1988; New Delhi bureau chief, current, 1988.

Deutsch, Claudia. *The New York Times*. Sunday Business Writer. B. 1947, NY. Cornell, 1968. American Management Association, reporter, to 1970. *Stores*, Assoc Editor, to 1972. *Purchasing*, reporter, to 1974. *BusinessWeek*, Environment & Management Editor, to 1982. *Chemical Week*, Sr Editor, to 1984. *The New York Times*, asst to Sunday Business Editor, to 1987; Sunday Business writer, current, 1987. Co-author *Reindustrialization of America*, 1980.

Dewar, Helen. *The Washington Post.* National Reporter. B. 1936, Stockton, CA. Stanford, BA-Political Science. *The Northern Virginia Sun,* reporter. *The Washington Post,* metro reporter, 1961-77; national reporter, current, 1977. American Political Science Association Award.

DeYoung, Karen. *The Washington Post.* National Editor. B. Chicago. U. of FL, 1971, BS-Journalism/Communications. *The St. Petersburg Times,* feature writer. *The Washington Post,* metro reporter, 1975-77; Latin America bureau chief, to 1980; Deputy Foreign Editor, to 1981; Foreign Editor, to 1985; London bureau chief; National Editor, current. *Sigma Delta Chi* Distinguished Service Award, 1980; Maria Moors Cabot Award, 1981.

Diamond, Edwin. *New York.* Contributing Editor, Media Columnist. B. 1925, Chicago. U. of Chicago, 1947, American History with honors; U. of Chicago, 1949. *Newsweek,* writer, Sr Editor, 1958-70. *New York,* contributor to 1977; Contributing Editor, media columnist, current, 1984. *Esquire,* contributor, 1970-77. Post-Newsweek TV, commentator, 1970-79. *Washington Journalism Review,* Co-founder, Sr Editor, 1977-80. *The* (NY) *Daily News,* Assoc Editor, to 1981. A/S/M Publications, NY, Editorial Director, to 1984. News Study Group, founder & Director, current, 1972. NYU, assoc prof, Dept of Journalism, current, 1984. Page 1 Awards, 1955, '56, '85; AAAS Westinghouse Award, Science Writing, 1962; Fairchild Award, Air Safety Writing, 1962; Communications Arts Award, Media Criticism, 1974; Lowell Mellet Award, Media Criticism, 1977. Author 12 books, including *The Spot,* 1988 (2nd edition).

Diaz, Tom. *The Washington Times.* Assistant Managing Editor. B. 1940, Ft. Olgethorpe, GA. U. of FL, 1963, BA-Political Science; Georgetown, 1972, JD; Law Journal. US Commerce & Defense Depts, staff, 1963-72. Law practice, to 1982. *Federal Times,* columnist, freelance, 1980-82. *The Washington Times,* "Barely Civil" columnist, Supreme Court correspondent, to 1985; national security reporter, to 1986; Asst National News Editor, 1986; Asst Managing Editor, current, 1986.

DiBenedetto, William. *The Journal of Commerce.* Reporter. B. 1950, NYC. U. of VA, 1972, English. Congressional Information Bureau daily newsletter, reporter/editor, 1975-88. *The Journal of Commerce,* DC reporter, current, 1988. Publisher's Award, 1st quarter, 1989.

Dickenson, James R. *The Washington Post.* Political Correspondent. B. 1931, McDonald, KS. San Diego State U., 1953, BA-History; U. of IA, 1959, MAJ. US Marines, 1953-57. *Huntington Park* (CA) *Daily Signal,* 1959-60. UPI, San Francisco, 1960. *The National Observer,* national political correspondent, 1962-74. *The Washington Star,* national political correspondent, National Editor, political columnist, to 1981. *The Washington Post,* Asst National Editor, politics, to 1984; political correspondent, current, 1984.

Diegmueller, Karen. *Insight.* Writer. B. 1950, Cincinnati, OH. U. of Cincinnati, 1977, BA-Political Science, *summa cum laude;* U. of WI, 1979, MAJ. *Boone County* (KY) *Recorder,* reporter, 1980. *The Daily Journal* (Kankakee, IL), reporter, to 1981. *The Home News* (New Brunswick, NJ), reporter, county bureau chief, statehouse reporter, to 1985. *Insight,* writer, current, 1985. Co-author *Effective Feature Writing,* 1982.

Diehl, Jackson. *The Washington Post.* Israel Correspondent. B. 1956, San Antonio, TX. Yale, 1978, English. *The Washington Post,* metro reporter, to 1981; foreign desk, 1981; South America correspondent, to 1985; Eastern Europe correspondent, Warsaw, to 1989; Israel correspondent, current, 1989. Inter-American Press Assn Award, 1984.

Dierdorff, John A. *BusinessWeek.* Managing Editor. B. 1928, Chicago. Yale, 1949, English. *Yakima* (WA) *Morning Herald,* writer, 1950-52. *The Oregonian,* writer, to 1956. *BusinessWeek,* Copy Editor, to 1960; Asst Editor, to 1961; Asst Managing Editor, to 1969; Sr Editor, to 1976; Asst Managing Editor, to 1977; Managing Editor, current, 1977.

Dillingham, Robert B. *Insight.* Publisher. B. 1932, Buffalo, NY. Columbia, 1955, Business. *Sports Illustrated,* sales rep, NY, Chicago, 1958-67; divisional manager, Cleveland, Detroit, to 1972; divisional ad manager, NY, to 1977; Eastern ad manager, to 1979; Assoc Ad Director, to 1981. *U.S.News & World Report,* Ad Director, to 1985. *Insight,* Publisher, current, 1985.

Dionne, Eugene J., Jr. *The Washington Post.* National Political Correspondent. B. 1952, Boston. Harvard, 1973, BA; Oxford, 1982, PhD-Political Sociology (Rhodes Scholar). *The New York Times,* consultant, Sunday *Magazine,* 1975-77; polling operations asst, 1976; reporter, to 1978; reporter, Albany, to 1979; national desk reporter, to 1981; Albany bureau chief, to 1983; foreign correspondent, to 1984;

Rome bureau chief, to 1986; national political correspondent, to 1989. *The Washington Post,* reporter, current, 1989.

Dixon, Michael. *Financial Times.* Jobs Columnist. B. 1932, Dukinfield, Cheshire, UK. *Skinner's Silk and Rayon Record* (UK), Asst Editor, 1960-63. *Paint and Wallpaper Retailer,* Exec Editor, to 1964. *Pet Store and Aquatic Trader,* Exec Editor, to 1964. *The Guardian* (UK), Sub-Editor, Deputy Editor, Manchester, to 1966; Commercial Editor, 1967; management correspondent, 1968. *Financial Times,* columnist, current, 1968.

Dobbs, Michael. *The Washington Post.* Moscow Bureau Chief. B. 1950, Belfast, UK. U. of York (UK), 1972, Economics. Reuters, correspondent, to 1975. Freelance, Africa, 1976. *The Washington Post,* special correspondent, Yugoslavia, to 1980; Eastern Europe correspondent to 1982; Paris correspondent, to 1987; on leave, to 1988; Moscow bureau chief, current, 1989. Nicholas Tomalin Award, London *Sunday Times,* 1975; Overseas Press Club Citation, Excellence, 1981. Co-author *Poland, Solidarity, Walesa.*

Dobrzynski, Judith H. *BusinessWeek.* Senior Writer. B. 1949, Rochester, NY. Syracuse U., 1971, Journalism. Trade magazine & cable TV work, to 1976. *BusinessWeek,* DC correspondent, to 1979; London correspondent, to 1983; Corporate Strategies Editor, to 1986; Assoc Editor, to 1988; Sr Writer, current, 1988. Deadline Club Award, 1987.

Doder, Dusko. *U.S.News & World Report.* Asia Correspondent. B. 1937, Yugoslavia. Washington U. (MO), 1962, Philosophy & Political Science; Columbia, 1964, MSJ, 1965, MA. Wilson Fellow, 1976-77, '85-86. AP, correspondent, to 1968. UPI, Moscow correspondent, to 1970. *The Washington Post,* Asst Foreign Editor, to 1972; State Dept correspondent, to 1973; foreign correspondent, to 1976; Moscow correspondent, 1978, '80; Canada correspondent, to 1980; Asst Foreign Editor, to 1981; Moscow bureau chief, to 1985; national reporter, to 1987. *U.S.News & World Report,* Asia correspondent, current, 1987. Overseas Press Club Citation, Excellence, 1983; Weintal Prize, Diplomatic Reporting, 1984. Author 2 books, including *Shadows & Whispers,* 1986.

Doherty, Shawn Michelle. *Newsweek.* Boston Correspondent. B. 1959, Madison, WI. Yale, 1982, Comparative Lit. *Newsweek,* correspondent, Boston, current, 1983.

Dombkowski, Dennis J. *Insight.* Senior Editor & Copy Desk Chief. B. 1950, Detroit. U. of Detroit, 1972, Journalism; U. of IL, 1982, PhD. Wayne State U. (Detroit), asst journalism prof, 1978-85. *Oakland* (MI) *Press,* Copy Editor, 1984-85. *The Washington Times,* Copy Editor, 1985. *Insight,* Copy Editor, to 1987; Sr Editor, Copy Desk Chief, current, 1987. *Insight* Blue Smoke & Mirrors Award, 1986, '87.

Donaldson, Samuel Andrew. ABC-TV News. "Prime Time Live" Co-Host. B. 1934, El Paso, TX. U. of TX, El Paso, 1955, BA; postgrad USC, 1955-56. US Army, to 1959. WTOP (Washington), radio & TV news reporter, anchor, 1961-67. ABC-TV News, Capitol Hill correspondent, to 1977; "World News Tonight," White House correspondent, to 1989; "Prime Time Live" co-host, current, 1989. Author *Hold On, Mr. President,* 1987.

Donne, Michael. *Financial Times.* Aerospace Correspondent. B. 1928, London, UK. U. of London, Birbeck College. Military, 1946-48. *Financial News of London,* 1945-46. *Financial Times,* from 1946; aerospace correspondent, current, 1953; defense correspondent, 1956-83; broadcasting correspondent, 1961-75. TV/radio, frequent broadcaster, aerospace & defense, current. Appointed Officer of the Order of the British Empire, 1986. Author *Leader of the Skies,* 1981; *Per Ardua Ad Astra,* 1984.

Donohoe, Cathryn. *The Washington Times.* Feature Reporter. B. Bronx, NY. Middlebury College, 1958, BA-American Literature, *cum laude;* Columbia, Russian Literature; American U., Journalism. Radio Liberty, research & policy advisor, 1963-74. Freelance, to 1985. *The Washington Times,* feature reporter, current, 1985. Co-recipient American Society of Magazine Editors' National Magazine Award, Public Service, 1985.

Dorfman, John R. *The Wall Street Journal.* Senior Writer. B. 1947, Chicago. Princeton, 1969, English; Columbia, 1972, MFA. *The Home News* (New Brunswick, NJ), reporter, 1970-72. AP, reporter, to 1973. *Consumer Reports,* Asst Editor to 1974; Exec Editor, 1984-86. Freelance, 1974-81. Syndicated columnist, 1974-81. *Forbes,* Assoc Editor, to 1984. *The Wall Street Journal,* Sr Writer, current, 1984. Author 8 books, including *The Stock Market Directory,* 1982.

Dorsey, James M. *The Washington Times.* Diplomatic Correspondent. B. 1951, USA. Gemeente Universite of Amsterdam, Economics/Tropical Agriculture. *Trouw,* Amsterdam, foreign affairs reporter, Middle East correspondent, 1974-81. *The Christian Science Monitor,* special Middle East correspondent in the Middle East, 1978-83. UPI, various foreign bureaus, to 1987. *The Washington Times*, diplomatic correspondent, current, 1987.

Dowd, Ann Reilly. *Fortune*. Associate Editor, Washington. Smith College; Northwestern, MSJ. Press secretary, Sen. Larry Pressler (R-SD). *Dun's Business Monthly*, Sr Editor, to 1983. *Fortune*, Assoc Editor, DC, current, 1983.

Dowd, Maureen. *The New York Times*. Washington Reporter. B. 1952, DC. Catholic U., 1973, English Literature. *The Washington Star*, editorial asst, sports columnist, metro reporter, feature writer, to 1981. *Time*, correspondent, writer, to 1983. *The New York Times*, metro reporter, to 1986; DC reporter, current, 1986.

Dowling, Robert J. *BusinessWeek*. Senior Editor. Villanova U. *The Sun*, business & financial reporter. *American Banker*, banking & monetary affairs correspondent, to 1980. *BusinessWeek*, Brussels bureau chief, to 1983; Sr Editor, international coverage, current, 1983.

Downie, Leonard Jr. *The Washington Post*. Managing Editor. B. 1942, OH State U., BA & MA-Journalism & Political Science. Alicia Patterson Foundation Fellow, 1971-72. *The Washington Post*, intern, summer 1964; investigative reporter, to 1971. '73-74; Asst Managing Editor, metro news, to 1979; London correspondent, to 1982; National Editor, to 1984; Managing Editor, current, 1984. 2 DC-MD Newspaper Guild Front Page Awards; ABA Gavel Award, Legal Reporting; John Hancock Award, Business & Financial Writing. Author 3 books, including *The New Muckrakers*, 1976.

Downs, Hugh Malcolm. ABC-TV News. "20/20" Co-Anchor. B. 1921, Akron, OH. Studied Bluffton (OH) College, 1938-39; Wayne State U., 1940-41; Columbia, 1955-56. WLOK (Lima, OH), radio announcer, 1939; program director, to 1940. WWJ (Detroit), radio announcer, to 1942. NBC-TV, Chicago, to 1954; "Today," 1962-72. Radio/TV freelance broadcaster, from 1954: "Home Show," to 1957; "Sid Caesar's Hour," 1956-57; "Concentration," to 1968; Jack Paar Show "Tonight," 1957-62, host. Raylin Productions, Inc, Chairman of the Board, current, 1960. UN, special counsel, Middle East refugee problems, 1961-64. ABC-TV News, "20/20" co-anchor, current.

Doyle, James S. Times Journal Company. Editorial Director, Army Times Group. B. 1935, Boston. Boston College, 1956, BS-English; Columbia, 1961, MAJ. Nieman Fellow, 1965. *Worcester* (MA) *Telegram*, reporter, 1956-57. *The Boston Globe*, reporter, to 1961; City Hall bureau chief, to 1963; State House bureau chief, to 1964; DC bureau chief, to 1970. *The Washington Star*, national correspondent, to 1973; Watergate Special Prosecution Force, spokesman, to 1975. *Newsweek*, deputy bureau chief, to 1983; chief political correspondent, 1978-83. Times Journal Company, Exec Editor, Editorial Director, current, 1983. Pulitzer Prize, Distinguished Public Service, 1966; Page 1 Award, 1978. Author *Not Above The Law*, 1977.

Dreman, David N. *Forbes*. Columnist. B. 1936, Winnipeg, Canada. U. of Manitoba, 1957, Bachelor of Commerce-Finance. Dreman Value Management Inc, founder, President, Managing Director, 1977-87. *Forbes*, columnist, current. Author 3 books, including *The New Contrarian Investment Strategy*, 1982.

Drew, Elizabeth. *The New Yorker*. "Letter from Washington" Columnist. B. 1935, Cincinnati. Wellesley, 1957, BA. *Congressional Quarterly*, writer, Editor, 1959-64. Freelance, to 1967. *The Atlantic Monthly*, DC Editor, to 1973. "Thirty Minutes With," host, interviewer, 1971-73. Agronsky & Co, Post-Newsweek TV/radio stations, commentator, current, 1973. *The New Yorker*, "Letter from Washington" columnist, current, 1973. Soc. Magazine Writers Award for Excellence, 1971; Wellesley Alumnae Achievement Award, 1973; DuPont Award, 1973; Mo. medal, 1979; Sidney Hillman Award, 1983; Ambassador of Honor Award, Books Across the Sea, 1984; Literary Lion Award, NY Public Library, 1985. Author six books, including *Campaign Journal*, 1985.

Du Bois, Peter C. *Barron's*. Foreign Editor. Princeton, 1952-56, English. RCA Records, writer. Union Carbide, technical writer. *The Journal of Commerce*, reporter. *BusinessWeek*, 1964-65. Securities analyst & salesman, 1967-73. *Barron's*, 1960-64, '65-67; Assoc Editor, 1973-82; creator, "International Trader" column, 1978; Foreign Editor, current, 1982.

Duffy, Michael. *Time*. White House Correspondent. B. Columbus, OH. Oberlin College, 1980. Military affairs reporter, to 1985. *Time*, Pentagon reporter; Capitol Hill reporter, to 1988; campaign reporter, 1988; White House Correspondent, current, 1989.

Duncan, Richard. *Time*. Assistant Managing Editor. B. 1935, Cincinnati, OH. Dartmouth, 1957, BA-English; Columbia, International Fellow, 1961, MSJ. Pulitzer Traveling Fellow, 1962. AP, to 1962. *Time*, correspondent, to 1966; Caribbean bureau chief, to 1968; Ottawa bureau chief, to 1970; DC News Editor, to 1972; Western regional bureau chief, to 1975; deputy chief of correspondents, to 1978; Chief of Correspondents, to 1986; Asst Managing Editor, current, 1986.

Dunn, Donald. *BusinessWeek*. "Personal Business" Editor. U. of MO, Journalism. *Sales Management*, Asst Managing Editor. *Television Magazine*, Managing Editor, Editorial Director, to 1967. *BusinessWeek*, Contributing Editor, to 1977; Media & Advertising Dept Editor, to 1980; "Personal Business" Editor, current, 1980. Author 3 books, including *Ripoff: The Corruption That Plagues America*, 1979; several musical books & lyrics. Co-author (with Thomas F. X. Smith) *The Powerticians of New Jersey*.

Dyson, Esther. *Forbes*. Columnist. B. 1951, Switzerland. Harvard, 1971, Economics. *Forbes*, reporter, 1974-77; columnist, current, 1987. New Court Securities, securities analyst, 1977-80. Oppenheimer Co, securities analyst, to 1982. *Release 1.0*, Editor, 1982; Editor, Publisher, owner, current, 1983.

Easterbrook, Gregg. *The Atlantic*. National Correspondent. *Newsweek*, Contributing Editor. B. 1953, Buffalo, NY. CO College, 1976, Political Science. *The Washington Monthly*, Editor, to 1981. *Newsweek*, Contributing Editor, current, 1987. *The Atlantic*, national correspondent, current. 2 Investigative Reporters & Editors Awards, 1980, '82; John Hancock Award, Business Writing, 1980; Livingston Award, National Reporting, 1986.

Eaton, William J. *Los Angeles Times*. Washington Staff. B. 1930, Chicago. Northwestern, 1951, BSJ, 1952, MSJ. City News Bureau, to 1953. UPI, to 1966. *Chicago Daily News*, to 1977. Knight-Ridder Newspapers, to 1978. *Los Angeles Times*, from 1978, Moscow staff, to 1987; DC staff, current, 1987. Pulitzer Prize, International Reporting, 1970.

Edsall, Thomas B. *The Washington Post*. Political Reporter. B. 1941, Cambridge, MA. Boston U., 1966, Political Science. *Providence* (RI) *Journal*, 1966-67. *The Evening Sun*, to 1974; *The Morning Sun*, DC staff, to 1981. *The Washington Post*, political reporter, current, 1981. Freelance, current. DC-Baltimore Guild Grand Prize, 1982; Bill Pryor Memorial Award, 1982. Author *The Politics of Inequality*, 1984.

Elias, Christopher. *Insight*. New York Writer. B. 1929, NYC. Hartwick, 1952, English & History; Columbia, 1955, Journalism. *BusinessWeek*, to 1963. *The Wall Street Journal & New York Herald Tribune*, to 1966. *The Exchange* (NYSE), Editor, to 1970. Freelance, to 1976. Champion Intl Corp, corp speechwriter, to 1977. Editorial consultant, freelance, speechwriter, to 1983 (founded *Fact* magazine). *Investment Dealer's Digest*, Editor, to 1985. *Insight*, NY writer, current, 1986. Author 2 books, including *The Dollar Barons*.

Elliott, John. *Financial Times*. Hong Kong Correspondent. B. 1939, UK. Christ's Hospital, UK. Building & architectural magazines, to 1966. *Financial Times*, to 1968; labor correspondent, to 1971; Labor Editor, to 1976; Management Editor, to 1978; Industrial Editor, to 1983; South Asia correspondent, New Delhi, to 1988; Hong Kong correspondent, current, 1988. British Institute of Management Journalist & Author of the Year Awards, 1977, '79, '83. Author *Conflict or Cooperation*, 1978.

Emery, Glenn D. *Insight*. Senior News Editor. B. 1954, Akron, OH. U. of VT, Math. *The Washington Times*, reporter, 1982-85. *Insight*, writer, 1985; Gen Editor, News, to 1988; Sr News Editor, current, 1988.

Engelberg, Stephen P. *The New York Times*. Domestic Correspondent. B. 1958, Princeton, 1979. *The Norfolk Virginian*, reporter, 1980-82. *The Dallas News*, to 1984. *The New York Times*, domestic correspondent, DC, current, 1984.

Epstein, Barbara. *The New York Review of Books*. Editor. B. 1929, Boston. Radcliffe, 1949, BA. *The New York Review of Books*, Editor, current, 1963.

Erickson, Stanford. *The Journal of Commerce*. Editor. Transportation communications. Various publications, journalist, 15 years. *The Journal of Commerce*, Editorial Director, to 1986; Exec Editor, to 1987; Editor, current, 1987.

Erlanger, Steven. *The New York Times*. Bangkok Bureau Chief. B. 1952, Waterbury, CT. Harvard, 1974, AB-Political Philosophy, *magna cum laude*, Phi Beta Kappa. Harvard, teaching fellow, 1975-83. *Nieman Reports*, Asst Editor, 1975. *The Boston Globe*, from 1976; Asst National Editor; Deputy National Editor; Asst Foreign Editor; Foreign Editor; London correspondent, 1983-87. *The New York Times*, reporter, to 1988; Bangkok bureau chief, current, 1988. Robert Livingston Award, 1981. Author, monograph, "The Colonial Worker in Boston, 1775," 1975.

Evans, Harold. *U.S.News & World Report.* Contributing Editor. B. 1928, Manchester, UK. Durham U. (UK), 1952, Economics; U. of Chicago, Stanford, MA. Ashton-under-Lyne Group (Lancashire, UK), reporter, 1944. *Manchester Evening News* (UK), Sub-Editor, editorial & political writer, to 1956; Asst Editor, to 1961. *Manchester Guardian* (UK), reporter. *The Northern Echo* (UK), Editor, to 1966. *The Sunday Times* (UK), chief asst to Editor, 1966; Managing Editor, to 1967; Editor, to 1981. *The Times*, Editor, 1981. *U.S.News & World Report*, Editorial Director, writer, to 1986; Contributing Editor, current, 1987. *Traveler*, Editor-in-Chief, current, 1987. Conde-Nast Publications, consultant, current, 1986. European Gold Medal, Institute of Journalists; International Editor of the Year, *World Press Review*, 1976. Author 8 books, including *Good Times, Bad Times*; co-author 2 books, including *We Learned to Ski*.

Evans, Medford Stanton. *Human Events.* Contributing Editor. B. 1934, Kingsville, TX. Yale, 1955, BA; postgrad, NYU, 1955. *Freeman*, Asst Editor, 1955. *National Review*, editorial staff, to 1956; Assoc Editor, 1960-68. *The Indianapolis News*, Chief Editorial Writer, 1959-60. *Human Events*, Managing Editor, 1956-59; Contributing Editor, current, 1968. Freedoms Foundation Award, Editorial Writing, 1959, '60, '65, '66; National Headliners Club Award, Outstanding Editorial Pages, 1960. Author several books, including *Assassination of Joe McCarthy*, 1970.

Evans, Rowland, Jr. North America Syndicate. "Inside Report" Columnist (with Robert Novak). B. 1921, White Marsh, PA. Studied Yale. US Marines. *Philadelphia Bulletin.* AP, DC staff, to 1953; Senate reporter, to 1955. *New York Herald Tribune*, assorted national magazines, to 1962. North America Syndicate. "Inside Report" columnist, current, 1963. *Evans-Novak Political Report*, co-author, current. *Evans-Novak Tax Report*, co-author, current. *Reader's Digest*, Roving Editor, current. Freelance, current. CNN, co-host, "Evans & Novak" & "Insiders", current. Frequent appearances "Meet the Press"; "Nightline." Co-author 3 books, including (with Robert Novak) *The Reagan Revolution*, 1981.

Fabrikant, Geraldine. *The New York Times.* "Business Day" Reporter. B. 1943, NY. Attended U. of WI; Brandeis, 1964. Film editor, 1966-72. Freelance writer, to 1976. *The Hollywood Reporter*, reporter, to 1978. *Variety*, reporter, to 1981. *BusinessWeek*, Media Editor, to 1985. *The New York Times*, "Business Day" reporter, current, 1985.

Fallows, James. *The Atlantic.* Washington Editor. B. 1949, Philadelphia. Harvard, 1970, BA, *magna cum laude*; Oxford, 1972, Economic Development (Rhodes Scholar). US-Japan Leadership Fellow, 1986-88. *The Washington Monthly*, Staff Editor, to 1974. Freelance, to 1976. *Texas Monthly*, Assoc Editor, to 1976. Chief speechwriter to President Carter, to 1979. *The Atlantic*, DC Editor, current, 1979. *U.S.News & World Report*, Contributing Editor, current. Author 2 books, including *More Like Us*, 1989.

Fanning, Deirdre. *Forbes.* Staff Writer. Middlebury College, 1982, BA-English Literature. *The American Lawyer*, staff reporter, 1984-86. *Institutional Investor*, "Corporate Financing," Sr Editor, 1986. *Forbes*, staff writer, current, 1986.

Farnsworth, Clyde. *The New York Times.* Financial Reporter. B. 1931, OH. Yale, 1952, BA-English. UPI, to 1959. *New York Herald Tribune*, to 1962. *The New York Times*, financial reporter, current, 1962. Overseas Press Club & *Sigma Delta Chi* Awards, Foreign Correspondence, 1968. Author 2 books, including *Out of This Nettle*, 1971.

Fein, Esther B. *The New York Times.* Moscow Correspondent. Barnard, 1961. *Newsday*, intern. *The New York Times*, sports office staff, 1983-84; reporter/trainee, to 1985; metro reporter, to 1986; DC correspondent, to 1988; Moscow correspondent, current, 1988.

Ferguson, Tim. *The Wall Street Journal.* Editorial Features Editor. B. 1955, Santa Ana, CA. Stanford, 1977, BA-Economics. *Orange County* (CA) *Register*, reporter; Asst Metro Editor; Editorial Page Editor, to 1983. *The Wall Street Journal*, Editorial Features Editor, current, 1983. Gerald Loeb Award, Business & Financial Journalism, 1980.

Field, David. *The Washington Times.* Reporter. B. 1948, NYC. Kenyon College, 1970, Classics; Oxford, 1976, Classics, History, Philosophy. Jack Anderson, reporter, 1981-82. *The Washington Tribune*, Assoc Editor, 1981-82. *The City Paper*, city desk, to 1983. *The Washington Monthly*, Copy Editor, 1985-87. *Aviation Daily*, Congressional Editor, 1986-87. *The Washington Times*, reporter, aviation & media, current, 1987. Numerous "Beltway" Awards.

Fields, Suzanne. *The Washington Times.* Columnist. B. 1936, DC. GWU, 1957, BA-English Literature; 1964, MA; Catholic U., 1970, PhD. *World Week Magazine*, writer, 1957. Freelance, from 1965. *Innovations*, Editor, from 1971. *Vogue*, columnist, 1980-81. *The Washington Times*, columnist, current, 1984. Los Angeles Times Syndicate, columnist, current, 1988. Author *Like Father, Like Daughter*, 1983.

Fineman, Mark. *Los Angeles Times.* Manila Bureau Chief. B. 1952, Chicago. Syracuse U., 1974, BA-Journalism & Philosophy. *Sun-Times*, writer, to 1978. *Allentown* (PA) *Call-Chronicle*, writer, to 1980. *The Philadelphia Inquirer*, Asia correspondent, to 1986. *Los Angeles Times*, Manila bureau chief, current, 1986. Amos Tuck Award, 1st prize, 1980; Overseas Press Club Citation, Excellence, 1985; George Polk Award, 1985.

Fink, Donald E., Jr. *Aviation Week & Space Technology.* Editor-in-Chief. B. 1935, Flint, MI. U. of MN, 1957, Technical Journalism. US Air Force, 1958-61. *Cedar Rapids* (IA) *Gazette*, police & aviation reporter, to 1962. *Aviation Week & Space Technology*, Engineering Editor, to 1963; Space Technology Editor, to 1966; Asst European Editor, Geneva, to 1969; Paris bureau chief, to 1972; Management Editor, LA, to 1975; LA bureau chief, to 1978; Asst Managing Editor, to 1981; Managing Editor, technical, to 1985; Editor-in-Chief, current, 1985. *Commercial Space*, current, 1985.

Finn, Edwin A., Jr. *Forbes.* Assistant Managing Editor. B. 1954, Whitinsville, MA. Tufts U., 1976, BA-English & Political Science; Columbia, 1983, MA-International Banking & Finance. *Blackstone Valley Tribune*, Asst Managing Editor, to 1977. *Southbridge* (MA) *Evening News*, Managing Editor, to 1979. *The Wall Street Journal*, International Editor, to 1984; reporter, Dallas, to 1986. *Forbes*, Sr Editor, international business, banking & finance, to 1989; Asst Managing Editor, current, 1989. New England Press Assn, Special Award, 1977, 3rd Prize, Community Service Reporting, 1979, 1st Prize, Business Reporting, 1979.

Fisher, Dan. *Los Angeles Times.* London Bureau Chief. B. 1941, Bedford, OH. Marquette U., 1963, BAJ. *Industry Week*, Assoc & Asst Editor, 1963-65; Detroit Editor, to 1969. *Los Angeles Times*, auto writer, to 1977; Moscow bureau chief, to 1980; Asst Financial Editor, to 1981; Warsaw bureau chief, to 1984; Jerusalem bureau chief, to 1988; London bureau chief, current, 1988. Times Editorial Award, 1981; New Israel Fund Lurie Award, 1988.

Fisher, Kenneth L. *Forbes.* "Portfolio Strategy" Columnist. B. 1950, San Francisco. Humboldt State U., 1972, Economics. Fisher Investments, Inc. founder, 1978; Chief Investment Officer, current. *Forbes*, "Portfolio Strategy" columnist, current. Author 2 books, including *The Wall Street Waltz*, 1987.

Flanagan, William G. *Forbes.* Senior Editor & "Personal Affairs" & "Careers" Columnist. B. 1940, Queens, NY. Brooklyn College, 1962, BA-English. *Bayonet* (US Army newspaper), Editor, 1963-64. *Electrical World*, reporter, Editor, to 1968. *BusinessWeek*, "Personal Business" writer & Editor, to 1976. *New York*, "Your Own Business" writer & Editor, to 1978. *Esquire*, "Personal Finance" writer & Editor, to 1980. *The Wall Street Journal*, "Your Money Matters" writer & Editor, to 1980. *Forbes*, Sr Editor, current, 1980; "Personal Affairs" columnist, current, 1980; "Careers" columnist, current, 1984. CNN, "Moneyline," Guest Editor, 1985; "Business Morning," Guest Editor, 1985. WABC-AM, NY, "Bill Flanagan Show," host, 1983-88. Author 4 books, including *The Takers*, 1984.

Flanigan, James. *Los Angeles Times.* Business Columnist. B. 1936, NYC. Manhattan College, 1961, History, English. *New York Herald Tribune*, copy, editorial asst. Paris edition correspondent, Desk Editor, finance & business reporter, 1958-66. *Forbes*, writer; bureau chief: DC, LA, London, Houston; Asst Managing Editor, to 1980, '81-82, '84-85. *Los Angeles Times*, writer; business columnist, 1980, '83-84, NY, current, 1986. Co-recipient Gerald Loeb Award.

Flint, Jerry. *Forbes.* Senior Editor. B. 1931, Detroit, MI. Wayne U., 1953, Journalism. Army Security Agency, 1953-56. *The Wall Street Journal*, reporter, Chicago, to 1958; Detroit bureau, to 1967. *The New York Times*, Detroit bureau chief, to 1973; asst to National Editor, to 1976; asst to Financial Editor, to 1978; national labor correspondent, to 1979. *Forbes*, DC bureau manager, to 1983; Asst Managing Editor, to 1985; Sr Editor, current, 1985. Author *The Dream Machine*, 1975.

Fly, Richard. *BusinessWeek.* Washington Correspondent. U. of TX, Austin. *The Houston Chronicle*, legislative reporter, 1975-80. *The Dallas Times-Herald*, White House reporter, to 1985. *BusinessWeek*, DC correspondent, White House & national politics, current, 1986.

Footlick, Jerrold K. *Newsweek.* Senior Editor. Gannett Center for Media Studies Fellow, Columbia, 1987. *Wooster* (OH) *Daily Record*, 1953-56. *Indianapolis Times*, 1961-63. *The National Observer*, News Editor, to 1970. *Newsweek*, Education Editor, 1970-73; Justice Editor, to 1978; Sr Editor, current, 1978. *Newsweek On Campus*, Editor, 1982-88. 3 ABA Silver Gavel Awards; NY Newspaper Guild Page 1 Award; Education Writers Assn Award; 3 National School Bell Awards. Author 2 books, including *The College Scene Now*, 1967; editor 2 books, including *Careers for the 70s*, 1969.

MediaGuide

Forbes, Malcolm S. Jr. *Forbes.* Deputy Editor-in-Chief & Editorial Writer. B. 1947, Morristown, NJ. Princeton, 1970, BA-History. *Business Today,* (Princeton business quarterly), Founding Editor. Forbes Inc, Director, 1971; VP, Secretary, 1973; President & CEO, current, 1980. *Forbes,* Assoc Editor, to 1978; Sr Editor, to 1982, Deputy Editor-in-Chief & editorial writer, current, 1982. 4 Crystal Owls, US Steel Award. Author *Fact & Comment,* 1974; "Some Call It Greed," 1977 (documentary).

Forbes, Malcolm S. Sr. *Forbes.* Chairman & Editor-in-Chief. B. 1919, NYC. Princeton, 1941. AB. *Fairfield Times* (Lancaster, OH), Owner, Publisher, 1941. *Lancaster Tribune,* founder, 1942. US Army, to 1945; Bronze Star, Purple Heart. *Forbes,* Assoc Publisher, to 1954; Publisher & Editor-in-Chief, current, 1957. NJ Senator, 1952-58. Forbes, Inc, President, to 1964; Chairman, current, 1980. 60 Fifth Avenue Corp, Chairman of the Board, current; Forbes Trinchera, Inc, President, current.

Forsyth, Randall W. *Barron's.* "Capital Markets" Editor & "Current Yield" Columnist. B. 1952, NYC. NYU, 1975. Economics, postgrad, Economics & Finance. *The New York Times,* financial news copyboy, 1970-72. *The Bond Buyer,* Asst Editor, to 1976. *Merrill Lynch Market Letter,* writer, to 1980. *Dow Jones Capital Markets Report,* reporter, to 1983. *Barron's,* "Capital Markets" Editor, "Current Yield" Columnist, current, 1983. NY Financial Writers Assn, President, 1987-88.

Fossedal, Gregory A. Copley News Service. Columnist. *Harper's* & *The American Spectator,* Contributing Editor. B. 1959. Dartmouth, 1981. BA-English Literature, *summa cum laude,* Phi Beta Kappa; U. of WI, 1977. Marxist Sociological Thought. Hoover Institute, Stanford, Media Fellow, current, 1986. *The Daily Dartmouth,* Editor-in-Chief, 1979-80. *The Dartmouth Review,* founder & Editor, to 1981. *Dallas Morning News,* editorial columnist, to 1982. *Charleston (NC) Daily Mail,* editorial writer, 1982. *The Washington Times,* editorial page writer, to 1983. *The San Diego Union,* editorial page writer, 1983. *The Wall Street Journal,* editorial page writer, to 1986. *Harper's,* Contributing Editor, current, 1986. *The American Spectator,* Contributing Editor, current, 1986. Ernest M. Hopkins Institute, Dartmouth, member, Board of Directors, current, 1986. Copley News Service, columnist, current, 1986. Author *The Democratic Imperative,* 1989; co-author 3 books, including (with Dinesh D'Souza) *My Dear Alex,* 1987.

Foster, Douglas. *Mother Jones.* Editor. U. of CA, Santa Cruz. San Francisco Center for Investigative Reporting, Editor. PBS-TV, Documentary Producer, 1985-87. *Mother Jones,* contributor, 1974-87; Editor, current, 1987. Emmy Award; World Affairs Council of Northern California Award, 1985.

Francis, Samuel. *The Washington Times.* Deputy Editorial Page Editor. B. 1947, Chattanooga, TN. Johns Hopkins, 1969, BA-History; U. of NC, 1971. MA; 1979. PhD. The Heritage Foundation, policy analyst, 1977-81. US Senate staff, to 1986. *The Washington Times,* editorial writer, to 1987; Deputy Editor, editorial page, current, 1987. ASNE Distinguished Writing Award, Editorials, 1988. Author 2 books, including *Power and History,* 1984.

Frank, Richard S. *National Journal.* Editor. B. 1931, Paterson, NJ. Syracuse U., 1953, BA; U. of Chicago, 1956, MA. *Evening Record* (Hackensack, NJ), local govt reporter, 1956-57. *The Evening Sun,* statehouse & City Hall reporter, to 1964. Admin Asst to Mayor of Baltimore, to 1965. *Philadelphia Bulletin,* state legislature, transportation, to 1968; DC staff, to 1971. *National Journal,* legal affairs, economics, trade, to 1976; Editor, current, 1976.

Frankel, Glenn. *The Washington Post.* London Correspondent. B. 1949, NYC. Columbia, 1971, History. Stanford, Professional Journalism Fellow, 1982-83. *Richmond Mercury,* writer, to 1975. *The Record* (Hackensack, NJ), writer, to 1979. *The Washington Post,* writer, to 1982; Southern Africa correspondent, to 1986; Israel correspondent, to 1989; London correspondent, current, 1989. Pulitzer Prize for International Reporting, 1988.

Frankel, Max. *The New York Times.* Executive Editor. B. 1930, Gera, Germany. Columbia, 1952, AB; 1953, MA-Political Science. *The Columbia Daily Spectator,* Editor-in-Chief. US Army, 1953-55. *The New York Times,* Columbia correspondent, to 1953; NY staff, to 1956; Austria correspondent, to 1957; Moscow correspondent, to 1960; UN correspondent, 1961; DC correspondent, to 1963; diplomatic correspondent, to 1966; White House correspondent, to 1968; chief DC correspondent & head of DC staff, to 1972; Sunday Editor, to 1976; Editorial Page Editor, to 1986; Exec Editor, current, 1986. Overseas Press Club Award, Foreign Reporting, 1965; George Polk Memorial Award, Foreign Affairs, 1970; Pulitzer Prize, International Reporting, 1973.

Freed, Kenneth J. *Los Angeles Times.* San Salvador Bureau Chief. B. 1937, Omaha, NE. U. of NE, 1959, BA-Government; LLB, 1961; U. of OK, 1963, MA-Government. AP, Charleston writer, 1963-65;

Asst Managing Editor, NY, to 1968; diplomatic reporter, to 1978. *Los Angeles Times,* metro writer, to 1980; Buenos Aires bureau chief, to 1983; Toronto bureau chief, to 1988; San Salvador bureau chief, current, 1988.

Friedman, Thomas L. *The New York Times.* National Security Correspondent. B. 1953, Minneapolis, MN. Brandeis, 1975, BA-Middle East Studies; St. Anthony's College, Oxford, 1978, MPhil. UPI, London & Beirut correspondent, to 1981. *The New York Times,* business reporter, to 1982; Beirut bureau chief, to 1984; Jerusalem bureau chief, to 1988; national security correspondent, current, 1989. Overseas Press Club Award, Business Reporting Abroad, 1980; Pulitzer Prize, International Reporting, 1982; George Polk Award, International Reporting, 1983; Livingston Award, Young Journalists, 1983. Author *From Beirut to Jerusalem,* 1989.

Fritz, Michael. *Forbes.* Reporter. B. 1959, Harvard, IL. Purdue, 1981. Agronomy. Miller Publishing, Staff Editor, Assoc Editor, 1982-84. *Progress,* Editor, to 1986. *Forbes,* reporter, current, 1986.

Frump, Robert R. *The Journal of Commerce.* Managing Editor. U. of IL, BAJ; Northwestern, MAJ. *The Philadelphia Inquirer,* reporter, Editor. Video Broadcasting Corp, co-founder, 1986; Exec VP. *The Journal of Commerce,* journalist, to 1988; Managing Editor, current, 1988. Gerald Loeb Award, 1983; George Polk Award, 1984

Fuerbringer, Jonathan. *The New York Times.* National Economics Correspondent. B. 1945, NYC. Harvard, 1967, BA-American History; Columbia, 1968, MSJ. *The Boston Globe,* Copy Editor; reporter; statehouse reporter; financial reporter. *The Washington Star,* reporter, national economics correspondent, to 1981. *The New York Times,* national economics correspondent, current, 1981. Barnet Nover Memorial Award for Congressional coverage, 1988.

Fuhrman, Peter. *Forbes.* European Bureau Correspondent. Tufts U., 1980, BA-Chinese History; Cambridge U., 1985, MPhil. *Forbes,* reporter, 1986-87; European bureau correspondent, current, 1987.

Galloway, Joseph L. *U.S.News & World Report.* Senior Editor, International. B. 1941, Bryan, TX. Victoria College, (TX) *The Victoria (TX) Advocate,* reporter, 1959-60. UPI, reporter, Editor, bureau chief, regional manager, to 1982. *U.S.News & World Report,* West Coast Editor, to 1984; special projects, 1984; Sr Editor, "Currents in the News," to 1987; Sr Editor, international news, current, 1987.

Gannes, Stuart. *Fortune.* Associate Editor. B. 1949, Detroit. U. of MI, 1971. History. *Change,* Asst Editor, 1972-73. Fairchild Publications, writer, 1973. Time-Life Books, reporter, then writer, from 1974; writer; Editor; book manager, to 1982. Time Teletext, News Editor, 1982-83. *Discover,* high-technology writer, 1984. *Fortune,* Assoc Editor, science & high-technology writer, current, 1984. Michigan AP Features Writing Award, 1971.

Garcia, Beatrice E. *The Wall Street Journal.* Reporter. Fairleigh Dickinson U., 1978, English. *Shopper's Guide,* reporter, 1977. Chase Manhattan Bank, public relations assoc, 1978. Munifacts News Wire, reporter, 1980. *The Wall Street Journal,* Capitol Markets reporter, 1982-88; "Abreast of the Market" columnist, 1985-88; Philadelphia reporter, current, 1989.

Gartner, Michael G. NBC-TV News. President. *Louisville (KY) Courier-Journal,* Editor, to 1984. Des Moines Register Company, President, to 1985. Gannett Co. Inc, Gen News Exec, to 1986. American Society of Newspapers Editors, to 1987. *Ames (IA) Daily Tribune,* Editor, to 1988; co-owner, current. *USA Today,* consultant, current. NBC-TV News, President, current, 1988.

Gelb, Arthur. *The New York Times.* Managing Editor. B. NYC. NYU, 1948. *The New York Times,* copyboy, reporter, asst drama critic, to 1962; chief cultural correspondent, to 1967; Metro Editor, to 1976; Asst Managing Editor, to 1977; Deputy Managing Editor, to 1986; Managing Editor, current, 1986. Co-author (with Barbara Gelb) *O'Neill.*

Gelb, Leslie. *The New York Times.* Deputy Editorial Page Editor. B. 1937, New Rochelle, NY. Tufts U., BA-Government & Philosophy; Harvard, 1961, MA, 1964, PhD. Wesleyan, asst prof, to 1966. Exec Asst, Sen. Jacob Javits, to 1967. US Defense Dept, Director of Policy Planning & Arms Control. International Security Affairs & Director Pentagon Papers project, to 1969. Brookings Institution, Sr Fellow, to 1973. State Dept, Asst Secretary of State (Director, Bureau of Politico-Military Affairs), 1977-79. Carnegie Endowment for International Peace, Sr Assoc, Security & Arms Control, to 1981. *The New York Times,* diplomatic correspondent, to 1977; national security correspondent, 1981-86; Deputy Editorial Page Editor, current, 1986; "Washington Report," syndicated commentator, current. ABC-TV, Sr Consultant, Producer, "Crisis Game," 1983; Sr Editor, "45/85," 1985; Panelist, "Capitol Journal," educational TV. Emmy, DuPont, Hood

Awards. Pulitzer Prize, Explanatory Journalism, 1985. Co-author 4 books, including *Star Wars*.

Gergen, David R. *U.S.News & World Report.* Editor-at-Large. B. 1942, Durham, NC. Yale; Harvard Law, 1967. John F. Kennedy Fellow, Harvard, 1984. Los Angeles Times Syndicate, columnist. American Enterprise Institute, Resident Fellow. White House staff; Communications Director, 1981-83. *U.S.News & World Report*, contributing columnist, 1985; Managing Editor, to 1986; Editor, to 1988; Editor-at-Large, current, 1988.

Germond, Jack. *The Sun*, Tribune Media Services. "Politics Today" Co-Columnist (with Jules Witcover). B. Boston. U. of MO, Journalism & History. *Post-Tribune* (Jefferson City, MO). *Monroe* (MI) *Evening News*. Gannett Newspapers, Albany, NY, DC bureau chief, 1953-73. *The Washington Star*, chief political writer, Asst National Staff Managing Editor, to 1981; co-columnist (with Jules Witcover), 1977-81. *The Sun*, "Politics Today" co-columnist (with Jules Witcover), current, 1981. Tribune Media Services, co-columnist (with Jules Witcover), current. "The McLaughlin Group," panelist, current. Co-author (with Jules Witcover) 3 books, including *Whose Broad Stripes and Bright Stars?* 1989.

Gerstenzang, James. *Los Angeles Times.* White House Correspondent. AP, White House correspondent. *The Detroit News*, Lansing correspondent, to 1985. *Los Angeles Times*, Pentagon correspondent, to 1987; White House correspondent, current, 1987.

Gerth, Jeff. *The New York Times.* Washington Reporter. B. 1944, Mansfield, OH. Northwestern, 1966, BS-Business Administration; postgrad Northwestern, Columbia. Freelance, 1969-77. McGovern Presidential Campaign, asst, 1972. Center for Corporate Responsibility, 1973. *The New York Times*, "Business Day" reporter, 1977-80; DC reporter, current, 1980. 3 *New York Times* Publisher's Awards; co-recipient Page 1 Award, George Polk Award.

Gertz, William David. *The Washington Times.* National Security Correspondent. B. 1952, Glen Cove, NY. Studied Washington College, English Literature, GWU, Journalism. *New York News World*, DC correspondent, 1979-80; State Dept correspondent, to 1981. Paragon House Publishers, Book Editor, to 1983. *New York City Tribune*, DC correspondent, to 1984. *The Washington Times*, national security correspondent, current, 1985.

Gest, Ted. *U.S.News & World Report.* Senior Editor, Legal Affairs. B. 1946, St. Louis, MO. Oberlin College, 1968, Government; Columbia, 1969, MSJ. *St. Louis Post Dispatch*, reporter, Editor, 1969-77. *U.S.News & World Report*, White House correspondent, to 1980; Sr Editor, Legal Affairs, current, 1981.

Geyer, Georgie Anne. Universal Press Syndicate. Columnist. Northwestern; Rhodes Scholar, Vienna. *Chicago Daily News*, society desk, reporter, 1959-64; Latin America correspondent, to 1967; roving foreign correspondent, columnist, to 1975. Los Angeles Times Syndicate, foreign affairs columnist, to 1980. Universal Press Syndicate, columnist, current, 1980.

Gibson, Paul. *Financial World.* Executive Editor. B. 1936. Leicester, UK. Southam Journalist Fellow, U. of Toronto, 1969. *Nottingham Guardian* (UK), reporter, 1954-57. British Force Network, commentator, to 1959. National Trade Press, News Editor, to 1963. *Montreal Star*, Copy Editor, to 1964. *Financial Post* (Canada), stock market columnist, Asst Financial Editor, to 1971. *Forbes*, Sr Editor, to 1981. Philip Morris Co. & Hill & Knowlton, public relations. *Financial World*, Exec Editor, current, 1986.

Gilmartin, Trish. *Aviation Week & Space Technology.* Reporter. B. 1955, Bronx, NY. St. Bonaventure U., 1977, Journalism. *Business Aviation*, reporter, Asst Editor, 1978-80. *Aviation Daily*, reporter, to 1982. *Aerospace Daily*, reporter, to 1985. *Defense News*, reporter, to 1989. *Aviation Week & Space Technology*, reporter, current, 1989.

Gilmore, Kenneth O. *Reader's Digest.* Editor-in-Chief. B. 1930, Providence, RI. Brown, 1953. *Reader's Digest*, DC staff, 1957-68; DC Editor, to 1973; Asst Managing Editor, to 1975; Managing Editor, to 1982; The Reader's Digest Assn, Inc, Exec Editor, VP; Board of Directors & Exec Committee, member, 1984; Editor-in-Chief, current.

Glaberson, William. *The New York Times.* Business Reporter. B. 1952, Brooklyn, NY. Tufts U., 1974, BA-Political Science; Albany Law School, Union U., 1977, JD; Columbia, 1982, MA. Westchester Legal Services, civil litigator, 1977-80. Matthew Bender, Inc, Editor/Sr Editor, to 1982. *New York Law Journal*, reporter, to 1983. *BusinessWeek*, Editor, Legal Affairs Dept, to 1987. *The New York Times*, business reporter, current, 1987.

Gladwell, Malcolm. *The Washington Post.* Business Columnist. B. 1963, Fareham, UK. Trinity College, U. of Toronto, 1984, History.

Ethics & Public Policy Center, Asst Editor, 1985. *The American Spectator*, Asst Managing Editor, 1984-85; contributor, current, 1986. *Insight*, writer, to 1987. *The Washington Post*, business columnist, current, 1987.

Glasgall, William. *BusinessWeek.* International Editor. Boston U. Walter Bagehot Fellow. AP, energy reporter. *BusinessWeek*, Energy Editor, 1981-86; International Money Editor, to 1988; International Editor, current, 1988.

Glasser, Samuel. *The Journal of Commerce.* Energy Editor. B. 1948, NYC. U. of Bridgeport, 1970, History. *The Star-Ledger* (Newark, NJ), Asst Sunday Editor, reporter, 1970-74. *The Journal of Commerce*, chemical desk, to 1977; Energy Editor, current, 1977. NY Financial Writers Assoc, President, 1981-82.

Gold, Philip. *Insight.* Defense Writer. B. 1948, Pittsburgh. Yale, 1970, History; Georgetown, 1981, PhD-History. *Insight*, defense writer, current, 1986. Author 3 books, including *Evasions*.

Goldman, John J. *Los Angeles Times.* New York Bureau Chief. B. 1936, NYC. Dartmouth, 1958, Government; Columbia, 1959, MSJ. *The Wall Street Journal*, writer. UPI, reporter, deskman, NY. *Newsweek*, writer, to 1966. *Los Angeles Times*, NY bureau chief, current.

Goldman, Peter. *Newsweek.* Contributing Editor. B. 1933, Philadelphia. Williams College, 1954, English Literature; Columbia, 1955, MSJ. Nieman Fellow, 1961. *The St. Louis Globe-Democrat*, writer, 1955-62. *Newsweek*, Assoc Editor, to 1964; Gen Editor, to 1968; Sr Editor, to 1988; Contributing Editor, current, 1988. Sigma Delta Chi Award, 1962; Page 1 Award, 1967, '72, '86; National Magazine Award, 1968, '82; Robert F. Kennedy Journalism Award, 1972; ABA Silver Gavel Award, 1972; Freedom Foundation Award, 1982; American Legion Fourth Estate Award, 1982, NY Bar Media Award, 1984; National Assn of Black Journalists Award, 1987. Author 3 books, including *The Death and Life of Malcolm X*, 1973; co-author 4 books, including (with Sylvester Monroe & others) *Brothers*, 1988.

Goodgame, Dan. *Time.* White House Correspondent. B. Pascagoula, MS. U. of MS; Oxford. (Tampa) *Tribune*. *The Miami Herald*, to 1984. *Time*, LA bureau writer, to 1988; White House correspondent, current, 1989.

Goodman, Ellen Holtz. *The Boston Globe.* Feature Writer, Columnist, & Associate Editor. Washington Post Writers Group, Columnist. B. 1941, Newton, MA. Radcliffe, 1963, BA, *cum laude*. Nieman Fellow, 1974. *Newsweek*, researcher, reporter, to 1965. *Detroit Free Press*, feature writer, to 1967. *The Boston Globe*, feature writer, columnist, current, 1967; Assoc Editor, current, 1987. Washington Post Writers Group, columnist, current, 1976. New England Press Assn Columnist of the Year Award, 1975, & Newspaper Woman of the Year Award, 1978; Pulitzer Prize, Commentary, 1980; ASNE Prize, Column Writing, 1980. Author 3 books, including *At Large*, 1981.

Gonzales, David L. *Newsweek.* Miami Correspondent. B. 1957, NYC. Yale, 1979, BA-Psychology; Columbia, 1983, MSJ. *Newsweek*, editorial asst, 1983-85; Detroit correspondent, to 1986; Miami correspondent, current, 1986.

Gordon, Michael R. *The New York Times.* Washington Reporter. B. 1951. Colgate U., 1972; Columbia, 1975, MA-Philosophy, 1976, MSJ. *The Inter Dependent*, Asst Editor; freelance writer, to 1980. *National Journal*, national security correspondent, to 1985. *The New York Times*, DC reporter, 1985.

Goshko, John M. *The Washington Post.* Writer. B. 1933, Swampscott, MS. U. of PA. BA; Columbia, MSJ. *The Minneapolis Star and Tribune*, reporter. *The Washington Post*, metro staff writer, 1961-64; Asst Foreign Editor, to 1966; Latin America correspondent, to 1970; Bonn correspondent, to 1975; national staff writer, current, 1975. National Press Club, Edwin M. Hood Award, 1985.

Gottlieb, Robert A. *The New Yorker.* Editor. B. 1931, NYC. Columbia, 1952, BA; Cambridge, 1954. Simon & Schuster, Editor-in-Chief, 1955-68. Alfred A. Knopf, Inc. Exec VP, 1968-73; Editor-in-Chief, current, 1968; President, from 1973. *The New Yorker*, Editor, current, 1987.

Graham, Bradley. *The Washington Post.* Buenos Aires Bureau Chief. B. 1952, Chicago, IL. Yale, 1974, MA; Stanford, 1978, MBA. *Yale Daily News*, Managing Editor, to 1974. *St. Petersburg Times*, intern, summers 1972, '73. *The Trenton Times*, city & statehouse reporter, to 1976. *The Washington Post*, intern, summers 1974, '77; business writer, to 1979; Bonn bureau chief, to 1982; Warsaw bureau chief, to 1985; Buenos Aires bureau chief, current, 1985. ASNE Award, Deadline Writing, 1986.

Graham, Donald Edward. *The Washington Post.* Publisher. B. 1945, Baltimore. Harvard, 1966, BA. US Army, to 1968. *The Wash-*

MediaGuide

ington Post, from 1971; Asst Managing Editor, Sports, 1974-75; Asst Gen Manager, to 1976; Exec VP & Gen Manager, to 1979; Publisher, current, 1979.

Graham, Katharine. The Washington Post Company. Chairman & Chief Executive Officer. B. 1917, NYC. Vassar, U. of Chicago, 1938. *San Francisco News*, reporter. *The Washington Post*, editorial & circulation depts, to 1969; Publisher, to 1979. The Washington Post Co, President, to 1973; Chairman & CEO, current, 1973.

Granat, Diane. *The Washingtonian*. Metropolitan Editor. B. 1954, Chicago. Northwestern, 1976, Journalism. Ford Foundation Fellow in Education Journalism, 1978. *Paddock Publications*, education & feature writer, 1976-79; DC correspondent, to 1981. *The Washington Post*, freelance, to 1982. *Congressional Quarterly*, reporter, to 1985. *The Washingtonian*, Metro Editor, current, 1986. Golden Hammer Award, 1982.

Gray, Patricia Bellew. *The Wall Street Journal*. News Editor. B. 1956, Fairfield, CT. U. of CT, 1978, Economics & Communications, *magna cum laude*. *The Miami Herald*, business reporter, 1980-84. *The Wall Street Journal*, San Francisco reporter, to 1986; legal affairs reporter, 1988; "Page One" Editor, to 1988; News Editor, current, 1988. NY State Bar Assn Merit Award, 1988.

Greenberg, Paul. Freelance Syndicate, Columnist. *Pine Bluff Commercial*, Editorial Page Editor. B. 1937, Shreveport, LA. U. of MO, 1958, BAJ, 1959, MA-History; Columbia, 1962, American History. US Army, to 1960; discharged 1961. *Pine Bluff* (AR) *Commercial*, Editorial Page Editor, to 1966; current, 1967. *Chicago Daily News*, editorial writer, 1966-67. Freelance Syndicate, columnist, current, 1971. Grenville Clark Memorial Award, 1st Place, 1964; National Newspaper Assn Editorial Award, 1st Place, 1968; Pulitzer Prize, Editorial Writing, 1969; ASNE Distinguished Writing Award, Commentary, 1981; Walker Stone Award, Scripps-Howard News Service, 1st Place, 1986.

Greenfield, James L. *The New York Times Magazine*. Editor. B. 1924, Cleveland, OH. Harvard, 1949, BA. *The Cleveland Press*. Voice of America. *Time*, correspondent, Korea, Japan, 1951-55; New Delhi bureau chief, to 1957; deputy London bureau chief, to 1961. *Life*, chief diplomatic correspondent, from 1961. Deputy Asst Secretary of State-Public Affairs, 1962-64; Asst Secretary of State for Public Affairs, to 1966. Continental Airlines, Asst VP-International Affairs, to 1967. Westinghouse Broadcasting, 1968. *The New York Times*, Metro News Desk Editor, to 1968; Foreign Editor, 1969-76; *Magazine*, Asst Managing Editor, to 1987; Editor, current, 1987.

Greenfield, Meg. *The Washington Post*, Editorial Page Editor. *Newsweek*, Columnist. B. 1930, Seattle, WA. Smith, 1952, BA, *summa cum laude*; Fulbright Scholar, Newnham College, Cambridge, to 1953. *Reporter*, to 1965; DC Editor, to 1968. *The Washington Post*, editorial writer, to 1970; Deputy Editorial Page Editor, to 1979; Editorial Page Editor, current, 1979. *Newsweek*, columnist, current, 1974. Pulitzer Prize, Editorial Writing, 1978.

Greenhouse, Linda. *The New York Times*. Supreme Court Reporter. B. 1947, NYC. Radcliffe College, 1968. American Government; Yale, 1978, MS-Law. *The New York Times*, asst to James Reston, 1968-69; metro reporter, to 1977; Albany bureau chief, 1976-77; Supreme Court correspondent, to 1985, current, 1988; chief congressional correspondent, 1986; congressional reporter, to 1987; reporter, legal issues, public policy, to 1988.

Greenhouse, Steven. *The New York Times*. Paris Financial Correspondent. B. Long Island, NY. Wesleyan U., 1973; Columbia, 1975, Economics Reporting; NYU, 1982, JD, valedictorian. *The Chelsea Clinton News* (NYC), reporter. *The Westsider* (NYC), reporter. *The Record* (Hackensack, NJ), labor & economics reporter, 1976. Law clerk, US District Court Judge Robert L. Carter, 1982-83. *The New York Times*, copyboy, 1973; reporter, 1983-84. Chicago financial correspondent, to 1987; Paris financial correspondent, current, 1987.

Grenier, Richard. *The Washington Times*, Columnist. B. 1933, Cambridge, MA. US Naval Academy. Engineering. *Agence France-Presse*, Paris, 1962. *Financial Times*, Paris, to 1969. Group W Broadcasting, Paris, 1968-70. *The New York Times*. Commentary. *The American Spectator*, Sr Editor, to 1988. *The Washington Times*, "Point Man" columnist, to 1987; columnist, current, 1987. Author 3 books, including *The Marrakesh One-Two*, 1983.

Griffiths, David. *BusinessWeek*. National Security & Defense Reporter. U. of VA, BA; U. of MO, MSJ. US Army. *The Kansas City Star*, reporter, 1973-77. *Aviation Week & Space Technology*, reporter, to 1981. *Defense Week*, reporter, to 1983. *BusinessWeek*, national security & defense reporter, current, 1983.

Griffiths, John. *Financial Times*. Motor Industry Writer. B. 1943, Staines, UK. *Surrey Herald* Group, reporter, Sub-Editor, 1962-65.

The Albertan (Calgary, Alberta), News Editor, to 1968. *Calgary Herald*, Night Editor, to 1970. *Financial Times*, Deputy Foreign News Editor, Night Foreign News Editor, to 1976; Joint Deputy Features Editor, to 1979; motor industry writer, current, 1980. C.T. Hoepner Prize for Journalism, 1987.

Grose, Peter. *Foreign Affairs*. Managing Editor. B. 1934, Evanston, IL. Yale, 1957, History; Pembroke College, Oxford, 1959, MA. Columbia, International Affairs Fellow, 1978-81. Council on Foreign Relations, Sr Fellow, 1982-84. AP, London, Africa, 1959-62. *The New York Times*, Paris, Vietnam, to 1965; Moscow bureau chief, to 1967; diplomatic correspondent, to 1970; Jerusalem bureau chief, to 1972; editorial board member, to 1976; UN bureau chief, to 1977. Dept of State, Policy Planning Staff, Deputy Director, to 1978. Rockefeller Foundation, research assoc, to 1981. *Foreign Affairs*, Managing Editor, current. Author *Israel in the Mind of America*, 1983; *A Changing Israel*, 1985.

Grover, Ronald. *BusinessWeek*. Los Angeles Bureau Manager. GWU, BA-Political Science, MBA; Columbia, MSJ. *The Washington Star*, reporter, to 1979. McGraw-Hill World News, energy correspondent, to 1982. *BusinessWeek*, economic & political correspondent, DC, to 1986; LA correspondent, to 1987; LA bureau manager, current, 1987.

Gruson, Lindsay. *The New York Times*. San Salvador Bureau Chief. B. 1952, Mexico City. Hampshire College, 1978. *The Greensboro* (NC) *Daily News*, reporter, to 1980. *The Washington Star*, reporter, to 1981. *The Gainesville Sun*, reporter, to 1982. *The New York Times*, metro reporter, to 1985; national correspondent, to 1988; San Salvador bureau chief, current, 1988.

Gubernick, Lisa. *Forbes*. Associate Editor. Bryn Mawr, 1978, BA. *Runner*, reporter, 1978-81. *Securities Week*, Wall Street correspondent, to 1984. *Vogue*, money columnist, 1981-83. *Forbes*, staff writer, to 1987; Assoc Editor, LA, current, 1987.

Gup, Theodore. *Time*. Congressional Correspondent. B. 1950, Lima, OH. Brandeis U., 1972, Classics & English; Trinity College, Dublin, 1970-71; Case Western Reserve U. Law School, 1978, JD. Thomas J. Watson Fellow, 1972. Fulbright Scholar to People's Republic of China, 1985-86. Freelance, to 1974. *Akron Beacon Journal*, staff writer, to 1975. *Virginian-Pilot*, summer intern, 1976. *The Washington Post*, summer intern, 1977; staff writer, 1978-87. *Time*, Congressional correspondent, current, 1987. George Polk Award, National Reporting, 1981; Worth Bingham Prize, 1981; Gerald Loeb Award, Business & Financial Writing, 1981, '84.

Gupte, Pranay. *Forbes*. Contributing Editor. B. 1948, Bombay, India. Brandeis U., 1970, BA-Economics & Politics. *The New York Times*, news clerk, 1970-71; staff correspondent, from 1973; UN correspondent, to 1979; African correspondent, Nairobi, to 1982. Freelance, to 1986. *Forbes*, Contributing Editor, current, 1986. *Newsweek International*, "Opinion" columnist, current. Population Institute Best Columnist, 1984; National Federation of Asian-Indian Organizations in America, Striving for Excellence Award, 1986. Author 3 books, including *A Silent Crisis: Children In A Troubled World*, 1988.

Guskind, Robert S. *National Journal*. Contributing Editor. B. 1958, Passaic, NJ. Georgetown, 1980, BA-Government, *magna cum laude*, Phi Beta Kappa. WGTB-FM, News Director, 1976-79. Freelance, current, 1980. Washington Post Writers Group. "The Neal Peirce Column" assoc, current, 1980. *National Journal*, contributor, 1982-84; Contributing Editor, current, 1984. *Planning*, Contributing Editor, current, 1987.

Gwertzman, Bernard M. *The New York Times*. Foreign Editor. B. 1935, NYC. Harvard, 1957, BA, 1960, MA-Soviet Affairs. *The Evening Star*, diplomatic correspondent, to 1968. *The New York Times*, State Dept correspondent, to 1969; Moscow bureau chief, to 1971; Washington diplomatic correspondent, to 1988; Deputy Foreign Editor, to 1989; Foreign Editor, current, 1989. Front Page Award, DC Newspaper Guild, 1966; Edward Weintal Award, Distinguished Diplomatic Reporting, 1984. Co-author *Fulbright: The Dissenter*.

Haas, Lawrence J. *National Journal*. Correspondent. B. 1956, Brooklyn, NY. U. of PA, 1978, American History; Princeton, 1980, MA-American History. *The Daily Register* (Shrewsbury, NJ), reporter, to 1982. *The Pittsburgh Post-Gazette*, statehouse correspondent, to 1983. UPI, Harrisburg bureau chief, to 1985. *The Bond Buyer*, DC correspondent, to 1987. *National Journal*, budget correspondent, current, 1987.

Haberman, Clyde. *The New York Times*. Rome Bureau Chief. B. 1945, Bronx, NY. CCNY, 1966, BA. *The New York Times*, campus stringer, to 1966; "The Week in Review" Editor, 1976-78; reporter, to 1983; Tokyo bureau chief, to 1988; Rome bureau chief, current, 1988. *New York Post*, reporter, 1966-76.

498

Hadar, Mary. *The Washington Post.* "Style" Assistant Managing Editor. B. 1945, NYC. U. of PA, 1965, English/Math; Columbia, 1966, BSJ. *The Sun,* Copy Editor, 1966-69. *Jerusalem Post,* Foreign Editor, to 1977. *The Washington Post,* "Style" Copy Editor, to 1979; "Style" Night Editor, to 1981; "Style" Deputy Editor, to 1983; "Style" Asst Managing Editor, current, 1983. JCPenney-MO Award, Editor of Best Feature Section, 1985, '86, '87.

Hagstrom, Jerry. *National Journal.* Contributing Editor. B. 1947, Bismarck, ND. U. of Denver, 1969, Economics. Loeb Fellow in Advanced Environmental Studies, Harvard, 1981. *Morning Pioneer* (Mandan, ND), reporter, Editor, 1972-73. Washington Post Writers Group, "The Neal Peirce Column" assoc, current, 1976. Freedoms Foundation at Valley Forge Medal, 1983. Author *Beyond Reagan* 1988; co-author (with Neal R. Peirce) *The Book of America,* 1983.

Haldane, David. *Los Angeles Times.* Writer. B. 1949, Long Beach, CA. Goddard College, 1970, Creative Writing. *Daily Southeast News,* reporter, 1979. *San Gabriel Valley Tribune,* reporter, to 1981. *Riverside Press-Enterprise,* feature writer, to 1985. *Los Angeles Times,* writer, current, 1985.

Hall, Alan. *BusinessWeek.* Senior Editor. Cornell, BSJ. *Plastics World,* bureau chief. *Modern Plastics,* Assoc Editor. *Chemical Week,* News Editor, to 1979. *BusinessWeek,* Research Editor, to 1985; Assoc Editor, Science & Technology, to 1986; Sr Editor, Science & Technology, current, 1986. AAAS Westinghouse Award, Science Journalism; Deadline Club Award, Science Writing; NYC Sigma Delta Chi. Author 2 books, including *Wood Finishing and Refinishing.*

Hall, William. *Financial Times.* Head of "LEX" Column. B. 1946, Birkenhead, UK. Cambridge, 1965-68, Economics. *The Banker,* Asst Editor, 1971-75. *Financial Times,* "LEX" column, to 1979; shipping correspondent, to 1981; banking correspondent, to 1983; NY correspondent, to 1988; "LEX" column, head, current, 1988.

Hallow, Ralph Z. *The Washington Times.* Political Writer. B. 1938, Pittsburgh. U. of Pittsburgh, 1960, AB; postgrad Law & History; U. of MO, Journalism. Ford Foundation Fellow, Northwestern. *The Pittsburgh Press,* Night City Editor, to 1969. *The Pittsburgh Post-Gazette,* editorial board member, to 1977. *Chicago Tribune,* Editorial Board, to 1982. *The Washington Times,* editorial writer, 1982; Deputy Editorial Page Editor, to 1984; financial writer, to 1985; political writer, current, 1985.

Hamilton, Joan O'Connell. *BusinessWeek.* San Francisco Correspondent. Stanford U. *The New York Times,* freelance. *The San Francisco Examiner,* freelance. *The San Francisco Bay Guardian,* intern. *Time,* correspondent intern. *BusinessWeek,* correspondent, San Francisco, current, 1983.

Hannon, Kerry. *Forbes.* Washington Writer. B. 1960, Pittsburgh. Duke, 1982, BA-Comparative Literature. *The Washingtonian,* editorial asst, 1981-82. *BusinessWeek,* correspondent, Pittsburgh, 1983-84. *Pittsburgh Business Times-Journal,* correspondent, to 1985. *The Pittsburgh Press,* correspondent, to 1985. *Pittsburgh Magazine,* contributor, 1983-85. *Advertising Age,* regional correspondent, Chicago, 1984-85. *Washington Business Journal,* Special Projects Editor, 1985. *Forbes,* reporter, to 1987; DC writer, current, 1987.

Harden, Blaine. *The Washington Post.* Warsaw Correspondent. B. 1952, Moses Lake, WA. Gonzaga U., 1974, BA-Philosophy & Political Science; Syracuse U., 1976, MAJ. *The Trenton Times,* reporter, to 1977. *The Washington Post,* metro reporter, to 1980; Sunday magazine reporter, to 1982; metro reporter, to 1983; Africa correspondent, to 1989; Warsaw correspondent, current, 1989. *The Washingtonian,* Sr Writer, 1983-84. Livingston Young Journalists Award, 1986. ASNE Distinguished Deadline Award, 1988.

Harries, Owen. *The National Interest.* Editor. B. 1930, Wales, UK. U. of Wales, 1950; U. of Oxford, 1952, Politics. U. of Sydney (Australia). Sr Lecturer, 1955-65. U. of New South Wales, prof, to 1975. Foreign Minister of Australia, special adviser, to 1977. Dept of Foreign Affairs, Head of Policy Planning, to 1979. Prime Minister, Sr Adviser, to 1981. UNESCO, Ambassador, to 1984. Heritage Foundation, Visiting Fellow, to 1984. *The National Interest,* Editor, current, 1985. Editor 2 books, including *Australia & The Third World,* 1979.

Harvey, Steve. *Los Angeles Times.* Reporter. B. 1946, Santa Monica, CA. USC, 1967, BAJ. *Los Angeles Herald Examiner,* sportswriter, 1966-67. *Los Angeles Times,* reporter, current, 1968. National Public Radio, commentator, current, 1981. United Press Syndicate, creator "The Bottom Ten," current, 1970.

Harwood, Richard. *The Washington Post.* Ombudsman. Vanderbilt U. Nieman Fellow, 1955. Carnegie Journalism Fellow, Columbia, 1965. *The Courier-Journal. The Trenton Times,* evening & Sunday editions, Editor, 1974-76. *The Washington Post,* national politics & public affairs reporter; Vietnam correspondent; National Editor; Asst

Managing Editor, national news, 1966-74; Deputy Managing Editor, 1976-88; Ombudsman, current, 1988.

Havemann, Judith Nicol. *The Washington Post.* National Reporter. B. Iowa. Michigan State U., BA. Nieman Fellow, 1979-80. *Chicago Sun-Times. Chicago's American. The Highland Park* (IL) *Herald. The Washington Post,* from 1973; metro reporter; Asst Editor, VA; Editor, VA, MD; Asst National Editor; Deputy National Editor, to 1986; national reporter, current, 1986.

Hayes, Thomas C. *The New York Times.* Western Economic Correspondent. B. 1950, Cincinnati, OH. Northwestern, 1973, BSJ; postgrad U. of MA, Amherst, & Xavier U. Walter Bagehot Fellow, 1978-79. *The Cincinnati Post,* sports reporter, summers 1968-70. *The Cincinnati Enquirer,* business reporter, to 1978. *The New York Times,* "Business Day" reporter, to 1981; Western economic correspondent, current, 1981.

Hector, Gary. *Fortune.* Associate Editor. Columbia, MSJ; NYU, MBA-Finance. *San Jose Mercury News,* reporter. *American Banker,* reporter. *Fortune,* writer, to 1982; Assoc Editor, CA, current, 1982. Gerald Loeb Award, Distinguished Business & Financial Journalism, 1981. Author *Breaking the Bank,* 1988.

Hedges, Michael B. *The Washington Times.* National Reporter. B. 1955, Muncie, IN. Northern KY U., 1978, Communications. Publishing industry, 1979-83. *Journal* (MD) newspapers, reporter, to 1985. *The Washington Times,* national reporter, current, 1985. Press Association Award, 1984, 1986; MD Health Care Association Award, 1985; Sigma Delta Chi Washington Dateline Award, 1985, 1986. Author *The Civil War, Soldiers and Civilians*; co-author *What a Civilian Needs to Know.*

Henkoff, Ronald. *Fortune.* Associate Editor. B. 1954, Boston. Carleton College, 1976, History; Columbia, 1977, MSJ; London School of Economics, 1984, MA-International History. *The Village Voice,* editing asst, 1976. *The Dispatch* (Hudson County, NJ), municipal reporter, to 1978. *Newsweek,* business reporter, NY, to 1979; Houston correspondent, to 1981; London correspondent, to 1984; European Economics Editor, London, to 1988. *Fortune,* Assoc Editor, Chicago, current, 1988. Media Award for Economic Understanding, 1979; JCPenney-MO Business Journalism Award, 1979; National Headlines Award, 1980; Overseas Press Club of America, 1983.

Henninger, Daniel P. *The Wall Street Journal.* Chief Editorial Writer/Senior Assistant Editorial Page Editor. B. Cleveland, OH. Georgetown, 1968, BA-Foreign Service. *The New Republic,* to 1971. *The National Observer,* writer, to 1977. *The Wall Street Journal,* editorial writer, to 1978; Arts Editor, to 1980; Editorial Features Editor, to 1983; Asst Editorial Page Editor, to 1986; Chief Editorial Page Editor/Sr Asst Editorial Page Editor, current, 1986. Gerald Loeb Award for Commentary, 1985.

Henriques, Diana. *Barron's.* Staff Writer. B. 1948, Bryan, TX. GWU, 1969, BA-International Affairs with distinction. Woodrow Wilson Visiting Fellow, Princeton, 1982-86. *Lawrence* (NJ) *Ledger,* Managing Editor, 1969-71. *Asbury Park* (NJ) *Press,* reporter, to 1974. *Palo Alto* (CA) *Times,* Copy Editor, to 1976. *The Trenton Times,* investigative reporter, to 1982. *The Philadelphia Inquirer,* correspondent, international economics, to 1986; Wall Street correspondent, 1985-86. *Barron's,* staff writer, current, 1986. The Bell Prize for Enterprise Reporting, 1977. Author *The Machinery of Greed,* 1986.

Hentoff, Nathan Irving. *The Washington Post.* "Sweet Land of Liberty" Columnist. B. 1925, Boston. Northeastern, 1945, BA, highest honors; Harvard, 1946, postgrad. Fulbright Fellow, Sorbonne, 1950; Guggenheim Fellowship, 1972. WMEX radio producer, announcer, 1944-53. *Down Beat,* Assoc Editor, to 1957. CBS-TV, "The Jazz Review" Co-founder, Co-Editor, to 1960. Copley News Service, radio commentator, current. *The New Yorker,* writer, current. *The Village Voice,* writer, current. *The Washington Post,* "Sweet Land of Liberty" columnist, current. *The Nation, Social Policy & The Wall Street Journal,* contributor. ABA Silver Gavel Award, 1980; American Library Assoc John Phillip Immroth Award, 1983; People for the American Way Lifetime Achievement Award, 1986. Author several books, including *The Day They Came To Arrest The Book,* 1982.

Herman, R. Thomas. *The Wall Street Journal.* Reporter. B. NY. Yale, 1968, BA. *Yale Daily News,* reporter, Political Editor. *The Wall Street Journal,* intern, DC, summer 1967; NY staff reporter, '74-76; Atlanta staff, to 1974; Hong Kong (*The Asian Wall Street Journal*) reporter, 1976-77; reporter, NY, current, 1980; co-author "Credit Markets" column, current, 1980.

Hershey, Robert D. Jr. *The New York Times.* Washington Reporter. B. 1939, Berlin, Germany. Gettysburg College, 1961, BA-Philosophy; NYU, American Civilization. *The New York Times,* copyboy, 1962; news clerk, 1963; news asst, to 1966; financial dept copy desk, to 1967; financial reporter, to 1973; Asst Editor, Deputy Editor, Sunday

Business section, to 1975; SEC & banking regulation reporter, to 1977; London business & economics correspondent, to 1980; DC reporter, current, 1980.

Hertzberg, Hendrik. *The New Republic.* Editor. B. 1943, NYC. Harvard, 1965, Government. US Navy, 1967-69. Harvard Institute of Politics Fellow, 1981-86. US National Student Assn, Editorial Director, 1965-66. *Newsweek,* San Francisco correspondent, to 1967. *The New Yorker,* writer, 1969-77. White House staff, chief speechwriter, to 1981. *The New Republic,* Editor, to 1985; Contributing Editor, 1985; 1988 Politics Editor; Sr Editor, to 1989; Editor, current, 1989.

Hewitt, Don. CBS-TV News. "60 Minutes" Executive Producer. B. 1922, NYC. Studied NYU, 1941. War Shipping Administration, special correspondent, WWII. 1st Kennedy-Nixon Debate, Producer, 1960. Producer-Director: "A Conversation with President Kennedy," 1962; "A Conversation with President Johnson," 1964. CBS-TV News, coverage of Eisenhower in Europe & India, 1960-61. President Kennedy in Europe, 1962-63, political conventions, inaugurations, producer-director; "CBS Evening News with Walter Cronkite," Exec Producer, 1961-64; Cape Canaveral, Producer, 1960-65; "60 Minutes" Exec Producer, current, 1968.

Hiatt, Fred. *The Washington Post.* East Asia Correspondent. B. 1955, DC. Harvard, 1977, BA-History. US-Japan program, Harvard, 1986-87. *Journal and Constitution,* City Hall reporter, 1979-80. *The Washington Star,* VA reporter, 1981. *The Washington Post,* VA reporter, to 1983; Pentagon reporter, to 1986; East Asia correspondent, current, 1987.

Hicks, Jonathan P. *The New York Times.* Business & Financial News Reporter. B. 1955, St. Louis, MO. U. of MO, 1979, BA-Political Science. Fellow for minority journalists, U. of CA, Berkeley, 1980. *The Arizona Daily Star,* reporter, to 1982. *The Plain Dealer* (Cleveland, OH), business reporter, to 1985. *The New York Times,* business & financial reporter, current, 1986.

Hiebert, Murray. *Far Eastern Economic Review.* Indochina Correspondent. B. 1948, Canada. Goshen College, 1970, History. *Indochina Issues,* Editor. *Far Eastern Economic Review,* Indochina correspondent, current.

Hillenbrand, Barry. *Time.* Tokyo Bureau Chief. B. 1941, Chicago. Loyola College, 1963, History. *Time,* Boston correspondent, 1968-70; LA, to 1972; Saigon, to 1974; Rio de Janeiro bureau chief, to 1977; Chicago correspondent, to 1980; Boston bureau chief, to 1982; Persian Gulf bureau chief, Bahrain, to 1986; Tokyo bureau chief, current, 1986.

Hiltzik, Michael. *Los Angeles Times.* Nairobi Bureau Chief. B. 1952, NYC. Colgate U., 1973, BA-English; Columbia, 1974, MAJ. *Buffalo* (NY) *Courier Express,* state capital correspondent, 1974-78. *Providence Journal,* environmental writer, to 1981. *Los Angeles Times,* business writer, Orange County edition, to 1982; business writer, 1983; NY staff writer, to 1988; Nairobi bureau chief, current, 1988. Co-recipient State Bar of CA Public Service Award for Distinguished Reporting, 1984.

Himmelfarb, Joel. *The Washington Times.* Editorial Writer. B. 1959, Baltimore. U. of MD, 1982, Political Science. *Human Events,* Assoc Editor, to 1986. *The Washington Times,* editorial writer, current, 1986.

Hitchens, Christopher. *The Nation.* Columnist. *Harper's,* Washington Editor. B. 1949, Portsmouth, UK. Balliol, Oxford, 1967, Philosophy, Politics & Economics; Honors Degree, 1970. *The Times* (UK) Higher Education Supplement, social science correspondent. London Weekend TV, "Weekend World," researcher, reporter. *The Daily Express,* foreign correspondent. *News Statesman,* writer, 1974-80. (London) *Times Literary Supplement,* "American Notes" columnist, current, 1982. *The Spectator,* DC columnist, 1981-86. *The Nation,* DC columnist, current. *Harper's,* DC Editor & columnist, current. *Newsday,* book reviewer, current. Author 4 books, including *Prepared for the Worst,* 1988.

Hitchens, Theresa. *Defense News.* Brussels Bureau Chief. Ohio U. Intern with Sen. John Glenn (D-OH), 1981. North Atlantic Assembly, intern, 1982. *Inside EPA,* Chief Editor. *Inside the Pentagon,* reporter. *Electronic Combat Report,* Editor. *Defense News,* Brussels bureau chief, current, 1988.

Hoagland, Jim. *The Washington Post.* Associate Editor & Chief Foreign Correspondent. B. 1940, Rock Hill, SC. U. of SC, 1961, Journalism. Ford Foundation Fellow, Columbia, International Affairs, 1968-69. *The New York Times* (International Edition), Copy Editor, Paris, 1964-66. *The Washington Post,* metro reporter, to 1968; Africa correspondent, 1969-72; Middle East correspondent, to 1975; Paris correspondent, to 1977; National Affairs reporter, to 1979; Foreign Editor, to 1981; Asst Managing Editor, Foreign News, to 1986; Assoc Editor

& chief foreign correspondent, Paris, current, 1986. Pulitzer Prize, International Reporting, 1971; Bob Considine Award, Overseas Press Club, International Reporting, 1977. Author *South Africa: Civilizations in Conflict,* 1972.

Hochschild, Adam. *Mother Jones.* Writer. B. 1942, NYC. Harvard, 1963, American History & Literature. *San Francisco Chronicle,* reporter, 1965-66. *Ramparts,* reporter, Editor, to 1968; 1973-74. *Mother Jones,* co-founder, 1974; Editor; writer, current. NPR, "All Things Considered" commentator, 1982-83. Freelance, current, 1966. Overseas Press Club of America Certificate of Excellence, 1981; Bryant Spann Award, 1984; Thomas M. Storke International Journalism Award, 1987. Author *Half the Way Home,* 1986.

Hoerr, John. *BusinessWeek.* Senior Writer. B. 1930, McKeesport, PA. Penn State, 1953, General Arts & Science. UPI, correspondent, Trenton & Newark, NJ, 1956-57; Chicago, 1958-60. *Daily Tribune* (Royal Oak, MI), police reporter, feature writer, 1957-58. *BusinessWeek,* correspondent, Detroit, 1960-63; Pittsburgh, 1965-69; Labor Editor; Assoc Editor; Sr Writer, NY, current, 1975. WQED-TV, Pittsburgh, on-air reporter, "Newsroom," documentary writer, Producer, to 1975. NY Newspaper Guild Page 1 Award, 1986. Author *And The Wolf Finally Came,* 1988.

Hoffman, David. *The Washington Post.* National Desk Writer. B. 1953, Palo Alto, CA. Attended U. of DE; Georgetown. The *News-Journal* Newspapers (Wilmington, DE). Capitol Hill News Service. States News Service, 1978-79. Knight Ridder Newspapers, DC Bureau, to 1982. *The Washington Post,* from 1982: reporter; national desk writer, current.

Hoffman, Ellen. *National Journal.* Contributing Editor. B. 1943, NY. U. of MN, 1964, BA-European History; Georgetown, 1966, MA. *The Washington Post,* reporter, to 1971. US Senate Subcommittee on Children & Youth, staff member, Director, to 1977. The Children's Defense Fund, Director of Governmental Affairs, to 1983. Freelance, current, 1983. Self-syndicated column, "The Resourceful Traveler," current, 1983. *National Journal,* Contributing Editor, current.

Hoge, Warren. *The New York Times.* Assistant Managing Editor. B. 1941, NYC. Yale, 1963, BA-English; GWU, Literature & Political Science. US Army Reserves, 1964. *The Washington Star,* police & courts reporter, to 1966. *New York Post,* DC correspondent, to 1970; Night City Editor, City Editor, Metro Editor, to 1976. *The New York Times,* metro reporter, 1976; Asst Metro Editor, Deputy Metro Editor, to 1979; Rio de Janeiro bureau chief, to 1983; Foreign Editor, to 1986; Asst Managing Editor, current, 1986.

Holley, David. *Los Angeles Times.* Beijing Bureau Chief. *Los Angeles Times,* metro writer, 1979-86; Tokyo & Hong Kong, intern, to 1987; Beijing bureau chief, current, 1987.

Holman, Michael. *Financial Times.* Africa Editor. B. 1945, Penzance, UK. U. College of Rhodesia, 1967, BA-English; U. of Edinburgh, 1971, MS-Politics. Freelance, Salisbury, Rhodesia (Harare, Zimbabwe), 1973-77. *The Financial Mail,* Rhodesia Editor, Johannesburg, South Africa, 1975-77. *Financial Times,* Africa correspondent, Lusaka, Zambia, to 1984; Africa Editor (London-based), current, 1984.

Holmes, John P. III. *Insight.* Senior Editor. B. 1955, Dalhart, TX. TX Tech U., 1977, Journalism. *The Corpus Christi Caller-Times,* reporter, to 1978. *The Lubbock* (TX) *Avalanche-Journal,* reporter, Regional Editor, to 1980. Press Secretary, Rep. Kent Hance (D-TX), to 1982. *The Washington Times,* "Capital Life" writer, to 1984; space, science & national news reporter, to 1985. *Insight,* science & space writer, to 1988; Sr Editor, Features, current, 1988. *Texas Business Magazine,* DC correspondent, current, 1982. *Home Team Sports,* Editor, current, 1985. H.L. Mencken Award, Investigative Journalism, 1985.

Holt, Donald Dale. *Fortune.* International Editor. B. 1936, Chicago. Wharton College, 1957, English. *Chicago Daily News,* 1961-64. *Newsweek,* to 1978. *Fortune,* International Editor, current.

Holusha, John. *The New York Times.* Detroit Bureau Chief. Newark College of Engineering, 1965, BS-Chemical Engineering; postgrad GWU, 1976-78, Economics. Walter Bagehot Fellow, 1975-76. *The Daily Record* (Morristown, NJ), reporter. *The Advance* (Dover, NJ), reporter. *The Star-Ledger* (Newark, NJ), reporter; Asst City Editor; Night City Editor, to 1970. *The Washington Star,* reporter; Asst National Editor; Asst Financial Editor, to 1979. *The New York Times,* asst to Financial Editor, to 1981; Editor, 1980 National & International Economic Surveys; Detroit bureau chief, current, 1982.

Holzman, David. *Insight.* Medicine & Science Writer. B. 1953, Cambridge, MA. U. of CA, Berkeley, 1975, Zoology. Center for Science in the Public Interest, researcher, writer, 1976-77. *People & En-*

ergy, writer, to 1978; Editor, to 1980. Freelance, to 1986. *Insight*, medicine & science writer, current, 1986.

Hornblower, Margot. *Time*. Paris Correspondent. B. 1950, NYC. Harvard, 1971, European History. *Charlottesville (VA) Daily Progress*, 1971-73. *The Washington Post*, metro reporter, to 1976; national environmental reporter, to 1979; foreign correspondent, South & Central America; political correspondent, 1976, 1980; Congressional correspondent, to 1983; New York bureau chief, to 1987. *Time*, NY correspondent, to 1988; Paris correspondent, current, 1988.

Hornik, Richard. *Time*. Washington Correspondent. B. 1948, NYC. Brown, 1970, Political Science. *National Journal*, researcher, to 1972. National Commission on Productivity, Writer, Editor, to 1974. *Eastwest Markets*, Contributing Editor, 1975; Assoc Editor, to 1978. *Time*, DC energy & economics correspondent, to 1980; Eastern Europe bureau chief, to 1983; Boston bureau chief, to 1984; Peking bureau chief, to 1988; DC correspondent, current, 1988.

House, Karen Elliott. *The Wall Street Journal*. International Editor. B. 1947, Matador, TX. U. of TX, 1970, BJ. *Dallas Morning News*, education reporter, 1970-71; DC correspondent, to 1974. *The Wall Street Journal*, regulatory agencies correspondent, to 1975; energy & environmental reporter, to 1978; diplomatic correspondent, to 1983; Asst Foreign Editor, NY, to 1984; Foreign Editor, to 1989; International Editor, current, 1989. Edward Weintal Award for Diplomatic Coverage, 1981; National Press Club Award, 1982; Pulitzer Prize International, 1984; Overseas Press Club Award, 1984, '88.

Hughes, David. *Aviation Week & Space Technology*. Boston Bureau Chief. B. 1947, Baltimore. Dartmouth, 1970, English. Northwestern, 1971, MSJ. (Charlestown, SC) *News & Courier*, 1973-76. MD Center for Public Broadcasting, scriptwriter, to 1979. Aerospace Corps, writer, to 1987. *Aviation Week & Space Technology*, Boston bureau chief, current, 1987. National ADDY Award.

Hume, Alexander Britton. ABC-TV News. White House Correspondent. B. 1943, DC. U. of VA, 1965, BA. Washington Journalism Center Fellow, spring 1969. *Hartford Times*, reporter, to 1966. UPI, 1967. *The Evening Sun*, 1968. Freelance, DC, 1969. Jack Anderson column, reporter, 1970-72. ABC-TV News, consultant, DC, to 1976; special correspondent, DC, to 1988; "Weekend Report, Saturday," anchor, 1985-87; White House correspondent, current, 1989. Author 2 books, including *Inside Story*, 1974.

Hunt, Albert R. *The Wall Street Journal*. Washington Bureau Chief. B. Charlottesville, VA. Wake Forest U., 1965, BA-Political Science. *Philadelphia Bulletin*. *Winston-Salem Journal*. *The Wall Street Journal*, NY staff; Boston staff; Congressional correspondent; DC bureau chief, current, 1983. "The Capitol Gang," panelist. Raymond Clapper Award. Co-author 3 books, including *The American Election of 1984*.

Ibrahim, Youssef M. *The New York Times*. Paris Reporter. B. Cairo, Egypt. American U. (Cairo), 1968, BA; Columbia, 1970, MAJ. *The New York Times*, foreign correspondent, to 1981; Paris reporter, current, 1987. *Mideast Markets*, Assoc Editor. *The Wall Street Journal*, Energy Editor, 1981-87. Overseas Press Club Citation, 1986.

Ignatius, David. *The Washington Post*. "Outlook" Associate Editor. B. 1950, Cambridge, MA. Harvard, 1972, Social Studies; Cambridge U., Economics. *The Washington Monthly*, Editor, 1975-76. *The Wall Street Journal*, steel reporter, Pittsburgh, to 1977; Justice Dept correspondent, to 1979; Senate correspondent, to 1980; Middle East correspondent, to 1983; diplomatic correspondent, to 1985; "Outlook" Assoc Editor, current, 1986. Edward Weintal Prize for Diplomatic Reporting, 1985. Author *Agents of Innocence*, 1987.

Ingrassia, Lawrence. *The Wall Street Journal*. Boston Bureau Chief. B. Laurel, MS. U. of IL, Champaign-Urbana, 1974, BS-Communications. *Chicago Sun-Times*, reporter, to 1978. *The Wall Street Journal*, reporter, to 1979; Minneapolis reporter, to 1983; News Editor, London, 1983; deputy London bureau chief, to 1986; Boston bureau chief, current, 1986.

Ingrassia, Paul. *The Wall Street Journal*. Detroit Bureau Chief. B. 1950, Laurel, MS. U. of IL, 1972, BSJ; U. of WI, 1973, MA. Lindsay-Schaub Newspapers, editorial writer, to 1976. *The Wall Street Journal*, Chicago reporter, to 1980; Chicago News Editor, to 1981; Cleveland bureau chief, to 1985; Detroit bureau chief, current, 1985.

Innerst, Carol. *The Washington Times*. Education Writer. B. York, PA. U. of MD, English. *The Gazette and Daily* (York, PA). *Allentown Call-Chronicle*. *The Philadelphia Bulletin*. *The Washington Times*, education writer, current.

Isaacson, Walter S. *Time*. Senior Writer. B. 1952, New Orleans, LA. Harvard, 1974, History & Literature; Oxford, 1976, MA-Philosophy & Politics. *Sunday Times* (London, UK), 1976-77. *New Orleans Times-Picayune*, to 1978. *Time*, staff writer, to 1980; political correspondent, to 1981; Assoc Editor, to 1985; Sr Editor, to 1988; Sr Writer, current, 1988. Overseas Press Club, 1981, '84, '88. Author *Pro & Con*, 1982; co-author *The Wise Men*, 1986.

Isikoff, Michael. *The Washington Post*. Reporter. B. 1952, NYC. Washington U. (St. Louis, MO). Capitol Hill News Service. States News Service. *The Washington Star*, reporter, to 1981. *The Washington Post*, metro reporter; reporter, current.

Iyer, Pico. *Time*. Contributor. B. 1957, Oxford, UK. Oxford, 1978, BA-English Language; 1982, MA-Literature; Harvard, 1980, AM. *Santa Barbara News and Review*, profile writer, 1980. *The Movies*, contributor, 1983. Freelance, current, 1977. *Time*, "World Affairs" writer, reviewer, 1982-87; contributor, current, 1987.

Jackson, Brooks D. *The Wall Street Journal*. Washington Reporter. B. 1941, Seattle, WA. Northwestern, 1964, BS; Syracuse U., 1967, MS. AP, reporter, NYC & DC to 1980. *The Wall Street Journal*, DC reporter, current, 1980. AP Reporting Performance Award, 1974; Raymond Clapper Award, DC Reporting, 1974; John Hancock Award, Business & Financial Reporting, 1978.

Jacoby, Tamar. *Newsweek*. Senior Writer. B. 1954, NYC. Yale, 1976, English. *New York Review of Books*, asst to Editor, 1977-81. *The New York Times*, Deputy Editor, Op-Ed page, to 1987. *Newsweek*, Sr Writer, to 1988, current, 1989; Justice Editor, 1988.

Jaffe, Thomas. *Forbes*. Associate Editor & "Streetwalker" Columnist. Yale, 1971, BA-Art History/Anthropology; Columbia, 1975, MSJ. *Forbes*, reporter/researcher, 1977-80; reporter, to 1984; staff writer, to 1983; "Streetwalker" columnist, current, 1983; Assoc Editor, current, 1986.

Jameson, Sam. *Los Angeles Times*. Tokyo Bureau Chief. B. 1936, Pittsburgh. Northwestern, 1958, BSJ, 1959, MSJ. US Army, *Pacific Stars & Stripes*, Tokyo, 1960-62. *Chicago Tribune*, 1959-60; Tokyo bureau chief, 1963-71. *Los Angeles Times*, Tokyo bureau chief, current, 1971. Loeb Award.

Janssen, Richard F. *BusinessWeek*. Senior Editor. B. 1933, St. Louis, MO. Washington U. (St. Louis), 1954, Political Science. US Army, to 1956. *The Wall Street Journal*, Chicago reporter, to 1963; DC economics correspondent, "Outlook" columnist, to 1972; London correspondent, European bureau chief, to 1978; financial & economic reporter, Editor, to 1981. *BusinessWeek*, Sr Editor, finance & personal business, current, 1981.

Jaroslavsky, Rich. *The Wall Street Journal*. Washington DC Features Editor. B. Santa Rosa, CA. Stanford, 1975, BA-Political Science. *San Francisco Chronicle*, campus correspondent. *Stanford Daily*, Editor-in-Chief, 1974. *The Wall Street Journal*, intern, summer 1974; Cleveland reporter, 1975-76; reporter, to 1981; White House correspondent, to 1985; DC Features Editor, current, 1985. Co-recipient Aldo Beckman Memorial Award, 1983.

Javetski, William. *BusinessWeek*. State Department Correspondent. Hunter College; U. of CA, Berkeley, MA. USC Journalism School, business journalism teacher. *The Merced (CA) Sun-Star*, reporter. *The San Jose Mercury News*, writer. *The Berkeley Gazette*, reporter. *BusinessWeek*, LA correspondent; Toronto correspondent, to 1983; Toronto bureau chief, to 1986; State Dept correspondent, current, 1986.

Jenkins, Holman W. Jr. *Insight*. Writer. B. 1959, Philadelphia. Hobart College, 1982, History; Medill School of Journalism, 1985. *Gas Daily*, DC Editor, to 1986. *Fed Fortnightly*, writer, to 1987. *Insight*, writer, current, 1987.

Jennings, Peter Charles. ABC-TV News. "World News Tonight" Anchor & Senior Editor. B. 1938, Toronto, Ontario. Studied Carlton U. (Ottawa, Ontario). CBC, Montreal. CJOH-TV, Ottawa. Canadian TV, Parliamentary correspondent, anchor. ABC-TV News, from 1964, anchor, national correspondent; "World News Tonight," London anchor, to 1983; anchor, Sr Editor, current, 1985.

Jereski, Laura. *Forbes*. New England Bureau Manager. Harvard, 1983, BA. *Marketing and Media Decisions*, Assoc Editor, 1983-85. Twentieth Century Fox, script writer. *Forbes*, reporter, to 1987; New England bureau manager, current, 1987.

Jewler, Sarah. *Manhattan, inc.* Managing Editor. B. 1948, DC. GWU, 1970, American Literature. Benwill Publishing, production coordinator, 1976-80. *Rolling Stone*, Asst Production Manager, to 1981. *Spring*, Art Production Manager, to 1983. *Cuisine*, Editorial Production Manager, to 1984. *Manhattan, inc.*, Managing Editor, current, 1984.

Johns, Michael. *Policy Review*. Assistant Editor. B. 1964, Allentown, PA. U. of Miami, 1986, BBA-Economics. *The Miami Tribune*

(U. of Miami), Editor-in-Chief, 1983-84, '85-86. Lyndon Baines Johnson Fellow. Rep. Don Ritter (R-PA), 1984. *The Miami Hurricane*, opinion columnist & reporter, 1982-83. *Human Events*, Capitol Hill reporter, 1983. *Policy Review*, Asst Editor, current, 1986. *Liberty Report*, Contributing National Security Editor, current, 1987. Iron Arrow Honor Society, U. of Miami; James Brady Press Award; Century III Leaders Scholarship, Shell Oil Co; US Achievement Academy National Award. Contributor *The Third Generation*, 1987.

Johnson, Haynes. *The Washington Post.* National Affairs Columnist. B. NYC. U. of MO, BSJ; U. of WI, Madison, MA-American History. Twice Ferris Prof of Journalism. *News Journal* (Wilmington, DE), reporter, 1956-57. *The Washington Star*, city reporter; Copy Editor; Night City Editor; national reporter, to 1969. *The Washington Post*, national reporter; Asst Managing Editor; national affairs columnist, current. Pulitzer Prize, Reporting, 1966; *Sigma Delta Chi* Award, General Reporting. Author 4 books, including *In The Absence of Power*, 1980; co-author 4 books, including *Lyndon*, 1973; editor *The Fall of a President*, 1974.

Johnson, Robert W. *The Wall Street Journal.* Reporter. B. 1947, Lakeland, FL. U. of South FL, 1972, BA-Mass Communications. *Tampa Tribune*, reporter, 1972-75. *Florida Trend*, reporter, to 1980. *Orlando Sentinel*, reporter, to 1982. *Wall Street Journal*, reporter, Chicago, current 1982. Co-recipient George Polk Award, 1982.

Johnson, Tom. *Los Angeles Times.* Publisher & Chief Executive Officer. B. 1941, Macon, GA. U. of GA, 1963, ABJ; Harvard, 1965, MBA. White House Fellow, 1965-66. *The Macon* (GA) *Telegraph And News*, sports stringer, reporter & state desk, 1956-65. Asst White House Press Secretary, 1966-67. Deputy Press Secretary to President Johnson, to 1968. Special Asst to President, to 1969. Exec Asst to President Johnson, to 1971. Texas Broadcasting Corp, Exec VP, to 1973. *Dallas Times Herald*, Exec Editor, to 1975; Publisher, to 1977. *Los Angeles Times*, President & Chief Operating Officer, to 1986; Publisher & CEO, current, 1987. Times Mirror Company Group, VP, 1984-85; Vice Chairman, current, 1987. *Adweek* US Publisher of the Year, 1984.

Johnston, Oswald, Jr. *Los Angeles Times.* Washington Writer. B. 1934, NY. Harvard, 1955, AB-History & Literature, *magna cum laude*; Cambridge, 1957, MA-English Literature. Yale, English instructor, 1962-63. *The Jersey Journal* (Jersey City, NJ), writer, 1964-65. *The Sun*, DC writer, 1965-1969; Rome bureau chief, 1970-72. *Washington Star-News*, national writer, 1972-75. *Los Angeles Times*, DC writer, current, 1975.

Jones, Alex S. *The New York Times.* Press Reporter. B. Greenville, TN. Washington & Lee U. *The Greenville* (TN) *Sun*, Editor, 1978-83. *The New York Times*, business reporter, to 1985; press reporter, current, 1985. Pulitzer Prize, Specialized Reporting, 1987.

Jones, Laurie Lynn. *New York.* Managing Editor. B. 1947, Kerrville, TX. U. of TX, 1969, BA. Columbia, asst to Director of College Admissions, 1969-70; asst to Director Office Alumni, to 1971. *Book World*, asst advertising manager, to 1972. *The Washington Post, Chicago Tribune*, 1971-72. *New York*, editorial asst, to 1974; Asst Editor, 1974; Sr Editor, to 1976; Managing Editor, current, 1976.

Jones, Tamara. *Los Angeles Times.* Denver Bureau Chief. San Diego State U., BSJ. *Los Angeles Times*, intern, 1978-79; Denver bureau chief, current, 1987. AP, NY, LA, San Diego, 1979-83; West Germany correspondent, to 1985; national correspondent, NY, to 1987.

Joseph, Gloria. *The Journal of Commerce.* News Editor. B. 1954, Terre Haute, IN. Indiana U., 1980, Journalism/Environmental Science. CBS-TV affiliates, reporter (Louisville, KY); anchor (Lexington, KY), to 1981. FNN, "Business Today" co-anchor, to 1982. *The Journal of Commerce*, Seattle bureau chief, to 1987; Asst Maritime Editor, to 1989; News Editor, current, 1989.

Kaiser, Robert G. *The Washington Post.* National News Assistant Managing Editor. B. DC. Yale; London School of Economics, MS; Columbia, International Reporting. Duke, Teaching Fellow, 1974-75. *The Washington Post*, intern, summer 1963; London correspondent, part-time, 1964-66; city reporter, to 1969; Saigon correspondent, to 1971; Moscow correspondent, to 1974; national news reporter, 1975-82; Assoc Editor, Editor "Outlook," to 1985; Asst Managing Editor, national news, current, 1985. Co-author 4 books.

Kamen, Albert J. *The Washington Post.* Metro Reporter & Columnist. B. 1946, Brooklyn, NY. Harvard, 1967, BA-Government. *The Washington Post*, from 1980: metro reporter, current; "Lawyers" columnist, current.

Kamm, Henry. *The New York Times.* Budapest Correspondent. B. 1925, Breslau, Germany. NYU, 1949, BA, *Phi Beta Kappa*. US Army, 1943-46. *The New York Times*, editorial index dept member,

Copy Editor, to 1960; Asst News Editor, *Times* International Edition, Paris, to 1964; foreign correspondent, to 1967; Moscow bureau chief, to 1969; Asia correspondent, to 1971; roving correspondent, to 1982; Rome bureau chief, to 1984; Athens bureau chief, to 1986; Budapest correspondent, current, 1986. George Polk Memorial Award, Foreign Reporting, 1969; Pulitzer Prize, International Reporting, 1978; co-recipient *Sigma Delta Chi* Distinguished Service Award, Outstanding Foreign Correspondence, 1968.

Kann, Peter Robert. *The Wall Street Journal.* Publisher. B. Princeton, NJ. Harvard, 1964, BA-Government. *The Harvard Crimson*, Political Editor, editorial board member. *The Wall Street Journal*, summer intern, 1963; Pittsburgh staff, to 1966; LA staff, 1966; Vietnam reporter, to 1968; roving Asia correspondent, to 1976; 1st Publisher & Editor of *The Asian Wall Street Journal*, to 1979; Dow Jones corp rep, Asia, to 1979; asst to Chairman & Chief Exec, 1979; Assoc Publisher, to 1988; Publisher, current, 1988; VP, Dow Jones, Management Committee member, to 1985; Exec VP, Dow Jones, current, 1985; President, International & Magazine groups, current, 1985. Pulitzer Prize Board member, current, 1987. Pulitzer Prize, Distinguished Reporting, International Affairs, 1972.

Kanner, Bernice. *New York.* Senior Editor. B. 1949, NYC. SUNY, Binghamton, English; English Literature. J. Walter Thompson, corporate communications division, 1974-77. *Advertising Age*, Sr Editor, to 1980. *The* (NY) *Daily News*, marketing columnist. *New York*, Sr Editor, writer, "On Madison Avenue" columnist, current. 2 Compton Advertising Journalism Awards; Public School Graduate of NY Award, 1986; Saatchi & Saatchi Advertising Journalism Award, 1989.

Kaplan, Roger. *Reader's Digest.* Associate Editor. B. 1946, Neuilly, France. U. of Chicago, 1970, Literature & History, 1974, MA. Freelance, to 1984. *Commentary*, to 1986. *The American Spectator*, to 1986. *The Detroit News*, editorial writer, Op-ed Editor, to 1986. *New York Post*, editorial writer, Op-ed Editor, to 1986. *Reader's Digest*, Assoc Editor, current, 1986.

Karmin, Monroe W. *U.S.News & World Report.* Senior Editor & Columnist. B. 1929, Mineola, NY. U. of IL, 1950, Journalism; Columbia, 1953, MSJ. *The Wall Street Journal*, NY, 1953-54; DC, to 1974. Knight-Ridder Newspaper Group, DC, to 1981. *U.S.News & World Report*, Sr Editor, "Economic Outlook" columnist, current, 1981. *Sigma Delta Chi* Award. Gen Reporting, 1966; Pulitzer Prize, National Reporting, 1967.

Katayama, Frederick H. *Fortune.* Reporter. B. 1960, LA, CA. Columbia, 1982, East Asian Languages & Cultures; Columbia, 1983, MSJ. East Asian Journalism Fellow, Columbia, 1982-83. Time Inc., *Fortune*, intern, Tokyo, 1983-84. AP, reporter, Tokyo bureau, to 1985. *Fortune*, Tokyo correspondent, to 1987; reporter, consumer electronics, current, 1988. Overseas Press Club Citation for Excellence, 1987.

Kaus, Mickey (Robert M.). *The New Republic.* Senior Editor. B. 1951, Santa Monica, CA. Harvard, 1973, Social Studies; Harvard Law School. *The Washington Monthly*, Editor, 1978-80. *American Lawyer*, Sr Editor, to 1981. *Harper's*, Politics Editor, to 1983. *The New Republic*, West Coast correspondent, to 1987. *Newsweek*, Sr Writer, to 1989. *The New Republic*, Sr Editor, current, 1989. ABA Silver Gavel Award, 1979; co-recipient NY State Bar Assn. Media Award, 1987.

Kaye, Steven D. *The Washingtonian.* Writer. B. 1960, Elizabeth, NJ. Brown, 1982, Political Science. *Houston City*, writer, 1986. *The Washingtonian*, writer, current, 1987. National Magazine Award, 1988; DC Dateline Award, 1988.

Kaylor, Robert. *U.S.News & World Report.* Associate Editor. *U.S.News & World Report*, Singapore bureau chief, to 1986; Assoc Editor, defense, current, 1986.

Keating, Susan Katz. *Insight.* Writer. B. Riverside, CA. U of CA, Davis, Medieval History. *Chattanooga Times*, reporter, 1978. *Dixon* (CA) *Tribune*, reporter, 1982; Editor, to 1985. *Insight*, reporter, to 1986; writer, current, 1986. Distinguished Achievement, Journalism Award, Air Force Assn. 1985; 1st Place, General Excellence Category, CA Newspaper Publishers Assn. 1985.

Keller, Bill. *The New York Times.* Moscow Bureau Chief. B. 1949. Pomona College, 1970. *The Oregonian* (Portland, OR), reporter, to 1979. *Congressional Quarterly*, lobbyist & interest groups reporter, to 1982. *Dallas Times Herald*, reporter, to 1984. *The New York Times*, domestic correspondent, DC, to 1986; Moscow correspondent, to 1988; Moscow bureau chief, current, 1988. Pulitzer Prize, International Reporting, 1988.

Kempster, Norman. *Los Angeles Times.* State Department Correspondent. B. 1936, Sacramento, CA. CA State U., Sacramento, 1957, Language Arts. Professional Journalism Fellowship, Stanford, 1967-68; Jos Alex Memorial lecturer, Harvard, 1983, honorary Nieman Fellow. UPI. Sacramento, to 1961; Olympia. WA, bureau chief, to 1966; deputy bureau chief, to 1968; DC economics, White House correspondent, to 1973. *The Washington Star*. White House correspondent, to 1976. *Los Angeles Times*, Pentagon correspondent, to 1981; Jerusalem bureau chief, to 1984; State Dept correspondent, current, 1984.

Kestin, Hesh. *Forbes*. Contributing Editor. B. 1943. NYC. *True*. Magazine Editor. *Newsview*, Magazine Editor, Israel. Freelance. *New York Herald Tribune*. *Newsday*. *Paterson* (NJ) *Call*. *Jerusalem Post*. *Forbes*, European correspondent, 1985-86; European bureau manager. London, to 1987; Contributing Editor, current, 1987.

Kilborn, Peter T. *The New York Times*. "Workplace" Correspondent. B. 1939, Providence, RI. Trinity College, 1961. BA-English; Columbia 1962. MSJ-Economics. Providence *Journal-Bulletin*, reporter, to 1963. McGraw-Hill World News & *BusinessWeek*. Paris correspondent, to 1968. *BusinessWeek*, writer, Asst Tech Editor, to 1971; LA bureau chief, to 1973; Companies Editor, to 1974. *Newsweek*, Sr Editor, to 1978. *The New York Times*, financial reporter, to 1975, '78; London economics correspondent, to 1977; Sunday Business Section Editor, to 1982; Economics Editor, DC, to 1983; economics correspondent, DC, to 1989; "Workplace" correspondent, DC, current, 1989.

Kilpatrick, James Jackson. Universal Press Syndicate. Columnist. B. 1920, Oklahoma City, OK. U. of MO, 1941. BJ-History. *Richmond News Leader*, reporter, to 1949; Editorial Page Editor, to 1951; syndicated columnist, to 1965. Washington Star Syndicate, columnist, to 1981. Universal Press Syndicate, columnist, current, 1981. William Allen White Award, U. of KS; U. of MO Medal of Honor, Distinguished Service to Journalism; Carr Von Anda Award, OH U., 1987.

Kinsley, Michael. *The New Republic*. "TRB From Washington" Columnist. B. 1951. Detroit. Harvard, 1972. Economics; Magdalen College; Oxford; Harvard Law. *The Washington Monthly*, Managing Editor, to 1975. *Harper's*, Editor, 1981-83. *The New Republic*, Managing Editor, to 1976; Editor, to 1979, 1983-89; "TRB from Washington" columnist, current, 1988. *Time*, contributor, current, 1988. *The Economist*, "American Survey" Editor, 1989. DC bar member.

Kirkland, Richard I., Jr. *Fortune*. Board of Editors Member & European Correspondent. Birmingham-Southern College, BA-English, *summa cum laude*, *Phi Beta Kappa*; Duke. AB-English. MA; NYU "Careers in Business" accelerated MBA program. *Fortune*, reporter/researcher, to 1981; Assoc Editor, DC, to 1985; Board of Editors member, European correspondent, London, current, 1985.

Kirkpatrick, David. *Fortune*. Associate Editor. B. 1953, St. Louis, MO. Amherst, 1976, English. *Time* Teletext, staff writer, 1982-83. *Fortune*, reporter, to 1988; Assoc Editor, current, 1988.

Kirkpatrick, Jeane J. Los Angeles Times Syndicate. Columnist. B. 1926, Duncan, OK. Stephens College, 1945, AA-Political Science; Barnard, 1948, AB; Columbia, 1950, MA, 1968, PhD; postgrad French Govt Fellow, *U. Paris Institute de Science Politique*, 1952-53. State Dept. research analyst, 1951-53. GWU, research assoc, to 1956. Georgetown, assoc prof, Political Science, 1967-73; prof, to 1978; Thomas & Dorothy Leavey U., Georgetown, prof, current, 1978 (on leave 1981-85). American Enterprise Institute, Sr Fellow, 1977-81 (on leave 1981-85); Counselor to President. Cabinet Member, US Permanent Rep to UN, 1981-85. Los Angeles Times Syndicate, columnist, current. Contributor, journals, current. Gold Medal of the Veterans of Foreign Wars; Commonwealth Fund Award; French Prize *Politique*, 1984; Presidential Medal of Freedom, 1985. Author 9 books, including *The Reagan Phenomenon*, 1982.

Klaw, Spencer. *Columbia Journalism Review*. Editor. B. 1920, NYC. Harvard, 1941, AB. *San Francisco Chronicle*, reporter, 1941. *Raleigh* (NC) *News & Observer*, DC correspondent, to 1943. UPI, DC correspondent, 1941-43; reporter, NY, 1946. *The New Yorker*, 1947-52. *New York Herald Tribune*, asst to Sunday Editor, to 1954. *Fortune*, Assoc Editor to 1960. Freelance, current, 1960. U. of CA, Berkeley, journalism lecturer, 1968-69. Columbia, journalism lecturer, current, 1970. *Columbia Journalism Review*, Editor, current, 1980. Author 2 books, including *The Great American Medicine Show*, 1975.

Klein, Joe. *New York*. Contributing Editor. B. 1946, NYC. U. of PA, 1968, American Civilization. *Beverly* (MA) *Times*, 1969-70. *The* (Boston) *Phoenix* 1971. WGBH-TV, "The Reporters," 1972. *The Real Paper* (Boston), News Editor, to 1974. *Rolling Stone*, DC bureau chief, to 1976; Assoc Editor, to 1978. *New York*, political correspondent, to 1987; Contributing Editor, current, 1987. Robert Kennedy Award, 1973; Deems Taylor Award, 1978. Author 2 books, including *Payback*, 1984.

Kleinfeld, Nathan R. *The New York Times*. "Business Day" Reporter. B. 1950, Paterson, NJ. Attended Clark U., 1968-69; NYU, 1972, BA, *cum laude*. *The Wall Street Journal*, reporter, 1972-77. *The New York Times*, "Business Day" reporter, current, 1977. Meyer

Berger Award, 1974; Gerald Loeb Award, 1979; Media Award for Economic Understanding. Author 6 books, including *Staying at the Top*, 1986.

Knight, Jerry. *The Washington Post*. Business Columnist. B. Iowa. Attended Iowa State U. *The Ames* (IA) *Daily Tribune*, reporter. *The Des Moines Register*, reporter. *National Home Center News*, Founding Editor. *The Trenton Times*, reporter; City Editor. *The Washington Post*, Deputy Financial Editor; business columnist, current.

Knight, Robin. *U.S.News & World Report*. Senior European Editor. B. 1943, Chalfout St. Giles, UK. Dublin U., 1966, Stanford, 1968, MA-Political Science (Hons). Rotary Foundation Fellowship, 1967-68. *U.S.News & World Report*. London reporter, to 1974; London bureau chief, to 1976; Moscow bureau chief, to 1979; African Regional Editor, Johannesburg, to 1981; Mediterranean Regional Editor, Rome, to 1983; DC, to 1984; Sr European Editor, London, current, 1985. Foreign Correspondents Assn of Southern Africa, chairman, 1980-81.

Knowlton, Christopher. *Fortune*. Associate Editor. Harvard, BA-English & American Literature, *cum laude*. Freelance, to 1985. *Fortune*, reporter/researcher, to 1988; Assoc Editor, current, 1989.

Kolata, Gina. *The New York Times*. Science Reporter. B. 1948, Baltimore, U. of MD, 1969; MS-Mathematics; attended MIT. *Science*, copy editor, 1973-74; writer, to 1987. *The New York Times*, science reporter, current, 1987.

Kondracke, Morton. *The New Republic*. Senior Editor. Dartmouth, 1960. Nieman Fellow, 1973-74. *Chicago Sun-Times*, 1963-68; DC staff, to 1973; White House correspondent, to 1977. NPR, "All Things Considered" & "Communique" commentator, 1979-82. WRC-AM, talk show host, 1981-83. United Feature Syndicate, columnist, to 1985. *The New Republic*, Exec Editor, 1978-85; Sr Editor, current, 1986. *Newsweek*, DC bureau chief, 1985-86. "The McLaughlin Group," panelist, current.

Koppel, Ted. ABC-TV News. Broadcast Journalist. B. Lancashire, UK. Syracuse U., BAJ; Stanford, MAJ. WMCA, news correspondent, writer, NY, 1963. ABC-TV News, correspondent, Vietnam; Miami bureau chief; Hong Kong bureau chief; diplomatic correspondent, DC; "Nightline" Anchor, current, 1980. Overseas Press Club Awards, 1971, '74, '75.

Koretz, Gene. *BusinessWeek*. "Economic Diary" Editor & Writer. B. 1931, NYC. U. of OK, BA-English Literature & Educational Psychology; U. of CT, MA; Columbia, MA. U. of CT, Robert College (Istanbul, Turkey). IN U., CCNY. English & Psychology teacher. Columbia, Economic Journalism teacher. *International Economic Letter*, Citibank, Editor. writer. *Newsweek*, Editor, writer. *BusinessWeek*, "Economic Diary" Editor, writer, current.

Kosner, Edward. *New York*. Editor & Publisher. B. 1937, NYC. CCNY, 1958, BA-English & History. *New York Post*, rewriteman, Asst City Editor, to 1963. *Newsweek*, "National Affairs" writer, to 1967; Gen Editor, to 1969; National Affairs Editor, to 1972; Asst Managing Editor, to 1972; Managing Editor, to 1975; Editor, to 1979. *New York*, Editor, to 1986; Editor & Publisher, current, 1986. Member, Exec Committee, ASME, 1977-86; President, 1984-86. Robert F. Kennedy Journalism Award, 1971; ABA Silver Gavel Award, 1971.

Kosterlitz, Julie. *National Journal*. Staff Correspondent. B. 1955, Chicago. U. of CA, Santa Cruz, 1979. History. *Williamette Week* (Portland, OR), business reporter, to 1980. Common Cause, to 1985. *National Journal*, staff correspondent, health & income security, current, 1985. *The Washington Monthly* Journalism Award, 1983.

Koten, John F. *The Wall Street Journal*. Chicago Bureau Chief. B. Kilteen, TX. Carleton College. AP-Dow Jones, 1977. *The Wall Street Journal*, Atlanta reporter, to 1980; Detroit, to 1984; Second Front's Marketing columnist, 1984; Chicago reporter, to 1988; Chicago bureau chief, current, 1989.

Kotlowitz, Alex. *The Wall Street Journal*. Reporter. B. 1955, New York. Wesleyan, Political Science. "MacNeil/Lehrer NewsHour," producer. NPR, reporter. Freelance, to 1984. *The Wall Street Journal*, reporter, current, 1984; on leave, current, 1989. Detroit Press Club Award for Magazine Reporting, 1980; George Polk Award, 1985; Robert F. Kennedy Journalism Award, 1988; Peter Lisagor Award, 1989.

Kozodoy, Neal. *Commentary*. Executive Editor. B. 1942, Boston, MA. Harvard, 1963, BA; Hebrew College, 1963; Columbia, 1966, MA. Woodrow Wilson Fellow, 1964-65; Danforth Fellow, 1965-67. *Commentary*, editorial staff member, current, 1966; Exec Editor, current, 1968. Library Jewish Studies, Editor, current, 1970.

Kraar, Louis. *Fortune*. Board of Editors Member. B. 1934, Charlotte, NC. U. of NC, 1956, History. Edward R. Murrow Fellow,

Council on Foreign Relations, 1968-69. *The Wall Street Journal*, reporter, 1956-58; Pentagon correspondent, to 1962. *Time*, Pentagon correspondent, to 1963; New Delhi bureau chief, to 1965; Bangkok bureau chief, to 1968; Asia correspondent, Singapore, to 1971. *Fortune*, Assoc Editor, Singapore, to 1974; Board of Editors member, current, 1975; Asian Editor, 1983-88. Overseas Press Club Citation, 1987.

Kraft, Scott. *Los Angeles Times*. Johannesburg Bureau Chief. B. 1955, Kansas City, MO. KS State U., 1977, Journalism & Economics. AP, writer, Jefferson City MO, 1977; writer, Kansas City, to 1979; Wichita correspondent, to 1980; national writer, to 1984. *Los Angeles Times*, national correspondent, to 1986; Nairobi bureau chief, to 1988; Johannesburg bureau chief, current, 1988. Top AP Reportorial Performance, AP Managing Editors Assoc, 1983; Peter Lisagor Award, Feature, Chicago Headline Club, 1985.

Kramer, Michael. *Time*. Special Correspondent. B. 1945, NYC. Amherst, 1967, Political Science; Columbia Law, 1970. *New York*, city political columnist, to 1976; Political Editor, 1979-87. *More*, Editor & Publisher, 1976-78. Berkeley Books, Publisher, 1978. *U.S.News & World Report*, chief political correspondent, 1987-88. *Time*, special correspondent, current, 1988. Overseas Press Club Award, Reporting from Central America, 1982. Co-author 2 books, including *"I Never Wanted To Be Vice-President of Anything,"* 1976.

Kramon, Glenn. *The New York Times*. Technology & Transportation Editor. B. 1953. Stanford, 1975, BA-Communications. *Kansas City Star*, copy editor/reporter. *San Francisco Examiner*, copy editor, 1977-79; Sunday News Editor, to 1984; Asst Business Editor, to 1986; Business Editor, to 1987. *The New York Times*, copy editor & business-health columnist, to 1989; Technology & Transportation Editor, current, 1989.

Kraus, Albert L. *The Journal of Commerce*. Editor Emeritus. B. 1920, NYC. Queens College (NY), 1941, BA-History; Columbia, 1942, Journalism. Nieman Fellow, 1954-55. *Journal-Bulletin* (Providence, RI), business & financial reporter, to 1956. *The New York Times*, business, financial, banking; asst to Financial Editor; Asst Financial Editor, to 1972. *Bond Buyer*, Sr VP, to 1978. *The Journal of Commerce*, Editorial Director; Editor, to 1987; Editor Emeritus, current, 1987.

Krauthammer, Charles. Washington Post Writers Group. Columnist. B. 1950, NYC. McGill U., 1970; Balliol College, Oxford, 1971, Political Science, Economics; Harvard Med, 1975, MD. MA Gen Hospital, Resident, Psychiatry, to 1977; Chief Resident, Psychiatric Consultation Services, to 1978. HEW, Dir, Div of Science, Alcohol, Drug Abuse & Mental Health Admin, to 1980. Speechwriter, VP Walter Mondale, to 1981. *Time*, contributor, current, 1983. *The New Republic*, Sr Editor, 1981-88. Washington Post Writers Group, columnist, current, 1985. Pulitzer Prize, Distinguished Commentary, 1987. Author *Cutting Edges*.

Kristof, Nicholas D. *The New York Times*. Beijing Bureau Chief. B. 1959, Chicago. Harvard, 1981, Government; Magdalen College, Oxford, Law (Rhodes Scholar). *The New York Times*, economic writer, to 1984; LA financial correspondent, 1984-85; Hong Kong bureau chief, to 1988; Beijing bureau chief, current, 1988.

Kristol, Irving. *The Public Interest*. Editor. *The National Interest*, Publisher. B. 1920, NYC. CCNY, 1940. US Army, to 1946. *Commentary*, Managing Editor, to 1952. *Encounter*, co-founder, Co-Editor, to 1958. *The Reporter*, Editor, to 1960. Basic Books, Inc, Exec VP, to 1969. *The Public Interest*, Co-Editor, 1965-88; Editor, current, 1988. *The National Interest*, Publisher, current. NYU, faculty member, current, 1969; prof, Social Thought, Grad School of Business Administration, current, 1979. American Enterprise Institute, Sr Fellow, current. Author 3 books, including *Reflections of a Neoconservative*, 1983.

Kriz, Margaret E. *National Journal*. Financial Correspondent. B. 1954, Chicago. U. of IL, Journalism; American U., MS-News Editorial. *Suburban Tribune* (*Chicago Tribune*), municipal reporter; county govt & courts reporter, 1976-79. Bureau of National Affairs, staff reporter; chemical regulations reporter; Asst Editor; special assgnmt. *National Journal*, financial correspondent, current. Author *Chemicals and the Community*, 1987.

Kronholz, June. *The Wall Street Journal*. Washington Deputy Bureau Chief. B. Pittsburgh. OH U., 1969, BS. National Endowment for the Humanities, Professional Journalism Fellow, U. of MI, 1974-75. *The Miami Herald*, intern, 1968; reporter, to 1974. *The Wall Street Journal*, Dallas reporter, to 1979; London reporter, to 1983; Boston bureau chief, to 1985; Hong Kong bureau chief, to 1987; DC deputy bureau chief, current, 1987.

Kucewicz, William. *The Wall Street Journal*. Editorial Writer & Editorial Board Member. B. Yonkers, NY. NYU, Economics, Politics.

NYU student newspaper, Editor-in-Chief. *The Public Interest*, Asst Editor, 1975-76. AP-Dow Jones, copyreader, 1975; reporter, London, to 1979. *The Wall Street Journal*, editorial writer, current, 1979; Editorial Board member, current, 1985. Overseas Press Club Citation, Excellence, 1981.

Kurtz, Howard. *The Washington Post*. New York Bureau Chief. B. 1953, Brooklyn, NY. SUNY, Buffalo, 1974, English; Columbia, 1975, MSJ. *The Record* (Hackensack, NJ), reporter, 1975-77. *The Washington Star*, reporter, to 1981. *The Washington Post*, urban affairs reporter, to 1984; Justice Dept reporter, to 1987; NY bureau chief, current, 1987. DC-MD Press Assn, 1st Prize, 1982; DC-Baltimore Newspaper Guild Front Page Award, 1982, '86.

Kuttner, Robert. *Washington Post* Writers Group. Economics Columnist. B. 1943, NYC. Oberlin, 1965, Government. Guggenheim Fellow, 1986-87. *The Village Voice*, DC Editor, to 1973. *The Washington Post*, national writer, to 1975. US Senate Banking Committee, Investigator, to 1978. *Working Papers*, Editor-in-Chief, to 1982. *The Boston Globe*, columnist, current, 1984. *BusinessWeek*, columnist, 1985-87. *The New Republic*, economic correspondent, 1982-88. *Washington Post* Writers Group, economics columnist, current, 1988. Author 2 books, including *The Economic Illusion*, 1984.

LaBarbera, Peter. *The Washington Times*. National Reporter. B. 1962, Chicago. U. of MI, 1985, BA-Political Science. *The Washington* (DC) *Inquirer*, reporter; Managing Editor, 1985-87. *The Washington Times*, business reporter, to 1988; national reporter, current, 1988.

Labaton, Stephen. *The New York Times*. Reporter. B. 1961, Queens, NY. Tufts, 1983, Philosophy & Political Science; Duke, 1986, JD; MA-Philosophy. *Newsday*, summer intern, 1981, 1982. *The New York Times*, summer intern, 1984; reporter, current, 1987. *The Washington Post*, summer intern, 1985.

Labich, Kenneth. *Fortune*. Associate Editor. B. Chicago. U. of San Francisco, BA. Columbia, MS. *Geo*, Senior Editor. *Newsweek*, General Editor. *Fortune*, Assoc Editor, current, 1983.

Laderman, Jeffrey M. *BusinessWeek*. Associate Editor. Rutgers; Columbia, MAJ. NJ newspapers, writer. *The Detroit News*, reporter, writer, to 1982. *BusinessWeek*, Markets & Investments Staff Editor, to 1985; Markets & Investments Editor, to 1988; Assoc Editor, current, 1988.

Lambro, Donald. *The Washington Times*, National Affairs Editor. B. Wellesley, MA. Boston U., Journalism. *The Boston Traveler*, reporter, to 1968. UPI, CT state legislature; DC correspondent. United Press Syndicate, DC columnist, current. *The Washington Times*, National Affairs Editor, current, 1987. AP Radio Network & Mutual Broadcasting System, commentator, current. Author 4 books, including *Land of Opportunity*; PBS-TV "Star Spangled Spenders."

Landro, Laura. *The Wall Street Journal*. Reporter. OH U., 1976, BSJ. McGraw-Hill World News, London, to 1977. McGraw-Hill Energy Newsletter Group, Asst Editor, to 1978. *BusinessWeek*, Staff Editor, to 1981. *The Wall Street Journal*, reporter, covering entertainment, cable & publishing. Gerald Loeb Award, Deadline Reporting, 1986.

Lapham, Lewis Henry. *Harper's*. Editor. B. 1935, San Francisco, CA. Yale, 1956, BA; postgrad, Cambridge, 1956-57. *San Francisco Examiner*, VA reporter, 1957-60. *New York Herald Tribune*, to 1962. USA-1 (NYC), author, Editor, 1962. *The Saturday Evening Post*, 1963-67. *Life*, writer, to 1970. *Harper's*, writer, 1967-70; Managing Editor, to 1975; Editor, current, 1975. PBS-TV, "Bookmark," creator, host, current, 1989. Author 2 books, including *High Technology and Human Freedom*, 1985.

Lappen, Alyssa A. *Forbes*. Writer. B. 1952, New Haven, CT. Tulane, 1974, English. *Phi Beta Kappa*. *The Western*, Editor, 1974-75. *The New Haven Register*, reporter, to 1977. *The Journal Of Electronics Purchasing and Distribution*, Managing Editor, 1978; *Forbes*, reporter/researcher, to 1981; Sr Reporter/Researcher, to 1983; reporter, to 1985; writer, current, 1985. Harvard Summer Poetry Prize, 1971.

Lardner, George, Jr. *The Washington Post*. National Reporter. B. 1934, Brooklyn, NY. Marquette, 1956, ABJ, 1962, MA. *The Worcester* (MA) *Telegram*, reporter, rewrite, night city desk, 1957-59. *The Miami Herald*, metro govt reporter, to 1963. *The Washington Post*, city staff, to 1964; local staff columnist, 1964-65; national reporter, current, 1966. Sigma Delta Chi National Reporting Award, Political Campaign Coverage, 1970; ABA Gavel Award Certificate of Merit, 1977; DC-Baltimore Newspaper Guild, Front Page Award, 1st Place, National Reporting, 1984.

Lau, Emily. *Far Eastern Economic Review*. Hong Kong Correspondent. B. 1952, Hong Kong. USC, 1976, BA-Broadcast Journalism; London School of Economics & Political Science, 1982, MS-International Relations. *South China Morning Post*, Hong Kong reporter, 1976-78. Hong Kong TV broadcasts, News Dept, reporter, Producer, to 1981. BBC, London, TV Current Affairs Dept, Asst Producer, to 1984. *Far Eastern Economic Review*, Hong Kong correspondent, current, 1984.

Lawrence, Richard. *The Journal of Commerce.* Reporter. B. 1928, NYC. Rensselaer Polytechnic Institute, Communications Engineering. McGraw-Hill, 1954-58. *Financial Times*, to 1959. *Agence France Presse*, to 1960. *The Journal of Commerce*, reporter, current, 1961.

Lawrence, Steve. *Forbes.* Assistant Managing Editor. B. 1942, NYC. U. of CA, 1964, BA-Philosophy; Northwestern, 1966, MSJ. *The* (NY) *Daily News*, special projects, Asst Business Editor. *Dallas Times-Herald*, Exec Business Editor. *The New York Times*, Enterprise Editor, "Business Day," to 1984. Time Inc, Sr Editor, Magazine Devlpmt, to 1986. *Forbes*, Sr Editor, to 1987; Asst Managing Editor, current, 1987.

Lawson, Dominic. *The Spectator.* Deputy Editor. B. 1956, London, UK. Westminster School & Christchurch, Oxford. BBC, researcher, reporter, 1979-81. *Financial Times*, correspondent; columnist, to 1987. *The Spectator*, Deputy Editor, current, 1987. Wincott Financial Columnist of the Year, 1987. Author *Korchnoi-Kasparov*, 1983.

Ledeen, Michael A. *The American Spectator.* Contributor. B. 1941, LA, CA. Pomona College, 1962, BA-History; U. of WI, 1969 PhD-Philosophy. Washington U., instructor & asst prof, history, 1967-73. U. of Rome, visiting prof, history, to 1977. *The New Republic*, Rome correspondent, 1975-77. *The Washington Quarterly*, Exec Editor, to 1981. *The American Spectator*, contributor, 1980-81, current, 1986.

Lee, Mary. *Far Eastern Economic Review.* Editorial Manager. B. 1948, Singapore. U. of Singapore, 1970, English. World Press Institute Fellow, 1974; Stanford Journalism Fellow, 1984. *Singapore Herald*, education reporter, to 1971. *New Nation* (Singapore), society columnist, Women's Page Editor, to 1974. *Sunday Nation* (Singapore), asst to the Editor, columnist, 1974-75. *The Guardian* (UK), foreign news, Sub-Editor, to 1977. *Far Eastern Economic Review*, Hong Kong correspondent, to 1983; Peking correspondent, 1984-86; editorial manager, current, 1986.

Lehrer, James Charles. PBS-TV. "MacNeil/Lehrer NewsHour" Associate Editor & Co-Anchor. B. 1934, Wichita, KS. Victoria College, 1954, AA; U. of MO, 1956, BJ. US Marine Corps, to 1959. *Dallas Morning News*, reporter, to 1961. *Dallas Times Herald*, reporter, columnist, City Editor, to 1970. KERA-TV (Dallas), Exec Producer, correspondent, to 1972. S. Methodist U., creative writing instructor, 1967-68. PBS-TV, Public Affairs Coordinator, 1972-73; NPACT-WETA-TV (DC), correspondent, from 1973; PBS-TV, "MacNeil/Lehrer NewsHour" Assoc Editor, co-anchor, current. Columbia-Dupont Award; George Polk Award; Peabody Award; Emmy Award. Author 2 books, including *We Were Dreamers*, 1975; 1 play, "Chili Queen," 1987.

Leinster, Colin. *Fortune.* Associate Editor. Polytechnic of North London, Journalism. Newspaper reporter, London. *Life*, Vietnam correspondent. Freelance, 1974-84. *Fortune*, Assoc Editor, current, 1984.

Lelyveld, Joseph. *The New York Times.* Deputy Managing Editor. B. 1937, Cincinnati, OH. Harvard, 1958, BA-English History & Literature, *summa cum laude*, 1959, MA-American History; Columbia 1960, MSJ. Fulbright Grant, 1960-61, Burma. *The New York Times*, copyboy, to 1963; financial writer, 1963; metro staff, to 1965; foreign correspondent, Africa, to 1967; India bureau chief, to 1969; NY reporter, to 1972; Hong Kong bureau chief, 1973-74; DC reporter, columnist, to 1977; Deputy Foreign Editor, to 1980; South African correspondent, to 1983; writer, 1984; London bureau chief, to 1986; Foreign Editor, to 1989; Deputy Managing Editor, current, 1989. Page 1 Award; George Polk Memorial Award; Byline Award. Author *Move Your Shadow* (Pulitzer Prize, 1986).

Lemann, Nicholas. *The Atlantic.* National Correspondent. B. 1954, New Orleans, LA. Harvard, 1976, American History & Literature. *The Washington Monthly*, Managing Editor, to 1978; contributor, current. *Texas Monthly*, Assoc Editor, to 1979; Exec Editor, 1981-83. *The Washington Post*, reporter, to 1981. *The Atlantic*, national correspondent, current, 1983. Freelance, current.

LeMoyne, James. *The New York Times.* On Leave. B. 1951, Heidelberg, Germany. Harvard, 1975, BA-Social Studies, 1977, BA-Philosophy & Political Theory; London School of Economics, 1979, MA-20th Century European Diplomatic History. *The Washington Post*, London stringer, to 1981. *Newsweek*, Contributor to 1981; Assoc Editor, Central American reporter, to 1983. *The New York Times*, metro reporter, to 1984; San Salvador bureau chief, to 1989; on leave, current, 1989. Co-recipient NY Newspaper Guild Page 1 Award, 1982.

Lerner, Marc. *The Washington Times.* Foreign Editor. AP. *The Denver Post*. *The Washington Times*, National Editor, Business Editor, 1983-87; special projects, 1987; SE Asia correspondent, to 1989; Foreign Editor, current, 1989.

Lerner, Max. *New York Post*, Los Angeles Times Syndicate. Columnist. B. 1902, Minsk, Russia. Yale, 1923, AB-Government; Washington U., 1925, AM; Robert Brookings Grad School of Economics & Government, 1927, PhD. Ford Foundation Grant, 1963-64. *Encyclopedia of Social Sciences*, Editor, Managing Editor, to 1932. Sarah Lawrence College, Social Science Faculty member, to 1935. Wellesley Summer Institute, Faculty Chairman, 1933-35. National Emergency Council, Director, Consumers Division, 1934. Harvard, Govt Dept lecturer, to 1936; visiting prof, 1939-41. *The Nation*, Editor, to 1938. Williams College, Political Science prof, 1938-43. *PM* (NYC), editorial director, to 1948. *The New York Star*, columnist, to 1949. Brandeis, American Civilization prof, to 1973 (Dean, Grad School, 1954-56); Prof Emeritus, current, 1974. *New York Post*, columnist, current, 1949. Los Angeles Times Syndicate, columnist, current, 1949. US International U. (San Diego, CA), Distinguished Prof, Human Behavior, current, 1975. Notre Dame, Prof, American Studies, 1982-84. Author 14 books, including *Ted and the Kennedy Legend*, 1980.

Lerner, Michael Alan. *Newsweek.* Los Angeles Correspondent. B. 1958, NYC. Harvard, 1981, History & Literature. *The New Republic*, writer, to 1982. *Newsweek*, Assoc Editor, national affairs, to 1983; Paris-based correspondent, to 1986; LA correspondent, current, 1987. Page 1 Award, 1982.

Lescaze, Lee. *The Wall Street Journal.* Foreign Editor. Harvard, 1960, BA-General Studies. *The Washington Post*, copyboy, 1963; reporter, to 1967; Vietnam correspondent, to 1970; Hong Kong correspondent, to 1973; Foreign Editor, to 1975; National Editor, to 1977; NY bureau chief, to 1980; White House correspondent, to 1982; "Style" Asst Managing Editor, to 1983. *The Wall Street Journal*, editing & writing, 1983; NY News Editor, 1984; Asst Foreign Editor, to 1988; Deputy Foreign Editor, to 1989; Foreign Editor, current, 1989.

Levin, Doron P. *The New York Times.* Detroit Bureau Chief. B. 1950, Haifa, Israel. Cornell, 1972, History; Columbia, 1977, MSJ. *St. Petersburg Times*, police & business, reporter, 1977-80; Pittsburgh & Detroit reporter, 1987-88. *The Wall Street Journal*, automotive reporter, 1981; 1987; Pittsburgh & Detroit reporter, to 1988. *The New York Times*, business & financial reporter, 1988; Detroit bureau chief, current, 1988. Author *Irreconcilable Differences*, 1989.

Lewis, Anthony. *The New York Times.* "Abroad at Home" Columnist. B. 1927, NYC. Harvard, 1948, English. *The New York Times*, Sunday dept, deskman, 1948-1952; reporter, DC. 1955-64; London bureau chief, to 1971; "Abroad at Home" columnist, current, 1969. *Washington Daily News*, reporter, 1952-55. Heywood Broun Award, 1955; Pulitzer Prize, National Reporting, 1955, '63. Author 2 books, including *Portrait of a Decade*, 1964.

Lewis, Ephraim A. *BusinessWeek.* Senior Editor. Brooklyn College. *BusinessWeek*, Asst Marketing Editor, 1962-67; Minneapolis bureau manager, 1967; Marketing Editor, to 1969; Assoc Editor, to 1976; sr correspondent, McGraw-Hill World News, Sr Editor, current, 1976, govt, energy, books, sports business, *BusinessWeek* Top 1000, other scoreboards, personal business supplement & *BusinessWeek*/Harris polls.

Lewis, Flora. *The New York Times.* "Foreign Affairs" Columnist. B. LA, CA. UCLA, 1941, Political Science; Columbia, 1942, MS. Arthur D. Morse Fellow in Communications & Society, 1977. *Los Angeles Times*, reporter, 1941. AP, DC, NY, London, to 1946. Freelance, to 1954. McGraw-Hill, NY, Editor, 1955. *The Washington Post*, bureau chief, Bonn; London; DC; NY to 1966. Syndicated columnist, Paris, NY, to 1972. *The New York Times*, Paris bureau chief, to 1976; European diplomatic correspondent, Paris bureau chief, to 1980; "Foreign Affairs" columnist, current, 1980. Overseas Press Club Award, 1956; Award for Best Reporting, Foreign Affairs, 1960; Award for Distinguished Diplomatic Reporting, Georgetown School of Foreign Affairs, 1978; *Chevalier de la Legion d'Honneur*, 1981; National Press Club, 4th Estate Award, 1985; NY Women in Communications, Matrix Award for Newspapers, 1985; NYU, Elmer Holmes Bobst Award in Arts & Letters, 1987. Author 3 books, including *Europe: A Tapestry of Nations*, 1987.

Lewis, Paul M. *The New York Times.* United Nations Bureau Chief. B. 1937, London, UK. Balliol College, Oxford, 1959-61. *Financial Times*, Common Market correspondent, to 1967; Paris correspondent, to 1971; DC bureau chief, to 1976. *The New York Times*, economic correspondent, to 1987; UN bureau chief, current, 1987.

Light, Larry. *BusinessWeek.* Corporate Finance Department Editor. B. 1949. Lafayette College, 1971, BA-English; Columbia, 1974, MSJ. *The Camden* (NJ) *Courier-Post*, municipal reporter, 1974-75. *The Record* (Hackensack, NJ), business reporter, to 1976. *The Philadelphia*

Bulletin, state govt correspondent, to 1978. *Congressional Quarterly*, political & economics reporter, to 1983. *Newsday*, government reporter & General Editor, to 1988; business reporter & Editor, to 1989. *BusinessWeek*, Corporate Finance Department Editor, current, 1989.

Limpert, John A. *The Washingtonian*. Editor. B. 1934, Appleton, WI. U. of WI, 1959, Philosophy, Psychology & Pre-Law. Congressional Fellow, Hubert Humphrey, 1968. UPI, Minneapolis reporter, 1960-61; Regional Exec, St. Louis, to 1963, Detroit, to 1964. *Warren (MI) Progress*, Editor, to 1965. *San Jose Sunpapers*, Managing Editor, to 1967. *Washington (DC) Examiner*, Editor, to 1968. *The Washingtonian*, Editor, current, 1969. American Political Science Assn Award for Distinguished Reporting of Public Affairs, 1970; 4 National Magazine Awards; *Sigma Delta Chi* Award.

Lindberg, Tod. *Insight*. News Executive Editor. B. 1960, Syracuse, NY. U. of Chicago, 1982, AB-Political Science. *The Public Interest*, Asst Editor, to 1983; Managing Editor, to 1985. *The National Interest*, Exec Editor, to 1986. *Insight*, Sr Editor, Asst Managing Editor, news, to 1987; Exec Editor, news, current, 1987.

Lingeman, Richard. *The Nation*. Executive Editor. B. 1931, Crawfordshire, IN. Haverford, 1953, Sociology. *Monocle*, 1960-69. *The New York Times Book Review*, to 1975. *The Nation*, Exec Editor, current, 1978. Author 3 books, including *Don't You Know There's A War On?*

Lipman, Joanne. *The Wall Street Journal*. Advertising & Public Relations Reporter. B. 1961, New Brunswick, NJ. Yale, 1983, History. *The Wall Street Journal*, summer intern, 1982; real estate reporter, 1983-86, advertising & public relations reporter, current, 1986.

Lipsky, Seth. *The Wall Street Journal/Europe*. Editorial Page Editor & Editorial Director, International Editions. B. 1946, Harvard, 1968, BA-English Literature. US Army, 1969-70: *Army Digest*, Pentagon reporter; *Pacific Stars and Stripes*, Vietnam combat reporter. *Anniston (AL) Star*, reporter, 1968-69. *Far Eastern Economic Review*, Asst Editor, 1974-75. *The Wall Street Journal*, reporter, Detroit, to 1974; Asia correspondent, to 1976; Assoc Editor, Editorial Page, NY, 1980-82; Foreign Editor, to 1984; Sr Editor, 1984. *The Asian Wall Street Journal*, founding reporter, 1976-78; Managing Editor, to 1980. *The Wall Street Journal/Europe*, Editorial Page Editor, current; Editorial Director, International Editions, current, 1986.

Liu, Melinda. *Newsweek*. Asia Regional Editor. B. 1951, Minneapolis, MN. Harvard, 1973, Sociology, *magna cum laude*. Michael Rockefeller Traveling Fellow, 1973. Freelance, 1976-78. *Far Eastern Economic Review*, to 1979. *Newsweek*, Beijing bureau chief, to 1982; Gen Editor, NY, to 1983; Hong Kong bureau chief, to 1986; Asia Regional Editor, Hong Kong, current, 1986.

Lochhead, Carolyn E. *Insight*. Writer. B. 1955, St. Louis, MO. U. of CA, Berkeley, 1979, Rhetoric & Economics; Columbia, 1983, Journalism. *St. Francisville (LA) Democrat*, Editor, 1979-81. *The Daily Press* (Paso Robles, CA), reporter, to 1982. *Chain Store Age Executive*, to 1984. *Insight*, writer, NY, current, 1987. LA Press Assn, 1980-81; CA Newspaper Publishers Assn, 1st Place Features, 1982.

Loeb, Marshall. *Fortune*. Managing Editor. B. 1929, Chicago. U. of MO, 1950, Journalism. UP, foreign correspondent, Frankfurt, 1952-54. *St. Louis Globe Democrat*, reporter, to 1956. *Time*, writer; Business Editor; Nation Editor; Economics Editor, columnist, to 1980; *Money*, to 1986. *Fortune*, Managing Editor, current, 1986. CBS Radio Network, commentator, current. U. of MO Award, 1966; Gerald Loeb Award, 1974; John Hancock Award, 1974; Champion Media Award, 1981; National Magazine Award, 1988. Author *Marshall Loeb's Money Guide*, annual; co-author (with William Safire) *Plunging Into Politics*.

Lohr, Steve. *The New York Times*. London Economic Correspondent. Colgate, 1974; Columbia, MSJ. Binghamton Press, business & financial reporter. Gannett News Service, business & financial reporter. *The New York Times*, Copy Editor, financial desk, reporter, to 1981; Tokyo correspondent, to 1984; Manila bureau chief, to 1985; London economic correspondent, current, 1985.

Long, William R. *Los Angeles Times*. Rio de Janeiro Bureau Chief. B. 1941, Denver, CO. Peace Corps, trainee, MI State U., 1965; volunteer, Santiago, Chile, to 1967. *The San Diego Union*, city hall reporter, Baja reporter trainee, to 1970. AP, Chile reporter, to 1971; Foreign Copy Editor, to 1973; Sao Paulo correspondent, to 1974; News Editor, to 1975; Brazil correspondent, to 1976; Chile & Bolivia bureau chief, to 1977. *The Miami Herald*, Latin America correspondent (Miami), to 1979; Managing Editor, *El Miami Herald*, to 1981; South America correspondent, to 1984; Day City Editor, to 1983; chief of correspondents, to 1984. *Los Angeles Times*, Caribbean bureau chief (Miami), to 1988; Rio de Janeiro bureau chief, current, 1988. Inter-American Press Assn Tom Wallace Award, 1979; Maria Moors Cabot Award, 1983.

Loomis, Carol Junge. *Fortune*. Board of Editors Member. U. of MO, Journalism. Maytag Co, Editor, to 1954. *Fortune*, research assoc, to 1958; Assoc Editor, asst to Chief of Research, to 1968; Board of Editors Member, current, 1968. 2 Gerald Loeb Awards; John Hancock Award; Newspaper Guild of NY Page 1 Award; National Magazine Award for General Excellence; NY State CPA Society Excellence in Financial Reporting Award.

Lopez, Laura Jean. *Time*. South America Bureau Chief. B. 1957, Inglewood, CA. CA State U., 1979, Information & Communication Sciences. *Time*, Mexico City stringer, 1981-83; "World" writer, 1984; NY correspondent, to 1985; correspondent, Managua, Mexico City, to 1987; South America bureau chief, current, 1987.

Lowenstein, Roger. *The Wall Street Journal*. "Heard on the Street" Columnist. B. 1954, NYC. Cornell, 1976, History. *Times Herald* (Newport News, VA), 1976-78. *Daily Journal*, Caracas, Venezuela, political reporter, to 1979. *The Wall Street Journal*, reporter, to 1989; "Heard on the Street" columnist, current, 1989.

Ma, Christopher Yi-Wen. *U.S.News & World Report*. Managing Editor. B. 1950, Columbus, OH. Harvard, 1972, Philosophy & English; U. of CA, Berkeley, 1978, JD. Michael Clark Rockefeller Traveling Fellow, China; Churchill Fellow, International Relations, Princeton. FCC, legal staff. *Newsweek*, DC correspondent, 1979-85. *U.S.News & World Report*, Asst Managing Editor, to 1986; Deputy Managing Editor, to 1988; Managing Editor, current, 1988. Co-author (with William J. Cook) *Teleshock*.

Machan, Dyan. *Forbes*. Staff Writer. Kent State U., 1980, BSJ, *cum laude*. *Money Management Letter*, Managing Editor, 1982-85. *Institutional Investor*, Contributing Editor, 1983-85. *Financial World*, Assoc Editor, to 1986. *Forbes*, staff writer, current, 1986.

Mack, Toni. *Forbes*. Southwest Reporter. Rice U., BA-Fine Arts & English. Deloitte Haskins & Sells, accounting, to 1978. *Forbes*, researcher, to 1981; reporter to 1984; writer, to 1986; Southwest bureau manager, to 1988; SW reporter, current, 1988.

Mackenzie, Richard. *Insight*. Senior Writer. B. 1946, Brisbane, Australia. El Centro (Dallas), 1974, Journalism & Criminal Science. Australian newspapers & TV, 1965-70. Mirror Newspapers (Toronto), Copy Editor, Layout Editor, to 1971. *Dallas Times Herald*, reporter, feature writer, to 1976. Freelance, to 1981. *Sydney Morning Herald* (Australia), NY North American Syn Manager, to 1985. *Insight*, Sr Writer, current, 1985.

MacNeil, Robert B.W. PBS-TV. "MacNeil/Lehrer NewsHour" Executive Editor & Co-Anchor. B. 1931, Montreal. Carleton U., 1955, BA. CBC (Halifax, Nova Scotia), radio actor, 1950-52; radio/TV announcer, 1954-55. CFRA (Ottawa), announcer; news writer, 1952-54. Reuters, Sub-Editor, 1955-60. NBC-TV, London news correspondent, to 1963; DC, to 1965; NY, to 1967. BBC, to 1971; 1973-75. National Public Affairs Center for TV, Sr Correspondent, 1971-73. PBS-TV, "MacNeil/Lehrer Report," Exec Editor, co-anchorman, current, 1975; "MacNeil/Lehrer NewsHour," current, 1983. Dupont Award, 1977. Author 2 books, including *The Right Place At The Right Time*, 1982.

Madison, Christopher. *National Journal*. Foreign Policy Reporter. B. 1951, Brooklyn, NY. Northwestern, 1973, BA-English, 1974, MSJ. *Independent Register* (Libertyville, IL), reporter, to 1975. McGraw-Hill, DC energy reporter, to 1978. *Legal Times*, DC energy & environment reporter, to 1980. *National Journal*, energy reporter, to 1981; trade reporter, to 1984; foreign policy reporter, current, 1984.

Maggs, John. *The Journal of Commerce*. Chemicals Editor. B. 1962, NYC. Columbia, 1984, English/Political Science. Fairchild Publications, energy reporter, 1984-87. McGraw-Hill, Inc. reporter, nuclear energy newsletter, 1987. *The Journal of Commerce*, from 1987, energy reporter; chemicals reporter; Chemicals Editor, current.

Magnet, Myron. *Fortune*. Board of Editors Member. Columbia, BA, PhD; Cambridge, MA. Middlebury College (VT), teacher, Columbia, teacher, English & Political Theory. *Fortune*, freelance, 1980-82; Assoc Editor, to 1983; Board of Editors Member, current, 1983.

Magnier, Mark. *The Journal of Commerce*. West Coast Editor. B. 1958, NY. Columbia, 1981, Literature; Columbia, 1984, MSJ. International Dateline newsletter, Editor, 1982-84. *American Shipper*, NY Editor, 1984. *The Journal of Commerce*, transportation reporter, to 1986; international trade reporter, 1987; West Coast Editor, current, 1987. Cavior Organization Award, 1984; *The Journal of Commerce* Publisher's Award, 1986.

Magnuson, Ed. *Time*. Senior Writer. B. St. Cloud, MN. U. of MN, 1950, Journalism. *Minneapolis Tribune*, reporter; Asst City Editor, to 1960. *Time*, correspondent, to 1961; Sr Writer, current, 1961.

Mahar, Maggie. *Barron's.* Writer. B. 1949, Syracuse, NY. Yale, 1971, English; 1975, PhD. Yale, prof. English, 1975-82. Freelance, to 1986. *Barron's,* writer, current, 1986.

Maher, Tani M. *Financial World.* Staff Writer. B. 1962, Campinas, Sao Paulo, Brazil. The American U., 1984, International Business & Finance. *The World Development Report* (World Bank), researcher, 1984-86. *Financial World,* reporter/researcher, to 1989; staff writer, current, 1989.

Main, Jeremy. *Fortune.* Board of Editors Member. B. 1929, Buenos Aires, Argentina. Princeton, 1950, AB-Politics. Ford Foundation Fellow, 1971-72. US Army, 1951-53; *Pacific Stars & Stripes,* Tokyo & Korea. International News Service, DC, 1950-51; Mexico City bureau chief, 1953-54; Madrid bureau chief, to 1956; West Berlin, to 1958. *Time,* defense & space correspondent, to 1961; Paris staff, to 1965. *Money,* writer, 1972-80. *Fortune,* Assoc Editor, 1966-71; Board of Editors member, current, 1980, management & productivity. U of MO Business Journalism Award, 1982.

Malabre, Alfred Leopold. *The Wall Street Journal.* News Editor. B. 1931, NYC. Yale, 1952, BA. Poynter Fellow, 1976. Hartford Courant, Copy Editor, to 1958. *The Wall Street Journal,* reporter, Bonn bureau chief, Economics Editor, News Editor, & "Outlook" columnist, 1958-69; News Editor, current, 1969. Author 4 books, including *Beyond Our Means,* 1987.

Mallet, Victor. *Financial Times.* Middle East Correspondent. B. 1960, Bonn, West Germany. Oxford, 1978, English. Reuters, correspondent, 1981-86. *Financial Times,* Africa correspondent, to 1989; Middle East correspondent, current, 1989.

Malcolm, Andrew H. *The New York Times.* Assistant National News Editor. B. 1943, Cleveland, OH. Northwestern, 1966, BSJ, Political Science & History; Northwestern, 1967, MSJ. UPI, Detroit, reporter, summer, 1963. *Press-Scimitar* (Memphis), reporter, summer, 1964. *La Derniere Heure* (Brussels), reporter, summer, 1965. *The New York Times,* International Ed, Paris, summer, 1966; asst to Foreign Editor, to 1969; metro reporter, UN bureau, to 1970; national correspondent, Chicago, to 1974; San Francisco, to 1975; South Vietnam correspondent, 1975; Japan correspondent, to 1978; Toronto bureau chief, to 1982; Chicago bureau chief, to 1987; First Asst National News Editor, current, 1987. George Polk Memorial Award, 1973; Penney-MO Award, 1975; Page 1 Award of NY, 1976, '83. Author 4 books, including *This Far and No More,* 1987.

Mann, James. *Los Angeles Times.* Washington Writer. B. 1946, Albany, NY. Harvard, 1968, AB-Social Relations; U. of PA, nondegree program in International Economics & History of the Middle East, 1975. *Journal-Courier* (New Haven, CT), writer, to 1969. *The Washington Post,* writer, to 1972. *Philadelphia Inquirer,* reporter, to 1975. *The Sun,* Supreme Court & Justice reporter, to 1978. *Los Angeles Times,* Supreme Court reporter, to 1984; Peking bureau chief, to 1987; DC writer, current, 1987. 1st Place Award, Humor. DC-Baltimore Newspaper Guild, 1970; Watergate articles contributed to *Post's* Pulitzer Prize, 1972.

Mann, Paul. *Aviation Week & Space Technology.* Washington Bureau Chief. B. Canandaigua, NY. Albany State U. US Congress, staff member, 1977-80. *Military Science and Technology,* DC Editor, 1980. *Military Electronics,* DC Editor, 1980. *Aviation Week & Space Technology,* Sr Congressional Editor, to 1988; DC bureau chief, current, 1988.

Mansfield, Stephanie. *The Washington Post.* On Leave. B. 1950, Philadelphia. Trinity College (DC), 1972, BA-English. *Daily Mail* (London), 1972-74. *Daily Telegraph* (London), 1974-76. *The Washington Post,* "Food" section, 1976-78; metro reporter, 1980; "Style" reporter, current, 1980; on leave, 1989. *Vogue,* contributor, current.

Marcial, Gene G. *BusinessWeek.* Senior Writer & "Inside Wall Street" Columnist. B. 1942, Manila, Phillipines. U. of St. Tomas, Manila, 1966, BLiterature in Journalism; NYU, 1976, MPolitics. *The Wall Street Journal,* "Abreast of the Market" & "Heard on the Street" columnist, Sr Special Writer, 1974-81. *BusinessWeek,* "Inside Wall Street" columnist, current, 1981; Assoc Editor, 1981-88; Sr Writer, current, 1988.

Marin, Richard. *The Washington Times.* TV Critic. B. 1962, Toronto, Canada. McGill U., English; U. of Toronto, MA; Columbia, MSJ. *Harper's,* Asst Editor, 1986-87. *The Washington Times,* TV critic, current, 1987.

Markoff, John G. *The New York Times.* "Business Day" Reporter. B. 1949, Oakland, CA. Whitman College, 1971. Freelance technology writer, 1977-81. *Infoworld,* reporter, to 1983. *Byte,* Technical Editor, 1984-85. *San Francisco Examiner,* reporter, to 1988. *The New York Times,* "Business Day" reporter, current, 1988.

Marsh, David. *Financial Times.* Bonn Correspondent. B. 1952, Shoreham, UK. Queen's College, Oxford, BA-Chemistry. Reuters, London, Frankfurt, Brussels, Bonn, 1974-78. *Financial Times,* economics staff, to 1982; Paris correspondent, to 1986; Bonn correspondent, current, 1986.

Marshall, Tyler. *Los Angeles Times.* London Bureau Chief. B. 1941, Detroit. Stanford, 1967, Political Science. *Sacramento Bee,* 1964-65. UPI, San Francisco, 1968. McGraw-Hill World News, San Francisco, to 1971; Bonn, to 1974; London, to 1979. *Los Angeles Times,* New Delhi, to 1983; Bonn, to 1985; London bureau chief, current, 1985.

Martin, Bradley K. *Newsweek.* Tokyo Bureau Chief. B. 1942, Buffalo, NY. Princeton, 1964, History. Stanford Professional Journalism Fellow, 1982-83. *The Charlotte Observer,* reporter, 1969-74. *The Sun,* reporter, to 1977; Tokyo bureau chief, to 1980; New Delhi bureau chief, 1980; Beijing bureau chief, to 1982. *The Asian Wall Street Journal,* Tokyo bureau chief, to 1986. *Newsweek,* Tokyo bureau chief, current, 1986.

Martin, Jurek. *Financial Times.* Foreign Editor. B. 1942, UK. Hertford College, Oxford, 1963, Modern History. Sabbatical, U. of SC, 1981-82. *Financial Times,* foreign desk, 1966-68; DC correspondent, to 1970; NY bureau chief, to 1972; Foreign News Editor, London, to 1975; DC bureau chief, to 1981; Tokyo bureau chief, 1982-86; Foreign Editor, current, 1986. David Holden Award, British Press Awards, Best Resident Foreign Correspondent, 1984.

Martin, Richard. *Insight.* Writer. B. 1958, Jackson, MS. Yale, 1980, Literature. *Arkansas Times,* Assoc Editor, to 1983. *Globescan,* Contributing Editor, 1984. *Insight,* writer, current, 1985.

Mason, Todd. *BusinessWeek.* Dallas Bureau Manager. U. of WI, BA. *The Marshfield* (WI) *News Herald,* reporter. *The Midland* (MI) *Daily News,* reporter. *The Miami News,* business writer, to 1978. *The Fort Lauderdale News,* Business Editor, to 1982. *BusinessWeek,* stringer, correspondent (Ft. Lauderdale, FL), 1980-82; Dallas bureau manager, current, 1982.

Mathews, Jay. *The Washington Post.* Los Angeles Bureau Chief. B. 1945, Long Beach, CA. Harvard, 1967, Government, 1971, MA-East Asian Studies. AP, intern, NY, 1966. US Army, to 1969. *The Washington Star,* intern, 1970. *The Washington Post,* metro reporter, to 1975; Asst Foreign Editor, to 1976; Hong Kong bureau chief, to 1979; Peking bureau chief, to 1980; LA bureau chief, current, 1981. National Education Reporting Award, 1983. Co-author (with Linda Mathews), *One Billion: A China Chronicle,* 1983.

Matlack, Carol. *National Journal.* Labor & Technology Correspondent. *Arkansas Gazette,* DC correspondent; DC bureau chief, to 1987. *National Journal,* labor & technology correspondent, current, 1987.

Matusow, Barbara. *The Washingtonian.* Senior Writer. B. Philadelphia. Penn State. French. TV Editor. Producer, 1968-78. Freelance writer, to 1985. *Washington Journalism Review,* Sr Editor, to 1987. *The Washingtonian,* Sr Writer, current, 1987. Author *The Evening Stars,* 1983.

Maxa, Rudy. *The Washingtonian.* Senior Writer. B. 1949, Cleveland, OH. Ohio U., 1971, BSJ. *The Washington Post,* reporter, 1971-83. *The Washingtonian,* Sr Writer, current, 1983. Author 2 books, including *Public Trust, Private Lust,* 1977.

May, Clifford. *The New York Times.* Political Correspondent. B. 1951, NYC. Sarah Lawrence, 1973, BA-Russian; Columbia, 1975, MSJ, 1975, MA-International Affairs. *The Record* (Hackensack, NJ), reporter, 1975. *Newsweek,* Assoc Editor, to 1977. Hearst Newspapers, roving foreign correspondent, to 1978. *Geo Magazine,* Sr Editor, to 1980. *The New York Times,* Science Editor, Sunday *Magazine,* to 1983; Africa correspondent, to 1985; domestic correspondent, to 1987; political correspondent, current, 1987.

May, Todd Jr. *Fortune.* Chief Economist & Board of Editors Member. Northwestern. Econometric Institute. Economic Analyst, Department Head, to 1952. Union Carbide, Assoc Economist, Economist, 1960-69. Economic Advisory Board member, US Secretary of Commerce, 1967-68. *Fortune,* Assoc Editor, 1952-60; Assoc Economist, 1969; Board of Editors, current, 1972; Chief Economist, current, 1980.

Maynes, Charles William. *Foreign Policy.* Editor. B. 1938, Huron, SD. Harvard, 1960, History. Rhodes Scholar, 1960. UN, foreign service officer, Laos, USSR, 1962-70. US Congress, legislative asst, to 1972. Carnegie Endowment for International Peace, Secretary, to 1977. International Organization Affairs, Asst Sec of State, to 1980. *Foreign Policy,* Editor, current. Olive Branch Award, Outstanding Magazine Coverage of Nuclear Arms Race, 1983.

MediaGuide

McCarthy, Colman. *The Washington Post.* Columnist. B. 1938, Old Brookville, NY. Spring Hill College (Mobile), AL, 1960, BS-English. GA farm worker, to 1966. Office of Economic Opportunity, to 1969. *The Washington Post,* editorial page staff, current, 1969; columnist, current. Faith & Freedom Award, 1970; Journalism Award, Legal Aid Society, 1971. Author *Disturbers of the Peace;* co-author *In the Name of Profit.*

McCarthy, Michael J. *The Wall Street Journal.* Reporter. B. 1962, St. Louis, MO. St. Louis U., 1984, Communications & Political Science. *St. Louis Globe-Democrat,* Copy Editor, 1984. *The Wall Street Journal,* news asst. to 1986; reporter, current, 1987.

McCartney, Robert J. *The Washington Post.* Central European Bureau Chief. B. 1953, Evanston, IL. Amherst College, 1975, American Studies, *magna cum laude. The Wall Street Journal,* Boston reporter, to 1976. *The International Daily News,* Business Editor, Rome, to 1978. AP-Dow Jones News Service, Rome correspondent, to 1980. AP, Rome correspondent, to 1982. *The Washington Post,* Asst Foreign Editor, DC, to 1983; Mexico City/Central America bureau chief, to 1986; Central European bureau chief, Bonn, current, 1986.

McCaslin, John. *The Washington Times.* Justice Department Correspondent. B. 1957, Alexandria, VA. Old Dominion U., 1980, Speech Communications & Journalism. KOFI radio (Kalispell, MT), News Director, to 1982. KJJR & KBBZ-FM (Kalispell), News Director, to 1984. UPI, correspondent, to 1984. *The Washington Times,* White House correspondent, to 1985; Justice Dept correspondent, current, 1985.

McCormick, John P. *Newsweek.* Deputy Chicago Bureau Chief. B. 1950, Dubuque, IA. Northwestern, 1972, Political Science & Journalism. *Chicago Daily News,* editorial asst, 1971. *Dubuque Telegraph Herald,* reporter & columnist, 1972-82. *Newsweek,* Chicago correspondent, 1982-84; deputy Chicago bureau chief, current, 1985.

McDaniel, Ann. *Newsweek.* Justice Department Correspondent. B. 1955, Charlottesville, VA. Vanderbilt, 1977, Political Science; Yale Law, 1983, MS. *Dallas Times Herald,* 1977-83. *Newsweek,* Justice Dept correspondent, current, 1984.

McGrory, Mary. *The Washington Post,* Universal Press Syndicate. Columnist. B. Boston, MA. Emmanuel College. Elijah Parish Lovejoy Fellow, 1985. *The Boston Herald,* 1947. *The Washington Star,* book reviewer, to 1954; national commentator, columnist, to 1981. Universal Press Syndicate, columnist, current, 1960. *The Washington Post,* columnist, current, 1981. George Polk Memorial Award, 1963; Pulitzer Prize, Commentary, 1975.

McGurn, William. *National Review.* Washington Bureau Chief. B. 1958, Camp Pendleton, CA. U. of Notre Dame, 1980, BA-Philosophy; Boston U., 1981, MSJ. *The American Spectator,* Asst Managing Editor, 1981-83. *This World,* Managing Editor, to 1984. *The Wall Street Journal/Europe,* Editorial Features Editor, to 1986. *The Asian Wall Street Journal,* Deputy Editorial Page Editor, to 1989. *National Review,* DC bureau chief, current, 1989. Editor *Basic Law, Basic Questions,* 1988.

McIntyre, Douglas. *Financial World.* President & Publisher. B. 1955, Erie, PA. Harvard, 1977, Religion. Time Inc, circulation, 1977; edit, 1977; marketing, to 1979; strategic planning, to 1980. *Penthouse,* asst to President, 1981. Veronis & Suhler, assoc, 1982. *Financial World,* Gen Manager, to 1983; President, Publisher, current, 1983.

McKillop, Peter. *Newsweek.* Acting New York Bureau Chief. B. 1957, Carthage, Tunisia. Wesleyan U., 1981, African Studies. *Paterson (NJ) News,* reporter, to 1984. *Newsweek,* correspondent, 1985; acting NY bureau chief, current, 1987.

McLaughlin, John. *National Review.* Washington Editor. Boston College, 1951, BA, 1952, MA-Philosophy, 1961, MA-English; Stanford, 1963, Communications; Columbia, 1967, PhD-Communications. Fairfield U. (CT), Director of Communications & educator, 1960-63. *America,* Assoc Editor, 1967-70. ABC-TV, consultant, 1969. Senate candidate, 1970. Special asst to the President, to 1974. McLaughlin & Co, Communications Consultants, President, to 1979. "The McLaughlin Group," moderator, current. "One on One," host & Producer, current. NPR, NBC Radio Network, CNBC-TV, commentator, current. *National Review,* DC Editor, current. Excellence in Journalism Award, Catholic Press Assn, 1970.

McManus, Doyle. *Los Angeles Times.* National Security/Foreign Policy Reporter. B. 1953, San Francisco. Stanford, 1974, History. Fulbright Scholar, U. of Brussels, 1975. UPI, foreign correspondent, 1975-78. *Los Angeles Times,* Los Angeles, to 1979; Beirut, to 1981; NY, to 1983; national security & foreign policy reporter, current, 1983. Co-recipient (with Robert C. Toth) Edwin M. Hood Award, 1986; Weintal Prize, 1986. Author *Free At Last,* 1981; co-author (with Jane Mayer) *Landslide,* 1988.

McManus, Jason. Time, Inc. Editor-in-Chief. B. 1934, Mission, KS. Davidson College, 1956, BA; Princeton, 1958, MPA; postgrad Oxford, 1958-59 (Rhodes Scholar). *Time,* Common Market bureau chief, Paris, 1962-64; Assoc Editor, to 1968; Sr Editor, to 1975; Asst Managing Editor, to 1978; Exec Editor, to 1983; Time, Inc, Corporate Editor, to 1985; *Time,* Managing Editor, to 1987; Time, Inc, Editor-in-Chief, current, 1987.

Mecham, Michael R. *Aviation Week & Space Technology.* Congressional Editor. B. 1946, LA, CA. Claremont Men's College, 1968, BA-Political Science; American U., 1979, MA-Communications. *Healdsburg (CA) Tribune,* reporter, editor, 1968-78. Gannett News Service, congressional correspondent, 1979-87. *Aviation Week & Space Technology,* Congressional Editor, current, 1987.

Meehan, John. *BusinessWeek.* Money & Banking Department Editor. B. 1952, CCNY, 1974, BS; Columbia, 1980, MS. *The Record* (Middletown, NY), reporter, 1974-76. *The Record* (Hackensack, NJ), reporter, to 1979. AP, Paris financial correspondent, 1981-84. *International Herald Tribune,* NY financial correspondent, to 1989. *BusinessWeek,* Department Editor, Money & Banking, current, 1989.

Meisels, Andrew. *The Washington Times & The* (NY) *Daily News.* Israel-based Correspondent. B. 1933, Budapest, Hungary. CCNY, 1955, English. AP, NJ & NY, newsman, to 1963. ABC-TV News, Israel correspondent, to 1982. Satellite News Channel, Israel correspondent, to 1983. *The* (NY) *Daily News,* Israel-based correspondent, current, 1985. *The Washington Times,* Israel-based correspondent, current, 1985. Overseas Press Club Award, Best Radio Spot News Reporting from Abroad, 1974. Author 2 books, including *Six Other Days;* contributor *Lightning Out of Israel.*

Meisler, Stanley. *Los Angeles Times.* Washington Reporter. B. 1931, NY. CCNY, 1952, English Literature; grad work, U. of CA, African Studies. AP, New Orleans, DC, 1954-64. *Los Angeles Times,* Nairobi, Mexico City, Madrid, Toronto, Paris, to 1988; DC reporter, current, 1988.

Melloan, George. *The Wall Street Journal.* Deputy Editorial Page Editor & "Business World" Columnist. B. Greenwood, IN. Butler U. (IN), BSJ. *The Wall Street Journal,* copyreader, 1952; reporter; "Page One" editing staff; Editor, "Business" column; Atlanta & Cleveland bureau manager; London correspondent, to 1970; Editorial writer, current, 1970; Deputy Editor, Editorial Page, current, 1973; "Business World" columnist, current, 1987. Gerald Loeb Award, Distinguished Business & Financial Journalism Commentary, 1982; Inter-American Press Assn Daily Gleaner Award, 1983, '87. National Conference of Editorial Writers, member. Co-author (with Joan Melloan) *The Carter Economy,* 1978.

Mendes, Joshua. *Fortune.* Personal Investing Columnist. B. 1962, NYC. Dartmouth, 1984, English Literature. *Fortune,* personal investing columnist, current, 1984.

Methvin, Eugene Hilburn. *Reader's Digest.* Washington Senior Editor. B. 1934, Vienna, GA. U. of GA, 1955, BAJ. US Air Force, 1955-58. *The Vienna (GA) News,* 1940-51. *Constitution,* reporter, 1952. *Washington Daily News,* reporter, 1958-60. *Reader's Digest,* DC editorial office from 1960, writer, Assoc Editor; Sr Editor, DC, current. Sigma Delta Chi National Award, Public Service, Magazine Reporting, 1965. Author 2 books, including *The Rise of Radicalism,* 1973.

Meyer, Cord. North America Syndicate. Foreign Affairs Columnist. B. 1920. Yale, 1942, BA, *summa cum laude;* Harvard, Society of Fellows, 1946-47, '49-51. US Marines, 1942-45, Bronze Star, Purple Heart, Presidential Unit Citation. Special asst to Harold Stassen as member US Delegation to Founding Conference of UN, 1945. United World Federalists, President, 1947-49. CIA, 1951-67; Asst Deputy Director for Plans, to 1973; Chief of Station, London, to 1976 (3 Distinguished Intelligence Medals). North America Syndicate, foreign affairs columnist, current, 1978. Georgetown, lecturer, 1982-85. Special Weintal Award, Foreign Affairs Column, 1986. Author 3 books, including *Facing Reality,* 1980.

Meyerson, Adam. *Policy Review.* Editor. B. 1953, Philadelphia. Yale, 1974, History, Arts & Letters. *The American Spectator,* Managing Editor, to 1977; Sr Editor, current. *The Wall Street Journal,* editorial writer, to 1983. *Policy Review,* Editor, current, 1983. Co-Editor (with David Asman) *The Wall Street Journal on Management.*

Michaels, James Walker. *Forbes.* Editor. B. 1921, Buffalo, NY. Harvard, 1943, Economics, *cum laude.* WWII, served India & Burma. State Dept. UPI, New Delhi bureau manager. *Buffalo Evening News, Forbes,* 1954-57; Managing Editor, to 1961; Editor, current, 1961.

Miller, Alan C. *Los Angeles Times.* Political Reporter. B. 1954, NYC. Wesleyan U., 1976, English; U. of HI, 1978, MA-Political Science. *The Times Union* (Albany, NY), govt reporter, 1978-80. *The Re-*

cord (Hackensack, NJ), political reporter, to 1986. *Los Angeles Times*, political reporter, current, 1987. NY State AP Award, 3rd Place, 1981; NY State Publishers Award, 1st Place, 1981; NJ Press Assn. 2nd Place, 1982; NJ Press Assn Citation, 1983.

Miller, Ericka. *The Washingtonian.* Assistant Editor. B. 1964, DC. Georgetown, 1987, English. *The Washingtonian*, Asst Editor, current, 1987.

Miller, Gay S. *The Wall Street Journal.* Markets Group News Editor. B. 1952, NYC. Yale, 1974. BA-Literature. *Milford* (CT) *Daily Citizen*, reporter, 1974-75. *New Haven Journal-Courier*, reporter, 1975. *The Wall Street Journal*, Pittsburgh reporter, to 1979; NY reporter, to 1981; editing assgnmts, Market Group News Editor, current, 1982.

Miller, Judith. *The New York Times.* Deputy Media Editor. B. 1948, NYC. Barnard College, 1969, BA-Economics; Center for European Studies, U. of Brussels; Princeton, 1972, MA. NPR, foreign affairs, national security specialist. *The Progressive*, DC correspondent, to 1977. Freelance, current. *The New York Times*, DC reporter, to 1983; Cairo bureau chief, to 1985; Paris correspondent, to 1986; DC deputy bureau chief, to 1988; Deputy Media Editor, current, 1989.

Miller, Marjorie. *Los Angeles Times.* Mexico City Bureau Chief. B. 1956. U. of CA, Santa Cruz, 1977, BA-American Studies with honors. *Los Angeles Times*, intern, LA, 1978; writer, San Diego County edition, 1983-85; San Salvador bureau chief, to 1988; Mexico City bureau chief, current, 1988. AP, Mexico City, 1979-80. *San Jose Mercury News*, 1981. *San Diego Union*, staff writer, to 1983.

Miller, Matt. *The Asian Wall Street Journal.* Reporter. Macalester College (St. Paul, MN), BA-Asian Studies; U. of Philippines. *Asia Travel Trade Magazine*, Deputy Editor. Freelance photographer, journalist. *The Asian Wall Street Journal*, Hong Kong reporter, 1981-85; New Delhi reporter, to 1988; Phillipines reporter, current, 1988. Journalist of the Year, Hong Kong Newspaper Society, 1984.

Miller, Michael W. *The Wall Street Journal.* Computer Correspondent. B. 1962, NYC. Harvard, 1984, English. *The Wall Street Journal*, intern, summer 1983; San Francisco computer industry correspondent, 1984-86; NYC M & A correspondent, to 1987; computer correspondent, current, 1987.

Minard, Lawrence. *Forbes.* Managing Editor. B. 1949, Seattle, WA. Trinity College (Hartford, CT), Economics. *Forbes*, reporter/researcher, 1974-75; reporter, writer, to 1978; special economic correspondent, Far East, 1978; European bureau manager, to 1983; West Coast/Asia bureau manager, to 1985; Asst Managing Editor, to 1986; Deputy Managing Editor, to 1989; Managing Editor, current, 1989. Gerald Loeb Award, Distinguished Economic & Financial Journalism, 1976. Editor *Forbes Numbers Game*.

Mitchell, Andrea L. NBC-TV News. "NBC Nightly News" White House Correspondent. B. 1946, NYC. U. of PA, 1967, BA. KYW Newsradio (Philadelphia), reporter, 1967-76. KYW-TV, political correspondent, 1972-76. WTOP-TV (DC), energy correspondent, to 1978. NBC-TV News, DC, to 1981; "NBC Nightly News" White House correspondent, current, 1981. Sigma Delta Chi, 1975; Women in Communications, Communicator of Year Award, 1976; AP Public Affairs Reporting Award, 1976; AP Broadcast Award, 1977.

Molotsky, Irvin. *The New York Times.* Congressional Correspondent. B. 1938, Camden, NJ. Temple, 1960, Political Science. *The Philadelphia Inquirer*, copyboy, 1956-60. *The Trentonian*, reporter, Editor, to 1963. *Newsday*, Editor, to 1967. *The New York Times*, reporter, Editor; congressional correspondent, current, 1967. Author *The Great Mail Order Bazaar*.

Monaghan, Nancy C. *USA Today.* Managing Editor. City Newspapers (Rochester, NY), Metro Editor, 1973-75. *Democrat And Chronicle* (Rochester, NY), legal affairs reporter; Metro Editor, 1977-82. *USA Today*, National Editor, to 1983; Managing Editor, current, 1983. NY State Press Assoc Award, 1973, '74, '75; Women in Communications, Matrix Award, 1981; NY State AP Award, 1981, '82.

Monroe, Bill. *Washington Journalism Review.* Editor. B. 1920, New Orleans, LA. Tulane, 1942, Philosophy. UPI, 1941-42. WNOE Radio (New Orleans), News Director, 1946-49. *New Orleans Item*, Assoc Editor, to 1956. WDSU-TV (New Orleans), News Director, to 1961. NBC-TV News, bureau chief, to 1969; "Today" DC Editor, to 1976; "Meet The Press" Exec Producer & moderator, to 1986. *Washington Journalism Review*, Editor, current, 1987. Peabody Award, 1972; Paul White Award (RTNDA), 1976.

Montalbano, William D. *Los Angeles Times.* Rome Bureau Chief. B. 1940, NY. Rutgers, 1960, BA-English; Columbia, 1962, MSJ. *The Star-Ledger* (Newark, NJ), reporter, to 1963. *Quincy* (MA) *Patriot-Ledger*, reporter/Editor, to 1963. *Buenos Aires Herald*, reporter, Editor, to 1965. UPI, NY Cables Desk, to 1967. *The Miami Herald*, Latin

America correspondent, sr correspondent, Projects Editor, founding Peking bureau chief, chief of correspondents, to 1983. *Los Angeles Times*, founding El Salvador bureau chief, to 1984; Buenos Aires bureau chief, to 1987; Rome bureau chief, current, 1987. Cabot Prize, Ernie Pyle, Overseas Press Club. Co-author 3 books.

Moody, John. *Time.* Central America Bureau Chief. B. 1953, Pittsburgh, PA. Cornell, 1975, Industrial & Labor Relations. UPI, Pittsburgh, NY; Moscow bureau chief, Paris bureau chief, to 1982. *Time*, Eastern Europe bureau chief, Bonn; NY writer; Central America correspondent, to 1988; Central America bureau chief, current, 1988.

Moore, Charles. *The Spectator.* Editor. B. 1956, Hastings, UK. Trinity College, Cambridge, History. *Daily Telegraph* (UK), editorial staff, 1979-81; leader writer, to 1983. *The Spectator*, Asst Editor, political columnist, to 1984; Editor, current, 1984. PPA Editor of the Year, 1988. Editor *The Church in Crisis*, 1986.

Moore, Molly E. *The Washington Post.* National Reporter. Georgetown, 1978, BA-American Government. *The Lake Charles* (LA) *American Press*, reporter, 1972-78. *The New Orleans Times-Picayune*, reporter, to 1981. *The Washington Post*, local & state reporter; national reporter, current, 1981.

Moore, W. John. *National Journal.* Staff Correspondent. B. 1950, Evanston, IL. Amherst College, 1972, History. *Coal Daily*, Editor, 1976-78. *Energy User News* (Fairchild Publications), DC reporter, to 1981. *Legal Times*, Assoc Editor, to 1986. *National Journal*, staff correspondent, current, 1986.

Mordoff, Keith. *Aviation Week & Space Technology.* Bonn Bureau Chief. B. 1956, Oakland, CA. San Jose State U., 1979, Aeronautical Operations. General Dynamics-Convair Division, flight test engineer, 1979-81. *Aviation Week & Space Technology*, Engineering Editor, to 1987; Bonn bureau chief, current, 1987. Co-recipient Jesse H. Neal Award, 1984.

Morgan, Dan. *The Washington Post.* National Reporter. B. 1937, NYC. Harvard, 1958, BA-English. *The Middleton* (CT) *Press*, reporter. *The Washington Post*, from 1963; city reporter; foreign correspondent; Sunday "Outlook" Editor; national reporter, current. Gerald Loeb Award; Champion Media Award; Hancock Award. Author *Merchants of Grain*, 1979.

Morgenson, Gretchen. *Forbes.* Senior Editor. B. 1956, State College, PA. Saint Olaf College (Northfield, MN), BA-History & English. *Vogue*, Asst Editor, NY, 1976-81. Dean Witter, stockbroker, to 1984. *Money*, writer, to 1986. *Forbes*, Assoc Editor, to 1988; "Forbes Informer" Editor, current; Sr Editor, current, 1988. Co-author (with Barbara Lee) *The Woman's Guide To The Stock Market*.

Morley, Jefferson M. *The Nation.* Washington Editor. B. 1958, NYC. Yale, 1980, History. *Worthington* (MN) *Globe* reporter, summer 1978. *Minneapolis Tribune*, reporter, summer 1979. *The Washington Post*, reporter, summer 1981. *Foreign Policy*, editorial asst, 1981. Asst to Bruce Cameron, human rights lobbyist, to 1982. *Harper's*, Asst Editor, 1983. *The New Republic*, Assoc Editor, to 1987. *The Nation*, DC Editor, current, 1987.

Morrison, David C. *National Journal.* National Security Correspondent. B. 1953, Minneapolis, MN. Columbia, 1978, History; Columbia, 1982, MSJ. Center for Defense Information, Sr Analyst, 1982-83. Freelance, current, 1976. *National Journal*, national security reporter, current, 1985. Olive Branch Award, 1987. Contributor 2 books, including *Outer Space — A Source of Conflict?* 1988.

Morrison, Donald. *Time.* Special Projects Editor. B. 1946, Alton, IL. U. of PA, 1968, Political Science; London School of Economics, 1970, M.Sc. *The Evening Telegraph* (Alton, IL), reporter, 1965-67. *The Daily Pennsylvanian* (U. of PA), Editor-in-Chief, to 1968. *Time*, reporter, to 1970; writer, to 1974; Assoc Editor, to 1978; Sr Editor, to 1988; Special Projects Editor, current, 1988. Editor & co-author 2 books, including *The Winning of the White House*, 1988.

Morrison, James. *The Washington Times.* London-based Correspondent. *Alexandria Gazette. The Washington Star. The Washington Times*, foreign desk reporter, to 1987; London-based correspondent, current, 1987.

Morrison, Mark. *BusinessWeek.* Assistant Managing Editor. U. of TX. *The Houston Post*, reporter, to 1974. *BusinessWeek*, correspondent, Houston, to 1978; Chicago bureau manager; Sr Editor, corporate strategies, management, marketing, people, to 1988; Asst Managing Editor, current, 1988.

Morrocco, John D. *Aviation Week & Space Technology.* Military Editor. B. 1952, Providence, RI. Boston College, 1974, History; London School of Economics & Political Science, 1976, MA-International History. *U.S.News & World Report*, Book Division, writer, 1980-82.

Boston Publishing, writer, to 1985. *Defense News*, writer, to 1986. *Investor's Daily*, aerospace & defense writer, 1986. *Aviation Week & Space Technology*, Military Editor, current, 1986. Author 4 books, including *Rain of Fire*, 1985.

Mortimer, Edward. *Financial Times*. Assistant Foreign Editor. B. 1943, Burford, UK. Balliol, Oxford, 1962, History. Fellow of All Souls, Oxford, 1965-72. Sr Carnegie Endowment, assoc, 1980-81. *The Times* (London), asst Paris correspondent, 1967-70; foreign specialist & leader writer, 1973-85. *Financial Times*, Asst Foreign Editor, current, 1987. Author 2 books, including *The World That FDR Built*, 1988.

Mosher, Lawrence. *National Journal*. Contributing Editor. B. 1929, LA, CA. Stanford, 1951, History, Journalism. *The Record* (Hackensack, NJ), reporter, 1958-59. *New York World-Telegram & The Sun*, reporter, to 1962. Copley News Service, foreign correspondent, Hong Kong, Beirut, to 1967. *The National Observer*, reporter, to 1977. Georgetown, Center for Contemporary Arab Studies, writer-in-residence, to 1979. *National Journal*, writer; Contributing Editor, current, 1979. *The Water Reporter* (newsletter), Publisher & Editor, current, 1984. Copley Ring of Truth Award, Best Foreign Reporting, 1965; National Wildlife Federation Communicator of the Year Award, 1982; George Polk Award, Environmental Reporting, 1986. Co-author 3 books, including *World Resources 1987*.

Mossberg, Walter S. *The Wall Street Journal*. International Economics Correspondent. *The Wall Street Journal*, reporter; deputy DC bureau chief, to 1987; Sr DC correspondent, to 1988; international economics correspondent, current, 1988.

Mudd, Roger H. PBS-TV. "MacNeil/Lehrer NewsHour" Commentator. B. 1928, Washington. DC & Lee U., 1950, AB; U. of NC, 1953, MA. Darlington School (Rome, GA), teacher, 1951-52. *Richmond News Leader*, reporter, 1953. WRNL (Richmond), News Director, to 1956. WTOP (DC), reporter, to 1961. CBS-TV, correspondent; Chief DC Correspondent, to 1980. NBC-TV News, broadcaster, to 1987. PBS-TV, "MacNeil/Lehrer NewsHour" commentator, current, 1987.

Munro, Ross H. *Time*. Bangkok Bureau Chief. B. 1941, Vancouver, Canada. U. of British Columbia, 1965, BA-Political Science; postgrad Stanford. *The Globe & Mail* (Toronto, Canada), 1967-71; DC bureau chief, to 1975; Peking bureau chief, to 1977. *Time*, Pacific, Asia economic correspondent, to 1980; Hong Kong bureau chief, to 1982; national security correspondent, DC, to 1985; South Asia bureau chief, New Delhi, to 1989; Bangkok bureau chief, current, 1989.

Murray, Alan S. *The Wall Street Journal*. Washington Economics Reporter. B. 1954, Akron, OH. U. of NC, Chapel Hill, 1977, English, highest honors; London School of Economics, 1980, MS-Economics, with distinction. Morehead Scholar, U. of NC, 1973-77; Luce Scholar, Japan, 1981-82. *The Chattanooga Times*, Business & Economics Editor, 1977-79. *Congressional Quarterly*, international economics reporter, 1980-81, '82-83. *Japan Economic Journal*, Tokyo reporter, 1981-82. *The Wall Street Journal*, DC economics reporter, current, 1983. Co-author (with Jeffrey Birnbaum) *Showdown At Gucci Gulch*, 1987.

Murray, Frank J. *The Washington Times*. White House Correspondent. B. 1938, NYC. FL newspapers, reporter. AP, reporter, 1967-70. *The Washington Star*, various editing slots, to 1978, 1979-85. *The Miami News*, City Editor, 1978-79. *Hollywood* (FL) *Sun-Tattler*, Managing Editor, 1986-87. *The Washington Times*, White House correspondent, current, 1987.

Nagorski, Andrew. *Newsweek*. General Editor. B. 1947, Edinburgh, Scotland. Amherst College, 1969. *Phi Beta Kappa*. *Newsweek*, writer, Assoc Editor, Gen Editor, to 1978 (*Newsweek International*); Asian Editor (International), Hong Kong bureau chief, to 1980; Moscow bureau chief, expelled 1982; Rome bureau chief, to 1985; Bonn bureau chief, to 1989; General Editor, current, 1989. Freelance, current. Co-recipient (with Peter Younghusband) Overseas Press Club Award, 1974; Overseas Press Club Award, Best Business Reporting from Abroad, 1978. Author *Reluctant Farewell*, 1985; contributor *Africa and the United States*, 1978.

Nasar, Sylvia. *Fortune*. Associate Editor. Antioch College, BA-Literature; NYU, MA-Economics. Institute for Economic Analysis, NYU, asst research scientist. Scientists' Institute for Public Information, Director of Energy Programs. Control Data Corp, Sr Economist. *Fortune*, Assoc Editor, current, 1983. Co-author (with Wassily Leontief, James Koo, Ira Sohn) *The Future of Nonfuel Minerals in the US and World Economy*, 1983.

Nash, J. Madeleine. *Time*. Senior Correspondent. B. 1943, NC. Bryn Mawr, 1965, Modern European History, *magna cum laude*. *Time*, clip girl, secretary, 1965-66; researcher-reporter, business, behavior, art, to 1970; stringer, to 1974; Midwest bureau correspondent, to 1988; Sr Correspondent, science & technology, current, 1988.

Freelance, 1970-74. Page 1 Award for Excellence in Journalism, 1981; Peter Lisagor Award for Magazine Features, 1982; Clarion Award, 1983; American Assn for the Advancement of Science, Magazine Award, 1988.

Nash, Nathaniel C. *The New York Times*. Business & Financial Reporter. *The New York Times*, from 1973; business/financial copy editor, to 1979; asst to business/financial news editor, to 1985; business/financial reporter, DC, current, 1985.

Navasky, Victor Saul. *The Nation*. Editor. B. 1932, NYC. Swarthmore College, 1954, AB-Political Science. *Phi Beta Kappa*; Yale, 1959, LLB. US Army, 1954-56. Guggenheim Fellow, 1974-75. Russell Sage Foundation, visiting scholar, to 1976. Ferris Prof of Journalism, to 1977. Special asst to Gov G. Mennen Williams (MI), 1959-60. *Monocle*, Editor, Publisher, to 1970. *The New York Times Magazine*, Manuscript Editor, to 1972. *The Nation*, Editor, current, 1978. American Book Award, 1982. Author 2 books, including *Naming Names*, 1980; co-author (with Christopher Cerf) *The Experts Speak*, 1984.

Neff, Robert. *BusinessWeek*. Tokyo Bureau Manager. B. 1947, St. Louis, MO. U. of MI, 1969, Political Science; U. of MO, 1974, MAJ. *Pacific Business News*, reporter, News Editor, Honolulu, 1975-76. *Kansas City Star*, reporter, to 1977. *BusinessWeek*, LA correspondent, to 1979; International Edition Editor, to 1988; Tokyo bureau manager, current, 1988. McGraw-Hill World News, Tokyo bureau chief, 1979-83. *International Management*, Managing Editor, London, to 1986. Inland Press Assn, First Place for Local Reporting, 1974.

Neilan, Edward. *The Washington Times*. Tokyo Bureau Chief. B. 1932, Torrance, CA. USC, 1954, BA-Journalism & Political Science; U. of London, Institute for International Education Scholarship, postgrad, summer 1956. Thomas Jefferson Fellow, Communications, U. of HI, 1973. *The Daily Trojan*, USC, Managing Editor, to 1954. *Evening Star-News* (Culver City, CA), Sports Editor, reporter, 1950-54; City Editor, reporter, to 1957. Consultant, Ministry of Information, Republic of Korea, to 1960. *The Christian Science Monitor*, contract Tokyo correspondent, 1960-62; Copley News Service, Tokyo correspondent, SE Asia bureau chief, 1962-70; diplomatic & national correspondent, DC, 1970-76. *The Asia Mail*, "American Perspectives on Asia & the Pacific," Editor, founder, 1976-82. The Alexandria Gazette Corporation, President, Editor & Publisher; columnist; CEO, 1979-82. *The Washington Times*, Asst Foreign Editor, 1982; Foreign Editor, to 1986; Tokyo bureau chief, current, 1986. Overseas Press Club Award, Excellence, 1974; UPI Award, 1981. Co-author (with Charles M. Smith) *The Future of the China Market*, 1974.

Nelson, John H. (Jack). *Los Angeles Times*. Washington Bureau Chief. B. 1929, Talladega, AL. GA State U., Economics; Harvard, Politics, History, Public Administration. Nieman Fellow. *Daily Herald* (Biloxi, MS), reporter, to 1949. *Constitution*, writer, to 1965. *Los Angeles Times*, Atlanta bureau chief, to 1970; DC investigative reporter, to 1975; DC bureau chief, current, 1975. PBS-TV, "Washington Week in Review", frequent appearances, current. Pulitzer Prize, 1960; Drew Pearson Award, Investigative Reporting, 1975. Author *Captive Voices — High School Journalism In America*; co-author 3 books.

Newport, John Paul, Jr. *Fortune*. Associate Editor. B. 1954, Fort Worth, TX. Harvard, 1977, English. *Fort Worth Star-Telegram*, reporter, 1980-82. *Fortune*, Assoc Editor, current. John Hancock Award, Excellence in Financial Journalism, 1981.

Noah, Timothy. *The New Republic*. Washington Correspondent. B. 1958, NYC. Harvard, 1980, English. *The New Republic*, writer, 1981-82. *The New York Times*, Asst Op-Ed Page Editor, to 1983. *The Washington Monthly*, Editor, to 1985. Freelance, to 1986. *Newsweek*, DC correspondent, to 1989. *The New Republic*, DC correspondent, current, 1989.

Nordland, Rod. *Newsweek*. Rome Bureau Chief. B. 1949, Philadelphia, PA. State, 1972, Journalism. *Philadelphia Inquirer*, investigative reporter, to 1978; Asia correspondent, Bangkok, to 1982; Central America correspondent, to 1984. *Newsweek*, Beirut & Cairo bureau chief, to 1986; Deputy Editor, roving foreign correspondent, to 1988; Sr Writer, 1986-89; Rome bureau chief, current, 1989; on leave, 1989. Pulitzer Prize, Local Reporting, 1978; George Polk Award, 1982; Thomas L. Stokes & Edward J. Meeman awards, 1982. Author *Names And Numbers*, 1978; editor, *The Watergate Files*, 1973.

North, David M. *Aviation Week & Space Technology*. Managing Editor. B. 1934, Oswego, NY. US Naval Academy, 1957, Engineering; Rensselaer Polytechnic Institute, 1965, MS-Communications. US Navy, fighter/attack pilot; PanAm, pilot. *Aviation Week & Space Technology*, since 1976. Transport Editor, Business Flying Editor, Senior Military Editor, DC bureau chief; Managing Editor, current, 1988.

Novak, Michael. *Forbes*. Columnist. B. 1933, Johnstown, PA. Stonehill College, 1956, AB; Harvard, 1965, MA; Gregorian U.

(Rome); Catholic U. Harvard, Teaching Fellow. Stanford, asst prof of Humanities, to 1968. SUNY, Old Westbury, prof, to 1973. Rockefeller Foundation, Humanities Program, to 1976. Syracuse, Ledden-Watson Distinguished Prof of Religion, 1976. *Catholicism in Crisis* & *This World*, co-founder. American Enterprise Institute, Resident Scholar, 1978-87; Director, social & political studies, current, 1987. Freelance, to 1987. Syndicated columnist, current. *National Review*, columnist, "Tomorrow & Tomorrow," to 1987; contributor, current. *Forbes*, columnist, current, 1989. George Washington Honor Medal, Freedoms Foundation, 1984; Award of Excellence, Religion in Media, 8th Annual Angel Awards, 1985; 1st US member Argentina National Academy of Sciences, Morals & Politics, 1985. Author 13 books, including *Will It Liberate*, 1986; co-author 2 books.

Novak, Robert D. S. North America Syndicate. "Inside Report" Columnist (with Rowland Evans Jr.). B. 1931, Joliet, IL. U. of IL, 1952, English. (Joliet, IL) *Herald-News*, reporter. (Champaign-Urbana, IL) *Courier*, reporter. *The Wall Street Journal*, reporter, 1958-61; Chief Congressional Correspondent, to 1963. *New York Herald-Tribune*, "Inside Report" columnist, to 1966. North America Syndicate, "Inside Report" columnist, current, 1966. *Evans-Novak Political Report*, co-author, current. *Evans-Novak Tax Report*, co-author, current. CNN, "Evans & Novak" & "Insiders," co-host, current. Host, "The Capitol Gang." Co-author 3 books, including (with Rowland Evans), *The Reagan Revolution*, 1981.

Nulty, Peter. Fortune. Associate Editor. B. 1943, NYC. Wesleyan U.; Columbia, MA-International Affairs. *Middle East Monitor*, Editor & *Middle East Journal*, Asst Editor, 1970-75. *Fortune*, reporter/researcher; Assoc Editor, current, 1976.

Oberdorfer, Don. *The Washington Post*. National Staff Writer. B. Atlanta, GA. Princeton, BA-International Affairs. Ferris Prof of Journalism, 1977. *The Charlotte Observer*, DC correspondent; local reporter. *The Saturday Evening Post*, Assoc Editor. Knight newspapers, national correspondent. *The Washington Post*, White House & diplomatic affairs correspondent, 1968-72; Tokyo correspondent, to 1975; national staff writer, current, 1977. Author *Tet!* 1971.

Oberfeld, Kirk E. Insight. Managing Editor. B. 1945, Orange, NJ. Kalamazoo College (MI), 1967, BA-Political Science; OH State U., 1971, MAJ. UPI, writer, summers 1970, '71. *Battle Creek* (MI) *Enquirer and News*, Editorial Page Editor, to 1973; City Editor, to 1975. *Philadelphia Bulletin*, NJ News Editor, to 1976; "Focus" Editor, to 1977; Director of News Technology, to 1978. *The Washington Star*, Principal Asst Metro Editor, to 1980; Principal Asst Features Editor, to 1981. *The Washington Times*, Deputy Features Editor, to 1983; Asst Managing Editor, to 1985; National Edition Editor, 1985. *Insight*, Managing Editor, current, 1985. National Design Awards.

O'Connor, Clint. Washington Journalism Review. Managing Editor. B. 1958, Evanston, IL. Boston College, BA-English. WVNH Radio, news director, 1982-84. *Washington Journalism Review*, writer, Asst Editor, to 1986; Assoc Editor, to 1988; Managing Editor, current, 1988.

O'Leary, Jeremiah. The Washington Times. Columnist. B. 1919, Washington, DC. GWU, 1941, English. *The Washington Star*, City Hall & State Dept reporter, nearly 45 years; Asst City Editor; Latin America; White House, to 1981. National Security Council, asst to William P. Clark, to 1982. *The Washington Times*, White House correspondent, to 1989; columnist, current, 1989. 1st Prize, National Reporting, DC Newspaper Guild, 1963, Kennedy assassination; Maria Moors Cabot Gold Medal, 1980.

Omestad, Thomas. Foreign Policy. Associate Editor. B. 1960, Minneapolis, MN. U. of MN, 1982, BS-Economics. AP, reporter, Pierre, SD, 1985. *Los Angeles Times*, reporter, LA, to 1987. *Foreign Policy*, Assoc Editor, current, 1987.

Oreskes, Michael. The New York Times. National Correspondent. B. 1954, NYC. CCNY, 1975. Dow Jones, 1974. *The (NY) Daily News*, Albany correspondent; Labor Editor; City Hall bureau chief, to 1981. *The New York Times*, metro correspondent; Albany bureau chief; DC correspondent; national correspondent, politics, current.

Ostling, Richard. Time. Associate Editor & Writer. B. 1940, Endicott, NY. U. of MI, 1962, AB; Northwestern, 1963, MSJ; GWU, 1970, MA-Religion. *Morning News* & *Evening Journal* (Wilmington, DE), copyreader, reporter, to 1965. *Christianity Today*, Asst News Editor; News Editor, to 1969. *Time*, staff correspondent, to 1974; writer & Assoc Editor, current, 1975. CBS Radio, syndicated "Report on Religion," 1979.

O'Sullivan, John. National Review. Editor. B. 1942, Liverpool, UK. London U., 1965, BA-Classics. Harvard, 1983, Fellow, Institute of Politics. Irish radio/TV, London correspondent, to 1972. *Daily Telegraph* (UK), "Parliamentary Sketch" writer, editorial writer, to 1977; Asst Editor, to 1979; Chief Asst Editor, to 1984, columnist, to 1986.

Policy Review, Editor, to 1983. *The New York Post*, Editorial Page Editor, to 1986. *The American Spectator*, columnist, to 1986. *The Times*, columnist, to 1986; Assoc Editor, to 1988. *National Review*, Editor, current, 1988.

Ott, James. Aviation Week & Space Technology. Senior Editor. B. 1938, Dayton, KY. Thomas More College (KY), 1961, English Literature; Xavier U. (Cincinnati), OH, 1973, MEd-Communication Arts. *Cincinnati Inquirer*, reporter, 1957-65; KY Editor, to 1969. Freelance, to 1978. *Aviation Week & Space Technology*, Sr Editor, air transport, current, 1978.

Ottaway, David B. The Washington Post. Diplomatic & National Security Correspondent. B. 1939, NY. Harvard, 1962, History; Columbia, 1972, PhD-Political Science. UPI, Paris & Algiers correspondent, 1962-63. *Time* & *The New York Times*, Algeria correspondent, to 1966; Africa correspondent, 1974-79; Cairo bureau chief & Middle East correspondent, 1981-85. *The Washington Post*, diplomatic & national security correspondent, current, 1985. 2 Overseas Press Club Awards 1974, '82. Co-author (with Marina Ottaway) 3 books, including *Afrocommunism*, 1981.

Paley, William S. CBS Inc. Consultant. B. 1901, Chicago. Studied U. of Chicago, 1918-19; U. of PA, 1922, BA. US Army, WWII, Dep. Chief Psychological Warfare Division. Congress Cigar Co, VP, secretary, to 1928. CBS Inc, President, to 1946; Chairman of the Board, to 1983; consultant, current, 1983. Whitcom Investment Co, Director, partner, current, 1983. Numerous Awards.

Parker, Laura. The Washington Post. Transportation Reporter. Nieman Fellow, 1986. *Seattle Post-Intelligencer*, reporter, 1979-86. *The Washington Post*, transportation reporter, current, 1987.

Parker, Maynard. Newsweek. Editor. B. 1940, LA, CA. Stanford, 1962, AB-History; Columbia, 1963, MSJ. *Life*, NYC reporter, to 1964; Hong Kong correspondent, to 1967. *Newsweek*, Hong Kong correspondent, to 1969; Saigon bureau chief, to 1970; Hong Kong bureau chief, to 1973; Managing Editor *Newsweek International*, to 1975; Sr Editor, National Affairs, to 1977; Asst Managing Editor, to 1980; Exec Editor, to 1982; Editor, current, 1982.

Parks, Michael. Los Angeles Times. Moscow Bureau Chief. B. 1943, Detroit. U. of Windsor (Canada), 1965, English Literature & Classics. *The Detroit News*, reporter, 1962-65. Time-Life News Service, correspondent, to 1966. *The Suffolk* (NY) *Sun*, Asst City Editor, to 1968. *The Sun*, political reporter, to 1970; Saigon bureau chief, to 1972; Moscow bureau chief, to 1975; Middle East correspondent, to 1978; Hong Kong bureau chief, to 1979; Beijing correspondent, to 1980. *Los Angeles Times*, Beijing correspondent, to 1984; Southern Africa correspondent, to 1988; Moscow bureau chief, current, 1988. Overseas Press Club citation, 1986; Pulitzer Prize, International Reporting, 1987.

Passell, Peter. The New York Times. Economics Columnist & Editorial Board Member. B. 1944, Pittsburgh. Swarthmore, 1966, Economics; Yale, 1970, PhD-Economics. Columbia, asst economics prof, 1971-76. *The New York Times*, Editorial Board Member, specializing in economics, current, 1977; economics columnist, current, 1988. Author 2 books, including *The Best*, 1987; co-author *A New Economic View of American History*.

Pear, Robert. The New York Times. Washington Reporter. B. 1949, DC. Harvard, 1971, BA-English, History & Literature, *magna cum laude*, Phi Beta Kappa; Henry Prize Fellow, Balliol College, Oxford, 1973; Columbia, 1974, MSJ. *The Washington Star*, Harvard correspondent, to 1971; summer intern; reporter, 1974-79; bureau chief, to 1979. *The New York Times*, DC reporter, current, 1979. Pulitzer Traveling Fellow, Henry Woodward Sackett Prize.

Pearlstine, Norman. The Wall Street Journal. Managing Editor & Vice President. B. 1942, Philadelphia. Haverford College, 1964, BA; U. of PA, LLB. *The Wall Street Journal*, reporter, Dallas, Detroit, LA, 1968-73; Tokyo bureau chief, to 1976; National News Editor, NYC, to 1982; Managing Editor, VP, current, 1983. *The Asian Wall Street Journal*, Managing Editor, Hong Kong, 1976-78. *Forbes*, Exec Editor, to 1980. *The Wall Street Journal/Europe*, Brussels, Editor, Publisher, 1982-83. Council on Foreign Relations, member, current.

Peirce, Neal R. National Journal. Co-Founder & Contributing Editor. B. 1932, Philadelphia. Princeton, 1954, History, *Phi Beta Kappa*. *Congressional Quarterly*, Political Editor, 1960-69. NBC-TV News, consultant, commentator, national elections, to 1966. CBS News, consultant, commentator, national elections, to 1976. Washington Post Writer's Group, columnist, current, 1975. *National Journal*, cofounder, 1969; Contributing Editor, current. American Political Science Assn Carey McWilliams Award, Political Reporting, 1986. Author *The People's President*, 1968; co-author (with Jerry Hagstrom) *The Book Of America*, 1983.

Pekkanen, John. *Reader's Digest.* Roving Editor. B. 1939, New Haven, CT. St. John's College, (MD), 1961, Philosophy. Nieman Fellow, 1970-71. *Middletown* (CT) *Press*, reporter, 1963-65. *Providence* (RI) *Journal*, reporter, 1966. *Life*, correspondent; bureau chief, to 1971. Freelance, to 1986. *Reader's Digest*, Roving Editor, current, 1986. National Magazine Award, 1982, '85; Penney-MO Award, 1982; National Headliners Award, 1982; National Press Club Consumer Reporting Award, 1984; Journalism Award of Excellence, 1986. Author 6 books, including *M.D.*, 1988.

Pennant-Rea, Rupert. *The Economist.* Editor. B. 1948, Harare, Zimbabwe. Trinity College (Dublin, Ireland), Economics; Manchester U., MA-Economics. Confederation of Irish Industry, 1970-71. General & Municipal Workers Union, 1972-73. Bank of England, to 1977. *The Economist*, Editor, current, 1973. Wincott Award for Financial Journalism, 1984. Author *Gold Foil*, 1979; co-author 3 books, including *The Economist Economics*, 1986.

Peretz, Martin. *The New Republic.* Editor-in-Chief. B. 1939, NYC. Brandeis, 1959, BA; Harvard, 1965, MA, 1966, PhD; Bard College, 1982, PhD-Hebrew Literature. Woodrow Wilson Fellow, 1959-61. Harvard instructor, 1965-68; asst prof, to 1972; Social Studies lecturer, current, 1972. *The New Republic*, Editorial Board Chairman, 1974-75; Editor-in-Chief, current, 1975. U. of MO Medal of Excellence, 1982.

Perle, Richard N. *U.S.News & World Report.* Contributing Editor. B. 1941, NYC. USC, 1964, BA-International Relations; Princeton, 1967, MA-Politics. Senate Committees, Govt Operations & Armed Services; Arms Control Subcommittee; personal staff, Sen Henry M. Jackson, 1969-80. Asst Secretary of Defense for International Security Policy, to 1987. American Enterprise Institute, resident scholar, current, 1987. *U.S.News & World Report*, Contributing Editor, current, 1987.

Perry, James M. *The Wall Street Journal.* Washington Political Reporter. B. 1927, Elmira, NY. Trinity, 1950, English. *Leatherneck Magazine*, 1946. *Hartford Times*, reporter, 1950-52. *Philadelphia Bulletin*, gen & rewrite, to 1962. *The National Observer*, politics, to 1977. *The Wall Street Journal*, DC political reporter, to 1985, current, 1987; London political reporter, 1985-87.

Peters, Charles. *The Washington Monthly.* Editor-in-Chief. B. 1926, Charleston, WV. Columbia, 1949, Humanities. Poynter Fellow, Yale, 1980. *The Washington Monthly*, Editor-in-Chief, current, 1969. Columbia Journalism Award, 1978. Author *Tilting at Windmills*, 1989.

Petranek, Stephen L. *The Washington Post Magazine.* Managing Editor. B. 1944, DC. U. of MD, 1970, Journalism. *The Diamondback* (U. of MD daily), Editor-in-Chief, 1969-70. *Rochester Democrat & Chronicle*, reporter, financial writer, investigative reporter. Asst Sunday Editor. Editor Upstate Magazine, to 1977. *The Miami Herald*, Editor, Tropic Magazine, to 1978. *The Washington Post*, from 1978, Deputy Editor, Acting Editor. *The Washington Post Magazine*, Managing Editor, current. Frank Tripp Newswriting Award, 1972; U. of MO-Ingaa Writing Award, 1972; John Hancock Financial Writing Award, 1973.

Pfaff, William W. III. *The International Herald Tribune*, Los Angeles Times Syndicate. Political Columnist. B. 1928, Council Bluffs, IA. U. of Notre Dame, 1949, Philosophy of Literature. Rockefeller Grant, International Studies, Sr Fellow, Columbia Russian Institute. Infantry, Special Forces Unit, US Army, Korean War & after. *The Commonweal*, Assoc Editor, 1949-55. ABC-TV News, 1955-57. Free Europe Organizations & Publications, Director of Research & Publications, to 1961. Hudson Institute, Sr Member, 1961-78. Hudson Research Europe, Ltd, Deputy Director, 1971-78. U. of CA, Regents Lecturer. Los Angeles Times Syndicate, political columnist, current. *The International Herald Tribune*, political columnist, current. *The New Yorker*, contributor, "Reflections" column, current, 1971. Author 2 books, including *Barbarian Sentiments*; co-author 3 books.

Phalon, Richard. *Forbes.* Contributing Editor. *New York Herald Tribune*, financial writer, 1954-64. *The New York Times*, metro desk; financial writer; columnist, to 1980. *Forbes*, reporter, to 1984; Tokyo bureau founder, 1985; Contributing Editor, current, 1985. NY Newspaper Guild Award, NY Newspaper Reporters Assn Award.

Picharallo, Joe. *The Washington Post.* Reporter. B. 1947, Newark, NJ. U. of CA, Berkeley, BA. *The North Carolina Journal*, 1972-77. *The Miami Herald*, to 1979. *The San Francisco Examiner*, 1979. *The Washington Post*, VA reporter; city reporter; investigative reporter, to 1987; reporter, current, 1987. Newspaper Guild, AP, Sigma Delta Chi Awards.

Pincus, Walter. *The Washington Post.* National Security Reporter. B. 1932, Brooklyn, NY. Yale. US Army, counter intelligence agent. *The New York Times*, copyboy. *The Wall Street Journal*, copy editor. NC newspapers, DC correspondent. *The Washington Star*, national

writer. US Senate Foreign Relations Committee, staff consultant. *The New Republic*, Executive Editor. *The Washington Post*, from 1975: national reporter; Editor, Sunday "Potomac" magazine; national security reporter, current.

Pine, Art. *Los Angeles Times.* Economics Correspondent. *The Wall Street Journal*, chief international economics correspondent, to 1987; agricultural reporter, 1987. *The International Economy*, Editor, to 1988. *Los Angeles Times*, economics correspondent, current, 1988.

Platt, Gordon. *The Journal of Commerce.* Financial Editor. B. 1949, Danbury, CT. Syracuse U., 1971, Journalism & Psychology. Newhouse Scholarship, 1967-71. *The Bond Buyer*, *The Money Manager*, Munifacts News Wire, Assoc Editor, to 1980. *The Journal of Commerce*, Asst Managing Editor, to 1986; Financial Editor, current, 1986. Gannett Award, 1971.

Plender, John. *Financial Times*, Leader & Feature Writer. B. 1945, Cardiff, UK. Oxford, 1966, BA-Modern Languages. Deloitte & Co, chartered accountant, 1967-70. *Investors Chronicle*, writer, to 1971. *The Times* (UK), reporter, feature writer, to 1974. *The Economist*, Financial Editor, to 1980. Policy Planning staff, Foreign Officer, to 1982. Channel 4-TV, presenter, current. *Financial Times*, leader & feature writer, current, 1982. Author 2 books, including *The Square Mile*, 1985.

Pletka, Danielle M. *Insight.* Staff Writer. B. 1963, Melbourne, Australia. Smith College, 1984, Modern European History; Johns Hopkins 1987, MA-International Studies. Reuters, intern, Jerusalem, 1984. *Los Angeles Times*, editorial asst, Jerusalem, to 1985. *Insight*, staff writer, current, 1987.

Podhoretz, John. *The Washington Times.* Assistant Managing Editor. B. 1961, NYC. U. of Chicago, 1982, Political Science. *The American Spectator*, movie critic, to 1982, 1984-85. *Time*, reporter, researcher, to 1984. *The Washington Times*, Features Editor, to 1985; "Critic at Large" columnist, to 1987; Asst Managing Editor, "life!", current, 1989. *Insight*, Exec Editor, to 1987. *U.S.News & World Report*, Contributing Editor, to 1988.

Podhoretz, Norman. *Commentary*, Editor. North America Syndicate, Columnist. B. 1930, Brooklyn, NY. Columbia, 1950; Cambridge, 1953, English. *Commentary*, Editor, current, 1960. Freelance, current. North America Syndicate, columnist, current, 1985. Author 6 books, including *The Bloody Crossroads*, 1986.

Pollack, Andrew. *The New York Times.* Reporter. Princeton, 1975, BSE-Civil Engineering; MIT, 1977, MS-Environmental Engineering. *The Dallas Times Herald*, reporter, to 1980. *The New York Times*, reporter, current, 1981.

Pollan, Michael. *Harper's.* Executive Editor. B. 1955, Long Island, NY. Bennington College, 1976, English; Columbia, 1981, MA. *Channels of Communications*, Contributing Editor, to 1983. *Harper's*, Exec Editor, current, 1983. Co-author *The Harper's Index Book*.

Pollock, Ellen Joan. *The Wall Street Journal.* Deputy Law Editor. B. 1955. Brandeis, 1977, BA-Politics. Author's asst, 1977-78. *New Times*, Asst Editor, to 1979. *The American Lawyer*, various editorial posts, including editorial director, to 1987. *Manhattan Lawyer*, editor, to 1989. *The Wall Street Journal*, Deputy Law Editor, current, 1989.

Poole, Isaiah J. *The Washington Times.* Assistant Metro Editor. B. 1954, DC. Howard U. *The* (NY) *News World*, DC correspondent, 1977-79. *Black Enterprise*, DC bureau chief, to 1982. *The Washington Times*, City Hall reporter, to 1985; national reporter, to 1989; Asst Metro Editor, current, 1989. Sigma Delta Chi Award, 1984.

Postrel, Virginia Inman. *Reason.* Editor. B. 1960, Asheville, NC. Princeton, 1982, English. *The Wall Street Journal*, summer intern, 1981; reporter, 1982-84. *Inc*, writer, to 1986. *Reason*, Asst Editor, to 1988; Assoc Editor, to 1989; Editor, current, 1989.

Pouschine, Tatiana. *Forbes.* Staff Writer. B. 1957, DC. Middlebury College, 1980, Political Science. Estee Lauder, marketing coordinator, 1980-81. Bankers Trust, lending officer, to 1984. *Forbes*, reporter, to 1989, staff writer, current, 1989.

Powell, Sally. *BusinessWeek.* Senior Editor. B. Budapest, Hungary. *Theatre Arts*, Managing Editor. *Brooklyn Eagle*, Editor, Entertainment Page. *World Telegram*, Copy Editor. *Electronics*, Chief Copy Editor; Assoc Managing Editor, to 1970. *BusinessWeek*, creator, book review section, 1970; Sr Editor, marketing, legal affairs, media, advertising, corporate woman, social issues, & transportation, current, 1980.

Power, William. *The Wall Street Journal.* Commodities Reporter. B. 1961, Philadelphia. Fordham, 1984, Journalism. *The Wall Street Journal*, NY state & federal courts reporter, 1986-87; commodities reporter, current, 1987.

Powers, Charles T. *Los Angeles Times*. Warsaw Bureau Chief. B. 1943, Neosho, MO. KS State U., 1966, BA-Journalism & English. Nieman Fellow, 1986-87. *Kansas State Collegian*, Editor, reporter, 1962-66. *The Kansas City Star*, intern, summers 1962-64; reporter, 1966-69. *Los Angeles Times*, writer, to 1971; "West Magazine" writer, to 1972; "View" writer, to 1975; writer, NYC, to 1980; Nairobi bureau chief, to 1986; Warsaw bureau chief, current, 1987. *Times* Editorial Award, 1973, '75 (co-recipient, 1982).

Prat, Marie. *The Journal of Commerce*. Reporter. B. 1960, New Orleans, LA. Loyola U., 1981, Communications. AP, New Orleans, reporter; Alabama, broadcast editor; legislative reporter, 1981-86. *The Journal of Commerce*, Gulf bureau chief, to 1989; reporter, current, 1989.

Prewitt, Edward. *Fortune*. Reporter. B. 1963, Atlanta. Duke U., 1985, English. *The News & Observer* (Raleigh, NC), metro reporter, 1983-84. *Triangle Business* (Raleigh, NC), staff writer, to 1986. *Fortune*, reporter, current, 1986.

Price, Joyce. *The Washington Times*. Health Reporter. B. 1945, Baltimore. Towson State U., 1967, English. *The News American*, reporter, 1968-86. *The Washington Times*, health reporter, current, 1986.

Prichard, Peter S. *USA Today*. Editor. Gannett Co, Inc, Senior Vice President/News. B. 1944, Auburn, CA. Dartmouth, 1966. Nieman Foundation, advisory committee member, current. DC Journalism Center, trustee, current. US Army, 1968-69. *The Time*, Greenwich, CT, 1970-72. *Democrat and Chronicle* (Rochester, NY), to 1975. WOKR-TV, assoc news director, to 1976. *The Times-Union* (Rochester, NY), reporter, TV columnist, to 1978. Gannett Co., Inc, asst to the president; director of communications for the Office of the Chief Executive, to 1982; *USA Today*, Columns Editor, to 1983; Deputy Editorial Director, to 1984; Assoc Editorial Director, to 1987; Managing Editor, cover stories & special projects, to 1988; Sr Editor, news, to 1988; Sr Vice President/News & Editor, current, 1988. Author *The Making of McPaper*, 1987.

Pruden, Wesley. *The Washington Times*. Managing Editor & "Pruden on Politics" Columnist. B. 1935, Jackson, MS. Little Rock (AR) Junior College, 1955, History. US Air Force, 1957. *Arkansas Gazette* (Little Rock), writer, 1952-56. *The Commercial Appeal*, writer. *The National Observer*, writer, from 1963, (Vietnam, 1965-68, '71; Middle East, 1969; London, 1970). Freelance, from 1976. *The Washington Times*, Managing Editor, "Pruden on Politics" columnist, current, 1985.

Putka, Gary. *The Wall Street Journal*. Boston Reporter. OH U., 1977, Journalism. *Journal Herald* (Dayton, OH), intern, summer 1975. AP, correspondent, intern, Israel, 1975-76. *Securities Week*, reporter, Editor, 1980. *The Wall Street Journal*, senior special writer, "Heard on the Market," to 1984; reporter, London, to 1987; education reporter, 1987; Boston reporter, current, 1988.

Quinn, Jane Bryant. *Newsweek*, Contributing Editor. Washington Post Writers Group, Financial Columnist. B. 1939, Niagara Falls, NY. Middlebury College, 1960, BA, *magna cum laude*, Phi Beta Kappa. *Insider's Newsletter*, Assoc Editor. 1962-65; co-Editor, 1966-67. Cowles Book Co, Sr Editor, 1968. *Business Week Letter*, Editor-in-Chief, to 1973; gen manager, to 1974. Washington Post Writers Group, columnist, current, 1974. *Women's Day*, contributor, financial columnist, current, 1974. NBC-TV News & Information Service, contributor, 1976-77. WCBS-TV (NYC), business correspondent, 1979; CBS-TV News, current, 1980. *Newsweek*, Contributing Editor, current, 1978. John Hancock Award, Excellence, Business & Financial Journalism, 1975; Janus Award, Excellence, TV Reporting, 1980; National Press Club Award, Consumer Journalism, 1980, '82, '83; Matrix Award, 1983; National Headliner Award, Consistently Outstanding Magazine Feature Column, 1986. Author *Everyone's Money Book*, 1979 (2nd ed, 1980).

Quinn, John Collins. *USA Today*. Editor-in-Chief. B. 1925, Providence College, 1945, AB; Columbia, 1946, MSJ. *The Journal-Bulletin* (Providence, RI), copyboy, reporter, Asst City Editor, DC correspondent, Asst Managing Editor, Day Managing Editor, 1943-66. Gannett Co., Inc, current, 1966; *Democrat and Chronicle & Times Union* (Rochester, NY), Exec Editor, to 1971; Gannett News Service, Gen Manager, 1967-80; VP, parent co, 1971-75; Sr VP, News & Information, to 1980; Sr VP Chief News Exec, parent co, 1980-83; President, current, 1980; Gannett Co, Exec VP, current; *USA Today*, Editor, 1983-89; Editor-in-Chief, current, 1989. Editor of the Year Award, National Press Foundation, 1986.

Quint, Michael. *The New York Times*. "Business Day" Reporter. Antioch College, 1973, BA. *American Banking Daily*, to 1980 *The New York Times*, "Business Day" reporter, current, 1980.

Rachid, Rosalind Kilkenny. *The Journal of Commerce*. Imports Editor. B. 1951, Georgetown, Guyana. CCNY, 1971, BA-French; U. of Madrid, 1971, Spanish Language & Literature Certificate; NYU, 1985, MAJ. English & French instructor, Uganda, 1973-74. English instructor, Zaire, to 1980. Bear Stearns & Co, Accounts Exec Asst, 1982-85. *Carib News*, freelance, 1982-85. *The Journal of Commerce*, international trade reporter, to 1987; Imports Editor, current, 1987.

Radcliffe, Redonia. *The Washington Post*. "Style" Staff Reporter. B. 1929, Republican City, NE. San Jose State U., BA. *The Salinas Californian*, reporter. Freelance writer. *The Washington Star*, reporter, 1967-72. *The Washington Post*, "Style" assgnmt editor, to 1976; "Style" staff reporter, current, 1976.

Raines, Howell. *The New York Times*. Washington Bureau Chief. B. 1943, Birmingham, AL. Birmingham-Southern College, 1964, BA; U. of AL, 1973, MA-English. *The Birmingham Post-Herald*, to 1965. WBRC-TV (Birmingham), to 1968. *The Tuscaloosa* (AL) *News*, to 1970. *The Birmingham News*, reporter, 1971. Constitution, Political Editor. *St. Petersburg Times*, Political Editor, to 1978. *The New York Times*, national correspondent, Atlanta, 1978; chief Atlanta correspondent, to 1982; White House correspondent, to 1985; Deputy Editor, DC, to 1986; London bureau chief, to 1988; DC bureau chief, current, 1988. Author 2 books, including *My Soul Is Rested*, 1977; contributor, *Campaign Money*, 1976.

Rainie, Harrison (Lee). *U.S.News & World Report*. Assistant Managing Editor. B. 1951, Long Island, NY. Harvard, 1973, Government; Long Island U., 1976, MA-Political Science. *The* (NY) *Daily News*, 1974-87. Sen Daniel Moynihan, chief of staff, 1987. *U.S.News & World Report*, Sr Editor, politics, to 1989; Asst Managing Editor, current, 1989. Author *Growing Up Kennedy*, 1983.

Raley-Borda, Laura. *The Journal of Commerce*. Reporter. B. 1966, Tuscaloosa, AL. U. of TX, 1987, Journalism. *Austin American-Statesman*, editorial asst, 1987. *Daily Texan*, reporter, 1987. *The Journal of Commerce*, reporter, current, 1987.

Ramirez, Anthony. *Fortune*. Associate Editor. B. Manila, Philippines. U. of CA, Berkeley, AB-Political Science. *The Wall Street Journal*, Atlanta reporter. *Los Angeles Times*, San Diego County Business Editor. *Fortune*, Assoc Editor, current, 1984.

Randal, Jonathan C. *The Washington Post*. Roving Correspondent. B. 1933, Buffalo, NY. Harvard, 1955, Romance Languages. UPI, France, Algeria, London & Geneva, 1957-60. *Agence France Presse*, English language desk, Paris, 1957. *International Herald Tribune*, Paris & N. Africa, 1960-61. *Time*, N. Africa, Congo, W. Africa, Middle East, to 1966. *The New York Times*, Dominican Republic, Haiti, Vietnam, Laos, Cambodia, Warsaw, E. Europe, to 1969. *The Washington Post*, European Economic correspondent, to 1971; Paris correspondent, to 1975; roving correspondent, Middle East, N. Africa & Asia, current, 1975. Edward Weintal Prize.

Randolph, Eleanor R. *The Washington Post*. Media Writer. B. 1943, Pensacola, FL. Emory U., 1964, History. *Pensacola News Journal*, 1968-70. *St. Petersburg Times*, to 1973. *Sun-Times*, 1974. *Chicago Tribune*, to 1979. *Los Angeles Times*, politics, environment, to 1984. *The Washington Post*, media writer, current, 1984.

Range, Peter Ross. *U.S.News & World Report*. Diplomatic Correspondent. B. 1941, Tiffon, GA. U. of NC, 1964, German. Universitat Gottingen, Germany, Exchange Fellow, 1961-62; Woodrow Wilson Fellow, 1964-65. *Time* & NBC-TV Radio, Berlin stringer, 1967-68. *Time*, Bonn correspondent, to 1970; Atlanta correspondent, to 1974; Saigon bureau chief, to 1975. Freelance, Paris, to 1976. *Playboy*, Chicago Senior Articles Editor, to 1977; Washington Contributing Editor, to 1985. *The Washington Post*, contract writer, to 1986. *U.S.News & World Report*, diplomatic correspondent, current, 1987.

Raspberry, William J. *The Washington Post* & Washington Post Writers Group. Urban Affairs Columnist. B. Okolona, MS. IN Central College, BA-History. US Army, 1960-62. *Indianapolis Recorder*, reporter, photographer, Editor, 1956-60. *The Washington Post*, various positions; urban affairs columnist, current. Washington Post Writers Group, columnist, current. Capitol Press Club Journalist of the Year Award, 1965.

Rather, Dan. CBS-TV News. "CBS Evening News with Dan Rather" Managing Editor & Anchor. B. 1931, Wharton, TX. Sam Houston State College, 1953, BAJ. Sam Houston State College, instructor, journalism, 1954. UPI, 1954. *Houston Chronicle*, 1954. KTRH (CBS), news writer; reporter; News Director, to 1958. KHOU-TV (CBS), Director of News & Public Affairs, to 1964; White House correspondent, 1964; London bureau chief, to 1966; 1974-76; Vietnam correspondent, 1966. CBS-TV News, "CBS Reports" anchor & correspondent, to 1975; "Who's Who" co-Editor, 1977; "60 Minutes" co-Editor, to 1981; "CBS News with Dan Rather" anchor, Managing Editor, current, 1981. CBS Radio Network, "Dan Rather Reporting" anchor, current, 1977. 5 Emmy Awards. Co-author 2 books, including *The Camera Never Blinks*, 1977.

Rawsthorn, Alice. *Financial Times*. Consumer Industries Correspondent. B. 1958. Manchester, UK. Clare College, Cambridge, History of Art; MA. Thomson, graduate trainee, 1980-82. *Marketing*, to 1984. *Campaign*, to 1986. *Financial Times*, consumer industries correspondent, current, 1986. Catherine Packenham Memorial Award, 1987.

Reasoner, Harry. CBS-TV News. "60 Minutes" Correspondent. B. 1923, Dakota City, IA. *Minneapolis Times*, reporter; drama critic, 1942-43, '46-48. Northwest Airlines, Asst Publicity Director, to 1950. WCCO (Minneapolis), newswriter, to 1951. USIA, Manila, Editor, to 1954. KEYD-TV (Minneapolis), News Director, to 1956. CBS-TV News, reporter, to 1970; "60 Minutes" correspondent, current, 1978. ABC-TV News, 1970-78. Peabody Award, 1967; Emmy Award, 1968, '74. Author 3 books, including *Before The Colors Fade*, 1981.

Redburn, Tom. *Los Angeles Times*. Washington Reporter. B. 1950, LA, CA. Pomona College, 1972, Sociology & History. *The Washington Monthly*, Editor, writer, 1974-75. *Environmental Action*, Editor, writer, to 1976. *Washington Newsworks*, reporter, 1976. *Los Angeles Times*, business staff, to 1984; DC reporter, current, 1984. Gerald Loeb Award, 1979; Greater LA Press Club Best Business Story, 1982.

Reed, Frederick Venable. *Harper's*, Washington Editor. Universal Press Syndicate, Columnist. B. 1945, Bluefield, WV. Hampden-Sydney College, 1970, BS-History, Minor Computing. *Fredericksburg (VA) Star*, stringer, Mid-East war, 1973. *Army Times*, stringer, Saigon, Phnom Penh, to 1975. *Soldier of Fortune*, 1980. *The Washingtonian*, staff writer, 1981. *The Washington Times*, science writer; military columnist, political & humor columnist, to 1986. Universal Press Syndicate, military columnist, current, 1986. *Harper's*, DC Editor, current, 1986. Freelance, current, 1986. Olive Branch Award, 1987.

Reed, J.D. *Time*. Associate Editor. B. 1940, Jackson, MI. MI State U., 1962, English; SUNY, Stony Brook, 1968, MFA-English. Guggenheim Fellowship, Poetry, 1969. U. of MA, English Dept, 1970-75. *Sports Illustrated*, writer, to 1980. *Time*, Assoc Editor, current, 1980. Author 2 books, including *Freefall*, 1974; co-author (with Christine Ree) *Exposure*, 1987.

Reid, T.R. *The Washington Post*. Denver Bureau Chief. B. 1944, Baltimore. Princeton; GWU, JD. US Navy, lieutenant. US Court of Appeals, DC circuit, law clerk. *The Trenton Times*, reporter; DC bureau chief. *The Washington Post*, national reporter, 1977-81; "Federal Report" Editor, to 1983; Denver bureau chief, current, 1983. ABA Journalism Award, 1975, 1976. Author 2 books, including *Congressional Odyssey*, 1980; contributor 2 books, including *The Pursuit of the Presidency*, 1981.

Reinhold, Robert. *The New York Times*. Los Angeles Bureau Chief. B. 1941, NY. Johns Hopkins, 1962, BS-Biology; Columbia, 1965, MSJ. *The New York Times*, copyboy, 1964-65; news clerk, to 1966; news asst, to 1967; science reporter, to 1965; national correspondent, various bureaus, to 1986; LA bureau chief, current, 1987. 13 *Times* Publisher's Awards; Educational Writer's Association Award; American Geographical Society Award.

Rensberger, Boyce. *The Washington Post*. Science Editor. B. 1942, Indianapolis, IN. U. of Miami, BS; Syracuse U., MS. *Detroit Free Press*, science writer, 1966-71. *The New York Times*, science writer, to 1979. "3-2-1 Contact," head writer, to 1981. *Science 81/84*, Sr Editor, to 1984. *The Washington Post*, science writer, to 1988; Science Editor, national news staff, current, 1988. AAAS-Science Journalism Award, 1986. Author 2 books, including *How the World Works*, 1986.

Reston, James. *The New York Times*. Senior Columnist. Cincinnati Reds traveling secretary, to 1934. AP, sportswriter, to 1937; London writer, to 1939. *The New York Times*, London, to 1945; national correspondent; diplomatic correspondent, to 1953; DC bureau chief, correspondent, to 1964; Assoc Editor, to 1968; Exec Editor, News & Sunday Depts, to 1969; VP, 1969-74; Board of Directors Member, 1973; "Washington" columnist, to 1987; Sr Columnist, current, 1987. *The Vineyard Gazette* (Edgartown, MA), owner, current, 1968. Pulitzer Prize, 1945, '57.

Revzin, Philip. *The Wall Street Journal*. Paris Bureau Chief. B. Chicago. Stanford, BA-English; Columbia, MA-English. *The Wall Street Journal*, intern, summer 1972; Cleveland reporter, 1974-77; London reporter, to 1980; asst NY bureau chief, to 1983; London bureau chief, to 1986; Sr Correspondent, Paris, 1986; Paris bureau chief, current, 1986. Overseas Press Club Citation, Best Business News Reporting from Abroad, 1978, '88.

Rich, Charles. *The Washingtonian*. Contributing Editor. B. 1952, DC. American U., 1973, Communication. WTOP Radio, news writer,

DC, 1975-80; film critic, 1979-80. WDVM-TV, "PM Magazine," film critic, DC, 1979-83. *The Washingtonian*, Contributing Editor, current, 1984. AP Radio Network, film & home video critic, current, 1984. Voice of America, writer, reporter, current, 1984.

Rich, Spencer. *The Washington Post*. National Desk Writer. B. 1930, NYC. NYU, BA-Modern European History; Columbia, MS-Russian & European History. *Congressional Quarterly*, reporter. *The Washington Post*, Asst National Editor, 1966-68; congressional reporter, to 1969; Senate reporter, to 1978; national desk writer, current, 1978.

Richburg, Keith. *The Washington Post*. Southeast Asia Correspondent. B. Detroit. U. of MI, 1980, Political Science; London School of Economics, 1984, MS-International Affairs & Development Studies. *Phi Beta Kappa*. *The Washington Post*, summer intern, 1978, 1979; political reporter, 1980-83; national reporter, 1984-86; SE Asia correspondent, current, 1986.

Richman, Louis S. *Fortune*. Associate Editor. Dickinson College, BA-History; Brandeis, MA-Modern & Contemporary History; MIT's Sloan School, MA-Management. *Sloan Management Review*, Editor. Brandeis & Hamilton College, History teacher. US Emergency Glass Co (Boston, MA), controller. Arlington, MA, Chamber of Commerce, Exec Director; Redevelopment Board member. *Fortune*, reporter, 1981; Assoc Editor, current, 1982; founded editorial office, Frankfurt, W. Germany.

Ricklefs, Roger. *The Wall Street Journal*. National Correspondent. B. 1940, San Rafael, CA. Harvard, 1961, History. *The Wall Street Journal*, NY reporter, 1964-66; London, to 1970; Editor Page One Dept, to 1972; NY special writer, 1982; Asst Second Front Editor, to 1983; Paris bureau chief, to 1986; national correspondent, NY, current, 1986.

Riding, Alan. *The New York Times*. Rome Correspondent. B. 1943, Rio de Janeiro, Brazil. Bristol U., (UK) 1964, Economics; Gray's Inn, (UK) Law, 1964-66. BBC, 1966. Reuters, London, NY, Buenos Aires, to 1971. *The New York Times*, *Financial Times*, *The Economist*, freelance, to 1978. *The New York Times*, Mexico City bureau chief, to 1984; Rio de Janeiro bureau chief, to 1988; Rome correspondent, current, 1988. Overseas Press Club Citation, Excellence, 1973; Maria Moors Cabot Prize, 1980.

Riemer, Blanca. *BusinessWeek*. Paris Economics Correspondent. B. Lima, Peru. Sorbonne (Paris, France), 1966, Literature diploma; *Institut d'Etudes Politiques* (Paris), 1968, International Relations. Walter Bagehot Fellow, 1983. *Agence France-Presse*, financial reporter, Paris; economics correspondent, NY; economics correspondent, DC. McGraw-Hill World News, correspondent, Bogota, Colombia, to 1983. *BusinessWeek*, DC correspondent 1983-87; economics correspondent, Paris, current, 1987.

Riley, Charles Allen II. *Fortune*. Money & Markets Reporter. B. 1958, Manhasset, NY. Princeton, 1979, English; 1981, MPhil; 1988, PhD. Doubleday & Co., Trade Editor, 1979-82. Hebei Teacher's U., Hebei, China, 1984. CUNY, College of Staten Island, Dept of English, 1983-87. *Fortune*, money & markets reporter, current, 1987. Author *A Season in Silence*.

Riley, Karen J. (Younquist). *The Washington Times*. Reporter. B. 1952, Minneapolis, MN. Cornell, 1974, Economics; postgrad, U. of MN, Journalism. WWTC radio, reporter, talk show host, 1977-79. *The Lakeview Life*, writer, Assgnmt Editor, columnist, 1979. *Housing Affairs Letter*, economics writer, to 1981. *U.S.News Washington Letter*, *U.S.News & World Report*, Assoc Editor. *The Washington Times*, reporter, current, 1985.

Rivard, Robert. *Newsweek*. Chief of Correspondents & Senior Editor. B. 1952, Petoskey, MI. *Brownsville (TX) Herald*, sports reporter, Desk Editor, 1977; city & county reporter, 1977. *Corpus Christi Caller*, investigative reporter, 1978. *The Dallas Times Herald*, Mexico & SW USA correspondent, to 1980; Central American bureau founder, to 1983. *Newsweek*, San Salvador bureau founder, to 1985; Sr Editor, chief of correspondents, current, 1985. Star Reporter of Year, Texas Headliners Award, 1979, '81; *Sigma Delta Chi* Distinguished Service, 1982.

Robbins, William H. *The New York Times*. Kansas City Bureau Chief. B. 1924, Lumberton, NC. Wake Forest College, 1948, BA, 1949, MA. Wake Forest College, English instructor, to 1950. *The Wilmington (NC) Star*, reporter. *The Richmond Times-Dispatch*, reporter. *The Sun*, reporter. *Motor Magazine*, Managing Editor, 1957-58. *The New York Times*, Copy Editor, business news dept; national copy desk; Asst Real Estate Editor, to 1969; Asst News Editor, agriculture reporter, DC bureau reporter, Chicago, to 1980; Philadelphia bureau chief, to 1985; Kansas City bureau chief, current, 1985. Author *The American Food Scandal*, 1973.

Roberts, Paul Craig. Scripps Howard News Service. Columnist. B. 1939, Atlanta, GA. GA Institute of Technology, 1961, Industrial Management; U. of VA, 1967, PhD-Economics; attended U. of CA at Berkeley, Oxford. Congressional staff, 1975-78. Asst Secretary of the Treasury for Economic Policy, 1981-82. *The Wall Street Journal*, Editor, columnist; contributor, current. Scripps Howard News Service, columnist, current. Meritorious Service Award, US Dept of Treasury, 1982; Legion of Honor, 1987. Author 3 books, including *The Supply-Side Revolution*, 1984.

Roberts, Steven V. *U.S.News & World Report*. Senior Writer. B. 1943, Bayonne, NJ. Harvard, 1964, Government. *The New York Times*, research asst to James Reston, 1964-65; metro staff, to 1969; LA bureau chief, to 1974; Athens bureau chief, to 1977; DC reporter, to 1980; Congressional correspondent, to 1986; White House correspondent, to 1989. *U.S.News & World Report*, Sr Writer, current, 1987. "Washington Week in Review," panelist, current. Everett McKinley Dirksen Award, Distinguished Coverage of Congress, 1985. Author *Eureka*, 1974.

Robertson, Sara. *Foreign Affairs*. Assistant Editor. B. 1956, Kansas City, MO. Stanford, 1978, International Relations; Columbia, 1984, MA-International Affairs. English teacher, Indonesia, 1978-79; China, 1980-82. *The Asia Record* (Palo Alto, CA), Production Editor, 1979-80. *The Asia Society* (NY), program/publications assoc, 1983-85. *Foreign Affairs*, Asst Editor, current, 1985.

Robinson, Linda. *Foreign Affairs*. Associate Editor. B. 1960, Pittsburgh. Swarthmore, 1982, BA-Political Science, high honors. *The Wilmington* (OH) *News-Journal*, reporter, part-time writer, 1977-79. *The Wilson Quarterly*, intern, 1981; Asst Editor, to 1983. *The New York Times Book Review*, book reviewer, current, 1983. *Foreign Affairs*, Sr Asst Editor; Asst Editor; Assoc Editor, current, 1986.

Rockwell, Keith M. *The Journal of Commerce*. Reporter. B. 1958, Boston. Tufts, 1980, History/Political Science. GWU, postgrad. *The Journal of Commerce*, reporter, 1980-84; Editorial Page Editor, to 1986; Enterprise Editor, to 1987; international economics reporter, current, 1987. Author *One Europe: 1992 and Beyond*.

Rogers, Michael. *Newsweek*. Senior Writer. B. 1950, CA. Stanford, 1972, Creative Writing. *Rolling Stone*, Assoc & Contributing Editor, 1972-82. *Outside*, Editor-at-Large, 1976-78. *Newsweek*, Gen Editor, 1983-89; Sr Writer, current, 1989. Freelance, current. AAAS-Westinghouse Distinguished Science Writing, 1976; Computer Press Assn Best Feature Article, 1988. Author 5 books, including *Forbidden Sequence*, 1988.

Rohter, William Lawrence (Larry). *The New York Times*. Mexico City Bureau Chief. B. 1950, Oak Park, IL. School of Foreign Service, 1971, *cum laude*; attended Columbia School of International Affairs, 1971-73. *The Washington Post*, "Style" reporter, to 1977. *Newsweek*, from 1977; Rio de Janiero correspondent; Latin America bureau chief; Beijing bureau chief; Asian Regional Editor, to 1984. *The New York Times*, reporter, to 1987; Mexico City bureau chief, current, 1987.

Romano, Lois. *The Washington Post*. "Style" Reporter. B. 1953, NYC. Emmanuel College, 1974, Political Science; GWU, MA-International Affairs. States News Service, 1977-79. *Women's Wear Daily*, to 1981. *The Washington Star*, feature writer, 1981. *The Washington Post*, "Style" writer, current, 1981. Author *Love and the Litmus Test*, 1983.

Rooney, Andrew A. CBS-TV News, "60 Minutes" Commentator. Tribune Company Syndicate, Columnist. B. 1919, Albany, NY. Colgate, 1942. CBS-TV News, writer, Producer, from 1959; "60 Minutes" commentator, current, 1978. Tribune Co Syndicate, columnist, current, 1979. Emmy Awards, 1968, '78, '81, '82. Author 7 books, including *Word For Word*, 1986; co-author *Air Gunner*, 1944.

Rose, Robert L. *The Wall Street Journal*. Airline Reporter. B. 1956, Passaic, NJ. Georgetown, 1977, Non-Western History & Diplomacy; Columbia, 1978, MSJ. *Toledo Blade*, labor reporter, 1978-82. Dow Jones Radio 2, gen assgnmt, to 1983. *Dow Phone*, stock market reporter, 1984. *The Wall Street Journal*, personal finance, NY, to 1986; financial futures, Chicago, 1987; airline reporter, Chicago, current, 1987.

Rosenbaum, David E. *The New York Times*. Washington Correspondent. B. 1942, Miami, FL. Dartmouth, 1963, AB; Columbia, 1965, MSJ. Borden Graduate Award, Pulitzer Traveling Fellow. *The St. Petersburg Times*, to 1966. *Ilford Recorder* (UK), 1966. *Congressional Quarterly*, to 1968. *The New York Times*, reporter, Editor, DC, to 1981; Enterprise Editor, NY, to 1984; correspondent, taxes, economic & domestic policy issues, DC, current, 1984.

Rosenblatt, Robert A. *Los Angeles Times*. Washington Correspondent. B. 1943, NYC. CCNY, 1964, BA-Economics; Columbia, 1966, MSJ. *Broadcasting Magazine*, reporter, to 1965. *The Charlotte* (NC)

Observer, reporter, 1966-69. *Los Angeles Times*, financial news reporter, to 1976; DC correspondent, aging & the elderly, current, 1976. Gerald Loeb Financial Journalism Award, 1978.

Rosenfeld, Stephen. *The Washington Post*. Deputy Editorial Page Editor, Columnist. B. 1932, Pittsfield, MA. Harvard, 1953, BA-European History & Literature. US Marines, 1953-55. Russian Institute, Columbia, 1957-59. *The Berkshire Eagle*, 1955-57. *The Washington Post*, city staff, 1959-62; editorial writer, to 1964, '66-82; Moscow correspondent, 1964-65; Deputy Editorial Page Editor, current, 1982; columnist, current. Author *The Time of Their Dying*, 1977; co-author (with Barbara Rosenfeld) *Return From Red Square*, 1967.

Rosenthal, Abraham Michael (A.M.). *The New York Times*. "On My Mind" Columnist. B. 1922, Sault Ste. Marie, Ontario. CCNY, 1944, BS-Social Science. *The New York Times*, UN correspondent, to 1954; India-based, to 1958; Warsaw, to 1959; Geneva, to 1961; Tokyo, to 1963; Metro Editor, to 1966; Asst Managing Editor, to 1969; Managing Editor, to 1977; Exec Editor, to 1986; Assoc Editor, to 1988; "On My Mind" columnist, current, 1986. G. P. Putnam, Editor-at-Large, current, 1988. Overseas Press Club Citation, 1956, '59; Pulitzer Prize, International Reporting, 1960; Number 1 Award, 1960; George Polk Memorial Award, 1960, '65; Page 1 Award, NY Newspaper Guild, 1960. Author *38 Witnesses*; co-author 3 books, including *One More Victim*.

Rosenthal, Andrew M. *The New York Times*. Washington Reporter. B. 1956, New Delhi, India. U of Denver, 1978, BA-American History. *The Rocky Mountain News*, police reporter, 1976-77. AP, sports stringer, 1976; Denver reporter, 1978-82; Foreign Copy Editor, to 1983; Moscow correspondent, to 1986; Moscow bureau chief, to 1987. *The New York Times*, DC reporter, current, 1987.

Rosenthal, Jack. *The New York Times*. Editorial Page Editor. B. 1935, Tel Aviv. Harvard, 1956, AB-History. *The Harvard Crimson*, Exec Editor. *The Oregonian* (Portland, OR), reporter, Editor. Press officer, State & Justice Depts, 1966-69. *The New York Times*, Asst Sunday Editor; editorial writer; Deputy Editor, Editorial Page, to 1986; Editorial Page Editor, current, 1986. Pulitzer Prize, Editorial Writing, 1982.

Rosentiel, Thomas. *Los Angeles Times*. Media Writer. B. 1956, Redwood City, CA. Oberlin College, 1978, English; Columbia, 1980, MSJ. Jack Anderson's "Merry Go 'Round" column, 1978-79. *Peninsula Times Tribune* (Palo Alto, CA), reporter, financial writer, Financial Editor, to 1983. *Los Angeles Times*, financial writer; media writer, current, 1983.

Rosett, Claudia. *The Asian Wall Street Journal*. Editorial Page Editor. B. 1955, New Haven, CT. Yale, 1976, Intensive English. Freelance, Chile, South America, 1981-82; NY, to 1984. *Policy Review*, 1984. *The Wall Street Journal*, Book Editor, to 1986. *The Asian Wall Street Journal*, Editorial Page Editor, current, 1986.

Rosewicz, Barbara. *The Wall Street Journal*. Energy & Environment Correspondent. U. of KS, 1978, BAJ. UPI, reporter, Dallas; reporter (Topeka, KS); Topeka bureau chief, to 1981; Supreme Court reporter; Congressional reporter, to 1984. *The Wall Street Journal*, NY staff, to 1985; Middle East correspondent, Cairo, 1985; Energy & Environment correspondent, DC, current, 1987.

Ross, Michael. *Los Angeles Times*. Cairo Bureau Chief. B. 1949. UPI, Middle East correspondent, Beirut, Lebanon, 1974-76; Editor, foreign desk, to 1982; Peking bureau manager, to 1984; Sr Editor, Tokyo, to 1985. *Los Angeles Times*, Cairo bureau chief, current, 1985.

Rothenberg, Randall M. *The New York Times*. Media Reporter. B. 1956. Princeton, 1978, BA-Classics, *magna cum laude*. *The News-Dispatch*, (NJ) stringer, 1974. *The Annapolis Evening Capitol*, stringer, 1974-75. *The Record* (Hackensack, NJ), stringer, 1977. *The Brooklyn Heights Press*, Features Editor, 1979-80. *Esquire*, "The New America" Editor, 1984-85; Contributing Editor, current, 1985. *The New York Times*, Sunday *Magazine* Assoc Editor, 1986-88; media reporter, current, 1988. Author *The Neoliberals*, 1984; co-author *Getting Angry Six Times a Week*, 1979.

Rowen, Hobart. *The Washington Post*. Economics Editor & Columnist. B. 1918, Burlington, VT. CCNY, 1938, BSS-Government & Sociology, Honors. *The New York Journal of Commerce*, reporter, to 1942. *Newsweek*, DC correspondent, "Business Trends" Editor, 1944-65. *The Washington Post*, Financial Editor, to 1969; Asst Managing Editor, to 1975; Economics Editor & columnist, current, 1975. Washington Post Writer's Group, columnist, current, 1975. PBS-TV, "Washington Week in Review," panelist, current. Sigma Delta Chi Distinguished Service Award, 1960; John Hancock Distinguished Service Award, 1966; Gerald Loeb Award, Business News Reporting, 1977; Journalist of the Year, National Economic Assn, 1984; *Washington Journalism Review*, Best in the Business, 1985. Author *The Free*

Enterprisers, 1964; co-author 2 books, including *The Fall of the President*, 1974.

Royko, Mike. *Chicago Tribune*, Tribune Media Services. Columnist. B. 1935, Chicago. Wright Junior College, 1951-52. US Air Force, to 1956. Chicago Northside Newspapers, reporter, 1956. Chicago City News Bureau, reporter, Asst City Editor, to 1959. *Chicago Daily News*, columnist, to 1978; Assoc Editor, 1977-78. *Sun-Times*, columnist, to 1984. *Chicago Tribune*, columnist, current, 1984. Tribune Media Services, columnist, current. Heywood Broun Award, 1968; Pulitzer Prize, Commentary, 1972; U. of MO School of Journalism Medal, Service, 1979. Author 4 books, including *Slats Grobnik and Other Friends*, 1973.

Ruby, Michael. *U.S.News & World Report*. Editor. U. of MO, BSJ. Nieman Fellow, 1974-75. *BusinessWeek*, correspondent, acting Chicago bureau chief, writer, 1966-71. *Newsweek*, business writer, to 1978; Sr Editor, business, to 1981; National Affairs Editor, to 1982; Managing Editor, international editions, to 1983; chief of correspondents; Asst Managing Editor, to 1986. *U.S.News & World Report*, Exec Editor; Editor, current, 1989.

Rudnitsky, Howard. *Forbes*. Senior Editor. CCNY, Baruch School, 1959, BBS. Moody's Investor Services, 1959-61. *Forbes*, statistical dept head, to 1969; writer; Assoc Editor; Sr Editor, current, 1978. Gerald Loeb Award, 1985.

Rule, Sheila. *The New York Times*. London Reporter. B. 1950, St. Louis, MO. U. of MO at Columbia, 1972, Journalism. *St. Louis Post-Dispatch*, reporter, to 1977. *The New York Times*, metro reporter, to 1984; temp assgnmt, Nairobi, to 1985; Nairobi bureau chief, to 1989; London reporter, current, 1989. Meyer Berger Award, 1985.

Rusher, William Allen. News Enterprise Association. Columnist. B. 1923, Chicago. Princeton, 1943, AB; Harvard, 1948, JD. US Army Air Force, 1943-46. Shearman & Sterling & Wright, NYC, assoc, 1948-56. NY Senate Finance Committee, special counsel, 1955. US Senate, Internal Security Subcommittee, assoc counsel, 1956-57. *National Review*, Publisher, to 1987; National Review, Inc, Director, VP, to 1987. Universal Press Syndicate, columnist, 1973-82. Newspaper Enterprise Assn. "The Conservative Advocate" columnist, current, 1982. Author 4 books, including *The Rise of the Right*, 1984; co-author (with Mark Hatfield & Arlie Schardt) *Amnesty?* 1973.

Russakoff, Dale. *The Washington Post*. National Reporter. B. 1952, Birmingham, AL. *The Alabama Journal*, reporter. *The Atlanta* (GA) *Journal*, reporter. *The Washington Post*, from 1980: metro reporter; national reporter, current. AP Newswriting Award for Public Service, 1980; UPI News Deadline Reporting Award, 1979.

Ryskind, Allan H. *Human Events*. Capitol Hill Editor. B. 1934, NY. Pomona College, 1956, BA-Political Science; UCLA, 1959, MA. City News Service, LA, summer 1959. *Human Events*, Asst Editor, to 1967; Capitol Hill Editor, current, 1967; co-owner, current. Author *Hubert*, 1968.

Safer, Morley. CBS-TV News. "60 Minutes" Correspondent. B. 1931, Toronto, Canada. U. of Western Ontario, 1952. Reuters, London, 1955. CBC, correspondent, to 1960; London correspondent, to 1964. BBC, correspondent, 1961. CBS-TV News, Vietnam correspondent, 1964-71; "60 Minutes" correspondent, current, 1971. *Sigma Delta Chi* Award, 1965; Peabody Award, 1965; Overseas Press Club Award, 1965, '66; 4 Emmy Awards.

Safire, William. *The New York Times*. "Essay" & "On Language" Columnist. B. 1929, NYC. Studied Syracuse, 1947-49. New York Herald Tribune Syndicate, reporter, to 1951. WNBC-TV-WNBT, Europe & Middle East correspondent, to 1951. US Army correspondent, to 1954. WNBC-TV (NYC), Radio & TV Producer, to 1955. Tex McCrary Inc, VP, to 1960. Safire Public Relations, Inc, President, to 1968. Special asst to President Nixon, to 1973. *The New York Times*, "Essay" columnist, current, 1973; "On Language" columnist (*The New York Times Magazine*), current, 1979. Pulitzer Prize, Distinguished Commentary, 1978. Author 9 books, including *Freedom*, 1987; co-author 2 books, including *What's The Good Word?* (with Leonard Safire), 1982.

Salpukas, Agis. *The New York Times*. Transportation Reporter. B. 1939, Kaunas, Lithuania. Long Island U., 1961, History. *The New York Times*, local staff, 1963-65; LI reporter, to 1970; Detroit, to 1976; "Business Day" reporter, to 1981; transportation reporter, current, 1981. *Sigma Delta Chi* Award, 1975.

Sancton, Thomas A. *Time*. Associate Editor. B. 1949, Jackson, MO. Harvard, 1971, American History & Literature; Oxford, 1978, DPhil-Modern History. *Time*, "World" writer, 1979-81; Assoc Editor, "World" Section, to 1982; Paris correspondent, to 1985; *Time* International, European-based Assoc Editor, to 1986; Assoc Editor, World, current, 1987. Bowdoin Prize, 1971; Helen Choate Bell Prize, 1971;

Gilbert Chinard Prize, 1979; Overseas Press Club, 1988. Co-author (with Donald Morrison) *Mikhail Gorbachev*, 1988.

Sanger, David E. *The New York Times*. Tokyo Financial Correspondent. B. 1960, White Plains, NY. Harvard, 1982, Government. *The New York Times*, college stringer, to 1982; news clerk, to 1983; technology reporter, to 1988; Tokyo financial correspondent, current, 1988.

Sanoff, Alvin P. *U.S.News & World Report*. Senior Editor. B. 1941, NYC. Harvard, 1963, Sociology; Columbia, 1964, MSJ. U. of MI, National Endowment for the Humanities Journalism Fellowship, 1974-75. Newhouse Newspapers, DC Desk Editor, 1965-66. *The Sun*, reporter, editorial writer, to 1971. *Dayton Journal Herald*, Editorial Page Editor, to 1977. *U.S.News & World Report*, Assoc Editor, to 1983; Sr Editor, current, 1983. AP Award Best Editorial Writing, 1974.

Sansbury, Timothy J. *The Journal of Commerce*. Reporter. B. 1955, Cincinnati, OH. Georgetown, 1977, Foreign Service. *The Piqua* (OH) *Daily Call*, 1979-80. McGraw-Hill, Inc, to 1986. *The Journal of Commerce*, energy reporter, current, 1986.

Sansing, John. *The Washingtonian*. Executive Editor. B. 1943, Memphis, TN. Amherst College, 1965, English; U. of VA Law School, 1968, JD. Private Law Practice, 1969-78. *The Washingtonian*, Exec Editor, current, 1978.

Saporito, Bill. *Fortune*. Associate Editor. B. Harrison, NJ. Bucknell, BA-American Studies; Syracuse U., MAJ. *The* (NY) *Daily News*, 1978. *Chain Store Age Supermarkets* Magazine, Sr Editor. Freelance, 1982-84. *Fortune*, Assoc Editor, current, 1984; founded Pittsburgh editorial office.

Saunders, Laura. *Forbes*. Associate Editor. U. of South Sewanee, TX, 1976, BA-English Language & Literature. National Fire Protection Assn, Boston, editorial dept, 1977-81. *Forbes*, reporter-researcher, to 1982; Sr Reporter-Researcher to 1984; reporter, to 1986; writer, to 1989; Assoc Editor, current, 1989.

Sawyer, L. Diane. ABC-TV News. "Prime Time Live" Co-Host. B. 1945, Glasgow, KY. Wellesley College, 1967, BA. WLKY-TV (Louisville), reporter, to 1970. White House, press office administrator, to 1974. Researcher, Richard Nixon's memoirs, to 1978. CBS-TV News, State Dept correspondent, to 1981; "CBS Morning News" co-anchor; "60 Minutes" correspondent, to 1989. ABC-TV News, "Prime Time Live" co-host, current, 1989.

Scardino, Albert. *The New York Times*. Press Reporter. B. 1948, Baltimore. Columbia, 1970, American History; U. of CA, Berkeley, 1976, MSJ. AP, Charleston, WV, 1971. *The Georgia Gazette*, Exec Editor, 1978-85. *The New York Times*, "The Week in Review," Editor, 1985; business/financial correspondent, 1986-88; press reporter, current, 1988. Golden Quill, International Society of Weekly Newspaper Editors, 1982; Silver Gavel, GA Bar Assn, 1984; Pulitzer Prize, Editorial Writing, 1984.

Schacter, Jim. *Los Angeles Times*. Business Writer. B. 1959, Glendale, CA. Columbia, 1980, BA-History. *Jacksonville* (FL) *Journal*, reporter, 1980-82. *Kansas City* (MO) *Star*, reporter, labor writer, to 1985. *Los Angeles Times*, business writer, current, 1985. Inland Daily Press Assn, 1st Place, 1983-84; American Public Planning Assn, 1st Place, 1983; San Diego County Bar Assn, 1st & 3rd Place, 1987.

Schanche, Don. *Los Angeles Times*. Caribbean Bureau Chief. B. 1926, New Brunswick, NJ. U. of GA, 1949, BAJ. US Navy. *Marietta* (GA) *Daily Journal*, reporter, City Editor, 1947-48. International News Service, Atlanta correspondent, 1949; Raleigh bureau chief, 1950; Miami feature writer, to 1951; Korean War correspondent, to 1952, Tokyo bureau, 1952. *Life*, reporter, 1953; Asst Editor, national affairs, 1955-56; DC correspondent, to 1958; writer, Mercury Astronauts, to 1960. *Sports Illustrated*, member, founding editorial group, 1953; staff writer, 1954. *Saturday Evening Post*, Assoc Editor, 1960; Contributing Editor, DC bureau chief, to 1962; Exec Editor, Managing Editor, to 1964. *Holiday*, Editor-in-Chief, to 1967. Communicaid, Inc, President, to 1968. Freelance, to 1975. *Los Angeles Times*, Cairo bureau chief, to 1981; Rome bureau chief, to 1988; Caribbean bureau chief, current, 1988. Author 2 books, including *Mister Pop*, 1970; co-author (with David Simmons) *Man High*, 1961.

Scheibla, Shirley Hobbs. *Barron's*. Senior Washington Editor. B. Newport News, VA. William & Mary, U. of NC, BA. *The Wall Street Journal*, DC correspondent. Founded & ran own DC news bureau. *Financial Times*, correspondent. *The Richmond News Leader*, correspondent. *Daily Press* (Newport News, VA), correspondent. *Barron's*, part-time writer, 1958-62; Assoc Editor, to 1967; Sr DC Editor, current, 1967. Author *Poverty Is Where The Money Is*, 1968.

Schifrin, Matt. *Forbes.* Associate Editor. Cornell, 1983, BS-Economics. Citicorp, management intern, 1983. FNN, reporter-researcher, Wall Street, to 1984. *American Banker,* freelance, to 1983-84. *Forbes,* reporter-researcher, to 1987; writer, to 1989; Assoc Editor, current, 1989.

Schmemann, Serge. *The New York Times.* Bonn Bureau Chief. B. 1945, France. Harvard, 1967. BA-English; Columbia, 1971, MA-Slavic Studies. AP, to 1980. *The New York Times,* metro staff, to 1981; Moscow correspondent, to 1984; Moscow bureau chief, to 1987; Bonn bureau chief, current, 1987.

Schneider, Keith. *The New York Times.* Washington Reporter. B. 1956, White Plains, NY. Haverford College, 1978. Freelance, to 1979. *Wilkes-Barre (PA) Times Leader,* reporter, 1979. *The News and Courier* (SC), reporter, to 1981. 2 independent news services. Editor, to 1985. *The New York Times,* DC reporter, current, 1985. George Polk Award, Investigative Reporting, 1984.

Schoenberger, Karl. *Los Angeles Times.* Tokyo Correspondent. Stanford, 1976, BA-Japanese Language & Literature. Kyoto U., Japan, Research Fellow, 1977-79. Freelance, to 1982. AP, reporter, Tokyo, to 1983; newsman, Philadelphia, to 1984. *Hartford Courant,* metro reporter, to 1986; reporter, projects desk, to 1986. *The Asian Wall Street Journal,* correspondent, to 1987; Tokyo bureau chief, to 1988. *Los Angeles Times,* intern reporter, 1982; correspondent, Tokyo, current, 1988. *Sigma Delta Chi* CT Journalism Award, 1985; UPI New England Newspaper Award, 1st place, 1985.

Schulz, William. *Reader's Digest.* Managing Editor. B. 1939, NYC. Antioch College, 1961, Political Science. Fulton Lewis Jr. King Features Syndicate, column ghostwriter, to 1966. *Reader's Digest,* Assoc Editor, to 1971; Sr Editor, to 1973; DC Editor & bureau chief, to 1988; Managing Editor, current, 1988.

Sciolino, Elaine. *The New York Times.* Washington Correspondent. B. 1948, Buffalo, NY. Canisius College (NY), 1970; NYU, 1971, MA-History. Edward R. Murrow Press Fellow, 1982-83. *Newsweek,* reporter, from 1971; Paris correspondent, to 1980; Rome bureau chief, to 1982; roving international correspondent, 1983-84. *The New York Times,* metro reporter, to 1985; UN bureau chief, to 1987; DC correspondent, current, 1987. Page 1 Award, 1978; Religious Public Relations Council Merit Award, 1979; Overseas Press Club Citation, Magazine Reporting from Abroad, 1983; co-recipient National Headliners Award, Outstanding Major News Event Coverage, 1981.

Scott, Gavin. *Time.* Midwest Bureau Chief. B. 1936, Montreal, Canada. Harvard, 1958, English. *The Gazette* (Montreal), 1959. *Time,* Montreal bureau chief, to 1960; Ottawa correspondent, 1961; Buenos Aires bureau chief, to 1966; Madrid correspondent, 1966; deputy bureau chief, London, to 1968; Boston bureau chief, 1969; Mideast bureau chief, Beirut, to 1972; Saigon bureau chief, to 1974; Madrid bureau chief, to 1976; Africa correspondent, Nairobi, 1977; San Francisco bureau chief, to 1981; South America bureau chief, Rio de Janeiro, to 1987; Midwest bureau chief, Chicago, current, 1987. Maria Moors Cabot Award, 1986.

Seaman, Barrett. *Time.* Deputy Chief of Correspondents. B. 1945, NY. Hamilton College, 1967, English Literature; Columbia, 1971, MBA. *Fortune,* reporter, researcher; 1972. *Life,* reporter, 1972. *Time,* NY correspondent, 1973; Chicago correspondent, to 1976; Bonn correspondent, to 1978; Detroit bureau chief, to 1981; DC News Editor, to 1983; State Dept correspondent, to 1984; White House correspondent, to 1988; deputy chief of correspondents, current, 1988. Co-author *Going for Broke,* 1981.

Seib, Gerald F. *The Wall Street Journal.* Washington Correspondent. U. of KS, 1978, BSJ. *The Daily Kansan,* Editor, fall 1977. Sears Foundation Congressional intern, Rep. Gillis Long (LA), spring 1978. *The Wall Street Journal,* Dallas intern, summer 1977; Dallas reporter, 1978-80; Pentagon & State Dept reporter, to 1984; Middle East correspondent, to 1987; DC correspondent, current, 1987. Merriman Smith Award, 1988; Aldo Beckman Award for 1987 Reagan-Gorbachev Summit Coverage, 1988.

Seligman, Daniel. *Fortune.* Contributing Editor. B. 1924, NYC. Rutgers; NYU, AB. *The New Leader,* 1946; labor columnist, 1949-50. *The American Mercury,* Asst Editor, 1946-50. *Fortune,* Assoc Editor, to 1959; Board of Editors member, to 1966; Asst Managing Editor, to 1969; Exec Editor, 1969-77; Assoc Managing Editor, to 1989; Contributing Editor, current, 1989; "Keeping Up" columnist, current. Time, Inc. Sr Staff Editor, 1969.

Semple, Robert B., Jr. *The New York Times.* Associate Editorial Page Editor. B. 1936, St. Louis, MO. Yale, 1959; U. of CA, Berkeley, 1961, MA-History. *The New York Times,* reporter, political reporter, White House correspondent, to 1973; Deputy National Editor, to 1975; London bureau chief, to 1977; Foreign Editor, to 1982; Editor, Op-Ed Page; Editorial Board Member, 1988; Assoc Editorial Page

Editor, current, 1989. NBC-TV News, "Meet the Press," panelist, current.

Seneker, Harry. *Forbes.* Senior Editor. B. 1941, Philadelphia. PA State U., 1967, BA-Psychology. Value Line, analyst, 1967-70. Trade papers, to 1976. *Forbes,* writer, to 1978; Assoc Editor, to 1982; Sr Editor, current, 1982. Developer, "Forbes 400."

Shabecoff, Philip. *The New York Times.* Washington Reporter. B. 1934, Bronx, NY. Hunter College, BA; U. of Chicago, MA. *The New York Times,* newsroom stenographer, 1959-60; news asst, business & financial dept to 1962; foreign trade reporter, to 1964; West Germany correspondent, to 1968; Tokyo correspondent, to 1970; DC reporter, current, 1970, environment. Contributor 2 books, including *American Government.*

Shales, Tom. *The Washington Post.* Chief TV Critic & TV Editor. B. 1944, Elgin, IL. American U., BA. *The DC Examiner,* Entertainment Editor. *The Washington Post,* "Style" writer, 1972-77; chief TV critic, current, 1977; TV Editor, current, 1979. Pulitzer Prize, 1988. Author *On the Air!;* co-author *The American Film Heritage.*

Shannon, Don. *Los Angeles Times.* United Nations Correspondent. B. 1923, Auburn, WA. Stanford, 1944, BA-Social Sciences; Stanford Law, 1947. Elementary Law. US Army, Pacific Theater, 1943-46. *Brazil Herald,* reporter, Rio de Janeiro, to 1948. UP, London correspondent, to 1951; Western Reporters, regional news bureau, DC, to 1954. *Los Angeles Times,* DC reporter, to 1961; Paris correspondent, to 1965; Africa correspondent, to 1966; Tokyo correspondent, to 1971; UN correspondent, to 1975; UN correspondent, DC, current, 1975.

Shapiro, Margaret. *The Washington Post.* Tokyo Correspondent. B. 1955, Newark, NJ. Harvard, 1977. *The Washington Post,* reporter, 1979-83; congressional reporter, to 1987; Tokyo correspondent, current, 1987.

Shapiro, Walter. *Time.* Senior Writer. B. 1947, NYC. U. of MI, 1970, BA-History, 1971, postgrad, European History. *Congressional Quarterly,* reporter, to 1970. *The Washington Monthly,* Editor, to 1976; Contributing Editor, current, 1976. Special asst, press secretary, to Secretary of Labor Ray Marshall, to 1978. Speechwriter to President Carter, 1979. *The Washington Post,* Sunday *Magazine* writer, to 1983. *Newsweek,* Gen Editor, national affairs writer, to 1987. *Time,* Sr Writer, current, 1987.

Shenon, Philip. *The New York Times.* Washington Reporter. B. 1959. Brown, 1981, English, *magna cum laude. The Brown Daily Herald,* Editor-in-Chief, President. *The New York Times,* James Reston's clerk, to 1982; copyboy, financial desk, to 1983; metro reporter, to 1985; DC reporter, current, 1985.

Shepard, Stephen B. *BusinessWeek.* Editor-in-Chief. B. 1939, NYC. CCNY, 1961, BS-Engineering; Columbia, 1964, MS-Engineering. Columbia, adjunct prof, 1970-75; founder, Walter Bagehot Fellowship Program in Economics & Business Journalism. *Newsweek,* Sr Editor, National Affairs, to 1980. *Saturday Review,* Editor, 1981-82. *BusinessWeek,* 1966-75; Exec Editor, 1982-84; Editor-in-Chief, current, 1984. National Magazine Award; *Sigma Delta Chi* Headliners Award; U. of MO Award.

Sherman, Stratford P. *Fortune.* Board of Editors Member. B. 1952, CT. Harvard, 1974, English/Comparative Literature, *cum laude. The Harvard Lampoon,* writer. Netherlands Antilles, teacher. William Morrow Co, editorial asst, to 1977. *Fortune,* reporter, researcher, to 1982; Assoc Editor, to 1988; Board of Editors member, current, 1988.

Shields, Mark. *The Washington Post.* Columnist. B. 1937, Weymouth, MA. U. of Notre Dame, 1959, Philosophy & History. Govt asst, various positions. *The Washington Post,* editorial writer, 1979-81; columnist, current, 1979. Mutual Radio Network, commentary, 1984. CBS-TV, on-air analyst, 1984 Republican & Democratic conventions, campaign & election night. WMAL Radio (DC), commentary, to 1986. "The Capitol Gang," panelist. DC Dateline Award, Local Journalism. *Sigma Delta Chi,* 1985. Author *On the Campaign Trail,* 1985.

Shiner, Josette Sheeran. *The Washington Times.* Deputy Managing Editor. U. of CO, 1976, BA-Communications. *New York City Tribune,* National Desk Editor, 1976-77; DC reporter, to 1982. *The Washington Times,* Asst Managing Editor, features, 1984-85; Deputy Managing Editor, current, 1985. *Sigma Delta Chi;* National Press Club Vivian Award & Meritorious Service recognition, 1981; U. of GA Atrium Award, 1984.

Shlaes, Amity. *The Wall Street Journal/Europe.* Editorial Features Editor. B. 1960, Chicago. Yale, 1982, English. Fellowship, W. Berlin, 1982-83. *The Wall Street Journal,* foreign desk, 1983-84; Cleveland reporter, 1984; Europe staff, 1985; Editorial Features Editor/Europe, current, 1985.

Shogan, Robert. *Los Angeles Times.* National Political Correspondent. B. 1930, NYC. Syracuse U., 1951, Journalism & American Studies. *Detroit Free Press,* 1956-59. *Miami News,* Telegraph Editor to 1961. *The Wall Street Journal,* Asst Editor to 1965. Peace Corps, evaluation officer, 1966. *Newsweek,* correspondent, to 1972. *Los Angeles Times,* national political correspondent, current, 1973. MI AP Sweepstakes, 1st Place Feature Writing, 1958. Author 3 books, including *None of the Above,* 1982; co-author (with Tom Craig) *Detroit Race Riot.*

Shribman, David M. *The Wall Street Journal.* National Political Reporter. Dartmouth, 1976, AB-History, *Phi Beta Kappa;* Cambridge, Graduate Fellow, to 1977. *Buffalo Evening News,* metro reporter, to 1979; DC reporter, to 1980. *The Washington Star,* style & national reporter, to 1981. *The New York Times,* feature writer; Congressional correspondent; national politics reporter, to 1984. *The Wall Street Journal,* national political reporter, current, 1984.

Sidey, Hugh. *Time.* Washington Contributing Editor & "The Presidency" Columnist. B. 1927, Greenfield, IA. IA State U., 1950, BS. US Army, 1945-46. *Adair City (IA) Free Press,* reporter, 1950. *The Nonpareil* (Council Bluffs, IA), reporter, to 1951. *Omaha World-Herald,* reporter, to 1955. *Life,* correspondent, to 1958. *Time,* correspondent, to 1966; columnist, to 1969; Chief, to 1978; DC Contributing Editor, current, 1978; "The Presidency" essayist, current. Author 4 books, including *Portrait of a President,* 1975.

Sieff, Martin. *The Washington Times.* Assistant Foreign Desk Editor. B. 1950, Belfast, N. Ireland. Exeter College, Oxford, Modern History; postgrad London School of Economics. *Jerusalem Post,* researcher, Middle East affairs analyst, to 1979. *Belfast Telegraph,* Copy Editor, Production Editor, to 1984. *Belfast Newsletter,* Copy Editor, Foreign News Editor, to 1985. *The Washington Times,* Asst Foreign Desk Editor & Soviet, Central Europe & Middle East Editor, current, 1987.

Siegal, Allan M. *The New York Times.* Assistant Managing Editor. B. 1940, NYC. NYU, 1962. *The New York Times,* copyboy, from 1960; foreign desk, 1963-68; asst to Foreign Editor, to 1971; Asst Foreign Editor, to 1977; Asst Managing Editor, current, 1987.

Sigal, Leon V. *The New York Times.* Editoral Writer & Board Member. Yale, 1964; Harvard, 1971, PhD. Wesleyan U., govt prof, 1974-89. State Dept, 1979-80. *The New York Times,* editorial writer & board member, current, 1989. Author 3 books; co-author (with John Steinbruner) *Alliance Security,* 1983.

Silk, Leonard. *The New York Times.* "Economic Scene" Columnist. B. 1918, Philadelphia. U. of WI, 1940, AB; Duke U., 1947, PhD. *Phi Beta Kappa.* Sr Fellow, Brookings Institution, 1969-70; Poynter Fellow, 1974-75. Duke, Economics instructor, 1941-42. US Army Air Force, to 1945. U. of ME, economics instructor, to 1948. Simmons College, asst prof, Economics, to 1950. US Mission to NATO, Asst Economic Commissioner, 1952-54. *BusinessWeek,* Economics Editor, to 1964; Sr Editor, 1959-66; Vice-Chairman & Economist, to 1967; Editorial Page Editor & Chairman of the Editorial Board, to 1969. *The New York Times,* editorial board member, to 1976; "Economic Scene" columnist, current, 1976. Loeb Award, Distinguished Business & Financial Journalism, 1961, '66, '67, '71, '72; Overseas Press Club Citation, Foreign Economic Reporting, 1967; Overseas Press Club Bache Award, Best Business Reporting from Abroad, 1972; Gerald Loeb Memorial Award, 1977; Elliot V. Bell Award, 1983. Author 11 books, including *Economics in the Real World,* 1985; co-author 4 books.

Silvers, Robert B. *The New York Review of Books.* Editor. B. 1929, Mineola, NY. U. of Chicago, 1947, AB; *Ecole des Sciences Politiques* (Paris), 1950. *Paris Review,* 1952-53. Press Secretary, Gov Bowles (CT), 1950. *Paris Review,* editorial board member, current, 1954. *Harper's,* Assoc Editor, 1959-63. *The New York Review of Books,* Editor, current, 1962. Teachers & Writers Collaborative, NYC, Director, current, 1966. Editor *Writing in America,* 1960; translator, *La Gangrene,* 1961.

Sims, Calvin. *The New York Times.* Technology Reporter. B. 1963, Compton, CA. Yale, 1985, Mechanical Engineering. *Yale Scientific Magazine,* Editor-in-Chief, 1984-85. *American Scientist,* intern, 1983. WEWS-TV (Cleveland, OH), 1984. *The New York Times,* "Science Times" reporter, to 1986; "Business Day" reporter, to 1987; technology reporter, current, 1987. National Society of Professional Engineers Award, Journalistic Excellence, 1986.

Singer, Daniel. *The Nation.* European Correspondent. B. 1926, Warsaw. *Bachelier es lettre* (Philosophy), BSc-Economics. *The Economist,* writer; Paris correspondent. *The Nation,* European correspondent, current. Author 2 books, including *The Road To Gdansk,* 1968.

Slutsker, Gary. *Forbes.* Senior Editor & "Science & Technology" Editor. B. 1955, NYC. Middlebury College, 1977, BA-Political Science, honors; Columbia, 1978, MAJ. *Electronic News,* reporter, 1978-80. *Venture,* Assoc Editor, to 1982; Sr Editor, to 1984. *Forbes,* staff

writer, to 1985; Editor, "Faces Behind The Figures," to 1987; Assoc Editor, to 1989; Editor, "Science & Technology," current, 1987; Sr Editor, current, 1989.

Smilgis, Martha. *Time.* New York Correspondent. B. 1946, Chicago. U. of CA, Berkeley, 1968, Political Science. *Sports Illustrated,* reporter, 1975-77. *People,* Sr Writer to 1980; LA bureau chief, 1983-86. *Time,* show business correspondent, LA, to 1983; Assoc Editor, 1986-88; NY correspondent, current, 1988.

Smith, Emily T. *BusinessWeek.* Science Department Editor. U. of WA, BA-Art History; U. of MN, MA-Mass Communications. *BusinessWeek,* Boston correspondent, 1980-82; Boston bureau manager, to 1984; Dept Editor, science & technology, to 1988; Science Dept Editor, current, 1988. National Assn of Education Writers Award, 1982.

Smith, Geoffrey N. *Financial World.* Editor. B. 1939, Cleveland, OH. Princeton, 1961, AB; NYU, 1970, MBA. US Army, Prentice-Hall, Harcourt Brace, Manuscript Editor, 1964. *Forbes,* writer, 1966-70; Asst Managing Editor, to 1976; European bureau chief, to 1978; Special Operations Editor, creator "Up & Comers" column, 1979; "The Numbers Game" columnist, 1980; "Taxing Matters" columnist, to 1986. *Financial World,* Exec Editor, to 1988; Editor, current, 1988. Author *Sweat Equity,* 1986.

Smith, James. *Los Angeles Times.* Buenos Aires Bureau Chief. B. 1953, Boston. Yale, 1976, BA-History, *magna cum laude.* AP, Hartford (CT) correspondent, from 1976; World Desk Editor, NY; Hague correspondent; Johannesburg correspondent, News Editor; 1982-87; Asian News Editor, to 1987. *Los Angeles Times,* Buenos Aires bureau chief, current, 1988.

Smith, Lee. *Fortune.* Washington Bureau Chief & Board of Editors Member. B. 1937, NYC. Yale, 1959, English. AP, Seattle & Olympia, WA, 1962-65. *Newsweek,* writer, back-of-the-book sections, to 1970. *Black Enterprise,* Managing Editor, to 1971. Freelance, to 1973. *Dun's Review,* Sr Editor, to 1978. *Fortune,* writer, Board of Editors, current, 1978; Tokyo bureau chief, 1983-85; DC bureau chief, current, 1986. Overseas Press Club Citation for Excellence, 1985.

Smith, R. Jeffrey. *The Washington Post.* National Security Correspondent. B. 1954, Chicago. Duke U., 1976, BA-Political Science & Public Policy Studies; Columbia, 1977, MSJ. *Sarasota* (FL) *Herald-Tribune,* summer intern, 1973. *Des Moines Register,* DC summer intern, 1974. *Milwaukee Journal,* summer intern, 1975. *Science,* DC Sr Writer, news & comment section, 1977-86. *The Washington Post,* national security correspondent, current, 1986. National Assn Of Science Writers Science-in-Society Journalism Award, 1979, '82; Overseas Press Club Award Citation, Excellence, 1984; American Society of Magazine Editors National Magazine Award, Public Interest, 1986.

Smith, Randall. *The Wall Street Journal.* "Heard On The Street" Columnist. B. 1950, Montclair, NJ. Harvard, 1972, Social Relations. US Navy, 1972-76. MBA Communications, to 1977. *New York Post,* city hall reporter, to 1980. The (NY) *Daily News,* real estate reporter, to 1981. *The Wall Street Journal,* real estate reporter, to 1983; institutional investing reporter, to 1985; computer reporter, to 1986; "Heard On The Street" columnist, current, 1986.

Smith, Richard M. *Newsweek.* Editor-in-Chief. B. 1946, Denorir, MI. Albion College, 1968, Political Science & Economics; Columbia, 1970, MSJ. *Newsweek,* Editor-in-Chief, current.

Smith, Stephen. *Newsweek.* Executive Editor. B. 1949, NYC. U. of PA, 1971, BA-History. *Daily Hampshire Gazette,* City Hall reporter, political writer, to 1973. *Amherst Times-Union,* special assgnmt reporter, to 1974. *The Philadelphia Inquirer,* reporter, to 1975; Deputy Regional Editor, to 1976. *The Boston Globe,* Asst Business Editor, 1976; roving New England reporter, 1979; Asst Metro Editor, to 1978. *Horizon,* Sr Editor, 1978. *Time,* staff writer, to 1980; Sr Editor, 1981; "Nation" Editor, to 1985; acting Asst Managing Editor, to 1986. *Newsweek,* Exec Editor, current, 1986. Ernie Pyle Memorial Award, 1977.

Snow, Tony. *The Washington Times.* Editorial Page Editor. *Greensboro* (NC) *Record.* The *Virginian-Pilot.* The *Newport News Daily Press.* The *Detroit News,* Deputy Editorial Page Editor, to 1987. *The Washington Times,* Editorial Page Editor, current, 1987.

Solomon, Burt. *National Journal.* Staff Correspondent. B. 1948, Baltimore. Harvard, 1970, Social Studies. *Texas Observer,* freelance, 1971-72. *The Danvers* (MA) *Times,* reporter, to 1973. *The Real Paper* (Cambridge, MA), reporter, to 1975. *The Energy Daily,* Editor, to 1985. *National Journal,* staff correspondent, current.

Sowell, Thomas. Scripps-Howard News Service. Columnist. B. 1930, Gastonia, NC. Harvard, 1958, Economics; U. of Chicago,

1968, PhD. Hoover Institution, Stanford Sr Fellow. *Los Angeles Herald-Examiner*, 1978-80. Scripps-Howard News Service, columnist, current, 1984. Author several books, including *Ethnic America*.

Spaeth, Anthony P. *The Asian Wall Street Journal*. India Reporter. Williams College (MA), 1977. *The Asian Wall Street Journal*, reporter, to 1984; Manila reporter, to 1988; India reporter, current, 1988.

Spevacek, Jennifer J. *The Washington Times*. Capitol Hill Reporter. B. 1961, Iowa City, IA. Wellesley College 1979-1981; U. of VA, 1983, BA-English. *The Washington Times*, VA capitol reporter, 1984-86; Capitol Hill reporter, current, 1986.

Stabler, Charles N. *The Wall Street Journal*. Assistant Managing Editor. B. 1925, Trenton, NJ. Swarthmore College, 1950, Economics. *Richmond Times-Dispatch*, reporter, to 1952. *The Wall Street Journal*, reporter, to 1955; founder Southeastern bureau, 1955; Managing Editor, Pacific Coast edition, to 1964; Dow Jones Books, Director, to 1966; News Editor, *The Wall Street Journal*, Banking & Finance Editor, to 1981; Asst Managing Editor, current, 1981. Loeb Award, 1967.

Stahl, Leslie. CBS-TV News. "Face the Nation" Moderator. B. 1941, Lynn, MA. Wheaton College (MA), 1963, BA, *cum laude*. Asst to speechwriter, NYC Mayor Lindsay, 1966-67. NBC-TV News, "Huntley-Brinkley Report" NY election unit researcher, to 1969. WHDH-TV (Boston), producer, reporter, to 1972. CBS-TV News, DC correspondent, from 1972; "Face the Nation" moderator, current, 1983. TX Headliners Award, 1973.

Stanfield, Rochelle L. *National Journal*. Staff Correspondent. B. 1940, Chicago. Northwestern, 1962, BSJ, 1963, MSJ. The Council of State Governments, to 1966. Voice of America, news writer, 1966. National Governors' Assn, to 1970. US Advisory Commission on Intergovernmental Relations, information officer. US Conference of Mayors, to 1976. *National Journal*, staff correspondent, current, 1976.

Stanley, Alessandra. *Time*. Senior Correspondent. B. 1955, Boston. Harvard, 1977, Comparative Literature. Freelance, Paris, 1978-81. *Time*, correspondent, to 1989; sr correspondent, current, 1989.

Steel, Ronald. *The New Republic*. Contributing Editor. B. 1931, Morris, IL. Northwestern, 1953; Harvard, 1955, Political Science. Scholastic Magazines, 1959-62. Freelance, current, 1962. *The New Republic*, Contributing Editor, current, 1980. Sidney Hillman Prize, 1968; Book Critics Circle Award, 1980; Bancroft Prize, American History, 1980; *Los Angeles Times* Book Award, 1980; *Sigma Delta Chi* Book Award, 1981; *The Washington Monthly* Book Award, 1981. Author 4 books, including *Walter Lippman And The American Century*.

Steiger, Paul E. *The Wall Street Journal*. Deputy Managing Editor. Yale, 1964, BA-Economics. *Los Angeles Times*, writer, 1968-71; DC economic correspondent, to 1978; Business Editor, LA, to 1983. *The Wall Street Journal*, San Francisco reporter, 1966-68; Asst Managing Editor, 1983-85; Deputy Managing Editor, current, 1985. 3 Gerald Loeb Awards, 2 John Hancock Awards, Economic & Business Coverage. Co-author *The 70's Crash*.

Stein, Benjamin. *The American Spectator*, *Barron's*. Contributor. B. 1944, DC. Columbia College, 1966, Political Science/Economics; Yale Law, JD. Presidents Nixon & Ford, speechwriter. *The Wall Street Journal*, Editor; Editorial Page; Arts & Culture. *Los Angeles Herald Examiner*, columnist, 1977-78. *GQ*, Contributing Editor, current. *The American Spectator*, Contributing Editor, current. *Barron's*, contributor, current. Pepperdine U. Best Professor of Journalism; Freedoms Foundation Award, 1978. Author many books, including *On The Brink*.

Stelzer, Irwin M. *The American Spectator*. "Business of America" Columnist. NYU, BA, MA. Cornell, PhD-Economics. National Economic Research Associates, founder & president. Stelzer Assoc, President, current. Harvard. Regulated Industries Group, chairman, current. *The Sunday Times*, US economic/political columnist, current. *Telematics*, editorial board, current. *The American Spectator*, "Business of America" columnist, current. Author *Selected Antitrust Cases*.

Stephens, Philip Francis. *Financial Times*. Political Editor. B. 1953, London. Worcester College, Oxford, 1971-74, Modern History. Fulbright Fellow, Economic Journalism. *Los Angeles Times*, 1986. Europa publications, Asst Editor, to 1976. *Commerce International*, writer; Editor, to 1979. Reuters, London, Brussels correspondent, to 1983. *Financial Times*, economics correspondent, to 1989; Political Editor, current, 1989.

Sterba, James P. *The Wall Street Journal*. Assistant Foreign Editor. B. 1943, Detroit. MI State U., 1966, BAJ. *The Evening Star*, DC reporter, to 1967. *The New York Times*, asst to James Reston, to 1968; reporter, 1968; war correspondent, Saigon, to 1970; bureau chief, Jakarta, Indonesia & roving Asian correspondent, to 1973; Denver bureau chief, to 1975; Houston bureau chief, to 1977; economic develop-

ment correspondent, 1978; Hong Kong bureau chief, to 1980; Peking bureau chief, 1981; science writer, 1982. *The Wall Street Journal*, reporter & Editor, foreign desk, 1982; Asst Foreign Editor & special writer, current, 1983. Distinguished Alumni Award, 1970.

Stern, Richard. *Forbes*. Senior Editor. B. 1941, NYC. Adelphi College newspaper, Editor. AP, Editor, 1970-74. *Securities Week*, Editor, to 1976. *Institutional Investor*, *The Wall Street Newsletter*, Editor, to 1979. *The (NY) Daily News*, business columnist, to 1980. *Forbes*, Sr Editor, current, 1980. Gerald Loeb Award, 1985.

Sterngold, James. *The New York Times*. Japan Reporter. B. 1954, Detroit. Middlebury College, 1977, BA-Philosophy. Columbia, 1980, MSJ. Time-Life Books, freelance, 1978-80. AP-Dow Jones Newswire, Hong Kong bureau founder, correspondent, to 1984. *The New York Times*, "Business Day" reporter, to 1989; Japan reporter, current, 1989. Publishers' Award, 1987.

Stevenson, Richard W. *The New York Times*. Los Angeles Correspondent. B. NYC. U. of PA, 1981, BA-English; London School of Economics, 1982, MA. *Ad Forum*, Sr Editor, 1983-84. *The New York Times*, business reporter, to 1984; LA correspondent, current, 1986.

Stewart, James B. *The Wall Street Journal*. "Page One" Editor. B. 1952. DePauw, 1973, BA-History; Harvard, 1976, JD. Cravath, Swaine & Moore, lawyer, 1976-79. *American Lawyer*, Exec Editor, to 1983. *The Wall Street Journal*, legal writer, to 1988; "Page One" Editor, current, 1988. Pulitzer Prize, 1988. Author *The Partners*.

Stewart, William Morgan. *Time*. Southeast Asia Bureau Chief. B. 1937, Dundee, Scotland. Johns Hopkins, 1958, History. US Foreign Service (DC, India, Vietnam), 1962-71. *Time*, New Delhi bureau chief, 1971-73; Beirut correspondent, 1974; Tokyo bureau chief, to 1977; deputy chief of correspondents, 1978; Assoc Editor, 1979; Middle East bureau chief, Beirut, to 1984; DC correspondent, 1984; diplomatic correspondent, to 1986; Hong Kong bureau chief, to 1989; SE Asia bureau chief, current, 1989.

Stillman, Whit. *The American Spectator*. New York Editor. B. 1952, DC. Harvard, 1973, US History. *The Harvard Crimson*, News Editor, 1970-73. *The American Spectator*, contributor, to 1978; Publisher, to 1979; NY Editor, current, 1979. *Access*, Daily News Briefing, Exec Editor, 1979-80.

Stockton, William. *The New York Times*. Sunday Business Editor. B. 1944, Raton, NM. NM Institute of Mining & Technology, 1966, BS-Chemistry. Nieman Fellow, 1972-73. AP, 1968-75. Physicians Radio Network, Exec Editor, to 1979. *The New York Times*, Director, science news & "Science Times" Editor, to 1982; asst to Exec Editor, to 1985; Mexico bureau chief, to 1986; NY reporter, to 1989, Sunday Business Editor, current, 1989. Author 2 books, including *Altered Destinies*, 1979; co-author (with John Noble Wilford) *Spaceliner*, 1981.

Stokes, Bruce. *National Journal*. International Economics Correspondent. B. 1948, Butler, PA. Georgetown, 1970, International Affairs; Johns Hopkins, 1975, MA. US Japan Leadership Fellow, 1987. Worldwitch Institute, 1975-82. National Public Radio, 1983. *National Journal*, international economics correspondent, current, 1984. Author *Helping Ourselves*, 1981.

Stout, Hilary. *The Wall Street Journal*. Economics Reporter. B. 1962. Brown, 1984, BA-European History & Literature. *The Vineyard Gazette* (Martha's Vineyard, MA), reporter, 1984-86. *The New York Times*, clerk, James Reston & freelance contributor, to 1988. *The Wall Street Journal*, economics reporter, current, 1988.

Strobel, Warren Paul. *The Washington Times*. National Desk Reporter. B. 1962, Camp Zama, Japan. U. of MO (Columbia), 1984, Journalism. *Maneater*, U. of MO, Editor, 1983. *Missourian* (Columbia, MO), state capitol reporter, spring 1984; city hall reporter, fall 1984. *The Washington Times*, intern, metro desk, summer 1984; metro reporter, to 1986; national desk reporter, current, 1986.

Struck, Myron. *Defense News*. Writer. B. 1953, NYC. Miami-Dade Community College, 1971-73; FL International U., 1973-75. *The Good Times* (FL International U. newspaper), founder, 1975. *The Miami Herald*, Sunday Features writer, Editor, 1974-75. Press asst to Michael Abrams, Chairman, Dade Cty Democratic Party, 1975. *Roll Call*, reporter, to 1976, 1979; Managing Editor, 1987. Press secretary, Rep. Phillip Burton (D-CA), 1977-79. States News Service, reporter, Desk Editor, to 1981. *The Washington Post*, reporter, "Federal Report" page, to 1985. *The Washington Times*, reporter, Asst National Editor, political coordinator, '86 elections, to 1987. *Defense News*, writer, current.

Sullivan, Allanna. *The Wall Street Journal*. Reporter. Queen's College (NY), 1971. BA-English; Columbia, 1977, MSJ. *Boating*, to 1975. *The Record* (Hackensack, NJ), Copy Editor, 1977. *Nucleonics*

Week, Wire Editor, to 1978. *Coal Age*, Asst Editor, Assoc Editor, to 1982. AP-Dow Jones, reporter, to 1984. *The Wall Street Journal*, reporter, current, 1984.

Sullivan, John Fox. *National Journal*. President & Publisher. B. 1943, Philadelphia. Yale, 1966, American Studies; Columbia, 1968, MBA. *Newsweek*, 1970-75. *National Journal*, President, Publisher, current, 1975.

Sullivan, Scott. *Newsweek*. European Regional Editor. B. 1937, Cleveland, OH. Yale, 1958, English; Cambridge, 1960, BA, 1964, MA. *The Sun*, reporter, 1964-66; City Editor, to 1970; Paris bureau chief, to 1973. *Newsweek*, Paris bureau chief, to 1975; Chief Diplomatic Correspondent, to 1978; Paris bureau chief, to 1983; European Editor, current, 1983. Front Page Award, 1979; Overseas Press Club Awards, 1981, '82, '83, '85. Author *The Shortest, Gladdest Years*.

Sulzberger, Arthur Ochs. *The New York Times*, President & Publisher. The New York Times Company, Chairman & Chief Executive. B. 1926, NYC. Columbia, 1951, BA. *The New York Times* Company, from 1951; asst treasurer, 1958-63; President, Publisher, current, 1963. *The Wall Street Journal* Bronze Award, 1988.

Summers, Colonel Harry G. Jr. *U.S.News & World Report*, Contributing Editor. Los Angeles Times Syndicate, Military & Political Affairs Columnist. B. 1932, Covington, KY. U. of MD, 1957, BS-Military Science; US Army Command & General Staff College, 1968, MS-Military Arts & Science; Army War College, 1981. Infantry Squad Leader, Korea; battalion & corps operations officer, Vietnam; negotiator with N. Vietnam on POW/MIA issues; negotiator, US withdrawal terms from Hanoi; Gen MacArthur Chair of Military Research, Army War College, 1947-85. Freelance, 1968-75. *U.S.News & World Report*, Sr Military Correspondent, 1985-87; Contributing Editor, current, 1987. Los Angeles Times Syndicate, military & political affairs columnist, current, 1987. Lecturer, military strategy & military-media relations, current. Author *On Strategy*, 1982 (OH State U. Furness Award); "Vietnam War Almanac," *Facts on File*, 1985.

Suro, Roberto. *The New York Times*. National Correspondent. Yale, 1973; Columbia, MSJ. *Chicago Sun-Times*, 1975-78. *Chicago Tribune*, 1978. *Time*, correspondent, Chicago, DC, Beirut, Rome, to 1985. *The New York Times*, Rome correspondent, to 1989; national correspondent, current, 1989.

Swardson, Anne. *The Washington Post*. Financial Desk Writer. Cornell, 1975, BA-Government; Ohio U., MSJ. *Business Week*, 1977-81. *The Dallas Morning News*, DC Bureau, to 1985. *The Washington Post*, financial desk writer, current, 1985.

Swartz, Steve. *The Wall Street Journal*. "Page One" Editorial Staff. B. 1962, Ridley Park, PA. Harvard, 1984, Government. *The Wall Street Journal*, reporter, 1984-86; securities industry reporter, to 1989; "Page One" editorial staff, current, 1989.

Swoboda, Frank. *The Washington Post*. National Reporter. B. Hanover, NH. Harvard, Nieman Fellow, 1974. UPI. White House reporter. *BusinessWeek*, DC reporter. *The Sun*, labor/economics reporter. *The Washington Post*, Asst Editor, business/financial news, 1978-82; Asst Managing Editor, business/financial news, to 1987; national reporter, current, 1987.

Tagliabue, John. *The New York Times*. Eastern Europe Correspondent. B. 1942, NJ. St. Peter's College; Catholic U. (Milan); U. of Bonn. *The Sun*, Bonn correspondent, to 1980. *The New York Times*, economics correspondent, Bonn, to 1988; Eastern Europe correspondent, current, 1988.

Talbott, Strobe. *Time*. Editor at Large & Columnist. B. 1946, Dayton, OH. Yale, 1968, BA; Oxford, 1971, MA (Rhodes Scholar). *Time*, Eastern European correspondent, to 1973; State Dept correspondent, to 1975; White House correspondent, to 1977; diplomatic correspondent, from 1977; DC bureau chief, to 1989; columnist, current, 1989; Editor at Large, current, 1989. Edward Weintal Prize, Distinguished Diplomatic Reporting, 1980; Overseas Press Club Award, 1983. Author 2 books, including *Deadly Gambits*.

Tanzer, Andrew. *Forbes*. Pacific Bureau Manager. B. 1957, DC. Wesleyan U., 1979, BA-East Asian Studies, *magna cum laude*; Columbia, 1980, MAJ. *Far Eastern Economic Review*, correspondent, Taiwan, 1980-83; China trade correspondent, Hong Kong, Editor, newsletter, to 1984. *Forbes*, LA writer, to 1985; Pacific bureau manager, current, 1985.

Taubman, Philip. *The New York Times*. Washington Deputy News Editor. B. 1948, NYC. Stanford, 1970, Modern European History. *Time*, Boston staff, 1970-73; writer, NY, 1976; DC staff, 1977. *Esquire*, Roving Editor, 1979. *The New York Times*, DC staff, 1985; Moscow reporter, to 1986; Moscow bureau chief, to 1989; DC Deputy

News Editor, current, 1989. Polk Award, National Reporting, 1982, Foreign Policy Reporting, 1984.

Taylor, Alex, III. *Fortune*. Associate Editor. B. 1945, Greenwich, CT. Middlebury College, AB-History; U. of MO, MAJ. Columbia Graduate School of Journalism, adjunct professor. *Detroit Free Press*, business writer. *Time*, business writer/editor. *Money*, business writer/editor. *Fortune*, Assoc Editor, current, 1986.

Taylor, Paul. *The Washington Post*. Reporter. B. 1949, Brooklyn, NY. Yale, 1970, BA-American Studies. *Yale Daily News*, Exec Editor, 1969-70. *Winston-Salem Journal and Sentinel*, reporter, to 1973. *The Philadelphia Inquirer*, reporter & columnist, to 1981. *The Washington Post*, reporter, current, 1981.

Tempest, Rone. *Los Angeles Times*. Paris Bureau Chief. B. 1947, Ely, NV. U. of CA, Berkeley, 1969. U. of Chicago, Urban Journalism Fellow, 1973. *Daily Oklahoman/Oklahoma City Times*, Norman bureau chief, 1970. *Oklahoma Journal*, reporter, to 1972. *Detroit Free Press*, gen assgnmt reporter, to 1976. *Dallas Times Herald*, gen assgnmt reporter, to 1977; Metro Editor, to 1981. *Los Angeles Times*, Houston bureau chief, to 1984; New Delhi bureau chief, to 1988; Paris bureau chief, current, 1988. Sigma Delta Chi Distinguished Service Award; UPI Award for Excellence; Dallas Press Club Best Feature Story Award, 1976; Best Investigative Story Award, 1977.

Theodonacopoulos, Taki. *Manhattan, inc.*, Columnist. B. 1937, Athens, Greece. U. of VA, 1959, Tennis. *Acropolis*, reporter, 1969-75. *National Review*, reporter, to 1976. *The Spectator*, columnist, current, 1977. *The American Spectator*, columnist, current, 1982. *Manhattan, inc.*, columnist, current. Author 2 books, including *High Life, Low Life*.

Thomas, Cal. *Los Angeles Times* Syndicate. Columnist. B. 1942, DC. American U., 1968, English Literature. KPRC-TV (Houston, TX), to 1969, '73-77. NBC-TV News, 1961-65, '69-73. WTTG-TV, DC commentator, current, 1985. NPR, commentator, current, 1985. *Los Angeles Times* Syndicate, columnist, current, 1984. AMY Writing Award, 1987; AP, UPI Spot News Awards, Headliners.

Thomas, Evan. *Newsweek*. Washington Bureau Chief. Harvard, 1973; U. of VA Law, 1977. *Time*, legal reporter, to 1979; Supreme Court & Justice Dept correspondent, to 1981; Congressional correspondent, to 1983; "Nation" writer, Assoc Editor, to 1986. *Newsweek*, DC bureau chief, current, 1986.

Thomas, Helen. United Press International. White House Bureau Chief. B. 1920, Winchester, KY. Wayne U., 1942, BA. UPI, DC reporter, 1943-74; White House bureau chief, current, 1974. 4th Estate Award, National Press Club, 1984. Author *Dateline White House*.

Thomas, Rich. *Newsweek*. Chief Economic Correspondent. B. 1931, Detroit. U. of MI, 1952, BA-English Literature; postgrad U. of Frankfurt, W. Germany, 1955. US Army, 1952-55. U. of MI, Teaching Fellow, 1957. Poynter Fellow, Yale, 1975. UPI, correspondent, Detroit, to 1959. McGraw-Hill, Public Affairs, to 1960. *New York Post*, Financial Editor, to 1962. *Newsweek*, writer, Editor, NY, to 1970; chief economic correspondent, DC, current, 1970. Gerald M. Loeb Award, 1969, 1979.

Thurow, Roger. *The Wall Street Journal*. South Africa Reporter. B. Elgin, IL. U. of IA, 1979, BA-Journalism & Political Science. *Daily Iowan*, to 1977. *The Wall Street Journal*, intern, summer 1979; Dallas reporter, to 1981; Houston staff, to 1982; Bonn reporter (principal East-West reporter), to 1986; South Africa reporter, current, 1986.

Tolchin, Martin. *The New York Times*. Washington Reporter. B. 1928, NYC. ID State College, U. of UT; NY Law School, 1951. US Army, to 1953. Law clerk, NYC, to 1954. *The New York Times*, reporter, NY, to 1970; City Hall bureau chief, to 1973; DC reporter, current, 1973; White House correspondent, 1978-79; regional reporter; currently covering Congress. The Women's Press Club, NY Reporters Assn, 1 Hundred Year Assn, NY Newspaper Guild, & Citizen's Budget Commission, 1966. Co-author 3 books, including *Clout*.

Tomlinson, Kenneth Y. *Reader's Digest*. Executive Editor. B. 1944, Grayson County, VA. Randolph-Macon College, 1966, History. *Richmond Times-Dispatch*, reporter, 1965-68. *Reader's Digest*, correspondent, Sr Editor, to 1982; European Editor, Paris, 1977-78; Managing Editor, 1984-85; Exec Editor, current, 1985. Voice of America, Director, 1982-84. National Voluntary Service Advisory Commission, 1981-83. Co-author *P.O.W.*

Toner, Robin. *The New York Times*. Reporter. B. 1954. Syracuse U., 1976, Journalism & Political Science. Trends Publishing, 1976-77. *Charleston (WV) Daily Mail*, reporter, to 1982. *Journal and Constitution*, reporter, to 1985. *The New York Times*, reporter, DC, current, 1985.

Toth, Robert C. *Los Angeles Times.* Washington Writer. B. 1928, Blakely, PA. Washington U., 1952. BS-Chemical Engineering; Columbia, 1955. MSJ. Nieman Fellow, 1960-61; Pulitzer Traveling Scholar, 1955. US Marines, 1946-48; US Army, 1952-53. *Rubber World,* Assoc Editor, 1953-54. *The Journal* (Providence, RI), reporter, 1955-57. *New York Herald Tribune,* writer, to 1960; writer, DC, to 1962. *The New York Times,* science writer, to 1963. *Los Angeles Times,* writer, DC, science & Supreme Court, to 1965; London bureau chief, to 1970; State Dept correspondent, to 1972; White House correspondent, to 1974; Moscow bureau chief, to 1977; science writer, DC, to 1979; writer, DC, national security affairs, current, 1979. *Sigma Delta Chi* Award, Foreign Correspondence, 1978; Overseas Press Club Award, Foreign Correspondence, 1978; George Polk Award, Foreign Correspondence, 1978; co-recipient *Times* Editorial Award, 1985; Edward Weintal Prize, Diplomatic Reporting, 1986.

Trachtenberg, Jeffrey. *Forbes.* Senior Editor. B. 1950, Mineola, NY. Franklin & Marshall College, 1972, BA-Literature. *Socio-Economic Publications,* labor reporter, 1974-77. *Lebhar-Friedman Publications,* business writer, to 1978. *Women's Wear Daily,* feature writer, business reporter, to 1984. *Forbes,* staff writer, to 1985; "Faces" Editor, 1985; "Marketing" Editor, current, 1985; Sr Editor, current, 1987.

Trainor, Bernard E. *The New York Times.* Military Correspondent. B. 1928, NYC. Holy Cross, 1951, History; U. of CO, 1963, MA. US Marines, from 1947. Lt. Gen. to 1986. *The New York Times,* military correspondent, current, 1986. Author *History of the Marine Corps,* 1968.

Treaster, Joseph B. *The New York Times.* Caribbean Bureau Chief. B. 1941. U. of Miami, 1963, Journalism. *The Miami Herald,* reporter, to 1963. US Army newspapers, reporter, Vietnam, to 1965. *The New York Times,* reporter, to 1984; Caribbean bureau chief, current, 1984. Freelance, current. 3 Overseas Press Club Awards, 2 Page 1 Awards & Inter-American Press Assn Award. Co-author *Inside Report on the Hostage Crisis.*

Trillin, Calvin. *The New Yorker,* Staff Writer. King Features Syndicate, "Uncivil Liberties" Columnist. B. 1935, Kansas City, MO. Yale, 1957, BA-English. US Army. *Time. The New Yorker,* staff writer, current, 1963; "U.S. Journal" series, 1967-82; "American Chronicles" columnist, current, 1984. King Features Syndicate, "Uncivil Liberties" columnist, current. Author many books, including *If You Can't Say Something Nice,* 1987.

Trimble, Jeff. *U.S.News & News Report.* Moscow Bureau Chief. *U.S.News & World Report,* Rome bureau chief, to 1986; Moscow bureau chief, current, 1986.

Truell, Peter. *The Wall Street Journal.* Reporter. Marlborough College (UK), 1973, Arts & Sciences; Pembroke College, Cambridge, 1977, MA-Modern History, (economics & business); St. Anthony's College, Oxford, 1979, MPhil. *Librarie Du Liban* (Beirut), Asst Editor, Dictionary dept, 1979. Orion Bank Ltd, London, junior exec, 1980. *Economist Financial Report,* London, Managing Editor, to 1982. *Middle East Economic Digest,* Deputy Editor, 1982. *The Wall Street Journal/Europe,* reporter, London, to 1987. *The Wall Street Journal,* reporter, NY, to 1988; DC reporter, current, 1989.

Tucker, William. *The American Spectator,* New York Correspondent. B. 1942, Orange, NJ. Amherst College, 1964, BA-English & Economics. *Rockland Journal-News,* reporter, to 1973. *The Record* (Hackensack, NJ), reporter, to 1975. *Rockland County Times,* writer-Editor, to 1976. *Harper's,* Contributing Editor, to 1982; current, 1983. *The American Spectator,* NY correspondent, current. John Hancock Award, Business Writing, 1977; Gerald Loeb Awards, 1978, '80; Amos Tuck Award, 1980. Author 2 books, including *Vigilante — The Backlash Against Crime in America,* 1985.

Tumulty, Karen. *Los Angeles Times.* New York Writer. B. 1955, San Antonio, TX. U. of TX, Austin, 1977, BJ, high honors; Harvard, 1981, MBA. *The Daily Texan,* staff member. Long News Service, part-time reporter, 1976-77. *San Antonio Light,* intern, summer 1976; Business Editor, reporter, to 1979. *Los Angeles Times,* intern, summer 1980; energy writer, to 1983; DC writer, to 1988; NY writer, current, 1988.

Tuohy, William. *Los Angeles Times.* Bonn Bureau Chief. B. 1926, Chicago. Northwestern, 1951, English. *San Francisco Chronicle,* copyboy; reporter; Night City Editor, to 1959. *Newsweek,* back-of-book writer, Assoc Editor, Asst National Editor, national political correspondent, 1964; Saigon bureau chief, 1965. *Los Angeles Times,* Saigon bureau chief, to 1968; Beirut bureau chief, to 1971; Rome bureau chief, to 1977; London, to 1985; Bonn bureau chief, current, 1985. Headliners Award, 1965; Pulitzer Prize, 1969; Overseas Press Club, 1969.

Turque, Bill. *Newsweek.* General Editor. B. 1954, NYC. U. of MI, 1977, English. *The Kansas City Star,* reporter, 1977-81. *The Dallas*

Times Herald, reporter, to 1985; national correspondent, to 1986. *Newsweek,* Detroit correspondent, to 1988; Gen Editor, current, 1988.

Tyler, Patrick E. *The Washington Post.* Middle East Correspondent. B. 1951, St. Louis, MO. U. of SC, 1974, Journalism. *The Hampton County* (SC) *Guardian,* Editor, 1974. *The Allandale County* (SC) *Citizen,* Editor, 1974. *Charlotte* (NC) *News,* reporter, 1975. *The St. Petersburg Times,* police & courts reporter, to 1978. *Congressional Quarterly,* 1978. PBS, WCET (Cincinnati, OH), host, "Congressional Outlook" documentary series, 1978. *The Washington Post,* metro, investigative, foreign staffs, to 1986; Middle East correspondent, current, 1986.

Tyrrell, R. Emmett, Jr. *The American Spectator.* Editor. B. 1943, Chicago. IN U., 1965, BA-History, 1967, MA. *The American Spectator,* founder, 1967; Editor, current, 1967. King Features Syndicate, "Public Nuisances" columnist, current.

Uchitelle, Louis. *The New York Times.* Business/Financial Reporter. B. 1933, Great Neck, NY. U. of MI, 1954, BA. Columbia, professor, from 1976. *The Mount Vernon* (NY) *Daily Argus,* reporter, to 1957. AP, from 1957; reporter, various bureaus; World Services Editor; San Juan correspondent, bureau chief; Buenos Aires bureau chief; Energy Editor; Supervising Editor; Business News Editor, to 1980. *The New York Times,* Asst Business/Financial Editor; Sunday Business Deputy Editor; Night News Editor; Business News Assgnmt Editor, to 1987; business/financial reporter, current, 1987.

Ungeheuer, Frederick. *Time.* Senior Correspondent. B. 1932, Frankfurt-am-Main, Germany. Harvard, 1956, Government Theory. Reuters, correspondent, to 1963. Time-Life News Service, correspondent, West Africa bureau chief, to 1969. *Harper's,* Contributing Editor, to 1971. *Eastwest Markets/Mideast Markets,* Editor, to 1977. *Time,* UN bureau chief, to 1973; European economic correspondent, to 1980; financial correspondent, to 1982; Sr Correspondent, current, 1982.

Unger, David C. *The New York Times.* Editorial Board Member. Cornell. U. of TX, 1979, PhD. *The New York Times,* editorial staff, from 1977; Editorial Page Day Editor; editorial board member, current, 1989.

Utley, Clifton Garrick. NBC-TV News. "NBC-TV Nightly News" Correspondent. B. 1939, Chicago. Carleton College, 1961, BA; postgrad Free U. of Berlin, 1963. US Army, 1961-62. NBC-TV News, correspondent, Brussels, to 1964; Vietnam, to 1965; Chicago, 1966; NYC, 1966, '71-73; Berlin, 1966-68; Paris bureau chief, to 1971; London correspondent, 1973-79; "NBC-TV Nightly News" correspondent, current, 1980; occasional anchor, current; "Meet the Press" host, current, 1989.

Utne, Eric. *Utne Reader.* Editor & Publisher. B. 1946, St. Paul, MN. U. of MN, 1968, Architecture. *East West Journal,* Ad Director, 1973-74. *New Age Journal,* Editor, Publisher, to 1977. *Utne Reader,* Editor, Publisher, current, 1984. National Magazine Award Nominee, 1988.

Van Voorst, Bruce. *Time.* Senior National Security Correspondent. U. of MI, 1955, MA-Soviet Studies. CIA, political analyst. Roving foreign correspondent, Europe & Latin America. *Time,* foreign correspondent; national security correspondent, to 1988; Sr national security correspondent, current, 1988.

Vobejda, Barbara. *The Washington Post.* Staff Writer. B. 1953, Englewood, CO. U. of CO, 1975; Georgetown, 1987, Government. *The Newburyport Daily News,* reporter. *The Honolulu Advertiser,* reporter. Congressional fellow, 1983. *The Washington Post,* reporter, 1984-86; staff writer, current, 1986.

Vultee, Fred. *The Washington Times.* Assistant Foreign Editor. *Columbus* (OH) *Dispatch,* Copy Editor, to 1988. *The Washington Times,* Asst Foreign Editor, current, 1988.

Walcott, John. *U.S.News & World Report.* Foreign Editor. *Newsweek,* to 1981; chief diplomatic correspondent, to 1986. *The Wall Street Journal,* national security reporter, to 1989. *U.S.News & World Report,* Foreign Editor, current, 1989.

Walczak, Lee. *BusinessWeek.* Washington Bureau Manager. U. of MD; U. of MO, MAJ. McGraw-Hill World News, health, transportation reporter, DC. *BusinessWeek,* NY; White House correspondent; Editor, "Washington Outlook;" Political News Editor; DC bureau manager, current, 1985.

Wald, Matthew L. *The New York Times.* "Business Day" Reporter. B. 1954, Cambridge, UK. Brown, 1976, BA-Urban Studies. *The Washington Post,* reporter, summer 1976. *The New York Times,* news clerk, DC, 1976-77; metro reporter, to 1978, 1982-88; Stamford reporter, to 1979; Hartford reporter, to 1982; "Business Day" reporter, current, 1988.

MediaGuide

Waldholz, Michael R. *The Wall Street Journal.* Science Reporter. B. 1950, Newark, NJ. U. of Pittsburgh, 1972, BA-English Literature, 1973, MA-English Literature. *The Wall Street Journal,* science reporter, current, 1980. Co-recipient National Assn of Science Writers' Science & Society Award, 1986.

Wallace, Charles P. *Los Angeles Times.* Nicosia Bureau Chief. B. 1950, NYC. NYU, 1970, BA-Communications & Fine Arts. Fawcett Publications, writer, 1970-71. UPI, reporter; Moscow reporter; Nairobi reporter, to 1981. *Los Angeles Times,* metro writer, to 1984; Beirut bureau chief, to 1985; Amman bureau chief, to 1987; Nicosia bureau chief, current, 1987. *Times* Editorial Award, 1985.

Wallace, Christopher. ABC-TV News. "Prime Time Live" Correspondent. B. 1947, Chicago. Harvard, 1969, BA. *The Boston Globe,* national reporter, to 1973. WBBM-TV, political reporter, to 1975. WNBC-TV-TV, NY, investigative reporter, to 1978. NBC-TV News, DC, political reporter, to 1981; "Today" anchor, to 1982; "NBC-TV Nightly News" White House correspondent, to 1989; "Meet the Press" host, 1987. ABC-TV News, "Prime Time Live" correspondent, current, 1989. Documentary writer, including "Nancy Reagan, The First Lady," 1984. Peabody Award, 1978; Emmy Award, 1981; Overseas Press Club, 1981.

Wallace, James N. *U.S.News & World Report.* Senior Editor, International. B. 1927, Sioux City, IA. U. of OR, 1950, Journalism. *Aberdeen* (Wash) *Daily World,* reporter, 1951-53. *The Wall Street Journal,* reporter, feature writer, to 1963. *U.S.News & World Report,* foreign correspondent, Sr Editor, international, current, 1963. Overseas Press Club, special citation, reporting from Soviet Union.

Wallace, Mike. CBS-TV News. "60 Minutes" Co-Editor & Correspondent. B. 1918, Brookline, MA. U. of MI, 1939, AB. Radio, from 1939. CBS-TV, commentator, 1951-54; TV interviewer, reporter, current, 1951. CBS News, correspondent, from 1963; "60 Minutes" Co-Editor & correspondent, current. Author 2 books, including *Close Encounters,* 1984. Emmy Award & Peabody Awards, 1963-71, DuPont Award, 1972.

Wallis, Claudia. *Time.* Senior Editor. B. 1954, Glen Cove, NY. Yale, 1976, Philosophy. *Time,* writer, 1979-84; Assoc Editor, to 1988; Sr Editor, current, 1988. Deadline Award 1982; William Harvey Award, 1983; NY Newspaper Guild Page 1 Award, 1984; National Magazine Award, 1984.

Walljasper, Jay. *Utne Reader.* Executive Editor. B. 1955, Fairfield, IA. U. of IA, 1976, English/Journalism. *In These Times,* Chicago, 1982-83. *Better Homes & Gardens,* Des Moines, to 1984. *Utne Reader,* Exec Editor, current, 1984.

Walsh, Edward. *The Washington Post.* National Staff Reporter. B. 1942, Chicago, IL. College of St. Thomas (St. Paul, MN), 1963, BA-Political Science & Journalism. Congressional Fellow, American Political Science Assn, 1970-71. Nieman Fellow, 1981-82. *The Catholic Messenger* (Davenport, IA), reporter, Asst Editor, 1965-67. *Houston Chronicle,* reporter, to 1970. *The Washington Post,* metro reporter, to 1975; White House correspondent, to 1981; Jerusalem correspondent, to 1985; national staff reporter, current, 1985. Merriman Smith Memorial Award, White House Correspondents Assn, 1979.

Walsh, Mary Williams. *The Asian Wall Street Journal.* Hong Kong News Bureau. B. Wausau, WI. U. of WI, 1979, BA-French & English. Walter Bagehot Fellow, 1982, '83. Western Publishing, editorial asst, 1978. *The Progressive,* Assoc Editor, 1979. *The Wall Street Journal,* Philadelphia reporter, 1982-85; Mexico bureau chief, to 1988. *The Asian Wall Street Journal,* Hong Kong news bureau, current, 1988.

Walters, Barbara. ABC-TV News. "20/20" Co-Anchor. B. 1931. Sarah Lawrence College, 1953. WCBS-TV & WPIX, writer, Producer. NBC-TV-TV News, "Today," from 1961, regular panel member, 1963-74, co-host, to 1976. ABC-TV News, "ABC Evening News" newscaster, from 1976; "20/20," co-anchor, current; occasional "Barbara Walters Special" interview programs, current. *Reader's Digest,* contributor, current. Emmy Award, 1975; other awards.

Wastler, Allen R. *The Journal of Commerce.* Reporter. B. 1962, Baltimore. Johns Hopkins, 1984, BA-Writing. *Traffic World,* Asst Editor; Assoc Editor, 1984-89. *American Sailings,* Managing Editor, July, 1989. *The Journal of Commerce,* reporter, current, 1989.

Wattenberg, Ben. Newspaper Enterprise Syndicate. Columnist. B. 1933, NYC. Hobart College, 1955, BA. US Air Force, to 1958. Asst to President Johnson, 1966-68. Business consultant, DC, to 1979. Aide to VP Humphrey, 1970. Campaign adviser, Sen. Henry Jackson, 1972, '76. Mary Washington College, Eminent Scholar, Prof at Large, 1973-74. Presidential Advisory Board on Ambassadorial Appointments, member, to 1980. US International U., Distinguished Visiting Prof, 1978, '79. International Broadcasting, Vice Chairman of the Board, 1981. Democracy Program, Vice Chairman of the Board, to 1983. Coalition for a Democratic Majority, co-founder, Chairman, current, 1972. Reading Is Fundamental, Board of Directors member, current, 1977. Hudson Institute, trustee, current, 1976. American Enterprise Institute, Sr Fellow, current, 1977. United Features Syndicate, columnist, 1977-87. Newspaper Enterprise Syndicate, columnist, current, 1987. *Public Opinion,* Co-Editor, current, 1977. Author 4 books, including *The Birth Dearth*; co-author 3 books.

Weberman, Ben. *Forbes.* Contributing Editor. B. 1923, NYC. CCNY, 1943, BS-Mathematics; NYU, School of Business, 1955, MBA. International Statistical Bureau, assoc economist, 1946-51. *The Journal of Commerce,* financial writer to 1954; Financial Editor, to 1956. *New York Herald Tribune,* bond market columnist, to 1961; Financial Editor, to 1964. *American Banker,* Financial Editor, to 1975. *Forbes,* Sr Editor, "Capital Markets: Money & Investments" columnist, to 1988; Contributing Editor, current, 1988. NY Financial Writers Assn Financial Journalism Award, 1983. Author *Interest Rate Futures - Profits and Pitfalls.*

Weiner, Steve. *Forbes.* Midwest Bureau Manager. U. of WA, 1970, BA-Communications. AP, reporter, correspondent, News Editor, desk supervisor, deputy bureau chief, 1970-79. *The Wall Street Journal,* reporter, commodity markets, agriculture, Midwest retail, to 1981; national retailing specialist, 1985. *Eugene* (OR) *Register Guard,* Asst City Editor, City Editor, 1981-85. *Seattle Times,* City Editor, City Editor, 1985. *Forbes,* Midwest bureau manager, current, 1987. Regional AP Awards; Alaska News Broadcaster of the Year, 1973.

Weinraub, Bernard. *The New York Times.* Washington Correspondent. B. 1937, NYC. CCNY, BA. US Army. *The New York Times,* copyboy, 1961; news clerk; news asst. UN Bureau; reporter, 1963-67; foreign correspondent, to 1968; metro staff, to 1970; London correspondent, to 1973, '75-77; India correspondent, to 1975; DC correspondent, 1977-87, current, 1988; Sen. Robert Dole presidential campaign correspondent, 1987. Newspaper Guild Award.

Weintraub, Richard. *The Washington Post.* Assistant Financial Editor. B. 1943, Valparaiso, FL. U. of Chattanooga, History. Fletcher School of Law & Diplomacy (Boston), AM, MA. *The Chattanooga Times,* copy editor. *The Boston Globe,* copy editor; reporter. *The Washington Post,* Asst Foreign Editor, 1974-84; Deputy Foreign Editor, to 1986; S. Asia bureau chief, to 1989; Asst Financial Editor, current, 1989. New England Newswriters Association Award, 1972.

Weisman, Steven R. *The New York Times.* Tokyo Correspondent. B. 1946, LA, CA. Yale, 1968, BA. *The New York Times,* metro reporter, 1970-74; politics & NYC's financial crisis, to 1976; Albany reporter, 1976; City Hall bureau chief, to 1978; Albany bureau chief, 1978; DC reporter, to 1979; White House correspondent, to 1981; Sr White House Correspondent, to 1985; New Delhi bureau chief, to 1989; Tokyo correspondent, current, 1989. Silurian Society Award, 1975.

Weiss, Gary. *BusinessWeek.* Markets & Investments Associate Editor. B. 1954, NYC. CCNY, 1975, BA; Northwestern, 1976, MS. *Hartford Courant,* reporter, 1976-81. States News Service, reporter, 1981. Network News Inc, reporter, to 1982; Business Editor, to 1983. *Barron's,* writer, to 1986. *BusinessWeek,* Staff Editor, to 1987; Markets & Investments Assoc Editor, current, 1988.

Weisskopf, Michael. *The Washington Post.* National Reporter. B. Chicago. GWU, BA-International Affairs; Johns Hopkins, MA. *The Montgomery* (AL) *Advertiser,* reporter. *The Sun,* reporter. *The Washington Post,* metro reporter, 1977-80; Beijing bureau chief, to 1985; Pentagon correspondent, to 1986; national reporter, current, 1986.

Welles, Chris. *BusinessWeek.* Senior Writer. B. 1937, Boston. Princeton, 1959, Politics, honors. US Navy, 1959-62. *Life,* reporter, 1962; Business Editor, 1965-68. *Saturday Evening Post,* Business Editor, to 1969. Freelance, to 1983. *Los Angeles Times,* staff writer, to 1986. Walter Bagehot Fellowship Program in Economics & Business Journalism, Director, 1977-85. *BusinessWeek,* Sr Writer, current, 1986. Gerald Loeb Award, 1979; U. of MO, 1972, '75, '77, '79; John Hancock Award, 1979; National Magazine Award, 1983. Author 2 books, including *The Last Days of the Club,* 1975.

Welling, Kathryn. *Barron's.* Managing Editor. B. 1952, Fort Wayne, IN. Northwestern, Journalism. *Barron's,* Assoc Editor, 1976-81; asst to Editor, to 1982; Managing Editor, current, 1982.

West, Woody. *Insight.* Associate Editor. B. 1934, MT. St. John's College, American U., 1961, History. *Lincoln* (NE) *Star,* reporter, 1961. *Omaha World-Herald,* Copy Editor, to 1962. *The Washington Star,* Asst National Editor, Asst City Editor, reporter, to 1980; editorial writer, 1975-81. *The Milwaukee Journal,* DC editorial writer, to 1982. *The Washington Times,* editorial writer, 1983. *Insight,* Managing Editor, to 1986; Assoc Editor, current, 1986.

522

Whalen, Bill. *Insight.* Writer. B. 1960, DC. Washington & Lee U., 1982, BAJ. *Compass Publications*, Assoc Editor, 1983-85. *Insight*, writer, current, 1985.

Wheeler, Charles. *The Washington Times.* Assistant "Commentary" Editor. B. 1947, Kansas City, KS. Emporia KS State U., 1972, Psychology; Unification Theological Seminary, 1977, M-Religious Education. *The Washington Times*, "Commentary" Production Editor, 1982-84; reporter, to 1987; Asst "Commentary" Editor, current, 1987. Free Press Assn. H. L. Mencken Award, 1985.

Whitman, David. *U.S.News & World Report.* Associate Editor. B. 1955, Philadelphia. Amherst College, 1978, Political Science. Harvard, John F. Kennedy School of Govt, case writer, 1978-85. *U.S.News & World Report*, Assoc Editor, current, 1985. Co-author 2 books, including (with Martin Linsky) *How The Press Affects Policymaking*, 1986.

Whitney, Craig R. *The New York Times.* London Bureau Chief. B. 1943, Milford, MA. Harvard, 1965, BA, *magna cum laude*. *The Worcester* (MA) *Telegram*, reporter, 1963-65. US Navy, to 1969. *The New York Times*, asst to James Reston, to 1966; metro news staff, 1969-1971; Saigon bureau chief, to 1973; Bonn bureau chief, to 1977; Moscow correspondent, to 1980; Deputy Foreign Editor, to 1982; Foreign Editor, to 1983; Asst Managing Editor, to 1986; DC bureau chief, to 1988; London bureau chief, current, 1988.

Whitworth, William. *The Atlantic.* Editor. B. 1937, Hot Springs, AR. U. of OK, 1960, BA. *Arkansas Gazette* (Little Rock), reporter, 1960-63. *New York ⁻Herald Tribune*, reporter, to 1965. *The New Yorker*, staff writer, to 1972; Assoc Editor, to 1980. *The Atlantic*, Editor, current, 1980.

Wicker, Thomas Grey. *The New York Times.* "In The Nation" Columnist. B. 1926, Hamlet, NC. U. of NC, 1948. Nieman Fellow, 1957-58. *Sandhill Citizen* (Aberdeen, NC), Editor. *The Daily Robesonia* (Lumberton, NC), Sports & Telegraph Editor. NC State Board of Public Welfare, Information Director. *The Winston-Salem Journal*, Copy Editor; Sports Editor, 1954-44; Editor, Sunday feature section, to 1957; editorial writer; city hall reporter, to 1959. US Naval Reserves, 1952-54. *The Tennessean* (Nashville, TN), Assoc Editor, to 1960. *The New York Times*, DC reporter; White House correspondent, to 1964; DC bureau chief, to 1966; "In the Nation" columnist, current, 1966. John Peter Zenger Award, Freedom of the Press, U. of AZ, 1984. Author 4 books, including *On Press*, 1978.

Wilford, John Noble. *The New York Times.* Science News Reporter. B. 1933, Murray, KY. U. of TN, 1955, Journalism; Syracuse U., 1956, MA. *The Wall Street Journal*, reporter, NY, 1956, '59-61. *Time*, Contributing Editor, to 1965. *The New York Times*, science reporter, to 1973; Asst National News Editor, to 1975; director of Science News, to 1979; science reporter, current, 1979. AAAS-Westinghouse Science Writing Award, 1983; Pulitzer Prize, National Reporting, 1984, '87. Author 3 books, including *The Riddle of the Dinosaur*, 1985; co-author 2 books, including *The New York Times Guide to Return of Halley's Comet*, 1985; Editor *Scientists at Work*, 1979.

Will, George F. *Newsweek*, Contributing Editor. Washington Post Writers Group, Political Columnist. B. 1941, Champaign, IL. Attended Trinity College, Oxford; Princeton. Teacher, Politics, MI State U., U. of IL, U. of Toronto. Congressional aide, Sen. Allot, (CO), to 1972. *National Review*, DC Editor, 1972. Washington Post Writers Group, columnist, current, 1972. *Newsweek*, columnist, current. ABC-TV, "This Week" commentary, current. Pulitzer Prize, Commentary, 1977. Author 5 books, including *Statecraft as Soulcraft*, 1982.

Williams, Dan. *Los Angeles Times.* Jerusalem Bureau Chief. B. 1949, Pittsburgh, PA. Yale, 1971, Political Science; Boston U., 1975, MS-Broadcast Journalism; Taiwan Normal U. Mandarin Training Center, 1975; US Army Defense Language Institute, Cantonese Program, 1972. *Miami News*, business writer, 1977-79. *Miami Herald*, 1979-83. *Los Angeles Times*, Central American bureau chief, 1983-85; Mexico City bureau chief, 1985-88; Jerusalem bureau chief, current, 1988.

Williams, Nick B., Jr. *Los Angeles Times.* Southeast Asia Bureau Chief. B. 1937, Santa Monica, CA. Claremont Men's College (CA), 1959, Business Administration. *San Diego Union*, metro reporter, Sunday desk, to 1964. *Sun-Times*, metro, financial & Sunday desks, to 1967. *Los Angeles Times*, Copy Editor, Metro News Editor, to 1972; Asst National Editor, to 1976; Asst & Deputy Foreign Editor, to 1985; SE Asia bureau chief, Bangkok, current, 1985.

Williamson, Chilton. *National Review.* Senior Editor. B. 1947, NYC. Columbia, 1969, History. *National Review*, Sr Editor, current. Author 3 books, including *Desert Light*, 1987.

Willoughby, Jack. *Forbes.* Staff Writer. Carleton U., Ottawa, Canada, 1977, BAJ; Walter Bagehot Fellow, 1983. *The Toronto Globe &*

Mail, business writer, 1977-83. *Forbes*, staff writer, current, 1984. National Business Writing Award, investigative journalism.

Wilson, George C. *The Washington Post.* National Staff. B. Orange, NJ. Studied Georgia Tech; Bucknell; *Alliance Francaise* (Paris, France). *The Washington Post*, from 1966; Pentagon reporter; Vietnam correspondent; national staff, military affairs, current. Mark Watson Memorial Award, Distinguished Military News Coverage, 1970. Co-author (with F. Carl Schumacher Jr.) *Bridge of No Return*.

Wines, Michael. *The New York Times.* National Security Correspondent. B. 1951, Louisville, KY. U. of KY, 1973, BA-Political Science & Journalism; Columbia, 1974, MSJ. *Lexington Herald*, reporter, 1974. *The Louisville Times*, reporter, to 1981. *National Journal*, DC reporter, regulatory affairs, to 1984. *Los Angeles Times*, DC economic correspondent, to 1988. *The New York Times*, national security correspondent, current, 1988.

Winter, Thomas S. *Human Events.* Editor. B. 1937, Hackensack, NJ. Harvard, 1959, Government, 1961, MBA. *Human Events*, Asst Editor, 1961-66; Editor, current, 1967.

Witcher, S. Karene. *The Asian Wall Street Journal.* Reporter. B. Monroe, GA. Davidson College (NC), 1975, BA-English; U. of Montpellier, France; U. of MO, 1977, MSJ. *The Asian Wall Street Journal*, reporter, Hong Kong, to 1979; reporter, to 1982, current, 1989. *The Wall Street Journal*, reporter, NY, 1982; foreign correspondent, Sydney, 1987-88.

Wolman, Clive R. *Financial Times.* Financial Services Correspondent. B. 1956, Sheffield, UK. Oxford, Philosophy, Politics & Economics, 1st Class Honors. *Reading Evening Post*, reporter, 1978-80. *Jerusalem Post*, Sub-Editor; economic & industry ministry correspondent, to 1981. *Financial Times*, company comments writer, to 1983; Personal Finance Editor, to 1985; financial services correspondent, current, 1985.

Wolman, William. *BusinessWeek.* Editor. B. Canada. McGill U.; Stanford, PhD-Economics. Citibank, VP, economic publications, 1969-71. Argus Research, economic trends forecaster, to 1974. ESPN, "Business Times," Exec Editor, 1983. *BusinessWeek*, economics staff, 1960-65; Economics Editor, to 1969; Sr Editor, economics dept, 1974-79; Deputy Editor, to 1983; Editor, current, 1984. PBS, "Nightly Business Report" commentary, current. U. of MO Journalism Award, 1978; National Magazine Award, 1981; Deadline Club Award, 1981; John Hancock Award, 1981; Champion-Tuck Award, 1984. Author 2 books, including *The Decline of U.S. Power*.

Wood, Lisa. *Financial Times.* Reporter. B. 1950, Penrith, Cumbria, UK. U. of Warwick, 1971, BA. BBC, researcher, 1973-74. *Birmingham* (UK) *Post & Mail*, to 1978. *Financial Times*, reporter, current, 1978.

Woodbury, Richard C. *Time.* Houston Bureau Chief. B. 1933, NYC. St. Lawrence U., 1956, English. Fairchild Publications, 1958-60. *Daily Sentinel Morning Sun* (Grand Junction, CO), to 1961. *The Denver Post*, reporter; bureau chief; Copy Editor, to 1965. *Life*, correspondent, NY, Chicago, LA, to 1972. *Time*, correspondent, Chicago, Miami, Denver, LA, Houston; Houston bureau chief, current, 1972.

Woodruff, Judy. PBS-TV. "MacNeil/Lehrer NewsHour" Chief Washington Correspondent. B. 1946, Tulsa, OK. Duke U., 1968, BA-Political Science. WAGA-TV (Atlanta), reporter, 1970-75. NBC-TV News, reporter, to 1977; White House correspondent, to 1982; "Today," chief DC correspondent, to 1983. PBS-TV, "MacNeil/Lehrer NewsHour" chief DC correspondent, current, 1983; "Frontline with Judy Woodruff" anchor, current. Outstanding Female Personality Emmy Award, 1975; Atlanta Women in Communications, Outstanding Communicator, 1976; Joan Shorenstein Barone Prize, 1986. Author *This Is Judy Woodruff At The White House*, 1982.

Woodward, Bob. *The Washington Post.* Assistant Managing Editor, Investigative. B. Geneva, IL. Yale, BA-English & History. US Navy, communications officer. *Montgomery County* (MD) *Sentinel*, investigative reporter, to 1971. *The Washington Post*, investigative reporter; Asst Managing Editor, investigative, current. Drew Pearson Foundation Award; Heywood Broun Award; George Polk Memorial Award; *Sigma Delta Chi* Award; co-recipient (with Carl Bernstein) Pulitzer Prize, 1973. Author 2 books, including *Veil*; co-author 3 books, including (with Scott Armstrong) *The Brethren*, 1979.

Wooster, Martin Morse. *Reason.* Washington Editor. B. 1957, DC. Beloit College (WI), 1980, BA-History & Philosophy. Northfield Associates, founder. *Harper's*, Asst DC Editor, 1981; DC Editor, 1983-87; Network News, writer, 1981-83. *The Wilson Quarterly*, Assoc Editor, 1987-88. *Reason*, DC Editor, current, 1989.

Woutat, Donald. *Los Angeles Times.* Energy Writer. B. 1944, Grand Forks, ND. U. of ND, 1969, English. (Fairbanks, AR) *News-Miner*, reporter, 1969-70. (Mankato, MN) *Free Press*, reporter, to 1971. *Minneapolis Star*, reporter, to 1974. (Wilmington, DE) *News-Journal*, reporter, Asst City Editor, to 1977. AP, reporter, Lansing, MI, to 1978; auto writer, Detroit, to 1979. *Detroit Free Press*, auto writer, to 1981. *Los Angeles Times*, Detroit bureau chief, to 1984; technology writer, 1985; energy writer, current, 1986. *The Wall Street Journal*, Detroit, 1984. AP-MI Award, 1980.

Wright, Michael. *National Journal*. Executive Editor. B. 1942, Fort Benning, GA. U. of AL, 1964. US Navy, to 1968. *Constitution*, city hall reporter, editorial writer, federal courts reporter, to 1970. *U.S.News & World Report*, regional correspondent, Atlanta, Congressional correspondent, to 1976; White House reporter, to 1978. *The New York Times*, "The Week in Review" Editor, to 1986. *National Journal*, Exec Editor, current, 1986.

Wright, Robin B. *Los Angeles Times*. National Security Correspondent. Poynter Fellow, Yale, 1985. Carnegie Endowment for International Peace, senior assoc, 1986. *The Washington Post*, special correspondent, to 1977. CBS-TV News, Africa correspondent, to 1980; Rome correspondent, 1981. *Sunday Times* (UK), Beirut correspondent, to 1985. Duke U., visiting prof, 1985-86. *The Christian Science Monitor*, correspondent, 1972-73; Asst Foreign Editor, to 1974; special correspondent, Africa, to 1975; Teheran, contributor, 1986-87. *Los Angeles Times*, national security correspondent, current, 1989. Author *In the Name of God*, 1989.

Wysocki, Bernard B. Jr. *The Wall Street Journal*. New York Staff. B. Waterloo, IA. Dartmouth, 1971. AB-Liberal Arts. *Amherst* (MA) *Record*, reporter, 1972. *Daily Hampshire Gazette* (Northampton, MA), 1973. *Albany* (NY) *Times-Union*, business & economics reporter, to 1975. *The Wall Street Journal*, Cleveland bureau, to 1978; Chicago reporter, to 1979; Philadelphia bureau chief, to 1982; News Editor, to 1983; NY News Editor, to 1985; Tokyo bureau chief, to 1989; NY staff, current, 1989.

Yoder, Edwin. Washington Post Writers Group. Columnist. B. 1934, Greensboro, NC. U. of NC, 1956. BA; Oxford, 1958. *Charlotte News*, editorial writer, to 1961. *Greensboro Daily News*, editorial writer, to 1964; Assoc Editor, to 1975. U. of NC, asst prof, history, 1964-65. *The Washington Star*, Editorial Page Editor, to 1981. Washington Post Writers Group, columnist, current, 1981. NC Press Assn Award, Editorial Writing, 1958, '61, '66; Walker Stone Award, Scripps-Howard Foundation, 1978; Pulitzer Prize, Editorial Writing, 1979.

Younghusband, Peter. *The Washington Times*. Special Correspondent, South Africa. B. 1931, Cape Town, South Africa. Educated in South Africa. *Northern Echo* (Darlington, UK), reporter, 1958. Reuters, London, desk rewriter, 1959. *Cape Times* (Cape Town), reporter, 1960. *Drum Magazine* (Johannesburg), feature writer, 1961. *London Daily Mail*, foreign correspondent (Africa, Middle East, Far East), to 1970; DC bureau chief. White House correspondent, 1970. *Newsweek*, special correspondent, South Africa, to 1986. *The Washington Times*, special correspondent, South Africa, current, 1986. Co-recipient (with Andrew Nagorski) Overseas Press Club Award, 1974.

Zucker, Seymour. *BusinessWeek*. Senior Editor, Economic News. Brooklyn College; New School for Social Research, PhD-Economics. Port Authority of NY & NJ, economist. NBC-TV Planning Dept, staff economist. *BusinessWeek*, Economics Editor, 1974-80; Sr Editor, Economic News, economics, Wall Street, markets & investments, current, 1980.

Zuckerman, Mortimer B. *U.S.News & World Report*, Chairman, Editor-in-Chief & Editorial Writer. *The Atlantic*, Chairman. B. 1937, Canada. McGill U., 1957, Economics & Political Theory, 1961, Law; U. of PA, 1961, MBA; Harvard, 1962, Master of Law. Boston Properties, Chairman & founder, current, 1970. *The Atlantic*, Chairman, current, 1980. *U.S.News & World Report*, Chairman, Editor-in-Chief & editorial writer, current, 1984.

Zweig, Jason. *Forbes*. Reporter. B. 1959. MA. Columbia College, 1981, Art History. *Africa Report*, editorial asst & Asst Editor, 1983-84. Freelance, W. Africa, 1985. *Time f.y.i.*, newsletter reporter, to 1986; "Economy & Business" reporter, researcher, to 1987. *Forbes*, reporter, current, 1987.

INDEX

Index

Annenberg School of

LIBRARY
THE ANNENBERG SCHOOL
OF COMMUNICATIONS
UNIVERSITY OF PENNSYLVANIA
3620 WALNUT STREET/C5
PHILADELPHIA, PA 19104